SCRIBNER LIBRARY OF DAILY LIFE

ENCYCLOPEDIA OF
CLOTHING
AND FASHION

EDITORIAL BOARD

SCRIBNER LIBRARY OF DAILY LIFE

ENCYCLOPEDIA OF CLOTHING AND FASHION

VOLUME 2:
Fads to Nylon

Valerie Steele, Editor in Chief

CHARLES SCRIBNER'S SONS
An imprint of Thomson Gale, a part of The Thomson Corporation

THOMSON
GALE

Detroit • New York • San Francisco • San Diego • New Haven, Conn. • Waterville, Maine • London • Munich

THOMSON
GALE
™

Encyclopedia of Clothing and Fashion
Valerie Steele, Editor in Chief

Library of Congress Cataloging-in-Publication Data

Encyclopedia of clothing and fashion / Valerie Steele, editor in chief.
p. cm. — (Scribner library of daily life)
Includes bibliographical references and index.
ISBN 0-684-31394-4 (set: hardcover: alk. paper) — ISBN 0-684-31395-2 (v. 1) —
ISBN 0-684-31396-0 (v. 2) — ISBN 0-684-31397-9 (v. 3) — ISBN 0-684-31451-7 (e-book)
1. Clothing and dress—History—Encyclopedias. I. Steele, Valerie II. Series.
GT507.E53 2005
391'.003—dc22

2004010098

This title is also available as an e-book.
ISBN 0-684-31451-7
Contact your Thomson Gale Sales representative for ordering information.

Printed in the United States of America
10 9 8 7 6 5 4 3 2

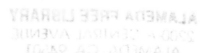

ENCYCLOPEDIA OF CLOTHING AND FASHION

FADS Here today, gone tomorrow. It is hard to identify a fad until it has fizzled. Fashion cycles, more generally, vary in speed; fads are those particular fashion cycles that "take us by surprise, but also fade very quickly" (van Ginneken, p. 161). The term "fashion" implies "strong norms" (Crane, p. 1), and although this criterion may also apply to fads, these norms are of shorter duration and within a more limited population. Fred Davis goes so far as to say that fashion itself "somehow manage[s] on first viewing to startle, captivate, offend," but ultimately "engage[s] the sensibilities of some culturally preponderant public, in America the so-called middle mass" (p. 15). By implication, a fad represents a temporary and limited divergence from a more general path of fashionability; the "so-called middle mass" may never approve.

A perusal of academic books in fashion studies over the last decade reveals that the term "fad" itself may have fallen out of style. Even Arthur Berger's text *Ads, Fads, and Consumer Culture* includes little mention of fads. Still, popular media feature lists of "what's hot" versus "what's not." Why aren't these called fads? Perhaps the time-space nexus associated with contemporary fashion cycles is at issue: Influencing the rapidity and scope of "what's hot" are factors such as a global economy, rapid technological change and media influence, "fast fashion" (or speed-to-market production), and a fashion system that combines branded commodities with stylistic diversity among consumers.

Nevertheless, a case can be made for interpreting the concept of fad for its historical, heuristic, and analytical significance. Issues of time, identity, stylistic detail, expression, and emotion all come into play in contemporary life, regardless of what we call the phenomenon in question. Historically, the term has been used to characterize collective behavior that may range from an article of clothing or an accessory (or how it is worn) to a hairstyle or other way of grooming. Or, it may describe toys or gadgets, or even activities or practices that do not require consumer purchase. Fads tend to be: (1) of a strikingly new or revolutionary quality that sets them apart from current fashion; (2) short-lived, with a rapid growth in popularity and demise; (3) accepted only in, and intensely popular within, small groups or subcultures; and (4) often "nonessential," "mostly for amusement," or a "passing fancy."

The concept of a fad seems to relate almost as much to who participates as it does to time. According to the *Oxford English Dictionary* the term is related to the earlier concept of fidfad (short for fiddle-faddle). A fidfad, dating back to 1754, was a person who gave "fussy attention to trifles." In the mid-nineteenth century, the terms "fad" and "faddish" were used to refer to shallow or unpredictable patterns of behavior or people.

It is interesting to note that the *Oxford English Dictionary* has not added new entries for the concept since its 1989 edition. However, it has generated related concepts that deserve careful attention: namely, "trendy" and "fashion victim." Trendiness implies the state of being fashionable and up to date; it also connotes following the latest trend ("sometimes dismissively"). Since the early 1960s, "trendy" and "trendiness" have begun to displace the concept of fad linguistically. By the 1980s, the concept of trendy had become well-entrenched in everyday speech. The connotation of being shallow or narrowly focused persisted; the term still does not describe individuals who are immersed in the larger, "mainstream" issues of the day. Dating back to the eighteenth and nineteenth centuries, the concept of a trend implied divergence from the mainstream—initially in the context of physical or geological manifestations (for example, streams, currents, or valleys). By the 1960s, the idea of trend analysis had taken hold in the social context as well. The idea of a fad was morphing into a "trend."

Aside from issues of intensified speed, media saturation, and identities and intentions, there is the question of who benefits from fads or trends, and how. Accordingly, Marx and McAdam made an analytical distinction between "spontaneous" and "sponsored" fads. The former appear and spread without the involvement (at least initially) of an entrepreneur or business. Usually a spontaneous fad can be pursued without an extensive monetary commitment; it tends to be behavioral in nature. Examples might include goldfish swallowing in the 1920s or "streaking" (running naked) in the 1970s; both of these fads spread and deceased rapidly as trends on college campuses. In contrast, a sponsored fad tends to be consciously promoted; this is probably most obvious when applied to toys or gadgets (for example, the "pet rock" fad of the mid-1970s or the Pog craze of the early 1990s).

Although there may be heuristic reasons for making distinctions between spontaneity and sponsorship in fads (just as there might be similar reasons for distinguishing fads from fashions), the two often become inextricably intertwined, especially in a commodified, branded, and celebrity-oriented consumer culture. First, it is difficult to ascertain in advance what will endure. Second, most fads or trends seem to include a commodity in some way, even (maybe especially) if it is somewhat affordable. Third, what may begin as a spontaneous fad (using the materials one has on hand to modify one's appearance, for example) can quickly become appropriated commercially. The phenomenon of trend spotters, or later, "cool hunters," took hold in the latter part of the twentieth century. Apparently, some analysts were able to spot or hunt trends so as to capitalize on them in some way.

Subcultural style, in particular, is open to such appropriation. In the mid-1970s, British working-class youth experimented with safety pins as accessories, with the use of Vaseline to spike their hair, and with ways of ripping their clothes. These looks were soon appropriated by top fashion designers and the apparel and beauty industries. Similarly, the hip-hop styles of inner-city (often African American) youth in the United States in the late 1970s became mainstream even in the suburbs of white, middle-class youth populations. Both of these examples were innovated by limited segments of society and then became more mainstream. But the time factor does not quite fit the classic definition of a fad. For example, the "sagging" trend associated with hip-hop male pants styles is still a way some young men of various ethnic backgrounds continue to wear their pants at the time of this writing. Whereas some adults might describe this look as a fad, younger people might simply characterize it as a longer-lasting fashion that resonates with some individuals and groups their age.

The approximately 250-year-old concept of fidfad reminds us that a fad is likely to be in the eye of the beholder. For example, when does the tendency to be trendy (or faddish) merge into that of becoming a fashion victim? Not surprisingly, the concept of fashion victim is usually used in a diminutive or depreciative way. The implication is that a fashion victim is susceptible to change, without devoting "serious" thought (as might a connoisseur) to the meaning of that change.

Michelle Lee's 2003 book *Fashion Victim*, intimates that fashion victim is an inclusive concept—not one confined to certain, limited groups within the population: "The Fashion Victim is all around us. The Hollywood startlet who's personally dressed by Donatella Versace is no less a Fashion Victim than the small-town salesgirl who hops on every fad at her local JC Penney" (p. xi). She goes on to say that a fashion victim is "anyone who has ever looked back at old pictures and cringed" (p. xii).

Fiddle faddle. The concept of a fad is frustrating and difficult to distinguish from fashion in general. Issues of time, identity, fun, commodification, appropriation, looking back, and moving forward all relate to the concept of fad as it has been used historically and analytically. None of these issues is without its own ambiguities. Still, fads, by any name or duration, are likely to remain a part of how we live and change.

See also **Fashion Advertising; Trendsetters.**

BIBLIOGRAPHY
Agins, Teri. *The End of Fashion: The Mass Marketing of the Clothing Business.* New York: William Morrow and Company, 1999.

Berger, Arthur Asa. *Ads, Fads, and Consumer Culture: Advertising's Impact on American Character and Society.* 2nd ed. Lanham, Md.: Rowman and Littlefield Publishers, Inc., 2004.

Crane, Diana. *Fashion and Its Social Agendas: Class, Gender, and Identity in Clothing.* Chicago: University of Chicago Press, 2000.

Davis, Fred. *Fashion, Culture, and Identity.* Chicago: University of Chicago Press, 1992.

George, Nelson. *Hip Hop America.* New York: Penguin Books, 1999.

Hebdige, Dick. *Subculture: The Meaning of Style.* New York: Routledge, 1979.

Hoffman, Frank W., and William G. Bailey. *Fashion and Merchandising Fads.* New York: Harrington Park Press, 1994.

Kaiser, Susan B., Richard H. Nagasawa, and Sandra S. Hutton. "Fashion, Postmodernity, and Personal Appearance: A Symbolic Interactionist Formulation." *Symbolic Interaction* 14, no. 2 (1991): 165–185.

———. "Construction of an SI Theory of Fashion: Part 1. Ambivalence and Change." *Clothing and Textiles Research Journal* 13, no. 3 (1995): 172–183.

Lee, Michelle. *Fashion Victim: Our Love-Hate Relationship with Dressing, Shopping, and the Cost of Style.* New York: Broadway Books, 2002.

Marx, Gary T., and Douglas McAdam. *Collective Behavior and Social Movements: Process and Structure.* Englewood Cliffs, N.J.: Prentice-Hall, 1994.

Meyersohn, R., and E. Katz. "Notes on a Natural History of Fads." *American Journal of Sociology* 62 (1957): 594–601.

More, Booth. "Going Von Dutch." *Los Angeles Times,* 2 January 2004.

Nystrom, Paul H. *Economics of Fashion.* New York: Ronald Press, 1928.

Sproles, George B., and Leslie D. Burns. *Changing Appearances.* New York: Fairchild, 1994.

Van Ginneken, Jaap. *Collective Behavior and Public Opinion: Rapid Shifts in Opinion and Communication.* London: Lawrence Erlbaum Associates, 2003.

*Susan B. Kaiser, Joyce Heckman,
and Denise Kastrinakis*

2   ENCYCLOPEDIA OF CLOTHING AND FASHION

FANCY DRESS

Celebrating festivals by wearing masks and disguises has been customary in Europe for many centuries. The eighteenth-century masquerade, forerunner of the fancy dress balls and parties of the nineteenth and twentieth centuries, owes its origin to the Venetian pre-Lent Carnival, developed in the seventeenth century. This was a public, open-air event in which all classes participated in dancing, feasting, and practical jokes. The revelers wore masks and either fanciful decorative costumes or all-concealing dark cloaks called dominoes, to enjoy flirtations and intrigue incognito.

Masquerading, or masking, was introduced as a public entertainment in London in 1710, held first in theaters and from the 1730s at the public pleasure gardens at Ranelagh and Vauxhall. In 1772, the Pantheon was built in Oxford Street to provide a winter indoor venue. Many masqueraders wore a mask and domino over fashionable evening dress, but others chose very diverse costumes. The dress of the commedia dell'arte characters Harlequin, Columbine, Punchinello, and Pantaloon was popular, as were nuns' and monks' habits (worn with subversive intent) and comic Scotsmen, sailors, and savages. Turkish dress for men and women, admired for its exoticism, appeared frequently at masquerades, and elements of *turquerie* were adopted in fashionable dress. Most outfits were probably hired, as advertisements show the existence of several London "habit-warehouses" engaged in this trade.

Romanticism

The morally questionable masquerade became unfashionable by 1820, but European society's love of fancy dress continued. To accord with the new mood of decorum, fancy balls became the fashion, given either in private houses or as large-scale civic fund-raising events. Masks disappeared, and costumes were based on historical characters (many from Shakespeare's plays or Sir Walter Scott's novels), Turkish and Greek dress inspired by Byron's poems, or the peasant dress of Spain, Italy, and Switzerland. The most admired romantic heroine was Mary, Queen of Scots, whose story combined legendary beauty, doomed love, and a tragic death; her popularity ensured that the "Marie Stuart" cap entered mainstream fashion in the 1830s.

Mrs. W. K. Vanderbilt at a fancy dress ball. In the latter half of the nineteenth century, fancy dress events became more common, and costumes could be found at department stores. © BETTMANN/CORBIS. REPRODUCED BY PERMISSION.

In France the masquerade was a fashionable way to celebrate state occasions. Louis XV attended the *bal masqué* at Versailles, celebrating the marriage of the Dauphin in February 1745, as one of a group of topiary trees.

Large civic balls were reported in detail in the press, with lists of costumes worn. Many women wore "a fancy dress," meaning fashionable evening dress with fanciful trimmings, particularly feathers. Local dressmakers or even the ballgoer herself created these outfits. Ladies' periodicals, especially *The World of Fashion* (first published 1828), included plates of historical or foreign dresses for inspiration. For more elaborate costumes and for men's dress, firms specializing in making and hiring fancy costumes advertised widely. London firms (including Nathan's, which still existed in the early 2000s), rented temporary premises in provincial towns where a ball was planned.

Imperial Pageants

From the 1860s onward, fancy dress opportunities multiplied. Society papers listed columns of private balls, often celebrating comings-of-age and housewarmings, as well as public balls hosted by lord mayors, children's parties, and clubs' and works' Christmas parties. Such was the demand for ideas for costumes that women's period-

Print of *La Saison*, showing women in fancy dress. Civic balls became popular in the mid-1800s, and the press often reported on the costumes of attendees. © Gianni Dagli Orti/Corbis. RE-PRODUCED BY PERMISSION.

icals, especially *The Queen*, published regular articles and correspondence columns, and from 1879, books were also available; Ardern Holt, *The Queen*'s columnist, produced *Fancy Dresses Described*, which ran to six editions by 1896. Popular costumes included "Vandyke" and rococo dress, Japanese dress (inspired by *The Mikado*, 1885), European peasant dress, and allegorical costumes such as Night, Winter, or Folly. By the 1880s, there was a demand for novel and inventive ideas (such as "The Front Hall" and "Oysters and Champagne"), and originality was important. As well as private dressmakers, the newly established department stores in London and provincial cities made fancy dresses for customers.

Queen Victoria's 1897 Diamond Jubilee inspired two of the most lavish fancy dress balls of the century: the Devonshire House Ball given in London by the duchess of Devonshire and attended by royalty and the cream of London society, and the Victorian Era Ball, given in Toronto by the governor general of Canada, Lord Aberdeen, and Lady Aberdeen. At Devonshire House, the guests dressed as famous people from history or fable; the hostess represented Zenobia, queen of Palmyra, and the countess of Warwick was Queen Marie Antoinette. Many of the costumes were couture creations, several by Jean-Philippe Worth (son of Charles). For the Canadian ball, the theme was the British Em-

pire, and many costumes were allegorical: the Aberdeens' daughter represented "The Forests of Canada," and other ballgoers dressed as "Electricity," "Postal Progress," and "Sports and Pastimes."

Bright Young Things

Fancy dress fitted the mood of 1920s party-going perfectly. Young people turned the social world topsy-turvy with all-night parties, jazz, cocktails, and exhibitionist behavior. Masks were reintroduced, and the most admired outfits were outrageous or bizarre, with good taste out-of-date. Theme parties became popular: Greek parties, baby parties, Wild West parties, and circus parties were held in London during the 1920s. The commedia dell'arte characters enjoyed a revival, especially Harlequin and Pierrot, given a contemporary twist. Fancy dress balls became annual events at universities and colleges and a popular feature of holiday cruises.

The press called the fancy dress ball given by Carlos de Beistegui, a Mexican millionaire, in the Palazzo Labia, Venice, in September 1951, the "Party of the Twentieth Century." The cream of international society dressed in sumptuous eighteenth-century costumes, many by French and Italian couturiers. In decline since the 1950s, fancy dress returned to fashion from the 1980s. Favorite characters in the 2000s include perennials such as monks, nuns, clowns, devils, joined by topical characters from films and TV. Themed parties are popular; Prince William of Wales celebrated his twenty-first birthday in June 2003 with an "Out of Africa" ball at Windsor Castle.

Children's Fancy Dress

Nineteenth-century children's costumes, apart from some nursery-rhyme characters, were usually miniature versions of adult dress, reflecting the mother's taste more than the child's. By the 1920s and 1930s, however, with more occasions for fancy dress, including pageants and street carnivals, and wider social participation, children's outfits were enormously varied, based on cartoon characters and cinema heroes, animals, storybook characters, even advertisements. Many were home-made: the paper pattern firm Weldon's produced catalogs of fancy dress

"I arrived at the Sutherlands' ball impenetrably disguised as a repulsive baby boy in rompers with a flaxen wig and a ghoulish baby-face mask, then I dashed home and returned as a Sylphide in white tulle with a wreath of gardenias."

Loelia, duchess of Westminster, 1927

patterns, and magazines suggested how to contrive costumes from everyday clothes or household furnishings.

In the early twenty-first century, dressing up is part of everyday play for three- to six-year-olds. Outfits are on sale in all toyshops and chain stores, to turn children into princesses, knights, nurses, policemen, Disney characters, or the popular fiction hero Harry Potter.

See also **Ball Dress; Masquerade and Masked Balls.**

BIBLIOGRAPHY

Cooper, Cynthia. *Magnificent Entertainments: Fancy Dress Balls of Canada's Governors General, 1876–1898.* New Brunswick, Canada: Goose Lane Editions and Canadian Museum of Civilization, 1997.

Finkel, Alicia. "Le Bal Costumé: History and Spectacle in the Court of Queen Victoria." *Dress* 10 (1984): 64–72.

Holt, Ardern. *Fancy Dresses Described, or What to Wear at Fancy Balls.* 5th ed. London, Debenham and Freebody, 1887, 6th ed., 1896.

Jarvis, Anthea. "'There was a Young Man from Bengal . . . ': The Vogue for Fancy Dress, 1830–1950." *Costume* 16 (1982): 33–46.

Jarvis, Anthea, and Patricia Raine. *Fancy Dress.* Aylesbury, U.K.: Shire Publications Ltd., 1984.

Ribiero, Aileen. "The Exotic Diversion: The Dress Worn at Masquerades in Eighteenth-Century London." *Connoisseur* (January 1978): 3–13.

Stevenson, Sara, and Helen Bennet. *Van Dyck in Check Trousers: Fancy Dress in Art and Life, 1700–1900.* Edinburgh: Scottish National Portrait Gallery, 1978.

Westminster (Duchess of), Loelia. *Grace and Favour: The Memoirs of Loelia, Duchess of Westminster.* London: Weidenfeld and Nicolson, 1961.

Anthea Jarvis

FANS Though already used for many centuries in other parts of the world, fans started becoming popular in Europe in the late sixteenth century, but experienced virtual demise in the early twentieth century.

Sixteenth-Century Rigid Fans
There were two distinct types of rigid fan in the sixteenth century: those of exotic feathers set in a fancy handle and those of vellum or plaited palm leaf also attached to a decorative handle.

A number of portraits from 1559 to 1603 show Queen Elizabeth I (1533–1603) holding feather fans. The identifiable feathers were ostrich. Fan handles ranged from handsome silver-gilt or silver set with fabulous jewels to plain-turned wood.

A well-known 1585–1586 portrait of Queen Elizabeth I attributed to John Bettes (c. 1585–1590) and now housed in the National Portrait Gallery, London, shows her with a large ostrich feather fan set in a superb jeweled handle. The fan is given the same prominence in the portrait as the jewelry and costume, indicating that it was valued. This is confirmed by the wardrobe inventories, which include numerous feather fans: "Item one Fanne of the feathers of the Birde of Paradise and other colored feathers thone set with sixe small starres and one great starre set with iiij or little Saphires the handle of sylver guilte." These are recorded in fascinating detail in the Stowe Inventory of 1600 and published in *Queen Elizabeth's Wardrobe Unlock'd* by Janet Arnold.

Rigid fans of vellum or plaited palm leaf were as a rule rectangular in shape and set into a handle in such a way as to look like small flags, and this is the term used to describe them.

Early Folding Fans
Mention the word "fan" in connection with dress and fashion, and the immediate mental image is likely to be that of the folding fan. A fashion accessory, it is easily held in the hand, whether open or closed.

The folding fan has found a niche in the popular history of fashionable dress as a pretty object that used to be carried by ladies of fashion, coupled with its reputation as a useful device in the art of flirtation. While its presence as an accessory in Western fashion has been taken for granted for over three hundred years, this is not a Western invention. It is generally acknowledged that the folding fan originated in Japan as long ago as the ninth century C.E. Its gradual dominance over the fashionable rigid feather fan of the late sixteenth and seventeenth centuries can probably be attributed to the convenience of being able to fold the fan away when not in use.

Folding fans probably made their first appearance in Europe between 1560 and 1600. It is likely that isolated examples were originally brought back by travelers or merchants as personal gifts for female friends or family and were probably treated as exotic curiosities. Proof of their existence in Japan prior to the 1560s can be seen in early Japanese paintings and manuscripts. One of the best known is the aristocratic hand scroll that illustrates *The Tale of Genji,* a romance of Japanese court life written by Lady Murasaki Shikibu in the tenth century C.E. The earliest surviving illustrated text dates from 1120 to 1130.

Not until the seventeenth century were significant quantities of folding fans imported into Europe from Japan and China. However, at some point before the end of the sixteenth century, European craftsmen appear to have taken up the challenge of making folding fans for their own market.

By the end of the seventeenth century, European fan makers had fully mastered the art of making folding fans. They used vellum or silk for the leaves and wood, ivory, tortoiseshell, mother-of-pearl, or bone for the sticks. In the sixteenth and seventeenth centuries, leather fan leaves and leather gloves were perfumed with orange water or other scents.

Nineteenth-century painted fan. The popularity of fans declined somewhat in the early 1900s, but revived again mid-century. Design continued to be moderated and simple, and pastoral and romantic scenes remained favorites. © V&A PICTURE LIBRARY, PHOTOGRAPHER: SARA HODGES. REPRODUCED BY PERMISSION.

Brisé Fans

Another type of folding fan known as brisé was contemporary with folding fans. The brisé fan does not have an attached leaf. In early European examples, the entire fan consists of very wide sticks. The brisé fan shown in this entry is made of quite thick pasteboard covered in silk and elaborately decorated with delicate straw appliqué designs. Straw work of this quality may have been of Italian or south German origin. Early brisé fans have one feature in common in the shape of the sticks—each one resembles a single, stylized, curled ostrich feather. Folding feather fans do not appear until the second half of the nineteenth century.

Seventeenth-Century European Fans

During the seventeenth century, European folding fans improved in technique and style. The leaf would be painted in gouache. The subject matter was usually taken from classical literature or allegories. The sticks became

finer and thinner; those that supported the leaf tapered to a point at the top. The two outer sticks, known as the guard sticks, were wider at the top and more bladelike. Fan painters of this period were influenced by the masters of the early and high baroque, copying or adapting their paintings for fan leaves. Literary tastes of the era, too, were reflected in the choice of subject: classical, biblical, and—to a lesser extent—conversation scenes predominated. Both sides of a fan leaf were decorated, the front (obverse) would be fully decorated with a painted scene while the back (reverse) was usually painted with a superb rendering of familiar flowers shown as a bouquet.

Eighteenth-Century Fans

The eighteenth century is considered a golden age for fans. The century began with the final flourish of the heavy baroque style of Louis XIV. His death in 1715 removed his overpowering influence, and breathed new life into fashion in France and Europe. It is no surprise that the ensuing rococo style, which predominated during the reign of King Louis XV (1715–1774), was a complete contrast. Characterized by its lightness and graceful, sinuous decoration, it was particularly well suited to decoration of fan sticks and fan leaves. Subject matter broadened to include pastoral, commemorative, and conversation themes—although classical subjects continued to be popular.

The major centers of fan production in Europe were France, Holland, England, and Italy. However, ivory fan sticks without leaves were imported in bulk from China as well as painted and plain brisé fans. The East India Company imported large quantities of fans and other goods into Europe from China in the seventeenth and eighteenth centuries. These traders would commission goods to their own specification for the European market. Such goods were designed to appeal to European rather than Asian taste, though they had a definite Asian influence, resulting in a style that became known as chinoiserie.

The most prolific fan production came from France during the eighteenth century. French influence on European fashion was profound at this time. Fan leaf design was influenced by painters such as Jean-Antoine Watteau (1684–1721), François Boucher (1703–1770), and Jean-Honoré Fragonard (1732–1806).

Many fan leaves were painted on paper or vellum throughout the eighteenth century, but from the 1730s onward, an increasing number were printed. Printing created some problems in the fan-making trade as it threatened to deprive fan painters of their livelihood. It had the advantage of being quick; a printer could produce huge numbers of just one design much faster than the fan painters.

The richness and exuberance of eighteenth-century design on fans and other forms of decorative art became increasingly restrained in the last quarter of the century. The affect of neoclassicism, with its strict adherence to classical form, caused fan designs to conform to minimal decoration in the approved style.

Nineteenth Century

Restrained decoration continued in the nineteenth century. Fashionable dress still retained the slim classical

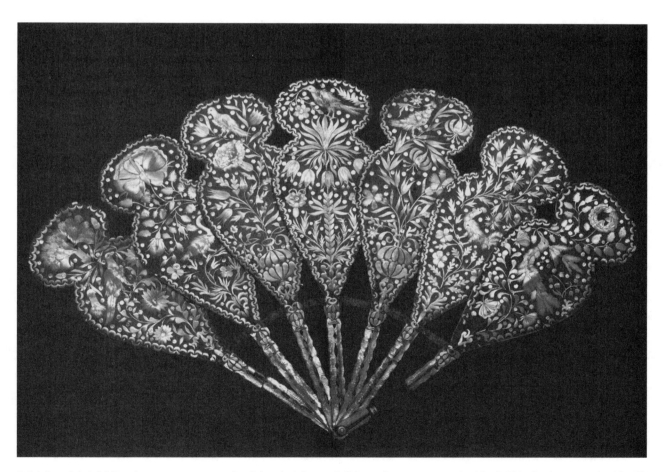

Brisé fan. Brisé folding fans were composed solely of sticks, and did not feature an attached leaf. This fan is covered with silk and accented with straw appliqué. © V&A PICTURE LIBRARY. REPRODUCED BY PERMISSION.

silhouette. Fans were small to the point of invisibility. Conveniently minute, they were held in the hand or could be popped into an equally small reticule. Decoration was slight; painted flowers and a little gilding usually sufficed. Many fans at this time were brisé made of pierced ivory, bone, wood, or tortoiseshell.

Inevitably women's fashions changed, and the elegant high-waisted styles moved to a more natural waistline in the 1820s. Decoration remained delicate but grew fussier. Fans became larger, and there was a fondness for silk or net leaves with appliquéd decoration in the form of gilt paper motifs and spangles. Other types of fan leaf were of painted or printed paper. Not until the mid-nineteenth century did fan making and fan design regain the panache of the previous century.

The second half of the nineteenth century saw a gradual decline in fan making and design. In France the firm of Duvelleroy dominated the European market with quality fans and had done so since it was established in 1827. Yet, the quality of their designs flagged during the second half of the century. Fan making in England fared no better despite attempts at holding competitions. Good-quality fans appeared briefly from the 1880s following a revival of interest in fans as fashionable accessories.

But World War I and the arrival of the "Modern Woman" completed the end of the fan. By the 1920s, fans had become attractive gimmicks to be given away as advertisements by well-known department stores, restaurants, or fashion houses.

See also **Asia, East: History of Dress; Europe and America: History of Dress (400–1900 C.E.).**

BIBLIOGRAPHY

Armstrong, Nancy. *A Collector's History of Fans.* London: Studio Vista, 1974.

Arnold, Janet. *Queen Elizabeth's Wardrobe Unlock'd.* London: W. S. Maney and Sons, 1988. The Stowe Inventory, p. 325, folio 91/8.

Bennet, A. G., and R. Berson. *Unfolding Beauty: The Art of the Fan.* Exhibition catalog. Boston: Museum of Fine Arts, 1988.

Cust, Lionel. *Catalogue of the Collection of Fans and Fan Leaves presented to the Trustees of the British Museum by Lady Charlotte Schreiber, 1893.*

Delpierre, M., and F. Falluel, eds. *L'eventail: Miroir de la belle époque.* Exhibition catalog, Musée de la Mode et du Costume. Paris: Palais Galliera, 1985.

Gostelow, Mary. *The Fan.* Dublin: Gill and Macmillan, 1976.

Hart, Avril, and Emma Taylor. *Fans.* London: V and A Publications, 1998.

Mayor, Susan. *Collecting Fans.* London: Christies/Studio Vista, 1980.

Rhead, George Woolliscroft. *History of the Fan.* London: Kegan Paul, Trench, Trübner, and Company, 1910.

Schreiber, Lady Charlotte. *Fans and Fan Leaves.* Vol. 1: *English;* Vol. 2: *Foreign.* London: British Museum, 1888–1890.

Avril Hart

FARTHINGALE. *See* **Skirt Supports.**

FASCIST AND NAZI DRESS Already in the decade preceding the Third Reich, female fashion had become a locus of contentious debate in Germany. In reaction to the "Garçonne" style that had become popular in the post-World War I years, conservative critics railed against "degenerate" cosmetics and clothing, which they described as "jewified," "masculinized," "French-dominated," and "poisonous." They also castigated the trend mongers who pushed such tasteless, unbecoming fashions onto unsuspecting female consumers. Short hair, shorter hemlines, pants, and visible makeup—all of these were purportedly causing the moral degradation of German women.

Vituperative commentaries claimed that French fashions were unhealthy for German women, both morally and physically, and that it was imperative for German designers to establish complete independence from the nefarious French influence on female fashion. Also denounced was the dangerous American vamp or Hollywood image that young German women were foolishly imitating with penciled eyebrows, darkly lined eyes, painted red mouths, and provocative clothing. Additionally, by the mid-1920s, Berlin had become an acclaimed world center of fashion, especially for ready-to-wear women's apparel and outerwear. Highly exaggerating the percentage of Jews in the German fashion industry, diatribes in pro-Nazi publications polemicized against the "crushing" Jewish presence, which was blamed for both ruining economic opportunities for the Aryan middle class and conspiring to destroy feminine dignity by producing immoral, whorish fashions for German women. This downward spiral in female appearance, critics asserted, could be halted only with the creation of a "unique German fashion." That term, however, was never fully defined.

Fashion Ideology and Policy

Such reactionary, anti-Semitic, and rabidly nationalistic messages were repeated on countless occasions throughout the 1920s and early 1930s, so that by the time the Nazi Party came to power in 1933 the argument was clear. Only German clothing, specifically Aryan-designed and manufactured, was good enough for females in the Third Reich. Racially appropriate clothing depended upon the elimination of French and, especially, Jewish influences from the German fashion industry.

To that end, an Aryanization organization named the *Arbeitsgemeinschaft deutsch-arischer Fabrikanten der Bekleidungsindustrie* (or Adefa), was established in May 1933 by several longtime German clothing manufacturers and producers. The group's aim was to systematically purge the Jews from all areas of the fashion industry. Through a combination of massive pressure, boycotts, economic sanctions, illegal buy-outs, forced liquidations, and the systematic exclusion and persecution of countless Jews, Adefa succeeded by January 1939 in ousting all Jews from the German fashion world. The *Deutsches Mode-Institut* (German Fashion Institute) was also founded in 1933, with strong backing from the Ministry of Propaganda and several other governmental agencies. Its mission was to attain fashion independence from French influence, to unify the various facets of fashion creation and fashion production in the German clothing industry, and to create a "unique German fashion" that would garner the Third Reich international acclaim and monetary rewards via its designs. Beset with internal conflicts throughout its existence and given little actual power, the German Fashion Institute never succeeded in fulfilling any of its goals.

Additionally, the Nazi state attempted to construct a female appearance that would mirror official ideology, uphold the government's autarkic economic policies, and create feelings of national belonging. This proposed female image would need to correlate to the Nazis' gender ideology, which urged women to return to their authentic role of wife and mother. Women's natural maternal instincts would thereby be satisfied, while also allowing them to fulfill the honorable duties of childbearer for the nation, significant consumer, and loyal citizen that Nazi Germany had bestowed upon them. As "mothers of the German *Volk*," women were assigned to correct the nation's sinking birthrate, guarantee the racial purity of future generations, and strengthen the economy by purchasing only German-made products. These were important tasks that required an image befitting the propaganda. For the ideal German woman, devoted to her family's well being, beauty stemmed not from cosmetics or trendy fashions, but from an inner happiness derived from her devotion to her children, her husband, her home, and her country.

The two images most often proposed and put into visual forms of propaganda were the farmer's wife in folk costume, usually referred to as *Tracht* or dirndl, and the young woman in organizational uniform. The rhetoric surrounding these two proposals advanced the "natural look" for women and condemned cosmetics and other "unhealthy vices," such as smoking and drinking, as unfeminine and un-German. Stress was placed on physical fitness and a healthy lifestyle, both of which

would facilitate a higher birthrate. Moreover, while the folk costume looked to the past and promoted an image that illuminated the Nazis' "blood and soil" ideology, and the female uniform spoke to the present and exemplified the idea of conformity over individuality, both images signified a rejection of international trends, again, as un-German. Both proposals also fit the state's anti-Semitic and anti-French agendas, as well as its "made-in-Germany" autarkic policy.

The Dirndl Fashion

The farmer's wife, labeled "Mother Germany," was offered as one female ideal. She was the link between the bonds of German blood and soil. Her natural looks, unsullied by cosmetics, her physical strength and moral fortitude, her willingness to bear hard work and to bear many children, and her traditional dress that recalled a mythical, untarnished German past, were deified through countless exhibits, paintings, and essays. In propaganda photos, rural women usually were shown with their hair braided or pinned up in a bun, no cosmetics, surrounded by children, and beaming with an inner glow that gave no hint of the difficult work that filled their days. And what was the ideal farmer's wife wearing? According to Nazi propaganda, she should dress herself in *Trachtenkleidung*, a folk costume that reflected Germany's rich cultural heritage. Promoted as an expression of the true German-Aryan character, the age-old *Trachtendirndl*—generally comprising a dress with tight bodice and full, long skirt, a white blouse with puffed and gathered sleeves, a heavily embroidered or crocheted collar, an embellished apron, and a variety of head pieces or hats—was viewed as the most suitable example of racially pure clothing and held up as a significant symbolic metaphor for pride in the German homeland.

To promote the resurrection of the folk costume, state-sponsored *Tracht* gatherings and folk festivals cropped up everywhere, even occasionally in metropolitan areas. Girls and women were told to proudly wear dirndls for Nazi Party-sponsored occasions and historic celebrations. And, farm women were encouraged to rediscover the many attributes of *Tracht*. They were also urged to sew their dirndls from fabric they had woven themselves, while caring for their flock of children and helping with the harvest. The problem was that most of them had ceased wearing anything resembling *Tracht* on a regular basis by this time, due to its impracticality and the difficult economic straits in which so many rural families found themselves. Farm women had long ago turned to dark fabrics that showed little dirt, looser clothes that allowed for greater movement, and sleeves that did not encumber them at their work. Except for the rare special occasion or celebration, rural women had not regularly worn the traditional dirndl for decades. Also problematic, the Nazis' extensive *Tracht* propaganda did not succeed in convincing urban women to embrace the folk costume. While dressing in dirndls for certain events was

German schoolgirls in peasant costume. The Nazi Party urged women to embrace their cultural heritage by adopting traditional German dress, but most found such clothing impractical and continued to wear modern fashions. © HULTON-DEUTSCH COLLECTION/ CORBIS. REPRODUCED BY PERMISSION.

considered fun, the majority of women living in large cities, such as Hamburg and Berlin, continued clothing themselves according to the latest international styles shown in German magazines, despite arduous efforts by some Nazis to convince them to dress otherwise.

The Female in Uniform

As an urban alternative to the farmer's wife in *Tracht*, the Nazis offered another female ideal: that of the young German woman in uniform, a reflection of the Party's attraction to organization and militarization. Much like *Trachtenkleidung*, the uniform offered yet another visible sign of inclusion into the Nazi-constructed German racial community. It also represented order and accommodation, as well as a rejection of international trends and individuality.

As organizations quickly proliferated in the Third Reich, so did female uniforms. Whether for girls, young

women, female youths in the labor service, or female auxiliary units, once World War II began, each group had a distinct uniform or, minimally, different insignia, badges, and armbands that specified rank or branch of service. Hair was to be kept neat and away from the face, preferably in braids for young girls and a bun for adult females. Cosmetics were shunned as unnatural and unnecessary for these young women who glowed from health and love of country. Physical fitness, self-sacrifice, obedience, and loyalty to the Nazi regime and its tenets were the most important components of all organizations, whose overriding purpose was to groom a generation of racially pure, healthy, ideologically sound females to become future "mothers of the *Volk*." No individual touches, no embellishments, nothing was allowed that might detract from the symbolic significance of the requisite clothing. The uniform sartorially expressed the Third Reich's demand for unity, uniformity, conformity, and community.

Clothing females in organizational uniforms, while fairly popular when the nation was at peace, became a political problem for the government once the conflict broadened throughout Europe and additional women were needed as war-essential auxiliaries. Uniforming increasing numbers of females and placing them in positions that had been designated as "male only," obviously upended the Nazi Party's "separate spheres" propaganda and its gender-specific work policies of the prewar years. The state's other concern was that extensive female uniforming would make clearly visible to the home population that the war was not going well. Furthermore, as the conflict continued and drastic textile shortages developed, some auxiliaries, who were only issued armbands indicating service affiliation in order to save material, openly complained and privately resented that they could not wear the full uniform others wore. Female auxiliaries stationed inside as well as outside of the Reich wanted, at the least, to look official as they risked their lives for the nation.

Popular Female Fashions

The image most widely embraced by German women not only competed with these two state-sanctioned offerings, but also often glaringly conflicted with either the Party's rhetoric or its policies. While "the natural look" was the beauty slogan pushed by Nazi stalwarts, and a "unique German fashion" was relentlessly advocated, neither was enthusiastically adopted by most women in the Third Reich. Instead, they bought the latest cosmetics, tried the newest hairstyles, and wore variations of the same fashions being worn by women in France, England, and America.

Reflecting the interests of their readership, popular magazines published articles that illustrated makeup techniques, advertised face creams, tanning lotions, and hair dyes, and offered tips on replicating the looks of Hollywood stars, such as Greta Garbo, Jean Harlow, and Katharine Hepburn. Photos in fashion journals depicted the newest styles by Parisian and American couturiers next to elegantly fashionable creations by Berlin's best designers. Well-known German fashion schools, such as the *Deutsches Meisterschule für Mode* in Munich and the *Frankfurter Modeamt* in Frankfurt, eschewed the dirndl image in favor of international influences and female consumer desires, much to the dismay of Nazi hard-liners. And for those women who did not have the means to purchase their clothing from dress salons or department stores, sewing patterns, with which to re-create popular fashions, were widely available and affordable.

Wartime Fashions and Rationing

On 14 November 1939, two months after the onset of World War II, the government issued the first *Reichskleiderkarte* (or Reich Clothing Card). This rationing system was designed to ensure an equitable means by which to supply the civilian population with sufficient shoes,

clothing, and textiles during the war. German Jews, deemed unworthy of receiving even minimal support, received no clothing coupons beginning in 1940. The clothing card was based on a point system, from which a recipient could not use more than 25 points in the time span of two months. Numerous other restrictions also applied. Hats were "points-free," which meant they could be acquired without ration vouchers or clothing cards and so would become the major fashion item of the war years. Once hat supplies were depleted, and thus unobtainable for purchase, women created their own turbans and hats from fabric remnants, lace scraps, netting, and felt pieces.

The first clothing card, good for one year, allotted 100 points, but severe shortages rapidly developed in several areas, particularly shoes and cloth. Because textile and leather production increasingly was geared toward the needs of the German army, many stores were soon emptied of their reserves. Consequently, material remnants replaced leather shoe uppers, and soles were often made from cork or wood. Additionally, the government quickly discovered that its autarkic economic policy had, in part, resulted in an unsuccessful scramble for a wide variety of viable synthetics that were urgently needed to keep Germans, military and civilian, clothed. Many of the textile and leather substitutes were of poor quality and disintegrated when washed or ironed.

The second clothing card, issued in the late fall of 1940, was worth 150 points, but the additional 50 points had no real value since, by then, extreme clothing and footwear shortages had developed in several major German cities. Widely circulated government brochures urged women to "make new from old," but a dearth of available sewing goods, such as thread and yarn, contradicted the state's catchy mottos. Despite admonishments by those who viewed pants as unfeminine and unacceptable female attire, women increasingly wore trousers as the war dragged on and shortages continued to mount. Pants were warmer than skirts, especially once supplies of stockings and socks had been exhausted. They were far more practical for women to wear as work attire in war-related factories. And, often, they were the only clothes item in the household still in plentiful supply, with so many absent husbands and brothers serving in the armed forces.

By 1943, drastic garment and shoe shortages rendered the clothing card virtually useless in some areas of Germany. In response, civilians turned ever more frequently to the burgeoning black market, even though this was a highly punishable offense. The inability of the regime to provide adequate clothing provisions throughout the war years was met with growing resentment and overtly expressed discontent, which belied the Nazis' depiction of a harmonious, supportive national community.

Summary

During the Third Reich, female fashion became a topic of much discussion and dispute. Instead of a unified view of what "German fashion" meant and a singular, consistently touted public image of the female, incongruities abounded. Additionally, no cohesive national fashion program was ever implemented successfully, despite tireless attempts by some officials. Women's fashion, which the Nazis had hoped would be a sartorial sign of inclusion into the national community, the *Volksgemeinschaft*, instead became a signifier of disjunction. Female appearance could and did circumvent Nazi ideological tenets and state regulations, sometimes flagrantly. Concurrently, ambiguous directives laid bare the government's obvious fear of losing both women's support on the home front and a lucrative fashion market abroad. In the end, fashion proved to be an unsuccessful tool in defining German womanhood and citizenship, partially through the dictates of clothing and appearance. This failure exposed the limits of state power in a highly visible manner. What was propagandized in the sphere of women's fashion had only a slight correlation to reality in Nazi Germany.

See also **Politics and Fashion.**

BIBLIOGRAPHY

Bundesarchiv R3101/8646 (regarding the papers of the aryanization organization "Adefa").

Bundesarchiv R55/692, R55/795, and other less voluminous files (regarding "German Fashion Institute").

Die Dame. One of the longest-running top contemporary German fashion magazines.

Deicke-Mönninghoff, Maren. "Und sie rauchten doch. Deutsche Moden 1933–1945." *Zeitmagazin,* supplement to *Die Zeit* 19 (6 May 1983): 30–40. Interesting German-language article about fashion in the Nazi period, with particular emphasis on the obvious contradictions between Nazi fashion rhetoric and reality.

Der deutsche Volkswirt and *Die deutsche Volkswirtschaft.* Contemporary trade journals filled with anti-Semitic essays regarding the role of Jews in the German economy.

Guenther, Irene. "Nazi 'Chic'? German Politics and Women's Fashions, 1915–1945." *Fashion Theory: The Journal of Dress, Body and Culture* 1, no. 1 (March 1997): 29–58. Overview of the subject of German fashion, with particular emphasis on the Nazi period and World War II.

———. *Nazi "Chic"?: Fashioning Women in the Third Reich.* Oxford: Berg, 2004. The only comprehensive English-language study of German fashion and the German fashion industry from World War I through the end of the Third Reich. All of the information quoted and summarized throughout this encyclopedia essay can be found in this source.

Jacobeit, Sigrid. "Clothing in Nazi Germany." In *Marxist Historiography in Transformation: New Orientations in Recent East German History.* Edited by Georg Iggers, 227–245. Translated by Bruce Little. Oxford: Berg, 1991. Translated overview of women's clothing developments and relevant state policies during the Third Reich. Jacobeit has published several German-language essays pertaining to fashion in the Nazi period, which include the issue of folk costume or *Tracht.*

Koonz, Claudia. *Mothers in the Fatherland: Women, the Family, and Nazi Politics.* New York: St. Martin's Press, 1987. Comprehensive study of Nazi gender ideology and policies, and the role of women as "mothers of the German *Volk.*"

Die Mode. High fashion German magazine begun in 1941, two years after the onset of the war. Because of wartime paper shortages, the journal ceased publication in 1943, along with all other fashion magazines.

Das Schwarze Korps. Newspaper of the Nazi SS, excellent source for condemnations of female fashions and cosmetics, as well as for anti-Semitic polemics.

Semmelroth, Ellen, and Renate von Stieda, eds. *N.S. Frauenbuch.* Munich: J. F. Lehmanns Verlag, 1934. Early Nazi anthology, the essays' themes pertain to the role of women in Nazi ideology and policy, fashion, autarky, and consumption.

Stephenson, Jill. "Propaganda, Autarky, and the German Housewife." In *Nazi Propaganda* 117–142*: The Power and the Limitations.* Edited by David Welch, London: Croom, Helm, 1983. In-depth essay about the Nazis' efforts to promote and implement the state's policy of autarky as it pertained to German women.

Sultano, Gloria. *Wie geistiges Kokain . . . Mode unterm Hakenkreuz.* Vienna: Verlag für Gesellschaftskritik, 1995. Excellent study of fashion during the Nazi period; however, sources are mostly Austrian-based, so study is focused more on Austria than on Germany.

Völkischer Beobachter. Pro-Nazi newspaper, excellent source for early diatribes against women's fashions.

Westphal, Uwe. *Berliner Konfektion und Mode: Die Zerstörung einer Tradition, 1836–1939.* 2d ed. Berlin: Edition Hentrich, 1986; 1992. Excellent examination of the early, important role of Jews in the German fashion world, and their persecution and exclusion from the fashion industry during the Third Reich.

Irene Guenther

FASHION According to the editorial policy of *Fashion Theory: The Journal of Dress, Body & Culture,* fashion is defined as "the cultural construction of the embodied identity." As such, it encompasses all forms of self-fashioning, including street styles, as well as so-called high fashion created by designers and couturiers. Fashion also alludes to the *way* in which things are made; to fashion something is to make it in a particular form. Most commonly, fashion is defined as the prevailing style of dress or behavior at any given time, with the strong implication that fashion is characterized by change. As Shakespeare wrote, "The fashion wears out more apparel than the man." There are fashions in furniture, automobiles and other objects, as well as in clothing, although greater attention is paid to sartorial fashion, probably because clothing has such an intimate relationship with the physical body and, by extension, the personal identity of the individual.

Fashion is most often thought of as a phenomenon of the Western world from the late Middle Ages onward;

but fashion-oriented behavior existed in at least some other societies and historical periods, such as Tang Dynasty China (618–907) and Heian Period Japan (795–1185). For example, at the eleventh-century Japanese court, it was a term of praise to describe something as *imamekashi* ("up-to-date" or "fashionable"). A regular pattern of stylistic change with respect to dress and interior decoration existed in Europe by the fourteenth century. The first fashion magazine is thought to have appeared in about 1586 in Frankfurt, Germany. By the seventeenth century, Paris was the capital of European fashion, and the source of most new styles in women's dress. By the eighteenth century, however, fashions in men's clothing tended to originate in London.

La mode is the French word for fashion, and many scholars believe there is a link between *la mode* (fashion) and *la modernité* (modernity, or the stylistic qualities of what is modern). Certainly, the number of people following fashion increased greatly in the modern era, especially beginning in the nineteenth century, due to the spread of democracy and the rise of industrialization. The later nineteenth century witnessed both the mass-production of ready-to-wear clothing and also the development in Paris of the *haute couture*. Although most dressmakers then were women, some of the most famous early couturiers were men, such as Charles Frederick Worth. Other famous Paris couturiers of the twentieth century include Gabrielle "Coco" Chanel, Christian Dior and Yves Saint Laurent.

It is popularly believed that there is a great difference between high fashion and ordinary clothes, but this is not the case. Designers such as Chanel and Dior sold expensive fashionable clothes to a relatively small number of people, but their designs were widely copied by manufacturers, who sold the "knock-offs" for a fraction of the price of the originals to a much more extensive clientele. Another popular myth is that men do not wear fashion. While it is true that men's clothing changes more slowly and subtly than women's clothing, it, too, follows the fashion. In the 1980s, for example, Giorgio Armani designed fashionable men's suits and jackets that had a profound influence on menswear generally. Finally, it is widely assumed that changes in fashion "reflect" societal change and/or the financial interests of fashion designers and manufacturers. Recent research indicates, however, that there also exist "internal taste mechanisms," which drive changes in fashion even in the absence of significant social change. Particularly relevant is Stanley Lieberman's research on fashions in children's first names, which are clearly unaffected by commercial interests. No advertisers promote the choice of names such as Rebecca, Zoe, or Christopher, but they have become fashionable anyway.

See also **Belgian Fashion; Fashion, Historical Studies of; Fashion, Theories of; Future of Fashion; Haute Couture; Italian Fashion; Japanese Fashion; Latin American Fashion; London Fashion; Paris Fashion; Ready-to-Wear.**

BIBLIOGRAPHY
Lieberman, Stanley. *A Matter of Taste: How Names, Fashions and Culture Change with Time.* New Haven: Yale University Press, 2000.
Steele, Valerie. *Paris Fashion: A Cultural History.* Revised ed. Oxford: Berg, 1999.

Internet Resource
Fashion Theory: The Journal of Dress, Body & Culture. Quarterly. Oxford: Berg, 1997—. Available from <www.fashiontheory.com>.

Valerie Steele

FASHION, ATTACKS ON While fashions in furniture and architecture have not generally been perceived as a problem, fashionable dress has been frequently criticized by clergy, philosophers, moralists, and academics for centuries. The condemnations have been numerous and varying; fashionable clothes are attacked for encouraging vanity, loose sexual morality, conspicuous consumption, and effeminacy (in men), and thus blamed for all manner of social breakdown and sexual and gender confusion. Further, the very idea of discarding clothes once they are no longer fashionable (rather than "worn out") has been seen by some as wasteful, frivolous, and irrational. The reasons fashion has been singled out for such condemnation are important and illustrative of the way in which fashionable dress intersects with wider social debates concerning gender, class, and sexuality. Perhaps the problem has to do with the close relationship of dress to the body, which bears the weight of considerable social, moral, sexual pressure, and prohibition (see Barcan 2004 and Ribeiro 2003). Further, given the close cultural associations between a woman's identity and her body, it is no surprise that fashion is subjected to such an onslaught of criticism: As feminists have argued, the things associated with women are likely to carry a lower social status than the things of men. This is not to say that men are exempt from criticisms concerning fashionable dress (indeed, they sometimes are), but such criticisms are less frequent in history and when they occur, it is the inappropriate nature of male interest in clothes, and fears about masculinity, that prompt such attacks.

Gender, Sexuality, and Morality
Understanding the historical condemnations of fashionable dress therefore necessitates an examination of attitudes toward gender, sexuality, and clothes. At the same time that women have long been associated with the making of clothes, with textiles, and with consumption, there has existed also a metaphorical association of femininity

and the very idea of fashion. According to Jones (1996, p. 35), "women had for centuries been associated with inconstancy and change," characteristics that also describe fashion. It is also the case that as Breward (1994) and Tseëlon (1997) note, up until the eighteenth century, fashion had been considered a sign of the weakness and moral laxity of "wicked" women. Tseëlon (1997) examines how ancient myths about femininity have informed Western attitudes toward women. She points out (1997, p. 12) that between them, archetypal figures, such as Eve, inform Western moral attitudes toward women. Within Judeo-Christian teachings, from the tales of the Old Testament through the writings of the apostle St. Paul, woman has been associated with temptations of the flesh and decoration. At the heart of this attitude toward women was a fear of the body that, in Christian teachings, is the location of desires and "wicked" temptations to be disavowed for the sake of the soul. Thus the decorated (female) body is inherently problematic to Judeo-Christian morality, as Ribieiro has also argued. So too, however, is the naked or unadorned body. As Tseëlon (1997, p. 14) notes, in Judeo-Christian teachings, nakedness became a shameful thing after the Fall and, since the Fall is blamed on woman, then "the links between sin, the body, woman, and clothes are easily forged" (see also Barcan 2004).

Given its associations with sexuality and sin, it is not surprising that female clothing is the subject of heated debate amongst moralists and clergy, and that feminine dress is the object of quite vitriolic attacks. One can find particularly misogynistic diatribes on femininity and dress in the medieval writings of clergymen, as well as in the writings of later moralists of the seventeenth and eighteenth centuries. For example, Edward Cooke in 1678 wrote,

> a double crime for a woman to be fashion'd after the mode of this world, and so to bring her innocence into disrepute through her immodest nakedness; because she her self not only sins against shame, but causes others to sin against purity, and at the same time, renders her self suspect. (Tseëlon 1997, p. 635)

To counter fears as to female sexuality and dress, Christianity produced "a discourse of modesty and chastity in dress" which became encoded into female sexuality (Tseëlon 1997, p. 12). Christian teachings held that redemption lay in the renunciation of decoration and modesty in dress, a moral duty born of Eve's guilt. Thus, while men's fashions were often highly erotic, it was women's immodest display that was the focus of religious and moral condemnation. Only a woman could be accused of seduction in dress. While such ideas may seem almost quaint by contemporary standards, where it seems all bodies can "shamelessly" flaunt bottoms, breasts, and bellies, in fact, evidence of the continuing associations between women, seduction, and morality today can be found in contemporary culture. In rape cases, for example, women are still implicitly and explicitly criticized for wearing "sexually revealing" clothes and what a woman wore at the time of attack can be given as evidence of her desires for sex and used as male defense in the form of "she was asking for it." The ghost of the temptress Eve still haunts contemporary culture.

Class, Morality, and Social Order

While sumptuary laws remained in place, fears about the breakdown of class distinctions were another source of anxiety for moral and social writers, particularly over the course of the eighteenth century. Here again, women's fashion exemplifies these concerns about class, along with familiar fears about female sexuality. Sumptuary laws attempted to regulate status but, in the case of women, they also attempted to differentiate between the good, gentile wealthy woman and her "fallen" sister, the prostitute. As Emberley (1998, p. 8) notes, the hierarchy of furs and social positions created by these regulatory acts also influenced notions of sexual propriety among different classes of women. At certain times prostitutes were forbidden to wear fur to differentiate them from "respectable women." However, it was not just sexual morality that was at stake in discourses on women and fashion. Women's supposed love of fashion, and all that glitters and shines, has been seen as problematic to the general social and moral order. This was true in the seventeenth and early eighteenth centuries when particular fears about the spread of luxury sometimes focused on women's supposed insatiable desires for such consumption and the threats they posed to the family, as this tract from 1740 illustrates: "although her children may be dying of hunger, she will take food from their bellies to feed her own insatiable desire for luxury, she will have her silk fashions at any cost" (Jones 1996, p. 37). Thus moral discourse gave way to other kinds of rhetoric: "sartorial offence moved from being defined as a moral transgression to being defined as a social transgression" (Tseëlon 1997, p. 16). While the former was considered indicative of character flaw, the latter indicates a lack of gentility and education and civility. Thus, while moral transgression through clothing was a matter for both sexes, a woman might transgress moral codes in more ways than a man. By being too highly decorated she might be seen to have fallen prey to the sin of vanity (Jones 1996, p. 36).

Masculinity and Morality

While men of aristocratic birth were at least as equally decorated as women, for much of the early modern period right through to the eighteenth century (and indeed, beyond, if one includes military dress), this simple fact did not dilute the association of fashion with femininity. Indeed, when male peacocks were criticized it was often on the grounds of "effeminacy," for showing too great an interest in fashion was deemed "inappropriate" to masculinity. Sometimes this criticism was leveled on the grounds that male interest in fashion transgressed the rightful division of the genders. At other times, effeminacy was seen as problematic to the image of a nation.

The equation of effeminacy in male attire with the diminution of national interests can be seen in Elizabethan England: In the sermon "Homily Against Excess," which Queen Elizabeth I ordered to be read out in churches, such associations are described as follows, "yea, many men are become so effeminate, that they care not what they spend in disguising themselves, ever desiring new toys, and inventing new fashions. . . . Thus with our fantastical devices we make ourselves laughing-stocks to other nations" (Garber 1992, p. 27).

As Garber notes, effeminacy here does not mean homosexuality (as it often does) but "self-indulgent" or "voluptuous" and therefore close to "womanly" things. Criticism is leveled at the money, time, and energy devoted by the effeminate man to the "feminine" and "trivial" frivolities of fashion. Similar criticism was directed at the "Macaroni" style (as in the rhyme "Yankee Doodle Dandy") that was popular among young aristocratic men of the eighteenth century. Macaronis appeared in the English lexicon of 1764 to describe ultra-fashionable young men of noble birth. It was a rather "foppish" style, Italianate and Frenchified, and was criticized on the grounds that this gentleman had "become so effeminate and weak, he became unable to resist foreign threats and might even admire European tyranny" (Steele 1988, p. 31). Men have, therefore, not been immune to sartorial criticism, because it was thought that they should be "above" fashion. However, while moralists and clergymen might hope to dissuade men from decoration, historical evidence illustrates that they, too, have been under the sway of fashion.

Fashion as Irrational
Over the nineteenth century, as fashionable clothing became more widespread, moving from the aristocracy to the new bourgeois classes as part of a more general opening up of consumption, other problems associated with fashion were singled out for criticism. For some, fashionable clothing was indicative of wastefulness associated with new forms of consumption. One key figure in this line of attack is Thorstein Veblen, whose *Theory of the Leisure Class*, first published in 1899, has remained a classic study of fashionable dress in late Victorian times and whose central theoretical tenants are still very much alive in contemporary critiques of consumption. Veblen argues that the newly emerging bourgeoisie express their wealth through conspicuous consumption, conspicuous waste, and conspicuous leisure. Dress is a supreme example of the expression of pecuniary culture, since "our apparel is always in evidence and affords an indication of our pecuniary standing to all observers at the first glance" (Veblen 1953, p. 119). Fluctuating fashions demonstrate one's wealth and transcendence from the realm of necessity. However, what motivates fashion change is that wastefulness is innately offensive and this makes the futility and expense of fashion abhorrent and ugly. He suggests that new fashions are adopted in our attempt to

escape this futility and ugliness, with each new style welcomed as relief from the previous aberration until that too is rejected. According to Veblen, women's dress displays these dynamics more than men's since the only role of the bourgeois lady of the house is to demonstrate her master's ability to pay, his pecuniary strength to remove her entirely from the sphere of work. The Victorian woman's dress was also an important indicator of vicarious leisure since she wore clothes that made her obviously incapable of work—elaborate bonnets, heavy and elaborate skirts, delicate shoes, and constraining corsets—testimony to her distance from productive work. Veblen condemns all these traits of fashionable dress, not just because they characterize women as men's chattel, but also because this fashionablity is inherently irrational and wasteful. He calls for dress that is based on rational, utilitarian principles, and his ideas are closely aligned to the principles of many dress reformers (Newton 1974).

Ugly, Futile, and Irrational: The Dress Reform Critiques of Fashion
Veblen was not alone in his condemnation of the fashions of his day. Numerous dress-reform movements emerged in the nineteenth century attacking fashionable dress. These movements were diverse and motivated by different concerns—social, political, medical, moral, and artistic—with some more progressive than others (Newton 1974; Steele 1985). For feminist dress reformers, the way in which narrow shoulders, tight waists, and expansive and awkward petticoats constrained the locomotion of the female body was a real political problem. However, more conservative medical discourses similarly attacked the corset for the way it constrained the reproductive organs, thus damaging women's reproductive capacities and preventing her from performing her "natural" duties. Indeed, the corset has excited considerable controversy, stimulating intense debate and outright condemnation: For some it is an instrument of physical oppression and sexual objectification (Roberts 1977; Veblen 1953 {1899}), for others, it is a garment asserting sexual power (Kunzle 1982; see also Steele 1988).

While women's dress, in particular, was singled out for criticism by these reform movements, men's dress, with its tight collars, fitted waistcoats and jackets, was also criticized by those, such as Flügel, associated with the men's dress reform movement. The dress of both men and women was seen by some to be "irrational" in that it contorted the body into "unnatural" shapes and was driven by the "crazy" rhythms of fashion considered to be not just archaic to a scientific age, but wasteful and unnecessary. For example, "aesthetic" dress of the late nineteenth century challenged the artificial constrictions of the fashions of the day with a new kind of dress for men and women that was free flowing and more "natural." At the same time health and hygiene campaigns often singled out women's dress as unhealthy or unhygienic: It was said that corsets damaged the spleen and internal organs, particularly the reproductive organs, and the long petti-coats picked up the mud, debris, and horse manure that were a constant feature of city streets in the nineteenth century (Newton 1974).

While fashion may be subject to much less criticism today, and no equivalents to the health and hygiene campaigns of the nineteenth century can be found, remnants of some criticisms linger in contemporary commentaries. For example, fashionable dress is still sometimes considered irrational and ugly, especially among intellectuals. Like Veblen, the contemporary philosopher Jean Baudrillard (1981, p. 79) condemns fashion as irrational and ugly, arguing that

> Beauty ("in itself") has nothing to do with the fashion cycle. In fact, it is inadmissible. Truly beautiful, definitely beautiful clothing would put an end to fashion. . . . Thus, fashion continually fabricates the "beautiful" on the basis of a radical denial of beauty, by reducing beauty to the logical equivalent of ugliness. It can impose the most eccentric, dysfunctional, ridiculous traits as eminently distinctive.

Wilson (1987) takes issue with Veblen and Baudrillard's account of fashion as wasteful and futile since both assume the world should be organized around utilitarian values; "there is no place for the irrational or the nonutilitarian; it was a wholly rational realm" (Wilson 1987, p. 52). A further problem with Veblen's and Baudrillard's accounts, according to Wilson, concerns their causal account of fashion change. The idea that fashion is constantly changing in an attempt to get away from ugliness and find beauty is reductive and over-deterministic. Both fail to acknowledge its ambivalent and contradictory nature, as well as the pleasures it affords, and their critique "grants no role to contradiction, nor for that matter to pleasure" (1987, p. 53).

Conclusion

Dress is still, perhaps, accorded less status than furniture, architecture, and other decorative commodities, which are similarly driven by fashion. There is something so intimate, sexual, and moral about what we hang at the margins of our bodies that makes dress susceptible to a kind of criticism that does not accompany the other objects we use. However, despite the fact that men and women wear fashionable dress, it is not considered a matter of equal male and female concern. Associations of fashion with femininity linger, and women's supposed "natural" disposition to decorate is still considered "trivial" and "silly," thus leaving women open to greater moral condemnation. While such ideas seem to be less obvious today, the lower status accorded to fashionable dress is evident in the sorts of criticism leveled at women, such as "mutton dressed up as lamb" (of which there is no equivalent term for men), and "fashion victim," (usually denoting the woman who is a "slave" to her wardrobe). As these phrases suggest, fashion still comes in for moral judgment and criticism.

See also **Dress Reform; Gender, Dress, and Fashion; Politics and Fashion.**

BIBLIOGRAPHY

Barcan, R. *Nudity: A Cultural Anatomy.* Oxford, U.K. and New York: Berg, 2004.

Baudrillard, J. *For a Critique of the Political Economy of the Sign.* St. Louis, Mo.: Telos, 1981.

Breward, C. *The Culture of Fashion.* Manchester, U.K.: Manchester University Press, 1994.

Garber, M. *Vested Interests: Cross Dressing and Cultural Anxiety.* London: Penguin, 1992.

Jones, J. "Coquettes and Grisettes: Women Buying and Selling in Ancien Regime Paris." In *The Sex of Things: Gender and Consumption in Historical Perspective.* Edited by V. de Grazia and E. Furlough. Berkeley: University of California Press, 1996.

Kunzle, D. *Fashion and Fetishism: A Social History of the Corset, Tight-Lacing and Other Forms of Body-Sculpture in the West.* Totowa, N.J.: Rowan and Littlefield, 1982.

Newton, S. M. *Health, Art and Reason: Dress Reformers of the 19th Century.* London: John Murray Ltd., 1974.

Roberts, H. "The Exquisite Slave: The Role of Clothes in the Making of the Victorian Woman." *Signs* 2, no. 3 (1977): 554–569.

Steele, V. *Paris Fashion: A Cultural History.* Oxford, U.K.: Oxford University Press, 1988.

Tseëlon, E. *The Masque of Femininity.* London: Sage, 1997.

Veblen, Thorstein. *The Theory of the Leisure Class: An Economic Study of Institutions,* (1899). New York: Mentor, 1953.

Wilson, E. *Adorned in Dreams: Fashion and Modernity.* London: Virago, 1985. Reprint, Piscataway, N.J.: Rutgers University Press, 2003.

Joanne Entwistle

FASHION, HISTORICAL STUDIES OF The earliest books on fashion history published in Europe date back to the Renaissance and the early modern period. Between 1520 and 1610, over two hundred books on dress were published in Germany, Italy, France, and Holland. These little books, designed for wealthy consumers, contained wood-engraved plates and minimal text, often in Latin and were focused on contemporary clothing. Curiosity about the foreign and the strange was as intense as ignorance was rife and publications contained fantasized images of the noble savage (the Peruvian, the Florida Indian, the African) set against plates of the fashionable clothes of European aristocracy and the dress of merchants, peasantry, and tradesmen. Between 1760 and 1820 interest in fashion and dress from wealthy consumers encouraged the publication of large folio-size costume books featuring hand-colored, etched copper plates and the new color printing technique of aquatint and, from the 1830s, lithography. Romanticism suffused all these luxury publications, with their emphasis on illustration with brief text, now no longer in Latin. Thomas Jefferys's ambitious four volumes, *Collection of the Dresses of Different Nations, Ancient and Modern* (1757 and 1772), covered dress of the entire known world, including "Old English Dresse after the Designs of Holbein, Vandyke, Hollar and Others." His view of women's fashions was that they were simply "a Decoration of Beauty, and an encitement to Desire."

"Antiquarian" Research into Fashions

A widening fascination with classical dress of ancient Greece and Rome in France led to Michel-François Dandré Bardon's *Costume des anciens peuples* of 1772 and André Lens's *Costume des peuples de l'antiquité* in 1776. These helped to fuel the eventual development of neoclassical fashions. The Gothic Revival too encouraged a wave of European interest in medieval dress history. These books provided "authentic" details of "Gothic" dress for dressmakers as well as artists, architects, and enthusiasts of fancy dress. Interest lasted into the nineteenth century and indeed beyond. The central dress historian of this period in England was Joseph Strutt, an artist and antiquarian. His major work was *A Complete View of the Manners, Customs, Arms, Habits etc. of the Inhabitants of England* (1774, 1775, and 1776) and *Complete View of the Dress and Habits of the People of England*, 1796 and 1799, which covered the Middle Ages through to the seventeenth century, using literary sources, and medieval manuscripts and monuments.

Dress of the Orient

The passion for an exotic, fantasy "Orient" encompassed Turkey, Arabia, India, China, and finally Japan, and fueled the imaginations of the makers of fashions and fancy dress throughout the eighteenth and nineteenth centuries. The vogue for Chinese decoration and chinoiserie infiltrated deeply into court and middling circles in Europe from 1680 to 1780 and much artistic and fashion inspiration was drawn from costume books of the period. Jean Baptiste Joseph Breton de la Martiniere's *La Chine en minature, . . . costumes, arts et métiers de cet empire*, with its seventy-four plates, was published in Paris, in 1811–1812. William Miller's *The Costume of China* of 1800 was reprinted in 1805, but with new plates drawn by William Alexander, official draftsman to the embassy of Earl Macarthy from 1792 to 1794 to China.

The elitist fashion vogue for *Turquerie* styles drew on plates from costume books such as William Miller's *The Costume of Turkey* of 1804 and, in 1814, on Jean Baptiste Joseph Breton de la Martiniere's *L'Egypt, et la Syrie au moeurs, usages, costumes et monuments des egyptians, des arabs, et des syriens*. Indian women became exoticized and sexualized, while modified Indian styling also filtered in to European fashionable dress. François Baltasar Solvyns's *Costumes of Indostan* was published in Calcutta in 1798–1799 and in London in 1804. Books with plates of Japanese dress were disseminated from the early nineteenth century. Thus, well before the tidal wave of publications of the 1880s and 1890s, Breton de la Martiniere's *Le Japon, ou moeurs, usages, et costumes des habitons de cet empire d'après les relations récentes de Krusenstern, Landsdorf, Titzing* was published in Paris by A. Nepveu in 1818.

Rural Europe

From the early nineteenth century a wave of descriptive books on the dress of European peasantry also exerted an influence on fashionable and fancy dress. Utopian notions and Romanticism turned to visions of a rural Europe peopled by a healthy peasantry in picturesque clothing. These costume books are informative and charming but also reveal period imperialist, gender, and stereotypic race and class prejudice. *The Costumes of the Hereditary States of the House of Austria* of 1804, for example, contains both sweet images of romanticized peasant women from all over central, southern, and eastern Europe set against textural and visual anti-Semitism in coverage of Polish Jewish dress. Twenty-three major French works were published between 1810 and 1830 on Breton peasant dress alone, such was the interest.

Books of Historical Dress for Theater and Fancy Dress

The role of historians undertaking research for theater costume and fancy dress purposes has been central to the development of fashion history since the eighteenth century. Thomas Hope's *Costumes of the Ancients* in 1809 was planned as a designer's dictionary, for "the theatrical performer, the ornamental architect and every other artist to whom the knowledge of classical costume is necessary." James Robinson Planché, the major early nineteenth-century British costume historian, not only republished volumes of Strutt but made the first attempt to design historically accurate costumes for a Shakespearean play in 1823. His 1834 *History of British Costume* became the first really popular costume history book, republished in cheaper versions in 1849 and in 1893.

Nineteenth-Century French Histories

In France, Camille Bonnard's *Costume historique des XIIe, XIIIe, XIVe et XVe siecles*, published in Paris by A. Levy fils in 1829–1830, became an important Pre-Raphaelite costume source book. Paris produced, too, Le Comte Horace de Viel-Castel's *Collection des costumes, armes, et meubles*, in four volumes, 1827–1845. Paul Lacroix's long list of publications includes his ten-volume *Costumes historiques de France* published from 1852. Laver declared that Raphael Jacquemin's *Iconographie du costume du IVe–XIXe siècle*, produced in three folio volumes in Paris between 1863 and 1869, was "superb and scholarly." In 1881, Augustin Challamel produced his *Histoire de la mode en France* translated into English and published in 1882 by Sampson Low, Marston, Searle and Rivington. In 1888, Firmin Didot published Auguste Racinet's famous and expensively produced six-volume *Le costume historique*.

Fashion, Sociology, and Psychology

While these early generations of descriptive dress history studies, all by male writers, laid the foundation stones of fashion history, it took Thorstein Veblen's *Theory of the Leisure Class* (1899) and George Simmel's *Philosophie der Mode* (1905) to launch lasting theoretical debate about the cultural meanings behind fashion development and the causes of variation in consumption patterns. Interestingly, however, their theories made virtually no impact on fashion history until at least sixty years after their publication. A selection drawn from the many new dress history books of the 1900 to 1930 period, including George Clinch's book *English Costume, from Prehistoric Times to the End of the Eighteenth Century*, for example, of 1909, showed little change from established antiquarian approaches. *Modes and Manners of the Nineteenth Century* by Oscar Fischel and Max von Boehn is a four-volume German study of fashion from the 1790s onward, first published in 1909, which used a lively choice of cartoons as well as the usual fashion plates. Hilaire Hiler's *From Nudity to Raiment* in 1929 took a painter's interest in the field. With M. Meyer, he produced one of two meticulous costume bibliographies of the 1930s. Theirs was a *Bibliography of Costume*, published by H. W. Wilson in 1939. This followed René Colas's *Bibliographie genérale du costume et la mode* of 1933. These carefully researched books were basically descriptive with little detailed study of garments.

Early Object-Centered Dress History

Elisabeth McClellan's unusually progressive study of 1904, however, *Historic Dress in America*, took markedly different approaches. It examined clothing worn in Spanish, French, English, Dutch, Swedish, and German settlements in early North America. This study, little discussed in the early 2000s, is remarkable on several counts. First it was written by a woman; and second, the author worked from a strongly object-based approach, declaring that "some relics of by-gone days have been preserved intact and placed in our hands for the preparation of this book—veritable documents of history on the subject of dress in America" (McClellan 1904, p. 5). Exceptional for studies of this period, hers took care to include everyday working clothes, such as her "Woman in Typical Working Dress 1790–1800" drawn from an original garment from the Stenton house in Philadelphia.

The second, major object-focused study is now a forgotten book by the painter Talbot Hughes, whose dress collection was accepted by the Victoria and Albert Museum in 1913. In that same year, interested in dress history for his own genre paintings, he published his *Dress Design—an account of Costume for Artists and Dressmakers—Illustrated by the author from old examples*. The book is illustrated with little line drawings, photographs, and even cutting patterns of surviving clothes from the mid-sixteenth century through the 1870s (Taylor, *Establishing Dress History*, pp. 47–49). Thalassa Cruso, the first cos-

tume curator at the Museum of London, basically a social history museum, also pioneered object-based fashion history. Her ideas were published in the museum's first dress catalog in 1933. She was probably the first woman costume curator to fuse theories related to issues of fashion production and consumption with close garment study.

The Psychology of Dress

The psychology of dress opened up further debates about the functions of dress and fashion. These debates were taken up by Frank Alvah Parsons in New York, whose study of that name was published in 1920, by J. C. Flügel, in his study *The Psychology of Clothes* of 1930, and in the work in England of the dress historians C. W. Cunnington and James Laver from the 1930s.

Thus by 1933, three diverging approaches to the study of fashion were in place—the descriptive, somewhat social history–oriented methods; object-focused research conducted largely but not exclusively by women curators; and the more detached, theoretical approaches developed by male specialists. These divisions remained firmly in place for another fifty years.

The Men Dress Historians

Drawing on Flügel, Dr. C. W. Cunnington, a medical doctor, and James Laver, Keeper of Prints and Drawings at the Victoria and Albert Museum, both took a deep interest in fashion history and in issues of women, style and sexuality, and fashion. Between 1931 and the late 1960s, they published books that successfully opened dress history to a wider popular audience. James Laver produced over fifty books dealing with art, prints, social, theater, and dress history. He understood well the problem of explaining the ephemeral character of fashion to those who still continued to dismiss the field as culturally worthless, defining fashion as "a spear head of taste, or rather it is a kind of psychic weathercock which shows which way the wind blows" (J. Laver 1945, p. 211). Laver's very real understanding of the creative and commercial processes of fashion were coupled with a detailed interest in social history and a profound knowledge of dress history. He died in 1975. By then, through lectures and radio and TV appearances, he had become the popular, articulate public face of British dress history. The Cunningtons' most lasting work was based on object analysis, though C. W. Cunnington also wrote up his own theories on women's motivation for wearing fashionable dress, now considered outdated (Taylor, *Establishing Dress History*, pp. 51–57).

The Women Fashion Historians

It is in this period too that women historians finally make their mark. It is significant within the history of the development of feminine approaches that they chose object-based approaches, much like those of Elizabeth McClellan and Thalassa Cruso. Directional, object-centered publications in the 1940s by Doris Langley Moore and from the 1950s onward by Anne Buck created methodological approaches that have remained lastingly valid.

Doris Langley Moore, whose personal costume collection formed the basis of the now famous Museum of Costume in Bath, published two much-neglected books: *The Woman in Fashion* of 1949 and *The Child in Fashion* of 1953. Using her own collection, these explored fashionable dress from 1800 on photographed on live models, (her famous actress and theater friends and their children) with carefully correct period hairstyles and in period settings. While this method of illustration is no longer used because of the danger to the garments, both her books contain directional debate that sought to explode popular sartorial myths, such that Regency dress was transparent and that Victorian women had tiny waists. Attacking Flügel and C. W. Cunnington for an overemphasis on women's sexuality as the most significant motivation for wearing fashionable dress, Langley Moore addressed the social and cultural codes hidden within fashionable dress, avoiding the trap of class generalization that Fischel and von Boehn and Cunnington fell into.

C. W. Cunnington's wife, Phillis, also a doctor, who had worked with him on the famous *Handbook* series, began, after his death in 1961, to collaborate with new researchers. Thus, she began producing a now-famous and well-reputed series of dealing with specialist dress histories, including her seminal study *Costume for Births, Marriages and Deaths.*

Anne Buck, as the first Keeper of the Gallery of English Costume at Platt Hall, from 1947 to 1972 quickly established an object-based approach that emphasized both the social function of dress and professional museological methods of conservation and display of clothing artifacts. This exerted a seminal influence in the dress history world after the 1950s. Her meticulously researched publications fused close analysis of clothing examples with archival study and are classic examples of "good practice." Her range of special interests included smocks and English lace making. In 1961 she published her *Victorian Costume and Costume Accessories* and in 1965, *Children's Costume in England from the Fourteenth to the end of the Nineteenth Centuries* (republished in 1996) and *Dress in Eighteenth Century England* of 1979. Once retired and with more time for archival research, she published a series of articles that incorporated new consumption approaches. That Buck centered her work on object-based approaches was rare enough, but rarer still is that her enthusiasms and expertise embraced the clothes of all levels of society.

Another group of women fashion historians developed the work of Talbot Hughes, studying surviving clothing through analysis of the cut and making up garments and specializing in producing cutting patterns of period clothing. Nora Waugh taught theater wardrobe design at the Central School of Arts and Crafts in London. She published *Corsets and Crinolines* in 1954, *The Cut of Men's Clothes* in 1964, and *The Cut of Women's Clothes* in 1969. Based on patterns drawn up from surviving garments, Waugh added details of style history and making up details but was vague on many sources.

This methodology was further developed by Janet Arnold and explained in her *Handbook of Costume* of 1973. Arnold spent a lifetime exploring dress history through meticulous analysis of the cut of male and female fashionable dress. She was frequently called on by museums on both sides of the Atlantic to advise on dating reconstructing damaged period clothing and often advised on film and theater productions.

New Approaches from the 1980s

From the 1980s, a great range of more open-minded theoretical approaches, derived from other academic fields, transformed the entire field of fashion history study These included analysis of the semiotics of fashion, new approaches to the coded body (fashionable, subcultural, and male/female, and gay/lesbian). Elizabeth Wilson's work is cited by many as seminal to the acceptance of "fashion" as a legitimate field of study. Wilson's *Adorned in Dreams* of 1985 (revised in 2003), which included a celebration of the enjoyment that women can derive on their own terms from fashionable dress, was a turning point. From the 1980s, interest in fashion history blossomed through new critical approaches flowing out from the developing fields of cultural and gender studies. These have had a dramatic impact on fashion history research as reflected since 1997 in the pages of *Fashion Theory: The Journal of Dress, Body and Culture*, founded and edited by Valerie Steele.

Object-Focused Study

Older, established fashion history methodologies have had to respond to these fresh approaches and have held their ground. Naomi Tarrant, of the Royal Museums of Scotland, Edinburgh, in her 1994 book, *The Development of Costume* stressed her conviction that artifact-based approaches remained a vital counterweight to theoretical analysis. Museum fashion history exhibitions in North America and across Europe spawned significantly new types of glossy yet informative and critical shows and catalogs, such as Richard Martin's and Harold Koda's study of orientalism and fashion at the Costume Institute of the Metropolitan Museum of Art in 1994. *Radical Fashion*, curated by Claire Wilcox at the Victoria and Albert Museum in London, placed contemporary radical couture and conceptual dress in front of the British public for the first time. Other "designer" exhibitions and catalogs have sparked debate about an overly close relationship between museums and global fashion companies through much-needed financial sponsorship. Some suggest that as the fashion world itself relies more and more on celebrity product endorsement, fashion history too must respond to the commercial and cultural realities that surround the fashion world in the early 2000s.

Studies on Fashion Designers

The history of the haute couture industry is thus subject to more intensive debate than ever before and studies now move far beyond the usual coffee-table books. Alexandra Palmer's *Couture and Commerce*, for example, is a seminal example of these new approaches. This beautifully illustrated study details the processes of the designing, making, and retailing of Paris couture clothes, as well as their social consumption and cultural meanings to Toronto society in the 1950s.

Conceptual Fashion

The advent of conceptual fashion has triggered new analytical debate in studies by, for example, Caroline Evans, Jennifer Craik, Richard Martin, Joanne Entwhistle, and Christopher Breward. The journal *Fashion Theory*, too, has been at the forefront of these developments. Breward writes that "the self constructed role of radical fashion design seems to be to present a very specialized commentary on the vicissitudes of contemporary taste and aesthetics, everything to do with internal fashion culture debate about genre, hierarchy, presentation and style" to be "showcased rather than sold" (Breward 2003, p. 229). Finally, Caroline Evans's seminal 2003 study *Fashion at the Edge* debates conceptual and couture fashion from the 1990s, using fashion development as a tool through which to "pathologize contemporary culture" and to examine its characteristics of "alienation and nihilism." She discusses conceptual and couture fashion as "a form of catharsis, perhaps a form of mourning and a coping stratagem. . . [It is] the dark side of a free market economy, the loosening of social controls, the rise of risk and uncertainty as key elements of 'modernity' and 'globalization.' She writes, "The dark history of twentieth century seems finally to have caught up with fashion design" (Evans 2003, p. 308–309).

Thus, fashion studies and fashion history are fields that positively incorporate critical approaches built around anthropology, psychology, history of technology, business, sociology, material culture, and cultural studies. The best examples of good practice are also finally filled with impressive color plates and intelligently fuse object and theory. It is serious debates such as these that confirm the fundamental and central cultural place of fashion within society and that clarify the future directions for the field of fashion history and fashion studies.

See also **Ancient World: History of Dress; Appearance; Fashion, Theories of.**

BIBLIOGRAPHY
The sections on the history of fashion publications are drawn from chapters 1 and 2 of Lou Taylor, *Establishing Dress History*, 2004, Manchester University Press, with their kind permission.

Arnold, Janet. *A Handbook of Costume*. London: Macmillan, 1973.

Bertin, Célia. *Paris à la Mode: A Voyage of Discovery*. London: Gollancz, 1956.

Breward, Christopher. *The Hidden Consumer: Masculinities, Fashion and City Life 1860–1914*. Manchester, U.K.: Manchester University Press, 1999.

———. *Fashion*. Oxford: Oxford University Press, 2003.

Buck, Anne. *Victorian Costume and Costume Accessories*. London: Jenkins, 1961.

———. *Thomas Lester, His Lace and the East Midlands Industry 1820–1905*. Bedford: Ruth Bean, 1981.

Craik, Jennifer. *The Face of Fashion: Cultural Studies in Fashion*. London and New York: Routledge, 1994.

Cunnington, Cecil Willett. *English Women's Clothing in the Nineteenth Century*. London: Faber, 1937.

———. *Handbook of English Costume in the Eighteenth Century*. London: Faber, 1957.

———. *Handbook of English Costume in the Nineteenth Century*. London: Faber, 1959.

Cunnington, Phillis. *Costume for Births, Marriages and Deaths*. London: Adam and Charles Black, 1972.

Entwistle, Joanne, and Elizabeth Wilson, eds. *Body Dressing*. Oxford: Berg, 2001.

Evans, Caroline. *Fashion at the Edge: Spectacle, Modernity and Deathliness*. New Haven, Conn., and London: Yale University Press, 2003.

Evans, Caroline, and Minna Thornton. *Women and Fashion: A New Look*. London: Quartet, 1989.

Davis, Fred. *Fashion Culture and Identity*. Chicago: University of Chicago Press, 1994.

Flügel, John Carl. *The Psychology of Clothes*. London: Hogarth Press Institute of Psycho-Analysis, 1930.

Habitus Praecipuorum Populorum tam Virorum quam Feminarum Singulari Arte Depicti. Nuremberg, Germany: Hans Weigel, 1577.

Langley Moore, Doris. *The Woman in Fashion*. London: B. T. Batsford, Ltd., 1949.

———. *The Child in Fashion*. London: B. T. Batsford, Ltd., 1953.

Laver, James. *Taste and Fashion*. London: Harrap, London, 1937. Reprint, London: G. G. Harrap, 1945.

———. *Costume and Fashion: A Concise History*. London: Thames and Hudson, Inc., 1982. Reprint, New York: Thames and Hudson, Inc., 1995.

Martin, Richard, and Harold Koda. *Orientalism and Fashion: Visions of the East in Western Dress*. New York: Metropolitan Museum of Art, 1994.

McClellan, Elisabeth. *Historic Dress in America, 1607–1800*. Philadelphia: George W. Jacobs and Company, 1904.

Palmer, Alexandra. *Couture and Commerce: The Transatlantic Fashion Trade in the 1950s*. Vancouver, Canada: University of British Columbia Press, 2001.

Parsons, Frank Alvah. *The Psychology of Dress*. New York: Doubleday, Page; London: B. T. Batsford, Ltd., 1920.

Planché, J. R. *History of British Costume*. London: George Bell, 1893.

Steele, Valerie. *Paris Fashion: A Cultural History.* New York and Oxford: Oxford University Press, 1988.

———. *The Corset: A Cultural History.* New Haven, Conn., and London: Yale University Press, 2001.

Strutt, Joseph. *A Complete View of the Manners, Customs, Arms, Habits etc. of the Inhabitants of England* (1774, 1775, and 1776) and *Complete View of the Dress and Habits of the People of England,* 1796 and 1799.

Tarrant, Naomi. *The Development of Costume.* London: Routledge, 1994.

Taylor, Lou. *The Study of Dress History.* Manchester, U.K.: Manchester University Press, 2002.

Troy, Nancy. *Couture Culture: A Study in Modern Art and Fashion.* Cambridge, Mass., and London: MIT Press, 2002.

Veblen, Thorstein. *Theory of the Leisure Class.* New York: Macmillan, 1899.

Wilcox, Claire. *Radical Fashion.* London: Victoria and Albert Museum, 2001.

Wilson, Elizabeth. *Adorned in Dreams: Fashion and Modernity.* New ed. London: I. B. Tauris, 2003.

Lou Taylor

FASHION, THEORIES OF Fashion involves change, novelty, and the context of time, place, and wearer. Blumer (1969) describes fashion influence as a process of "collective selection" whereby the formation of taste derives from a group of people responding collectively to the zeitgeist or "spirit of the times." The simultaneous introduction and display of many new styles, the selections made by the innovative consumer, and the notion of the expression of the spirit of the times provide impetus for fashion. Central to any definition of fashion is the relationship between the designed product and how it is distributed and consumed.

Fashion systems model. The study of fashion in the twentieth century has been framed in terms of a fashion systems model with a distinct center from which innovations and modifications radiate outward (Davis 1992). Designers work from the premise of one look, one image for all, with rules about hem lengths and what to wear with what. In this model, the fashion-consuming public develops from an innovative central core, surrounded by receptive bands of fashion consumers radiating outward from the center.

Within this system innovation can originate from a select grouping of designers, such as Christian Dior who introduced the "New Look" in 1947. Influential factors can range from individual tastes, to current events, to marketing and sales promotions. The ultimate qualifier of the fashion systems model is the scope of influence, urging, even demanding, one look for all. The element of conformity is instrumental.

Populist model. An alternative model to the fashion systems model is the "populist" model. This model is characterized as polycentric, where groups based upon differences of age, socioeconomic status, location, and culture create their own fashion. Such groups might include teenagers in a certain school or senior citizens in a retirement community. Polhemus (1994) describes "styletribes" as a distinct cultural segment that generates a distinctive style of dress and decoration. Such "styletribes" may create their own looks from combining existing garments, creating their own custom colors by tie-dyeing or painting, mixing and matching from previously worn and recycled clothing available in thrift shops and vintage markets. They are not so concerned with one style of dressing as with expressing themselves, though there is an element of conformity that derives from the processes used and the resulting social behavior. Polhemus reflects that such "styletribes" have flourished at "precisely that time in history when individuality and personal freedom have come to be seen as the defining features of our age" (p.14).

The Flow of Fashion
The distribution of fashion has been described as a movement, a flow, or trickle from one element of society to another. The diffusion of influences from center to periphery may be conceived of in hierarchical or in horizontal terms, such as the trickle-down, trickle-across, or trickle-up theories.

Trickle down. The oldest theory of distribution is the trickle-down theory described by Veblen in 1899. To function, this trickle-down movement depends upon a hierarchical society and a striving for upward mobility among the various social strata. In this model, a style is first offered and adopted by people at the top strata of society and gradually becomes accepted by those lower in the strata (Veblen; Simmel; Laver). This distribution model assumes a social hierarchy in which people seek to identify with the affluent and those at the top seek both distinction and, eventually, distance from those socially below them. Fashion is considered a vehicle of conspicuous consumption and upward mobility for those seeking to copy styles of dress. Once the fashion is adopted by those below, the affluent reject that look for another.

Trickle across. Proponents of the trickle-across theory claim that fashion moves horizontally between groups on similar social levels (King; Robinson). In the trickle-across model, there is little lag time between adoption from one group to another. Evidence for this theory occurs when designers show a look simultaneously at prices ranging from the high end to lower end ready-to-wear. Robinson (1958) supports the trickle-across theory when he states that any social group takes its cue from contiguous groups in the social stratum. King (1963) cited reasons for this pattern of distribution, such as rapid mass communications, promotional efforts of manufacturers and retailers, and exposure of a look to all fashion leaders.

Trickle up. The trickle-up or bubble-up pattern is the newest of the fashion movement theories. In this theory the innovation is initiated from the street, so to speak, and adopted from lower income groups. The innovation eventually flows to upper-income groups; thus the movement is from the bottom up.

Examples of the trickle-up theory of fashion distribution include a very early proponent, Chanel, who believed fashion ideas originated from the streets and then were adopted by couture designers. Many of the ideas she pursued were motivated by her perception of the needs of women for functional and comfortable dress. Following World War II the young discovered Army/Navy surplus stores and began to wear pea jackets and khaki pants. Another category of clothing, the T-shirt, initially worn by laborers as a functional and practical undergarment, has since been adopted universally as a casual outer garment and a message board.

Thus how a fashionable look permeates a given society depends upon its origins, what it looks like, the extent of its influence, and the motivations of those adopting the look. The source of the look may originate in the upper levels of a society, or the street, but regardless of origin, fashion requires an innovative, new look.

Product Innovation

A new look may be the result of innovations in the products of dress, the way they are put together, or the type of behavior elicited by the manner of dressing. A fashionable look involves the form of clothing on the human body and its potential for meaning (DeLong 1998). Meaning can derive from the product, but meaning can also develop from ways of wearing the product, or from the body itself (Entwistle 2000). Fashionable dress embodies the latest aesthetic and what is defined as desirable at a given moment.

Lehmann (2000) describes fashion as a random creation that dies as an innovation is born. He views fashion as contradictory, both defining the ancient and contemporary by randomly quoting from the past as well as representing the present. Robinson (1958) defines fashion as pursuing novelty for its own sake. Lipovetsky (1994) claims that determining factors in fashion are the quest for novelty and the excitement of aesthetic play, while Roche (1994) describes fashion as dynamic change.

Though fashion implies continual change, certain products have persisted over long periods of time, such as blue jeans, which were made a staple of dressing in the United States in the twentieth century. Though blue jeans are a recognizable form, there is the potential for great variety in the product details, including stone washing, dyeing, painting, tearing, and fraying. Blue jeans epitomize the growth of casual fashion and endure because they can change to resonate with the times.

The way products are combined can define a fashionable look. For example, the idea of buying "separates" to mix and match instead of buying complete ensembles has increased the separate purchases of jackets, trousers, shirts, or blouses. The advent of the concept of separates coincided with the advent of the desired casual look. Mass production of sizes began to reflect a "one size fits all" model of fitting; more consumers could be fitted by choosing among the separate parts than would occur with the purchase of an ensemble with head-to-toe sizing requirements. Acceptance of separates and the growth of leisure was accompanied by a profound change, reflecting the restructuring of consumer societies and an increase in non-work lifestyles (Craik, p. 217).

The Fashion Life Cycle

An innovation is perceived as having a life cycle, that is, it is born, matures, and dies. Rogers's (1983) classic writing spells out rate of change, including characteristics of the product, the market, or audience, the distribution cycle, and those characteristics of individuals and societies where innovation takes place.

Diffusion of innovations. Diffusion is the spread of an innovation within and across social systems. Rogers (1983) defines an innovation as a design or product perceived as new by an individual. New styles are offered each season and whether an innovation is accepted depends upon the presence of five characteristics:

1. Relative advantage is the degree an innovation is seen as better than previous alternatives, in areas such as function, cost, social prestige, or more satisfying aesthetics.
2. Compatibility is the degree to which an innovation is consistent with the existing norms and values of the potential adopters. An innovation is less likely to be adopted that requires a change in values.
3. Complexity concerns how difficult it is to learn about and understand the innovation. An innovation has a greater chance of acceptance if easily learned and experienced.
4. Trialability is the extent to which an innovation may be tested with a limited commitment, that is, easily and inexpensively tried without too much risk.
5. Observability is the ease with which an innovation may be communicated to others.

The individual's role. The fashion adoption process results from individuals making a decision to purchase and wear a new fashion. Rogers (1983) suggests that this process involves five basic stages: awareness, interest, evaluation, trial, and adoption. The individual becomes aware of the fashion, takes an interest in it, and evaluates it as having some relative advantage that could range from a new fabric technology or simply as being consistent with self concept or what one's friends are wearing. If the individual evaluates the fashion positively, the process proceeds to trial and adoption.

The study of the pattern of consumers' adoption of a fashion is often represented by a bell-shaped curve. The life cycle of a specific fashion represented graphically indicates duration, rate of adoption, and level of acceptance.

The graph depicts the rate and time involved in the diffusion process, with the horizontal axis indicating the time and the vertical axis indicating the number of adopters or users (Sproles and Burns 1994). Such graphically portrayed data can be used to calculate the level of acceptance for a fashion. For example, the curve for a fashion that is rapidly adopted but also rapidly declines will show early growth and quick recession. The curve resulting from plotting the data in this way leads to characteristic patterns of fashion adoption, applicable for fads or classics. The graph is also useful to identify type of consumer in terms of when each adopts a fashion within its life cycle. The consumer who adopts the fashion at the beginning of the curve is an innovator or opinion leader; at the peak, a mass-market consumer; after the peak, a laggard or isolate.

Fashion leaders and followers. Theories of fashion distribution all have in common the identification of leaders and followers. The fashion leader often transmits a particular look by first adopting it and then communicating it to others. Fashion followers include large numbers of consumers who accept and wear the merchandise that has been visually communicated to them.

A distinction exists between the role of the innovator and leader. The leader is not necessarily creator of the fashion or the first to wear it. The leader seeks distinction and dares to be different by wearing what the innovator presents as new. By adopting the look, the leader influences the flow or distribution of fashion. But the innovator within a group is also influential in serving as the visual communicator of the style. Historically the leader has been influential in some desirable way and possible leaders include athletes, movie stars, royalty, presidents, or fashion models.

Characteristics and Influencing Factors

Basic tensions addressed by fashion in Western culture are status, gender, occasion, the body, and social regulation. Craik (1994) suggests potential fashion instabilities, such as youth versus age; masculinity versus femininity; androgyny versus singularity; inclusiveness versus exclusiveness; and work versus play (p. 204). Fashion systems generally establish means for self-formation through dress, decoration, and gesture that attempt to regulate such tensions, conflicts, and ambiguities.

Social change and fashion. Social change is defined as a succession of events that replace existing societal patterns with new ones over time. This process is pervasive and can modify roles of men and women, lifestyles, family structures, and functions. Fashion theorists believe that fashion is a reflection of social, economic, political, and cultural changes, but also that fashion expresses modernity and symbolizes the spirit of the times (Lehmann, 2000; Blumer 1969; Laver 1937). Fashion both reflects and expresses the specific time in history.

The tension of youth versus age has influenced dress in the twentieth century. The trend has been toward separate fashionable images for the younger and older consumer, especially with the burgeoning baby population that followed World War II. Fashions for the young have tended to take on a life of their own, especially with the parade of retro looks of the last decades of the twentieth century that increasingly borrow images of recent time periods. Roach-Higgins (1995) reasons that because fashionable dress requires an awareness of change in the forms of dress within one's lifetime, the older consumer who has experienced that look before may choose not to participate (Roach-Higgins, Eicher, and Johnson, p. 395).

How one dresses for work and play has changed over time. A persistent trend of the twentieth century has been toward coveting leisure time coupled with an increasing need to look leisurely. Wearing casual clothing and leisurewear increased in the 1950s because families moved to the suburbs and engaged in many outdoor activities and sports. Clothing for spectator sports has increased, as has clothing for participation in many sports, such as tennis, golf, jogging, cycling, skiing, and rock climbing. In the 1970s the number of women who adopted pantsuits encouraged the trend to more casual dressing. In the 1990s the workplace was infiltrated by casual dress on Fridays. The formal-informal nature of dress reflects how much importance is placed on dress for work and play, but also the ambiguity and tension involved.

Appearance and identity. Clothes are fundamental to the modern consumer's sense of identity. That criticism of one's clothing and appearance is taken more personally and intensely than criticism of one's car or house suggests a high correlation between appearance and personal identity (Craik, p. 206).

People may buy a new product to identify with a particular group or to express their own personality. Simmel (1904) explained this dual tendency of conformity and individuality, reasoning that the individual found pleasure in dressing for self-expression, but at the same time gained support from dressing similarly to others. Flügel (1930) interpreted paradox using the idea of superior and inferior, that is, an individual strives to be like others when they seem superior but unlike them when they seem inferior. In this way fashion can provide identity, both as an emblem of hierarchy and equalizer of appearance.

Whether or not fashion and the way products are combined upon the body can be considered as a visual language has been a source of discussion in recent years. Barthes (1983) insists that fashion be perceived as a system, a network of relationships. Davis (1992) concludes that it is better to consider fashion as a code and not as a language, but a code that includes expression of such fundamental aspects of an individual as age, sex, status, occupation, and interest in fashion.

Culture, observer, and wearer. Fashion favors the critical gaze of the knowing observer, or the one "in the know," and the wearer who arranges the body for his own delight and enjoyment. Perceptions of the observer and wearer of fashion are sharpened based upon the many potential variations in lines, shapes, textures, and colors. For example, clothing of French inspiration and origin emphasized contour and cut of dress historically. Fashion changes occurred in the layout of the garment, which in turn focused attention on the silhouette and details, such as bias cutting and shaping (DeLong 1998). In contrast, societies where traditional dress has been worn, Korea, for example, fashion in traditional dress has derived more from the colors, motifs, and patterns adorning the surfaces, with the layout of the garments holding relatively constant. Thus subtle meaning derives not from the proportions of the *chogore* and *chima*, but from the variations found in the treatment of the surfaces (Geum and DeLong 1992).

Dress, agency, and popular culture. Popular culture can be defined loosely as those elements of entertainment that run alongside, within, and often counter to the elite structures of society. In the seventeenth century civilizing agents of aristocratic society included courtly entertainment, tournament, masque ball, and opera. But at the same time, popular culture became subject to increasing entrepreneurial control and commodification, with widening appeal to the urban merchant class (Breward 1995, p.97).

A new conception of popular culture was pertinent to the potential of dress as a communicator of social distinction and belonging. This movement preceded and contributed to the consumer and technological revolutions of the eighteenth century. Today popular culture is enhanced by the influence of mass media, and the medium has become the message, in many ways. According to Wilson (1985), fashion has become the connective tissue of the cultural organism and is essential to the world of mass communication, spectacle, and modernity.

Pursuit of modernity. Fashion is an accessible and flexible means of expressing modernity. The fashionable body has been associated with the city as a locus of social interaction and display (Breward, p. 35; Steele 1998). In the nineteenth century fashion was identified with a sense of contradiction of old and new. Modernity resulted in part from new technologies and a sense of the modern resulting from new ideas of design and consumption. Tensions from a growing commodification of fashionable trends emphasized the worldly and metropolitan. In the twentieth century modernity was identified through various but subtle means, from the way the dress contoured the body, to obvious product branding.

As a means of expressing modernity, Western fashions have been adopted by non-Western societies. In some societies where traditional styles of dress were prevalent, the men were quick to adopt Western business suits. Women have been slower to adopt Western dress in favor of traditional styles that express historical continuity. This creates an ambivalent message related to gender: Are women excluded from the modern world or

are they simply the purveyors of tradition? Traditional dress in South Korea is more often seen on older women on occasions of celebration (Geum and DeLong). Both Chinese men and women have been encouraged recently to adopt Western styles of dress (Wilson 1985).

Gender and dress. A tension exists when women have been assigned the dual role of being fashionable as well as the subordinate gender (Breward 1995). In the last two centuries fashion has been primarily assigned to women, and it follows that fashionable dress and the beautification of the self could be perceived as expressions of subordination. Male dress has been somewhat overlooked. Veblen (1899) in the nineteenth century described separate spheres of the male and female, with feminine sartorial dress as a symbol of enforced leisure and masculine dress a symbol of power. Display and appearance of the body were considered innately feminine pursuits and thus the model was constructed in which overt interest in clothing appearance implied a tendency toward unmanliness and effeminacy. This gave rise to ultra-conservative, non-expressive male dress codes that prioritized the uniformity of the city suit as the model for respectable middle classes for males in most of the nineteenth and twentieth centuries (Breward, p. 170). This model does not entirely explain the way men consumed fashion, for example, the aesthete of the 1880s and dandy of the 1890s.

Such expressions of difference in gender roles and fashionable appearances of men and women also occur in other historical periods. Within medieval culture, the display of masculinity and femininity varied according to class, age, wealth, and nationality. Clothing, fashionably cut, moved toward overt display of the body and its sexual characteristics (Breward, p. 32). Interpretations of a male and female ideal permeated visual and literary interpretations of the human body. The male ideal focused upon proportion, strength, nobility, and grace; the female ideal included diminutive size, delicacy, and heightened color.

In medieval society, concepts of femininity included monopoly on production and maintenance of textiles, clothing, and accessories and the display of patriarchal wealth and status. When the monopoly of women was broken, production of clothing moved from the home to the public sphere. Male-dominated systems of apprenticeships emerged for weavers, cloth cutters, and tailors; the mass production and marketing system was born.

Market Forces and Momentum
The fashion industry has led the way, or followed, depending upon the nature of the fashion and its origins (Wilson 1985). Fashions serve as a reflection of their time and place and can be determined by society, culture, history, economy, lifestyle, and the marketing system. The market for fashion ranges from the world of couture to mass-produced clothing called ready-to-wear.

The couture fashion system and the couturier, who regularly presents a collection of clothing, originated in Paris, France. The couturier caters to the handmade, made-to-measure, exquisite product. In some ways the couturier functions as an artist, but when the product fails that designer ceases to exist. In this way the couturier walks a fine line between artist and industrialist (Baudot, p.11). The dominance of Paris as an international center depends as much on its sophistication as a fashion center as on the superiority of its clothing (Steele 1998).

Other countries beside France have taken on fashion leadership—notably, Italy, the United Kingdom, and the United States—and each country has placed its unique stamp on fashion (Agins 1999). For example, Milan, the hub of the Italian fashion industry is close to the country's leading textile mills in the Lake Como region. The Italians not only produce beautiful fabrics, they also design beautiful clothes as exemplified by such notable talents as Giorgio Armani and Krizia.

Though some may consider fashion frivolous, it is also considered a serious, lucrative business in capitalist society. The United States has been a leader in the technologies required for mass production and mass marketing of apparel, making fashion a democratic possibility, available to all.

Mass production and democratization of clothing. To provide clothing at moderate cost for all citizens took two primary developments, mass production and mass distribution (Kidwell and Christman 1974). Mass production required developing the technology for middle-quality clothing that could be made available for the majority. Mass distribution required the retailing of ready-made clothing and innovations in salesmanship and advertising. Department stores sprang up in every city following the Civil War and by the end of the century, mail-order houses were developed sufficiently to reach all citizens in the United States.

The clothing revolution that occurred in the twentieth century in the United States was a double revolution. The first was the making of clothing, from the homemade and custom-made to the ready-made or factory-made; the second was the wearing of clothing, from clothing of class display where clothing was worn as a sign of social class and occupation, to the clothing of democracy where all could dress alike. According to Kidwell and Christman (1974), in the eighteenth century anyone walking in Philadelphia or Boston could easily have distinguished towns people from country folk by the striking differences in their clothing. Clothing was distinctive because of differences in textiles and clothing construction. America was dependent upon England's textile industry so the rich purchased fine-quality silks, woolens, and cottons while others had limited access to fabrics that were coarse and middle to low grade. The tailor and dressmaker made clothing for the rich and the amateur made clothing for the average person.

In the nineteenth century, the industrial revolution brought the machine, the factory, and new sources of power. A series of great inventions mechanized the making of yarn and cloth. By 1850 machines included the invention and distribution of a practical sewing machine that was quickly adopted for men's shirts and collars and women's cloaks, crinolines, and hoopskirts. By the end of the nineteenth century, machine cutting was standard; pressing became more efficient. Men began to look and dress alike, and the sameness of their dress made multiple production by machine entirely possible.

Ready-made clothing for women lagged behind what was available for men. In 1860 ready-mades for women included only cloaks and mantillas, and dressmakers continued to supply women's fashions. Women of limited income made their own clothing, thus saving their clothing dollars for male family members. The department store and mail order were established means of distribution in the latter half of the nineteenth century.

In the early twentieth century, the mass-manufacturing process was organized and capable of producing clothing for both men and women. Thus was born an industry of industries, each with a system of organization to create ready-made clothing for everyone (Kidwell and Christman 1974). Though fashion always was an identifier of person, mass production equalized every person's opportunity to identify.

Marketing and distribution systems. Entwistle (2000) describes fashion as the product of a chain of activities that includes industrial, economic, cultural, and aesthetic. Changes in production and marketing strategies allowed for the expansion in consumer activity during the second half of the eighteenth century that led to increased consumption and the speeding up of the fashion cycle. This led to an increase in fashions that could be selected to reflect specific and individual circumstances.

In the twentieth century consumer choice was affected by means of mass distribution including chain stores, mail order, and Internet shopping. Chain stores have made fashion accessible within a relatively short drive for most consumers. Mail order has enabled a consumer in a remote area to follow fashion trends, select an appropriate garment, and place an order for ready-made clothing. Internet shopping relies on a person's access to a computer. Chain stores, mail order, and Internet shopping have extended the reach of fashion and created new consumer groups.

A Historical Perspective

Fashion is viewed broadly as a chronology of changing forms and a critique of wider cultural influences and their historical interpretation (Carter 2003; Johnson, Tortore, and Eicher 2003). The history of fashion reveals the importance of changes in appearance, but also the way fashion is conceived, who participates, and for what and how many occasions. The middle years of the fourteenth century have been identified as the first period of significant fashion change, generally related to the rise of mercantile capitalism in European cities (Lipovetsky 1994; Roche 1994; Breward 1995; Tortore and Eubank 1998). At that time, fashion became a practice of prestigious imitation among social groups and changes in tastes occurred often and were extensive enough for people to gain an appetite for new fashions in dress (Lipovetsky 1994; Roche 1994; Breward 1995). With class distinctions on the wane and an accelerated rate of stylistic change, the specific character of dress was associated with gender and the circumstance of different lifestyles. In the history of fashion, modern cultural meanings and values, especially those that elevate newness and the expression of human individuality to positions of dignity have allowed the fashion system to come into being and establish itself (Lipovetsky, p. 5).

The rise of fashion is associated with "the civilizing process" in Europe. The medieval woman engaged in what became the feminine pursuits of weaving, textile work, and fashion. Fashion in medieval society had a direct impact on the emerging of the individual, on self-knowledge, and understanding one's place in the world (Breward, p. 34). The body provided a principal means of expression through clothing; for example, to throw down one's glove was an act of defiance that committed a person to certain actions. The deliberate manipulation of the social meanings attached to clothing helped initiate a heightened sense of the significance of fashion.

Though fashion was first created for the privileged few, in the late nineteenth and twentieth century mass production made fashion accessible to the majority. In the nineteenth century the distinguishing feature of fashion was its imposition of an overall standard that nevertheless left room for the display of personal taste. Fashion change accelerated with major apparel changes occurring in twenty-year intervals.

The twentieth century is characterized as the age of mass production, mass consumption, and mass media. Mass fashion became a form of popular aesthetics and a means of self-enhancement and self-expression. Advances in technology and materials used for clothing production provided more comfortable, cheaper, and more attractive items to a larger proportion of the population. In the early twentieth century, mass consumption of fashionable dress increased within the sphere of fashion promotion and advertising, leading to unlimited diversification. The fashion industry became more complex and fashion intervals shortened to ten years (Tortore and Eubank 1998).

Mass media has allowed for wide dissemination of fashion information and opportunities for the stimulation of a more homogeneous public imagination. The fashion magazine and the Hollywood film brought fashionable models to a hugely expanded audience from the 1920s onward. Examples of fashionable dress were often made available through the expansion of chain stores and mail-order companies. At the same time, a reorganization of business practices, of marketing and advertising, prioritized certain strands of society as fashion leaders. A cult of the designer, revolving around ideals of couture and high fashion or strong subcultural identities, ensured the survival of hierarchies based on notions of quality, style, and individuality (Breward, p. 183).

Steele (2000) surmised that in 1947 when Christian Dior launched his "New Look," it was still possible for a fashion designer to transform the way a woman dressed. The postwar transformation was remarkable, from the war years of boxy shoulders, rectangular torso, and short skirts to the postwar look of narrow shoulders, nipped-in waist, padded hips, and long, full, flowing skirts. You could like it or hate it, but the look was the fashion, regardless (Steele 2000, p. 7).

Today major fashion changes occur frequently, but the choices and selections have increased so that mainstream fashion is one choice among many, including recycled clothing, vintage clothing, and wearable art. Also the easily recognizable rules of fashion, such as rigid proportions, hem lengths, and silhouettes now relate more to the particular look of one group than to a fashionable look for all. Agins (1999) has declared the end of fashion, but only as it has been known historically.

See also **Fashion, Historical Studies of; Trickle-Down.**

BIBLIOGRAPHY

Agins, T. *The End of Fashion.* New York: William Morrow, 1999.

Barthes, R. *The Fashion System.* New York: Hill and Wang; Farrar, Straus, and Giroux, 1983.

Baudot, F. *Fashion, The Twentieth Century.* New York: Universe, 1999.

Benedict, R. "Dress." *Encyclopedia of the Social Sciences.* New York: Macmillan, 1931.

Blumer, H. "Fashion: From Class Differentiation to Collective Selection." *The Sociological Quarterly* 10, no. 3 (1969): 275–291.

Brannon, E. *Fashion Forecasting.* New York: Fairchild Publications, 2000.

Breward, C. *The Culture of Fashion.* Manchester, U.K.: Manchester University Press, 1995.

Carter, M. *Fashion Classics: From Carlyle to Barthes.* Oxford: Berg, 2003.

Craik, J. *The Face of Fashion.* New York: Routledge, 1994.

Davis, F. *Fashion, Culture, and Identity.* Chicago: University of Chicago Press, 1992.

DeLong, M. *The Way We Look, Dress and Aesthetics.* 2nd ed. New York: Fairchild Publications, 1998.

Entwistle, J. *The Fashioned Body, Fashion, Dress and Modern Social Theory.* Cambridge, Mass.: Polity Press, 2000.

Flügel, J. *The Psychology of Clothes.* London: Hogarth Press, 1930.

Geum, K., and M. DeLong. "Korean Traditional Dress as an Expression of Heritage." *Dress* 19 (1992): 57–68.

Johnson, K., S. Tortore, and J. Eicher. *Fashion Foundations: Early Writings on Fashion and Dress.* Oxford: Berg, 2003.

Kidwell, C., and M. Christman. *Suiting Everyone: The Democratization of Clothing in America*. Washington, D.C.: Smithsonian Institution Press, 1974.

King, C. "Fashion Adoption: A Rebuttal to the 'Trickle Down' Theory." In *Toward Scientific Marketing*. Edited by S. Greyser. Chicago: American Marketing Association, 1963.

Laver, J. *The Concise History of Costume and Fashion*. New York: Harry N. Abrams, 1969.

Lehmann, U. *Tigersprung: Fashion in Modernity*. Cambridge, Mass.: MIT Press, 2000.

Lipovetsky, G. *The Empire of Fashion*. Princeton, N.J.: Princeton University Press, 1994.

McCracken, G. "Meaning Manufacture and Movement in the World of Goods." In *Culture and Consumption*. Bloomington: Indiana University Press, 1988.

Nystrom, P. *Economics of Fashion*. New York: Ronald Press, 1928.

Polhemus, T. *Streetstyle: From Sidewalk to Catwalk*. London: Thames and Hudson, Inc., 1994.

Roach-Higgins, M. E. "Awareness: Requisite to Fashion." In *Dress and Identity*. Edited by M. E. Roach-Higgins, J. Eicher, and K. Johnson. New York: Fairchild Publications, 1995.

Robinson, D. "The Rules of Fashion Cycles." *Harvard Business Review* (November–December 1958).

——. "Style Changes: Cyclical, Inexorable, and Foreseeable." *Harvard Business Review* 53 (November–December 1975): 121–131.

Roche, D. *The Culture of Clothing*. Translated by J. Birrell. Cambridge, U.K.: Cambridge University Press, 1994.

Rogers, E. *Diffusion of Innovations*. 4th ed. New York: Free Press, 1995.

Simmel, G. "Fashion." *International Quarterly* 10 (1904): 130–155.

Sproles, G., and L. Burns. *Changing Appearances*. New York: Fairchild Publications. 1994.

Steele, V. *Paris Fashion: A Cultural History*. Rev. ed. Oxford: Berg, 1998.

——. "Fashion: Yesterday, Today and Tomorrow." In *The Fashion Business*. Edited by N. White and I. Griffiths. Oxford: Berg, 2000.

Tortore, P., and K. Eubank. *Survey of Historic Costume*. 3rd ed. New York: Fairchild Publications, 1998.

Veblen, T. *The Theory of the Leisure Class*. New York: Macmillan, 1899.

Wilson, E. *Adorned in Dreams: Fashion and Modernity*. London: Virago Press, 1985.

Marilyn Revell DeLong

FASHION ADVERTISING Fashion advertisements have their own stylistic modes and spheres of production and consumption, involving the interrelationship of word and image among other things. Yet, technological and social changes in clothing and retailing, and the impact of class, gender, and race politics, also have to be taken into account. Early forms of fashion promotion that originated in the eighteenth century, for example, overlapped with the rise of urban culture and shopping and embraced diverse forms of promotion, some of which we might not strictly recognize today as advertising. In the first instance, the majority of retailers regarded the creation of an enticing shop façade and interior as sufficient means for attracting and establishing a suitable clientele. This would subsequently be complemented by the circulation of handbills and trade cards, and to a lesser extent by press advertising, all of which were used to reinforce the reputation of the shop in question rather than to publicize the sale of particular wares. In the *London Evening Post* for 24 April 1741, for example, the haberdasher John Stanton placed an advertisement, not to tell the public about the goods he sold but to inform them of a change of trading address. Otherwise, newspaper advertisements were occasionally used by large-scale retailers and manufacturers to promote both new and secondhand goods at fixed prices, and from the 1760s tailors also began to advertise different items of male and female clothing. The emphasis of such publicity was the printed word and the general format was the list, enumerating the items on offer and how much they cost. By contrast, more alluring pictorial representations of the latest fashions were available as engraved or etched plates, displayed for sale in print sellers' windows and also incorporated into such volumes as Heidelhoff's *Gallery of Fashion* (1794–1802) and intermittently in magazines like the *Lady's Magazine*.

During the late eighteenth and early nineteenth centuries, the nexus between what Roland Barthes refers to as image-clothing and written clothing in *The Fashion System* became more evident in French and British publications, such as the *Cabinet des Modes*, *La Belle Assemblée*, and Ackermann's *Repository of Arts*, where illustrations were accompanied by captions and editorials concerning changes in the styles of fashion. These titles were the forerunners of such popular illustrated weeklies as the *Illustrated London News* (ILN), *Graphic*, *Lady's Pictorial*, and *Ladies' Home Journal*, which had sprung up by the mid-nineteenth century on both sides of the Atlantic to cater to middle-class readers and in which the first distinctly recognizable alpha-pictorial advertisements for clothing retailers appeared. Many of these promotions, however, were similar in approach to the "reason why" format of their antecedents since they consisted of straightforward wood-engraved illustrations of women—and men—wearing the garments alongside text that relates the cost of the clothing represented and where it could be purchased. Occasionally more suggestive or atmospheric forms of advertising, in which the product appeared in a situational context, cropped up. Thus press promotions during the 1880s and 1890s in *Lady's Pictorial* and *Graphic* for "My Queen" Vel-Vel, a velvet for dressmaking, resorted to the trope of Queen Victoria as consumer. In them, she is embodied in a domestic setting as a saleswoman unfurls the fabric before her. Yet, Victoria's detached gaze and demeanor transcend the material situation, and it is rather

her majestic aura that symbolically bestows favor on the fabric and invests it with value.

By the turn of the century, the color lithographic poster, pioneered by Jules Chéret in France, had also become a popular form of advertising internationally, although there are few extant examples relating directly or exclusively to fashion promotion. In 1900, for instance, H. G. Gray produced a poster to publicize the latest fashions on sale at the Parisian department store Prix Unique. Publicity for some manufacturers also tended to a form of double symbolism; hence an 1885 poster for the American company New Home Sewing Machine, representing a mother painting and a daughter playing with a cat in their new clothes, not only represented the products that such domestic technologies enabled but the leisure time that they also afforded middle-class women.

The seeds for a modern, atmospheric form of fashion advertising, therefore, were sown by the late nineteenth century. Not until the twentieth century, and especially the interwar period, did an evident quantitative and qualitative shift take place in the promotion of fashion and clothing for women and men. This was due in no small measure to the expansion of the ready-to-wear and bespoke markets, as well as the professionalization of the advertising industry itself, which had begun to get involved more systematically with market segmentation and to probe what made different types of consumers tick in terms of sex, age, and class. At the same time, the impact of modernist aesthetics, the role of the copywriter, and the deployment of avant-garde designers and photographers also greatly transformed fashion advertising.

Prussian-born Hans Schleger (alias Zéró) was probably the most renowned of this new breed of commercial artists, and he worked both in Europe and America. Between 1925 and 1929, he was hired by outfitters Weber and Heilbroner of New York to transform their advertising campaigns. To this end he devised press advertisements that dynamically conveyed a sense of rhythm and proportion, such that the layout of asymmetric or expressive typeforms into wave or wedge formations was complemented by the shape and directional thrust of the illustrations or photographs. In 1929, he struck up an association with the pioneering British advertising agency W. S. Crawford (founded 1914), which held accounts for Wolsey hosiery and Jaeger amongst others. Working in collaboration with the copywriter G. H. Saxon Mills, he created imaginative promotions for Charnaux corsets that appeared in *Vogue* during the 1930s and that used sporting metaphors to emphasize the idea of health and freedom in the design and wearing of undergarments.

America took the lead in pioneering the evolution of photographic advertising during the early 1920s, with Clarence White, who had founded a school of photography in New York in his own name in 1914 and the Art Center in 1921, becoming one of the first apologists for its application. The modern style he advocated was based on sharp focus, simple geometry, and oblique perspectives, and manifested itself in the photography of the school's most well-known graduates, Edward Steichen and Paul Outerbridge. The former promulgated the idea of straight photography in advertising campaigns for Realsilk hosiery in *Ladies' Home Journal* between 1927 and 1937, and the former in his campaign for the Ide Shirt Collar, which was photographed in stark isolation against a checkerboard and published in *Vanity Fair* in November 1922. In Europe, similar ideas had taken root during the 1920s with the advent of the Neue Sachlichkeit (New Objectivity). Thus, László Moholy-Nagy, in "How Photography Revolutionizes Vision" (1933), espoused a battery of different techniques, including photomontage and the photogram, and a range of different stylistic approaches to the object, such as the introduction of the greatest contrasts, the use of texture and structure, and the use of different or unfamiliar perspectives that offered "new experiences of space." All of these formal concerns are evident in an advertisement in *Punch* in 1933 for Austin Reed shirts featuring a color photograph of bales of material, which invites us to contemplate everyday objects from a fresh vantage point.

The photographic forms of fashion advertising that had begun to supplant the use of hand-drawn illustrations during the 1930s continued unabated after World War II. By the mid-1950s the market for teenage and youth fashions had also influenced the sexual iconography of many advertisements. A common motif in press promotions during the 1960s for designers as diverse as Mary Quant and Dior, and garments from miniskirts to coats and trousers to tights, was the woman-child, represented clowning in playful poses or pouting provocatively. Between 1961 and 1963, photographs by David Olins of "the girl" wearing a man's shirt were also deployed in poster and press ads to promote the Tootal brand. At the same time, the male consumer was drawn into this ornamental realm of desire and in promotions for Newman Clothing during the 1960s was depicted as the object of the adoring female admirers who surrounded him. But it would be erroneous to argue that men had not been objectified in this way before; in poster advertisements for Pope and Bradley in 1911–1912 and in many of those by Tom Purvis for Austin Reed during the 1930s, as well as press advertisements for multiple tailors like the Fifty Shilling Tailors, the fashionable peacock was connoted as someone who could turn women's heads.

Since the 1960s it is probably more casual forms of dress, and jeans in particular, that have made an appeal on television and in the press to both men and women in terms of sexual desire. As competition between brands and designer labels heated up in the late 1970s and early 1980s, advertisers began to fetishize the contour-hugging nature of denim. Thus press ads for Calvin Klein, featuring Brooke Shields, and for Jordache traded on close-ups of pert buttocks clad in jeans. In this vein, the retro British television campaign for Levi 501's (masterminded by Bartle, Bogle and Hegarty and screened in 1985–1986), which featured Nick Kamen stripping down to his boxer shorts in a launderette, initiated a more subtle and ambiguous form of sexual objectification.

Interestingly, although Levi's are sold across the world, publicity for the brand has not been orchestrated on a multinational basis. In comparison with the retro-styled British television and press campaigns of the 1980s, for instance, in America the "501 Blues" television advertisements traded on the idea of nonconformity by associating the product with contemporary street-smart individuals and blues music, while press advertisements tended to foreground the idea of jeans as leisure wear on a more conventional or "reason-why" level with images of men playing pool or dressing down for the weekend. At the same time, in Japan, the retro association of Levi's and the 1950s was symbolized by images of James Dean.

One company that has promoted itself on a multi-national basis is Benetton, and in doing so, it has transformed the way that clothing can be publicized. Under the banner "United Colors of Benetton," the company's artistic director Oliviero Toscani mobilized fashion advertising to promote historical and ideological consciousness of issues as wide as race and national identities, religion, and HIV/AIDS. Between 1985 and 1991, he juxtaposed young people of disparate ethnic origins in the hope of encouraging racial tolerance, and since that time he has manipulated existing news photographs, such as a man shot dead by the Mafia, or created politicized images, such as his photograph of blood-stained garments worn by a dead militant in the Serbo-Croat conflict, to connote a similar message of national and international harmony. Such events have little or nothing to do with Benetton per se, whose exploitative production methods have themselves been subject to moral scrutiny, and it is debatable whether they draw more attention to the company rather than raising awareness of the issues with which they purport to be concerned. Nonetheless Benetton advertising remains at the cutting edge artistically and ideologically, and not least in the way that it has encouraged other fashion advertisers to deal with the ambiguities of sexual and racial identities.

The leitmotiv of many promotions for clothing at the turn of the millennium, therefore, has been the queering of femininities and masculinities, such that the normative dynamics of spectatorial pleasure and the gaze are leitmotiv problematized (much as they had been earlier in the twentieth century in the homoerotic advertisements designed by J. C. Leyendecker for the Arrow Shirt Collar). Key examples of this kind of promotion since the 1990s include advertisements for Versace, Calvin Klein, Dolce & Gabbana, Diesel, Ben Sherman, Northwave Shoes, and Miss Sixty, all of which exploit the tension between straight and gay identities for men and women,

and white and nonwhite spectators alike. At the same time, some designers like Vivienne Westwood and Yves Saint Laurent, and companies like Diesel have made postmodern intertextual references between well-known works of art or the cult of media celebrity and their own products not only to deconstruct the meaning of personal identities but also to undermine the distinction between the representation and reality of fashion itself.

See also **Art and Fashion; Economics and Clothing; Fashion Magazines; Fashion and Homosexuality; Retailing.**

BIBLIOGRAPHY
Goffman, Erwin. *Gender Advertisements.* London: Macmillan, 1979.
Loeb, Lori-Anne. *Consuming Angels: Advertising and Victorian Women.* New York: Oxford University Press, 1994.
Moholy-Nagy, László. "How Photography Revolutionizes Vision." *The Listener* (November 1933): 688–690.
Mort, Frank. *Cultures of Consumption: Masculinities and Social Space in Late Twentieth-Century Britain.* London: Routledge, 1996.

Paul Jobling

FASHION AND HOMOSEXUALITY Throughout the twentieth century, clothing has been used by lesbians and gay men as a means of expressing self-identity and of signaling to one another.

Male Cross-Dressing

Even before the twentieth century, transvestism and cross-dressing among men were associated with the act of sodomy. By the eighteenth century, many cities in Europe had developed small but secret homosexual subcultures. London's homosexual subculture was based around inns and public houses where "mollies" congregated. Many of the mollies wore women's clothing as both a form of self-identification and as a means of attracting sexual partners. They wore "gowns, petticoats, head-cloths, fine laced shoes, furbelowed scarves, and masks; [and] some had riding hoods; some were dressed like milk maids, others like shepherdesses with green hats, waistcoats, and petticoats; and others had their faces patched and painted" (Trumbach, p. 138).

Male homosexuals continued to cross-dress in both public and private spaces throughout the nineteenth century. In the 1920s, the Harlem drag balls offered a safe space for gay men (and lesbians) to cross-dress. Similarly the Arts Balls of the 1950s in London offered an opportunity denied in everyday life. Cross-dressing performers, commonly known as drag queens, used women's clothes to parody straight society and create a gay humor. One of the greatest American drag performers was Charles Pierce, who began his career in the 1950s, and was best known for his impersonations of film stars such as Bette Davis and Joan Crawford. The tradi-

***Una, Lady Troubridge,* 1924.** The period between the two world wars saw a rise in the visibility of lesbians. This oil-on-canvas portait by artist Romaine Brooks typifies the masculinized lesbian dress of the period. Note the wing collar, monocle, and men's jacket. © SMITHSONIAN AMERICAN ART MUSEUM, WASHINGTON, DC/ART RESOURCE, NY. REPRODUCED BY PERMISSION.

tion has been carried on by gay drag performers such as American performers Divine and RuPaul and British television star Lily Savage.

Effeminacy

Overt gay men, who did not want to go so far as to cross-dress, sometimes adopted the most obvious signifiers of female mannerisms and dress: plucked eyebrows, rouge, eye makeup, peroxide blond hair, high-heeled shoes, women's blouses. In America it was illegal for men (and women) to cross dress unless attending a masquerade. At least three items of clothing had to be appropriate to the gender. Adopting such an appearance was dangerous, for it was risky to be overtly homosexual. In his autobiography, *The Naked Civil Servant* (1968), Quentin Crisp recalls being stopped a number of times by police because of his effeminate appearance. However, the risks were worthwhile for many. Dressing as a "flaming queen" was a means of entering into the subculture of gay society. Also, by adopting female characteristics and by adhering to strict gendered rules of sexual behavior, queens could attract allegedly "normal," straight sexual partners. The adoption of effeminate dress codes began to wane with the rise of gay liberation, but has continued to play a role in gay life.

Masculinity and Lesbian Dress

In the late nineteenth and early twentieth centuries, the adoption of male dress was a means for many women, including many lesbians, to protest the status of women and the roles assigned them by patriarchal societies. Cross-dressing had been and continued to be utilized by women to allow them to "pass" as men and be accepted. Some, like writer George Sand and painter Rosa Bonheur utilized the methods in order to have their professional work be taken seriously. The period between the two World Wars saw a rise in lesbian visibility. The typical masculinized lesbian dress of the period is typified by the wing collar, monocle, and man's jacket worn by Lady Una Troubridge (lover of Radclyffe Hall, author of *The Well of Loneliness*) in her portrait by Romain Brooks. In America, lesbian performers such as Ma Rainey and Gladys Bentley wore men's top hat and tails to express their identity, while bisexual film stars Greta Garbo and Marlene Dietrich wore masculine clothes both on- and offscreen.

Until the 1970s, the public image of lesbians was very much centered on masculinity. As a means of asserting difference and signaling to other lesbians, many women-loving women adopted certain "masculine" markers, such as a collar and tie or trousers. In America, it was illegal for women to dress completely in men's clothes, and they were required to wear "three pieces of women's clothing" (Nestle, p. 100). Public reaction was not sympathetic to "butch" lesbians. American lesbian writer and activist Joan Nestle "walked the streets looking so butch that straight teenagers called [her a] bulldyke" (Nestle, p. 100).

Not all lesbian women felt drawn to the adoption of male clothing, preferring instead more conventional female attire: makeup, high-heeled shoes, and skirts. Many accounts of lesbian bar life note the prevalence of "butch" and "femme" identities and behavior, where butch lesbians were expected to form relationships only with femme lesbians, and lesbians were expected to identify with one role or the other.

Subtle Signifiers

The illegality of homosexuality and the moral disapproval that it attracted forced gay men and lesbians to live virtually invisible lives in the first part of the twentieth century. Up until the gay liberation movement of the late 1960s, the most important criterion of dressing in public, for the mass of gay men and lesbians, was to be able to "pass" as heterosexual. Despite this need, many were aware of the dress codes and items that could be used to signal sexual orientation. These symbols of identity often took the form of a specific type or color of accessory and, like other secret symbols, developed and changed over time. The primary signifier at the time of the Oscar Wilde trials in the 1890s was the green carnation. Indeed, the color green had been associated with the effeminate and sometimes sodomitical macaronis of the 1770s and continued to have gay associations in clothing through the first part of the twentieth century. George Chauncey notes that in 1930s New York City, green suits were the badge of open "pansies." Other signifiers for gay men included a red necktie (worn in New York City before World War II) and suede shoes (one of the most international and enduring gay signifiers). Lesbian signifiers included accessories such as ties and cufflinks, short haircuts (particularly the "Eton crop" of the 1920s), and the color violet.

Menswear Revolution

During the "menswear revolution" of the 1960s, the association of fashion and homosexuality began to diminish. With the rise in subcultural fashions and the dissemination of Carnaby Street fashions around the world, it was suddenly acceptable for young men to be interested in fashion, and to spend time and money on clothes and appearance. Carnaby Street fashions were initially sold to a gay "theatrical and artistic" clientele by a former physique photographer by the name of Vince from a shop near Carnaby Street. John Stephen, who was later to be known as the "King of Carnaby Street," had worked at Vince's shop and produced the clothes faster, cheaper, and for a younger market. In America, too, a close-fitting "European style." worn primarily by gay men, was sold from "boutiques" in Greenwich Village, New York, and West Hollywood in Los Angeles.

Gay Men and Masculinity

By the late 1960s, lesbians and gay men throughout the Western world had begun to question their position as second-class citizens and their stereotype as effeminate "queens" or "butch dykes." Along with the demands for equality and recognition, lesbians and gay men began to address their appearance. There had always been gay men who dressed in a conventionally masculine style, but in the early 1970s, gay men in New York and San Francisco looked to the epitomes of American masculinity—the cowboy, the lumberjack, the construction worker—for inspiration for a new dress style. The clones, as they were known, adopted the most masculine dress signifiers they could find—work boots, tight Levi's, plaid shirts, short haircuts, and moustaches. Their clothes were chosen to reveal and celebrate the contours of the male body.

Some clones also developed their sexual tastes by experimenting with sadomasochism. Consequently, they sometimes adopted a "leatherman" appearance and lifestyle, which involved a strict codification of dress and a new system of signifiers, most notably colored handkerchiefs in a back pocket, specifying particular sexual interests. The hypermasculine image has continued to be important even after the supposed death of the clone in the late 1980s, when the image became associated with an older generation of pre-AIDS gay men. Gay men have interpreted and demonstrated their masculine looks through the celebration of muscular "gym" bodies and clothing that shows off those bodies, as well as the emergence of other masculine subcultural styles such as the shaven-headed, boots and braces wearing, but not necessarily racist skinhead.

Post-Liberation Lesbian Style

The advent of both the women's and gay-rights movements led to a questioning of the stereotyped dress choices previously available to lesbians. Trousers had become increasingly acceptable for women from the 1950s, and during the 1960s it became more difficult to identify lesbians on the grounds of trouser-wearing. "Androgyny" became a key word in fashion, and this manifested itself in various ways. Initially, the move was toward a feminine look for men, but the radical lesbian and gay community rejected this in favor of a more masculine look for both men and women.

The rise of radical feminism saw a rejection of fashion-forced femininity. Flat shoes, baggy trousers, unshaved legs, and faces bare of makeup made a strong statement about not dressing for men. Radical feminist politics during the 1970s took this to an extreme as a new stereotype was born—that of the dungaree-wearing, crew-cut lesbian feminist.

The 1980s and 1990s saw a new diversification in lesbian dress. The breakdown of the old butch and femme divides, the changes instigated in women's dress by feminism and punk, and the increasing visibility in public life of lesbians opened up the debate about what lesbians could and should wear. One of the most significant developments was the appearance of the lipstick lesbian (also known as glamour or designer dyke). Dress styles signaled a move away from the traditional butch or radical-feminist styles and allowed out gay women to develop a fashionable urban look that combined signifiers of lesbianism or masculinity with fashionable women's dress. However, critics accused lipstick lesbians of hiding behind a mask of heterosexuality.

The Fashion Industry

The large proportion of gay men who have worked in creative fields of fashion and the theater and service industries, such as catering, has been well documented by historians such as Ross Higgins, whose study highlighted the involvement of gay men at all levels of the fashion industry in Montreal.

Throughout the twentieth century, many of the top couture fashion designs were gay, even though social pressure called for them to keep their sexuality quiet if not secret. Indeed, many of the greatest names in twentieth-century fashion were gay or bisexual, including such figures as Christian Dior, Cristobal Balenciaga, Yves Saint Laurent, Norman Hartnell, Halston, Rudi Gernreich (who was one of the founding members of the first American homophile organization, the Mattachine society), Calvin Klein, and Gianni Versace.

As designers took over from traditional tailors and gentleman's outfitters in men's fashion, a new gay influence became evident. Because gay men were often more willing to experiment with new ideas, styles, and fabrics in clothing, designers such as Jean-Paul Gaultier began to look at what was happening at street level and in gay clubs for ideas for their men's collections. Moreover, gay men bought clothes that were influenced by and styled toward a gay aesthetic, so their taste influenced fashion in both obvious and subtle ways.

The advent of the "new man" (as a media icon) in the 1980s was a result of men's reaction to major social changes brought about by a second wave of feminism. As a consequence, it became acceptable for straight men to be interested in their appearance, clothes, and grooming products. New magazines aimed at a wider, heterosexual male consumer were published, but even here a gay influence could be perceived. It was not just that gay designers were creating the looks, but gay stylists, hairdressers, and photographers all exerted a fashion influence. For example, stylist Ray Petri (featured in *The Face*, *i-D*, and *Arena* magazines) drew on looks that he saw in gay clubs to create a whole new style known as Buffalo. Buffalo style dressed black and white, gay and straight models in an unlikely mix of elements such as cycling shorts, flight jackets, skirts, hats, and boots.

The early 1990s saw the advent of "lesbian chic" in the fashion world. This manifested itself most visibly in a series of photographs in *Vanity Fair* in 1993, including a cover that featured lesbian singer k. d. lang cavorting with supermodel Cindy Crawford.

Homosexual men in cowboy clothing. In the 1970s, gay men began to look to traditional icons of masculinity for fashion inspiration, donning rugged clothing that showed off the physique. PHOTO BY LEONARD FINK, LESBIAN, GAY, BISEXUAL & TRANSGENDER COMMUNITY CENTER. REPRODUCED BY PERMISSION.

Today it is perfectly acceptable for straight men to be interested in fashion and to be obvious consumers of clothes, grooming products, and fashion or "lifestyle" magazines. Popular figures, such as soccer player David Beckham, are avid consumers of clothes and even acknowledge their debt to gay men's influence on fashion. In an age where homosexuality is tolerated and to a great extent accepted in major urban centers, it has become increasingly difficult to distinguish gay and straight men, and lesbians and straight women, on the basis of their dress. Acknowledging this, Elizabeth Wilson poses the following question: "Throughout the queer century we have disguised and revealed our deviant desires in dress, masquerade, disguise. Now that everyone's caught on in a postmodern world, what do we have to do to invent new [gay and] dyke style?" (Wilson, 177)

See also **Fashion and Identity; Gender, Dress, and Fashion.**

BIBLIOGRAPHY

Ainley, Rosa. *What is She Like: Lesbian Identities from the 1950s to the 1990s*, London: Cassell Academic Publishing , 1995.

Blackman, Inge, and Kathryn Perry. "Skirting the Issue: Lesbian Fashion for the 1990s." *Feminist Review* 34 (Spring 1990): 67–78.

Chauncey, George. *Gay New York: Gender, Urban Culture and the Making of the Gay Male World, 1890–1940*. New York: Basic Books, 1994.

Cole, Shaun. *Don We Now Our Gay Apparel: Gay Men's Dress in the Twentieth Century*. Oxford: Berg, 2000.

Fischer, Hal. *Gay Semiotics*. San Francisco: NSF Press, 1977.

Higgins, Ross. "A la Mode: Fashioning Gay Community in Montreal." In *Consuming Fashion: Adorning the Transnational Body*. Edited by Anne Bryden and Sandra Nieman Oxford: Berg, 1998.

Levine, Martin P. *Gay Macho: The Life and Death of the Homosexual Clone*. New York and London: New York University Press, 1998.

Nestle, Joan. *A Restricted Country: Essays and Short Stories*. London: Sheba, 1988.

Schuyf, Judith. "'Trousers with Flies!': The Clothing and Subculture of Lesbians." *Textile History* 24, no. 1 (1993): 61–73.

Trumbach, Randolph. "The Birth of the Queen: Sodomy and the Emergence of Gender Equality in Modern Culture, 1660–1750." In *Hidden From History: Reclaiming the Gay and Lesbian Past*. Edited by Martin Baum Duberman, Martha Vicanus, and George Chauncey Jr. London: Penguin, 1991.

Wilson, Elizabeth. "Dyke Style or Lesbians Make an Appearance." In *Stonewall 25: The Making of the Lesbian and Gay Community in Britain*. Edited by Emma Healey and Angela Mason. London: Virago, 1994.

Shaun Cole

FASHION AND IDENTITY Identity is one of the most compelling and contentious concepts in the humanities and social sciences. Fashion becomes inextricably implicated in constructions and reconstructions of identity: how we represent the contradictions and ourselves in our everyday lives. Through appearance style (personal interpretations of, and resistances to, fashion), individuals announce who they are and who they hope to become. Moreover, they express who they do *not* want to be or become (Freitas et al., 1997). Appearance style is a metaphor for identity; it is a complex metaphor that includes physical features (for example, skin, bodily shape, hair texture) as well as clothing and grooming practices. Because the latter are especially susceptible to change, they are prone to fluctuating and fluid ways of understanding oneself in relation to others within the larger context of fashion change.

Appearance style visually articulates multiple and overlapping identities such as gender, race, ethnicity, social class, sexuality, age, national identity, and personal interests, aesthetic, and politics. Not all of these identities are consciously present at any given moment; power relations influence one's awareness of one identity or another. Privileged identities (such as whiteness, masculinity, heterosexuality) are often taken for granted as being "normal" or "natural." But because identities intersect and overlap, their representation is seldom simple. From a cultural studies perspective, identities have not only histories but also futures: They come from somewhere, they are complex and contradictory, and they enable us to express who we might become (Ang 2000).

Expressing who we are and are becoming in words can be a challenge; appearance style seems to offer a way of articulating a statement that is difficult to put into words—that is, emerging and intersecting identities. In fact, it is easier to put into words who we want to *avoid* being or looking like (that is, not feminine, not too slutty, no longer a child) than it is to verbalize who we are (Freitas et al., 1997). Moreover, one identity blurs or blends into another identity (for example, gender into sexuality). And, articulations of identity are often ambivalent. Davis (1992) argued that identity ambivalences provide the "fuel" or ongoing inspiration for fashion change. Fashion-susceptible ambivalences include the interplay between youth versus age, masculinity versus femininity, or high versus low status, among many other possibilities within and across identities.

The study of identity in the social sciences and humanities can be traced to a longer history of the self, personality, and subjectivity, especially in modern Western cultures. Breward (1995) identifies the middle to late sixteenth century as a time when there was a heightened self-consciousness about identity as something that could be individually "fashioned" (p. 69). By the eighteenth century, philosophers (such as Hume and Rousseau) were questioning what constitutes one's true selfhood, when traditional societies were breaking down (Kellner 1994). (It is important to note that this questioning still assumed the subjectivity of a white, bourgeois male.) Also in the eighteenth century, consumers began to establish more personalized relationships with individuality, modernity, culture, and clothing (Breward 1995, p.112). For example, the "molly" culture of eighteenth century London provided a means for males to transgress traditional boundaries of masculinity by experimenting with feminine clothing and accessories. By the nineteenth century, consumption linked identity directly to one's possessions, especially among bourgeois Western women. At the same time, new ways of expressing identifications and disidentifications in city life were emerging (for example, bohemians, dandies; Breward 2003, p. 218).

The modern fashion consumer was moving away "from a concern with elaborate artifice" toward one of individual expression (Breward 2003, p. 200). Crane (2000) describes this as a shift from class fashion to consumer fashion. This was not a smooth process. Modernity itself created fragmentation and dislocation, producing a paradoxical sense of what it meant to be an individual. Wilson (1985) theorizes that a modern sense of individuality functions like a wound that generates fear about sustaining the autonomy of the self; fashion somewhat assuages that fear, while also reminding us that individuality can be suppressed (p. 12).

Although for centuries clothing had been a principal means for identifying oneself (for example, by occupation, regional identity, religion, social class) in public spaces (Crane, 2000), the twentieth century witnessed a wider array of subcultural groupings that visually marked "their difference from the dominant culture and their peers by utilizing the props of material and commercial culture" (Breward 2003, p. 222). In the 1960s, sociologist Gregory Stone (1965) argued that identity has many advantages over the more fixed, psychological concept of personality, and that identity is not a code word for "self." Rather, identity is an announced *meaning* of the self—one that is *situated* in and negotiated through social interactions. He argued that appearance is fundamental to identification and differentiation in everyday life. The "teenage phenomenon" of the 1950s and 1960s made this very apparent by fostering an awareness of age identity as it intersected with a variety of musical and personal preferences—all coded through appearance styles. The social movements (civil rights, feminist, gay and lesbian rights) of the late 1960s and early 1970s further accentuated stylistic means for constructing and transgressing racialized, ethnic, gender, and sexual identities.

From the post-1960s to the present—a period described as everything from post-industrial to postmodern—an advanced (global) capitalist marketplace has produced an eclectic array of commodities from which individuals can select, mix, and match to produce their identities (Kaiser 1999; Kaiser, Nagasawa, and Hutton, 1991). Wilson (1992) reminds us that despite modern (or postmodern) fragmentation, we ultimately do not choose our bodies, "so postmodern playfulness can never entirely win the day" (p. 8). In the context of ongoing fashion

change, appearance style functions ambiguously both to (a) resist "older" ideas about fixed personality or true self and (b) fix identity (for example, ethnicity, sexuality, religion) more firmly. As the global and local penetrate one another, style and fashion afford strategies for articulating the "contradictory necessity and impossibility of identities . . . in the messiness of everyday life" (Ang 2000, p. 11).

See also **Afrocentric Fashion; Ethnic Dress; Gender, Dress, and Fashion.**

BIBLIOGRAPHY

Ang, Ien. "Identity Blues." In *Without Guarantees: In Honour of Stuart Hall.* Edited by Paul Gilroy, Lawrence Grossberg, and Angela McRobbie, London: Verso, 2000.

Breward, Christopher. *The Culture of Fashion.* Manchester, U.K.: Manchester University Press, 1995.

———. *Fashion.* Oxford, U.K: Oxford University Press, 2003.

Crane, Diana. *Fashion and Its Social Agendas: Class, Gender, and Identity in Clothing.* Chicago and London: The University of Chicago Press, 2000.

Davis, Fred. *Fashion, Culture, and Identity.* Chicago: University of Chicago Press, 1992.

Freitas, Anthony, et al. "Appearance Management as Border Construction: Least Favorite Clothing, Group Distancing, and Identity . . . *Not!*" *Sociological Inquiry* 67, no. 3 (1997): 323–335.

Kaiser, Susan B., Richard N. Nagasawa, and Sandra S. Hutton. "Fashion, Postmodernity and Personal Appearance: A Symbolic Interactionist Formulation." *Symbolic Interaction* 14, no. 2 (1991): 165–185.

Kaiser, Susan B. "Identity, Postmodernity, and the Global Apparel Marketplace." In *The Meanings of Dress.* Edited by Mary Lynn Damhorst, Kimberly A. Miller, and Susan O. Michelman. New York: Fairchild Publications, 1999.

Kellner, Douglas. "Madonna, Fashion, and Identity." In *On Fashion.* Edited by Shari Benstock and Suzanne Ferriss. New Brunswick, N.J.: Rutgers University Press, 1994.

Stone, Gregory P. "Appearance and the Self." In *Dress, Adornment, and the Social Order.* Edited by Mary Ellen Roach and Joanne B. Eicher. New York: Wiley, 1965.

Wilson, Elizabeth. *Adorned in Dreams: Fashion and Modernity.* Berkeley, Calif.: University of California Press, 1985.

———. "Fashion and the Postmodern Body." In *Chic Thrills: A Fashion Reader.* Edited by Juliet Ash and Elizabeth Wilson. Berkeley, Calif.: University of California Press, 1992.

Susan B. Kaiser

FASHION DESIGNER A fashion designer is responsible for creating the specific look of individual garments—including a garment's shape, color, fabric, trimmings, and other aspects of the whole. The fashion designer begins with an idea of how a garment should look, turns that idea into a design (such as a sketch), and specifies how that design should be made into an actual piece of clothing by other workers (from patternmakers to finishers). The category of fashion designer includes people at different levels of the fashion business, from well-known couturiers, to anonymous designers working for commercial ready-to-wear houses, to stylists who might make only small modifications in existing designs. Fashion designers hold a special place in the world. Their talent and vision not only play a major role in how people look, but they have also made important contributions to the cultural and social environment.

The Origin of Fashion Designers

Charles Frederick Worth is considered the father of haute couture. An Englishman, he opened his couture house in Paris in 1846. Along with Worth, the Callot sisters, Jeanne Paquin, Jacques Doucet, and Jeanne Lanvin are considered to be among the first modern fashion designers, as compared with the dressmakers of earlier generations. Paris was the center of international fashion for more than one hundred years, with French couturiers setting the trends for Europe and the Western world. But the position of Paris as the undisputed leader of fashion was disrupted by World War II.

During that war, with Paris occupied by the Nazis, American designers and manufacturers were cut off from the fashion leadership of Paris. As a result, American designers began to receive more serious recognition. Claire McCardell, known as the creator of the "American Look," drew some of her inspiration from the vernacular clothing of industrial and rural workers as inspiration. Other American designers such as Hattie Carnegie, Vera Maxwell, Bonnie Cashin, Anne Klein, and Tina Leser had flourishing careers; they helped shape the development of sportswear that reflected the casual American lifestyle.

In the postwar economy, as fashion became big business, the role of the designer changed. Increasingly, especially in the United States, fashion designers worked closely with store buyers to identify customers' preferences and lifestyle needs. Customer demographics influenced designers to create fashions targeted to specific customer profiles. Through sales events known as "trunk shows," designers traveled to stores with their latest collection in a trunk. This simple and inexpensive marketing technique allowed customers to preview and respond to the designer's new collection, and to buy clothes. Bill Blass was one of many designers who used trunk shows to gain customers, profits, and a growing reputation.

The Role of the Fashion Designer

From the 1950s through the 1980s, the design room in the United States became the equivalent of the European atelier. With a staff of assistant designers, sketchers, patternmakers, drapers, finishers, and sample makers, American designers worked in their design rooms to create a collection each season. "First samples" were produced in the design room and later shown in a fashion show or in the company showroom. Design rooms are extremely costly to maintain and have been downsized due to the fact that most manufacturing is now done offshore. In the early 2000s, most designers work with an assistant and a technical designer to create tech packs. A tech pack contains a designer's original idea, which is then re-sketched by the technical designer whose responsibility is to detail all garment specifications and construction information. Tech packs are sent directly to factories in China, Hong Kong, India, or other countries where labor costs are low and where, increasingly, first samples are made and production takes place.

As the apparel industry grew, fashion schools were established to train designers and other industry professionals. Design schools in New York City include Parsons (1896) and Fashion Institute of Technology, or FIT (1914). These schools train students in specializations like children's wear, sportswear, evening wear, knitwear, intimate apparel, and activewear, for both the men's and women's market. Design schools have been established in Paris, London, Antwerp, and throughout Italy. Some American institutions have partnerships with other design schools in China, India, and elsewhere around the world.

Although designers in the twenty-first century are to some extent still responsible for creating trends, the notion of designers dictating fashion has been replaced with lifestyle designing. Each season, designers follow a process of identifying trends and searching for inspiration, researching fabrics and colors. They then focus on creating a collection that will appeal to their specific target customers' lifestyle. Although fashion trends continue to emanate from Europe, many designers look to the street for inspiration. Fashion designers, working in tandem with the film and music industries, have launched or helped popularize such fashion trends as mod, punk, grunge, hip-hop, and cholo. Fashion designers are both creators and trend trackers. Much of what they now design is a response to street styles.

With the help of marketing and advertising, designers promote themselves to the world. Some designers market their look through runway shows, as well as maintaining their own retail stores. The concept of lending their name to other licensed products is yet another vehicle to expand their brand identity. Many celebrity designers actually do very little designing of the collections that bear their name.

A major trend in the fashion business is the iconic use of sports and music idols to sell product. With the hope of increasing sales, manufacturers hire anonymous designers to create apparel bearing celebrity names. Television, the Internet, personal appearances, film, print ads, and editorial coverage used as marketing tools for fashion, have become as important, if not more so, than the clothing itself. New entrepreneurial designers rely on editorial coverage to launch collections while established

Edith Head surrounded by some of her fashion designs. During her 58-year career in Hollywood, Edith Head designed costumes for many films and influenced popular fashion with some of her designs, such as with Elizabeth Taylor's lilac-strewn gown in *A Place in the Sun* (1951). AP/WIDE WORLD PHOTOS. REPRODUCED BY PERMISSION.

companies spend millions of dollars each year on advertising, marketing, and promotion.

Mass retailers and manufacturers enlist the services of market-research firms to predict consumers' changing tastes so as to make appropriate product. Fashion designers utilize data for design purposes that is collected from focus groups and consumer behavior studies. The business of fashion has morphed into the science of fashion.

The Future of the Fashion Designer

Designers in the twenty-first century are beginning to adopt new technologies such as body-scanning for custom fit, along with seamless and whole garment knitting technologies, which can manufacture garments with the push of a button. Both are forerunners in a movement toward automation that will once again revolutionize the fashion industry. Just as the sewing machine changed the face of fashion in the past, technology will change it in the future. Designers of the future, as they have in the past, will continue to serve their customer's needs but will do so utilizing new resources and tools. To create new product lines, designers in the future will utilize high-tech textiles, including those that possess healing, sun protection, and other unique qualities. Designing clothes in the future may have more to do with function than with fancy, in response to new consumer demands and preferences.

See also **Callot Sisters; Color in Dress; Fashion Advertising; Haute Couture; Ready-to-Wear; Worth, Charles Frederick.**

BIBLIOGRAPHY

Baudot, Francois. *Fashion: The Twentieth Century.* New York: Universe Publishing, 1999.

Frings Stephens, Gini. *Fashion: From Concept to Consumer.* 7th ed. Englewood Cliffs, N.J.: Prentice-Hall, 2001.

Payne, Blanche, Jane Farrell-Beck, and Geitel Winaker. *The History of Costume.* 2nd ed. New York: Harper Collins, 1992.

Francesca Sterlacci

FASHION DOLLS "Fashion doll" must be considered a very loose term. Sometimes it is used to indicate decorative figures usually produced as a series. Many times they are attired in historical dress. Additionally, notable people dress these dolls for charitable purposes. But there are other candidates for the term as well.

Historically the primary role of a doll has been as a companion and teaching tool for the young. Doll-like figures have additionally played roles in religious, artistic, and fashion-related endeavors. Neither methods nor materials of construction, nor supporting devices, are indicators of possible primary intention. Except for the earliest examples, dolls and figures addressing the subject of fashion range in height from under an inch to, in rare exceptions, nearly three feet.

What in the early twenty-first century might be recognized as a true "fashion doll" were those figures that were sent around to the wealthy and stylish individuals and centers of Europe and, later, American colonies. According to Max von Boehm, the first recorded wardrobed fashion doll—she was life size—went from the French to English court in 1396. By the seventeenth century, when these French figures were known as "Pandora," the dressing of the head and hair was as important as the garment. And by the eighteenth century the British were not only receiving but also sending their own versions of these figures, which seem from the records to have continued the tradition of being life, or near-life, size. The size perhaps explains why attempts to relate surviving play-dolls from the late seventeenth and eighteenth centuries to fashion dolls has been unsuccessful.

With the introduction of printed images of fashion, the need for the expensive creation and transport of a fashionably dressed three-dimensional figure diminished. Picking up on speed with which printed fashion illustrations could be distributed, French publishers began issuing both boxed sets and serialized accessorized paper dolls. For nearly a generation, circa 1825–1850, this type of doll was an important purveyor of fashion information.

While commercially assembled play-dolls continued to be dressed in current styles, it was not until the mid-nineteenth century that French doll distributors took a renewed interest in offering a variety of outfits and accessories based on the latest modes. Known to doll collectors as French Fashion dolls, these dolls—whatever their body material and articulation—feature a nipped-in waist that makes the dolls suitable for dressing in the waves of latest fashions for toddlers, children, men, and women between about 1850 and 1900. Produced in a defined section of Paris, most of the apparel for these dolls is so finely constructed that they are truly fashions in miniature, even down to the stamped waistband and hat labels found in Maison Huret apparel.

It was these play dolls that inspired the *Tina Cassini,* a doll whose wardrobe was the creation of the American designer Oleg Cassini, and her contemporary, *Barbie,* the iconic fashion doll of the twentieth century. Not only has *Barbie* been dressed by a studio of personal designers, including Bob Mackie, but other internationally recognized fashion designers from time to time outfitted her and her family for purposes of charity, publicity, and pure promotion. Indeed, since about 1890 French and other fashion designers have dressed dolls in their creations for purposes of international exhibitions and fund-raising. Jeanne Lanvin, in the 1910s, dressed dolls with porcelain heads made by Sévres, while Margaine-Lacroix dressed those with heads designed by Albert Marque. In the 1930s a consortium of French fashion houses dressed *France* and *Marianne* in up-to-the-minute detail for the British princesses.

On a parallel track beginning in France in the early 1890s was the fashionable dressing of dolls and specifically designed figures solely for the purpose of display and not play. Usually these display figures in series were, in the traditional French manner, attached to a base. The series frequently illustrated the history of fashion especially as drawn from lifetime or imagined portraits of notables, usually women. The trend was begun by Mme Piogey in 1892 with a thousand years of French fashion shown on sixteen dolls, the 1893 Columbian Exhibition display of twenty-five French queens, and the sixteen dolls exhibited by Mme Charles Cousson, whose creations in the early 2000s can be found at Paris's Musée des Arts Decoratif. Respected museums on both sides of the Atlantic would add such figures to their collection, with New York's Metropolitan Museum of Art, under the museum's textile curator, Frances Morris, accessioning the now deaccessioned representations of seven centuries of feminine fashion. As part of the 1949 French Gratitude Train, forty-nine mannequin dolls attired to represent two centuries of French fashion were created, to complement Theatre de la Mode figures by members of the Syndicat de la Couture de Paris. These figures are currently found in the collection of the Brooklyn Museum of Art. In the United States, the tradition of dressing figures in historical fashion has been carried on by a number of artists/designers, including Jacques and France Rommel and John Burbridge.

By the second decade of the twentieth century, the wax-headed figures in contemporary dress of Mmes Lafitte and Désirat were featured in international press. At this time other concerns lured or interpreted the creations of contemporary French designers, such as Jacques Doucet and Paul Poiret. In the early twenty-first century

Woman with doll collection. In the 1890s, clothing designers began creating fashions specifically for dolls, often for promotional, exhibition, or fundraising purposes. © BETTMANN/CORBIS. REPRODUCED BY PERMISSION.

the best-recognized effort to document a moment of fashion is found at Maryhill, a school in Oregon. There reside the figures for the Theatre de la Mode created by members of the French haute couture and related trades—Dessès, Molyneux, Grès, Patou, Fath, Balenciaga, Dior, etc. Assembled just after World War II, these figures represent an attempt to remind the world of the artistic uniqueness of all the components of French fashion.

During the American Civil War, as raffle items at Sanitary Fairs, a variety of dolls were dressed and outfitted with complex and elaborate wardrobes. Many of these were called Flora McFlimsey, after the subject of a pe-

riod poem who was convinced she had nothing to wear, thus leading her to undertake frantic shopping trips to Paris. In the early 2000s, such charitable work continued as fashion designers were asked to dress dolls in signature outfits; sometimes they chose the doll, sometimes the doll was chosen for them—which returns this article to the original dilemma of what exactly constitutes a "fashion doll." Now add to the mix fashion dolls designed specifically for a new category: collectors. Current collectors' fashion dolls include most prominently those of Mel Odom, *Gene;* and Robert Tonner, *Tyler Wentworth.* These dolls, and their attendant "family" members have been created specifically as models for high-fashion garments: *Gene*, the World War II and postwar model and *Tyler Wentworth*, the contemporary spirit.

See also **Barbie.**

BIBLIOGRAPHY

Barbie: A Visual Guide to the Ultimate Fashion Doll. London; New York: Dorling Kindersley, 2000.

Charles-Roux, Edmonde, et al. *Théâtre de la mode: Fashion Dolls: The Survival of Haute Couture.* Portland, Ore.: Palmer-Pletsch Associates, 2002.

Mac Neil, Sylvia. *The Paris Collection.* Cumberland, Md.: Hobby House Press, 1992.

Parrot, Nicole. *Le stiff et le cool: une histoire de maille, de mode et de liberté.* Paris: Nil, 2002.

Elizabeth Ann Coleman

FASHION EDITORS The title "fashion editor" evokes images of fashionable women, those arbiters of style and taste, who pronounce and decree what's new and what's next. They've appeared on stage and screen—from the indecisive Liza Elliot of *Lady in the Dark* ("the circus cover or the Easter cover?") to the very decisive Maggie Prescott of *Funny Face* ("Think pink!").

With the advent of the fashion magazine, the fashion editor emerged as the tastemaker in the early twentieth century. The first and most enduring of these women was Edna Woolman Chase of Conde Nast's *Vogue*, who rose from assistant in the circulation department in 1895, three years after *Vogue* was founded, to editor in chief in 1914. She remained in that venerable position until retirement in 1952. Through the 1940s and 1950s, the most visible of her fashion editors was the tasteful and talented Bettina Ballard. An earlier colleague, Carmel White (later Snow) had left *Vogue* to head Hearst's *Harper's Bazaar*. Her longtime fashion editor was a flamboyant eccentric (her outrageous column *Why Don't You … ?* was notorious) named Diana Vreeland, who in 1963 was tapped by Conde Nast's new owners to become editor in chief of their flagship, *Vogue*.

These grandes dames of fashion publishing were there at the creation. At first they filled their pages with news of what fashionable and wealthy women were wearing and doing. Actually, they were covering and reflecting their own worlds, as each had come from, or married into, families of wealth and society; and most of their staffers served in their low-paying but prestigious jobs as stop-offs between finishing school and marriage. Coverage of the Paris couture, the wellspring of fashion, and of the emerging American designers established these two magazines as the ultimate authorities—the innovators of fashion and fantasy.

They also discovered and encouraged such talents as Richard Avedon, Irving Penn, Martin Munkacsi, Edward Steichen, Louise Dahl-Wolfe, art director Alexey Brodovitch, Cecil Beaton, and more. The arts were covered, distinguished writers wrote for every issue, and an environment for fashion was carefully integrated.

By the mid-1950s, a new breed of editor was being sought. The competition coming from the newer, younger fashion magazines devoted to the emerging working woman, the post-war suburbanite, and the "youth market" of the sixties, brought into the editors' chairs a more pragmatic, reality-based editor. *Vogue* had tapped its merchandizing editor, Jessica Daves, to succeed Mrs. Chase. Diana Vreeland followed as editor in chief, after being passed over at *Bazaar*. Those qualities ultimately did her in at *Vogue*, when she was replaced by her assistant, Grace Mirabella, a down-to-earth market-trained fashion editor. Mrs. Snow's niece, Nancy White, who'd been editor at Hearst's service magazine, *Good Housekeeping*, followed her at *Bazaar*.

Of the booming "younger" books, *Mademoiselle*, edited first by Betsy Blackwell, then Edie Raymond Locke, was the first to "merchandise" each fashion shown, informing the reader of its price and where to buy it. *Charm, Glamour,* and *Mademoiselle* mounted promotions with editors making appearances in retail stores, as the link between the editorial and advertising departments grew stronger. A fashion editor, covering her assigned market, learned to dutifully cover the advertisers' "lines." She even collaborated with designers and manufacturers, developing ideas for new looks for her readers.

Fashion was beginning to reverse itself—starting on the streets and then inspiring designers—so it was important to keep an eye on a magazine's younger staff and the streets of New York, Paris, Milan, and Saint-Tropez to spot the trends. Paris couture (made-to-order for private customers) no longer dominated; ready-to-wear (prêt-a-porter), started in 1969 in Paris and later in Milan, was manufactured for and sold directly to American and European retailers. These collections became the trendsetters. American fashion editors sat side by side with store executives in the front rows of the overcrowded showings, their photographers jockeying for position along the runways, shooting the photos for the next issue, while space was being held until the last minute before deadline.

The fashion editor's job was to report the news, making choices from the season's offerings, whether from Europe or America; to play a major role in the selection of the photographers and models for each "portfolio," or series of pages; and often to oversee the "sitting" in the studio or the "shoot" on location. High-profile "stars" were Polly Mellen of *Vogue* and Carrie Donovan of the *New York Times*.

New media brought new opportunities, and in the 1980s Elsa Klensch, a former *Vogue* and *Harper's Bazaar* fashion editor, convinced CNN that women the world over would be eager to view the designers' collections within weeks of their showings. Her viewers numbered in the millions, but CNN canceled *Style* in 2000. Successors include *Full Frontal Fashion* and cover not just the collections but the "fashionistas" and front-row celebrities attending.

The technology of the information age has made all things possible on demand. Fashion editors can now view the collections online (not the same as being there in the tents of New York, Milan, London, and Paris); they oversee the selections for their own magazine's popular Web sites, such as *Vogue*'s Style.com.

Communicating with and serving the reader are duties of today's fashion editors, who have a whole new world of titles such as "fashion news editor," "fashion market editor," "editor-at-large," "stylist," and more. Many appear regularly on TV "what's in" and "how to" segments. They still watch the streets, but mostly they watch the New York and Los Angeles clubs, music videos, and the red carpets to spot the trends. Perhaps the first star of the 2000s is Anna Wintour of *Vogue*, who, in the tradition of earlier grandes dames, pronounces and decrees what's new and what's next.

See also **Fashion Journalism; Fashion Magazines; Fashion Online; Fashion Television; Vogue; Vreeland, Diana.**

BIBLIOGRAPHY

Ballard, Bettina. *In My Fashion.* New York: David McKay, 1960.

Chase, Edna Woolman, and Ilka Chase. *Always in Vogue.* New York: Doubleday, 1954.

Esten, John, and Katherine Betts. *Diana Vreeland: The Bazaar Years.* New York: Universe Books, 2001.

Mirabella, Grace, and Judith Warner. *In and Out of Vogue.* New York: Doubleday, 1995.

Snow, Carmel, and Mary Louise Aswell. *The World of Carmel Snow.* New York: McGraw-Hill 1962.

Lenore Benson

FASHION EDUCATION Because the design and retailing of fashion is a global phenomenon, it should come as no surprise that learning institutions around the world prepare graduates for careers in the international fashion industry. Training ranges from vocational to creative to theoretical and results in certificates and diplomas (one to three years), which include associate (two years), baccalaureate (four years), master (master of arts, M.A.; master of fine arts, M.F.A.; and master of sciences, M.S.) and doctoral (doctor of philosophy, Ph.D.; doctor of education, Ed.D.; and doctor of art, D.A.) degrees.

Programs that offer certificates and diplomas tend to exist as part of vocational institutions, and curriculum is focused exclusively on preparing students for industry employment. Baccalaureate programs, in contrast, tend to vary in scope. While some colleges and universities balance a major in fashion design or retailing with re-quired general or liberal education courses that expose students to a broader worldview, other four-year institutions concentrate solely on the theory and practice of art and design and all curriculum offerings stem from that singular mission. Graduate work is meant to be more focused, and degrees are offered in the areas of retailing, design, textile science, and history. Many universities around the world also offer more flexible graduate programs under such names as Fashion Studies or Clothing and Textiles.

Education Options
The fashion industry reaches around the world, with degree-earning opportunities that provide training on every continent in fashion design and retailing.

The United States
The United States is home to over 250 institutions of higher learning that include programs in fashion design and retailing. Many of these offerings are housed in colleges or departments that have evolved from the home economics tradition. Consequently, virtually every state in the United States has a university with undergraduate and graduate curriculum in retailing and fashion design. As programs have expanded and contracted, a variety of names have emerged. Such college or department names as Human Ecology, Environmental Sciences, and Family and Consumer Sciences represent a general definition of the changing disciplines included in the mission. Design, Housing, and Apparel, Apparel Merchandising and Interior Design, and Merchandising and Hospitality Management represent more specific program orientation. When searching for fashion design and retailing programs at the university level, these are among the many terms and phrases to consider. Within this type of university system, the retailing or fashion design major program is enriched with required general or liberal education courses that introduce students to a broader perspective on the global community. Students are able to earn a bachelor's degree, and many departments also offer master's and doctoral degrees.

Within the United States, there are also colleges, schools, and universities of art and design, with four years of curriculum that refine and focus students' individual vision and aesthetics related to fashion design, complementing the development of creative skills with an expanded understanding of design theory. Graduates of these institutions have the opportunity to earn a variety of degrees, including an associate of arts (A.A.), bachelor of arts (B.A.), bachelor of fine arts (B.F.A.), master of arts (M.A.), and master of fine arts (M.F.A.) degrees.

In addition, an abundance of vocational and technical schools and art and design institutes offer focused one- to three-year programs in the areas of retailing and fashion design. Degrees earned include associate of arts (A.A.) and associate of applied sciences (A.A.S.), and students are prepared for specific positions within the fashion industry.

Canada

Six Canadian provinces have more than ten notable educational institutions that offer programs in fashion design or retailing. Students are able to earn bachelor, master of science, and doctoral degrees within departments of Human Ecology in the general areas of Clothing and Textiles. Bachelor of applied arts or bachelor of design degrees are also available at technical universities. Several vocational and technical institutions offer certificates and two-year diplomas that prepare students for the business and creative sides of the fashion industry.

Europe

There are well over one hundred learning institutions in twenty-seven countries across Europe that include fashion design or retailing in their curriculum. Because London, Paris, and Milan continue to function as celebrated international fashion centers, the United Kingdom, France, and Italy warrant individual consideration. There are also significant and interesting educational opportunities in Scandinavia, Central and Eastern Europe, and the other Western European countries.

United Kingdom. With London as one of the premier world fashion centers, it makes sense that more than forty educational institutions offering programs in fashion design or retailing are situated throughout England, with one or two in Scotland, Wales, and Northern Ireland. Learning opportunities range from vocational and technical training to prestigious art schools and universities. Completion is designated by National Diploma/Certificate (ND/C), generally a one-year technical degree; Higher National Diploma (HND), an additional year beyond earning of a certificate; and Bachelor of Arts Honors (B.A. Hons.) or Bachelor of Science Honors (B.S. Hons.), typically a three- or four-year advanced degree comparable to a four-year degree earned at a U.S. institution. Master and doctoral degrees can be earned at a few institutions, including more traditional university systems as well as those focused specifically on art and design.

France. Paris is home to France's five premier learning institutions with programs in fashion design and retailing. Two institutions offer curriculum in English and are organized for international students who desire short-term (four weeks) or long-term (three years) study-abroad opportunity in the areas of retailing or fashion design. Certificates and bachelor degrees can be earned, and credits may be transferred to colleges and universities at both the graduate and undergraduate levels. The other specialized schools are organized in the manner of art and design schools and offer one-, two-, or three-year programs in textile design and fashion design.

Italy. Italy has more than twenty design and retailing academies and institutes scattered around the country, with several more prominent programs in such vibrant international fashion centers as Florence, Milan, and Rome. Students are presented with a range of opportunities: one-, two-, three-, and four-year programs, summer short courses, workshops, and practical training in all facets of the fashion industry. Several academies offer programs of varying lengths for international students who choose to study fashion in Italy. All programs, regardless of length, are part of academies or institutes that focus solely on the practical and theoretical aspects of design and retailing. Many of the learning institutions are directly linked with professionals in the Italian fashion industry, providing students with opportunities to train and network with potential employers.

Other Western European countries. While not as heavily concentrated, over thirty-five institutions offering fashion design and retailing are distributed throughout the remainder of Western Europe in such countries as Austria, Belgium, Germany, Greece, Ireland, the Netherlands, Portugal, Spain, and Switzerland. Diplomas, bachelor, and a few graduate programs are available throughout the region.

Central and Eastern European countries. There are several opportunities for earning degrees in retailing and fashion design in such countries as the Czech Republic, Estonia, Hungary, Latvia, Lithuania, Poland, Romania, Russia, Slovakia, Slovenia, and the Ukraine. Lithuania, Poland, Slovakia, and Russia have particularly impressive and extensive offerings, with bachelor and graduate programs.

Scandinavia. Scandinavia has long enjoyed a rich craft tradition, which continues to be nurtured through university curriculum offerings. Norway, Sweden, and Denmark have institutions that offer two- and four-year degrees in both fashion and textile design. In Finland, students can earn bachelor, master, or doctoral degrees in textiles, clothing, or craft design within such departments as Textiles and Clothing and Home Economics and Craft Science.

Asia

Fashion education is prominent and tremendously active in China, India, and South Korea and is the focus of this section. However, exciting educational opportunities also exist in Japan, Malaysia, Philippines, Singapore, and Vietnam.

China. Including the People's Republic, Taiwan, and Hong Kong, China has much to offer in the educating of professionals in the areas of clothing design and textile technology. Students are able to earn certificates and diplomas, bachelor of arts, bachelor of science, masters, and doctoral degrees at several institutions. Some institutions focus on textiles and apparel programs that include studies in textile science and textile technology. College names such as Home Economics and Human Ecology emerge in institutional literature, suggesting that some Chinese clothing and textiles programs are modeled after U.S. offerings.

India. The country of India is a hotbed of international apparel and footwear manufacturing companies. Educational institutions have responded to the need to train professionals and over fifty-five institutions offer programs in fashion design and retailing. The majority of curriculum focuses on fashion design and technology, although a few programs offer degrees focused on the business side of the apparel industry. Degree opportunities range from technical diplomas and certificates in such areas as apparel production competencies (garment fabrication, sketching, cutting, tailoring, embroidery, and computer-aided design [CAD]) and fashion retail management, to four-year bachelor degrees in fashion design.

South Korea. Within South Korea, more than forty universities and colleges offer two-year, four-year, master's, and doctoral degrees in the areas of fashion design and retailing. These programs emerge from such divisions as Human Ecology, Home Economics, Clothing and Textiles, Fashion Design, and Fashion Marketing. Two- and four-year degrees prepare students for careers in the textile and apparel industry. Graduate curriculum focuses specifically on textile and apparel industry issues, including technological expertise and economic trends.

Oceania

There are more than twenty institutions located in the Oceanic region, with programs that focus on fashion design, retailing, and textile technology. Australia boasts several programs with certificates and diplomas, bachelor's, master's, and doctoral degrees. New Zealand is home to a dozen universities, institutes of technology, polytechnics, and colleges of art and design with a focus on fashion design and retailing. A degree in apparel merchandising and fashion design is also available in Papua New Guinea. Within these Oceanic countries, certificates and diplomas are earned in such areas as clothing production, textiles, footwear production, and fashion design. Bachelor of science degrees are available in Textile and Apparel Management and bachelor of arts degrees are available in Fashion and Textile Design.

Other World Locations

Iraq, Israel, Saudi Arabia, and United Arab Emirates in the Middle East; Argentina, Brazil, Chile, Uruguay in South America; Mexico in North America; and the African countries of Congo, South Africa, and Zimbabwe also have universities and colleges that offer stimulating two- and four-year degrees in fashion design and fashion marketing.

Conclusion

This overview on fashion education reveals three important points: (1) fashion education is offered on every continent around the world, (2) training professionals for the international apparel industry takes many forms, and (3) there exists a reciprocal relationship between the inter-national fashion industry and educational training in the areas of fashion design and retailing. In geographic regions around the world where design is celebrated, there are fashion design schools (Italy, France, and England). Locations with a multitude of apparel manufacturing sites tend to be breeding grounds for training in technical and creative competencies (China, India, and South Korea). Educational institutions continue to recognize and address the essential needs of the fashion industry.

See also **Fashion Advertising; Fashion Designer; Fashion Editors; Fashion Illustrators; Fashion Industry; Fashion Journalism; Fashion Models; Fashion Photography.**

BIBLIOGRAPHY

The World of Learning: The Definitive Guide to Higher Education World-wide. London: Europa Publications, 2003.

Internet Resources

Education Institutes in India: Fashion and Design. 2003. Available from <http://www.webindia123.com/career/fashion/list.asp?action=Fashion+Technology>.

International Directory of Design. 2003. Available from <http://www.penrose-press.com>.

International Textiles and Apparel Association Directory. 2003. Available from <http://www.itaaonline.org>.

Jane Hegland

FASHION, HEALTH, AND DISEASE The relationship between fashion and health is a complex one, with fashion sometimes being shaped by current beliefs about health and disease and, at other times, acting as the cause of illness.

Early Beliefs

For many centuries, those in the Western world believed that human illness was primarily related to the disposition of "humors," vapors coming from deep inside the body and released at the skin surface (Renbourn and Rees 1972, p. 401). The ancient Greeks believed that a damp, cold environment prevented these humors from passing out through the skin, being turned back instead toward the internal organs. There, they caused inflammation and every imaginable disease. The belief that damp cold was almost solely responsible for most human illness persisted until the middle of the nineteenth century, when the science of bacteriology began to link disease to the spread of infectious organisms.

The fear of damp cold led to multiple theories about dressing for health. There was, of course, the fear that the very clothing worn to protect the body from damp cold, could itself block the passage of humors outward. Arguments were made in favor of each of the natural fibers as being the most healthy to be worn, with wool being believed by many to be the most healthy because it was found to be the greatest absorber of water.

The human body does actually release vapors from the skin surface in a continual drying out of the skin called insensible perspiration. Research in the mid-1800s established for the first time that wool had the ability to absorb insensible perspiration and later condense it under cooler conditions, sending the resulting heat from condensation back toward the body (Renbourn and Rees, p. 40). Cotton and linen appeared to have no such capacity to produce heat; they continued to cool until dry, leading to a dangerous chilling of the body.

These findings caused many health practitioners to advocate wool in the years that followed. One, a German physiology professor named Jaeger, touted his all-woolen system of dress as the key to revolutionizing the health of all ages in all climates (Renbourn and Rees, p. 46). Many believed that wool also served as a "filter" to prevent impurities from reaching the body. Wool later was discovered to have another prized quality—it retained an electric charge. In the middle of the eighteenth century, many believed that a strong positive electrical charge led to male virility (Renbourn and Rees 1972, p. 33). During the nineteenth century, electric and magnetic garments were in vogue, and statically charged undergarments were credited with having powers from curing rheumatism to affecting the bowels (Renbourn and Rees, p. 39).

Wool, however, had its detractors, particularly among those who worked and lived in the tropics. A number of physicians in the seventeenth and eighteenth centuries noted that because wool was not easy to clean, it housed and propagated fleas, lice, and other carriers of disease. Excessive swaddling of infants in wool in the tropics by British nurses working there was thought to be one cause of infant mortality. Many believed cotton to be healthier than wool in warm climates because it provided more continual cooling and was more easily cleanable and less irritating to the skin.

From the seventeenth to nineteenth centuries, an almost irrational fear of exposure to drafts existed in many countries. Exposure to air currents was believed to be responsible for a wide range of conditions, including head colds, sore throats, and rheumatism. This concern contributed to excessive coverage of the body, even in warmer weather. During the French Revolution, when women ignored traditional admonitions for body coverage, the supposed link between diseases like consumption and revealing garments made of the sheer muslins of the time even led to new labels, such as "muslin disease" and "pneumonia blouses" (Renbourn and Rees, p. 34).

Color was believed to have had magical properties that affected human health. Various colors have been thought to best intercept dangerous rays of the sun or attract or repel toxins. While there has been considerable debate about the importance of specific hues in protecting the body, many cultures that exist in desert climates have long accepted that most whites and lighter colors reflect more sunlight than most blacks and darker colors. The white robes of desert dwellers, for example, offer thermal protection by reflecting the radiant heat of the sun away from the body.

Fashion as Detriment to Health

One of the main reasons early fashion was detrimental to health was that dressing in many layers and bathing infrequently combined to make clothing a breeding ground for infectious organisms and vermin. Some fashions also seemed to attract infected refuse. A medical paper of 1900 reported on a bacteriological examination of the trailing voluminous skirts of the time in which the author "found large colonies of germs, including those of tuberculosis, typhoid, tetanus, influenza" (Rudofsky 1947, p. 181).

Fashion has often involved modification of the body. The professed reasons for this range from ceremonial to practical, among them: influencing the morality of a wearer's behavior, communicating social status, increasing sexual allure, and establishing an aesthetic ideal. Harold Koda states that "Shoes have been the most persistent example of fashion's imposition of an idealized form on the natural anatomy" (2001, p. 140). He notes that the portion of the shoe that contained the toes has rarely, if ever, reflected the shape of the human foot but that the shape of a shoe, "consistently worn eventually molds the foot" (p. 140).

There has been much controversy about the health effects of modified feet. The most extreme example of foot modification is the Chinese bound, or lotus, foot. Dorothy Ko states that while Chinese footbinding shifted the placement of the bones of the foot, it broke no bones. It simply shortened the length of the foot and changed the locus of its support of body weight (p. 60). Many lotus shoes were designed to allow the axis of support of body weight to pass through the heel alone, alleviating any painful pressure on the folded toes (p. 152). Koda states that the spiked heel that was first made popular in the 1950s has acted to place the foot of its wearer in almost the same vertical position as the lotus foot. (2001, p. 159). In addition to precipitating ankle injury, the "tiptoe" stance of the foot in high heels "has been known to shorten the leg muscles, and in creating a destabilized stance, it can precipitate problems at the small of the back" (p. 163).

In the nineteenth century, physicians argued that the "wasp waist" of the corseted woman was detrimental to health, producing various conditions such as fainting, cracked ribs, miscarriage, difficulties in breathing, and abnormally functioning internal organs (Renbourn and Rees 1972, p. 11). More recent research on the effects of the corset have found few, if any, permanent health effects for adult women once a corset is removed (Steele 2001). However, Steele acknowledges that because corsets interfered with respiration, they did create "a disincentive" for Victorian women to exercise (p. 71). Indeed, one of fashion's primary negative effects on health in the past may have been limiting the types of activities in which individuals have felt able to participate.

Current Approaches

The belief that cold, damp weather and exposure to drafts are responsible for the common cold and flu has persisted to modern times, despite the assertions of clothing physiologists that "cold stress" is only one of dozens of stresses of modern life that lead to these illnesses.

During the second half of the twentieth century, dressing to protect the body from thermal conditions in the environment generally involved one of two approaches: using clothing to insulate the body against sudden heat loss or using it to shield the body from excessive heat gain. While much has been made of the healthful effects of specific fibers, it is well accepted that the fiber used in garments is only one factor in the ability of clothing to provide thermal balance. Watkins cites multiple factors: the fiber, yarn type, fabric construction, fabric finish, garment design, and the way of wearing a garment (1995, p. 26). Even when the same garments are worn in a different layering order, or freed or tucked in differently, the thermal balance of the wearer can be greatly affected.

New processing methods for fibers and fabrics have markedly improved insulation materials, and a variety of methods of protecting insulations from wind and water have emerged. The development of a material with micropores, Gore-Tex, in the mid-twentieth century brought the advent of waterproof materials that "breathe." These fabrics exclude liquid water, but allow vapor such as insensible perspiration to migrate out of an ensemble. Supple aluminized coatings on materials enable the reflection of radiant heat from the sun, fires, or high-heat industrial settings.

Despite technological advances that have created the potential for healthy clothing, some cultural norms may still dictate the use of garments that negatively affect health. Muslim women continue to wear the chador, the heavy, full-length veil that has been said to have caused fainting and serious long-term health problems such as osteoporosis. Western men continue to wear improperly sized business shirts with collars that cut off proper blood flow, leading to a variety of conditions from fainting to decreased visual acuity (Langan and Watkins 1987).

Other cultural norms focus on what is believed to be healthier approaches to dressing. Some Western professionals wearing high fashion walk to the office in running shoes, donning fashionable footwear only for meetings. Elderly women in nursing home wheelchairs are increasingly seen, not in the socially acceptable dresses from their pasts, but in nonbinding jogging suits.

The growing interest in alternative medicine has also revived a number of clothing practices that have met with great skepticism in the past. Experiments with the effect of color on the immune system continue. Proponents believe that magnetic clothing items may relieve pain and cure a number of different conditions. Citing new evidence relating copper to the body's enzyme production, proponents have revived interest in copper jewelry as a cure for arthritis.

The Future

Clothing has been designed to shield the body from all sorts of hazards of modern life. During the Gulf War in 1991, it was not unusual to see Israeli civilians of all ages carrying gas masks as constant accessories. Filtration masks to prevent the spread of respiratory diseases or protect asthmatics from pollution have become familiar sights. The U.S. Occupational Safety and Health and Administration (OSHA) has established educational programs to teach laborers who work with toxic chemicals the dangers of exposing the skin and respiratory system to those hazards and help them select appropriate protective suits and respirators. Space suits have been miniaturized to allow immune-deficient patients to venture into the world. Sheer, supple stainless-steel undergarments have been marketed particularly to pregnant women who work at computers, to protect them from electromagnetic radiation. There are few occupational hazards for which health-protective apparel has not been developed. Many of these have been reshaped into fashionable forms; others themselves establish a new fashion aesthetic.

All of these approaches to protection are essentially passive design concepts, working to shield the body somehow from the environment. Advances in technology are making it increasingly possible to use active approaches to protection, where clothing contributes to thermal balance or other forms of protection. For example, electrically heated and water-cooled systems have existed for decades, but the increasing miniaturization of power sources will make these more available and easily incorporated into everyday clothing. Clothing fibers have been impregnated with chemicals that absorb body heat when the wearer is warm and release it when the body begins to cool. These advances allow clothing to serve not just as a barrier, but as an active provider of thermal balance without an external power source.

Some proposed clothing designs incorporate mechanisms that will massage and stimulate blood flow to an ailing body part or trigger an automatically inflated airbag should the wearer start to fall. Others, for example a wristband worn to prevent seasickness, simply help the body heal itself, operating on centuries-old knowledge based on alternative treatments such as acupuncture.

Garments have been impregnated with bacteria-deterring agents to actively fight organisms that attempt to make their way toward a wearer. Undergarments have been developed that monitor multiple aspects of body function and send signals that stimulate medical devices or trigger the release of medications into the body. Many of these have been connected to computerized body-monitoring systems allowing clothing to respond automatically to each individual's needs. These garments allow patients formerly tied to hospital beds to move into the world. Many are wireless, so that doctors can monitor a patient's health at a distance and make adjustments in treatment accordingly. As the body's most intimate environment, clothing has enormous potential to help individuals meet the health challenges of the future.

See also **Color in Dress; Corset; Footbinding; High Heels.**

BIBLIOGRAPHY

Ko, Dorothy. *Every Step a Lotus.* Berkeley: University of California Press, 2001.

Koda, Harold. *Extreme Beauty.* New York: Metropolitan Museum of Art, 2001.

Langan, Leonora, and Susan Watkins. "Pressure of Menswear on the Neck in Relation to Visual Performance." In *Human Factors* 29 no. 1 (1987): 67–72.

Renbourn, E. T., and W. H. Rees. *Materials and Clothing in Health and Disease.* London: H. K. Lewis and Company, 1972.

Rudofsky, Bernard W. H. *Are Clothes Modern?* Chicago: Paul Theobold, 1947.

Steele, Valerie. *The Corset.* New Haven, Conn.: Yale University Press, 2001.

Watkins, Susan. *Clothing: The Portable Environment.* Ames: Iowa State University Press, 1995.

Susan M. Watkins

FASHION ICONS The term "fashion icon" has recently replaced the slightly antiquated notion of "fashion leaders." During the second half of the twentieth century, fashion became less hierarchical, more meritocratic, and media-dominated. Indeed, the media itself created its own icons of style, while scrutinizing those proffered up by journalists, stylists, and others involved in the professional process of promoting fashion. The "trickle-down," designer-led fashions of the past were joined by the concept of "bubble-up," where fashions are created on the streets and fed upward through the fashion system. "Style is not fashion until it has reached the street," is a statement popularly attributed to Coco Chanel, herself a leader; she was also part of the democratization of fashion.

The "fashion leaders" of past generations were those in the very highest society—royalty, aristocrats, and their wives and mistresses. The Bourbon courts of pre-Revolutionary France were famous for their fashion excesses, while in the 1790s Napoleon's wife, Josephine, embraced the new "Empire-line dresses," which quickly crossed the Channel. In England, at precisely the same moment in history, the Prince Regent, who gave his name to an architectural style, was consorting with the dandies of the day, including the famous Beau Brummel.

At the start of the twentieth century, magazine journalism had been enlivened by still photographs, and cinema was in its infancy. Much of the newsreel footage from the first decade of the new century showed King Edward VII and his elegant wife, Alexandra; many of his mistresses were also fashion leaders, such as Madame Standish of Paris, who was the first to wear the new "tailor-mades" by Creed to the Paris racecourse; and Lillie Langtry, the music-hall actress, who was a favorite of the popular press. It was her amply curved figure that was the fashionable silhouette, as seen in the popular illustrations of the "Gibson Girls," created by the American, Charles Dana Gibson.

Chanel set up her fashion business before World War I and, in its aftermath, a radically altered society found her designs suited its new needs. During the War, many women had experienced the freedom of wearing trousers for manual work—and freedom of movement was Chanel's aim. She liked wearing men's sweaters and put women in soft jersey and fluid garments. She popularized costume jewelry, the little black dress—and the suntan. She was emulated in every way, and when she came back from the Riviera to display her suntan at the Opera, a new craze began.

The war annihilated a generation of young men; the women who survived wanted to forget, rather than to mourn. Economic independence and changing mores meant new fashion icons were needed for the 1920s—the "Bright Young Things" of London and the stars who personified the Jazz Age: Clara Bow, the "It Girl" of cinema; and the idol of Paris, singer Josephine Baker. In the Roaring Twenties, too, stage actresses—such as Gertrude Lawrence—were still relevant; they, too, had shingled hair, short skirts, and cigarette holders.

There was still a role for royalty—men and women were fascinated by the dress of Edward, Prince of Wales, and his Oxford bags, plus fours, and Argyle sweaters were widely copied. He even had a fabric pattern named after him—Prince-of-Wales check. His long-term mistress, Freda Dudley Ward, embodied the flapper look of the 1920s, but in the following decade he abandoned her to marry the stylish American divorcée, Wallis Simpson. It was she who formulated the fashion dictum, "A woman can never be too rich or too thin." Although the public was distressed by his abdication, they nevertheless bought mass-market copies of her Molyneux wedding dress.

Technological changes now meant that fashions could be copied at moderate prices, and, at last, ordinary women could copy their icons. This was the decade when Hollywood moguls allowed women to imitate the dresses of their favorite stars, as well as their makeup—Adrian's outfits for Joan Crawford were highly influential, and Travis Banton's dressing of Marlene Dietrich made trousers seem sexy rather than merely functional. Joan Crawford's famous puff-sleeved dress, created by Adrian for the film *Letty Lynton* in 1932, was instantly copied, and inspired young girls' party dresses for the next ten years. Dietrich in *Morocco* (1930) was the first woman to don men's evening wear, and created a sensation when she appeared on screen in her tuxedo and top hat.

World War II meant fashion was curbed—and economic recovery was slow in the postwar period of shortages and rationing. The most famous couture collection ever was Dior's New Look of 1947, with its long skirts and nostalgic elegance—it filtered down to high-street level and was popular well into the 1950s with Hollywood costume designers. Edith Head dressed leading stars Grace Kelly, Audrey Hepburn, and the young Elizabeth Taylor in outfits inspired by the New Look.

The 1950s saw a sea change with the advent of youth-oriented fashions, linked to music and to the newly discovered and largest consumer group, the "teenagers." Economic power meant that young people wanted their own fashions and music, and their own icons. Marlon Brando created a particular look with his T-shirt in *A Streetcar Named Desire* (1951) and his leather jacket in *The Wild One* (1953). James Dean put the two together—as did Elvis Presley. The changing mood was reflected by the antifashion look of Brigitte Bardot in *And God Created Woman* (1956)—with untidy hair, short cotton dresses, and bare feet, she was the antithesis of groomed Hollywood glamour.

Jackie Kennedy presented a very different fashion picture in the early 1960s; copies of her suits, dress-and-coat outfits, and pillbox hats were very popular. But taste had changed—and fashion became, for the first time, completely youth-led, with London at the epicenter of the "youthquake." Models such as Jean Shrimpton and Twiggy, film stars like Julie Christie and, above all, musicians, were the new icons. Whether dressed in sharp suits, like the Beatles, or wearing their own eclectic mix of clothes, like Jimi Hendrix and Keith Richards of the Rolling Stones—whatever they did was picked up immediately. Designer Ossie Clark famously dressed Mick Jagger in a white tunic and trousers in 1969, and in the 1970s the male stars of "glamrock" wore makeup.

The economic difficulties of the 1970s produced the hedonism of Studio 54—where Bianca Jagger appeared, attired by Halston—and the confrontational androgyny of punk. In 1977, the Sex Pistols wore clothes designed by Vivienne Westwood—torn, provocative, and fetishistic.

In the 1980s, as economic prosperity returned, so did conventional icons, like the young Princess Diana, and more glamorous icons; the "supermodels" were dressed and lionized by Gianni Versace. Rap stars, like Run-DMC, made active sportswear fashionable; designers copied their look. In the 1990s, there was a need for less "glitzy" icons; fashion followed music into "grunge," photographers like Corinne Day created "waifs" such as Kate Moss, and sports stars became emblems of style. In 2003, there is no shortage of icons—"celebrity culture" has provided, perhaps, too many. This could mean that the notion of a "fashion icon," like that of a "fashion leader," needs to be redefined.

Jacqueline Kennedy. Though she was First Lady for only a few years, Jackie Kennedy's modern elegance had a long-lasting influence on the fashion world. © UPI/CORBIS-BETTMANN. REPRODUCED BY PERMISSION.

JACKIE KENNEDY

Jacqueline Lee Bouvier was born into a wealthy family and raised to a life of privilege. Her 1953 marriage to Senator Jack Kennedy at the wealthy enclave of Newport, Rhode Island, was one of the most glittering social events of the decade. Mrs. Kennedy became a popular figure during the 1960 presidential campaign; after her husband's election, her beauty, love of clothes, and sense of style set her apart from her rather plain predecessors as First Lady, Bess Truman and Mamie Eisenhower. Criticized in some quarters for wearing European fashions, she patronized American designers, particularly Oleg Cassini (whose designs, however, owed much to European originals). Her inauguration outfit of a fawn-colored woolen coat with matching pillbox hat was instantly copied by thousands of women; a red dress (by Chez Ninon after a Marc Bohan for Dior original) that she wore for a televised tour of the White House became another iconic "Jackie Look."

In 1968, five years after her husband's assassination, Mrs. Kennedy married wealthy Greek shipowner Aristotle Onassis; after his death in 1975 she returned to New York City and lived there until her death in 1994. Throughout those years she dressed with elegance and style; but her time as a true fashion icon came during her brief years in "Camelot," the Kennedy White House.

See also **Actors and Actresses, Impact on Fashion; Celebrities; Fashion Models.**

BIBLIOGRAPHY

Bailey, David, and Peter Evans. *Goodbye Baby and Amen.* London: Conde Nast, 1969.

Beaton, Cecil. *The Glass of Fashion* London: Weidenfeld and Nicholson, 1954.

Bruzzi, Stella, and Pamela Church Gibson. *Fashion Cultures: Theories, Explorations, Analysis.* London: Routledge: 2000.

Garland, Madge. *The Changing Face of Fashion.* London: Dent and Sons, 1970.

Pamela Church Gibson

FASHION ILLUSTRATORS Fashion illustration, although often considered quaint and recherché, cannot, in fact, be separated from the development of printing technologies and the growth of fashion journalism.

The appearance of the first costume books (records of regional and ethnic dress) in the sixteenth century, is linked, as Alice Mackrell confirms in her book, *An Illustrated History of Fashion*, to: "The invention of movable printing types by Johannes Guttenberg in Munich in 1454" (p. 14). The development of engraving techniques further propagated the distribution of fashion art, even as the computer is doing today.

The advent of fashion photography, however, has had as great an impact on fashion illustration as any printing technologies. Today, illustration exists in a symbiotic, and secondary, relationship to the lens, where once it was king.

Photography—no matter how altered or retouched—has become irrevocably equated with what is real and true. The photographic image is seen to provide a "customer service"—to show the clothes, just as the fashion plate once did. In contrast, in the twentieth century, fashion illustration has become more and more expressive, conveying an idea or an attitude, the fragrance of a look, as it were.

In some ways the predominance of photography is very logical. During a time of fashion dictatorship (through the 1950s) fashion illustration existed alongside photography as a sort of couture art form that mirrored in many ways the production, presentation, and style of the clothes. The 1960s' emphasis on youth and street influences was well suited to the immediacy of photography and its by-now iconic pioneers, like the rough-and-tumble David Bailey–type parodied in Michelangelo Antonioni's *Blow-Up*. Illustrators, in contrast, are mostly anonymous, working as they do, alone.

The all-star list of fashion artists might be topped by the seventeenth-century artists Jacques Callot (1592–1635) and Abraham Bosse (1602–1676), both of whom exploited improving engraving techniques to produce realistic details of the clothes and costumes of their times. A litany of fashion magazines appeared between the seventeenth and nineteenth centuries in France and England—among them *Le Mecure Gallant, The Lady's Magazine, La Gallerie des Modes, Le Cabinet des Modes,* and *Le Journal des dames et des modes*—all of which propelled the fashion plate to its nineteenth-century efflorescence.

The fashion plate, which captured trend-driven information as well as provided general dressmaking instruction, came into its own in the eighteenth century, flourishing, finally, in *fin de siècle* Paris. A shining example of this flowering is Horace Venet's *Incroyables et Merveilleuses*, a series of watercolor drawings by Venet of fashions under Napoleon I, engraved by Georges-Jacques Gatine as a series of fashion plates. France's position as the arbiter of fashion insured that there was a constant demand, at home and abroad, for fashion illustration. This demand was met by such talented artists as the Colin sisters and Mme. Florensa de Closménil.

The focus of nineteenth-century illustrators was on accuracy and details. They conformed to static, iconographic conventions in order to provide information and instruction to their viewers. In contrast, contemporary fashion illustration, which dates to the turn of the twentieth century, is highly graphic and focuses more on the artist's individual filter of the world. For example, Charles Dana Gibson's (1867–1944) scratchy renderings of the modern American woman, with upswept hair and shirtwaist, defined a type as well as provided a humorous, sometimes satirical, commentary on contemporary American life.

In Paris, Paul Poiret was commissioning limited edition albums by artists like Paul Iribe (1883–1935), known for his jeweled-tone palette and clean graphic line, as pure artwork. In this way Poiret aligned his new uncorseted and exotic silhouettes with the elite and exclusive world of art.

Iribe was part of a cabal of fashion illustrators who contributed to the celebrated *La gazette du bon ton*, which was published from 1912–1925 and included work by such greats as: Charles Martin (1848–1934); Eduardo Garcia Benito (1892–1953); Georges Barbier (1882–1932); Georges Lepape (1887–1971); and Umberto Brunelleschi (1879–1949). The now highly collectible plates they produced for the gazette show the influence of Japanese wood-block prints as well as the new sleek geometry of Deco styling.

Vogue and *Harper's Bazaar* magazines also kept the art of fashion illustration alive, featuring from about 1892 through the 1950s the work of fashion illustrators like Christian Berard (1902–1949), Eric [Carl Erickson] (1891–1958), Erté [Romain de Tirtoff] (1892–1990), Marcel Vértes (1895–1961), Rene Bouché (1906–1963), and René Gruau (1908–). Berard and Vértes in particular are famous for their friendships and collaborations with designers such as Coco (Gabrielle) Chanel and Elsa Schiaparelli, who also worked with fine artists like Jean Cocteau and Salvador Dalí (who illustrated several *Vogue* covers). Both Berard and Vértes had a soft line, similar to that of Andy Warhol's fashion illustrations. René Gruau, on the other hand, is famous for his work for Christian Dior. His bold calligraphic style is among the most distinguished of the first half of the twentieth century.

One illustrator dominated the century's second half: Puerto Rican-born Antonio Lopez (1943–1987). Inspired as much by the street as by experiments with art historical styles (Deco, Op, etc.) his sensual renderings of personalities from friends like Pat Cleveland and Jerry Hall to urban break-dancers, all drawn from life, had relevance and resonance even in a photographic age. "When Antonio died," says fellow illustrator Tobie Giddio, "it's as if he took illustration with him."

Indeed, in spite of the contributions of artists like Jeffrey Fulvimari, Joe Eula, Lorenzo Mattotti (1954–), Mats Gustafson (1951–), Thierry Perez, and Tony Viramontes (1960–1988), the métier was not to see a re-

vival of any scale until the 1990s. However, *Vanity*, a short-lived illustrated magazine founded in Milan by Anna Piaggi (for which François Berthoud [1961–] illustrated most of the covers), deserves mention.

Credit for a renewed interest in illustration at the turn of the twenty-first century goes to Barneys New York for their 1993–1996 advertising campaign. Conceived of by Ronnie Cooke Newhouse, with copy by Glenn O'Brien and squiggly, indeterminate—yet bitingly satirical illustrations—by Jean-Philippe Delhomme (1959–), these bizarre advertisements stood in direct, and effective, contrast to the aesthetics of the time, especially the supermodel phenomenon and the penchant for the grungy, often androgynous "heroin chic" look.

The next blip in the history of contemporary fashion illustration came via a lifestyle—not a fashion—book: Tyler Brulé's *Wallpaper*. In *Wallpaper* illustration was considered an extension of design, and the magazine's out-sized pages were given over to such talents as Anja Kroenke, Liselotte Watkins, and the magazine's illustrative mascot of sorts, Jordi Labanda. Fashion magazines, with the notable exception of *Vogue Italia*, which often features the work of Mats Gustafson, the Swedish-born master of minimalism, continue to relegate illustration to spots—often on cooking or horoscope pages. *Vogue Nippon*, founded in 2000, also proves an exception to the rule, favoring the work of such artists as Ruben Toledo and Piet Paris.

Most recently, illustration has come into vogue through collaborations between designers and illustrators/artists. Marc Jacobs at Louis Vuitton has partnered with Julie Verhoeven and Takashi Murakami, and Stella McCartney with David Remfy.

At the turn of the twenty-first century, illustration is being revolutionized by technology—again—this time via the computer. While the late nineties saw the rise of slick computer-based drawing by such pioneers as Ed Tsuwaki, Graham Rounthwaite, Jason Brooks, and Kristian Russell, there has been a backlash in favor of work that is, or looks like it is, hand-drawn. Charles Anaste's realistic, biographical illustrations are much in demand, but so are the hyperrealist work of René Habermacher, the surreal stylings of Richard Gray, and Julie Verhoeven's erotic fashion drawings. Mixed media work is also popular, as virtual collages are made possible by new technology.

Technology's greatest impact, though, is on the actual production of artwork. What fashion illustration is, must be reconsidered. It is a strange, strange irony, too, that the fashion plate, an early form of fashion illustration, was mechanically produced and hand-colored, whereas contemporary illustration usually starts with a hand sketch and is finished—and colored—by hand. "I am curious about what is going to happen," muses Habermacher, whose work fully exploits digital processes. "In recent years," he said, "I have realized that the direction of my work is different from what you can describe as classical fashion illustration. Continuing on that road will necessarily lead to a new definition."

However difficult a definition of fashion illustration might be, its existence, and importance, is without question. The world has need of what art director Davis Schneider refers to as "visual luxuries"—illustrated fashion art.

See also **Barbier, Georges; Fashion Plates; Fashion Magazines; Fashion Models; Fashion Photography; Iribe, Paul.**

BIBLIOGRAPHY

Borrelli, Laird. *Fashion Illustration Now.* London: Thames & Hudson, Inc., 2000.

Holland, Vyvyan. *Hand Coloured Fashion Plates: 1770–1889.* London: B. T. Batsford, Ltd., 1955.

Mackrell, Alice. *An Illustrated History of Fashion: 500 Years of Fashion Illustration.* New York: Quite Specific Media Group Ltd., 1997.

Packer, William. *Fashion Drawing in Vogue.* London: Thames & Hudson, Inc., 1989.

Steele, Valerie. *Paris Fashion.* New York: Oxford University Press, 1988.

Weill, Alain. *Paris Fashion: La gazette du bon ton: 1912–1925.* Paris: Bibliotèque de l'image, 2000.

Laird Borrelli

FASHION INDUSTRY The fashion industry is unique from other fields of manufacturing in that it is ruled largely by the same intention as its end product: change.

What defines the fashion industry is largely based on the functions of the individuals who comprise it—designers, stores, factory workers, seamstresses, tailors, technically skilled embroiderers, the press, publicists, salespersons (or "garmentos"), fit models, runway models, couture models, textile manufacturers, pattern makers, and sketch artists. In simplest terms, the fashion industry could be described as the business of making clothes, but that would omit the important distinction between fashion and apparel. Apparel is functional clothing, one of humanity's basic needs, but fashion incorporates its own prejudices of style, individual taste, and cultural evolution.

The notion of fashion as solely fulfilling a need is past, as the modern apparel industry finds its purpose in the conception, production, promotion, and marketing of style on the basis of desire. It reflects the changing wants of consumers to be defined by their attire, or more commonly to be accepted, which has precipitated change throughout fashion history—from iconic silhouettes referred to in the patronizing language of the early twentieth century, the Gibson Girls and Floradora Girls, to the enlightened New Look (a term coined by Carmel Snow, the editor of *Harper's Bazaar*, in 1947) and evolving right on through an ever-changing lexicon of haberdashery. Changing styles always necessitate change through industry, notably in the ever-specialized fields of manufacturing and merchandising, as well as through the promotion of designs and designers, expanding their scope into what are known in the early 2000s as "lifestyle brands," encompassing more than just fashion—incorporating the vernacular of fragrance, accessories, home furnishings, automobiles, jewelry, and writing instruments as well.

Even limited to the business of making clothes, its components have continually adapted to the changes of fashion and prevailing consumer demands, whether for casual clothes or formal suits, American sportswear, or celebrity-endorsed street wear. Over the decades, crinoline makers have become bra manufacturers, suit makers have adapted to the rise of separates, and textile mills have discovered the comfort of stretch. Meanwhile, new advancements in fabric development, manufacturing, and information management have become as important commodities as cotton and wool in the ever more complicated and competitive field. Throughout it all, the industry has developed classifications of pricing and style to facilitate its basic functions of designing and selling clothes along the traditional dividing line of wholesale and retail, one that has become much less distinct in recent years.

Following the traditional view of fashion's infrastructure, as referenced in the textbook *The Dynamics of Fashion*, there are four levels of the fashion industry: the primary level of textile production, including mills and yarn makers; the secondary level of designers, manufacturers, wholesalers, and vendors; the retail level, which includes all types of stores and distribution points of sale; and also a fourth level—the auxiliary level—which connects each of the other levels via the press, advertising, research agencies, consultants, and fashion forecasters who play a part in the merchandise's progression to the end consumer. While the relationship between the levels is more or less symbiotic—they need one another to survive—historically, the competitive spirit of capitalism has also created a tension between retailer and manufacturer, where the balance of power is usually tipped to one side in the race to capture profits and margins. The degree to which each side benefits financially from the sale of apparel has changed gradually over the decades, subject to many factors from social advancements to economic swings to cults of designer personalities to wars—both between countries and conglomerates. Over the century, the retailer, in many cases, has taken on the role of the manufacturer, and manufacturers have become retailers of their own designs.

The mass production of clothing began roughly in the mid-nineteenth century, when some manufacturers began to produce garments that did not require fitting, but fashion did not become an established industry in the institution sense of the word until the twentieth century, when networks of neighborhood tailors casually evolved into manufacturing businesses, factories grew from necessity during the world wars, and the ensuing social and cultural changes signified the dawn of less restrictive and unilateral codes of dress. Changes in the business of fashion, and the establishment of designers as arbiters of taste, began to take shape in the early part of the century, although largely led by European houses. As the French designer Paul Poiret said during a presentation at the Horace Mann School in 1913, "Elegance and fashion have been the pastime of our ancestors, but now they take on the importance of a science" (quoted in *Women's Wear Daily* in its ninetieth anniversary issue, 16 July 2001).

Just as French couture houses were beginning to gain an international reputation in the late nineteenth century, following the styles introduced by Charles Worth, Jeanne Lanvin, Paquin, and Poiret, the fast rise of garment factories, meanwhile, was largely an American phenomenon. It was most visible as an industry in New York City, where more than 18,000 workers were employed in the manufacture of blouses by 1900 at the time of the founding of the International Ladies Garment Workers Union (ILGWU), a precursor to the modern-day apparel union UNITE (Union of Needletrades, Industrial and Textile Employees), formed in 1995 with the merger of the Amalgamated Clothing and Textile Workers Union. The rapid shift of custom-made to ready-made clothes during the industrial revolution was stimulated by the growth of the middle class and a large increase in foreign labor, mostly Jewish and Italian immigrants who brought their tailoring skills from Europe and first organized themselves in tenements on the Lower East Side. However, the immigrant connection and overcrowded conditions generally associated with the industry led to zoning restrictions that quickly pushed production from apartment buildings into lofts and away from increasingly sophisticated showrooms. For twenty years, manufacturers continued to migrate north and west, often driven by law, such as when the Save New York Committee campaigned to move apparel factories out of the neighborhood known as Madison Square—where Broadway and East 23rd Street converge—because of fears that the factories would be a detriment to the atmosphere of nearby Fifth Avenue, known as the Ladies' Mile.

Working conditions declined as manufacturers took advantage of the increasing pools of immigrants, influencing the rise of sweatshop labor as well as the move to unionize workers. The industry grew exponentially—by 1915, apparel was the third largest in America, after steel and oil. The Triangle Shirtwaist fire of 1911, in which 146 workers were killed, had finally led to the regulation and scrutiny of garment industry working conditions.

The industry moved again beginning in 1920, when two sites along Seventh Avenue between 36th and 38th Streets were developed by the Garment Center Realty Co., an association of thirty-eight of the largest women's clothing makers, sparking the first influx of apparel businesses in a neighborhood that has become the early twenty-first-century home to New York's garment district. Yet change is still occurring, as most production has moved offshore to factories in cheaper locales and many designers have moved their offices to more "refined" neighborhoods away from the bustle of rolling racks and button shops.

In the 1930s, though, as the unified center for garment production, and the most highly concentrated apparel manufacturing capital in the world by this point, Seventh Avenue from 30th to 42nds Streets began to reflect the need for categorization within fashion. Although the industry can broadly be divided into two primary functions—wholesale and retail—the growing prevalence of department stores necessitated further distinctions. Certain buildings, in a tradition that continues in the early 2000s, house bridal firms, and others specialize in furriers, dress vendors, or coat companies, and within those categories grew distinctions of price or targeted demographic. The modern industry divides its pricing into four general categories of moderate, better, bridge, or designer apparel, from the least to most expensive, and within those categories are even more specialized distinctions, such as the relatively new silver and gold ranges (for prices that are too high to be considered bridge or too low to be called designer). There are also categories geared toward types of customers, such as juniors (a more generic classification for sportswear in the 1960s that is used to define teen-oriented labels), contemporary (geared toward young women and relating commonly to smaller sizes), and urban (reflecting the growing market for street wear).

For much of the twentieth century, the industry continued its evolution along familial lines, as the descendants of poor immigrants who had once operated those small factories along Orchard and Mulberry Streets on the Lower East Side began to establish serious businesses on Seventh Avenue, along with impressive fortunes behind companies with names that were for the large part inventions. Apart from the few pioneers of the first half of the century—Adrian, Bonnie Cashin, and Claire McCardell among them—the personalities behind the American fashion industry operated largely in anonymity compared with their counterparts in Paris, where Coco Chanel, Alix Grès, and Madeleine Vionnet had already become celebrities of international acclaim. Until World War II, it was common for American manufacturers to travel to the seasonal Paris shows, where they would pay a fee known as a caution to view the collections, usually with a minimum purchase of a few styles. They were legally permitted to copy these styles in the United States, where department stores began a tradition of lavishly presenting their copied collections with their own runway shows.

In the 1950s and 1960s, however, a growing number of entrepreneurial designers—many striking out in the business following their service in the war—began to make their way out of the backrooms to feature their own names on their labels, a development facilitated in part by the curiosity of the press and also by the ambitions of manufacturers to capitalize on designer personalities. Licensing a designer name into other categories became a common practice, and by the 1980s, propelled by an economic boom, designers had become celebrities—led by such ambitious and charismatic personalities as Oscar de la Renta, Bill Blass, Calvin Klein, and Halston. Meanwhile, the advent of the modern designer business stood in stark contrast to the overall industry, which remained largely characterized by independent companies, with as many as 5,000 businesses then making women's dresses, helmed by a prosperous but aging second generation. Since the 1980s, the apparel industry has come to be defined by consolidation, globalization, and the economics of publicly traded companies, where the biggest news stories have been the rush of many designers to Wall Street and the retail industry's continual merging into only a handful of remaining department store companies—giants encompassing the majority of retail nameplates.

Change continues to come. The fashion industry of the early 2000s is global, with luxury conglomerates taking stakes in American businesses and production constantly moving to countries that offer the most inexpensive labor. Garments are conceived, illustrated, and laser-cut by computers, and replenished automatically by a store's data system alerts. Designers compete directly with their biggest customers by opening flagships around the world, and stores compete with designers by sourcing and producing their own private label collections, often based on the prevailing runway looks. Magazine editors and stylists have gone on to become designers, while Hollywood actors and pop stars have gone from wearing designer clothes to creating them. At the outset of the twenty-first century, what defines the fashion industry has little to do with the artisan's craft of a century ago, but would be better described as the pursuit of profitable styles by multinational conglomerates with competitive technology and the most efficient delivery of timely merchandise.

But change in fashion—or the fashion industry—is nothing new. It seems fitting to refer to the opening line on page 1 of the first issue of *Women's Wear Daily*, which was founded as *Women's Wear* in June 1910, in response to the rise of the women's apparel industry: "There is probably no other line of human endeavor in which there is so much change as in the product that womankind wears."

See also **Economics and Clothing; Fashion Education; Fashion Marketing and Merchandising; Globalization.**

BIBLIOGRAPHY

Friedman, Arthur. "New York's Lucky Seventh." *WWD Century, Women's Wear Daily Special Edition* (September 1998): 162.

———. "Garment Town's Rise to Fashion Avenue." *WWD Ninety, Women's Wear Daily Special Edition* (16 July 2001): 226.

Stone, Elaine. *The Dynamics of Fashion*. 2nd ed. New York: Fairchild Publications, 2004.

Stegemeyer, Anne. *Who's Who in Fashion*. 3rd ed. New York: Fairchild Publications, 1996.

Wilson, Eric. "The Early Years." *WWD Ninety, Women's Wear Daily Special Edition* (16 July 2001): 58–60.

Eric Wilson

FASHION JOURNALISM Until Virginia Pope of the *New York Times* made fashion the topic of serious newspaper coverage with the attendant responsibilities for accuracy, objectivity, and fairness, the words "fashion journalism" were an oxymoron.

During her tenure at the *Times* (1925–1955), she raised the bar not only for fashion journalism, reporting on the Paris haute couture collections beginning in 1934 in addition to her regular New York coverage, she also introduced the idea of live theatrical fashion presentations, which she produced for the public each fall under the auspices of the *Times*.

Many other U.S. papers of that era ran occasional photos of the latest Paris creations and counted on their society editors to report on who-wore-what to the local charity ball. There was little or no regard for the business of fashion, its sociological implications, or news from designers.

In 1943, the New York fashion publicist Eleanor Lambert, who represented many New York designers of that era, initiated "press weeks," inviting fashion editors from newspapers throughout the country to attend capsule presentations of her clients' collections—showings that took place in New York hotel meeting rooms months after those same collections had opened to buyers in Seventh Avenue showrooms. Similar "press weeks" were held in Los Angeles, sponsored by the California Fashion Creators, a loose coalition of designers there.

The general tenor of the fashion writing in the 1940s and early 1950s was a labored accounting of skirt lengths, jacket cuts, color choices, and fabric descriptions. In 1956, Eleanor Nangle of the *Chicago Tribune*, together with fashion editors from the *Milwaukee Journal* (now the *Milwaukee Journal Sentinel*), the *Buffalo News*, and the *Fort Worth Star-Telegram* decided that fashion should be covered as sports are covered—at the time the games are played, in this case, at the time the seasonal collections opened to buyers, and not from hotel suites months later. (New York papers had "always" covered the showroom openings, but the out-of-town press had not, as few newspapers considered fashion an important enough subject to justify the expense of a week in New York.)

Lambert's press weeks continued, but more and more fashion editors from metropolitan newspapers began to attend the buyer openings and report, on the spot, from New York. And as they came, their competitors followed. A few—the *New York Times*, the *New York Times Magazine*, the *New York Herald-Tribune*, the *Chicago Tribune*, the *Washington Post*, the *Boston Globe*, the *Chicago Sun-Times*, and the *Los Angeles Times*—also reported on the Paris haute couture openings, as did the trade publication *Women's Wear Daily*.

Eugenia Sheppard, then at the *New York Herald-Tribune* and later at the *New York Post* and *Women's Wear Daily*, was one of the first to make fashion writing entertaining. She also proved her resourcefulness as a journalist by once sneaking into a Balenciaga show as a buyer in order to get immediate coverage. (Balenciaga and Hubert de Givenchy showed one month after the other couturiers and put embargos on news coverage for a month after their openings.) Her coverage got her banned from the next season's show, but she managed to cover that one, and others from which she would eventually be barred, by interviewing buyers who were in attendance. Such ingenuity also made her one of the first to be a fashion journalist celebrity.

By 1969, Paris ready-to-wear was becoming more and more important to American retailers, and newspaper fashion editors gradually started reporting on these twice-yearly events, later expanding that coverage to include Florence, Milan, and London. One editor, Nina Hyde of the *Washington Post*, made an exceptional contribution to fashion journalism by her efforts to discover new talent.

Bill Cunningham, first a columnist for *Women's Wear Daily* and later a freelance contributor to the *Chicago Tribune*, *Los Angeles Times*, and *Details* magazine, was the first fashion photojournalist to point out design copying. His photos of original designs juxtaposed with his photos of the copies left readers of *Details*, the *Los Angeles Times*, and the *Chicago Tribune* with little doubt of the design's provenance, and his witty texts became classroom examples of how to make fashion writing interesting. Cunningham's photo essays of the New York fashion scene for the *New York Times* are a weekly documentary of what real people really wear on the streets and in the social arena.

That so much fashion coverage in the 1970s, 1980s, and 1990s centered on the seasonal shows in Europe was a reflection of the Eurocentric nature of fashion at that time. The news—the trends that set the scene for the direction of fashion—was, for the most part, coming from Paris, Milan, or London. Americans were generally known as fashion marketers or stylists. Europeans, especially Paris designers, were the *créateurs*. As some have said: Americans make clothes; Europeans make fashion.

Increasingly aware that a lot of the fashion space they usually garnered was being taken by the European coverage, New York designers began to join the trend to more theatrical shows by leaving their showrooms in favor of larger hotel venues. Many upgraded their presentations from models instructed to bring their own shoes and the announcing of style numbers to buyers seated in rented-for-the-day little gold chairs to choreographed shows with music, never-seen-before, never-worn-before accessories crafted especially for the collection, hair and makeup professionals creating beauty looks, backstage booze, and, eventually, "supermodels."

In 1980, television fashion coverage, which until then had been limited to an occasional fashion "special," makeovers, and sixty seconds or so at the end of a morning show during collection openings, got its biggest boost when Elsa Klensch went on the air for CNN, her shows televised around the world. Given her international audience and her interviewing style—always respectful, never critical—Klensch was able to attract all the top designers for interviews and to gain access to their shows. For the first time, a viewer could watch the runway shows of all the major fashion players in New York, Tokyo, Paris, Milan, London, and Klensch's native Australia. *Style with Elsa Klensch* truly brought fashion to the masses. When the show was discontinued in 2000, it had an estimated 120 million viewers in 210 countries. *Edie Raymond Locke's Show* was another groundbreaking TV show from that time (1981–1986). The show was hosted by Edie Raymond Locke, who brought the magazine format she had pioneered as editor-in-chief of *Mademoiselle* magazine to USA Network. Her half-hour weekly shows concentrated on fashion, beauty, decorating, finances for women, makeovers, and model of the month. In the early 1990s, Geoffrey Beene became the first American designer to forsake the runway for the stage—first a mise-en-scène at Lincoln Center, then Broadway-type shows at the Equitable Building with elaborate stage sets, music created just for the show, and models interspersed with ballet dancers.

By 1993 the Council of Fashion Designers of America (CFDA) decided to try to compete with the European cities as a fashion capital by creating 7th on Sixth (7th on Sixth was the CFDA's way of saying Seventh Avenue—typically known as Fashion Avenue—had moved over a block to Sixth Avenue where Bryant Park is located) and producing shows under tents in Bryant Park. As the showmanship increased, fashion coverage increased, and designers attracted movie and rock stars to sit front row, some exchanging clothes for appearances. Journalists from Europe and Japan attended, providing a global audience for New York designers, a few of whom had begun to sell to European stores and open their own boutiques there. Madonna became a regular. Barbra Streisand, Whitney Houston, David Bowie, Mariah Carey, Lenny Kravitz—all brought their star power to the tents, juicing the entertainment element and thereby increasing newspaper readership and television viewers. The Bryant Park shows inspired a television show, *Full Frontal Fashion*, which went on the air with New York's Metro Channel in 1998, featuring footage taken during the shows and designer interviews, many of them with the show's founder, Judy Licht. Producer John Filimon says the object of the show, which was being broadcast on the WE channel in the early 2000s, was, and is, to make the designer the star.

During the 1980s and 1990s, most newspaper fashion editors had a laissez-faire approach to their coverage, writing about trends rather than critiquing individual collections. The exceptions, notably Eugenia Sheppard, Hebe Dorsey of the *International Herald Tribune* and her replacement Suzy Menkes, and Amy Spindler and Cathy Horyn, the first and second fashion critics at the *New York Times*, treated (and treat) the subject of fashion, especially the openings, as critics covering other fields would do—with opinions as well as facts.

The role of fashion journalism has obviously changed with the times. It also changes with the type of medium involved. Most magazine fashion editors do not write. They cover markets, making recommendations to the top editors for specific garments for specific shoots, and they style photography. The oldest fashion magazines, *Vogue* and *Harper's Bazaar*, have traditionally defined their fashion coverage not only by their audience demographics—upper-income adults—but also by their conviction that fashion begins in Europe and is homogenized in America. By encouraging American designers to "adapt" the designs of Cristóbal Balenciaga, Jacques Fath, and Christian Dior, for example, editors in the 1930s, 1940s, and 1950s discouraged design innovation in America, effectively relegating the New York designer to the backrooms of Seventh Avenue. And until the mid-1980s and 1990s, before it joined Paris, Milan, and London as a fashion capital, New York was generally considered a digester of fashion, not a feeder. The media effect of those two magazines, plus the editorial slant of *Women's Wear Daily* during the years John Fairchild was publisher, was to place Europe at the top of the fashion chain and to convince many American designers that their role was to assimilate, not innovate.

In many respects, Fairchild revolutionized the way fashion was covered—with great irreverence. He and his staff mixed fact with opinion, encouraged controversy, baited designers, followed them, scared them, coined phrases ("the lunch bunch" was code for rich socialites), made some of them heroes and destroyed others. *WWD*, as it is known, even created a new syntax, using . . . as a way of separating thoughts instead of as an ellipse to indicate an omission.

Like magazine fashion coverage, television fashion coverage is more subject-friendly than confrontational or critical. The entertainment element is fundamental.

In many ways, the advent of television fashion coverage has influenced fashion in a way few predicted. As Malcolm McLaren was quoted as saying in the May 1995 issue of *W Magazine*: "Fashion is a television spectacle now. But at the same time, it has become voyeuristic. Because if people watch it enough, and read about it enough, to some extent they don't have to wear it. They've already consumed the idea." This raises the question: Is the widely circulated immediate coverage of the seasonal openings giving people too much advance knowledge of the season and thereby making the clothes look old by the time they reach the stores?

The Internet's biggest impact on fashion journalism in the early twenty-first century is to enable users to see images of the collections here and abroad and read capsule reviews within hours after the runway show. For manufacturers inclined to copy, this is a great service. For designers eager to see what their competition is doing, it is far more valuable than an occasional photograph in a newspaper or trade publication. For consumers eager to see for themselves what lies ahead, and thereby help them plan their seasonal purchases, it is a boon. For someone hoping to see the season synthesized and trended, it is a boondoggle. For journalists who cover the shows and for stylists who will be responsible for accessorizing the clothes with the point of view of their magazine or their advertising client, it is a quick reference for planning future stories or avoiding the seasonal clichés. For magazine editors accustomed to making their own runway sketches as notes, it is a great backup.

With the beginning of fashion on television, some, like McLaren, were concerned with its potential long-term impact on the subject. The same questions are being asked now about the Internet. Fashion can now be conveyed in a variety of ways, from print to live satellite feeds to video conferencing with designers.

The question now remains: Why does a fashion journalist have to be there—wherever *there* is—to get the story?

See also **Fashion Advertising; Fashion Designer; Fashion Magazines; Fashion Models; Fashion Online; Fashion Shows; Fashion Television.**

BIBLIOGRAPHY
Wood, Dana. "Modus McClaren." *W* (May 1995): 49.

Marylou Luther

FASHION MAGAZINES Fashion magazines are an essential component of the fashion industry. They are the medium that conveys and promotes the design's vision to the eventual purchaser. Balancing the priorities has led to the diversity of the modern periodical market.

Fashion, except in its lifestyle sense or as a byword for vanity, played no part in early periodical literature. In 1678, however, Donneau de Visé first included an illustrated description of French fashions with suppliers' names in his ladies magazine, *Le Mercure galant*, which is considered the direct ancestor of modern fashion reports. Thereafter, fashion news rarely reappeared in periodical literature until the mid-eighteenth century when it was included in the popular ladies handbooks and diaries. Apparently in response to readers' requests, such coverage to the popular *Lady's Magazine* (1770–1832) was added to the genteel poems, music, and fiction that other journals were already offering to their middle-class readers.

By the end of the eighteenth century, *Lady's Magazine* had been joined by many periodicals catering to an affluent aspirational society. Interest in fashion was widespread and it was included in quality general readership journals such as the Frankfurt *Journal der Luxus und der Moden* (1786–1827) and Ackermann's *Repository of the Arts, Literature, Commerce, Fashion and Politics* (1809–1828) as well as those specifically for ladies. Despite the continental wars, French style was paramount and found their way into most English journals. Very popular with dressmakers was *Townsend's Quarterly* (later *Monthly*) *Selection of Parisian Costumes* (1825–1888), beautifully produced unattributed illustrations with minimal comment. The journals were generally elite productions, well illustrated and highly priced, though cheaper if uncolored. John Bell's *La belle assemblée* (1806–1821) was edited by Mary Anne Bell between 1810 and 1820, also proprietor of a fashion establishment. Dressmaker's credits are rare, perhaps because fashion establishments were dependent on personal recommendation and exclusivity.

By the middle of the nineteenth century, the magazine, like other popular literature, profited from improvements in printing methods, lower paper costs, and lower taxation. Literacy levels had risen and readership increased. Many new titles were produced and fashion for all types and ages were generally included in those for the women's market. Circulation figures were high; *Godey's Lady's Book* (1830–1897) issued 150,000 copies in 1861 and Samuel Beeton's *The Englishwoman's Domestic Magazine* (1852–1897) issued 60,000. Advertisement increased but the revenue rarely inhibited editorial independence. The key to circulation was innovation, and Godey and Beeton both added a shopping service and additional paper patterns to those already available within the magazine. Up-to-date fashion news was an essential and fashion plates as well as embroidery designs came direct from Paris sources, though in America they were often modified for home consumption.

The wide-ranging informative articles, typical of the "new journalism" were often written by women beginning to be well established in the newspaper profession. By the end of the century, there had been women editors at *Godey*, the Demorest publications, 1860–1899, *The Queen* (c. 1860s) and *Myra's Journal of Dress and Fashion* (1875–1912).

Entertaining and practical guides for the average family, this type of mid-market magazine had a long life, only recently losing its popularity. Its main competitors were shop catalogs and store magazines.

High-fashion Paris news was most easily accessible in the large format society journals, the weekly illustrated

Former *Cosmopolitan* editor-in-chief Helen Gurley Brown. *Cosmopolitan* was originally conceived for the whole family, but when Brown took the reins in 1965, she reformatted it into a woman's magazine. AP/WIDE WORLD PHOTOS. REPRODUCED BY PERMISSION.

newspapers, and *La mode illustrée* (1860–1914), of which there was an English edition. Semi-amateur fashion cum gossip columnists were a feature of Gilded Age society, but the couture concerned with their expanding international market were increasingly professional about their publicity, and well-kept house guard books were probably as useful for press promotion as they were to designers and clients.

Through its Chambre Syndicale, the couture was organizing its own fashion journal, *Les modes* (1901–1937). Its innovative and informative photographic illustrations made it an anthology of high status Paris design by the end of the century. In 1911 Lucien Vogel offered the couture an even more modern shop window in the elitist *Gazette du bon ton* (1911–1923), the precursor of the small *pochoir* (stencil) illustrated fashionable journals

1929 *Vogue* cover. Revamped by Condé Nast in the early twentieth century, *Vogue* is global in its coverage of the world of high fashion. © CONDÉ NAST ARCHIVE/CORBIS. REPRODUCED BY PERMISSION.

characteristic of the avant-garde press of the early twentieth century.

It is a tribute to their vision that a men's style publication was included. *Monsieur* (1920–1922) was a complete break with the stereotyped format and trade jargon of the tailoring journals. It was not followed until *Esquire* (1933–), described as the male counterpart to *Vogue* and *Harper's Bazaar*, updated the male fashion image, stressing a harmony between clothes and lifestyle.

High fashion was reinterpreted for the American market when *Vogue* was taken over by Condé Nast Publications in 1909. His publishing experience had shown that a rich and aspirational American society wanted practical fashion guidance and a direct line to Paris. *Vogue* coverage is global in the early 2000s, and foreign editions make their own assessments of the fashionable and the salable. Until his death in 1942, Condé Nast maintained meticulous control of the quality and service he believed were owed to his readers. *Vogue* archives provide insight into the management of quality fashion publication in a twentieth-century world. The contributors, editors, designers, photographers, and artists who have enriched the *Vogue* pages over the years add another essential layer of information.

As fashion pace increased, the fashion publication scene was stimulated by developments at *Women's Wear Daily* (*WWD*), after the Fairchild family purchased it in 1909 as a conventional trade paper for the garment trade. Its offshoot, *W* (1972–) was developed by John Fairchild, the son of the founder, to have "the speed of a newspaper . . . with the smart look of a fashion magazine" and significantly, its survival depended on advertisement. News "scoops" were competed for ruthlessly. *Vogue* secured the designs for Princess Elizabeth's wedding dress in 1947, *WWD* obtained Princess Margaret's in 1960, plus the annual Best-Dressed List. Assessment of style change was more problematic and it was the role of the fashion editor to balance designer's contribution and public acceptance. It was a tribute to both when magazines and public supported Dior's New Look in 1947, despite trade and government opposition.

Increasingly dependent on advertising, the conventional magazine is challenged if fashion deviates from established trends. The "lead in" time for a quality, full-color journal is generally two months—too long for the speed of street fashion and its high-spending, young, and trendy clientele. This readership was not targeted until 1976 when Terry Jones, originally from *Vogue*, developed the U.K. magazine *i-D*, with its apparently spontaneous fanzine look. Its original message, "It isn't what you wear but how you wear it," had little appeal for the clothing trade but it has found its niche market in the early 2000s and is the prototype "young fashion" magazine.

Despite the number of fashion magazines currently available, it is probable that most people appreciate fashion through the daily press, the popular lifestyle and celebrity magazines, television, and the Web. With advertising pressures and the sheer volume of clothing choices in an affluent society, it is not unexpected that these popular magazines react by judging celebrities not by their designer clothes, but by the way that they wear them.

See also **Vogue; Women's Wear Daily.**

BIBLIOGRAPHY

Breward, Christopher. "Feminity and Consumption: The Problem of the Late Nineteenth Century Fashion Journal." *Journal of Design History* 7, no. 2 (1994): 71–89. Perceptive survey of late nineteenth-century editorial attitudes.

Fairchild, John. *Chic Savages.* New York: Simon and Schuster, 1989. Personal account of *Women's Wear Daily* and *W.*

Finley, Ruth E. *The Lady of Godey's: Sarah Josepha Hale.* Philadelphia and London: J. B. Lippincott, 1931. Useful for early American periodical publishing history.

Seebohm, Caroline. *The Man Who Was Vogue.* New York: Viking Press, 1982. Full biographical account of Condé Nast.

White, Cynthia L. *Women's Magazines 1693–1968.* London: Michael Joseph, 1970. Clear account based on U.K. sources.

Madeleine Ginsberg

FASHION MARKETING AND MERCHANDISING The goal of fashion marketing and merchandising, for both manufacturers and retailers, is to sell merchandise at a profit. This requires careful planning and coordination.

In ancient times, people "shopped" in open-air markets and bazaars, finding not only necessities but also products that were unique and gave excitement to their everyday lives. Today, we shop and buy in much the same way, but open-air markets and bazaars have evolved into department and specialty stores, discount outlets, and huge malls that continue to excite and entice the shopper. The difference is that fashion marketing and fashion merchandising are now the watchwords of successful fashion businesses. In the early twenty-first century, the customer has become the most important ingredient in successful fashion retailing. Determining the needs and wants of the targeted customer has become very important, and this challenge has led to the creation of specific goods and stores for specific categories of customers.

For many years, fashion producers were concerned only with what was economical and easy for them to produce. They would spend considerable time and money trying to convince the consumer that what they produced was what the consumer wanted. The fashion producer had little or no interest in the needs and wants of the consumer. However, marketing proved so successful in the growth of consumer goods such as automobiles, packaged foods, and health and beauty aids that it was eventually adopted by the fashion businesses. Under the classic definition of marketing, the key task of the organization is to determine the needs and wants of target markets and adapt the organization to deliver the desired satisfactions more effectively and efficiently to the ultimate customer.

Through the use of sophisticated marketing techniques such as focus groups, surveys, data mining, and market segmentation along with systematic approaches such as electronic data information (EDI), inventory tracking, and constant evaluation of advertising results for determining consumer tastes, the industry's awareness of the importance of pleasing the target customer has greatly increased. Every step—design, production, distribution, promotion—is geared to consumer demand.

"Fashion marketing" includes all of the activities involved from conceiving a product to directing the flow of goods from producer to the ultimate customer. Activities of marketing include product development, pricing, promotion, and distribution. If a fashion retailer or manufacturer is to make a profit, the firm must have a product that consumers perceive as desirable, and the product must be presented to potential customers in a way that makes them want to buy it.

The first step in a fashion marketing approach is to define the company's target customers, those persons the company most wants to attract as customers. Fashion

marketers determine their target customer's needs and wants by examining various market segments, identified by geographics, demographics, psychographics, and behavioral studies. Fashion marketers also track trends in population growth and diversity. Changing patterns of immigration bring with them new influences from different parts of the world. Products that will meet the needs and desires of these customers are then developed or selected. Most fashion manufacturers and retailers recognize that following a consumer-marketing approach leads to a profitable business.

"Fashion merchandising" is defined as the buying and selling of goods for the purpose of making a profit. Merchandising is the planning involved in marketing the *right* merchandise at the *right* price at the *right* time in the *right* place and in the *right* quantities. Commonly known as the 5Rs, merchandising is concerned with all the activities necessary to provide customers with the merchandise they want to buy, when and where they want to buy it, and at prices they can afford and are willing to pay. This includes making buying plans, understanding the customer, selecting the merchandise, and promoting and selling the goods to the consumer.

Fashion merchandising is practiced by both manufacturers and retailers. For manufacturers, merchandising begins with estimating consumer demand in terms of styles, sizes, colors, quantity, and price. Merchandising also involves designing the goods and selecting the fabrics and findings, designing the packaging, pricing, advertising, and other sales promotion activities.

For fashion retailers, merchandising also begins with forecasting the needs and wants of their target customer. The retailer must first project sales in terms of dollars and units of merchandise. Just as the manufacturer must anticipate the needs of the retailer, the retailer must also anticipate the needs of the consumer by reviewing past sales, keeping up on trends, and knowing where on the fashion cycle their customer falls. The retailer must also know what colors, sizes, styles, and prices of merchandise that their target customers want to purchase. After planning what and how much to buy, merchandising for the fashion retailer includes determining resources from which to purchase, selecting from their assortments, and purchasing the goods for sale to the consumer. Another factor of merchandising is presenting the merchandise attractively and effectively to the consumer and promoting the merchandise so that the target customer will want to buy it.

In the early 2000s, technology has been a major factor in helping fashion manufacturers and retailers to successfully satisfy the needs and wants of the targeted customer, with body scanning being just one example. Body scanning software customizes patterns for an individual's body. This results in the kind of fit previously available only to couture customers. As technology continues to improve and become less costly, scanning of the entire body will become more common, resulting in the kind of fit previously available only in expensive made-to-measure fashion products.

The development of fashion marketing and merchandising as distinct professions with their own expertise, insights, and techniques, has made them the cornerstone of the modern world of fashion. The use of sophisticated marketing and merchandising methods and techniques has given rise to some of the most exciting and innovative strategies: among them are entertainment-oriented shopping malls, themed environments, designer and manufacturer retail flagship stores, brands, off-site retailing and e-tailing and packaging, now viewed as the science of temptation.

Fashion marketing and merchandising present a unique problem because of the ever-changing nature of fashion and the difficulty of predicting consumer demand. The fashion world is famous for its fast-moving, do-or-die success or failure rate. With a need to respond quickly to consumer purchasing, sophisticated processes are required for quick decision making that will support the fashion marketers and merchandisers in satisfying the customer.

See also **Fashion Industry; Retailing.**

BIBLIOGRAPHY

Harris, Louis. *Merchant Princes.* New York: Harper and Row, 1979.

Kotler, Philip, and Gary Armstrong. *Principles of Marketing.* 9th ed. Upper Saddle River, N.J.: Prentice Hall, 2001.

Stone, Elaine. *The Dynamics of Fashion.* New York: Fairchild Publications, 2004.

Traub, Marvin. *The Bloomingdales' Legend and the Revolution of American Marketing.* New York: Random House, 1993.

Elaine Stone

FASHION MODELS In the nineteenth century, the first living mannequins, or "manikins," took their name from the static dummy or lay figure they were soon to replace as the principal form of display in the dressmaker's salon. While the word "mannequin"—in French, *le mannequin*—described the woman, the word "model"—*le modèle*—designated the gown she exhibited in the salon. The model gown was a one-off that did not go into production; it was thus both an exclusive dress for sale to an individual client, and a prototype (hence the term model) sold to a fashion buyer for adaptation to the mass market. Both model gowns and model women were at the heart of the commercial development of the French couture industry and its global markets, and there was always some confusion in the terminology. The dual meaning of the word "model" also signals the ambivalent status of the earliest fashion models, hovering uneasily between subject- and object-hood. They invoked both admiration and disapproval, disconcerting their critics precisely be-cause they wore fashionable dress in public for money rather than for its own sake.

Origins
Charles Frederick Worth is generally thought to be the first couturier to use live models. However, many nineteenth-century dressmakers had a young woman available to put on a dress for a client, although their primary mode of display was a wooden or wicker dummy. Indeed, Worth met his future wife, Marie, while she was employed to model shawls to customers on the shop floor of their mutual employer, the mercer Gagelin et Opigez. The couple set up their first *maison de couture* in 1858, and Marie modeled in the Worth salons until the 1870s, after which she remained responsible for training the house mannequins. Maison Worth's real innovation was thus to institutionalize the profession within the increasingly bureaucratic structure of a couture house, having several trained house mannequins, rather than using the occasional *petit main*, or seamstress, as a model.

The Early Twentieth Century
Lady Duff Gordon, trading as Lucile, claimed to have started the first mannequin parades in London in the late 1890s. She trained her mannequins in carriage and deportment and gave them stage names such as Hebe, Gamela, and Dolores. Often six feet tall, they struck dramatic poses during the parades but barely smiled and never spoke. When Lucile opened in New York in 1910 and then Paris in 1911, she took with her four of her London mannequins whose glamour was widely reported in the press of both continents. Dolores later joined the Ziegfeld Follies, and there are many parallels between the fashion model and the chorus girl.

In the same period, fashion magazines began to use photography alongside fashion illustrations, but the women in these photographs were often actresses and, later, society women, rather than professional mannequins, and, with some notable exceptions, the two career paths—photographic and catwalk models—remained separate until well into the 1960s.

Catwalk modeling was always a specialist option. Mannequins were full-time employees of the house and sometimes even lived in. In Paris, both Paquin and Poiret were in the vanguard in showing their fashions on live mannequins, but between 1900 and 1910 most couture houses had their *cabine*, or studio, of mannequins. Although poorly paid and barely respectable, they were also considered exceptionally glamorous. From behind the scenes, they would be summoned several times a day to model gowns for private customers and professional buyers alike, under the direction of the *vendeuse*. Until approximately 1907, they wore a high-necked and long-sleeved black satin sheath, or *fourrure*, beneath the luxury gowns; although generally believed to designate their lack of respectability, the *fourrure* must also have facilitated the rapid costume changes required.

The appearance of three paid mannequins with an unnamed couturier at the Auteil racecourse in 1908 caused outrage, but the practice rapidly became common. In 1910, Poiret made a film of a mannequin parade, and in 1911 he toured Europe with a troupe of uniformed mannequins. In 1913, both he and Paquin undertook mannequin tours of the United States; in one town, the host department store responded to Paquin's mannequins with a matching parade of American male mannequins. Department stores in the United States were, if anything, ahead of Parisian couturiers in pioneering the use of models in dramatic fashion shows. In 1924, Jean Patou traveled to New York to recruit six American mannequins to model in Paris for his American customers whose physique, he claimed, was longer and leaner than that of the "rounded French Venus." Paquin, Poiret, and Patou understood the importance of showing on live models in the marketing of modern fashion. All were able to harness innovative publicity techniques to the early twentieth-century desire to see fashion in motion.

The Mid-Twentieth Century

John Powers opened the first American model agency in 1923; the Ford modeling agency was founded in 1946. By contrast, the first French model agency opened only in 1959, perhaps because French fashion houses had always employed their own models. In New York in the 1920s, there was also a mannequins' school dedicated to teaching fashion modeling techniques.

By the 1920s, fashion journalists were beginning to report not only on the seasonal fashions, but equally on individual mannequins from the Paris "openings." Captain Molyneux's principal mannequin, Sumurun (Vera Ashby), was well known; in the 1930s, the in-house mannequins of the London department store Selfridges were popular figures, while Schiaparelli's mannequin Lud was reputed to be married to a lion-tamer.

After World War II, the profession of model acquired some respectability, perhaps due to cinematic representations of models in films such as *Cover Girl* (1944), *Funny Face* (1957), and *Blowup* (1966). The social status of models improved as several married into the aristocracy.

Modeling styles changed. From the early twentieth-century the mannequin had been required to move sedately in the salon, notwithstanding the risqué connotations of Lucile's "goddesses" and Poiret's undulating mannequins. By contrast, when, in 1947, Christian Dior showed his "New Look," he encouraged his models to do theatrical turns, knocking over ashtrays in the audience as their coats swung round. However, in general modeling styles remained staid and the 1950s' model was required to look haughty and disdainful. Paris fashion houses maintained a *cabine* of fourteen to eighteen models, and there tended to be a "house style" of modeling, although each model was a different physical type to represent the range of clients' looks. It was therefore, revolutionary when, in the late 1950s, the British designer Mary Quant first showed on photographic mannequins who danced frenetically to jazz music and then froze in graphic, static poses on the catwalk.

The 1960s to the Early 2000s

Quant laid the path for the innovations of the 1960s when the development of ready-to-wear required a different kind of presentation. Now models were required to dance, act, and clown on the catwalk. In Courrèges's futurist collection of 1965, grinning models danced in experimental kinetic movement to *musique concrète*. Marie Helvin recalled that haute couture modeling in the 1960s and 1970s was about contact with hand-made, one-off clothes, whereas showstopping modeling techniques, photogenic beauty, and the showgirl instinct were the prerequisites of the ready-to-wear show.

Until then, models had been poorly paid, but their compensation went rocketing up in this period; top models could command $1,000 for a one-hour show in Milan and even a little more for one in Paris. The strict separation between house mannequins and photographic models began to be eroded and the proliferation of media images of the young, beautiful, and fashionable in the 1960s ensured that photographic models like Jean Shrimpton ("the Shrimp") and Twiggy became iconic figures of their times.

The rise of the supermodel in the early 1990s was followed by a fashion for more waiflike models with slighter frames and quirkier looks. Their salaries, however, did not shrink correspondingly. By the end of the twentieth century, models were firmly established as the new celebrities. Feted in gossip columns and highly compensated, they were far removed from their early twentieth-century predecessors with their dubious status and poor pay. Nevertheless, and despite the high visibility of the black model Naomi Campbell, models of color continue to be underrepresented in the industry at the beginning of the twenty-first century.

See also **Mannequins; Patou, Jean; Quant, Mary; Twiggy; Worth, Charles Frederick.**

BIBLIOGRAPHY

Ballard, Bettina. *In My Fashion.* London: Secker and Warburg; New York: David McKay Company, 1960.

Balmain, Pierre. *My Years and Seasons.* Translated by Edward Lanchberry with Gordon Young. London: Cassell, 1964.

Bertin, Célia. *Paris à la Mode.* Translated by Marjorie Deans, London: V. Gollancz, 1956.

Castle, Charles. *Model Girl.* Newton Abbot, U.K.: David and Charles, 1977.

De Marly, Diana. *Worth: Father of Haute Couture.* London: Elm Tree Books, 1980.

Evans, Caroline. "Living Dolls: Mannequins, Models and Modernity." In *The Body Politic.* Edited by Julian Stair, 103–116. London: Crafts Council, 2000.

———. "The Enchanted Spectacle." *Fashion Theory* 5, no. 3 (2001): 271–310.

Etherington-Smith, Meredith, and Jeremy Pilcher. *The "It" Girls*. London: Hamish Hamilton, 1986.

Gordon, Lucy Wallace Duff, Lady. *Discretions and Indiscretions*. London: Jarrolds, 1932.

Gross, Michael. *Model: The Ugly Business of Beautiful Women*. London and New York: Bantam, 1995.

Helvin, Marie. *Catwalk*. London: Pavilion Books, 1985.

Kaplan, Joel H., and Sheila Stowell. *Theatre and Fashion: From Oscar Wilde to the Suffragettes*. Cambridge, U.K.: Cambridge University Press, 1994.

Keenan, Bridget. *The Women We Wanted to Look Like*. London: Macmillan, 1977.

Leach, William. *Land of Desire: Merchants, Power, and the Rise of a New American Culture*. New York: Vintage Books, 1994.

Liaut, Jean-Noël. *Cover Girls and Supermodels 1945–1965*. Translated by Robin Buss. London and New York: Marion Boyars, 1996.

Poiret, Paul. *My First Fifty Years*. Translated by Stephen Hayden Guest. London: V. Gollancz, 1931.

Seebohm, Caroline. *The Man Who Was Vogue: The Life and Times of Condé Nast*. London: Weidenfeld and Nicolson, 1982.

Caroline Evans

FASHION MUSEUMS AND COLLECTIONS

Clothing has been collected and exhibited by a variety of individuals and institutions. Already in the eighteenth century, Madame Tussaud of wax-museum fame, was acquiring and displaying the clothing of celebrities. Today, a wide variety of museums collect dress and textiles, including anthropological and ethnological museums, history museums, art museums, design museums, and specialized fashion and textile museums.

In Paris, still the international capital of fashion, there are two important fashion museums: the Musée de la Mode et du Costume at the Palais Galliéra, which was formerly known as the Musée du Costume de la Ville de Paris, at 10 Avenue Piere-1er-de-Serbie in the 16th arrondisement; and the Musée de la Mode et du Textile at 107 Rue de Rivoli in the 1st arrondisement , which is affiliated with the Louvre. The former was founded in the 1920s and is funded by the city of Paris; it has been at its present location in the Galliéra since 1977. The latter opened its doors in 1986 and is more lavishly funded by the state. For simplicity's sake, we might refer to them, respectively, as the Galliéra and the Louvre. The Galliéra possesses an extensive collection of historical dress, while the Louvre is stronger in contemporary fashion. The Louvre also houses, but does not own, the collections of the Union Française des Arts du Costume. Among the Galliéra's best exhibitions was the late Guillaume Garnier's *Paris Années Trentes* (1987). Pamela Golbin, one of several curators at the Louvre's fashion museum, has organized innovative exhibitions, such as *Lumière*.

The fashion designer Yves Saint Laurent is organizing his own museum in Paris. Elsewhere in France, the Textile Museum in Lyons has an important collection, while nearby Romans is home to a small shoe museum.

In London, the most important collection of fashion belongs to The Victoria & Albert Museum, one of the world's most important museums of the applied arts. As early as 1913, The V&A exhibited eighteenth-century fashions. In the 1970s Cecil Beaton obtained many examples of high fashion for the museum. A permanent exhibition of historic costume, arranged chronologically, has been on display for many years in the costume gallery. In 1994, the V&A mounted an important exhibition, *Streetstyle: From Sidewalk to Catwalk*, curated by Amy de la Haye, which compared subcultural styles such as punk with high fashion. Another curator, Claire Wilcox, has organized *Fashion in Motion*, a monthly event that includes a live fashion show. Wilcox also curated the 2001 exhibition *Radical Fashion*.

In 2002, after years of effort, the fashion and textile designer Zandra Rhodes opened the Museum of Fashion and Textiles in London. Judith Clark's tiny eponymous gallery has also presented innovative fashion exhibitions. Elsewhere in Great Britain, there are a number of other fashion museums, which were founded by individual collectors. For example, Dr. and Mrs. C. Willett Cunnington created the Gallery of English Costume in Manchester, and Mrs. Doris Langley Moore created the Museum of Costume in Bath. Mrs. Hélène Alexander founded the Fan Museum in Greenwich.

Oddly enough, there exists no full-scale fashion museum in Italy, although the Galleria del Costume in the Palazzo Pitti (Florence) has a significant collection and mounts occasional exhibitions. There are also a number of private collections in Italy, such as that of Enrico Quinto in Rome. Many fashion designers have their own archives, as well.

In the United States, many art museums have important costume collections. The most famous is the Costume Institute of the Metropolitan Museum of Art in New York City. Diana Vreeland, formerly editor-in-chief at *Vogue*, became Special Consultant to the Costume Institute in 1972. She organized more than a dozen exhibitions on themes such as the *The 18th-Century Woman* (1981), *Romantic and Glamorous Hollywood Design* (1974), and *Yves Saint Laurent* (1983). Although subject to criticism on the grounds of commercialism and historical inaccuracy, Mrs. Vreeland's shows were undeniably glamorous, and they succeeded in abolishing the aura of antiquarianism that had previously surrounded most "costume" exhibitions.

The Museum at the Fashion Institute of Technology is the only museum in New York dedicated primarily to fashion. It owns some 50,000 examples of clothing and accessories, with their greatest strength in modern and contemporary fashion. Richard Martin and Harold

Koda organized a number of important exhibitions at FIT, including *Fashion and Surrealism* (1987), before they moved uptown to the Costume Institute. Martin's premature death in 1999 at the age of 52 robbed the field of a brilliant intelligence. In 1997 Valerie Steele became chief curator of the Museum at FIT. Among her many exhibitions are *The Corset: Fashioning the Body* (2000), *Femme Fatale: Fashion and Visual Culture in Fin-de-Siècle France* (2002), and *London Fashion* (2001), which received the first Richard Martin Award from the Costume Society of America. The Brooklyn Museum of Art also has impressive holdings in fashion and has mounted exhibitions, such as *The Genius of Charles James* (1982). The Museum of the City of New York has another important collection, which focuses on clothing made and/or worn in the metropolis. It is especially strong in fashions of the Gilded Age and in theatrical costumes. Other North American museums with important fashion collections include the Boston Museum of Fine Arts, the Los Angeles Museum of Art, and the Royal Ontario Museum.

The Kyoto Costume Institute is a private museum in Japan founded by the Wacoal Company, which manufactures foundation garments. The chief curator, Akiko Fukai, has organized a number of important exhibitions, including *Japonism Fashion* (1994), which has traveled to museums worldwide. Fashion museums have recently been opened or are planned in many places around the world, including Belgium (the Moda Museum in Antwerp, curated by Linda Loppe), Chile, and Goa.

See also **Belgian Fashion; Cunnington, C. Willett and Phillis; Fashion Education; Japonisme; Moore, Doris Langley; Rhodes, Zandra; Saint Laurent, Yves; Vreeland, Diana.**

BIBLIOGRAPHY
Ribiero, Aileen. "Re-Fashioning Art: Some Visual Approaches to the Study of the History of Dress." *Fashion Theory* 2, no. 4 (December, 1998).
Steele, Valerie. "A Museum of Fashion Is More than a Clothes-Bag." *Fashion Theory* 2, no. 4 (December, 1998).
Taylor, Lou. "Doing the Laundry? A Reassessment of Object-Based Dress History." *Fashion Theory* 2, no. 4 (December, 1998).

Valerie Steele

FASHION ONLINE Fashion was first propelled onto the Internet (c. 1994) by what María Contreras refers to in *Vogue España* as that old refrain "adapt or die." A decade into Web history, it has become clear the Internet is used for gathering information, communication, and entertainment. Rather than becoming a world, the Web has become an essential tool for living.

Theoretically, if not culturally, fashion is well suited to the new media. As the photographer and showStudio.com founder Nick Knight observes, "speed of change" is the essential nature of fashion and new media. Both promote image in an era where perception (branding) is as important, if not more so, than the fashion object.

The Web does not threaten print media. Even the founders of the online zine, Itfashion.com, assert that "the existence of paper magazines is necessary." Vanity sites have, however, become an essential part of public relations and brand-building strategy. The primary purpose of a vanity site is to communicate the brand. Unlike a television or commercial, a Web site offers "bidirectional communications" (Deborah Kania) and invites dialogue between the brand and the consumer. Almost all sites have a "Contact Us" or e-mail function built into their architecture. Some sites integrate the feedback function into their content/identity. Thus on emilio-pucci.com users are encouraged to "sign in" on the guest book section where they are asked: "Do you have a Pucci story of your own?" and encouraged to share it, which maximizes the emotional bond that is unique to the brand. On johngalliano.com, users can "Whisper sweet words to John Galliano or confide in Miss Galliano" via the "Love Letters" section.

The vanity site provides the brand a means to create a multisensory experience that creates a bond between the brand and user resulting in "stickiness"—the desire to come back—and encourage consumer loyalty and possibly profitability.

Fashion is a hard sell on the Web, but not an impossible one. What we have learned so far is that e-commerce is more easily adaptable to certain sectors than others. Shopping at the Gap or Banana Republic online, for example, is essentially the same as ordering from the catalog, and these chain stores have the back-end operations already in place to support large-scale e-commerce ventures. Vintage clothing also sells well on the Web, because it provides unique accessibility to one-of-a-kind items (think ebay).

Gradually, shopping on the Web is becoming a desirable form of entertainment, not to mention convenience. (Colette.fr reports that one of their first orders came from a client who "lived but five minutes from the store.") Web demographics—above-average income and education—suggest that this is an area that will continue to be developed.

The most exciting, and potentially, revolutionary impact of the Web on fashion is its inherent democratic nature. Whereas high fashion is built upon exclusivity, the Web offers full-access, twenty-four hours a day, seven days a week: both grandma and Gucci have equal access to the virtual world. In the 1960s the legendary *Vogue* editor Diana Vreeland celebrated "youthquake," ostensibly the end of fashion dictatorship. The ingress of the Web beyond the velvet ropes into the theater of fashion—usually the bailiwick of international press and celebrities—is significant. It suggests that the Web might be the tool that incites a twenty-first-century shake-up. In a virtual world, a camel can, in fact, pass through the eye of a needle.

See also **Fashion Advertising; Fashion Editors; Fashion Journalism; Fashion Magazines; Fashion Models; Vogue.**

BIBLIOGRAPHY

Borrelli, Laird. *Net Mode: Web Fashion Now.* London: Thames and Hudson, Inc., 2002.

Kania, Deborah. *Branding.com: On-line Branding for Marketing Success.* Lincolnwood, Ill.: NTC Contemporary Publishing Company, 2000.

Laird Borrelli

FASHION PHOTOGRAPHY A fashion photograph is, simply, a photograph made specifically to show (or, in some cases, to allude to) clothing or accessories, usually with the intent of documenting or selling the fashion. Photographs of fashionable dress, in existence since the invention of photography in 1839, are not fashion photography. The distinguishing feature—and the common denominator in the enormous diversity of style, approach, and content—is the fashion photograph's intent to convey fashion or a "fashionable" lifestyle. At the end of the twentieth century, the Calvin Klein advertisement featuring only Calvin's portrait changed the very definition of a fashion photograph from a picture of the featured clothing to the selling of a glamorous lifestyle identified with a specific logo.

Fashion photography has sometimes been called ephemeral, commercial, and frivolous, and its importance has been called into question. That fashion photography has a commercial intent implies to some that it lacks photographic and artistic integrity. In reality, it has produced some of the most creative, interesting, and socially revealing documents and revealed the attitudes, conventions, aspirations, and taste of the time. It also reflects women's image of themselves, including their dreams and desires, self-image, values, sexuality, and interests.

The psychology behind a fashion photograph as a selling device is the viewer's willingness to believe in it. No matter how artificial the setting, a fashion photograph must persuade individuals that if they wear these clothes, use this product, or accessorize in such a way, the reality of the photograph will be theirs. The fashion photograph can offer a vision of a certain lifestyle (from glamorous to grunge), sex, or social acceptance (via the most current, the most expensive, or the most highly unattainable), but it is the viewer's buy-in that makes the photograph successful.

Early Fashion Photography

The earliest fashion photographs were made, probably in the 1850s and 1860s, to document fashion for Parisian fashion houses. Reproduction in fashion journals occurred much later, between 1881 (with the invention of the halftone printing process by Frederic Eugene Ives) and 1886 (when the refinement of the process made it financially practicable). This breakthrough made it possible to reproduce photographs and sell to a large audience through the medium of the printed page.

In the late nineteenth and early twentieth centuries, distinctions between fashion photography, portraiture, and theater photography were often blurred. The idea of using professional models was initially considered shocking, and it thus became fashionable in the early years of the century for society celebrities, such as Gertrude Vanderbilt Whitney, to model. The result was that fashion photographs were strikingly similar to society portraits. The idea of using an actress such as Sarah Bernhardt is not unlike the vogue in the early 2000s for using Gwyneth Paltrow or Madonna or the tennis stars Venus and Serena Williams to model current fashion.

That nineteenth-century fashion photography did not exist is a misconception. Many believe that Americans were first in this field, perhaps based on Edward Steichen's claim that he was the first fashion photographer. This has obscured the contributions of such important Parisian fashion photographers as Maison Reutlinger, Talbot, Felix, Henri Manuel, and Boissonnas et Taponnier as early as 1881. They worked in the studio, but charming outdoor fashion photography was also shot on the Parisian boulevards and at the races by the Seeberger Frères in the first decade of the twentieth century.

American Fashion Photography, 1900–1930

The first important American photographer of fashion was European-born Baron Adolf de Meyer, who had entered fashionable London society through his marriage to Donna Olga Alberta Caracciolo (the daughter of the duchess of Castelluccio and reputed to be the illegitimate daughter of King Edward VII) and was knighted by the king of Saxony. De Meyer changed fashion photography by disintegrating form and bathing his pictures in a limpid atmosphere and shimmering light, creating what *Vogue* in 1914 termed "artistic" photography. This approach changed the idea of what a fashion photograph should be, from an exacting depiction of a garment's detail to an evocation of mood.

In 1924, Edward Steichen replaced the soft-focus effects of de Meyer's style with the clean geometric lines of photographic modernism. Steichen rejected the rococo backdrops used by de Meyer in favor of unadorned, sleek settings and showed modern woman in the sports clothes that reflected a new, liberated sense of herself and her freedom from the corset. Many of Steichen's most important photographs featured his signature model Marion Morehouse, who epitomized the look of the "contemporary" woman, the flapper. Other important photographers who benefited from and were influenced by Steichen's innovations were George Hoyningen-

Photograph of model at Lincoln Memorial. The true fashion photograph is not one that simply records a clothing design, but one that conveys a desirable lifestyle suggested by that design. PHOTOGRAPH BY TONY TINSELL. THE LIBRARY OF CONGRESS. REPRODUCED BY PERMISSION.

Huene, known for his extraordinary use of negative space and passion for the Greek ideal, and his student Horst P. Horst, who used theatrical lighting and trompe l'oeil effects to great advantage.

Realism and Surrealism
Another startling change—and one that would have profound impact on future fashion photography—was the

1933 introduction of out-of-door realism by the Hungarian sports photographer Martin Munkacsi. Munkacsi's *Harper's Bazaar* photograph of the model Lucile Brokaw running down the beach—blurred, in motion, and possessing the naturalness of amateur snapshots—changed the course of fashion photography. The spontaneity was revolutionary, particularly when contrasted to Steichen's posed and static style that preceded it. Realistic fashion photography offered the modern woman a vision that she could apply to her own life. Munkacsi's snapshotlike realism influenced a long line of photographers, including Toni Frissell, Herman Landshoff, and Richard Avedon.

The artistic ferment of Paris in the 1930s, particularly the fantastic, mysterious, and dreamlike aspects of surrealism, had a profound influence on fashion photography. The painter and photographer Man Ray produced fashion photography as a way of earning money that enabled him to pursue "serious" painting and experimental photography. He was able to chart a new direction for fashion photography because he disregarded the conventions of fashion depiction, instead producing elongations, double exposures, and a "fashion rayograph" that simulated what a fashion would look like when radioed from Paris to New York. Other fashion photographers who incorporated surrealist-influenced ideas in their work were Peter Rose-Pulham, André Durst, George Platt Lynes, and Cecil Beaton.

Constant experimentation and technical virtuosity marks the fashion work of Erwin Blumenfeld, who used solarization, overprinting, combinations of negative and positive images, sandwiching of color transparencies, and even drying the wet negatives in the refrigerator, resulting in crystallization, to achieve his extraordinary effects. Also important in the 1930s was the appearance of Kodachrome, which arrived on the market in 1935. Louise Dahl-Wolfe was one of the first and most important practitioners of color in fashion photography, creating striking photographs of American fashion with the new color technology.

Fashion Photography after World War II

Fashion photography was severely affected at the outbreak of World War II in 1939, not only because of the lack of materials, models, and safe locations, but also because of a demoralization in attitude toward the medium: because fashion was seen as a frivolous and unnecessary form of luxury, fashion magazines stressed women's role in the war, rationalized fashion as morale building, published war reports instead of society columns, and featured the tailored, plain, and often drab clothing more suitable for a world subjected to daily reports of death and destruction. Studio photography with its complicated props and setups was almost eliminated. In general, photographers such as Lee Miller in Paris and Cecil Beaton in London turned to a straightforward documentary approach. Louise Dahl-Wolfe produced some of the most important American fashion photography of the 1940s using a clear, straightforward style.

With the end of the war, New York replaced Paris as the mecca of fashion photography. America's fashion design and ready-to-wear industry achieved its first international success in the postwar period. The time was thus ripe for the emergence of two young American talents who would dominate fashion photography for many years to come: Richard Avedon and Irving Penn.

The charming ease of Richard Avedon's fashion style of the 1950s was perfectly suited to a war-weary society. In this decade, Avedon staged his models as glamorous but "real" girls whose carefree exuberance was both sophisticated and appealing. Each was an actress of sorts, creating both a fashion look and a dialogue of emotions. By the 1960s, Avedon's fashion work had moved from the outdoor locations and softly beautiful natural light of this early work to his signature style of models running and jumping across a plain white background, illuminated with the harsh, raking light of the strobe.

The other major fashion leader whose work started in the 1940s is Irving Penn. Penn's work has no rival in terms of formal complexity, in the rich beauty of constructed shape, elegance of silhouette, and abstract interplay of line and volume. Compared with the white-hot moment of immediacy of Avedon's photographs, Penn's work aimed at the values of monumentality, formal clarity, and quiet truth. Perhaps his most extraordinary shots are those done in collaboration with his wife, the model Lisa Fonssagrives-Penn.

Both Avedon and Penn have each sustained careers over a period of five decades, a record of remarkable range and consistency. Avedon's ability to take inventive risks and his creative inspiration, with its kaleidoscope of techniques and ideas, are unequaled in the field of fashion photography. He always captures the "look" of the moment, in part because of his choice of the model who best epitomizes the time, from Dorian Leigh, Dovima, and Suzy Parker to Verushka, Twiggy, Jean Shrimpton, Brooke Shields, and Nastassja Kinski.

Fashion Photography in the 1960s

Fashion photography in the 1960s yielded to more socially oriented and exotic themes. In part this was due to the fact that fashion design began to show the influence of many diverse sources, from peasant and "street" styles to the women's liberation movement, the space program, and pop art. There was a break with convention, both in social mores and fashion itself: outrageous, seemingly unwearable outfits were designed, models reflected a new diversity of "look" and race, and fashion was redefined toward a defiant market dominated by the youth culture.

The 1960s was also a time when certain fashion photographers, including Bert Stern and David Bailey, enjoyed high-voltage lifestyles, skyrocketing fees, and lavish studio setups. At the opposite extreme, the influence of Penn and Avedon continued to attract serious young photographers from the world over to New York. Yasuhiro Wakabayashi, known professionally as Hiro, developed a monumental, clear, and memorably vivid style while Bob Richardson's work flirted with social concerns such as lesbianism. Other photographers working in the field of fashion in the 1960s included William Klein, Art Kane, and Diane Arbus, whose photography for the *New York Times Magazine* was among the most disturbing and uncharacteristic children's fashion images ever published.

Fashion Photography in the 1970s

In the 1970s, the tide again turned: Diana Vreeland resigned from her influential reign as editor-in-chief of *Vogue*, and in January 1977, American *Vogue* reduced the actual trim size of the publication. Meanwhile, French *Vogue* took the creative lead in fashion photography in this decade and offered their two leading photographers, Helmut Newton and Guy Bourdin, complete creative autonomy. Deborah Turbeville produced work that reflected psychological dislocation in the modern world, in part through her slouching and stylized poses. She was the first to use overweight and "ugly" models, pioneering a more diverse standard of model. Her "bathhouse" photographs published in *Vogue* (May 1975) created a furor by evoking the grisly aura of a concentration camp or the frightening vacuousness of drugged stupor.

Fashion Photography in the 1980s

Some of the most important editorial and advertising fashion photography of the 1980s continued to be done by Richard Avedon. His brilliant advertising campaign "The Diors," a story spun weekly in the pages of the *New York Times Magazine*, created the enduring vogue for narrative in fashion photography. Avedon's shot of Nastassja Kinski, her nude form sensuously entwined with a gigantic snake, has become a classic. Women's strength and independence was emphasized, from sporty and athletic to domineering and brutalizing. Numerous photographers, including Denis Piel, Bruce Weber, and Bert Stern pictured women threatening men with everything from pocketbooks to knives and chains. Fashion itself, particularly in the work of such designers as Jean Paul Gaultier, Azzedine Alaïa, and Issey Miyake (whose work was notably photographed by Penn), helped form the look of the decade's photography

Fashion Photography in the 1990s

In the last decade of the century, Herb Ritts, Steven Meisel, and Bruce Weber continued to produce some of the most interesting and innovative work, including Weber's hilarious hip-hop version of a black Snow White and the Seven Dwarfs and his seminal spread dealing with the impact of grunge on fashion in the 1990s (including the first post-punk nose ring in a *Vogue* fashion spread). Two of the greats of fashion photography, Irving Penn and Helmut Newton, continued to dominate the field. Ellen von Unwerth's romantic individualism and Sheila Metzner's spare but sumptuous style were also widely evident. Models were increasingly racially diverse, with a number of black models, such as Iman, Naomi Campbell, and Karen Alexander, achieving the status of celebrity superstars. As to the early years of the twenty-first century, one must await the knowledge of hindsight to assess the importance of very recent fashion photography as well as the development of such young talents as Christophe Kutner, Glen Luchford, Javier Vallhonrat, and Craig McDean. What seems certain is that fashion photography—whether published in *Vogue, W, Dazed and Confused*, or *Sleaze Nation*—will continue to reflect the society and the times in which it was made.

See also **Actors and Actresses, Impact on Fashion; Art and Fashion; Avedon, Richard; Beaton, Cecil; Hartnell, Norman; Hoyningen-Huene, George; Newton, Helmut.**

BIBLIOGRAPHY

Brooke-Adler, Isabel. "Baron von Meyer." *Art Journal* (1899): 270–272.

Chase, Edna Woolman, and Ilka Chase. *Always in Vogue*. Garden City, N.Y.: Doubleday and Company, 1954.

Edwards, Owen. "Blow-Out: The Decline and Fall of the Fashion Photographer." *New York* 6, no. 22 (28 May 1973): 49–56.

Ewing, William A., and Nancy Hall-Duncan. *Horst*. New York: International Center of Photography, 1984.

Frenzel, H. K. *Hoyningen-Huené: Meisterbildenisse*. Berlin: Verlag Dietrich Reineer, 1932.

Garner, Philippe, and David Alan Mellor. *Cecil Beaton, 1920–1970*. New York: Stuart, Tabori and Chang, 1995.

Goldberg, Vicki, and Nan Richardson. *Louise Dahl-Wolfe*. Foreword by Dorothy Twining Globus. New York: Harry N. Abrams, 2000.

Hall-Duncan, Nancy. *The History of Fashion Photography*. New York: Alpine Press, 1978.

Harrison, Martin. *Appearance: Fashion Photography since 1945*. New York: Rizzoli International, 1991.

Hayden-Guest, Anthony. "The Return of Guy Bourdin." *New Yorker* 70, no. 36 (7 November 1994): 13–46.

Kramer, Hilton. "The Dubious Art of Fashion Photography." *New York Times*, 28 December 1975.

Lehmann, Ulrich. *ChicClicks: Creativity and Commerce in Contemporary Fashion Photography*. Boston: The Institute of Contemporary Art in collaboration with Hatje Cantz Publishers, 2002.

Liberman, Alexander. *The Art and Technique of Color Photography: A Treasury of Color Photographs by the Staff Photographers of Vogue, House and Garden, and Glamour*. New York: Simon and Schuster, 1951.

Ray, Man. *Self-Portrait: Man Ray*. London: Andre Deutsch, 1963.

Sargeant, Winthrop. "Profiles: Richard Avedon." *New Yorker* 34 (8 November 1958): 49–50.

Steichen, Edward. *A Life in Photography*. New York: Doubleday and Company, 1963.

Thornton, Gene. "Turbeville Gives Fashion a Torture Treatment." *New York Times*, 24 January 1977.

Nancy Hall-Duncan

FASHION PLATES Fashion plates are small printed images, often hand-colored, of people wearing the latest fashions and depicted in conventional minimally narrative social contexts. They flourished from the late eighteenth to the early twentieth centuries, and were usually distributed with fashion magazines either as integral parts of the editorial content or as supplementary plates. The poet Charles Beaudelaire, in his essay *The Painter of Modern Life*, described fashion plates as an image of the "ideal self" and thus a reflection of the artistic, historical, moral, and aesthetic feeling of their time. He wrote in 1863, when fashion plates were reaching a peak in their development. Although the basic purpose of the fashion plate was to illustrate new styles and sell more clothes, their charm gives them an established place among the minor graphic arts. Sadly for the student, fashion plates are often removed from the magazines in which they appeared and sold as collectors' pieces; divorced from their original context they lose much value as historic sources.

Origins

People attractively or unusually dressed have been popular graphic subjects at least since the sixteenth century, when the *Costume Book* or *Trachtenbuch* brought them into popular publishing. By the middle of the seventeenth century, the graphic artist Vaclav Hollar had given such illustrations new artistic status and Bosse, Callot, and de Hooghe began to group their fashionables in suitable settings.

Not until the last quarter of the seventeenth century did the series of popular prints (usually termed *Les Modes*) of fashions and fashionable people appear. Published by the Paris print sellers, the Bonnarts, with plates by Saint Aubin, Bérain, and Arnoult, they promoted French taste to a wide international market. Nevertheless, such illustrations did not take on a commercial role as advertisements until Jean Donneau de Vizé introduced them into the *Mercure Extraordinaire* and the *Mercure Galant* of 1678 and 1681, noting suppliers as well as garments.

The Eighteenth Century

Thereafter the fashion plate fell into disuse until the 1750s, reappearing in ladies pocketbooks, diaries, almanacs, and magazines. Occasionally credited to dressmakers, they were popular as fashion guides. The small monochrome plates were often by well-known artists and engravers.

By the last quarter of the eighteenth century, the ending of French Guild restrictions in 1777 made fashionable clothing available to many more consumers, and so opened the market to a flood of illustrated fashion material. The best known, an anthology of some 200 to 400 colored fashion plates compiled from several sources by the publishers Esnaut and Rapilly between 1778 and 1787, is the *Galerie des Modes et Costumes Francais*, illustrated most notably by Watteau le Jeune and Desrais. The fine *Suite d'Estampes pour servir à l'Histoire des Moeurs et du Costume* (1778), drawn by J. M. Moreau, had as its stated aim the promotion of French taste. Though often regarded as the quintessence of French fashion, it is more a complete guide to the world of fashionable people in their material context.

The Nineteenth Century

The publishing boom of the late eighteenth and early nineteenth centuries stimulated the flow of fashion illustrations. Despite the Revolution and the Napoleonic wars, French plates continued to dominate the market, though equally fine examples were produced in England and Germany. Le Brun Tossa in the *Le Cabinet des Modes*, 1785–1789, and La Mésangère in *Le Journal des Dames et des Modes*, 1797–1839, featured high-quality plates by excellent artists, as did John Bell in the English *La Belle Assemblée* 1806–1832, but Bell's illustrations were often pirated and adapted to local taste.

La Mésangère extended the range of his artist illustrators by publishing them in a series of fashion and genre prints, such as Debucourt's *Modes et Manières du Jour*, 1810, and the Vernets' *Incroyables et Merveilleuses* and *Le Bon Genre*, 1818. They are a precedent for the more intimate picture series by Gavarni and Deveria, whose fashion plates were such a feature of the periodicals of the 1830s and 1840s. A successful formula, it was followed by the *pochoir* fashion illustrators of the twentieth century, most notably George Barbier.

The most prestigious early nineteenth-century British contribution to the art of the fashion plate was *Heideloff's Gallery of Fashion*, 30 aquatint plates, 1797–1801, published by subscription to an aristocratic clientele. Focused on fashions worn by anonymous noble ladies, it also included the creations of named dressmakers. With the aquatint plates of British popular venues crowded with fashionable men, women, and children, published by London tailor Benjamin Read between the 1820s and 1840s, the fashion plate was decisively democratized. Prints and full-scale patterns were sold through Read's establishments in London and New York, where American versions soon appeared.

By the mid-nineteenth century, with the expansion of popular and pictorial publishing as well as the clothing trade, the fashion plate proliferated. To satisfy demand, engraving establishments, especially in Britain and Germany, provided type images easily grouped and amended for the cheaper fashion and advertising market. The male fashion figure largely disappeared from fashion plates at this time; however arranged and accessorized, he lacked the vivacity of fashionable men as drawn by Paul Gavarni and the Vernets.

Quality fashion plates remained available through large-scale French publishers and agents for publications abroad, such as Goubaud and Mariton. The best documented and most prolific artists during the middle of the nineteenth century were the Colin sisters—Heloise Leloir, Anais Toudouze, and Laure Noel—who, together with their rival Jules David, were skillful in showing the requisite dress detail in conventional evocative settings. American fashion plates, sometimes modified from French originals, as in *Godey's Ladies' Book* and the publications of Mme Demorest, could be more practical, even featuring domestic appliances.

The Artist and the Photographer

By the end of the century, the earlier romanticizing tradition was challenged by avant-garde black-and-white work, dramatic rather than representational. An idealized realism also became fashionable, and A. Sandoz, especially for the House of Worth, produced Tissot-like groupings set in the wider world of the modern woman of the twentieth century.

His source material probably included photographs from the house archives, but although promotional photographs had been occasionally used in fashion publications since the 1860s, and press pictures of fashionable scenes, such as those by the Seeberger brothers, were popular, the detailed color reproduction expected by the quality market was expensive. Retouching was easy but the photographs from *Les Modes*, their speciality, illustrate the problems. Idealization, the core of fashion illustration, was problematic, and fashion artists were available, adaptable, quicker, and cheaper.

Confronted by advances in printing and photographic technology and the easy availability of the conventional graphic image, in the early twentieth century the artistic avant-garde retreated to the craft technique of *pochoir* (stencil) printing and hand coloring, producing formal, modernist, *faux naives* fashion plates in exotic or romantic settings reminiscent of the early nineteenth century. The genre was pioneered by Paul Iribe for Poiret's 1909 collection in *Les Robes de Paul Poiret*, 1909, and by Georges LePape in *Les Choses de Paul Poiret*, 1911. Their work and others of the group, such as Charles Martin and George Barbier, was brought to a wider public by the publisher Lucien Vogel, who launched the elitist *Gazette du Bon Ton* in 1911, the precursor of several similar art and fashion magazines. The general public became aware of the style and technique through prestige advertising, such as *Art Gout Beauté*, 1920–1936, published by the textile firm Albert Godde Bedin.

In general the advertising agencies were very open to modern trends. Not without reference to the cinema, by the early 1930s they had revived the male fashion image illustrating active realistic men in glamorized everyday settings. *Esquire* adopted this style in 1933 and subsequent men's fashion advertisements and magazines would continue it well into the 1960s.

By 1923, the *Gazette du Bon Ton* and its artists had been taken over by *Vogue*. Fashion narrative illustrations were not part of *Vogue*'s format, and the work of the *Bon Ton* artists, like that of established *Vogue* artists such as Helen Dryden and Douglas Sutherland, was confined to the elegantly decorative covers. By the late 1920s and 1930s, a new generation of fashion artist, Eric (Carl Erickson), H. Bouet Willaumez, Bouché, and Christian Bérard had begun to convey the essence of style, scene, and above all movement, in vivid and impressionist plates, though occasionally their lack of detail was deplored.

It is the ability to convey the soul of the garment as well as the seams, the ambience and the dynamic of fashion, and the essence of its modernity, which keeps the fashion plate an element of publishing in the early twenty-first century.

See also **Fashion Illustrators; Vogue.**

BIBLIOGRAPHY

Cornu, Paul, ed. and preface. *Galeries des Modes et Costumes Francais, dessinés d'après nature, 1778–1787*. New, collected edition. Paris: E. Lévy, 1911–1914.

Gaudriault, Raymond. *La Gravure de Mode Feminine de France*. Paris: les editions de l'amateur, 1988.

Ginsburg, Madeleine. *An Introduction to Fashion Illustration*. London: V & A/Compton/Pitman, 1980.

Hay, Susan. "Paris to Providence: French Couture and the Tirocci Shop." In *From Paris to Providence*. Edited by Susan Hay. Providence: Museum of Art, Rhode Island School of Design, 2000. An admirable study that illustrates the practical use of fashion illustrations.

Packer, William. *Fashion Drawing in Vogue*. New York: Coward McCann, 1983.

Steele, Valerie. *Paris Fashion: A Cultural History*. Oxford: Berg, 1998.

Madeleine Ginsberg

FASHION SHOWS The fashion show has evolved from an exclusive in-house presentation of haute couture held for a private clientele, to a biannual spectacle of both couture and ready-to-wear clothing that is seen by a vast cross-section of consumers, the mass media, and the fashion industry. A number of cultural and social forces are responsible for this evolution, including the increased consumer awareness of Parisian couture, the rise of the ready-to-wear industry after World War II, the growth of the modeling profession, and the increasing attention paid to the runway by the popular press. While the fashion show today is different from its early-twentieth-century incarnation, it does retain links to its origins in theatrical display and the couture salon shows of that period.

Origins

In nineteenth-century Paris, it was common practice for dressmaker houses to use their assistants or saleswomen (*desmoiselles du magasin*) to wear the designer's creations while working at the shop. To reach a broader clientele, many couturiers extended this display to the public arena as well, with figures such as Charles Frederick Worth dressing his wife in the latest styles to promenade in socially important areas of the city such as the Bois du Boulogne. In the late nineteenth and early twentieth centuries in London and Paris, the custom-dressmaking trade also maintained important and effective links to the world of theater and advertised its wares by dressing famous actresses both on and off the stage. The couture

Model backstage at a fashion show. Since their inception in the early 1900s, fashion shows have evolved from relatively simple in-house events to highly publicized worldwide spectacles. © LANGEVIN JACQUES/CORBIS SYGMA. REPRODUCED BY PERMISSION.

houses of Doucet and Paquin, for example, were very successful promoters through this medium and their clientele included such popular stars as Sarah Bernhardt, Réjane, and Cecile Sorel. The theater, particularly in France and England, became a place to see the most avant-garde styles and eventually a "fashion play" genre developed that revolved around the presentation of the latest couture creations. Dressing members of the fashionable demimonde and house mannequins (the term for models in this period) for the races, opera, and theater premieres, and resort areas were another means of advertising up-to-the-minute designs.

In the first decade of the century, social display was supplemented by organized shows at a fixed time in the couture house. Although a number of designers and fashion personalities claim responsibility for the first fashion show, it was not one person who started the trend, but rather a gradual evolution toward more formal presentations of seasonal clothing lines. By the mid-1910s many designers, including Paul Poiret, Lucile, and Paquin, were using the fashion show as a promotional vehicle. In 1910 Lucile promoted the opening of her New York branch with a spectacular fashion show in a city theater. The presentation had an Arabian Nights theme inspired

by vaudeville revues. Lucile was one of the first to promote her mannequins as public personalities, giving them exotic names such as Dinarzade and Sumurun, and training them to walk with a distinctive gait.

For Paris haute couture, the shows were first presented in Paris or London and then sometimes traveled to America on well-publicized tours. Paul Poiret followed this pattern, organizing a tour in 1911 in which he and his mannequins showed his exotic creations in venues such as charity bazaars, theaters, and department stores throughout Europe. In 1913 he also conducted a heavily promoted tour of the United States with his mannequins, and other designers followed suit, including Jeanne Paquin in 1914 and Jean Patou in 1924. Another innovative mode of presentation in the 1910s was the organization of a *thé dansant*, a popular pastime that showcased new dances such as the tango and the fox-trot. Designers including Lucile and Paquin showed their new designs in such a context, often using theaters as a show venue.

In America, department stores, such as Wanamakers in Philadelphia, started holding regular fashion shows in 1910 and gradually broadened the audience for such fashion display. The advent of the fashion newsreel in the same period also served to bring the fashion show to a wider clothes-buying public. Beginning in 1910, a number of French, English, and American film companies began to show fashion reels as part of their weekly newsreel production. In 1913 a New York–based film company started documenting the biannual fashion shows in New York that now took place in February for the spring–summer collections and July for fall–winter collections. At this point, modeling was not an evolved routine and both film and fashion magazines often used actresses, opera singers, and dancers as mannequins.

In the United States during World War I, a number of fashion shows were organized to benefit the war effort and toured across the country. In 1914, a Fashion Fête was organized by Edna Woolman Chase, the editor of *Vogue*, to showcase New York designers. Also in that year a number of couture houses banded together to form Le Syndicat de defense de la grand couture francaise with Paul Poiret as president. In an effort to fight design piracy, the organization charged a standard copyright fee for business customers who wished to reproduce couture designs. The syndicate also placed more stringent rules on who could attend the couture shows and wholesalers and retailers were barred from couture showings unless they were invited.

By 1918 the couture industry had fixed dates for two major shows per year for the foreign buyers that were coming to Paris. The shows were becoming organized presentations using in-house mannequins and by the 1920s, the House of Patou, for example, was employing 32 mannequins to model 450 dresses at each showing. Other contemporary references document between 7 and 15 mannequins regularly employed in the couture houses at this time. One 1920s commentator wrote that the mannequins were still considered "demimondaine" but they did have paid salaries, bonuses, and some had season contracts. In 1923 John Robert Powers established the first modeling agency in New York, which served to professionalize the industry and positioned modeling as a more socially acceptable career. In the 1920s designers also had a set routine and started by showing sports and day clothes, then evening wear.

In the 1930s Elsa Schiaparelli was the first to create themed collections, including "Circus," "Commedia dell'Arte," and "Astrology," among others. These themes added a theatrical flair to her shows between 1936 and 1939 by incorporating music, special lighting, and dance into the presentation. Her 1938 "Circus" collection, for example, included circus performers who jumped, skipped, and flipped all over the couture house.

The Postwar Era
An increasingly formal presentation style marked the postwar era and at this point the show evolved into the essential organization that is still associated with it in the early 2000s. The show took place in the couture salon, the crowded audience consisted of invited buyers with important journalists at the front, and there was a specific sequence for the type of dress shown (for example, the wedding dress at the end). Fashion shows often lasted seventy-five minutes and approximately sixty ensembles were presented on between eight and ten models. This period also witnessed the association of particular mannequins with specific couture houses. Mannequins, such as Bettina at Jacques Fath or Praline at Pierre Balmain, with their distinctive saunters, visually represented the designer's philosophy and often acted as the designer's muse. While Paris had successfully reestablished itself as the style leader in the postwar era, countries such as the United States, England, and Italy also held regular fashion shows.

It was still common practice to hold fashion shows in department stores and hotels and the *Vogue* editor Edna Woolman Chase recorded in her 1954 memoirs:

> Now that fashion shows have become a way of life, now that a lady is hard put to it to lunch, or sip a cocktail, in any smart hotel or store from New York to Dallas to San Francisco without having lissome young things in the most recent models, swaying down a runway six inches above her nose—it is difficult to visualize that dark age when fashion shows did not exist. (Chase and Chase 1954, p. 119)

By the mid-1950s, fashion shows were common in urban centers in semiannual department store displays and, at the local level, they were often incorporated into charity events.

Ready-to-Wear Market
In the late 1950s the rise of the ready-to-wear market had a significant impact on the organization, number, and scale of fashion shows. In 1959 Pierre Cardin showed his ready-to-wear collection in the *Printemps* department store in Paris and by the mid-1960s, ready-to-wear was regularly included in the fashion calendar. The growth of the ready-to-wear market was also related to the decline in interest in haute couture by the younger generation, who did not want to follow the fashion dictates of Paris. New designers responded to this cultural phenomenon by adding a youthful energy to their fashion shows. The English designer Mary Quant, for example, presented her mod ready-to-wear designs to jazz music and her mannequins skipped and danced down the runway. Quant opted to use print models rather than runway models because she liked the way they moved and the fast pace allowed her to show forty garments in fourteen minutes. The distinction between the runway and photography model was on the wane.

This growth of the ready-to-wear market eventually changed the function of the haute couture fashion show, shifting its targeted audience from private clientele to one consisting mainly of press and buyers. The 1960s also mark the beginnings of the use of the fashion show as a marketing tool to promote the licensed products associated with the house.

Fashion Show as Spectacle

In the 1970s and 1980s the public visibility and magnitude of fashion shows increased dramatically. In 1973 the designer Kenzo presented a large-scale ready-to-wear show on a stage rather than a runway, indicating a break with haute couture tradition and the increasing emphasis on spectacle. In the 1980s Thierry Mugler and Claude Montana staged theatrical events that further removed the fashion show from the couture salon. Mugler hired a rock impresario to stage his fashion show, an audience of six thousand people attended, and half of the show's tickets were available for purchase by the public. This was the first time that the public was allowed to attend a couture show and marks a trend toward the fashion show as mass entertainment. In the mid-1980s the regular broadcasting of the ready-to-wear shows on cable television further broadened the viewing public. The increased public awareness of the catwalk shows led to the promotion of "supermodels" in the early 1990s. By this time, modeling had long been a socially acceptable profession and the increasing cult of personality in various cultural arenas served to promote models as celebrities on a par with movie actors.

While the majority of fashion designers hold traditional runway shows during the fashion weeks in Paris, London, New York, and other cities, many now have specific themes, mood music, and special lighting and other effects. In the 1990s there were a number of designers, including John Galliano and Alexander McQueen, who became renowned for producing extravagant shows in unusual spaces with narratives and fictional characters. These theatrical stagings have pushed the fashion show beyond the garment and into the realm of the conceptual fantasy. These types of shows function primarily to promote brand recognition and to sell the ready-to-wear lines and the licensed products.

See also **Department Store; Fashion Designer; Fashion Models.**

BIBLIOGRAPHY

Bertin, Célia. *Paris à la Mode: A Voyage of Discovery.* Translated by Marjorie Deans. London: Victor Gollancz Ltd., 1956.

Castle, Charles. *Model Girl.* Newton Abbott, U.K.: David and Charles, 1977.

Chase, Edna Woolman, and Ilka Chase. *Always in Vogue.* New York: Doubleday, 1954.

Evans, Caroline. "The Enchanted Spectacle." *Fashion Theory* 5, no. 3 (September 2001): 270–310.

Michelle Tolini Finamore

FASHION TELEVISION Fashion television has revolutionized the dissemination of fashion information to a mass audience; it has become a major marketing vehicle, helping to launch fashion trends and enhance the cult of personality surrounding fashion designers and models. With immediacy that only television can offer, following fashion has become a source of entertainment for millions. The evolution of fashion television into a distinct genre of broadcasting parallels, but is not limited to, the development of cable and satellite television.

Cable television was developed as a localized service in Pennsylvania in the late 1940s in response to a growing need for improved television reception and better access to existing channels in more remote geographical regions. Since then, it has expanded into a competitive, multibillion-dollar industry; pay television and the launch of satellite broadcasting, first used by the Home Box Office (HBO) network in the early 1970s, contributed to its rapid growth and popularity. Satellite broadcasting, which receives signals from space, transformed cable programming into a global, cost-efficient transmission system, and led to the creation of specialized cable networks that provide viewers with 24-hour news, weather, music, movie, sports, shopping, and entertainment channels.

The 1970s and 1980s saw a boom for cable and satellite broadcasting. It was during this time that fashion television emerged as a genre of broadcasting, with certain networks and television personalities becoming key players in its development. In 1976, Videofashion News, a video version of a fashion magazine, was created and has been produced continuously since, carried by a number of distributors internationally. The series provides viewers with a front-row seat and backstage pass to runway shows around the world, profiling designers, models, and celebrities and reporting on the latest trends.

Elsa Klensch, the preeminent television fashion journalist, got her start in 1980 on the newly created Cable News Network (CNN). Her daily segments and half-hour weekend program, *Style with Elsa Klensch*, which have been broadcast worldwide to millions of viewers, were the first regularly scheduled fashion reports on network television in the United States. *Style*, which continually ranked as one of CNN's highest-watched weekend shows, has covered designer collections from around the world, profiling both designers and models, and the latest trends in interior design.

Klensch's straightforward, comprehensive reporting on international fashion and design has earned the respect of those within the fashion industry as well as the viewing public. She has won numerous awards, including an honor in 1987 from the Council of Fashion Designers of America for bringing fashion to a mass audience; authored the 1992 fashion how-to book, *Style with Elsa Klensch: Developing the Real You*; and made a cameo in Robert Altman's 1994 fashion film *Prêt-à-Porter*. In 2001 and 2002, Klensch collaborated with Videofashion News to produce the hour-long segments, *Trio World Fashion Tour*, for the popular arts channel Trio, which featured top designer collections from the runways of the world's fashion capitals.

Another key personality in fashion television has been the Canadian journalist Jeanne Beker, who launched

Fashion Television (FT) on Video Hits One (VH1) in 1985, now a leading style program. Beker began her career as a music industry journalist in the late 1970s, which informed her approach to reporting on the fashion world. She considers herself an entertainment, not a fashion, reporter. FT started as an intermittent series of one-hour specials and grew into a full series of thirty-nine, half-hour shows a year, broadcast in over one hundred nations with numerous satellite providers, and has since become its own 24-hour network. FT has covered the latest runway collections from around the world, profiled designers and models, offered viewers a peek into post-fashion show parties, and presented FT through the eyes of a psychologist and a rabbi.

According to Beker, fashion executives in the 1980s wanted to add video to fashion coverage with the hope that it could do for fashion what Music Television (MTV) did for music. MTV, which premiered in 1981 as a 24-hour music video channel targeting young adults, has been a launching pad for celebrities and fashion trends. "Madonna wannabes" emerged after her appearance on MTV in 1984; retailers sold Madonna-licensed fashions and accessories. Designer Tommy Hilfiger dispensed his logo-laden sportswear to musicians, who became walking advertisements in music videos; he also collaborated on a fashion show and CD for MTV.

As part of its shift away from 24-hour broadcasting of music videos, MTV attempted to sell clothes in the manner of The Home Shopping Network; and in 1989, launched its fashion program, *House of Style*, with model-host Cindy Crawford, who accepted the position without pay in order to gain more exposure. The show has also helped the careers of subsequent model-hosts including Daisy Fuentes, Rebecca Romijn-Stamos, and Molly Sims. The show, resembling music videos with pumping sound tracks and quick splicing of images, has featured the latest fashions and youth trends. Regular features like "Todd Time" with fashion designer Todd Oldham helped boost designers' profiles. *House of Style* has also hosted *Fashionably Loud*, a fashion show featuring top models walking the runway in the latest fashions to the beat of the newest music acts. The fusion of music, fashion, and celebrity spawned an awards show on MTV Network's other music channel VH1; the VH1 Fashion Awards, in collaboration with *Vogue* magazine, first premiered in the mid 1990s.

In the 1990s E! Networks, arguably the largest distributor of entertainment news and lifestyle programming, became a leader in fashion television. By 1998, E! offered almost thirty half-hour fashion segments a week including "Fashion Week," "Fashion File," "Video Fashion Weekly," and "Model TV." The network also owns The Style Network—a 24-hour channel devoted to fashion, beauty, decorating, and entertaining. Their fashion programming includes makeover shows like "Fashion Emergency" and "Style Court" and covers celebrity fashion with special segments like the popular "Academy

Awards Pre-Show" and "Golden Hanger Awards" both hosted by Joan and Melissa Rivers.

Much of E!'s programming reflects the growing popularity in recent years of lifestyle and makeover shows and programs that focus on celebrity style. Programs such as "Full Frontal Fashion" on Women's Entertainment (WE), much like the magazine *In Style*, show viewers who's wearing what by which designers and how to get the look for yourself. Makeover shows like *What Not to Wear* on The Learning Channel (TLC) and *Queer Eye for the Straight Guy* on Bravo have been popular in 2002 and 2003. *The Isaac Mizrahi Show* on the Oxygen network helped put the network on the map while resuscitating designer Mizrahi's fashion career.

Fashion television has had far-reaching effects on the fashion industry. Fashion reporting like that of Klensch and Beker has brought high fashion into the homes of millions and helped define it for the mainstream. Not only has fashion television launched trends, it has also made designers more attuned to the "telegenic" qualities of their runway shows. It has boosted the profiles of designers and models—even launching the acting careers of many models—putting greater pressure on both to perform well in front of a camera. The proliferation of fashion television programming that exists today attests to the immense appetite of the viewing public to follow fashion, particularly celebrity fashion, as entertainment.

See also **Film and Fashion; Hollywood Style; Music and Fashion.**

BIBLIOGRAPHY
Agins, Teri. *The End of Fashion: How Marketing Changed the Clothing Business Forever.* New York: Quill, 2000.
Gross, Michael. "Rock Videos Shape Fashion for the Young." *New York Times,* 27 December 1985.
Horyn, Cathy. "Vogue Paints a Face on VH1 Awards." *New York Times,* 7 December 1999.
Klensch, Elsa, with Beryl Meyer. *Style.* New York: Berkley Group, 1995.
La Ferla, Ruth. "All Fashion, Almost All the Time." *New York Times,* 29 March 1998.
Menkes, Suzy. "Fashion's TV Frenzy." *New York Times,* 2 April 1995.
Parsons, Patrick R., and Robert M. Friedman. *The Cable and Satellite Television Industries.* Boston: Allyn and Bacon, 1998.
Sheehy, Maura. "No Frills, Meet Fash Dancer." *New York Times,* 19 July 1992.
Spindler, Amy M. "Look Who's Talking." *New York Times,* 15 May 1994.

Tiffany Webber-Hanchett

FASTENERS A fastener is the essential part of a fastening system used to hold together at least two pieces of material. It is typically a single item (button) that often works in concert with another device (buttonhole).

Apparel fasteners may be permanent or temporary. Permanent fastenings, such as stitching and fusing, create form and shape in tailored garments. Temporary fasteners take many forms, including basting used to hold fabrics in place before permanent machine stitching is applied. Temporary fasteners, such as hook and eye closures for bras, can adjust garment size. Zippered fly front openings in men's trousers provide access for bodily functions. However, one most often thinks of apparel fastening as providing a method of "donning and doffing" garments for everyday dressing (Watkins 1995).

In physics terms, friction is the basis for holding solid materials together using one of two methods, applied force or restraining force (Kammermeyer 1967, p. 19). Applied forces are either bidirectional, like the two opposing threads of a lockstitch holding fabric layers together, or radial, like the circular pressure exerted by the female side of a snap fastener (or, in the United Kingdom, press stud). Restraining forces for apparel follow mechanical principals relying on either random surface texture as used in hook-and-loop tape, more commonly known as Velcro, or on functionally configured parts like the teeth of a zipper.

The earliest apparel fastenings can be traced to the Mesolithic era, when needles were used to stitch materials together, and to the age of metals, when evidence of bone buttons and a safety pin–like device are found. The Bronze Age introduced forerunners of the buckle with the brooch and pin concept and the penannular, a sliding pin on a U-shaped element. The first written record of buttons is from the twelfth century (Epstein and Safro 1991). Modern developments have improved on old concepts and added ease and efficiency in fastening garments. The sewing machine increased the speed of stitching fabric pieces together and facilitated production. The zipper, introduced in the late 1800s, has evolved from a bulky mechanism made of metal hooks and eyes, to interlocking metal teeth, to plastic coils, to extruded all-in-one devices. Velcro was invented after World War II and has applications in industry and fashion. New technologies in adhesives and fusibles have influenced the speed of apparel production and the appearance of apparel.

There are many fasteners used in clothing in the early 2000s. Garments are "stitched" together with thread, glue, or fusible substances. Lacing through grommets or eyelets is used in shoes and corsets. Tied or tucked-in fabric ends secure sarongs, saris, and wrap skirts. Clamping devices are used to fasten jewelry to the body. Hook and eye fasteners may be used to add an industrial look to outerwear. Fashion apparel borrows fasteners like C-clamps and D rings from industrial products. Zippers have metal, plastic, or cut-crystal teeth. Buttons, the long-standing epitome of the fashion fastener, provide function with unlimited options in form, color, and texture. Fasteners provide function in garments and often provide the finishing fashion touch.

See also **Closures, Hook-and-Loop.**

BIBLIOGRAPHY
Epstein, Diana, and Millicent Safro. *Buttons.* New York: Harry N. Abrams, 1991.
Kammermeyer, Michael. "Towards a Theory of Fastening Systems." Master's thesis, California State College at Long Beach, 1967.
Watkins, Susan. *Clothing: The Portable Environment.* Ames: Iowa State University Press, 1995.

Karen L. LaBat

FATH, JACQUES A key figure in the revival of the Paris fashion industry after World War II, Jacques Fath (1912–1954) created colorful and inventive designs catering to a young and sophisticated international clientele who identified with the vitality of his label. Though Fath was regarded as one of the "big three" Paris designers in the early 1950s—along with Christian Dior and Pierre Balmain—his untimely death at the age of forty-two meant that the impact and importance of his work was often overlooked in comparison to that of his contemporaries. While Fath's designs were right on the mark of the glamorous postwar look, it was his attitude toward business and his understanding of the power of publicity and marketing that helped to place this charismatic and flamboyant designer apart from his peers.

Fath was born just outside Paris into an artistic family in 1912. His grandfather was a successful artist named René-Jacques Fath. Although Fath's great-grandmother had also been an artist who occasionally worked in fashion illustration, the designer did little to suppress the rumor that she had been a couturière to the Empress Eugénie. Encouraged by his family to enter the business world, Fath worked for a stockbroker for two years upon finishing his education. After completing a required year of military service, however, he realized that a more creative career lay in store. He spent some time in drama school and also took evening courses in drawing and pattern cutting. During this period Fath met Geneviève Boucher de la Bruyère, a photographer's model and fellow drama student, who became his wife in 1939. She modeled many of Fath's early creations and came to epitomize the elegantly finished style of the Jacques Fath woman.

At the end of 1936, Fath established a couture house in the rue de la Boetie and showed his first collection of just twenty garments in the spring of 1937. The collection was well received and enabled Fath to build up a steady clientele, although he still had something of a hand-to-mouth existence in the 1930s. Guillaune notes that in later years Fath recalled how he often used the money from a deposit on a garment to purchase the fabric to make it.

Fath served in the French Army during World War II. After he was demobilized following the fall of France to the Germans in 1940, however, he continued to run his house on a small scale. Having already moved once, Fath secured a permanent home for his label in an imposing eighteenth-century building on the avenue Pierre Premier de Serbie. In 1945 he created four designs for the Théâtre de la Mode, a traveling exhibition of fashion dolls that showcased the work of the top Parisian couturiers.

An astute businessman, Fath decided to add a line of perfumes to his fashions. He launched his first perfume, Chasuble, in 1945 and his second, Iris Gris, a year later. Recognizing the incredible potential to expand his business in the United States, he signed a contract with the New York manufacturer Joseph Halpert in 1948. Fath contracted to provide two collections a year, each comprising about twenty models to be marketed in large department stores throughout the United States. His popularity in America was further increased when Rita Hayward chose him to design her wedding dress and trousseau for her marriage to Prince Aly Khan in 1949. Fath had a loyal following in Hollywood, and designed the costumes for several movies both in the United States and Europe. His costumes for Moira Shearer in the celebrated film *The Red Shoes* (1948) were considered classics.

An attractive and gregarious person, Fath recognized the importance of associating his label with fantasy and marketing images of a lavish lifestyle that his clients could share. He was often photographed with his beautiful wife at evening events in Paris or basking in the sun on the Riviera. He threw large, sumptuous, themed costume parties at his château, inviting an international mix of socialites, actors, and fellow couturiers—which ensured maximum publicity in the press.

The year 1950 was eventful for the designer, with both the launch of his perfume Canasta and the opening of his boutique. Fath's boutique offered more affordable items, such as accessories, scarves, ties, and stockings. He was also chosen by the Chambre Syndicale de la Haute Couture to become one of five designers, alongside Carven, Desses, Paquin and Piguet, to make up a group of associated couturiers. Later that same year he set up a separate company, Parfums Jacques Fath, to market his growing line of scents. In 1953, preempting similar moves from other designers to target a larger market, Fath made the decision to launch a ready-to-wear collection. The Jacques Fath Université range was inspired by the fast and efficient mass-production methods that the designer had seen in the United States.

Fath's love of the dramatic was evident in his clothes. He drew much of his inspiration from historic costume, the theater, and the ballet. These influences are apparent in his use of the bustle and corsetry as recurring motifs, and in his playful and undulating lines. He perfected a clean and tailored hourglass shape, enhancing it with plunging necklines, sharp pocket details, or dramatic

Jacques Fath altering dress. Fath's designs, which frequently drew on historic costumes, were known for their youthful energy and touch of the dramatic. © GENEVIEVE NAYLOR/CORBIS. REPRODUCED BY PERMISSION.

pleats. Fath experimented with asymmetry, pleating, and volume, designing huge voluminous skirts for both day and evening attire. These skirts cascaded from beneath his signature constricted waistline, or appeared as explosions of fabric under large enveloping coats and jackets. Fath's clever use of color ran from discreet juxtapositions of soft colors to loud prints in strong shades. His designs often featured a tartan patterned fabric and a plain fabric combined in one garment and he was unafraid to use bold modern prints to add an extra dimension to the controlled lines of his tailored garments.

Fath's collections of 1948 were notable for rejecting the full New Look silhouette in favor of severe tubular skirts and dresses cut along diagonal lines. His spring collection of 1950 caused a sensation when it was displayed, with dresses featuring a plunging décolletage accompanied by starched wing collars fastened with a bow tie—a suggestive look that later became identified with Playboy bunnies. Fath was extremely fond of fine wool tweed and jersey fabrics for daywear, often draping these materials directly onto a mannequin to create a new design. Rich satins, taffetas, and fine chiffons were his fabrics of choice for evening gowns, and he often used fur, both in trimmings and as full garments, to dramatic effect.

In 1954 Jacques Fath died tragically early at the age of forty-two. He left behind him a fashion empire at the height of its success, with over six hundred employees.

Geneviève Fath valiantly took over the business for a few years, but closed the clothing line in 1957. The Fath name continued as a perfume label until 1992, when it was acquired by a succession of different companies. The most recent owner of the Fath label was the France Luxury Group, who resurrected the clothing line in 2002 in an attempt to restore the success of this once great house.

See also **Fashion Marketing and Merchandising; Film and Fashion; Haute Couture; New Look; Paris Fashion; Perfume; Tartan; Theatrical Costume.**

BIBLIOGRAPHY

Balmain, Pierre. *My Years and Seasons.* London: Cassell and Co.,1964.

Charles-Roux, Edmonde, et al. *Théâtre de la Mode: Fashion Dolls: The Survival of Haute Couture.* Portland, Ore.: Palmer-Pletsch Associates, 2002.

Guillaume, Valérie. *Jacques Fath.* Paris: Adam Biro et Paris Musées, 1993.

Lynam, Ruth, ed. *Paris Fashion, The Great Designers and Their Creations.* London: Michael Joseph, 1972.

Millbank, Caroline Rennolds. *Couture: The Great Fashion Designers.* London: Thames and Hudson, 1985.

Steele, Valerie. *Paris Fashion: A Cultural History.* 2d ed. Oxford, New York, and Tokyo: Berg/Oxford International Publishers, 1998.

Watson, Linda. *Vogue: Twentieth Century Fashion.* London: Carlton Books, 2000.

Oriole Cullen

FEATHERS Feathers are the horny outgrowth of skin found on birds. They serve a protective function for birds similar to the scales for fish and hair for mammals. Protecting birds from temperature extremes, feathers also help them fly and differentiate between the sexes.

Feathers are made up of a spiny central structure called the axis and flat side branches called barbs. The axis consists of a quill and a shaft. The quill is the hollow, colorless portion rooted in the skin, from which the feather derives nourishment while it is growing. From the quill to the tip of the feather is the shaft. It is solid and serves as an anchor to millions of barbs or interlocking hooks. This is where most of the color is found.

Feathers come in two main types: contour and down. Contour feathers, the most conspicuous of these types, are found on the wings and tail. The down feathers, considerably softer and fluffier than the contour feathers, are located at the base of the contour feathers.

Uses of Feathers

Feathers have had a wide range of uses for thousands of years. Pillows have been filled with feathers and down since around 400 C.E. Until the advent of steel pens in the mid-nineteenth century, the best writing instruments were made from the quill of goose feathers. Feathers have been used for toys for cats, magic, and medicine bags. But of most relevance to this volume is the use of feathers in personal adornment across time and culture.

Feathers and symbolism. In a number of cultures, feathers have assumed great symbolism, often being associated with spirituality. Feather bonnets have been worn in religious ceremonies and ritual dances since the sixteenth century in Brazil.

Feathered spirit masks, made by the Tapirapé of the Amazon, play an important role in dry-season ceremonies performed by the Bird Societies as they circle their village and sing the songs of their respective bird species. For Yanomamö men of the Amazon, their feathered armbands worn high on their upper arms gave them the appearance of having wings, thereby bringing them closer to bird spirits.

The Native American war bonnet was made out of feathers from a golden eagle's tail. This headdress was a symbol of honor, accomplishment, and bravery.

In ancient Egypt, the ostrich feather was a symbol of truth. It was often seen in depictions of Ma'at, the goddess of truth and justice, who passed judgment over the souls of the dead.

Feathers and fashion. The Chinese of 500 C.E. used feathered fans. Robin Hood of merry old England wore a feather in his hat. By the late nineteenth century, feathers had become a must-have fashion item around the world, primarily for muffs and hats. The demand for feathers seemed to know no bounds. In 1886, Frank Chapman, an American Museum of Natural History ornithologist, counted feathers or even whole birds adorning 542 out of 700 hats he observed being worn by ladies from New York City. An estimated 5 million birds were killed each year to supply feathers for fashion items according to the American Ornithologists' Union. Bird species were plundered in the United States, Burma, Malaya, Indonesia, China, Australia, New Zealand, and throughout Europe. As a result, some bird species were greatly threatened and several became extinct. The nineteenth-century popularity of the feather muff led to the extinction of the bittern. The huia of New Zealand was extinct by the early twentieth century as well. Populations of snowy egrets and other wading birds were greatly reduced.

The Future of Feathers

As a result of the decimation of bird populations all over the world, some environmental concern began to emerge and bird protection laws began to be enacted in the early twentieth century. Queen Alexandra of England made a statement by getting rid of all of her own hats with feathers on them in 1906. In 1918, the Federal Migratory Bird Treaty Act was signed between the United States and

Canada. This treaty limits sportsman to shooting migratory birds no more than three and a half months a year. In 1937 a similar treaty was established between the United States and Mexico. The Endangered Species Act of 1973 contains important provisions for the protection of migratory birds. In addition, international treaties between the United States and Japan and the former Soviet Union protect migratory birds that spend part of their year in the different countries. In the early 2000s most wild birds are protected. It is illegal to use feathers from songbirds (such as chickadees), marsh birds (such as egrets), and birds of prey (such as eagles) in the United States for clothing and accessories.

While the laws undoubtedly helped reduce the number of birds being killed for use in clothing and accessories, perhaps the biggest reason that birds on the endangered species list made a comeback was a change in fashion. In the 1920s, young women cut their hair so short that it could not properly support the large hats that had been decorated with many feathers just a few years earlier. Feathers did reappear on hats in the 1930s, 1940s, and 1950s. By the late 1960s, very few women wore hats on a regular basis. In the early 2000s, less colorful feathers from chickens and ducks are dyed vivid colors. Also, technology has allowed fake feathers and fur to look very realistic.

Feather Purchase and Care

For those with a passion for feathers, there are many Web sites where customers can buy feathers that look like a golden eagle, which is illegal to kill, but are really dyed and trimmed from legal feathers. Other businesses assure their customers that the feathers were obtained by natural molting and not by killing of birds. The following types of feathers are generally available: duck, goose, guinea hen, macaw, pheasant, turkey, peacock, ostrich, and rooster.

Since cleaning feathers can be quite damaging to them, it is best to take preventive measures to ensure their longevity. Feathers should be stored away from dust, light, and insects in pH neutral boxes, which can be obtained from businesses that sell archival storage materials. Ideal temperature for storage is 60 degrees Fahrenheit to 75 degrees Fahrenheit, with a humidity of 45 to 55 percent. Handling of feathers should be kept to a minimum.

See also **America, North: History of Indegenous Peoples Dress; Fur; Inuit and Arctic Dress; Trimmings.**

BIBLIOGRAPHY
Braun, B., ed. *Arts of the Amazon.* London: Thames and Hudson, Inc., 1995.
Callan, G. O. *The Thames and Hudson Dictionary of Fashion and Fashion Designers.* London: Thames and Hudson, Inc., 1998.
Gillow, J., and B. Sentence. *World Textiles: A Visual Guide to Traditional Techniques.* Boston: Little, Brown and Company, 1999.
Thomas, N. *Oceanic Art.* London: Thames and Hudson, Inc., 1995.
Tortora, P. *The Fairchild Encyclopedia of Fashion Accessories.* New York: Fairchild Publications, 2003.

Elizabeth D. Lowe

FELT Felt is a fabric with a long history. It is a wonderfully versatile material. Felt with precise technical specifications is created in factories for industrial use, and yet the same material can be made by hand into beautiful clothing and exquisite works of art.

Felt can only be made from wool (the hair of sheep, camel and goat) or from fibers from the coats of certain other animals including beaver and rabbit. When these fibers are moistened, compressed, and agitated by rolling, beating, or rubbing, they move and become tangled together and form felt fabric. Scales on the outside of the fibers allow them to move in only one direction and prevent untangling. Hot water, soap, and various other chemicals speed the felting process—in fact, the reason why wool sweaters often shrink during washing is because the fibers become felted.

The origin of felt is unknown but is believed to date back to prehistoric times in Central Asia. Felt may have been discovered when wool, shed from wild sheep, was used to soften sleeping areas, and it formed a cohesive fabric, or when the wool on skins used for clothing became matted.

Felt is a good insulator. It is windproof and rain will run off it. It can be cut and will not fray because it has no yarns to unravel. Dense felt is remarkably strong and cannot be pierced by arrows. This property was appreciated by many warriors in the past, who used felt for lightweight shields and armor. Thin felt may tear when stretched, but dense felt can be stretched and molded into various shapes for uses such as hats, boots, and bags.

The Land of Felt

As in the past, felt plays an integral part in the lives of Eurasian nomads, who live in lightweight felt tents, known in the West by their Turkish name, yurts, but called *gers* in Mongolia. Yurts are domed structures usually sixteen to twenty feet in diameter, made from a wooden framework covered with felt. A yurt can be erected or dismantled in less than an hour and can easily be carried by two camels or yaks. Nomads also use felt for clothing, boots, hats, bags, carpets, blankets, horse paraphernalia, idols, and toys. This practice continued as the nomads settled in villages, and in Mongolia, many nomads now settled in towns and cities still choose to live in yurts.

Traditionally, nomads make felt by spreading wool fibers on a yak skin and wetting them. The wool and skin are wrapped around a pole and rolled by hand or pulled across the ground by a yak or other animal. After the

THE LAND OF FELT

From about 400 B.C.E., felt was used so extensively in Central Asia that the area was known to the Chinese as "the land of felt." The goal of Genghis Khan was to unite "the people who live in felt tents," and by 1206 he ruled the second-largest empire in human history.

wool has formed a cohesive sheet, it is removed from the mat and rolled further until a strong piece of fabric is created. Decorative designs may be added by appliquéing colored felt pieces or by the use of dyed wool in the felting process.

Before the time of the Roman Empire, felt was made in areas north of a line from Scandinavia, down to Italy, across Greece and Turkey, down the Persian Gulf, across Northern India, and up to the northeast tip of China. There is mention of felt in the works of Homer and pictures of felt production in the ruins of Pompeii. Felt was not known in Africa, Australia, or the Americas.

Until the 1960s, handcrafted felt continued to be used in many Middle Eastern areas for hats, boots, clothing, rugs, and wall hangings. The Turkish military wore felt boots until the 1950s. In Iran and Turkey, felt is now associated with an unsophisticated rural lifestyle.

Felt in the West

Little is known about felting in Europe prior to the Middle Ages. Felt was generally a low status fabric used for men's hats, saddle covers, and the linings of helmets. When Charles VII of France wore a beaver felt hat in 1449 after defeating the English at the Battle of Rouen, such hats became so popular (and an indication of a wearer's social status) that by the late 1500s beavers were extinct in Western Europe. This led to the development of the North American fur trade by British and French explorers and settlers.

To improve the felting properties of beaver fur, pelts were soaked with a mercury compound before the hair was cut from the skin. The mercury evaporated during hat making and was inhaled by the hatters, causing damage to their nervous systems that eventually resulted in madness. This is the origin of the term "mad as a hatter."

Hats were so much a part of life that, by the 1820s, there were over 200 hat manufacturing companies in London alone. Beaver felt hats declined in popularity at about that time, but until the 1950s, fashion dictated that men should wear wool felt hats and caps outside, and even in many indoor situations.

Modern Felt

The development of felting machines in the mid-1800s increased the uses of felt as both a consumer and an industrial material. Machine-made wool felt has been used for hats, slippers, toys, the linings of silverware cases, carpet underlay, washers, gaskets, filters, polishing wheels, drum sticks, piano parts, and felt pens. It is not generally used for clothing in the West, because thick felt is stiff and does not drape well while thin felt will stretch out of shape. One notable exception is the circular skirts with appliquéd poodle designs that were popular in the 1950s. For crafts, ladies' hats and many other uses, nonwoven fabrics made from synthetic fibers replaced felt in the late twentieth century.

As traditional felt-making is declining and commercial production of wool felt is decreasing, there has been a revival in interest in the study of traditional felt and the production of felt by hand as a craft or an artistic endeavor. Because of its unique properties and the way it can be made by hand, there will always be uses for felt.

See also **Appliqué; Nonwoven Textiles.**

BIBLIOGRAPHY
Burkett, Mary E. *The Art of the Felt Maker.* Kendal, U.K.: Abbot Hall Art Gallery, 1979.

Gordan, Beverly. *Feltmaking.* New York: Watson-Guptill Publications, 1980.

Laufer, Berthold. "The Early History of Felt." *American Anthopologist,* n.s. 32, no. 1 (1930): 1–18.

Sjöberg, Gunilla Paetau. *Felt: New Directions for an Ancient Craft.* Translated by Patricia Sparks. Loveland, Colo.: Interweave Press, Inc., 1996.

Pufpaff, Suzanne, ed. *Nineteenth-Century Hat Maker's and Felter's Manuals.* Hastings, Mich.: Stony Lonesome Press, 1995.

Julia Sharp

FELTING. *See* **Felt.**

FENDI Fendi is a synonym of fur and revolution, two apparently contradictory concepts. Having accepted the idea of mass consumption, Fendi attempted to provide furs for women of every social position, or nearly so, demystifying the luxury connotations that have always characterized this type of garment.

The story begins at the corner of the Piazza Venezia in Rome in 1925, where there was a small Fendi boutique and, next door to it, a fur and leather workshop, owned by Edoardo and Adele Fendi. By the 1930s they had expanded the business considerably. But the true protagonists of Fendi's success are their daughters—Paola (b. 1931), Anna (b. 1933), Franca (b. 1935), Carla (b. 1937), and Alda (b. 1940)—who made the Fendi label famous throughout the world. All five daughters began working in the family business at an early age—between fifteen and eighteen—assuming different responsibilities as required. In 1964 they opened the office on the via Borgognona in Rome, with a large picture of their mother, Adele, in the entrance. In 1965 they began their collaboration with Karl Lagerfeld, the designer who, together with the Fendi sisters, helped develop a renewed interest in furs. During this time, the famous black and brown double "F," one of the first company logos, was created.

During the second half of the 1950s, ownership of a fur garment was the dream of many women, but following the social changes that occurred in the 1960s and 1970s, fur came to be seen as old-fashioned and bourgeois. An illustration by the well-known painter Giuseppe Novello, outstanding illustrator of Italy's postwar bourgeoisie, shows a woman at two different stages of her life. In the first image she is young and thin and wears a fitted coat. In the second she is weighted down by the years and stuffed into a large fur. The caption reads "When I first started wanting a fur coat . . . and when I finally had one" (Novello, p. 32).

Lagerfeld, under the sisters' direction, experimented with materials, patterns, finishes, weight, tanning methods, and colors, so that furs would be seen as something completely new, supported by advanced technological craftsmanship, suited to the needs of a public that wanted more accessible and wearable fashion. In 1966 he scandalized the fashion world by introducing color as a design element: "A colorful fur coat that was not precious but original" (Aragono, p. 92).

One of the characteristics of the Fendi label is the company's unusual way of working with traditional skins. Fendi designers were continually experimenting on furs and in 1969, with the introduction of their Pret à Porter line, besides the exclusively artisan manufacturing, Fendi succeeded in producing a product accessible to the ordinary consumer: beautiful furs at a limited price.

Fendi used furs that were considered to be of "poor" quality, which the company then reworked and reinterpreted, and expensive skins, such as fox, ermine, mink, and astrakhan, which it transformed using different finishes and colors, so that they no longer were seen as stiff and conservative but as fashionable outerwear.

The same approach was used in the treatment of leather, especially handbags, which although they were luxury items, were made more versatile through the addition of printed patterns, unusual colors, and new designs. In 1968 Classic Canvas was launched, an alternative to leather; then striped colored rubber—beige and black—that became Fendi's classic colors.

In 1977 Fendi introduced a line of ready-to-wear, known as "365—a dress for every day of the year, for a woman who wants her fur and purse to match her dress." (Villa). In 1978 they brought out a line of shoes, pro-

Fendi advertisement. Italian fashion-house Fendi is best known for bringing furs back into vogue and creating coveted handbags featuring the distinctive double "F" trademark. THE ADVERTISING ARCHIVE LTD. REPRODUCED BY PERMISSION.

duced by Diego Della Valle. In the 1970s Fendi also launched new artisan-made lines: Giano, Astrologia, Pasta, and Selleria, all in limited edition and numbered.

When Adele died in 1978, each of the five Fendi children took over a different part of the business: Paola was primarily interested in furs; Anna, in leather goods. Franca handled customer relations, Carla coordinated the business, and Alda was responsible for sales. In the 1980s, as was the case with many Italian fashion houses, Fendi underwent a period of considerable expansion, involving product diversification and especially licensing. A wide range of products now bore the Fendi label—sweaters, suits, jeans, umbrellas, clocks, ceramics, and household decorations. Stores and boutiques were opened around the world. In 1985 Fendi even produced the uniforms for the Rome police department. That same year they launched their first perfume. In 1987 they introduced the Fendissime line, conceived by the third generation of the Fendi family: Silvia, Maria Teresa, Federica, and Maria Ilaria Fendi. The new line included sportswear, furs, and accessories for younger buyers. In 1989 they opened their first store in the United States, located on Fifth Avenue in New York City. The following year they introduced a men's perfume and ready-to-wear line.

In 1997 they began making a series of handbags that quickly became cult objects. The most famous is the Fendi "Baguette," inspired by the shape of French bread, and conceived by Silvia Venturini Fendi. A small, minimalist jewel produced in a wide range of materials from horsehide to pearls, in six hundred different versions, it was an extraordinary success, chosen by Madonna, Julia Roberts, Naomi Campbell, and Gwyneth Paltrow. A special baguette called Lision was produced in limited edition, embroidered with an eighteenth-century loom at the speed of only five centimeters per day. The Rollbag, which was wrapped in a transparent case, followed in 1999. The Ostrik bag appeared in 2002 and the Biga Bag, favored by Sharon Stone, in 2003.

Silvia Venturini Fendi, together with Karl Lagerfeld, pursued the Fendi tradition of research in furs. For their Winter 2003–2004 collection they launched, among other furs, the "Vacuum Persian Fur," that is, a fur put into a PVC packaging, a fox fur cut into small stripes and then reassembled with small rubber bands, and depilated mink coats.

Meanwhile a number of licenses that had weakened the company's image were sold and Fendi focused on its core business, leather and fur. The Dark Store is the Fendi concept store based on the company's realignment. Dark Stores could be found in Paris, on rue François 1er and in the Galeries Lafayette on boulevard Haussmann, and on Sloane Street in London in the early 2000s.

Also in the early 2000s Silvia Venturini Fendi, Anna's daughter, was in charge of the style department as creative director of accessories and Man's Line.

In 2001, after considerable legal maneuvering associated with the mergers and acquisitions that typified the fashion world early in the twenty-first century, Fendi became part of the LVMH group, a giant in the world of luxury goods.

Over the years Fendi has designed costumes for both cinema and theater and has worked with a number of directors, including Luchino Visconti (*Gruppo di Famiglia in un Interno* 1975, *L'Innocente* 1976), Mauro Bolognini (*La Dame aux camélias* 1980), Franco Zeffirelli (*La Traviata* 1983), Sergio Leone (*C'era una Volta in America* 1983), Lina Wertmuller (*Scherzo*), Marco Ferreri (*Futuro di Donna* 1984), Dino Risi (*Le bon roi dagobert* 1984), Liliana Cavani (*Interno Berlinese* 1985), Francis Ford Coppola (*The Godfather III* 1999), Martin Scorsese (*The Age of Innocence* 1993, a film that won the Oscar for costumes, in which Michelle Pfeiffer was wearing Fendi furs designed by the costumist Gabriella Pascucci), and Alan Parker (*Evita* 1996, starring Madonna). Wes Anderson's *Royal Tenenbaums* (2001) featured a fur coat worn by Gwyneth Paltrow, that became popular.

See also **Fur; Lagerfeld, Karl; Leather and Suede; Tanning of Leather.**

BIBLIOGRAPHY

Aragono, Bonizza Giordani, ed. *Moda Italia: Creativity and Technology in the Italian Fashion System.* Milan: Editoriale Domus, 1988.

Bianchino, Gloria, ed. *La moda Italiana.* Milan: Electa, 1987.

Laurenzi, Laura. "Fendi." In *Dizionario della moda 2004.* Edited by Vergani Guido and Gabriella Gregorietti. Milan: Baldini and Castoldi, 2003.

Novello, Giuseppe. *Sempre più difficile.* Milan: Mondadori, 1957.

Villa, Nora. *Le regine della moda.* Milan: Rizzoli International, 1985.

Simona Segre Reinach

FERRAGAMO, SALVATORE Salvatore Ferragamo (1898–1960) was an artisan and an innovator during his fifty-year career in footwear design. His family name evokes beauty, traditional craftsmanship, and an assurance of quality and comfort. Born in Bonito, Italy, a remote hill town not far from Naples, Ferragamo was the eleventh in an agricultural family of fourteen children. Since poverty limited the resources needed to sustain a family, many Italians made their own shoes. Young Salvatore was determined to be a shoemaker and served an apprenticeship in a shop where each step was accomplished by hand. Intent on refining his knowledge and craftsmanship, he moved to Naples—at that time a hub for dressmakers, milliners, and shoemakers—in 1909, with the goal of learning accurate methods of measuring, fitting, and aesthetics. While still an adolescent, the imaginative and entrepreneurial Ferragamo returned to Bonito and set up a workshop with six assistants; under his leadership they produced custom-fitted, distinctively designed shoes.

Success in the United States

An older brother encouraged Salvatore to join him in Boston, where the Queen Quality Shoe Company hired him in 1914. Although modern technology mass-produced basic footwear, it was, in Ferragamo's opinion, heavy and clumsy. Subsequently he relocated to Santa Barbara, California, where he established a shoe-repair shop with the intent to create custom shoes by hand. Commissions included custom-designed boots and sandals for celebrities and silent film stars from 1914 to 1927.

In 1923 Ferragamo opened the legendary Hollywood Boot Shop in Los Angeles. Celebrities often commissioned outrageous footwear, such as pumps with appliqué patterns or sandals decorated with pearls or feathers. During the 1920s Ferragamo labels could be found in stores like Gimbel's and Saks Fifth Avenue. Ferragamo's standards for measuring and sizing, combined with his originality, influenced the entire industry. Although handmade shoes became an exclusive product for discerning clientele, he collaborated with American manufacturers to design mass-produced shoes as well.

Return to Italy

Following fifteen successful and creative years in southern California, Ferragamo returned to Florence, Italy, in 1927 to organize assembly-line production of handcrafted shoes. He took advantage of the inherent qualities of Italian craftsmen and the availability of superior materials to create legendary footwear. In 1940 he returned to his hometown to marry Wanda Miletti, the daughter of the village doctor. Their life together produced a family of six children, all of whom became involved in the family business.

The American stock market crash of 1929 devastated the Italian economy, resulting in Ferragamo's bankruptcy. An undaunted entrepreneur, he managed to reestablish himself in Florence, and by 1937 he was able to purchase the elegant thirteenth-century Palazzo Spini-Feroni, one of the most historic buildings of the city, which became his workplace and showroom. By 1939 four hundred employees produced two hundred pairs of handmade shoes per day. Florence was once again a popular tourist destination by 1950, and international clientele frequented the elegant Ferragamo shop on via Tornabuoni.

A Family Business

Although Ferragamo's eldest daughter, Fiamma, had studied classics at the university, she observed all stages of her father's business from an early age. Following his death in 1960, she assumed responsibility for 700 workers who produced 350 pairs of shoes a day. The labor-intensive practice of making shoes by hand vanished by the end of the 1960s. Her sister Giovanna had studied fashion design in Florence, preparing for the eventuality of apparel as a new direction for the family business. Motifs from classic Italian art inspired her patterns and colors for an early signature collection of ready-to-wear for women in 1959. In the 1970s the company expanded into producing small leather goods, luggage, scarves, and perfume for the international market, in addition to footwear.

In the early twenty-first century the heirs continued to conduct business from the Palazzo Spini-Feroni. Wanda presided as chairman, and her son Ferruccio was the chief executive officer. Fiamma died prematurely in 1998 after almost forty years as the vice president responsible for product design. Her visionary initiatives built the company from a custom-made shoe business for the privileged few to a global, privately owned corporation. Today the company produces high-quality ready-to-wear and fashion accessories in addition to men's and women's footwear, all of which is available in exclusive and flagship stores around the world through joint ventures and licensing agreements. In addition the company subsidizes cultural restorations and sponsors international competitions for young shoe designers.

Personal Image and Acknowledgments

Wanda Ferragamo recalled that her husband was motivated by faith in his abilities. He was strong-willed and optimistic, determined to prosper. His workers remember that he transmitted confidence, and although he demanded discipline, he also recognized merit. He did not sketch his ideas, but as a great improviser and engineer, he intuitively cut samples and draped materials on wooden shoe forms to convey original ideas to his production staff.

In 1948 an exhibit at the Palazzo Strozzi in Florence, displaying two hundred models of Ferragamo's footwear produced between 1927 and 1960, was installed. Each pair was presented as a work of art. The exhibition traveled internationally and became the foundation of the archives in the Museo Ferragamo at the corporate headquarters. In 1999 the company won the Guggenheim Enterprise and Culture Prize for its investments in the sphere of culture.

Clothing Designs and Artistic Hallmarks

Ferragamo's autobiography, *Shoemaker of Dreams*, first published in England in 1957, details his career. As a true artist, Ferragamo found ways to create even under the most limited conditions. During World War II, restricted to using only the poorest of materials, he became known for his inventive use of what was at hand. Hemp cord and the strong, multicolored cellophane wraps of candy and cork were readily available in this region of wine making. He ingeniously placed the supportive metal shank precisely in the instep of the shoe, freeing the joints and heels from supporting body weight. Weightless qualities of both design and construction became Ferragamo's hallmark. He sculpted cork into wedge platforms and heels and dyed raffia to be woven for upper constructions. In 1947 he appropriated the clear filament wire used by fishermen to create straps around the foot and ankle to create the illusion of a seductive, feminine "Invisible Shoe."

In 1938 Ferragamo tapped into the allure of the prevailing theme of Orientalism. He created an upturned toe that he called the Oriental mule. He patented shoes with heels fabricated in steel. He coined the term *shell soling* for upturned soles. Narrow toes and slim high heels counterbalanced the voluminous gowns of designer Christian Dior, creator of the New Look of 1947. Ferragamo introduced a sculptural high heel carved into an F, his signature letter. In 1961 Fiamma collaborated with the up-and-coming Florentine noble, Emilio Pucci, on a display that accessorized colorful and vivacious garments with footwear. Fiamma Ferragamo is the creator of the most popular shoe style ever produced by the company: the *Vara*, a practical, midheel pump adorned with a signature metal buckle and stamped with the family signature and grosgrain bow, remains a wardrobe staple today.

Ferragamo stressed that his success was based in technical expertise and a discerning sense for materials, combined with a knowledge of anatomy and his admiration for the allure of the female leg and foot. In the early 2000s the company continued to produce high-quality products made of superior materials with the same sophisticated standards originally established, sustaining the legacy of a truly unique man.

See also **Orientalism; Shoemaking; Shoes.**

BIBLIOGRAPHY

Angioni, Martin. *Fashion and Art Newspaper*, no. 76, December 1997, p. 21.

Ferragamo, Salvatore, Stefania Ricci, and, Edward Maeder. *Salvatore Ferragamo: The Art of the Shoe, 1898–1960.* New York: Rizzoli, 1992. An exhibition catalog.

———. *Shoemaker of Dreams: The Autobiography of Salvatore Ferragamo.* New York: Crown Publishers, 1972.

Stengel, Richard. "The Shoes of the Master." *Time* 139, no. 18 (4 May 1992): 72.

Gillion Carrara

FETISH FASHION Fetishism is a term with a long and complicated history, encompassing religious, anthropological, economic, and sexual meanings. Missionary tracts with titles such as *Fetishism and Fetish Worshippers* denounced the "barbarous" religions of "primitive" people who worshiped "idols of wood or clay." The term fetish was then extended to refer not only to objects allegedly possessing magic powers, but also to anything that was irrationally worshiped. Karl Marx famously coined the term "commodity fetishism" to describe the way objects produced through human labor acquired an exaggerated exchange value. Sexologists and psychiatrists traditionally described fetishism as a sexual "perversion." Today, fetishism is usually characterized as a type of variant sexuality, in which arousal is associated with a (nongenital) part of the body, such as hair, or an inanimate object, such as a shoe.

Experts tend to agree that the majority of sexual fetishists are men. Indeed, the psychiatrist Robert Stoller argued, "fetishizing is the norm for males, not for females." However, the subject of female fetishism is of interest to cultural theorists. There are also thought to be degrees of fetishism. Many men may be sexually aroused by high-heeled shoes, for example, but only a minority require the presence of such shoes for sexual arousal—and even fewer women have such a directly sexual relationship with shoes. Fetishism has also been associated with sadomasochism and transvestism. Leather fetishists, for example, may be involved in sadomasochistic sexuality. Sigmund Freud argued that fetishism was caused by castration anxiety, but this theory is not widely accepted today.

High-heeled shoes, so-called "kinky" boots, corsets, lingerie, and garments made of leather or rubber are among the most common clothing fetishes. Sometimes

Woman modeling Thierry Mugler rubber dress. Rubber clothing is a standard of fetish fashion, as are kinky, extremely high-heeled shoes or boots. © PIERRE VAUTHEY/CORBIS. REPRODUCED BY PERMISSION.

individual clothing fetishes are combined; thus, a black leather corset might be worn with high-heeled boots and long rubber gloves. Fetishes are associated with particular sexual fantasies. Or as Stoller put it: "A fetish is a story masquerading as an object." In the nineteenth and early twentieth centuries, fetish clothing was utilized in secret sexual scenarios; for example, in brothels or the staging of pornographic imagery. Since the 1970s, however, clothing fetishes have played an increasingly important role in fashion and popular culture. As early as the 1960s, the television program *The Avengers* featured a character, Mrs. Peel, who wore a black leather catsuit that was modeled on an authentic fetish costume. Mrs. Peel's costume was a precursor of Michelle Pfeiffer's latex catsuit and mask in the film *Batman Returns.*

Fetishism moved from the sexual underground into mainstream popular culture via subcultural groups such as punks and leathermen. A youth subculture associated with bands like the Sex Pistols, the punks appropriated fetish clothing as part of their own "style in revolt." The fashion designer Vivienne Westwood, herself a punk, opened a shop in London called Sex, where she sold bondage trousers, rubber stockings, corsets, and extreme shoes to a clientele divided between real fetishists and young people attracted by the idea of breaking taboos. Westwood herself wore "total S&M as fashion" in the early 1970s, not just in private or at clubs, but on the street, as a way of subverting accepted social values.

The 1970s saw the spread of sexual liberation, women's liberation, and gay liberation—all movements that provided a context for the emergence of fetish fashion. Although many feminists regard fetish fashion as exploitative and misogynistic, the iconography of sexual fetishism unquestionably focused on images of powerful women. The image of the dominatrix or phallic woman was especially pronounced in the work of Helmut Newton, a very influential fashion photographer of the 1970s. As a result of his controversial pictures in magazines such as the French edition of *Vogue*, Newton is often credited with having made fetishism "chic." One of his fashion photographs of 1977, for example, was titled "Woman or Superwoman?" It showed a woman wearing a leather trench coat by French designer Claude Montana, accessorized with riding boots to convey the image of an Amazon, a subcategory of the dominatrix.

Jean Paul Gaultier is another designer who pioneered fetish fashion in the 1980s. Gaultier has told interviewers that, as a child, his grandmother's flesh-colored corsets fascinated him, and he describes the process of lacing a corset as ritualistic. Many of his designs for both men and women have featured corset-style lacing. He is probably most famous for the corset that he designed for Madonna's Blonde Ambition tour, which helped launch the trend for underwear-as-outerwear. Lingerie, of course, has become a ubiquitous influence on fashion

Perhaps even more than Gaultier, Thierry Mugler has focused on corsetry and on fetishized materials such as rubber and leather to create costumes that evoke the image of "the phallic woman." One of his couture ensembles was entirely handcrafted of leather, including a leather neck-corset. It resembled the carapace of an insect. Other hard-bodied styles include metal corsets and entire ensembles made of metal and plastic, which transform the wearer into a kind of armored cyborg. Indeed, there is virtually no fetish ensemble—from the clothing of the equestrienne to the military uniform—that has not appeared on Mugler's runways.

Leather is the material most often utilized in fetish fashion. Claude Montana was among the first to become known for fetish leather, to be followed in the 1990s by the Italian designer Gianni Versace, who caused a sensation with his leather fashions. Is it "chic or cruel?" asked *The New York Times*. Similar styles had been pioneered by sadomasochists, especially gay leathermen. Designers such as Thierry Mugler and John Galliano for Dior have also incorporated other second-skin materials, such as latex, into high fashion. All of the designers mentioned are also known for their "kinky" shoes and boots, which are the most important accessories in the wardrobe of fetish fashion. Fetish shoes typically feature extremely high heels and sometimes also high platforms and ankle straps or lacing that allude to bondage. Fetish boots tend to be either very high (to mid-thigh) or overtly aggressive-looking.

See also **Fashion and Homosexuality; Film and Fashion; Galliano, John; Gaultier, Jean-Paul; Madonna; Mugler, Thierry; Versace, Gianni and Donatella; Westwood, Vivienne.**

BIBLIOGRAPHY

Gammon, Lorraine and Merja Makinen. *Female Fetishism*. New York: New York University Press, 1994.

Kunzle, David. *Fashion and Fetishism*. Totowa, N.J.: Rowman & Littlefield, 1982.

Lafosse-Dauvergne, Geneviève. *Mode et fétichisme*. Paris: Éditions Alternatives, 2002.

Steele, Valerie. *Fetish: Fashion, Sex & Power*. New York: Oxford University Press, 1996.

Stoller, Robert. *Observing the Erotic Imagination*. New Haven, Conn.: Yale University Press, 1985.

Valerie Steele

FIBERS According to the American Society for Testing and Materials (ASTM), a fiber is a unit of matter that has a length of at least 100 times its diameter. If fibers are to be used in textile products, they must have characteristics of fineness, strength, cohesiveness, and flexibility appropriate to the projected end use. Chemically, fibers are composed of long chains of molecules called polymers.

Fibers may be found in nature or manufactured. Fibers may be short and noncontinuous or of indefinite length, long and continuous. Short fibers are called staple fibers, while long, continuous fibers are called filament fibers. All natural fibers except silk are staple fibers. Manufactured fibers and silk can be filament fibers or can be cut into staple lengths.

Humans have used natural fibers since prehistoric times. Fibers are often classified according to their chemical structure. Natural fibers obtained from plants are generally made of cellulose. Others, generally obtained from animal hair, are protein. One mineral fiber, asbestos, is obtained from rock deposits. Asbestos products are no longer manufactured in the United States because the fibers can be carcinogenic if inhaled.

Natural cellulosic fibers are classified as seed hair fibers (cotton and kapok) because they grow on seeds. Bast fibers are obtained from the stems of plants (linen from the flax plant, ramie, jute, hemp, and kenaf). Fibers from plant leaves and other vegetable sources include agave, coir, henequen, sisal, yucca, piña, and sacaton. Many of these fibers, and others that are even more rare, have only limited use for industrial products or for local crafts. Cotton, linen, ramie, and hemp are the cellulosic fibers most often used in apparel. Piña comes from the leaves of the pineapple plant and is used for traditional costumes in some Asian and Pacific areas.

Protein fibers are generally obtained from the hair of animals. Silk, another protein fiber, is extruded by the silkworm and obtained from its cocoon. Widely used animal hair fibers include sheep's wool, cashmere, camel hair, mohair, and alpaca. Other animal hair fibers have more limited use. Eskimo women knit qiviut, the soft, fine underhair of the musk ox, into very expensive accessories and garments, using patterns characteristic of their village. Llama and guanaco, Andean animals that are similar to alpaca, and *huarzio* and *misti*, cross-bred llamas and alpacas, produce hair harvested for textiles. Attempts to domesticate the vicuña, a wild Andean ruminant, have had limited success. Most of this very soft and costly fiber comes from animals that have been hunted, and strict limits are placed on the number that can be taken each year. In New Zealand, cross-breeding female cashmere goats and male angora goats has produced "cashgora," but marketing efforts for this fiber have had limited success.

Manufactured fibers (sometimes called man-made fibers) can be either regenerated fibers, those formed from natural materials that are not useable as fibers in their natural form, or synthetic fibers from chemical substances. Most manufactured fibers are formed either by melting or dissolving the polymer in a chemical solution, then forcing this solution through holes in a metal plate, called a spinneret, in order to form long, continuous fibers.

The manufacture of a regenerated fiber begins with such diverse substances as cotton fibers too small to be formed into a yarn, wood chips, corn or milk protein, or seaweed. These materials are subjected to chemical processing that allows them to be dissolved and then reformed into filament fibers. The most widely used regenerated fibers include rayon, lyocell, and acetate.

Synthetic fibers are created (synthesized) from chemical substances. The Federal Trade Commission classifies synthetic and manufactured fibers according to their chemical composition. Manufacturers may also give their fibers trade names. The most widely used synthetic fibers are acrylic and modacrylic, elastomers, nylon, polyolefins, and polyester.

Metallic fibers have been used in fashionable apparel for thousands of years, often to make lavish garments to display status. Thin sheets of metal can be cut into narrow strips or a thin filament of metal can be wound around a central core of another material. Except for gold, metal fibers are likely to tarnish unless provided with a protective coating.

Some high-tech fibers with limited use in apparel are aramid, PBI (Polybenzimidazol), melamine, and sulfar.

These are used for protective clothing or gloves. Bicomponent fibers are made from two different polymers, combined in various configurations in order to take advantage of the special characteristics of each fiber.

Fibers are made into textiles by techniques in which the fibers are held together or formed into a yarn and the yarns formed into a fabric by any of a number of techniques.

See also **Acrylic and Modacrylic Fibers; Alpaca; Camel Hair; Cotton; Elastomers; Hemp; Nylon; Polyester; Silk; Techno-Textiles.**

BIBLIOGRAPHY

Annual Book of ASTM Standards, Volume 07: *Textiles—Yarns, Fabrics, and General Test Methods.* (Standard Terminology Relating to Textiles.) Philadelphia: American Society for Testing and Materials, 2002.

Collier, B., and P. Tortora. *Understanding Textiles.* 6th ed. Upper Saddle River, N.J.: Prentice Hall, 2001.

Hongu, R., and G. Phillips. *New Fibers.* Manchester, U.K.: Woodhead Textile Institute, 1998.

Lewin, M., and E. Pearce. *Handbook of Fiber Chemistry.* New York: Marcel Dekker, 1998.

Moncrieff, R. W. *Man-Made Fibres.* London: Newnes Butterworth, 1975.

Tortora, P., and R. Merkel. *Fairchild's Dictionary of Textiles.* New York: Fairchild Publications, 1996.

Phyllis Tortora

FILM AND FASHION The couturier and designer of surreal hats, Elsa Schiaparelli once declared, "The film fashions of today are your fashions of tomorrow" (Prichard 1981, p. 370). Besides planning haute couture collections, Schiaparelli also designed costumes for such stars as Mae West (*Every Day's a Holiday* [1937]) and the British stars Margaret Lockwood and Anna Neagle (*The Beloved Vagabond* [1936], *Limelight* [1936]). Since then, the interrelationship between film and fashion has become more complex. Schiaparelli's belief in the direct influence of the "dream factory" on what ordinary people wore is borne out by a number of examples from the classical Hollywood period: one of Adrian's robes for Joan Crawford in *Letty Lynton* (1932) was widely copied, as was Edith Head's white party dress for Elizabeth Taylor in *A Place in the Sun* (1951). However, since then various factors have enriched and diversified fashion's interaction with film. First, there was—in the wake of Audrey Hepburn's successful collaboration with the then young and relatively unknown Paris couturier Hubert de Givenchy from *Sabrina* (1954) onward—the growing use of fashion as opposed to costume design on a number of key movies. Second, alongside this industrial shift and commensurate with the expansion within the couture industry into prêt-à-porter, there was an escalation of fashion's influence over film as well as the other way round. Third (and a far more contemporary factor) is the rise in celebrity culture and a burgeoning interest in movie stars, what they wear both on and off the screen.

From the 1920s through the 1940s, relatively few fashion designers demeaned themselves by working for moving pictures. The most notable Parisian export was Coco Chanel who, in 1931, was lured to Hollywood by Sam Goldwyn for $1 million, only to find that Hollywood costume design—because she was too meticulous, too precise—was not for her. When she returned to France, Chanel did return to costume designing, working on the films *Les Amants* (1958) and *L'année dernière à Marienbad* (1961). Despite the phenomenal impact on cinema as well as fashion of his New Look in 1947, Christian Dior lent his designs to a relatively small and eclectic series of films: René Clair's *Le silence est d'or* (1946), for example, some of the costumes for Jean-Pierre Melville's *Les enfants terribles* (1950), and Marlene Dietrich's costumes for Alfred Hitchcock's *Stage Fright* (1950). It was Givenchy's collaboration with Hepburn that changed everything.

Called in reputedly at Hepburn's behest, Givenchy's first film costumes were the ball gowns in *Sabrina*. The details of this story are muddled because Givenchy's account of his input in the film at times directly contradicts the version proffered by the film's overall costume designer, Edith Head. Head, who had designed the costumes for Hepburn's Oscar-winning role as the princess in *Roman Holiday* just the previous year, was clearly hurt by the star's—and director's—decision to acquire an actual Paris wardrobe for Sabrina. In *The Dress Doctor*, Head comments: "I had to console myself with the dress, whose boat neckline was tied on each shoulder—widely known and copied as 'the *Sabrina* neckline'" (Head and Ardmore 1959, p. 119). Elsewhere, Givenchy queried Head's claim to the *bateau* neckline design. Certainly it is a more eye-catchingly cut than one might expect from Head who, having found her so-called breadline, rationing-conscious costumes of World War II made to look démodé by the immediate impact of Dior's opulent New Look, declared herself to be a "fence-sitter" who would follow rather than lead fashion. This claim by Head that she intentionally occupied the middle of the road crystallizes the difference between the couturier and the straightforward costume designer. While the couturier might be more expressive and daring when designing for the screen, costume designers opted for safer styles that remained secondary to character and narrative and never, as the Hollywood director George Cukor commented, "knocked your eye out" (Gaines and Herzog 1990, p. 195). The inherently spectacular quality of Givenchy's designs for Hepburn is frequently accentuated by the nature of the narratives the costumes serve. In both *Sabrina* and later *Funny Face*, the story revolves around the Hepburn characters' Cinderella-esque rags-to-riches tales, transformed from a chauffeur's daughter to a millionaire's wife in one, bookshop assistant to an icon of glamour and

sophistication in the other. The joke in *Funny Face*—in which Hepburn's character models clothes on a Paris catwalk—is ultimately that, for all the appeal of high fashion, Hepburn is happiest (and most iconic) when dressing down in black leggings, turtleneck, and flats.

There have been other significant collaborations between stars and designers—Adrian's partnerships with Greta Garbo and Joan Crawford, or Jean Louis's designs for Doris Day's comedies of the late 1950s and early 1960s—and following these, couturiers contributed more regularly to film costume design. Hardy Amies (Queen Elizabeth's favorite fashion designer) designed the wardrobe for films such as *The Grass Is Greener* (Stanley Donen, 1960) and *2001: A Space Odyssey* (Stanley Kubrick, 1968). Giorgio Armani later became the most prolific couturier costume designer, working on a number of films, ranging from *American Gigolo* (1980) to the remake of *The Italian Job* (2003). However, the way in which Armani has approached costume design—and this holds for several classic designers such as Nino Cerruti, Yves Saint Laurent, Donna Karan, Calvin Klein—is in a likewise classic way. His costumes occupy a traditional, servile role in relation to the narratives and characters they serve; they remain stylishly unobtrusive and do not "knock your eye out," as arguably Givenchy's extravagant ball gowns for Hepburn do. Cinema's most popular couturier costume designers, it seems, are those who follow the underpinning conventions of costume design.

From the 1970s onward, a schism has become increasingly apparent between the classic and the spectacular look in film. Peter Wollen has argued that only the latter kind of extrovert costume design (such as those in William Klein's 1966 film *Qui êtes-vous, Polly Maggoo?*) can be considered art, thus echoing Saint Laurent's belief that "Art is probably too big a word for fashion. Fashion is a craft, a poetic craft" (Saint Laurent 1988, p. 20). The "art" of fashion in film would be exemplified by the film work of Jean Paul Gaultier, who has designed costumes for various art-house movies including *The Cook, the Thief, His Wife and Her Lover* (1989) and *Kika* (1993). In both, exaggerated versions of Gaultier's signature styles—his cone bras, his use of corsetry as outer clothing, his asymmetrical cutting, his persistent predilection for classic tailoring alongside much more radical designs—are evident with a pervasive, more nebulous interest in creating outlandish costumes in their own right. Gaultier's designs are intrinsically fashionable and extend the boundaries of costume and style (as Chanel once explained, there is an essential distinction to be drawn between "fashion," which is ephemeral, and "style," which endures). Although Gaultier trained with Pierre Cardin and Jean Patou (thereby explaining his residual interest in traditional tailoring), in *The Cook, the Thief* alone one can find a string of witty, audacious juxtapositions—there are echoes of Courrèges's space-age costumes (far more outlandish than Amies's designs for *2001*), the influence of the effete cavaliers and more than a whiff of seventeenth-century cardinals. In

Kika, the smooth surface of classicism—exemplified by Victoria Abril's black bias-cut dress—is ruptured by radical flourishes, such as the prosthetic breasts bursting out of it.

The creation of self-consciously spectacular costumes (less "over the top" than drawing attention to themselves in whatever way) has persisted through a variety of eclectic movies. Gaultier's own wardrobe for Luc Besson's *The Fifth Element* (1997) is incontrovertibly spectacular; the clothes are ostentatious, wildly colorful, eclectic and, again, overtly sexual, as in Leeloo's artful stretch-bondage gear. Once more, these costumes flagrantly come in the way of character identification as one cannot help but notice them, and in their very styles (asymmetric, clashing) and man-made fabrics, they proclaim their ephemerality. This is only one, obvious, use of the spectacular; other more subtle examples from within contemporary film of costumes that draw attention to themselves and so intrude upon the seamlessness of the classical narrative form would be *The Talented Mr. Ripley* (1999), *Far from Heaven* (2002), and *Dolls* (2002). Like Luis Buñuel's *Belle de jour* (1967) before them, *Ripley* and *Far from Heaven* in particular make use of costumes that are only slightly out of the ordinary. The cardigan trimmed with thick, swirling braid that Cate Blanchett is wearing when she bumps into the only slightly less ostentatiously dressed Paltrow is a further example of a costume's overt fashionableness being used to prevent the spectator's unthinking identification with the characters and the scene. Fashion (and it is important that the character Blanchett plays here is a textiles heiress) creates an alternative dialogue between text and spectator.

However, it is perhaps not altogether surprising that the dominant tendency in cinema has been to follow the Armani route, using fashion to denote stylishness and class but not to be too spectacular and so interrupt the flow or balance of a scene. For *The Italian Job* (2003), Armani's costumes are used, very traditionally, as a means of interpreting character. Essential differences between the principal characters are signaled through costume, in much the same way as Edith Head created a shorthand for understanding her characters through dress (a high-buttoned neckline for a repressed woman, a shimmering décolleté dress for a more sexually available one). So, Donald Sutherland's sensuous, unstructured wool coat and warm turtleneck sweater serve as coded references to his innate charm and old-school heist-master values (he has had enough of the criminal life and the "job" at the start of the film is meant to be his last before going straight), while Mark Wahlberg's tighter-fitting, slightly spivvy black leather jacket quickly makes him out to be eager and on the make. Armani had used a similar system of typage for the four protagonists in *The Untouchables* (1987)—the friendly father-figure in chunky knits, the nerd in a coat slightly too big, the cop from the wrong side of the tracks in his rather-too-jazzy brown leather jacket, and the dependable leader (again) in his flowing Armani coat and tailored three-piece.

The dressing of Gwyneth Paltrow in many of her films conforms to a similar pattern. Apart from her period films (*Emma*, *Elizabeth*) and latterly *The Royal Tenenbaums* (2001), in which she appears to be signaling her desire to break free of her previous typecasting, Paltrow has exemplified a certain well-groomed, affluent but slightly frigid and repressed look, given to her in films such as *Sliding Doors* (1998) or Alfonso Cuaròn's modern-day *Great Expectations* (1998) by the elegant but unexceptional designs of Calvin Klein and Donna Karan respectively. These designers, like Ralph Lauren before them, exemplify a specific kind of safe but sophisticated New York fashion. Like costumes in Hollywood's heyday, the clothes in these films accomplish the easy, unobtrusive creation of Paltrow's characters' social identity. The straight lines, modern fabrics, and neutral colors do more than suggest the characters' fashionableness, they mark them out as coming from a specific milieu, in much the same way as Head's costumes for Grace Kelly in her Hitchcock films of the 1950s (*Rear Window*, *Dial M for Murder*, *To Catch a Thief*) had done.

The refined, slightly aloof elegance of Grace Kelly could perhaps have been expected to make a bigger impact on fashion itself than it did. The relationship between fashion and film is a two-way process: fashion designers get involved in films in part to showcase their designs and perhaps influence fashion outside cinema along the way. Armani, for example, has denied that his film designs are product placement, although the association with movies is a tidy way of giving his designs exposure. Films, even the less clearly fashionable ones, have frequently influenced fashion. There are multiple examples throughout cinema history of items of clothing in films making a significant intervention into fashion on the street. Some films (such as Michelangelo Antonioni's quintessentially 1960s' *Blowup*) are notable as "time capsules" of the fashions of their times, while others might add a look, a garment, or accessory to the contemporary fashion scene. The latter are more intriguing, as they are actively rather than passively engaged with fashion. Sometimes, though, the precise reason for a film having a significant impact on fashion might remain elusive; it simply captures the zeitgeist.

An early example of a single garment changing the course of fashion occurs in *It Happened One Night* (1934) in which Clark Gable takes off his shirt to reveal that he is not wearing an undershirt underneath (reputedly because he felt that taking off another shirt would prove ungainly). Undershirt sales in the United States plummeted by 30 percent. Male underwear sales went up again in the 1950s when the white T-shirt became a fashionable item of male clothing, with Marlon Brando sporting one in *The Wild One* (1953) and James Dean another in *Rebel without a Cause* (1955). Later examples of films directly impacting on fashion are *Annie Hall* (1977) and *Out of Africa* (1985). Just months after the respective releases of both films, the pages of American and British

Vogue were awash with derivative images. The distinctive, ditsy look Ralph Lauren created for Diane Keaton as Annie Hall was swiftly mimicked in fashion magazines and in department stores as women were urged to mix up masculine and feminine styles as Annie had done—a big tweed jacket over a feminine shirt, or a waistcoat and tie over peg-top trousers to accentuate rather than obscure the feminine form. In the wake of *Out of Africa*, both in the pages of glossy magazines and on the street, the safari look dominated women's and men's fashions alike. Fashion shoots had safari settings and ensembles featuring billowing linen, cotton shirts, wide skirts, breeches, and leather riding boots. A clear reason for the fashion success of both these films was that their looks were easily attainable; the British store Top Shop tempted shoppers to its *Out of Africa*–inspired collection with the tag line "Out of Oxford Circus, into Top Shop." Likewise, women and girls could achieve the androgynous Annie Hall look by simply raiding the wardrobes of their older, more traditional male relatives or by visiting thrift shops.

Two issues emerge from the impact a film such as *Out of Africa* had on fashion: that it still, despite being a period film, exerted considerable influence on contemporary fashion and that its wardrobe manifestly illustrated the importance of accessibility and democratization when it comes to film's influence on fashion. Few costume films have influenced fashion—although Edward Maeder makes a case for the 1933 version of *Little Women* leading to the popularization of such items as the gingham pinafore, and John Fairchild, publisher of *Women's Wear Daily*, waged a personal crusade in the late 1960s to have hemlines drop after enjoying *The Damned* (1962), *Doctor Zhivago* (1965), and *Bonnie and Clyde* (1967) (Prichard, 216). It is tempting to presume that any period piece that influences fashion must contain elements of inauthenticity: Julie Christie's "swinging sixties" makeup and hair in *Far from the Madding Crowd* (1967) or the anachronistically colorful gowns Michelle Pfeiffer wears in *The Age of Innocence* (Hollander 1993). If such period films have affected contemporary fashion, there has tended to be a manifest overlap between the fashions of the historical period and the fashion trends at the time the film is made. This mutuality was evident in the safari clothes of *Out of Africa* and was logically the reason for *Moulin Rouge*, with its basques and retro-new romantic styles, having been readily emulated in shop windows. While costume films have indirectly influenced designers (Kubrick's *Barry Lyndon* [1975] has been cited more than once as an inspiration by modern couturiers), the films rarely impact upon clothes styles as a whole.

The accessibility of film fashion has become a hugely significant factor in their appeal. In the 1970s and 1980s, fashion had become about what people wear, not what they might fantasize about wearing, a transition that altered the relationship with film. Quentin Tarantino's *Reservoir Dogs* (1992), which inspired London department store windows and led to an increase in the wearing of dark suits and shades amongst younger men, is just such an example of film's democratization of fashion; the costume designer Betsy Heimann had bought the suits cheaply. As *Reservoir Dogs* became successful as a movie, however, so did the clean-silhouetted French gangster look (Tarantino readily admitted to having emulated the look created by the French director Jean-Pierre Melville for his gangsters). By the time Tarantino came to make his second film, *Pulp Fiction* (1994), the idea that his films were trendy was cemented, and this time he bought suits for Samuel L. Jackson and John Travolta and Uma Thurman's black trousers and white shirt duo at *Agnès b*. Audiences now somewhat randomly scavenge films for fashion ideas, so Thurman's Chanel Rouge Noir nail polish in *Pulp Fiction* was much in demand, as earlier Tom Cruise's sunglasses from *Top Gun* (1986) had been. The overall attractiveness of the film is only partly responsible for its potential impact on fashion; sometimes just a single garment or accessory becomes popular, such as Keanu Reeves's mobile phone and long black coat in *The Matrix* (1999) or Nicole Kidman's half-fitted, half-loose teddy in *Eyes Wide Shut* (1999), which sold out everywhere. As Schiaparelli noted back in the 1930s, cinema is inevitably going to influence fashion. Since then, a more fluid, flexible interaction has emerged—sometimes fashion borrows from film, but often the exchange is reversed. Film actors are inevitably dressing up, and this use of clothes as fantasy comes out in audiences' acquisitions of particular on-screen looks, whether this be women using patterns to make up their favorite costume designs in the 1940s or their granddaughters going to Agnès b. in the 1990s to find Uma Thurman's trousers. Likewise, as Jean Paul Gaultier has remarked, film lets the designer's imagination run riot in a way fashion, because of its commercial constraints, does not. In the early twenty-first century, there is the added dimension of what stars wear off-screen becoming as important in influencing cinema audiences. Film and fashion will continue to serve each other.

See also **Actors and Actresses, Impact on Fashion; Celebrities; Hollywood Style.**

BIBLIOGRAPHY
Bruzzi, Stella. *Undressing Cinema: Clothing and Identity in the Movies.* London and New York: Routledge, 1997.
Gaines, Jane. "Costume and Narrative: How Dress Tells the Woman's Story." In *Fabrications: Costume and the Female Body*, 180–211. London and New York: Routledge, 1990.
Gaines, Jane, and Charlotte Herzog, eds. *Fabrications: Costume and the Female Body.* London and New York: Routledge, 1990.
Head, Edith, and Jane Kesner Ardmore. *The Dress Doctor.* Boston and Toronto: Little Brown and Company, 1959.
Hollander, Anne. *Seeing Through Clothes.* Berkeley: University of California Press, 1993.
Maeder, Edward, ed. *Hollywood and History: Costume Design in Film.* Los Angeles: Thames and Hudson, Inc., 1987.

Prichard, Susan Perez. *Film Costume: An Annotated Bibliography.* Metuchen, N.J., and London: Scarecrow Press, 1981.

Saint Laurent, Yves. *Yves Saint Laurent: Images of Design.* With an introduction by Marguerite Duras. London: Ebury Press, 1988.

Wollen, Peter. "Strike a Pose." *Sight and Sound* 5, no. 3 (March 1995): 10–15.

Stella Bruzzi

FIRST LADIES' GOWNS For over one hundred years, one of the Smithsonian Institution's most visited exhibitions has been a display of gowns worn by the First Ladies of the United States. An unofficial title, "first lady" has been in popular use since the 1860s to refer to the president's official hostess who is usually, but not always, the president's wife.

Many people think of the first family as the United States' version of royalty who are expected to fulfill ambiguous and evolving ideals of how to act and look. New first ladies have often discovered that they will have to learn how to dress to belong in this national spotlight. If a first lady fails to achieve this elusive goal, she is vulnerable to the political consequences of media criticism; but when a first lady does succeed, she may popularize a fashion.

Political Implications

While Americans want their first lady to look as if she represents an affluent and powerful country, citizens do not want her to look too regal—spending excessive amounts on high-fashion clothing. For example, in the early 1860s the southerner Mary Todd Lincoln was severely criticized for her extravagant fashions and entertainment as the nation dealt with the horrors of the Civil War. A hundred years later, Jacqueline Kennedy's love of expensive clothes, particularly French couture, became a political liability during the 1960 presidential campaign between her husband and Richard Nixon. To avoid these hazards, attractive Pat Nixon restrained herself from buying anything too special. The fur coats she purchased in the past did not support the public persona of a "good Republican woman in a cloth coat."

Some presidents' wives have only slightly refined their wardrobe for their public role. For example, in 1998, self-assured Barbara Bush had no intention of becoming more concerned with her appearance while first lady; but she came to appreciate her American designers, Arnold Scaasi and Bill Blass. They transformed her into a glamorous grandmother who felt pretty even as she endured treatments for Graves disease.

As the first president's wife to have been born after World War II, Hillary Rodham Clinton was part of a generation who paid more attention to their achievements than to their appearance. She eschewed the fash-

ionable trappings of traditional "well-bred" ladies and focused on her education and professional career. Mrs. Clinton was first criticized for this lack of attention to her appearance and then judged for all the "fine tuning" she attempted, particularly changes in hairstyles. When a first lady's appearance is continually criticized, it seems more likely that she is being attacked because she acts different rather than just because she looks different. Never was this truer than for Mrs. Clinton—a lawyer, a public servant, and a new kind of first lady.

Fashion Popularizer

Although a successfully dressed first lady is not a fashion innovator, a favorite color—Mamie (Eisenhower) pink—or accessory—Barbara Bush's three-strand imitation pearl necklace—or even a single dress style could become more popular because of her well-publicized role in the White House. In 1993, Mrs. Clinton wore to her first official White House event a Donna Karan turtleneck, long-sleeved, long black dress with cutouts that bared her shoulders. This glamorous dress was not a new style; it had already been seen on celebrities such as Liza Minnelli and Candice Bergen. Nevertheless, within a week of Mrs. Clinton's stunning appearance, manufacturers copied it by the thousands for the mass market.

Dolley Madison and Jacqueline Kennedy were two first ladies who popularized more than a dress style. They each embodied a unique way of dressing that influenced women in their own time. In the early nineteenth century, Dolley Madison's love of French fashions and elegant furnishings encouraged conservative American women to more fully embrace the latest foreign fashions. The popularity of the lively Mrs. Madison blunted the effect of the critics who accused her of aristocratic behavior unsuitable for the first lady of a republic. In contrast, two months before the election in 1960, Jacqueline Kennedy was directed by her husband's advisers to stop buying French couture. Taking into account the best of French fashions, she crafted a simple, youthful, made-in-America glamour. She exemplified a new, and soon-to-become classic, American look.

Collection and Exhibition

In the early twentieth century, the Smithsonian Institution, along with other museums presenting American history, celebrated the accomplishments of notable people, most of whom were important white men. Intended as a way to educate the public in the values of hard work and good citizenship, the focus was on traditional masculine achievements. As Edith Mayo, curator emeritus First Ladies Collection, reported in her 1996 publication, *The Smithsonian Book of the First Ladies*, a volunteer supporter of the Smithsonian, Mrs. Cassie Myers James "introduced the idea of women as historical role models by building a collection of clothing that showed 'the fashions of the women of the United States from colonial times . . . and their sphere in home life'" (p. 279).

Smithsonian exhibit of First Ladies. First Ladies often walk a fine line when choosing their dress, as the public wants them to look sophisticated and elegant, but not extravagantly so. © RICHARD T. NOWITZ. REPRODUCED BY PERMISSION.

The inspiration to acquire and exhibit dresses of the first ladies came about when a descendant of President James Monroe, Mrs. Rose Gouverneur Hoes, was invited to contribute to the collection. In 1912 the success of this effort was assured when Mrs. William Howard Taft, the current first lady, and descendants of five other presidents, promised gowns for the collection. By 1915 the display of dresses in rows of cases was called "Historical Costumes, Including those of the Mistresses of the White House."

These collections and the exhibition were radical innovations. For the first time, women were made visible in the nation's museum, creating a precedent for future collections about women. Over time, the Smithsonian's presentation of the first ladies has changed. In the 1950s the dressed mannequins were reinstalled in elaborate room settings resembling public spaces in the White House during different periods. In March 1992 a new exhibition, "First Ladies: Political Role and Public Image" opened. In a break with tradition, the first ladies are reinterpreted as historical agents in their own right within the context of the American presidency and the history of women in America. The continued popularity of the Smithsonian's First Ladies Hall demonstrates both the American fascination with first ladies and the power of dress to evoke the personality and life experiences of the wearers.

See also **Blass, Bill; Celebrities; Fashion Icons.**

BIBLIOGRAPHY

Mayo, Edith, ed. *The Smithsonian Book of the First Ladies: Their Lives, Times, and Issues.* New York: Henry Holt, 1996.

Claudia Kidwell

FLANNEL Flannel is a light to heavyweight fabric woven as a plain or twill weave that originated in Wales. Some sources claim the name is derived from the Welsh word "gwalen," which means literally a piece of clothing or material made of wool. Another possible etymological origin of the word is from the Old French "flaine," which refers to a blanket or coverlet. Flannel is finished with napping to increase its insulating properties. After the fabric is woven, it is brushed so that the staple fiber ends are loosened from the weave to form a fuzzy surface.

Napping also contributes to the soft hand of the fabric. Flannel may be made from wool, cotton, synthetic fibers, or blends that incorporate a synthetic fiber with a natural fiber to add to the overall strength of the fabric and increase resistance to abrasion. Flannel-back satin refers to a type of silk satin that has spun yarns in the weft (crosswise yarn) and is brushed or napped on the back.

Cotton flannel is made with loosely spun filling yarns to ensure a dense nap. It may be napped on one or both sides. After the untreated fabric or greige goods are napped, the fabric is dyed or printed and finished again by brushing or being run through the napping machine a second time to restore the nap. Variations of cotton flannel include outing flannel, Canton flannel, dommet flannel, flannelette, and suede cloth, which is shorn after napping. Outing flannel, which is heavier than flannelette, is used for lightweight jackets, shirts, dresses, and upholstery. Flannelette is used for bedding and sleepwear.

Wool flannel may be made of either worsted or woolen yarns, the latter producing a denser nap. It is typically napped on one side only. Flannels made of woolen yarns are usually plain woven, and those made of worsted yarns are usually twill. Worsted flannel is lighter and firmer than woolen and will wear better. Pure wool flannel is a favorable fabric for tailoring because it shapes easily with the use of steam and heat. Wool flannels are used to make trousers, skirts, suits, and coats. French flannel is a variation of wool flannel that has a more fluid drape.

See also **Napping; Worsted.**

BIBLIOGRAPHY
American Fabrics Encyclopedia of Textiles. 2nd ed. Englewood Cliffs, N.J.: Prentice Hall, 1972.
Gioello, Debbie Ann. *Profiling Fabrics: Properties, Performance and Construction Techniques.* New York: Fairchild Publishing, 1981.
Humphries, Mary. *Fabric Glossary.* 3rd ed. Upper Saddle River, N.J.: Pearson Prentice Hall, 2004.
Kadolph, Sara J., and Anna L. Langford. *Textiles.* 9th ed. Englewood Cliffs, N.J.: Prentice Hall, 2002.
Linton, George E. *The Modern Textile and Apparel Dictionary.* 4th ed. Plinfield, N.J.: Textile Book Service, 1973.

Marie Botkin

FLAPPERS The flapper was an important figure in the popular culture of the 1920s and helped to define the new, modern woman of the twentieth century. She was the embodiment of the youthful exuberance of the jazz age. Although she defied many of society's taboos, she was also seen by many as the ideal young woman and was described by author F. Scott Fitzgerald as "lovely, expensive and about nineteen."

It is commonly assumed that the term "flapper" originated in the 1920s and refers to the fashion trend for un-fastened rubber galoshes that "flapped" when walking, an attribution reinforced by the image of the free-wheeling flapper in popular culture. Despite this potent imagery, the word has its origins in sixteenth-century British slang. Deriving from the colloquial "flap," the word indicated a young female prostitute and likely referred to the awkward flapping of a young bird's wings when learning to fly. By the nineteenth century the term had lost most of its lewd connotations and instead was used to describe a flighty or hoydenish adolescent girl. In the years following World War I, the word was increasingly used to describe a fashionably dressed, impulsive young woman and by the 1920s, it was used to describe "modern" young women who broke traditional rules of both appearance and behavior.

The "fast living" ethos of the 1920s was widely perceived to be a direct consequence of World War I. During wartime, many young women experienced freedoms previously unheard of, such as taking jobs, shortening skirts, driving cars, and cutting their hair. Competition for male attention was paramount since the pool of eligible men had been depleted during the war, and this probably contributed to the flashier fashions and aggressive behavior of many young women. Outrageous behavior and dress was seen as an investment against spinsterhood or, at the very least, boredom.

The Flapper Image
The common perception of the flapper had as much to do with behavior as it did with appearance. Flappers displayed a carefree disregard for authority and morality. They drank heavily in defiance of Prohibition, smoked, embraced new shocking dances like the Charleston, the Shimmy, and the Black Bottom, used slang, drove fast, and freely took lovers and jobs. Posture and motion were important elements of the flapper persona. The fast, jerky motions characterized by these popular dances emphasized bare arms, backs, and legs. The posture of the flapper was an affected "debutante slouch," often with hand on hip. This limp, listless pose was not possible on a traditionally corseted body and was meant to imply the aftereffects of the previous night's debauchery.

Accordingly, flapper styles blatantly disregarded established fashions in exchange for the new and daring. Popular styles of the 1920s focused on the display of the slim, youthful body through the use of short skirts and dropped waists. Gabrielle "Coco" Chanel and Jean Patou were particularly known for this youthful, sporty style. The flapper took this fashionable ideal to the extreme and wore the shortest skirts possible, low cloches, and negligible underwear. Evening dresses were sleeveless, flashy, and frequently featured slit skirts meant to enable active dancing. She bobbed her hair, wore obvious makeup, and sunbathed in skimpy, one-piece bathing suits.

A common element of the flapper style was the tendency to misuse clothing and accessories—a way of thumbing noses at high fashion and polite society. Examples of this phenomenon were the rolling of stockings below the knees, the wearing of unhooked rubber galoshes that "flapped" when walking, evening shoes worn with daywear, and occasionally even the natural waist worn in defiance of the dictates of high fashion. Flappers were also rumored to rouge their knees, and this is a part of the greater emphasis on legs crucial to the flapper persona. Besides the previously mentioned galoshes and rolled stockings, flappers were associated with elaborate garters and anklets. A daring minority rejected stockings altogether when the weather was warm, but many opted for stockings in fashionable "suntan" shades. Accessories that flaunted outrageous behavior, like the jeweled cigarette holder and ornate compact, were also popular.

The Rise and Fall of the Flapper
The creation of the flapper image is largely credited to the writings of F. Scott Fitzgerald and the drawings of John Held Jr., which frequently featured skinny, stylized flappers in comical situations. Fitzgerald's writings focused on the fast pace of modern life, but when he was given the credit for popularizing the movement, he responded, "I was the spark that lit up Flaming Youth and Colleen Moore was the torch. What little things we are to have caused that trouble."

Fitzgerald shrewdly understood the power of the motion picture to spread the flapper image to a mass audience. Colleen Moore, Joan Crawford, Anita Page, and Clara Bow were some of the many actresses who specialized in flapper roles during this period. The flapper had been a popular screen type since the 1910s, and by the mid-1920s, films featured titles like *Flapper Fever, The Painted Flapper, Flapper Wives, The Perfect Flapper,* and *The Flapper and the Cowboy.*

Although viewers were unlikely to adopt the fast living and flamboyant dress seen on screen, it is quite likely that they incorporated elements into their lives. The 1928 film *Our Dancing Daughters,* which starred Joan Crawford and Anita Page, was particularly influential. The film was mentioned repeatedly in the Payne Fund Studies commissioned to determine the effects of film on the youth of the United States. One respondent claimed that after seeing *Our Dancing Daughters,* "I wanted a dress exactly like one she had worn in a certain scene. It was a very 'flapper' type of dress, and I don't usually go in for that sort of thing" (Massey, p. 30).

As early as 1922, it was suggested that the term "flapper" be divided into three levels: the semi-flapper, the flapper, the superflapper. By the end of the decade, most young women could easily be classed as a semi-flapper since flapper styles and behaviors were gradually being adopted into mainstream life. Bobbed hair, lipstick, and short skirts no longer were the sign of a flapper, just that of a modern fashionable woman.

With the stock market crash of 1929, the frivolity and excess characterized by the flapper and the jazz age

Joan Crawford models a flapper dress. The emphasis of flapper fashion was on the feminine figure, and garments such as this showcased a woman's bare arms, slim waist, and legs. © BETTMANN/CORBIS. REPRODUCED BY PERMISSION.

were replaced with frugality and a return to a more traditional view of feminine behavior and dress. Although the stock market crash signaled the flapper's demise, she remains a potent symbol of flaming youth.

See also **Chanel, Gabrielle (Coco); Patou, Jean; Subcultures.**

BIBLIOGRAPHY
Evans, Mike, ed. *Decades of Beauty.* New York: Reed Consumer Books Limited, 1998.
Hall, Lee. *Common Threads: A Parade of American Clothing.* Boston: Little, Brown and Company, 1992.
Hatton, Jackie. "Flappers" In *St. James Encyclopedia of Popular Culture* Vol. 2: *E–J.* Edited by Tom Pendergast and Sara Pendergast. Detroit: St. James Press, 2000.
Latham, Angela J. *Posing a Threat: Flappers, Chorus Girls, and Other Brazen Performers of the American 1920s.* Hanover, Conn.: Wesleyan University Press, 2000.
Massey, Anne. *Hollywood Beyond the Screen: Design and Material Culture.* Oxford: Berg, 2000.
Rosen, Marjorie. *Popcorn Venus: Women, Movies and the American Dream.* New York: Avon Books, 1974.

Clare Sauro

FLIPFLOPS. *See* **Sandals.**

FLOCKING Flocking is a method to apply very short (1/10″ to 1/4″) fibers called flock to a substrate, such as fabric, foam, or film, coated with an adhesive. Flocking is an inexpensive method of producing an imitation extra-yarn fabric, flocked in a design, or a pile-like fabric where the flock has an overall pattern. Examples of end use of flocked fabrics for home furnishings include carpeting, upholstery fabrics, blankets, bedspreads, wall coverings, and window coverings. For clothing, flocked fabrics are used for shoes, hats, and apparel fabrics. Industrial uses include automotive fabrics, conveyor belts, air filters, books, and toys.

The flock is applied to the fabric using a mechanical or electrostatic process. Depending on the process and fibers used, the effect may be a velvety or suede-like appearance.

Natural or synthetic fibers such as cotton, rayon, nylon, and polyester can be used depending on the particular end use. There is an advantage to using first-quality filament synthetic materials, because the flock can be cut square and in uniform lengths. Cotton is the least expensive and the softest but does not have good abrasion resistance. Rayon has the advantage of being low cost and uniform, but also has low abrasion resistance. Nylon has the best abrasion resistance. Present-day adhesives, such as aqueous acrylic, polyester, and nylon, have excellent bond and usually have the same flexibility and wear resistance as the substrate. The high-quality adhesives have excellent fastness to laundering, dry cleaning, or both, but it is important that testing is conducted to ensure that the cleaning method listed on the label is accurate.

The Processes

After the flock is cut, it is then cleaned. The fibers and the substrate are dyed if they are to be colored. The adhesive is applied to the substrate in the desired design. The flock is then prepared depending on what method will be used to apply the flock to the adhesive. In the mechanical process, a simpler and less-expensive means of flocking, the fibers are placed in a hopper and sifted onto the substrate where beater bars vibrate the flock. The vibration helps the fibers become erect on the adhesive. The fibers randomly adhere to the substrate at different depths forming an irregular surface. Shedding occurs because not all the fibers adhere to the adhesive.

In the electrostatic process the fibers are chemically treated to allow the fibers to receive an electrical charge. The moisture content is specified. Again the flock fibers are placed in a hopper where they are given an electric charge. A grounded electrode plate under the substrate orients the fibers in an upright position when they imbed into the adhesive. Electrostatic flocking is more expensive and slower, but the flock is more uniform and denser.

It is also possible to flock both sides of the fabric. Although there is a difference in the two processes, most consumers are unable to tell what method was used on the flocked fabric.

See also **Fibers; Yarns.**

BIBLIOGRAPHY
Carty, Peter, and Michael S. Byrne. *The Chemical and Mechanical Finishing of Textile Materials.* 2nd ed. Newcastle upon Tyne: Newcastle upon Tyne Polytechnic Products, 1987.
Slade, Philip E. *Handbook of Fiber Finish Technology.* New York: Marcel Dekker, 1998.

Robyne Williams

FLÜGEL, J. C. John Carl Flügel (1874–1955) was an English academic psychologist, a prominent member of the British Psychoanalytical Society, and a leading figure in the movement for liberal social reform between the two world wars (1918–1939). A member of the Men's Dress Reform Party, in 1930 he published *The Psychology of Clothes*, the first Freudian-inspired analysis of dress and fashion. In this work he advances the idea that clothing is a "compromise-formation" that mediates between the desire of children to exhibit their naked bodies and the later social prohibition that the body be covered for the sake of modesty. For Flügel the story of clothing is the story of the relative strength of these two forces.

Freud, Flügel, and Politics

Flügel makes little use of Freud's ideas of clothing as either fetish objects or as sexual symbols in dreams. Central to his analysis of clothing is the sociopolitical interpretation he gives to Freud's model of the human psyche. Freud argues for a three-part division of the mind into id, superego, and ego. The id is the dimension of primitive instinct and the ultimate propelling force of the organism. The superego is an equally primitive inhibitory mechanism that operates as a crude controller of the desires of the id. The ego has the difficult task of establishing a compromise between the demands of the id, the superego, and the outside world so that the individual can exist as a functioning entity. Flügel assigns a general political value to each of these dimensions of the mind. He relates his program of reform to lessening of the power of an overbearing superego, which he regards as the driving force of authoritarian conservatism. As he comments, "The troubles that we experience in adjusting ourselves to civilized social life seem to be due, not merely, as earlier moralists had supposed, to the strength of our a-social instincts [the id], but also, in no inconsiderable degree to the power of the primitive moral factors embodied in the superego" (Flügel 1934, p. 296).

Clothing, for Flügel, comes into being so as to reconcile the demands that these opposing forces place upon the human body and psyche. Dress, therefore, is a prime area of dispute between political liberals and conservatives over what sort, and how much, clothing is appropriate in civilized society.

The Psychology of Clothes

Flügel's theory of clothing attempts to answer two questions. First, why do human beings wear clothes at all? Second, why do the ways in which human beings dress vary so greatly?

The conventional answer given by European thinkers to the first question proposed the existence of three "fundamental motives" out of which clothing was thought to have arisen—bodily protection, modesty, and decoration. Flügel concentrates on the motives of modesty and decoration. Using a version of Freud's model of how the child becomes a socialized adult, he argues that we are born in a condition of narcissistic self-love. The consequence is a "tendency to admire one's own body and display it to others, so that others can share in the admiration. It finds natural expression in the showing off of the naked body and in the demonstration of its powers, and can be observed in many children" (Flügel 1930, p. 86).

This state of idyllic infantile nudity ceases with the arrival of the somatic prohibitions associated with the forces of modesty. The infant relinquishes its pleasurable self-absorption. The body is covered, and shame is triggered when too much of it is inappropriately revealed. However, neither of these tendencies is ever able fully to cancel out the other. As Flügel observes:

> The exhibitionistic instinct originally relates to the naked body, but in the course of individual development it inevitably (in civilised races) becomes displaced, to a greater or lesser extent onto clothes. Clothes are, however, exquisitely ambivalent, in as much as they both cover the body and thus subserve the inhibiting tendencies that we call "modesty," and at the same time afford a new and highly efficient means of gratifying exhibitionism on a new level.
> (Flügel 1932, p. 120)

Clothes simultaneously both hide and draw attention to the body.

Variations of Dress

Flügel realizes that while all humans are dressed, the manner in which this is achieved varies greatly with time and place. His explanation of this is the following:

> to understand the motives that lead to different kinds of clothing, to changes in our clothing and to the changes in our whole attitude towards clothes, we shall have to be constantly on the look out for changes in the manifestations of these two fundamental conflicting tendencies, the one proudly to exhibit the body, the other modestly to hide it. (Flügel 1928)

The most striking of these dress variations, certainly to Flügel and his contemporaries, are those between men and women. Indeed, contemporary European clothing presented Flügel with an added complication, in that it seemed to run against the "normal" situation encountered in nature as well as the evidence of "primitive peoples." There the man "is more ornamental than the female" and almost always the most "adventurous and decorative" in his appearance. In explaining this anomaly, Flügel argues that a profound reorganization of masculinity took place during the political and economic revolutions of the late eighteenth and nineteenth centuries. The tendency to modesty increased at the expense of "male sartorial decorativeness," and the result was a set of simplified garments, less colorful and with a greater degree of uniformity than had existed in previous historical epochs. Flügel named this dramatic shift "The Great Masculine Renunciation" (Flügel 1930, p. 110ff). Against this, he greatly approved of the development taken by European female dress. Beginning with the extremely modest clothing styles of the Middle Ages, female dress had gradually reformed itself. Flügel claimed that female clothing now exhibited a more rational integration of the antagonistic forces operating on dress than was the case in male dress. Indeed, it was his respect for what he saw as the positive mental benefits provided by contemporary forms of female dress that lead him to advocate the reform of men's clothing.

The Nude Future

Near the end of his book *The Psychology of Clothes*, Flügel speculates about a future in which clothing could become obsolete. He argues that, the three main reasons for wearing clothes—bodily protection, modesty, and adornment—will all be surpassed as humans evolve a more "developed" and "rational" way of life. The need for protection will diminish as the control of the environment—for example, by the heating engineer—increases (Flügel 1930, p. 235). The urge to cover our bodies out of a sense of modesty will evaporate once we understand how irrational our fears of nakedness are. Finally, decorative modification and alteration of our bodies would cease as we become reconciled more and more to the natural human form (Flügel 1930, p. 235). As a species we will achieve a "complete reconciliation with the body [which] would mean that the aesthetic variations, emendations, and aggrandizements of the body . . . produced by clothes would no longer felt [to be] necessary" (Flügel 1930, p. 235). Clothing would just fade away.

See also **Fashion, Theories of; Nudity.**

BIBLIOGRAPHY

Burman, B. "Better and Brighter Clothes: The Men's Dress Reform Party, 1929–1940." *Journal of Design History* 8, no. 4 (1995): 275–290. A fascinating account of the men's dress reform movement, in which Flügel was an important participant.

Carter, Michael. "J. C. Flügel and the Nude Future." In *Fashion Classics from Carlyle to Barthes*. Oxford and New York: Berg, 2003. An examination of Flügel's ideas on clothing, particularly as they pertain to his liberal social beliefs.

Flügel, John C. Unpublished transcript of a talk given by Flügel on BBC Radio, 26 June 1928.

———. *The Psychology of Clothes.* London: Hogarth Press, 1930.

———. *An Introduction to Psycho-Analysis.* London: Victor Gollancz, 1932.

———. "A Psychology for Progressives—How Can They Become Effective?" In *Manifesto: Being the Book of the Federation of Progressive Societies and Individuals.* Edited by C. E. M. Joad. London: George Allen and Unwin, 1934.

Michael Carter

FOGARTY, ANNE Anne Fogarty is best remembered for designing quintessential 1950s fashions for young women that emphasized femininity and for espousing the concept of "wife-dressing," the title of her 1959 book. Born Anne Whitney in Pittsburgh, Pennsylvania, on 2 February 1919, Fogarty moved to New York City in her early twenties to pursue acting. While working as a fitting model for the dress manufacturer Harvey Berin, she decided to become a fashion designer. In the late 1940s and 1950s, she designed clothing for the teenage and junior markets, creating her signature "paper doll" dress while working at Youth Guild in 1948, for which she won

the Coty award in 1951 and the Neiman-Marcus Award in 1952. In 1954, while working for Margot Dresses, she introduced her "tea cozy" dress, a variation on the paper doll silhouette.

With its tight bodice, wasp waist, and full, ballet-length skirt supported by layers of stiffened petticoats, the paper doll dress was a simplified and inexpensive adaptation of Christian Dior's 1947 "New Look." Its silhouette was nostalgically romantic and playful and reflected Fogarty's first principle of wife-dressing: "Complete Femininity—the selection of clothes as an *adornment,* not as a mere covering" (p. 10). In her book, *Wife-Dressing: The Fine Art of Being a Well-Dressed Wife,* Fogarty instructed wives to wear their corsets and never to let their husbands see them in pin curls or dungarees. Wife dressing was about dressing to please husbands and aiding their social advancement; for Fogarty, a wife was an appendage and her marital roles were of foremost importance (Fogarty herself was married three times). The book also contains advice for husbands—"If you adore her, adorn her. There lies the essence of a happy marriage" (p. 9) and tips on pruning one's wardrobe, multipurpose dressing for day and evening, and how to be disciplined and discerning in creating one's own look—not unlike tips found in the pages of 1950s fashion magazines.

The ideas expressed in Fogarty's book reflect and reinforce the centrality of women's domestic lives just after World War II. Women were to be in character and properly outfitted, maintaining the feminine mystique as wife and mother. An emphasis on femininity, exemplified in fashions and accessories that exaggerated the female figure, emerged in the late 1940s and 1950s as many women returned to the home front after having worked during the war. Even successful career women like Fogarty maintained the centrality of home life.

As social norms and fashions changed in the following decades, Fogarty expanded as a designer. By the end of the 1950s, she was the exclusive designer for Saks Fifth Avenue, designing more casual, versatile styles. In 1962 she opened her own business, Anne Fogarty, Inc., which ran successfully for eight years. Throughout the 1960s and 1970s she experimented with different silhouettes (her favorite being the Empire) and targeted a more mature audience. After closing her business in 1970, she did freelance designing until her death on 15 January 1980.

Anne Fogarty was, at least in part, a woman and designer of her time. The fashions for which she is best remembered reflect the prevailing ethos of postwar femininity. Yet she was also part of a generation of American designers who tapped into the burgeoning youth culture of the 1950s and 1960s and whose fashions speak to a versatility and youthfulness that are part of a distinctly American vernacular of fashion.

See also **Dior, Christian; New Look; Paper Dresses.**

Model in Anne Fogarty design. Fogerty's fashions focused on femininity and the role of the woman in domestic life. AP/WIDE WORLD PHOTOS. REPRODUCED BY PERMISSION.

BIBLIOGRAPHY

Fogarty, Anne. *Wife-Dressing: The Fine Art of Being a Well-Dressed Wife.* New York: J. Messner, 1959.

Milbank, Caroline Rennolds. *New York Fashion: The Evolution of American Style.* New York: Harry N. Abrams, 1989.

Steele, Valerie. *Women of Fashion: Twentieth Century Designers.* New York: Rizzoli International, 1991.

Williams, Beryl. *Young Faces in Fashion.* Philadelphia: J. B. Lippincott, 1956.

Tiffany Webber-Hanchett

FOLK DRESS, EASTERN EUROPE Folk dress in eastern Europe distinguished shepherds and peasants from fashion-following townspeople and landowners. In regions where peoples of different ethnic origins coexisted, folk dress could also function as ethnic dress. The general characteristics of eastern European folk dress resembled those of western Europe. However, historical and cultural influences created some remarkable folk costumes and customs.

Historical Overview

Eastern Europe has experienced centuries of change as a result of shifting political boundaries. Tribal groups inhabited many northern and central regions until Germanic crusaders arrived during the Middle Ages. Thereafter, a landowning class developed that oversaw agricultural production by peasant-serfs. Ottoman Turkey ruled much of southeastern Europe, stretching as far north as Hungary. Russia, poised on the edge of Europe, melded ideas from both east and west. During the tumultuous twentieth century, eastern European countries became part of the Russian Soviet Federative Socialist Republic. The breakup of the Soviet Union in 1991 brought a period of ethnic conflict, still not fully resolved in the early 2000s.

For the study of folk dress, divisions are cultural rather than political. Distinctive styles for peasants appeared as early as the sixteenth century. Influences came from both Europe's fashion capitals and the Ottoman Turks. Several older tendencies already in clothing practices solidified. While some elements came and went, others continued in use and became long-standing components of regional folk dress. In the eastern- and southernmost regions, the wearing of folk dress lasted until the middle of the twentieth century.

As in western Europe, Romanticism and nationalism encouraged the early collection of folk material. Ethnographers carefully recorded facts about the costumes that they collected, including the many local names for the various components. State-run museums harbor rich collections of folk costumes and related textiles. Much of the literature published during Soviet domination is in Russian, although some texts are translated into two or three languages. With the breakup of the Soviet Union,

Russian peasant girls. Peasant clothing, which represented close ties to the land, remained popular in several eastern European countries until the end of the nineteenth century. © SCHEUFLER COLLECTION/CORBIS. REPRODUCED BY PERMISSION.

folk dress gained new status as a symbol of independent nationhood. The many active folk-dance troupes of eastern Europe and abroad maintain a lively interest in creating accurate replicas of costumes.

Baltic Countries

The three independent states that border the Baltic Sea—Estonia, Latvia, and Lithuania—display great affection for their folk dress. Ethnic celebrations, at which singing of folk songs is an important activity, provide opportunities to wear folk costumes.

Women's folk costumes consisted of skirts, white blouses, and vests; shawls with decorative borders; and headgear to distinguish young unmarried women from matrons. The latter wore crowns, coronets, or floral wreaths to signal their availability, while married women covered their hair with caps or cloths. Brooches and pins made with Baltic amber fastened blouses and shawls. Men's costumes included a shirt, breeches, coat, and hat. Men often secured their stockings with narrow sashes.

Baltic women excelled in weaving complex patterns for belts, sashes, and trims. The following Lithuanian folk song tells of dowry preparation:

> Weave, dear mother, the finest linen cloth
> While I, still young, weave sashes.
> A young man from a distant land
> Is eager for my hand.

Albanian women in native dress. Heavy wool fabric is commonly used in the Balkans, as are linen, hemp, and cotton. Jewelry and headdresses made from metal coins are also prevalent. © LUCIEN AIGNER/CORBIS. REPRODUCED BY PERMISSION.

Women also knitted many pairs of patterned mittens and gloves. The motifs in the weaving and knitting are considered mythological signs by some authorities. Archaeological evidence from the eighth to the thirteenth centuries reveals that some of these costume features predate the arrival of Teutonic crusaders, and thus Christianity.

Some controversy exists about which are the "real" national costumes. In each of the Baltic countries, folk dress based on regional divisions went through several iterations. While some groups look to the ethnographic material collected in the nineteenth and early twentieth centuries, others propose going further back in time to the dress worn prior to foreign occupation. Folk dress in the Baltics continues to evolve.

Russia, Belarus, and Ukraine

Western ideas about dress came to Russia, Belarus, and Ukraine rather late in history. In 1700, Peter the Great of Russia forced adoption of European fashions through imperial decree in an attempt to bring refinement to his court. Yet peasants continued to wear folk dress until the end of the nineteenth century. The late arrival of Christianity to this area, combined with the peasants' connection to the land, preserved ancient agricultural beliefs evident in both style and embellishment of folk dress.

In both Russia and Ukraine, a woman wore a woolen back-apron over her chemise. Called a *plákhta* or *panjóva*, it signaled marital status. Another archaic dress form is a shirt with ultra-long sleeves. Worn by young girls during ritual dances, the fluttering sleeves helped them simulate bird maidens known as *víly* or *rusálki*. Embroidery motifs also link to pre-Christian beliefs. Predominantly geometric, the motifs include known fertility and protection symbols. One example is the hooked lozenge, said to represent a fertile field. The use of the primordial colors of red and black (blood and earth) further connect folk dress with pre-Christian religious practices.

Some dress traditions, such as the economical use of cloth, date from the Middle Ages. Lengths of wool and linen were joined with minimal piecing, not cut up for Renaissance-influenced tailored clothing. Both men and women wore linen shirts as the first layer of clothing. Men wore two shirts—the top one of better fabric—over trousers tucked into boots. The shirts were girdled at the waist. In some areas of Russia, women wore a *sarafan*, a long overdress resembling a jumper. As elsewhere, young girls wore crowns, or diadems, while married women covered their hair. Caftans, capes, and furs provided warmth for both sexes during the cold winter months.

Central Europe

The central European countries have a long, rich history of folk dress. The middle and upper ranks sometimes wore elaborate versions of what could be termed a national style in the seventeenth and eighteenth centuries. Such styles were influenced by European fashions as well as by Ottoman dress. Other components of folk dress in these regions have antecedents that stretch back hundreds, if not thousands, of years.

One such garment is the Hungarian *szür*, a man's hooded or collared mantle with hanging sleeves. Scholars believed that it developed from the first sleeved coat—the Persian *kandys*—in the sixth century B.C.E. The Magyars, forerunners of the Hungarians, brought it with them to the central European plains in the ninth century where it developed and flourished as a man's outer garment. Made from coarse fulled wool in either black or white, the decorated *szür* remained popular with peasants and herdsmen into the early twentieth century. A related garment is the *suba*, a shaggy woolen cape favored by shepherds.

In Hungary, men's folk dress is just as ornamental as women's. Men wore jackets (*dolman*), overcoats (*mente*), fitted pants, and knee-high boots decorated with oriental patterns in embroidery or braid. Even the boot tops could be decorated. Women's dress, which depended heavily on Western fashion, featured Ottoman-influenced tulips and carnations. Frog closures are a design feature of Hungarian coats and jackets for both sexes. Hungarian dress was influential beyond its borders, reaching north to Poland and west to Austria and Switzerland.

Folk dress in the Czech Republic and Slovakia, called *kroje*, had many local variations. The most distinctive women's costumes are characterized by blouses with large extended sleeves, short full skirts, and prominent headdresses. Lace, cutwork, and embroidery embellished both men's and women's folk dress. During the eighteenth century, the monarchy was charmed by peasant costumes and orchestrated court appearances of peasants in their local dress. The real flowering of folk dress occurred in the late eighteenth and early nineteenth centuries and lasted until 1848 when serfdom was abolished. Some of the older ritualistic uses of folk dress prevailed, specifically the capping of the bride in marriage ceremonies and the isolation of new mothers behind large linen shawls.

In Romania and Moldavia, embroidered linen blouses are among the most treasured components of folk dress. Two types exist based on cut. The first, which dates to the adoption of horizontal looms, has a T-shape and

FUNCTIONS OF FOLK DRESS

In 1971, Petr Bogatyrev published his influential study *The Functions of Folk Costume in Moravian Slovakia*. A proponent of structuralism, Bogatyrev argued that peasant clothing may be interpreted as a language that communicates a number of functions. These functions express attitudes within the community regarding social, aesthetic, moral, and nationalistic ideals. His observations regarding the wearing of folk dress, some of which are summarized below, apply to all of eastern Europe.

Folk dress signifies a special day, such as Sunday, holiday, or ceremonial day. Clothing for brides and grooms are among the most elaborate.

Folk dress indicates the occupation of the wearer (for example, shepherd).

Folk dress distinguishes wealth and social status, typically through the number and quality of clothing items.

Components of folk dress have a "magical" function. For example, the ritual marriage cap placed on a new bride brought fertility and good fortune.

Folk dress signifies regional and national affiliation.

Folk dress may indicate religious affiliation.

Age and marital status is communicated by folk dress. Contradictory situations in peasant society, such as single motherhood, are visible in a woman's appearance.

Folk dress has approved aesthetic qualities that attract available members of the opposite sex.

no shoulder seams. The second type is gathered at the neck with a drawstring and has full sleeves. Its origins are in Renaissance shirts. The embroidery of these blouses is remarkable—sleeves are covered in geometric motifs of Slavic origin. Romanians wore a variety of outer woolen garments similar to those found in the Balkans: pieced trousers, vests, and coats.

Poland's folk dress is more like that of western Europe: women's outfits consist of white blouses, fitted vests, and full skirts, while men's ensembles include breeches, coats, and hats. Folk-dress traditions were formed in the early seventeenth century, appropriating the braiding and cording so popular among the Hungarians. Older folk beliefs about the allure of women's hair kept matron's heads covered with a variety of cloths and caps.

Albanian boys. White, full-sleeved shirts and felt hats such as those seen here are major components of the Albanian traditional dress for males, which is influenced heavily by Turkish fashions. © SETBOUN/CORBIS. REPRODUCED BY PERMISSION.

Balkan Countries

The Balkan countries include Albania, Bosnia-Herzegovina, Croatia, Slovenia, Serbia, Montenegro, Macedonia, and Bulgaria. The former Yugoslavia is in the Balkan region. Mainland Greece belongs geographically to the Balkans, but the country was never part of Europe's Soviet bloc.

Competing ethnic and religious groups, whose clothing differs from one another in form or decoration, inhabit specific regions in the Balkans. Turkish influence is strong, as these countries were once part of the Ottoman Empire. Women of the Muslim faith wore Turkish-style trousers while Christian women wore ankle-length chemises. Fez caps identified Muslim males. Embroidery in curvilinear Islamic designs is seen on costumes in all the countries once ruled by the Turks. This work was done by professionals with couched threads of gold or black silk on fine wool or velvet.

Heavy woolen fabric known as *saya* or *tsocha* was common to both male and female costumes. Women spun the wool, which they collected from their flocks, then wove on simple two-harness looms. Sometimes they dyed the fabric black or dark blue; other times it was left white. Then they sent the fabric to water mills near mountain streams for fulling. This process made the wool dense and thick, suitable for village tailors to cut and sew coats, trousers, vests, and jackets.

The women also wove linen, hemp, or cotton for men's shirts, women's chemises, and head cloths. They sewed them with a minimum of cutting and seaming so that no cloth was wasted, then embroidered them with silk or wool threads in dense geometric motifs, some of which are known fertility symbols. In some districts long red or black fringes protected brides and newly married women from the "evil eye," a malevolent force feared throughout the region. In western Macedonia, these fringes can be found on aprons, sleeves, jackets, belts, and headscarves. In her book *Women's Work*, Elizabeth Barber proposes that fringes on folk dress signaled a woman's availability for marriage just as they did in Neolithic times. Customs such as those in parts of Albania—where a woman who is divorced must cut the fringes from her garments to signify her changed social status—confirm this assumption.

A garment that interests dress historians is the Albanian *xhubleta*, a bell-shaped skirt constructed from narrow bands of homespun cloth that resembles Minoan women's dress. Another is the white *foustanella* costume of the Albanian resistance fighters, one of the few skirts worn by men in Europe. More often, men wore baggy pants cut in the Turkish fashion.

Another component common across the Balkan countries is the use of metal coins made into necklaces and headpieces. Large ornamental belt buckles are used for women's festival dress. Commercially printed yellow or white kerchiefs replaced the older white head cloths in recent years.

See also **Ethnic Dress; Folk Dress, Western Europe; Folklore Look.**

BIBLIOGRAPHY

Barber, Elizabeth Wayland. *Women's Work: The First 20,000 Years: Women, Cloth, and Society in Early Times.* New York: W. W. Norton and Company, 1994.

Bogatyrev, Petr. *The Functions of Folk Costume in Moravian Slovakia.* The Hague, Netherlands: Mouton, 1971.

Burnham, Dorothy. *Cut My Cote.* Toronto: Royal Ontario Museum, 1973.

Földi-Dózsa, Katalin. "How the Hungarian National Costume Evolved." In *The Imperial Style: Fashions of the Hapsburg Era.* New York: Metropolitan Museum of Art, 1980.

Gervers-Molnár, Veronika. *The Hungarian Szür: An Archaic Mantle of Eurasian Origins.* Toronto: Royal Ontario Museum, 1973.

Kennett, Frances. *Ethnic Dress.* New York: Facts On File, 1995.

Paine, Sheila. *Embroidered Textiles: Traditional Patterns from Five Continents.* New York: Rizzoli International, 1990.

Petrescu, Paul, and Elena Secosan. *Romanian Folk Costume.* Bucharest, Romania: Meridiane Publishing House, 1985.

Snowden, James. *Folk Dress of Europe.* New York: Mayflower Books, 1979.

Tilke, Max. *Costume Patterns and Designs.* New York: Hastings House, 1974.

Turnau, Irena. "The Main Centres of National Fashion in Eastern Europe from the Sixteenth to the Eighteenth Centuries." *Textile History* 22, no. 1 (1991): 47–66.

Welters, Linda, ed. *Folk Dress in Europe and Anatolia: Beliefs About Protection and Fertility.* Oxford and New York: Berg, 1999.

Linda M. Welters

FOLK DRESS, WESTERN EUROPE Folk dress in Western Europe refers to the clothing of rural populations engaged in farming, fishing, or herding. Variously termed peasant, rural, or regional dress, it may also be considered ethnic dress in regions with more than one ethnic group. In all cases, folk dress identified people with a place.

Swedish couple in wedding finery. Swedes, like all Scandinavians, still honor their country's traditional folk dress, donning it frequently for festivals and special occasions. © BETTMANN/CORBIS. REPRODUCED BY PERMISSION.

Historical Overview

From the fourteenth to the eighteenth centuries, the dress of rural dwellers reflected the fashionable styles worn by those from the middle and upper ranks of society, albeit in simplified form. In many parts of Europe, sumptuary laws limited decoration and restricted use of materials so that peasants would easily be distinguished from those of higher social standing. The elimination of sumptuary laws, combined with land reforms, brought about a true flowering of folk dress in some, but not all, Western European countries in the late eighteenth and early nineteenth centuries.

Around the same time, political changes in Europe spawned nationalist movements in many countries. Early ethnologists began systematically collecting songs, legends, myths, and examples of regional dress to bolster the argument for the existence of a national character in the "folk." The romanticism of the era contributed to the invention of traditions not based in historical fact.

British Isles

The concept of invented traditions fits easily with the so-called folk dress of Scotland, Wales, and Ireland. Scotland is known for the man's kilt made from clan tartans. Historically, the Celts in Ireland and Scotland wore shirts and plaid mantles, which they arranged on their bodies in various ways. Sometime after 1727, Thomas Rawlinson, an Englishman living in Scotland, separated the plaid

GREEK CUSTOMS

Katerina Stamou, born in 1892 in the Greek village of Peania, spoke about the wearing of folk dress in her youth, underscoring the importance of signifying marital status through appearance: "The newly married ones wore their jewelry for about a week after the wedding to show it off. They went to pick olives with all that jewelry on. They held the *kordoni* [necklace of many chains with coins attached] with one hand and picked olives with the other. Now we laugh about these things, but then that's how things were." (Interview with Katerina Stamou, Peania, Attica, Greece. 29 June 1983)

into the pleated kilt, or *philabeg*, and shoulder wrap. It became so popular that the English banned it after the rebellion of 1745, which served to strengthen its association with Scottish culture. After 1780, the mythology surrounding the kilt expanded to include the assignment of certain "setts," or plaid patterns, to specific clans.

Wales and Ireland offer more recent examples of invented traditions. As Welsh language and culture faded in the early nineteenth century, intellectuals promoted the preservation of customs and traditions. This extended to dress. In 1843, Lady Llanover invented a Welsh "national" dress loosely based on rural clothing of the 1780s: short gown, petticoat, and cloak of checked or striped wool worn with a tall beaver hat. In actuality, no one had ever worn that type of hat. A similar situation occurred in Ireland in the late nineteenth century when cultural leaders proposed a tunic and mantle combination inspired by the "ancient" dress of *brat* and *léine*. It became more Irish by adding Celtic embroideries.

England did not suffer the same crisis of identity as did Scotland, Wales, and Ireland; thus it did not have a folk dress. Certain occupational dress styles, such as the farmer's smock, were worn over breeches or trousers in rural areas.

Scandinavia

The Scandinavian countries of Norway, Sweden, and Finland have strongly developed folk-dress traditions encouraged by the Romantic revival. Denmark's folk dress is not so well known, because the Danes did not systematically collect folk material in the nineteenth century as did the Swedes and Norwegians. Today, all of the Scandinavian countries actively preserve their folk dress. In America, descendants of Swedish and Norwegian émigrés don folk dress for festive attire.

In Sweden, each local parish has its own costume, which is still worn as festival dress. The authors of *Folk Costumes of Sweden: A Living Tradition* identified over 400 local costumes in use in the 1970s. While the parish costumes of some provinces such as Skåne, Dalarna, and Hälsingland have a long history, others are "reconstructed" based on old costume material in museums. Local costumes are seen as an expression of identification with one's home community. Some of the jackets have features dating to c. 1600, such as shoulder wings and pickadils.

Norway was under Swedish rule until 1905. The country's mountains and fjords promoted the development of independent communities organized around church parishes, each of which had distinctive sartorial customs. Sunday and festival dress was decorative while everyday clothing was quite plain. During the nationalist movement of the late nineteenth century, the folk dress of the Hardanger region came to symbolize Norway. It consisted of a long skirt, embroidered vest, and cut-work linen blouse in the heraldic colors of black, red, and white. Hardanger brides wore elaborate crowns, which they exchanged for marital caps during the wedding ceremony. Around 1900, the bunad movement promoted the wearing of other regional costumes for folk festivals, thereby expanding the Norwegian folk-dress repertoire.

Lapland, an area north of the Arctic Circle, is an ethnic area rather than a political entity. Its people, known as the Saami, are reindeer herders who roam across northern Norway, Sweden, and Finland into Russia. Not surprisingly, their clothing is made from reindeer skins and the fur of the Arctic hare. The colorful dress of the Saami, still worn for festive occasions, consists of a wool tunic worn over trousers and ear-protecting caps. Curled boots made from reindeer hide and stuffed with straw keep feet warm during the cold winters. The dominant colors are rich blue accented with red. Braids, tassels, and pom-poms in red, green, and yellow further enliven this unique costume.

Common to all Scandinavian countries is the wearing of silver brooches and pins, believed to ward off evil. The shiny metal protected people of all ages from legendary supernatural forces such as trolls and gnomes.

Northern and Central Europe

The Netherlands, France, Germany, Austria, and Switzerland have well-developed folk dress traditions. In the Netherlands, rural clothing from various districts is preserved in museums. Simplified versions are worn at events commemorating Holland's association with the sea, as well as in tourist areas such as Volendam and Marken. A typical man's outfit consists of blue woolen trousers and jacket worn with a flat cap and wooden shoes. Winged white caps are characteristic of women's dress.

Tyrolean men in native costume. While Austria has eight separate costume districts, Tyrolean clothing is often considered representative of its traditional dress, known as *tracht*. © TIZIANA AND GIANNI BALDIZZONE. REPRODUCED BY PERMISSION.

In France, the proximity of peasants to fashionable Paris stunted development of a folk dress with the exception of a few distinctive customs in distant regions based on long-defunct historical styles. In Brittany, women continued to wear stiffened high lace caps with lappets hanging down the back into the nineteenth century. In the Savoie region bordering Italy and Switzerland, women wore white fluted headdresses and ruffled collars. The women of Provence sported quilted petticoats made from beautiful hand-printed cottons manufactured in the region.

In Germany, Austria, and Switzerland, the folk dress of certain districts is better known than others, thanks to the Romantic movement. German societies formed in the 1880s revived the costumes of the Black Forest and Upper Bavaria. Bavarian costume is still worn today at Munich's Oktoberfest. Austrian folk dress, known as *tracht*, is often synonymous with Tyrolean costume, even though

Austria is divided into eight costume districts. The Tyrolean costume has influenced fashionable dress at various times. In Switzerland, the National Federation of Swiss Costumes was founded in 1926 to preserve regional dress. Swiss folk dress is categorized by canton (geographical division). In the fifth edition of *Ardern Holt's Fancy Dresses Described; or, What to Wear to Fancy Balls* (1887) the most characteristic Swiss dress was that of Berne. Holt recognized that Swiss costumes varied by canton, but dismissed some of them as "not picturesque" (p. 215).

In all three of these countries, women's costumes featured dirndl skirts, fitted vests, white blouses, and distinctive caps, while men's displayed colorful vests and coats worn with knee breeches or leather hose. The latter are known as lederhosen—short leather trousers with suspenders—and are worn in both Germany and Austria. A fulled woolen fabric known as loden was used for men's clothing in Austria. Woolen embroideries of hearts and

GENERAL CHARACTERISTICS OF FOLK DRESS

Folk dress on the European mainland typically reflected fashionable dress from various historical periods. Specific features may be traced to medieval, Renaissance, baroque, rococo, neoclassic, or Victorian sources. A basic woman's outfit consisted of a white shift, tight-fitting vest or sleeved jacket, full skirt, apron, shawl, and headgear. Headgear was often the most distinctive part of the costume because it signified marital status; unmarried women wore wreaths or crowns, while married women covered their hair with caps or draped cloths. A typical male folk costume included a simple shirt, a pair of breeches or trousers, a vest or jacket, leather boots or shoes, and a hat. Folk dress varied locally, particularly that of women, depending on availability of raw materials and knowledge of specialized techniques of manufacture peculiar to a region. Most people in a particular district dressed alike because conformity was prized over individuality. Clothing signified membership in a community.

Home production of cloth was integral to folk dress. Both sexes were involved in flax and wool production. Women knew how to spin, weave, knit, and embellish the cloth peculiar to their region. They learned embroidery from pattern books featuring curvilinear patterns such as hearts and flowers. Occasionally special materials (silk ribbons and fabrics) were purchased to trim garments. Some regions specialized in particular textile techniques, for example lace making or tablet weaving. Local tailors sewed garments of more complicated cut, that included vests, jackets, and coats, and hard-to-handle materials like leather and fur. Women sewed the garments cut from rectilinear pieces of cloth, such as shirts, shifts, skirts, and aprons.

Bast fibers such as flax and hemp grew easily in the moist cool climates of northern Europe; thus, they became the fibers of choice for shirts and cloths for the head and neck. Woolens in medium to dark colors were made into skirts, trousers, breeches, vests, jackets, and coats. In a few regions, leather was used for breeches or trousers. Shoes were of leather, too, although sometimes other available materials like bark or wood substituted for leather. Silk fabrics were a luxury, appearing only in accessories and trimmings.

The industrial revolution made commercially produced fabrics and clothing widely available for moderate prices, gradually replacing hand-woven fabrics and ultimately the homemade clothing itself. In most areas of Western Europe, people stopped wearing distinctive rural styles by 1850. In the early twenty-first century, some Europeans and European Americans wear folk dress to festivals and celebrations as "costume" to signify their affiliation with a particular country or region. The making of accurate reproductions is of great interest to these people.

---

flowers are common to both men's and women's folk dress in these areas.

Mediterranean Countries

One of the most distinctive ensembles of the Mediterranean area is the Andalusian dress of Spain. Situated in the southernmost region, Andalusia absorbed Moorish influence. In the eighteenth century, women began wearing *maja* (female dandy) and *gitano* (gypsy) costumes inspired by the region's machismo culture that glorified bullfighting. The maja look incorporated jackets and skirts trimmed with black lace or fringe, mantillas, and hair combs. The *gitana* outfit included ruffled skirts and Manila shawls with colorful embroidery. Men wore tight-fitting jackets and trousers, frilly shirts, and wide-brimmed hats. These popular outfits spread to Madrid and then to the rest of Spain. Eventually Andalusian dress came to represent Spain itself.

Neither Portugal nor Italy has a well-known folk-dress tradition, although regional styles existed in rural communities in both countries. Portuguese folk dress is characterized by fine embroidery on linen garments.

Greek folk dress has more in common with the Balkan countries than with western Europe. Over the course of its long history, Greece has absorbed influence from Byzantine, Italian, and Turkish culture, resulting in great diversity in the form and decoration of its folk dress. After the Revolution of 1821, islanders and city dwellers abandoned traditional dress in favor of fashionable dress. Like their European compatriots, in the 1840s the bourgoisie developed a national folk costume consisting of the skirted *foustanella* for men and a fitted jacket, skirt, and fez cap for women. These outfits remain popular to this day as a symbol of Greece and are worn by Greek school-children in Greece and abroad for national celebrations. In the more geographically isolated farming and herding communities, the wearing of regional folk dress continued until the onset of World War II.

See also **Folk Dress, Eastern Europe; Folklore Look; Roma and Gypsy; Scottish Dress; Spanish Dress.**

Women wearing Andalusian dresses. In the eighteenth century, Andalusian fashion began to draw inspiration from gypsies and the bullfighting culture, creating a distinctive look that quickly spread across the country. © RICHARD KLUNE/CORBIS. REPRODUCED BY PERMISSION.

BIBLIOGRAPHY

Arnö-Berg, Inga, and Gunnel Hazelius-Berg. *Folk Costumes of Sweden.* Translated by W. E. Ottercrans. Västerås, Sweden: ICA bokförlag, 1975.

Dunlevy, Mairead. *Dress in Ireland.* London: B. T. Batsford, Ltd., 1989.

Fochler, Rudolf. *Trachten in Österreich [Costumes in Austria].* Wels-München, Germany: Verlag Welsermühl, 1980.

Kennett, Frances. *Ethnic Dress.* New York: Facts on File, 1995.

Nelson, Marion, ed. *Norwegian Folk Art: The Migration of a Tradition.* New York: Abbeville Press, 1995.

O'Kelly, Hilary. "Reconstructing Irishness: Dress in the Celtic Revival, 1880–1920." In *Chic Thrills: A Fashion Reader.* Edited by Juliet Ash and Elizabeth Wilson. London: Pandora Press, 1992.

Sichel, Marion. *Scandinavia.* London: B. T. Batsford, Ltd., 1987.

Snowden, James. *Folk Dress of Europe.* London and New York: Mayflower Books, 1979.

Stevens, Christine. "Welsh Peasant Dress—Workwear or National Costume?" *Textile History* 33(1) (2002): 63–78.

Trevor-Roper, Hugh. "The Invention of Tradition: The Highland Tradition in Scotland." In *The Invention of Tradition.* Edited by Eric Hobsbawm and T. Ranger. Cambridge, U.K.: Cambridge University Press, 1982.

Welters, Linda, ed. *Folk Dress in Europe and Anatolia: Beliefs About Protection and Fertility.* Oxford and New York: Berg, 1999.

Worth, Susannah, and Lucy R. Sibley. "Maja Dress and the Andalusian Image of Spain." *Clothing and Textile Research Journal* 12(4) (1994): 51–60.

Linda M. Welters

FOLKLORE LOOK A folklore look is a style inspired by peasant dress. The term "folklore look" came into use around 1970. However, fashions drawn from peasant costumes have appeared numerous times in the last one hundred years.

Antecedents in Exoticism

Fashion has a long history of borrowing from other "exotic" or "primitive" cultures to create new looks that perfectly express the moment. Western fashion's fascination with exoticism dates to the eighteenth century when wealthy Europeans and Americans donned Turkish-inspired ensembles for masquerade and to sit for portraits. The love of things oriental continued into the nineteenth century with the popularity of cashmere shawls, fez caps, and kimonos.

In the first decade of the twentieth century, exoticism found a new proponent—the Paris couturier Paul Poiret. Inspired by the Ballets Russes, he created widely copied ensembles based on middle Eastern and Asian prototypes, often shown with turbans. Soon several constituencies—intellectuals, designers, and politicians—borrowed clothing styles from rural communities to represent specific cultural ideals, thus ushering in the first peasant looks in fashion.

HOMEMADE CLOTHING

Living on the Earth (Random House, 1971) was written as a guide for those who had rebelled against industrial society by turning to self-sufficient communal living. Author Alicia Bay Laurel showed readers how to raise vegetables, build dwellings, and give birth at home. She also explained how to make clothes. Her hand-lettered book gave simple directions for making your own patterns, remaking secondhand clothes, tie-dyeing, and embroidering. Many of her patterns were based on the simple shapes of folk clothing including a burnoose, a smock shirt, a djellaba, and a Mexican blouse.

Early Peasant Looks

Artists, writers, and political activists who settled in New York City's Greenwich Village after 1910 adopted peasant blouses and farmer's smocks to signify their leftist sympathies. Embroidered blouses, sold in Hungarian and Russian shops, became almost a uniform for bohemian women. The city's fashion industry picked up on these new Greenwich Village styles, featuring them in *Women's Wear* (predecessor of *Women's Wear Daily*) and leading department stores like Bonwit Teller.

Similar peasant looks appeared in Paris following the 1917 Bolshevik Revolution, when aristocratic Russian émigrés arrived in the city. In need of money, they began to embroider traditional peasant designs for Kitmir, a company founded by Grand Duchess Marie Pavlovna, daughter of Grand Duke Paul Alexandrovitch. Kitmir's two major clients were Jean Patou and Gabrielle (Coco) Chanel, who produced simple tunics and waistcoats with Russian embroideries for their first postwar collections.

The trend for geometric embroideries on gauzy fabrics coincided with a period in fashion history of clothes with simple shapes and elaborate decoration. Many blouses, delicately embroidered with Slavic motifs, survive from this period in museum collections.

Folk-inspired motifs and shapes appeared in other apparel as well. Sweaters frequently took their inspiration from folk designs, such as the Fair Isle patterns popularized by the Prince of Wales in the 1920s. In the 1930s, skiwear designers looked to Scandinavian, Swiss, and Austrian models for trousers, jackets, sweaters, and caps to wear for this newly fashionable sport. The designer Elsa Schiaparelli included Austrian Tyrol looks in her collections. Peasant styles occasionally sprang from resorts frequented by the rich and famous, such as men's embroidered shirts from Mexico, or ponchos suitable for wearing as beach cover-ups or on board ship.

Rise of the Hippies

After World War II ended, the popularity of clothing inspired by folk dress faded. The sophisticated lines and elegant fabrics preferred by the two leading postwar couturiers, Christian Dior and Christóbal Balenciaga, were the antithesis of folk looks. Peasant styles found a new home, however, among dissenters who rejected the blandness of the 1950s. Folk music aficionados wore rural-inspired ponchos and peasant shirts. Beatniks added eclectic elements from cultures around the world—Mexican shirts and huaraches, Peruvian vests, Indian sashes, and ethnic jewelry—to signal their marginal social position.

The folk and beat looks of the 1950s signified the beginnings of a rebellion against mainstream society that blossomed into the full-blown "flower power" of the later 1960s. This social transformation, fueled by the coming-of-age of the baby boomers, incorporated the antiwar movement and the new youth culture of sex, drugs and rock and roll. Hippies, as they were known, wore anti-establishment looks borrowed from India, Morocco, Mexico, and Native American communities. The hippie movement foreshadowed the ecology movement; once again the clothes of peasants seemed right for the time. In the 1970s peasant looks merged with ethnic looks, forming the immensely popular "folklore look."

Authentic folk and ethnic patterns became available to home sewers in the mid-1970s, when three California women founded *Folkwear*. Their first two patterns were for a Syrian dress and a Turkish coat. In the early 2000s, the company offers patterns for smocks, various peasant blouses, shirts, vests, and dirndls.

Designers and the Folklore Look

Designers inspired by street styles brought the folklore look to high fashion in the 1970s. The English designer Zandra Rhodes observed that in the late 1960s, with the Beatles in India and the Rolling Stones in Morocco, "folklore was appealing." She found the peasant embroidery and the simple shapes of ethnic clothes "infinitely pleasing" and began creating dresses with ethnic shapes for her hand-painted textiles. Before long, the Paris couture got in on the act, particularly Yves Saint Laurent. His Russian collection of 1976–1977 featured rich peasant looks with full skirts, corselet-type bodices, and short decorated jackets in luxurious fabrics trimmed with fur. This collection introduced colorful scarves, shawls, ruffled skirts, and boots to mainstream fashion.

Since the 1980s any number of designers regularly revived the folklore look. Jennifer Craik describes this process as "bricolage"—the creation of new patterns and styles from a variety of sources, including non-Western dress. Mixing high fashion and everyday clothing is consistent with the postmodern, multicultural world that emerged in the 1980s. At the couture level, Christian Lacroix is known for incorporating peasant elements from Provence into his exotic outfits. John Galliano mixes

Model in Yves Saint Laurent design. The folklore look met high fashion in the 1970s, when several well known designers incorporated peasant dress into their clothing lines. © Pierre Vauthey/Corbis. Reproduced by permission.

historical and cultural influences to create innovative designs for Dior. The appropriation of themes from peasant cultures is characteristic of ready-to-wear collections from designers such as Anna Sui, Vivian Tam, Miu Miu, Arden B., and Dolce & Gabbana. Such looks are easily recognizable and move rapidly across the fashion landscape. Indeed, in the spring of 2002, the embroidered peasant blouse was featured by the fashion press as the "look of the moment," and was soon copied at all levels. Donatella Versace was photographed for the March 2002 issue of *Vogue* wearing jeans and an embroidered peasant blouse purchased from The Ukrainian Shop in New York City. Barely a season later the look was declared passé.

See also **Chanel, Gabrielle (Coco); Ethnic Dress; Folk Dress, Eastern Europe; Folk Dress, Western Europe; Hippie Style; Lacroix, Christian; Patou, Jean; Rhodes, Zandra; Saint Laurent, Yves.**

BIBLIOGRAPHY

Craik, Jennifer. *The Face of Fashion: Cultural Studies in Fashion.* London and New York: Routledge, 1994.

Etherington-Smith, Meredith. *Patou*. New York: St. Martin's Press/Marek, 1983.

Parker, Mary S. *The Folkwear Book of Ethnic Clothing: Easy Ways to Sew and Embellish Fabulous Garments from Around the World*. New York: Lark Books, 2002.

Polhemus, Ted. *Street Style: From Sidewalk to Catwalk*. London: Thames and Hudson, 1994.

Rhodes, Zandra, and Anne Knight. *The Art of Zandra Rhodes*. Boston: Houghton Mifflin, 1985.

Saint Laurent, Yves, Diana Vreeland et al. *Yves Saint Laurent*. New York: The Metropolitan Museum of Art, 1983.

Linda M. Welters

FONTANA SISTERS Zoe (1911–1979), Micol (b. 1913), and Giovanna (b. 1915) Fontana were born in Traversetolo, near Parma, Italy. They learned sewing and tailoring from their mother, Amabile Fontana, who opened her own tailor shop in 1907. The three sisters became apprentices as soon as they were old enough to handle needles and scissors. Legend has it that the work was hard and unpaid and that the sisters worked Saturdays and Sundays. Despite the long hours, the sisters' memories of childhood are happy ones, and they look back with fondness on the years spent in the large, quiet house surrounded by greenery. Micol writes often of her childhood experiences in her memoir, *Specchio a tre luci*. "We were never alone, but always accompanied by our mother's love" (p. 20).

Apprenticeships

In the 1930s Zoe, the eldest of the three, left Traversetolo to become an apprentice in Milan. Micol joined her there, while Giovanna remained in the countryside. Shortly after her marriage in 1934, Zoe moved with her husband to Paris, where she continued her apprenticeship in an atelier. After returning to Italy in 1936, Zoe, excited by her experiences in Paris, moved to Rome. In her memoirs she treats this major turning point in her life casually: "I took the first train that arrived. . . . It could have gone north or south. It happened to be going south, to Rome" (2001, p. 14). After her sisters joined her in Rome, Zoe went to work for Zecca and Micol for Battilocchi; Giovanna sewed garments at home. Based on their experiences in Milan and Paris, the sisters felt they were ready to go into business for themselves. Although French fashions were still dominant in the world of haute couture, the sisters opened their own workshop in Rome in 1943, changing the name from "Fontana" to "Sorelle Fontana" and leading members of the Italian aristocracy soon began patronizing it.

International Fame

However, their Roman clientele would not have been sufficient to cement the Fontana sisters' reputation if Hollywood had not discovered Italy and *la dolce vita romana*

in the 1950s. One of the events that helped secure their international reputation was the marriage of the Hollywood actors Tyrone Power and Linda Christian, whose wedding gown the Fontana sisters designed. The ceremony was held in the basilica of Santa Francesca Romana in Rome in 1949. The gown was constructed of white satin, with a five-yard train, and was covered with embroidery; it resembled a dress that might have been worn by a fairy tale princess. The international press covered the event, and photographs of the ceremony and a radiant Linda Christian appeared in papers around the world. A magazine published for foreign tourists in the 1950s proclaimed, "Rome? Twenty minutes in St. Peter's, twenty in the Coliseum, and at least two days in the Fontana sisters' studio" (Soli, p. 75).

In 1951 the Fontana sisters participated in the first fashion show held in Florence, which was organized by Giovanni Battista Giorgini, the promoter of Italian fashion and organizer of catwalk shows at Sala Bianca, Palazzo Pitti. That same year Micol Fontana left for Hollywood, arriving in the United States as the guest and personal friend of Tyrone Power and Linda Christian. Power organized a show for her because he wanted to introduce other members of the Hollywood community to the Fontana sisters' designs. From that moment on, the Fontana sisters began designing for many of Hollywood's best-known stars, from Ava Gardner to Elizabeth Taylor, and started developing a varied international following as well. Margaret Trujillo (the Santo Domingo dictator's wife who ordered Sorelle Fontana's atelier 150 dress), Grace Kelly, Margaret Truman (President Harry S. Truman's daughter), Jackie Kennedy, Soraya Esfandiary, Marella Agnelli (of the family that runs the Fiat), and Maria Pia di Savoia, (one of the daughters of last king of Italy, Umberto of Savoia) were some of their regular customers. From Linda Christian Marriage, they also specialized in celebrities' wedding dress: Margaret Truman (1956), Janet Auchincloss, Jacqueline Kennedy's sister (1966), Maria Pia di Savoia (1955), whose dress is now shown at the Museum of Art and Costume in Venice, and Angelita Trujillo, the daughter of the Santo Domingo dictator (1955), are some examples.

In 1957 the Fontana sisters were received by Pope Pius XII to mark fifty years of tailoring begun by their mother, Amabile. In 1958 they were invited to the White House as Italy's representatives to the Fashion around the World conference. In 1960, at the request of American customers, they introduced a line of ready-to-wear. This product launch was followed by a line of furs, umbrellas, scarves, costume jewelry, and table linen. Because of the careful division of labor among them, the three sisters were invincible: Micol traveled around the world—Japan, Europe, and ninety-four trips to the United States, Zoe handled public relations, and Giovanna monitored work in the studio.

In 1972, while continuing their work in couture and ready-to-wear, the sisters withdrew from most of the official fashion shows. In 1992 the Fontana label and the company itself were sold to an Italian financial group. In 1994 Micol created the Micol Fontana Foundation, the mission of which is to promote fashion and the training of talented newcomers.

Inspiration for Designs

The Fontanas' designs, although they referred to French models, were inspired by eighteenth-century modes of dress, which were based on designs of the early Renaissance. The sisters were able to navigate between Parisian haute couture, an essential reference point, and the originality of the Italian fashions with which American women had become enamored. The sisters' designs were known for craftsmanship and intuition. Embroidery, lace, and impeccable tailoring were characteristic of their garments. They specialized in formal wear and evening gowns and used the most precious materials, including silk and velvet. Their ideas came from a wide variety of sources, but their designs, for the most part, were Italian in inspiration. Quintavalle remarked that the Fontana sisters "redeemed the Italian culture that Fascism had disfigured, restricting it within the confines of a local culture" (Bianchino, p. 43).

Innovations

The sisters' love for America continued to deepen. In her diary Micol writes that she felt more at home in America than in Italy and that public relations was not the only reason she traveled. Micol was a close observer of the way Americans dressed, and she tried to determine exactly what they wanted to wear. The sisters' relations with the international jet set, and especially with Hollywood and the film industry, were one of their strengths; in fact, Nicola White remarks that it is unlikely they would have been able to achieve such fame without their connection to Ava Gardner, as well as to other stars like Myrna Loy, Grace Kelly, Audrey Hepburn, and Kim Novak. However, their skill as couturiers, which allowed them to compete with Dior's Paris, cannot be overlooked. The clothing they created was designed for the individual client. Zoe, known as the "golden scissors," could cut and drape as well as the best designers in Paris.

Renato Balestra and Alain Reynaud, the creators of Biki, are among the designers who had worked with Sorelle Fontana. By presenting some of their designs in newspapers—an innovation resulting from their ability to intuit future developments in fashion—they took another step in consolidating their fame, completely altering their relationship with the public. Unlike other designers, their relations with their clients did not develop through frequent customer visits to their studio, which had typified the role of the designer until then. Most of their clients learned of them through the media and wanted to meet the sisters so they would design something for them. In this sense they helped lay the foundations for the star designers of the future.

Woman modeling Sorella Fontana design. The Fontana Sisters exported Italian fashion to the rest of the world, especially to the United States, where they designed clothing for some of Hollywood's most famous stars. AP/WIDE WORLD PHOTOS. REPRODUCED BY PERMISSION.

Italian cinema put the atelier of the Sorelle Fontana under the spotlights when it became the set for the film *Le ragazze di piazza di Spagna* by Luciano Emmer (1953). The Fontana sisters also designed the costumes for Ava Gardner in *The Barefoot Contessa*, a film released in 1954. One of their designs, the "cassock dress," which was made for Gardner in 1956, was used by the costume designer Danilo Donati for Anita Ekberg in Federico Fellini's film *La dolce vita*. The Fontana sisters' work has been presented in several exhibitions and designs are exposed in the museums internationally: the Metropolitan Museum of Art in New York, the Metropolitan Museum of Art in San Francisco, the Museo d'Arte e Costume in Venice, and the private library of Harry Truman.

See also **Evening Dress; Haute Couture; Wedding Costume.**

BIBLIOGRAPHY

Bianchino, Gloria. *Moda dalla fiaba al design.* Novara, Italy: De Agostini, 1989.

Fontana, Micol. *Specchio a tre luci.* Roma: Rai Radiotelevisione Italiana, 1992.

Gastel, Minnie. *50 anni di moda italiana.* Milan: Vallardi, 1995.

Giordani Aragno, Bonizza. *900 Il Secolo Di Moda: Sorelle Fontana.* Roma: Fondazione Micol Fontana, 2001.

——, ed. *Storia di un atelier: Sorelle Fontana 1907–1992.* Rome: Logart Press, 1992.

Pisa, Paola. "Sorelle Fontana." In *Dizionario della moda.* Edited by Guido Vergani. Milan: Baldini and Castoldi, 1999.

Soli, Pia. *Il genio antipatico.* Milan: Arnoldo Mondadori, 1984.

White, Nicola. *Reconstructing Italian Fashion.* London, New York: Berg, 2000.

Simona Segre Reinach

FOOTBINDING Footbinding was specific to and unique to traditional Chinese culture. Its various names conveyed its multifaceted image in Chinese eyes: *chanzu* (binding feet) called attention to the mundane action of swaddling the body with a piece of cloth; *gongwan* (curved arch) described a desired shape of the foot similar to that of a ballerina in pointe shoe; *jinlian* (golden lotus, also gilded lilies) evoked a utopian image of the body that was the subject of fantastical transformation. A related poetic expression of *lianbu* (lotus steps) suggested that footbinding was intended to enhance the grace of the body in motion, not to cripple the woman.

Body Modification
The much-maligned practice has often been compared to corsetry as evidence that women were oppressed in cultures East and West, modern and traditional. The comparison is apt albeit for different reasons. The goal of both practices was to modify the female figure with strips of carefully designed and precisely positioned fabric, and in so doing alter the way the wearer projected herself into the world. During its millennium-long history, footbinding acquired various cultural meanings: as a sign of status, civility, Han Chinese ethnicity, and femininity. But at its core it was a means of body modification, hence its history should be sought from the foundational garments of binding cloth, socks, and soft-heeled slippers.

The materials needed for binding feet were specialized articles made by women (binding cloth, socks, and shoes) together with sewing implements readily available in the boudoir (scissors, needle, and thread). Alum and medicinal powder were sprinkled between the toes as an astringent. Women often wove the cotton binding cloth; its average width was three inches, and its length ranged from seven to ten inches. Skillful wrapping of the cloth allowed the woman to reshape the foot into desirable shapes in accordance to footwear fashion. The method and style of binding feet varied greatly with geography, age, and occasion. A moderate way involved compressing the four digits into a pointy and narrow tip; an extreme regiment required both the folding of the digits and the bending of the foot at midpoint into an arch. The tendons and extensors of the toes were stretched to the point of breakage, but the breakage did not, at least in theory, require fracturing the bones. The binding of feet altered the shape of the foot and the woman's gait. Slender slippers and dainty steps signified class and desirability.

Similar to tattooing, footbinding bespeaks an attitude that viewed the body as a canvas or a template—a surface or "social skin" on which cultural meanings could be inscribed. Yet the effect of binding was more than skin deep. It signaled an extreme form of self-improvement and mastery; the contemporary body-piercer's motto of "no pain, no gain" is equally apt for Chinese women.

Unlike tattooing and body-piercing, however, footbinding was only practiced by females, and its connections with the female handicraft traditions of textile, embroidery, and shoemaking rendered it a quintessential sign of feminine identity. It is paradoxical that footbinding, supposedly a signal of the woman's family status as "conspicuous leisure," was in itself a result and expression of a strenuous form of female labor.

Early Beginnings
The earliest material evidence for the binding of feet is several pairs of shoes from twelfth- to thirteenth-century tombs in south-central China. Scholar Zhang Bangji (fl. 1147) provided the first known textual reference to footbinding as an actual practice: "Women's footbinding began in the recent times; it was not mentioned in any books from the previous eras." By the twelfth century, footbinding was a common but by no means mandatory practice among the wives and daughters of high-status men, as well as courtesans and actresses who entertained this same group of privileged scholar-officials.

Song-dynasty China (960–1279) enjoyed a prosperous commercialized economy. The Northern Song capital of Kaifeng and the Southern Song capital of Hangzhou, with populations of over a million each, were the largest cities in the world at the time. Indeed, historians have suggested that the beginnings of Chinese modernity can be traced back to the Song. A taste for novelty, together with status-anxiety—the same factors that gave rise to fashion in early modern Europe—also facilitated the birth of footbinding. Adoration for small feet ran deep in Chinese culture: the story of Ye Xian, China's Cinderella, appeared in a ninth-century story collection *Youyang zazu* (Ko, pp. 26–27), and poets eulogized dainty steps and fancy footwear from the sixth to tenth centuries. But these fantasies gave rise to the actual practice of binding feet only in the urban culture that emerged after the fall of the Tang aristocratic empire.

The style of women's shoes from the twelfth to fifteenth centuries conforms to two subtypes: one is long and narrow with pointy toes, like a kayak; the other, with turned-up toes, is like a canoe with a high stem. These shoes are made of monochrome silk and decorated with embroidered abstract floral or cloud patterns. The length of archaeological specimens ranges from 5.9 inches to 9.4 inches (15 to 24 cm). Both styles feature flat fabric soles, suggesting that in this early stage women swaddled their four digits together with a binding cloth to achieve a sleek, pointy look.

Paintings show these pointy toes or the more dramatic upturned toes peeking out from long, flowing silk trousers, creating an aesthetic of subdued feminine elegance. The most credible origin myth attributes footbinding to Yaoniang, a dancer in the court of the last ruler Li Yu (r. 969–975) of the Southern Tang kingdom, who beguiled Li with her graceful dance and shoes that "curl up like the new moon." In the beginning, footbinding was not meant to cripple.

The Cult of the Golden Lotus

A more extreme regime of beauty arose around the sixteenth century with the invention of high heels. One type of shoes was elevated on a cylindrical heel; another featured a curved sole supported by a piece of silk-covered wood from the heel area to the instep. Not only did heels afford an optical illusion of smallness, they also enabled an extreme way of binding that pushed the base of the metatarsal bones and the adjoining cuneiforms upward, forming a bulge on the top of the foot. A crevice was formed on the sole due to the compression of the fifth metatarsal bone toward the calcaneus or heel bone. The high heel redirected the wearer's body weight into a tripod-like area consisting of the tip of the big toe, the bent toes, and the back of the heel. However unsteadily, heeled footwear provided better support for the triangular foot than flats.

This strenuous regimen bespeaks heightened female competition in a fashion-conscious society. In the sixteenth century, the Ming Empire (1368–1644) enjoyed the largest trade surplus in the world. Buoyed by a net inflow of New World silver, the money economy spread to the countryside. In a world of material abundance and social fluidity, there was intense pressure on women to display the status of their fathers and husbands. The incessant drive for small feet and their attendant eroticization in this atmosphere gave rise to a cult of the golden lotus.

Silk Ginlein shoe. Footbinding is a form of body modification mainly practiced by Han Chinese women. One of the two popular styles of shoes available to women with bound feet in the twelfth to fifteenth centuries was made of silk with embroidered patterns and pointed toes. Shoes in this style averaged in length between 15 and 24 centimeters. COURTESY OF THE BATA SHOE MUSEUM, TORONTO. PHOTO BY HAL ROTH. REPRODUCED BY PERMISSION.

Cantonese boots. High-heeled shoes were introduced to women's fashion in China during the Ming Dynasty. The heels created the illusion of smallness and, due to the shoes' design and the weight and balance modifications resulting from footbinding, they actually provided more support to women with bound feet than did flat shoes. COURTESY OF THE BATA SHOE MUSEUM, TORONTO. PHOTO BY HAL ROTH. REPRODUCED BY PERMISSION.

Female footwear—often store-bought—became fanciful. Some women hired famous carpenters to carve their heels, often of fragrant wood. Floral cutouts were made on the surface of hollowed heels; perfumed powder inside the heels would leave traces of blossoms on the floor as the wearer shifted her steps. The shoe uppers were fashioned from red, white, or green silk with increasingly elaborate embroidered motifs of auspicious symbols. The earlier flat socks evolved into contoured and footed soft "sleeping slippers" which women wore to bed on top of the binding cloth. The erotic appeal of the golden lotus

The Fetishism of Bound Feet and Tiny Shoes

William Rossi has suggested the bound foot was "the organ of ultimate sexual pleasure"; the soft fleshy cleavage on the underside of the foot was "the equivalent of the labia" for men (pp. 29–30). Although this view is corroborated by Chinese erotic paintings from the nineteenth and twentieth centuries, no premodern Chinese sources depict footbinding in this light.

Novels, poetry, and prose by premodern Chinese male scholars suggest that embroidered slippers and partially undressed, but still concealed, feet served as the locus of their erotic imagination. The first credible connoisseur of bound feet was the Yuan dynasty scholar-poet Yang Weizhen (also known as Yang Tieya, 1296–1370), who in his later years retired from the court and dallied in the garden city of Suzhou. To add to the merry-making, Yang drank from wine cups fashioned from courtesans' tiny shoes. Brothel drinking games involving the tiny shoe persisted and became more fanciful, as evinced by the connoisseur Fang Xuan's (probably a pseudonym) treatises first published in the last decade of the Qing dynasty (Levy, pp. 107–120).

The connoisseur Li Yu (c. 1610–1680)—no relation to the Southern Tang ruler—described the sexual appeal of the bound foot in both visual and tactile terms. In a bedroom scene in Li's erotic novel *The Carnal Prayer Mat*, the protagonist Vesperus removed all the clothes of Jade Scent but left her leggings on, because "in the last resort tiny feet need a pair of dainty little leggings above them if they are going to appeal" (p. 50). Li recounted his own experience of removing courtesans' stockings to fondle feet so soft that they feel "boneless" in an essay collection, *Casual Expressions of Idle Feeling.* Presum-ably the binding cloth was not removed. Li added: "Lying in bed with them, it is hard to stop fondling their golden lotus. No other pleasures of dallying with courtesans can surpass this experience" (Hanan, p. 68).

The most vivid Chinese account of the fetishism of shoes and feet during the height of the cult of the golden lotus is the erotic novel *The Plum in the Golden Vase,* first published in 1618. Presiding over a polygynist household, the protagonist Simen Qing is the paragon of male privileges and excesses. Females vie to get his attention, hence their heart's desires, by a parade of tiny shoes they designed and assembled. Simen was partial to red sleeping slippers; his love for them—and their wearer—was transference for his own desire to wear red shoes (chapter 28). Simen, a merchant, personifies the commodity culture that enabled new economies of pleasure and desire in seventeenth-century China.

Chinese fetishism assumes different meanings than that which crystallized in Europe in the second half of the nineteenth century, in part because the association of pleasure and guilt is absent in Confucian morality. But in China as in Europe, the fetishism of the foot found its most graphic expression in the spectacular details lavished onto high heel shoes. As a vessel for wine, plaything, or token of exchange, embroidered slippers were receptacles of boundless fantasy.

The very subject of footbinding has been fetishized in the West. As a stand-in for the exotic and erotic Orient, footbinding has continued to fascinate modern observers and collectors after its demise in China as a social practice.

was wrought of layered footwear as instruments of concealment.

Even at the heyday of the cult, many women did not have bound feet. Footbinding was more a privilege than a requirement. Women of Manchu descent, an ethnic minority group, eschewed footbinding, as did Hakka women, who shouldered back-breaking manual labor. After the Manchus became the rulers of China in 1644, they issued prohibition edicts that only served to make footbinding more popular among the subjugated Han Chinese majority.

The Anti-Footbinding Movement
The decline of footbinding can be attributed to internal and external factors. Domestically, it became a victim of its own success. As footbinding spread geographically outward and socially downward during the Qing dynasty (1644–1911), it lost its raison d'être and ceased to be a sign of exclusivity. Externally, Christian missionaries and merchants brought an imported concept of the natural God-given body as well as a new sartorial regime in the second half of the nineteenth century. Footbinding became so dated that it was synonymous with "feudal and backward China" in the Republican period (1912–1949). Although coastal women gave up the practice in the early decades of the twentieth century, girls in the remote southwestern province of Yunnan were forced to stop by the Communist regime only in the 1950s.

Ironically, on the eve of footbinding's decline, the paraphernalia of footbinding reached the height of its glory, surpassing previous centuries in rapidity of stylistic changes and ornamental techniques. Each region developed its own distinct footwear styles. New genres of patterns, snow clogs, and rain boots served the growing number of working-class women with bound feet. Footwear innovation continued into the 1920s and 30s, when women with bound feet updated their wardrobes with such Western styles as the Mary Jane, fastened with buttons and flesh-colored silk stockings.

In sum, there is not one footbinding but many. During each stage of its development the way of binding, shoe styles, social background of the women and their incentives are different; the regional diversities are also pronounced. But in the final analysis, the binding of feet was always motivated by a utopian impulse to overcome the body and to elevate one's status in the world.

See also **China: History of Dress; Fetish Fashion.**

BIBLIOGRAPHY

Feng, Jicai. *Three-Inch Golden Lotus.* Translated by David Wakefield. Honolulu: University of Hawaii Press, 1994. A realistic novella that explores the complex female psychology during the anti-footbinding period.

Hanan, Patrick. *The Invention of Li Yu.* Cambridge, Mass., and London: Harvard University Press, 1988. An introduction to the life and times of Li Yu, maverick writer and connoisseur of bound feet.

Ko, Dorothy. *Every Step a Lotus: Shoes for Bound Feet.* Berkeley and Los Angeles: University of California Press, 2001. Includes an illustrated chart of regional footwear styles and a discussion of shoemaking tools.

Levy, Howard S. *Chinese Footbinding: The History of a Curious Erotic Custom.* Taipei: Nantian shuju, 1984. A convenient summary of the six-volume *Caifei lu*, a Chinese encyclopedia on footbinding, and early Japanese scholarship on the subject.

Li Yu. *The Carnal Prayer Mat.* Translated by Patrick Hanan. Honolulu: University of Hawaii Press, 1990.

The Plum in the Golden Vase, or *Chin P'ing Mei.* Volume 2: *The Rivals.* Translated by David Tod Roy. Princeton, N.J.: Princeton University Press, 2001.

Rossi, William A. *The Sex Life of the Foot and Shoe.* Ware, Hertfordshire, U.K.: Wordsworth Editions, 1989.

Steele, Valerie. *Fetish: Fashion, Sex and Power.* New York and Oxford: Oxford University Press, 1996.

Wang, Ping. *Aching for Beauty.* Minneapolis: University of Minnesota Press, 2000. A Chinese woman's poetic evocation of the male and female desires that sustained the thousand-year custom.

Zhang, Bangji. *Mozhuang manlü.* In *Congshu jicheng chubian,* nos. 2864–2866. Changsha: Shangwu, 1939.

Dorothy Ko

FOOTWEAR. *See* **Shoes.**

FORD, TOM In his role as creative director for the Gucci Group, designing collections for both Gucci and Yves Saint Laurent, Tom Ford was central to early twenty-first-century fashion. Under Ford's direction,

Tom Ford. Ford began designing for Gucci in 1990, rescuing the company from serious financial trouble partly by placing greater emphasis on its line of accessories. AP/WIDE WORLD PHOTOS. REPRODUCED BY PERMISSION.

creativity and innovation shared equal value with marketing and promotion in the positioning of the brands.

Born in 1962 and raised in San Marcos, Texas, and Santa Fe, New Mexico, Ford first began his career as a model for television advertisements before studying interior design at Parsons School of Design in New York City. In his final year of school, he changed his focus to fashion design. As a freelance designer on Seventh Avenue, he first worked for Cathy Hardwick and then in 1988 in the jeans department of Perry Ellis, under the short-lived direction of Marc Jacobs.

In 1990, the company's worst year financially, Ford was appointed womenswear designer at Gucci. Because of loss of strategic and creative direction and in-house family feuding, the company was losing 340 billion lire annually. In 1992 Ford was appointed design director, and in 1994, creative director; by the first six months of 1995, the company's revenues had increased by 87 percent. This financial turnaround was largely achieved by a consolidation of the company's product range, editing out weak licenses for vulgarly branded goods and redesigning core items, typified by the reappearance of the classic Gucci loafer in rainbow hues (1991) and the success of the Gucci platform snaffle clog (1992).

The international recognition of Gucci as a producer of prêt-à-porter collections was crystallized by the autumn/winter season of 1995–1996. From the prevailing aesthetic of pared-down minimalism and understated luxury, Ford presented a sleek, retro-inspired collection evoking a somewhat louche sexuality. The look was defined by velvet hipster trousers with a kick at the heel and a narrowly cut silk shirt, accessorized with a large, unstructured shoulder bag and matching platform court shoes in patent leather with a metallic shine normally associated with car chassis.

The collection was pivotal, as it established a trend for the consumption of seasonal fashion defined not so much by a total look as by how the look could be attained through buying the "must-have" accessory. As Ford later suggested, "You have to get the product right, it's the most important aspect." Much of this success was achieved through the advertising campaigns the company produced with fashion photographer Mario Testino, where the glamorous proposition of the dressed models was matched on the opposite side of the spread by an isolated close-up of the accessory. The close relation between the image of Gucci and its advertising campaigns eventually produced a lapse in confidence, when for the spring/summer collections in 2003 the company ran an image of a model who had her pubic hair shaved into the Gucci "G." The image was widely criticized for being too blatantly sexual and in dubious taste. Meanwhile, the Gucci Group had acquired the Yves Saint Laurent (YSL) brand after the legendary designer retired from the couture. From an uncelebrated opening collection (largely due to the French press berating an American ready-to-wear designer for having the audacity to step into the most hallowed of shoes), the brand developed consistently and confidently, particularly from Ford's gaining access to the YSL archive.

Through his close relation to Domenico de Sole, CEO of the Gucci Group, Tom Ford was central to the increasing dominance of the company in the designer fashion and luxury goods market, as Gucci acquired stakes in Balenciaga, Alexander McQueen, Stella McCartney, Bottega Veneta, and Sergio Rossi. The unexpected 2003 announcement of Ford's departure from the Gucci group, effective in April 2004, shook the fashion world, and speculation immediately began about his successor as well as about his own future plans.

See also **Gucci; Saint Laurent, Yves; Shoes.**

BIBLIOGRAPHY

Ford, Tom, for Gucci. *Light. Visionaire* 24. New York: Visionaire Publishing, 1998. Unique, multiformat album of fashion and fine art published three times yearly in numbered, limited editions. Artists are given freedom to develop a theme. In issue 24 *Visionaire* and Tom Ford created the first such publication that is battery-operated. Only 3,300 copies were made.

Forden, Sara Gay. *The House of Gucci: A Sensational Story of Murder, Madness, Glamour, and Greed.* New York: Perennial, 2001.

Alistair O'Neill

FORMAL WEAR, MEN'S The quintessence of uniform elegance in men's wear must surely be those nearly unchanging garments described as "formal." The exact opposite of "casual" clothes, men's formal garments are as curiously elevating and ennobling as they are utilitarian and leveling. This might seem a contradiction in terms at first, but one has only to think of a "black-tie" event to realize that at least en masse, the uniform nature of the clothes—coded and easily recognizable globally—places all men in the same category, much like a uniform does for the army, navy, or air force. But like the armed forces, which have panoplies of different ranks, a tangible difference in provenance can be evinced in evening or formal clothes. Is this suit custom-made? Is that rented? Is that a hand-me-down? Is this a lucky find in a vintage market?

A black-tie event is a sea of ebony and ivory—all men, although from different ranks in society, at least visually and superficially are united by convention. Formal wear not only functions as a social leveling device for the men at a gathering, but it also provides a uniform backdrop (or perhaps, "black-drop") for the female guests who are of course, not restricted to the color black for their gowns. Formal clothes have an air of assured authority and confidence about them and are generally resistant to fashion, although of course some designers attempt to play with their strictures from collection to collection. But customers always seem to revert to the history, tradition, and timeless style of the unshakable classics.

The most recognizable formal wear costume is the black-tie—in the United States, usually referred to as the tuxedo and frequently shortened to "tux." In 1896, a mischievous, iconoclastic dandy, Griswold Lorillard, wore a shorter, black formal jacket (without tails) to a country club in Tuxedo Park, New York—and the name was established. The jacket part of the black-tie ensemble is sometimes referred to as a "dinner jacket," though that appellation is too limiting to encompass all its myriad social functions. Essentially, the terms all refer to the same costume, though some contend that the classic tuxedo jacket must have a shawl collar rather than peaked lapels, and many would permit no color other than black (some will allow cream). But these distinctions have more to do with the wearer's upbringing and taste as opposed to the outfit itself.

There are generally five styles to choose from: single-breasted, double-breasted, peaked lapels (usually double-breasted) and single- or double-breasted shawl collared. Basically, it is a black suit but ennobled by a silk or gros-grain facing on the lapels, the better to provide a suggestion of luxury and attention to detail. And black-tie is, and should only ever be, black—or perhaps midnight blue, which the late royal couturier Sir Hardy Amies always maintained looked blacker than black itself, under artificial light. A corresponding black silk or grosgrain stripe runs down the sides of the trouser—again echoing uniform pants.

The shirt is always white. It can be made in anything from the finest zephyr cotton to polyester—but it must always be white. Pearl buttons or studs are the norm and a wing collar a matter of choice and taste, although if one is sported it should be buttoned on or studded through—not ready-made. And the bow tie is not considered one if it is not hand-tied. Aficionados frown upon the ready-made examples with elastic and hooks. Cummerbunds are reserved for the most formal of occasions, but they do have a small function which rescues them from being pure items of conspicuous consumption; in their pleats is concealed a tiny pocket for small essentials.

While the basic elements of formal wear are conveniently precise, the wearer is able to exert his individuality through the sporting of discreet (or not so discreet) items of jewelry—these for the most part being concealed by the jacket cuff in the form of links or by the jacket itself if a spirited watch chain or fob is attached to a waistcoat.

The luxe de luxe of formal wear is white-tie, an ensemble that includes tails, wing-collared shirt, hand-tied white bow tie usually in a cotton pique or fine grosgrain, and corresponding white waistcoat—traditionally three buttoned and cut low to expose maximum shirt front. For the feet, nothing but glacé, glossy pumps will suffice, topped off with a pair of silk, decorative bows. And at the other end of the body, a top hat—in glossy black silk—is the point finale. This look was established as a sartorial must by the early 1920s. Whether formal or extremely formal, the basic sonorous quality of the ensemble is the color black As the costume historian James Laver has pointed out, since the eighteenth century, all attempts to introduce color to male formal attire have failed or have been derided. A shiny, colorful, patterned male evening ensemble is unthinkable; such is the continuing power and influence of tradition.

Formal daywear is now found primarily in the world of sports, and especially of horse racing and boat racing. Royal Ascot, Goodwood, and Henley are social institutions where formal clothes are demanded and specific dress code requirements are imposed on all who attend. Formal wear for Royal Ascot would be full morning dress (dove gray or black); the groom or the bride's father at a formal daytime wedding would wear the same ensemble. The coat is sometimes referred to as a cutaway coat (being a frock coat with the corners removed), not to be confused with a tailcoat, which is cut to the waist in the front, and sports a pair of tails behind. A gray, buff, or for the more fashion conscious, brightly colored and pat-

Man in formal attire. Elegant and sleek, a man's Black Tie costume, or tuxedo, is comprised of jacket, pants with matching stripe, white shirt, and hand-tied bow tie. © JOSE LUIS PELAEZ, INC./CORBIS. REPRODUCED BY PERMISSION.

terned silk waistcoat, is worn beneath and teamed with a tie, cravat, or some other individualistic neck wear—but never a bow.

The origin of formal wear is open to discussion and challenge, but one name forever associated with formality, uniformity, and simplicity was Beau Brummell—king of the dandies and a one-time favorite of King George IV. He is often referred to as the "father of modern male formal costume" as he eschewed the brightly hued silken finery and powdered wigs generally worn at court for a sober suit of midnight blue-black with minimal jewelry (a signet ring was permissible), no wig, no perfume but plenty of shaving and washing—a well-scrubbed appearance being the natural partner to formal dress.

It is the Beau whom many think invented or at least popularized the under-the-foot strapped pantaloon (from the French—*Pend en talon*—to the heel) and set the standard for what would become the ubiquitous tailcoat. Brummell was belligerently exact when it came to matters of formal and what came to be "court dress." To

Men's formal wear. Formal attire for men has seen little change since the nineteenth century. These men are modeling the fashions of 1932, ranging from the highly formal tuxedo on the right to less formal business attire at left. © BETTMANN/CORBIS. REPRODUCED BY PERMISSION.

a would-be dandy seeking sartorial approval he snapped, "Do you call that *thing* a coat?" Brummell made formality look simple—challenging the brightly colored costumes in feminine fabrics like silk and velvet for the sharp masculinity of well-cut wool and flannel. Thus formal wear showed and still does show its class by line, not content.

In the twenty-first century, the reduction of occasions on which to wear formal clothes has curiously thrown a sharper light on these style stalwarts. Not even a hundred years ago, BBC radio announcers were required to wear black-tie—the premise being that the stiff formality of the shirt, bow tie, and exact-fit jacket aided the gravitas of the voice and the assurance of the delivery. At weddings and funerals, formal clothes were obligatory and many other social situations demanded this "civilian uniform" as a means of maintaining a required ambiance, from balls and tea dances to memorials and visits to the opera. Just a hundred years ago, dressing for dinner in one's own home could have meant having to wear full formal dress—even if it was just with family members. A visit to almost any vintage clothing fair or market will reveal several yesteryear formal garments for men—a clue as to how vital they were and perhaps how few the occasions for which they are needed in the early 2000s.

In the mid-1950s, everyone who could afford to have at least one formal outfit owned one, which would most often be mothballed until needed. Those who did not own formal wear relied on borrowing from relatives or renting. The formal rental market is still hugely successful with providing formal wear for weddings to royal garden parties and theatrical opening nights. The respect that formal wear lends to the occasion is thus implied—even if not required or requested—and many will opt for formality to suggest this. Those who have chosen casual attire will be thrown into sharp contrast. Perhaps formal wear represents the last bastion of constancy in clothing with a conspiratorial nod to time, not trend.

See also **Brummell, George (Beau); Tuxedo.**

BIBLIOGRAPHY

Curtis, Bryan, and John Bridges. *A Gentleman Gets Dressed Up: Knowing What to Wear, How to Wear It, and When to Wear It.* New York: Rutledge Hill Press, 2003.

Flusser, Alan. *Dressing the Man: Mastering the Art of Permanent Fashion.* New York: HarperCollins Publisher's Inc., 2002.

Hollander, Anne. *Sex and Suits: The Evolution of Modern Dress.* Tokyo and New York: Kodansha International, 1995.

Robin Dutt

FORTUNY, MARIANO Although Mariano Fortuny considered himself a painter, he pursued various critical and aesthetic interests. He is primarily remembered for remarkable layers of dyed and patterned fabrics, which he created between 1906 and 1949. Born in Granada, Spain, to an upper-class family of distinguished painters, Mariano Fortuny y Madrazo (1871–1949) is more often associated with the city of Venice, Italy, where he lived and worked most of his life.

As a child, Fortuny was surrounded by eclectic assemblages of ephemera: antique textile remnants, carpets, costumes, vestments, furniture, armor, and implements of war collected as art objects. Following the untimely death of his father, the painter Mariano Fortuny y Marsal, in 1874, young Mariano, his mother, and his sister moved to Paris in 1875. Although he considered himself self-taught, he was guided toward the arts by his uncle Raymundo, a painter, and informally by the sculptor Auguste Rodin. He later expanded his education in Germany, where he studied physics and chemistry. In 1889 the Fortuny family traveled to Venice; finding it a romantic and artistic center, they moved there permanently in 1890.

Business Innovations
Fortuny's garments and textiles fuse history, anthropology, and art. By blending various dyes he achieved luminous, unique colors. Resurrecting the ancient craft of pleating fabric, artistically symbolizing a reflection of the sun's rays, Fortuny developed his own interpretation of this craft and registered his heated pleating device in 1909. Between 1901 and 1933 he registered twenty-two patents, all of which related to garments and printing methods. Prolific in artistic pursuits, he printed etchings, invented a type of photography paper, designed lamps and furniture, bound books, and maintained an extensive, private reference library. He displayed his own artistic creations in the ground floor showroom of his residential palazzo.

An interest in Richard Wagner's operatic productions drew Fortuny to Bayreuth, Germany, in 1892. Fascinated by the dramatic spectacle unfolding before him, he developed a revolutionary, indirect lighting system that transformed cumbersome stage scenery and obsolete gas lamps, significantly changing the atmosphere onstage. Commissioned by an art patron, he constructed two enormous, vaulted quarter spheres of cloth, expanded over a collapsible metal frame, which amplified color and sound. The spheres were 225 square meters (269 square yards) in area and 7 meters (7.6 yards) high. His first theatrical costume was a figure-enveloping, border-printed scarf titled the Knossos, presented in a private theater in 1907. Isadora Duncan was the first to wear the Knossos scarf. At the home of his patron Cotesse de Bearn in 1906 in Paris, his stage lighting system first appeared as well as his first textile creation printed with geometric motifs. This theatrical endeavor transformed his awareness and appreciation of materials into a tactile form, quite separated from his representational works.

Fortuny preferred working alone to avoid conflict, illustrating his theory that an artist must control all aspects of the creative act, but he did allow collections of his fabrics, gowns, and accessories to be sold in a Paris boutique operated by Paul Poiret. His gowns were also available at Liberty of London and his shops in Paris, London, and New York.

Personal Image and Acknowledgments
Throughout his life Fortuny maintained a striking figure, dressing in artistic combinations, even regional and ethnic dress. He married Henriette Negrin, an accomplished French seamstress who designed patterns for his garments. Together, they developed methods and practices in the atelier of their Palazzo Orfei residence. Driven by spirited curiosity rather than training as a couturier, Fortuny depended on ancient and regional styles that became the foundation of his modern and comfortable styles for women, costumes for the theater, and yardage for interiors.

In an atmosphere of antiquated splendor, Fortuny dressed Venice's artistic community at the turn of the century, where Americans and Europeans—including the actress Sarah Bernhardt, the dancer Isadora Duncan, and the poet Gabriele D'Annunzio—were among those who sought cultural legitimacy with the notion that the classical and the beautiful were one. Artists of the theater and American travelers were the first to wear his gowns in public.

Artistic Hallmarks
Among the garments viewed in museum collections, the loosely twisted, pleated gowns labeled Delphos and Peplos, of Greek origin, are exhibited more frequently than any others. His diagrams of the Delphos and the wooden structure fitted with ceramic tubes that heat-set his signature pleats are also popular museum exhibits. Similar avant-garde dresses, referred to as tea gowns, enhanced Fortuny's popularity with the wave of orientalism that dominated the arts in the years before World War I.

Echoing his knowledge of textile history, Fortuny produced his imaginative manipulations through printed and applied methods, freeing him to experiment. His vertical pleating and undulating silk and cotton yardage yielded natural elasticity, flowing effortlessly over the contours of female forms. Delicate Murano glass beads were laced onto silk cording and hand-stitched along hems, seams, and necklines, giving weight to an even edge, similar to the ancient Greek method of weighting fabric with metal. His method was to piece-dye cut lengths, frequently layering natural and, later, aniline dyes and occasionally incorporating agents to resist previously applied colors, which resulted in random, transparent irregularity. Clients were required to return the garment to the island factory of La Giudecca in order to clean and pleat the material.

For his imported silk, cotton, and velvet surfaces, Fortuny studied Japanese and Southeast Asian methods of hand-printing, including the *pochoir* method, for precise color transfer to cloth. Block printing and silk screening, positioned on seams in central areas of a garment and along edges, provided striking effects. Fortuny combined metal powder with pigments to simulate shimmering metallic thread, inspired by sixteenth-century velvets. On occasion, more than a dozen processes—including paintbrushes, sponges, and decolorization—were implemented on each unique length. The paintbrushes and sponges were used to create a marbled effect, already a method known in Lyon, to create the same effect of patchiness. Artisans were directed to incorporate various methods to correct or retouch the yardage. Textile patterns and motifs reflected his studies in the art museums of Venice, where he made note of the dress depicted in canvases. When he adapted the traditional practice of goffering, realizing a relief in velvet pile, he may have used block-printing methods and silk screening. His pattern adaptations of regional dress, hand-stitched with one of three labels (Mariano Fortuny Venise, Fabriqué en Italie, or Fortuny de Pose), can be identified as variations inspired by ancient Greek dress for men or women, dress of the Renaissance and the Middle Ages, the Moroccan djellaba, North African *bournous*, Arabic *abaia* (a kind of caftan), Japanese kimono, Coptic tunic, and Indian sari.

Fortuny in the Twenty-first Century

In 1922 Fortuny, Inc., was established in collaboration with the American interior designer Elsie Lee McNeill, later Countess Gozzi. Henriette remained in the palazzo to oversee the production of silk and velvet garments, while Fortuny moved production to a factory on the island of La Giudecca. After his death in 1949, garments were no longer produced. Gozzi continued to promote the mysteries of his textiles for almost forty years, until she sold her rights to printing yardage to her friend and attorney, Maged Riad, in 1998. In the early twenty-first century, Riad's children became responsible for the firm in New York, and his brother took over as the artistic director of production on La Giudecca. Appointments for research in the Palazzo Fortuny are limited, though the building is frequently the venue for art exhibitions, managed by the city of Venice.

The company's contemporary collection of yardage contains approximately 260 original patterns and color combinations printed on silk, velvet, and Egyptian cotton, including irregular application by artisans, who give each length an aged and artistic patina. Antique textile dealers and international specialists represent original yardage.

Since Fortuny creations were originally an attraction for travelers, interpretations of his artistry have been faithfully recovered by Venetia Studium, directed by Lino Lando and available to the visitor to Venice. Connois-

seurs, collectors, historians, and antique dealers agree that Mariano Fortuny achieved an elegant, impressive balance, fusing art and science. His legacy proves his relevance.

See also **Art and Fashion; Clothing, Costume, and Dress; Orientalism; Proust, Marcel.**

BIBLIOGRAPHY

Deschodt, Anne-Marie, and Doretta Davanzo Poli. *Fortuny.* Translated by Anthony Roberts. New York: Harry N. Abrams, 2001.

D'Osma, Guillermo. *Fortuny: Mario Fortuny, His Life and Work.* New York: Rizzoli International, 1980.

Fortuny, Mariano. *Fortuny.* New York: Fashion Institute of Technology, 1981. Published in conjunction with the exhibition *Fortuny*, shown at the Fashion Institute of Technology and the Art Institute of Chicago.

Fuso, Silvio. "Fortuny the Magician." *FMR* 120 (February/ March 2003).

Steele, Valerie. *Paris Fashion: A Cultural History.* 2nd rev. ed. New York: Berg, 1998.

Gillion Carrara

FULLING Fulling, or milling, is a finish that produces a wool fabric softer, denser, heavier, and thicker than greige goods (fabric from the loom). Wool greige goods are reedy (loosely woven). Because fulled fabric is more compact, it has better cover and appearance. The fabric is shrunk under controlled conditions to make it compact. Shrinkage may be by as much as 50 percent, and it must be controlled or the fabric will become hard and harsh. Almost all wool woven fabric will be fulled to some degree; many knit fabrics will also be fulled. The amount of fulling will depend on the characteristics of the finished fabric.

Woolen fabrics, made from yarns with fibers that have been only carded are often heavily fulled. Carding and combing are yarn processes. Carding aligns the fibers somewhat where combing further aligns the fibers before spinning. Combed yarns have longer staple fibers and fewer fiber ends than carded yarns. Melton cloth is an example of fabric of such considerable fulling as to have a feltlike texture. Melton cloth is so heavily fulled that the warp and filling yarns are not seen. The fabric is smooth with a very short nap. Napping is a finishing process where the fiber ends are brushed to the surface of the fabric, producing a softer fabric. Melton and loden cloth are used for cold weather coating. Other fabrics that are heavily fulled are duffel—which is used in overcoats and blankets—kersey, and boiled wool. Boiled wool is not actually boiled but heavily fulled.

Worsted fabrics, made from yarns in which the fibers have been carded and combed, are lightly fulled. Since worsteds are firmly woven, they tend not to shrink as easily as loosely woven fabrics. The fibers in worsteds are less mobile and thus are unable to interlock as easily as soft, fluffy fabrics. Knitted sweaters are also lightly fulled.

The Process

The fulling process takes advantage of the microstructure of wool fabric. The outer layer of the wool fiber consists of overlocking scales that can be seen under a microscope. The scales on the surface of the fiber point toward the tip and will move only in one direction. In the presence of moisture, heat, and friction, these scales will open up, move, and become interlocked. Once these scales interlock, the change is permanent and the fabric shrinks and thus becomes more compact.

The wool fabric is scoured to remove any processing oils that may be on the fabric. Then the fabric is placed in a rotary fulling or jig machine. The fabric is passed between stainless steel rollers pounded by clappers. Water with a mild alkaline soap and sodium carbonate or a weak acid dampens the fabric. Wool fibers need moisture, mechanical action, and heat for the scales on the fibers to interlock, and the friction from the pounding produces the necessary heat.

The fabric is carefully dried after the fulling process. To give it additional softness, the fabric may be brushed or napped.

See also **Wool.**

BIBLIOGRAPHY

Carty, Peter, and Michael S. Byrne. *The Chemical and Mechanical Finishing of Textile Materials.* Newcastle upon Tyne, U.K.: Newcastle upon Tyne Polytechnic Products, 1987.

Slade, Philip E. *Handbook of Fiber Finish Technology.* New York: Marcel Dekker, 1998.

Robyne Williams

FUR Fur garments occupy a long and significant place in European history. From the fourteenth to seventeenth century, the kings and queens of England, for example, issued royal proclamations in order to regulate furs and fur apparel and, especially, to reserve the more exclusive furs of marten, fox, gray squirrel, and ermine for the aristocratic and clerical elite. These royal proclamations became part of what is known as "sumptuary legislation" in which everyday practices involving clothing, drinking, and eating were subject to public governance and scrutiny. Thus, from very early on furs and fur garments were regulated, not only in order to establish a hierarchy of desirable fur, but also to create recognizable codes of social status in the wearer of fur. While by law the most exclusive furs were reserved for the higher nobility, the middle class wore less costly furs such as beaver, otter, hare, and fox, and the peasantry wore the hardier, rougher furs of wolf, goat, and sheepskin.

Very little appears to have changed in six hundred years. In the global economy of the twenty-first century, the luxurious full-length fur coat is subject to various processes of identification, as a commodity and sign of elite standing and material wealth from England to Japan. What is markedly different at the turn of the twenty-first century, is that fur garments, especially those worn by women, now come under intense scrutiny for the dangers and risks they pose to the planet's ecological stability. Politics and fur fashions have become so intertwined in the contemporary setting that it is impossible to discuss fur fashions without reference to ecological struggles, not to mention the challenges faced by indigenous peoples in Canada, Greenland, and Alaska whose very livelihood, in some cases, still depends on the fur trade initially created by Europe's early modern industrial economy and mercantile trade.

Class, Gender, and Sex Distinctions

In the Middle Ages the exclusivity of some furs meant that they were used sparingly. The practice of "purfling" was invented in which the more expensive furs were reserved for decorative trim, while cheaper furs were used to finish the lining. There are some examples of excessive expenditures on the part of nobles such as Charles VI of France who apparently used 20,000 squirrel pelts to line a garment. It was not until the fur trade was established in the sixteenth century between France, and then England, and the New World (what is now Canada), that furs were available to European consumers in newer and larger supplies. Beaver fur was especially important to this new trade initiative and, in fact, became the primary economic unit from the mid-sixteenth century to the 1870s. In England, the technologically innovative process of felting beaver fur was used to produce the broad-brimmed beaver hats worn by the opposing religious and political groups of the seventeenth century, the Puritans and Cavaliers. One of the most significant promoters of the cavalier style of beaver hat was Charles II. With his restoration to the throne in 1660, the beaver hat emerged as a dominant fashion article supported no less than by Charles II's incorporation of the Hudson's Bay Company by royal charter. Thus, the English fur trade was firmly established and once again fur circulated in abundance among the nobility as well as among a rising mercantile class of consumers as a distinctive sign of class and imperial wealth.

In Russia, similar motivations to expand colonial governance and mercantile wealth were carried out through fur trading. From the mid-eighteenth century and throughout the nineteenth century, Russian frontier merchants traded in sea otter pelts from northern Pacific waters to fulfill the clothing demands of the Chinese elite. Competition from China and eventually the United States and Britain led to various economic and territorial accommodations that resulted in a treaty with the United States and the formation of the Russian-American company in 1824, and between the latter and the Hudson's Bay Company in 1839.

The history of the fur trade and fur garments is in many ways a history of imperial class distinctions but one that is also marked by gender and cultural differences.

Influenced by the Russian fur market, in the earlier period in England the fur coat was worn both by men and women. The fur was mostly on the inside, visible as trim on the collar and cuffs. But during the late nineteenth century and throughout the twentieth century, fur became increasingly identified with elite women's fashions and the fur coat was "reversed" in the sense that fur was now worn almost exclusively on the outside.

The 1920s saw the image of the fur-clad woman emerge as a sign of unevenly distributed economic wealth. From debates in the British House of Commons in February of 1926 over the benefits of socialism in providing women with practical and affordable cloth coats against the excesses of capitalism represented by a luxury fur coat, to G. W. Pabst's brilliant silent film *Joyless Streets* (*Die Freudlose Gasse*, 1925) in which Greta Garbo plays the heroine who is offered a fur coat in exchange for her sexual services, the image of the fur-clad bourgeois woman not only signified material wealth; it also came to represent, in contradictory fashion, feminine passivity and female sexual power.

Political Protests and Fur Fashion Design

The symbolic power associated with the fur garment in the Middle Ages ensured its value for contemporary fashion as a mark of distinction in the making of luxury commodities. Since the late nineteenth century and the publication of Leopold von Sacher-Masoch's novel, *Venus in Furs*, the fur coat's value increased with its strong identification with sexual fetishism. However, by the 1970s the fur coat was transformed from desirable female commodity to a symbol for animal rights' activism. Efforts to ensure that the international trade in specimens of wild animals, including fur by-products, did not threaten their survival resulted in the national and international legislation of the Endangered Species Act (1973) in the United States and the Convention on International Trade in Endangered Species of Wild Fauna and Flora (1975). The antisealing campaigns off the coast of Labrador in Canada in the 1970s anticipated the antifur protests of the 1980s and 1990s, headed by organizations such as People for the Ethical Treatment of Animals (PETA) in the United States and LYNX in England, which were successful, momentarily, in diminishing fur sales. More recently, the European Union tried to introduced a ban on the import of wild fur from countries using the leg-hold trap. The ban was temporarily postponed pending an international agreement on humane trapping standards among Canada, the United States, Russia, and the European Union. In response to the global politicization of fur garments, fur manufacturers developed new dyeing and tailoring techniques in order to change the conventional image of the elite fur-clad woman as well as to "disguise" fur, although the Federal Fur Products Labeling Act requires that all fur products bear a label indicating, among other things, whether the fur product was artificially colored. The fashion for fur knitting, popularized in the 1960s, was rejuvenated as a

INUIT DRESS AND SOCIAL CLASS

Inuit now use combinations of traditional and southern-style garments to convey group affiliation, gender, age, role, status, social organization, interaction with neighboring groups, and changing technology. . . . Contemporary Inuit clothing provides an intriguing unwritten essay reflecting the social, economic, and technological changes to which Inuit have adapted over the last generation.

Judy Hall, Jill Oakes, and Sally Qimmiu'naaq Webster, eds., *Sanatujut, Pride in Women's Work: Copper and Caribou Inuit Clothing Traditions.*

result of these new design strategies. The synthetic textile manufacturers benefited from the antifur media campaigns and developed "fake fur" alternatives. In an interesting twist on the environmental implications of natural fur products, the Montréal-based fashion designer Mariouche Gagné recycled fur into fashion accessories, arguing that fur was a biodegradable product and, therefore, more ecologically friendly than the synthetic alternatives offered by the "green" marketplace.

In the early 1990s more established fashion designers such as Jean Paul Gaultier and Isaac Mizrahi tried to give their turn on fur fashion an edge of political correctness by creating designs that incorporated Inuit and First Nations motifs and images. First Nations and Inuit communities responded to this politics of appropriation, as well as to the economic devastation of their participation in the contemporary fur trade, by forming their own political organizations, for example, Indigenous Survival International. They also made use of public institutions—the British Museum in London, and the Canadian Museum of Civilization in Ottawa—to exhibit traditional as well as contemporary fur fashions in an effort to educate the general public about the symbolic and practical dimensions of fur in northern societies and economies.

See also **Muffs.**

BIBLIOGRAPHY

Emberley, Julia. *The Cultural Politics of Fur.* Ithaca, N.Y.: Cornell University Press, 1997. Comprehensive historical and cultural overview of the history of fur and fashion.

Hall, Judy, Jill Oakes, and Sally Qimmiu'naaq Webster, eds., *Sanatujut, Pride in Women's Work: Copper and Caribou Inuit Clothing Traditions.* Hull, Quebec: Canadian Museum of Civilization, 1994. Excellent book on fur, clothing, and Inuit culture and society.

Pelts: Politics of the Fur Trade. Dir. Nigel Markham. Videocassette. National Film Board of Canada, 1989. An example of the environmental movement's critique of fur fashion industry.

Steele, Valerie. *Fetish: Fashion, Sex, and Power*. New York: Oxford University Press, 1996. Authoritative text on fetishism and fashion, including fur fetishes.

Julia Emberley

FUTURE OF FASHION Predicting the future of fashion can be as analytical as market research and statistical analysis allow, or as speculative as the predictions William Norwich of the *New York Times* received when in April 2003 he playfully asked the fashion world's favorite psychic the question, "Where is the future of fashion?" Attempts to influence the future of fashion—made at times by dress reformers, moralists, and social thinkers—have invariably had little effect. Actual influences on fashion have typically stemmed from changing technologies, political events, and the creativity of certain individuals.

The manufacturing of clothes has always been affected by technological advances. The sewing machine revolutionized the clothing industry in the nineteenth century, and zippers altered clothing construction when they were perfected for use in the 1930s. In the early 2000s, technological innovations in fabrics influence how designers think about clothing, with textiles being developed that have properties unheard of in natural fibers. The abilities of these high-tech fabrics to stretch to overwhelming sizes or change their structure according to temperatures inspire clothing designers and blur the lines between fashion and industrial design. The Italian firm Corpo Nove designed a shirt woven with titanium that reacts to shifts in temperature. Wrinkles in the fabric are released when the shirt is exposed to hot air. Another item from the firm is a nylon jacket with a cooling system. The changing face of communications is also influencing styles of the future. A nylon jacket, manufactured by Industrial Clothing Design, a venture of Philips Electronics and Levi Strauss and Company, features a "fully integrated communications and entertainment system" (Lupton, p. 153).

Designers are also looking at ways of incorporating clothing with other functions of daily life. The C.P. Company has produced jackets that transform into chairs, tents or sleeping mattresses. Ixilab, a Japanese firm, designed plastic shorts with a cushion in the rear that inflates for the wearer to have a place to sit. New ideas for multifunctional clothing are also coming from industrial designers. A class called Weaving Material and Habitation at Harvard's Graduate School of Design "has been experimenting with Lycra-spandex type materials that can stretch out to four times their original size. A poncho or sweater might expand into a 7-foot-by-4-foot tarp" (Stevenson, p. 28).

Throughout fashion history, shifts in styles have been attributed to political and historical events. America's war with Iraq has elicited reactions from fashion designers ranging from antiwar sentiments to militaristic overtones. Proponents of various political and social issues attempt to influence what people wear and how clothes are produced. Antifur organizations frequently disrupt fashions shows featuring animal fur. The exploitation of labor is another controversial issue. Some politically minded consumers boycott clothes produced in factories and countries considered to have unfair labor practices. For some designers, these issues resonate; Katharine Hamnett has said that her goal is "the hope of making clothing that is environmentally friendly" (Jones and Mair, p. 209).

Primarily the fashion designers, in their roles as creators, determine the course of fashion. As a result, clothing designers are often asked to look into the future. Over time, their ideas and themes relating to these predictions remain almost constant. In 1968, André Courrèges described the future of fashion: "Women have become liberated little by little through thought, work, and clothes. I cannot imagine that they will ever turn back. Perhaps they will continue to suffer occasionally to be beautiful, but more than ever they seek to be both beautiful and free" (*Fashion, Art, and Beauty*, p. 140). He might have said the same in the early 2000s.

In her 1982 book *Fashion 2001*, Lucille Khornak asked fashion designers to each select a garment that would reflect fashions in 2001, and she interviewed them about how fashions would change by 2001. Many of the predictions made were unlikely to be achieved in that short period: "Paco Rabonne predicts that the clothes of the future will be premolded, bound or welded—no longer will they be sewn" (Khornak, p. 7). Issey Miyake is one designer rethinking how to make clothes for the future. Miyake's A-POC (A Piece of Cloth) features knitted tubes of fabric with markings for an outfit. When purchased, the fabric is cut by the wearer to make different articles of clothing. But ideas such as these are beyond the realm of mainstream fashion in the early twenty-first century.

One of the ongoing influences on fashion is the shift in women's roles in society. Fashion designers look at these changes from various angles and possibilities: the approach of unisex or androgynous clothing; the working woman's wardrobe as compared with men's wear; or the validity of femininity now that women are supposedly equal. The result is a spectrum of styles that caters to a diverse group of women, yet retains many stereotypes. Fashion continues to represent female sexuality as both demure, with pleats and bows and flowing chiffon, and as aggressive, with leather, corsetry, and body-revealing shapes. This dichotomy was featured in a 20 July 2003 *New York Times Magazine* fashion editorial of "good girl/bad girl" clothing.

The human body plays as integral a role as the clothes for many fashion designers working in the early 2000s. The idea of clothing as a "second skin" is often discussed when designers speak of the future of clothing. This concept has yet to be achieved with the wearing of only body stockings, or as Jean Paul Gaultier predicted in 1982 that we "spray on a latex body suit" (Khornak, p. 62). Yet this idea of a second skin continues to interest Gaultier and other designers. For his Fall 2003 collection, Gaultier created patterned bodysuits, worn under clothes, including one outlining the body's arteries. More often fashion designers attempt to mold the body into other shapes. While the concept differs little from bustles of the nineteenth century, the results found in the early twenty-first century differ greatly. As Walter van Beirendonck, the Belgian designer for Wild and Lethal Trash, said, "the body of the future will be different" (Lupton, p. 187).

How fashion designers will manifest their ideas depends partly on the changing structure of the fashion industry and the evolving needs, and demands, of consumers. There remains the ongoing question regarding the demise of French couture and the stimulus to fashion from street styles. In *The End of Fashion*, Teri Agins argues that street style, consumer demands, and profit making have changed and will continue to alter the fashion industry. "In today's high-strung, competitive marketplace, those who will survive the end of fashion will reinvent themselves enough times and with enough flexibility and resources to anticipate, not manipulate, the twenty-first century customer" (Agins, p. 16). While Agins's theories apply to the marketplace, fashion in the twenty-first century still belongs to the elusive world of luxury, status, sex, and glamour. While fashion is known to be fleeting, many predictions about its future are slow to arrive.

See also **Fashion, Historical Studies of; Fashion Designer; Fashion Industry; Gaultier, Jean-Paul; Miyake, Issey.**

BIBLIOGRAPHY

Agins, Teri. *The End of Fashion.* New York: HarperCollins, 1999.

Braddock, E. Sarah, and Marie O'Mahony. *Techno Textiles: Fabrics for Fashion and Design.* New York: Thames and Hudson, Inc., 1999. Reprint 2001.

Breward, Christopher. *The Culture of Fashion.* Manchester, U.K.: Manchester University Press, 1995.

Fashion, Art, and Beauty. Metropolitan Museum of Art Bulletin 26, no. 3 (November 1967).

Jones, Terry, and Avril Mair, eds. *Fashion Now.* Köln, Germany: Taschen, 2003.

Khornak, Lucille. *Fashion 2001.* New York: Viking Press, 1982.

Lupton, Ellen. *Skin: Surface, Substance + Design.* New York: Princeton Architectural Press, 2002.

Norwich, William. "Change Your Life, Boost Your Aura." *New York Times Magazine,* 27 April 2003, 63–67.

———. "The Mirror Has Two Faces." *New York Times Magazine,* 20 July 2003, 48–54.

Stevenson, Seth. "Gimme Temporary Shelter." *New York Times Magazine,* 18 May 2003, 26–30.

Donna Ghelerter

FUTURIST FASHION, ITALIAN Futurism in fashion is not limited to the artistic movement alone. The pervasive conceptual and visual influence of futurist art at the beginning of the twentieth century accounts for the fact that the term "futurism" continues to be applied—in the case of fashion to designs that are made from unorthodox materials, demonstrate new technologies and shapes, and display colorful dynamism. Futurism as a modernist movement was born on 20 February 1909 when Filippo Tommaso Marinetti published his manifesto "Manifeste du Futurisme" in the Paris daily *Le Figaro*. His aim was to extol the shock of the new (as cubism had done previously). However, whereas the provocation had previously been limited to museums or books, Marinetti wanted to extend it to social and political life. While futurist paintings mixed stylistic idioms from cubism and divisionism, its poetry, music, photography, film, and drama expanded along more abstract principles like speed, novelty, violence, technology, nationalism, and urbanity, which were often expressed according to prior formulated declarations. For fashion the programs were written by Giacomo Balla in the form of the "Futurist Manifesto of Men's Clothing" of 1914, followed by his "The Anti-Neutral Clothing: Futurist Manifesto" of the same year; in 1920 the "Manifesto of Futurist Women's Fashion" by Volt (pseudonym of Vincenzo Fanni); 1932 saw the "Manifesto to Change Men's Fashion" by the brothers Ernesto and Ruggero Michahelles; then Marinetti collaborated with Enrico Prampolini and a couple of second-generation futurists on "Futurist Manifesto: The Italian Hat," and in 1933 the "Futurist Manifesto: The Italian Tie" was formulated by Renato di Bosso and Ignazio Scurto.

The trajectory of these various programs can be constructed parallel to changes in futurist art from the avant-garde protest of its first generation, through the drama of World War I and sobriety of the time after the conflict, and the decorative subjectivism of the interwar years, to the rise in nationalist culture that would lead to the close association in the early 1930s between futurism and fascist Italy. The manifestos about fashion accordingly move from the direct intervention into culture by transforming the appearance of man—and to a lesser extent woman—in the street, where it was hoped that manners and mores would follow radical alterations in the bourgeois dress code, via a utilitarian attitude to dress as expression of communal principles, and the design of decorative and colorful costumes, to the fervent declaration of a nationalist dress. These various attitudes are not dissimilar to those that other art movements displayed vis-à-vis fashion, for example, aesthetic dress in Vienna or Proletkult clothing in 1920s U.S.S.R. Only futurism, however, ran through the entire range of oppositional clothing, from radical individualism to collective uniform, from decadent subjectivity of sartorial expression to formal invention in the construction of clothes.

Despite the founding role of poetry (with its onomatopoetic "parole in libertà") futurist aesthetics were disseminated markedly through painting. This implies a leaning toward decorative rather than structural solutions. And it favors the alteration of visual appearances and style (artistic, mode of living) rather than changing the sociopolitical foundation of artistic production proper. Similarly, fashion in futurism was often conceived as decorated surfaces of fabrics and textiles, where the introduction of color functioned as a novel element. An actual change in the cut and construction of clothes was comparatively rare.

From its very beginning futurism had a strong performative quality. Through the primacy of speed and dynamics, the representation of objects in movement became paramount. This was demonstrated not only through actual performances—although the poetry readings, musical soirées, and theater pieces, as well as demonstrative excursion in the motorcar, initiated an early concept of "performance art." Significantly, futurist photographs and canvases aimed at showing successive stages of an object moving through space. This in turn accounts for the early significance of fashion, as an aesthetic expression that is directly—and almost exclusively—applicable to the active and activated body. Futurists like Balla and Fortunato Depero, who both designed costumes for the Ballets Russes in Paris, realized the opportunity of playing with volumes, density of material, and animated objects. Balla's early designs between 1912 and 1914 show the attempt to break the surface of the body into fractions and lend movement to even heavy and static cloth. He hoped that the painted "speedlines" and colorful beams on the fabric would render even the most conservative and immovable individual a model of dynamism. Balla himself sported his designs well into the 1930s and conceived a rapid manner of walking and moving appropriate for the aesthetic principles of his dress. In contrast Marinetti, Depero, and others favored more staid sartorial expressions, wherein brightly colored waistcoats or ties offered the habitual outlet for individualism (1920s). Whereas men's bourgeois suits, as the somber constructed mainstay of modernity, offered the most obvious target for a futurist reform of the dress-code, women's fashion with its seasonal changes and decorated surfaces did not appear to require the same reformist zeal. Thus the futurist contribution to female dress is to be found outside Italy, in the "simultaneous" dresses by Sonia Delaunay created in Paris in the 1920s and the cubo-futurist costumes by Alexandra Exter and Liubov Popova made in Moscow from 1915 onward.

Balla had attempted to provide new patterns for the cut of shirts and suits that were based on geometric principles of nonobjective paintings, but it took Ernesto Michahelles, who worked under the pseudonym Thayaht,

to innovate a utilitarian and unisex dress that was based on the progressive notion that form and volume were to follow only inherent constructive principles. His "Tuta" of 1918 was designed as a cheap and uniform overall that due to its simple pattern could be tailored at home from a variety of fabrics. The aim was to provide "sportswear" that maximized freedom of movement for the body and directed an active lifestyle and corporeal ideal that would feed later into the fascist glorification of athleticism. In the early 2000s "tuta" is used in Italy to denote a tracksuit and Thayaht, who went on to illustrate haute couture for Madeleine Vionnet, thus designed a template for the emancipation of the body in the time between the wars. More decorative solutions for the embellishment of dress came from Depero, whose contribution lies in the commercial viability of his designs for fashion boutiques, posters, and the theater, from Tullio Crali who continued Balla's efforts to redesign the jacket and suit, and from Pippo Rizzo's textiles.

Balla's first Manifesto of 1914 had proclaimed: "We must invent futurist clothes, hap-hap-hap-hap-happy clothes, daring clothes with brilliant colors and dynamic lines. They must be simple, and above all they must be made to last for a short time only in order to encourage industrial activity and to provide constant and novel enjoyment for our bodies." It was a sartorial call to arms that mixed progressive aesthetics in dress with a shrewd understanding of its commercial and industrial basis, thus perfectly fitting as a credo for the artist engaging in modernity.

See also **Art and Fashion; Theatrical Costume.**

BIBLIOGRAPHY

Balla, Giacomo. "Futurist Manifesto of Men's Clothing." In *Futurist Manifestos*. Edited by Umberto Apollonio. London: Thames and Hudson, Inc., 1973.

Crispolti, Enrico. *Il Futurismo e la moda*. Venice: Marsilio, 1986.

Fiorentini Capitani, Aurora. "Tra arte e moda." *Imago Moda* no. 1, Florence 1989.

Hulten, Pontus, ed. *Futurism & Futurisms*. London: Thames and Hudson, Inc., 1987.

Lapini, Lia, ed. *Abiti e costumi futuristi*. Pistoia, Italy: Edizioni del Comune, 1985.

Lista, Giovanni. *Balla*. Modena, Italy: Galleria Fonte d'Abisso, 1982.

———. "La Mode Futuriste." In *Europe 1910–1939*. Edited by Valérie Guillaume. Paris: Les Musées de la Ville de Paris, 1996.

Ruta, Anna-Maria. *Arreddi Futuristi*. Palermo, Italy: Il labirinto, 1985.

Scudiero, Maurizio. *Fortunato Depero*. Trento, Italy: Il Castello, 1995.

Stern, Radu. *Against Fashion*. Cambridge, Mass., and London: MIT Press, 2003.

Ulrich Lehmann

119

G

G-STRING AND THONG The G-string, or thong, a panty front with a half- to one-inch strip of fabric at the back that sits between the buttocks, became one of the most popular forms of female underwear in the early twenty-first century. Its sources are manifold; the thong bikini designed by Rudi Gernreich in 1974, launched with a matching Vidal Sassoon hairstyle, is one which in turn spawned the more popular Brazilian string bikini brief, or tanga, of the late 1970s. This tiny bikini—dubbed the *fio denta*, or dental floss—ensured that the buttocks achieved maximum exposure to the sun and openly displayed an erogenous zone that was a particular favorite in Latino culture.

The stripper's G-string is another influence and has been an important part of the striptease artist's—or, more latterly, lap dancer's—wardrobe since the 1950s, when the taboo of displaying the vagina or any degree of pubic hair was paramount. The G-string was comprised of an elastic string that went around the waist and up between the buttocks and is popularly believed to have been originally added to the stripper's accoutrements on the occasion of the 1939 World's Fair in New York when Mayor Fiorello La Guardia demanded that the city's nude dancers cover themselves as a mark of respect for the thousands of visitors thronging the city. However, these types of coverings could be described as derivations of male underwear or garments associated with sports, such as jockstraps, which tend to reveal the muscle power of the legs and buttocks. Posing pouches worn by nude models in life classes since the Renaissance and in the nineteenth and early twentieth century in magazines promoting "health culture" and featuring body builders could be seen as types of G-string in that they have a front part that covers the genitals and a string at the back that exposes the bottom.

The thong was incorporated into the vocabulary of women's underwear in the 1980s in response to tighter and tighter trousers, especially jeans worn by women to display more of their gym-honed bodies in an era that emphasized muscled body shape. Women demanded underwear that would remain invisible under outerwear and combat what became known as VPL, or Visible Panty Line. Frederick Mellinger, of popular underwear manufacturer Frederick's of Hollywood, realized the potential of this form of underwear; Frederick's began to mass-market the thong, at first known as the "scanty panty," as an erotic item alongside crotchless or edible underwear. By the mid-1980s, however, the thong began to be appreciated as a practical garment in its own right. By 2003, it had become the fastest growing segment of women's underwear, making "full-bottomed" panties almost obsolete. In order to persuade the few reluctant women left to wear the thong, a "training" garment was invented called the Rio, or "starter" thong, which rose more sedately up the sides to expose less of the buttocks.

In the 1990s, the thong became a garment of folkloric proportions after the White House intern Monica Lewinsky's affair with U.S. president Bill Clinton was outlined in the Starr Report. Lewinsky admitted initiating her liaison with Clinton by flirtatiously lifting the back of her formal suit jacket to reveal the straps of her thong underwear. This indicated the irony of the thong for, in its original incarnation as underwear, it was designed to remain invisible so as to reveal the contours of a shapely bottom under the tightest of trousers. By the early 2000s, it became fashionable to wear low-cut hipster jeans that revealed the back of the thong, which became a focal point reinforced by diamanté-covered straps by such designers as Agent Provocateur and Frost French and the manufacturers Gossard. This fad, believed to be initiated by glamour model Jordan in England and singers Britney Spears and Mariah Carey in the United States, also showed a cultural shift in the sexual zoning of women's bodies. The prominent, fleshy bottom mythologized in African American culture by songs such as "The Thong Song" by American rhythm and blues star Sisqó, who exhorted, "Let me see that thong," and eulogized in the shape of actress and singer Jennifer Lopez, began to take over from the breasts as the primary erogenous zone. The popularity of the thong spread across all ages and sexes (although the man in the thong is mainly popular in certain gay circles), and by 2003, a moral panic had ensued as parents and the media saw the thong as responsible for sexualizing girls at too young an age. According to provisional figures compiled by manufacturers' sales of thongs to *tweenage* girls, the marketing definition of twelve- to fourteen-year-olds, jumped 33 percent from 2002 to 2003 in the United Kingdom. In 2003, an estimated ten million thongs worth about sixty-five million pounds were sold in the United Kingdom. The British shop Tammy Girl came under particular fire for marketing thongs to pre-teenaged girls with logos such as "Cupid Rules" and "Talent" printed on them. A further attack on the thong came in 2002, when the authorities at Daytona Beach, Florida, using anti-nudity laws to dissuade the use of the thong, threatened to arrest anyone displaying more than a third of their buttocks in public.

See also **Lingerie; Underwear.**

BIBLIOGRAPHY

Cox, Caroline. *Lingerie: A Lexicon of Style.* London: Scriptum Editions, 2001.

Craik, Jennifer. *The Face of Fashion: Cultural Studies in Fashion.* London: Routledge, 1994.

Caroline Cox

GABARDINE Gabardine is a tightly woven warp-faced twill weave fabric. Warp-faced fabrics have more warp or lengthwise yarns on the surface of the fabric than filling or crosswise yarns. Twill weave fabrics show a diagonal wale, or raised line, on their surface. The fine wale is closely spaced, slightly raised, distinct, and obvious only on the fabric's face. The wale angle in gabardine is 45 or 63 degrees. Gabardine always has many more warp than filling yarns, often twice as many warp yarns as filling yarns. Fabric weights range from 7 ounces per square yard to 11 ounces per square yard. Fabric density ranges from 76 warp ends per inch (epi) by 48 filling picks per inch (ppi) to 124 epi by 76 ppi. The combination of the weave structure, yarn size, and warp to filling ratio creates the wale angle. A steep (63 degree angle) twill gabardine is often used in men's wear while a regular (45 degree angle) twill gabardine is often used in women's wear. In the most common interlacing patterns the warp crosses two filling yarns before going under one filling (2 x 1) or the warp crosses two fillings before going under two fillings (2 x 2) to create right-hand twills in which the wale line moves from the lower left to the upper right.

Gabardine is a firm and durable fabric with a hard or clear finish. Singeing and shearing remove projecting surface fibers, fuzz, and nap and make the yarn and weave structure visible. Gabardine is available in several fiber types, weights, and qualities. Gabardine is usually made of wool. The best-quality gabardine uses two-ply worsted yarns, but single-worsted yarns, two-ply, and single woolen yarns are also used. Better quality fabrics are soft with a beautiful drape. Lower-quality fabrics are harsh, rough, and stiff. Two-ply worsted yarns, the warp-faced structure, and the fabric's hard finish produce a long-wearing and durable fabric. Gabardine is found in medium (dress) to heavy (suiting) weights in all wools, wool and synthetic blends, and acrylics. Gabardines made of cotton or silk are strong, compact, and elegant, but not very common. Gabardine can also be 100 percent

GLOSSARY OF TECHNICAL TERMS

2 x 1; 2 x 2: The number of filling yarns crossed over by the warp is represented by the first digit. The number of filling yarns the warp passes under before returning to cross the filling again is represented by the second digit.

Filling picks: Textile industry term for a crosswise yarn in a woven fabric.

Right-hand twill: Twill weave fabrics in which the wale line moves from lower left to upper right.

Wale: A raised line visible on the face of the fabric.

Warp-faced: Fabric in which the lengthwise (warp) yarns predominate on the surface of the fabric.

Warp yarns: Lengthwise yarns in a woven fabric.

textured polyester or a cotton-polyester blend. Cotton and textured polyester gabardines are usually made with a left-hand 2 x 2 twill weave.

Gabardine has a dull sheen. It is usually piece dyed for solid color fabric. It also may be fiber (stock) dyed for heather fabrics or yarn dyed for stripe or plaid fabrics. Because of its compact structure and hard finish, it sheds soil and water and does not wrinkle easily. It works best with tailored designs that have clean and simple lines or gentle curves because the tight weave makes easing in large quantities of fabric difficult. Gabardine is used for such apparel as slacks, jackets, and suits for men and women, uniforms, skirts, raincoats and all-weather coats, sportswear, riding habits, skiwear, hats, and fabric shoes. Lighter-weight gabardine is used for sportswear and dresses while heavier-weight gabardine is used for slacks and more tailored suits. Excessive wear or overworking when ironing or pressing may produce a shine on the fabric.

An alternate spelling is gaberdine. Gabardine is Spanish or French in origin. In the Middle Ages, gabardine described a loose mantle or cloak of a coarse woven twill.

See also **Weave, Twill.**

BIBLIOGRAPHY

Humphries, Mary. *Fabric Glossary.* Upper Saddle River, N.J.: Prentice Hall, 1996.

Parker, Julie. *All About Wool: A Fabric Dictionary and Swatchbook.* Seattle, Wash.: Rain City Publishing, 1996.

Tortora, Phyllis G., and Robert S. Merkel. *Fairchild's Dictionary of Textiles.* 7th ed. New York: Fairchild Publications, 1996.

Sara J. Kadolph

GALANOS, JAMES Often hailed as one of the few American designers to rival the great French couturiers in craftsmanship and exquisite finish, James Galanos achieved his position as one of America's premier designers through his commitment to exquisite fabrics and perfect workmanship throughout his long career. An uncompromising individualist, he established Galanos Originals in Los Angeles rather than New York's Seventh Avenue and went on to create a successful ready-to-wear business, catering to a discerning clientele.

Galanos was born in 1924 in Philadelphia, the third child and only son of émigrés from Greece. He knew at a young age that he wanted to design dresses and was fortunate to have the support of his family throughout his early struggling career. After graduation from high school in 1942, Galanos enrolled at the Traphagen School of Fashion, one of the oldest schools of its kind in New York City. He lasted only two semesters, having grown bored with the curriculum despite coursework that included design, draping, and construction. Hoping to gain actual design experience, Galanos took a job at the firm of Hattie Carnegie. This turned out to be another disappointment, so he left and began selling his sketches to ready-to-wear firms on Seventh Avenue, with limited success.

Galanos's acquaintance with the entrepreneur Lawrence Lesavoy led to his relocation to Los Angeles in 1946. After his failed business venture with Lesavoy left him unemployed, he made sketches for Columbia Pictures' head designer Jean Louis. Lesavoy compensated Galanos a year later by offering to underwrite his study and travels in Europe. In 1947 Galanos went to Paris, where he secured a position as apprentice designer at the House of Robert Piguet. Galanos stayed for just one year, yet the lessons in French fabrics and couture construction he learned at Piguet had a lasting impact on his later career.

Galanos Originals

Galanos returned to New York in 1948 and accepted a design position with another Seventh Avenue dressmaking firm, Davidow, but the venture was unsuccessful, and Galanos headed back to California. With the encouragement and financial backing of his former employer Jean Louis, Galanos designed a line of dresses, which was purchased by the Beverly Hills buyer for Saks Fifth Avenue, and thus Galanos Originals was launched in 1951.

From the start Galanos garments were unique. Although they were ready-to-wear garments, Galanos Originals included many features more commonly associated with custom dressmaking—hand embroidery, beadwork, rolled hems, tucking, piping, and luxurious fabrics. Integrally involved with all aspects of production, Galanos continued to run his design business through the years. Even into the twenty-first century he traveled twice a year to Europe, where he selected fabrics. He also designed the collection, consulted with technical assistants, oversaw the workroom, and had a hand in marketing the lines.

James Galanos altering a dress. Trademarks of Galanos's ready-to-wear collection include expensive, luxurious fabrics and meticulous details more often found in custom dressmaking. © BETTMANN/CORBIS. REPRODUCED BY PERMISSION.

Galanos designs range from meticulous day wear to exquisite evening dresses, but all feature fabrics of exceptional quality. His perfectly cut suits and day dresses, fashioned from expensive wools, silks, cottons, and linens, featuring such fine detailing as welted seams and tucking that produce a sculptural quality akin to the designs of Cristóbal Balenciaga, one of Galanos's favorite designers. His simple wool dresses appear to be carved out of the fabric through virtuoso pleating. Galanos also has distinguished himself with his copious and accomplished use of chiffon throughout his design career. Pleating, draping, and *bouillonné* gathering are some of the labor-intensive hand techniques he has employed with this fabric. At times using up to fifty yards of chiffon in a skirt, Galanos has been credited with contributing to the postwar revival of the chiffon industry in France.

Galanos's evening dresses have emphasized finesse and luxury rather than innovation. During his career he explored many different silhouettes, including full, bell-shaped skirts and dropped-waist "ballerina" dresses in the 1950s, miniskirts and caftans in the 1960s and 1970s, and off-the-shoulder sheaths in the 1980s and 1990s. His trademark silhouette, however, is a columnar sheath shape, featuring wide shoulders and a long, slim skirt. This simple, understated form offers the perfect foundation for another of Galanos's trademarks—exquisite embroidery. In the mid-twentieth century, Galanos began to collaborate with the Los Angeles firm of D. Getson Eastern Embroidery in the creation of intricate, hand-applied beadwork, sequins, and embroidery. This collaboration produced some of the most elaborate, labor-intensive ready-to-wear garments on the market.

Despite the modest size of his business, Galanos's adherence to quality and detail always ensured him a devoted fan base. Nancy Reagan, who became a client when her husband was governor of California, is perhaps his most famous customer. She wore Galanos gowns to four inaugural balls and countless receptions. Her selection of a fourteen-year-old Galanos gown for the presidential inauguration ball in 1981 highlighted the timelessness of his designs while bringing Galanos a new level of national attention formerly accorded only by the fashion congnoscenti.

From fashion critics Galanos has received almost every possible award. He won his first Coty American Fashion Critics Award in 1954, followed by awards from Neiman Marcus, Filene's, the Fashion Group, the *Sunday Times*, and the Council of Fashion Designers in America. Galanos designs are represented in the permanent collections of many major museums, and he has been the subject of retrospective exhibitions organized by such institutions as the Los Angeles County Museum of Art (in 1975), the Fashion Institute of Technology in New York (in 1976), the Smithsonian Institution, the Metropolitan Museum of Art, the Brooklyn Museum, the Philadelphia Museum of Art, Ohio State University, the Dallas Museum of Art, and the Western Reserve Historical Society in Cleveland, in collaboration with the Los Angeles County Museum of Art (in 1996).

Galanos is considered one of America's great designers. His independent vision, rigorous work ethic, and continued insistence on preserving the use of quality fabrics and thoughtful cut and construction in his garments made him a unique living link between the French couture tradition and American ready-to-wear.

See also **Ball Dress; Balenciaga, Cristóbal; Beads; Embroidery; Ready-to-Wear.**

BIBLIOGRAPHY

Bradley, Barry W. *Galanos.* Cleveland, Ohio: Western Reserve Historical Society, 1996.

Diamonstein, Barbaralee. *Fashion: The Inside Story.* New York: Rizzoli International, 1985.

Milbank, Caroline Rennolds. *Couture: The Great Designers.* New York: Stewart, Tabori and Chang, 1985.

Williams, Beryl. *Young Faces in Fashion.* Philadelphia: J. B. Lippincott Company, 1956.

Lauren Whitley

GALLIANO, JOHN John Galliano (1960–) is widely considered one of the most innovative and influential fashion designers of the early twenty-first century. Known for a relentless stream of historical and ethnic appropriations, he mingled his references in often surprising juxtapositions to create extravagant yet intricately engineered and meticulously tailored clothes. His continual interest in presenting fashion shows as highly theatricalized spectacles, with models as characters in a drama and clothes at times verging on costumes, won him applause as well as criticism. With his respective appointments at Givenchy and Christian Dior, Galliano rose to international celebrity status as the first British designer since Charles Frederick Worth to front a French couture house. He has been a member of France's Chambre Syndicale de la Haute Couture since 1993 and is the winner of many prestigious awards, most notably British Designer of the Year in 1987, 1994, 1995, and 1997, and International Designer of the Year in 1997.

Education and Early Career

Galliano, christened Juan Carlos Antonio, was born in Gibraltar in 1960. He moved to Streatham, South London, with his Gibraltan father and Spanish mother at the age of six. Galliano had a brief period of work experience with Tommy Nutter, the Savile Row tailor, during his studies at St. Martins School of Art in London (since renamed Central St. Martin's), as well as a part-time position as a dresser at the National Theatre. He graduated from St. Martins with first class honors in fashion design in 1984. His hugely successful final collection, Les Incroyables, was based on fashion motifs of the French Revolution and was immediately bought by the London boutique Browns, where it was featured in the entire window display. Galliano launched his label in the same year and has designed in his own name ever since.

Despite Galliano's rapid securing of a cult following and critical acclaim with such collections as Afghanistan Repudiates Western Ideals, The Ludic Game, Fallen Angels, or Forgotten Innocents, the business part of his early design career was most challenging. With inadequate and unstable financial backing—the Danish businessmen Johan Brun and Peder Bertelsen were among his first backers—Galliano had to produce several collections on a limited budget; some seasons he was not able to show at all. Galliano's shows of this period sometimes relied on last-minute improvisations for the final effect—as in his Fallen Angels show when he splashed buckets of cold water over the models just before the finale. Galliano began to work with the stylist Amanda Harlech, who worked closely with him until 1997. Other long-term associates include the DJ Jeremy Healy, the milliner Stephen Jones, and the shoemaker Manolo Blahnik.

In 1990 Galliano designed the costumes for Ashley Page's ballet *Currulao*, performed by the Rambert Dance Company. In 1991 he launched two less expensive, youth-oriented diffusion lines, Galliano's Girl and Galliano

Genes. By the early 1990s, Galliano had become firmly rooted in London's club scene. This, combined with his first-hand knowledge of the theater, channeled his interests toward experimentation and rarefied eccentricity, while it also fed the self-styled reinventions of his personal image. Both remain Galliano trademarks.

From London to Paris

Galliano moved to Paris in 1990, hoping for better work prospects. His acclaimed 1994 spring–summer collection, inspired by his personalized fairy-tale version of Princess Lucretia's escape from Russia, opened with models rushing down the catwalk, tripping over their giant crinolines supported by collapsible telephone cables. Thanks to the support of (U.S.) *Vogue's* creative director Anna Wintour and the fashion editor Andre Leon Talley, Galliano's breakthrough 1994–1995 autumn–winter collection was staged in an *hôtel particulier*, the eighteenth-century mansion of the Portuguese socialite São Schlumberger. The show re-created the intimate mood of a couture salon, with models walking through different rooms in the house that held small groups of guests. The interior of the house was transformed into a film set, evoking an aura of romantic decadence, with unmade beds and rose petals scattered about. Despite being composed of a mere seventeen outfits, the show used choreography and its exotic location to mark a momentous mid-1990s shift toward fashion shows as spectacles. A comparable mode of presentation was developed by Martin Margiela and Alexander McQueen around the same time.

In 1995 the president of the French luxury conglomerate LVMH, Bernard Arnault, appointed Galliano as Hubert de Givenchy's replacement as principal designer at Givenchy. Here Galliano had an excellent opportunity to study the archives of a major Parisian couture house. He developed his skill for merging—within one collection or a single outfit—traditional feminine glamour with a distinctly contemporary element of playfulness. He was also able to do justice to the breadth of his vision as one of fashion's most spectacular showmen. During and after Galliano's brief tenure at Givenchy, the house acquired an air of "Cool Britannia," and received unparalleled publicity. Alexander McQueen took over at Givenchy in 1996, while Galliano was installed as chief designer at another LVMH label, Christian Dior, as Gianfranco Ferré's successor. Four years later, Galliano's creative control over Dior's clothes was extended to the house's accessories, shop design, and advertising. Meanwhile, Galliano has continued to design under his own label. In 2003 he opened his first flagship store on the corner of the rue Duphot and the rue du Faubourg-Saint Honoré in Paris. The building's interior was designed by the architect Jean-Michel Wilmotte. Galliano launched his first signature men's wear collection since 1986 for autumn–winter 2004.

Galliano creates eclectic clothes, which are based on sources from fashion, film, art, and popular culture, and

John Galliano. Bold and imaginative, Galliano often presents his fashion shows as highly theatrical affairs, with models playing characters and clothing inspired by historical costumes. AP/WIDE WORLD PHOTOS. REPRODUCED BY PERMISSION.

modernizes his borrowings to varying degrees. Inspired by extensive travel experiences as well as thorough research in libraries, museum exhibitions, and archives, Galliano interprets not only exotic and historical looks but also construction techniques—most significantly the body-flattering elastic bias cut popularized by Madeleine Vionnet in the 1920s. His approach has been described variously as magpie-like, history-book-plundering, romantic escapism, and postmodern pastiche. Galliano's first haute couture Dior collection for spring–summer 1997, which coincided with Dior's fiftieth anniversary, juxtaposed quasi-Masai jewelry and quasi-Dinka beaded corsets with hourglass silhouettes reminiscent of the Edwardian era and Dior's own New Look. In the same collection, innocent white leather doily-like dresses and hats were shown alongside 1920s Chinese-inspired dresses styled with a menacing edge.

Unlike the androgynous creatures who paraded avant-garde shapes in Galliano's London shows of the 1980s, the heroines of his 1990s Paris period were luxurious icy divas by day and exotic opium-fueled seductresses by night—as represented in his Haute Bohemia collection for spring–summer 1998. For most of the decade he found inspiration in mysterious and sexually ambiguous women, ranging from real historical aristocrats, showgirls, and actresses to imagined characters and female stereotypes: Indian princess Pocahontas, Lolita (stemming from Vladimir Nabokov's fictional character), Edwardian demimondaines, the actress Theda Bara as Cleopatra, the artist and model Kiki de Montparnasse, the Russian princess Anastasia Nicholaevna, the Duchess of Windsor, the film character Suzie Wong, other prostitutes, and trapeze artists. Galliano's real clients in this period included Béatrice de Rothschild, Madonna, Nicole Kidman, and Cate Blanchett.

Since around 2000, in addition to Galliano's multicultural cross-referencing, he has placed new emphasis on shaking up the high and low of fashion. He has returned to the excesses of his earlier work and "dirtied" traditional elegance with over-the-top chaotic mixes of punk and grunge trashiness, 1980s–1990s street culture, clown-like infantilism, and spoofs of "rock'n'roll chic." While the designer maximized the concepts of couture and ready-to-wear alike as a masquerade and "laboratory of ideas," with clothes as "showpieces," he has reinforced the identities of Givenchy and particularly Dior as leading luxury brands with a tongue-in-cheek twist. The creative identity of his own label, which makes up for two of the six collections he produces yearly, has been closely linked to that of Dior.

See also **Blahnik, Manolo; Dior, Christian; Givenchy, Hubert de; Grunge; London Fashion; Margiela, Martin; McQueen, Alexander; Paris Fashion; Punk; Vionnet, Madeleine.**

BIBLIOGRAPHY

Arnold, Rebecca. *Fashion, Desire and Anxiety: Image and Morality in the Twentieth Century*. London and New York: I. B. Tauris, 2001.

Barley, Nick, Stephen Coates, Marcus Field, and Caroline Roux, eds. *Lost and Found: Critical Voices in New British Design*. Basel, Boston, and Berlin: Birkhäuser Verlag AG and The British Council, 1999.

Bradberry, Grace. "From Streatham to Dior." *The Times* (London), 15 October 1997.

Breward, Christopher. *Fashion*. Oxford: Oxford University Press, 2003.

Evans, Caroline. *Fashion at the Edge: Spectacle, Modernity, and Deathliness*. New Haven, Conn., and London: Yale University Press, 2003.

Frankel, Susannah. *Visionaries: Interviews with Fashion Designers*. London: V and A Publications, 2001.

McDowell, Colin. *Galliano*. London: Weidenfeld and Nicolson, 1997.

Menkes, Suzy. "Dior's Aggression Misses the New Romantic Beat." *International Herald Tribune*, 10 October 2001.

Tucker, Andrew. *The London Fashion Book*. London: Thames and Hudson, Inc., 1998.

Marketa Uhlirova

GARMENTS, INTERNATIONAL TRADE IN

Garments have been perhaps the most international of consumer products dating back to the late 1800s when Paris couturiers—led by the House of Worth—dictated the styles that affluent women around the world wore. Those garments were composed of rich, imported fabrics and trimmings: silks from China, woolens and velvets from England, damasks and lace from Italy. Back then, representatives from the first department stores in the United States, Chicago's Marshall Field's, R. H. Macy's in New York, and John Wanamaker in Philadelphia, voyaged to Paris in order to purchase haute couture samples, that their workrooms translated into styles suitable for America's growing consumer society.

In the 1980s, the fashion boom popularized designer jeans and athletic shoes and accelerated the globalization of fashion, as licensing became a lifeline to the fashion business, especially couture fashion houses. In fashion licensing, a design house collects a royalty payment between 3 percent to 10 percent of wholesale volume, from an outside manufacturer who produces and markets the merchandise. Licensing enabled designers to put their trademarks on clothes, handbags, jewelry, shoes, and perfume quickly and relatively painlessly. Licensing turned designers like Pierre Cardin and Calvin Klein into household names as they built billion dollar empires marketing sofas, bedsheets, clocks, and even frying pans to an international marketplace.

Modern fashion houses have no national borders. For example, an outfit that carries an Italian fashion label might have well been created in Milan, by a team of British, French, and American designers, and manufactured by contractors from countries in China, Korea, and Mexico.

This shift toward globalization is evident in trade statistics. In 1999, the five leading exporters of clothing were China ($30.08 billion), Italy ($11.78 billion), Hong Kong ($9.57 billion), the United States ($8.27 billion), and Germany ($7.44 billion). The five largest importers of clothing were the United States ($58.79 billion), Germany ($20.77 billion), Japan ($16.40 billion), the United Kingdom ($12.53 billion), and France ($11.58 billion). France, despite the continuing prominence of Paris in the world of fashion design, had only $5.69 billion in clothing exports in 1999 (International Trade Centre, World Trade Organization, 2001).

Like McDonald's and Starbucks, fashion marketers have been forced to think globally in order to cater to a cross section of international shoppers whom they now serve directly. No longer do consumers have to travel abroad to find the top brands, as Giorgio Armani, Valentino, and Polo Ralph Lauren have blanketed the world with boutiques from Buenos Aires to Tokyo.

Thanks to the Internet, Hollywood, and cable television, there is not much difference between consumers in Spain and those in the United States, who are all exposed to the same trends, celebrity role models, and popular music simultaneously. Furthermore, globalization has leveled the playing field, enabling retailers from the Gap to Zara to Target to compete in the multibillion-dollar fashion game, as these discount chains have learned to master the mechanics of delivering fast fashion at rock bottom prices.

Fashion entered a new era in the 1990s, as the world's buoyant high-tech industries broke the pattern for formal dress codes. Jeans, khakis, and knitwear replaced suits as the new corporate uniform. Seeking higher ground, the high fashion industry could no longer bank on dress-up clothes. Marketers thus found a new hook to captivate consumers: accessories like handbags, shoes, and watches, which could be plastered with showy designer logos and coordinated with casual clothes. Furthermore, accessories delivered higher profit margins than apparel, making them even more attractive to fashion marketers.

Luxury accessories thus became the focal point of such European conglomerates as Gucci, Prada, and LVMH Moët Hennessy Louis Vuitton, which scooped up dozens of faded fashion brands like Givenchy, Yves Saint Laurent, and Fendi. By owning a roster of fashion brands, these clothing giants have benefited from economies of scale. The luxury fashion boom began in the late 1990s as women began collecting status trinkets, the $1,000 Fendi baguette handbags, for example, that they wore to dress up their casual clothes. The accessories boom underscored how international fashion trends have become as shoppers in Tokyo, Paris, and New York all flocked to buy the hot designer handbags of the season.

Industry experts agree the next frontier is the Internet, which takes globalization to new heights. With the click of a mouse from their laptop computers, the world's consumers can conveniently shop the shelves of Harrods in London, L.L. Bean in Maine, Neiman Marcus in Texas, as well as Ebay, the auction Web site that features fashion merchandise offered by millions of individuals from around the world.

More than anything, the Internet has exposed the world's consumers to an infinite range of choices at all price ranges. It is the ultimate example of globalization, built on the back of rapidly changing media, which has further democratized fashion, shrinking the world into a single, accessible marketplace.

See also **Fashion Industry; Globalization.**

BIBLIOGRAPHY

Dickerson, Kitty G. *Textiles and Apparel in the Global Economy.* 3rd ed. Englewood Cliffs, N.J.: Prentice Hall, 1998.

Hyvarinen, Antero. "The Changing Pattern of International Trade in Textiles and Clothing." Geneva: International Trade Centre, World Trade Organization, 2001.

Teri Agins

GAULTIER, JEAN-PAUL Jean-Paul Gaultier was born in 1952 in the Paris suburb of Arcueil. An autodidact, he discovered fashion at a very early age. In childhood and adolescence, television and fashion magazines fed his imagination; he was particularly fascinated by the fashion features in *Elle.* He served his apprenticeship as a designer from 1970 to 1975 in the most innovative couture houses of the time: Pierre Cardin, Jacques Esterel, Jean Patou, and Angelo Tarlazzi. He soon struck out on his own and presented his first show of women's fashion in 1976.

Noticed and financed at first by the Japanese consortium Kashiyama, Gaultier established his own business in 1982, the success of which was continuous into the early 2000s. He developed a men's fashion line in 1984 and attracted a broader clientele through his Junior Gaultier collections, replaced in 1994 by a new JPG line. In 1992 he introduced Gaultier Jean's creations, and accessories and perfumes completed the lightning-fast rise of his business. Gaultier's fashion consecration arrived with his first haute couture collection in 1997. Investment support from Maison Hermès in 1999 enabled him to increase his reputation and his distribution, notably with the establishment of a network of boutiques bearing his name.

A Parisian designer, Gaultier was deeply attached to his city, which provided the backdrop to his inspirations. Neighborhoods such as Pigalle and Saint-Germain, monuments like the Eiffel Tower and the Moulin Rouge, and the most emblematic Parisians, from Toulouse-Lautrec to Juliette Greco, fueled his imagination. In the tradition of Chanel and Saint Laurent, his clothing has made it possible for women to assert their independence in an emancipated city.

From the beginning of his fashion career, London was Gaultier's second city. It very early became an immense source of inspiration, with the punk and ska movements, the allure of James Bond, and especially the flea markets and the eccentricities of Londoners. He felt a deep and enthusiastic admiration for his elder, Vivienne Westwood. The street fascinated him, providing him with the means of attaching fashion to the present and amplifying the echoes of the world around him. He has reinterpreted and made his own uses of the wardrobe of the past and its legacy in order to provide clothing for the future.

The Gaultier style of the 1980s was identifiable by the famous silhouette of broad and sloping shoulders and

Jean-Paul Gaultier and Vivienne Westwood. Gaultier's eclectic and often controversial designs found acceptance in pop culture, and in 1990 he designed for Madonna's Blonde Ambition tour. AP/WIDE WORLD PHOTOS. REPRODUCED BY PERMISSION.

narrow hips that emphasized stockinged legs. In the 1990s his palette of colors and materials was enriched by contact with many cultural worlds. The silhouette became more balanced, and comfort and protection took on added importance. His shows, with their exuberant and provocative staging, long obscured the fact that his clothes are designed to be worn. At the beginning of the millennium, he attained a certain classicism without renouncing the original image of his talent as the enfant terrible of fashion.

Gaultier's work has been characterized by a stylistic consistency since 1976: jacket and pants constitute the basic link between male and female wardrobes. The masculinity of double-breasted jacket, fitted coat, leather jacket, overalls, trench coat, smock, and down jacket is inflected by the femininity of corset, stockings, and garters, or is enriched by Eastern touches, by the influence of caftans and djellabas.

Mixtures and superimpositions make lingerie an item of clothing in itself, so that hybrid costumes like chemise-jackets and pants-skirts make up an unexpected wardrobe. Some accessories, such as ties and leotards, sewn together, become new textile materials. While women have adopted masculine attire, men are not far behind, and in Gaultier's shows they have worn skirts, corsets, and dresses with trains, increasing their masculinity. Gaultier has brought great care to textiles and employed the most luxurious materials; wool, taffeta, and velvet, for example, are blended with rayon, latex, imitation leather, and synthetic tulle. Lycra blended with traditional materials provides comfort in his designs. His designs often give fabrics a worn, faded look, as though they had already been worn. Knitwear in every form, always present, sea-

son after season, has been one of his distinctive signs. Precious fabrics enhance work clothes or military uniforms, and denim flourishes in evening dresses.

Navy blue, khaki, brown, red, and deep purple—Gaultier's original colors—have in the course of time been joined by salmon and powder pink, orange, turquoise, beige, and bronze. His motifs make up a distinctive repertoire: astrology, including the bull's head from his own sign; tattoos, writing, escutcheons, Celtic symbols, and faces; and religious themes like the cross, the star of David, and the hand of Fatima, all appear in a variety of forms on his fabrics, and are printed or sewn on accessories, particularly on jewelry. Stripes, plaids, and polka dots have been fetish designs for Gaultier. Certain details are trademarks, such as fastenings for his clothes: his designs feature distinctive zippers, laces, hooks, tortoiseshell buttons, or buttons with an anchor design.

A creator of images and atmospheres, Jean-Paul Gaultier could not avoid the cinema. He has created costumes for films of Peter Greenaway, Jean-Pierre Jeunet, Pedro Almodóvar, and Luc Besson. He has made stage costumes for Madonna and the dancer and choreographer Régine Chopinot. In 1993 he hosted a television show on Channel 5 in England.

Jean-Paul Gaultier's strong personality and his multifaceted universe have for decades influenced the worlds of both fashion and street clothes. He has enabled people to think about the place of clothing in contemporary society. Breaking the last taboos of the late twentieth century, his designs have exalted the theme of androgyny, brought men and women closer, moved to put an end to the prejudice against age, given sublime expression to the encounter between worlds and cultures, and associated memory with the strictly contemporary.

See also **Caftan; Corset; Djellaba; Extreme Fashions; Hermès; Punk; Unisex Clothing.**

BIBLIOGRAPHY

Chenoune, Farid. *Jean-Paul Gaultier*. New York: Universe Publishers, 1998.

McDowell, Colin. *Jean-Paul Gaultier*. New York: Viking Press, 2001.

Xavier Chaumette

GENDER, DRESS, AND FASHION Clothing for both men and women is culturally defined. Cultural norms and expectations are related to the meaning of being a man or woman and are closely linked to appearance. In Indonesia, parts of West Africa, and in traditional Scottish dress, men wear an article of clothing that closely resembles a Western definition of a skirt. In Indonesia, both men and women wear the sarong, a length of cloth wrapped to form a tube. The wrapper, a rectangular cloth tied at the waist, is worn by both sexes in parts of West

Africa. The Scottish kilt, still worn at many social gatherings to establish a social and cultural identity, represents the height of masculinity (Kidwell and Steele 1989). In North American culture, the sarong, wrapper, or kilt would rarely be seen on men except within the theater, film, or in the context of couture or avant-garde fashion. For example, the grunge style of the early 1990s had fashions for men designed to be worn with skirts. However, there was nothing particularly feminine about these styles; rather, they were purely a fashion statement.

Sex, Gender, and Socialization

What is meant by the terms "sex" and "gender"? Although many people use the terms interchangeably, the two words do not have the same meaning. While gender is a social, psychological, and cultural construct, our reason to polarize gender is influenced by sex, that is, the biological dichotomy of male and female. The biological continuum of genes, chromosomes, hormones, and reproductive physiology helps produce a script for appearing and behaving male and female. Viewing gender as a fluid concept allows scholars studying clothing and appearance to understand gender relations as more than men and women "dressing their parts" (Michelman and Kaiser 2000). Gendered dressing is more than complementary role-playing; power relations are inextricably involved. Otherwise, women's adoption of trousers represents an important readjustment of the definition of femininity, but not necessarily a change in the existing balance of power (Paoletti and Kregloh 1989).

A person's sex is determined on the basis of primary sex characteristics, the anatomical traits essential to reproduction. One may assume that determining biological sex is a clear-cut process, but a significant number of babies are born intersexed. This is a generic term used by the medical profession to classify people with some mixture of male and female biological characteristics (Newman 2002). For example, a true hermaphrodite is a person born with ovaries and testes. Parents, with the help of professionals in the medical field, make the decision to assign their child to be recognized as either male or female. One of the critical cues that these parents would use is dressing the baby in clothing appropriate to its assigned gender.

Secondary sex characteristics distinguish one sex from another. These are physical traits not essential to reproduction (for example, breast development, quality of voice, distribution of facial and body hair, and skeletal form). Gendered appearance and how we construct our identity are closely tied to these sex characteristics. A body ideal is a size, age, and a combination of physical attributes that society deems to be the most desirable for each gender. For example the early-twenty-first century popular ideal for Western women emphasizes a youthful, slim, athletic, and well-toned physique. Fashion requires women to slavishly conform to this image despite the fact that recent studies have found that the

Actress Marlene Dietrich in suit. Women are often less limited than men in their clothing options, as it is generally acceptable for women to wear suits and pants, but not for men to wear dresses. © Bettmann/Corbis. Reproduced by permission.

average American woman is 5 feet 4 inches tall, weighs 142 pounds, and wears a size 14.

Color is a cue that effects how people interact with a child. The response of others to gender-specific colors of attire encourage what is socially designated as gender-appropriate behavior by that child (Stone 1962). Stone observed that dressing a newborn in either blue or pink in America begins a series of interactions. Norms governing gender-appropriate attire are powerful. Gender-specific attire enhances the internalization of expectations for gender-specific behavior. Through the subtle and frequently nonverbal interactions with children regarding both their appearance and behavior, parents either encourage or discourage certain behaviors often related to dress that lead to a child's development of their gender identity. When a boy decides he wants to play dress-up in skirts or makeup or a daughter chooses to play aggressive sports only with the boys, it would not be surprising to find the parents redirecting the child's behavior into a more socially "acceptable" and gender-specific activity. Even the most liberal and open-minded parents can be threatened by their child not conforming to appropriate gender behaviors. Research has shown that children as young as two years of age classify people into gender categories based on their appearance (Weinraub et al. 1984).

A person or behavior that deviates from these scripts of gender can be defined as unnatural or pathological (Bem 1993, p. 81). For example, in the movie *Mrs. Doubtfire*, Robin Williams is discovered cross-dressing as a woman. It is at this point in the movie that he is regarded as being suspiciously deviant for such a behavior. What starts as a comedy quickly turns to more serious issues regarding his psychological stability. He is punished for his success at transcending proper gender appearance and behavior.

Gender as a Social Construction

Gender is a socially constructed phenomenon, and not all cultures aspire to the same physical ideal for men and women as those in Western societies. Likewise, dress can symbolically convey meanings about gender specific to a culture. For example, research on the Kalabari people of Nigeria (Michelman and Erekosima 1992) found that indigenous Kalabari men's attire demonstrates social and political achievement and does not emphasize the procreative aspect of social development, as does women's dress. Men's dress emphasizes social power and responsibility, and women's dress draws attention to moral and physical development. An example of dress emphasizing power is shown by the vertical lines and emphasis on the head in men's dress. Kalabari females progress to full womanhood wearing distinctive styles of dress with ascending values of complexity that mark physical and social maturity. Also of note, is that the ideal adult Kalabari female body is substantial, thick, and plump (Daly 1999) in contrast to an American thin ideal. Researchers have used several critical frameworks to analyze body ideals and dress.

Cultural Ideals of Body and Dress

One approach to critically analyzing gender and dress is to examine cultural ideals of beauty. In Western culture, a slim waist for women and men is emphasized, along with large breasts and hips for women and broad shoulders and slender hips for men. Greek ideals of beauty are still present in Western culture. The Greek ideal of perfect body proportions has stood the test of time in Western culture (Etcoff 1999). Minoan artifacts, which date from 2900 to 1150 B.C.E., illustrate men and women with extremely tiny waists. Some scholars speculate that this was the result of artistic convention while other authorities suggest that young men around the age of twelve or fourteen wore belts that constricted the waist (Tortora and Eubank 1998, p. 48). There have been periods in history when men adopted the corset to achieve the fashionable silhouette of the time (Kidwell and Steele 1989). As a result, neither Western men nor women have escaped Greek beauty ideals.

Given this long-standing Western ideal of body proportions, the continuation of America's obsession with the body comes as no surprise. Common phrases regarding the body include: One can never be too rich or too thin; no pain, no gain; thin-but-toned; and tall, dark, and handsome. Bodies depicted in magazines are often modified by using computers or airbrushing, allowing models to appear unrealistically beautiful and thin. Body doubles in popular movies mean that viewers might see two or more people standing in for an actor in a leading role. In magazines, the hand putting on the mascara of a beautiful model in an ad might be that of a hand model and not the model herself. The models themselves cannot attain the ideal, as can almost no one else. Some models have admitted to eating-disordered behaviors in the early 2000s. This is largely because clothing, in order to sell, must have "hanger appeal," and fashion models must be walking hangers. Many individuals try to approximate ideals through diet, exercise, and sometimes plastic surgery. Although these ideals are prevalent in American culture, at least one study has indicated that white and African American adolescent girls respond differently to these social pressures (Parker et al. 1995). African American girls get community feedback for developing a style of their own, while the white group gets support for their success in copying the unattainable ideal.

Codes of Dress and Gender

Through an examination of historical changes in Western men's and women's dress during the twentieth century, it is possible to gain a greater understanding of the changes in the social meanings of clothing and its relationship to gender. Through the 1950s, men followed a restricted code for appearance, limited to angular design lines, neutral and subdued color palettes, bifurcated garments (for example, pants) for the lower body, natural but not tight silhouettes, sturdy fabrics and shoes, and simple hair and face grooming (McCracken 1988). This simple and restricted dress "code" related well to a focus on work and on social, economic, and political accomplishments rather than attention to changes in fashion (Davis 1992). Dress (except for the necktie) did not impede physical activity. The negative impact of this uniformity and conformity is that men may dress to conceal aspects of their identity, which Spindler feels is not always true of women (1994). Men's business attire has been linked to a display of power facilitated by the uniform nature of dress. Joseph (1986) pointed out that uniforms exert a degree of control over those who must carry out the organization's work, encouraging members to express the ideas and interests of the group rather than their own, thus promoting the group's ability to perform its tasks. The opportunity for men to relax at work on "casual Fridays" has not released them from burdens of conformity, as they frequently adopt a Gap or Levi's uniform of polo shirt and khaki pants. This symbolic allegiance to work and career also signals a privileged access to economic and political power in postindustrial society, namely, occupational success. Women's conservative dress-for-success appearance of the 1980s can be analyzed as an appearance cue that announced women's intention to ascend the corporate ladder.

Women, in contrast, have had a more elaborated fashion code, which meant that they could wear some of what men wore, and a lot more. For example, although men always wear pants, women wear both pants and skirts. They have an unlimited choice of fabrics, colors, design lines, and silhouettes. Women also have worn corsets, tight or flowing skirts, high heels, and nylons that have restricted their freedom of movement. Historically, women have been more engrossed than most men in an emphasis on beauty rituals, including fashion, hair, weight control, and makeup, although recent studies indicate that men are catching up with women in their overall concern with their appearance (Garner 1997).

As early as the turn of the twentieth century, both Simmel (1904) and Veblen (1899) noted that with the rise of the urban bourgeois, women without title or other claims to social status were denied access to business, politics, and government. They demonstrated their rising status through clothing, interior decorating, and other consumer activities (Davis 1992). In other cultures, layering of body supplements frequently can indicate an elaborated code related to gender, but it can also serve to demonstrate social rank (Eicher, Evenson, and Lutz 2000). For example, in India, most married women wear bangle bracelets on each wrist. The type of bracelet (plastic, glass, conch shell, silver, ivory, or gold) is appropriate gendered dress as well as an indication of that woman's place in the social hierarchy.

More recently this "code" for men and women was examined in an intra-societal and cross-cultural context (Lynch, Michelman, and Hegland 1998). This research explored the potential of using a system of visual analysis of dress (DeLong 1998) to explore social construction of gender. In three research projects, the investigators found relationships between aesthetic choices and culturally determined gender roles. Lynch found that form and meaning worked together to express either commitment to tradition or openness to change in dress worn by Hmong American women to the New Year's celebration. Michelman concluded that dress worn in the context of traditional women's societies of the Kalabari of Nigeria was linked to cultural ideals of beauty. In contrast, dress worn by women in Nigerian national and international organizations provided a visual challenge to women's constructed gender through the incorporation of visual effects typically found in Kalabari men's dress. Hegland was able to discern degrees of difference in dress among transvestites, transsexuals, and drag queens who are typically placed in one broad category.

Historic Perspective

Historically, dress and gender have not always been fixed and have enjoyed some latitude. Researching dress and gender from a historical viewpoint stimulates awareness of the shifts regarding appropriate dress for males and females. For example, the expectation of blue is for boy babies and pink for girl babies has not always been the case.

Paoletti and Kregloh (1989) discussed how the color "rule" in 1918 was pink for the boy and blue for the girl. Pink was interpreted then as a stronger and more assertive color and blue as more dainty and delicate.

After World War II, the color preferences for boys and girls reversed. Parents often put elastic pink satin headbands on their hairless girl babies, so that no one is confused about their gender. Babies are also often "color coded" prior to their arrival. Once parents know the sex of their baby, nursery rooms are painted in blue colors for boys and pink for girls. If wallpaper is selected, the themes are often coded by gender, for example, frog, snake, and turtle designs for boys and flower, unicorns, and fairy princess designs for girls. Parents describe their newborns in terms of gender (Cahill 1989). In a study of girl and boy babies of the same weight and length, twenty-four hours after birth, parents were asked to describe the newest addition to their family (Rubin, Provenzano, and Luria 1974). Boys were described as strong, having large hands or feet, and demanding. Girl babies were described as sweet, cuddly, and cute.

In American culture of the twenty-first century, adolescents are often allowed leeway in experimentation with gender and dress, as some adolescent girls may shave their heads and some adolescent boys may have shoulder-length or longer hair. Adults are generally expected to adhere to their societies' rules regarding appropriate gender dress. But gender dress has not always been polarized. For example, during the seventeenth century, adult men's and women's dress shared many of the same elements. A painting of Henri, Duc de Guise by Van Dyck (c. 1634) gives us a glimpse of how aristocratic masculine dress was defined during the first half of the seventeenth century. De Guise's hair is past shoulder length and styled with a "lovelock." He is wearing a profusion of lace at the collar and cuff areas of his doublet and below the knee of his breeches, his doublet opening is held together with a bow, and he carries a wide-brimmed hat decorated with a large plume. His knee-high boots are also elaborately decorated. De Guise's portrait appears especially feminine when compared with contemporary American male dress.

Queen Henrietta Maria in a portrait by Van Dyck (*Queen Henrietta Maria with Sir Jeffrey Hudson*, 1633) has similar details to her costume as de Guise's in that she is wearing her hair in a "lovelock" style, a large brimmed, plumed hat, and her collar and three-quarter-length sleeves are decorated with a profusion of lace. However, Queen Maria's portrait in some respects is more streamlined and less fussy than de Guise's in that the line of her skirt is not broken up and her legs and feet are hidden while de Guise's lacy knee breeches and decorated boots break up the line of his lower body.

According to Davis (1992), the dress of the European aristocracy changed in the 1800s when men's dress became a means of communicating economic success and women's dress continued to follow an elaborate dress code. As a result, men assumed a highly restricted dress code as the European aristocracy began to decline and the advent of industrial capitalism began. Therefore, we see fewer similarities between men's and women's dress in modern culture at the start of the twenty-first century compared with the seventeenth-century dress of European aristocrats.

Gender, Dress, and the Self

Eicher (1981) proposed a model for viewing dress and the different aspects of the self. She stated that the public self is the part of the self we let everyone see, the private self is the part of the self we let only family and friends see, and the secret self we let no one or only intimates see. One hypothesized disparity between men and women in American culture is that dress for the secret self (what Eicher calls fantasy dress) is more restricted for men than women. In other words, women are allowed to purchase fantasy dress for the secret self more so than men. In order to test Eicher's hypothesis, Miller (1997, 1998) surveyed historic reenactors regarding their use of costume during living history events and reenactments.

In 1997, Miller found that women reenactors have more sexual fantasies about dress than men, supporting Eicher's (1981) hypothesis that American women feel more freedom to dress out fantasies than men. Female reenactors also reported more childhood memories about dress than men, indicating that boys and girls are socialized differently about dress (Vener and Hoffer 1965).

In 1998, Miller reported that among costumed reenactors surveyed, females dress in costume primarily to assume another persona, whereas males dress in costume primarily because of their love of history. In written responses to open-ended questions, male reenactors distanced themselves from such descriptions of their hobby as "fantasy," "costume," and "dress-up." Women on the other hand embraced these terms and indicated that people don't dress in costume only on the weekends (for reenactments), but for every day. As a result of these two studies by Miller (1997, 1998) and in collaboration with Eicher, a new grid model was developed for dressing the public, private, and secret self (Eicher and Miller 1994).

Gender Markers

Some aspects of dress mark the gender of an individual more than others, for example, a corset, footbinding, interest in fashion, a codpiece, and maternity apparel. Corsets have been associated with female morality, with the tight-laced woman as moral and the unlaced woman as "loose" and immoral. In addition, corsets have been blamed for displacement of internal organs and disfigurement of the female body during the 1800s; however, these accounts are generally considered few in occurrence and possibly overstated (Steele 1999). One cannot deny the erotic appeal of corsets, and Steele (1999) has used representations of the corset in art, illustrations, and ad-

vertising to discover that the corset shares a close association with female erotic beauty.

Corsets have also been worn by men, although less frequently than by women. For example, during the nineteenth century, the ideal for a fashionably dressed male included a rounded silhouette. These illustrations show the areas of the body that were to be rounded by padding (shoulder, chest, hip, and calf). Tight corseting created a small waist and emphasized the padded areas of the body by contrast.

Footbinding, once performed in China, was a disfiguring and socially acceptable practice performed exclusively on females and was closely linked with eroticism (Jackson 1997). Women in China followed a centuries-old tradition of breaking and binding their feet to achieve a lotus bud shape. This shape was purportedly sexually attractive to males and created high social status while increasing the likelihood of marriage among Chinese women.

Women are often accused of being excessively interested in fashion. But throughout history one can find examples of men who were also extremely interested in fashion. During the late 1700s, the king of France, Louis XVI, was very interested in fashion; he wore hose and high heels to call attention to his calves, and he wore a high wig to increase his height. Attention to fashion among men reached its zenith between 1796 and 1816 when Beau Brummell became the undisputed arbiter of men's fashions in England: "Brummell was famous for his impeccable dress. . . . [H]e personified the Regency 'dandy,' a fashionable man who dressed well, circulated in the 'best' society, and who was always ready with a witty comment" (Tortora and Eubank 1998, p. 265).

The codpiece is one gender marker exclusively for men. In the sixteenth century, a small pouch of fabric was needed to join separate legs of hose to create trousers. This small piece of fabric was used to place emphasis on the male genitalia. From 1500 to 1560 the codpiece would grow in size, be padded, slashed, decorated, and used by men to carry coins, keys, and tobacco.

Maternity apparel, like the codpiece, is gender specific, and illustrations of pregnant women over time show that the public perception of pregnancy has greatly influenced the style of maternity apparel available. For instance, maternity career apparel became available during the last half of the twentieth century largely because popular opinion found it acceptable for women to work while pregnant (Belleau, Miller, Elliott, and Church 1990). This approach is in contrast to the Victorian era when pregnant women were said to be "in a family way" and were expected to remain at home and out of public view. Juxtapose the Victorian image of a pregnant woman with a more recent image of Demi Moore, nude and pregnant, on the cover of *Vanity Fair* in the early 1990s and you begin to see how society's perception of pregnancy has changed over time (Damhorst, Miller, and Michelman 1999).

Social Resistance

Dress can be a powerful, nonverbal indicator of political beliefs. Examples demonstrating this relationship include uniforms, religious garb, and fashion. Political dress can convey a clear and positive message regarding the wearer's beliefs and affiliation. Sometimes this dress can also be closely associated with the "politics of gender." Feminism has challenged what is taken for granted about gender with a political goal of changing the world and transforming gender relations so that women and men alike can fulfill their human potential (Ramazanoglu 1989, p. 8). Feminists examine gender as a fluid concept that shifts in its meaning and expression according to time, place, social class, race/ethnicity, sexuality, age, and other variables. Issues of gender and power are part of the feminist analysis of dress and fashion. The fashion and image industries build their sales by playing with the boundaries of gender and power. For example, the semi-masculinized fashions designed for women by Ralph Lauren, Giorgio Armani, and Calvin Klein can be interpreted as sexy, assertive, urbane, and most decidedly upper class but never something that would be worn by a man.

Athletic dress. Dress can be an important way to express political resistance and frequently is associated with the power relations of gender. Examples can be found in many cultures around the world. The history of women's athletic dress from gym suit to the current athletic fashions provides a study in the power of the gendered resistance of dress. The early gym uniform was more than just attire for physical education; rather, it symbolized the long, slow process of adoption of the trouser form for women. Warner believes that the clothing for women's athletics has had a wider influence on women's clothing in the twentieth century than any other, except dance (1993, p. 191). In 1972, Title IX legislation demanded equal funding of athletic programs for females and males in schools across the United States. Since then, increasing numbers of girls and women participate in sports that have traditionally been seen as out of bounds for them, including lacrosse, wrestling, soccer, rugby, and ice hockey. As women's opportunities in athletics have multiplied, so has their chance to expand the "boundaries" of their dress. Serena Williams, the American tennis star, exemplifies resistance to the boundaries of gender and femininity. She is comfortable in designer dresses that display her muscular arms and legs as well as tennis clothing and a physical appearance that was once reserved for only the most accomplished male athletes. She is highly feminine and simultaneously supremely athletic, an appearance resistant to a frail, feminine ideal of beauty.

Religion and resistance. Recent events in other cultures provide examples of dress as resistance. From a Western perspective, Muslim women's veiling appears a form of great social repression. Indeed, in some cases, this may be true, such as the 1990s rules of public appearance for women under the Taliban rule of Afghanistan. The *burqa,*

a total body covering, clearly represents a type of oppression to many Afghani women, although its long-standing place in Afghan culture is complicated. What may have been more distressing were the Taliban rules that prevented women from working or attending school. In the Muslim countries of Algeria, Egypt, and Iran, the return to veiling practices indicates a return to more traditional values of modesty, religious values, family virtue, and an aversion to Western consumerism—that is, fashion. For many women, veiling is resistant to certain prevailing social norms and an assertion of their personal and social identity (El Guindi 2000).

Conservative Holdeman Mennonite women also use dress to combat patriarchal control. Young women are allowed some leeway when it comes to the strict dress code of the Mennonites, and the older women who police the behavior of the younger women often overlook deviations in young women's dress. Arthur (1993) found that young Mennonite women used lightly applied makeup, worldly clothing hidden in school lockers, and dyed high-heel shoes in black or brown to bend rules established by the male ministers. Even though Mennonite communities maintain strict dress codes, most men defer to their wives when raising daughters. Women help keep each other in line while overlooking some deviations. Both behaviors were considered "a double nature to the agency of Mennonite women" (p. 83).

Conclusion

Clearly, gender as a social and cultural construction needs—demands—the appropriate props to successfully convince the audience that one's gender presentation is authentic. The dress we wear is layered with many meanings, such as culturally appropriate gender behavior, gender socialization via dress, codes of dress and gender, historical perspectives of dress and gender, dressing parts of the self, social resistance, and gender markers.

See also: **Codpiece; Cross-Dressing; Fashion and Homosexuality; Maternity Dress; Reenactors; Religion and Dress; Unisex Clothing**

BIBLIOGRAPHY

Arthur, L. B. "Clothing, Control, and Women's Agency: The Mitigation of Patriarchal Power." In *Negotiating at the Margins.* Edited by S. Fisher and K. Davis, 66–84. New Brunswick, N.J.: Rutgers University Press, 1993.

Barnes, Ruth, and Joanne B. Eicher, eds. *Dress and Gender: Making and Meaning.* London: Berg, 1992.

Belleau, B. D., K. A. Miller, P. Elliott, and G. E. Church. "Apparel Preferences of Pregnant Employed Women." *Journal of Consumer Studies and Home Economics* 14 (3): 291–301.

Bem, S. *The Lenses of Gender: Transforming the Debate on Gender Inequality.* New Haven, Conn.: Yale University Press, 1993.

Cahill, S. E. "Fashioning Males and Females: Appearance Management and the Social Reproduction of Sex." *Symbolic Interaction* 12 (1989): 281–298.

Daly, M. Catherine. "'Ah, a Real Kalabari Woman!': Reflexivity and the Conceptualization of Appearance." *Fashion Theory* 3(3) (1999): 343–361.

Damhorst, M. L., K. A. Miller, and S. O. Michelman, eds. *The Meanings of Dress.* New York: Fairchild Publications, 1999.

Davis, F. *Fashion, Culture, and Identity.* Chicago: University of Chicago Press, 1992.

DeLong, M. R. *The Way We Look: Dress and Aesthetics.* 2d ed. New York: Fairchild Publications, 1998.

Eicher, J. B. "Influences of Changing Resources on Clothing, Textiles, and the Quality of Life: Dressing for Reality, Fun, and Fantasy." *Combined Proceedings: Eastern, Central, and Western Regional Meetings of Association of College Professors of Textiles and Clothing* (1981): 36–41.

Eicher, J. B., S. L. Evenson, and H. A. Lutz. *The Visible Self: Global Perspectives on Dress, Culture, and Society.* 2nd ed. New York: Fairchild Publications, 2000.

Eicher, J. B., and K. A. Miller. "Dress and the Public, Private, and Secret Self: Revisiting a Model." *ITAA Proceedings.* Proceedings of the International Textile and Apparel Association, Inc. (1994): 145.

El Guindi, F. *Veil: Modesty, Privacy and Resistance.* Oxford: Berg, 2000.

Etcoff, N. *Survival of the Prettiest.* New York: Doubleday, 1999.

Garner, D. M. "The 1997 Body Image Survey Results." *Psychology Today* 30 (1) (January/February 1997): 30–44, 75–76, 78, 80, 84.

Jackson, B. *Splendid Slippers.* Berkeley, Calif.: Ten Speed Press, 1997.

Joseph, N. *Uniforms and Nonuniforms: Communicating through Clothing.* New York: Greenwood Press, 1986.

Kidwell, C., and V. Steele. *Men and Women: Dressing the Part.* Washington, D.C.: Smithsonian Institution Press, 1989.

Lynch, A., S. Michelman, and J. Hegland. "Cross-cultural and Intra-societal Application of DeLong's Framework of Visual Analysis." *Clothing and Textiles Research Journal* 16(4)(1998): 145–156.

McCracken, G. *Culture and Consumption.* Bloomington: Indiana University Press, 1988.

Michelman, S., and T. Erekosima. "Kalabari Dress: Visual Analysis and Gender Implications." In *Dress and Gender: Making and Meaning.* Edited by R. Barnes and J. Eicher, 164–182. Oxford: Berg, 1992.

Michelman, S., and S. B. Kaiser. "Feminist Issues in Textiles and Clothing Research: Working through/with the Contradictions." *Clothing and Textiles Research Journal* 18(3) (2000): 121–127.

Miller, K. A. "Gender Comparisons within Reenactment Costume: Theoretical Interpretations." *Family and Consumer Sciences Research Journal* 27 (1) (1998): 35–61.

Miller, K. A. "Dress: Private and Secret Self-Expression." *Clothing and Textiles Research Journal* 15 (4) (1997): 223–234.

Newman, D. *Sociology: Exploring the Architecture of Everyday Life.* Thousand Oaks, Calif.: Pine Forge Press, 2002.

Paoletti, J., and C. Kregloh. "The Children's Department." In *Men and Women: Dressing the Part.* Edited by C. Kidwell and V. Steele, 22–41. Washington, D.C.: Smithsonian Institution Press, 1989.

Parker, S., M. Nichter, et al. "Body Image and Weight Concerns among African American and White Adolescent Females: Differences That Make a Difference." *Human Organization* 54 (2) (1995): 103–114.

Ramazanoglu, C. *Feminism and the Contradictions of Oppression.* London and New York: Routledge, 1989.

Roach-Higgins, M. E., and J. B. Eicher. "Dress and Identity." *Clothing and Textiles Research Journal* 10 (1992): 1–8.

Rubin, J., F. Provenzano, and Z. Luria. "The Eye of the Beholder: Parent's Views on the Sex of Newborns." *American Journal of Orthopsychiatry* 44 (1974): 512–519.

Simmel, G. "Fashion." *American Journal of Sociology* 62 (1957): 541–558 (originally published in 1904).

Spindler, A. "Men in Uniformity." *New York Times Magazine. Men's Fashions of the Times* (1994, September 25): 16, 18.

Steele, V. "The Corset: Fashion and Eroticism." *Fashion Theory* 3(4) (1999): 449–474.

Stone, G. "Appearance and the Self." In *Human Behavior and Social Processes: An Interactionist Approach.* Edited by A. Rose, 86–118. New York: Houghton Mifflin, 1962.

Tortora, P., and K. Eubank. *Survey of Historic Costume.* 3rd ed. New York: Fairchild Publications, 1998.

Veblen, T. *The Theory of the Leisure Class.* New York: Mentor Books, 1953 (originally published in 1899).

Vener, A. M., and C. R. Hoffer. "Adolescent Orientations to Clothing." In *Dress, Adornment and the Social Order.* Edited by M. E. Roach and J. B. Eicher, 76–81. New York: John Wiley and Sons, 1965.

Warner, P. "The Gym Suit." In *Dress in American Culture.* Edited by P. Cunningham and S. V. Lab, 140–179. Bowling Green, Ohio: Bowling Green State University Popular Press, 1993.

Weinraub, M., et al. "The Development of Sex Role Stereotypes in the Third Year: Relationships to Gender Labeling, Gender Identity, Sex-Typed Toy Preference, and Family Characteristics." *Child Development* 55 (1984): 1493–1503.

Susan O. Michelman
Kimberly A. Miller-Spillman

GERNREICH, RUDI Rudi Gernreich was born on 8 August 1922 in Vienna and died in 1985. Gernreich's family came from the nonreligious Jewish middle class and had ties to the Social Democrats. One of his mother's sisters ran a fashion salon in Vienna where the newest French designs were translated with high-quality craftsmanship.

In 1933 Austria, having affiliated itself with Nazi Germany, became the scene of rampant anti-Semitic violence. Rudi Gernreich and his mother were able to flee to Los Angeles. Gernreich studied art for a few semesters and quickly made a connection in Los Angeles with The Modern Dance Studio of Lester Horton, whose choreography was concerned with antifascist themes and racial discrimination. In the mid-1940s, his first sketches for dance costumes appeared. For a few years, Gernreich

Rudy Gernreich on the cover of *Time* magazine, December 1, 1967. Born in Vienna, Austria, Gernreich was well known for using provocative fashion designs, such as the "monokini," to express the 1950s and 1960s generations' desire for freedom. TIME LIFE PICTURES/GETTY IMAGES. REPRODUCED BY PERMISSION.

was a fashion designer for Adrian and others before developing his first small collection in 1948. In the late 1940s he worked for a short time in the garment district of New York's Seventh Avenue, returning eventually to California. Around 1950 he developed a collection of sportswear for Morris Nagel, which featured interchangeable pieces. Hattie Carnegie engaged Gernreich for a few months during which he provided her with design sketches. In 1950 he met Harry Hay (1912–2002), who was a member of the California Communist Party and an activist union organizer. Hay and Gernreich founded the secret Mattachine Society, one of the first organizations to agitate for homosexual rights.

In 1952 Gernreich began work for Walter Bass, and his first designs were an immediate success. The newly founded Beverly Hills boutique, JAX, as well as department stores like Lord and Taylor in New York and Joseph Magnin in San Francisco, sold Gernreich's sportswear. Gernreich developed jersey tube dresses and printed nylon stockings and used synthetic materials. Starting in 1955 Gernreich also designed knitted bathing suits. In 1954 he met Oreste Pucciani, the future chairman of the UCLA French department, and began a relationship that would last until Gernreich's death in 1985. Finally in 1960, Gernreich established his own company: Rudi Gernreich Incorporated. In 1964, the monokini, or topless bathing suit, brought the name Gernreich into the headlines. In 1968 Gernreich closed his company but continued his work as a designer.

From the beginning of his career, Gernreich also designed costumes for various film productions, such as Eva Marie Saint's wardrobe in Otto Preminger's 1960 film *Exodus*. In 1970 he designed "Dress Codes" of the new decade for the January issue of *Life* magazine. Gernreich's fashion concept of the future was "unisex." In 1971 he presented an ironic military collection: jersey pieces in uniform colors, mounted pockets, and models armed with guns. In 1972 Gernreich developed a perfume, which came in a bottle shaped like a chemical laboratory beaker. Gernreich never thought of his activity as a designer as limited to fashion alone; clothing was only one possible expression of a freely chosen lifestyle.

Gernreich's 1950s bathing suits were influenced by the work of the American designer Claire McCardell. Gernreich's suits, conceived as an expression of a new body consciousness, were unstructured and emphasized the body's natural form. In 1965, Gernreich accessorized his bathing suits with visors, over-the-knee vinyl boots, and even fishnet stockings. In 1961 Gernreich's bathing suits and clothes featured cutouts, and in 1968 he used transparent vinyl inserts, which integrated the skin and silhouette of the wearer into the clothing.

The monokini, or topless bathing suit, first presented in 1964, finally made Gernreich internationally famous. Gernreich's monokini consisted of a rib-cage-height bottom, held up with shoulder straps. Gernreich had wanted to liberate the bosom from its status as something that had to be kept concealed. He also used this idea in his underwear collection "No." The bras from the collection, the "no bra," the "maybe bra," or, later, the "almost bra," were distinguished by their transparency and lightness. The thong, presented in 1974, is part of the standard repertoire of clothing in the early 2000s.

Gernreich used patterns—bold animal skins or graphic decorations—in clothing, accessories, and even underwear. The body became, in the Total Look, an abstract, aesthetic element, and clothing became a conscious field of aesthetic experimentation, like architecture or furniture design. The fall collection of 1964 featured a suit of a top and skirt and matching stockings, with dark-blue and gray (oyster) vertical stripes, completed by garish green patent-leather pumps. In 1966, three models, Peggy Moffit, Léon Bing, and Ellen Harth, appeared in William Claxton's short film *Basic Black*, which focused on Rudi Gernreich's fashions. All three mannequins wore suede suits, with dalmatian, giraffe, and tiger-skin patterns complete with matching patterned accessories: caps, gloves, pumps, stockings, and even underwear.

Gernreich's collections often featured uncommon color combinations, such as black and white, orange and yellow, or red and purple, and the juxtaposition of differing graphic motifs, such as stripes with polka dots, checks with diagonal stripes, zigzags with cubes. On the one hand, the influence of the Vienna Workshops is apparent, on the other hand, Gernreich was responding to the antifashion of the 1960s and 1970s, whose signals and messages he transformed. "Real T-shirts are worn with slogans or Mickey Mouse figures or letters. All of these deliver messages. I have abstracted these signals into symbols, conveying them by various inserts: panels, stripes, or circles" (*Topeka State Journal*, 23 February 1972). Instead of extravagant tucks, folds, or piping, Gernreich accentuated and molded particular body parts through the optical effect of colors and patterns. With refined trompe l'oeil effects, the illusion of a multiple-piece suit was created.

Gernreich's collections often included elements of folklore, quoted and freshly adapted: the pattern mixture of Austrian dirndl, the hussar's uniform with embroidery on black vinyl, or elements of Chinese and Japanese clothing, such as obis or colorfully patterned silks. The 1968 collection was criticized by the press at the time as not contemporary enough and seemed to many to even contradict Gernreich's modernism. But the designer had not intended to offer romantic dress-up as an escape from reality, but rather as a medium for a continual self-exploration or role-play. According to Gernreich, such a repertoire of historical and national style elements could only be successfully introduced in a free society whose members were capable of personal exploration and experimentation with a confident mastery of existing dress codes.

Gernreich always advocated the interchangeability of men's and women's clothes. In the Unisex Project of 1970, for example, Gernreich arranged for a woman and a man to be shaved completely of body hair. Then the pair modeled identical clothing: both in bikinis or miniskirts , both topless. In the conception of his unisex-style, Gernreich chose abstract, unromantic, democratic clothing which was intended to be available to all—in Gernreich's words: "an anonymous sort of uniform of an indefinite revolutionary cast" (*Michigan News*, 15 July 1971).

"We have to take this terrible world and make fun of it with fun clothes, functional clothes" (*Los Angeles Herald Examiner*, 29 September 1966). Already in 1954 Gernreich had used white vinyl for an evening dress. He tried to break through the traditional boundaries of clothing manufacture by using new materials. He was not only interested in the aesthetic characteristics of synthetic materials, but also in their manufacturing possibilities. He hoped to produce seamless clothing, but was frustrated due to the inability, at the time, to overcome technical problems. In addition to synthetic materials, Gernreich favored mechanical elements like zippers or metal fasteners, and he incorporated elements of both motorcycle clothes and dance leotards in his designs. He designed overalls with detachable pants legs, sleeves, or skirts, which could be altered at will.

"I consider designing today more a matter of editing than designing," said Gernreich describing his aesthetic method (*Los Angeles Times*, 30 January 1972). During the course of his career Gernreich utilized various styles, drawing upon austere secessionist patterns for casual slacks, reworking the simple cut of a sleeveless dress, season after season, with new materials and color combinations, introducing industrial materials like vinyl, or historical costumes for greater social flexibility. The exclusivity of expensive craftsmanship, the value of a particular material, or the refined solution to a particular technical sewing problem—be it sleeve holes or folds—would not have harmonized with Gernreich's design intentions. He reduced clothing to an inventory of functional pieces, which could be infinitely varied with colors, materials, or patterns.

Fashion magazines ignored, for the most part, his taboo-breaking, subversive fashion strategies. Gernreich, however, always saw his fashion concepts as carriers of a total, aesthetically formulated worldview. With the monokini he succeeded in pushing the fashion envelope. He utilized the success and fame awarded by his first collections in the 1950s to introduce his new aesthetic concepts about contemporary and futuristic clothing theory to the public eye. Art and fashion, thus, were never separated worlds for him. In the 1950s and 1960s, Gernreich was accepted in artistic circles because he had utilized fashion to radically question societal conventions. He rejected the idea of fashion as a corset of socially relegated hierarchy and rigid gender polarization. He used ironically provocative concepts such as the monokini, topless, uni-

sex, and the Total Look to articulate a generation's desire for freedom as program.

See also **Ethnic Style in Fashion; McCardell, Clare; Unisex Clothing.**

BIBLIOGRAPHY
Faure, Jacques, ed. *Rudi Gernreich. A Retrospective.* Los Angeles: Fashion Group Foundation, Inc., 1985.

Felderer, Brigitte, ed. *Rudi Gernreich: Fashion Will Go Out of Fashion.* Catalog for eponymous exhibition from Oct. 7 to Nov. 26, 2000. Künstlerhaus Graz, Cologne: Dumont, 2000.

Lobenthal, Joel. *Radical Rags: Fashions of the Sixties.* New York: Abbeville Publishers, 1990.

Moffitt, Peggy. *The Rudi Gernreich Book.* New York: Rizzoli, 1991. Photography by William Claxton. Essay by Marylou Luther.

Brigitte Felderer

GIGLI, ROMEO The designer Romeo Gigli was born in 1949 in Castelbolognese, near Faenza, Italy, into a family of antiquarian booksellers with a collection of more than twenty thousand volumes from the fifteenth and sixteenth centuries. The region of Faenza has a rich cultural and historical heritage. It was there, in the Byzantine mosaics of Ravenna and in the rare books in his family's library, that Gigli found the initial inspiration for his future art.

Gigli studied architecture in Florence. At the end of the 1970s, after ten years spent traveling around the world, during which time he collected objects, fabrics, and clothing, he began to take an interest in fashion. In 1979 he went to New York, where Pietro Dimitri, a tailor who made custom clothing for men, asked Gigli to design a line of women's clothing. It was a defining moment for Gigli, who, after returning to Italy and settling in Milan, decided to enter fashion on a full-time basis. In 1983 he launched the Romeo Gigli label, which was produced by Zamasport beginning in 1985.

Gigli broke with existing conventions, revolutionizing the approach to women's fashion common in the 1980s. During a period characterized by padded shoulders and aggressive sexuality, Gigli introduced a new look for women—one that was romantic and intimate. He turned away from the hard-edged contours that were then prevalent and based his designs on classic proportions, which he updated, sometimes radically. He made use of contrast and asymmetry and combined simplicity with luxurious fabrics, sometimes pairing smaller, microlength designs with long, full garments. He made use of unusual combinations of colors, such as sand and pink, dark blues, verdigris, saffron, red, and gold, and of fabrics, such as stretch linen, silk, chiffon, cotton gauze, wool, and cashmere. And he was one of the first designers to use Lycra.

The Gigli woman is ethereal and silent, fragile and poetic; her conical silhouette, with its long, narrow sleeves and layered overcoats, jackets, and scarves, emphasizes the sensuality of a woman's arms and shoulders, her gestures and bearing. Even Gigli's men's collection, begun in 1986, broke with the traditional schema and returned to classical proportions and uncommon pairings of materials. He reintroduced the three-button jacket and the natural, or Neapolitan, shoulder; his pants were narrow and his shirts colorful. The Gigli man is neither aggressive nor a dandy; he is an intellectual, casual in appearance only, careful in his choice of colors and fabrics.

In 1987 Gigli signed an agreement with Takashimara—the Japanese department store specializing in luxury and quality goods—for the exclusive production and distribution of the women's ready-to-wear collection and men's and women's accessories.

For several years Gigli showed his clothes in Paris, where he was received with considerable enthusiasm. In Milan his showrooms at 10 corso Como, Spazio Romeo Gigli, which opened in 1988 in a former automobile repair shop in the working-class Garibaldi neighborhood, have become a place of cult worship for intellectuals and fashion rebels, for whom Gigli is the undisputed leader.

One of his women's perfumes, Romeo di Romeo Gigli, received the International prize Accademia del Profumo for the best packaging of 1989 and the award of the American Fragrance Foundation for the best packaging of 1991.

In 1990, he launched the G Gigli line, produced by Stefanel for a younger market. From 1987 to 1996 he designed Callaghan for Zamasport, a collection of richly decorated ethnic clothing. In 1993 he started a cooperation with Christopher Farr's Handmade rugs for the carrying out of carpets in a limited edition.

Because of disagreements with his associates, Gigli decided to completely redefine his activity. He continued as the artistic director of Gigli Spa, a part of IT Holding, which was founded in 1999 and which produces and distributes products associated with the Gigli name. Romeo Gigli, considered Italy's poet-designer, has been a forerunner of minimalism and understatement in modern clothing design. His stylistic and conceptual innovations have been widely imitated.

See also **Elastomers; Ethnic Style in Fashion; Italian Fashion.**

BIBLIOGRAPHY

Borioli, G. "Gigli." In *Dizionario della moda*. Edited by Guido Vergani. Milan: Baldini and Castoldi, 1999.

Giordani Aragno, Bonizza. *Callaghan: 1966. La nascita del prêt-à-porter italiano*. Milan: Mazzotta, 1997.

Simona Segre Reinach

GIRDLE Mary Brooks Picken defined girdle as a "flexible, light-weight shaped corset, made partly or entirely of elastic. Worn to confine the figure, especially through the hip line." Merriam-*Webster's Collegiate Dictionary* offered: "A woman's close-fitting undergarment often boned and usu. [*sic*] elasticized that extends from the waist to below the hips." Neither definition does full justice to the undergarment that changed shape, materials, and functions through its six decades of prominence in women's wardrobes, from the 1910s through the 1960s. Girdles evolved continuously to take advantage of new fibers and fabric structures and to respond to each new silhouette in women's outerwear. Pantie girdles came on the scene when substantial numbers of women began to wear pants. Initially, girdles appealed to younger women and teen girls, but women of all ages eventually wore some type of girdle, before control-top panty hose supplanted the girdle's functions for all but the most conservative women.

The modern girdle's origin may be traced to the short hip-confiners worn over corsets during the early 1900s, but the term itself began to assume its contemporary meaning in the mid-1910s. Treo, an early manufacturer, applied the term girdle to its flexible Para rubber corsets without laces. Competing terms to describe girdles included the French ceinture, belt, and sash. In 1916, Stanford Mail Order Company, New York, marketed girdles to "Misses and Small Women." At the outset, girdles were associated with youth and informality, in part because their light control suited the figures and activities of a younger clientele. However, rubber "reducing girdles" were sold to weight-conscious women of all ages.

Flappers and Girdles

In the famously unconstrained 1920s, teens and young women, collectively termed flappers, generally abhorred the heavy corsets on which their mothers depended for figure control. Fashionable young women often rolled their stockings and limited underwear to a wispy bandeau and step-in panties. By the mid-1920s, as a contoured silhouette began gradually to return to women's fashions, flappers and other fashionables accepted garter belts and light girdles. The advertising agency J. Walter Thompson reported the views of a Manhattan department store buyer thus: "widely talked of abandon [*sic*] of corsets was a myth. Even flappers wear something, if it's only a garter belt or corselette." Girdles of the 1920s usually extended from natural waistline to hipline, came in white or peach-tone knit elastic, and were worn over step-ins. More conservative girdles included woven brocade panels over the tummy and derriere. Generally priced from $1 to $6 dollars, girdles appealed to the budgets of young women.

Thriving During the Depression

In the 1930s, technology and fashion converged to produce styles of girdles that sold by the millions, despite the persistence of the business depression. Unit sales of girdles topped 20.6 million in 1935 alone ("The Corset," *Fortune*, March 1938). Technological innovation arrived in the form of Lastex, an extruded (spun) rubber latex yarn covered by mercerized cotton. Put on the market in autumn 1931, Lastex made possible the lightweight two-way stretch girdles that gained wide appeal, especially with young customers, for their ability to move with the body. Lastex hand-washed easily and provided control without boning, though some girdles added a few bones and often had panels of woven fabric to tame front and rear bulges.

Warner made knitted Lastex girdles, whereas Kops Brothers specialized in woven two-way stretch fabrics. By the end of the 1930s, makers had devised tubular, seamless knitted girdles and knits of differential density and tension for molding different parts of the wearer's anatomy.

Fashion also contributed to the survival of girdles. Throughout the 1930s, dress silhouettes gradually became fuller in the bust, slimmer and higher in the waist, and gently curved and elongated in the hips. Compared with the changes in bust contours and bras, where aggressive uplift held sway by 1939, girdle shapes altered only subtly. Fashion's overall trimness of line meant that all but the very young and slender needed a girdle (or corselette) to wear a chic dress well.

Fashionable women's 1930s wardrobes began to include pants, primarily for active sports, gardening, and strictly informal social events. Enter the pantie girdle. Beginning about 1934, pantie girdles constituted a staple in the lines of many manufacturers. Most panties had garters, because stockings continued to be worn under pants, but a few styles featured removable garters or special leg bands to hold down the girdle when socks were worn or the woman went barelegged. Regular girdles were marketed for all purposes, from housework to evening parties, and at prices that ranged from 59 cents to $15 dollars.

Like bras, girdles sold mainly in peach (like present-day nude) or white, but by 1939 at least a couple of makers offered black girdles. "Talon slide fasteners"—zippers—appeared in slightly heavier or fancier girdles. Talon argued that roll-on girdles caused frustrating tugging matches. A girdle could be as short as eight inches—like a glorified garter belt—but most came in ten-, twelve-, fourteen- and sixteen-inch lengths, varying with both the height of the wearer and her need for control at the hip and waist.

Girdle manufacturing was widely dispersed during the 1930s, with many of the 240 corset companies ("The Corset," *Fortune*, March 1938) producing some type of girdle. Some stores featured private-brand girdles, but generally the industry divided between prestige-brand makers and small, marginal firms. Even the better-known companies split between those grounded in corset-making, such as Maidenform and Formfit, and those derived from knit underwear makers, including Carter, Kayser, and Munsingwear.

A 1920s girdle. Girdles of the 1920s usually extended from waistline to hipline, came in white or peach-tone elastic, and were worn over step-in panties. Priced from $1.00 to $6.00, they appealed to young women shoppers. © HULTON-DEUTSCH COLLECTION/CORBIS. REPRODUCED BY PERMISSION.

Wartime Retrenchment and Postwar Expansion

New fibers and innovative marketing might have constituted the core of the girdle story in the 1940s but for the hiatus of World War II. Nylon, introduced for hosiery in 1939, was offered in girdles in 1940; Formfit and other companies marketed all-nylon and blended-fiber girdles by that autumn. Nylon and Lastex created strong, light powernet, so effective in girdles for the junior market. Latex film Playtex all-way-stretch girdles offered another route to smooth control.

As war approached, the U.S. government took possession of strategic textiles, including nylon and latex. Regulation L90 stipulated allowable amounts of elastic in girdles and other undergarments; however, neither Lastex nor nylon wholly disappeared from girdles or bras. Small sections of elastic provided some relief from rigidity. Knitted fabrications helped too, but wartime girdles often looked and felt dowdy to young customers. Pantie girdle sales held up well, because women working in armaments factories often wore pants or coveralls, which looked better over a pantie girdle. Slim and fit girls just wore garter belts or inexpensive briefs with garters.

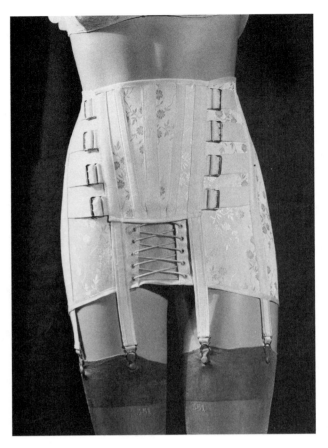

Girdle displayed on a mannequin. In the 1930s, technological innovations such as Lastex and other lightweight, easily washable stretch fabrics helped account for a boom in girdle production that, except for a brief period during World War II, lasted through the 1950s. © BETTMANN/CORBIS. REPRODUCED BY PERMISSION.

Late in the war, synthetic rubber neoprene appeared in girdles, but was overshadowed by the newly plentiful nylon and Lastex. With wartime seriousness forgotten, pink, blue, rose, black, and plaid girdles gladdened consumers' hearts. Embroidered touches, including custom sorority emblems from the new Olga Company, lent glamour to formerly stodgy foundations. The biggest news, however, came from the outerwear silhouette. American dress and girdle styles were moving tentatively toward fuller hips and smaller waists as early as fall 1945, but the 1947 French New Look took the trend much further, faster. Girdles rose in the waistline, swelled in the hip, and even returned to selective lacing to achieve the newly desired hourglass effect. American brands pursued a more moderate line, in order not to alienate customers—especially the all-important teenagers, who demanded comfort, easy care, and flexibility in their girdles.

Far longer-lasting than the New Look was the new marketing, presaged before the war by Playtex's packaging of its Living Girdles in tubes for self-service. Other girdle and bra makers followed suit after 1945, and the old tradition of corsetieres fitting customers began a slow decline.

1950s' Heyday
Sheath dresses, popular periodically through most of the 1950s, kept various types of girdle in adult women's wardrobes. Many girdles sported waists as much as four inches above the natural line, supported by boning, wires, and Lastex reinforcements. Snug pants, a fashion of the mid- to late 1950s, augmented the need for long-legged pantie girdles. However, as early as 1952, hints of eased fit in some dress and suit styles foretold the coming of shift dresses in the 1960s. Blousons, Empire-waisted dresses, and the ill-fated chemise of 1957–1958 offered women escape from the stifling embrace of the sheath and its confining foundations.

During the 1950s, very short girdles and pantie girdles proliferated, designed for informal wear and appealing to older teens and young adults. Some merited the nickname "postage stamp" that Jantzen applied to its 1952 style. Some makers featured girdles proportioned for tall women. Companies tried to serve varied customers, though some, including Jantzen, Olga, and Hollywood Vassarette, specialized in a young clientele.

Young or mature, women made their complaints about girdles known, because companies repeatedly trumpeted improvements in comfort. Several firms began to cut the lower front edge in a high upward curve to reduce discomfort in walking. Sarong famously brought out a crisscrossed lower front to move with the wearer's stride. Legs of panties were redesigned for ease in wearing, and both top and bottom of the rear of the girdle were engineered to prevent riding up—a major lament. Removable, even disposable, crotches remedied the panties' laundry problems.

Throughout the decade, manufacturers trumpeted their girdles' lightness, at no sacrifice of shaping power. Girdles, like their wearers, seemed to be on a diet. Nylon in Powernet and woven materials subtracted ounces. Openwork fishnet improved ventilation—crucial in selling girdles for warm-weather wear. By 1954, Dacron polyester appeared in girdles, alone and in blends with cotton. Less-clammy textured nylon came to market under the brand names of Helanca and Ban-lon. Most successful of the weight-reducing textiles, however, was Dupont's Fiber K, which in 1959 produced a two-ounce girdle! Spandex was born.

Comfort alone did not suffice; beauty was also required. Colors proliferated—from subtle almond and pale gray to vibrant red, purple, and salmon. Individual styles came in as many as eight colors by 1957. Embroidery, lace, and appliqués gratified the desire for luxury. All of this cost money. Although $2.95 could purchase a down-market girdle, typical prices ranged from $5 to $25 dollars.

Girdles reportedly contributed 39 percent to total 1956 sales dollars in foundation departments, but those sales were highly seasonal, peaking in April, September, and December, and hitting troughs in January, July, and August (*Merchants Trade Journal*, January 1957; *Merchants Trade Journal*, September 1955). Despite blandishments about comfort, women lost interest in girdles in hot weather.

Surviving the 1960s

Like the 1920s, the 1960s had an exaggerated image of uncorseted, braless freedom. In fact, the early 1960s produced waist-hugging dresses and tight pants that drove some women to retain their girdles. Constraint was achieved by machine-washable powernets of Fiber K, christened Lycra in 1960, and joined by rivals Vyrene and Numa in the 1960s. Every girdle company used proprietary shaping in front and side panels to tame tummies and thighs. Derrieres, however, came into fashion, and girdles that uplifted the gluteus maximus moved from racy Frederick's of Hollywood into mainstream companies in the mid-1960s.

Other aspects of girdle shape evolved through the decade. Snug waists in the early 1960s were gradually replaced by dipped waists. By 1962, so-called "hip-hangers" or "hipbone pants" came into fashion, producing low-slung panty girdles. As skirts rose, girdles shortened, ending the decade at crotch level. Tights and panty hose drove girdle makers to promote their products as panty-hose mates. Taste ran to riotous colors in outerwear, and innerwear followed suit: Floral swirls, polka dots, checks, butterflies, and leopard prints enlivened girdles and coordinating innerwear.

Frantic pursuit of fashion and novelty availed little. A 1963 report showed that girdles constituted only 23.6 percent of foundation-department sales, compared with 71.8 percent for bras. Fashion reportage stressed the nude look, and played up Yves Saint Laurent's statement "underwear is dead." Despite howls from the trade press, girdles seemed to be in terminal decline. By 1970, a mere scattering of ads for panty-sized "smoothers" appeared. But fashion has taken many turns through the years, and in 2003 at least a few companies still produced nylon and spandex "body slimmers." Under such euphemisms, the girdle lives.

See also **Brassiere; Corset; Petticoat; Underwear.**

BIBLIOGRAPHY

"The Corset." *Fortune* (March 1938): 95–99, 110, 113, 114.

Corset and Underwear Review, various issues, 1916–1969.

Dry Goods Merchants Trade Journal (title varies), various issues, 1929–1959.

Field Sales Guide. 1 May 1963. Maidenform Archives, Box 27, Folder 3. National Museum of American History.

"Girdles Contributed 39 Percent to 1956 Foundation Sales." *Merchants Trade Journal* (January 1957): 90.

Harper's Baza(a)r, various issues, 1935–1968.

"How Do Your Bra and Girdle Sales Compare?" *Merchants Trade Journal* (September 1944): 104.

Kops Brothers Account Record; transcript of Interview No. 6. J. Walter Thompson Archives, John Special Collections, Duke University.

Mademoiselle, various issues, 1940–1975.

MaidenForm Mirror, various issues, 1931–1966.

Picken, Mary Brooks. *The Fashion Dictionary*. New York: Funk and Wagnalls, 1957, p. 149.

Vogue, various issues, 1935–1975.

Merriam-Webster's Collegiate Dictionary. 10th ed. Springfield, Mass.: Merriam-Webster, Inc. 1980.

Jane Farrell-Beck

GIVENCHY, HUBERT DE Hubert de Givenchy was born on 21 February 1927 in Beauvais, France. The son of a prosperous family, he attended college at Beauvais and then moved to Paris. In 1944 he took a position as an apprentice designer at the couture house of Jacques Fath while studying at the École des Beaux-Arts in Paris. In the late 1940s and early 1950s he took a series of jobs as an assistant designer—first with Fath, then with Lucien Lelong, Robert Piguet, and Elsa Schiaparelli. Givenchy's years as an assistant designer encompassed the period of the New Look and perhaps instilled in him a sense of romanticism that was to characterize his work for over four decades.

Givenchy opened his own couture house in 1951 and made an immediate mark with his design of the "Bettina blouse," a simple white cotton shirting blouse named for Fath's favorite model, Bettina Graziani. Givenchy was quickly recognized as an innovative talent for his system of designing his creations—including evening gowns—as compositions of separate and interchangeable elements. In 1953 he met Cristóbal Balenciaga, who quickly became his mentor and lifelong friend. Givenchy moved his business in 1955 to 3, avenue George V, across the street from Balenciaga's atelier, and the two men were in almost daily contact thereafter. In 1954 Givenchy opened his fragrance business, Société des Parfums Givenchy. He designed his first outfits for the actress Audrey Hepburn that same year. She quickly became his most famous model and muse and looked so enchanting in his creations in a series of films—beginning with *Sabrina* in 1954 and continuing with *Funny Face* (1957), *Breakfast at Tiffany's* (1961), *My Fair Lady* (1964), and others—that she made Givenchy a household name. The designer was generous in acknowledging Hepburn's role in his career, remarking that "often ideas would come to me when I had her on my mind. She always knew what she wanted and what she was aiming for. It was like that from the very start." Givenchy also became known as one of Jacqueline Kennedy's favorite designers; he designed the dress that she wore to President Kennedy's funeral.

Hubert de Givenchy at his last show, Paris, 1996. De Givenchy was perhaps best known for designing dresses for Audrey Hepburn for a number of acclaimed film roles and for designing the dress that Jaqueline Kennedy wore to President John F. Kennedy's funeral. AP/WIDE WORLD PHOTOS. REPRODUCED BY PERMISSION.

Givenchy's style was characterized by bright cheerful colors and a youthful femininity. Yet his simple tailleurs, cocktail dresses, and evening dresses were also the height of chic, emphasizing line more than decoration. "You have to know when to stop," he once said. "That is wisdom."

Givenchy expanded his business in the late 1960s and into the 1970s to include women's ready-to-wear clothing as well as a line of menswear. He sold his company to the French luxury conglomerate LVMH in 1988 but continued to serve as head designer until his retirement in 1995. His first successor was John Galliano, who departed in 1996 and was replaced by Alexander McQueen. McQueen in turn left the company in 2001 and was succeeded as artistic director by Julien McDonald.

See also **Balenciaga, Cristóbal; Fath, Jacques; Galliano, John; McQueen, Alexander; New Look; Paris Fashion; Perfume; Schiaparelli, Elsa.**

BIBLIOGRAPHY
Benbow-Pfalzgraf, Taryn, ed. *Contemporary Fashion.* 2nd ed. Farmington Hills, Mich.: St. James Press, 2002.

Buxbaum, Gerda, ed. *Icons of Fashion: The 20th Century.* Munich, London, and New York: Prestel Verlag, 1999.

Join-Diéterle, Catherine, Susan Train, and Marie-José Lepicard. *Givenchy: 40 Years of Creation.* Paris: Musée de la Mode et du Costume, 1991.

Milbank, Caroline Rennolds. *Couture: The Great Designers.* New York: Stewart, Tabori and Chang, 1985.

Mohrt, Françoise. *The Givenchy Style.* New York: Vendome Press, 1998.

John S. Major

GLAZING Glazing is a textile finish that adds luster and smoothness to the surface of the fabric. Many glazed fabrics are plain-woven cotton. A specialized calender (set of metal rollers) called a friction calender, literally rubs the fabric lustrous. Glazed chintz and polished cotton are examples of glazed fabrics.

The Process

The fabric is first impregnated with wax, starch, or a resin solution using a pad machine. The fabric passes through the solution in a bath, then through pad rollers. Pressure is applied so that the solution is forced into the fabric. The pressure on the pad roller squeezes the excess solution out of the fabric. The fabric is partially dried and passed through a friction calender. The friction calender is made up of three rollers. One roller is a padded roller that moves the fabric slowly between two metal rollers. As the fabric moves slowly between the rapidly moving heated metal rollers, the friction creates heat. The fast moving metal rollers polish the fabric. The glaze will be temporary if the fabric has been treated with wax or starch. The finish will be durable if the fabric has been treated with resins. The glazing will be durable on thermoplastic (heat sensitive) fiber fabrics because the friction rollers produce heat.

Ciré

A specialized finish, ciréing (sometimes called the "wet look") is similar to glazing. The difference is that very hot rollers in the friction calender are used to add a highly lustrous surface. Again, waxes, starches, or thermoplastic resins are added to the fabric. When thermoplastic fibers are used in the ciré process the fibers slightly fuse, melt, and flatten. The ciré finish on thermoplastic fibers is permanent. When hydrophobic fiber fabrics are given a ciré finish the resultant fabric is water repellent. Typical fabrics that are ciréd are taffeta (a filament unbalanced ribbed fabric), tricot (a warp knit), and satin.

Glazing can occur accidentally when fabrics are over-pressed. Glazing occurs when a too hot iron is used on a fabric made from a fiber that is heat sensitive. The heat is not enough to melt the fabric completely but does slightly fuse and flatten the fibers. An undesirable sheen that may resemble an oil stain will appear. The damage will be permanent.

Another definition for glazing is the pressing of fur to develop a desirable sheen. The pressing aligns the hairs in the fur, thus generating a natural luster and additional softness to the fur. Often a glazing solution using a spray gun is applied.

See also **Chintz; Cotton; Fibers.**

BIBLIOGRAPHY

Needles, Howard L. *Textile Fibers, Dyes, Finishes, and Process: A Concise Guide.* Park Ridge, N.J.: Noyes Publications, 1986.

Slade, Philip E. *Handbook of Fiber Finish Technology.* New York: Marcel Dekker, 1998.

Robyne Williams

GLOBALIZATION In a certain sense, the Western economy has been "global" since the sixteenth century. After all, the African slave trade, colonialism, and the intercontinental trade in sugar and coffee made capitalism possible. But since the early 1980s, transnational corporations, cyber technology, and electronic mass media have spawned a web of tightly linked networks that cover the globe. Taken together, these forces have profoundly restructured the world economy, global culture, and individual daily lives. Nowhere are these changes more dramatic than in the ways dress and fashion are produced, marketed, sold, bought, worn, and thrown away.

For consumers in dominant Western countries, globalization means an abundance of fashions sold by giant retailers who can update inventory, make transnational trade deals, and coordinate worldwide distribution of goods at the click of a computer. It means that what people are consuming is less the clothing itself than the corporate brand or logo such as Nike, Victoria's Secret, or Abercrombie & Fitch. Consumers are purchasing the fantasy images of sexual power, athleticism, cool attitude, or carefree joy these brands disseminate in lavish, ubiquitous, hyper-visible marketing on high-tech electronic media. But much less visible is the effect of globalization on the production of fashion.

As fashion images in magazines, music videos, films, the Internet and television speed their way around the world, they create a "global style" (Kaiser 1999) across borders and cultures. Blue jeans, T-shirts, athletic shoes and base ball caps adorn bodies everywhere from Manhattan to villages in Africa. Asian, African and Western fashion systems borrow style and textile elements from each other. Large shopping malls in wealthy countries

house all these styles under one roof. Like high-tech global bazaars, they cater to consumers of every age, gender, ethnicity, profession, and subculture.

According to Susan Kaiser, "This tendency toward both increased variety within geographic locations and a homogenizing effect across locations represents a global paradox" (Kaiser 1999, p. 110). On the one hand, shopping malls in every city have the same stores, and sell the same fashion items. Yet if we take the example of jeans, we find a seemingly infinite and often baffling array of cuts and fits: from stretched tight to billowing baggy, from at-the-waist to almost-below-the-hip; from bell-bottom to tapered at the ankle; from long enough to wear with stiletto heels to cropped below the calf. While a somewhat baggy, "relaxed" cut can signify dignified middle-aged femininity, a baggy cut taken to excess can signify hyper-masculine ghetto street smarts. Each variation takes its turn as an ephemeral and arbitrary signifier of shifting identities based on age, gender, ethnicity, or subculture.

While marketing campaigns encourage us to associate fashion consumption with pleasure, power, personal creativity, and individual fulfillment, business economists and corporate finance officers have a different view. Contrary to fashion magazines, business organs like *The Wall Street Journal* anxiously watch over consumer behavior as minutely measured by the Consumer Confidence Index managed at the University of Michigan (Weiss 2003). In this view, consumption is neither personal nor individual, but necessary for upholding a vast, intricate global capitalist economy. Dependent on massive fashion consumption in the wealthier countries, this economy depends equally on massive amounts of cheap labor in poorer countries.

The Global Assembly Line

No longer manufactured by the company whose label it bears, clothing from large retailers is manufactured through a network of contractors and subcontractors. Pioneered by Nike, the largest retailer of athletic shoes and fashions, the outsourcing or subcontracting system was quickly taken up by giant retail chains like Express and The Gap, and big-box stores such as Wal-Mart. These companies do not manufacture their own goods, but rather source and marketing goods produced on contract in low-wage environments. Because they make large profits, they can force manufacturers to contract with them at lower and lower prices. To reduce their costs, manufacturers subcontract much of the sewing, and even the cutting, to sweatshops in countries such as Mexico, China, Thailand, Romania, and Vietnam, where poverty is high and wages can be as low as 23 cents per hour. Manufacturers can also subcontract to sweatshops in the vast underground economies of immigrant communities in cities like Los Angeles, New York, or London. There is a huge contrast, but a tight relation, between production in sweatshops, where

Employees making shoes at a Reebok factory, 1996. Since the early 1980s, globalization has become an increasingly dominant force in the production of fashion goods. In the early twenty-first century, to take advantage of costs, fashion corporations outsourced much of their manufacturing to factories in countries such as China, Thailand, Mexico, and Vietnam. © MICHAEL S. YAMASHITA/ CORBIS. REPRODUCED BY PERMISSION.

young women workers are often subjected to physical and sexual abuse, and consumption in retail chains filled with glamorous images. Jobs come without even the most basic worker safeguards and benefits.

Since retailers can lower their prices to consumers by lowering their labor costs, consumers have unwittingly participated in intensifying a system of competition among manufacturers that drives wages and working conditions downward. According to the World Bank, one of the most powerful institutions of globalization, "the competitive intensity of the U.S. retailing industry has increased significantly" (Biggs et al., p. 1). As a consequence, it says, "new emerging retail strategies" include "the drive to offer more value-oriented, low-priced goods to their customers, utilizing a global sourcing network that increasingly favors low wage, quota free countries," and the "liberalization of labor regulations" (Biggs, p. 2). This "liberalization" means relaxing worker protections for health and safety, lowering and also enforcing less stringently the minimum wage, and prohibiting workers from organizing for better wages and working conditions.

Immigrant Labor

By contrast to the World Bank's optimism about globalization, in 1998, the California Labor Commissioner said: "Global competition results in a feeding frenzy in which local producers compete against one another and against foreign factories in a brutal race to the bottom" (Rabine, p. 118). Referring to one among countless examples of production on the global assembly line, he was speaking on the occasion of the closure of a garment factory in Los Angeles that owed its workers $200,000 in unpaid wages. To meet a contract for T-shirts from the Disney Corporation, it had to reduce its profit margin and keep accelerating its production schedule in a downward spiral to closure.

One effect of globalization is increased immigration from third-world countries to all the countries of the world. Immigrants to the United States provide a labor pool for local versions of third-world sweatshops. In 1997, Southern California came to lead the nation in garment production. By 1999, hourly wages for garment workers in Los Angeles had dropped below minimum wage of $5.75 to as little as $3.00. Often workers were not paid at all. The California Labor Commissioner estimated in 1999, right before a new anti-sweatshop law was passed, that the industry accumulated $72,620,000 in unpaid wages to mostly immigrant garment workers.

Responses to the Global Assembly Line

Until 1997, CEOs of the giant retailers, such as Philip Knight of Nike, claimed that they had no responsibility for the working conditions in the sweatshops because the owners were independent contractors. But by this time consumer groups, religious groups, and student groups, including the National Labor Committee in New York, Global Exchange in San Francisco, the Los Angeles Jewish Commission on Sweatshops, the national organizations of United Students Against Sweatshops and Sweatshop Watch, as well as garment workers' unions like Unite, began campaigning for reforms. By bringing publicity to the practices of the giant retailers, these groups persuaded corporations to pledge themselves to accept fair labor standards and to have independent monitors in the factories that supply their fashions. These groups have also promoted legislation in California and New York that aims to hold the retailers responsible for the wages and working conditions of the workers who produce the products they sell.

Informal Global Networks

While the global assembly line and mass consumption form the dominant circuits of globalized fashion, other, less visible circuits span the globe. These shadow networks concern fashion production and consumption in third-world countries. The global economy of high-tech, large-scale networks also works by exclusion. In third-world countries, globalization has resulted in the destabilizing and dismantling of official economies, massive unemployment, and the rise of informal or underground economies. As part of the restructuring and deregulation of global capital, the World Bank and International Monetary Fund have imposed on debtor nations in the third world Structural Adjustment Programs. These programs dismantled state economic controls on basic necessities and social programs for health, education, housing, and sanitation, in favor of free-market strategies, austerity programs, and privatization of basic utilities like electricity and water. These measures have resulted in a disintegration of formal institutions of the government and economy. Out of desperation, people have devised means of surviving in informal economic networks. In Africa and Latin America, this has had two effects on fashion.

One is that the numbers of artisanal producers, especially tailors, dyers, weavers, and jewelry makers, have increased dramatically. In an alternative global network, suitcase vendors sell to tourists, or they travel to diasporic communities in Europe and the United States, where they sell their fashions in people's homes, at eth-

nic festivals, or on the street. They also sell in the boutiques and on the Web sites of nonprofit organizations dedicated to helping third-word artisans.

A second effect concerns global networks of used-clothing dealers and consumers. Large wholesalers buy masses of used clothing from charity thrift shops such as Goodwill in the United States, Canada, and Europe. In giant warehouses, dealers sort the clothes, bale them, and send them by container to smaller wholesalers in countries of Asia, Africa, and Latin America. Small retailers then sell the clothes for affordable prices at open-air stalls in cities and tiny rural towns. Jeans, T-shirts, and athletic shoes thus become the most visible symbol of globalization in virtually every corner of the world.

See also **Sweatshops; Textiles and International Trade.**

BIBLIOGRAPHY

Anderson, Sarah, John Cavanagh, and Thea Lee. *Field Guide to the Global Economy.* New York: New Press and the Institute for Policy Studies, 2000.

Biggs, Tyler, Gail R. Moody, Jan-Henrik van Leeuwen, and E. Diane White. *Africa Can Compete!: Export Opportunities and Challenges for Garments and Home Products in the U.S. Market.* World Bank Discussion Papers, no. 242. Washington, D.C.: The World Bank, 1994.

Bonacich, Edna, and Richard Appelbaum. *Behind the Label: Inequality in the Los Angeles Apparel Industry.* Berkeley: University of California Press, 2000.

Brydon, Anne, and Sandra Niessen, eds. *Consuming Fashion: Adorning the Transnational Body.* Oxford: Berg, 1998.

Hansen, Karen Tranberg. *Salaula: The World of Secondhand Clothing and Zambia.* Chicago: University of Chicago Press, 2000.

Kaiser, Susan. "Identity, Postmodernity, and the Global Apparel Marketplace." In *Meanings of Dress,* edited by M. L. Damhorst, K. Miller, and S. Michelman. New York: Fairchild, 1999.

Rabine, Leslie W. *The Global Circulation of African Fashion.* Oxford: Berg, 2002.

Ross, Andrew, ed. *No Sweat: Fashion, Free Trade, and the Rights of Garment Workers.* New York: Verso, 1997.

Stiglitz, Joseph E. *Globalization and Its Discontents.* New York: W. W. Norton and Company, 2002.

Internet Resources

Global Exchange. Available from <http://www.globalexchange.org/campaigns/sweatshops.htm>.

Los Angeles Jewish Commission on Sweatshops. Available from <http://www.pjalliance.org/SweatrshopReport.pdf>.

National Labor Committee. Available from <http://www.nlcnet.org.htm>.

Sweatshop Watch. Available from <http://swatch.igc.org/swatch/industry/cal/.htm>.

United Students Against Sweatshops. Available from <http://www.studentsagainstsweatshops.org>.

Leslie W. Rabine

GLOVES Over time, shifts in production methods and patterns of consumption in relation to gloves have been paralleled by a shift in their primary role. Today, gloves may broadly be considered as a form of protective hand covering for use in cold weather. Within the context of fashion, gloves belong to the family of small accessories that includes fans, scarves, and hats. They are closely related to the mitten and muff. For several centuries gloves were highly symbolic garments, often worn for reasons other than protection. This changing conception illustrates the varied roles gloves have played within the discourse of fashion.

The Origin of Gloves

Gloves have been made since ancient times. Over the course of history gloves have served both utilitarian and decorative functions. Early cave paintings depict people wearing primitive leather gloves, and gloves have also been recovered in the remains of ancient Egyptian tombs. In both instances gloves came to be out of a need for protection. Similarly, ancient Greek and Roman peoples wore gloves for protection in battle and agricultural work. Gloves have also been an indicator of social status and power. Traditionally, the clergy wore gloves while performing the sacraments. In this case they communicated the power of the church and its representatives.

The development of the European gloving industry did not begin until the tenth century, and it was not until the eleventh century that it extended throughout Britain. Originally, the use of gloves within Britain was confined to the realm of warfare. Gloves were typically made of local deer, sheep, or imported kidskins. Knights and military officials wore protective hand coverings fashioned out of linked iron. Women did not generally include gloves as part of their dress until the Reformation period. The widespread use of gloves as fashion accessories did not commence until the early seventeenth century.

Seventeenth-Century Gloves

During the seventeenth century, fashion and status-oriented motivations for wearing gloves emerged. Within Britain the use of gloves was primarily confined to the elite social classes and signified the wearer's wealth and superior rank. Glove styles of the period were designed to complement the highly decorative and patterned styles of clothing that were in vogue. These gloves were not gender specific, and the styles worn by both sexes were almost identical in terms of shape, decoration, and color. They were typically made from deer, sheep, and kidskins in a natural color palette. As the century progressed, however, gloves became decorative garments in their own right. Gloves adorned with elaborate gold and silver silken embroideries, often bejeweled with precious stones, became popular, as did the attachment of a patterned and fringed gauntlet at the wrist. The seventeenth century also witnessed the birth of fabric and knitted gloves. However, fabric gloves did not communicate the social status and prestige that highly decorated leather gloves and gauntlets did. These gloves were elegant, fashionable, and expensive objects of desire that often served little or no utilitarian or protective function.

This new perspective brought with it new conventions concerning the trade of gloves. The newly established connection between gloves and the social status of their wearers led to the practice of offering gloves as symbolic gifts and even methods of payment. Within courts of law judges and official dignitaries were often presented with gloves not only as payment for services but also as symbols confirming the power of the State. The value of the gifts was commonly increased by inserting gold coins into the body of the glove, or by perfuming the material.

New behaviors emerged concerning the correct etiquette for wearing and removing gloves. It was not considered appropriate, for instance, to be wearing gloves when accepting objects or in the presence of a judge. Institutions such as the courts and the church continued to regard gloves as symbolic garments. Indeed, gloves were not only worn by the clergy, but became an integral element of what was considered proper church dress.

The latter years of the seventeenth century saw the emergence of distinct men's and women's styles. Elbow-length versions in different colors became popular for women while men opted for more basic styles. It was at this time that the practice of wearing gloves began to extend to the middle classes as the range of materials and styles increased. The distinction between men's and women's gloves, the proliferation of styles, and their broadening social appeal continued into the eighteenth century.

Eighteenth-Century Gloves

As a consequence of technical advances and new forms of fashionable dress, the consumption of fabric and knitted gloves began to increase during the eighteenth century. The lower cost of these materials meant that gloves soon became accessible to a wider section of the populace. Changing fashions, along with the high cost of elaborate gauntlet styles, led to the emergence of shorter, wrist-length gloves. Such styles were often constructed of finely embroidered and printed leather or multicolored woven cloth. Gloves of this type were designed to complement the popular fashions of long ruffled or lace-trimmed sleeves.

Toward the end of the eighteenth century, gloves no longer formed an essential part of the male wardrobe. Men's use of gloves was becoming confined to sporting pursuits. Gloves were thus employed only while riding, hunting, or driving, and styles emerged which catered specifically to these activities.

Nineteenth-Century Gloves

The beginning of the nineteenth century saw men return to wearing gloves for reasons other than sporting. The established preference for simple, wrist-length styles for both sexes continued throughout the early nineteenth century. Popular choices for men and women were generally constructed of pale-colored leather or white silk and cotton. The continued preference for short gloves was a consequence of the prevailing trend in clothing for long ruffled or lace-trimmed sleeves.

A clear dichotomy began to appear by the end of the century between the forms of gender-defined dress. As clothing became more elaborate for women and simplified for men, so too did the respective designs of their gloves. For women, gloves once again emerged as highly decorative fashion accessories, and specific styles were designated for day and evening wear. These were constructed either of white silk and knitted fibers or of pale-colored embroidered and finely printed leather. For men, styles became increasingly plain and well fitting. These gloves were designed to properly accompany the fine tailoring that came to dominate male dress during the early decades of the nineteenth century. For day gloves, yellow emerged as a popular color choice for men along with black, brown, and navy blue. White gloves remained de rigueur for evening wear.

By the end of the century, it became fashionable to wear tightly fitting gloves that were molded to the specific contours of the hand. Wrist-length gloves that fastened with buttons came to be worn by both sexes. For women, buttoned elbow-length evening gloves became available in a range of color and fabric variations.

The nineteenth century saw the development of social codes that prescribed the types of gloves to be worn during particular day and evening engagements. To appear in public without gloves in situations that called for glove wearing was to invite censure or ridicule. Maintaining one's gloves was also very important, as soiled gloves were reflective of poor etiquette. As pale-colored gloves were popular at the time, people had to purchase their gloves in multiple quantities and carry spare pairs with them on outings should one pair become soiled.

Twentieth-Century Gloves

In sharp contrast to the preceding century, the twentieth century was marked by the gradual demise in the social importance of gloves. Although technological advancements made in glove production meant that greater varieties could now be made, the significant social upheaval following World War I profoundly affected the way they were consumed. After World War II, previously held standards of social etiquette concerning the wearing of gloves no longer seemed appropriate. Since clothing was rationed and became rather standardized in design, highly fashionable gloves were largely deemed unnecessary. As a consequence, gloves reverted to a more utilitarian role as garments to be used for protection against cold weather. Practical, durable styles were produced for both sexes in conservative color choices of black, brown, and navy. Leather versions were often lined with wool and fur for extra warmth.

Throughout the 1950s, however, something of a glove renaissance occurred within the realm of female fashionable dress. Styles gradually emerged that were constructed from synthetic fibers, such as satin and netting, in a wide range of colors. Women began to wear gloves that either sharply contrasted or closely matched the color of their clothing, jewelry, and other small accessories. This trend was short lived, and by the 1960s the use of gloves became increasingly less frequent, except as protection against cold weather or for work, such as gardening.

Conclusion

The fact that gloves have been widely preserved within museum collections indicates our appreciation of the important role gloves have played throughout history. Gloves were once highly symbolic garments used to convey important social messages. Since the twentieth century, however, this has changed. Within the contemporary fashion discourse gloves assume a limited role and function. Their status has been reduced to utility and they are worn only as means of protection. It is highly unlikely that gloves will ever assume the symbolic significance they once had in the past.

See also **Muffs.**

BIBLIOGRAPHY

Boehn, Max Von. *Modes and Manners: Ornaments; Lace, Fans, Gloves, Walking Sticks, Parasols, Jewellrey & Trinkets.* London and Toronto: J. M. Dent and Sons Ltd., 1929.

Cumming, Valerie. *Gloves.* London: B. T. Batsford Ltd., 1982.

Dent, Allcroft & Co. *A Brief Description of the Manufacture, History and Associations of Gloves with illustrations from Dent, Allcroft & Co's Manufactory.* Worcester, England: Worcester, Baylis, Lewis and Company.

Ellis, Eldred B. *Gloves and the Glove Trade.* London: Pitman and Sons, 1921.

Norton-Kyshe, J. W. *The Law and Customs Relating to Gloves.* London: Stevens and Haynes, 1901.

Kristina Stankovski

GODEY'S LADY'S BOOK *Godey's Lady's Book,* first published in Philadelphia in 1830 as *Godey's Ladies' Handbook,* was the leading women's magazine in mid-nineteenth-century America. Similar publications had been produced in Europe since the late eighteenth century and *Godey's* was closely patterned after its English and French counterparts. Several variations of the periodical's name occurred over time, including *Godey's Magazine and Lady's Book,* but the magazine is generally known by its most familiar title, *Godey's Lady's Book.*

The magazine's founder and first publisher, Louis Antoine Godey (1804–1878), provided his female audience with a wide range of articles designed to educate and entertain. *Godey's* topics included fashion, travel

Fashion plate from *Godey's Lady's Book,* October 1852. Founded by Louis Antoine Godey in 1830, *Godey's* was the leading women's magazine in mid-nineteenth-century America. It ceased publication in 1898. PUBLIC DOMAIN.

notes, exercise regimens, practical advice for the house-wife on home decoration, recipes, gardening, and crafts, plus fiction, poetry and essays by celebrated nineteenth-century authors, such as Harriet Beecher Stowe, Edgar Allan Poe, and Nathaniel Hawthorne. In the 1850s,

Godey's had the highest circulation of any American women's magazine, reaching a peak of 150,000 subscriptions by the early 1860s. The periodical's success during these years was largely due to Sarah Josepha Hale (1788–1879), *Godey's* editor from 1837 to 1877. Before coming to *Godey's*, Hale edited her own literary journal, an experience that influenced her work at Godey's and strengthened the magazine's content, making it more appealing than its competitors.

Fashion illustrations were part of *Godey's* from its first number. Single hand-colored fashion plates were issued until 1861, when folded double-page plates were introduced. The magazine also included descriptions of the outfits in the fashion plates, detailing fabrics, trims, and accessories. Additional uncolored plates illustrating accessories or individual garments were also found in most issues, along with needlework and craft projects, and occasionally, patterns.

Godey's was not the first American publication to use hand-colored fashion plates—that distinction goes to a competitor started in 1826, *Graham's American Monthly Magazine of Literature, Art and Fashion*. The fashion plates in American magazines through the 1840s were generally inferior copies of designs that initially appeared in English or French periodicals. By the 1850s, the quality of the images improved because some of the metal engraving plates used in French publications were imported to the United States. The original captions on these plates were removed and new ones, such as "The Latest Fashions, only to be found in Godey's Lady's Book," were substituted. While tactics like these obviously resulted in illustrated fashions some months behind the latest European modes, they did give *Godey's* subscribers direct contact with such styles.

Although homemakers were *Godey's* targeted audience, the magazine's fashion information and illustrations were invaluable tools for professional dressmakers in determining what was stylish and for tips in achieving the newest look. The resulting garments, however, were generally much less elaborate than those in the fashion plates. Beginning in 1870s, *Godey's* fashion influence was eclipsed by new publications like the high-style fashion magazine *Harper's Bazaar*, or others with a practical focus, such as *What to Wear and How to Make It: Madame Demorest's Semi-Annual Book of Instructions on Dress and Dressmaking*. It was also in the 1870s that Godey sold the magazine and Hale retired, accelerating *Godey's* decline as a quality publication. After passing through several owners, *Godey's Lady's Book* ceased publication in 1898.

See also **Fashion Illustrators; Fashion Magazines; Fashion Plates.**

BIBLIOGRAPHY

Finley, Ruth Elbright. *The Lady of Godey's, Sarah Josepha Hale.* Philadelphia and London: J. B. Lippincott, 1931. Laudatory biography of the remarkable life of *Godey's* edited by Sarah Josepha Hale.

Godey's Lady's Book, 1830–1898. A full run of this title can be found at the Library of Congress.

Holland, Vyvyan. *Hand Colored Fashion Plates, 1770 to 1899.* London: B. T. Batsford Ltd., 1955. A history of hand-colored fashion plates that details the uncredited use of European plates in American magazines.

Kunciov, Robert, ed. *Mr. Godey's Ladies: Being a Mosaic of Fashions and Fancies.* New York: Bonanza Books, 1971. A compendium of fashion illustrations and quotations from *Godey's Lady's Book* issues from 1830 to 1879, with an introductory history of the magazine.

Mott, Frank Luther. *A History of American Magazines.* 6 vols. Cambridge, Mass.: Harvard University Press, 1938–1968. Comprehensive history of American magazines.

Colleen R. Callahan

GOLF CLOTHING Although golf had existed in Scotland since the Middle Ages, as a popular game it dates to the end of the nineteenth century. The first North American golf club, founded by a Scot in Montreal in the 1870s, and soon followed by others in Quebec and Ontario, was the outcome of Scottish immigration. The earliest U.S. club was founded in Brookline, Massachusetts, in 1882. From the beginning, the clothing for golf was practical fashion wear, based primarily on the new men's sporting models appearing for use for bicycling or shooting at the time. It consisted of tweed suits with vests and, if knickers were chosen as trousers, knee-high stockings to complete the outfit. For women, who participated from the outset, a nod to practicality appeared in the slight shortening of skirts, some four to six inches off the ground, but dress for golf generally remained the clothing of the New Woman of the turn of the century: skirt, shirtwaist blouse, jacket, hat and gloves, and of course, a corset. The overall effect was conservative but comfortable for the time. It was clothing suitable for women to wear while interacting in public with men. This remained the model well into the 1920s, and indeed, given inevitable changes in design, the general tone for golf wear from that time on.

In the 1920s, Edward, Prince of Wales (later Edward VIII and duke of Windsor), influenced golf fashion with his dashing personal style, especially in his choice of traditional Fair Isle patterned knit pullover sweaters and argyle socks. The knickerbockers of the previous century were the preferred trousers at this time, but now were cut four inches longer than the older version, making them baggier at the knee; hence the name, "plus fours." Two-colored shoes and soft-peaked tweed caps completed the look, which became the uniform of choice throughout the 1930s. Even in the early 2000s, knickers, though rare, continue to be worn. Cleated shoes then were often two-toned, much in the style of the saddle shoes that became the signature footwear of bobby-sox teenagers everywhere in the late 1930s. In addition, golf shoes often had a fringed kiltie flap that covered the laces. Bobby Jones, the Tiger Woods of his day and founder of the Masters, codified the fashion set by the Prince of Wales in the United States.

Throughout this time, women remained skirted. Tailored sports dresses that were the precursors to the shirtmaker dress emerged in the late 1920s and 1930s;

tailored separates alternated with the dresses into the post–World War II years. Skirts were in keeping with the fashions of the time, hovering around the knee in length, usually gored or relaxed with inverted tailored kick pleats front and back to allow movement and ease. They were coupled with tailored shirts and sweaters. Bermuda shorts, the sportswear darlings of the mid-1950s, hitting just above the knee and worn with knee socks, became preferred garments for both men and women at that time and continue to be worn for golf in the first years of the twenty-first century, though women usually wear them with short socks or sockees that come only to the ankle. Shorts and skorts (shorts with a skirt-like flap extending from the side seam three-quarters of the way across the front of the garment to give the appearance of a skirt) are also part of a woman golfer's wardrobe. Professional golfers, both male and female, wear long, loose, comfortable trousers or long shorts, with belt loops and belts. Most golf clubs have a policy of a collared shirt, whether woven or knit. Most frequently, these are polo shirt style. The club name or emblem is traditionally embroidered on the left breast, and it also appears on the baseball caps or sun visors that have been adopted for golf.

Most clothes for golf were practical cotton, particularly if worn in warm or moderate climates. Of course, golf fanatics who play as much as they can throughout the year, even in the north, wear layers that keep them warm, with sweaters and zipper-front waterproof jackets. With the introduction of manufactured fibers, notably polyester in the 1960s that spawned the ubiquitous "no care" polyester/cotton fabrics, golf clothes took on a more daring coloration in keeping with the fashions of the 1960s, giving golf clothing the reputation, that continues to linger, of colorful, often garish clothing that makes no attempt to be stylish. Even the greatest sartorial symbol of golf, the highly coveted Master's jacket, is a bright, unforgettable green that few would choose to wear off the links.

Overall, golf clothing might be termed fossilized fashion, becoming almost a parody of itself in its adherence to conventional forms. Golfers are stereotypically known to wear clothes that are codified by past traditions rather new fashions. They choose outfits that are practical, loose, and pragmatic in keeping with long outdoor walks that are broken periodically by the need to swing a golf club.

Although stars such as Tiger Woods maintain a casual elegance in their golf dress, their choices still fall into the general categories of loose and comfortable. The contrast between dark conservative business suits worn during the workweek and the colorful, loose, and comfortable clothing worn for golf on the weekends has become, at the beginning of the twenty-first century, virtually a cliché.

See also **Sportswear.**

BIBLIOGRAPHY

Armitage, John. *Man at Play Nine Centuries of Pleasure Making.* London and New York: Frederick Warne and Company, Inc., 1977.

Chenoune, Farid. *History of Men's Fashion.* Paris and New York: Flammarion, 1993.

Lee-Potter, Charlie. *Sportswear in Vogue since 1910.* New York: Abbeville Press, 1984.

Tortora, Phyllis, and Keith Eubank. *Survey of Historic Costume.* 3rd ed. New York: Fairchild Publications, 1998.

Patricia Campbell Warner

GORE-TEX. *See* **Techno-Textiles.**

GOTHS Having emerged in the wake of punk during the 1980s, the contemporary goth scene has existed for more than two decades, as a visually spectacular form of youth culture, whose members are most immediately identified by the dark forms of glamour displayed in their appearance.

Goth or Gothic Revival?

Extensive links are sometimes drawn between goth style and various "gothic" movements and individuals throughout history associated with themes such as elegance, decadence, and death. Gavin Baddeley has detailed a linear progression of gothic culture that ends with present-day goths, having journeyed through twentieth century horror genres in television and cinema, through various examples of literature and fashion from the preceding two hundred years and finally back to the "grotesque" art and sculpture credited to the original fourth century goths. The notion that what is known as goth fashion in the early 2000s is merely the latest revival of a coherent centuries-old tradition has undoubted appeal and convenience, even to some enthusiasts for the subculture. The reality, though, is that they owe a greater debt to post-1960s developments in popular music culture than to literary, artistic, or cinematic traditions.

Origins

A selection of British bands that appeared prior to, during, and after the late 1970s punk era set the tone for the goth subculture that was to emerge. Crucial ingredients were provided by the deep-voiced feminine glamour of David Bowie, the disturbing intensity and eclecticism of late 1970s Iggy Pop, and the somber angst-ridden despair of Joy Division. The key direct founders of goth, though, were former punks Siouxsie and the Banshees, whose style began to take on a decidedly sinister tone toward the early 1980s, and Bauhaus, whose self-conscious emphasis upon funereal, macabre sounds and imagery was epitomized in the now legendary record "Bela Lugosi's Dead." As the dark, feminine appearance and imagery associated with such bands began to be taken up by their fans, the new "scene" received extensive coverage in the music press. By the mid-1980s, the deep vocals, jangling guitars, and somber base lines of The Sisters of Mercy alongside black clothes, long coats, and dark shades, had established them as the archetypal "goth rock" band. A period of chart success for the Sisters, alongside The Mission, Fields of the Nephilim, The Cure, and Siouxsie and the Banshees, would ensure that toward the end of the 1980s goth enjoyed significant international exposure. Through the 1990s, however, the subculture existed in a rather more underground form, with occasional moments of mass exposure provided by high-profile artists such as Marilyn Manson and through the borrowing of goth style by emerging metal genres and, intermittently, by major fashion labels.

Horror Fiction
Consistent with this emphasis upon sounds and appearances emerging from the music industry, the goth scene has consistently been focused, first and foremost, around a blend of music, fashion, pubs, and nightclubs. As such, it would be more usefully seen in the context of punk, glam, skate, and other contemporary style subcultures, than that of ancient tribes or nineteenth-century poets. Yet this should not be taken to imply that previous "gothic" movements are somehow irrelevant here. Most notably, it is clear that goth musicians and fans have drawn—sometimes "ironically," sometimes not—upon imagery associated with horror fiction in both literary and cinematic forms. Beyond a general emphasis upon black hair and clothing, this has manifested itself, for both males and females, in the form of ghostly white faces offset by thick dark eyeliner and lipstick. As if the vampire link were not clear enough, some have sported even more overt signifiers, from crosses to bats, to plastic fangs. For others, there has been a tendency to adapt elements of the traditional bourgeois fashions associated with vampire fiction, something often mediated through the wardrobes of such cinema blockbusters as *Bram Stoker's Dracula* (1992) and *Interview with the Vampire* (1994). Obvious examples here would include corsets, bodices, and lacy or velvet tops and dresses. Furthermore, although it is seldom regarded as pivotal to subcultural participation, many goths enjoy directly consuming and discussing horror fiction in both its literary and cinematic forms.

Contemporary Influences
Yet there is more to goth fashion than this. The subculture's emphasis upon the somber and the macabre has been accompanied by consistent evidence of other themes that fit rather less neatly with the notion of a linear long-term history of gothic. For example, an emphasis upon particular forms of femininity, for both sexes, goes far beyond the macabre angst and romanticism associated with vampire fiction. Notably, for some years, PVC skirts, tops, corsets, and collars have been among the most popular styles of clothing for goths of both genders, something that borrows more from the contemporary fetish scene

Goth clothing. Inspired by the somber and the macabre, goth fashion in the late twentieth and early twenty-first centuries owed much to horror fiction and punk/glam icons such as David Bowie, Joy Division, and Siouxsie and the Banshees. COPYRIGHT SARAH LOUISE HODKINSON, 2003. REPRODUCED BY PERMISSION.

than it does from traditional gothic fiction. Links with fetishism, punk, and rock culture more generally can also be demonstrated by the consistent display of facial piercing, tattoos, dyed hair, and combat pants by goths. Indeed, one of the most popular types of clothing among goths has consistently been T-shirts displaying band logos, something distinctive to the goth scene in the specific artist name and design, but otherwise comparable with other music cultures. During the course of the 1990s, another contemporary influence from music culture established itself as central to the evolving goth style, particularly in Europe. In search of new directions in which to take a well-established set of looks and sounds, bands and their fans increasingly began to appropriate and adapt elements of dance culture into the goth sound and appearance. In addition to the incorporation of mechanical dance beats and electronic sequences into otherwise gloom-ridden, sinister forms of music, "cybergoth" involved the juxtaposition of more established elements of goth fashion with reflective or ultraviolet-sensitive clothing, fluorescent makeup, and braided hair extensions.

Distinctiveness and Identity
In spite of its variety of influences, goth fashion is a contemporary style in its own right, which has retained significant levels of consistency and distinctiveness for over two decades. Put simply, since the mid 1980s, goths have always been easily recognized as such, both by one another and by many outsiders to their subculture. Attempts to interpret their distinctive appearance as communicating a morbid state of mind or a disturbed psychological makeup are usually misplaced. What *is* symbolized,

though, is a defiant sense of collective identity, based upon a celebration of shared aesthetic tastes relating primarily to music, fashion, and nightlife (Hodkinson 2002).

See also **Occult Dress; Punk; Street Style; Subcultures.**

BIBLIOGRAPHY

Baddeley, Gavin. *Goth Chic: A Connoisseur's Guide to Dark Culture.* London: Plexus, 2002.

Hodkinson, Paul. *Goth: Identity, Style and Subculture.* Oxford: Berg, 2002.

Mercer, Mick. *Gothic Rock Black Book.* London: Omnibus Press, 1988.

———. *Gothic Rock: Everything You Wanted to Know but Were Too Gormless to Ask.* Birmingham: Pegasus, 1991.

Thompson, Dave. *The Dark Reign of Gothic Rock.* London: Helter Skelter, 2002.

Paul Hodkinson

GRÈS, MME. Madame Alix Grès is widely regarded as one of the most brilliant couturiers of the twentieth century. She employed innovative construction techniques in the service of a classical aesthetic, creating her hallmark "Grecian" gowns as well as a wide range of simple and geometrically cut designs based on ethnic costume. Her garments are noted for their three-dimensional, sculptural quality.

Mme. Grès's life, like the creation of her gowns, was unconventional. Born Germaine Emilie Krebs on 30 November 1903 in Paris, France, she became a couturier after her bourgeois Catholic parents discouraged her desire to pursue a career first as a professional dancer and then as a sculptor. Around 1933, during a brief apprenticeship of three months at the couture house of Premet, she learned the basics of dressmaking and changed her first name to Alix. That same period she began to work for a couturier named Julie Barton, who renamed her house Alix to reflect the astounding success of her assistant.

On 15 April 1937 Grès married a Russian-born painter, Serge Anatolievitch Czerefkow. It was then that she became Alix Grès, Grès being an anagram of her husband's first name, which he used to sign his paintings. In August 1939 their only child, Anne, was born. Months earlier, however, Serge had left France and relocated to Tahiti.

In the spring of 1940 the Nazis occupied Paris. After a falling out with Barton, Grès fled the city, like many other Parisians, and moved south with her infant daughter. The one enduring legacy of her exile was the donning of a turban; she took to wearing the headdress initially because she could not go to a hairdresser. It became her personal trademark.

In 1941 Grès returned to Paris and opened her own salon. After refusing to accommodate the Nazi's insistence that she reveal her trade secrets and adhere to the regime's fabric restrictions, she was forced to close the shop in January 1944. Finally, in the early summer of 1944, she was authorized to resume her business in time to show a final collection before the liberation of Paris. This now legendary group of garments was made using only the red, white, and blue of the French flag.

The most famous and recognizable design of Mme. Grès was her classically inspired floor-length, pleated gown. In the 1930s these "Grecian" garments were primarily white in color, made from uncut lengths of double-width matte silk jersey, most often sleeveless, and cut to enhance the female body without physically restricting its movement. By the onset of World War II, because of textile restrictions, Grès focused on the manipulation of the bodices, sleeves, and necklines of much shorter garments.

In the late 1940s Grès resumed the use of larger quantities of fabric as well as a tighter and finer style of pleating. She also employed inner reinforcement or corseting. By the 1970s Grès has eliminated the corset and, simultaneously, cut away portions of the bodice, thus exposing large areas of the nude torso.

In the 1950s and 1960s Mme. Grès's business and her designs thrived. She engaged in several licensing agreements, the most successful of which was her perfume, Cabochard, released in 1959. Literally meaning "pigheaded," it describes the tenacity of the couturier. Madame Grès's ethnic-inspired garments were an important part of her oeuvre during this time. Non-Western art was a major source of inspiration to her beginning in the 1930s, with the proliferation of exhibitions and expositions that displayed the products of France's colonies. Although her output of such garments was to drop off significantly during the 1940s and 1950s, she responded to a strong revival of ethnic influences during the mid-1960s, creating caftans, capes, and pajamas for "couture hippies." These gowns were different from her prewar creations in that Grès relied on construction techniques she observed in non-Western dress. This change occurred after a 1959 trip to India, where Grès studied ethnic costume and took note of Eastern cultures' aversion to the cutting of textiles. She also experimented with fabrics, using faille and brocaded silks as well as more pliable materials such as fine wool knits and djersakasha, a cashmere jersey that could be woven as a tube, eliminating the need for seams.

In 1972 Mme. Grès was unanimously elected president of the Chambre Syndicale de la Couture. Four years later she became the first recipient of the Dé d'Or (Golden Thimble award), the highest honor given by the Chambre Syndicale. By the mid-1980s, however, the house of Grès had fallen into decline. After entrusting both her business and her trademark to a businessman-cum-politician named Bernard Tapie, Grès lost both. In April 1986 Maison Grès was expelled from the Chambre Syndicale for nonpayment of dues. Difficulties continued until the official retirement of Madame Grès, after the presentation of her 1988 spring/summer collection. The exit of one of the greatest figures in the world of haute couture took place quietly, with no official press release from the house of Grès. She died in the south of France on 13 December 1994.

No figure in French couture used the elements of classicism so completely or so poetically as Madame Grès, who used this aesthetic in her creation of seemingly limitless construction variations on a theme. Often referred to as the great "sculptress" of haute couture, Grès used the draping method to create her most dramatic designs, often consisting of puffed, molded, and three-dimensionally shaped elements that billowed and fell away from the body. Examples included capes made with yards of heavy wool manipulated into deep folds, taffeta cocktail dresses that combine finely pleated bodices balanced with full balloon-shaped skirts puffed sleeves, and evening gowns with enormous circular sleeves and trains that could rise like sails. Although volumetric, her sculpted garments are supple and pliable and have no reinforcement such as an attached inner facing. The end result was sensual fashions that stood away from the body rather than falling next to it.

See also **Ethnic Style in Fashion; Haute Couture.**

BIBLIOGRAPHY

Aillaud, Charlotte. "Legend: Madame Grès." *Architectural Digest* (August 1988).

Ardisson, Thierry, and Jean Luc Maitre. "The Greatness of Grès." *Interview* (February 1981).

Brantley, Ben. "Mme. Grès on Finely Chiseled Couture." *Women's Wear Daily* 7 (November 1979).

Charles-Roux, Edmond. "Madame Grès, a Romantic View without Nostalgia." *Vogue* (September 1964).

Cooper, Arlene. "How Madame Grès Sculpts with Fabric." *Threads Magazine* (April/May 1987).

Hata, Sahoko, ed. *L'Art de Madame Grès.* Tokyo: Bunka Publishing Bureau, 1980.

Hollander, Anne. "A Sculptor in Fabric." *Connoisseur* (August 1982).

"Madame Grès, Hellène de Paris." *Jardins des Modes* (December 1980–January 1981).

Nemy, Enid. "Timeless Styles by Madame Grès." *New York Times* (10 October 1979).

Villiers le Moy, Pascale. "The Timeless Fashions of Madame Grès." *Connoisseur* (August 1982).

Patricia Mears

GRUNGE The term "grunge" is used to define a specific moment in twentieth-century music and fashion. Hailing from the northwest United States in the 1980s, grunge went on to have global implications for alternative bands and do-it-yourself (DIY) dressing. While grunge music and style were absorbed by a large youth

Nirvana singer/guitarist Kurt Cobain, Seattle, Washington, 1990. Fueled by a back-to-basics ethic, the grunge movement started in the Pacific Northwest in the late 1980s. Its simple way of dress became a fashion phenomenon after the multiplatinum success of bands like Nirvana, Pearl Jam, and Soundgarden. © S.I.N./CORBIS. REPRODUCED BY PERMISSION.

following, its status as a self-conscious subculture is debatable. People who listened to grunge music did not refer to themselves as "grungers" in the same way as "punks" or "hippies." However, like these subcultures, grunge was co-opted by the music and fashion industries through its promotion by the media.

Grunge Music

The word "grunge" dates from 1972, but did not enter popular terminology until the birth of the Seattle sound, a mix of heavy-metal, punk, and good old-fashioned rock and roll, in the late 1980s. Many musicians associated with grunge credit their exposure to early punk bands as one of their most important influences.

Like San Francisco in the 1960s, Seattle in the 1980s was a breeding ground for music that spoke to its youth. The independent record label Sub Pop recorded many of the Seattle bands inexpensively and was partly responsible for their garage sound. Many of these bands went on to receive international acclaim and major record label representation, most notably The Melvins, Mudhoney, Green River, Soundgarden, Malfunkshun, TAD, and Nirvana. Nirvana's second album, *Nevermind*, was released in 1991, making Nirvana the first of this growing scene to go multiplatinum and Kurt Cobain, Nirvana's lead singer, the reluctant voice of his generation.

(Sub)Cultural Context

The youth movements most often associated and compared to grunge—hippie and punk—were driven both by music and politics. Punks and hippies used music and fashion to make strong statements about the world and are often referred to as "movements" due to this political component. While the youth of 1980s Seattle were aware of politics, grunge was fueled more by self-expression—sadness, disenchantment, disconnectedness, loneliness, frustration—and perhaps was an unintentional movement of sorts. There does not appear to have been a common grunge goal, such as punk's "anarchy" or the hippies' "peace." Despite this lack of unifying intentionality, grunge gave voice to a bored, lost, emotionally neglected, post-punk generation—Generation X.

Grunge Fashion

If punk's antifashion stance can be interpreted as "against fashion," then that of grunge can be seen as "nonfashion." The grunge youth, born of hippies and raised on punk, reinterpreted these components through their own post-hippie, post-punk, West Coast aesthetic. Grunge was essentially a slovenly, thoughtless, uncoordinated look, but with an edge. Iconic items for men and women were ripped and faded jeans, flannel shirts or wool Pendletons layered over dirty T-shirts with outdated logos, and black combat-style boots such as Dr. Martens. Because the temperature in Seattle can swing by 20 degrees in the same day, it is convenient to have a wool long-sleeved button-down shirt that can be easily removed and tied around one's waist. The style for plaid flannel shirts and wool Pendletons is regional, having been a longtime staple for local lumberjacks and logging-industry employees—it was less a fashion choice than a utilitarian necessity.

The low-budget antimaterialist philosophy brought on by the recession made shopping at thrift stores and army surplus outlets common, adding various elements to the grunge sartorial lexicon, including beanies for warmth and unkempt hair, long underwear worn under shorts (in defiance of the changeable weather), and cargo pants. Thrift-store finds, such as vintage floral-print dresses and baby-doll nightgowns, were worn with oversized sweaters and holey cardigans. Grunge was dressing down at its most extreme, taking casualness and comfort dressing to an entirely new level.

Grunge Chic

The first mention of grunge in the fashion industry was in *Women's Wear Daily* on 17 August 1992: "Three hot looks—Rave, Hip Hop and Grunge—have hit the street and stores here, each spawned by the music that's popular among the under-21 set." The style that had begun on the streets of Seattle had finally hit New York and was heading across the Atlantic. Later that same year, Grace Coddington (editor) and Steven Meisel (fashion photographer) did an eight-page article and layout for *Vogue* with the help of a Sub Pop cofounder and owner Jonathan Poneman: "Flannels, ratty tour shirts, boots, and baseball caps have become a uniform for those in the know, and their legions are growing" (p. 254). The fashion machine was drawn to the utilitarian aspects of grunge as well as the juxtapositions of textures and the old against the new. Marc Jacobs is credited with bringing grunge to the runway with his spring 1993 collection for Perry Ellis. He was later followed by such designers as Calvin Klein, Christian Francis Roth, Armani, Dolce & Gabbana, Anna Sui, and Versace who all came out with layered and vintage looks made out of luxury fabrics.

Ultimately, grunge failed as a high-fashion trend because its vitality came from the unique and personal art of combining clothes and accessories from wildly disparate and idiosyncratic sources. Grunge was not easily repackaged and sold to the people who related to it because it was out of their price range and the upscale consumer was not taking the bait. Where grunge worked well was at low to moderate price points as middle-class kids across America were buying pre-ripped jeans, beanies, and flannels all the while dancing to Nirvana.

Post-Grunge World

Repackaging was also the fate of grunge music as every major record label tried to find the next Nirvana, and bands like Pearl Jam and Bush filled stadiums but paid little homage to grunge's punk roots. Nevertheless, grunge ultimately managed to revive rock and roll, redefine the music of the 1990s by bringing the focus back to the guitar, and make the word "alternative" meaningless in the twenty-first century as alternative music is now the music of the masses.

What grunge did for music it also did for fashion. Grunge opened the door to recycled clothes for everyone as a fashionable, and even a chic, choice. Grunge defined a new approach to dressing that included layering and juxtapositions of patterns and textures. The DIY approach to dress has become the norm, giving the consumer the freedom to choose, to not be a slave to one look or designer, and the confidence to create personal ensembles with the goal of self-expression through style.

See also **Hip-hop Fashion; Hippie Style; Punk; Street Style; Subcultures.**

BIBLIOGRAPHY

Coddington, Grace. "Grunge and Glory." *Vogue* (December 1992): 254–263.

de la Haye, Amy, and Cathie Dingwall. *Surfers, Soulies, Skinheads, and Skaters: Subcultural Style from the Forties to the Nineties.* London: V&A Publications, 1996.

Polhemus, Ted. *Street Style: From Sidewalk to Catwalk.* London: Thames and Hudson, Inc., 1994.

Sims, Joshua. *Rock/Fashion.* London: Omnibus Press, 1999.

Steele, Valerie. *Fifty Years of Fashion: New Look to Now.* New Haven, Conn., and London: Yale University Press, 1997.

Shannon Bell Price

GUCCI From modest beginnings at the end of the nineteenth century, the Gucci company became one of the world's most successful manufacturers of high-end leather goods, clothing, and other fashion products. As an immigrant in Paris and then London, working in exclusive hotels, young Guccio Gucci (1881–1953) was impressed with the luxurious luggage he saw sophisticated guests bring with them. Upon returning to his birthplace of Florence, a city distinguished for high-quality materials and skilled artisans, he established a shop in 1920 that sold fine leather goods with classic styling. Although Gucci organized his workrooms for industrial methods of production, he maintained traditional aspects of fabrication. Initially Gucci employed skilled workers in basic Florentine leather crafts, attentive to finishing. With expansion, machine stitching was a production method that supported construction.

Together with three of his sons, Aldo, Vasco, and Rodolfo, Gucci expanded the company to include stores in Milan and Rome as well as additional shops in Florence. Gucci's stores featured such finely crafted leather accessories as handbags, shoes, and his iconic ornamented loafer as well as silks and knitwear in a signature pattern. The Gucci loafer is the only shoe in the collection of the Museum of Modern Art in New York.

The company made handbags of cotton canvas rather than leather during World War II as a result of material shortages. The canvas, however, was distinguished by a signature double-G symbol combined with prominent red and green bands. After the war, the Gucci crest, which showed a shield and armored knight surrounded by a ribbon inscribed with the family name, became synonymous with the city of Florence.

Gucci clothing and accessories for sale. The Gucci company, which began as a single Italian leather goods shop founded in 1920, expanded to become one of the most successful international purveyors of fashion © JACQUES M. CHENET/CORBIS. REPRODUCED BY PERMISSION.

Aldo and Rodolfo Gucci further expanded the company's horizons in 1953 by establishing offices in New York City. Film stars and jet-set travelers to Italy during the 1950s and 1960s brought their glamour to Florence, turning Gucci's merchandise into international status symbols. Movie stars posed in Gucci's clothing, accessories, and footwear for lifestyle magazines around the world, contributing to the company's growing reputation.

Gucci's distinctive lines made its products among the most frequently copied in the world in the early 2000s. Pigskin, calf, and imported exotic animal skins were subjected to various methods of fabrication. Waterproof canvas and satin were used for evening bags. Bamboo was first used to make handbag handles by a process of heating and molding in 1947, and purses made with a shoulder strap and snaffle-bit decoration were introduced in 1960. In 1964 Gucci's lush butterfly pattern was custom-created for silk foulards, followed by equally luxuriant floral patterns. The original Gucci loafer was updated by a distinctive snaffle-bit ornament in 1966, while the "Rolls-Royce" luggage set was introduced in 1970. Watches, jewelry, ties, and eyewear were then added to the company's product lines. A particularly iconic touch, introduced in 1964, was the use of the double-G logo for belt buckles and other accessory decorations.

The company prospered through the 1970s, but the 1980s were marked by internal family disputes that brought Gucci to the brink of disaster. Rodolfo's son Maurizio took over the company's direction after his father's death in 1983, and dismissed his uncle Aldo—who eventually served a prison term for tax evasion. Maurizio proved to be an unsuccessful president; he was compelled to sell the family-owned company to Investcorp, a Bahrain-based company, in 1988. Maurizio disposed of his remaining stock in 1993. Tragically, Maurizio was murdered in Milan in 1995, and his former wife, Patrizia Reggiani, was convicted of hiring his killers. Meanwhile, the new investors promoted the American-educated Domenico De Sole from the position of family attorney to president of Gucci America in 1994 and chief executive in 1995.

The company had previously brought in Dawn Mello in 1989 as editor and ready-to-wear designer in order to reestablish its reputation. Well aware of Gucci's tarnished image and the value of its name brand, Mello hired Tom Ford in 1990 to design a ready-to-wear line. He was promoted to the position of creative director in 1994. Before Mello returned to her post as president of the American retailer Bergdorf Goodman, she initiated the return of Gucci's headquarters from the business center of Milan to Florence, where its craft traditions were

rooted. There she and Ford reduced the number of Gucci products from twenty thousand to a more reasonable five thousand.

Tom Ford came to the foundering company with vision and style. Having the strong support of Dominico De Sole, Ford wished to maintain a sense of the company's history while updating Gucci's trademarks. In 1994 Ford became responsible for creative direction, and by 1996 he directed all aspects of the company—including ready-to-wear clothing, visual merchandising, packaging, interior design, and advertising. Ford and De Sole struggled to restore the former reputation of Gucci, while redirecting the growing brand to a new level for the market of the late 1990s.

There were seventy-six Gucci stores around the world in 1997, along with numerous licensing agreements. Ford was instrumental in the process of decision-making with De Sole when the Gucci Group acquired Yves Saint Laurent Rive Gauche, Bottega Veneta, Boucheron, Sergio Rossi, and, in part-ownership with Stella McCartney, Alexander McQueen and Balenciaga. By 2001 Ford and De Sole shared the responsibility for major business decisions, while Ford concurrently directed design at Yves Saint Laurent as well as at Gucci.

The French conglomerate Pinault-Printemps-Redouté, however, gained ownership of 60 percent of the Gucci Group's stock in 2003. *Women's Wear Daily* then announced the departure of both Domenico De Sole and Tom Ford from the Gucci Group when their contracts expired in April 2004. The last spring collection under the direction of Ford and De Sole was a critical and commercial success. Amid widespread speculation in the fashion press about Ford's heir, the company announced in March 2004 that he would be replaced by a team of younger designers promoted from the ranks of the company's staff.

See also **Brands and Labels; Ford, Tom; Italian Fashion; Leather and Suede; Saint Laurent, Yves; Shoes.**

BIBLIOGRAPHY

Bianchino, Gloria, et al., eds. *Italian Fashion*. Vol. 1, *The Origins of High Fashion and Knitwear*. Milan: Electa SpA, 1987.

Forden, Sara Gay. *The House of Gucci: A Sensational Story of Murder, Madness, Glamour, and Greed*. New York: William Morrow, 2000.

Horyn, Cathy. "Tom Ford Goes Out with a Roar." *New York Times*, 26 February 2004.

Steele, Valerie. *Fashion, Italian Style*. New Haven, Conn.: Yale University Press, 2003.

Gillion Carrara

H

HAIR ACCESSORIES Hair accessories are functional or ornamental objects wrapped, tied, twisted, inserted, or otherwise attached to the hair. Throughout history, types of ornamentation and the materials from which they were made indicated religious significance, social class, age group, and level of fashion awareness. Infinitely varied in shapes, sizes, and materials, examples of hair accessories include: hair rings or bands, ribbons and bows, hairpins, hair combs, barrettes, beads, thread or string, hair spikes and sticks, and other affixed miscellaneous objects (shells, jewels, coins, flowers, feathers) perceived to have aesthetic or social and cultural value. Hair accessories have been worn by people of all ages and by both genders.

Hair rings and hair bands are cylindrically shaped hair accessories wound around the hair, designed to hold hair away from the face, or otherwise confine strands of hair. Some of the earliest hair rings were found in Great Britain, France, and Belgium at the end of the Bronze Age. These objects were solid gold or gold-plated clay, bronze, or lead. Ancient Egyptians wore similar rings during the New Kingdom Dynasties 18–20. Examples have been found in Egyptian tombs. Worn in wigs rather than hair, these hair rings were made of alabaster, white glazed pottery, or jasper, and were a sign of social ranking or authority (*Antiquity* 1997). In North America, hair binders were made of pliable materials such as silk or cotton covering lead wire (Cox 1966). In the twentieth century, the use of rubber and other manufactured elastomeric fibers made hair rings (now called hair bands or ponytail holders) more flexible. They were covered with thread or fibers to make them less likely to break strands of hair. "Scrunchies" were some of the most popular hair bands during the 1980s. These fabric-covered elastic decorative bands were used to create ponytails in the hair of young girls and women (Tortora and Eubank 1998).

Ribbons and bows are narrow fabric strips of closely woven yarns or braid wrapped and knotted around the hair, also used to bind the hair. They were especially popular during the seventeenth and eighteenth centuries in Europe. In the 1600s in France, ribbons were worn by women of all ages, from young girls to elderly dowager duchesses, and were specifically chosen to color coordinate with their dresses (Trasko 1994). Fashionable men also adorned their long tresses with ribbons and bows. A "love lock" was a lock of a man's hair grown longer than the rest, and then accentuated with a ribbon (Tortora and Eubank 1998). During the 1700s in France and England, both a man's queue (a lock or pigtail on a wig) and women's elaborate coiffures were decorated with ribbons and bows. In Mexico in the early 2000s, women in Venustiano Carranza and San Pablito intertwine their hair with brilliantly colored rayon ribbons, woolen cords with pom-poms and beading, and hand-woven tapes (Sayer 1985).

Hairpins are single-pointed pins used to dress or fasten the hair. They serve both a functional and decorative purpose, as in central Africa where copper, wood, ivory, and bone hairpins are used to fasten the hair (Sagay 1983). The elaborate hairstyles worn by ancient Roman women were often set with long hairpins hollow enough to double as containers for perfume or even poison. In Japan, during the seventeenth century, hair ornaments of lacquered wood or tortoiseshell began to be used. The *kanzashi* (a hairpin with a decorative knob, tassel, or bead on the end) was worn by fashionable courtesans. In fact, a conspicuous mark of a courtesan during this time was her "dazzling array of hair ornaments, radiating like a halo from an often dramatically sculptured coiffure" (Goodwin 1986, Introduction). Other Japanese women wore hairstyles decorated much more simply, perhaps with a floral or pendant hairpin (Goodwin 1986). Hairpins were also necessary for maintaining a fastidious appearance in France during the late 1600s. The large "periwigs" worn by men required them to shave their head or pin their hair tightly to the head. The use of *bobbing pins* included both large, straight pins and U-shaped hairpins. The "bobbed" hair then allowed the wig to be donned more easily, as well as confined the underlying hair to present a neat, well-groomed appearance (Trasko 1994). Hairpins continued in popularity as a means of fastening long hair into chignons. According to Trasko (1994), it was considered indecent for Victorian women to be seen with an abundance of loose, streaming hair. She states, "Hairstyles continued to be as constrained as women's lives" (p. 102). In the early twentieth century, hairpins were also necessary for creating waves in the hair (marcel waves during the 1920s) and pin curls in the 1940s. During the 1920s the bobby pin, with its tight spring clip, replaced the older style (open hairpins) allowing women to bob their hair more effectively under tight-fitting cloche hats (Tortora and Eubank 1998).

Barrettes are metal pins approximately three inches long with a beaded head and guard cap, used to secure the hair. Some of the first barrettes were used during the mid-nineteenth century. This bar-shaped hair accessory typically has a decorative face with an underlying spring clip to fasten to the hair (Cox 1966). Often made of metal or plastic in a variety of colors, this hair clip could be viewed as a modified version of the bobby pin, combining the pin's functionality with a more decorative outer appearance. And the appeal is not solely Western. In Mexico, Totonac and Tzelta girls who live near Papantla and Ocosingo, wear a colorful array of plastic slides and ornamental hair combs (Sayer 1985).

Headbands are hair accessories that also go back to ancient times, and combine aesthetics and functionality. As early as 3500 B.C.E., Mesopotamian men and women wore fillets or headbands to hold their hair in place. These circlets were placed on the crown of the head. In the Middle Ages, royal European ladies wore fillets of metal in the shape of a crown or cornet with various types of veils. Metal fillets gradually lost favor and were replaced by strips or bands of fabric (Tortura and Eubank 1998). During the neoclassical revival of the early 1800s, women imitated ancient Greek hairstyles by holding back their hair with fabric bands. As hats and bonnets became more fashionable in the mid-to-late 1800s, headbands lost popularity (Trasko 1994). It was not until the 1920s that headbands reappeared, when women began wearing headache bands for evening events. These bands were often ornamented with jewels or had tall feathers attached to them. Contemporary headbands often have a plastic U-shaped core covered in foam or fabric. These headbands fit closely over the top of the head and behind the ears. They emerged onto the fashion scene once again in the late 1980s and early 1990s, when the First Lady Hillary Clinton began wearing them during and after her husband's election in 1992 (Tortora and Eubank 1998).

Men as well as women wore headbands. During the Jin Dynasty (1139–1163 C.E.), Chinese men tied their long hair up with a silk band (Xun and Chunming 1987). In Mexico during the sixteenth century, priests on the Yucatan Peninsula wore bark cloth headbands. The practice continues in present-day ceremonies. Red bark cloth headbands, known as "god-hats," are wrapped around the heads of worshipers (Sayer 1985). For everyday purposes, hair adornments are rare among male Mexicans, who have followed the Western lead for "civilized" haircuts (Sayer 1985, p. 204). However, there are exceptions. Older men from Amatenango occasionally wear factory-made bandanna handkerchiefs (known as *paliacates*) to tie back their hair from their faces. The Huichol wear a headband of purchased cotton cloth called a *coyera* to fasten their hairstyle in place. The narrow folded headband is wrapped about the head with the ends trailing and is often wound with ribbons or decorated with safety pins (Sayer 1985).

Hair combs have been used since the Stone Age to confine and decorate the hair. Boxwood combs, dating back to 10,000 B.C.E. have been found as some of the earliest hair ornaments (*Antiquity* 1997). Ancient Roman women set their hair with tortoiseshell combs. In China during the Tang Dynasty (621 C.E.–907 C.E.), women held their buns in place with decorative golden and emerald hairpins or combs made of rhinoceros horn (Xun and Chunming 1987). During the Song Dynasty (960–1279 C.E.), hairpins and combs were made into elaborate shapes of phoenixes, butterflies, birds, and flowers pinned on top of women's buns. Around the twelfth year of the Republic, Chinese women began wearing an extremely elaborate hair accessory called a "coronet comb." The coronet was made of painted yarn, gold, pearls, silver, or jade, and had two flaps hanging over the shoulders. A long comb, nearly one foot long and made of white horn, was placed on top. The arrangement required the wearer to turn her head sideways if passing through a door or entering a carriage (Xun and Chunming 1987). During the seventeenth century in Japan, tortoiseshell or lacquered wood combs embellished with gold or mother-of-pearl were worn by fashionable courtesans, who often combined them with *kanzashi* (decorative hairpins). During the nineteenth century, women often used hair combs decorated with gemstones or "paste" (imitation) jewels. The twentieth century saw the continued use of hair combs for long hair, made of a variety of new manufactured materials such as celluloid and plastics. Hair combs also were used to attach small hats and veils to the head during the 1950s. The 1980s created new forms of hair combs, including a circular-shaped hair comb that acts like a headband and the large double-sided comb called a "banana clip" that fastened women's hair into a ponytail.

Beads used as a decorative means of accentuating plaited hair have long been worn by cultures in Africa. Cornrowing is a traditional West African method of arranging the hair into numerous small braids. It can take from two to six hours to arrange, depending on the complexity of the style. Beads were also used to accentuate the plaited strands (Sagay 1983). Used for hundreds of years in Africa, during the 1970s this African-inspired hairstyle penetrated the Western mass market when the movie actress Bo Derek wore her hair in cornrow braids in the movie *10* (Eubank and Tortora 1998). Decorating cornrow braids with beads is still an important part of West African hair traditions in the early 2000s.

Thread may also be used to wrap hair and is a more recent method of braiding used by men and women in the tropical areas of West Africa. The thread-wrapped hair causes the strands to raise from the head like spikes, creating a decorative hairstyle as well as keeping the head cool (Sagay 1983). The "trees" hairstyle is one style popular in West and Central Africa. The hair is parted into five sections, secured with rubber bands, and braided into cornrows. Each center section is wrapped with thread, covering three-quarters of the entire hair's length. Different colored threads are sometimes used for an even more decorative effect (Thoman 1973). String has a similar decorative, fastening history. During the Ming Dynasty (approximately 1393 C.E.), Chinese women laced up their hair with gold and silver strings, decorated with emeralds and pearls (Xun and Chunming 1987).

Thread or yarns that are assembled into an open, gauzelike fabric creates a netting. Netting was used during the ancient Roman Empire and again during medieval times in Western Europe as a means to bind hair. In the middle of the nineteenth century, nets called snoods were a fashionable way for women to confine long hair at the base of the neck. They were revived once again during the 1940s. Older Chinese women also used netting during the Song Dynasty (960 C.E.–1279 C.E.) A black hair net covered their buns, and then jade ornaments were pinned in a random arrangement onto the net. It became known as *xiao yao jin* or "random kerchief" (Xun and Chunming 1987, p. 130).

Hair forks, hair spikes, and hair sticks have been used in diverse cultures, from Native Americans to Far Eastern nations such as China and Japan. Long hair was wrapped and knotted around the head, and then held in place by long hair spikes, sticks, or sometimes forks. The Native American hair forks or sticks were made from a variety of materials, but were often elaborately carved or polished (*Antiquity* 1997). Japanese women during the seventeenth century often fastened their buns with *kogai*, a straight bar used to pierce a topknot and hold it in place. During the twentieth century, mostly geisha and courtesans wore hair sticks, as most Japanese women had begun to adopt European costumes, hairstyles, and attitudes (Goodwin 1986).

Additional miscellaneous ornaments have been inserted into the hair over time and in numerous cultures, including (but not limited to): shells, coins, jewels, flowers, feathers, cow horns, bones, and sheepskin. In portions of North and West Africa, women would create intricate hairstyles that took three to four hours to decorate. If the woman's husband was away from home, hair ornaments were omitted as unnecessary. In South and East Africa, cow horns, bones, and sheepskin was used to adorn hair. Many of these totemic ornaments were worn by men rather than women (Sagay 1983).

During Egypt's New Kingdom, women typically plaited their hair rather than wearing wigs. These braids were then intertwined with colorful ribbons and flowers. The lotus flower was used frequently, as it symbolized abundance (Trasko 1994). In China during the Qin (221–207 B.C.E.) and Han (206 B.C.E.–7 C.E.) Dynasties, female dancers and aristocratic women alike adorned their buns with gold, pearls, and emeralds (Xun and Chunming 1987). In Western Europe during the medieval period, hairpieces and accessories were uncommon, due to strong Christian beliefs about covering women's hair for modesty and to indicate one's piety.

Adornments for the hair were discouraged, as they indicated an "unhealthy regard for personal vanity" (Trasko 1994, p. 27). In contrast, the Renaissance period focused on humanism rather than Christianity, prompting a renewed interest in hair ornaments. Women often adorned their hair to indicate their social status or for aesthetic purposes. Some of the more famous examples are the wigs worn by Queen Elizabeth in 1558. In portraits from this period, the queen visually portrays her power by wearing wigs adorned with large emeralds and rubies set in gold, as well as chains of large pearls. Women of lesser economic means wove flowers in their hair as a means of decorative ornamentation.

Perhaps the most fantastical hair arrangements for women in France, England, Spain, and Russia were found in the 1700s. During the rococo period, pink roses were desirable as hair accessories as they exemplified the graceful, feminine curves found in furniture and other decorative arts. Hair was accented with a *pompon*, or the placement of a few flowers or a feather amidst a hair arrangement (Trasko 1994). In Spain, women "fixed glow worms by threads to their hair, which had a luminous effect" (Trasko 1994, p. 66). These elaborate coiffures were status symbols in courts throughout Europe's fashionable cities, and were meant to be the "talk of the town" (Trasko 1994, p. 64). In the twenty-first century, most flower-adorned hairstyles for Westerners are worn only by brides on their wedding day. Real or artificial flowers may be used.

Native North American Indians often used feathers, as well as other parts of birds. In Mexico, colorfully feathered breasts of small birds were tied to the back of married Lacandon women's heads (Sayer 1985). The Minnesota Chippewa male Indians in the 1830s wore skins of birds as part of their "war bonnets." The bird was associated with spiritual powers during wartime, and the men attached them to the "top of their heads, letting the beak bounce up and down on their foreheads. All kinds of accessories trim it so as to produce a general effect of hideousness likely to terrify the enemy" (Penny 1992, p. 215). In 1868, the Lakota recognized Sitting Bull as "head-chief" by presenting him with an eagle-feathered bonnet. Consisting of a beaded brow band, ermine pendants, and a double tail of black and white eagle tail feathers trailing down the back, each one of the feathers was a reward of valor, representing a brave deed performed by the Northern Teton Sioux warrior who had contributed it (Penny 1992, p. 215).

Lack of hair ornamentation seems to be the overall trend for the twentieth and twenty-first centuries. With the exception of the 1980s when hair accessories had a strong resurgence (Tortora and Eubank 1998), most modern styles seem to rely on haircuts and hair color to make visual statements rather than dressing coiffures with additional accessories. Perhaps this is best exemplified by the famous hairstylist Vidal Sassoon. In 1963, he told fashion press, "I'm going to cut hair like you cut material. No fuss. No ornamentation. Just a neat, clean, swinging line" (Trasko 1994, p. 129).

See also **Costume Jewelry; Hairstyles; Jewelry.**

BIBLIOGRAPHY

Anderson, Ruth M. *Hispanic Costume 1480–1530.* New York: The Hispanic Society of America, 1979.

Antiquity. Vol. 71. Gloucester, England: Antiquity Publications, 1997, pp. 308–320.

Cox, J. S. *An Illustrated Dictionary of Hairdressing and Wigmaking.* London: B. T. Batsford Ltd., 1966.

Goodwin, Shauna J. *The Shape of Chic: Fashion and Hairstyles in the Floating World.* New Haven, Conn.: Yale University Art Galleries, 1986.

Penny, David W. *Art of the American Indian Frontier.* Seattle: University of Washington Press, 1992.

Sagay, Esi. *African Hairstyles.* Portsmouth, N.H.: Heinemann Educational Books, 1983.

Sayer, Chloe. *Costumes of Mexico.* Great Britain: Jolly and Barber, Ltd, 1985.

Thoman, V. M. *Accent African: Traditional and Contemporary Gari Styles for the Black Woman.* New York: Col-Bob Associates, 1973.

Tortora, Phyllis, and Keith Eubank. *Survey of Historic Costume* 3rd ed. New York: Fairchild Publishing, 1998.

Trasko, Mary. *Daring Do's: A History of Extraordinary Hair.* Paris and New York: Flammarion, 1994.

Xun, Zhou, and Gao Chunming. *5,000 Years of Chinese Costumes.* San Francisco: China Books and Periodicals, 1987.

Julianne Trautmann

HAIRDRESSERS Hairdressers seem to appear with civilization itself. Comparatively little is known about history's earliest coiffeurs, those who curled the beards of Sumerian princes and built the fabulous headdresses of Egyptian princesses, except that the Egyptian deities included a barber god. The market squares of ancient Greek cities included barbershops, where people could laze and gossip. Roman towns also contained hairdressing salons, visited mostly by the middle classes, while slaves dressed the heads of upper-class women. These practices survived in the Byzantine east, long after they had been destroyed in the Latin half of the empire.

The Viking hordes and Arthurian nobility of the Dark Ages doubtless continued to cut their hair and trim their beards, but hairdressers as such disappeared along with the cities where they had always practiced their trade. They return to recorded history with the revival of urban life and fashion in the Middle Ages. Medieval towns organized guilds of barber-surgeons who, in addition to shaving clients, lanced boils and pulled teeth. The hairdressing profession continued to develop during the Renaissance, particularly as women's headdresses became more popular and elaborate. More often than not, the ladies' hairdresser was principally a wig maker.

The modern era of splendid hairdos and celebrity coiffeurs, like "Champagne," who opened the first beauty salon in Paris, emerged with the development of court society in the seventeenth century. The courts of Charles II and Louis XIV were among the last places where men's coiffures were as important as women's, but as the elaborate headdresses of the era depended on the skills of wig makers—the French court contained more than forty of them in 1656—barbers became superfluous.

The eighteenth century belonged even more decidedly to the wig makers. While men's wigs generally took on more modest proportions, by the middle of the 1700s women's headdresses reached unprecedented dimensions and raised their architects to a new level of prominence. Léonard became the most famous of his peers, under the patronage of Marie-Antoinette. So much confidence did the queen place in her coiffeur that in 1791, as the royal family tried to flee Revolutionary France, she sent him ahead to Brussels with a collection of crown jewels—although she and the king were arrested before they could reach him there. The French Revolution hurt hairdressers by repressing extravagant coiffures and the taste for wigs and by hastening the destruction of the guilds that had protected barbers' monopoly on shaving and bleeding.

The fashions for clean-shaven faces for men and long, natural hair for women, made the century of industrialization and urbanization an unspectacular one for hairdressers. Barbers sunk to being among the poorest and worst paid of tradesmen. The appearance of King Gillette's remarkable safety razor in 1903 threatened them with the loss of much of their remaining business. As for ladies' hairdressers, the mass of working women in cities and on farms had neither need nor money for their services. Society dames might call on a hairdresser-artiste for a very special occasion, but most of the daily work of arranging hair fell to their ladies' maids.

It was only near the end of the century, with the appearance of the "marcel" wave, that the hairdressing profession began to take on its contemporary shape. The beautiful, long-lasting waves that Marcel and his imitators created attracted women to beauty salons in unparalleled numbers and gave hairdressers a huge new source of revenue. The success of "marcelling" also reflected important social changes, in particular women's growing independence and the expansion of the market for fashionable things among the popular classes, especially among young women. Ladies' hairdressers became pioneers on the frontier of mass-consumer society.

World War I further revolutionized the hairdressers' trade. First, by adding to women's economic and personal autonomy, it increased the market for hairdressers' services. Second, by pulling men out of the salons, it set in motion a process that feminized what had always been a predominantly male trade. The vogue for women's short hairstyles that swept through Western societies in the 1920s accelerated these developments. The majority of ladies' hairdressers initially rejected what they considered a threat to their "art," but they soon came to embrace the radical new fashion for the revenue it brought. For short hair was not only cut, it was shampooed, "permed," and often colored, making salons more profitable even as they became more numerous. As the fashion for short hair spread beyond Europe and America, modern hairdressing salons began to open in Shanghai, Tokyo, and other major non-Western cities.

Although most shops remained very small, the number of large, chic salons multiplied. These usually belonged to the profession's luminaries and often were established in the more fashionable department stores. Antoine, the most luminous of all, expanded his operations to the United States through an agreement with Saks Fifth Avenue, which also sold a line of beauty products bearing his name.

In an era when new fashions and products gave ladies' hairdressers fresh business and artistic opportunities, barbers' fortunes continued to decline. Men's conservative haircuts proved barren ground for the sort of value-added services that fueled ladies' hairdressing, while, at least before the 1960s, the ethic of maleness sharply limited the market for cologne and cosmetics.

The consumer revolution that followed World War II carried more women than ever into the hairdressing salons. At the top of the profession, a host of new stars, led by Alexandre, the Duchess of Windsor's protégé, joined Antoine in the hairdressers' pantheon. Yet even as the trade became increasingly feminized, few women rose to the summit. The Carita sisters and Rose Evansky are rare exceptions.

In the 1950s, the modish styles of Vidal Sassoon and the "poodle cut" of the campy Raymond made London the second capital of hairdressing. Beginning with Jacques Dessange in 1976, the best-known coiffeurs began to attach their names not only to products but to salons, as well. In the 1980s and 1990s the practice spread rapidly, and in the early 2000s franchises bearing the names of Jean-Louis David, Jean-Claude Biguine, and others control a large portion of the hairdressing business all over the world.

Other fashion capitals turned out their own prodigies, who performed in international competitions and opened chic salons far from home in what by the end of the millennium had become an international society of hair fashion.

See also **Barbers; Hair Accessories; Hairstyles.**

BIBLIOGRAPHY

Cooper, Wendy. *Hair: Sex, Society, Symbolism.* New York: Stein and Day, 1971.

Corson, Richard. *Fashions in Hair: The First Five Thousand Years.* London: Peter Owen, 1965.

Cox, Caroline. *Good Hair Days: A History of British Hairstyling.* London: Quartet Books, 1999.

Graves, Charles. *Devotion to Beauty: The Antoine Story.* London: Jarrold's, 1962.

Willet, Julie T. *Permanent Waves: The Making of the American Beauty Shop.* New York: New York University Press, 2000.

Steve Zdatny

HAIRSTYLES Standards of beauty have varied enormously according to time and place. Yet as long as people have ordered their social relations, hairdressing has had a role in the struggle for status and reproduction. "Humans," writes Robin Bryer, "are unique in two aspects of their behavior: wearing clothes and having their hair cut voluntarily" (p. 9). Hairdressing is part of the human condition.

One presumes that the first hairdos were long, scraggly, and filthy. Even given the general squalor atop primitive heads, however, it is likely that some hair was considered more attractive and admirable than others. What is certain is that wherever primitive society congealed into civilization, it produced a culture of hairdressing.

Archaeological evidence suggests that the early Egyptians wore their natural hair in tight braids. That changed with the discovery of the art of wig making. Hair was then cut short or shaved. Young boys retained their queues, but adults who could afford them wore wigs, especially for special occasions. Specialists made up elaborate headdresses filled with jewels and expensive accessories and splashed with oils and perfumes. The Mesopotamian civilizations preferred heavy beards and long hair, often frizzed or waved. At Knossos, Cretan women wore elaborate coiffures, with golden hairpins, and lots of makeup. As always, different codes distinguished elites—kings, nobles, priests—from commoners.

In *Fashions in Hair: The First Five Thousand Years,* the author Richard Corson quotes a seventeenth-century source describing a teenage noblewoman attempting to turn her hair blonde. After exposing it to the hot sun for hours and anointing it with a coloring substance that seemed to produce the effect, she was afflicted with a near-daily nosebleed and

> being desirous to stop the Blood by the pressing of her Nostrils, not farr from her right Eye toward her Temple, through a pore, as it were by a hole made with a needles point, the Blood burst out abundantly, and ... shee was diseased by the obstruction of her courses (p. 173).

Advertisement for Solco Human Hair Products, 1924. Since the dawn of civilization, hair styles have reflected every aspect of the human condition and often give important clues about the societies and cultures that spawned them. © CORBIS. REPRODUCED BY PERMISSION.

The ancient Greeks invented the beauty salon, where women had their cheeks blanched with white lead and their naturally blonde hair artistically dressed. Sometimes it was dyed red or blue. Spartan brides cropped their hair; Athenians wore veils over their dressed hair. They cut it as a sign of mourning. Beginning in the fifth century B.C.E., Greek men began to wear their hair short. It was Alexander the Great who insisted that his soldiers shave their beards in order to deprive their foes of a handle during combat.

Typically, the Romans at first copied the Greeks and then developed more elaborate hairstyles to match the imperial ethic. Men often wore their hair short, in what came to be called the "Titus," after the Emperor. Attended to by the barbers who worked at the marketplaces and public baths, or by their slaves (who were shaved bald), both men and women curled their hair and dyed it red. They applied costly oils and pomatums or wore expensive wigs. The most extravagant powdered their hair with gold dust. In the East, Byzantine hairstyles

blended Greco-Roman culture with oriental. Men wore moderately short hair, mustaches, and beards. Feminine coiffures incorporated pearls and precious metals, which were also used for ecclesiastical costumes. Sometimes the fashion was for bare heads, sometimes for ribbons or ornamented turbans. Turbans became standard in Moorish culture—although the Islamic injunction against "graven images," like that of the Jewish religion, means that documentation of Islamic hairstyles remains sparse before the Christian Middle Ages.

The paintings of the Pre-Raphaelites have provided a certain image of Arthurian damsels and knights. A small amount of evidence suggests that the period between the departure of the Romans and the arrival of the Normans in England favored flowing locks and facial hair for men. But, in fact, very little documentation about hairstyles during the Dark Ages survives.

The revival of European culture in the Middle Ages also brought back something like international fashion, of which coiffures were a part. Hairstyles differed between northern and southern Europe. And if the return of fashion meant anything, it was that coiffures popular at one moment became *démodées* in the next—although the fashionable "moment" in the Middle Ages could be rather long by later standards. The bobbed styles for men of the twelfth century were still around in the fifteenth, when smart Venetian gentlemen were also sporting yellow silk wigs. Depending on the time and place, women wore long braids or huge, horned headdresses. Or they packed their hair into a variety of bonnets and bags, often adorned with jewels and expensive knickknacks. The expanding middle class ordinarily adopted "quieter" versions of these noble styles. Poorer women wore their hair long and enclosed. Their men folk cut theirs short or shoulder length, while beards and mustaches came and went.

By the Renaissance, whatever the particular arrangement, hairstyles had become one of those idioms of international art that allowed fashion to circulate across the continent. Variety and inventiveness were the rules. Hair was frizzed, or not. Some women plucked or shaved their foreheads—thus becoming "highbrow," in the manner of Elizabeth I, who was also reputed to own a hundred perukes. Blonde was the hair color of choice, and women bleached their hair by sitting in the sun and using saffron or medicated sulphur. Blonde wigs became the vogue in France and Italy, and nobles—Marguerite de Valois, most notably—would engage blonde maids in order to command their hair for wigs. Mary, Queen of Scots possessed many beautiful curled wigs and adorned her head with lace. Other ladies used pads and wire frames to give their coiffures volume.

Contemporary illustrations of the early sixteenth century depict Englishmen with long hair and clean chins. Beards were more popular on the Continent. By the end of the century, English courtiers had cut their hair and adopted stylish beards with precious names such as the "swallowtail" and the "spade."

The portraits of the great Flemish painter Sir Anthony Van Dyke capture the Cavalier style that reached its height in the 1630s and 1640s, with men sporting long hair and neat, pointed beards under wide-brimmed hats. Hair became politicized briefly, during the English Civil War, when the more austere Protestant Roundheads battled the more elegantly coiffed forces of the English king, Charles I. The Pilgrims of the Colony of New Plymouth condemned long hair for men as prideful.

The Puritan position on hair must have softened, for later portraits of Cromwell depict him with longer hair, although not nearly as long as the styles coming out of the French court and brought back to England with the Restoration of Charles II in 1660. This was the great age of periwigs for men. Indeed, the French court imported so much blonde hair that Louis XIV's finance minister Colbert tried to ban wig making in France so as to stem the outflow of French gold.

The most popular women's styles of the period were the "hurluberlu"—unevenly cut and crimped, with two long curls over the shoulders—worn by Louis's favorite, Madame de Maintenon, and the "Fontange"—with its high curls secured by ribbon and bow—invented by the king's new mistress, the Duchess de Fontange. The fashions of Versailles traveled to all the other courts of Europe, and from there to the modish classes of every country.

In the eighteenth century, women's hair became the principal focus of art and conspicuous consumption. The massive headdresses of the middle decades serve as both the symbol of the Old Regime and the classic image of excess in fashion. It was in the 1770s that coiffures reached their most exaggerated form. Wendy Cooper describes "a certain Madame de Lauzun," whose "enormously high headdress," stuffed with the usual assortment of trash, was topped with "modeled ducks swimming in a stormy sea, scenes of hunting and shooting, a mill with a miller's wife flirting with a priest, and a miller leading an ass by its halter" (p. 95). Coiffures grew so immense that doorways had to be enlarged, and in two instances ladies were killed when their headdresses were set on fire by chandeliers. Men of weight and fashion in the Enlightenment wore modest, powdered wigs, although George III made enemies of English wig makers when he took to powdering his own natural hair.

The powdered look disappeared altogether in England when the Younger Pitt imposed a one-guinea tax on hair powder. Events in France had an even more revolutionary effect on hairstyles, as the fall of Louis XVI swept aside the fashion habits of the Old Regime. An era that admired the civic virtues of classical antiquity found men and women wearing their hair *à la Titus*. Those with a sharper sense of political irony adopted the mode *à la victime*, with their hair pulled up off the neck in imitation of those about to be guillotined. In the aftermath of the Terror, women wore their hair long and loose over di-

Billie Jones Kana describes her disappointing first trip to a beauty shop to have a "perm" in 1928:

As I recall, I couldn't have cared less about curls, but went along and was tortured beyond my wildest imagination … first our hair was washed and cut, then we waited and waited. There were women everywhere in different stages of getting beautified. Everyone was waiting. My hair was wound up on spiral rods so tight that I thought I would never blink again [and] after the machine that looked like a milking machine was attached to the rods, I couldn't move. [Then] it began to steam and tears rolled down my cheeks.... Someone got a blower and cooled my head here and there, but my scalp was scalded (Willet, pp. 92–93).

aphanous dresses. No one in Revolutionary France wanted to look like an aristocrat.

In the nineteenth century, men's hairstyles tended to the short and simple. Common in one decade, facial hair vanished in the next, only to return thereafter. In mid-century Naples, the government so objected to mustaches that it instructed police to shave them off offenders. While men's hair became increasingly tame and standardized, women's coiffures retained their complexity, if not their old proportions. The early part of the century saw a vogue for concatenations of natural hair adorned with feathers, rich combs, and other items. Other moments featured puffs of curls or ringlets. Powder reappeared briefly on the hair of fashionable dames under the Second Empire. Chignons vanished in the 1870s; jeweled pins became popular in the 1880s. In general, the pace of fashion quickened, and intricate coiffures made ladies more dependent than ever on their hairdressers, even though the daily work of brushing and arranging a lady's hair fell to her lady's maid.

Wigs no longer played the dominant role in coiffure, as they had in the past. Still, the century admired long, luxurious hair, and since most women did not possess hair of sufficient quality or quantity, they made generous use of false hair. In fact, the taste for *postiches* (bits of false hair) drove the international market in hair to new heights. By the turn of the twentieth century, the United States was importing more than half a million tons of hair per year—a $3 million business. Most of this stuff came from European peasant women in the poorer rural areas, who used their long tresses as a sort of cash crop.

The wheel of hair fashion took its next dramatic turn in the mid-1880s, when Marcel Grateau, a hitherto unknown hairdresser in Paris, perfected a technique for giving hair soft, beautiful, durable waves and thereby launched the modern era of hairdressing. Replacing the nests of postiches and fancy bijoux, the "marcel" wave radically simplified ladies' hairstyles. Many of the most celebrated coiffeurs hated the "marcel" for precisely this reason, but women loved it. An insatiable popular demand soon forced its opponents to capitulate, and the "marcel" wave became the basis of a fashionable coiffure for the next twenty-five years—although, to be sure, enterprising hairdressers found ways to dress "marceled" hair with the traditional assortment of feathers, flowers, and pricey doodads. The "négligé" styles of the Belle Epoque, often colored with henna or dusted with white or gray powder, featured ribbons, enameled combs, and big chignons.

When the dean of French coiffeurs, Emile Long, complained about the cheap waves he saw on the *midinettes* (working girls) on the streets of Paris, he was pointing to the fact that the stunning success of "marceling" depended on a fundamental change in the social contours of fashion. It coincided with the early stages of a big expansion in the market for fashionable things in Western society.

In effect, three developments combined to create the modern beauty salon and the culture associated with it. First, rising wages gave women more disposable income, while greater autonomy freed them to spend it as they pleased. Second, a loosening of social constraints made it more acceptable for women to move in public spaces, that is, to take their toilettes out of the boudoir and into the hairdressing salon. Third, a critical series of technological developments expanded the services available in the salon.

New sensibilities about hygiene, combined with water heaters and hair dryers, encouraged women to have their hair shampooed. Non-toxic dyes helped dissolve old taboos about hair coloring. Most critically, the invention of the permanent-wave machine enabled women to alter their hair dramatically, while it brought hairdressers a huge new source of revenue. For a few hours hooked up to this contraption, a woman would pay anywhere from ten to fifty times the cost of an ordinary haircut. These new consumer habits were nourished by the growing number of magazines aimed at middle- and working-class women, and especially by the movie stars who were coming to dominate popular ideas of beauty and fashion.

All of this paved the way for the "bob," which proved to be a seminal moment both for coiffure and for Western society more generally. From the lacquered "garçonne" of Josephine Baker to the more fluid "Eton crop," the bob had many incarnations. Some of them had appeared on some stylish young heads before World War I, especially in the United States. But the vogue took off only in the 1920s, when it became part of the aesthetic turnabout associated with "flappers." As the "androgynous" clothes of Coco Chanel surpassed the curvaceous styles of the great Edwardian couturiers, so the bob became the badge of the so-called Modern Woman.

No other hairstyle in history provoked so much comment and controversy. Cultural conservatives hated it for its challenge to inherited gender verities. Stories abound of outraged men locking up, even murdering, their newly shorn wives and daughters. On the other side, women endorsed it by the millions. Observers generally saw the short hairstyles and women's spontaneous taste for them as evidence of a significant "emancipation" of women. It is true that the bob provided some relief from the arduous regimes of Edwardian coiffures. At the same time—permed, dyed, in need of frequent retouching, and often requiring a postiche for evening wear—it was hardly carefree or cheap.

At the end of the day, however, the bob was more fashion than political statement, and by the close of the Roaring Twenties, women had begun to tire of it. The hairstyles of the 1930s, created by such international stars as Antoine and Guillaume, were longer and more "feminine," although there was no return to the massive, superfluous hairdos of the pre-bob era. The Platinum Blonde, curvy and sexy, defined the new "New Woman" of the depression decade. Men in the period between the wars continued to favor short, neat haircuts, accompanied sometimes by a thin moustache (never by a beard) in the manner of Rudolph Valentino or Clark Gable.

The war years, rich in misery, were poor in new hair fashions. *Haute coiffure* survived mostly in Hollywood, where, for example, Veronica Lake became famous for the silky blonde hair that fell across half her face in the "bad-girl" style that alarmed some moralists. More commonly, millions of women involved in the war effort tucked their short, simple hairdos under military caps or hard hats. If the war brought the world one distinctive hairstyle, however, it would have to be the shaved heads belonging to camp survivors and "horizontal" collaborators.

The consumer revolution, born out of the ashes of war, once again transformed hairdressing. Stylistically, the postwar years promoted the so-called petite tête, the compact hairdos that fit so well with Christian Dior's fashion revolution, the New Look. Long styles made a partial comeback in the 1950s, led by the "artichoke" cut that Jacques Dessange created for the nubile Brigitte Bardot. The clear trend, however, was toward more compact coiffures. In the United States, ponytails became the classic expression of 1950s adolescence.

In the end, the 1950s may be less important for stylistic innovation than for the changes in the structures of consumption that occurred. While disposable incomes rose steadily, a growing mass media of movies, television, women's magazines, and broadcast images of beauty and stimulated the demand for fashionable commodities. More and more women indulged themselves in a weekly visit to the beauty parlor. In the United States, this became one of the defining rituals of middle-class femininity and an important communal event. At the same time, new hair care products—"cold" perms, do-it-yourself hair coloring, and setting—allowed women to exercise much of their expanding beauty regimen at home.

Men continued to provide a much poorer field for art and profit. Their haircuts became, if anything, plainer in the 1950s. Yet change was in the air. Rebellious teenagers began to turn away from crew cuts and flattops by wearing the "duck ass" cut associated with the likes of James Dean, Elvis Presley, and Johnny Halliday. In France, George Hardy achieved a small breakthrough in 1956 when he introduced the razor cut. Beards and mustaches turned up on the chins and lips of "beatniks" and other nonconformist types.

"Anti-fashion" hair spread over the next few decades, following the prominence of rock stars and hippies. Blacks in America and Europe put aside the hair-relaxing agents they associated with self-loathing and began to sport voluminous Afros. In the 1970s, "Mohicans," dreadlocks, and the sinister skinhead became the protest hairstyles of choice. Throughout, sales of personal grooming products for men increased, and the men who visited the new "unisex" hair salons paid more than the proverbial "two bits." But hairdressing remained an overwhelmingly female preoccupation.

The "beehive," made possible by the invention of lacquered hairspray and the copious use of false hair, carried the 1950s ideal of femininity into the sixties. However, that raucous decade really belonged to the geometrical cuts that Vidal Sassoon created to fit the latest styles of Mary Quant, creator of the miniskirt. *Haute coiffure* survived, as the profession's contemporary stars coiffed movie stars, society dames, and runway models. But the rule for the last quarter of the twentieth century was variety and innovation. Hairstyles were long or short, flowing or spiked, natural or tinted, straight or permed.

The diversity of coiffures also reflected a critical change in the trajectory of fashion. In the days of Marie Antoinette or Marcel, a small, privileged elite made the laws that ruled taste. In the twentieth century, the masses gained a larger and larger say in the success of this vogue or that. By the end, masses of women were not merely endorsing (or not) the choices made by a select group of the fashionable. "The street" produced its own styles, which then permeated the formal structures of fashion.

The ceaseless evolution of hairstyles has produced a lot of speculation, both casual and academic, on their etiology and meaning. Numerous speculations have linked coiffures, not coincidentally but organically, to their historical moment. The many observers who attributed the popularity of the bob to women's emancipation provide the most pointed example of this. Others have gone further and tried to find the deeper meaning of forms. The French critic Roland Barthes offered an entire science, semiotics, dedicated to deconstructing those forms.

Hairstyles can unquestionably supply important clues about the societies that produce them. Once again, the bob is the perfect illustration. Permed, tinted, cre-

ated in commercial establishments with electricity and hot running water, and consumed by millions of women spending considerable sums of money, it has a lot to say about Western civilization in the 1920s. Sometimes the meaning of coiffures is not hidden at all, but openly proclaimed, as it might be in a punk band, a neo-Nazi rally, a hippies' commune, or a lesbian rights parade.

Yet, in many ways, those who assert the free-flowing nature of fashionable "signifiers" have the stronger argument. After all, "liberated" women of the 1960s often sported long, straight hair, while the sainted defender of a medieval French king, Joan of Arc, wore a bob. It seems fair to say that in a historical world where Charles II and Cher look alike from behind, the forms of fashion obey an elusive logic of their own.

See also **Afro Hairstyle; Barbers; Hair Accessories; Hairdressers.**

BIBLIOGRAPHY

Asser, Joyce. *Historic Hairdressing.* Bath: Pittman Publishing, 1966.

Bryer, Robin. *The History of Hair: Fashion and Fantasy Down the Ages.* London: Philip Wilson, 2000.

Cooper, Wendy. *Hair: Sex, Society, Symbolism.* New York: Stein and Day, 1971.

Corson, Richard. *Fashions in Hair: The First Five Thousand Years.* London: Peter Owen, 1965.

Cox, Caroline. *Good Hair Days: A History of British Hairstyling.* London: Quartet Books, 1999.

Keyes, Jean. *A History of Women's Hairstyles, 1500–1965.* London: Methuen, 1967.

Louis, M. *Six Thousand Years of Hair Styling.* New York: M. Louis, 1939.

McKracken, Grant. *Big Hair: A Journey into the Transformation of the Self.* Woodstock, N.Y.: The Overlook Press, 1995.

Rambaud, Rene. *Les fugitives. Precis anecdotique et historique des coiffures feminines a travers les ages, des Egyptiens a 1945.* Paris: Rene Rambaud, 1947.

Reynolds, Reginald. *Beards: Their Social Standing, Religious Involvements, Decorative Possibilities and Value in Offense and Defense through the Ages.* New York: Doubleday and Co., 1949.

Severn, Bill. *The Long and the Short of It: Five Thousand Years of Fun and Fury over Hair.* New York: David McKay and Co., 1971.

Trasko, Mary. *Daring Do's: A History of Extraordinary Hair.* New York: Flammarion, 1994.

Willet, Julie T. *Permanent Waves: The Making of the American Beauty Shop.* New York: New York University Press, 2000.

Steve Zdatny

HALLOWEEN COSTUME The wearing of Halloween costumes in America reaches back into the country's cultural history. This shared American folk ritual is a window on the diverse ethnic and religious heritage of the people who settled the United States.

Children trick-or-treat on Halloween. The concept of the Halloween costume traces its roots back to the ancient Celtic festival of Samhain, during which revelers wore disguises to foil restless spirits. © Ariel Skelley/Corbis. Reproduced by permission.

Halloween itself has deep folk roots. It originates with the Celtic Day of the Dead autumn festival of Samhain, celebrated by Celts throughout Europe in ancient times and celebrated still in northern France, Ireland, Scotland, Wales, and other regions where the Celtic heritage is preserved. The Celts used a lunar calendar and divided the year into two seasons. Winter, the season of the dying, began on Samhain (which roughly translates as "summer's end"), which fell on the full moon closest to 1 November after the harvest was complete.

Samhain was the first day of the Celtic New Year, and it was believed that the souls of those who had died were extremely restless this night, which marked the porous border between the living and the dead, the old and new year, and summer and winter. At Samhain, people disguised themselves in feathers and furs so as not to be recognized by the spirits wandering the earth that night. When the Celts converted to Christianity, Samhain was amalgamated with All Hallows' Eve, the evening before All Saints' Day, the night that is now called Halloween. (All Saints' Day is followed by All Souls' Day, 2 November.)

Originally a feast marking the departure of souls from the material world to the spiritual world of the dead, All Hallows' Eve was widely celebrated throughout the European world, and particularly in countries with a Catholic tradition. In America, the seeds of the distinctively American festival of Halloween date back to the 1840s. The arrival in the country of large numbers of Irish immigrants, following the disastrous potato famine in Ireland, helped establish the feast in America. Their celebrations of All Saints' and All Souls' Days still preserved many of the ancient rites of Samhain. For example, the carving of pumpkins comes from the Irish legend of Jack, a man so evil that when he died he was rejected by both heaven and hell and was condemned to roam the countryside with nothing but a glowing turnip for a head.

Halloween in America became a folk holiday sanctioned neither by the church nor the state. Ancient roots in European culture, the arrival of many different groups of immigrants, and the constantly evolving nature of U.S. culture have continued to shape this distinctly American celebration. Contemporary celebrations of Halloween reflect many different cultural traditions, such as England's Guy Fawkes Day and Mexico's *El dío de los muertes*. During colonial times Americans gathered for harvest festivals that (like the Celtic Samhain) acknowledged the end of the bountiful summer; these festivals also gave rise to the distinctive American festival and rituals of Thanksgiving. At these harvest festivals, ghost stories were often told, a reminder of the bridge between the living and the dead. Divination games, often with unremembered but very ancient roots, were played; for example young women bobbed for apples to determine whom they would marry.

During Victorian times, Halloween began to become a quaint holiday with rituals that emphasized children's participation; the festival's folk and religious roots were downplayed. By the early twentieth century, Halloween had become a celebration for children. Community organizations arranged parades and haunted houses. During the 1940s trick or treat was added to the traditions; this custom of begging in costume had very old roots in European culture, and was explicitly transgressive, forgiving behavior that would otherwise be frowned upon. Children would sing or perform mimes in exchange for a treat; they also implicitly threatened to play tricks on householders if a treat was not forthcoming. Homemade masquerade costumes appeared as early as the nineteenth century. Women's magazines printed instructions for making costumes at home. Later these homemade costumes increasingly gave way to commercially produced costumes, a trend that began at the time of the industrial revolution. During the second half of the nineteenth century, advances in technology made commercially produced costumes cheaper, better made, and more varied. The earliest costume themes, all of which continue to the early 2000s, were ghosts, skeletons, devils, and witches. Otherworldly creatures such as Frankenstein, the Mummy, and Dracula are drawn from popular culture.

The Dennison Manufacturing Company in Massachusetts began making paper costumes in 1910. Collegeville, located in Pennsylvania, began as a company that produced flags and later used the scraps to create costumes around 1910 and continued to make early clown and jester costumes. Its namesake founded the Ben Cooper Company in 1927. Based in Brooklyn, New York, Cooper created theatrical sets and costumes for the Cotton Club and the Ziegfeld Follies, and expanded into Halloween costumes in 1937. The company later joined with A. S. Fisbach, a New York City–based costume company that held the license to Disney characters, such as Donald Duck, Mickey and Minnie Mouse, and the Big Bad Wolf, and packaged them under the name Spotlight. Cooper sold his company in the 1980s to Rubies, also in New York, which has become one of the largest producers of Halloween and Purim costumes in the United States.

Many of the masks for the early costumes were produced by U.S. Mask Company in Woodhaven, New York. Their earliest gauze masks, made of buckram, were sprayed with starch and steamed over a mold. Themes included witches, clowns, and animals. In the 1950s vacuum-formed latex masks appeared. Figures from popular culture, such as the Beatles and John and Jacqueline Kennedy, joined TV and film personalities such as Laurel and Hardy, and dolls and action figures such as Barbie and G.I. Joe, in being molded in latex. Other major costume companies in America included Halco, in Pennsylvania; Bland Charnas Company on Long Island, New York; and E. Simons and Sons, in New Orleans, Louisiana.

The costumes produced in America are testaments to the creative powers of ordinary people. The makers demonstrate a technical and aesthetic skill that reflects the handmade techniques used in home production and in factories before mass-machine production took over. These costumes express the personal, social, and cultural identity of the people, and transcend the barriers of class and ethnicity. Halloween has become a uniquely American ritual, not only for children but for adults as well, and it grows in popularity from year to year. (Halloween has also become an important holiday for the gay community, with large, elaborate costume parades in San Francisco, New York's Greenwich Village, and other gay centers.) Halloween allows individuals to experience and explore the shared ethnic, cultural, and folk celebrations that have engaged diverse peoples since ancient times.

The Jewish festival of Purim, which commemorates the Biblical story of Esther, is celebrated on the fourteenth and fifteenth days of the twelfth month of the Jewish calendar, usually in March. In America, Purim celebrations have taken on many of the trappings of Halloween, with costumed children wielding noisemakers and giving gifts of food or donating to charity.

See also **Occult Dress.**

BIBLIOGRAPHY

Galembo, Phyllis. *Dressed for Thrills: 100 Years of Halloween Costume and Masquerade.* New York: Harry N. Abrams, 2002.

Rogers, Nicholas. *Halloween: From Pagan Ritual to Party Night.* New York: Oxford University Press, 2002.

Santino, Jack. *Halloween and Other Festivals of Death and Life.* Memphis: University of Tennessee Press, 1994.

Phyllis Galembo

HALSTON The designer Roy Halston Frowick (1932–1990) was born in Des Moines, Iowa, and began his career as a milliner. He subsequently rose to become one of the most important American designers of the 1970s, whose influence was still being felt into the twenty-first century.

HALSTON'S CLIENTELE

Halston's most famous saying was "You're only as good as the people you dress." If that is true, he was better than good. He was good enough, in fact, to win five coveted Coty Fashion Critics Awards, the Oscars of the fashion industry. Halston's clientele list reads like a who's who of celebrities and socialites: Lauren Bacall, Marisa Berenson, Candice Bergen, Princess Grace of Monaco, Katherine Graham, Margaux Hemingway, Bianca Jagger, Liza Minnelli, Jackie Kennedy Onassis, Elsa Peretti, Barbara Cushing "Babe" Paley, Lee Radziwill, Elizabeth Taylor, and Barbara Walters.

Biography

While studying fashion illustration at the Art Institute of Chicago in 1952, Halston began designing hats in his spare time. Eventually, he started to sell his designs at André Basil's hair salon at the Ambassador Hotel. Halston moved to New York City in 1958 to design hats for the legendary milliner Lilly Daché and then began working in the custom millinery salon of the prestigious retailer Bergdorf Goodman in 1959. While there, he designed the famous pillbox hat worn by the First Lady Jacqueline Kennedy for the 1961 presidential inauguration of her husband, John F. Kennedy.

Moving beyond hats, Halston went on to design his first clothing collection for Bergdorf Goodman in June 1966. Two years later he left the retailer to form his own company, Halston Ltd. In December of 1968 Halston showed his first namesake collection in his new Angelo Donghia–designed showroom at 33 East Sixty-Eighth Street in New York City. As his business grew, Halston took over the entire building, creating a retail boutique in 1972 that took up three floors of the building, with each floor selling a different collection (and at a different price point). Later that year a ready-to-wear company, Halston Originals, was formed with two partners and headquartered on New York's Seventh Avenue.

In a first-of-its-kind deal for a fashion designer, Halston and his partners sold both the Halston businesses and the Halston trademark to Norton Simon Industries (NSI), a large multibrand corporation, in 1973. Halston's success soared during the mid-1970s, and so did his fame. An article in *Esquire* magazine asked the question: "Will Halston take over the world?" (p. 69).

As the success continued, NSI started signing a multitude of licensees—thirty existed at one point. In 1978 the company moved its design studio to a spacious venue on the twenty-first floor of the Olympic Tower at Fifty-first Street and Fifth Avenue. With the bigger space once again came an increased workload. Eventually, Halston was designing four ready-to-wear, four sportswear, and two made-to-order collections per year. All this was in addition to furs, shoes, swimwear, robes, intimate apparel, men's wear, luggage, and uniforms for both Avis Rent A Car System and Braniff Airline employees. Halston also continued to design costumes for his celebrity friends, including the performer Liza Minnelli, and for Martha Graham's dance company.

By the early 1980s, however, Halston's influence was waning, and his social life began to garner more attention than his fashions. The beginning of the end, according to many, came when, in 1982, Halston signed a multimillion dollar deal with the J. C. Penney discount chain to create products under the Halston label. Many prestigious retailers voiced concern about the deal, and Bergdorf Goodman dropped the designer's ready-to-wear line from their store.

Before signing the deal with Penney's, things had started to unravel for the designer. Many cite the pressure of his workload and his inability to delegate responsibility as major faults. Others noted that as he spent more time socializing, allegedly using drugs, and as his increasingly difficult temperament became apparent, his business started to fail. In 1984, with tension mounting between the designer and NSI, Halston took a two-week vacation and never returned to Halston Enterprises. Until 1988 he kept trying to buy back a part of the company that bore his name from the various owners of the trademark, but he was unsuccessful. While negotiating one such buyback with Revlon, the owners of the trademark, in 1988, Halston tested positive for HIV. He died of complications from AIDS on 26 March 1990.

Mr. Clean

Halston was known for his minimalistic approach to fashion, and his signature looks were spare, fluid, and often deceptively simple. He married the ease and comfort of sportswear with ready-to-wear and then raised the bar with luxurious fabrics and his distinct eye for cut and proportion. Halston has been credited with creating a unique new look, an original American way of dressing. His clothes were a representation of his own pared-down lifestyle. Many say that his life and his work were one and the same. In simplifying fashion for modern lifestyles without sacrificing glamour and luxury, he influenced many other designers. "Halston was one of the most influential designers of our time," said Donna Karan, quoted in Gross and Rottman (p. 225). "I say that on a personal level, because when I was young, he was the designer I aspired to be like. He understood luxury, glamour, simplicity, fit and the importance of uniform. To me, he represented all that was modern and pure. What more could a designer hope to be?" Narciso Rodriguez, also a fan, said, "Halston changed the face of fashion and the way women dressed with a clean and pure look. Within its purity there was extreme femininity and sexiness. His slink dress as well as his doublefaced coats both maintained his clean, sensual line with brevity of construction. He is one of my heroes!" (Gross and Rottman, p. 225.)

In her book *The Fashion Makers*, Bernadine Morris wrote, "A nod from Halston and a fashion is flashed around the world" (p. 90). After Halston fell in love with Ultrasuede in 1971, he went on to use the fabric in everything from suits and coats to his famous shirtdress. As a result, Ultrasuede became as famous as Halston himself.

When he tied a sweater around his models' shoulders, the look was adopted by fashionable women everywhere. Other designs also became Halston trademarks: the strapless dress, dresses made of draped rayon matte jersey, cashmere knits, caftans, one-shoulder and halter dresses, and asymmetrical necklines. He was well known for his love of the bias cut and his single-seamed spiral and wrapped dresses. In 1976 the designer created his first perfume, the enormously successful Halston. The Elsa Peretti–designed tear-shaped bottle was so recognizable that Halston insisted that it not be stamped with his name. The only branding was a small paper band with the name "Halston" that was wrapped around the neck. It broke off when the bottle was opened.

See also **Dance and Fashion; Flocking; Hats, Women's; Ready-to-Wear; Retailing; Sportswear.**

BIBLIOGRAPHY

Berkin, Lisa. "The Prisoner of 7th Avenue." *New York Times Magazine*, 15 March 1987.

Bowles, Jerry. "Will Halston Take Over the World?" *Esquire*, August 1975, p. 69.

Gross, Elaine, and Fred Rottman. *Halston: An American Original*. New York: HarperCollins Publishers, Inc., 1999.

Herald, Jacqueline. *Fashions of a Decade: The 1970's*. New York: Facts on File, 1990.

Milbank, Caroline Rennolds. *Couture: The Great Designers*. New York: Stewart, Tabori and Chang, 1985.

Morris, Bernadine. *The Fashion Makers*. New York: Random House, 1978.

Fred Rottman

HANDBAGS AND PURSES The handbag is much more than a functional alternative to the pocket. In the course of time it has become a design object in its own right, a signature mascot for the major French couture houses (surpassing the role of perfume as a brand identity) and a powerful symbol of growing female independence. Until the late 1700s, both men and women carried bags. When the directoire fashions of 1800 streamlined the female silhouette, the need for an exterior pocket created a permanent role for the woman's handbag.

In antiquity, bags were used to carry weapons, flint, tools, food, and eventually money. Egyptian burial chambers of the Old Kingdom (2686–2160 B.C.E.) contain

Actress Charlize Theron holds a Fendi handbag, February 9, 2004. Major fashion accessories in the late twentieth and early twenty-first centuries, handbags were originally conceived for very practical concerns, such as storing flint and money. © Frank Trapper/Corbis. Reproduced by permission.

double-handled leather bags designed to be suspended from sticks, as well as bags made from linen and papyrus. The ancient Greeks used leather bags called *byrsa* as coin pouches; this is the source of the English word "purse." The rise of coin currency gave birth to the drawstring purse, an item always worn close to the body and most often suspended from a belt or secreted within folds of clothing. Judas sealed the fate of Jesus with a purse full of silver coins. Roman women used net purses; the Latin term *reticulum* (meaning net) was revived in the 1790s. One of the earliest ornamented leather purses to be recovered from Anglo-Saxon Britain came from the burial mounds of Sutton Hoo in Suffolk, assumed to be the burial site of King Roewald, who died in 625 C.E. The leather body of the bag had deteriorated but its gilt ornaments remained intact. The purse had a lavish lid decorated with gold, silver, garnets, and millefiore glass. Containing forty gold coins and hung from hinged straps on a waist belt fastened by a large gold buckle, the purse was part of a suite of regal accoutrements.

The heraldic symbol for Saint Matthew, the tax-gatherer, was a ruched moneybag and this symbol was emblazoned upon the crests of treasurers and titled families with large landholdings. Ritual contents also made bags precious and many trends for the ornamentation of secular fashion began with bags made for the church. A Byzantine relic pouch of the ninth century stored at St. Michaels in Beromunster, Switzerland, was lined in red silk and worked with intricately embroidered lions on a blue silk ground. By the thirteenth century, the popular term for a bag in Western Europe was an almoner. This term referred to an alms bag, that is, a purse to hold coins to be given as charity. Almoners lent a rather showy side to Christian charity; the richer the purse the more generous the social image of the Lady who carried it. Such pomp gave rise to thievery, the term "cut-purse" came into use in 1362.

The purse was also an important offering in the ritual of courtly love. The most amusing and sophisticated bags of the fourteenth and fifteenth centuries were made as gifts to lovers, decorated with allegorical scenes and mottoes alluding to the trials of romance. One bag dating from the mid-fourteenth century (housed in the Musée Historique des Tissues, Lyon) depicts a lady posing as a falconer and her lover as the falcon, a witty reversal of the roles of hunter and prey. On another fourteenth-century French bag (from the Troyes Cathedral Treasury) two female rivals are depicted sawing a human heart in half. The tradition of the wedding or betrothal bag originated in the medieval custom of a groom presenting his bride with a sack of coins. In art, the drawstring purse came to connote female sexuality. Albrecht Dürer, Lucas Cranach, and others depicted many a lascivious older man reaching for the drawstring pouch of a younger woman. Female genitalia were referred to in Shakespearean slang as a purse. The eroticism of the bag was heightened by the way almoners, purses, and "harmondeys" were worn, suspended from a girdle that tightly straddled the belly or swayed suggestively about the hips.

In the fifteenth century, large and elaborate bags with cast-metal frames became more common and were carried by men of the ruling class. In the late sixteenth and early seventeenth centuries, the size and shape of bags diversified, and the tiniest bags denoted the greatest status. Small, square embroidered "swete" bags containing perfumed pomanders, rose petals, rare spices, and oils were worn to scent skirts and cuffs and used as containers for personal gifts. Over time, swete bags and coin purses assumed increasingly ornamental shapes. One small purse from the Museum of London is a life-sized crocheted frog that fits snugly into the palm of the hand. Made of cream silk with silver mesh, the mouth of the frog forms the opening of the bag just large enough for a tiny coin. The Elizabethans had a taste for visual conceits and allegory. A bag in the shape of an acorn symbolized thrift, but was likely to be worn in the manner of a precious jewel, wound about the wrist or bouncing against full skirts. Satchels and sacks worn across the body were for peasants and pilgrims; often made from recy-cled socks or scraps of cloth; these bags are now known mainly from paintings and etchings as few actual examples survived their heavy daily use.

The rise of the evening bag can be dated from the seventeenth century, when men and women used gaming bags to carry their chips and coins. Designed to sit flat upon a table, these bags reflected a new sophistication in form. With a shallow tightly ruched drawstring body attached to a circular base stiffened with cord or leather, the bases of these bags were often decorated with the initials or coat of arms of their owner to avoid any confusion over the night's winnings. The square shape that had dominated bag design for two centuries or more was now sprouting into three dimensions. Bags were made of interlocking panels in the shape of crescents, shields, and pentagons and told little stories (of heroic colonial enterprise or secret love) on each individually embroidered panel. The idea of the bag as a narrative in itself or a formal social badge for its owner expanded in the eighteenth century when leather folding wallets featured one's name and title boldly embossed on the front, usually in gold letters. By the middle of the seventeenth century, bags and purses for women became smaller and tended to be obscured within the folds of large skirts made even more voluminous by hoops and farthingales. Increasingly, the bag had to compete with its much more practical rival: the pocket.

At the beginning of the eighteenth century, the role of the bag for men and women began to divide. Men might resort to slipping a small, netted purse into their sleeve or slung over the belt buckle, but they no longer dangled leather or cloth bags from a long drawstring at the waist. The notion of an elaborate bag with a drawstring or handle became more and more feminized as the century progressed. As masculine fashion became even more streamlined with tight breeches and cutaway coats, men were forced to compress their needs into custom-made wallets that contained everything from a compass to nail scissors and a snuff bottle. Eighteenth-century women carried small purses on the wrist, toted large silk and cotton workbags for knotting and personal effects on the arm and had the additional storage space of large pear-shaped pockets worn laced around the hips beneath their petticoats.

All of this extra room gave birth to a culture of the handbag long before the handbag proper came into existence. Women grew accustomed to carrying their workbags about socially, slipping extra items in for evening such as fans, smelling salts, cosmetics, and opera glasses. In their dimity pockets they carried small leather-bound pocketbooks whose printed pages included calendars, recipes, songs, and Saint days as well as engravings of the latest dress and hat models. A precursor to the modern fashion magazine, the pocketbook added depth to the idea that a woman carried the world in her pocket.

Despite the capacious generosity of pockets and knotting bags, small purses for women remained popular, and their decorations reached a peak of worldly topicality. A woman could advertise her love of science or a political allegiance with the elegant flick of a wrist. The fine sable beaded bags produced in Paris from the 1770s on, wove up to 1,000 tiny glass beads onto each square inch of the bag's surface, lending a remarkable clarity to color, lettering, figures, and detail. One such beaded bag from 1784 was decorated with hot-air balloons and the face of Jean-Francois Pilâtre de Rozier, the French balloonist who made his maiden voyage the year before. Printed images on silk also offered swift production of commemorative and novelty bags.

By 1799, hand-netted bags were referred to in England as "indispensables" and in France as reticules, after the netted bag (*reticulum*) carried by Roman ladies. Handbags were in existence even before chemise-style dresses became fashionable, but bags became permanently established as a feminine accessory once the long, sheer and close-fitting dresses of the directoire eliminated the space for pockets altogether. As with all new fashions there was a period of adjustment, and fashionable women of Paris and London were reported to be secreting small coin purses into their décolletage or slipping important letters into the leaves of their fans. The need for an alternative to the pocket gave birth to early bags that looked very similar to the pear-shaped pockets of the late 1700s, simply grafted onto a silken drawstring. There was some social outcry at the notion of wearing such an intimate article in public but demand soon replaced dissent. The Parisian *Journal des modes* quipped, "One may leave one's husband but never one's bag."

The prevailing shape of the first decade of the nineteenth century was the drawstring reticule but frame bags began to come into use. Bag size is always contingent on the shape, cut, and proportion of clothes; as skirts grow larger bags tend to shrink. In the mid-nineteenth century, alternative containers such as muffs, link metal chain purses, knitted miser bags, and chatelaines (a range of miniature domestic trinkets worn hung from a belt) competed with the hand-held bag for carrying coins and small personal articles. Unlike the deliciously worldly style of the eighteenth century, the Victorian era idealized domesticity and sentimentality. Bags reflected these themes with hand-beaded patterns of home and hearth (bought commercially or made at home), hand-painted scenes of mourning on black satin, and arrangements of flowers encoded with private messages for loved ones. Bags made at home advertised the skill of their maker and were given to eccentric almost esoteric detail, commercially made leather frame bags for shopping and train travel were far plainer, designed for security, respectability, and privacy. These two trends were to echo the split identity in handbags into the next century and beyond. The idea became established that a woman could own several very different bags for different occasions and different personae.

By the 1880s the handbag had become a fashion fixture. Based on the design of much larger luggage and the traveling carpetbag (first executed in tapestry fabric by Pierre Godillot in France in 1826), necessity had bred a very plain, useful bag that became the blueprint for all to come. Most of the classic bags known today were invented and developed by the great luggage and saddlery houses of Paris in the late nineteenth century. Louis Vuitton made traveling trunks for Napoleon III. In 1896 he had logos based on his initials hand-painted onto his trunks and hand luggage to defy counterfeiters. His steamer trunk of 1901, designed to hang on the back of a cabin door with a long canvas body and short, strong leather straps, is the precursor to the tote bag. Emile Maurice Hermès had the vision to transform feed and saddle bags into elegant travel accessories. The genesis of the Kelly and later the Birkin bags were in tall leather satchels designed to hold saddles: the Haut a Courroies. Hermès was also the first to apply the Canadian army cargo zipper as a modern fastening, bringing it back to Paris in 1923 to create the Bolide, a driving bag for his wife. Travel in the early years of the century was not about expedience but studied luxury, and the grand French houses created classics out of an ingenuity for stylish living. The Noe bag was designed by Vuitton in 1932 as a satchel to carry exactly five bottles of champagne. This design formed the basis of all shoulder strap bucket bags to follow. The Plume bag designed by Hermès in 1933 was based on a square horse blanket bag and updated with thin central straps and a zip that encircled the body of the bag. An heir to the Hermès Bolide of 1923, this simple square bag was the model for the gym bag including the Adidas tennis bag of the 1980s and the Prada bowling bag of the 1990s. The tote, the bucket, and the box are the geometrical foundations of twentieth-century design. Bags have gone to every extreme since but their origins always return to these three templates.

From 1900 to 1914 handbags swung like a pendulum between exotic fantasy and pragmatic reality. In one last nostalgic bid against the fully mechanized age, there was a brief vogue for tiny silver mesh bags, large velvet chatelaine bags with hand-carved silver frames, and elaborately beaded German and Italian bags depicting fairy-tale castles, Renaissance landscapes, and rococo ladies in hoop skirts. The influences of orientalism and art nouveau spread the desire for bags cut from antique textiles, ecclesiastic velvets, tapestry, and handmade lace. Leather shoulder bags were pioneered by the suffragette movement, and when war came in 1914 this style gained serious ground. During the 1920s there was a trend for bags that were androgynous, sleek, and held close to the body. The Exposition of Decorative Arts held in Paris in 1925 influenced every aspect of handbag design from the geometric abstraction of their hardware and decoration to the streamlining of their form and function. Lancel, the French luxury leather goods firm, presented a sleek purse in 1928 that included a mirror, makeup case, and minuscule umbrella. The mesh bags of the 1920s echoed perfectly the sinuous lines of the chiffon and net dresses worn

HOW THE KELLY BAG GOT ITS NAME

A Hermès Kelly bag takes over eighteen hours to create and is hand-stitched by a single craftsman. Based on a bag originally designed to carry a saddle, the original name for the Kelly was the *Haut a Courroies* (meaning literally "bag with tall handles"), and the first model was refined for use in car and air travel in the early 1930s. Famous women who have carried the bag include Marlene Dietrich and Ingrid Bergman, but these are not the women who made it a household name. In 1956 Grace Kelly was photographed getting out of a limousine holding her Hermès bag in a white-gloved hand. In fact, she was using the bag to shield her pregnant belly from prying photographers. The image ran on the cover of *Life* magazine in 1956 making the Kelly the most famous bag in the world. Luxury accessories were slower to catch the public's imagination in midcentury America than in Europe, where an expensive handbag was expected to last a lifetime. In France it has long been a bourgeois ritual to present a Kelly bag on a young woman's twenty-first birthday. In America, the Kelly has also come to represent a treasured prize for a rite of passage and has remained the last word in conservative chic for almost half a century.

by the flappers, and were just large enough to contain a pack of cigarettes, a lipstick, and some coins. While the average office girl of 1930 was content with her enameled Whiting and Davis mesh bag decorated with a deco flower for $2.94, socialites carried bags studded with pavé diamonds, jade, and emeralds by Cartier, or Van Cleef and Arpels minaudières, evening box bags made of solid gold.

By the late 1930s the spirit of surrealism and Hollywood screwball comedies infused handbag design with a last blast of witty sophistication before the war. Suddenly a bag could be shaped like a Daimler automobile, a Scotty dog, or a model of the SS *Normandie*, complete with miniature metal steam vents (this bag was sold as a souvenir aboard the ship in 1935). The designer who embodied this irreverent spirit best was Elsa Schiaparelli. She was the first designer to link the handbag to the concept of celebrity: She decorated a pochette in 1934 with a print of newspaper clippings about herself! Subsequent bags were shaped like bouquets and inverted balloons. During World War II, handbag design took a sober turn, with practical styles prevailing; the return of frankly masculine shoulder bags dominated the decade. Ingenuity and improvisation dominated this decade. Rationing saw women recycling nineteenth century bags for evening

and using everything from men's suiting to crocheted wool and upholstery cord to craft their own handbags at home. Stealth influenced style and bags were designed with secret pockets, stacked compartments, sliding metal panels and riveted mesh clasps.

As if in reaction to the solidity of 1940s bags, 1950s bags were small, saucy, and (due to the development of plastic technology) quite often completely see-through. Transparent bags were made possible by a new form of hard plastic Perspex known as Lucite. But the lifespan of Lucite as a luxury item was cut short by the invention of injection molding, a process that could make hard plastic bags quickly and cheaply. By 1958 the Lucite bag was available at chain stores and no longer a coveted status symbol. Wealthy ladies had moved on to luxury bags made of crocodile and alligator. The next generation would care for neither.

The handbag in the 1960s seemed eager to shrug off the hang-up of structure and tradition. Bags were made in simple shapes and elaborate inexpensive materials such as wood, straw, cotton, and PVC. Bags could be whimsical, like Enid Collins' sequined baskets, or psychedelic as in the case of Emilio Pucci's patterned handbags, but they were rarely staid. Bonnie Cashin's design mantra "make things as lightweight as possible—as simple as possible—as punchy as possible—as inexpensive as possible" summed up the spirit of the era. The American sportswear designer spearheaded a return to soft, unstructured bags. She coined the term "Cashin Carry" for her 1967 shopper with a coin purse self attached; she made a lunchbox shaped bag with pockets that flipped open on either end, and a hobo bag that included an extra pouch—just in case. She took the everyday tote and dolled it up in acid-bright leather piping and Harris tweed. Designing for Coach from 1962 to 1972, her ideas spawned the slouchy egalitarian style of the 1970s and continue to speak to the preppy elegance of contemporary sports bags. The handbag in the seventies was influenced by the divergent forces of feminism, global travel, status fashion and sport. Unisex styling gave the 'man-bag' its brief moment and many rough hewn embroidered denim and handtooled leather shoulder bags were worn by both sexes. Utility style had an impact on materials and both the rip stop nylon 'Le Sportsac' tennis bag and the canvas L. L. Bean tote were worn as badges of egalitarian chic and career equality. Designer status bags by Gucci, Dior, and Fendi established jetset style but over-licensing and widespread counterfeiting diluted the power and exclusivity of the logo as the decade progressed. Luxury evening bags of the late seventies and early eighties were exquisite and small. The disco bags by Carlos Falchi, Halston and Judith Leiber were worn almost like jewelry. Prada, the Milanese leather house, was substantially revived when Miuccia Prada introduced a simple leather and rip-stop nylon backpack to their line in 1985. Monochrome and subtly monogrammed, the bag and its' practical accessories (small wallets and purses) gave the designer bag a fresh dose of street credibility. The late eighties saw a return to the surrealist spirit in fashion with many French designers approaching the handbag as a witty found object or subverted status symbol. Jamin Puech suspended a marabou powder puff on a satin strap, Christian Lacroix fashioned a gold clutch into the shape of a Byzantine bible, and Karl Lagerfeld shrank the Chanel bag to the size of a bon bon to bounce off the hip. The nineties was perhaps the centuries richest decade for handbag design, almost every year saw the birth of an iconic new bag. In 1993 Lulu Guinness launched her flower pot, a surreal basket bag festooned with silk roses. The following year Kate Spade's top handled square tote became an instant American classic. In 1995 Madame Chirac presented Lady Diana with a small bag of embossed leather with loose gold letters hanging like a charm bracelet from its handles, the 'Lady Dior.' In 1996 Moschino dripped rich brown calfskin over a pristine white handbag, effectively dipping the bag like a strawberry in chocolate. The most famous bag of the decade was launched the following year. The Fendi baguette tucked under the arm (inspiring its title) and was made of rich and unexpected materials: tapestry, handloomed velvet, embroidered denim and exotic skins. The bag changed the fortunes of the company and the face of the handbag in fashion history, as the first bag since the Kelly to become a household name, a cult object and a celebrity in its own right.

Designers have tried to predict what the bag would look like in the twenty-first century. In 1999 Karl Lagerfeld designed the Chanel 2005 bag: a vacuum-formed ovoid handbag with a hard body flocked in neoprene. The all-in-one design of this bag with a handle punched out of its body like a doughnut hole resembled both a laptop case and a futuristic cartoon character. Houses such as Fendi, Prada, Gucci, and Vuitton created dramatic sequels to their best-selling bags.

The logo itself came up for review with aggressive revision and reinvention. Marc Jacobs's first contribution to his post as creative director at Louis Vuitton was to have the 1980s artist Stephen Sprouse tag the name of the house in graffiti lettering across a zip-topped structured bag. Released in 2000, this bag led the charge for staid houses to revise their image radically. John Galliano's designs for Dior from 2000 on, have evoked Cadillac dashboards, car headlights, punk rock kimonos, and miniature riding saddles in arresting materials like red patent leather and acid-washed denim.

The impetus behind the capital and artistic risk of issuing radical bags for the classic labels has been both prestige and money. When a label launches a successful bag the corporation's stock can rise dramatically in value. Handbags have also become the stylistic mascots for designer culture. In the 1940s one wore the perfume of Chanel; in the early 2000s one wears the bag to attain the same cachet. The quest for an "it" bag dominates the field. After the initial long-running success of the

baguette since its launch in 1997, Fendi presented the croissant (shaped like a crescent moon) in 2000, followed in 2002 by the Ostrik, a 1970s-inspired shoulder bag with zipped side panels and a beaten metal panel something like a Roman breastplate, and a succession of bags that mimiced the bouffant folds of a chef's hat or fanned outward in concentric tiers of leather, fabric, and skins. Outlandishly organic designs have vied for attention by creating a sexy alternative to the top handle bag. Tom Ford for YSL's "Nadja" bag (2003) resembled a massive suede rosebud or ruffled labia depending on your view. The studded Domino bag by Sonia Rykiel (2001) squashed under the arm like a comfortable designer dim sum, and Marc Jacob's "Venetia" with its massive buckles, chunky pockets, and top stitching set a powerful trend for utilitarian bags with cartoonish proportions in saturated colors.

The first four years of the twenty-first century saw the most intense diversity in handbag design and equally intense competition between designers. When Madonna, Gwyneth Paltrow, and Kate Moss began to carry the saddlebag designed by Nicholas Ghesquiere for Balenciaga, the rather plain distressed leather hobo with front zips and trailing tassels became a cult. When characters on the TV show *Sex and the City* obsessed about owning a red Hermès Birkin bag, the yearlong waiting list for the bag doubled and then tripled. In terms of fame, the Hermès Birkin bag has now eclipsed the Hermès Kelly or perhaps it has simply become the Kelly bag of its generation, being softer, larger, and slightly louder than its predecessor.

While famous designer label bags lead the trends for mass-market fashion, there is room for a backlash or a return to one-of-a-kind bags made by hand. In the Victorian era bags assumed a split identity. The formality of a leather shopping bag or traveling case and the eccentricity of a little silk evening purse stitched from remnants or decorated with a hand-embroidered poem struck the contrast between social duty and private pleasure, professional production and home crafts. As the handbag grows more and more commodified, streamlined, and hyped, a return to more individual shapes and materials seems increasingly possible. The bag began as a simple vessel for private needs. Despite the advances of technology and the far-reaching tentacles of advertising, this is where the handbag may return. A rejection of luxury culture might produce the most original bags of the twenty-first century, and the most personal.

See also **Cashin, Bonnie; Europe and America: History of Dress (400–1900 C.E.); Ford, Tom; Hermès; Pucci, Emilio.**

BIBLIOGRAPHY

Ettinger, Roseann. *Handbags.* Atglen, Pa.: Schiffer Publishing, 1999.

Hagerty, Barbara G. S., and Anne Rivers Siddons. *Handbags: A Peek Inside a Woman's Most Trusted Accessory.* New York: Running Press, 2002.

Johnson, Anna. *Handbags: The Power of the Purse.* New York: Workman Publishing Company, 2002.

Steele, Valerie, and Laird Borelli, *Handbags: A Lexicon of Style.* New York: Rizzoli International, 2000.

Wilcox, Claire. *Bags.* London: Victoria and Albert Museum, 1999.

Anna Johnson

HAND SPINNING. *See* **Homespun; Spinning.**

HANDWOVEN TEXTILES The category handwoven textiles encompasses a broad spectrum of woven fabrics formed by interlacing two sets of elements—warp and weft—with the aid of a loom, which is a device for maintaining tension on the warp elements. Whether the loom is primitive, mechanized, or computer-driven, it is considered a handloom if it is operated directly by the weaver. Even though various types of power looms have been developed since the industrial revolution, handweaving persists in many parts of the world as an expression of ethnic culture, as a cottage industry or small-scale artisan workshop, as an avocation, and as an art form.

Handwoven Textiles in Interior Design

Handwoven cloth contains irregularities not usually present in industrially-produced cloth—a quality often considered desirable by contemporary artists and designers. The rich colors and designs of traditional cultural textiles are appreciated by collectors and continue to provide sources of inspiration to handweavers and artists, as well as to designers in the textile industry. Noted textile designers such as Jack Lenor Larsen formed unique collaborations with traditional handweavers around the world to produce unique and distinctive fabrics for interiors, using traditional design elements and woven by traditional means. Such collaborations not only produce exciting new textiles; they also help the cultures involved to maintain art forms that are struggling to survive in the current global economy.

Handwoven rugs are popular items of interior decor that may be imported from traditional textile workshops in countries such as Turkey and China, or they may be unique works of art designed by contemporary artists. Liturgical fabrics specially handwoven to adorn houses of worship comprise a specialized market for this specialized group of artist-weavers. Other handwoven items created for interiors include afghans or throws, table linens, and wall hangings. A few handweavers specialize in reproducing historic fabrics for historic dwellings and reenactments.

Many artist-weavers are attracted to using hand-manipulated weaves, such as tapestry and supplementary-weft techniques, that allow for the creation of free-form and pictorial designs to create tapestries and wall hangings for art galleries and collectors. A growing field for artist-weavers is the application of digital technology to handweaving to produce computer-generated designs on complex looms.

Traditions and Looms

Cultures with living traditions in handwoven textiles made on simple looms are numerous and can still be found in many parts of the world, including Mexico and Guatemala, Peru, Bolivia, Ghana, Nigeria, Morocco, Turkey, China, Burma, Japan, Thailand, Vietnam, Indonesia, and the Philippines.

Fabrics woven on simple two-bar looms such as the backstrap loom, tend to be narrow widths (12–14 inches) of warp-dominant or warp-faced plain weave, for ease in operating the loom. The so-called primitive fabrics produced on these looms, usually by women, are often decorated with elaborate supplementary-weft techniques (brocade) inserted between the rows of the plain-weave ground; or with supplementary-warp techniques (pickup weaves) worked in a similar manner. Such patterns involve hand-manipulating selected threads during the weaving, and their complexity is limited only by the weaver's patience and imagination.

Many cultures make use of simple, two-bar looms to create their traditional folk costumes. Such weavings are often pieced together from rectangles of narrow, four-selvage cloth and may be further embellished after assembly. Two-bar looms may also be used to create shawls, cloths for wrapping and carrying, bags, rugs, tent fabrics, and other utilitarian fabrics. From the brocaded huipil, or blouse, worn by indigenous women of Guatemala and Mexico, to the sarongs of Indonesia, traditional handwoven garments are associated with personal identity and cultural pride.

Weft-faced weaves such as tapestry can be woven on an upright version of the two-bar loom. Well-known products of upright looms include Turkish rugs in various weaves such as pile, kilim (tapestry), and soumak; and the Navajo rugs of the Southwest United States made in tapestry weave.

A simple foot-manipulated loom, the tripod loom, is used by men in West African countries such as Nigeria, Senegal, and the Ivory Coast, to weave narrow cotton strips for kente cloth. These strips are pieced together to make large cloths for men's ceremonial dress.

Handwoven fabrics created on mechanized handlooms such as treadle looms can range from simple, textured effects achieved with novelty yarns in plain weave, to fabrics with pattern repeats that become increasingly complex as the available number of loom shafts increases. India, China, Japan, and Thailand are well-known for their production of handwoven silks, cottons, and other natural fibers. Guatemala and Mexico produce handwoven cotton fabrics. Cottage-industry handweaving of woolens persists in Scotland and Ireland.

CONTEMPORARY HANDWOVEN CLOTHING

Artists who create art-to-wear garments often prefer the distinctive texture and character that handwoven cloth adds to their expressive works. Contemporary handwoven clothing has undergone an evolution in sophistication since it became popular as an art form during the 1960s. As a greater variety of threads became available, and as handweaving equipment became more sophisticated, so did handwoven clothing design. Woven fashions in the 1960s and 1970s were inspired by ethnic clothing styles and were usually designed using rectangular shapes that could be put together with minimal cutting or sewing. Weavers at that time also challenged themselves to create garments "shaped on the loom" by weaving pattern pieces to shape according to a predrawn cartoon. By the 1980s, the increasing availability of fine yarns and luxury fibers combined with the increased availability of complex looms, inspired handweavers to create drapeable fabrics for fashionable, tailored garments and to explore the expressive possibilities of weave structures in fashion design and wearable art. Handweavers today create complex textiles through creative combinations of weave structure and use of textured yarns. They may also employ techniques such as warp painting or ikat dyeing of the threads before weaving, or may apply surface design techniques such as painting, printing, and foil transfer to embellish the finished fabric.

Markets for Handwovens

In addition to textiles produced for the interior design trade mentioned above, commercial markets for handwovens in the United States and Europe include folk art galleries, museum shops, craft galleries and art and craft fairs, wearable art galleries, and contemporary art galleries. In the many countries with cultural textiles traditions, sales are realized through tourist markets, specialty shops, and government-supported handcraft outlets. Artisan cooperatives may export textile products through fair trade markets, which guarantee the artisans a fair wage for their work. Export and import of handwoven yardage occurs through the international textile trade or through specialty importers.

See also **Ikat; Kente; Loom; Tapestry; Weave, Double; Weave, Pile; Weave Types; Weaving.**

BIBLIOGRAPHY
Alderman, Sharon. *Handwoven Tailor Made.* Loveland, Colo.: Interweave Press, 1982.

Brown, Rachel. *The Weaving, Spinning and Dyeing Book,* New York: Alfred A. Knopf, 1984.

Collingwood, Peter, and Ann Sutton. *The Craft of the Weaver.* Asheville, N.C.: Lark Books, 1983.

Hecht, Ann. *The Art of the Loom: Weaving, Spinning and Dyeing Across the World.* New York: Rizzoli International, 1989.

Karen Searle

HARTNELL, NORMAN Norman Hartnell (1901–1979) was Britain's most successful and distinguished mid-twentieth-century couturier. He was the first in a wave of London-based designers to emerge in the 1920s and 1930s who offered wealthy British women an alternative to patronizing a court dressmaker or purchasing a Paris-designed model. His graceful, feminine designs, which combined dreamy nostalgia with fairy-tale glamour, appealed to English sensibilities. He excelled at making dresses for grand entrances and was equally at ease designing court-presentation dresses for debutantes and stage costumes for actresses. The latter were sophisticated and sexy as well as glamorous, but Hartnell is remembered for the romantic, quintessentially English gowns that he designed for the upper classes and the royal family. His role as dressmaker to Queen Elizabeth, consort of King George VI, and Queen Elizabeth II won him international recognition and honors. He was nominated an *officier d'académie* by the Institut de l'education nationale de France in 1939 and was given a Neiman Marcus Award for contemporary influence on fashion in 1947. In 1977 he became the first fashion designer to be knighted.

Norman Hartnell. Britain's most successful mid-twentieth-century couturier, Norman Hartnell was best known for designing glamorous dresses for Britain's upper class and royal family. He was the first fashion designer to be honored with knighthood, in 1976. © HULTON-DEUTSCH COLLECTION/CORBIS. REPRODUCED BY PERMISSION.

Queen Elizabeth, the Queen Mother (1900–2002). Taken in the mid-twentieth century by Cecil Beaton, this photo shows Queen Elizabeth wearing a silk tulle crinoline dress. Sequins decorate this elegant, fairytale-like gown, designed by Norman Hartnell. © V&A PICTURE LIBRARY. REPRODUCED BY PERMISSION.

The theater, ballet, fine art, and the natural world inspired Hartnell. As an undergraduate at Cambridge University, he neglected his architectural studies to design for the university's amateur dramatic societies and then dropped out of school to try his luck as a dress designer. After working briefly as a sketch artist, he set up on his own in 1923 and in 1934 moved to 26 Bruton Street. He made his name designing for debutantes, society weddings, and charity galas, many of which required fancy dress and Hartnell's talents as a stage

designer. In 1942 he was a founding member of the Incorporated Society of London Fashion Designers and was named president several times. After World War II, Hartnell was the largest couture house in London, employing a staff of 385.

Hartnell designed clothing for members of the royal family from 1935. His most legendary commission was the all-white wardrobe he designed for Queen Elizabeth for her 1938 state visit to France, when she was still in mourning for her mother. Hartnell and the photogra-

Commenting on how the creative impulse is evoked, Hartnell remarked, "Who can say exactly . . . ? A wax-white magnolia in the moonlight is a debutante dancing at Hurlingham. Swans on the lake may turn into a young woman in white arriving to cut the cake at Queen Charlotte's Ball, and a farmyard is redolent of sporting tweeds." (Hartnell, p. 82)

pher Cecil Beaton created a lasting image for the queen that was fresh and feminine but unmistakably regal. In 1947 he designed Princess Elizabeth's wedding dress and, six years later, her coronation robes. Hartnell relished the symbolism and pageantry of British ceremonial and found embroidery, which had already become his signature, the perfect medium for conveying the gravity and glamour of monarchy.

Drama, color, and light suffused Hartnell's designs. He enjoyed working with soft, floating fabrics, particularly tulle and chiffon, and with plain, lustrous silks, which provided the perfect foil for his spectacular, eye-catching embroideries. He was the master of the special-occasion dress that flatters and dignifies both wearer and occasion with consummate tact. His legacy to the future lay in his Englishness, in his creative and romantic engagement with history and tradition, and in his love of spectacle.

See also **Court Dress; Embroidery; Fancy Dress; Royal and Aristocratic Dress; Theatrical Costume; Wedding Costume.**

BIBLIOGRAPHY

Brighton Art Gallery and Museums and the Museum of Costume. *Norman Hartnell.* Haslemere, U.K.: South Leigh Press, 1985. Well-illustrated and an excellent overview of Hartnell's career.

Hartnell, Norman. *Silver and Gold.* London: Evans Brothers, 1955.

McDowell, Colin. *A Hundred Years of Royal Style.* London: Muller, Blond and White, 1985.

Edwina Ehrman

HATS, MEN'S Protection, status, and vanity have always been the prime reasons for wearing hats. A hat is much more than a piece of clothing; it is a cerebral fashion accessory that can mark personality, social etiquette, and lifestyle. The twenty-first century is a relatively hatless age, with the exception of the baseball cap and modern hoods. This might be just a passing fad, but it is socially as significant as trends of the previous era, when men wore proper hats all the time.

There have been hatless periods in history before. Eighteenth-century wigs replaced hats and coiffeurs eclipsed the hatter, but the nineteenth century dictated hats for men again with many important styles still remembered with nostalgia. Post–World War I democratic ideologies, modern infrastructure, and, most importantly of all, the car, all caused the gradual demise of hats. World War II changed social values even more, resulting in youth's imperative right of wanting to look radically different from the previous generation. Yet fashion's pendulum never ceases to swing, and there might well be a time in the future when fashion will demand that heads need to be covered again. Why the fashion for wearing or not wearing a hat fluctuates at different times can only be explained with hindsight of historical and social developments.

The ancient Romans lived in a hatless age but showed their status by wearing metal fillets over their brows. The exceptions were military helmets, worn over a leather cap and held in place by a chinstrap. Northern European tribes wore leather caps before the Roman occupation. An eight-section leather cap, said to be over 2,000 years old, is preserved at the National Museum in Copenhagen, Denmark, which must be the oldest existing man's hat in history.

When Christianity arrived in Europe, the church demanded that the body be covered up with a hooded cloak called *bardocucullus*. Faces were overshadowed by all kinds of hoods as well as by beards, the fashion in England until the Norman conquests over the Saxons in 1066. The French invasion imposed a fashion for clean-shaven faces and short hair, which was often covered by a coif, a close-fitted linen cap, tied under the chin. A variation was the phrygian cap, a soft, close-fitting and pointed hat, inspired by the Phoenician fashion, brought into Europe by traders from the Mediterranean.

Early medieval pointed hoods and capes merged into gorgets (a hood and neckpiece) and coif-de-maille (a metal chain-mail hood). Professional people, such as doctors, wore richly decorated round skullcaps. The first hats with brims, made of straw or felt, were utilitarian and worn by field laborers, shading their eyes from the sun and rain. A soft linen coif, tied under the chin was usually worn underneath a hat, thus keeping long hair in place. In the late thirteenth century, the *chapeau a bec*, a brimmed hat, cocked into a beak shape pointing to the front, became the fashion for young men and was also always worn over a coif. Later on, the *chapeau de fer*, a divergence from the closed metal helmet, provided shade and protection with its cap, brim, and chinstrap.

Headwear became more eccentric in the fourteenth century, with meek and humble hoods developing ever-longer and longer drooping points. The soft lengthy tubes, worn over a gorget, were called liripipes and often matched the then fashionable four- or five-piece outfits. The tube could be up to two feet in length with a long

Roman legionaire wearing helmet. Hats, though rarely worn by ancient Romans, were used by the military. They were made of leather and held in place by a chinstrap. © BETTMANN/CORBIS. REPRODUCED BY PERMISSION.

houppeland, a stiff collar cradling the head and tucked under the liripipe or rondelet at the back of the head. The coif was relegated to be worn as a nightcap called cuffie, cappeline, benducci, or bendoni and replaced by close-fitting lined linen caps without chinstraps. Worn under expensive velour or plush hats, this was a practical solution for keeping the inside of a hat clean from sweat and grease. As hoods and liripipes could not be taken off in greetings, they had to be raised by two fingers while bowing, a gesture called "*riverenza di cappuccino.*" The Vatican influenced social etiquette and with it men's fashion. The becca replaced the liripipe and became a social attribute with its long and flat band, hanging down over the right shoulder, draped over the chest, or tucked into the belt. To greet a lady, a man had to raise his hat with his right hand, while holding the streamers of the becca with his left. The becca's practical advantage was in securing the hat when it was slung over a man's shoulder, a custom still used on ceremonial robes of the Order of the Garter.

Men's fashion changed from a slim, tall medieval silhouette to a short, stocky look in the sixteenth century, established in England by King Henry VIII. Flat, wide berets complimented the style best. Worn straight or at an angle with six- or eight-sided stiff brims underneath, they were known as "bonetes." Brimmed hats developed into quite flamboyant styles, generally called "beavers" after the fur used for felting. These felt hats were often trimmed with real fur, which was also used for rondelets and under brims.

Plumes of swan feathers and ornamental brooches, gold plaques and crests enhanced a look of prosperity. The coif changed to the caul, a wide-netted snood to be worn under the hat or inside the house. Young men liked hoods with very long points down to the floor, which could be wound around the head. Prosperous merchants wore cushion hats, stuffed berets with voluminous rondelets, while older men preferred high, flat birettas, usually in bright scarlet red.

During the Elizabethan era, men's hats changed to capotains, brims with high crowns, lavishly decorated with gold and silver braids, Vandyke lace, as well as exotic plumes from the newly discovered Americas. In England, all men above the age of six had to wear a hat by law. This court edict was proclaimed in order to foster the hat trade.

In the seventeenth century, hats diversified even more extravagantly. Wide cocked-up brims with diamond studded ostrich feathers drooping over the edges were the fashion for the new romantic male idol, "the cavalier," an image immortalized in numerous paintings. The cavalier's beaver hat, posed on long, flowing love locks was the perfection of elegance, a peacock look, that took time and wealth to perfect, which might possibly have been the reason why wigs came into fashion. Wearing a periwig, made of human or of horse hair under one's hat, was a simpler, less time-consuming option, allowing even

ribbon added, which could be wound around the head in infinite variety. The coif, the gorget, and the liripipe were collectively called the chaperon. A round, stuffed band, called a rondelet, was sometimes added by fashionable jongleurs, the wandering musicians and medieval trendsetters. Further variations were achieved by rolling the gorget up over the forehead or by winding the liripipe around the head, creating a kind of turban style. Added to this complicated arrangement could be a felt bycock hat, a style worn by men and women, which allowed even more variations by splitting or slashing the brims, or by wearing the hat back to front. Diversification seemed infinite with soft tammy berets worn over coifs or draped over brims. Materials varied from robust leather and felt to furs and precious silk velvets in lush colors, matching or contrasting the extravagant medieval outfits.

Hoods and gorgets for warmth continued into the fifteenth century, with hat shapes adding personal identity. Occasionally, the soft gorget was replaced by a

more variations in color and style. The perfect new stylish hat was the tricorn, which like wigs was in fashion up to the end of the eighteenth century. An individual note was achieved by wearing the hat either pointing to the front or to the side and by adding different decorations like feather fringes and cockades; very important in all military headwear.

Fashion in the eighteenth century was dominated by hair and wigs leaving hats to be carried in the hand and raised in greetings rather than worn. Coiffeurs created wigs of great varieties, powdered toupees or center-parted curls with queues and pigtails hanging down at the back. The tricorn was still worn, but changed shape by being flattened or "pinched" at the front, which was a foretaste to the two-cornered "bycocked" hat. Beaver fur, (*castor* in French) was still used as the raw material for felting, but was often mixed for economical reasons with rabbit fur and then called "*demi-castors.*" Both tricorns and elaborate wigs lost their appeal at the end of the century. European fashion was influenced by the French Revolution, when men shedded notions of aristocracy in favor of egalitarianism. Round, small-brimmed and light-colored felt hats, trimmed with simple bands and buckles, worn over natural-colored hair were "de rigueur."

Curiously, the start of the nineteenth century heralded a new age for men's hats in the Western world, which reached its zenith at the turn of the twentieth century, when no gentleman would ever step out of his house without wearing a hat. Men's clothing was dictated by sobriety and egalitarianism and hats fulfilled an important role in subtly marking differentials, personal and professional ones, as well as social class distinction. Top hats, bowlers, derbies, boaters, fedoras, panamas, and cloth caps were all created during this century and lasted well into the twentieth century.

The black silk topper was the first in line. Developed from the high felt stovepipe hat, it became the hat worn by postrevolution aristocracy and an emblem of conservative capitalism. Its origins were far less formal. Like many other hats in history, the topper, also known as "*chapeau haut de forme,*" was a French design, at first causing outrage and dismay in London in the 1790s. According to the *Mayfair Gazette*, this new tall black hat "frightened people, made children cry, and dogs bark." John Heatherington, the London haberdasher who dared to wear it, was arrested and charged with "inciting the breach of the peace." Despite this turbulent beginning, the high black hat was gradually adopted by gentlemen of distinction in the West.

The construction and making of the high topper was innovative, too. The hat was not shaped in beaver felt but constructed from stiffened calico, which was covered with silk plush fabric and brushed around repeatedly until smooth and shiny. Mercury was used to enhance the hat's blackness and was later discovered to cause mental disorder, hence the popular term "mad as a hatter." The height and the shape of the crown varied, the tallest being the "kite-high dandy," with a height of 7¾ inches (21cm). The diameter of the flat top varied as well and with it the "waisted" shape of the chimney crown. Toward the end of the nineteenth century, a collapsible version of the hat was devised, known as "chapeau claque" or "chapeau Gibus," after its French inventor. This ingenious design could be folded flat—concertina-fashion—and sprung back into shape by the flick of the fist, thus making storage much easier.

Stetson hats on display. Established in the late nineteenth century, the well-known Stetson company produces hats that evoke a masculine feel and a sense of history in the wearer. © DAVE G. HOUSER/CORBIS. REPRODUCED BY PERMISSION.

The bowler hat, called derby in the United States, was designed in 1849 at the height of the industrial revolution in Britain. Like the top hat, it quickly became a classic wardrobe item and a quintessential badge of Englishness. Named after John and William Bowler, hatters from Stockport, an industrial city in the north of England, it was to become the first mass-produced hat in history. A young English aristocrat who wanted a new hunting hat ordered the original design. Lock and Company, hatters of St. James's in London, since 1676, had been given a brief to supply a brown, round-crowned felt hat, practical and hard wearing, but also dashing and modern. Most importantly, the hat was to be hard and protective as it was to be used for riding. The making of felt hats was traditionally done by small factories in South London, who experimented with stiffening of felt in various ways. A substance called shellac was perfected by mixing a dark treacle-like extract from a parasite insect found in Southeast Asia with methylated spirit. The felt hoods were manually rolled and beaten in the hot and steaming mixture, before being blocked and dried on wooden hat blocks. The procedure was arduous and dirty, but the key to mass production, making the hat affordable to the middle-classes.

The industrial revolution in Britain and all over Western Europe brought important social changes and a shift from agriculture to factories. Factories needed not

Actor Maurice Chevalier in Boater hat, ca. 1930s. Men's hats have long served a variety of functions, from head protection to fashion statement. Their form and function have largely been determined by the age and culture in which they developed. © JOHN SPRINGER COLLECTION/CORBIS. REPRODUCED BY PERMISSION.

only workers but also managers, bookkeepers, and accountants, all new middle-class men who traveled on the newly invented railways wearing black bowler or "iron hats." With its sturdy, solid look the hat was the perfect fashion and style accessory for social climbers in Victorian Britain: a smart, discreet hat that turned every man into a gentleman. The earl of Derby introduced the hat to the United States, hence the name given to it there.

The bowler held its place in fashion for over one hundred years, its distinctive silhouette making it the most widely recognized hat image in history. The bowler hat was immortalized in art, comedy, and literature, and it is still exploited in advertising today. Charlie Chaplin made the hat famous in his satiric silent films of the early 1920s, a comedy act, which was followed by Laurel and Hardy a few years later. Samuel Beckett put bowler hats on the tramps in his famous play, *Waiting for Godot* ("He can't think without his hat," says one of the characters.) Bertolt Brecht's *Threepenny Opera* features bowler hats and Stanley Kubrick's anarchist in *Clockwork Orange* also wears a bowler. René Magritte's paintings are famous because of the bowler hats on his surrealistic figures. Sculpture has immortalized the hat's image too, in a famous bronze statue with a bowler hat called *The Man in the*

Open Air by Ellie Nadelman at the Museum of Modern Art in New York. It epitomizes the link between the Old and the New World, the transition between convention and modernity.

During the early twentieth century, a black bowler hat became synonymous with financial affairs and was the headwear for German businessmen during the years of the Weimar Republic (1918–1933), but the Nazi regime branded it "*Judenstahlhelm,*" outlawed it, and used it in anti-Semitic propaganda. The bowler remained the recognizable attire of bankers in the City of London until the 1970s and is still worn by a few city lawyers today.

The homburg was a German hat, similar to the bowler, but with a higher and lightly dented crown and is named after its city of origin. It is said that King Edward VII of Britain saw the hat worn by his German cousin Kaiser William and thus started the fashion in England. British politicians like Winston Churchill and Anthony Eden also liked to wear this hat. The American fedora and the slightly smaller British version, the trilby, are felt hats with dented crowns and brims turned up at the back, and down at the front, shading the eyes. Soft felt hats brought a more casual look to men's fashion, which had changed from black frock coats to suits and raincoats. Franklin D. Roosevelt's fedora helped to change the image of his presidency after the assassination of President McKinley, who had always worn a black top hat. The soft felt trilby was originally a bohemian hat, worn by artists and modern thinkers who wanted to make a stand against the old conservative values of the previous century. In the 1930s and 1940s the hat took on a gangster role in the United States, which was exploited by many moviemakers and film stars. It was also the hat worn by newspapermen, crime reporters, and Mafia bosses, whose shady expressions were obscured beneath the stylish brim.

The panama hat was the summer hat for the modern man around the turn of the twentieth century. The hat was woven using the finest jipijapas straw, flexible enough to be rolled into a narrow tube for packaging and transportation. Panamas were handwoven in Ecuador and shipped through the Panama Canal, which gave the hat its name. Growing and preparing the straw was a lengthy procedure and so was the weaving of a hat, which could take a skilled worker up to four weeks. The finest and costliest panama hat is called a Montecristi fino-fino. With not many skilled hat weavers left in Ecuador, this hat has become a collector's item. Cheaper versions and paper panamas are very popular and commercially massproduced in many other countries today.

The boater was another popular straw hat of the nineteenth and the twentieth centuries. The straw was plaited, sewn in a spiral, stiffened and blocked hard into its distinct shape of a flat crown and stiff flat brim. The design of the boater is derived from the shape of sailor's hats and suited to the debonair informal look men liked around the turn of the twentieth century.

The Stetson is a truly American hat, stylish, protective, and unmistakably masculine; a hat of the prairie and the most treasured possession of a cowboy, it evokes silver-screen bravery and passion of the Wild West. Its origins are in Philadelphia, where John Batterson Stetson established his first hat factory in the1880s, which was to grow into one of the great American enterprises of the twentieth century. Having learned the principles of hat making from his father, John Stetson first sought fame and fortune by trekking 750 miles to the west, and felting and making hats by the campfire for his fellow travelers. He did not find gold, but his skills and tenacity helped him build the largest hat empire in the world. The making of a modern Stetson is still based on the old techniques of felting and blocking, requiring thirteen different stages in production, thus making the hat the costliest item of a rancher's clothing. The image of the battered cowboy hat has given way to a range of stylish models for Texan businessmen, topped by the famous "Boss of the Plains," as worn by J.R. of the famous 1980s TV series *Dallas*.

Cloth caps are flat hats with visors traditionally cut and sewn from woolen cloth. The image of the cap was a modest, practical one in keeping with a workingman's life. The saying, "cap in hand," illustrates the social position of the cap—as does the Russian poet Alexander Blok's verse, "Caps tilted, fag drooping, everyone looks like a jailbird on the run." The cap, like other hats, changed its image and is worn in the early 2000s by wealthy gentlemen when shooting grouse or playing golf rather than by laborers going to work at a factory. Capmakers or cappers, also made livery caps, military caps, and various styles for sports caps, like the baseball cap, which has become the universal hat of youth culture in the twentieth and twenty-first centuries.

Finally, the beret, which was in existence long before the twentieth century, has evolved from a French Pyrenean shepherd's hat to the most widely worn military hat in the world. The colors and badges may vary, but the beret is now a universal soldier's hat as well as the favorite hat of revolutionary guerrilla groups. A French mountain regiment, *les chasseurs alpines* always wore dark red berets and presented one to the British Field Marshal Montgomery after World War I. He wore this beret, called *"tarte alpine"* during his command of the British forces during World War II.

See also **Hats, Women's; Headdress; Helmet.**

BIBLIOGRAPHY

Amphlett, Hilda. *Hats, A History of Fashion in Headwear.* Mineola, N.Y.: Dover Publications, Inc., 2003.

Hopkins, Susie. *The Century of Hats.* London: Aurum Press, 1999.

McDowell, Colin. *Hats, Status, Style and Glamour.* London: Thames and Hudson, Inc., 1992.

Robinson, Fred Miller. *The Man in the Bowler Hat: His History and Iconography.* Chapel Hill: University of North Carolina Press, 1993.

Whitbourn, Frank. *Mr. Lock of St. James's Street.* London: Frank Heinemann Ltd., 1971.

Susie Hopkins

HATS, WOMEN'S

Hats are head coverings with a crown and usually a brim. They are distinguished from caps that are brimless but may have a visor. Hats are important because they adorn the head, which is the seat of human rational powers, and they also frame the face. Women's hats have often been differentiated from men's headwear, although in modern times, many women's hat styles have been copied from men's.

Hats are material communicators that indicate gender, age, social status, and group affiliation. They also serve as ceremonial symbols and enhancers of sexual attractiveness. As a sculptural art form, hats may be described and interpreted in terms of shape, color, textured materials, adornments, proportion, and scale to the wearer.

While hats have been universally worn, their historical development within the Western European fashion world will be the focus here. Women's hat fashions began in the Renaissance and grew dramatically with the nineteenth-century industrial revolution, sometimes called the "Golden Age" of millinery, which lasted until the mid-twentieth century.

Origins

The woman's hat may have its origin with a turbanlike head wrap or pointed cap as documented in Neolithic cave paintings at Tassili, Algeria (c. 8000–4000 B.C.E.) and later Mesopotamian sculptures (c. 2600 B.C.E.) Evidence for a variety of shaped hats comes from Crete (c. 1600 B.C.E.) via polychrome terra-cotta female figures wearing several types: the high sugarloaf style, the flat beret, and the tricorne with rosettes, curled plumes or ribbon decorations, which may have association with fertility rituals.

According to Classic, fifth-century B.C.E. painted vases, Greek women were more likely to wear their hair on top of the head secured by a bandeau or net caul. The Greek wide-brimmed straw petasos, worn by both women and men as a sun protector, was also adopted by Romans. Because of modesty and religious reasons stemming from Saint Paul's admonition to the Corinthians that women must cover their hair while praying, wealthy Christian women in the Middle Ages wore draped veils, hoods, or wimples indoors and practical wide-brimmed hats over the wimple for traveling. Peasants wore wide hats over skullcaps or hoods while working in the fields.

Renaissance Humanism: Fashion Begins

With the emergence of Renaissance humanism in fifteenth-century Italy came capitalism stimulated by overseas trade and increased bourgeoisie wealth accompanied by an appreciation of secular portraiture and clothing as art forms. Thus was born the phenomenon of Western

Young Woman with a Pink, **by Hans Memling, 1485–80.** Throughout history, women's hats have served numerous functions, including communicating gender, age, social status, and group affiliation. THE METROPOLITAN MUSEUM OF ART, THE JULES BACHE COLLECTION, 1949. (49.7.23) REPRODUCED BY PERMISSION.

cone-shaped, silk-and-velvet steeple hat with draped veil (hennin), depicted in modern publications of medieval fairy tales, and the brocaded silk, stuffed bourrelet created into enormous horns, reproduced with proto-feminist writings by Christine de Pisan as *The Book of the City of Ladies* (1405). Other contemporary styles included the large, round, beehive-shaped hat popular in Germany and an English silk-gold braid with pearls covered by a wired gauze wimple. Scholars have noted the possible cross-cultural source for these excessive headpieces as coming from Turkish styles at a time when the Ottomans were expanding their control into eastern Europe not far from Vienna. In response to these feminine excesses, Catholic churchmen were known to encourage Christians to yell insults aimed at humiliating women wearing such outlandish headwear. In some places, sumptuary laws were issued limiting the size, number, and materials that could be devoted to women's hats in an effort to control excesses and maintain class social structure.

Court Fashions

From the sixteenth century on, hat styles were largely influenced by royal tastes, from the English Tudor gable hood to the Elizabethan wigs and a wide variety of velvet, taffeta, silk, felt, leather, and beaver hats, many based on men's styles.

The seventeenth century saw a white lace wired or starched "Mary Stuart" hood as popular for indoors, and the wide-brimmed, plumed felt or beaver hat for outdoor riding associated with Queen Henrietta Maria. The English Restoration Queen Catherine of Braganza, Portugal, still wore this "cavalier" style for riding in 1666.

In portraits, court ladies during the reign of Charles II were frequently depicted in pastoral costume as "shepherdesses" holding contrived sun-protector hats made of heavy fabric, like velvet. A century later, the pastoral look was still in vogue, but the hats had changed to more realistic, broad-brimmed straw versions called bergère, decorated with ribbons, artificial flowers, and large plumes, reaching their zenith with Marie Antoinette as painted by Vigée Lebrun. Although many of these hats were made locally from country-style materials, the finest smooth straw was imported from Leghorn, Italy, to northern markets and widely used by fashion milliners.

During the late seventeenth century, France became Europe's fashion center under the leadership of Louis XIV. One of the most visually striking headpieces of this era was named for the king's mistress. Supposedly Mlle. Fontanges was out riding when her hair became caught on a tree branch. When she tied it up with ribbon (possibly her lace garter), the *fontange* was born. It metamorphosed into a complex tiered and ruffled architectural-like structure of muslin, lace, and ribbons built up onto a round wire base. Masked balls and carnival festivals provided a venue for women in Venice, Rome, France, and England to wear fantasy headwear, including tricornes, flower basket hats, and exotic Eastern tur-

fashion, whereby individuals aspiring to privileges enjoyed by nobles acquired clothing and hats, not just for functional reasons, but capriciousness. Within a short time, this emphasis on individual materialism spread to many regions of northern Europe.

Some of the most elaborate hats women have ever worn appeared in the late-medieval and Renaissance courts of France, Flanders, and Bavaria, including the tall bans. After living in Turkey for two years as wife of Britain's ambassador, Lady Mary Wortley Montagu was influential in popularizing the turban as an aristocratic women's style in England.

Throughout the eighteenth century, milliners competed with wigmakers for setting headwear fashions. This may be why in Georgian England, enormous crowned hats with stiff lining and gigantic plumes became the mode, copied from French styles set by Marie Antoinette. Some were associated with unusual events, such as the balloon hat, named for Vincenzo Lunardi who in 1784 ascended in a hot-air balloon. Nevertheless, interest in fashionable hats continued to be stimulated by the early hand-colored fashion-plate publications such as *The Lady's Magazine* (London, c.1760–1837) and *Galerie des Modes* (Paris, 1778–1787).

Middle-Class Fashions

With the social upheavals of the French Revolution, aristocrats lost their political, social, and economic privileges; those who survived were careful to distance themselves from the wigs and extravagance of the ancien régime. New, simpler hats associated with prevailing middle-class values became popular, although exotic turbans continued, with possible influences from African head wraps.

Throughout the nineteenth century, reflecting ideals of Romanticism, the ubiquitous chin-tied bonnet, with its numerous variations prevailed, from the calash and its folding hoops like a covered wagon, to the poke bonnet that extended far outward. With elaborate silk, lace, floral, feather, and artificial fruit trimmings, bonnets by mid-century reflected the married woman's status as queen of her home and symbol of her husband's financial success. The man's top hat communicated the same message, and added social status. This fashion persisted through the remainder of the nineteenth century and into the twentieth.

Large emporiums such as Bloomingdale's in New York, Marshall Field's in Chicago, and Gorringes in London began to spring up in cities providing ready-made and custom-designed hats in their millinery departments to a growing middle-class clientele. Rural dwellers in the United States could learn of new fashions from magazines such as *Godey's Lady's Book* (1830–1898) and obtain ready-made hats and bonnets at reasonable prices through mail-order catalogs, beginning with Montgomery Ward in 1872 and Sears Roebuck after 1886.

Millinery Industry

Beginning in the sixteenth century, "millinery" referred to fine artifacts for women, such as ribbons, gloves, and straw hats sold by men around Milan, Italy. By 1679, milliners were dressmakers who also made or sold women's hats, bonnets, headdresses, and trims. Newspaper advertisements indicate that millinery shops abounded by the eighteenth century in European and American cities, although owners were usually only known locally.

Jacqueline Kennedy in pillbox hat. Jacqueline Kennedy made the pillbox hat famous during her brief tenure as First Lady, and its popularity swept across the country. © BETTMANN/CORBIS. REPRODUCED BY PERMISSION.

The first internationally recognized milliner was Rose Bertin (1744–1813), *marchande de modes*, whose luxurious salon, Le Grand Moghul, on rue Faubourg Saint-Honoré, Paris, became the focal place for attractive designs with ribbons, laces, and trimmings along with the latest social gossip. Her most important client was Queen Marie Antoinette until the royal execution in January 1793. Bertin's business records preserved at the University of Paris reveal clientele to include nobility from Russia and England.

The industrial revolution of the nineteenth century affected the millinery industry in many ways. A new sewing machine, introduced in America and sold abroad, meant large quantities of hats could be produced quickly at low prices. Manufactured hats could be stored and sent to wholesalers for sales in department stores or for overseas export. While trains and ships assisted mass-marketing distribution, overall Paris was still considered the center for elite, high-fashion hats. Wealthy women traveled to Paris for purchases, and store milliners from London and New York made annual pilgrimages to

Marie-Antoinette. This portrait of Marie-Antoinette by Elisabeth Vigée-Lebrun illustrates the pastoral "shepherdess" look of French court ladies during the eighteenth century. The look was typified by broad-brimmed straw hats decorated with ribbons, flowers, and large plumes. VIGEE-LEBRUN, ELISABETH. MARIE-ANTOINETTE, TIMKEN COLLECTION, IMAGE © 2004 BOARD OF TRUSTEES, NATIONAL GALLERY OF ART, WASHINGTON. REPRODUCED BY PERMISSION.

bring back the "latest" modes and trimmings for their home customers. Millinery ideas and advice were also made available to wide audiences from subscription magazines as *Harper's Bazaar* (1867–) in the United States, *Townsend's Monthly Magazine* (1823–1988) in England, and *Le Follet* (1829–1892) in France.

Folk Costume Hats

Another clothing-and-hat trend took place in Europe outside aristocratic fashion circles during the nineteenth century. With the relaxation of sumptuary laws regarding clothing, particularly after the French Revolution, European peasant artisans, encouraged by nationalism, began to express their ethnic affiliation through elaborate outfits worn for Sunday religious services, dancing, and festivals. These colorful costumes and hats, still worn by villagers and townspeople, serve as visual representations of community and marital status to be worn on special occasions. The women's hats are usually straw, felt, or other natural materials, and because of their multicolored festive styles, they have served as inspiration over decades for twentieth-century fashion milliners, who may re-create the styles with new, synthetic materials. Occasionally referred to as "ethnic-chic," examples include the bead-and-sequin velvet Basque beret, the Tyrolean felt sport hat, the "pakable" rayon knotted turban, Central Asian styled velvet-and-pearl pillbox, and the cellophane Breton.

Unisex Sports Headwear

Beginning in the 1860s, as the middle class was growing and enjoying increased leisure activities, men's tailoring techniques were first applied to women's dress. Slightly flared skirts replaced the older crinolines and were complemented by formal suit jackets. Likewise, the fanciful, highly decorated bonnet of earlier decades gave way to more simple, masculine-style headwear. These styles represented for the "New Woman" a sense of physical freedom through sports and political independence via the suffrage movement.

For outdoor sports, women wore the white linen peaked cap while rowing and yachting; and the plain flat-top, hard straw boater for cycling and later automobile driving. Boaters could be adapted for formal wear embellished with bird feathers or plumes.

Other hat styles shared by both genders included the stiff felt, round-crown bowler, or derby, and black silk top hat for horseback riding; the woolen tam-o'-shanter for lawn tennis, badminton, or cycling; the fore-and-aft as a hunting cap; and the fedora for archery or golf. In winter, knitted stocking caps served for bobsledding, ice sailing, and skating. Indoors, the Breton was considered appropriate for bowling or roller skating, known as "rinking." This trend of women's involvement with sports by wearing unisex hats or caps continues to the present. As spectators, they wear the contemporary baseball cap to league games, and as golfers, on the links.

Twentieth Century

World War I (1914–1918) brought about dramatic changes in women's clothes, hairstyles, and hats, creating a lucrative environment for entrepreneurial designers. Throughout the 1920s, short skirts, bobbed hair, and the cloche, or bell-shaped hat, were the mode on both sides of the Atlantic.

Paris, however, remained the fashion center with trend-setting designers as Elsa Schiaparelli, Cristóbal Balenciaga, and Agnès introducing synthetic materials and abstract shapes. New York and Hollywood also began attracting millinery talent from Europe. Hattie Carnegie from Austria first worked in New York at Macy's before opening her own shop and eventually creating a millinery empire with a thousand employees. French-born Lilly Daché trained with Suzanne Talbot and Caroline Reboux in Paris before arriving in 1925 at New York, where she, too, worked for Macy's before opening her own salon, which led to a multimillion-dollar, international business and fame for her turbans, floral designs, and the "half hat." John-Frederic's hats resulted from the partnership of John Piocelle (who studied in Paris at École des Beaux Arts) and the businessman Frederic Hirst (1929–1947). Their designs gained notoriety through Hollywood stars like Marlene Dietrich, Gloria Swanson, and Greta Garbo who wore the slouch hat.

Oleg Cassini, son of a Russian count, first worked in Paris before a long career designing for Hollywood studios. While individual designers maintained their own salons for one-of-a-kind headpieces, they also mass-produced less expensive styles for sales through urban department stores.

Sally Victor also got her millinery start at Macy's and by the 1930s branched out into her own business with her husband, Victor Serges. Her hats combined fashion styling with modest pricing aimed at a wide middle-class clientele, including Mamie Eisenhower. A number of twentieth-century couturiers either began as milliners (Coco Chanel) or designed hats, purses, and handbags as complementary accessories to their clothing line (Christian Dior). Throughout much of the twentieth century, hats and gloves were required for attending social events.

During the World War II Nazi occupation of Paris (1940–1944), when rationing curtailed the fashion industry and sales abroad, French women boosted their morale by defiantly wearing outlandish structures on their heads made out of scraps. With the armistice came rebuilding and the renewed claim that Paris would again become the fashion center of the world. By the 1950s, a cadre of influential wholesale and retail millinery clients from abroad attended Paris fashion shows, purchasing rights to copy the latest hat designs for home markets at inexpensive prices.

In New York, Bergdorf Goodman was known to have the best millinery department; its custom-made Halston hats were top of the line. Roy Halston Frowick created the now-famous deep pillbox hat that Jacqueline Kennedy wore to her husband's 1961 inauguration. The hat, designed to be worn back on the head, accommodated the First Lady's bouffant hairstyle. Within months, the pillbox became the rage across America, boosting the millinery industry, and was thereafter known as Jackie's signature hat.

Some historians see President John F. Kennedy's predilection for hatlessness as leading the trend toward eliminating men's toppers for formal attire. Others see the civil rights movement also effecting this change since hats over centuries had served as visible symbols of the class system. Whatever the cause, in the late 1960s, the custom for both men and women of wearing hats to social events began to disappear. "Informality" became the key to clothing modes. Hats were seen as irrelevant, particularly to the younger generation bent on social change and personal independence. Milliners were replaced by professional hairdressers who created self-expressing new hairstyles such as the Afro and cornrows for African Americans. Simultaneously, middle-class women were in-

troduced to the comfort of pantsuits that had no precedents or hat-wearing fashion requirements.

In contrast to the white community, urban African American women never stopped wearing hats. They continue the African tradition that survived slavery of adorning the head for worship celebrations. Combining glamour and holiness, their Sunday hats are colorful, flamboyant, enormous, and plentiful (some own up to 100), made of straws, felts, furs, starched fabrics, adorned with plumes, sequins, artificial flowers, and rhinestones extending the head upward and outward. Their designers, such as Shellie McDowell of New York, whose clientele includes Oprah Winfrey, understand the tastes of black women and their desire for recognition. This unique tradition of black women in church hats has been documented in the book *Crowns* (2000) and an off-Broadway production of the same title.

In England, after a two-decade hiatus, Princess Diana helped to re-popularize the wearing of attractive hats in the 1980s. Her London-based milliner John Boyd and others (Simone Mirman and Graham Smith) continued designing hats for royal family members, while also producing popular ready-to-wear lines; and the talented Stephen Jones struck out into another surrealistic, trend-setting direction related to the shocking punk styles of colored Mohican-spiked hair and the rock generation.

Festivals have also helped popularize hats. From the 1880s to 1940s, supported by the millinery manufacturers, Easter Sunday parades were held in American cities. These encouraged American women to annually buy or re-trim their Easter bonnets, dress-up their daughters, and walk down main streets. The Hollywood film *Easter Parade* (1948) had Fred Astaire and Judy Garland participate in a re-enactment of this New York Fifth Avenue event.

In England, the historic Ascot, weeklong series of horse races, held annually in June and featured in the musical *My Fair Lady*, still reaches its peak of excitement on Gold Cup Day, known since 1807 as Ladies Day, when the men wear traditional top hats, and the Queen, along with hundreds of women from all classes wear spectacular chapeaux. Large picture hats (also called "cartwheels") are the most common, but what gets attention and appears in press coverage are photos of the most novel hats, featuring intriguing images, such as a dartboard, cellular telephone, flying saucers, Astroturf, or a birdcage.

Paris celebrates Saint Catherine of Alexandria, patroness of maidens and milliners, on 25 November. Unmarried women, especially those working in the millinery trade, who are known as "Catherinettes," wear extravagant hats to parties held in their honor. In earlier times, their goal was to catch a husband with the saint's assistance.

A notable effort at reigniting interest in millinery was the 1983 opening of the Hat Making Museum in Chazelles-sur-Lyon, France, center of the former hair felt hat industry. Its permanent exhibition presents a chronological display of hats from 1850 on, and temporary shows include the results from its biennial International Contest of Hat Designers, which in 2003 drew 176 hats from 16 countries, including Canada, the United States, Australia, and Japan.

See also **Beret; Hairstyles; Hats, Men's; Headdress; Turban; Veils.**

BIBLIOGRAPHY

Bates, Christina. "Women's Hats and the Millinery Trade, 1840–1940: An Annotated Bibliography." *Dress* 27 (2000): 49–58.

Clark, Fiona. *Hats.* The Costume Accessories Series. London: B. T. Batsford Ltd., 1982.

Daché, Lilly. *Talking Through My Hats.* New York: Coward-McCann, 1946.

deCourtais, Georgine. *Women's Headdress and Hairstyles in England from A.D. 600 to the Present Day.* London: B. T. Batsford, Ltd., 1973.

Ginsburg, Madeleine. *The Hat: Trends and Traditions.* Hauppauge, N.Y.: Barrons's Educational Series, 1990.

Langley, Susan. *Vintage Hats and Bonnets, 1770–1970.* Paducah, Ky.: Collector Books, 1998.

McDowell, Colin. *Hats: Status, Style and Glamour.* New York: Rizzoli International, 1992.

Reilly, Maureen, and Mary Beth Detrich. *Women's Hats of the Twentieth Century.* Atglen, Pa.: Schiffer Publishing, Ltd., 1997.

Stein, Gail. "Mr. John, 'Emperor of Fashion,'" *Dress* 27 (2000): 37–48.

White, Palmer. *Elsa Schiaparelli: Empress of Paris Fashion.* London: Aurum Press Ltd., 1986.

Wilcox, R. Turner. *The Mode in Hats and Headdress, Including Hair Styles, Cosmetics and Jewelry.* New York: Charles Scribner's Sons, 1959.

Beverly Chico

HAUTE COUTURE Historically, aristocratic and upper-class women's fashionable Western dress was created by an intimate negotiation between the client and her dressmaker. The investment in the design was principally in the cost of the luxurious textile itself, not in its fabrication. The origins of the haute couture system were laid by the late seventeenth century as France became the European center for richly produced and innovative luxury silk textiles. Thus the preeminent position of France's luxury textile industry served as basis and direct link to the development of its haute couture system. The prestigious social and economic value of an identifiable couturier, or designer's name, is a development of the late nineteenth and early twentieth centuries.

Beginning in the mid-nineteenth century, the Paris-based haute couture created a unique fashion system that validated the couturier, a fashion designer, as an artist and established his or her "name" as an international authority for the design of luxurious, original clothing.

Couturiers were no longer merely skilled artisans, but creative artists with identifiable names printed or woven into a petersham waist tape that was sewn discreetly into the dress or bodice. This was the beginning of designer labels in fashion. The client was required to visit the couture house where a garment was made to measure to high-quality dressmaking and tailoring standards.

The couture house workrooms are carefully distributed according to sewing techniques. The sewing staff are divided between two areas: dressmaking (*flou*), for dresses and draped garments based upon feminine dressmaking techniques, or tailoring (*tailleur*), for suits and coats utilizing male tailoring techniques of construction. The staff work according to a hierarchy of skills ranging from the *première*, head dressmaker or tailor, to apprentices. The selling areas, salons, are equally controlled and run by the *vendeuse*, saleswoman, who sells the designs to clients and negotiates the fabrication and fittings with the workrooms.

The British-trained tailor and dressmaker Charles Frederick Worth is commonly credited as being the "father" of haute couture. What was radical in the mid-nineteenth century was that a male was creating women's fashion, a situation that required intimacy between a dressmaker and client, and had previously been a female-dominated profession. Worth's designs also commanded high prices that were a substantial investment in the garment itself and his associated and recognizable design style. This significant shift established the profession of fashion designer of women's garments as a suitable and profitable one for men. Worth worked directly with the French silk weaving industry to access and promote the original, luxury textiles that were a signature of his production. His clientele included the nobility of European courts as well as the new haute bourgeoises who followed his advice on appropriate dress for day to evening wear. Worth and his contemporaries, particularly Doucet, introduced innovations that have become standards for haute couture establishments. They created luxurious Paris salons to which wealthy clients came rather than the couturier visiting his patrons at their homes; they created artistic designs from which clients could select and that were made to measure; they also employed live mannequins who modeled the designs for private individuals. Thus the haute couture system of luxury dressmaking production was created.

In 1868, Worth instigated a new group called *La Chambre Syndicale de la confection et de la couture pour dames et fillettes.* This body, an outgrowth of the medieval guild system, was formed as a collective or type of union that could lobby and deal with issues related to labor, taxes, administration, and production for dressmakers. At this time there was little distinction between *couture*, clothing made to measure, and *confection*, ready-made clothing. In 1910, the two activities were clearly divided and the nomenclature *la haute couture* was strictly reserved for couture salons that produced collections for private clients, not solely for professional buyers. The newly named *Chambre Syndicale de la haute couture parisienne* outlined specific rules for membership that evaluated the creativity of designs and the quality of fabrication that had to be made to measure for the client, and also instituted regulations concerning the sale of designs and reproductions. The issue of copying and design piracy was of constant concern to the haute couture industry that relied upon exclusivity to retain design supremacy and its resultant high prices. The creation of PAIS (*L'Association de protection des industries artistiques saisonnières*) in 1921 by Madeleine Vionnet aimed to protect individual haute couture designs. Designs were photographed on a mannequin, front, back and side, and these documentary design records were registered with PAIS, thereby intending to discourage piracy and could be used as evidence if required. Allegations of design piracy were dealt with under the French penal code. This service was later taken over by the *Chambre Syndicale* in 1943. By 1930, the *Chambre Syndicale* established a formal calendar of fashion shows that were coordinated, consecutive, not concurrent, and able to accommodate the increasing numbers of foreign buyers and journalists to the collections.

In 1929, the *Chambre Syndicale de la haute couture parisienne* established vocational sewing and design training in its associated schools under the Ministry of National Education. The school offered an apprenticeship of three years that began with practical sewing skills in the first year, garment construction techniques in the second, and women's tailoring and draping in the third year. Two more years were available to a select few thought capable of working as first hands within a couture salon and who could train heads of workrooms and potentially be creative designers. These schools and courses continue to operate in the early 2000s.

In 1939, there were seventy haute couture salons. However, World War II (1939–1945) and particularly the German Occupation of Paris, created a crisis in the industry. The Nazis wanted to move the Paris haute couture industry to Berlin or Vienna, but the president of the *Chambre Syndicale*, the couturier Lucien Lelong, successfully negotiated to keep it in operating in Paris. After the Liberation of Paris the haute couture industry needed to recapture the North American buyers and manufacturers in order to reinstate France's historical position as the center of fashion design and also in order to rebuild a fragile economy and industry. Even before the war, the principal client was no longer the private client, but the commercial buyer and the attendant fashion press, and this situation was heightened after the war. This was clearly reflected in the schedule of showings of the collections set by the *Chambre Syndicale* that showed to the North American commercial buyers, then the European buyers, and finally to private clients. Postwar recognition of the importance of the Paris haute couture for fashion design leadership was internationally recognized after 1947 with the acclaim of the new house of Christian Dior

THE USE OF TOILE

A couturier's design was usually first created in inexpensive muslin, called a *toile,* so as to perfect the design, cut, and fit. These *toiles* record the exact cut and sewing techniques, and include samples of the interlinings, linings, and fabric required in the final garment. Paper patterns were also used to replicate designs.

(founded in 1945) by Carmel Snow in the American fashion magazine *Harper's Bazaar.*

In 1945, the *Chambre Syndicale* introduced more rigorous regulations intended to further control the quality and prestige of the haute couture industry in the difficult immediate postwar years. Haute couture was divided into two classes: *Couture,* and the more prestigious *Couture-Création.* An haute couture house had to apply for membership that was reviewed annually. The application made by a couturier for the classification *Couture-Création* covered several areas: at least twenty-five designs had to be created in-house, spring and fall, and made up on a live mannequin. The collection was then to be presented on live mannequins, and in an "appropriate" setting in the haute couture house located in Paris. The rules also covered the technical execution of the original models, the repetitions to be made in-house to clients' measurements, the number of fittings required and at what stage in the making, and the sales of the designs.

The 1950s were years of huge profits and press and the continuation and emergence of new haute couture salons. The most important, and largest, houses in terms of production were those of Christian Dior, Pierre Balmain, and Jacques Fath. The postwar years continued and consolidated the prewar situation that was shifting the economic basis of the houses from private sales to the commercial buyers. The large market for haute couture was as a design source. Couture was copied and adapted to limited editions, or line for line copies, a process that began in the 1930s, as well as for mass-market fashions. Haute couture houses sold the original models as well as *toiles* (muslins) and paper patterns, all of which was regulated by the *Chambre Syndicale.*

This situation stimulated many new initiatives from the Paris couture to control their designs and for the design houses to directly profit from them. Christian Dior began his own licensing arrangements with Christian Dior, New York, and Jacques Fath entered into the American ready-to-wear market with Joseph Halpert. Increasingly couturiers opened boutiques within their cou-

Haute couture evening dress, circa 1894. Dresses designed by the House of Worth, one of the first couture houses, were known for their luxurious textiles and were worn by wealthy society ladies. This Worth dress was worn by the wife of renown architect Stanford White. © MUSEUM OF THE CITY OF NEW YORK. REPRODUCED BY PERMISSION.

ture salons in order to sell less expensive versions of their haute couture lines as well as accessories, a development begun by Paul Poiret in the early twentieth century. The society *Les Couturiers associés*, founded in 1950 by Jacques Fath, Robert Piguet, Jean-Marc Paquin, Marie-Louise Carven, and Jean Dessès, was a precursor to the creation of prêt-à-porter designed by couturiers who sold ready-made designs to French department stores. A similar initiative, *Le Prêt-à-porter Création* (1958–1962) was directly aimed at international buyers and press. It ceased as ready-to-wear collections by couture houses became firmly established. However, the successful governance of the *Chambre Syndicale* over the couture houses, and its huge success during the 1950s is reflected in prosperity of the haute couture that in 1959 exported garments worth 20 million francs, and 3,000 workers were employed on a full-time basis, totaling 100,000 hours per week for most of the year.

The Paris haute couture system was such a successful formula for attracting sales, prestigious clients, commercial buyers, and international press that all other couture organizations were based upon this French

model. In 1942, the Incorporated Society of London Fashion Designers was formed in England; in Spain during World War II the Cooperativa de Alta Costura was formed in Barcelona; the first Italian couture collective was shown in Florence in 1951; and the Association of Canadian Couturiers was founded in 1954. However, no other nation managed to create a haute couture industry that was as prestigious or economically important as Paris. The French system was historically based on its luxury textile industry and its ancillary industries of beading, embroidery, ribbons, and lace as well as its highly skilled artisans

The craft base of haute couture was financially difficult to maintain in an increasingly industrialized society. The numbers of couture house fell from 106 in 1946 to 19 by 1970. The establishment of quotas and high custom duties resulted in radical declines of haute couture exports and served to intensify the commercialization of rights for reproduction and licensing agreements. In 1953–1954, Pierre Cardin presented his first prêt-à-porter collection and made it a separate department within the house in 1963. In 1966, Yves Saint Laurent created Saint Laurent Rive Gauche, the first freestanding couture boutique. Sociocultural shifts and an emphasis on youthful fashion instead of designs for mature women caused the breakdown of uniformity in the women's wear market, and resulted in the haute couture's departure as the only or leading source for international fashion design. The more profitable ready-to-wear market necessitated new initiatives for the haute couture houses, which began to create new, less expensive non-couture lines marketed with labels associated with the prestige of the haute couture house.

The 1970s and 1980s were years of crisis and reconstruction for the haute couture, as the United States was no longer the primary market that it had been since the 1930s. In 1973 the *Chambre Syndicale de la couture parisienne* joined with the Prêt-à-porter federation, and became *La Fédération français de la couture, du prêt-à-porter des couturiers et des créateurs de mode*, and in 1975 joined with the *Fedération de l'union nationale des artisanale de la couture et des activités connexes*. In the early 2000s the organization has approximately 500 members and promotes French fashion at home and abroad. The consortium of French luxury products led by the group LVMH (Louis Vuitton Moët Hennessy) created by Bernard Arnault, bought out the leading names of the haute couture. In the early 1980s, Christian Lacroix renewed the 1930s house of Jean Patou, where he was artistic director from 1981 to 1987, and Parisienne haute couture was front-page fashion news as it had been in the 1950s and early 1960s. Karl Lagerfeld designed for Chloé and resuscitated the house of Chanel by cleverly employing all the Chanel hallmarks of design (logo, chains, cardigan suit jacket, loose tweeds, and so forth) and updating them for a younger market. The designer signature and logo became ubiquitous and familiar on an enormous range of products from fashion to home furnishings. Once again haute couture was worn and promoted by international celebrities and equally famous and highly paid super models. In 1987, Arnault invested millions in the new haute couture house of Christian Lacroix, which had a similar impact on the revitalization and public interest in the haute couture industry that Marcel Boussac's investment in the opening of the house of Christian Dior had immediately after World War II in 1946. During the 1990s, LVMH purchased Dior, Lacroix, Givenchy, Celine, Kenzo in a restructuring aimed at reclaiming French fashion design leadership, which had been overtaken by Italian and Japanese high-end ready-to-wear fashions. Celebrity designers were selected to design the Paris haute collections. Claude Montana worked for the house of Jeanne Lanvin from 1990 to 1992, and young, radical, Brits John Galliano and Alexander McQueen designed for Givenchy. In 1996, Galliano was placed as the chief haute couture designer for the most prestigious house of Christian Dior as a replacement for Gianfranco Ferre. Few couture houses have kept their independence in an increasingly global and conglomerate economy. The houses of Pierre Cardin, André Courrèges, Patou, and Phillipe Venet all ceased haute couture production, leaving only eighteen haute couture establishments by 1996. The 2002 retirement of Yves Saint Laurent closed one more establishment, but the new couture collection of Jean Paul Gaultier resulted from success as a ready-to-wear designer, a twenty-first-century inversion of the couture tradition.

In the early 2000s the business of haute couture is viewed as a costly and luxurious design laboratory that attests to and sustains France's international cultural position as a taste leader. Though haute couture posts enormous financial losses and produces less than 10 percent of the French clothing industry, the salons garner fantastic international press and prestige for the house name, which fuels lucrative licensing agreements for ready-to-wear collections, perfumes, accessories, and domestic products.

See also **Balmain, Pierre; Cardin, Pierre; Courrèges, André; Dior, Christian; Doucet, Jacques; Lagerfeld, Karl; McQueen, Alexander; Patou, Jean; Worth, Charles Frederick.**

BIBLIOGRAPHY

Antoine-Dariaux, Geneviève. *Elegance: A Complete Guide for Every Woman Who Wants to Be Well and Properly Dressed on All Occasions.* Garden City, N.Y.: Doubleday, 1964.

Dior, Christian. *Dior by Dior.* Translated by Antonia Fraser. London: Weidenfeld and Nicolson, 1957.

Fraser-Cavassoni, Natasha, and Jennifer Jackson Alfano. "Couture's Big Spenders." *Harper's Bazaar*, October 2002, pp. 88ff.

Grumbach, Didier. *Histoires de la Mode.* Paris: Seuil, 1993.

Lynam, Ruth, ed. *Couture: An Illustrated History of the Great Paris Designers and Their Creations.* New York: Doubleday, 1972.

Palmer, Alexandra. *Couture and Commerce: The Transatlantic Fashion Trade in the 1950s.* Vancouver: University of British Columbia Press, 2001.

Picken, Mary Brooks. *Dressmakers of France: The Who, Why and How of French Couture.* New York: Harper and Brothers, 1956.

Steele, Valerie. *Paris Fashion: A Cultural History.* New York and Oxford: Oxford University Press, 1988.

Troy, Nancy J. *Couture Culture: A Study in Modern Art and Fashion.* Cambridge, Mass.: MIT Press, 2003.

Veillon, Dominique. *La mode sous L'Occupation: Débrouillardise et coquetteries dans la France en guerre (1939–1945).* Paris: Payot, 1990.

Alexandra Palmer

HAWAIIAN SHIRT Hawaii's aloha shirt has become a visible manifestation of the state's multicultural population, and in Hawaii, wearing these shirts represents both an attitude and Hawaiian identity. The style lines and design motifs of the aloha shirt developed from the interaction of several of Hawaii's immigrant groups. The aloha shirt took its shape from the shirts worn by the first Caucasian men to appear in the islands—British and American sailors. In addition, the looseness of the shirts worn by Filipino men, the *barong tagalong*, was incorporated as a key element of the aloha shirt as an adaptation to Hawaii's tropical environment. The early aloha shirts (1920s–1930s) were made of Japanese kimono fabric by Chinese tailors, and the early customers were *haole* (Caucasian) residents and tourists, or *hapa haole* (part Caucasian) residents of Hawaii. It was not until World War II that the local population embraced the wearing of aloha shirts.

The early aloha shirts were made of silks and kabe crepe, with Asian design motifs. Ellery Chun trademarked the aloha shirt in 1935, and from that time on designs took on a tropical Hawaiian theme for quite some time. Rayon of good quality was not available until the early 1940s. When it was adopted for use, vibrant colors and designs were the result and these shirts were called "silkies" due to the feel of the fabric. Silkies are the most highly collectible of the aloha shirts, and were produced until the mid 1950s when they went out of style. The 1950s featured abstract designs and cotton fabrics, and in the 1960s the reverse-print aloha shirt was created to look like faded shirts worn by surfers. While tourists ignored these shirts, locals immediately adopted them as a badge of Hawaiianness. Synthetic fabrics with ethnic designs became popular in the 1970s aloha shirts. Tropical designs of flora and fauna have consistently been featured, and the 1990s favored retro styles in rayon and silk. Manufacturers have brought back some of the original designs of the famous "silkies" of the 1940s and 1950s.

The aloha shirt has had an impact on American business attire. The production of reverse-print shirts worn for work by most men in Hawaii have kept pace with more vibrant shirts that are worn for more casual occasions.

Hawaii's aloha shirt began America's movement toward business casual attire in 1962 when Hawaii's government required men to wear it throughout the summer, and then later on, Aloha Friday was declared, and workers were (and still are in the early 2000s) expected to dress in aloha attire every Friday. One could say that Aloha Fridays led to Casual Fridays on the U.S. mainland. Throughout the mid-twentieth century, tourists and soldiers brought the aloha shirt to the U.S. mainland but more importantly, the aloha shirt migrated to California on the backs of surfers who brought the relaxed shirt and lifestyle to the mainland. This was the beginning of the business casual movement, as many of the young California surfers grew up to become Silicon Valley executives who shed three-piece suits for more relaxed attire at work and instituted Casual Fridays into the world of business.

See also **Colonialism and Imperialism; Cotton; Rayon.**

BIBLIOGRAPHY

Arthur, Linda. *Aloha Attire: Hawaiian Dress in the Twentieth Century.* Atglen, Pa.: Schiffer Publications, 2000.

Brown, David, and Linda Arthur. *The Art of the Aloha Shirt.* Honolulu, Hawaii: Island Heritage, 2002.

Hope, Dale, and Gregory Tozian. *The Aloha Shirt.* Hillsboro, Ore.: Beyond Words Publishing, 2000.

Linda B. Arthur

HAWES, ELIZABETH Elizabeth Hawes (1901–1971) belonged to the first generation of American designers who succeeded in making a name for themselves as individuals outside the sphere of the Parisian couture. In 1925 Hawes graduated from Vassar College, where she was an economics major sympathetic to socialism, but she pursued an interest in fashion by participating in school theatricals and making her own clothes. By graduation she had decided to go to Paris and learn fashion design. Hawes spent the next three years in various positions within the couture business: as a design copyist, journalist, and assistant designer. During this time she wrote a fashion column for *The New Yorker*, using the pen name "Parisite." She also worked briefly for Nicole Groult, the sister of the designer Paul Poiret. Her life in Paris was divided between socializing with her wealthy Vassar friends and engaging in the bohemian life; she spent much of her time with an artistic crowd, including the sculptors Alexander Calder and Isamo Noguchi.

Hawes's Vassar education gave her the critical faculty to dissect the couture industry and the fashion press, while her social connections and her exposure to couture at the highest levels left her ambivalent about fashion, a feeling that grew all the stronger for her love of its creative potential. In 1928 Hawes returned to New York and started her own custom dressmaking business with a Vassar classmate, Rosemary Harden. Harden left the business one year later, and Hawes decided to continue on her own as Hawes, Inc. Advertising, for which Hawes herself wrote the copy, helped business pick up significantly. Calder and Noguchi designed decorative objects for her New York showroom and influenced Hawes's own work. In 1930 Hawes married the artist Ralph Jester, whom she had known in Paris; they divorced in 1934.

Fashion and Politics

In 1932 Hawes and two other young American designers were promoted by the Lord and Taylor department store. This was one of the earliest attempts (if not the first) to prove that there was homegrown talent worthy of the public's notice. Hawes fully understood the power of publicity and exploited it. The ensembles in her collections were named according to themes: Spring/Summer 1933 was political, and the collection included such ensembles as "The Five Year Plan," a cotton nightgown and bed jacket; "the Yellow Peril," a silk afternoon dress; and "Disarmament," an embroidered evening dress. Her work was characterized by a bold use of fabrics—wide strips and large prints were used in simple, comfortable silhouettes. Hawes was an early advocate of trousers for women and wore them often herself.

In 1935 Hawes traveled to the Soviet Union to explore her growing interest in mass-produced clothing; as part of this trip, she showed some of her designs to members of the Soviet State Clothing Production Board, known as the Soviet Dress Trust. During her trip to the Soviet Union, she was accompanied by the theatrical director Joseph Losey, whom she married in 1937. The next year brought the birth of their son, Gavrick, and the publication of her first major work as an author: *Fashion Is Spinach*. This was Hawes's manifesto, and in it she expounds on the difference between "style" and "fashion" and how women are manipulated by the fashion industry:

> Style . . . gives you the fundamental feeling of a certain period in history. Style doesn't change every month or every year. . . . Fashion is that horrid little man with an evil eye who tells you that last winter's coat may be in perfect physical condition, but you can't wear it. (pp. 5–6)

Hawes's criticism was not limited to women's clothing; she maintained that men needed to be freed from their conservative attitudes toward clothing. She staged an all-male fashion show in 1937, showing brightly colored clothes of her own design. This led to her next book, *Men Can Take It*, published in 1939. She could be considered the Dorothy Parker of fashion criticism, with her snappy tone and tell-it-straight attitude.

Career Change

Hawes, Inc., closed early in January 1940. The onset of World War II had firmly awakened Hawes's social conscience, and she felt that being a fashion designer was not an appropriate career for her at that time. She became committed to her career as a writer, becoming involved in writing for the new left-wing paper, *PM*. In 1943 she took a job in a munitions factory for three months and then relocated to Detroit to work for the United Auto Worker's Union, where she also wrote for the *Detroit Free Press*. The result of her war work was her fifth book, *Why Women Cry; or, Wenches with Wrenches* (1943).

In 1948 Hawes made a last attempt at the fashion business and reopened Hawes, Inc., for eleven months. To demonstrate the timelessness of her designs, she played a game at the inaugural show, making guests guess which designs were new and which were from 1930s collections. Hawes settled in Southern California in the early 1950s. While she experimented with the production of knitwear, creating simple shapes decorated with abstract patterns, she spent the majority of her time writing. Her most rewarding experience during this period was her association with the young designer Rudi Gernreich, in whom she found a kindred spirit. In 1967 a retrospective of their work was mounted at the Fashion Institute of Technology.

Hawes moved back to New York in 1967 and lived in the Chelsea Hotel until her death on 6 September 1971. In total, she published nine books on fashion and culture as well as numerous articles in journals ranging from the left-leaning *PM* to the *Ladies' Home Journal*. In reality, her clothes did not appear radical for their time; it was her outspoken philosophy that set her apart.

See also **Fashion Designer; Fashion Journalism; Paris Fashion; Politics and Fashion.**

BIBLIOGRAPHY

Berch, Bettina. *Radical by Design: The Life and Style of Elizabeth Hawes*. New York: E. P. Dutton, 1988.

Hawes, Elizabeth. "The American Designer Has Not Yet Been Born." *Magazine of Art* April 1937.

———. *Fashion Is Spinach*. New York: Random House, 1938.

Mahoney, Patrick. "In and Out of Style." *Vassar Quarterly* 82, no. 2 (Spring 1986): 8–10.

Steele, Valerie. *Women of Fashion: Twentieth-Century Designers*. New York: Rizzoli International, 1991.

Melinda Watt

HEAD, EDITH Edith Head (1897–1981) was born in San Bernardino, California. In 1923, after a brief career as a schoolteacher, Head answered an advertisement for a sketch artist at Famous Players–Lasky (soon to be renamed Paramount Studios). Although she had very little artistic training, her versatility impressed Howard Greer, the chief costume designer, who hired her immediately. When Greer left Paramount in 1927, he was replaced by his assistant designer, Travis Banton. As chief designer, Banton costumed the stars at Paramount, while Head, who had been promoted to assistant designer, costumed the B-movie players and extras. When Banton left the studio in 1938, Paramount named Edith Head chief de-

Edith Head tailors a dress for Sophia Loren. Head was well known for her ability to work with difficult personalities and to camouflage figure problems. © BETTMANN/CORBIS. REPRODUCED BY PERMISSION.

signer; she remained at the studio in this capacity until 1967. That same year she received a contract with Universal Studios, where she worked until her death in 1981. From the 1950s on, Head became a media personality through her regular appearances on the television show *Art Linkletter's House Party*. She also published two books: *The Dress Doctor* (1959) and *How to Dress for Success* (1967).

During her fifty-eight-year career, Head received more than one thousand screen credits, garnered thirty-five Oscar nominations, and won the Academy Award for costume design an unprecedented eight times. She was legendary for her ability to please difficult personalities and to camouflage figure problems. She was considered particularly skilled at defining character through costume, and her "character" costumes were among her most successful, including those for *Double Indemnity* (1944), *The Heiress* (1949), and *Sunset Boulevard* (1950). Head was especially proud of her work on *The Heiress*, for which she had traveled to the Brooklyn Museum of Art to conduct period research, winning her the first of her many Academy Awards. Her collaborations with the director Alfred Hitchcock were renowned, since Head shrewdly understood the importance of costume to Hitchcock's creative vision in his films *Rear Window* (1954), *To Catch a Thief* (1955), and *Vertigo* (1958).

Head's designs were also occasionally responsible for influencing popular fashions. Her costumes for the Mae West film *She Done Him Wrong* (1933) reputedly set off a flurry of Gay Nineties–inspired fashions, while the sarong worn by Dorothy Lamour in the film *The Jungle Princess* (1936) continued to influence styles well into the next decade. Her costumes for Barbara Stanwyck in *The Lady Eve* (1941), which featured bare midriffs and fringed bolero jackets, are said to have popularized Latin American styles. Her most influential design by far was the lilac-strewn gown worn by Elizabeth Taylor in *A Place in the Sun* (1951). The dress was a sensation in the teen market, and thousands of copies were sold.

Throughout her career, Head was criticized for taking credit for costumes she did not design and for exaggerating her influence on popular fashion. Despite these flaws, Head was undeniably one of the hardest-working talents in costume design and certainly one of the most versatile. Her intelligence and dedication secured her position both in the Hollywood studio system and in the history of fashion.

See also **Costume Designer; Film and Fashion.**

BIBLIOGRAPHY

Chierichetti, David. *Edith Head: The Life and Times of Hollywood's Celebrated Costume Designer.* New York: HarperCollins Publishers, Inc., 2003.

Epstein, Beryl Williams. "Edith Head." In *Fashion Is Our Business.* Philadelphia: J. B. Lippincott, 1945.

Head, Edith, and Jane Kesner Ardmore. *The Dress Doctor.* Boston: Little, Brown and Company, 1959.

Head, Edith, with Joe Hyams. *How to Dress for Success.* New York: Random House, 1967.

LaVine, W. Robert. *In a Glamorous Fashion: The Fabulous Years of Hollywood Costume Design.* New York: Charles Scribner's Sons, 1980.

Clare Sauro

HEADDRESS Headdress is an elaborate, ornamental, or practical covering for the head, as differentiated from the hat, which has a crown, and includes many varieties such as the hairnet, headband, head wrap, wreath or chaplet, mantilla, turban, crown, and others. Headdresses incorporate complex meanings including religious symbolism, political power and affiliation, social status or rank, and fashion consciousness. Made of numerous materials, designs, shapes, and embellishments, headdresses can also serve practical purposes—protecting the head against natural elements, carrying objects like weapons, baskets, or water pots—and are often associated with ceremonies, particularly rites of passage.

Hairnets

Hairnets may be the oldest headdresses worn by humans. A mammoth-ivory figurine dated circa 36,000 B.C.E. and found at Brassempouy (Las Landes), France, shows a human face with hair possibly braided and covered with what appears to be a netting. Bronze Age second millennium B.C.E. hairnets of horsehair using the sprang or twisted-thread technique were found in Borum Eshøj, Denmark, and are preserved in the National Museum, Copenhagen. Complementing long, unfitted robes, a fashionable silk hairnet, known as a crespine, was worn with head and chin bands by upper-class women during the late thirteenth century C.E. in medieval Europe. By the 1500s, as Renaissance styles spread from Italy to northern Europe, ornate gold cord mesh, pearl-studded nets called cauls became fashionable. A modern version of the Renaissance-style silk-knobbed hairnet, Goyesca, which cascades down to a tassel is still worn at Spanish festivals. It commemorates Francisco Goya (1746–1828) who painted celebrating peasants of both sexes wearing tasseled hairnets. By the 1920s, new cropped and wavy hairstyles on European and American women led to the mass production and marketing of fine human hairnets, particularly for outdoor wear. Within a few years, international designers such as Elsa Schiaparelli (1930s) and Sally Victor (1940s) popularized the "snood" style hairnet, often made of chenille, cord, or ribbon and attached to a hat.

Headband Bandeau

Modern headbands, originally made of knitted wool, cotton, and later of natural and synthetic fiber mixtures, have many functions besides holding the hair in place. Athletes such as marathon runners, skiers, basketball, and tennis players wear them across the forehead to absorb perspiration. Political advocates use them like earlier hatbands to make public statements. In 1893, native Hawaiians in Western clothing appeared on Honolulu streets wearing hatbands with the words Aloha Aina ("Love of Country") indicating their loyalty to Queen Liliuokalani and opposing U.S. annexation. World War II Japanese kamikaze pilots wore white samurai headbands (hachimake), with a red rising-sun emblem and the words "Absolute Victory" in black Japanese calligraphy, while participating in rituals before flying off on suicide missions against U.S. targets; and in 2003, exiled protesters demonstrating against their country's ruling military dictatorship wore red headbands with white stars, symbolizing the Burmese peoples, outside Burma's Embassy in Bangkok, Thailand.

Aesthetically, headbands are part of many ethnic costumes. On the Indonesian islands of Bali and Sulawesi, men wear cotton batikked headbands (formed from a folded square of cloth) for everyday, ornamented brocades for festivals. Reflecting social rank, lace-edged cotton headbands were part of a maid's uniform in Europe and America, representing nineteenth- and twentieth-century middle-class gentrification, a carryover from earlier aristocratic livery customs.

Metal headbands worn across the top of the head hold earmuffs in place. Over centuries, in cold climates, earflaps on fur hats could be tied over the head or let down as desired. By the early twentieth century, with outdoor recreational sports gaining popularity, mass-produced metal-headband fur earmuffs came to be marketed for adults and children. The industrial revolution had another impact on ear protection, namely, against noise. By the 1920s, pilots flew open-cockpit planes wearing cloth "helmet" caps designed with inner pockets over the ears to hold noise-absorbent material. More recently, responding to concerns for worker safety, industrial earmuffs were introduced for preventing hearing loss caused by loud machinery noises. In the early 2000s, there are noise-reduction, liquid-foam filled cushioned earmuffs, cap-mounted earmuffs, a Velcro-adjustable type, and three-position version (over-the-head, behind-the-head, and under-the-chin). Most contemporary flight or firefighting helmets are additionally equipped with wired earmuffs allowing communication between the wearer and coworkers. Cyclers, hunters, and other sports enthusiasts can enjoy musical CDs, tapes, and radio broadcasts through ear covers, computer designed for lightweight comfort, portability, and noise attenuation.

Kerchief and Head Wrap

The kerchief, a cloth covering the head, from the French *couvrir* (to cover) and chief (head), is usually worn by women. Traditionally, European peasants wore a small cloth tied under the chin while working outside; thus, the kerchief became associated with rural women and later with lower-class city residents. As late as the 1950s, a domestic servant girl in Madrid, Spain, was considered breaking social barriers by wearing a hat rather than the kerchief assigned her class. Also called a bandanna, the kerchief did become a practical middle-class head cover used for riding in open automobiles.

The head wrap, a kerchief worn by tying over the forehead, is believed to have traveled with women from Senegal and Gambia (West Africa) along the slave trade routes to Caribbean Islands and ports in North and South America. The falla, a strip of cotton cloth tied around the head in eighteenth-century Gambia, may be the precursor to the head wrap later identified with adult female slaves. Imported into New Orleans possibly by way of the French colonies Martinique and St. Dominique, the head wrap when worn by free women of color, became a nineteenth-century fashion called Tignon, created from brightly-colored madras, occasionally adorned with jewels and feathers.

Spanish Mantilla

Usually black or white, the mantilla may derive from *manton* (mantle or cape) worn both indoors and outdoors during the Muslim rule of Spain. Mantillas (small capes) were originally head coverings of handmade silk lace, often imported from Chantilly, France, and worn by aristocratic women, as documented in portraits by Velasquez (c. 1625) and Goya (1792). By the nineteenth century, a

Yemenite bride in wedding finery. Headdresses are part of the costume for special occasions in many cultures, such as this elaborately crafted bridal hood. © RICHARD T. NOWITZ/CORBIS. REPRODUCED BY PERMISSION.

popular hairstyle, the chignon, provided suitable positioning for high, decorative combs (tortoiseshell, silver, ivory) to support larger mantillas—some measuring 7 x 3 feet—which drape over the shoulders. This style is commonly worn for special events such as Holy Week processions and community fiestas. Red-silk knobbed mantillas are occasionally worn by unmarried young women to bullfights. Romantic myths transported to Spanish colonies in Latin America (Mexico) and the Philippines depict señoritas in white mantillas on balconies listening to guitar-playing suitors. Because of their cost, mantillas are often passed down from mother to daughter as family heirlooms. The lace mantilla, without a comb, was a French fashion during the 1920s and 1930s.

Royal Headdresses

Since antiquity, rulers have worn impressive and costly headdresses, visible symbols of their power and claims to divinity. Prehistoric peoples stressed survival; their practical head coverings were made of animal skins in northern

Masai woman with traditional headdress and jewelry. Head-dresses have many styles, including the headband, hairnet, headwrap, mantilla, and turban. They can serve various practical purposes, but also connote religious symbolism, political power, and social status. © YANN ARTHUS-BERTRAND/CORBIS. REPRODUCED BY PERMISSION.

regions, twisted straws in warm climes. With the evolution of complex population centers, textile production and class stratification emerged in Mesopotamia, which resulted in Sumerian turbans and head wraps (3000 B.C.E.), and later splendid regal twisted hair and headbands during the Akkadian era (2250 B.C.E.). Egyptian royal ceremonial headdresses of the New Kingdom (c. 1580–1085 B.C.E.) were extremely precious, some made of gold decorated with inlaid carnelian, colored glass, and ostrich feathers.

The Ancient Greek korone (crown), a golden circlet or gold wreath, symbolized political and military power during the fourth century B.C.E. Macedonian era, while Olympic champions were crowned with nature cult headpieces: laurel, olive, pine, or celery wreaths. Adopting Greek depictions of gods, especially Apollo, many Roman emperors were portrayed on coins wearing the laurel wreath. Christian monarchs since Charlemagne have worn bejeweled crowns with a cross symbolizing their power as God-given.

Gigantic turbans, three to four times the head size, usually wrapped around a tall hat, adorned the heads of Ottoman sultans including Süleyman I in early sixteenth-century Istanbul. For public occasions, Manchu royalty in China wore ornate cone-shaped, silk-covered headpieces, with imperial insignia above a tall gold finial intricately decorated with dragons, Buddhas, and pearls. But the nonofficial headdress worn by the Empress

Dowager Cixi and her courtiers (1903) was more striking. Bat-wing shapes of false hair and black satin were arranged over a wide frame with large artificial flowers and long silk tassels dangling from the sides.

For centuries, Japanese emperors have worn the black lacquered ceremonial headpiece (kanmuri) with a birdlike tail made of fine horsehair, associated with Shinto priests and courtiers. Because of his role as intermediary between humans and gods, only the emperor wore the tail vertically.

Glass beads, cowrie shells, and feathers are the precious materials used for elaborate headdresses of many African chieftains. A Yoruba king in Nigeria, who represents the collective destiny of his people, wears a tall conical beaded headdress asserting his authority in social, political, and religious matters. Numerous strands of beads hang from the royal headdress hiding his face, which is considered powerful and dangerous. The headdress, which represents the king, must be given reverence in his absence.

A 46-inch-high Aztec headdress (kopilli ketzalli), popularly called "Montezuma's Crown" and adorned with over 400 Quetzal bird feathers, is exhibited at Vienna's Hofburg Museum of Ethnology in the early 2000s. For Aztecs, the number 400 represented eternity; only the highest-ranking ruler could wear 400 feathers of this sacred bird, associated with wisdom, peace, and freedom. The headdress supposedly was taken by Spanish invaders under Cortez and sent in 1524 as a present to Hapsburg ruler Charles V, then Holy Roman Emperor and king of Spain. Since the early 1990s, Yankuikanahuak, an association fostering revival of native Indian cultures supported by the Mexican government, has been lobbying the United Nations and the Austrian government to return this sacred relic to its rightful homeland. Similar efforts have taken place in the United States. Under the Native American Graves Protection and Repatriation Act, an eight-foot-long war bonnet, made of thirty-five sacred bald and golden eagle feathers each measuring one foot, and claimed to have belonged to the renowned nineteenth-century Apache Chief Geronimo, came under government protection for return to tribal ownership.

Wedding Headdresses

In many cultures and religious traditions, elaborate wedding headdresses become ritual objects. The Mien mountain tribal peoples of Laos and Thailand in the Golden Triangle emphasize a complex structure on the bride's head. Her hair, coated with beeswax, is pulled through a tube projecting from a large board on her head above which a vault (like a roof truss) is created from bamboo sticks. A red-embroidered patterned fabric covers the whole ensemble. After two days of ceremonies, the head-dress is removed indicating the bride's acceptance as a full member of the groom's household.

For festivals, including weddings, Hmong (Miao) women in China's Yunnan Province wear an elaborate black scarf measuring to 35 feet long that is wrapped around the head creating a plate shape. The headdress features an embroidered belt with dangling tassels or coins around its edge. Decorations include amuletic symbols: a spiral motif representing family; triangular patterns as "sacred mountains" protecting against evil spirits.

Traditional Japanese brides wear an elaborate hairstyle called Bunkin-Shimada. Hair decorations include a comb (*kushi*) and gold or silver multithreaded string folded in back in an elaborate shape. Hand-painted, lacquered floral-motif hairpins (*kanzashi*) may depict good-luck symbols such as pine trees for durability. Matching comb-and-hairpin sets are sold or rented in bridal stores. A white brocade band or hood (*tsuno-kakushi*), matching a white kimono, covers the elaborate bridal-adorned coiffure. White symbolizes the bride's willingness to "color herself as the husband wishes." The term "tsuno-kakushi" combines the words for "horn" and "concealer." It is said the white hood hides horns of jealousy or hatred the wife might have toward her husband, in-laws, or neighbors. At ceremony's end, the bride removes the white headdress signifying she has left her family and adopted his.

In imitation of Ming empress crowns, Chinese brides wear an ornate phoenix headdress made of tiny gilded silver butterflies, flowers, and fruits dangling from wires, with inlaid kingfisher feathers (fertility and good-luck symbols) and embellished with strings of pearls hiding the bride's face. A large red veil completely covers the bride's head. Symbolism of the phoenix headdress and dragon motif on her robe associates the couple with the royal family, suggesting they are "emperor and empress" for the day.

Jewish wedding headgear incorporates local ethnic variations. One ornate example is the Yemenite bridal gargush, or hood, with its elaborate metallic ornamentation. Everyday gargushes are black cotton or velvet with a band of jewelry pendants (*agrat*), tiny silver rings, discs, and balls dangling over the forehead. Costly bridal gargushes are crafted from gold brocade decorated with golden agrats, golden chains (*khneishe, salsa*), valuable coins, and fine filigree pins (*koubleh*) of geometric shapes.

Crowns, wreaths, and veils are wedding head wear popularly used for Christian rituals. In Russian Orthodox ceremonies, ornate royal-style crowns with Christ and the Virgin icons are held over the bride and groom's heads. The couple is recognized as ruling a new kingdom, the home, where they are urged to live together as moral Christians.

Throughout Europe, peasants held spring flower festivals (Christian substitutes for earlier pagan fertility rites) and some groups adopted them for wedding celebrations. The white lace veil with orange blossom wreath became a classic after Queen Victoria's attire worn at her 1840 wedding to Prince Albert.

In the twenty-first century, Greek Orthodox couples wear wreaths of real, fabric, or artificial flowers joined together by a long ribbon representing their marital union. A similar practice of combining wedding headpieces is used by Buddhist couples in Thailand, where round white "Circles of Eternity" are joined by long strings.

See also **Crowns and Tiaras; Hats, Men's; Hats, Women's; Helmet; Turban; Veils.**

BIBLIOGRAPHY

Arnoldi, Mary Jo, and Christine Mullen Kreamer. *Crowning Achievements: African Arts of Dressing the Head.* Los Angeles: Fowler Museum of Cultural History, University of California, 1995.

Biebuyck, Daniel P., and Nelly Van den Abbeele. *The Power of Headdresses.* Brussels, Belgium: Tendi, 1984.

Boucher, François. *20,000 Years of Fashion: A History of Costume and Personal Adornment.* New York: Harry N. Abrams, 1967.

Cocuzza, Dominique. "The Dress of Free Women of Color in New Orleans, 1780-1840." *Dress* 27, (2000): 78–87.

Foster, Helen Bradley. *New Raiments of Self and African American: Clothing in the Antebellum South.* Oxford and New York: Berg, 1997.

Garrett, Valery M. *Chinese Clothing, an Illustrated Guide.* Hong Kong: Oxford University Press, 1994.

Kilgour, Ruth Edwards. *A Pageant of Hats, Ancient and Modern.* New York: Robert M. McBride, 1958.

Lewis, Paul and Elaine. *Peoples of the Golden Triangle.* London: Thames and Hudson, Inc., 1984.

Rubens, Alfred. *A History of Jewish Costume.* New York: Crown Publishers, 1973.

Wilcox, R. Turner. *The Mode in Hats and Headdress.* New York: Charles Scribner's Sons, 1959.

Beverly Chico

HELMET A helmet—a defensive covering for the head—is made of hard materials for resisting blows so as to protect ears, neck, eyes, and face. Helmets have been worn over centuries for military combat and ceremonies, later for hazardous occupations, and recently for sports. Helmet design fluctuated with changes in warfare and technology.

Ancient Helmets

Prehistoric peoples probably wore woven basketry or hide head protectors; ancient Ethiopians used horse skulls, manes, and tails. Archaeological evidence reveals that rawhide caps and copper helmets, protecting ears and neck nape—with chin straps and padded wool or leather lining—were worn by Sumerian, Babylonian, and Assyrian warriors during the third to first millennia B.C.E. Early Greek helmets were usually bronze hemispherical crowns. The Corinthian version incorporated a movable face mask; the Attic style had cheek guards (mentioned by Homer). Romans used Greek designs, including elaborate horsetail plumes; crested gladiator helmets were made of hammered bronze.

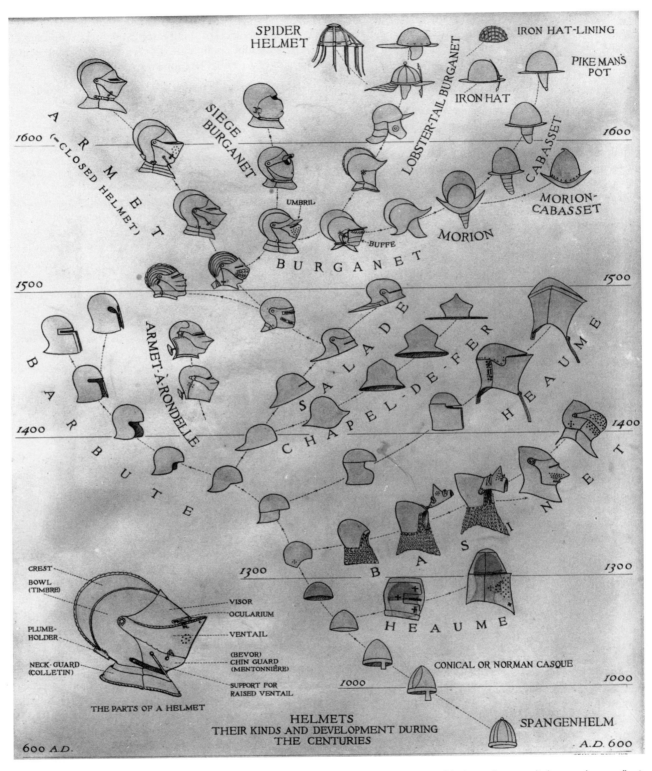

SPIDER HELMET

IRON HAT-LINING

PIKE MAN'S POT

LOBSTER-TAIL BURGANET

IRON HAT

CABASSET

MORION-CABASSET

MORION

BURGANET

UMBRIL

BUFFE

SIEGE BURGANET

ARMET (=CLOSED HELMET)

SALADE

CHAPEL-DE-FER

HEAUME

BARBUTE

ARMET-À-RONDELLE

BASINET

HEAUME

CONICAL OR NORMAN CASQUE

SPANGENHELM

1600

1500

1400

1300

1000

600 A.D.

1600

1500

1400

1300

1000

A.D. 600

CREST
BOWL (TIMBRE)
PLUME-HOLDER
NECK-GUARD (COLLETIN)

VISOR
OCULARIUM
VENTAIL
(BEVOR) CHIN GUARD (MENTONNIÈRE)
SUPPORT FOR RAISED VENTAIL

THE PARTS OF A HELMET

HELMETS
THEIR KINDS AND DEVELOPMENT DURING THE CENTURIES

Evolution of European medieval helmets. Over the course of the Middle Ages, armored helmets became lighter and more flexible to adapt to different styles of warfare. THE METROPOLITAN MUSEUM OF ART. REPRODUCED BY PERMISSION.

Middle Ages

European medieval helmets evolved from the seventh to seventeenth centuries as part of body armor, beginning with a boiled leather conical casque (*spangenhelm*) worn by tribal warriors over a hood of mail. During the feudal era, a large, heavy iron pot (*heaume*) protected the head from lances in chivalry tournaments, and the towering steel snouted visor (*basinet*) was worn in battle. Archers and pikemen used lighter, more flexible helmets with neck guards during the Hundred Years' War (c. 1337–1453).

By 1550, the Italian-invented *armet*, with its thin laminated iron or steel plates and joints providing ease of movement, was adopted by many armies in Europe. The crescent-shaped morion, copied from Moorish designs, protected sixteenth-century Spanish conquistadores in the New World against Indian bows and arrows.

Armor and helmet production reached its artistic zenith for knights and nobles during the sixteenth and seventeenth centuries; ornamental parade pieces often had embossed relief decorations reflecting Renaissance-style, Biblical, and mythological motifs, along with ostrich or peacock panaches. By the eighteenth and nineteenth centuries, when the ultimate weapon was a cannon, metal helmets were displaced by lighter, felt tricorne hats, lamb's fur busbys, and beaver-with-leather shakos.

Another head protector came into widespread use after the 1850s mutinies in Bengal, India, where British troops encountered light, strong helmets made from the dried pith of the solah or sponge wood plant. Subsequently, the "pith sun helmet" was adopted by England and other countries for overseas military campaigns and sports.

Modern Military

World War I technologically revolutionized warfare and weaponry. Shallow-crowned, felt-padded steel helmets protected combatants in trenches against automatic machine guns, replacing earlier spiked and plumed headgear. M-1 steel helmets of World War II infantry were more comfortable with an internal sweatband liner that rested lightly on the soldier's head. Serving multiple functions for the troops, helmets were used as washbasins, eating bowls, and cooking pans. Throughout the twentieth century, at military funerals, a soldier's helmet often sits atop a rifle symbolizing personal heroism and patriotism.

From 1970 to 1997, the U.S. Army Natick Research, Development, and Engineering Center in Massachusetts developed the standard Personnel Armor System Ground Troops (PASGT) helmet; its shell is a one-piece composite molded structure made of multiple levels of Kevlar aramid fiber. Inside is a cradle-type suspension providing space between the helmet and head for ventilation and deformation during impact. Cotton and nylon twill camouflage reversible covers reflect different environments: woodlands, snow, and daylight desert.

Continuing innovation, the twenty-first-century U.S. Army incorporates the most advanced high-tech fea-

tures in its standard bulletproof Integrated Helmet Assembly Subsystem (IHAS). Its attachments, including night-vision goggles, allow for viewing the battlefield via digitized maps, messages, and sensor imagery generated from a personal computer and weapon sights, while receiving audio communications through a computer/radio subsystem composed of components embedded into the ballistic helmet shell. Defensively, the headgear also includes a chemical/biological protection mask and ballistic/laser eye protection.

Occupation Helmets

With nineteenth-century urban growth, larger police and fire units wearing military-style uniforms and helmets including chin straps, badges, and spikes encouraged esprit de corps. In 1863, London's Metropolitan Police began wearing the high-crowned dark serge-covered cork helmet (called "bobby hat" after the Tory prime minister Robert Peel, founder of the Metropolitan Police), similar to the lightweight pith helmet. Around 1900, a more practical, modern peaked hat was adopted in many countries, complemented decades later by titanium or plastic helmets with transparent anti-riot shields. Despite the changes, the English bobby hat survived.

Parisian fire brigades in the 1830s were outfitted with metal, gendarmerie cavalry visor casques. Wide-brimmed leather fire helmets, which (unlike metal) resisted retaining heat, were first used in New York (1740s) and spread to many areas over the next century. By 1959, U.S. government safety regulations began requiring the use of polycarbonate-plastic helmets that are impact, penetration, and water resistant, insulated against electrical charges, and self-extinguishing. Fire helmets of 2004 have transparent plastic face masks.

Coal and ore mining, which grew exponentially during the nineteenth century, gave little attention to head protection for workers. Leather or cloth caps had dangerous oil wick lamps attached for lighting. They were replaced by tin and fiber-compound helmets with carbide lamp attachments, which sometimes still caused explosions. The safest contemporary helmets have battery-powered electric lamps. The U.S. Department of Labor's Occupational Safety and Health Administration (OSHA) establishes regulations for industrial workers' hard hats, which come in varying types for use in construction, welding, electrical work, and mining, with appropriate accessories.

Sports Helmets

Protective helmets for sports were largely introduced in the twentieth-century Western world. Earlier, horseracing jockeys, polo players, and fencers wore head protectors. Advertisements for English bicycle manufacturers in the 1880s show cyclers wearing dark pith helmets. By 1915, bicycle racers wore heavy, round leather helmets, similar to those of aviators and American football players, although recreational cyclists went bareheaded. After World War II, the "hairnet" made of leather strips attached to a round base became popular for racers; its style was later incorporated into Styrofoam and plastic headgear providing increased comfort and protection.

As bicycle technology and design produced faster, more efficient vehicles and the number of cyclers grew to the millions, issues related to safety came to public attention. Beginning in 1957, the nonprofit Snell Memorial Foundation promoted helmet safety after the head-injury death of internationally renowned car racer Pete Snell the previous year. This foundation developed car racing helmet standards and later bicycle helmet criteria, which are used complementing rules set by the American National Standards Institute (A.N.S.I.). Legislation followed that mandated government-approved, laboratory-tested, head-protecting helmets, effective since the 1990s in many countries including Australia, New Zealand, Canada, and the United States

Also in the 1990s, participants in other individual sports, such as motorcycling, skateboarding, and snowboarding, began adopting helmets. Ski helmet use proliferated in 1998 after the accidental deaths of the celebrities Sonny Bono and Michael Kennedy.

Design and durability for recreation sport helmets is usually classified by motorized and nonmotorized sports, including specifications for adults, children, and toddlers. Car racing helmets have neck braces, like those designed for pilots. Rollerblading helmets have ear covers but an open aerodynamic design for air circulation. Helmets for the more dangerous sport of skateboarding incorporate additional padding and snug fit, and bicycle helmets vary according to use—road racing, mountain biking, or touring.

Many ski helmets incorporate a plastic shell over an inner Styrofoam liner with venting system for thermal protection. A few are made from lighter carbon or platinum materials. In the early 2000s ski racer, hockey, and football helmets have large extending chin protectors. Accessories include headphones or built-in speakers for radio communication, CDs, tapes, MP3 or mini disc listening, and cameras. Appealing to youth, helmet manufacturers produce a wide range of helmet colors and novelty decals.

Space Helmets

The most complex helmets ever created are for National Air and Space Administration (NASA) astronauts. They protect the wearer in alien environments against extreme temperatures (250° F to 250° below zero); micrometeoroids traveling up to 64,000 miles per hour; solar ultraviolet, infrared, and light radiation from the sun; and zero gravity conditions. The pressure helmet consists of a transparent polycarbonate (plastic) shell with aluminum neck ring that fits into and locks with the space suit neck ring. The helmet left side contains a feed port where water and food enter, and a purge valve. A vent port of synthetic elastomer foam is bonded in back with a ventilation

opening. The helmet functions as an integral part of the astronaut's life-support system. Oxygen, warmed to avoid fogging the visor, enters the helmet rear and travels over the head downward to the front. Carbon dioxide exits, via a fan and tubing, along with respiration- and perspiration-caused humidity. These are also integrated with the Feedwater and Liquid Transport Systems, which cool the astronaut, and radio transmitter/receivers. Recent "micro display" technology provides a visual image inside the helmet allowing technical diagrams to be beamed the astronaut.

See also **Hats, Men's; Hats, Women's; Headdress; Military Style; Protective Clothing.**

BIBLIOGRAPHY

Alderson, Frederick. *Bicycling, a History.* New York: Praeger Publishers, 1992.

Howell, Edgar M. *United States Army Headgear to 1854.* Vol. I (1969); *United States Army Headgear 1855–1902.* Vol. II (1976). Washington, D.C.: Smithsonian Institution Press.

Les casques de combat: du monde entier de 1915 à nos jours. Paris: Lavauzelle, Vol. I, 1984. (Paolo Marzetti, *Combat Helmets of the World,* 3 vols.)

Nickel, Helmut, Stuart W. Pyhrr, and Leonid Tarassuk. *The Art of Chivalry, European Arms and Armor from the Metropolitan Museum of Art.* New York: American Federation of Arts, 1982.

Reynosa, Mark A. *The Personnel Armor System Ground Troops (PASGT) Helmet.* Atglen, Pa.: Schiffer Publishing Ltd., 1999.

Beverly Chico

HEMLINES The term "hemline" entered fashion-speak in the 1930s. Prior to that time, the fashion press referred to skirt lengths and, since the 1920s, when hems first became a focus of fashion, slavishly reported on how many inches above the floor the latest season's models were hemmed. While the press and fashionable women of the twentieth century obsessed about hemlines, throughout most of Western fashion history, skirt length was not an issue. Skirts reached the floor, except in clothing worn by members of the working class whose shortened garments facilitated their work, and, for brief periods of time during the 1780s and 1830s, when ankles were revealed. The history of the hemline is then one of twentieth-century dress, when the raising and lowering of women's skirts made headlines, occasioned protest marches, and served as a symbol of revolution.

1915—Hemlines Rise

Designers and couturiers first raised hemlines several inches above the floor in 1915 when they created the wartime "crinoline" with a full, shortened skirt. Many women greeted this new look with pleasure and saw it as more practical and better suited to a time when women were entering the workforce at unprecedented levels. After the war, as skirt lengths continued to rise—ten to twelve inches above the floor in 1925 to fifteen inches in 1927—so did the outrage against them by more conservative parties such as religious leaders, politicians, and university presidents, who tried to preserve the moral order of the previous century when women did not smoke or bob their hair and stayed at home to raise a family. The *New York Times* reported on 27 December 1925 that Mrs. John B. Henderson, a prominent Washington hostess announced the inauguration of a campaign to reform modern tendencies in dress and that, following the efforts of high dignitaries of church and education, her movement would frown on cigarette smoking by women and call on them to abandon immodest attire. However, changes in society accelerated by World War I fostered increasing economic independence for women and a focus on youth culture with which the shorter skirts became identified; thus the fashion for short skirts prevailed. In fact, attempts by designers to introduce longer skirts between 1922 and 1924 were met with protests by many women who felt the shorter skirts were more youthful and modern.

Skirts continued to rise until 1927, when they reached just below the knee. Not surprisingly, in the following year, designers began to lower hemlines, sensing that women were more amenable to change than they had been in the early 1920s. This news was a relief to textile manufacturers, to whom one inch of added skirt length meant they could sell millions of yards of additional cloth. While manufacturers heralded this change, consumers protested. The *New York Times* reported on 27 October 1929 that some women claimed that the effort to put them back in long skirts was "an insidious attempt to lure women back into slavery." Other, more practical women refused to discard their current wardrobes in which their hemlines could not be lowered to the new fashionable standard, and buy new garments.

During the 1930s, hemlines did fall, but only for evening dress did they reach the floor. Women continued to wear shorter skirts during the day, now hemmed just above the ankle. This long, lean silhouette prevailed until the war years when regulations like L-85, issued by the U.S. government in April 1942, set skirt lengths at 17 inches above the floor and regulated other aspects of the cut of garments in an effort to conserve textiles. Evening dress remained more feminine, with floor-length full skirts made of tulle and marquisette that were not regulated under L-85. The "duration" silhouette survived throughout the war and suited women who, in even greater numbers than during World War I, entered the workforce and supported their families.

1947—The New Look
Following the war, the French designer Christian Dior brought the focus of fashion back to Paris when he introduced his 1947 collection dubbed "The New Look"

Christian Dior measuring a hemline. Dior's New Look line, introduced in 1947, substantially increased the length of women's skirts. © Bettmann/Corbis. Reproduced by permission.

by Carmel Snow, editor of *Harper's Bazaar*. The collection featured long, very full skirts that were a complete reversal of the wartime silhouette. While many greeted Dior's new look with pleasure and a chance to regain their femininity, others protested the profligate use of material after the deprivations of the war. Despite the protests, the New Look gained popularity on both sides of the Atlantic and helped revive the fashion industry in Paris. Dior became known as the tyrant of the hemlines, and he and his fellow couturier's collections were avidly followed and their efforts to raise and lower hems of singular importance to fashionable women.

By the beginning of the 1960s, couture's fashion dominance began to diminish. American and Italian designers had more prominence and the postwar, baby boom generation was beginning to reach their teen years and enjoy an independence and economic freedom not known in the past. Their rejection of their parents' look, exemplified by the Paris couture, led to an increasing interest in street fashion. Young designers, especially those in London, began to introduce clothes more suited to their generation. Mary Quant opened her own boutique on Carnaby Street in London in 1955, and when she couldn't find what she wanted wholesale, she began to design her own pieces, featuring short skirts worn with tights. Skirts continued to rise throughout the 1960s, and by 1966, the miniskirt was at the height of its popularity with the young. By 1968, most established designers in New York and Paris showed short skirts as well.

Of course, as in the 1920s, this evolution in fashion caused an uproar among the more conservative members of society. Also, as in the 1920s, designers tried to reintroduce skirts with longer hemlines, the midi and the maxi, and met, this time, with fierce resistance.

1970—The Midi

In 1970, designers, along with manufacturers and retailers, introduced the midi-skirt, originally defined as anything hemmed below the knee or above the ankle. An intense marketing campaign was waged, in which retailers such as Bergdorf Goodman forced their salesgirls to wear the new-length skirt. Despite the effort, most women rejected the midi, refusing the dictates of fashion designers and retailers. Women organized into groups such as POOFF (Preservation of Our Femininity and Finances), FADD (Fight Against Dictating Designers), and GAMS (Girls Against More Skirt) to protest the new look and encourage others to not buy the midi.

Although longer skirts prevailed in the 1970s and shorter skirts in the 1980s, since the battle of the midi, the length of a women's skirt is no longer dictated by fashion designers but rather is a personal choice.

See also **Quant, Mary; Skirt.**

BIBLIOGRAPHY
Most fashion histories do not address the story of hemlines in any depth. The best source of information is to be found in newspapers and magazines that covered its month-to-month and even day-to-day rise and fall. The source most easily searchable is the *New York Times*. Articles that proved particularly useful in writing this history are included below.

"The Day the Hemlines Went Down at Bonwit's." 4 August 1970.

"Dior, 52, Creator of 'New Look' Dies," 24 October 1957.

"Let the Hemlines Fall Where They May." 7 June 1967.

Morris, Bernadine. "The Rise of the Hemline Is Recounted." 5 April 1965.

Nemy, Enid. "Petitions and Parades: War of Descending Hemline Escalates." 28 April 1970.

Pope, Virginia. "Fashions for 1943 Feel War Effects." 2 January 1943.

"Society Women Hit at Immodest Dress." 27 December 1925.

Pamela A. Parmal

HEMP Hemp is a soft bast fiber from the stem of a plant, as are flax, jute, and ramie. Hemp plant fibers are three to twelve feet long and are made up of bundled cellular fibers. The plant itself, *Cannabis sativa*, is hardy and can be grown in most locations and climates around the world and requires moderate water. Its recorded use for food, shelter, and fiber dates from at least to 8000 B.C.E. Although ethnobotanists and others cannot be absolutely sure, it is thought that hemp was first grown in Asia.

Hemp can be fabricated for clothing, canvas, rope, and other uses. While hemp is not as soft as cotton, it is stronger than other cellulosics, such as flax, and more absorbent than cotton. Due to hemp's coarse and tough attributes it must be retted (rotted), a process by which the fibers are broken down microbially or chemically, decomposing the pectins that attach the bast fibers to the woody inner part of the stem known as the hurd or shive. Natural retting can be accomplished by simply allowing the cut stems to lie in damp fields for several weeks or by placing the stems in running water. The process of separating the bast fibers from the hurd is extremely difficult even when mechanized. The hurd is cleaned from the fiber by scutching (beating) and the fiber is further refined by hackling (combing). Thus, the retting, separating, and cleaning processes are lengthy and, therefore, expensive compared with other natural fibers. Overall, the production and processing of hemp is prohibitively expensive for routine consumer products.

Because hemp is naturally resistant to ultraviolet light, mold, and mildew, and to salt water, it has been used extensively for centuries by ships for sail canvas and rope. Farmers in the United States were encouraged to grow industrial hemp when, during World War II, the United States was denied access to abaca (called Manila hemp) from the Philippines. The U.S. Department of Agriculture produced a film titled "Hemp for Victory" and subsidized hemp cultivation by farmers. After World War II, industrial hemp cultivation was outlawed due to its association with marijuana hemp, a different variety of *Cannabis sativa*. In 1999, Hawaii became the first state since 1957 in the United States to plant hemp seeds legally. Hawaii's hemp project ended on 30 September 2003, when the Drug Enforcement Agency (DEA) ended Hawaii's attempt to grow industrial hemp. Industrial hemp is harvested in Canada, China, and most of Europe.

Hemp was reputedly used by Levi Strauss for the first Levi trousers sent to miners during the U.S. gold rush in the mid-1800s. Hemp fibers and yarns can be successfully combined with other natural fibers and yarns, including silk, and with synthetic fibers and yarns. Processed hemp is imported into the United States for use in industrial carpeting and upholstery as well as light supple dress weights.

In 2003, there were several businesses in the United States selling hemp fabrics or hemp blend fabrics for various uses. There were a large number of retailers who sold hemp and hemp blend products ranging from knitted T-shirts to woven and printed aloha shirts. Hemp fabrics become softer with repeated use and washing. Home products and accessories such as upholstery and table linens made from hemp are found to have strong market appeal to those seeking natural textile products.

At the turn of the twenty-first century, consumer use of hemp fabrics could be seen as a novelty touched by hemp's arcane association with forbidden marijuana.

See also **Hawaiian Shirt; Levi Strauss.**

BIBLIOGRAPHY

Barber, E. J. W. *Prehistoric Textiles.* Princeton, N.J.: Princeton University Press, 1991.

Blair, C. "Hemp Dies in Hawaii." *Honolulu Weekly,* 8 October 2003.

Kadolph, Sara J., and Anna L Langford. *Textiles.* 8th ed. Upper Saddle River, N.J.: Prentice-Hall, 1998.

Zimmerman, Malia. "Some See Profit in Hawaii Hemp." *Pacific Business News,* 9 July 1999.

Carol Anne Dickson

HERMÈS The world's most acclaimed maker and purveyor of status goods, Hermès has evolved from its days supplying harnesses to coach builders. The firm has been in family hands since it was begun in 1837, when Thierry Hermès (1801–1878), who had moved to France from Prussia in 1821, established his wholesale business near the old city wall on the rue Basse du Rempart in Paris.

In 1879 his son Émile-Charles Hermès (1835–1919) acquired the current flagship building at 24, rue du Faubourg Saint-Honoré and expanded the business into retailing by manufacturing and selling saddles along with related equestrian accoutrements. At the time the phrase "carriage trade" connoted the uppermost level of the haute monde: those who could afford to commission, equip, and maintain exquisite horse-drawn carriages, not to mention stables of purebred horses. Thus the Hermès clientele came to be composed of the upper crust of international society.

Somewhat unusually for a company associated with the stately past, Hermès adapted astutely to a rapidly changing world as the early twentieth century witnessed enormous changes in modes of transportation. Émile-Maurice Hermès (1870–1951), understood that people's preferred methods of travel had increasingly become an expression of their personae and position in society. Thus the company developed luggage, folding portable furniture, and other articles made specifically for travel by ocean liner, airplane, safari, or automobile. Nor was the world of the horse ignored, as riding became even more glamorous as a sport than it had been as a means of transportation.

Émile-Maurice's son-in-law Robert Dumas (1905–1978) was the next director of the company. Robert was succeeded by one of his sons, Jean-Louis Dumas (1938–), who held the reins after 1978. Numerous Hermès family members continued to be closely involved with the company, and the fact that it remained a family-run firm made all the difference in its continuing reputation for superb quality. At Hermès tradition and innovation were almost paradoxically intertwined; what might have seemed like mechanical precision was achieved by carefully nurtured and trained artisans working entirely by hand. Besides a level of quality against which all other quality goods were measured, Hermès came to be best known for several of its products that progressed from practical items to best-sellers to classics to cultural icons.

Hermès Handbags

Few articles of women's attire carried the significance of a Hermès handbag in the early 2000s. The Hermès Kelly and Birkin bags entered modern consciousness as icons laden with status. As a plot element in Diane Johnson's novel *Le Divorce,* the Kelly bag was instantly recognizable to those conversant in the language of status and society as a sign that the American-in-Paris Isabel Walker had acquired a well-heeled older lover. And Martha Stewart's carrying two Birkin bags—not just a black bag but a brown one as well—received international attention at her 2004 trial and might have contributed to the distance the jurors perceived between her lifestyle and theirs.

The haphazard path of the Kelly bag's journey to icon status was part of its appeal. Originally a large bag for holding a saddle when it was introduced around 1892, the prototype of the Kelly bag was known as the Haut à Courroies, indicating that it had a high handle. During the 1930s the Haut à Courroies joined the Mallette and Bollide as roomy Hermès travel bags. An early depiction in the July 1937 issue of the French high-fashion magazine *Femina* showed two women waiting as a curved aerodynamic train pulled into the station. Both women were dressed in typically chic travel clothes of the period—sober and tailored. One carried a light-colored Mallette bag; the other, a dark and soft rather than stiff Kelly bag in dark leather. Both handbags represented a departure from the dominant purse of the 1930s, which was a simple flat small envelope.

The boxy Kelly bag got its nickname, famously, when Princess Grace of Monaco was shown on the cover of *Life* magazine in 1956 shielding her stomach with her handbag so as to ward off rumors (which would have been front-page news the world over) of her first pregnancy. In the 1950s Princess Grace was more than a fascinatingly beautiful style-setting woman; she was romance incarnate. She represented two types of American aristocracy—East Coast upper-class families and Hollywood celebrities—married to European royalty. Sales of the Kelly bag took off; it began to be used as a town bag, appropriate to wear with a tailored dress or suit.

Thirty or so years later, Jean-Louis Dumas chanced to sit next to the actress Jane Birkin on an airplane. Dismayed by the unkempt appearance of her straw carry-all, Dumas asked Birkin if she would help develop a new tote for the company. The much-coveted result was introduced in 1984. Like the Kelly, the Birkin bag had its origins in the world of luggage. An early version of the bag

THE ORANGE BOX

Appropriately for a firm that can be said to have invented the nonprecious status object, the Hermès box itself became a coveted item, decorating glamorous foyers and boudoirs, and being auctioned off on Internet websites. The box's distinctive color and texture were originally designed to resemble pigskin, one of the most popular sporty materials used for Hermès products of the 1920s and 1930s.

had appeared in a 1963 advertisement on top of a stack of small Hermès suitcases. That women of the early twenty-first century required the equivalent of antique luggage to help contain a day's necessities spoke volumes about their lives having become more rather than less complicated.

Many of the hundreds of Hermès handbags became classics, including Jacqueline Kennedy Onassis's favorites—the casual Trim, the more formal Constance with its large H-shaped clasp, and the Mangeoire, made like a horse's feed bucket with holes through which a scarf could be threaded. The Bollide, however, deserves special mention for its use of zippers. While in Canada during World War I, Émile-Maurice Hermès was intrigued by the sliding fastener used to close the top of his Cadillac convertible. Although Elsa Schiaparelli usually gets the credit for having discovered zippers, Hermès used them throughout the 1920s for all sorts of sports clothes, luggage, and purses, including the zippered and padlocked precursors of the Bollide and Plume handbags.

Hermès Scarves

The famous Hermès scarf, known as a silk carré or square, was launched in an advertisement in December 1936 as a coming attraction of 1937. Called "*Jeu des omnibus et dames blanches*," its pattern was based on a woodcut of an eighteenth-century game. Hermès scarves of the 1930s tended toward modernist geometric patterns. By designing a large square of silk printed with boldly scaled figural scenes, Hermès invented a whole new genre of fashion accessory, one that maintained its popularity for more than seventy years. Although all sorts of patterns came later—the stable of designs hovered around a thousand in the early 2000s—the typically bold scale of the patterns never wavered, and also influenced the design of high-fashion prints during the late 1980s. Besides the patterns, many based on Hermès's private museum holdings of art and antique objects, what made the scarves instantly recognizable as Hermès products was the quality of the

crisp silk twill, woven in Lyons from raw silk from China, and the precision printing. Each scarf design made use of as many as forty-five screens and 75,000 tones, resulting in unparalleled brilliance of color.

Hermès Ties

The first Hermès ties for men were dark, with discreet geometric designs, and made their debut in 1953. After the 1960s Hermès ties were designed by Henri d'Origny. They typically featured small repeated equestrian or sailing-inspired patterns in dazzling colors not usually associated with menswear. Hermès ties were steadily popular for more than forty years, no small feat in the fickle world of fashion.

Hermès Fashions

At the turn of the twenty-first century, the global brand conglomerates that dominated the market for luxury goods vacillated between emphasizing star designers and brand names. Hermès had offered clothes for sport, both custom-made and ready-to-wear, since the 1920s, but the firm's typical style was better known than the contribution of any particular designer. Since the 1980s, the names of designers associated with Hermès included Eric Bergère and Martin Margiela—whose most lasting contribution may have been an accessory rather than a line of clothing, namely a double-wrapped watch strap. Jean Paul Gaultier, who presented his first collection for Hermès in the fall of 2004, tapped a mien conspicuously lacking from contemporary fashion—the insouciance of the aristocrat born with a good seat. Designs in this mood included fringed cashmere coats fitted like horse blankets that had been thrown around the shoulders and belted, and a leather corset reminiscent of a saddle fastened with the famous Hermès padlock in the style of a chastity belt.

See also **Celebrities; Gaultier, Jean-Paul; Handbags and Purses; Leather and Suede; Margiela, Martin; Scarf; Schiaparelli, Elsa; Silk.**

BIBLIOGRAPHY

Nadelson, Reggie. "Out of the Box." *Departures* (May–June 2002): 142–178.

Remaury, Bruno, ed. *Dictionnaire de la mode au XXe siècle.* Paris: Editions du Regard, 1994.

Reynolds, C. P. "Hermès." *Gourmet*, February 1987, 42–122.

Caroline Rennolds Milbank

HEROIN CHIC At the U.S. Conference of Mayors on 21 May 1997, President Bill Clinton triggered a media furor on both sides of the Atlantic with his comments about the dangers of so-called heroin chic in contemporary fashion imagery. "You do not need to glamorize addiction to sell clothes," he asserted. "The glorification of heroin is not creative, it's destructive. It's not beautiful, it's ugly" (White House Briefing Room p.1). The photographs in question showed emaciated models, eyes half-closed, skin pale and clammy, heads twisted in apparent abandon against a backdrop of seedy, anonymous hotel rooms and dirty apartments. Clinton's fears had been heightened by fashion photographer Davide Sorrenti's death at twenty-one, from a drug overdose on 4 February 1997. The gap between image-makers' and models' real lives and constructed fashion photographs blurred. Since the 1970s fashion designers' struggles with drug addiction, for example, Yves Saint Laurent and Roy Halston, had been related alongside discussions of their work and influences. In the 1990s media coverage merged actual drug abuse and fashion scenarios created to suggest decadent and nihilistic rejections of conventional notions of beauty. Clinton decried what he saw as fashion's glamorization of heroin use, and his words were reinforced by fashion journalists such as Amy Spindler of the *New York Times*, who felt that fashion insiders were irresponsible, that they ignored drug use by models and photographers, and that they made images that spoke of dark addictions in order to promote clothing and fashion ideals.

The ensuing media debate was further fueled by revelations of heroin abuse within the fashion industry. It is notable, though, that heroin chic existed only at the level of representation, in photographs and in styling for catwalk shows, rather than in actual clothing. It was a conjuring of signifiers that were frequently intended to evoke a more realistic idea of beauty and which its creators felt linked to their everyday lives in a way that more traditional fashion photographs, which relied upon sanitized visions of artificially enhanced perfection, never could.

This realist aesthetic had evolved since the early 1990s, with the London-based photographers Corinne Day and David Sims, and German-born Juergen Teller highly influential in its formation. They worked with like-minded stylists, most importantly Melanie Ward (with Day) and Venetia Scott (with Teller), who sought out secondhand clothes to mix with designer and high street garments to create a mood or atmosphere that related to their own experiences. Their work responded to post-rave youth culture, disenchantment with politics, and the impact of the global recession. It drew upon the intensity and fluidity of the rave scene and the darker obsessions and sense of alienation of rock bands such as Nirvana.

They were influenced by 1960s and 1970s fashion photographers who had experimented with notions of morality and acceptability, such as Bob Richardson and Guy Bourdin, and combined their images' often jarring, filmic quality with the raw emotion and intimate expositions of Larry Clark and Nan Goldin. In the 1990s, fashion photographers locked into a tradition of documentary photography that drew significance from traces of the everyday and sought to express the intensity of the moment. Goldin and Clark had both photographed real scenes of sex and drug use. They used the camera as a visual record, an external memory of their lives, and that is what 1990s photographers—Sorrenti, Teller, and Day—integrated into their own work.

They mainly worked for style magazines such as *The Face*, *Dazed and Confused*, and *i-D* in London, and therefore drew a young audience that responded to the stripped-down settings and light touch of Ward's and Scott's styling, which created outfits that seemed to have been thrown together from old favorites rather than crisp, new clothes. The models they chose, Emma Balfour, Rosemary Ferguson, and Kate Moss among them, were skinny and androgynous, and embodied a challenge to the more Amazonian physiques of previous models. However, their thinness at times seemed acute, and their glazed, Vaseline-lidded eyes and pale faces were jarring among glossier beauty ideals shown in advertisements in the same magazines.

Although other areas of culture were equally preoccupied by images of youthful rebellion, through drugs and partying, the models' fragile bodies appeared bruised and vulnerable. Their delicate features seemed blurred by smudged makeup and incongruous in the context of dirty rooms or overgrown countryside. They recalled the emaciated style shown in the 1981 cult film, *Christiane F.*, which depicted the life of a teenage heroin addict. Models were often shown lying prone, perhaps asleep, perhaps passed out.

Irvine Welsh wrote about heroin addiction in *Trainspotting*. Films, such as the one inspired by his book made in 1996; *Drugstore Cowboy*, 1989; *Pulp Fiction*, 1994; and *The Basketball Diaries*, 1995, were all far more graphic in their scenes of drug abuse; they were also able to show their protagonists' suffering and turmoil. Fashion images, however, presented snapshots that covered perhaps eight magazine pages, a mini-narrative that was ambiguous, with drugs never actually explicit but implied to some onlookers by gestures, settings, and facial expressions.

By the time Clinton spoke out about so–called heroin chic, a term that had been circulating, along with "junkie chic," in the press for the past year, many felt the style was over, and fashion had moved on. It had been a strand within fashion that had grown up over the previous years, coming to fruition in 1993, as evidenced by, for example, fashion shoots for *The Face* of that year, and it gradually shifted, into more straightforward documentary work for Day and Teller, into a darker, more erotic fantasy for photographers such as Sean Ellis, or into more explicit imagery for Terry Richardson. Camilla Nickerson and Neville Wakefield's book, *Fashion, Photography of the Nineties* (1996), brought together many of the key images of the period and showed the breadth of the realist style, of which heroin chic was only a part. The outcry came as mainstream labels appropriated the aesthetic, Calvin Klein included, adding an edge to their brand. As it shifted context, and therefore reached a wider audience, heroin chic's suggestions of internalized violence and illicit pleasures became increasingly controversial.

Heroin chic was a symptom of cultural anxiety, and fashion's contradictory position within Western culture meant that its exploration of uncomfortable themes of alienation, deathliness, and beauty were problematic, especially at a time when representations of reality and fiction were ever more blurred.

See also **Extreme Fashions; Fashion Photography.**

BIBLIOGRAPHY

Arnold, Rebecca. "Heroin Chic." *Fashion Theory, The Journal of Dress, Body and Culture* 3, no. 3 (September 1999): 279–295.

———. *Fashion Desire and Anxiety: Image and Morality in the 20th Century.* New Brunswick, N. J.: Rutgers University Press, 2001.

Nickerson, Camilla, and Neville Wakefield, eds. *Fashion: Photography of the Nineties.* Zurich, Berlin, and New York: Scalo, 1996.

Internet Resource

White House Briefing Room. "White House Press Release: Remarks by the President at the U.S. Conference of Mayors." Available from <http://www.treatment.org/news/mayors.html>.

Rebecca Arnold

HIGH HEELS High-heeled shoes, perhaps more than any other item of clothing, are seen as the ultimate fashion symbol of being a woman. Little girls, who raid their mother's closets for dressing-up props, gravitate toward them. A first pair of high heels was often a rite of passage into womanhood.

Vivier/Christian Dior red satin stilettos. Known for their slim, elegant high heels, stilettos were extremely popular into the early 1960s. NORTHAMPTON MUSEUMS AND ART GALLERY. REPRODUCED BY PERMISSION.

Fetish footwear. High heels have long been associated with the fetish and bondage scenes because of their ability to convey the image of power and authority to the wearer. NORTHAMPTON MUSEUMS AND ART GALLERY. REPRODUCED BY PERMISSION.

To be so fashionably shod is often detrimental to one's feet, but a high-heeled shoe is widely perceived as the sexiest, most feminine shoe a woman can wear. High heels have the ability to change radically the wearer's posture and appearance. Heels make the leg look longer, slimming calves and ankles. A woman's silhouette changes. Her breasts are thrust forward and her bottom pushed out to create a seductive S-shape that helps to create that sexy walk. These physical changes influence how a woman feels and often how she is perceived, so creating the paradox of wearing heels. On the one hand, high heels are all powerful. A woman becomes taller, striking a defiant pose that signifies sexuality and power. In heels she can take on the world. Yet, high heels can also create a helpless woman, teetering and unsteady, unable to run for the bus, passive and weak.

High heels have had a long association with sexual fetishism—from the dominatrix in black leather high-heeled boots to the submissive in bondage shoes.

Origins
Heels were first introduced in the 1590s. In the 1660s Louis XIV of France made high heels fashionable for men. As a relatively short man he coupled high heels with tall wigs to create an illusion of height. Royal customization gave rise to red heels, a symbol of status and power, initially only worn by those in the royal court. High red heels continued to be fashionable into the 1770s.

The Eighteenth Century
The French fashion of the 1770s and 1780s saw high heels placed under the heel arch of the foot, causing the wearer's toes to be crushed in the upturned pointed toe, yet tilting the wearer forward in a provocative manner.

The resulting pain was worth it for the very fashionable look. A satirical poem of the time says it all: "Mount on French heels/ When you go to a ball /'Tis the fashion to totter/ and show you can fall!" Toward the end of the eighteenth century, heels became lower or wedged, disappearing altogether by around 1810.

The Nineteenth Century

From the 1850s women's heels began to make a comeback, and by the 1860s fashionable heels could measure 2.5 inches. In June 1868 the *Ladies Treasury* told its readers: "High-heel boots are universal, notwithstanding that medical men have been writing very severely against them. They say the fashion causes corns, cramps, lameness at an early age, lessens the size of the calf and thus makes it lose its symmetry" (Swann, p. 48). From 1867 there was also the introduction of a straight, slender high heel known as the Pined PINET, after the French shoemaker Francois Pinet.

In the 1890s some courtesans wore a style known as the Cromwell shoe, based on the Victorians' rather fanciful ideas of the shoes worn by Oliver Cromwell and his followers; this style had a heel of up to 6.5 inches.

Early heels were carved from wood and covered with leather or fabric used for the upper shoe. To strengthen the area between the sole and the heel the leather sole often ran down the heel breast.

The Twentieth Century

The Cuban heel with straight sides appeared in 1904. It was usually constructed using pieces of leather stacked to create its height. The bar shoe was the classic style of the 1920s, sporting a high Louis or Cuban heel. Jewelled heels decorated with paste, diamante, and enamels were featured on evening shoes.

A significant development in the history of high heels came on the wave of Christian Dior's New Look in 1947. This style required a correspondingly slim and elegant high heel. Previously high slim heels were prone to breaking. The problem was solved when a steel rod was inserted through a molded plastic heel. Stilettos were first mentioned in the *Daily Telegraph* on 23 September 1953. Initially high fashion, made popular by the French shoe designer Roger Vivier, all women were soon wearing them until the early 1960s. Stilettos caused many practical problems, including the pitting of wooden floors and getting caught in street gratings.

It was also in the 1960s that for the first time since the 1720s, the high heel was reclaimed by men in the form of the Cuban heel on what were known as Beatle boots, a style made popular by the the Beatles. In the 1980s high stiletto heels made a comeback, as power dressing for women at work became de rigueur. Coupled with a shoulder-padded masculine tailored suit and red lipstick, the high heel symbolized sexual power and dominance, a "don't mess with me" visual attitude.

French mule, 1720. From its origins in the seventeenth century to the early twenty-first century, the high heel connotes strength, authority, and sexuality. NORTHAMPTON MUSEUMS AND ART GALLERY. REPRODUCED BY PERMISSION.

Since then the high heel has never really disappeared. Its resurgence in the early 2000s was reflected in the popularity of Manolo Blahnik's shoes in the TV show *Sex and the City*. Some women only wear high heels for special occasions as formal wear, while others wear them all the time. Whatever the preference is, the high heel will never go away.

See also **Blahnik, Manolo; Boots; Shoes; Shoes, Women's.**

BIBLIOGRAPHY

McDowell, Colin. *Shoes: Fashion and Fantasy.* London: Thames and Hudson Inc., 1989.

Pattison, Angela, and Nigel Cawthorne. *Shoes: A Century of Style.* London: The Apple Press, 1998.

Pratt, Lucy, and Linda Woolley. *Shoes.* London: V&A Publications, 1999.

Swann, June. *Shoes.* London: B.T. Batsford, Ltd., 1982. Excellent historical overview.

Rebecca Shawcross

HIGH-TECH FASHION High-tech fashion uses advances in science and technology to design and produce fashion products. Methods used in high-tech fashion borrow from technologies developed in the fields of chemistry, computer science, aerospace engineering, automotive engineering, architecture, industrial textiles, and competitive athletic wear. Fashion projects an image of rapid change and forward thinking—a good environment for use of the latest technologies in production methods and materials. As technology becomes more integrated with one's everyday life, its influence on the fashion one wears continues to increase.

Airplane Dress. Designed by Hussein Chalayan, the Airplane Dress is representative of how advances in science and technology are used to create fashion products. COURTESY OF CHRIS MOORE. REPRODUCED BY PERMISSION.

High-tech fashion. A Pioneer Corp. employee demonstrates the latest in Japanese streetwear—the wearable PC. In the early 2000s, Pioneer was attempting to showcase more functions to the heat-proof, fabric-like display on the sleeve. © REUTERS/CORBIS. REPRODUCED BY PERMISSION.

Historic technological innovations such as the development of the sewing machine, the zipper, and synthetic fibers have influenced how garments are made, how they look, and how they perform. Elsa Schiaparelli was a noted designer of the 1930s and 1940s who had an eagerness to experiment with synthetic fibers. She introduced the first zipper to Paris couture. World events delayed advancements in techno fashions until the race for space began to influence designers in the 1960s. André Courrèges's use of bonded jersey, Paco Rabanne's experimentation with metal-linked garments, and Pierre Cardin's pioneering vacuum-formed fabrics began to push the boundaries of fashion through experimentation with technology and innovative materials. Plastics, foam-laminated fabrics, metallic-coated fabrics, and a sleek fashion silhouette launched fashion into a new realm.

Technological advances continue to influence fashion with new developments in materials, garment structuring and sizing, methods of production, and the quest for fashion that reflects the look and lifestyle of the future.

Techno Materials

Techno materials include fibers, textiles, and textile finishes engineered for a specific function or appearance. The U.K. designer Sophia Lewis believes that "the greatest potential for the future lies in experimental fashion using advanced synthetics to promote new aesthetics and methods of garment construction" (Braddock and O'Mahony, 1999, p. 80). While most synthetics of the twentieth century were developed to mimic natural fibers, the new synthetics are engineered to be strong and durable even when lightweight, transparent, or elastic. Blending natural fibers with synthetics in new ways to produce "techno-naturals" is adding to the aesthetic and performance advantages of textiles.

Recent fiber developments include microfibers, fibers regenerated from corn and milk proteins, metallics, and fiber optics. Microfibers can be produced at a thickness less than that of a silk filament to create fabrics that are soft and fluid with great strength and capabilities of performing under extreme environmental conditions.

New processes and experimentation have lead to eco-friendly fibers made from renewable resources such as corn and soybeans. Another eco-friendly advancement is the genetic development of naturally colored cotton, eliminating the need to use caustic dyes. Shape memory alloys (SMAs) made of nickel and titanium can be produced in wire or sheet form to be incorporated into fabrics that retain memory of their original shape.

Holographic fibers can be used to reflect colors and images from the wearer's surroundings. Fiber optics incorporated into fabrics can be used to transmit messages.

While traditional fabrication methods of weaving and knitting remain, new fabric technologies are emerging. Knits are being fashioned to form seamless garments that are shaped to fit any figure. Nonwovens are inexpensive to produce and are adaptable to multiple end uses. Experimentation with a variety of finishing techniques for nonwovens has introduced a new aesthetic option for designers such as Hussein Chalayan, who fashioned dresses of Tyvek nonwoven fabrics. Foams give options of developing sculptural shapes for the body as well as providing insulation. Synthetic rubber allows garments to fit close to the body with freedom of movement in many applications, from wet suits to evening gowns.

Fabric finishes are providing new options for designers. Fabrics can be coated with microencapsulated substances such as vitamins, fragrances, insect repellents, or bacteriostats. As the tiny capsules burst, the substance is released onto the skin. Phase-change technology, originally developed by NASA, produces fabrics that adapt to changes in temperature with the potential of providing garments that heat and cool the body. Phase change materials (PCMs) can be incorporated into fibers or sandwiched between layers of fabrics. The PCM can absorb and distribute excess heat throughout the fabric before storing it. As the environment cools, the PCM solidifies and releases the stored heat to the wearer.

Textile designers have a heightened interest in combining both chemical and mechanical processes to develop beautiful and practical fabrics. Experimentation with high-tech interpretations of simple finishing techniques, such as calendering or mercerization, can give fabrics a variety of textures, from smooth and lustrous to crinkled or sculpted. The finish can dramatically transform a fabric's visual and tactile qualities as well as performance characteristics like stain resistance, wind resistance, or permanent-press features. Thermoplastic fibers can be molded with heat to create permanent three-dimensional surfaces.

Printing is another method of transforming the surface of a textile that has been advanced through experimentation with new technology. Computer Aided Design (CAD) is a tool that enables textile designers to create modern print patterns, including the feeling of three-dimensional space. The computer has replaced many of the labor-intensive production demands needed to create surface pattern. It provides flexibility and speed, and can be used with a range of printing options to create a new visual aesthetic. Ink-jet printing can move a design from the computer screen to the fabric with speed and flexibility. Heat-transfer allows for great experimentation by developing a design on special paper and then transferring it to a synthetic fabric with heat and pressure. Relief printing with synthetic rubbers and metallic powders creates textural surfaces that are modern and functional.

In addition to looking at technology for direction, many designers have a renewed interest in traditional finishing techniques such as pleating, shibori, and resist-dyeing. The strength of the pioneering Japanese textile industry is based on the combination of new technologies with traditional craft. Rei Kawakubo, Issey Miyake, Yohji Yamamoto, Junya Watanabe, and Michiko Koshino have been leaders in combining traditional craft techniques with cutting edge technology. These designers pioneered a trend toward cooperative partnerships between textile designers and fashion designers, enhancing the development of textiles and garments in a synergistic fashion. This is a model copied worldwide.

In contrast to the strong trend to use technological advances, a sentiment echoed by many designers worldwide is for a more balanced perspective. It is the belief that a design is enhanced by evidence of the hand that created it; thus imperfection, individuality, and an honest approach to materials is highly valued. In many respects, this effort to reject the uniformity of mass-produced garments has been attributable to rapidly evolving technology and move toward fashion that expresses individuality. The explosion of the Internet at the millennium added to this shift by presenting new possibilities in fashion.

Garment Production
The last quarter of the twentieth century saw rapid development of computer technology. Computer-aided design and computer-aided manufacturing (CAD/CAM) dramatically changed the process of designing and manufacturing garments by reducing many labor-intensive processes, increasing speed and accuracy, and lowering costs. Garments can be developed with CAD from sketch to pattern and cutting, either locally or globally, in a fraction of the time it took.

Designers research trend and development information, communicate with clients and suppliers, and sell and market designs in a wireless Internet environment where yesterday is too late. Fashion news is available hours after an event occurs, and the Internet has even replaced some live fashion events. Walter Van Beirendonck, Helmut Lang, and Victoria's Secret have used Internet methods of showing designs. This rapid flow of information, an interest in individuality, and the technology to support rapid production have led to the development of mass customization.

Mass customization is a design, manufacturing, and marketing concept that allows a customer to order a garment to specifications for approximately the same cost as off-the-rack. Part of the specifications may include custom sizing that is achieved with the use of a body scanner, which records measurements that are translated to individualized patterns. This scanned measurement information, along with personal preferences and shopping history, can all be stored on a credit card to facilitate the shopping experience. There are many benefits to this method of operation, including a satisfied customer, less wasteful production, and sales made at full price.

Customization concepts may also support the development of new apparel production technology in molding materials, industrial fusing methods, and seamless knitting technology—providing a glimpse at forming garments without needle and thread. Hussein Chalayan's remote control dress uses composite technology borrowed from the aerospace industry to form molded panels that are clipped together and can move to reveal different parts of the body. The forerunner of this molding technology was the molded bra cup developed in the 1960s. Designers have worked with lasers for cutting patterns and creating intricate, cut designs, or ultrasound to fuse the seams of thermoplastic fabrics. New developments in circular knitting machines move from simple tube knits to entire garments shaped to the body on the machine. Industrial materials that include metals, glass, plastics, and industrial mesh are providing inspiration from architecture for many clothing designers. Traditional apparel production methods are revised or even abandoned according to the needs of the new materials and the way they interact with the body.

Fashions for New Lifestyles
Sports and active lifestyles have influenced fashions of the early 2000s. Apparel technologies developed for competitive sports are incorporated into fashions for everyone. Research and innovative thinking have advanced sportswear with attention to both performance and aesthetics. Garments that maintain body temperature, cool the body, and improve performance are researched and engineered with a new aesthetic that has moved the garments out of the gym and into everyday life.

Current fashion is making accommodations for the consumer's changing electronic lifestyle, including garments with pockets for cell phones, jackets with connections for electronic music players, and stylish bags to tote laptops. Researchers are developing "intelligent" fashions incorporating wearable computers, communication systems, global positioning systems, and body sensors. Systems may have the capability to allow the wearer to surf the Internet, make phone calls, monitor vital signs, and administer medication. While much research remains to be done, initial exploration has begun at MIT's Media Lab, Starlab, Charmed Technology, and International Fashion Machines. The goal of these groups is to develop prototypes of wearable electronics and to explore the synergy required between computer science, fashion, health

care, and defense to produce marketable, user-friendly products. Advances and innovative thinking in the production of apparel and communication platforms and networks will be required to move these concepts forward.

The changing world political climate and the continuing challenges of world health present new opportunities for science to address wearable solutions. Development of protective apparel against bioterrorist attack and spread of infectious disease commands research dollars from governments worldwide. These investments will most likely lead to exciting new materials that ultimately result in new fashion.

Fashion is a reflection of the times, and thus incorporates current scientific and technological developments. Change is a constant in fashion, and one can look forward to ever-developing advanced materials and methods and perhaps even new purposes for fashion.

See also **Extreme Fashions; Futurist Fashion, Italian.**

BIBLIOGRAPHY
Braddock, Sarah E., and Marie O'Mahony. *Techno Textiles: Revolutionary Fabrics for Fashion and Design.* London: Thames and Hudson, Inc., 1999.
O'Mahony, Marie, and Sarah E. Braddock. *Sportstech: Revolutionary Fabrics, Fashion and Design.* London: Thames and Hudson, Inc., 2002.
Quinn, Bradley. *Techno Fashion.* Oxford and New York: Berg, 2002.

Elizabeth K. Bye and Karen L. LaBat

HIJAB Equating the terms *hijab* and "veil" is a common error. "Veil" is an easy, familiar word used when referring to Arab women's head, face, and body covers. *Hijab* is not the Arabic equivalent of veil—it is a complex and multilayered phenomenon.

"Veil" has no single word equivalent in Arabic. Instead many different terms refer to diverse articles of women's and men's clothing that vary by region, era, lifestyle, social stratum, stage in the life cycle, and gender. Adding to this complexity is the fact that some covers and wraps worn by both sexes have multiple usages and are manipulated flexibly to cover the face when socially required. For example, women use head covers or large sleeves to hide the face in ways that can communicate kinship, distance, or social stratum of a person they encounter. Men, as well, can use their head covers in the same way.

"Dress" is a more inclusive word and has an Arabic equivalent, *libas*, that in Arab-Islamic culture connotes meanings beyond material form and function. *Libas* extends conceptualization to notions of family and gender implying haven-shelter-sanctuary—a protective shield, as it were. Dress is integral to Islam's sacred beginnings and explicit Qur'an references reveal a role for *libas* (dress) in Islam's conceptualizations.

Dress in Arab and Islamic culture can be viewed in two ways: the traditional-secular dress (clothing adopted through customary practices over time without religious connotation) and religious dress (clothing forms justified or believed to be justified or prescribed by religious sources or authorities). The Christian example of the latter would be the nun's habit. The Afghan burqa, the object of scrutiny and attack by some feminists preceding the Afghan invasion by the United States, exemplifies the traditional or secular form of dress. Hijab is the religious kind of cover in an Islamic context. The English word "veil" can apply to either secular or religious kind of cover. Hijab is more culturally specific than veil, but embodies multiple cultural levels of meaning and is better understood when embedded in wider sociocultural and sociopolitical contexts. Muslims use Qur'anic references to support their adoption of practices or in taking positions regarding related issues, and there are indeed some references to hijab in the Qur'an.

Qur'anic References

In the Qur'an (considered the primary and divinely revealed source), but mostly according to the *Hadith* (Prophetic Narrative, a secondary worldly source), evidence suggests that the Prophet Muhammad had paid much attention to dress style and manner for Muslims in the emerging community, gradually developing a dress code. There was a specific focus on Muslim men's clothing and bodily modesty particularly during prayer, but reference to women's body cover is negligible.

Within the Qur'an's references to hijab, only one concerns women's clothing. Muslim men and women who argue in the early 2000s for the Islamic dress and behavioral code usually cite two chapters in support of modesty for women and for an Islamic basis for wearing the hijab.

As Islam gradually established itself in the Madina community, after it had been chased out of its place of origin in Makka, the interpretation of "seclusion" for Muhammad's wives originated from sura (chapter) 33, ayah (verse) 53 in which hijab is mentioned:

> O believers, enter not the dwellings of the Prophet, unless invited. . . . And when you ask of his wives anything, ask from behind a hijab. That is purer for your hearts and for their hearts. (33:53)

Evidence suggests that this sura is ultimately about privacy of the Prophet's home and family and the special status of his wives in two ways—as Prophet's wives and as leaders with access to Islamic information and wisdom who are increasingly sought by community members. There was a need to protect their privacy by regulating the flow of visitors and the comportment of the men who entered upon the women's quarters. Here "hijab" refers not to women's clothing, but to its use as partition or curtain to provide privacy for women.

Sura al-Ahzab (33), ayah 59 enjoins the Prophet's wives, daughters, and all Muslim women to don their *jilbab* for easy recognition and protection from molestation or harassment:

> O Prophet tell your wives, daughters and believing women to put on their *jilbabs* so they are recognized and thus not harmed (33:59).

Jilbab refers to a long, loose shirtdress, and does not connote head or face cover. This verse distinguishes the status of the Prophet's wives from the rest of the believers, and the other (33:53) protects their privacy from growing intrusions by male visitors.

Sura 24 refers to *khimar* (head cover) in the general context of public behavior and comportment by both sexes. In it ayah 31 (24:31) has been widely cited in scholarly works, often in isolation from the rest of the verse, distorting the meaning, implying that women are singled out for "reserve" and "restraint." Preceding it, ayah 30 addresses men first:

> Tell the believing men to lower their gaze and conceal their genitals; for that is purer for them, God knoweth what they do.

Ayah 31 follows, continuing the same theme:

> And tell the believing women to lower their gaze and conceal their genitals, and not reveal their beauty, except what does show, and to draw their *khimar* over their bosoms, and not to reveal their beauty except to ... etc. (emphasis added).

Evidence from the usage of hijab in the Qur'an, from early Islamic discourse, and subjected to anthropological analysis, supports the notion of hijab as referring to a sacred divide or separation between two worlds or two spaces: deity and mortals, good and evil, light and dark, believers and nonbelievers, or aristocracy and commoners. The phrase "*min wara' al-hijab*" (from behind the *hijab*) emphasizes the element of separation and partition.

When referring to women's clothing, the terms often used are *jilbab* (long, loose-fitting shirtdress) and *khimar* (head cover). Neither hijab nor *niqab* are mentioned. *Niqab* and *lithma* are terms that unambiguously refer to face cover. Hijab, which only refers to head (shoulder) cover and to the general Islamic attire, is not mentioned in these two suras either. In other references to comportment and modest way of dressing appropriate to the new status of the Prophet's wives, hijab is not mentioned either. When it is used in other suras, the word conveys more the sense of separation than veiling or covering.

The Qur'an and the contemporary Islamic movement make clear that Muslim men and women are to carry themselves in public with a sense of reserve and restraint. Exhibitionist public comportment, through behavior, dress, voice, or body movement, is frowned upon, and becomes associated with *Jahiliyya* (pre-Islamic era) that is not confined to a historical moment, but rather becomes a state and a condition of society that can oc-

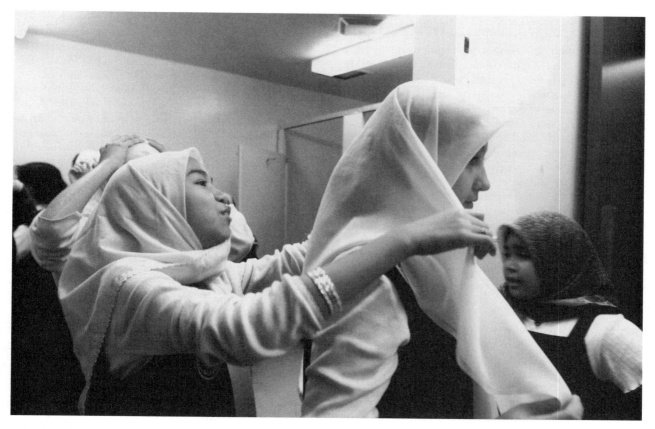

Hijab. The *hijab* is used as women's headcover in the Islamic world. Although it is commonly, and mistakenly, referred to simply as a veil, it serves the higher purpose of representing Islamic identity and morality. © JULIE PLASENCIA/SAN FRANCISCO CHRONICLE/CORBIS. REPRODUCED BY PERMISSION.

cur at any time when social and moral controls are abandoned. But overall the contemporary movement is not simply about clothing but about a renewal of a cultural identity and traditional ideals and values.

Etymology and Meaning

The cultural and linguistic roots of "hijab" are integral to Islamic (and Arab) culture. "Hijab" translates as cover, wrap, curtain, veil, screen, partition. The same word is used to refer to amulets carried on one's person (particularly for children or persons in a vulnerable state) to protect against harm.

By the nineteenth century, upper-class urban Muslim and Christian women in Egypt wore the *habarah*, which consisted of a long skirt, a head cover, and a *burqa*, a long rectangular cloth of white transparent muslin placed below the eyes, covering the lower nose and the mouth and falling to the chest. When veiling entered feminist nationalist discourse during British colonial occupation, "hijab" was the term used by feminists and nationalists and secularists. The phrase used for the removal of urban women's face and head cover was *raf'* (lifting) *al-hijab* (not *al-habarah*: the term used for cloak or veil

among upper-class Egyptian women up to the early 1900s).

Three Arab Feminisms

Muslim and Christian women of the upper and middle classes described the Egyptian feminist movement at the turn of the century as a secular movement. Some observers linked European colonialism and feminism, distinguishing two feminist trajectories: a Westward-looking feminism and a more local one. In neither form have women made veiling or unveiling the central issue. Rather, some prominent men advocated feminist programs and called for reform centering on women's veiling. Removing the veil was not part of the official feminist agenda of the Egyptian Feminist Union. Importantly, when the most prominent Arab feminist, Huda Sha'rawi, "lifted the hijab" as the famous public gesture came to be described, she had only removed the face cover (*burqa* or *yashmik*), which was worn by upper-class women at the turn of the century, but kept the head covering. Technically, therefore, Huda Sha'rawi never "lifted the hijab," since "hijab" refers broadly to the whole attire, but more commonly to the head covering. Some attribute her success in feminist nationalist leadership, compared with other contemporaries, to the fact that she had respect for the traditional attire. In her memoirs she mentions being congratulated for "my success in . . . lifting the hijab . . . but wearing the *hijab shar'i* (lawful or Islamic hijab)" (Sha'rawi 1981, p. 291). This distinction is important and assumes special significance because the other prominent feminist, Malak Hifni Nasif, opposed mandatory unveiling for women. Her agenda in early 1900 stressed two elements absent in Sha'rawi's feminist agenda: the opening of all fields of higher education to women and demanding space accommodation for public prayer by women in mosques. These local elements contrast to French-influenced agendas by other feminists. A third movement developed through the seeds sown since 1908 calling for the importance of Islam and the wearing of the hijab, formed under the initiative of Zaynab al-Ghazali in the 1970s espousing Islamic ideals and supporting family values. None of the three feminisms espoused calling for abandoning the hijab.

Contemporary Movement

Beginning in the 1970s in Egypt an Islamic movement emerged. The Islamic movement reasserted a cultural historical identity and stood for resisting hegemonic colonial occupation. It centered initially on youth and college-level young adults and broadened across generations and social strata and spread throughout the region. The public appearance of an innovative form of dress for men and women without exact historical precedent characterized the movement. This new style was not a return to any traditional dress form, and had no tangible model to emulate, and no industry behind it—not one store in Egypt carried the new garb in the 1970s. In the early 2000s there are many stores that sell this outfit throughout the region, on the Internet, in Europe, and in the United States. The dress was referred to as "the Islamic dress," in Arabic called *al-ziyy al-Islami* or *al-ziyy al-Shar'i*, or more commonly *al-hijab*.

This new fashion seemed incomprehensible and bewildering to observers. The strong, visible appearance of young Egyptian women going to college dressed in a manner unfamiliar to their own parents, completely "veiled" from head to toe, sometimes covering the face and hands as well, disturbed many. Some young women had switched almost overnight from wearing sleeveless dresses and miniskirts to becoming a "veiled" doctor, engineer, or pharmacist. Confused observers speculated about the cause. Was it an identity crisis, a version of America's hippie movement, a fad, a youth protest, an ideological vacuum, an individual psychic disturbance, a life-crisis, a social dislocation, or protest against authority?

Dress Code

The contemporary dress code translates materially this way: men and women wear full-length *gallabiyyas*, loose-fitting to conceal body form, in solid or otherwise aus-

tere colors made out of opaque fabric. The wearers lower their gaze in cross-sex public encounters and refrain from body or dress adornment that draws attention to their bodies. The dress code for men consists of sandals, baggy trousers with loose-top shirts in off-white or, alternatively (and preferably) a long, loose white *gallabiyya* and a white or red-checkered *kufiyya*. They grew a *lihya* (full beard trimmed short). Women wear the hijab, which consists of *al-jilbab* (ankle-length, long-sleeved, loose-fitted dress) and *al-khimar*, a head covering that covers the hair and extends low to the forehead, comes under the chin to conceal the neck and falls down over the chest and back. During the first decade of the movement, women wore solid colors such as beige, brown, navy, burgundy, or black. The *muhajjabat* (women wearing hijab) engaged fully in daily affairs and public life. That is, austerity in dress and reserve in public behavior are not accompanied by withdrawal or seclusion and neither communicates deference nor sexual shame. Modern hijab is about sanctity, reserve, and privacy.

Colonialism and Resistance

The role of the veil in liberating Algeria from French colonial occupation is popularly known. When the French landed in Algeria in 1830 most inhabitants were Arabic-speaking Sunni Muslims, with a large Berber population that was by then bilingual Berber Arabic speaking. Administratively, Algeria was a France populated by "the Muslims"—a majority of second-class citizens. France began a gallicization process on many fronts: French law was imposed on Islamic law, French social plan was imposed on local custom, French education substituted for Arab education, and the French language replaced Arabic. Many Algerians were excluded from education altogether. The French conquest of Algeria represented a deformation of the social, moral, legal, and cultural order. Economically the French monopolized the best land and the top jobs, exploited labor, harnessed local energies, and cultivated crops for French consumption (grapes for wine) while violating Islamic morality. Another strategy was to assimilate upper-class Algerians by gallicizing the woman and uprooting her from her culture. The target of the colonial strategy became to persuade the Muslim woman to unveil. Thus, Arabs and Muslims often link the deveiling of Muslim women with a colonial strategy to undermine and destroy their culture. The effect was the opposite: it strengthened the attachment to the veil as a national and cultural symbol, and gave it a new vitality.

Since 1948 Palestinian women who were uprooted from their homeland, particularly the older ones, wore a dress and head covering that communicated their rural origins and their contemporary status in refugee camps. After the 1967 Six-Day War, women wore white or black shawls (*shasha*) and had no access to their traditional fabrics and tools to embroider their clothing. In the late 1970s, as militant Islamic consciousness began to arise,

Palestinians attempted to restore the hijab. Women affiliated with the movement began wearing long, tailored overcoats and head covers now known as *shari'a* or Islamic dress. As in Egypt, the Islamic dress had no precedent in indigenous Palestinian sartorial history, but is an innovative tradition in form and meaning.

Conclusion

The hijab worn by Muslim women in Arab, Muslim, European, or United States society is largely about identity, about privacy of space and body. In specific social settings, veiling communicates exclusivity of rank and nuances in kinship, status, and behavior and also symbolizes an element of power and autonomy and functions as a vehicle for resistance.

Hijab in the early twenty-first century is politically charged in France and Belgium, countries that are taking measures to ban the wearing of headscarves (hijab) to schools purportedly for maintaining the integrity of secularism, but the issue is considered to be fraught with anti-Islamic implications. To many young women the hijab represents an identity of choice and a freedom of expression they do not want to lose.

See also **Burqa; Djellaba; Islamic Dress, Contemporary; Jilbab; Kaffiyeh; Middle East: History of Islamic Dress.**

BIBLIOGRAPHY

Sha'rawi, Huda. *Huda Sharawi: Muthakkirat Ta'idat al-Mar'a al-Arabiyya al-Hadith* (Memoirs of Huda Shawari, Leader of Modern Arab Women). Introduction by Amina al-Said. Kitab al-Hilal, Silsial Shahriyya. Cairo: Dar al-Hillal, 1981. In Arabic.

Fadwa El Guindi

HILFIGER, TOMMY The ubiquity of Tommy Hilfiger's fashions, particularly among urban youth, is a testament to the marketing and image branding that has characterized contemporary American fashion. Hilfiger was born in 1952, one of nine children raised by a jeweler and nurse in upstate New York; he described his childhood in his 1997 stylebook, *All American*, as living in "Leave it to Beaver-land" (p. 2). In his senior year of high school Hilfiger and two friends opened People's Place, a clothing shop in their hometown of Elmira that sold candles and bell-bottom jeans; Hilfiger enjoyed decorating the windows and designing in-store merchandise displays. People's Place thrived for nearly eight years, with additional stores opening in other towns, until it went bankrupt in the late 1970s.

In 1980 Hilfiger moved to New York City to pursue a career in fashion. He had a brief stint designing for Jordache jeans before joining forces with a woman's clothing manufacturer and starting 20th Century Survival, a junior-sportswear company that offered a variety of clothes in western and nautical styles, as well as Vic-

toriana dresses, khakis, and camouflage gear. In the mid-1980s Hilfiger contemplated job offers from Perry Ellis and Calvin Klein but instead accepted an offer from Mohan Murjani of Murjani International (the clothing manufacturer behind the fame of Gloria Vanderbilt jeans) to fund his own men's wear company. Murjani was looking to create a "name" designer like Calvin Klein and Ralph Lauren, and in 1985 Tommy Hilfiger was launched.

The building of Tommy Hilfiger was as much about marketing as it was about the clothes. Hilfiger embodied this approach, referring to himself in a 1986 *New York Times* article as a "natural, all-American-looking, promotable type of person with the right charisma.... I'm a marketing vehicle" (Belkin p. D1). Shortly after the debut of his first collection of preppy classics like chinos, oxford shirts, and polo knit tops and the opening of his Manhattan flagship store on Columbus Avenue, Murjani boldly put Hilfiger's name in lights. A billboard in Times Square read, "The 4 Great American Designers for Men Are: R—L—, P—E—, C—K—, and T—H—," referring to Ralph Lauren, Perry Ellis, Calvin Klein, and Hilfiger. Hilfiger's name did not appear in the ad, just his red, white, and blue flag logo and the address of his newly opened store. A 1987 advertising campaign for Tommy Hilfiger polo knit shirts pictured the Lacoste alligator, the Lauren polo player, and the Hilfiger flag logo type.

From the outset Hilfiger has been compared to Ralph Lauren. He has been criticized for copying Lauren's preppy style but gearing his signature red, white, and blue styles toward a younger market at more popular prices. Hilfiger, like Lauren, has appeared in advertisements for his clothing line; both men have used the American flag as an important marketing tool. Hilfiger has also replicated Lauren's business model, even employing former Lauren executives to help build Tommy Hilfiger, which Hilfiger, with backing from Silas Chou and Laurence Stoll of Novel Enterprises, bought from Murjani in 1989; Chou and Stoll then incorporated Tommy Hilfiger in Hong Kong. Following Lauren's lead in "lifestyle merchandising," Hilfiger expanded his franchise by opening a number of stores whose interiors reflect the all-Americanness of his clothing; by signing licensing agreements around the world; and by offering a range of lines, such as underclothing, accessories, fragrances, home décor, designer jeans, women's wear, children's wear, and a higher-end men's wear collection. Hilfiger spent $15 million in advertising to launch his men's fragrance "tommy" in 1995, which, at the time, was the most money spent on a campaign for men's fragrance.

Unlike Lauren and other big-name American designers, Hilfiger tapped into hip-hop street styles, making him one of the hippest and wealthiest designers of the 1990s. Hilfiger had always been interested in music, and he saw the potential for musicians to dictate fashion trends. He sponsored a Pete Townsend tour; designed stage costumes for Mick Jagger and Sheryl Crow, among others; and wrote the 1999 book *Rock Style: How Fashion Moves to Music* to accompany an exhibition cosponsored by the Costume Institute of the Metropolitan Museum of Art and the Rock and Roll Hall of Fame and Museum. However, Hilfiger's biggest coup in the music world occurred in 1994 when the rapper Snoop Doggy Dogg appeared on *Saturday Night Live* wearing a rugby shirt with the word "Hilfiger" running down the sleeve, which Hilfiger's brother Andrew had given the musician; the shirt sold out the next day at many New York department stores. Andrew, who worked in the music industry, acted as a goodwill ambassador for Tommy, handing out logo-emblazoned shirts and bags to musicians when he arrived on sets for concerts and music videos.

Hilfiger's logo-laden street styles of the 1990s came about after he saw that counterfeiters were knocking off logos, enlarging them, and sporting them on oversized shirts, sweatshirts, and outerwear; they looked like walking advertisements. He also realized the huge possibilities in the status-symbol-conscious hip-hop movement that revolutionized the music scene in the 1990s. Hilfiger made regular in-store appearances, learning what young consumers wanted. Multiculturalism played a big part in his advertising campaigns; he employed stylists from hip-hop record labels, such as Rashida Jones, to appear in his ads and style his runway shows, which often featured such rappers as Treach, who mentioned Hilfiger in their songs.

In 1995 his once skeptical peers recognized Hilfiger with the Menswear Designer of the Year Award from the Council of Fashion Designers of America. Hilfiger made a name for himself by prominently putting his name and logo on his clothes and marketing them to urban youth in a way that other American designers had not done. He harnessed a diverse following of consumers with his oversized, street-style sportswear and his relaxed, all-American style of jeans, khakis, and polos that fit into the more casual approach to dressing that began to be taken at the end of the twentieth century. Hilfiger invested a great deal in advertising to keep his name and logo prominent; his packaging of the product has surpassed any originality in the clothes themselves. He has raised the bar for the fashion merchandising and image branding that have come to define American fashion.

See also **Fashion Advertising; Fashion Marketing and Merchandising; Hip-hop Fashion; Logos; Music and Fashion.**

BIBLIOGRAPHY

Agins, Teri. *The End of Fashion: The Mass Marketing of the Clothing Business.* New York: William Morrow, 1999.

Belkin, Lisa. "Big Campaign for Hilfiger." *New York Times*, 18 March 1986.

Collins, Glen. "Campaign for Fragrance Plans to Assure That Men See It, Hear It, Sniff It." *New York Times*, 18 May 1995.

Hilfiger, Tommy. *Rock Style: How Fashion Moves to Music.* New York: Universe Publishing, 1999.

Hilfiger, Tommy, with David A. Keeps. *All-American: A Style Book.* New York: Universe Publishing, 1997.

McDowell, Colin. *Fashion Today.* London: Phaidon Press Ltd., 2000.

White, Constance. "The Hip-Hop Challenge: Longevity." *New York Times*, 3 September 1996.

———. "If It Sings, Wear It: The Hilfiger Ploy." *New York Times*, 26 October 1997.

Tiffany Webber-Hanchett

HIP-HOP FASHION Hip-hop is both the voice of alienated, frustrated youth and a multibillion-dollar cultural industry packaged and marketed on a global scale. Hip-hop is also a multifaceted subculture that transcends many of the popular characterizations used to describe other music-led youth cultures. One of the important considerations about hip-hop is that since its conception in the early 1970s, hip-hop has arguably become more potent and efficient in galvanizing black social identity than the civil rights movement of the 1960s.

The evolution of hip-hop has developed from a self-conscious rumination of words and music to an obstinate expression of contemporary urban life through corporal gestures and apparel. From the beginning, hip-hop fashion has been on a trajectory of relentless flowering. Developments have been primarily in the men's wear sector; early clothes were functional and included conventional items—multicolored appliqué leather jackets, sheepskin coats, car coats, straight leg corduroy or denim jeans, hooded sweatshirts, athletic warm-up pants, mock turtlenecks, and sneakers and caps. Less functional items included designer jeans and moniker belts, gold jewelry, Kangol caps, Pumas with fat laces, basketball shoes, and oversized spectacles by Cazal.

Baggy apparel shapes that disguise the contours of the body were introduced in the 1980s. During the early 2000s, the archetypal hip-hop look consisted of baseball caps emblazoned with insignia from the Negro leagues and football teams and well-known fashion designers. Woolen beanie hats and bandannas were worn singularly or together. Goose down jackets or other foul-weather outerwear teamed with hooded sweatshirts. During the late 1990s the ubiquitous oversized white T-shirt, basketball vests, and hockey shirts became staples of the expression. Baggy denim jeans or camouflage cargo pants worn in a low-slung manner, backpacks, combat- or hiking-styled boots or sports shoes were complemented with tattoos and shaved, plaited, or dreadlocked hairstyles. Initially hip-hop women's wear consisted of inconsequential looks that reflected contemporary women's wear and were accompanied with items such as Gloria Vanderbilt jeans, bamboo earrings, Fendi and Louis Vuitton handbags, name chains, midriff tops, bra tops, short skirts, tight jeans, high boots, straight hair weaves and braids, tattoos, and false fingernails and oversized gold jewelry. In addition, some women wore apparel that consisted of items similar to those worn by men during the 1990s. Female rappers such as Lil' Kim and Foxy Brown displayed provocative apparel and outlandish sexual gesturing that would eventually become a raison d'être for hip-hop women's wear.

From within the postindustrial environment, hip-hop has emerged as an articulation of an affirmative "otherness," which is at times unpopular and misunderstood by politically conservative and socially moralistic groups, and especially by those who regard the modernist, antipluralist perspective to be sacrosanct.

Consequently, hip-hop tends to be unpopular with establishment agencies who wish to censor the expression and supervise the conduct and morals of the young; however, hip-hop is understood by mass media agencies and is exploited as a symptom of the volatility between the pull of materialism and the stagnancy of the urban underclass. The precarious state of this condition forces hip-hop to become a project concerned with the mastery of urban survival, and therefore has a global appeal that is demonstrated in hip-hop from New Zealand, Japan, Africa, France, and Great Britain.

A centrifugal force, hip-hop has contributed to the conceptualization of an alternative perspective in the wider society; this includes materialism, manners, morals, gender politics, language, gesture, music, dance, art, and fashion. Hip-hop music and fashion have attained an essential position in culture, though they oscillate on the periphery of conformity and general acceptability, but because of the notion of outsider status, and building upon the popularity of rock music, hip-hop has been admired and emulated by teenagers of most ethnicities and social classes.

Where Hip-hop Began

Hip-hop has at times become synonymous with a constellation of products in the luxury goods market, though such a situation would have been absurd at hip-hop's genesis. Hip-hop was formed in the culture of the basement parties that took place in the Bronx in New York City. These parties became formalized when the DJs Kool Herc, Grandmaster Flash, and DJ Starski began to play at impromptu parties in parks, streets, and community centers. Jamaican DJ Kool Herc, the credited founder of hip-hop break-beats based his Herculords discotheque system on the Jamaican reggae sound systems that played in Jamaica and New York. The art form of rapping emerged as the way of communicating narrative to the audience. Rapping is similar to "toasting," a long-established feature of reggae music.

Toasting and rapping are delivered in the style of the African oral tradition. The DJ, or toaster in Dancehall, and the MC, or rapper, in hip-hop are the progeny of the African griot (storyteller), each offering a narration of everyday events.

A NEW YORK HOME BOY IN THE MID-1990s

The wearer is dressed in iconic mainstream American classics, a white T-shirt, and Levi's 501 jeans. Either he is ignorant of that or his other clothes and the way he wears them are chosen to offset their status: Kangol golf hat, Nike sneakers, and the ubiquitous boxer shorts.

However, the key device of the display is achieved in wearing boxer shorts with jeans in a manner that the elastic edge of the boxer shorts peeps over the jeans waist causing the designer branded elastic to be visible. As a consequence the jeans are restructured, to the extent that the form of the pants begins to affect the wearer's stride. Bundles of fabric collect around the lower legs, causing bulk and restrictive movement. This precarious way of wearing jeans creates the foundation for the expression.

It is from rap and music video that followers are able to determine and validate their assumptions about their lifestyle decisions, including apparel expressions. Followers of hip-hop have created apparel expressions that are comparable to the utterances of hip-hop music. Hip-hop fashions reflect the energy and resonance of the urban experience while omitting illusory signs that demonstrate the metamorphosis of the subaltern individual into street luminary.

Influence on Other Styles

"B-boy" and "Flyboy" were designations used to differentiate those focused on music and dance, and those who were focused on fashion. B-boys and B-girls were the former, and Flyboys and Flygirls the latter. B-boys have derived their designation from break-dancing. Break dancers dressed in sportswear like Puma sneakers, Adidas track pants, T-shirts, and padded nylon or leather jackets. They specialized in making poetic, gravity-defying acrobatic and explosive body-popping movements to the accompaniment of the interrupted, repeated, and overlaid phrasing of break-beat recordings.

The subtrends that followed break-dancing became the forerunners to rap-influenced fashion. For example, there are direct correlations to the fashion associated with hardcore rap, gangsta rap, and Afrocentric/cultural rap.

The B-boy expression has successfully crossed the subcultural divide. Skate boarders, who are predominantly white, also embraced much of the B-boy expression and have adapted it for their lifestyles. The Daisy Agers were exemplified by rappers De La Soul, who drew

Rap star Lil' Kim wearing Chanel clothing and hat. With hip-hop fashion a booming industry, many manufacturers are attempting to cash in, often using hip-hop personalities as spokespeople. © PACE GREGORY/CORBIS. REPRODUCED BY PERMISSION.

The genesis of fashion hip-hop had been skillfully articulated by the B-boys of the 1970s who created a path for subsequent hip-hop groupings (Daisy Agers, New Jacks, Sportifs, Nationalist [neo-Panthers]), who all added their own unique expressions to the fashion. As unofficial designers, such groups breached and corrupted many of the extant propositions about fashion and provided the template that a new generation of hip-hop fashion wearers should have committed. Like hip-hop music, hip-hop fashion edits, samples, repeats, unites, and creates new fashions—sometimes from nonsense and sometimes from deep-felt sentiment that defines the bona fide experiences of hip-hop wearers. In many instances B-boys are found to have enthusiasm for mainstream fashion labels. A feature of hip-hop fashion expressions is a predilection for American, Italian, and English designer labels such as Tommy Hilfiger, Ralph Lauren, Gucci, and Burberry. For the B-boy, consumption of clothes is part of a rite of consumption and exhibition which reaffirms the formula, "I am = what I have and what I consume" (Fromm p. 36).

The overstated stylization of the B-boy is articulated in humorous, exaggerated, and outlandish clothes that are sometimes similar to an animated cartoon character. This visual aesthetic replaces and dispels any idea that alienation renders individuals invisible. The "standardized" version of hip-hop fashions has become locked into parody. During the 1980s, fashion labels became ensconced in hip-hop culture. The adoption of counterfeit Gucci and Fendi apparel and bona fide Nikes and Timberlands represented attempts to create fashion that has resonance beyond the context of hip-hop community.

During the 1980s, the Harlem store Dapper Dan became renowned for the idea of exalting "exotic" conspicuous fashion labels such as Fendi and Gucci. Much of the appeal to consumers was in the distillation of the logotypes of these high fashion brands on to *their* clothing and on to the streets of Harlem. Typically, fabric printed with the logotypes of these brands would be made into apparel that would not be found in the bona fide collections of Fendi or Gucci. Ultimately Dapper Dan was a postmodern project that included the development of hip-hop fashion.

Designers and Producers

In part, hip-hop fashion came about by default. Designers of active sportswear and sports shoes did not target the streets, nightclubs, or music videos as the primary location for their products. In particular, branded sportswear such as Adidas, Reebok, Nike, and British Knights had been appropriated by hip-hop and became precursors to the dedicated fashion sportswear hip-hop brands of Troop, Cross Colors, Mecca, Walker Wear, and Karl Kani. However, apparel companies have never surpassed the preeminence of the sportswear shoe brand. Nike and Adidas sneakers are indicators of hip-hop's distance from the mainstream; for many wearers the sneaker and the

on the Afrocentric characteristics demonstrated by various black consciousness movements since the 1960s. Neo-Panthers, Afrocentrics, Sportifs, and Gangstas represent developments that enjoyed widespread followings. Indeed these characterizations contain apparel objects that demonstrate complicity in virtually every diaspora expression since hip-hop defined itself during the early 1980s. Many of the fashion objects utilized by the 1980s B-boy were affirmations of the pre-1980s. Much of the gangsta expression borrowed from the 1970s pimp style, while the mid-1980s look of the archetypal B-boy fused a Black Panther aesthetic with a sportswear look flavored by Jamaican Rude *Bwoys*. B-boys and Flyboys have succeeded as a result of the intercultural exchange between "the cultural imperatives of African-American and Caribbean history and identity" (Rose p. 21).

During the mid-1980s and early 1990s, hip-hop fashion gathered importance as hip-hop music became successful around the world. As a consequence, B-boys are no longer black and working class.

Nike Swoosh were potent objects in the urban rite of passage. Nike Air Force 1s and Air Jordans became iconic and fetishistic. The Nike logotype has been worn as jewelry, cut into hair, and tattooed onto skin.

Hip-hop has created its own trends and consumption patterns, with cultural networks that mutate at an intimidating rate. Its collusion with mainstream fashion is well established. Many of the raps by major hip-hop stars exalt the importance of wearing Gucci, Prada, Versace, Tommy, Earl, Burberry, Timberland, Coogi, and Coach. Such raps are usually arrogant brags condoning one-upmanship such as Lil' Kim's request on her song "Drugs" on the album *Hardcore*, "Call us the Gabbana girls, we dangerous, bitches pay a fee just to hang with us" or "Yes indeed, flows first class and yours is coach like the bag, the Prada mama."

Motifs, fabrics, color, and the drama of wearing apparel dramatically altered during 1998 when hip-hop leaders began to recognize the mainstream fashion quartet of Versace, Prada, Dolce & Gabbana, and Gucci as the ultimate in fashion expression. The materialist focus set by the hip-hop gangstas, players, and hip-hop celebrities populated the idea of "ghetto fabulousness" (the juxtaposition of "fabulously" expensive objects placed in the context of the impoverished ghetto) as a replacement for hip-hop fashions that did not rely upon endorsements of glamorous and expensive mainstream fashion brands.

Such new inflections prompted another revision of hip-hop fashion. Although branded performance sportswear was initially popular in hip-hop culture, its displacement was prompted when Lil' Kim—among other hip-hop stars—used important designer labels to create an image of privilege and status. Ordinary hip-hop fans and fashion companies alike understood this idea. The raps of Lil' Kim and other rappers have injected retail, advertising, and promotion strategies of fashion companies with a new thematic source and a previously unexploited marketplace. Hip-hop fashion represents a subversive discourse; fashion companies recognize this standpoint as being favorable if they wish to affect values and attitudes that are urban and therefore cool. However, some companies fail in this ambition and have all suffered from "myths" about consumers that are "incompatible" with the companies branding.

In their attempts to achieve postmodern relevance, fashion companies such as Asprey, Puma, Versace, and Iceberg have used the formal recommendation offered in strategies of cross-marketing. This can range from a celebrity appearing in an advertising campaign or just sitting in the front row of a designer's runway show.

To counter this, a number of hip-hop music moguls—Russell Simmons, P. Diddy, and Master P—have all have owned apparel companies. Their companies produce creative fashion collections that are synchronized with the musical output of their recording enterprises. These companies separate into those that follow an ac-

curate rendition of hip-hop fashion and those companies that seek to cross over and produce designs that have broad mass fashion appeal rather than a specialist hip-hop appeal.

In attempting to model the direction and content of hip-hop fashion, hip-hop's moguls have disregarded the life experiences, economic means, and self-creative tendencies of hip-hop followers in favor of a personal ideology.

How Hip-hop Crosses Boundaries
In the early 1990s, a group of Brooklyn hip-hop followers began to reuse Ralph Lauren garment labels, and to sew them on apparel not made by Ralph Lauren. The action of the Lo-lifer subculture was to challenge the commercially aggressive opposition of Ralph Lauren and to counteract the "antagonism" of the fashion label. The deconstruction of the fashion company's well-maintained branded image creates a reversal in hierarchy. When Ralph Lauren's Polo label is hand-painted onto a wall, or even a towel, as the Lo-lifers did, a question is asked about commercial branding and the mythological representation of the fashion logotype.

A characteristic of hip-hop fashion is the multiple themes that are filtered through the aspirations of wearers and designers alike. The American mainstream designer Tommy Hilfiger has successfully captured an understanding of hip-hop culture and has produced very specific fashion items, which fit the market place without being apologetic.

During the mid-1990s, new cuts of Hilfiger's jeans were given titles such as "Uptown," which refer to the geographical placements of Harlem and the Bronx, two New York districts with large African American populations. The Uptown cut of the jeans are ostensibly the same as extra-baggy, low-slung jeans manufactured by any other hip-hop designer or popular mainstream manufacturer addressing the hip-hop marketplace; however, the degree of hip-hop enthusiasm for Hilfiger made the brand very popular.

Hip-hop fashion is regarded as a delineator of "cool." Indeed aspects of hip-hop have become the characterization of dissonance; that is why British royal princes William and Harry were happy to adopt homeboy gestures while wearing baseball caps. Probably having never met a real live B-boy, cool gesturing postures are no doubt gleaned from music videos.

In one of the most informative studies of the cool expression, Majors and Billson suggest that cool adds value to the disenfranchisement of the individual. Its practice is constructed through attitude and implies status for the wearer through an attributed importance of fashion objects. The phenomenon of cool emerges as the compelling ingredient to hip-hop life; it is effected by the attachments of self. Cool, or to use other evocations, "fly" or—in Britain—"styling it out" is a creative procedure of stealth serving as a badge of belonging, though it allows wearers the scope to make minor adjustments to their apparel configuration.

See also **Hilfiger, Tommy; Lauren, Ralph; Music and Fashion.**

BIBLIOGRAPHY

Fricke, Jim, and Ahearn Charlie. *Yes, Yes, Y'all: The Experience Music Project Oral History of Hip-Hop's First Decade.* Cambridge, Mass., Da Capo Press, 2002.

Fromm, Erich. *To Have or to Be?* New York: HarperCollins Publishers, Inc., 1976.

Lil' Kim. "Drugs." *Hardcore.* (Sound recording.) New York: Undeas/Big Beat, 1996.

Lusane, Clarence. "Rap, Race and Politics." *Race and Class: A Journal for Black and Third World Liberation* 35, no. 1 (July–September 1993): 41–56.

Majors, Richard, and Janet Mancini Billson. *Cool Pose: The Dilemmas of Black Manhood in America.* New York: Touchstone Books, 1993.

Perkins, William Eric, ed. *Droppin' Science: Critical Essays on Rap Music and Hip Hop Culture.* Philadelphia: Temple University Press, 1995.

Rose, Tricia. *Black Noise: Rap Music and Black Culture in Contemporary America.* Middletown, Conn.: Wesleyan University Press, 1994.

Van Dyk Lewis

HIPPIE STYLE In the mid-1960s, the hippies—the rebels and dropouts of the Haight-Ashbury community of San Francisco—generated one of the most influential of history's dress reform movements. Their style was so outrageous and anomalous that it alone could have made the hippie movement impossible to ignore. As did their lifestyles, their fashion built upon San Francisco and California's tradition of iconoclasm; important, too, was the precedent provided by the young ready-to-wear designers of London, whose international impact began in the late 1950s.

The hippies' protest against capitalist society informed their impunity to all received strictures or etiquettes about clothes. They coordinated garments so that harmonies and homogeneity were fractured. Mad, anarchic mélanges resulted. They simulated acid phantasmagoria in their color schemes and paraded recycled old clothes, proclaiming them not as cast-off rags but proudly worn pedigree. They disguised and revealed themselves in costumes that were avatars of theatrical or historical or mythological identities, rather than the easily legible roles recognized by contemporary society. Their clothes were a paean to sexuality and sensuality: texture and tactility were foregrounded in their favorite fabrics, which ranged from slinky satin and stretch to all variety of embroidered and figured surfaces. Sometimes their fashion became not a second skin, but the exposure of their own nude bodies, painted and pat-

terned in tribal fashion; this was a celebration of instinctual expression that they believed had been obliterated by industrialization.

Ecological Fashion
The hippies built on the generic silhouettes that prevailed during the 1960s—the miniskirt, the pantsuit—but they transmogrified Mod fashion at the decade's midpoint by the way they put their clothes together, by their choices of fabric, and by the way they accessorized. Folkloric motifs, style, and fabrics were ubiquitous in hippie fashion. Their adoption of long peasant skirts helped move fashion back to longer hemlines. The generally loose and unconstructed silhouette of the 1960s became even more flowing with the adoption of mideastern tent shapes. The hippies' infatuation with the ensembles of Native Americans demonstrated solidarity with their plight as well as well an aesthetic appreciation.

Another prong of hippie fashion likewise proclaimed common cause with the workers of the world: this was the utilitarian fare that came to be known as "anti-fashion." It was fashion at its least overly decorative, most rugged, and basic: blue jeans worn with T-shirts, work shirts, and other commonplace attire. Decorative appeal was provided instead by the contours outlined by these body-clinging garments. Thus the youthful counterculture promulgated an allure that could not be achieved by expenditure alone.

The hippies generated an ecological consciousness of fashion by their recycling of vintage clothes as well as their cannibalizing of old fabrics and hangings, out of which they cut new garments. They drew attention to the way that all clothes costume the wearer into roles, some—businessman, housewife—so integrated into the warp of society that they were no longer recognized as constructed characterization. Their pacific appropriation of military uniform likewise showed a determination to mock and denature the pieties vented by the opposite side of the ideological divide.

Los Angeles, New York, and London also became important citadels for hippie fashion. On Los Angeles's Sunset Boulevard and in New York's Greenwich Village were clustered constellations of independent boutiques. London's contribution to hippie fashion was indebted to the art and crafts movement of a century earlier. More than San Francisco, the city's secondhand clothes stores and bazaars were more likely to be filled with heirloom couture. London raided its storage vaults, disgorging into the city's auction house fabulous caches of vintage clothing as well as theatrical and ballet costumes.

The Rich Hippies
"We got pretty scathing about store-bought hip that didn't come from the soul," said Linda Gravenites (interview with the author, November 1986), who made clothes for many residents in the Haight-Ashbury com-

munity and the rock bands based there. Nevertheless the purists or the ideologues were powerless to stop the inevitable co-opting, the proliferation of hippie fashion within the mainstream fashion industry. From 1967 to 1971, the hippie's fashion was grist for the couture and upscale ready-to-wear mills. The "rich hippie" look upgraded hippie style into fabrics that were largely well beyond the economic reaches of the financially marginal denizens of Haight-Ashbury.

The fashion of the hippies was as much threat as influence to the fashion establishment. The hippie's open-ended pluralism threw down the gauntlet to the seasonable revisions proffered to women by the mainstream fashion industry. Savoring vintage garments established a continuum between past and present, a rejoinder to the forced amnesia of customers told that each year marked a tabula rasa of consumption.

Perhaps what above all made hippie fashion so subversive to the mainstream industry was its tacit message that the time had come to abolish the fashion designer. It resonated as well with the burgeoning women's liberation movement: women would no longer be told what to wear by a designer, who was usually male. After Rudi Gernreich decided to close his ready-to-wear business in 1968, he told reporters that he was now disenchanted by clothes that bore the imprint of the individual designer. The very act of designing, in fact, seemed to him to be an a priori dictate that no longer fit the needs and aspirations of the clothes-wearing public.

With every question of identity in Western civilization of the late 1960s being debated, fashion exploded with costume and fantasy, thanks in large part to the inspiration provided by the hippies. "Today nothing is out, because everything is in," Marshall McLuhan wrote in 1968. "Every costume from every era is now available to everyone." (*Harper's Bazaar*, April 1968, p. 164)

Hippie fashion continued to steep throughout fashion during the 1970s. Even as fashion retreated from the utopian threshold advanced during the late 1960s, the hippies' ideas were disseminated to many more people than they had been during the 1960s. By the end of the decade, it seemed to have become exhausted. But since the mid-1980s, hippie style has enthralled designers and the public again and again, becoming a recurrent influence in every echelon of fashion.

See also **Music and Fashion; Politics and Fashion; Social Class and Clothing.**

BIBLIOGRAPHY

Lobenthal, Joel. *Radical Rags: Fashions of the Sixties.* New York: Abbeville Press, 1990.

Reich, Charles A. *The Greening of America: How the Youth Revolution Is Trying to Make America Livable.* New York: Random House, 1970.

Joel Lobenthal

HISTORICISM AND HISTORICAL REVIVAL

Prior to the rise of the bourgeoisie, historical revivals in dress were the preserve of the aristocratic classes, principally employed as costume either for masquerade and pageantry, portraiture or professional function (courtly and legal uniform), and always as a distinguishing mark of timelessness and status—of both power and beauty.

From the sixteenth to eighteenth centuries, fashions in the choice of historical focus were mainly informed by divisions between town (the urban powerful) and country (the Arcadian idyllic), and received ideas of morality and immorality. The meaning and embodiment of the latter coupling shifted most frequently—morality at some stages implied by Anglo-Saxon mythologies of status and structure. The body coverings most frequently represented by fashions were crinolines, hoops, bustles, and corsetry for women, and armor and padded upper bodies for men. In turn, however, the looser costume of Greco-Roman mythology and the reverence for the ideal physique, and the beauty of nature that they represented, were also held up as archetypes of morality in different periods—although they were usually quite swiftly decried for their immorality in openly revealing the female body. As with all the revivals to follow, these trends were rarely based on historical accuracy, relying primarily on a nostalgic imagination and secondhand source material.

Gothic

The original fifteenth-century Gothic dress for women combined thirteenth-century ideals of fitness for purpose and an ecclesiastical sensibility (headdresses in particular bore direct reference to the wimple) with beauty of line and sumptuous fabrics (velvets and brocades). Gothic revivalism was already taking place in the mid-seventeenth century (the Puritans drew on the religious overtones of the Gothic in the face of Royalist decadence), and was popularized again in the mid-eighteenth century as a decorative and architectural movement (Gothick), its leading proponents including Batty Langley (1696–1751) and Horace Walpole, whose Strawberry Hill project (1750–1770) came to epitomize the period. The eighteenth-century revival was a movement driven by romance, and one that stood against the perceived rigidity and rules of the classical style; the medieval appeared more natural, fantastical, and foreign compared to the worlds of Greece or Rome. In dress, its expression was principally neomedieval, somber in tone and concentrated on flat, embroidered pattern on sleeve and bodice panels. It was notoriously inaccurate and widely ridiculed until the 1830s when A.W. N. Pugin (1812–1852) proposed an accurate and faithful return to Gothic style as a nationalist, moral, and spiritual bulwark in the face of advancing industrialization. Pugin's work heavily influenced the Victorian aesthetic and later, the flat printed pattern of William Morris (1834–1896) and the Arts and Crafts movement. In the late twentieth century, the Gothic style returned again as an addendum to punk, drawing on but darkening the punk movement's oppositional stance and twisting the spiritual meaning of Gothic style to embody older, more mystical religions (such as Wicca, paganism, and Buddhism). But, as with previous Gothic revivals, 1980s' goths embraced the romanticism of the movement, combining the PVC and rubber of punk with the velvets and brocades of their eighteenth- and nineteenth-century predecessors.

Neoclassicism

The taste for what became known as neoclassical style has its roots in the 1750s, emerging in opposition to the exoticism and opulence of the rococo (promoted by the launch of the Dilettanti Society in 1734 and the Society of Arts in 1754). Much of the literature (Rousseau) and painting (Gainsborough, Reynolds, and Hogarth) in the decades leading up to the neoclassical movement was directed toward proposing a romanticized classicism as a moral tendency linking the purity of nature with purity of spirit. It was possible for both the neoclassical and the Gothic to exist in much the same space, due both to the opening up of society to fashion and to the shared beliefs of each movement.

The movement achieved prominence in the 1780s and is most closely associated with Thomas Hope (1769–1831), whose *Costumes of the Ancients* (1809) and *Designs of Modern Costumes* (1812) were pivotal to popularizing the looser, unstructured Greco-Roman dress styles. Dresses were made principally from muslin with waistlines rising to the bust, which was still firmly secured by stays and highlighted by a sash and knotted scarf. The effect was naïve and childlike, best expressed in the popular 1880s' illustrations of Kate Greenaway. In keeping with antique statuary and notions of the ideal physique for men, tightly fitting breeches and cutaway jackets revealed more of the body.

Hope was also an exoticist and hosted Turkish-inspired parties at his home, similar to those favored by the Parisian designer Paul Poiret (1879–1944) in the early twentieth century. Poiret and two other designers of the period, Madeleine Vionnet (1876–1975) and Mariano Fortuny (1871–1949), were the principle players in the revival of the neoclassical in the 1920s and 1930s (also known as vogue regency).

The Aesthetic Movement

As with neoclassicism, the aesthetic movement studied and celebrated beauty. The movement took hold in the United Kingdom in the 1870s. Its proponents in the decorative arts (William Morris), literature (Walter Pater, Charles Baudelaire, Oscar Wilde), and fine arts (James McNeill Whistler, Aubrey Beardsley, and the Pre-Raphaelite painters) proposed elegance in everything. Nature (flora, fauna, and the athletic human body) was eulogized in all its glory as the epitome of beauty, a manifestation of God on Earth. What separated Gothic and aesthetic was the latter's belief of "art for art's sake" as

shifts in understanding over the nature of morality gave rise to an intense dispute between the Philistines (art as a medium for social and moral purpose) and aesthetics (art as beauty and truth) that raged throughout the 1860s and 1870s.

The proponents of grace, athleticism, and activity for women had to wait for the Rational Dress Society, launched in 1881, to put forward their case. The Healthy and Artistic Dress Union swiftly followed it in 1889 pronouncing Victorian restraint unhygienic and spiritually detrimental. Women's clothing became looser, more opulent in texture and heavily influenced by medieval styling, folklore, fairytale, and Arthurian legend. The figure of woman as represented in painting was most commonly sleeping—a state of innocence and purity that also implied the awakening, or liberation (sartorial and sexual), into womanhood that was to follow in the fin de siècle era of decadence. The legacy of the aesthetic movement is most clearly seen in the artistic circles of the Bloomsbury Set in the early twentieth century and the hippie movement of the 1960s.

Neo-Edwardianism

The Teddy boy (derived from the nickname of Edward VII) grew out of a sensibility fostered in post–World War II Britain that the shared hardships of war and rationing would result in a more egalitarian society (Polhemus, p. 34). The expectations of the young working class were manifested in the reworking of a neo-Edwardian style that had been pioneered by London's Savile Row tailors for their upper-class clients—single-breasted, long, and fitted jackets with velvet collars were worn with drainpipe trousers and brocaded waistcoats. Young men from the East End paired similar clothing with a cowboy's tie and the extravagant sentiments of American East Coast, black Zoot style. The adoption of these specific signifiers served to ally Britain's working classes simultaneously with the American Dream, and the outsiders who challenged it. In doing so, the Teds presented a challenge to establishment British society, particularly by subverting aristocratic dress codes, and this subcultural style served as blueprint for all the street style that followed in the latter half of the twentieth century.

Retro

The fashion for retro styling had often left the industry open to accusations of moribund nostalgia. Both at street level—the Teds by the Edwardians, the mods by the Italians, glam-rock by the aesthetics, the casuals by the mods, the goths by the punks—and at the level of high design, the speed and influence of revivalism has increased incrementally over the last forty years, to the point that even futurism is retro. But critics ignore the importance of sociopolitical and cultural context in the process of selection. This is particularly apparent in high design. Walter Benjamin, in *Theses on the Philosophy of History*, speaks of the creative "tiger's leap" into the past, the aggressive and specific selection of historical reference to serve contemporary comment. Historical revivalism is most often used as a tool to create a pervasive, and recognizable, environment for fashion that responds very pertinently to the times in which it is created. Arguably, there is nothing new to create, only creative ways of reinterpreting the past. As the designer John Galliano points out, "What's modern? . . . Gucci? Or Prada? That's just their interpretation of modern but it's still an historical take. . . . I think reinterpreting things with today's influences, today's fabric technology is what it's all about" (Frankel, p. 176).

See also **Aesthetic Dress; Goths; Retro Style.**

BIBLIOGRAPHY
Burman Baines, Barbara. *Fashion Revivalism: From the Elizabethan Age to the Present Day.* London: B. T. Batsford, Ltd., 1981.
Frankel, Susannah. *Visionaries: Interviews with Fashion Designers.* London: V and A Publications, 2001.
Lambourne, Lionel. *The Aesthetic Movement.* London: Phaidon Press Ltd., 1996.
Polhemus, Ted. *Fashion and Anti-Fashion: An Anthropology of Clothing and Adornment.* London: Thames and Hudson, Inc., 1978.

Internet Resource
Benjamin, Walter. "Theses on the Concept of History." Available from <http://www.tasc.ac.uk/depart/media/staff/ls/WBenjamim/CONCEPT2.html>.

Alice Cicolini

HOLLYWOOD STYLE

In 1974, Diana Vreeland organized an exhibition at the Metropolitan Museum of Art, devoted to studio designs. The exhibition's title, *Romantic and Glamorous: Hollywood Style*, sums up perfectly the way in which traditional "Hollywood style" is perceived. It is seen as synonymous with glamour and opulence. Vreeland emphasized this in the exhibition's catalog: "Everything was larger than life. The diamonds were bigger, the furs were thicker and more luxurious . . . silks, satins, velvets and chiffons, miles and miles of ostrich feathers . . . everything was an exaggeration" (p. 5).

Certainly this is true of archetypal "Hollywood style." But, arguably, there is another important factor—the way in which cinema can be used to sell most products and, in particular, to disseminate new fashions. As Charles Eckert argues, Hollywood gave consumerism its "distinctive bent"—it influenced the way men and women wanted to look, as well as the cars they chose to drive, and the cigarettes they decided to smoke. Gradually, this influence became globalized.

This potential power was not immediately perceived. However, as early as 1907 there was widespread public interest in the rumored disappearance of Florence Lawrence, the "Biograph Girl." A desire to know about the private lives and off-screen activities of the first identifiable stars was apparent at an early stage.

With the identification and growing popularity of stars such as Mary Pickford, Gloria Swanson, and Irene Castle before, during, and after World War I, women began to see the star "image" as something to emulate. During the radical sartorial changes that took place in the 1920s, Hollywood was a vital part of the process through which it became both desirable and socially acceptable for women to wear makeup, after a century of taboo. The carbon lighting of early films meant makeup was a necessity—pink cheeks became gray and skin bleached. Max Factor, a makeup artist for the Moscow State Theatre, arrived in Los Angeles in 1908, and by 1914 he had perfected a product called Supreme Greasepaint for all the studios, along with newly developed eye shadows and pencil liners. This product was packaged in a compact tube and manufactured in several colors, and in a very short time he was selling directly to the public, for it was the faces of the stars that had the most impact on the public at this early stage.

Clara Bow was the first star that women set out to imitate, copying her "Cupid's bow" mouth and penciled brows. Furthermore, her bobbed hair made the new cuts desirable. Bow portrayed the sort of girl who, although unusually pretty, was not too far removed from the world of her female fans.

This kind of popularity with a female fan base meant that a star could popularize not one, but several fashions. Just as in the next decade Garbo would make berets, trench coats, and men's pajamas simultaneously desirable, so Clara Bow persuaded women to shorten their skirts, bare their legs, and adopt the cloche hat, which had been in fashion for some time. And in 1928 Jean Harlow, the "Platinum Blonde," prompted many women to experiment with peroxide; hence, safe home hair dyes were swiftly produced. Harlow also made a Paris fashion popular—the backless, bias-cut dress she wore in *Dinner at Eight* (1933) was instantly copied.

Retailing Tie-ins

Hollywood studios were beginning to appreciate their power. The studio system, which lasted until the 1950s, meant that stars and costume designers were under contract to a particular studio, which could profit from their work. The studios owned distribution rights in cinemas across America, and it was easy to export Hollywood films, first to Europe and later worldwide, despite the existence of national cinemas elsewhere. In the early 2000s, despite the vast size of the Hindi film industry, American cinema was still dominant.

The fashion industry had been swift to recognize the commercial possibilities of the cinema—in 1923 Salvatore Ferragamo, founder of the firm, provided every single pair of sandals for *The Ten Commandments*. Couture designers became involved—Paul Poiret designed the clothes worn by Sarah Bernhardt in *Elizabeth I* (1912) and Sam Goldwyn lured Chanel to Hollywood. Meanwhile, the studios, becoming aware of the appeal of the costumes designed by Adrian and his peers, worked speedily to prevent unauthorized copying and to maximize profit.

In 1930 the Movie Merchandising Bureau was established, and Macy's had a Cinema Shop. During the 1930s different studios would issue their own licenses, so that by the end of the decade there were various different retail outlets within department stores across America. This was the age of the "tie-in," when promotional campaigns linked to particular films were highly successful—window displays featured not only clothes and accessories from a particular film but also other themed goods. *Queen Christina* (1933), for example, was used to promote "hostess gowns" and Swedish flatware.

The fan magazines were at the height of their popularity—and discussions raged in their pages. Dorothy Lamour conducted a dialogue with her fans as to whether or not she should make another "sarong" film. In fact, she would always be associated with this garment, designed for her by Edith Head—and now a wardrobe staple. At the same time, glossy magazines were debating the question of whether Hollywood could lead fashion, or merely follow Paris.

Gone with the Wind (1939) influenced bridal wear for decades—and it was suggested that Dior had the popularity of the film's costumes in mind when he created the New Look. The decade had also made lingerie an enormously profitable business through the slips, negligees, and marabou slippers seen on screen.

The Postwar Period
The influence of Hollywood did not end in 1939—and included body shape. The busty stars of the 1950s meant enormous profits for the underwear industry, and Marilyn Monroe was arguably the most influential star of all time, as women sought the different components of her "look."

With the emulation of Marlon Brando and James Dean in the 1950s, and the gym culture, which resulted from the sight of well-muscled male bodies in the action pictures popular from the 1980s onward, it seems that men in the postwar period have been more influenced by Hollywood than ever before. Men's wear designers responded quickly, and continue to remain heavily involved. Ralph Lauren's designs for Robert Redford in *The Great Gatsby* (1974) were not as heavily covered in the press as his women's wear for Diane Keaton in *Annie Hall* (1977). However, it had been clearly demonstrated that a mainstream Hollywood film could be used to showcase clothes not unlike those in the designer's current ready-to-wear range, and Armani was the first to manipulate this opportunity by dressing Richard Gere for *American Gigolo* (1980); Cerruti followed his lead by dressing

Michael Douglas for a number of influential films in the 1980s, including *Wall Street* (1988). Much of what we wear is a legacy of Hollywood—trousers for women, tennis shoes for everyday, leather jackets, jeans, and T-shirts. Yet some designers were never convinced—Elsa Schiaparelli complained that Joan Crawford's shoulder pads were copied from her collections and that Adrian had simply stolen the concept. Vivienne Westwood's one foray into cinema—she designed the collection supposedly produced by Richard E. Grant in the box-office debacle *Prêt-à-Porter* (1995)—has obviously made some other designers wary of involvement. But attempts to use film as a way of presenting new ideas continue; Uma Thurman's yellow trainers for *Kill Bill* (2003) did not impress audiences, but Samuel L. Jackson's Kangol beret in the same hue, worn in *Jackie Brown* (1997) meant that their already buoyant sales figures virtually doubled.

See also **Actors and Actresses, Impact on Fashion; Film and Fashion.**

BIBLIOGRAPHY
Bruzzi, Stella. *Undressing Cinema: Clothing and Identity in the Movies.* London: Routledge, 1997.

Eckert, Charles. "The Carole Lombard in Macy's Window." In *Fabrications: Costume and the Female Body.* Edited by Jane Gaines and Charlotte Herzog. London: Routledge, 1990.

Fox, Patty. *Star Style: Hollywood Legends as Fashion Icons.* Santa Monica: Calif.: Angel City Press, 1999.

Maeder, Edward. "Hollywood and Seventh Avenue." In his *Hollywood and History: Costume Design in Film.* Los Angeles: Thames and Hudson, Inc., 1987.

Pamela Church Gibson

HOMESPUN The word "homespun" connotes both a rough fabric worn by country people and the human qualities, good or bad, associated with it. In English literature, "homespun" can mean boorish behavior or wholesome simplicity. In Shakespeare's *Midsummer Night's Dream*, for example, Puck dismisses the comic bumpkins Bottom and Snout as "hempen homespun." Writing a century later, John Dryden contrasted "harlot-hunting" foreigners with an "honest homespun countrey Clown" of English make. In the eighteenth century, political writers on both sides of the Atlantic adopted the personae of a wise but plainspoken countryman or -woman, signing themselves "Dorothy Distaff" or "Horatio Homespun." In the nineteenth-century United States, poets, novelists, and preachers celebrated an idealized "age of homespun" that symbolized the virtues of self-sufficiency and egalitarian simplicity.

Because "homespun" had such a powerful literary existence, it is sometimes difficult to define its actual use in times past. Commercial production of cloth was well developed on the European continent and in Great Britain by the seventeenth century. Before industrialization, the opposite of homespun was not factory spun but market spun. Most spinners did, in fact, spin in their own or their masters' homes, but merchant clothiers managed the steps in production. Spinning, weaving, and finishing sometimes took place in different regions or even in different countries, sometimes mixing wool from different colored sheep to produce the rough hodden, russet, or country gray that poets praised, but that fewer and fewer people actually wore.

In the earliest years of settlement, North American colonists had little incentive to spin. It made more sense to devote energy to developing crops for export. But as farms and plantations developed and as the population grew, more families began to raise sheep and sow flax for their own use. By the middle of the eighteenth century, in New England and in the Chesapeake, women took up weaving, an occupation that had belonged to men in commercial textile-producing areas of Europe. In Pennsylvania, high immigration from England, Scotland, and Germany kept looms in male hands. Rural families used locally made fabrics for towels, sheets, grain bags, everyday petticoats, work shirts, and aprons, but they were never self-sufficient. English woolens and Indian calico were prized for outer clothing, and in the plantation South, most slave clothing was still made from cheap imported linens like osnaburgs or from coarse Welsh woolens.

Homespun took on political connotations in the years leading up to the American Revolution. A writer in the 16 October 1769 *Boston Gazette* claimed that if "Hellen wrought the Fate of ancient Troy," then New England's daughters, through household industry, could "make us Blest and Free." As political leaders urged boycotts of British goods, New England women gathered in "spinning meetings" and southern planters like George Washington improved sheep herds and diverted some slave labor to spinning. Although true self-sufficiency was never a realistic possibility, the boycotts did for a time put pressure on Parliament.

Before a second war with England in 1812, a Rhode Island poet, nostalgic for revolutionary days, lamented in the 1 December 1810 (Providence) *Columbian Phoenix*:

There was a time—Columbia's gothic days—
When maidens spun their wedding gowns and linen:
But no, so tasty, so refin'd our ways—A homespun
   gown no wench will stick a pin in.
The veriest dowdy now is too genteel,
To waste a moment at the whirling wheel.

The poet was wrong in thinking American women had ever spun their "wedding gowns," though many women continued to spin a great deal of household linen, and newspapers once again reported patriotic spinning bees during this war.

The federal census of 1810 counted spinning wheels and yards of cloth as well as people. On average, Americans were making ten yards of cloth per capita, though the state averages ranged from twenty-eight yards in New Hampshire to five in Maryland and Delaware. The early

Homespun gown. As the United States developed, and as its population grew, more and more families began to raise sheep and sow flax for their own use. In this sense, the term *homespun* often conjures images of wholesome simplicity and self-sufficiency. IRMA BOWEN TEXTILE COLLECTION, UNIVERSITY MUSEUM, UNVERSITY OF NEW HAMPSHIRE. REPRODUCED BY PERMISSION.

stages of industrialization actually stimulated household production. When water-powered carding mills assisted in the tedious task of preparing wool for spinning, housewives increased their output of spun yarn. They also learned to mix factory-spun cotton thread with homespun flax or wool. In much of the United States, though, household production declined rapidly after 1830. It persisted, however, in isolated pockets of the Northeast and South, in newly settled areas of the West, and in eastern Canada, where it was still an important part of the agricultural economy in 1870.

In the southern United States, homespun also had a brief revival during the Civil War. Again poets and politicians linked patriotism with female industry, as in the popular song "The Homespun Girl."

The homespun dress is plain, I know,
My hat's palmetto, too;
But then it shows what Southern girls
For Southern rights will do.

Again, the mystique of homespun was probably more powerful than the reality. Women who already knew how to spin took their wheels out of the attic, but families with no prior experience found it difficult to take up cloth making. Furthermore, many white women refused to wear homemade fabric because it seemed too much like the rough "negro cloth" worn by slaves.

The United States was not the only place where homespun acquired political meaning. When Mohandas Gandhi returned to India from South Africa in 1914, he wore an approximation of peasant clothing. Soon he was preaching the gospel of *swadeshi*, or self-sufficiency, urging Indians to burn imported fabrics and adopt simple clothing made from *khadi*, or homespun. Ironically, there were so few peasants who still spun by hand that he had to search out those who could revive the dying craft, and because *khadi* was so much more expensive than industrially produced fabrics, it was difficult to persuade people to use it. Gandhi's promotion of *khadi* had two objectives—to assert India's economic independence and to unify the nation by establishing a national dress common to all classes. Gandhi wore a simple loincloth to demonstrate his solidarity with poor peasants who could not afford more elaborate clothing. Although few of his followers went to that extreme, the *khadi* cap he designed did become an emblem of national unity.

See also **Europe and America: History of Dress (400–1900 C.E.); Fashion and Identity; Handwoven Textiles; Politics and Fashion; Spinning.**

BIBLIOGRAPHY

Baumgarten, Linda. *What Clothes Reveal: The Language of Clothing in Colonial and Federal America.* New Haven, Conn., and London: Yale University Press, 2002.

Faust, Drew Gilpin. *Mothers of Invention: Women of the Slaveholding South in the American Civil War.* Chapel Hill and London: University of North Carolina Press, 1996.

Inwood, Kris, and Phyllis Wagg. "The Survival of Handloom Weaving in Rural Canada, circa 1870." *Journal of Economic History* 53 (2) (1993): 346–358.

Tarlo, Emma. *Clothing Matters: Dress and Identity in India.* London: Hurst and Company, 1996.

Ulrich, Laurel Thatcher. *The Age of Homespun: Objects and Stories in the Creation of An American Myth.* New York: Alfred A. Knopf, 2001.

Laurel Thatcher Ulrich

HOOP SKIRT. *See* **Crinoline.**

HORST, HORST P. Horst Paul Albert Bohrmann (1906–1999) was one of the most creative and prolific fashion photographers of the twentieth century. (He took the name of Horst P. Horst during World War II and was known professionally simply as Horst.) From the beginning of his career in 1931 until 1992, when failing eyesight forced him to abandon his work, his photographs graced the pages of American, French, British, German, Spanish, and Italian editions of *Vogue, Vanity Fair, House and Garden*, and a host of photography magazines, books, and catalogs. Horst came to prominence in the 1930s, by which time the power unique to the medium of photography was dramatically apparent to promoters of fashion. He is appreciated in the twenty-first century not only for the spare elegance and refined glamour of his fashion work, which produced icons of the genre, but also for his myriad portraits, male and female nudes, flower studies, and pictures of homes and gardens.

Early Life and Training

Horst Bohrmann was born in Weissenfels-an-der-Saale, Thuringia, in 1906, the second son of prosperous, middle-class, Protestant parents. The family suffered financial hardships as a result of World War I but eventually recovered in the 1920s, enabling Horst to attend the Hamburg School of Applied Art, where he studied furniture making and carpentry. Exposure to Bauhaus principles and personalities led him to seek an apprenticeship in Paris with Le Corbusier. However, Horst was disappointed both with the projects and the great architect himself and soon quit. Wandering about Paris in search of something more vital, he encountered the fashion photographer George Hoyningen-Huene, by then well-established at Condé Nast. Soon Horst was a familiar figure at the studio, helping his older friend arrange sets and lighting, as well as serving as a male model for some of Huene's most striking swimwear images, and even starring in a short film with Natasha Paley (now sadly lost).

First Photographic Assignments

In the spring of 1931 Horst was given a sudden chance to try his own hand at the métier. Dr. Mehemed Agha, American *Vogue*'s celebrated art director, was then visiting Paris and thought Horst might have the required talents. Horst passed his initial tests, which required still lifes of accessories and jewelry, with flying colors, these first photographs being published in the November and December issues of *Vogue*. An invitation to work from American *Vogue* soon followed, but the engagement was short-lived: he was sent back to Europe for insubordination. When Hoyningen-Huene later left Paris for an assignment for *Vanity Fair* in Hollywood, Horst shouldered his work, and when his friend and mentor left *Vogue* for good in 1935, it was Horst who inherited the mantle as photographer-in-chief. Almost immediately, Condé Nast recalled him to New York, though he was allowed to continue to photograph the Paris collections each season. By 1937 he was firmly established in New York.

In 1942 Horst volunteered to serve in the United States Army, and despite being initially classed as an enemy alien, he was called up in July 1943 as a photographer. His assignments, however, remained on American

Horst P. Horst. One of the most prolific and inventive fashion photographers of the twentieth century, Horst P. Horst first came to prominence in the 1930s. During a sixty-year career in photography, his photographs appeared in numerous magazines, including *Vanity Fair* and *Vogue*. COURTESY OF FAHEY/KLEIN GALLERY, LOS ANGELES, @ WWW.FAHEYKLEINGALLERY.COM. REPRODUCED BY PERMISSION.

soil. At war's end he was invited to the White House for a portrait commission of President Truman.

Postwar Life and Work

The postwar decades were filled with fashion and portrait assignments on both sides of the Atlantic, as well as trips to Mexico, Syria, Iran, and the new state of Israel. Moreover, he moved in the same circles as luminaries such as the film director Luchino Visconti, the artist Leonor Fini, Coco Chanel, Salvador Dali, Marlene Dietrich, Gertrude Stein, President and Mrs. Eisenhower, Gore Vidal, Yves St. Laurent, and Jacqueline Bouvier. He became close friends with a number of these people.

In 1952 Horst began to fall out of favor at *Vogue*, whose new editor, Jessica Davies, imposed rigid rules on the photographers. His fortunes were restored in 1962, however, when the much more supportive Diana Vreeland arrived to head the magazine. In 1971, on the latter's departure from *Vogue*, Horst gravitated to *House and Garden*, where he had occasionally worked beginning in

1947. He returned to Europe for an extensive cruise-wear assignment with French *Vogue*, which led to renewed work for the magazine.

Notable Exhibitions and Publications

From the early 1930s Horst exhibited both his professional and personal work, at first in European galleries, then more gradually in museums, most of which were hesitant to accept fashion photography as a legitimate domain of art. Significant group exhibitions include *Fashion 1900–1939* at the Victoria and Albert Museum, London, 1975; *Fashion Photography* and *Fleeting Gestures*, at the International Center of Photography, New York, in 1977 and 1984, respectively; *Lichtbildnisse: Das Porträt in der Fotografie*, at the Rheinisches Landesmuseum in Bonn in 1982; and *Das Akfoto*, at the Fotomuseum in Munich in 1985. Major gallery exhibitions were held at the Galerie la Plume d'Or, Paris, in 1932; at the Germain Seligman Gallery, New York, in 1938; at the Sonnabend Gallery, New York, in 1974 and 1980; at Hamilton's

Gallery, London, in 1986 and 1999; at the Staley-Wise Gallery, New York, in 1984; and at the Galerie Thierry, Paris, in 1999.

Horst's major retrospective of his fashion work was organized by the International Center of Photography, New York, in 1984; it then traveled to the Fortuny Palace, Venice, in 1985. A retrospective look at his fashion photography was held at the Musée des Arts de la Mode, the Louvre, Paris, in 1991. A major retrospective of his portraits was shown at the National Gallery, London, in 2001.

Horst's own books include *Photographs of a Decade*, 1944; *Patterns from Nature*, 1946; *Salute to the Thirties*, 1971; *Return Engagement: Faces to Remember—Then and Now* (with writer James Watters), 1984; and *Horst: Images of Elegance*, 1993.

Horst's Legacy

Most critics consider Horst's prewar fashion photographs, together with a select number of portraits from the same era, to be his finest work. His style, consistent across the various genres he explored, was characterized by a high degree of eclecticism. There are manifold references to art history, and he made liberal use of classical, baroque, and surrealist props and decor along with witty trompe l'oeil effects. Appreciative of historical precedents, he was as able to fabricate pictorial images in the style of Baron de Meyer as easily as he could cool modernist pictures in the style of Edward Steichen and Hoyningen-Huene. Horst's women subjects, in fashion studies or in portraits, project the power of their sex rather than the power of sex; they are bold, poised, and serene. Horst saw the body in architectonic terms, so that appendages of the body could be severed and reassembled to striking effect. Above all, he is known for his exquisite compositional sense, prompting an early admirer, Janet Flanner, to characterize his work as "a linear romance." His work influenced many younger photographers of fashion, portraiture, flowers, and the nude, including Robert Mapplethorpe, Bruce Weber, and Herb Ritts.

See also **Fashion Photography; Hoyningen-Huene, George; Vogue; Vreeland, Diana.**

BIBLIOGRAPHY

Deal, Joe. "Horst on Fashion Photography." *Image* 18 (September 1975): 1–11.

Ewing, William A. *The Photographic Art of Hoyningen-Huene.* New York: Rizzoli International, 1986.

Flood, Richard. "Horst." *Artforum* (October 1980): 81.

Hall-Duncan, Nancy. *The History of Fashion Photography.* New York: Alpine Book Company, 1979. This publication gives an overall context for Horst's contribution to fashion photography.

Horst, Horst P. *Photographs of a Decade.* New York: J. J. Augustin, 1944.

———. *Patterns from Nature.* New York: J. J. Augustin, 1946.

———. *Salute to the Thirties.* New York: Viking Press, 1971.

Lawford, Valentine. *Horst: His Work and His World.* New York: Alfred A. Knopf, 1984.

Liberman, Alexander. *The Art and Technique of Color Photography.* New York: Simon and Schuster, 1951.

Pepper, Terence. *Horst Portraits: 60 Years of Style.* New York: Harry N. Abrams, 2001. An exhibition catalog. This publication, accompanying the retrospective exhibition of Horst's photographs, *Horst Portraits: Sixty Years of Style*, includes a detailed chronology of Horst's life by Robin Muir.

Rose, Barbara. "Horst in Fashion." *Vogue*, May 1976, 175–176, 208.

William Ewing

HOSIERY, MEN'S The term "hosiery" in contemporary usage is generally defined as stockings or socks, more specifically as tight-fitting knit goods that cover men's feet and varying portions of the lower leg, or as knitted feet and leg coverings for women (such as pantyhose or tights). The related term "hose," while used synonymously, is even more specifically historically defined as a man's garment that fully covers the legs, like tights, and is tied to the doublet (a short, close-fitting jacket). The origin of the word "hose" is the Old English "hosa" or leg covering, or Middle English "hose" for stocking. A related German term, "hosen," is also often seen in historical use. In the history of Western dress, the term "hose" has been used to refer to a wide range of men's leg coverings, with or without a footed portion, from early centuries C.E. through the early nineteenth century. These include the Roman lower leg wrappings called *feminalia*, the early northern European footed or ankle-length woven trousers, and medieval criss-crossed leg wrappings sometimes referred to as *chausses*.

Early Development

Men's hosiery is a garment in which technology and fashion are interlinked in terms of both meeting demand for and inspiring changes in styles. From the Middle Ages through the early Renaissance, there are numerous images in art that portray the bagginess, sagging, and wrinkling of ill-fitting hose worn under tunics or *houppelandes*. As clothing construction technology such as tailoring improved to allow a closer fit over the body, men's legs and leg coverings became more prominent, and hose were the predominant lower body garment for men throughout the fifteenth and sixteenth centuries. For instance, fourteenth- and fifteenth-century Italian tailoring techniques created full-length parti-colored hose for men from woven fabrics cut in panels on the bias. They were sewn with curved seams to tightly fit the leg and lower torso. These techniques also allowed hose to get longer, and by the last quarter of the fourteenth century the two separate legs of hose reached the waist and were joined into one garment, similar to what we today call tights. They were seamed up the back and closed over the crotch with an overlapping panel or a codpiece. Various trends in color and patterning were seen in men's hose throughout each period of their predominance. Many fashionable hose in the seventeenth century were embroidered with gold and silver thread for a type of embellishment around the ankles called clocks or clocking. Early hose were sometimes constructed with leather soles on the foot that could be worn instead of shoes, and the fourteenth-century fashion for soled hose with long pointed toes is the best example of this.

Knitted Hosiery

Knitted socks were recovered from Egyptian burial excavations dating to the fourth or fifth century C.E., the same period that knitting was introduced to Europe. Hand knitting of socks was an important industry in medieval Europe and by the sixteenth century had advanced to a fine craft. Silk hose for those who could afford them were hand knitted in the round on needles as fine as wire with very fine silk threads. Well-fitted hose were an important fashion item for men of the gentry and nobility during the sixteenth and seventeenth centuries. Hose worn by lower status men were coarser, knitted by hand in the round from wool or linen fibers, or still made from bias-cut woven fabrics. The production of hose to meet the demands of men's fashion sparked important innovations in knitting. The first knitting machine (called a flatbed frame) was invented in late-sixteenth-century England to make hose. It produced coarse, flat pieces of knitted cloth with eight stitches per inch. Although it could be knit ten times faster than by hand, the cloth was considered suitable only for peasant hose. By century's end this technology was refined to make silk stockings using approximately twenty stitches per inch, creating a very active industry and market for higher quality, high-priced hose that lasted until the end of the eighteenth century. Innovations to the knitting machine in the eighteenth century included refinements in shaping hosiery on the frame during the knitting process. Cotton, from India, was introduced for knitted hosiery in England in 1730. By the beginning of the nineteenth century, fashion changes in men's dress resulted in legs covered by long pantaloons or trousers instead of hose, and knitted hosiery industries declined.

Later Development

Until the late sixteenth century, both woven and knitted hose were held up by being tied to the waist of a man's doublet with laces called points. By 1540, the full-length style of men's hose was broken up into two or three different sections up the leg called stocks. Each section was sewn or tied to the one above it in order to hold it up on the leg. The lower hose, from toe to knee, were predominantly held up by garters, and, after the 1540s, were almost exclusively knitted. Through the seventeenth and eighteenth centuries, knee-length hose or stockings were worn with breeches. Garters were the most popular method for holding up one's hose until new develop-

ments created highly elastic manufactured fibers in the mid-twentieth century. From the 1770s until into the 1820s, many men padded their hose with "artificial calves" strapped to their legs, if needed, to create the shapely leg demanded by fashion ideals.

By the early twentieth century, men's hosiery was a fully diversified industry, producing a wide range of knitted garments completely shaped and finished on the frame. In the apparel industry, the term "half-hose" refers to socks or stockings that end at mid-calf or lower, and the term "hose" refers to those that end above the knee.

See also **Breeches; Doublet.**

BIBLIOGRAPHY

Brackenbury, Terry. *Knitted Clothing Technology.* Oxford: Blackwell Scientific Publications, 1992.

Chenoune, Farid. *A History of Men's Fashion.* Translated by Deke Dusinberre. Paris: Flammarion, 1993.

Payne, Blanche, Geitel Winakor, and Jane Farrell-Beck. *The History of Costume: From Ancient Mesopotamia through the Twentieth Century.* 2nd ed. New York: HarperCollins Publishers Inc., 1992.

Tortora, Phyllis G., and Keith Eubank. *Survey of Historic Costume: A History of Western Dress.* 3rd ed. New York: Fairchild Publications, 1998.

Susan J. Torntore

HOSIERY, WOMEN'S. *See* **Stockings, Women's.**

HOSPITAL GOWNS. *See* **Nonwoven Textiles.**

HOYNINGEN-HUENE, GEORGE George Hoyningen-Huene (1900–1968) is remembered as one of the finest fashion photographers of the 1920s and 1930s. He was born in St. Petersburg, Russia, to a Baltic nobleman, the chief equerry to Tsar Alexander III, and an American mother whose own father had been the United States Minister Plenipotentiary and Envoy Extraordinary to the Russian court. Huene's early upbringing was one of privilege, though the revolution brought those advantages to an abrupt end: the family's properties were confiscated, and they were forced to flee for their lives.

Huene settled in Paris. Dreaming at first of reclaiming his rightful heritage, he participated briefly in the British Expeditionary Force's disastrous campaign against the Reds in 1918. However, the fiasco taught him that there was no turning back the historical clock and that he would have to forge a new life for himself in the West.

While the family chose exile in London, Huene settled in Paris, where he supported himself with a series of odd jobs, the most interesting being the role of an extra in cinema. Delighted to be in a city that so valued art, for which he had long harbored a passion, Huene decided to pursue drawing and painting, signing up for classes with the famed cubist instructor André Lohte. Huene was instinctively attracted to the world of couture, which he saw as another manifestation of art, and he was quick to grasp that a topflight fashion illustrator like Georges Lepape or Edouard Benito could command a high salary. Huene first put his drawing talents to work for Yteb, his sister Betty's dressmaking business, and by 1925 he had expanded his clientele considerably, selling illustrations to *Harper's Bazaar*, *Women's Wear*, and *Le Jardin des modes*.

Never one to be chained to a desk, Huene teamed up with his new friend, the photographer Man Ray, to produce a portfolio of "the most beautiful women in Paris." Huene's role had only been to recruit the women, but *Vogue*'s Main Bocher (later the couturier Mainbocher) was impressed with the ambitious project, and while he didn't accept it for *Vogue*, he took it upon himself to introduce the young man to Edna Chase, the editor-in-chief of the magazine. This led to his "first real job," as he put it, as an illustrator, though Huene always suspected that Chase's decision had more to do with Huene's access to the world of glamorous women than it did with his drawing skills.

Huene fell into photography literally by chance, though in retrospect he seems to have been slowly gravitating toward the métier. He took every opportunity at the *Vogue* studio to help photographers with their sets and lighting, and when one of the photographers did not appear one morning in 1926, Huene stepped in. Thus begun a ten-year photographic collaboration with *Vogue*.

Huene brought a neoclassical style, lightly inflected by cubism, to the magazine, a mix perfectly attuned to the zeitgeist. H. K. Frenzel's introduction to a slim volume of Huene's portraits, published in 1932, notes how

> Ionic columns rose alongside factory smoke-stacks, Greek temples alongside railroad tunnels and depots . . . and the ladies and gentlemen of Paris, London, New York and Biarritz enjoyed the sunshine among pedestals from which the gods of ancient Greece looked down in naked silence, between snorting stallions and muscular heroes.

Greek columns, temples, and statuary were common motifs in Huene's imagery; thus enobling the clothes. Not surprisingly, he admired the couture of Madame Grès ("fluid, harmonious and sculptural"), Madame Vionnet ("Her clothes were built like great architecture"), and Coco Chanel, whom he appreciated for her "absolute assurance of her own talent, competence and authority."

At *Vogue* Huene had the chance to study the contributions of his predecessors, and in the case of Edward Steichen—then chief photographer at *Vogue*—even to watch him work. From Baron de Meyer's early twentieth-century fashion photography he learned the power of suggestion, "the mysterious air of making every woman look

like a vision in a dream," and from Steichen he learned the importance of psychology:

> In addition to directing the activities of his assistants the photographer plays the clown, the enthusiast, the flatterer. He acts and talks about other things while his mind is watching the building up of the picture—its lights, shadows and lines; its essential fashion photograph requirements—distinction, elegance, and chic.

Huene also absorbed a great deal from painters, and two friends made particularly strong impressions: the painter and fellow Russian Pavel Tchelitchev, who accepted commissions for magazine covers in addition to his own personal art work and could be as enthusiastic about workman's clothes and army surplus gear as he was about haute couture; and Christian Bérard, an artist famed for his Dionysian temperament that was poles apart from Huene's own more own Apollonian sensibilities.

Huene also followed developments in cinema and photography. He rubbed shoulders with personalities as diverse as the French photographer Henri Cartier-Bresson, the American dancer Josephine Baker, and the Armenian mystic G. I. Gurdjieff. He played bit roles in movies and even tried his hand at making three films, all of which were subsequently lost. Although his fashion work has long been given its due, his exquisite portraiture has not received the attention it deserves. His photographs of his great friend and fellow photographer Horst P. Horst, the authors Jean Cocteau and Janet Flanner, the composer Igor Stravinsky, the photographers Baron de Meyer and Cecil Beaton, the actor Johnny Weismuller, the painter and sculptor Alexander Calder, Coco Chanel, and dozens of other celebrities of the day, never resort to formulaic poses or superficial flattery but always find a way of signifying their subjects' originality.

The second significant period of Huene's fashion photography (though it could never match his Paris output) was spent at *Harper's Bazaar* in New York, where he arrived in 1935. Although Huene continued to innovate, the magazine's art director, Alexey Brodovitch's, penchant for bleeding photographs off the page and overlaying graphic elements on the image undermined the integrity of Huene's exquisitely balanced compositions. Gradually he began to lose interest in his photographic work. American fashions could never match their French counterparts; the problem solving that had once given him so much pleasure no longer did so, and the business-is-everything climate of New York was increasingly discouraging.

Huene escaped, temporarily, to the ancient world of the Middle East, looking for spiritual renewal. He found solace on grand voyages across Africa and Arabia. One beautifully written book, *African Mirage, the Record of a Journey* (1938), came of his travels, and other journeys resulted in equally fine photographic albums (*Hellas* in 1943; *Egypt* in 1943; *Mexican Heritage* in 1943; and *Baalbek/Palmyra* in 1946).

In the mid-1940s Huene abandoned fashion photography, leaving it to a new generation less committed to his prewar ideal of elegance. He famously greeted the young Richard Avedon, just beginning his own career in photography, with the words, "Too bad, Too late!" His mind was increasingly set on travel—especially spiritual explorations—and he was willing to try new ways of earning a living. He taught photography at the Art Center School in Pasadena, California, experimented briefly with drugs under the guidance of Aldous Huxley, and served as a color coordinator for several filmmakers such as Jean Negulesco, Michael Kidd, Michael Curtiz, and most notably, George Cukor, who became a great friend.

Hoyningen-Huene first exhibited in a Parisian group show in 1928, in the *Premier Salon indépendant de la photographie*, and was invited to show several works at the seminal *Film und Foto* exhibition in Stuttgart in 1929. He did not show his work again until 1963, when he was selected for Cologne's influential *Photokina* exhibition. However, it was only after his death that he was acknowledged by two important collective exhibitions: *Fashion Photography: Six Decades*, shown at the Emily Lowe Gallery at Hofstra University, Hempstead, New York in 1975, and *History of Fashion Photography*, held at the International Museum of Photography in Rochester, New York, in 1979, and with a full retrospective, *Eye for Elegance*, at the International Center of Photography in New York. In the interim, fashion photography had been treated as a minor commercial vein, and books and exhibitions rare, though one exception should be noted: *Glamor Portraits*, held at the Museum of Modern Art in 1965.

George Hoyningen-Huene died of a heart attack at his home in Los Angeles in 1968. His outstanding contribution to fashion photography is unquestioned, and he broadened this field with his erudition and his flair. In the final analysis the full range of his photography must be considered in any appreciation. His legacy is as a coherent system of images, chiefly of fashion and portrait studies, which were characterized by precision, economy of means, harmony, elegance, and psychological acuity.

See also **Fashion Photography; Film and Fashion.**

BIBLIOGRAPHY
Beaton, Cecil. *The Magic Image: The Genius of Photography from 1839 to the Present Day.* Boston: Little Brown, 1975.
Chase, Edna Wollman, and Ilka Chase. *Always in Vogue.* New York: Doubleday, 1954
Devlin, Polly. *Vogue Book of Fashion Photography 1919-1979.* New York: Simon and Schuster, 1979.
Ewing, William. *Eye for Elegance: George Hoyningen-Huene* (exhibition catalog). New York: Congreve Press; International Center of Photography, 1980
———. *The Photographic Art of Hoyningen-Huene.* London and New York: Thames and Hudson, Inc.; Rizzoli International 1986
Frenzel, H. K.. *Hoyningen-Huene: Meisterbildenisse.* Berlin: Verlag Dietrich Reineer, 1932
Harrison, Martin. *Appearances: Fashion Photography since 1945.* London: Jonathan Cape, 1991.
Horst, Horst P. *Salute to the Thirties*, foreword by Janet Flanner. New York: Viking Press, 1971
Maloney, Tom. "Hoyningen-Huene." *U.S. Camera Annual*, 1950
Pepper, Terence. *Horst Portraits, London, Paris, New York.* London: National Portrait Gallery, 2001
Pucciani, Oreste, ed. *Hoyningen-Huene* (exhibition catalog). Los Angeles: Los Angeles University Press, 1970

William Ewing

HUGO BOSS At the start of the twenty-first century Hugo Boss AG was among the biggest companies producing menswear in Germany and, in the last decade of the twentieth century, dominated the German menswear designer market through the distribution of various lines and licenses. In 1923 Hugo Boss founded the clothing company in Metzingen, near Stuttgart in the south of Germany. At first the company specialized in the production of work clothes, overalls, raincoats, and uniforms. From 1933 onward it made uniforms for German storm troopers, Wehrmacht, and Hitler Youth. Boss brought forced laborers from Poland and France to his factory to boost output in the following years. When Boss died in 1948, the factory returned to making uniforms for postal and police workers. In 1953 it produced its first men's suits.

By the early 1970s, after several changes in the management and ownership since the founding of the company, Jochen and Uwe Holy, the grandchildren of Boss, took over work-wear manufacturing, and the duo started to manufacture fashion-conscious men's suits and sportswear. In the following years the new owners turned Hugo Boss from a work-wear manufacturer into a stylish clothes company for formal men's wear. Hugo Boss was the first German company to construct a brand identity within the men's wear sector.

After the relaunch of the Boss brand in the early 1970s, the company developed steadily into an international fashion designer house. In the 1980s, Hugo Boss constructed a high degree of brand awareness through the distribution of licenses and brand extension in fragrances, dress shirts, sportswear, knits, and leatherwear. Boss went public in Germany in 1985. Their formal menswear, in particular, became strongly associated with the Yuppie.

Family control ended in 1992, and since 1993 Mazzotto S.p.A. in Valdagno, Italy, has held majority control of Hugo Boss AG. The company operates in more than ninety countries with a product range including bodywear, cosmetics, evening wear, eyewear, fine clothing, formal wear, fragrances, hosiery, leisurewear, shoes, and watches. Since control by Mazzotto began, Hugo Boss

AG has applied a three-brand strategy for the men's wear market under the labels Boss Hugo Boss, Hugo, and Baldessarini. Boss Man, the company's core brand is divided into three subsidiary labels—Black Label (business and leisure wear), Orange Label (urban sportswear), and Green Label (outdoor activewear).

The Hugo brand encompasses an avant-garde collection, which is designed for business and leisure, and which combines unconventional details with new materials. The Baldessarini brand is the most sophisticated label, featuring the finest Italian fabrics and hand stitching. As a traditional men's wear manufacturer, Hugo Boss made an unsuccessful attempt to start a women's wear line in 1987. Eleven years later Hugo Boss successfully launched the female counterpart to the male Hugo label. In 2000 the designer brand introduced Boss Woman, designed for the sophisticated female businesswoman. The Hugo Boss brand is clearly defined by a dynamic design with an emphasis on functionality, clean lines, and attention to details.

The Hugo Boss collections are distributed on the international market through selected specialty stores and Hugo Boss monobrand shops. The collections are designed and managed according to a standardized concept that reflects the clean, stylish brand image applied at monobrand shops worldwide. Nevertheless, the company opened a 20,000-square-foot store in New York City in 2001 that presented all brands and collections under one roof for the first time.

See also **Formal Wear, Men's; Suit, Business; Uniforms, Military; Uniforms, Occupational.**

BIBLIOGRAPHY

Clark, Andrew. "Dressed for Success." *Guardian*, 24 February 2001. Available from <http://guardian.co.uk>. Interview with Werner Baldessarini, the chairman of Hugo Boss.

Givhan, Robin. "Fashion Firm Discovers Its Holocaust History: Clothier Hugo Boss Supplied Nazi Uniforms with Forced Labour." *Washington Post*, 14 August 1997.

Thomas Hecht

IKAT Ikat is a resist dye technique used to pattern textiles. The more common methods of resist dyeing involve covering parts of a fabric to shield the reserved areas from penetration of the dye, as in tie-dyeing, where threads are wound around the fabric, or in batik, where wax is applied to the surface of the cloth. The term "ikat" by contrast, is used for a process where prior to weaving, warp (lengthwise yarn) or weft (crosswise thread) or sometimes both are tied off with fiber knots that resist absorbing color and are then dyed. To facilitate the pattern tying, the threads are set up on a frame. They are then grouped into bunches of several threads to be tied at once; this results in the creation of knot units from which the overall pattern is built up. Resist ties are removed or new ones added for each color; their combinations create the design. After dyeing is completed, all resists are opened, and the patterned yarns are woven.

The word "ikat" comes from the Malay-Indonesian word for "tie"; it was introduced into European sources of textile technology and history in the early twentieth century when Dutch scholars began paying attention to the rich textile traditions of the Netherlands Indies, the present-day Indonesia. Depending on whether the tied fibers are applied to the warp or weft, the technique is identified as either warp ikat or weft ikat. A third variety, double ikat, combines both warp- and weft-tied resist. For the pattern to be visible, the resist-dyed thread system has to be the prominent one, so for warp ikat, the weave has to be warp-faced, and weft ikat needs a weft-faced structure, which means that either warp or weft is predominantly visible. Plain weave is especially suitable for showing the ikat's design, but for weft ikat, a twill weave may also be used. Double ikat, where the design is built up from both systems, should ideally by woven in a balanced weave, with warp and weft equally visible. All textile fibers may be used for ikat, although silk and cotton are the most common ones. For the seminal study of ikat as a resist dye technique, its history and geographic distribution, see Alfred Bühler (1972).

History of the Technique

While it is not known when and where the resist technique first developed, Asia has several cultural regions with a particularly strong ikat tradition. Maritime Southeast Asia, India, and Central Asia are all potential candidates for the origin of the technique, but it may also have evolved independently in several locations. Ikat may have spread at an early age through many parts of the Austronesian-speaking world, as technical similarities exist between Indonesian ikat production and that of Madagascar, which was settled by maritime Southeast Asians early in the first millennium C.E. As Malagasy weavers also use a distinctly Austronesian version of a horizontal back-strap loom, the technique may have arrived simultaneously with the spread of loom technology. Ikat patterning is probably represented in garments shown in the Ajanta cave paintings of India (from the fifth to the seventh century). A fragment patterned in the technique, kept for centuries in the Horyuji temple at Nara but now in the Tokyo National Museum, was apparently brought there from China during the Tang period (618–907 C.E.), but was probably produced in Central Asia. Cotton textiles with relatively simple warp ikat stripes were made in Yemen by the eighth or ninth century and were traded to Egypt, where they have survived.

Early ikat production is also testified for pre-Columbian South America, in particular Peru, where a few examples of ikat survive from before the common era. The Mapucha of Chile still produce indigo-dyed warp ikat textiles. Guatemalan ikat, on the other hand, may have been introduced originally as trade textiles brought by the Spanish from the Philippines and could ultimately have a Southeast Asian source. West African weavers also make use of the technique, in particular in Ghana, the Ivory Coast, and Nigeria. In the Mediterranean world and Europe, ikat apparently developed in response to Islamic textiles; it first appeared in Italy in the seventeenth century as an influence from warp-ikat striped *mashru* cloth (a warp-faced satin weave with silk warp and cotton weft) made in Syria and Turkey. For its spread through Europe, especially France, Majorca, and Spain, see Marie-Louise Nabholz-Kartaschoff.

Nineteenth- and twentieth-century evidence show that at least during the last two hundred years, Asia produced the most varied and highest quality ikat textiles, and a survey of the technique will inevitably have the continent as its main focus, although the occurrence of ikat worldwide needs to be acknowledged. Particularly fine

GLOSSARY OF TECHNICAL TERMS

Balance weave: A textile structure in which the number of yarns in the lengthwise direction and the number of yarns in the crosswise direction are similar in size and number.

Warp/warp yarn: Lengthwise yarns in a woven fabric.

Warp-faced: Fabric in which the lengthwise (warp) yarns predominate on the surface of the fabric.

Weft/weft yarn: Crosswise yarns in a woven fabric. Synonyms: filling, woof.

Weft-faced: Fabric in which the crosswise (weft) yarns predominate on the surface of the fabric.

material survives from India, Central Asia, Southeast Asia, and Japan. China, otherwise of course a producer of quality textiles, apparently has not developed the technique to any degree, at least outside its Central Asian provinces.

Regional Characteristics in Asia

India and Southeast Asia are the geographical regions with the greatest diversity of ikat weaving, with all three technical versions present and developed to an unrivalled variety of designs. In India, Andhra Pradesh, Orissa, and Gujarat are best known for their ikat traditions, but Tamil Nadu in southern India also once had an active production. The most famous, and complex, of ikat textiles are the *patola* (sing. *patolu*) of Gujarat. These double-ikat, sari-length silk cloths are in the early 2000s only made by a small group of weavers in Patan. Their designs require great precision in planning and setting up of warp and weft, as the desired effect is a clear outline of patterns, rather than the softly blurred appearance characteristic of many ikat traditions. Patola are still worn as saris in India, but they also have ceremonial functions, such as at weddings, where they may be used to drape the bride and bridegroom.

For centuries, patola were not only made for an Indian clientele, but were also luxury trade items. Their international reputation as high-quality export textiles was already established in Southeast Asia when the first Europeans became involved with the maritime trade of Asia in the early sixteenth century. The Portuguese and later Dutch and English traders discovered that patola were essential exchange items for establishing local contacts in the lucrative spice trade. Patola made for the Southeast Asian market were usually smaller in size than the sari-

length textiles found in India, and they had distinctly different designs.

Patola imitations in weft ikat are produced in Rajkot in Saurashtra, western Gujarat; these use conventional patola designs but are garish in colors and technically less ambitious. Andhra Pradesh and Orissa produce both cotton and silk warp and weft ikat, sometimes using both in a single cloth, such as the *telia rumal* handkerchiefs made in Chirala, Andhra Pradesh. Warp and weft may be matched to create simple double ikat patterns, but more often warp and weft ikat are placed separately in different parts of the textile. Tamil Nadu and Karnataka in southern India formerly produced fine cotton and silk sari with very simple ikat bands.

Southeast Asia has a strong warp ikat tradition, usually worked on cotton. Particular highlights are found in Sarawak (Borneo) among the Iban, the Toba Batak of northern Sumatra, and throughout eastern Indonesia, specifically on Sumba, Roti and Savu, Flores, and the Solor Islands. Weft ikat is most commonly associated with silk weaving and is found predominantly in mainland and western maritime Southeast Asia; it occurs in Cambodia among the Khmer, in southern Sumatra, and (as a cotton version) on Bali. Double ikat is only found in Bali in the village of Tenganan, where the ceremonially important cotton *geringsing* cloths are woven. The designs used in Southeast Asian ikat combine indigenous motifs with outside influences, as they incorporate patterns that go back to the region's prehistory, with a response to Indian textiles. Particularly relevant are the patola formerly traded from Gujarat, which had a major impact on local ikat textiles.

Central Asia produces silk warp ikat garments, in particular coats worn by men and women until the early twentieth century. These were made by specialist weavers and dyers in the city-states along the Silk Road, often involving the local Jewish communities, and were worn as heavily quilted outer garments, as well as undercoats without cotton padding. These robes are characteristically dyed with vibrant colors and large-scale designs; unlike some other ikat traditions that may place importance on a precise outline of patterning (the patola of Gujarat and warp ikat textiles from Borneo and eastern Indonesia), the bold effect is the desired aesthetic achievement, rather than a clearly defined motif. In East Asia, ikat continues to be commonly produced in Japan. It was traditionally only dyed with indigo, although other colors have become used as well. One finds both warp and weft ikat, often combined into double ikat patterns.

While ikat production in India, Central, and East Asia is done in commercial or craft industry–oriented workshops and is mainly carried out by men, the tying and weaving of ikat in Southeast Asia is definitely a female activity. The textiles of the region are often associated with ritual and ceremonial functions that concern both individuals and the community. They may be presented as gifts at marriage and funerals, or may be essential paraphernalia for ritual cycles and ceremonies. Even when they are made to be used by men, their production is inevitably closely linked to the female aspect of society, both in mainland and maritime Southeast Asia.

Production and Function

Ikat continues to be produced in the early 2000s, especially in Southeast and East Asia. It may also have a revival in India, as traditional crafts there experience a certain renaissance. Ikat textiles are used for both dress and display purposes. They can be appreciated for their decorative beauty alone, but because a complicated pattern is difficult to achieve in this technique, especially when several colors are part of the design, ikat garments may carry a high prestige value as well. This is apparent in the use of patola as costly sari fabrics worn by women in India; it also contributed to the local appreciation of ikat garments in Central Asia, where the robes were considered most prestigious if they included several colors, as this implied the repeated tying of the warp threads and further dyeing, which is both time-consuming and technically demanding.

Although most ikat textiles produced in Southeast Asia are used as garments, such as the wrap-around sarong or an open shoulder cloth, they may in addition acquire a considerable ceremonial importance. They are produced by women and therefore have become closely associated with the status females have in the region, which in general is high and inevitably is linked to concepts of fertility. The ikat textiles are frequently a prescribed part of elaborate gift exchanges accompanying a wedding. Textiles with a ceremonial function often use designs and color combinations that are considered traditional in the local context; comparing current patterns to those found in early museum collections can provide confirmation that designs have been established for several generations and continue to follow certain conventions. Ikat textiles made for daily wear, on the other hand, display local fashions in both design and color and may change relatively quickly.

See also **Dyeing; Dyeing, Resist; Weave, Plain; Weave, Twill.**

BIBLIOGRAPHY

Bühler, Alfred. *Ikat Batik Plangi.* 3 vols. Basel, Switzerland: Pharos Verlag, 1972.

Bühler, Alfred, and Eberhard Fischer. *The Patola of Gujarat: Double Ikat in India.* 2 vols. Basel, Switzerland: Krebs Verlag, 1979.

Crill, Rosemary. *Indian Ikat Textiles.* London: Victoria and Albert Museum, 1998.

Fitz Gibbon, Kate, and Andrew Hale. *Ikat: Silks of Central Asia.* The Guido Goldman Collection. London: Laurence King, 1997.

Gittinger, Mattiebelle. *Splendid Symbols: Textiles and Tradition in Indonesia.* Washington, D.C.: The Textile Museum, 1979.

Maxwell, Robyn. *Textiles of Southeast Asia: Tradition, Trade and Transformation.* New York: Oxford University Press, 1990.

Nabholz-Kartaschoff, Marie-Louise. *Ikatgewebe aus Nord- und Südeuropa.* Basler Beiträge zur Ethnologie Band 6. Basel, Switzerland: Pharos Verlag, 1969.

Tomita, Jun, and Noriko Tomita. *Japanese Ikat Weaving.* London: Routledge and Kegan Paul, 1982.

Zerrnickel, Maria "The Textile Arts of Uzbekistan." In *Uzbekistan: Heirs to the Silk Road.* Edited by Johannes Kalter and Margareta Pavaloi. London: Thames and Hudson, Inc. 1997.

Ruth Barnes

IMPLANTS An implant is the introduction of a material or object under the skin that changes the shape of the body in that area. Implants create temporary, semipermanent, and permanent body modifications that transform the volume, space, and mass of a body area. Implants require an invasive procedure or surgery, often plastic or cosmetic surgery.

Plastic surgery refers to surgical techniques aimed at reconstructing, correcting, or modifying parts of the human body. Cosmetic surgery is a subdivision of plastic surgery, which refers to any surgery that modifies a person's appearance, but is not necessarily for a health-related reason. Cosmetic surgery makes it possible to replace, reconstruct, or reshape every external part of the body, from the cheeks to the buttocks. Examples of cosmetic surgery that utilize implants include facial, chest, buttock, and calf augmentations.

Facial Augmentation

Changing of the facial structure can involve a wide variety of implant practices, such as soft tissue, cheek, dental, and chin implants. These implants are used for reconstructive and cosmetic purposes. A common facial augmentation is to remove or improve the appearance of existing scars and facial lines. In the latter part of the twentieth century, many rigid and injection implants were developed; the most successful and popular types were soft tissue implants.

Soft Tissue or Injection Implants

Soft tissue implants include collagen, human fat and tissue, Botox, and Gortex. A common type of collagen implant is made from the deep surface of bovine skin. Bovine collagen implants consist of sterile, purified, reconstituted bovine collagen, which is injected into the dermal layers of the skin. The body absorbs collagen, resulting in a smoother skin surface. This type of implant lasts from four to ten months.

Excess fat removed from the body can be injected into areas with wrinkle lines to reduce their depth. This procedure is called "fat grafting," which utilizes a strip of a deep layer of underlying fatty tissue, which may be taken

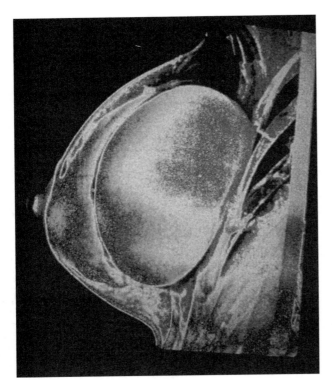

X-ray of breast implant. Silicone gel was used in breast implants until 1992, when medical concerns led to its replacement with water-filled silicon bags. © Howard Sochurek/Corbis. Reproduced by permission.

from any location on the body. The fatty tissue is then injected below or threaded into the wrinkle lines, where it may last for several years.

Botox is a safe liquid derived from botulism toxin. This type of implant paralyzes the muscles underneath facial wrinkles, thereby producing a smooth skin surface. Botox is effective for up to five months.

Gortex, a Teflon implant, is injected below wrinkle lines to produce a permanently smooth transformation of the skin's surface. This substance is nontoxic and does not need additional surgery. This type of implant does not need to be repeated, but it can be removed whenever desired or if complications arise.

Cheek and chin implants have been used to reconstruct and reshape the face since the mid-twentieth century. The most common implants for these augmentations include both injection and rigid implants.

Rhinoplasty is a surgical procedure that modifies the size or shape of the nose. Early records, from about 600 B.C.E., refer to Sushruta, an Indian surgeon who implanted necessary cartilage structures and reconstructed noses that were amputated as a result of punishment.

Dental implants are used to replace, reconstruct, or enhance teeth or the jawbone. There is evidence that den-

tal implants were used in early Egypt, where the upper classes replaced their teeth with those extracted from slaves, poor people, or animals. A wide variety of dental implants existed during the twentieth and early twenty-first century, and most involved surgical procedures.

Hair Grafts or Implants

One type of hair replacement is to use small hair grafts or implants, which typically vary in size from two to ten hairs. The grafts are placed in the scalp according to the natural hair patterns. Originally punch grafts were used that placed about ten hairs with each punch. By the late twentieth century, mini- and micro-grafts placed groups of one to four hairs at a time.

Chest Augmentation

While both males and females have chest augmentation, the primary difference is that female augmentations are referred to as breast implants, whereas males have pectoral implants. Breast implants typically replace or enhance and increase the size of a female's breast. Pectoral implants push the chest muscles outward, creating the appearance of a larger, more muscular chest.

Chest augmentation involves inserting implants into the chest. Silicone gel chest implants were invented by the plastic surgeons Thomas Cronin and Frank Gerow in the early 1960s. This silicone gel implant was developed into a commercial product by Dow Corning in 1962. Other manufacturers introduced chest implants in the late 1960s. Chest implants were once filled with silicone gel, but it was banned in 1992 due to health risks. The Federal Drug Administration (FDA) reported that silicone was linked to connective tissue diseases, such as arthritis and lupus. As a result, chest implants were modified to silicone bags filled with saline. Saline implants are shaped and sized according to the desired appearance, and the implant surface can be smooth or textured. Breast implants are either round or teardrop-shaped, while pectoral implants are more flat and circular. The type of implant used will usually depend on individual preferences.

Penile Implant

First used in the 1950s, the penile implant or prosthetic is a treatment for impotence. The penile implant is a set of prosthetic tubes within the penis designed to mimic the creation of an erection. There are three types of penile implants: the semirigid implant, the inflatable implant, and a self-contained inflatable implant.

Calf Augmentation

Calf augmentation enhances the calf muscle of the leg with the placement of a solid silicone rubber implant on the back of one or both calves. Men and women have calf augmentation to create more shapely calves or to produce symmetry, when one calf is significantly smaller than the other.

Top: **Fan painted with *The Toilette of Cupid.*** During the seventeenth century, European fans saw a great increase in quality of design and technique. (*See* Fans) © V&A Picture Library, Photographer: Sara Hodges.

Middle: **Reverse of fan depicting *The Toilette of Cupid.*** Fans of the seventeenth century often featured scenes from works of art created during the baroque period, and both sides of the fan were generally painted. (*See* Fans) © V&A Picture Library

Bottom: **Mid-eighteenth-century French fan.** France was the primary producer of fans in the eighteenth century. The rococo style had a profound effect on fans during this time, and the decorations became lighter and more graceful. (*See* Fans) © V&A Picture Library, Photographer: Sara Hodges.

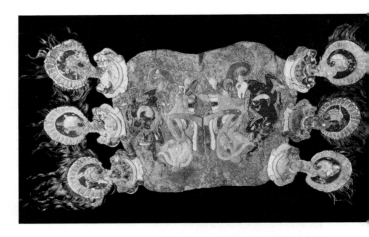

Top: **Felt saddle covering, Russia, 400 B.C.E.** Made mostly from wool, felt is a good insulator and a remarkably strong and versatile material that can be stretched and molded for various uses. (*See* Felt) © The State Hermitage Museum, St. Petersburg. Reproduced by permission.

Bottom: **Machine for producing synthetic fiber.** Synthetic fibers, including nylon and polyester, are created from chemicals substances. Synthetic fibers and regenerated fibers are known as manufactured, or man-made, fibers. (*See* Fibers) © John Madere/Corbis.

Below: **Thierry Mugler 1997–1998 fall/winter haute couture collection.** The Paris haute couture system, which garners international attention and prestige, generates profitable deals on ready-to-wear clothing, perfume, and more. (*See* Haute Couture) AP/Wide World Photos.

Inset: **Roberto Capucci with one of his designs, 1993.** Capucci began his career early, opening his first *atelier* when he was not yet twenty years old. His designs often exhibited unusual structure and volume. (*See* Haute Couture; Capucci, Roberto)
© Vittoriano Rastelli/Corbis.

Top, right: African women wearing headdresses. Headdresses are worn for both decorative and practical purposes. Depending on design, they can indicate religion, social rank, political affiliation, or a combination of all three. (*See* Headdress) Hulton/Archive by Getty Images.

Below: Performers at Aztec dance. Feathers from birds such as the quetzal and the eagle have long been used in the tribal headdresses of the Aztecs. (*See* Headdress) © Wolfgang Kaehler/Corbis.

Top, left: **Indian** *ikat* **coat.** All three varieties of *ikat* dyeing techniques were prevalent in India, and the garments featured an extensive array of designs and colors. (*See* Ikat) Ashmolean Museum, Oxford. Reproduced by permission.

Middle, left: **Sari designer Paul Satya with customers.** The *sari,* a wrapped garment, is among the most prevalent form of dress in India. Wrapping methods and decorative embellishments can vary widely from region to region. (*See* India: Clothing and Adornment) © John Van Hasselt/Corbis Sygma.

Below: **Indian designer Seerat Narindra.** Narindra worked together with Indian women whose lives had been devastated by a 1996 earthquake to bring their traditional handiwork to her contemporary fashion designs. (*See* India: Clothing and Adornment) © Lindsay Hebberd/Corbis.

Top, left: Portrait of a Gentleman, by Bartolomeo Veneto. In the sixteenth century, round brooches called *enseigne* were pinned by Italian men on the upturned brim of their hats. (*See* Jewelry; Brooches and Pins) © Massimo Listri/Corbis.

Below: **Indian woman wearing elaborate jewelry.** By the beginning of the twenty-first century, decorative jewelry was worn almost exclusively by Indian women, although men from royal families sometimes wore jewels for special occasions. (*See* Jewelry; India: Clothing and Adornment) © Robert Holmes/Corbis.

Top, left: **South Korean model in Swatch ensemble.** By the late twentieth century, the materials that could be used to create jewelry knew little boundary, and items such as watches were not restricted to the traditional placement on the wrist. (*See* Jewelry; Korean Dress and Adornment) Getty Images.

Below: **Korean baby in traditional clothing.** Korean children's clothing is similar to that of adults, except that the colors may be brighter and warmer. For special occasions, children may wear a rainbow-striped *chogori*. (*See* Korean Dress and Adornment) © Nancy Brown/Corbis.

Above: **Evil-bunny Halloween mask.** Despite being sanctioned by neither church nor state, Halloween is a major holiday in the United States. It has its origins in the ancient Celtic tradition of Samhain, a day in which it was believed that the souls of the dead were especially restless. (*See* Masks; Halloween Costume) Photo by Phyllis Galembo.

Right: **Indian "Elephant March" mask.** A man wears an intricate mask during the Great Elephant March, a celebration that takes place each January in India. (*See* Masks) © Hans Georg Roth/Corbis.

Below: **Masked revelers.** The emphasis of carnivals is on spectacle, and the more eye-catching the costume, the better. Many festivals even feature competitions, with judges awarding prizes for the most inventive costumes, many of which include masks. (*See* Masks; Carnival Dress) AP/Wide World Photos.

Buttock Augmentation

Buttock implants augment a flat posterior. The implant is placed in between the gluteal muscles, increasing and changing the shape of the buttocks. There are two types of implants to be used for this procedure: solid and cohesive implants. The solid buttock implant is made from a dense silicone, which is uncomfortable and lacks a natural appearance. The cohesive implant is made from a lighter, less-dense silicone gel, with additional flexibility. Both types of implants resist rupture, but the FDA has approved only the latter.

Teflon and Surgical Steel Implants

Teflon and surgical steel implants are primarily subcutaneous body art used by the Modern Primitive subculture. These implants take shape as horns, beads, gauged jewelry, organic shapes, and the like. Steve Haworth is a "3-dimensional body modification artist," who invented the specialized instruments and procedures to place the Teflon implants just under the surface of the skin. The procedures used for these types of implants are invasive, but do not require any anesthesia (occasionally local anesthesia is used for more extensive implants). In 1999, the *Guinness Book of World Records* recognized Steve Haworth as the "Most Successful 3-Dimensional Artist" in the world.

Health Risks

As with most body modifications that require surgery, implants have associated health risks. Common risks include pooling of serum or blood, blood clots, infection, prolonged swelling, rupture, and loss of sensation. Cosmetic problems can also occur, such as rippling of the skin or undesired settling.

See also **Body Building and Sculpting; Plastic and Cosmetic Surgery.**

BIBLIOGRAPHY

Babbush, Charles, ed. *Dental Implants: The Art and Science.* Philadelphia: W. B. Saunders, 2001.

Camphausen, Rufus C. *Return to the Tribal: A Celebration of Body Adornment.* Rochester, Vt.: Park Street Press, 1997.

Engler, Alan. *Body Sculpture: Plastic Surgery for the Body of Men and Women.* 2nd ed. New York: Hudson Publishing, 2000.

Haiken, Elizabeth. *Venus Envy: A History of Cosmetic Surgery.* Baltimore: Johns Hopkins University Press, 1999.

Mercury, Maureen. *Pagan Fleshworks: The Alchemy of Body Modification.* Rochester, Vt.: Park Street Press, 2000.

Theresa M. Winge

INDIA: CLOTHING AND ADORNMENT

Contemporary Indian dress is based upon a rich history of fashion development through 4,000 years (Ghurye 1966). The country contains one-sixth of the world's population, divided into three language families—Sanskrit, Dravidian, and Proto-Munda—each contributing its own dress traditions. Dress varies by region, whether it is a difference in how a woman's sari or man's dhoti is wrapped; the cut of the design; the use of the headdress or hair dressing; or the use of temporary or permanent body markings. Caste, religious, regional, or ethnic identity of most rural dwellers and some urbanites is revealed in the design of their tattoos, jewelry, or headdress. Clothing style often communicates the same information. This entry focuses on popularly worn garments and major fashion trends of the recent era.

If an individual lives in rural India—particularly as a member of a low-income, minority, or low-caste group—choices will be smaller than those of urban, mainstream, or elite compatriots. Limitations in rural choice result, too, from a higher saliency of caste, ethnicity, and religion, and lower expectations of involvement in the fashion system.

In urban areas, comprising 30 percent of the population, and among elites, choices in dress are much greater. Though the dress traditions of minorities seeking upward mobility are giving way to the dress of dominant regional and national communities, the latter is developing into a fast-moving fashion industry. Regional and national styles of dress provide some anonymity to the wearer regarding social origins. Additionally, world dress provides further alternatives in cities to elite women and men of all classes.

Wrapped Garments

Wrapped garments constitute the national wardrobe mainstay. Great complexity and varieties of garments and wrapping styles lie behind India's stereotypic sari. Wrapped garments for the torso—primarily women's sari and *veshti* and men's dhoti, *lungi*, and *veshti*—include cloths 2.5 to 12 yards long, with women wearing the longer garments. Additional wrapped garments include shawls; veils for women, for example, *dupatta*, *chunri*, and *orhni*; 4–7.5-yard-long *pagri* turbans and shorter informal head wraps for men; men's *kamar band* "waist ties"; and other items worn within minority groups, whose populations typically run to millions.

Wrapped garments are surface designed or woven to size on the loom with border designs on all four sides. The distinctive design of a garment, as wrapped on the body, results in the pattern of creases, pleats, and folds that the cloth makes. Women's sari borders are wide. Their placement on the body defines the main lines of each wrapped style. With a glance at fabric characteristics and border placement, an onlooker can tell from which ethnic region an individual, or at the least, her sari originates.

Preshaped Garments

Preshaped garments are not as ancient in India as wrapped forms of dress. Yet the *orhni* worn with *ghaghra* skirt and *choli*, a bodice front and sleeves secured across the back by ties, first appeared in pre-Muslim Gujarat in the tenth century (Fabri 1977). Both cut and sewn and

Indian women in fashion show. Wrapped garments such as these are the oldest form of clothing in India and are still considered the traditional dress. Fitted garments were not readily available until the 1970s. © REUTERS/CORBIS. REPRODUCED BY PERMISSION.

knitted garments are now broadly incorporated into Indian dress practice.

Women have largely retained wrapped forms of dress despite the move into fitted clothing by many rural and most urban men. Yet women combine their wrapped saris with cut and sewn blouses. Still, among the elder population in parts of the rural East and South and in minority rural communities in central and southern India, bare-chested female dress sporadically occurs. For example, very orthodox Brahmin women still cook meals for auspicious occasions wearing only their sari (Boulanger 1997).

The movement under Muslim rule, from the twelfth to nineteenth centuries, toward cut and sewn clothing was strongest in the North and West. Women wear ensembles of *salwar* (narrow-ankle loose pants), *kameez* (tunics fitted with darts and inset sleeves), and *dupatta*; or *ghaghra*, *choli*, and *orhni*. Men of these regions wear *salwar* and *kurta* tunics. Men, who did not adopt pants, still donned tunics of various styles for upper-body dressing. Well-to-do and formal men's apparel expand this variety in tunics with the knee-length *achkan* and other long tunics, coordinating them with a variety of drawstring waist pants—straight-legged *pajama*, *churidar pajama* and *sal-*

war—to create ensembles specifying the wearer's social identity and occasion of wear. In the North and West, turbans are broadly worn with these ensembles. Everywhere shawls are worn in winter.

British and European trade and rule, from the sixteenth to nineteenth centuries, introduced more styles of fitted clothing. Sari-wearing women added petticoat underwear and adopted British styles of fitting for their blouses. Men, no longer working in the agricultural or handicraft economy, adopted shorts or trousers and Western styles of shirts, including varieties of cotton knit under and outer shirts. Sweaters became popular—cardigans for women and pullovers for men.

Jewelry

Typical locations for jewelry include the ears, neck, upper arms, wrists, and fingers. Women additionally wear jewelry on the hair, nose, forearms, waist, ankles, and toes. Turban-wearing noblemen include jewelry in their headdress.

Gold and silver jewelry are worn by both genders and by individuals of all ages, except for orthodox Hindu widows. Following the aesthetic of India's former colonial rulers, strictly decorative jewelry is now worn almost exclusively by women; *raja* "kings" may wear rich jewels for formal appearances. Expensive jewelry is made from natural, polished, or carved items like pearls, coral, and ivory (now replaced with plastic) as well as local and imported diamonds, rubies, sapphires, and emeralds cut and set in India. Indeed, Indian kings and queens taught the European nobility to wear jewels.

In hotter regions of the country, a toddler may wear only a piece of jewelry, but one providing spiritual protection or marking entrance into community membership. Adults wear protective jewelry, too. Among urban middle and upper classes, jewelry has disappeared almost entirely from male dress, except for that which provides spiritual protection, such as rings with stones prescribed from horoscope readings. Women wear such rings as well, but they continue, like their rural sisters, wearing decorative jewelry. Upper-class women are now likely to wear styles of jewelry from a variety of regions. Their consumption of ethnic jewelry as changeable fashion items, not indicators of ethnic identity, marks them as members of the national upper class and global society.

Scenting the Body

Essential oils for scenting the body are extracted in northern and western India from fragrant plant and animal sources. A broader proportion of women, particularly in southern India, scent themselves by wearing fragrant flowers like jasmine in their hair. The most common methods of scenting the body are daily bathing with fragrant soaps and application of scented bath powder. Middle-class and rural women use face powder to lighten the complexion, in pursuit of a wheat-colored appearance.

Treatment of Head and Body Hair

Cultural norms of hair treatment stress uncut hair for women and global style short hair for men. Very orthodox high-caste Hindu men maintain one long uncut lock of hair from the crown. Long, thick, very black hair is a highly valued component of an attractive woman. Approaching puberty, if not before, a girl learns to take special care combing and oiling her hair to grow it into an asset as she approaches the marriage market. Women in southern India and girls throughout the country keep their hair in one or two braids, respectively. Northern Indian women usually tie their hair in a bun, with styles differing through history and across regions. Exceptions to these male and female practices are found in minority groups of central and far-eastern India. Among the Bondo of central India, for example, women cut their hair close to the scalp and wear a headband, while men grow their hair long and tie it up (Elwin 1950). Also, long, uncut and matted locks identify the holy man or woman who has given up worldly cares for a life of meditation. In the last twenty years, women in cities and wealthier classes have begun cutting their hair in neck- and shoulder-length styles.

Indian musicians. The most prevalent wrapped garment for Indian men is the *dhoti*. Turbans fashioned of varying lengths of cloth are also frequently worn. © LINDSAY HEBBERD/CORBIS. REPRODUCED BY PERMISSION.

Facial hair is treated in a variety of ways, depending on caste, religion, and region. Most men shave their beards, but Hindu men often maintain a mustache. Up-turning mustaches are claimed by high-caste men; in rural areas a low-caste man who turns his mustache up may be severely beaten. Full, uncut beards and mustaches are a religious must for orthodox Sikhs, who usually roll the beard under the chin, securing it with a net. Sikh men and women both leave their hair uncut, the men tying it into a bun at the top of the head and covering it with a cloth and turban. Older Muslim men tend to grow a full beard and, if they have made the pilgrimage to Mecca, dye the beard red with henna.

Many Indian men shave their armpits as part of their regular grooming, but women's body hair removal varies a lot by region and subculture. Some indigenous beauty saloons advertise thread work hair removal treatments as a bridal service. The goal is to make a woman's skin as smooth as a child's.

Contemporary Indian wedding attire. A male and female model, wearing contemporary Indian wedding fashion, show off the fashions of Indian designers Kalpesh and Purobi Dresswala in 2003. AP/WIDE WORLD PHOTOS. REPRODUCED BY PERMISSION.

Application of Color to the Body

Adults and children across rural northern India wear *kajal* eyeliner. Users say the eye-black, made from the soot of burned camphor, is cooling and promotes eye health. Black-lined eyes are aesthetically appreciated, too, so kajal is not strictly medicinal. Exaggerated kajal-lined eyes are essential makeup for male and female classical Indian dancers.

A code of symbols marked on the foreheads of devout men and women in red *sindur* powder or pastes of saffron, rice, or sandalwood mark an individual not only as a Hindu, but also communicates the particular deity to which a person is devoted. Young women concerned with adornment in some fashion periods make the Hindu *bindi* dot on the forehead in a myriad of sari-matching colors and decorative designs. Some designs are available as stick-on bindis.

Brides and grooms are massaged with a mixture of oil and turmeric in preparation for marriage. In addition

to the benefits of purification and spiritual blessing, turmeric also makes the skin glow golden. Some southern women regularly apply turmeric facials to enhance beauty. The faces of brides, and some bridegrooms, are decorated with designs in sandalwood paste. Additionally, lyrical designs in reddish *mehendi* are painted on the bride's hands, and on the feet, even if only the minimal design of a red line around the outside edge of the foot. As long as her husband lives, a married woman of eastern India wears red *sindur* in the part of her hair.

Age and Gender Differentiation

Babies and toddlers wear little or no clothing in rural areas, particularly when temperatures rise, but in urban areas and among the elite they are clothed in the full range of world dress garments for babies. Children under five years of age are dressed in bright, solid colors, especially red. Brighter colors continue for girls thereafter while boys begin dressing down in color. Girls wear dresses with a bodice, dropped waist, and skirt. Boys wear shirt and pants. Adolescent girls wear *salwar-kameez-dupatta* ensembles, though the short-sleeved top, long skirt, and half-sari veil tied over the developing chest continue in popularity in southern India. Adolescent boys wear shorts and later long pants, with a shirt. The clothing of children attending private schools is codified into uniforms.

Gender difference is boldly announced in Indian dress. In extreme western Gujarat, for example, women's blouse design draws attention to breasts, through embroidered circles or panels of bright cloth over the bosom. The tightly wrapped dhotis holding male genitalia in high relief in one region of western India perform a similar function. When outside the home, orthodox Muslim women always wear a two-piece *burqa* over their clothes, covering themselves entirely. Tinkling anklets and bangles, always worn in matched left-right pairs, audibly announce a woman's presence.

Yet even where gender is not so baldly announced, dress clearly distinguishes gender through a variety of means. These include major differences in garment form; the restriction of most of men's dress to somber and neutral colors—especially since contact with colonial dress norms; using rich color, texture, or surface design on every aspect of a women's clothing; and restriction of decorative jewelry to women.

A woman's marital and socially sanctioned reproductive status—unmarried, married, or widowed—is marked in dress. *Sindur* use was described above. Veiling practices vary by area. In some places all females cover their head; in others only married women cover up, and then only in the presence of their husband's senior relatives. Local and caste-specific designs of jewelry mark the status of a woman married to a husband who remains living. In each region, a loose code of garment colors communicates the marital and reproductive status and age of a woman. Absence of adornment in a woman's dress in very orthodox high-caste Hindu families indicates that

Fashion show by designer J.J. Valaya. Indian designer J.J. Valaya takes a bow after his runway show in 2003. A number of Indian designers create ensembles that blend traditional elements of Indian dress with modern fashion codas. AP/WIDE WORLD PHOTOS. REPRODUCED BY PERMISSION.

her husband is away or deceased or that she is menstruating (Leslie 1992). Widows wear white, or at least neutral colors.

History and the Indian Fashion Industry
For 4,000 years India has exported elaborately designed apparel and houseware textiles to the world, especially cottons but also some wools and silks. Importing markets, following their own cultural aesthetic, requested particular patterns and colors, introducing into India new design ideas. Indian textiles also attracted travelers from Europe, middle and central Asia, and China, as well as conquering armies from those same quarters and tourists. Such intrusions also expose Indians to new designs. Under colonialism, British rulers even invented Indian dress traditions, for example, the codification of the Sikh headdress (Cohn 1989).

At the end of the nineteenth century, the broad array of garments described above and rich textiles—everything from gold-embroidered velvets to transparent cotton muslins and brocaded silks—were still being made by hand to dress the Indian elite. Middle and lower classes wore a decreasing number of indigenous hand-loomed cottons, favoring cheaper industrially produced cotton garments from British, European, and Indian mills.

During the struggle for liberation from British rule, nationalists abandoned industrially produced cloth and overtly European or luxurious forms of Indian dress. Mahatma Gandhi encouraged production of *khadi*—cloth hand-loomed from hand-spun yarn—and designed a nationalist garment ensemble sewn from *khadi*. This *pajama*, *kurta*, and Gandhian cap outfit communicated a unified identity, replacing the divisive caste and religious identifications of conventional dress. The less ardent continued wearing traditional ensembles, but made from *khadi*. India's luxurious textiles as well as conspicuous displays of jewelry fell out of fashion among urban educated elites and political leaders.

However, diversity in Indian dress continued after the 1947 liberation, in part because 75 percent of the population still earned their livelihood in relatively unchanged agricultural villages. Government restructuring of the textile and apparel industry also played a major role. To keep employment high in the textile industry, the government developed a bifurcated policy. It facilitated mechanized spinning to feed the hand looms, which clothed the nation and supported revival of waning weaving traditions. Industrial weaving was reserved for export, and suffered severely, but bifurcation gave new life to local styles of hand-loomed saris.

Then in the late 1980s, the generation born after Independence came into power and reassessed its relationship to the global economy as well as sober forms of dress. Reversal of textile policies encouraged industrialization of both weaving and spinning, including production of synthetics. Cotton-polyester blends became popular among the working and middle classes. *Khadi*-producing societies now weave *polyvastra* cotton-poly *khadi*. Foreign-educated designers like Ritu Kumar (1999) began mining the luxurious clothes of Indian heritage for inspiration.

The government established a chain of National Institutes of Fashion Technology (NIFT) in seven of its major cities. NIFT students study local textile technology and design traditions and incorporate them into designs aimed at national and export markets, including the huge Indian diaspora ringing the globe. Richly embellished textiles and apparel are the mainstay of modern fashion design, drawing on India's wealth of skilled hand labor for block-printing, varieties of embroidery, beading, tie-dyeing, and other indigenous textile crafts.

Indian and foreign entrepreneurs and business owners are contributing to the growth of the Indian fashion industry. As late as the 1970s, wrapped forms of dress remained the only available ready-to-wear items. For fitted garments, individuals purchased yardage and had it tailored. Housewives began designing and manufacturing fitted and woven garments, eventually opening boutiques to retail them to urban elites (Castelino 1994). Fashion cycles of design development arose within various sari-weaving traditions (Nag 1989). In New Delhi and Bombay these small beginnings grew into destination shopping areas filled with designer boutiques.

NIFT and the growth in boutiques support a cadre of Indian designers who experiment with India's garment and textile traditions, particularly in surface design in the early 2000s. Even the *ghaghra-choli-orhni* ensemble worn by some women construction laborers has been gentrified into haute couture for a season of the Ethnic Chic trend. The industry has converted *salwar-kameez-dupatta* dressing into the national urban outfit for teenage girls. Women wear their first saris at graduation and marriage (Banerjee and Miller 2003). Ethnic Chic men's wear provides contemporary designs of heritage garments for elite and diaspora bridegrooms.

In the early twenty-first century, the *salwar-kameez-dupatta* ensemble has been globalized. Flared pants with outside hem slits replace the *salwar*. The *kameez* is cut briefer and shorter. The *dupatta* has been altogether dropped. A stylish woman in an elite society anywhere in the world could wear this ensemble.

The boutique ready-made movement has developed into national chains of stores reaching into all the main cities of India, and into the Indian diaspora via foreign branches and Internet sales sites (Bhachu 2003). In 2004 Anokhi and Fab India occupied the middle rank providing designs for everyday wear in multiple sizes and colors. The Ensemble and Ritu Kumar chains straddled the haute couture and ready-made markets. For the first time, a variety of sized apparel were being retailed to Indian women. Haute couture customers found one-of-a-kind outfits designed, like the ready-made, in garment silhouettes drawn from both Indian heritage and world dress.

Foreign businesses are helping bring world dress to India. By 1995 at least thirty-five agreements between Indian and foreign textile and apparel-producing firms had been made, including Lee and Levi Strauss. These are deals to produce denim in India and sew it into apparel to reach the lucrative Indian jeans market. Several foreign retailers of men's wear have branches in all of India's major cities.

Indian fashion is falling in step with its Western counterpart. The lengths of women's *kameez* and end border of the sari have risen and fallen with Western skirt lengths. Trends in hairstyles started by Elvis Presley, the Beatles, and more recent global media heartthrobs have spread to India, popularized in film by heroes like Raj Kapoor, Rajesh Khanna, and Shah Rukh.

Television programs from the United States and Britain, Bombay films produced as much for the Indian diaspora as for national audiences, and Indians' active maintenance of ties with relatives settled abroad encourage growth in world dress among young women as never before. Young elite women are beginning to catch up with the world dress trend of their male peers. Fashionable young urban women in tight jeans and midriff-baring tank tops are challenging modesty norms requiring that a woman's lower torso be covered by loose clothing.

Changing economic realities and rural television and film viewing are eliciting fashion experiments outside cities, too. Young men are giving up dress that marks low caste, ethnic, or regional identity. Young women, who have been altering the designs of their embroidered trousseau skirts for two generations, are now abandoning them altogether for saris; lower-caste groups are taking up their skirt-embroidering traditions. In western Gujarat state, young women recombine garments from their own and neighbors' traditions to create astonishing *choli-salwar* outfits as revealing as those of their elite urban sisters. The supposedly tradition-bound dressers of rural India are as caught up in fashion changes as their urban compatriots.

See also **Nehru Jacket; Salwar-Kameez; Sari.**

BIBLIOGRAPHY

Abreu, Robin. "Weaving a New Survival Strategy." *India Today* 20, no. 23 (15 December 1995): 119.

Bala Krishnan, R. Usha, and Meera Sushil Kumar. *Dance of the Peacock: Jewellery Traditions of India.* Mumbai, India: India Book House Limited, 1999.

Banerjee, Mukulika, and Daniel Miller. *The Sari.* Oxford: Berg, 2003.

Bhachu, Parminder. "Designing Diasporic Markets: Asian Fashion Entrepreneurs in London." In *Re-Orienting Fashion: The Globalization of Asian Dress.* Edited by Sandra Niessen, Ann Marie Leshkowich and Carla Jones, 139–158. Oxford: Berg, 2003.

Boulanger, Chantal. *Saris: An Illustrated Guide to the Indian Art of Draping.* New York: Shakti Press International, 1997.

Brij Bhushan, Jamila. *The Costumes and Textiles of India.* Bombay: Taraporevala's Treasure House of Books, 1958.

Castelino, Meher. *Fashion Kaleidoscope.* Calcutta: Rupa and Company, 1994.

Chishti, Rta Kapur, ed. *Saris of India: Bihar and West Bengal.* New Delhi: Wiley Eastern Ltd.; National Institute of Fashion Technology and Amr Vastra Kosh, 1995.

Chishti, Rta Kapur, and Amba Sanyal. *Saris of India: Madhya Pradesh.* Gen ed. by Martand Singh. New Delhi: Wiley Eastern Ltd., and Amr Vastra Kosh, 1995.

Cohn, Bernard. "Cloth, Clothes, and Colonialism: India in the Nineteenth Century." In *Cloth and Human Experience.* Edited by Annette B. Weiner and Jane Schneider, 305–353. Washington: Smithsonian Institution Press, 1989.

Dasgupta, Sunil, and Sudeep Chakravarti. "On the Cutting Edge: New Players Are Coming in and Old Ones Are Reshaping Their Strategies." *India Today* 19, no. 9 (15 May 1994): 130.

Dhamija, Jasleen, ed. *The Woven Silks of India.* Bombay: Marg Publications, 1995.

Dhamija, Jasleen, and Jyotindra Jain, eds. *Handwoven Fabrics of India,* Ahmedabad, India: Mapin Publishing Pvt. Ltd., 1989.

Elwin, Verrier. *Bondo Highlander.* Bombay: Oxford University Press, 1950.

Fabri, Charles. *Indian Dress: A Brief History.* New Delhi: Sangam Books; Orient Longman Limited, 1977.

Frater, Judy. *Threads of Identity: Embroidery and Adornment of the Nomadic Rabaris.* Ahmedabad, India: Mapin Publishing, Pvt. Ltd., 1995.

Ghurye, G. S. *Indian Costume.* Bombay: Popular Prakashan, 1966.

Kumar, Ritu. *Costumes and Textiles of Royal India.* Edited by Cathy Muscat. London: Christie's Books, 1999.

Leslie, Julia. "The Significance of Dress for the Orthodox Hindu Woman." In *Dress and Gender: Making and Meaning.* Edited by Ruth Barnes and Joanne B. Eicher, 198–213. Oxford: Berg, 1992.

Nag, Dulali. "The Social Construction of Handwoven Tangail Sari in the Market of Calcutta." Ph.D. diss., Michigan State University, 1989.

Sahay, Sachidanand. *Indian Costume, Coiffure and Ornament.* New Delhi: Munshiram Manoharlal Pub. Pvt. Ltd., 1973.

Singh, K. S. *The Anthropological Atlas: Ecology and Cultural Traits, Languages and Linguistic Traits, Demographic and Biological Traits.* People of India series, vol. 11. Delhi: Oxford University Press for Anthropological Survey of India, 1993.

Tarlo, Emma. *Clothing Matters: Dress and Identity in India.* Chicago: University of Chicago Press, 1996.

Untracht, Oppi. *Traditional Jewelry of India.* New York: Harry N. Abrams, 1997.

Hazel Lutz

INDIGO Indigo is a dyestuff known for its blue hue. The color comes from indigotin, a dye derived from the glucoside indican found in some fifty related plants, mostly in the leaves. Of these, *Indigofera tinctoria*, native to India, has the highest concentration of indican that makes deep, dark blues practicable. Less well-endowed varieties grow in Mexico and South America, Europe, Egypt, West Africa, Sumatra, Central Asia, China, and Japan where from ancient times they were used, it is thought, with varying degrees of influence from India.

Woad and Indigo

Woad (*Isatis tinctoria*) was used as a blue dye from as early as the fifth century B.C.E. in Europe where a textile fragment from a Celtic grave has been verified as having been dyed with this source of indigotin. The East India companies introduced indigo into Europe in the 1500s; although Europeans recognized its virtues, they outlawed it because it threatened economic disaster to their woad-based economies.

Indigo Manufacture

Separating indican, the basis of the dye, from the rest of the plant and changing it into indigotin, the dye, was a laborious undertaking begun by fermenting plant material in vats of water. One hundred pounds of plants yielded about four ounces of the insoluble, granular blue precipitate called "indigo," containing from 10 percent to 80 percent indigotin. The best came from Bengal.

Spices and calico were the focus of the India trade, but traders established hundreds of indigo plantations in the East Indies to supply the growing demand. The Spanish introduced indigo production to Central and South America and the West Indies, where it flourished. In America, the English colonists found indigo to be a lucrative crop, and during the difficult period of the Revolution, for lack of stable currency, lumps of indigo served the purpose.

Supplies of processed indigo dyestuff are nearly nonexistent in the early 2000s because its manufacture is labor intensive and expensive; there is little profit in it now that synthetic indigo prevails.

Indigo's Distinction

Unlike madder and most other natural dyes, indigo permanently attaches to fibers, particularly cotton, without mordant (a chemical that fixes a dye). Silk, wool, linen, and cotton may be successfully dyed with indigo. The dyestuff, however, cannot simply be stirred into the vat because indigo is insoluble. This property confers permanence, but carries the challenge of getting it onto the cloth in the first place.

Indigo Vats

Undissolved indigo does not adhere to fibers. The purchased chunk must be laboriously ground to a very fine powder and placed in a vat of water containing an agent to reduce, or chemically remove, oxygen molecules from the indican suspended in the liquid. The color of the indigo then changes from blue to a near white known as "indigo white." In this state the indican may be dissolved, but only if the liquid is alkaline. The art of indigo dyeing lies in maintaining the vat in a state of balance between reduction and solution in such a way that the cloth is successfully dyed without suffering alkali damage.

The earliest method of reducing indigo was to induce fermentation by the introduction of vegetable matter such as seeds into the vat. Later, woad, bran, or madder were used, but the fermentation vat was slow to "come on." Because it was effective and worked faster than fermentation, orpiment (arsenic trisulphide) came into favor although it was a deadly poison. When ferrous sulphate, or copperas, was found to work better and safely, it became the reducing agent of choice. Toward the end of the nineteenth century, a form of glucose was preferred. For all of these methods, lime was added to the vat to raise the alkalinity sufficiently to allow the white indigo to completely dissolve. The well-known urine vat was best suited to dyeing on a domestic scale; fermenting nutrients in the urine simultaneously generated a reducing and an alkaline solution.

As dyed cloth is removed from the vat, atmospheric oxygen immediately combines with the white indigo to restore the insoluble blue form again, thereby fixing the color mechanically within and upon the surface of the fibers and forming a weak chemical bond. If the dye is not completely reduced, it is not completely dissolved, and in that state cannot adhere to the fibers. An excess of undissolved—hence, unattached—indigo would crock, or rub off. The deepest shades of blue are achieved by successive dips so that the color will be even and rich.

Patterned Indigo

The Indians are recognized as the originators of resist dyeing with indigo, accomplished by applying wax to protect the cloth wherever it was not to be colored blue, even if that meant most of the cloth. The Japanese and Indonesians employed tie-dye and clamping techniques to resist indigo.

Europeans developed a resist paste made of starch mixed with copper or lead salts that were best applied by block. Discharge pastes that bleached or removed the blue color to make white designs came into use on in-

digo in the 1820s. These were more suitable than resists for cylinder printing. Resist and discharge pastes bearing mordants or lead salts for chrome colors were later developed, permitting the incorporation of colored shapes neatly fitted into the blue ground.

Obtaining a white ground with fine or small blue designs posed a problem. To do so, "pencil blue" —indigo mixed with lime and orpiment—was applied like watercolor with a brush or "pencil." Variations called China or Fayence blue were repeatedly revised for block and cylinder printing, but never produced a very dark or even color and usually gave trouble.

Synthetic Indigo

Adolph von Bayer first synthesized indigo in 1880, but it was not until the end of the century that a commercially viable process became available. The synthetic indigo was chemically identical to the natural form, minus the organic impurities. It was very much cheaper and little reason remained to resist; by 1920, natural indigo was little more than a memory in commercial print works.

Summary

The efficiently aggressive East India traders launched the final three hundred years of intensive commercial exploitation of all aspects of indigo production. By 1900, the venerable role of the "drug" that had shaped cultures and ages was usurped by a distinctly unromantic, synthetic replacement. The ubiquitous blue jeans of the early 2000s testify, undaunted, to the endurance of a global heritage called "indigo blue." Natural indigo is used only by artisans producing special custom yarns and fabrics. Most distinctively, the Japanese continue to employ age-old tie-dyeing, resist, and stencil techniques to make masterful indigo-patterned fabrics for kimonos.

See also **Dyeing; Dyeing, Resist.**

BIBLIOGRAPHY

Irwin, John, and P. R. Schwartz. *Studies in Indo-European Textile History.* Ahmedabad, India: Calico Museum of Textiles, 1966.

Liles, J. N. *The Art and Craft of Natural Dyeing.* Knoxville: University of Tennessee Press, 1990.

Pettit, Florence. *America's Indigo Blues.* New York: Hastings House, 1974.

Sandberg, Gosta. *Indigo Textiles: Techniques and History.* Asheville, N.C.: Lark Books, 1989.

Susan Greene

INUIT AND ARCTIC DRESS People throughout the circumpolar region, including Inuit and Inuvialuit in Canada, Yup'ik and Inupiat in coastal Alaska, Inuhuit in Greenland, Saami in northern Europe, and many groups from Siberia such as the Khanty, Nenets, Evenki, and Siberian Yupik, are recognized as the first people to make tailored garments. In ancient times, rather than wrapping skins around themselves, pieces were cut and laced together to provide protection from the weather and from spirits, which enabled these northern peoples to thrive. Each region developed its own styles, and people could tell where someone was from by looking at their clothing.

Generally, children wore miniature versions of adult clothing styles. Clothing was beautifully sewn and elaborately decorated with light- and dark-haired skins, skin tassels, beading, hair embroidery, stained or dyed skins, and different types of animal skins. Decorative treatment reflected the individuality of each seamstress, the regional identity or group affinity, and it also helped women appease the spirits, enabling the animal spirits to offer animals to hunters. Hunters saw skin clothing as their most important hunting "tool," without it they were unable to protect themselves from harm, bad weather, evil spirits, and show the respect needed for animals to wish to give up their lives to the hunter.

Inuit and Inuvialuit from Canada wore hooded pullover skin parkas. In the eastern and central Canadian Arctic women's parkas had a sculptured hemline creating

Inuit woman and baby. In many Arctic regions, a pouch is sewn onto the back of a woman's parka to hold her child. © RICK RIEWE. REPRODUCED BY PERMISSION.

front and back tongues or flaps. The length and silhouette of these pieces changed as a young woman entered puberty. A pouch-like area was sewn into the back of parkas worn by women of all ages and used to carry children. Parkas worn by women who were not carrying children had a much smaller pouch than those worn by mothers of young children. A small piece of polar bear or bull caribou skin was placed at the base of the pouch and cleaned when soiled by an infant. Men's pullover parkas were usually about thigh-length and had either a center front or side splits to allow for extra maneuverability. Men and women wore skin pants; in the eastern Canadian Arctic women wore shorts with leggings.

In the western Canadian Arctic and coastal Alaska women's parkas were much longer and had a relatively straight hemline. The back panel was cut extra large creating enough space to carry a baby; a sash tied around the waist of the parka prevented the child from falling out. Men's parkas were shorter, often hip-length. Both men's and women's parka hoods were finished with a large "sunburst" ruff made from strips of wolverine and wolf.

Siberian Yupik women wore a pant-top combination suit, which they put on by slipping through the extra-large neck opening. In other areas of northern Siberia

Inuit child. The hooded pullover parka is probably the most basic component of Arctic dress. The hood is generally lined with fur, creating a sunburst effect. © RICK RIEWE. REPRODUCED BY PERMISSION.

Inuit woman's parka with embroidery. Inuit clothing is often elaborately decorated with beads, tassels, dyes, and colored thread. Styles vary from region to region, and often a person's locale can be deduced from details of their clothing. © ROB HOWARD/CORBIS. REPRODUCED BY PERMISSION.

and Europe, women wore unhooded parkas with center-front openings. Infants were bundled up separately and carried in carrying boards. Men wore hoodless parkas with distinctly styled hats.

Inuhuit men and women from northern Greenland wore short, waist-length pullover hooded parkas. Women's parkas had a small narrow tab or flap at the front and back and a pouch for carrying children. They wore skin shorts with long boots. Men wore polar bear skin pants.

In the early 2000s, people from each of these regions wear traditional styles made from contemporary fabrics. Some seamstresses have developed new styles, such as waist-length "packing" parkas made from lightweight fabric for carrying young children around modern homes. As transportation systems shift from dog sled to snow-mobile to automobiles, styles used by women carrying children have changed so it is more comfortable to sit in a car seat. Hunters, herders, and other people who travel on the land extensively continue to wear traditional skin clothing as it provides the best long-term cold weather protection. They wear an inner parka with the fur next to their bodies and slip on an outer parka with the fur to the outside in extremely cold weather. Although the styles change regionally, each region's style works together with each of the components to trap warm air. For example, hot air rises up the pant legs, circulates around the torso, and exits at the face opening. When someone gets too warm, the outer parka is removed, along with the waist sash and hood to allow more hot air to escape.

Materials

In the past and today, caribou and ringed sealskin are the most commonly used materials for skin clothing throughout the circumpolar region. Caribou skin is ideal for cold, dry weather as each hair has a honeycomb core that traps air, which is an excellent insulator. Sealskin is ideal for milder, damp weather as the hair provides very little insulation, however, sealskins are wind and water-resistant. Arctic hare, fox, muskrat, ground squirrel, birds, and other northern animals are used for parkas in areas where caribou is scarce. These skins are more fragile than caribou, but they are extremely warm and lightweight. Wolf, wolverine, and dog skins are preferred for hood ruffs; sometimes parkas that are only worn around the village are trimmed with fox. Fish skins and intestines are used for waterproof clothing in a few areas, especially in southern coastal Alaska. For example, commercial herring fishers from Tooksook Bay in Alaska still prefer intestine parkas to heavy-duty raincoats, as they are lighter and allow body vapor to pass through the skin membrane while preventing rain from entering.

Technology

Most skins are dried, scraped, wrung and twisted by hand to soften, and then used for skin clothing. Skins are stained red with a variety of mixtures, including shred-

Man in Arctic dress. Most clothing in the circumpolar regions is made from animal skins. Depending on the relative dryness of the climate, caribou or seal is the most popular choice. © RICK RIEWE. REPRODUCED BY PERMISSION.

ded and boiled alder bark, powdered ocher (red clay), and, more recently, red dye leached out of wet crepe paper and concentrated red fabric dye. In northern Greenland, skins are de-haired and then painted with acrylic paints, creating a wide range of vibrant colors; plant dyes were used in the past. Special techniques are used for specific skins, for example, fat is sucked from bird skins to protect the quill end of each feather from being damaged by a scraper. Intestines are scraped to remove the inner layer, blown up, and dried before scraping and wringing them until soft. Fish skins are soaked in prepubescent male urine to remove some of the oils, dried, and then scraped until soft.

Skins are sewn together using sinew or connective tissue collected from caribou, muskrat, birds, and other animals. Sinew is cleaned, dried, rumpled by hand until soft, and then split into threads, which are either twisted or braided before being used. Today a synthetic waxed thread is often used as a substitute for sinew on most skins. Needles were made from bone or stone; today fine steel needles are commonly used with a metal thimble. A few still use the skin thimbles, which were passed down from one generation to the next. A few seamstresses use sewing machines to sew their skin clothing today.

See also **Inuit and Arctic Footwear; Parka.**

BIBLIOGRAPHY

Oakes, Jill and Rick Riewe. *Spirit of Siberia: Traditional Native Life, Clothing, and Footwear.* Washington, D.C.: Smithsonian Institution Press, 1998.

———. *Our Boots: An Inuit Women's Art.* New York: Thames and Hudson, Inc., 2000.

Oakes, Jill, et al. *Pushing the Margins: Native and Northern Studies.* Manitoba, Canada: University of Manitoba, 2001.

Jill Oakes

INUIT AND ARCTIC FOOTWEAR Throughout the circumpolar region, from coastal Alaska, northern Canada, Greenland, and northern Europe to northern Siberia, people protected their feet with layers of inner and outer stockings, inner and outer boots, and inner and outer slippers. Customarily, these layers were made from skins, often with grass or skin insoles. Traditional northern people can identify where you are from and what you do by looking at your skin boots. The styles and materials used to make footwear changed seasonally, regionally, and from one usage to another. Many northern people see footwear as an extremely important part of their clothing because it is the one item that helps humans make the transition from earth to air, from the spirit world to the present world. For example, northerners who move into urban centers or move south often bring a pair of skin boots and carefully store them in the freezer compartment

Yupik boots from Siberia. In order to make their *kamiks* (boots) waterproof, Inuits scraped the hair from the animal hide before the tanning process. © RICK RIEWE. REPRODUCED BY PERMISSION.

of the refrigerator, even though these items might be impractical when used in centrally heated buildings and on paved sidewalks. People continue to use traditional footwear for ceremonial and other special occasions.

Cross-Cultural and Historical Overview

Arctic footwear generally includes a sole, vamp, and leg section. Soles are either flat or pleated. Pleated soles vary from fine, diffused pleating to one or two large, rounded pleats per centimeter. Vamp silhouettes range in breadth and length, as well as curvature. Leg sections can be a narrow strip only a few centimeters high up to a long, thigh-high panel. In addition, straps are used on some boots and range from narrow skin laces to broad bands; as well, decorative features range from skin embroidery, hair embroidery, beading, tassels, and much more. Each of these characteristics is distinct to individual seamstresses and specific regions. Men's and women's boots are often decorated differently; children's styles are miniature versions of adult styles.

Inuit from northern Quebec, and the eastern and central Canadian Arctic generally prefer flexible boot soles that extend well up over the heel and toe with fine, diffused pleating. Narrow strips of skins are sewn to the bottom of soles for extra traction on some boots. Leg sections are decorated with floral and geometric inlaid skin work. In general, men's boots are decorated with a center front vertical design; women's are decorated with a horizontal design that encircles the boot, possibly representing fertility. Men's and women's boots are usually shin- or knee-high.

In Greenland flexible boot soles wrap only slightly around the heel and toe with fine, diffused pleating. Leg sections are painted black or red, or bleached white. In western and eastern Greenland, men and widows generally use black leg sections; red leg sections are used for married women, and white leg sections with lace and floral embroidery around the top are used for unmarried women. In northern Greenland, women's leg sections are often thigh-high and stiffened. The upper edge is decorated with a narrow strip of polar bear skin. Men's boots are generally shin- or calf-high. In some areas of Greenland, both men's and women's boots are decorated with elaborate skin embroidery designs, which are traced back to specific families and communities. Undecorated boots are also used for kayakers and hunters. Indigenous Greenlanders wear their traditional footwear at special ceremonies such as confirmations, weddings, first day of school, and official community events.

In the western Canadian Arctic and coastal Alaska, stiff, boatlike boot soles are pleated with fine pleats in the northern communities and coarser pleats in the South. Some seamstresses manufacture many pairs of the finely pleated boatlike soles and sell them to seamstresses from other areas who use them for their own footwear. Leg sections are generally shin- or knee-high. Thigh-high boots are worn by trappers in areas where they might encounter deep water caught on top of the ice and covered by snow. Dance boots are decorated with red yarn, fur and yarn tassels, beaded panels, pom-poms, and strips of different-colored skins or bias tape.

The variety of styles used in each Alaskan community is exceptional. For example, over fifteen distinct styles are used in coastal Alaskan communities, while just a few miles away across the Bering Strait in coastal Siberian communities only a few styles are used. In Siberia, seamstresses were required to produce at least 100 pairs of skin boots per year for their collective reindeer farms; in Alaska, seamstresses produced footwear for their family and friends, their handiwork was recognized and appreciated by other community members, and occasionally purchased by tourists or cultural institutes. In Siberia, boots are made shin-, knee- or thigh-high from the skins of reindeer legs. Several panels are sewn together to encircle the herder's leg and then attached to a flat, unpleated sole, with a narrow strip of skin sewn in the sole seam. Boots worn by shamans have skeletal lines painted on them using ocher (red clay) mixed with fish eggs or blood. This helps the shamans communicate with the underworld, to show respect, and to appease the spirits thereby protecting people from danger and hunger.

In northern Europe, Saami footwear is unpleated with a firmly stuffed curved toe. The curvature, width, length, and overall shape of the toe vary regionally. Saami slip the toe extension under their ski strap, preventing the ski strap from slipping off their footwear. Leg sections usually extend up to just above the ankle and then a handwoven sash is wrapped around the ankle and up the leg. The sash is decorated with gender-specific designs passed along from one generation to the next. Footwear is decorated with narrow strips of red, yellow, blue, and green fabric sewn into the seams.

Materials

Caribou, or reindeer (domesticated caribou), and ringed sealskins are the most common materials used for northern footwear. Caribou or reindeer skins are used for winter footwear; sealskins are used for summer. When bearded sealskin is available locally or through trade, this large, thick skin is often used for boot soles needed for all seasons. Caribou or reindeer bull skins are used for soles when extra insulation is needed. These soles are less durable than bearded sealskin but provide much greater insulation. For example, hunters or fishers wearing footwear with caribou or reindeer soles can stand all day on the ice waiting for a seal or fish without getting cold feet. Caribou- or reindeer-leg skins are sewn together to make leg sections for boots. These skins last many years, the soles are replaced as they wear out, and the leg sections reused.

Sealskins are either left with the hair on or de-haired by shaving (produces a black skin) or rubbing the hair off (produces a yellowish skin). Some skins are dried and hung outside in the early spring sun to be bleached white. Black

Koriak fur boots. Boots are worn year round by Inuits and are usually made from sealskin, with the hair left on in the winter for added warmth. © RICK RIEWE. REPRODUCED BY PERMISSION.

and yellowish skins are used for waterproof or water-resistant boots, white skins are used in the winter for cold, dry conditions. Some boots are made from sealskins, which are first made into a bag used to store seal fat. Once all the fat is used the bag is reused to store wild berries mixed with fat. Once that is eaten, the bag is fully impregnated with oils and used to make waterproof leg sections on boots used in unfrozen wet areas during the winter.

Other skins used in footwear include a wide variety of species used for the leg sections, including black bear, brown bear, polar bear, wolf, wolverine, fox-leg skins, sea otter, moose, elk, fish, bird, muskrat, beaver, musk ox–leg skin, mountain goat, and mountain sheep. In the early 2000s, some women also use fabric for leg sections.

Technology

Footwear is made from pieces measured using a complex hand-span system passed down from one generation to the next. Pieces are cut out of skins in a preplanned manner that makes the best use of the skin grain, skin thickness, hair color, and hair direction. They are sewn together using animal sinew or artificial sinew and a steel needle and thimble. Traditionally, bone or stone needles and skin thimbles were used. In most cases an overcast or running stitch is used. On some seams a waterproof stitch is used to ensure the boot stays waterproof. When sewing this stitch, the needle penetrates all the way through one skin and only partway through the other skin. The work is then turned over and resewn with the needle going all the way through the second skin and partway through the first skin, preventing the seamstress from making a hole through all layers in any one place.

In Greenland, elaborate skin embroidery is applied around the top of the leg section. This is done by removing the hair from sealskin, bleaching the skins, and then painting them with bright colors. These skins are then cut into very narrow, straight strips and stitched to the leg section. Once it is stitched in place, the strip of skin is cut, allowing the seamstress to sew much smaller pieces than if she had cut the pieces first and then tried to stitch them in place. Many different-colored skins are used for skin embroidery. Today few seamstresses make this type of footwear; they usually purchase these boots from a local business.

Conclusion
Footwear and clothing used throughout the circumpolar region has several common characteristics in that it is generally made from caribou and sealskin, protects individuals from the weather and terrain, and enables seamstresses to communicate to their helping spirits. In addition, footwear and clothing depicts the relationship individuals and groups have to their local environment within the distinct cultural frameworks throughout the circumpolar region.

See also **Boots; Inuit and Arctic Dress.**

BIBLIOGRAPHY

Oakes, Jill and Rick Riewe. *Spirit of Siberia: Traditional Native Life, Clothing, and Footwear.* Washington D.C.: Smithsonian Institution Press, 1998.

———. *Our Boots: An Inuit Women's Art.* New York: Thames and Hudson, Inc., 2000.

Oakes, Jill et al. *Pushing the Margins: Native and Northern Studies.* Manitoba, Canada: University of Manitoba, 2001.

Jill Oakes

IRAN, HISTORY OF PRE-ISLAMIC DRESS

Our knowledge of dress in pre-Islamic Iran comes from pictorial depictions mainly on rock reliefs, metalwork (including coinage), seal impressions, and, from about the second century C.E., wall paintings. Information is fragmentary and episodic, and relates to the ruling households, the military, divinities, and occasionally priests; depictions of women (even female goddesses) are rare.

Elamite Dress (c. 2750–653 B.C.E.)
In its heyday the Elamite empire controlled the region from eastern Mesopotamia to central Asia and Pakistan, but after 1100 B.C.E. its political influence waned. Early Elamite cylinder seals show bearded men (possibly princes or priests), wearing multi-layered skirts—perhaps of hanging feathers, leather strips, or sheepskin—similar to those found in certain votive statues from Mari (an ancient Syrian city), and clay tablets reveal that wool and flax were being exported to neighboring lands. A few seals (c. 2200–1600 B.C.E.) include female figures wearing similar but fuller skirts. However, a bronze statue (now in the Louvre) of Queen Napirasu (d. 1333 B.C.E.) from Susa shows a diagonally necked bodice with elbow-length sleeves, a long, bell-shaped skirt with wide decorated bands around the hips and down the left front, fabric flaps on the right hip, and a deep fringe (possibly of sheep wool) around the hem. Later Elamite rock reliefs (e.g., Kuh-i Farah, c. 800 B.C.E.), although seriously eroded, record ankle-length, long-sleeved robes worn with projecting shoulder collars.

Achaemenid Dress (c. 550–330 B.C.E.)
The Persian Achaemenid family triumphed over the Medes of northwest Iran, seizing land stretching from the Balkans to the Tian Shan mountains in central Asia and China, until its destruction by Alexander the Great. The ceremonial capital of Persepolis provides most costume pictorial evidence; scholastic opinion is divided regarding whether details on the so-called Oxus Treasure (British Museum) and surviving clothing from other central Asian sites such as Pazyryk should be considered Iranian Achaemenid or central Asian dress.

The Persepolis reliefs and the Susa tile revetments (Louvre) reveal nothing of women's and children's dress but show two distinct male costumes: the "Median" dress of long trousers tucked into ankle boots, a tunic under a knee-length, a long-sleeved coat (*kandys*) draped over the shoulders, and a rounded soft cap encircled by metal fillet; and the "Persian" dress of an ankle-length, draped skirt, a top with four deep pleats at the elbow, and a tall, fluted cap (possibly of feathers or padded felt). It is this latter garment that has provoked discussion. Rejecting a theory from the 1930s that the garment was made of an unseamed rectangle of fabric folded on the shoulders and belted to form drapery folds, Anna Roes argued for a sophisticated construction of two separate pieces: a waist-length cape with a triangular insert at the elbow creating four sleeve pleats, and a sari-like skirt with hanging fabric bands down the front, back, and sides. Two decades later, P. Beck (1972) proposed another structure based on two lengths joined at the shoulder, both differently cut to produce the curves and pleats of the distinctive sleeves. Neither theory is entirely satisfactory regarding the skirt as detailed on seated figures. At court, men's hair was worn behind the ears to shoulder-length, tightly curled, while the beards (which may have been false) were carefully arranged into ringlets, interrupted by rows of tight curls.

Parthian or Arsacid Dress (c. 250 B.C.E.–224 C.E.)

The various Silk Roads crossing Asia flourished in the Parthian period, bringing Chinese silk to the West in exchange for horses, wool, and linen. Short-staple cotton was perhaps being cultivated in eastern Iran but was available from east Africa and the Persian Gulf regions. Most detailed information about the dress from this period is gleaned from pictorial art from the ancient cities Palmyra, Dura Europos, Hatra, and Nimrud Dag—as well as from central Asian regions of ancient Syria, ancient Iraq, and ancient Anatolia—but modern specialists in these regions often evaluate such clothing as "national" rather than Parthian "imperial" dress.

The man of rank wore a hip- or thigh-length belted tunic with narrow, long sleeves, although the Palmyran sculptures show a long fabric tie, knotted and looped. There were various methods of fastening tunics, possibly denoting differences in rank, status, or, perhaps, office: wide diagonal openings right to left, small and deep rounded necks, square necks, and extended neck lapels fastening below the front left shoulder. The tunic sometimes had heavy drapery folds forming a U-shaped apron, and a long-sleeved, calf-length, narrow-fitting jacket was worn over this. Loose trousers, often heavily patterned and banded down the center of the leg, were gathered at the ankle or into calf-length boots. A long folded stole, or strip of silk, on the left shoulder, shown on figures in some images, may indicate priestly attire. Regarding head covering, gods, kings, and generals (as those at Hatra and Nimrud Dag) are shown with tall helmets with a narrow front profile, decorated with "pearl" beading.

Information regarding female attire is sparse. The Greek *chiton* is said to be the inspiration behind the Palmyran dress, but ladies' bodices in Khaltchyan wall-reliefs are close-fitting with a deep or shallow neck, with additional material flaring from the breast band. Below this a trailing pleated skirt was worn, and a long, wide stole covered the shoulders or was draped over the arms.

Sasanid Dress (224–658 C.E.)

From the fifth century, Iranian cotton was being exported to China along with linen flax and wool. Chinese imperial histories record that silkworms were smuggled into central Asia in 419 C.E., but the Arab histories and Iranian poetry suggest sericulture was established in Sasanid lands around 300 C.E.. Draw-loom technology was known from eastern Mediterranean lands, but most dress fabrics were still made on the narrow back-strap loom. Tapestry (slit) weave and compound twill weave are mostly associated with Sasanid wool and silk dress fabrics, respectively.

The rock carvings near Shiraz show shahs in fitted bodices, perhaps of molded leather, together with full-length trousers or chaps with long wavy curls of either sheepskin or very fine fabric. By the mid-fourth century a draped apron-like tunic, reaching to the lower calf in front, was worn, and some later silver dishes depict another type of tunic with stiffly pointed side corners. By the late fifth or early seventh century—depending on the date of a carving at Taq-i Bustan—the royal dress was a long-sleeved, knee-length tunic in heavily patterned woven silk, or decorated with padded appliqué forms; the belt had hanging lappets signifying status (the more numerous, the higher the rank). A double row of beading decorated the central front fastening, neck, cuffs, and hem edges. Underneath, ample trousers were gathered into soft ankle boots fastened with long ribbon ties. Each shah wore a distinctive crown often incorporating a large "balloon" (possibly of hair), while princes and generals had tall caps with a slight Phrygian curve ending in a bird or animal head, or decorated with a stylized emblem.

A few images of the Zoroastrian goddess, Anahita, and court entertainers provide most information about women's dress. In a late-third-century relief at Naqsh-i Rustam, Anahita has an ankle-length robe, falling in diaphanous folds and girded by a creped ribbon belt. However, at Taq-i Bustan, carved at least 150 years later, her long-sleeved robe falls from a shoulder clasp with a sleeved coat (possibly felt) draped over her shoulders. Her tall, tasseled headdress is more elaborate than those of female musicians in the hunting compositions beneath. On Sasanid metalwork female dancers are noticeable for their long stoles draped across the front at hip level. In the rare depictions of royal ladies, the dress is similar to those of Anahita, while the children wear miniature versions of the regal ensembles.

In Sasanid times, Zoroastrianism was officially promoted, and Zoroastrian priestly dress was probably formalized in this period. Ritual regulations concerning the lambswool *kusti* (girdle) and cotton *sudra* (shirt), worn by all adult believers, were also probably codified during this period.

See also **Islamic Dress, Contemporary; Middle East: History of Islamic Dress.**

BIBLIOGRAPHY

Beck, P. "A Note on the Reconstruction of the Achaemenid Robe." *Iranica Antiqua* 9 (1972): 116–122. Refers to earlier garment-structure theories, with bibliography.

Colledge, Malcolm A. R. *The Parthian Period*. Leiden, Netherlands: Brill, 1986. Best illustrative overview, with good bibliography.

Fukai, S., and K. Horiuchi. *Taq-I Bustan*. Volume 2. Tokyo: Yamakawa Publishing Company, 1972. Detailed photographs but not comprehensive as it omits lower "hunting" reliefs carved in main grotto.

Herrmann, G. "The Daragird Relief." *Iran* 7 (1969): 63–88. Argument concerns identification of shahs and gives clear drawings of most Sasanid rock reliefs. Contains useful bibliography.

Hofkunst van die Sassanieden. Brussels: Koninklije Musea voor Kunst en Geschiedenis, 1993. An exhibition catalog. Excellent illustrations of Sasanid art including helmets, textiles, metalwork, and full bibliography.

Potts, Daniel T. *The Archaeology of Elam: Formation and Trans-formation of an Ancient Iranian State.* New York: Cambridge University Press, 1999. Little accessible information on dress but comprehensive bibliography.

Roaf, M. "Sculptures and Sculptors at Persepolis." *Iran* 21 (1983). Entire issue devoted to this topic; good illustrations and drawings with thorough bibliography.

Roes, A. "Achaemenid Influence Upon Egyptian and Nomad Art." *Artibus Asiae* 15 (1952).

Patricia L. Baker

IRIBE, PAUL Paul Iribe (1883–1935) was born in Angoulême, France. He started his career in illustration and design as a newspaper typographer and magazine illustrator at numerous Parisian journals and daily papers, including *Le temps* and *Le rire*. In 1906 Iribe collaborated with a number of avant-garde artists to create the satirical journal *Le témoin*, and his illustrations in this journal attracted the attention of the fashion designer Paul Poiret. Poiret commissioned Iribe to illustrate his first major dress collection in a 1908 portfolio entitled *Les robes de Paul Poiret racontées par Paul Iribe*. This limited edition publication (250 copies) was innovative in its use of vivid fauvist colors and the simplified lines and flattened planes of Japanese prints. To create the plates, Iribe utilized a hand-coloring process called *pochoir*, in which bronze or zinc stencils are used to build up layers of color gradually. This publication, and others that followed, anticipated a revival of the fashion plate in a modernist style to reflect a newer, more streamlined fashionable silhouette. In 1911 the couturier Jeanne Paquin also hired Iribe, along with the illustrators Georges Lepape and Georges Barbier, to create a similar portfolio of her designs, entitled *L'Eventail et la fourrure chez Paquin*.

Throughout the 1910s Iribe became further involved in fashion and added design for theater, interiors, and jewelry to his repertoire. He continued to illustrate fashion, opened a store of decorative art on the rue du Faubourg St.-Honoré in Paris, and created textiles for the firm Bianchini Ferier and for designer André Groult. His association with the theater resulted in several publications related to the renowned dancer Vaslav Nijinsky, including the album *Prélude à l'aprés-midi d'un faune*, which captured Nijinsky's choreography for the Claude Debussy composition in photography by Adolph de Meyer.

Iribe is perhaps best recognized for his contributions to the *Gazette du bon ton*. Started in 1912 by the publisher Lucien Vogel, the fashion journal featured the creations of the top couture houses illustrated by the leading visual artists of the day, including Iribe, Georges Barbier, Georges Lepape, A. E. Marty, and Charles Martin. Like Iribe's earlier work, the magazine was a deluxe limited-edition journal. The publication included between eight and ten *pochoir* plates in each issue and helped position fashion graphics as a modern medium. While the *Gazette*

du bon ton slowed its publication during World War I, it resumed putting out monthly editions from the end of the war until 1925, and a total of sixty-nine issues were printed. In 1925, the publisher Condé Nast purchased the *Gazette* and it merged with *Vogue*.

In 1919 Iribe moved to New York, and his art deco style was further disseminated to the American fashion-buying public through his continued work in fashion illustration and interior design. His work was published in seven issues of American *Vogue*, and he also opened a store on Fifth Avenue called Paul Iribe Designs New York–Paris. Iribe was one of the first French fashion figures to work in Hollywood. Cecil B. DeMille commissioned him to create clothing for Gloria Swanson in the 1919 film *Male and Female*. This film marked the beginning of a six-year collaboration with the Hollywood studio, during which Iribe acted as artistic director for eight DeMille films.

Iribe moved back to France in 1930 and became involved in numerous design projects, including the publication of *Choix*, a book that showcased his designs for furniture, decorative arts, and jewelry. He continued to design jewelry, working with Coco Chanel in 1932 to create a line that her couture house produced. In 1933 Iribe was awarded *la Légion d'honneur* for his work as an artist-illustrator. He died of a heart attack in 1935 at Chanel's villa in Roquebrune Cap Martin, France.

See also **Art and Fashion; Art Nouveau and Art Deco; Dance and Fashion; Fashion Illustrators; Fashion Magazines.**

BIBLIOGRAPHY
Lelieur, Anne-Claude. *Paul Iribe: Précurseur de l'art déco.* Paris: Bibliothèque Forney, 1983.

Mackrell, Alice. *An Illustrated History of Fashion: 500 Years of Fashion Illustration.* New York: Costume and Fashion Press, 1997.

Robinson, Julian. *The Golden Age of Style: Art Deco Fashion Illustration.* New York: Harcourt Brace Jovanovich, 1976.

Michelle Tolini Finamore

ISLAMIC DRESS, CONTEMPORARY For both insiders and outsiders, dress is often at the center of debates concerning how Muslims should live in the rapidly changing, globally interconnected world of the early 2000s. Should women cover their heads? Is the *hijab*, the veil, a sign of oppression or a symbol of liberation? Who decides what Muslims should wear? Are Western styles of dress appropriate? Are they necessary for modernization? And what is acceptable for Muslims living in the West?

Islamic dress is layered with overt and subtle symbolic meanings. Many individual men and women dress as Muslims for the purpose of showing their devotion to God. The word Islam means "submission"—not to the religion itself, but to the guidance and will of God. A

Muslim, therefore, is literally "one who submits," and Islamic dress displays that commitment. At the same time, specific styles of dress have been shaped by other factors such as climate, cultural aesthetics, economics, trade patterns, and political ideologies.

The "five arkan," or pillars, of Islam have fundamentally shaped what Muslims believe and practice, including how they dress. These pillars include the *shahada* (a declaration of faith that "there is no god but God and Muhammad is the prophet of God"), *salat* (five daily prayers), *zakat* (the giving of charity; which is sometimes regarded as a religious tax), *Sawm* (the annual month of daytime fasting known as Ramadan), and the *Hajj* (the pilgrimage to Mecca). Cleanliness of the body and clothing is highly valued. Muslims must wash their face, hands, and feet before prayer. Loose clothing makes it easier to bow and kneel. Men and women who have completed the *Hajj* are called "Hajji" or "el-Hajj" and frequently wear garments that display their new status. There is also a special form of dress called *ihram* that is worn during the pilgrimage. For men, this consists of two lengths of white cloth that are wrapped around the upper and lower body. Women on the pilgrimage are expected to wear a simple form of dress from their own culture. One of the major purposes of *ihram* is to eliminate the display of rank and wealth. This is a reflection of the philosophy that all Muslims are equal before God.

Detailed discussions about the five pillars are provided in the Qur'ān (believed to be the literal word of God), the *hadith*s (sayings and traditions of the prophet Muhammad), and codes of *Shari'ah* (Islamic law). Unlike the Catholic church, there is no central authority in Islam. Muslims often follow the pronouncements of reli-

DRESS AND THE REJECTION OF WESTERN INFLUENCES

"A Muslim who wears Western dress cannot but betray his preference for Western civilization and all it stands for. If a man truly loves Islam, is it not logical that he should express that love in his physical appearance?" (Samuillah, pp. 24–25)

gious scholars and leaders, but there is no barrier for individuals who want to study the religion for themselves. There are many different interpretations about the "correct" practice of Islam in everyday life, including how Muslims should be dressed. Many choose to adopt practices that are *sunna* (meaning "encouraged" in religious law as well as "following the path of the prophet Muhammad") and avoid practices that are *haram* ("forbidden" or "dirty"). It is considered *sunna* for men to grow a beard and dye it with henna. Devout men avoid wearing silk and gold, including anything dyed yellow (because it might look like gold). Women avoid wearing perfume that contains alcohol, which Muslims are also not allowed to drink.

Often, these ideals are tempered by more worldly concerns. Although beauty is closely connected with *haya* or "modesty," some simple forms of dress are actually very expensive. In oil-rich states around the Persian Gulf, women from wealthy families can buy a designer Islamic dress that looks modest but costs hundreds of dollars. Under these layers of clothing (or at private parties segregated by gender) they might also wear couture from Europe. Some fashion houses, such as Chanel and Dior, have many clients in the Middle East. In communities where people are not as wealthy, there are often other forms of dress—such as the *chaadaree*, or *burqa*, in Afghanistan—that can be worn to display a higher level of social and economic status. Clothing that covers a woman from head-to-toe is not only costly but makes it physically difficult for her to perform manual labor. Many families cannot afford the expense or loss of income. This is equally true in the United States and Europe, where discrimination against women who are visibly Muslim can make it difficult to hold a job outside of the home.

Forms of Dress

In the Middle East, the most common form of dress for men consists of several layers of clothing including trousers, a *dishdasha* (an ankle-length shirt that buttons down the front), and a cloak called an *aba* or *abaya*. This outermost layer is usually white or brown and is worn

A COMMON INTERPRETATION OF ISLAMIC DRESS

- Men and women should not dress the same
- Clothing should not be tight or reveal the form of the body underneath
- The design, texture, or scent of clothing should not attract undue attention
- A man should cover his body from knees to navel
- A woman should cover everything except for her hands and face
- These rules for men and women apply in public places and private gatherings where both men and women are present; bodies are not for display
- Modesty is appropriate at any age, but particularly important after a girl or boy has reached puberty

with a close-fitting cap called a *kufi*. Over this, men wear a loose head covering known as a *ghutra* that is held in place with a thick cord called *agal*. The *agal* once had a functional purpose (used by Bedouins for tying the legs of camels together), but is now manufactured specifically as an item of dress. Women also wear the *abaya*, but this outer layer is frequently black or gray. Other items of dress vary depending upon the location. Since the Iranian Revolution in 1979, women in that country have been required to wear a head covering and are encouraged to wear the *chador*, a waist-length (or longer) tailored garment that fits closely around the face. In Saudi Arabia, many women wear a *niqab* (a kind of veil), along with dark gloves and socks, leaving only their eyes visible in public. In Oman and the United Arab Emirates, women traditionally wear a mask (also called *niqab*) that covers the face but leaves the hair and neckline showing. This practice is falling out of favor, as many young women prefer to wear the *chador* or the style of *niqab* that is common in Saudi Arabia. These forms of dress are generally made out of wool or cotton cloth and are not only modest but offer protection from the piercing sun and blowing sand.

In Palestine, Syria, and Turkey, many women wear a head covering called *khimar*. This is simply a large triangle of cloth (or a square folded into a triangle) that covers the head and is wrapped around the neck or pinned under the chin. A new style of *khimar* that is easy to wear (particularly for children) is sold in packages of two pieces. The first one covers the hairline; the second one fits under the chin and covers the head and shoulders. This head covering is often worn with a buttoned overcoat called the *jilbab*, or *jellabib*.

Among Muslim women in Malaysia, Indonesia, and East Africa (including immigrants from these areas who live in the United States and Europe), the jilbab is used as a plain, "Arab" style of dress that covers the entire body except for the feet and hands and fits closely around the face. For men, a garment that has spread from the Middle East to many parts of the world is the *kaffiyeh*, a black-and-white or red-and-white checkered shawl that can be draped over a shoulder, wrapped around the head as a turban, or secured over the head with an *agal*. In the West, the *kaffiyeh* is one of the most recognizable symbols of Islam, worn by many political leaders including Yassir Arafat.

In Pakistan and India, men and women wear *salwar kameez*, loose pants covered by a long shirt. This style of dress is originally from Persia. Women also wear the *dupatta*, a long piece of cloth that can be draped over a shoulder or wrapped around the head and body depending on the situation. Men cover their heads with a turban. Many of these items are lightweight and made out of silk, cotton, or a synthetic material like polyester—practical for a hot and humid climate. Unlike clothing in the Middle East, these textiles can be very colorful.

In North and East Africa, religious men often wear headgear, such as a turban or *kufi*, particularly for communal prayers on Friday. (In the United States, many African American Muslim men wear just the *kufi* along with more ordinary Western clothing.) Women in Tanzania, Kenya, and Somalia wear colorful cotton textiles imported from India. These are sold in lengths of six to ten yards that are later cut into pieces—one for a long, loose-fitting dress, and one that is draped over the head and around the shoulders (respectively called *dirac* and *garbasaar* in Somalia). In Morocco, Algeria, and Tunisia, men wear a *burnoose*, a loose cloak with a hood unique to that area. In West Africa, men and women both wear a long, simple gown known by various names including *boubou*, *bubu*, and *baba riga*. Women are not expected to cover their heads, but many do wear a piece of wrapped cloth to signify that they are married. Coverings similar to the *dupatta* and *garbasaar* are limited to use by women who have completed the *Hajj* or live in Niger, northern Mali, and Mauritania, or other areas where many communities have begun to enforce Islamic law. In rural areas of East and North Africa, southern Arabia, and Central Asia, where many people still live a nomadic or semi-nomadic lifestyle, it is also not uncommon for women to go without a head covering.

Political and Economic Context

Over the last century, the Islamic world has gone through many dramatic changes—the discovery of oil ("black gold") in the Middle East and Southeast Asia; the introduction (and sometimes rejection) of Western-style education, markets, technology, and dress; a series of revolutions and wars; and a rapid expansion in population. Although the Islamic religion began in the Middle East, in the early 2000s there are far more Muslims outside that area, in countries such as Pakistan, India, Indonesia, and China. The total number of Muslims has grown to more than 1 billion people.

The production and sale of oil has given some countries incredible wealth. In Brunei, Bahrain, Qatar, and the United Arab Emirates, there are no personal income taxes. Education and health care are provided free of charge. A number of governments have used oil money to build roads, irrigation systems, universities, and other public buildings—sometimes not just for the nation, but also for Muslims in other parts of the world. Farmers, laborers, teachers, and doctors from Egypt, East Africa, and South Asia have been drawn to the Middle East for jobs that pay much more than similar positions at home. Although the media is often closely monitored for sexual and political content, many people have access to videos, satellite television, and the Internet. The Arab television network Al-Jazeera competes with CNN and the BBC.

At the same time, there have been downsides to this economic windfall. Long-standing relationships and tensions that began when Great Britain and France colonized many parts of Africa, Arabia, and South Asia have intensified. The United States has been involved in two wars with Iraq and built or used military bases in Kuwait, Saudi Arabia, Turkey, Afghanistan, and Djibouti. Oil money has brought a new wave of entrepreneurs and professionals from Europe and the United States. In Cairo, anthropologists Elizabeth and Robert Fernea have observed that colonization and contacts with the west have been accompanied by social changes that many Muslims (not only the fundamentalists) have found objectionable.

> Along with our technology go our sales techniques, administrative methods, ideas about investment and economic growth . . . [as well as] rock music, bars and nightclubs full of alcohol and fashionably dressed women. . . . [This is often viewed as] the loss of Egyptian, Arab, and/or Muslim ways of life—a shameful loss of independence, respectability, and honor (p. 440).

In the early 1900s, many Egyptian feminists adopted Western dress and removed their veils as a sign of liberation. In the early 2000s, a new generation has returned to covering their heads. This practice offers some protection from sexual harassment on overcrowded city streets and buses, but it also signals a resurgence of pride in Islam and Islamic practices in everyday life.

In the late 1800s and early 1900s, people in many parts of the Islamic world turned to religion as a source of guidance and unification in their efforts to resist colonization. Remnants of these movements, such as Wahhabism in Saudi Arabia and Mahdism in the Sudan, still exist. Similar approaches are reemerging as a response to cultural and military invasion and to counteract the excesses of globalization. In Afghanistan, where the population has been involved in continuous warfare for more than two decades, the Taliban made an effort to establish order by imposing a very strict interpretation of Islamic law. Girls were forced out of schools; professional women were dismissed from their jobs, required to wear the *chaadaree*, or *burqa*, and could appear in public only if accompanied by a male relative. Many feminists in the West were horrified by these practices and circulated petitions over the Internet begging the Taliban to stop. During the invasion of Afghanistan after 11 September 2001, the United States government and media networks made use of these sentiments by citing the "liberation of women" as one justification for overthrowing that regime.

A more moderate version of political Islam is gaining support from both intellectuals and ordinary citizens in many countries. In Turkey, where the government has tried to "modernize" the nation by banning Islamic dress in public buildings, women who are sympathetic to the Islamist movement have been forced to leave universities and even elected positions in Parliament for expressing their religious and political beliefs through dress. In France, the children of immigrants from Turkey and North Africa have sometimes been expelled from public schools for violating a strict separation of church and state by wearing head coverings. Unfortunately, many

people view Islam (and Islamic dress) as being incompatible with democracy. This has become a very sensitive issue in Turkey as that country is trying to become part of the European Union.

Outside of the Middle East—in areas such as Malaysia, Indonesia, and Somalia—men and women are beginning to wear the *kaffiyeh* and *jilbab* to signal that they are looking to Islam for social and political change. In Malaysia and Indonesia, the government has provided money to build mosques and support religious education, but political Islam is forbidden. Approximately 15 percent of Indonesians are Hindu, Catholic, or Protestant (a designation that must be recorded on official documents such as a driver's license), but there are also more than 180 million Muslims—the largest number of Muslims in a single nation (Farah, p. 273). Indonesia has oil resources and is a member of OPEC, but millions of people live in absolute poverty. Some would like to replace what they view as a corrupt government with one founded on Islamic principles. In East Africa, Somalia has been in a state of chaos since the last government collapsed during a civil war in 1991 without being replaced. Some Somalis would like to initiate a new government based on Islamic law. Others see this as "Arabization"—a non-Somali influence from the Middle East. The rebuilding of that government is complicated by internal differences as well as accusations from Ethiopia and the United States that Somalia is a harbor for terrorists.

The events following September 11th—including the passage of the Patriot Act and military action in Afghanistan and Iraq—have brought intense scrutiny to Islam and Muslims. The visibility of Islamic dress has led many women in particular to feel they must make a choice between personal safety and religion. A report by the Council on American-Islamic Relations notes that many Muslims have been effected by religious and ethnic profiling in public places and at airports, often based on their dress. "The experiences of Muslims in the post–September 11 climate have been unmatched by any previous period. . . . A Muslim woman from Lincoln, Nebraska, was ordered to remove her *hijab* [head covering] before boarding an American Airlines flight. She was frightened by the guard with a gun, so she complied" (pp. 4–5).

At the same time, the number of Muslims in the United States is continuing to grow through immigration as well as conversion. For many people, these difficult times have renewed their sense of commitment to the religion and religious dress. An awareness of Islam in the general public is also growing as more people than ever read books and attend lectures in an effort to gain a better understanding of what is going on in the world.

See also **Burqa; Ethnic Dress; Jilbab; Middle East: History of Islamic Dress.**

BIBLIOGRAPHY

Abbas. *Allah O Akbar: A Journey Through Militant Islam.* London: Phaidon Press Ltd., 1994.

Arthur, Linda, ed. *Undressing Religion: Commitment and Conversion from a Cross-Cultural Perspective.* Oxford: Berg, 2000.

El Guindi, Fadwa. *Veil: Modesty, Privacy and Resistance.* Oxford: Berg, 1999.

Farah, Caesar E. *Islam: Beliefs and Observances.* 7th ed. Hauppauge, N.Y.: Barron's, 2003.

Fernea, Elizabeth W., and Robert A. Fernea. *The Arab World: Forty Years of Change.* New York: Anchor Books, 1997.

Haddad, Yvonne Y., and John L. Esposito, eds. *Muslims on the Americanization Path?* Oxford: Oxford University Press, 2000.

Khan, Maulana W. *Women in Islamic Shari'ah.* New Delhi, India: The Islamic Centre, 1995.

Lindisfarne-Tapper, Nancy, and Bruce Ingham, eds. *Languages of Dress in the Middle East.* Surrey, U.K.: Curzon Press, 1997.

Samiullah, Muhammad. *Muslims in Alien Society: Some Important Problems with Solution in Light of Islam.* Lahore, Pakistan: Islamic Publications, 1982.

Internet Resource

The Status of Muslim Civil Rights in the United States. Washington, D.C.: Council on American-Islamic Relations Research Center, 2002. Available from http://www.cair-net.org/civilrights2002/civilrights2002.doc.

Heather Marie Akou

ITALIAN FASHION During the Renaissance, Italian city-states such as Florence were centers of fashion innovation. For centuries thereafter, however, Paris dominated the world of fashion. Of course, fashions were produced in Italy during that time, but they were usually derivative of French styles. Only since the 1950s has Italy achieved its own independent identity as a source of fashionable clothing for the rest of the world.

The emergence of the "Italian look" drew on important historical advantages, such as the existence of fine craft traditions in textile production, luxury leather goods, high-quality tailoring, and other trades crucial to the fashion system. The artistic textiles and garments of Mariano Fortuny were well known internationally in the decades before World War II, as were the superb men's woolen suiting fabrics woven by Ermenegildo Zegna and fine accessories made by Ferragamo and Gucci. Still, it is symbolic of Italy's relative invisibility on the international fashion scene that Italy's most famous prewar designer, Elsa Schiaparelli, was based in Paris.

Modern Italian fashion first came to international prominence with the rapid post-World War II war reconstruction of the textile industry and the rise of ready-to-wear clothing production, as Nicola White documents in her important book *Reconstructing Italian Fashion.* The postwar rise of Italian fashion was not accidental. A number of Italian manufacturers, with the support of the Italian government, made a systematic effort to create an export-oriented fashion industry that would play a significant role in Italy's postwar economic reconstruction. Beginning in 1949 fashion shows designed to emphasize Italy's heritage of art and culture were staged to capture the attention of foreign journalists. In July 1951 a pivotal fashion show in Florence attracted almost two hundred American buyers and journalists, along with another hundred from Italy and elsewhere in Europe. Soon journalists and department store buyers attending the Paris fashion shows began to take the train down to Florence. There, fashion presentations were conceived, in part, to cater to the demand for creatively constructed, well-made ready-to-wear combining distinction and informality, adapted to the American fondness for sunny weather and colorful, affordably priced garments. Originally, the Italian *alta mode* (couture) houses also showed in Florence, but soon the couturiers for a variety of reasons began to show instead in Rome, where many of them were members of Roman society. There they organized and presented their own singular creations for *la dolce vita.*

American journalists enthusiastically promoted "the Italian Look," identifying it with casual yet aristocratic elegance. Italian designers were said to have a special knack for resort wear; capri pants, sandals, gold jewelry, and chic sunglasses were essential elements of Italian style. Italian fashion offered an appealing (and less expensive) alternative to the more formal Paris couture.

The commercial and cultural relationship between Italy and America played an important role in the postwar development of Italian fashion. One manifestation of this was the close connection between the worlds of film and fashion. For example, the Fontana Sisters, who had opened their couture house in Rome in 1944, became closely associated with Hollywood glamour. Ava Gardner wore Fontana dresses in the 1953 film *The Barefoot Contessa.* Other film stars, including Audrey Hepburn, Elizabeth Taylor, and Kim Novak, wore Fontana Sisters evening dresses, and Margaret Truman was married in a Fontana Sisters wedding dress in 1956. Also important in the glamorous world of film was Emilio Schuberth, who was born in Naples in 1904 and opened a couture house in Rome in 1938. Among his clients were Gina Lollobrigida and Sophia Loren.

Emilio Pucci entered the fashion business in 1948 and quickly became known for his kaleidoscopic textile designs, which were made up into "featherweight" jersey scarves, shirts, and other separates. Pucci helped establish the reputation of Italian designers for easy, comfortable, body-conscious clothing. His brightly colored fashions were part of a broader range of Italian products, such as Vespa motor scooters and Olivetti typewriters, that became icons of modern style. By the early 1960s, it was clear that Italy had changed the way the world looked; the word "Italian" had become synonymous with "good design."

Another important Italian designer was Roberto Capucci, born in 1930, who opened his own atelier in Rome in 1950 and quickly gained a reputation as a master of both silhouette and color. Capucci approached his work as an artist, pleating and manipulating fabric into fluid, sculptural forms. Probably the single most important and successful Italian designer to emerge during the 1960s was Valentino. Valentino Gavarni studied couture in Paris before opening his own *alta moda* house in Rome in 1960; his career now spans more than four decades. He designs both ready-to-wear and couture, and is known for his fondness for brilliant red fabrics. His opulent gowns have appealed to many celebrities, from Sophia Loren to Gwyneth Paltrow, but his most famous client was Jacqueline Kennedy, who wore a lace-trimmed Valentino dress for her marriage to Aristotle Onassis.

The Italian Look that had such a profound impact on women's fashions extended to men's wear as well. Even before World War II, Italy had an international reputation for the highest quality bespoke shirts and men's accessories. By the 1950s, tailoring firms such as Brioni created the "Continental look" in menswear. Italian tailors created luxurious, body-conscious suits that offered a clear alternative to the dominant Ivy League look of American men's wear and the traditional styles of London's Savile Row.

The persistent, unresolved competition between Florence and Rome, each with its own schedule of fashion shows, contributed to the rise of Milan, which emerged in the 1970s as the center of Italian fashion for both men and women. Some of the most innovative Italian houses, including Krizia and Missoni, shifted their collections to Milan, as did the influential stylist Walter Albini, who designed for several different firms that showed in Milan, as well as producing clothing for his own label.

A northern Italian industrial city, Milan lacked the historic allure of Rome and Florence, but was able to draw on the established Italian tradition of fine textiles. Textile producers in northern Italy provided financial backing to Italian clothing manufacturers who showed in Milan. Moreover, Milan was known for modern product design, and *Vogue Italia* had been published there beginning in 1961. The rise of a ready-to-wear clothing industry was a natural consequence of these circumstances. Two designers in particular rose to prominence and worldwide fame in this milieu: Giorgio Armani and Gianni Versace.

Armani revolutionized men's wear in the 1970s, creating unstructured jackets that were as comfortable as sweaters and that radiated an air of seductive elegance. Armani's clothes were prominently featured in the 1980 film *American Gigolo*; by 1982 his picture was on the cover of *Time* magazine. His women's wear was also characterized by an easy elegance and luxurious minimalism. Meanwhile other Italian firms long known for fine fabrics and superb workmanship, such as Ermenegildo Zegna, also benefited from the rise of Italian tailoring to

a position of world leadership from the 1970s onward.

Very different from Armani was Gianni Versace, who founded his own label in 1978. Where Armani emphasized understated luxury, his rival Versace grounded his designs in an aesthetic of flamboyance and display; he produced, for both men and women, some of the most sexually expressive clothing ever made within the mainstream of fashion. After Gianni Versace was murdered in 1997 in Miami, his sister Donatella became the company's head designer. Having collaborated closely with her brother for many years, she was able to build on his aesthetic, while also making her own contributions to the Versace style. Popular music, for example, had always been a passion of Gianni's, but became even more central to Donatella's style. Her body-revealing and consciously outrageous dresses, worn by top singers and actresses, became by the early 2000s an eagerly awaited feature of the annual Oscar and other entertainment business award ceremonies.

Franco Moschino was overshadowed commercially by Armani and Versace, but his witty send-ups of the fashion system were popular with women who wanted to be seen as stylish but not as "fashion victims." Other important Italian designers of the late twentieth and early twenty-first centuries include Romeo Gigli; Gianfranco Ferré; knitwear designer Laura Biagiotti; and Renzo Rosso, founder of the irreverent sportswear firm Diesel.

Among the most remarkable success stories of Italian fashion in the late twentieth century are the revival of Gucci under the direction of the American Tom Ford, the rise of the firm of Prada, and the impact of Dolce & Gabbana. After Miuccia Prada took charge of her grandfather's small, respected leatherwear firm in the 1980s, it burgeoned into an international phenomenon in accessories, shoes, and clothing. Her first big success was a black nylon backpack with a triangular silver label that became a must-have cult item among fashion-conscious women. By the mid-1990s, Prada bags and shoes were setting the international standard for cool. Meanwhile, Gucci, founded in the 1920s as a leather-goods firm, and famous among jet-setters in the 1960s, had lost prestige until its reinvention in the 1990s as a source of ultrasexy fashions and accessories. Domenico Dolce and Stefano Gabbana founded Dolce & Gabbana in 1982, and skyrocketed to fame with fashions that recall the sex-bomb stars of 1950s Italian cinema.

Italy's success as a center of modern fashion derives in large part from a uniquely Italian model of the fashion industry, quite different from that in other countries. It is immediately apparent, for example, that the family unit remains an important feature of the Italian fashion system. Craft traditions also remain strong. At the same time, the most up-to-date technology is readily available. While a handful of star designers from Milan and Rome attract public attention, hundreds of anonymous but highly trained creative talents work at family firms and large companies throughout the country. A skilled workforce is available both for factory employment and in small-scale production by independent contractors. Florence, Rome, and later Milan have all been important fashion centers, but the geography of Italian fashion is widely dispersed, and different regions of Italy specialize in different materials and goods. In addition to the regional segmentation of production in specific geographic areas known as "the Districts," the Italian fashion system is also characterized by the vertical integration of production from fiber to finished product.

The Italian fashion system in the early 2000s integrates state-of-the-art production of modern apparel, relaxed tailoring, luxury leather goods and knitwear, and research into new modes of design and production together with thread, yarn, and fabric innovations. Italian style is characterized by understated luxury and modernism, as well as glamour and sensuality. Fashion designers in Italy are not considered "artists" so much as skilled workers within an industrial system. One of the dominant characteristics of the Italian fashion industry is its interdisciplinary nature: the seamless blend of product development, new materials and technology, new communications methods, celebrity, tradition, and art.

Since the Biennale di Firenze in 1997, which included a city-wide exhibition that posed the relationship between art and fashion, further opportunities of this kind of convergence have been created; for example, the Fondazione Prada in Milan has an exhibition policy of promoting contemporary art. Nothing could be more representative of a designer's aesthetic spirit than a flagship store. In 2000, Prada Group hired the eminent architect Rem Koolhaas to conceive of new and technologically innovative retail spaces for the presentation of products in new and ultra-modern ways. And, as Guy Trebay wrote in the *New York Times*, Carla Sozzani, proprietor of Corso Como 10 in Milan, presents Italian and international luxury brands in a "true theater of commerce."

Italian fashion has evolved to supply the market with styles based on both the latest technology and traditional craftsmanship. Designers concur that imagination, research and experimentation are the basis for the Italian Look.

See also **Armani, Giorgio; Capucci, Roberto; Dolce & Gabbana; Moschino, Franco; Prada; Pucci, Emilio; Valentino; Versace, Gianni and Donatella.**

BIBLIOGRAPHY

Bianchino, Gloria, et al. *Italian Fashion.* Milan: Electa, 1987.

Gastel, M. *50 anni di moda italiana.* Milan: Vallardi, 1995.

Giacomoni, Silvia. *The Italian Look Reflected.* Milan: Mazzotta, 1984.

Malossi, Gino, ed. *Il Motore della moda.* Florence: Monacelli Press, 1998.

Menkes, Susy. "Are Italian Designer Brands Having an Identity Crisis?" *International Herald Tribune,* 1 March 2000.

Steele, Valerie. *Fashion: Italian Style.* New Haven, Conn., and London: Yale University Press, 2003.

Trebay, Guy. "Fashion Diary; A Model and Her Traitorous Stilettos." *The New York Times,* 5 March 2002.

White, Nicola. *Reconstructing Italian Fashion: America and the Development of the Italian Fashion Industry.* Oxford: Berg, 2000.

Valerie Steele and Gillion Carrara

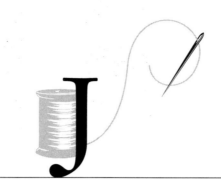

J

JACKET A jacket is short coat, worn by both men and women. Apart from the suit, the jacket is one of the most important pieces in a man's wardrobe. If cut and styled well, and if made in a fairly neutral color palette, this versatile piece of outerwear is suitable for both formal and leisure activities. A jacket should never be exaggerated in the shoulder or tight-fitting in the body, but cut proportionately to a man's height and width in single- or double-breasted versions, with notched lapels or Nehru collar revers. There are countless styles and shapes of jackets through history, but each fits neatly into formal and semiformal styles.

History

In April 1857 the women's magazine *Corriere delle dame* announced the arrival of the jacket (a shortened version of the morning coat with shorter jacket skirts), a style that would go on to become an essential item for both men's and women's wardrobes. The *Adam Magazine* stated in its July 1935 issue "The jacket, a type of coat that is neither tail coat nor redingote, will be the general fashion in a single-breasted version with skirts that do not reach the knee." Adam went onto say how the jacket "barely covers the buttocks and is shaped like a sack."

The jacket seems to have originated during the Middle Ages or early Renaissance as the jerkin, a more fitted version of the older short tunic worn by working-class men. By the early eighteenth century, the jacket became standard working dress for those employed both in agriculture as well as by servants in urban settings.

From the late 1830s, fitted single-breasted lounge jackets (as opposed to more loosely cut jackets of the previous century), with darts beneath the arms, small revers, and waisted pockets became popular with middle-class men, with a double-breasted version appearing about 1862 (which would later become known as the reefer jacket). At that time the single-breasted Norfolk jacket, which buttoned high to the neck, became very fashionable, particularly for country sporting activities.

But by the end of the nineteenth century, only three-buttoned styles were deemed fashionable, with the lounge jacket remaining the most popular. One version, made with silk-fronted lapels, was often worn to dinner parties and would become known simply as a dinner jacket (part of the formal suit known as a "tuxedo").

Similar styles to those worn in the nineteenth century were worn for most of the twentieth century and into the present century as well. Sports jackets are still worn with flannels, the Norfolk remains a sporting favorite, and blazers with brass buttons are popular summer attire when worn with white pants. The upper garment of a man's suit is known as a jacket, and "dinner jacket" remains an alternative term for the ensemble known as "black tie."

Jackets in the Early 2000s

The term "jacket" has assumed a much wider meaning. No longer simply associated with more formal styles, "jacket" has become an umbrella term for many styles, including sports jackets, Harringtons, anoraks, blazers, and even bomber jackets. Originally cut in wool, tweed, and cotton, current styles incorporate nylon, leather, suede, and hemp.

See also **Blazer; Coat; Outerwear; Sports Jacket; Windbreaker.**

BIBLIOGRAPHY

Amies, Hardy. *A,B,C of Men's Fashion.* London: Cahill and Company Ltd., 1964.

Byrde, Penelope. *The Male Image: Men's Fashion in England 1300–1970.* London: B.T. Batsford, 1979.

Chenoune, Farid. *A History of Men's Fashion.* Paris: Flammarion, 1993.

De Marley, Diana. *Fashion for Men: An Illustrated History.* London: B.T. Batsford, Ltd. 1985.

Keers, Paul. *A Gentleman's Wardrobe.* London: Weidenfeld and Nicolson, 1987.

Roetzel, Bernhard. *Gentleman: A Timeless Fashion.* Cologne, Germany: Konemann, 1999.

Schoeffler, O. E., and William Gale. *Esquire's Encyclopedia of 20th Century Fashions.* New York: McGraw-Hill, 1973.

Wilkins, Christobel. *The Story of Occupational Costume.* Poole, U.K.: Blandford Press, 1982.

Tom Greatrex

JAMES, CHARLES Charles Wilson Brega James was born 18 July 1906, in Camberley, Surrey, England. He was described by a friend, Sir Francis Rose, as temperamental,

Charles James fitting a dress for Mrs. Randolph Hearst. Known for his obsessive attention to the fit of garments, James created gowns for several prominent socialites during his career. © JERRY COOKE/CORBIS. REPRODUCED BY PERMISSION.

artistic, and blessed even in childhood with the ability to escape the mundane chores of life like a trapeze artist. His mother's family was socially prominent in Chicago and his father was a British military officer, so young Charles experienced an international upbringing. He was educated at Harrow, a British public school, where he met the fellow fashion enthusiast and fashion photographer Cecil Beaton, whose images later defined James's work.

While still in his teens James initiated his design career in Chicago, where friends of his mother supported him. He began by making patterned scarves that he modeled and sold from his office desk at the architectural division of a utilities company, where he was employed. When he was fired from his job, he turned to millinery.

He sculpted hats directly on the heads of clients in the shop he had named after a school friend, Charles Boucheron. In 1928 James left Chicago in a swirl of financial confusion and relocated in New York City. He was there long enough for Diana Vreeland to observe and comment on his hats, to have his hats merchandised through a prominent department store of the time, and to begin designing dresses before heading to London in 1929. For the next ten years he divided his time between London and Paris, with brief promotional journeys to Chicago and New York. During this period he opened his first salon in London, located in Mayfair, but he quickly declared bankruptcy. In 1933 he reopened the business.

James, who was never afraid to try new materials, spiraled a zipper around the torso in 1929, thus designing his famous taxi dress. The taxi dress and several other of his designs were licensed in the early 1930s so that manufacturers in both England and the United States could copy them. Marketed in famous department stores of the day—most notably Best and Company, Marshall Field's, and Fortnum and Mason—these garments gave his designs, if not his name, wide visibility. Friends of James's mother on both sides of the Atlantic were counted among his most enthusiastic clients for his increasing output of couture garments, at least until her death in 1944. Additionally, his designs intrigued actresses such as Gertrude Lawrence and women with artistic leanings such as Anne, countess of Rosse, and Marit Guinness Aschan. By this time, however, the twin nemeses of James's career were obvious: his desire to receive outsized financial rewards for his designs, coupled with perfectionism and his insistence on total control, eventually destroyed him.

The late 1930s were a period of great and lasting creativity for James. He produced the Corselette or L'Sylphide evening dress (1937); the two-pattern piece halter gown (1937); La Sirène evening dress with a pleated front panel (1938); a raised, pouf-fronted gown (1939); and the Figure-8 wrapped skirt (1939). In 1937 James held his first showing in Paris; included among the garments were striking wraps made of old silk ribbons from the firm of Colcombet. For the remainder of his design career, James produced variants of the ribbon gowns he first fashioned for this Paris show. The gowns were initially in two pieces, bodice and skirt, with the winglike skirt featuring tapering tips of ribbon ending in infinity at the waistline; later examples featured one-piece skirts constructed of cut fabric terminating in a much less graceful manner. Indeed, James continually reused many of the designs that he first created in the 1930s. For example, the garment made for Austine Hearst that James himself identified as his thesis in dressmaking, the 1953 Clover Leaf or Abstract gown, actually evolved from a trilobed, skirted gown created in 1938 and a cloverleaf crown hat designed in 1948. Excluding mass-produced designs of the 1930s, for which no records are known to exist, James created just over one thousand designs during his career. Only a few of James's designs are titled; those that generally identify a unique cut rather than a single garment.

Because of various financial escapades that skirted the limits of legality, James found himself in 1939 no longer welcome in England. The next year he opened Charles James, Incorporated, at 64 East Fifty-seventh Street, New York City. Virtually ignoring wartime rationing, he began designing collections for Elizabeth Arden and redesigning her couture collection in 1944; their relationship was severed in 1945 because of financial overruns. However, the Arden-James partnership spawned a Cecil Beaton drawing of several of James's greatest designs, including a variant of the Sirène gown, which is associated with the collaboration.

Following his year-long stint at Arden, James established himself at 699 Madison Avenue, the address where he remained longer than any other in his career. One observer quipped that it was James's perpetual house of torture, not couture. The majority of extant James couture creations came from the Madison Avenue workrooms. James did not let go of his creations easily. He made his clients pay, sometimes twice for the same gown, and sometimes for a garment he had also promised another client. He was notorious for not having garments delivered on time. He was known to cut completed garments off of clients because he was unhappy with either the product or the client. Despite his volatile and often outrageous behavior, his clients acknowledged his genius for cut and color, and many of them supported him financially until the end of his career.

James was obsessed with understanding exactly how clothes worked on the body. He spent thousands of dollars in 1950 and 1951 trying to understand how a sleeve worked. The result was an arced sleeve that drew an editorial observation that James's interest in a sleeve was equivalent to an engineer's interest in a bridge. The writer had it right, for James worked not only with tools associated with dressmaking but also construction tools like calipers, a compass, and a plumb line, among others. During his later years James tried teaching his theories, which related to the proportion of the female figure and how it intersected with apparel construction. In the end, some of his clients found his clothes a joy to wear, while others were tortured. One even bought two opera seat tickets, one for the skirt of her "Butterfly" gown, the other for its sweeping, layered tulle back panel.

So sure was James of the cut of his garments that only rarely does one find him using either patterned fabrics or surface embellishment. Indeed, one of the joys of looking at a James creation is following the flow of seams, seams that seem to go in previously unexplored directions. He made this indulgence easy by selecting contrasting fabrics, such as silk jersey, satin, and taffeta or velvet, organdy, and satin to meld in skirts of black, gar-

net, and tobacco brown or rose red, white, and ruby. He enjoyed blending cool celadon and celery greens, as well as contrasting warm moss and cool bottle greens. When combinations of purple, pink, and green were all the rage in the mid-1940s, James never blended such colors; rather, he would meld dusty rose and pale gold; mustard and maroon; and oranges and blacks in different materials. On a garment's surface he treated the two sides of the fabric equally, playing the color and texture of the one against the other.

For roughly a decade, from 1947 to 1954, James achieved success and recognition. His garments were acquired by many of the fabled socialites of the period, including Mrs. William (Babe) Paley, Mrs. William Randolph (Austine) Hearst Jr., Mrs. Harrison (Mona) Williams, Mrs. Cornelius Vanderbilt Whitney, Mme. Arturo Lopez-Willshaw; by fabled theatrical personalities such as Gypsy Rose Lee and Lily Pons; and by notable collectors of art such as Dominique de Menil. But the most important client of his career was Millicent Huddleston Rogers, a Standard Oil heiress. In her he found a perfect figure to dress, a client with whom he could discuss art and design. Moreover, she was able to pay his inflated prices. She arranged an exhibition of James's work at the Brooklyn Museum in 1948; the show featured the garments he had made for her during the previous ten years. These formed the nucleus of the unequaled collection of Charles James material at this institution, which includes not just garments but half and full toiles and card patterns. Of all James's clients, Rogers is the only one with whom he is known to have codesigned a garment, an eighteenth-century inspired, open-robe gown.

Even while the manager Kate Peil was keeping his dress salon on an even keel, James was becoming restless and demanding more recognition of his talents as well as increased financial reward. To this end he rapidly entered into contractual arrangements with a variety of manufacturers. In 1951 he began by working with the Cavanaugh Form Company, a mannequin manufacturer, to produce his uniquely proportioned, papier-mâché dress form that he called Jenny. In 1952 he began designing collections of dresses and separates for Seventh Avenue's Samuel Winston and suits and coats for William Popper that were retailed by Lord and Taylor. In 1953 James designed furs for Gunther Jaeckel and belts for Bruno Belt based on his "floating line" principle—that is, the waist is not a true oval but has depth as well as dimension. In 1954 he added a line of jewelry to be manufactured by Albert Weiss and agreed to design for another Seventh Avenue concern, Dressmaker Casuals. By the time this last contract was signed, however, previously signed agreements were unraveling due to James's inability to deliver designs on time and his convoluted business practices. Two Coty awards in 1950 and 1954 for "great mystery of color and artistry of draping" and "giving new life to an industry through his sculpturesque ready-to-wear coats designed for Dressmaker Casuals" did nothing for the ensuing courtroom battles that effectively ended the most productive and potentially profitable period in James's career.

He tried in 1956 to design a line of Borgana synthetic fur coats with Albrecht Furs as well as a coat for off-the-rack distribution by E. J. Korvette. Most astonishingly, he designed a line of infant wear to be manufactured by Alexis Corporation of Atlanta. James married Nancy Lee Gregory in 1954 and soon had a young family. His success with the baby garments surely lay in the fact that once again he had at his disposal a live model on which to experiment, his son, Charles Junior. As with so many other early designs that evolved over the years, James transformed some of the baby clothes into adult attire.

By 1958 James was a beaten man, unwelcome on Seventh Avenue, and mentally, physically, and financially drained. His marriage ended in 1961, and in 1964 he moved into New York's bohemian hotel, the Chelsea. Here he worked with the illustrator Antonio to document his career. Old clients joined with his protégé Halston in 1969 in a bravely attempted salute to his career. James attempted to document the creations of a lifetime, whether they were in public or private holdings. He accomplished some design work with Elsa Peretti and Elizabeth de Cuevas. Above all, during those final years of his life, Charles James was fanatical about securing his proper place in the history of twentieth-century fashion.

His fellow fashion designers, potentially his most severe critics, left no question regarding their assessment of his talent. Poiret passed his mantle to James, and Schiaparelli and Chanel dressed in his clothes. Dior praised him for being the inspiration for the New Look, and Balenciaga saw James as the greatest and best American couturier; moreover, he believed that James was the only couturier who had raised dressmaking from an applied to a pure art form.

See also **Art and Fashion; Halston; Milliners.**

BIBLIOGRAPHY

Coleman, Elizabeth A. *The Genius of Charles James*. New York: Holt, Rinehart and Winston, 1982.

Martin, Richard. *Charles James*. London: Thames and Hudson, 1997.

Elizabeth Ann Coleman

JAPANESE FASHION The appearance of Western clothing and fashion during the Meiji era (1868–1912) represents one of the most remarkable transformations in Japanese history. Since the United States' 1854 treaty allowing commerce, negotiated by Commodore Matthew Perry, the Japanese have enthusiastically and effectively borrowed and adapted styles and practices from Western countries. Until then, Japan had isolated itself economically, politically, and culturally from the West as well as

Children in traditional Japanese costume. During the Meiji period, the T-shaped *kosode* became known as the *kimono,* and it is now recognized as the national dress of Japan. The *hakama,* as worn by the young boy, can be worn as an outer garment over the *kimono.* © JOHN DAKERS; EYE UBIQUITOUS/CORBIS. REPRODUCED BY PERMISSION.

neighboring countries for two hundred years. The new Meiji era heralded hope for the future, and government officials felt change necessary for the system to quickly convert Japan into a modern state. Emperor Meiji instituted a parliamentary form of government and introduced modern Western educational and technological practices. The Japanese were then exposed widely to Western influences, and its impact on people's lives has been impressive.

This new modern phenomenon encouraged and expedited the spread of Western clothing among ordinary people, and it became a desirable symbol of modernization. It was first adopted for men's military uniforms, with French- and British-style uniforms designed for the army and navy, as this style was what Westerners wore when they first arrived in Japan. Similarly, starting in 1870, government workers, such as policemen, railroad workers, and postal carriers, were required to wear Western male suits. Even in the court of the emperor, the mandate to dress in Western clothing was passed for men in 1872 and for women in 1886. The emperor and empress, as public role models, took the lead and also adopted Western clothing and hairstyles when attending official events, and

Japanese socialites were also participating in lavish balls in Western-style evening gowns and tuxedos.

By the 1880s, both men and women had more or less adopted Western fashions. By 1890, men were wearing Western suits although it was still not the norm, and Western-style attire for women was still limited to the high nobility and wives of diplomats. Kimonos continued to dominate in the early Meiji period, and men and women combined Japanese kimonos with Western accessories. For instance, for formal occasions, men wore Western-style hats with *haori*, a traditional waistcoat, *hakama*, an outer garment worn over the kimono that is either split like pants between the legs or nonsplit like a skirt.

Conversely, there was also a trend for Japanese goods in the West. The opening of Japan's doors to the West enabled the West to significantly come into contact with Japanese culture for the first time. New trade agreements beginning in the 1850s resulted in an unprecedented flow of travelers and goods between the two cultures. By the

end of the nineteenth century, Japan was everywhere, such as in fashion, interior design, and art, and this trend was called *Japonisme*, a term coined by Philip Burty, a French art critic. Western appreciation for Japanese art and objects quickly intensified, and World Fairs played a major role in the spread of the taste for Japanese things. In an age before the media, these fairs were influential forums for the cultural exchange of ideas: London in 1862, Philadelphia in 1876, and Paris in 1867, 1878, and 1889.

Fashion after World War II

During the Taisho period (1912–1926), wearing Western clothing continued to be a symbol of sophistication and an expression of modernity. It was in this period that working women such as bus conductors, nurses, and typists started wearing Western clothes in everyday life. By the beginning of the Showa period (1926–1989), men's clothing had become largely Western, and by this time, the business suit was gradually becoming standard apparel for company employees. It took about a century for

Western-style clothing for sale in Japan. In the mid-nineteenth century, Japanese dress began to be influenced by the West, and by the late twentieth and early twenty-first centuries, most urban Japanese only wore traditional clothing on special occasions. © MICHAEL S. YAMASHITA/CORBIS. REPRODUCED BY PERMISSION.

Table 1: Japanese Designers' Year of First Collection in Paris

Japanese Designers	First Collection in Paris
Kenzo	1970
Issey Miyake	1973
Kansai Yamamoto*	1974
Yuki Torii	1975
Hanae Mori	1977
Junko Koshino	1977
Yohji Yamamoto	1981
Comme des Garçons by Rei Kawakubo	1981
Junko Shimada	1981
Hiroko Koshino*	1982
Zucca by Akira Onozuka	1988
Mitsuhiro Matsuda*	1990
Trace Koji Tatsuno	1990
Atsuro Tayama	1990
Yoshiki Hishinuma	1992
Masaki Matsushita	1992
Junya Watanabe	1993
Shinichiro Arakawa	1993
Naoki Takizawa**	1994
Koji Nihonmatsu	1995
Miki Mialy	1996
Junji Tsuchiya	1996
Yoichi Nagasawa	1997
Keita Maruyama	1997
Oh!Ya? By Hiroaki Ohya	1997
Gomme by Hiroshige Maki	1997
Hiromichi Nakano	1998
Yuji Yamada	1999
Undercover by Jun Takahashi	2002

*Hiroko Koshino, Kansai Yamamoto, and Mitsuhiro Matusda are no longer showing their collections in Paris but continue to design in Japan.
**Takizawa started designing for Issey Miyake's menswear in 1994 and, after Miyake withdrew from his women's wear in 1999, Takizawa took over the collection.

Western clothing to completely infiltrate Japanese culture and for people to adopt it, although women were slower to change.

After World War II, the strong influence from the United States caused Japanese ways of dressing to undergo a major transition, and people began to more readily follow the trends from the West. Japanese women were starting to replace the loose-fitting trousers called *monpe*, required wear for war-related work, with Western-style skirts. By the early 2000s, the kimono had virtually disappeared from everyday life in Japan. Kimonos were worn only by some elderly women, waitresses in certain traditional Japanese restaurants, and those who teach traditional Japanese arts, such as Japanese dance, the tea ceremony, or flower arrangement. Furthermore, special events at which women wear kimonos included *hatsumode* (the new year's visit to shrines or temples), *seijinshiki* (ceremonies celebrating young people's reaching the age of twenty), university graduation ceremonies, weddings, and other important celebrations and formal parties.

Fashion information from Europe, such as Christian Dior's New Look, was disseminated by way of the United States. The new trends and fashion were generated pri-

marily from the American and European movies shown to the Japanese public. For instance, when the English film *The Red Shoes* was first screened in Japan in 1950, red shoes became fashionable among young people. Similarly, when the film *Sabrina*, starring Audrey Hepburn, was shown in 1954, young Japanese women became fond of tight-fitted Sabrina pants, and flat low-heel Sabrina sandals became trendy. After the mid-1960s, Japanese men adopted the new "Ivy Style," which paid homage to the fashions of American Ivy League university students. This style supposedly came from the traditional fashions of America's elite class and spread from young students to middle-aged Japanese men.

As Japan's economy prospered in the 1980s, the Japanese fashion and apparel industries expanded rapidly and became very profitable as consumers were becoming fashion-conscious. A new fashion movement called the "DC Burando" was focused on brands of clothing with insignia or with clearly identified styling of specific fashion designers. Famous brands, such as Isao Kaneko, Bigi by Takeo Kikuchi, and Nicole by Hiromitsu Matsuda, among many others, had cult-like followings. Some of the women's fashion trends diffused during this decade were *bodikon* (body-conscious) style, emphasizing the natural lines of the body, and *shibukaji* (Shibuya casual), originating among high school and college students who frequented the boutiques of Tokyo's Shibuya Ward shopping streets.

While Japanese create their own unique trends, they are at the same time voracious followers of Western fashion. They are eager to dress themselves in the latest designs from such names as Chanel, Yves Saint Laurent, Christian Dior, and Gucci. Even in the traditional corporate world, many companies implemented the trend "Casual Friday" that originated in the United States, allowing workers to wear casual clothing on Fridays.

Japanese Youth Fashion
In Japanese society of the early twenty-first century, the uncontested arbiters of fashion, street fashion in particular, were high school and junior high school students.

"The widespread popularity of the 'Japanese fashion' in the 1980s was a decisive factor in placing Tokyo on the list of international fashion capitals. A number of Japanese designers ... established the Tokyo Designers' Council in the early 1980s to handle the inflow of foreign editors covering the local collections."

Lise Skov, in "Fashion Trends, Japonisme and Postmodernism."

Among them, loose, baggy white knee socks deliberately pushed down to the ankles like leg warmers were all the rage. Fashion-conscious girls have took the lead in setting fashion trends. Young Japanese embraced Western fashion in a unique Japanese way. While Japan produced its own distinctive fashion, it drew on a mix of the latest trends from the United States and Europe. They became the new breed of young Japanese who were not afraid to break and challenge the traditional values and norms.

In the early twenty-first century, it became common on the streets of Tokyo to see groups of young girls with long, dyed-brown hair, tanned skin, and miniskirts or short pants that flare out at the bottom. Their natural black hair was often replaced with hues of bleached-blond and red. It became fashionable to have a light suntan with heavy makeup. Many of them wore thick-soled mules in the summer and white boots with towering platform soles in winter. As in the West, tattoos were also part of the latest fashion. Previously, tattoos held a connection to the Yakuza, the Japanese mafia, who adorned themselves with elaborate tattoos as a badge of membership.

As Japan faced the worst economic recession in history, the younger generation's value system had become changed—the result of a deliberate move away from traditional ideology and ways of life. The previous generation's Japanese values, such as selfless devotion to their employers, respect for seniors, and perseverance, were breaking down. The decline of traditional way of thinking had accelerated in the teenage generation. Attending cram schools after their regular school hours was no longer the norm. The Japanese shifted from deeply disciplined, industrial attitudes to much freer consumerist ways. The doctrine of long study hours and single-minded focus on exams and careers that helped build Japan were disappearing and evaporating. The Japanese youth post–World War II became more hedonistic and wanted to have fun and live moment to moment, and their attitude was reflected in their norm-breaking fashion and styles.

Designers and Their Influence

As Japanese began to consume Western fashion, Japanese designers were becoming prominent in the West, especially in Paris. They are said to have created the Japanese fashion phenomenon and influenced many Western designers. Kenzo in 1970, Issey Miyake in 1973, Hanae Mori in 1977, Rei Kawakubo of Comme des Garçons and Yohji Yamamoto in 1981, first appeared in the Western fashion world and have since solidified their positions. Fashion professionals recognize and accept their achievements because of their "Japaneseness" reflected on their designs, and many called it "the Japanese fashion" only because these clothes were definitely not Western in regard to constructions, silhouettes, shapes, prints, and combination of fabrics. The Japanese public is reminded of its racial and ethnic heritage every

"When I first began working in Japan, I had to confront the Japanese people's excessive worship of things foreign and fixed idea of what clothes ought to be. I began … to change the rigid formula for clothing that the Japanese followed."

Issey Miyake, quoted in *Issey Miyake: Bodyworks.*

fashion season with the references to Japanese cultural products and artifacts. Fashion journalists and critics in the West used everyday Japanese vocabulary familiar to Westerners to describe their designs. The source of their design inspiration undoubtedly came from symbols of Japanese culture, such as Kabuki, Mount Fuji, the geisha, and cherry blossoms, but their uniqueness lies in the ways they deconstructed existing rules of clothing and reconstructed their own interpretation of what fashion is and what fashion can be. These Japanese first proved to Paris, and then to the world, that they were masters of fashion design, prompting Western societies to reassess the concept of clothing and fashion and also the universalism of beauty. They shocked fashion professionals in the West by showing something none of them had seen before.

The Japanese designers were the key players in the redefinition of clothing and fashion, and some even destroyed the Western definition of the clothing system. Rather than being isolated as deviant and left outside the French fashion establishment, they were labeled as creative and innovative and were given the status and privilege that, until then, only Western designers have acquired. These Japanese managed to stay within the territory that is under the authorization of the system and the fashion gatekeepers.

After the first generation Japanese designers, other Japanese were flocking to Paris one after another. The second, the third, and the fourth generations were emerging in Paris. There were formal and informal connections among almost all the Japanese designers in Paris, some through school networks and others through professional networks. They can be traced back directly or indirectly to Kenzo, Miyake, Yamamoto, Kawakubo, and Mori as they have learned the mechanism of the fashion system in France.

These Japanese acquired the means to enter the French fashion system and at the same time used their ethnic affinity as a strategy. They achieved insider status in the realms where artistic power is concentrated and where gatekeepers, such as editors and critics, participate. The line between inside and outside the system is an issue about status and legitimacy, and the inside bound-

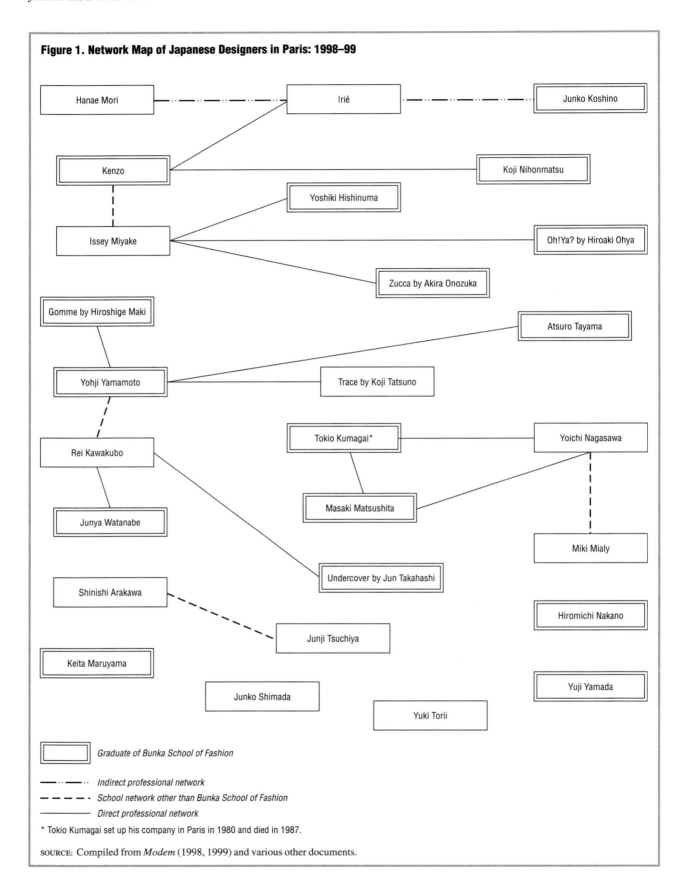

Figure 1. Network Map of Japanese Designers in Paris: 1998–99

Hanae Mori

Irié

Junko Koshino

Kenzo

Koji Nihonmatsu

Yoshiki Hishinuma

Issey Miyake

Oh!Ya? by Hiroaki Ohya

Zucca by Akira Onozuka

Gomme by Hiroshige Maki

Atsuro Tayama

Yohji Yamamoto

Trace by Koji Tatsuno

Tokio Kumagai*

Yoichi Nagasawa

Rei Kawakubo

Masaki Matsushita

Junya Watanabe

Miki Mialy

Undercover by Jun Takahashi

Shinishi Arakawa

Hiromichi Nakano

Junji Tsuchiya

Keita Maruyama

Yuji Yamada

Junko Shimada

Yuki Torii

Graduate of Bunka School of Fashion

—··—·· Indirect professional network

– – – – School network other than Bunka School of Fashion

———— Direct professional network

* Tokio Kumagai set up his company in Paris in 1980 and died in 1987.

SOURCE: Compiled from *Modem* (1998, 1999) and various other documents.

aries provide privilege and status whose boundaries in the world of fashion can be expanded and manipulated through style experiments and innovation. Fashion professionals accept and welcome designers who push and test the boundaries, signs of creativity. Once the designers are acknowledged as insiders, although recognition is never permanent, they slowly gain worldwide attention. Fashion design is an occupation where prestige necessarily antedates financial success. Prestige, image, and name bring financial resources. Until designers reach that stage, they struggle to achieve it; once it is achieved, they struggle to maintain it.

Due to the structural weaknesses of the fashion system in Japan, Japanese designers have continued to mobilize in Paris, permanently or temporarily, to take part during the Paris Collection. Though Kenzo's appearance in Paris in 1970 through Yamamoto's and Kawakubo's in 1981 had some impact, in the early 2000s Tokyo still fell far behind Paris in the production of "fashion"—that is, setting the fashion trends, creating designers' reputation, and spreading their names worldwide. Tokyo as a fashion city lacked the kind of structural strength and effectiveness that the French system had. Thus, lack of institutionalization and of the centralized fashion establishment in Japan forced designers to come to Paris, the battlefield for designers, where only the most ambitious can compete and survive.

Acceptance of the new Japanese styles led to the success of a group of Belgian designers, who also utilized the French fashion system to their advantage. From the mid-1980s to the early 1990s, a group of radical Belgian designers trained at the Royal Academy of Fine Arts in Antwerp followed the path that the Japanese had taken: Dirk Bikkembergs in 1986, Martin Margiela in 1988, Dries Van Noten in 1991, and Ann Demeulemeester in 1992, among others. By tracing the success of new designers, such as the Japanese and the Belgians, in Paris, one can see whether they are promoting and reinforcing the existence of the French fashion authority and the system, or are impeding the stability of the system and proposing the emergence of a new institutional system.

Influence in Western Fashion

Exhibitions such as *Orientalism* at the Costume Institute of the Metropolitan Museum in 1994, *Japonisme et Mode* at the Palais Galliéra costume museum in 1996, *Touches d'Exotisme* at the Art Museum of Fashion and Textile in Paris in 1998, and *Japonisme* at the Brooklyn Museum of Art in 1998, show that Western designers have long been inspired by the Eastern textiles, designs, construction, and utility, including Japanese kimonos. For instance, Jeanne Lanvin's dress with its bolero jacket in the 1930s simulated kimono sleeves. Similarly, in the beginning of the twentieth century, as boning and corsetry were reduced to a minimum, a loose fitting kimono sleeve of Paul Poiret came in, and the high-neck collar was abandoned for an open V-neck resembling a kimono. Chrysanthemum

prints or the exotic fabrics were used by many couturiers, such as Charles Worth and Coco Chanel. Those fascinated by the kimono's geometry, such as Madeleine Vionnet, cut dresses in flat panels and decorated only with wave-seaming, a Japanese hand-stitching technique. The East remained a fashion influence through World War I. Western designers incorporated Japanese elements into Western clothing with Western interpretation while remaining within the normative definitions of clothing and fashion.

See also **Japanese Traditional Dress and Adornment; Kimono; Miyake, Issey; Mori, Hanae; Yamamoto, Yohji.**

BIBLIOGRAPHY

Dalby, Liza. *Kimono: Fashioning Culture.* New Haven, Conn.: Yale University Press, 1993.

Kawamura Yuniya. *The Japanese Revolution in Paris Fashion.* Oxford: Berg Publishers, 2004.

Kenzo. Tokyo: Bunka Publishing, 1995.

Mendes, Valerie, and Amy de la Haye. *20th Century Fashion.* London: Thames and Hudson, 1999.

Modem. Collections femme printemps-été, 1999 (Women's Spring–Summer Collection, 1999), 1998.

———. Collections femme automne-hiver 1999–2000 (Women's Fall-Winter Collection, 1999–2000), 1999.

Mori Hanae. *Hanae Mori Style.* Tokyo: Kodansha International, 2001.

Skov, Lise. "Fashion Trends, Japonisme and Postmodernism." *Theory, Culture and Society* 13, no. 3 (August 1996): 129–151.

Steele, Valerie. *Women of Fashion: Twentieth-Century Designers.* New York: Rizzoli International, 1991.

Sudjic, Deyan. *Rei Kawakubo and Comme des Garçons.* New York: Rizzoli International, 1990.

Tsurumoto Shozo, ed. *Issey Miyake: Bodyworks.* Tokyo: Shogakkan Publishing Co., 1983.

Wichmann, Siegfried. *Japonisme: The Japanese Influence on Western Art since 1858.* London: Thames and Hudson, Inc., 1981.

Yuniya Kawamura

JAPANESE TRADITIONAL DRESS AND ADORNMENT Japan, an archipelago consisting of four principal islands situated off the east coast of the Asian mainland, was a relative latecomer in terms of both receiving from the outside and nurturing at home a rich and sophisticated material culture. Whereas ample archaeological evidence exists in China of extant garments, ceramic sculptures, and tomb paintings, giving a credible view of Chinese costume history across several centuries before the advent of the Common Era, a verifiable history of Japanese dress does not begin until the eighth century C.E.

Speculative Early History

Apart from its indigenous peoples, Japan was populated by successive waves of immigrants from China, Korea,

Woman modeling Japanese formal court ensemble. While it varied from period to period, female imperial court dress often featured voluminous sleeves, overlapping panels, and many layers of fabric. © REUTERS/CORBIS. REPRODUCED BY PERMISSION.

Southeast Asia, Central and North Asia, and possibly Polynesia. Native textile fibers were processed from the inner bark of trees and plants, and weaving was done on a backstrap loom. Textile technology continually advanced as the result of immigration, with the production of silk presumably established by the third century. Silk remains the fiber of choice for traditional Japanese dress.

The archaeological record in Japan yields little in the way of human imagery until the fifth century C.E. Prior to that time representations of stick figures found on pottery shards and bronze bells allow for the hypothesis that a long tunic-like garment, belted at the waist, may have been a common form of dress.

In the fifth and sixth centuries, large quantities of *haniwa*, terra-cotta tomb sculptures, were produced for important burials. Male figures are often depicted wearing tight, body-hugging, long-waisted jackets flared at the sides with long tubular sleeves and baggy pants secured with ties just above the knees. Such garb is reminiscent of the practical wear of horse-riding, nomadic steppe peoples from the Asian mainland. The horsemen required

full mobility of arms and legs to guide their mounts and tightly fit garments for warmth in the cold, wind-swept northern latitudes. Loose-fitting, wide-sleeved, floor-length Chinese robes, the other dominant elite mode of dress on the continent, were the antithesis of this kind of nomadic clothing.

Typical female *haniwa* figures wear an upper garment resembling the men's jacket and a skirt, rather than trousers. It is important to note that *haniwa* jackets tend to be fastened in a sequence that places the right front panel over the left panel, after which the ties are secured at the right side of the jacket. This was considered a barbaric practice by the Chinese, whose robes were closed left side over right. Japanese dress was to mimic the Chinese mode in this and in other ways soon thereafter.

It is doubtful that *haniwa* dress was widespread in Japan during the fifth and sixth centuries. Such dress would not be suitable for Japan's long months of warm and humid weather, and a life on horseback would have been unlikely in mountainous Japan. Judging from the large number of extant *haniwa* horse figures, a horse-riding elite may well have established itself in Japan during this period, perhaps after an incursion from the Asian mainland, but their way of dressing was not to prevail.

Asuka and Nara Periods

The year 552 is considered the official date for the introduction of Buddhism in Japan and marked the first year of the Asuka period (552–710). Buddhism had its origins more than a thousand years earlier in India, spread to China by the beginning of the Common Era, and finally reached Japan by way of Korea. One of the important cultural advances that arrived with Buddhism was literacy. The Japanese employed the Chinese writing system based on ideograms.

Japan's native religion, Shintoism, coexisted with Buddhism, in keeping with a continuous theme in Japanese history of borrowing from the outside while preserving the most valued native traditions and ultimately transforming foreign ways into something uniquely Japanese.

The history of Buddhist dress in Japan, as embodied in the religion's principal ritual garment, a patchwork mantle (*kesa*), illustrates the theme of importation and adaptation. *Kesa* are among the oldest extant garments in Japan. As the physical manifestation of Buddhist teachings, examples were brought from the Asian mainland in order to aid in the implantation of the religion on Japanese soil. In later times, certain *kesa* tested the limits of the garment's parameters in a uniquely Japanese way.

Another early group of costumes in Japan were used during performances and ceremonies commemorating an enormous bronze Buddha completed in 752, midway through the Nara period (710–794). Dignitaries from various Asian countries came to Nara, then the capital of Japan, to attend. These costumes, along with most of the early *kesa*, have been preserved in the famous temple storehouse known as the Shôsôin.

The Shôsôin performance wear is mostly left-closing and includes both knee-length sleeveless vests and long-sleeved full-length robes. Collars are either narrow and round or V-neck, with front panels that either abut or overlap. Both figural and geometric decorations, in either woven or dyed patterns, are part of the rich legacy of this diverse group of silk robes. Also included are trousers and accessories such as leggings, socks, shoes, and aprons.

Other costumes in the Shôsôin include robes worn by craftsmen, similar in cut to the full-length robes with the round collars mentioned above, but in hemp rather than silk; robes with wide flaring sleeves; and even archaic, right-closing *haniwa*-style costumes.

The Shôsôin costumes are very likely representative of diverse types of Asian dress then in use, and any number of them may well have been made outside of Japan. In later Japanese traditional dress, several of these early modes of clothing were to be reflected in the costumes of the Nô theater.

According to period documents, dress at Japan's imperial court followed that of China's at this time, with rank indicated by color. Contemporary pictorial representations depict both male and female courtiers in long flowing robes with voluminous sleeves ample enough in length to cover the hands. A characteristic of male dress was a close-fitting, narrow, round collar, while female dress featured wide front panels that overlapped in the left-over-right sequence. Women's court dress also included one or more underrobes that closed in the same manner.

Heian Period

Kyoto became the new imperial capital at the end of the eighth century, marking the beginning of the long and relatively peaceful Heian era (794–1185). Japan's previous periods of intensive cultural absorption from the Asian mainland was followed by the internal development and refinement of foreign ways combined with native sensibilities.

A costume history of this period cannot be based on extant garments, as extremely few examples have survived. Knowledge of Heian dress is largely derived from pictorial representations, wardrobe records, and two of the earliest novels in world literature—the *Tale of Genji*, by Lady Murasaki Shikibu, and the *Pillow Book* by Sei Shônagon.

The novels describe the insular world of the imperial court and its daily life full of intrigue, poetry, wit, romance, and a remarkably refined way of dressing. Women wore layer upon layer of silk robes, with only the edges of individual robes being revealed at the sleeve ends, collar, and hem, and the outermost robe setting the overall tone for the color scheme. A woman's taste and sensitivity was displayed by her choice of color combinations in

selecting the various robes for the ensemble in accordance with the season, an occasion, or a prevailing mood. Further articles of clothing, such as a jacket, skirt-like pants (*hakama*), and an apron worn at the back completed women's court dress.

The robe, presumably worn closest to the body in this ensemble, is considered the precursor to the Edo period (1603–1868) *kosode* in terms of construction and shape. This innermost garment had an overall T-shape composed of square- or rectangular-shaped sleeves with narrow openings for the hands. These sleeves attached to long, straight lengths of cloth composing the body of the robe. A relatively wide, flat collar and lapels were sewn to the inner edges of the body panels at the front of the garment. This article of clothing conforms to the present-day kimono.

Male dress of the Heian period retained the narrow, round tunic-like collar reflecting the earlier period of influence from the Asian mainland, and men also wore a skirt-like trouser and an underrobe or two. Sleeve shape departed from previous mainland models in that a square or rectangular shape came to dominate, and a single sleeve could be as wide as the entire body of a garment. In the wearing of such a robe, the bottoms of the sleeves, which were unsewn at their extremities, could practically sweep the ground.

It is also during this period that family crests are thought to have first appeared on clothing. Some Heian costume types have persisted to the present day as seen in imperial court wear, religious dress, and costumes of the Nô theater.

Kamakura Period

During the latter part of the twelfth century, the base of power in Japan shifted away from the increasingly decadent, self-absorbed imperial court in Kyoto to provincial military clans who chose the town of Kamakura as their headquarters. There are few extant garments from the Kamakura era (1185–1333), and the period literature is not very rich on the subject of costume. However, well-detailed surviving paintings do give an idea of dress at that time.

Women's clothing was less encumbered by exaggerated multilayering, and large-scale dyed patterns appear on some female outer robes. Pattern-dyed designs were to become one of the most important creative expressions in later Japanese dress. Expressions of originality in men's clothing also began to be manifest through the use of outscaled motifs and the splicing together of pieces from two completely different robes in order to create a startling new costume. Buddhist sects (such as Zen), previously unknown in Japan, were introduced from the Asian mainland, which resulted in the importation of *kesa* made from certain luxurious types of textiles otherwise unavailable to the Japanese. Earlier *kesa* were, on the whole, more humble in appearance.

Nambokuchô, Muromachi, and Momoyama Periods
The imperial city of Kyoto became the capital again with the advent of the Nambokuchô era (1333–1392), a period marked by clashes between rival military clans. Warfare continued during the subsequent Muromachi period (1392–1568). Since the advent of the Kamakura era, the imperial family had ruled in name only; the shogun, as the supreme military power, wielded the real power.

In regard to cultural matters, the imperial court ceased to be in the vanguard. Elite members of the military class and high-ranking Buddhist monks were the leading practitioners of the newly established and extremely aesthetic tea ceremony. The shogun Ashikaga Yoshimitsu (1358–1408) was the first important patron of the No theater.

Costumes of the No theater continued to exist in a wide variety of different types through the early twenty-first century. During the initial centuries of the all-male theatrical form, actors wore garments donated from the wardrobes of their elite patrons. By the Edo period (1603–1868), No costumes were being made specifically for use on the stage; however, for the most part the costume styles did not change and continued to reflect the clothing of earlier periods.

Within the broad category of No robes called *ôsode*, a term referring to tall and wide sleeves that are left unsewn at their ends, are certain types of robes long since obsolete in Japan, except within the most conservative and traditional spheres of Japanese life, such as imperial court rites and Shinto rituals.

Often making use of gold threads in the form of flat, gilded narrow strips of paper, along with silk threads, *ôsode* costumes always have woven designs. These designs can be quite bold in scale and composition, though their coloration is more reserved, usually limited to just one color for the silk. The No theater also preserves the skirt-like trousers (*hakama*) of earlier times, and the layered wearing of costumes, with an *ôsode* robe typically worn as an outer robe.

The other principal category of No costumes features robes with sleeves shorter in height and width relative to *ôsode* sleeves. The sleeves are also rounded off at their bottommost outer edges rather than having a right angle as in *ôsode*. Sleeve ends are sewn up, allowing just enough of an opening for the hands to pass through. The name for this general category of No costumes is *kosode*. The same term had been used for the plain silk robe worn next to the skin and under layers of voluminous garments in the Heian period.

During the Muromachi period, the *kosode* literally emerged as acceptable outerwear. What had previously been private intimate wear was now permissible outside of domestic interiors. This form of dress became the principal vehicle for the expression of changing fashions and styles.

During the Edo period, most *kosode*-category costumes still preserved Muromachi and Momoyama period styles. Archaic styles that persisted included the use of heavy, ornate brocade fabric, extensive gilding, the splicing together of two completely different kinds of fabric in one robe, and an empty-center composition that concentrates the design motifs at the shoulders and hem of the robe. Such costumes did, however, change their overall sleeve shape from oblong to squarish in response to an Edo period trend, and certain No robes with embroidered designs were occasionally influenced by contemporary fashion styles.

Extant No costumes date as far back as the latter part of the Muromachi period. No robes were still being made in the early twenty-first century, and some of the modern producers made use of traditional hand weaving and natural dyeing techniques.

For the purpose of providing comic relief from the tragedy and melancholy of No, *kyôgen* plays were traditionally performed along with No plays. Costumes for *kyôgen* reflect lower-class dress and are made of bast fibers (usually hemp or ramie) rather than silk, use no gold threads or gilding, and are patterned by means of dyeing—unlike No robes with their woven, embroidered, or gilded designs. Extant *kyôgen* costumes do not predate the Edo period.

In the 1540s, when the first Europeans reached Japan, the country was in the midst of protracted civil war. This combination of turbulent times and a new wave of foreign influence led to the creation of some astonishing examples of samurai-class dress. Western-style tailoring and the newly imported "exotic" fabrics of European woolen cloth, Indian cotton chintz, and even Persian silk tapestry can be seen in several extant *jimbaori* (a type of vest worn over armor).

Further creativity in male dress is evident in some short *kosode*-shaped garments (*dôfuku*) associated with the leading military figures of the sixteenth century. These robes exhibit unconventional motifs and surprising color combinations.

Edo Period
Three successive military leaders were to emerge as unifiers of war-torn Japan. An enduring peace was finally established by the last of the three, Ieyasu Tokugawa. A new capital was established in Edo (later known as Tokyo), and all of the subsequent shoguns were supplied by the Tokugawa clan ruling from Edo while the imperial court remained in Kyoto. Japan entered a period of isolation, during which time the new religion of Christianity was suppressed, travel to and from Japan was prohibited, and foreign trade came under strict controls.

Conservative dress became the norm for the samurai class. Men's formal wear consisted of a short vest with winglike shoulders and the traditional *hakama*, with both

Man in samurai clothing. The traditional samurai costume consists of armor, *hakama* (skirt-like pants), and a short vest worn over the armor. The *hakama* and vest, both typically dyed blue, were made from a bast fiber. © HISTORICAL PICTURE ARCHIVE/CORBIS. REPRO-DUCED BY PERMISSION.

garments made from a bast fiber patterned with tiny repeat motifs and invariably dyed blue. The samurai had no more wars to fight, though armor and its associated vest continued to be made. Although creative examples of the vest were still produced, samurai were not encouraged to dress like dandies.

The greatest creativity in dress during the Edo period was manifest in the *kosode*. Much of the impetus for transforming this garment into such a fashion-conscious form of dress came from the newly rich merchant class, which was, nevertheless, at the bottom of the social hierarchy.

Whereas the No theater was the preserve of the upper classes, Kabuki theater was the performance art for the nouveau-riche merchants. Most Kabuki costumes have the standard T-shape of *kosode*; however, their coloration tends toward the garish and their design motifs can be overwhelming in scale. For example, a giant lobster might cover the entire back of a robe.

Leading Kabuki actors (also an all-male theatrical form) became wildly popular, their faces and dress disseminated in myriad woodblock prints. However, their costumes tended to be too outlandish to influence fashion, other than by popularizing a particular shade of a color or a certain motif. Kabuki costumes of the early twentieth century continued to resemble those of the Edo period.

Buddhist clergy ranked high on the social scale and were given administrative powers and official support under the Tokugawa government, enabling them to share in the general prosperity. The most unusual tendency seen in *kesa*, the patchwork garment, was a pictorial impulse that resulted in examples being woven, embroidered, or painted with such narrative representational imagery as birds and animals in landscape settings, gatherings of divinities, and even flower arrangements. Two of the methods used to satisfy token adherence to the patchwork tradition involved the stitching of cording or the drawing of lines onto the garment in order to create the impression of a pieced construction. As the *kesa* is a flat, wide, horizontal-oriented, usually rectangular-shaped garment, an inspiration for this new style in surface design was quite likely to have been the broad painted screens widely in use during the Edo period.

The *kesa* also reflected fashionable taste in a more indirect way as a result of the custom for lay Buddhists to donate valuable clothing to temples. The garments would be unstitched, cut up, and remade into Buddhist robes. Other *kesa* were assembled from rich brocades, which were being woven domestically, as the Japanese textile industry had, by this time, absorbed the foreign skills and technology necessary for the weaving of luxury textiles.

The extravagant tendencies in *kesa* led at least one Buddhist sect to make an austere, monochromatic, unpatterned vestment in a bast fiber. Although there were no new innovative styles, *kesa*—in the early 2000s—reflected all of the variety seen in the Edo-period examples. However, several early twenty-first-century textile artists in the West have made creative works inspired by the traditional form of the *kesa*.

Meiji Period

Japan was forced to end its isolation in the 1850s when Western powers with advanced military technology demanded trading concessions. The Tokugawa Shogunate collapsed, and power shifted to the imperial family, which moved the court to Tokyo in 1868 and proclaimed a new era, the Meiji (1868–1912). Once again, the Japanese realized the need to keep pace with more developed nations, and embarked upon a policy of rapid Westernization.

Western dress was adopted, with the emperor and empress helping to set an example for the rest of the country by occasionally wearing Western clothing. Buddhists and elite samurai families sold off quantities of *kesa* and No costumes, ultimately enriching museum and private collections in Japan and the West. For the more sophisticated urban population, and especially men, traditional Japanese dress ceased to be a part of everyday wear until eventually the use of traditional dress was relegated to Buddhist temples and monasteries; Shinto shrines; No, *kyôgen*, and Kabuki theater; tea ceremony and other traditional arts such as flower arranging; and the imperial court. Geisha, still an institution in Japan at the start of the twenty-first century, were still expected to entertain in kimono.

In the early 2000s, rites of passage such as children's coming-of-age ceremonies, school graduations, and weddings are occasions for members of the general public to wear traditional dress. A Japanese family also might don kimono when participating in special national and regional festivals or when relaxing after bath time at a traditional inn. It was not uncommon for a Japanese housewife to attend kimono school in order to better understand how to select and properly wear a kimono and its most important accessory, the obi.

During the Meiji period, terms were coined in order to distinguish the old Japanese way of dressing (*wafuku*) from the newly adopted Western dress (*yofuku*). Kimono (derived from the verb for wearing clothes and the word for "thing") became the new term for the T-shaped garment formerly known as the *kosode*. The word has entered the dictionaries of languages the world over and commonly serves as the designation for the national dress of Japan, just as "sari" is universally recognized as the timeless Indian garment.

During the early Taishō (1912–1926) and late Taishō (1926–1989) periods, the *mingei* movement was founded by artists and intellectuals for the purpose of preserving and perpetuating the folk crafts of Japan, especially as practiced by farmers and ethnic minorities. Those who championed the idea of *mingei* can be thought of as the East Asian inheritors of the Arts and Crafts movement, although they did not have to insist on the importance of handicraft, as did their Western predecessors, because in the traditional Japanese distinctions between fine and decorative arts were not emphatic. However, the elevation of handcrafted works made by simple-living country people and minorities on the fringe of Japanese society did not fit with conventional ideas of social hierarchy in Japan.

Examples of costumes collected and studied by *mingei* enthusiasts include the bast fiber and cotton robes of the indigenous Ainu tribe, specially dyed costumes from Okinawa, heavily stitched farmers' jackets, and fishermen and firemen's garb.

See also **Kimono; Japanese Fashion.**

BIBLIOGRAPHY

Bethe, Monica, and Iwao Nagasaki. *Patterns and Poetry: Nô Robes from the Lucy Truman Aldrich Collection at the Museum of Art, Rhode Island School of Design.* Providence: Rhode Island School of Design, 1992.

Bethe, Monica, and Sharon Sadako Takeda. *Miracles and Mischief: Noh and Kyôgen Theater in Japan.* Los Angeles: Los Angeles County Museum of Art, 2002.

Dalby, Liza Crihfield. *Kimono: Fashioning Culture.* New Haven, Conn.: Yale University Press, 1993.

Dusenbury, Mary. "Textiles." In *Kodansha Encyclopedia of Japan.* Vol. 8. Tokyo: Kodansha International, 1983, 16–20.

Kennedy, Alan. *Japanese Costume: History and Tradition.* Paris: Editions Adam Biro, 1990.

Kirihata, Ken. *Noh Costumes.* Kyoto: Kyoto Shoin, 1993.

Liddell, Jill. *The Story of the Kimono.* New York: E. P. Dutton, 1989.

Matsumoto Kaneo, ed. *The Treasures of the Shôsôin: Musical Instruments, Dance Articles, Game Sets.* Kyoto: Shikosha, 1991.

Minnich, Helen Benton. *Japanese Costume and the Makers of Its Elegant Tradition.* Tokyo: Charles E. Tuttle, 1963.

Noma Seiroku. *Japanese Costume and Textile Arts.* New York and Tokyo: Weatherhill/Heibonsha, 1974.

Yamanobe Tomoyuki. *Textiles.* Rutland, Vt., and Tokyo: Charles E. Tuttle, 1957.

Alan Kennedy

JAPONISME Prior to the 1800s, Japan was a nation isolated from the West. The arrival of its wares in Europe and America in the second half of the nineteenth century precipitated a new creative surge in art and design that became known as *Japonisme*. While many scholars have studied the influence of Japonisme, or the assimilation of Japanese aesthetic principles on European painting and decorative arts, few have addressed its influence on Western dress. And yet fashion, which differs from traditional dress in that it stresses urbanity and constant change, eagerly absorbed the principles of Japanese design.

In the mid-nineteenth century, European and American garments were ornamented with Japanese motifs or made of fabrics exported from Japan while conforming to fashionable Western silhouettes. Later, in the early twentieth century, some costume items, ranging from tea gowns to opera coats, were constructed with elements adapted from the construction of kimonos. More recently, some of the world's most influential designers have emerged from Japan to redefine contemporary fashion.

Although some Japanese objects had been arriving in Europe since the 1600s, it was not until after the American commodore Matthew Perry opened this island nation to international trade in 1854 that Japonisme began in earnest. Its popularity accelerated when many Europeans and Americans saw Japanese artworks and design objects for the first time at the world's fairs of 1862 in London, 1867 in Paris, and 1876 in Philadelphia. These expositions exerted a profound influence on innumerable nineteenth-century artists, artisans, designers, and manufacturers. Everything from paintings to porcelain began to be produced in the Japanese manner. In the 1870s and 1880s, such designs—then considered avant-garde—developed into a distinctive style that came to be associated with the aesthetic movement.

While nineteenth-century critics had reservations about artists' adopting Japanese conventions in paintings and prints, this was not true in the arena of fashion. French textile designers in the 1890s, for example, readily appropriated new and "exotic" floral motifs from Japan, and these fabrics were readily used by couturiers like Charles Frederick Worth. The most popular item of dress exported to the West in the late nineteenth century was a modified version of the kimono, worn as a dressing gown. Both fully finished garments and unsewn components were sold at small boutiques and at large firms such as Liberty of London. Kimonos for export were often constructed with elements to suit the European market; these might include a set-in box pleat to accommodate the bustle; a collar lining instead of an under kimono; the addition of a knotted and tasseled trim; and a variety of sleeve styles.

In the decade prior to World War I, the construction of women's garments began to change dramatically. As early as 1908, revolutionary couturiers, such as Marie Callot Gerber and Paul Poiret, took inspiration from the drapery-like quality of kimonos. Loosely cut sleeves and crossed bodices were incorporated into evening dresses, while opera coats swathed the body like bat-winged cocoons.

One of the twentieth century's greatest couturiers, Madeleine Vionnet was inspired by the kimono, with its reliance on uncut lengths of fabric, and raised dressmaking to an art form. From the onset of World War I to the late 1920s, she abandoned the traditional practice of tailoring body-fitted fashions from numerous, complex pattern pieces, and minimized the cutting of fabric. A "minimalist" with strict aesthetic principles who rarely employed patterned fabrics or embroidery, Vionnet relied instead on surface ornamentation through manipulation of the fabric itself. For example, the wavy parallel folds of a pin-tucked crepe dress evoked the abstracted image of a raked Zen rock garden, itself a metaphor for the waves of the sea.

Although the influence of the kimono on the construction of garments was extremely important in the 1910s and 1920s, surface ornamentation remained a vital force. During the art moderne, or art deco, era, French textiles in the Japanese style developed a more sophisticated use of both abstract motifs and recognizable images. Examples range from metallic lamé dresses that replicate the appearance of black lacquer inlaid with gold particles, to garments of brocaded silk woven with a pattern of crashing waves and fish scales. Also appropriated was the *mon*, or family crest. While the *mon* is usually an abstracted image drawn from nature, such as a bird or flower, it can also represent a man-made object, such as the *nara bi-ya*, or parallel rows of arrows; or celestial bodies such as the *mitsuboshi*, an abstraction symbolizing the three stars of Orion's belt.

The influence of "exotic" cultures on fashion began to diminish in the late 1930s. Instead, American and European designers created modern versions of historical Western dress, and this trend dominated fashion from the late 1930s through the 1950s. The revival of historical styles offered an escape from the pressures of the Great Depression of the 1930s and helped assert the growing sense of nationalism in Europe at that time. Also a factor in the United States was strong anti-Japanese sentiment during and after the war. Nonetheless, some of this country's most innovative designers remained open to Japanese influence. One of the best was Elizabeth Hawes, who designed a variety of Asian-inspired garments in the late 1930s and early 1940s using modern Japanese kimono fabric.

The use of Japanese elements became the cornerstone for another revolutionary American ready-to-wear designer, Bonnie Cashin. Born in California in 1915, Cashin was one of a handful of female American designers who made clothes for the modern and active woman. By using the loose construction of the *nakajuban*, or informal kimono worn by peasants, and discarding Western tailoring, Cashin created functional fashions that fit a broad range of sizes and later seemed decades ahead of their time. Not only were her garments in sharp contrast to the couture creations of her French contemporaries, they had little in common with the designs of her American counterparts. Cashin's use of indigenous Japanese textiles, like double *ikat* silks with their subtle geometric designs, did much to advance the notion of modern luxury in American fashion.

Although by 2004 Japonisme was no longer a major force in fashion, the influence of Japanese design and aesthetics continued to be important. One of the main reasons was the dramatic impact of creators such as Issey Miyake, Rei Kawakubo, and Yohji Yamamoto. Born just before and during World War II, they became some of the most important fashion figures to chart a new course since the 1970s. Their use of oversized silhouettes, cutting-edge textiles, and the appropriation of Japanese aesthetic principle like *sabi/wabi* have made them leaders of the avant-garde.

See also **Asia, East: History of Dress; Cashin, Bonnie; Europe and America: History of Dress (400–1900 C.E.); Kimono; Vionnet, Madeleine.**

BIBLIOGRAPHY

Evett, Elisa. *The Critical Reception of Japanese Art in Late Nineteenth Century Europe.* Ann Arbor, Mich.: UMI Research Press, 1982.

Fukai, Akiko, and Jun Kanai. *Japonism in Fashion.* Kyoto, Japan: Kyoto Costume Institute, 1996.

Grand, France. *Comme des Garçons.* New York: Universe Publishing, 1998.

Hiesinger, Kathryn B., and Felice Fisher. *Japanese Design: A Survey Since 1950.* New York: Harry N. Abrams, 1995.

Issey Miyake: Ten Sen Men. Hiroshima: Hiroshima City Museum of Contemporary Art, 1990.

Kirke, Betty. *Madeleine Vionnet.* San Francisco: Chronicle Press, 1998.

Kondo, Dorinne. *About Face: Performing Race in Fashion and Theater.* New York: Routledge, 1997.

Koren, Leonard. *New Fashion Japan.* Tokyo: Kodansha International, 1984.

———. *Wabi Sabi for Artists, Designers, Poets and Philosophers.* Berkeley, Calif.: Stone Bridge Press, 1994.

Martin, Richard, and Harold Koda. *Orientalism.* New York: Metropolitan Museum of Art, 1994.

Martin, Richard, Harold Koda, and Laura Sinderbrand. *Three Women: Madeleine Vionnet, Claire McCardell, and Rei Kawakubo.* New York: Fashion Institute of Technology, 1987.

Sudjic, Deyan. *Rei Kawakubo and Comme des Garçons.* New York: Rizzoli International, 1990.

Vreeland, Diana, and Irving Penn. *Inventive Paris Clothes: 1909–1939.* New York: Viking Press, 1977.

Wichmann, Siegfried. *Japonisme: The Japanese Influence on Western Art in the 19th and 20th Centuries.* English translation. New York: Harmony Books, 1981.

Patricia Mears

JEANS "Blue jeans" are the archetypal garment of the twentieth century. They are traditionally ankle-length, slim-fitting trousers made of blue denim worn for labor and casual dress. The term "jeans," or "blue jeans," has been in widespread usage since the mid-twentieth century.

The word "jeans" comes from the word *Génes*, the French word for Genoa, Italy, where sailors were known to wear sturdy pants of fustian, a sturdy twill of cotton, linen, or wool blend. By the sixteenth century, the fabric was being referred to as "Jene Fustyan." By the eighteenth century, jean fabric was made entirely of cotton and was being used to make work clothes. Jean was available in many colors, but often dyed with indigo. Pants made from jean were often referred to as "jean pants," the origin of the contemporary jeans.

Jeans, however, are made of denim. Denim is also a sturdy cotton twill, similar to jean, but even stronger. Denim is traditionally yarn-dyed and woven with an indigo-blue face and a gray or unbleached fill. This method of manufacture enables denim to develop distinctive areas of fading and wear with usage. It is commonly believed that the name "denim" is an Anglicised name for *serge de nîmes*, a French fabric dating back to the seventeenth century. While this attribution has been popular and widely disseminated, it has recently been called into question. *Serge de nîmes* and a second French textile known simply as "nim" were mainly wool, not cotton. The sturdy cotton twill now recognized as denim was originally given the name "denim" in eighteenth-century England. It has been theorized that the French name was given to an English product to add prestige.

To confuse the matter even further, jeans are sometimes referred to as dungarees. This term refers to a coarse calico fabric that was often dyed blue and used to make work pants. The word "dungaree" would later describe the pants as well.

Miners and the Workingman
The first true "jeans" were created in 1873 by Jacob Davis, a Nevada tailor, who went in with Levi Strauss, a San Francisco merchant, for the patent. The pair received a patent for the addition of copper rivets at the pocket joinings of work pants to prevent tearing—a boon to the many California miners and laborers. The first jeans Levi-Strauss and Co. produced were available in brown cotton duck and blue denim and were known as waist overalls (the name jeans not adopted until the mid-1900s). In the late nineteenth century, Levi's (as they became known) began to acquire their hallmarks: the leather "Two Horse Brand" patch, lot numbers, and back patch pockets with distinctive stitching. The Levi's "501," which originated in 1890, is considered by many to be the archetypical pair of blue jeans.

Levi-Strauss had cornered the market with their denim pants, but competitors moved quickly. Companies manufacturing similarly styled denim work pants entered the market. These included OshKosh B'Gosh in 1895 and Blue Bell in 1904, which later became Wrangler. The Lee Mercantile began production of their waist overalls in 1911 and enjoyed their first great success with the Lee Union-All in 1913. During World War I, Union-Alls were standard issue for all war workers, and the design was modified for the doughboy uniform.

Hollywood, Cowboys, and Wartime
During the 1920s and into the 1930s, the image of the waist overall was given a glamorous spin by handsome cowboy movie stars like Tom Mix, John Wayne, and Gary Cooper. In 1924 H. D. Lee Mercantile Co. introduced their 101 cowboy pants, which were designed to meet the needs of cowboys, rodeo riders and others looking for authentic western garb. The 101 cowboy pant was given a facelift in 1941 when Sallie Rand, the wife of famous rodeo champion Turk Greenough, recut them for a tighter fit. These new and improved cowboy pants were then called Lee Riders. The romanticized view of the cowboy life seen onscreen brought about an enthusiasm for dude-ranch vacations, and tourists brought back comfortable waist overalls as souvenirs. This glamorous new image was reinforced by publicity photos featuring actresses like Ginger Rogers and Carole Lombard wearing the humble waist overalls while camping and fishing. Through these glamorous associations, the waist overall became associated with leisure and rugged individualism rather than manual labor. Young people began to adopt them into their casual dress, wearing them rolled up and baggy.

World War II would change the image of the waist overall forever. Raw materials were restricted for the war effort, and the general silhouette was slimmed down to reduce fabric consumption. As a result of these restrictions, Levi's lost their back cinch and copper crotch rivet while the stitching on the back pocket was painted on to conserve thread. Denim began to be used as a fashion fabric by fashion designers like Claire McCardell, whose denim wrap dress, the "popover," sold in the thousands.

American GIs brought jeans overseas with them to wear while off-duty. This had an important impact on the international reputation of jeans; they became associated with American leisure and abundance, especially in countries devastated by the war. To many, blue jeans were an important symbol of freedom and wealth.

Post–World War II Leisure and Rebellion
Blue jeans would continue to be associated with leisure in the post–World War II period. The term "jeans" became widely adopted during this time, and jeans began to be marketed specifically to the youth market. In 1947, Wrangler introduced the slim "body fit" jeans, which emphasized fit and appearance over traditional qualities like durability. In 1949, Levi Strauss and Co. opened an outlet in New York, and began nationwide promotion of their waist overalls, which they grudgingly began to call "jeans" in 1960. In 1953, H. D. Lee (formerly Lee Mercantile Co.) began an advertising campaign aimed at teenagers. Lee Riders were transformed into a slimmer "drainpipe" style popular with teens.

Once again, Hollywood films had an important role in the reinvigoration of the image of the utilitarian waist overall. While young children continued to idolize the cowboy, teenagers found new denim-clad idols in Marlon Brando (*The Wild One*, 1953) and James Dean (*Rebel*

Actor James Dean in jeans. The entertainment industry did much to promote the popularity of blue jeans in the 1950s, associating them with rock stars and sexy film rebels. © SUNSET BOULEVARD/CORBIS SYGMA. REPRODUCED BY PERMISSION.

Without a Cause, 1955). Denim now had a dangerous element and a healthy dose of sex appeal. Exciting new rock'n'roll musicians like Eddie Cochran, a Levi's devotee, also played a role in the popularization of denim. This rebellious association caused jeans to be banned from many high schools throughout the 1950s, but this only strengthened their popularity.

The 1960s saw an explosion of the production and acceptance of jeans as leisure wear. Denim as a fashion fabric also became widely accepted, and the important contribution denim jeans had made to fashion and popular culture began to be acknowledged. In 1964, it was boldly stated in *American Fabrics* magazine:

> Throughout the industrialized world denim has become a symbol of the young, active, informal, American way of life. It is equally symbolic of America's achievements in mass production, for denim of uniform quality and superior performance is turned out by the mile in some of America's … most modern mills. (American Fabrics, No, 65, 1964, p. 30)

With this mass acceptance came the need for distinction. Early in the 1960s, slim-fitting styles dominated but were superceded by the well-worn bell-bottom styles popularized by the hippie movement. The wearing of jeans was both a political and social statement and the baby boomers embraced the aesthetic of customized decorated denim. Embroidery, paint, and appliqué on faded bell-bottom jeans became a powerful symbol of anti-establishment ideals around the world.

Designer Jeans

Since jeans and denim-inspired fashions were everywhere in the 1970s, this period has been called "the golden age of denim." The customization of jeans continued and reached its pinnacle with Levi's Denim Art Contest of 1973. Mass-produced jeans echoing the earthy styles worn by political activists and rock stars, and the traditional workingman's garb, the overall, became popular.

Increasingly though, denim jeans reflected a new sophistication. Early inroads were made by the Italian company Fiorucci with their Buffalo 70 jeans. Buffalo 70 jeans were skintight and dark, the opposite of the faded bell-bottoms worn by most consumers. Since they were also expensive and difficult to find, they became a status symbol among the Studio 54 set. Their success paved the way for the high-end designer jean market of the early 1980s. American socialite Gloria Vanderbilt introduced her jeans in 1979. Similar in styling to the Fiorucci Buffalo 70 jeans, they also featured dark denim, a slim fit that emphasized a woman's curves and a bold designer logo on the rear pockets. They were significantly more expensive than other jeans and were promoted as being "high fashion." The jeans used the glamour and celebrity of socialite Gloria Vanderbilt to promote them, rather than emphasizing their practicality or styling.

This type of marketing strategy would become increasingly important during the 1980s, since there soon was a deluge of similarly styled "designer" jeans on the market. Advertising had the ability to make or a break a brand's success, and this trend has continued. Designer jeans lines from this period included Jordache, Sassoon, Sergio Valente, and the legendary Calvin Klein Jeans. In 1980, Calvin Klein Jeans embarked on a now-legendary ad campaign featuring fifteen-year-old model Brooke Shields, who cooed provocatively, "Nothing comes between me and my Calvins." The public outcry was great, but Calvin Klein Jeans sales rose from $25 million to $180 million in the span of one year. During the next decade, sexy marketing campaigns became standard. Some of the most successful were advertisements for Guess? Jeans that featured sultry models like Claudia Schiffer in seductive poses.

The jeans market grew increasingly fragmented during the 1980s. What had been the uniform of youthful rebellion and social protest during the 1950s and 1960s was now seen as a wardrobe basic and worn by all age groups. The many different styles offered included pinstriped, acid-washed, stonewashed, cigarette cut, twotoned, stretch, and pre-ripped. With this focus on innovation and novelty, many traditional denim manufacturers languished. The designer denim movement continued into the 1990s when well-established fashion

Advertisement featuring Brooke Shields in Calvin Klein jeans. In 1976, designer Calvin Klein became the first fashion designer to showcase blue jeans on the runway. AP/WIDE WORLD PHOTOS. REPRODUCED BY PERMISSION.

houses like Versace, Dolce & Gabbana, and Donna Karan branched out into denim.

Vintage Denim and Retro Styling

After more than a decade of designer jeans of various finishes, denim saw a return to classic styles, dark denim, and dangerous rebellion. Dark denim returned to mainstream popularity during the 1990s, a dramatic change from the pale, fluffy denim being produced throughout the 1970s and 1980s. Dark denim was stiff and was often worn with cuffed hems in the style of a 1950s bobbysoxer. Dark denim was seen as intellectual and ironic, a deliberate throwback to the essential elements of mid-century jeans. Traditionally styled dark denim was given an additional boost by the popularity of hip-hop. The hip-hop styles of the early 1990s were characterized by oversized, low-slung baggy jeans, associated with convicts forced to turn in their belts. Manufacturers like Ben Davis and Carhartt prospered since their no-frills, dark denim work clothes appealed to this hard-edged prison aesthetic and were prominently featured in music videos and lyrics by artists such as Dr. Dre and Snoop Dogg. Based on styles popularized by the hip-hop community, urban sportswear labels like FUBU, Rocawear, and Phat Farm

emerged. Mainstream labels like Tommy Hilfiger and Polo Jeans were also appropriated in this style.

At the same time, vintage denim was experiencing a renaissance. By the late 1980s, the simple garment of the mid-century had been bastardized by the glut of fashion jeans on the market. To many consumers, vintage denim symbolized strength and integrity, a direct challenge to the perceived corruption of the 1980s. Increasingly the wearing of vintage denim became popular, and prices for original Levi's, Wranglers, and Lees soared. Others turned to faithful modern renditions of vintage denim. Evis Jeans, a Japanese company, made their name during the early 1990s by producing modern versions of classic denim, like the Levis 501 and the Lee 101 with a twist. In 1999, Levi Strauss and Co. launched the "Red" line, a successful series of high-priced reproductions of vintage styles. Likewise, Lee jeans produced a replica of their highly collectible "hair on hide" cowboy pants for the Japanese market. Jeans, at least for the moment, had returned to their roots.

During the 1980s, smaller, higher-priced lines began to experiment with vintage-styled denim, paving the way for the vintage-inspired denim explosion of the

1990s. Adriano Goldschmied, founder of the influential "genius group" of denim innovators, was an early proponent of sandblasted knees and painted on "cat's whiskers" (the wear pattern at the crotch of vintage jeans). The genius group would become hugely influential, spawning many denim labels, such as Diesel and replay, whose higher priced lines provided finishes that the coveted striations and fading that characterized vintage denim. By the mid-1990s this aesthetic had gone mainstream as seen by success of "Dirty Denim" produced by designers such as Helmut Lang and Calvin Klein. The denim craze has continued into the twenty-first century with cult denim lines like Mavi, Paper Denim and Cloth, Seven, and Blue Cult all competing in the marketplace with perfectly faded, whiskered, and creased jeans.

Jeans, the ubiquitous twentieth-century garment, will undoubtedly continue to have a permanent place in twenty-first-century wardrobes around the world. Their iconic status will remain intact, largely since they will be reinterpreted by each passing generation. In 1983, legendary French couturier Yves Saint Laurent told *New York Magazine*, "I have often said that I wish I had invented blue jeans. They have expression, modesty, sex appeal, simplicity—all that I hope for in my clothes" (*New York Magazine*, November 28, 1983, p. 53).

See also **Denim; Klein, Calvin; Strauss, Levi.**

BIBLIOGRAPHY

Downey, Lynn, et al. *This Is a Pair of Levi's Jeans: The Official History of the Levi's Brand.* San Francisco: Levi Strauss and Co. Publishing, 1997.

Finlayson, Iain. *Denim: An American Legend.* New York: Simon and Schuster Inc., 1990.

"The Genius of Yves Saint Laurent." *New York Magazine* (28 November 1983): 53.

Gordon, Beverly. "American Denim: Blue Jeans and Their Multiple Layers of Meaning." In *Dress and Popular Culture.* Edited by Patricia A. Cunningham and Susan Voso Lab. Bowling Green, Ohio: Bowling Green State University Popular Press, 1991.

Hall, Lee. *Common Threads: A Parade of American Clothing.* Boston: Little, Brown and Company, 1992.

Harris, Alice. *The Blue Jean.* New York: Powerhouse Books, 2002.

Hay, Ethan. "Jeans." In *St. James Encyclopedia of Popular Culture,* vol. 2: E–J. Edited by Tom Pendergast and Sara Pendergast. Detroit: St. James Press, 2000.

Marsh, Graham, and Paul Trynka. *Denim: From Cowboys to Catwalks: A Visual History of the World's Most Legendary Fabric.* London: Aurum Press Limited, 2002.

Musées de la Ville de Paris. *Histoires du jeans de 1750 à 1994.* Paris: Paris Musées, 1994.

"Stretch Denim: Bright Star in the Modern Family of Stretch Fabrics" (Special merchandizing insert). *American Fabrics,* no. 65 (Fall 1964): 30.

Clare Sauro

JERSEY Jersey is a weft-knit fabric that is also called plain knit or single knit. Some sources claim the term "jersey" is used loosely to refer to any knitted fabric without a distinct rib. It is called jersey because it was manufactured on the island of Jersey off the coast of England. This early version of the fabric was used for fishermen's clothing and was a heavier weight fabric than the jersey fabrics of the early 2000s. The related term in current usage used to describe athletic shirts is from a similar origin. The tight-fitting, knit tunic-style sweaters worn by seamen were also known as jerseys.

Jersey can be made by hand or on flat and circular knitting machines. Jersey knits are made from the basic knitting stitch, in which each loop is drawn through the loop below it. The rows of loops form vertical lines, or wales, on the face of the fabric and crosswise rows, or courses, on the back. Jersey knits are lightweight in comparison with other knits and are the fastest weft knit to produce. Jersey stretches more in the crosswise direction than in length, may be prone to runs, and curls at the edges because of the difference in tension on the front and the back.

Historically, jersey was used mainly for hosiery and sweaters. However, as early as 1879 the actress Lillie Langtry, "the Jersey Lily," made jersey fashionable for daywear. Her costume was made up of a tight-fitting, hip-length jersey top that was worn over a pleated skirt. In the 1920s Gabrielle Chanel popularized the fabric for comfortable womenswear, constructing dresses and suits out of it.

Jersey may be finished with napping, printed, or embroidered. Variations of jersey include pile versions of the knit and jacquard jersey. Pile jerseys have extra yarns or sliver (untwisted strand) inserted to make velour or fake-fur fabrics. Jacquard jersey incorporates stitch variations to create complex designs that are knitted into the fabric. Intarsia fabrics are jersey knits that use different colored yarns to produce designs and are more costly to produce than printing the design as a finish.

Jersey is used to make hosiery, T-shirts, underwear, sportswear, and sweaters. It has also been incorporated into the home furnishings market and is used for bedding and slipcovers.

See also **Napping.**

BIBLIOGRAPHY

American Fabrics Encyclopedia of Textiles. 2nd ed. Englewood Cliffs, N.J: Prentice Hall, 1972.

Calisbetta, Charlotte M., and Phyllis Tortora, eds. *The Fairchild Dictionary of Fashion.* 3rd ed. New York: Fairchild Publishing, 2003.

Gioello, Debbie Ann. *Profiling Fabrics: Properties, Performance and Construction Techniques.* New York: Fairchild Publishing, 1981.

Jerde, Judith. *Encyclopedia of Textiles.* New York: Facts on File, 1992.

Kadolph, Sara J., and Anna L. Langford. *Textiles.* 9th ed. Englewood Cliffs, N.J.: Prentice Hall, 2002.

Wingate, Isabel, and June Mohler. *Textile Fabrics and Their Selection.* 8th ed. Englewood Cliffs, N.J.: Prentice Hall, 1984.

Internet Resource

"Plain Stitch." *Encyclopedia Britannica.* Available from <http://search.eb.com/eb/article?eu=61814> (subscription required).

Marie Botkin

JEWELRY Jewelry is often associated with treasure—gold, gemstones, valuable materials—and is considered to be objects of intrinsic beauty, though the early beginnings were very different. In prehistoric times, long before humans worked metals, jewelry was made of non-precious materials. Burials of 30,000 B.C.E. in Europe show that at the time people used local materials available to them, such as shells and pebbles, and, in hunting societies, also animal teeth and claws, to make jewelry. Existing examples reveal that pieces were engraved with intricate geometric patterns and, later, zoomorphic images. Thus, jewelry was an early form of decorative art. The study of some primitive cultures gives evidence that organic materials, which have since disintegrated, would have also undoubtedly been utilized in the past. It was not until a later stage of human development that people chose precious and possibly scarce materials from faraway for jewelry.

Jewelry is as old as humankind. Whether coming from a primitive culture or modern civilization of the West or East, and regardless of material and style, humans of both genders and all age groups have the need for self-adornment. The significance of jewelry transcends time limits and geographic boundaries; similarities in the use of jewelry for personal adornment become apparent in the study of various cultures.

In prehistoric times, as well as in contemporary cultures, jewelry is not only ornamentation for the body, but also a means of communication. Hierarchy, prestige, and power are expressed through jewelry, which can affirm the status of an individual in society. What initially appears to be an ornament can mark allegiance to a society or individual. Men and women can impress each other through jewelry. Yet possibly the most powerful qualities attributed to jewelry are the amuletic and talismanic functions of warding off evil or giving luck. These properties go back to the origins of jewelry and continue well into the nineteenth century. Even in contemporary cultures people carry good-luck charms. Jewelry also played an important role in protecting against the dangers of life, and was given in burials for the afterlife of the deceased. In addition, jewelry was also worn as a sign of personal affection and fidelity, and marked special occasions in life, such as coming of age, association to a religion through communion or confirmation, nubility, marital status, and motherhood. Jewels in their aesthetic expression are not only signs of wealth and taste, but also reflect—and communicate—the personal character and temperament of the wearer.

Throughout its history until about the mid-twentieth century, when jewelry experienced a radical change, it had been dependent on the fashions of the day, with the exception of finger rings. Varying necklines, sleeve lengths, hemlines, and fabrics determined the type of jewelry worn, while the choice of materials and symbolism determined its function and usage. The creativity of the goldsmith is boundless, as are the types and styles of wearable objects for the body.

If not passed on as a family heirloom or given for the person's afterlife and found in excavations of burials, many types of jewels that are known to have existed have not survived. Jewelry made of precious materials, regardless of century or culture, have been destined to be dismantled, the gemstones reused and the metals such as silver and gold melted down for bullion, either to become a financial resource or to be remodelled in a new fashion. Jewels with enamel have withstood this destiny, as it was too complicated and costly to remove the enamel, whereas golden chains with a considerable weight in metal were the first to be melted down. Few images of jewelry types and how they were worn survive from antiquity. Mummy masks and wall paintings of the ancient Egyptian era, ancient Greek statues of gods and vase painting, Etruscan tomb sculpture, Roman tombstones, and the informative mummy portraits of Fayum from the Roman period all give valuable evidence. In the Middle Ages, tomb effigies and even religious paintings of the Virgin Mary and saints illustrate jewelry of the time. More importantly, the development of portrait painting and the depiction of the individual from the fifteenth century onwards (supplemented after the mid-nineteenth century by photography) enables a comprehensive study of jewelry, and makes possible the reconstruction of many types that are no longer in existence.

In prehistoric times people chose materials from their immediate environment. A statuette dating back to 20,000 B.C.E., the so-called "Venus of Willendorf," shows a fertility statue wearing a bracelet, and burials give evidence of the use of necklaces made of snails and shells—both fertility symbols and a sign of motherhood. Men wore animal teeth and claws to signify their strength over the animal kingdom and their ability to hunt and, in turn, feed and protect their families. Such objects would possibly have marked their position within the community. In its early stages, jewelry was predominantly amuletic—its function was to guard its wearers in a life of hardships.

Until recently, and even to a limited extent in the early 2000s, among traditional peoples who managed to resist the impact of Western religion and culture, it is possible to discern elements of these more traditional attitudes toward personal adornment. Tattoos, makeup, and jewelry were in many cases, in such societies, not simply matters of personal adornment, but also conveyed specific messages about social and gender roles; they were used to ward off disease and other evils, and sometimes also to work magic against opponents; and as acts and signs of prayer and devotion to divinities. A widespread, if attenuated, example of the magical power of jewelry can be found throughout the Middle East and in parts of Africa, where the wearing of blue glass beads as a means of warding off the "evil eye" is very common.

In some societies, Western-style jewelry has still not completely effaced the wearing of more traditional forms of jewelry. The use of natural materials in jewelry in ways that probably preserve a very long continuous tradition of craftsmanship can be found, for example, among the highland peoples of New Guinea, where shell, bird-of-paradise feathers, boar tusks, and other animal products are commonly employed in personal adornment. Until the second half of the twentieth century these elements of jewelry were ubiquitous in the absence of alternative materials (for example, metal objects); in the early twenty-first century their continued use represents a choice among a wide range of possibilities.

In other contemporary non-Western societies, jewelry can still be seen as fulfilling another of its ancient functions, that is, it acts as a repository of wealth while also retaining its amuletic properties. Among pastoral nomadic peoples in the steppelands of Asia, throughout the Middle East, and in North Africa, women commonly wear very heavy silver jewelry, including headdress ornaments, earrings, necklaces, bracelets, belts, and frontlets, sometimes including actual silver coins (of many eras and many countries) worked into the jewelry. These coins also had an amuletic function, because their jingling sound was believed to ward off evil. Such jewelry not only displays the status of the family to which the woman belongs, but also acts as a highly portable form of wealth that can be converted to monetary use at any time it is needed. Likewise, in cities and agricultural regions of the Middle East, India, and Southeast Asia, gold jewelry acts as a repository of wealth as well as being beautiful and prestigious. In many Indian communities, for example, the conspicuous wearing of gold jewelry by a bride is an essential element of a wedding ceremony.

Jewelry found in western Asia in the cradle of civilization from about 5000 to 2500 B.C.E. illustrates a society with a taste for refined and decorative jewelry, as well as a trade network in supplying rare materials for their goldsmiths and differing local traditions. The earliest examples were necklaces made of obsidian from Turkey and cowrie shells with red stain from the nearby coastal areas. The most splendid jewels found in the area were from the royal graves of the Sumerian city of Ur in southern Mesopotamia, where the king and queen lay buried accompanied by their soldiers and attendants. Men wore beads to keep their headdress in place, whereas women's jewelry was more elaborate with dress pins, headdresses, and necklaces made of embossed and repouseé gold, probably from the areas currently known as Iran and Turkey. The motifs were stylized flowers and foliage, interspersed with beads in varying geometric shapes cut from lapis lazuli imported from Afghanistan and carnelian from India. The designs are intricate with signs of inlay, filigree, and the use of alternating colors.

Like the Sumerians, the ancient Egyptians from 3100 B.C.E. till the Graeco-Roman period in the first century B.C.E. showed a preference for lapis lazuli and carnelian, and typically, in Egyptian jewelry, turquoise is added to this combination. The resources in the area were vast and the choice of materials for the Egyptian jewelry-maker amazing as they also included a variety of organic materials. Gold and many other metals were found in the surrounding areas as were agates, amethysts, garnets, jaspers, malachite, and steatite, to name but a few. Glazed faience, and glass imitations in substitution, were applied to achieve colorful compositions, forming a contrast to the rather plain clothing the Egyptians wore, which was essentially made of white linen. Pectorals and necklaces were the most popular of jewelry types, but bracelets and head ornaments of all sorts are characteristic for the culture. The motifs ranged from the animal world (including fish and lions), the magical scarab, sphinxes, the udjat eye, and deities, either signifying rank or serving an amuletic purpose. Other designs are of a more decorative nature with vivid color combinations achieved through varied bead shapes and stones. Pharaohs, princesses, peasants, and artisans alike wore jewelry in life and in death, many surviving types were in fact funerary objects. The jewelry-making techniques were most sophisticated, such as inlaying in cloisons and granulation, and we even have pictorial records of craftsmen from ancient Egypt demonstrating technical processes in their workshops.

In the eastern Mediterranean of about 2500 B.C.E. there was the Minoan culture in Crete, which was taken over by the Mycenaeans in about 1450 B.C.E. The jewelry of that period and area is characterized by an abundance of gold; their styles were greatly influenced by the jewelry of the Babylonians and Egyptians. The Phoenicians were traders who colonized the eastern and western Mediterranean from Syria to Spain, and their choice of jewelry was influenced by the ancient Egyptians. Near Eastern designs also had influence on the later Greeks, as seen in the Orientalizing style of the Archaic period (700–480 B.C.E.), and in Etruscan jewelry (seventh to fifth centuries B.C.E.). The Etruscans were known for their technical perfection in goldsmithing and most of all for their outstanding technique of granulation with almost pulverized granules of gold. By the seventh century B.C.E., however, forms and decorative elements in jewelry were dominated by Greek designs and symbols.

Greek goldsmiths of the classical to Hellenistic periods were renowned for their technical skills and fine craftsmanship mainly in gold—a reputation that would be retained in future centuries. Greece was not rich in gold resources until its empire was extended as far as Persia in the fourth century B.C.E. In the classical period, from the Crimea to as far west as Sicily, Greek men wore more jewelry in some areas than others. In certain places it was even considered to be effeminate. Jewelry were gifts presented at birth, birthdays, and weddings, or even as votive offerings to cult statues. Rings and hair wreaths adorned men, both men and women wore rings, and the main forms of adornment for women were necklaces, earrings, bracelets on their upper arms or thighs, and diadems or golden nets in their hair. Fibulae were widespread and not only a decorative feature, but functional in as much as they held the drapery of the chiton on the shoulder. As the iconography of Greek jewelry confirms, it was intended for women, mainly to attract the opposite sex. This may explain the numerous images of Aphrodite, the goddess of love, in gold, as three-dimensional figures suspended from necklaces or earrings, possibly given at the birth of a child. Eros, symbolic of desire, was equally popular and given as a token of love. Deities such as Athena or Dionysus or other figures from mythology referred to religious beliefs and the power of the deities during life. Bracelets worn in pairs on the upper arm or rings with elaborately coiling snakes functioned as amulets, calling on the sacred creatures of the underworld to protect against evil. Antelopes and goats would attract the opposite sex, whereas lions were worn as emblems of fertility and royal power. These decorative motifs were all rendered in a naturalistic manner in gold sheet metal with intricate filigree wires and granulation, as were the interspersed motifs from nature such as seeds, nuts, and different shapes of foliage. Enamels, garnets, emeralds, and glass pastes became fashionable during the Hellenistic period as beads or inlay to add color to the previously predominantly gold jewelry.

With the loss of Greek independence and the victory of the Romans over Macedonia in 168 B.C.E, Rome became a strong military and political power. The wealth of the new empire attracted many Greek craftsmen to come to the capital, where they were most successful. Essentially the Romans followed Greek styles until about the first century B.C.E., when the aesthetics of their jewelry began to change. The jewelry became unpretentious, the gold techniques less elaborate, the designs simplified, and more emphasis was laid on the choice of stones and the use of color—a new taste had developed, it was the beauty of the material to which one aspired. Regional differences are evident: jet was fashionable in Britain, where it was found in Whitby, and amber from the Baltic Sea was cut in Aquileia in Roman Italy. Emeralds from the newly discovered mines in Egypt—what was then recently acquired Roman territory—became fashionable and their abundance led to the natural hexagonal crystal

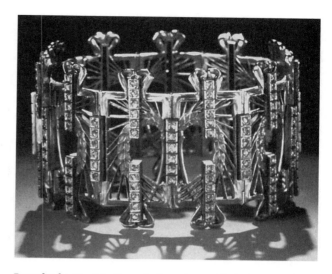

Bracelet by René Lalique. Lalique began designing jewelry in the late 1880s and was known for his unique combinations of metals, glass, and gemstones. AP/WIDE WORLD PHOTOS. REPRODUCED BY PERMISSION.

shapes being drilled, strung on thread, or connected with simple gold links to be worn as necklaces. Garnets were imported from the Middle East, and sapphires from Sri Lanka. Pearls were considered to be an expression of luxury and indulgence. Apart from the Romans showing a preference for gemstones, each has a special significance, described in the *Historia naturalis* by Pliny the Elder (23–79 B.C.E). Specific gemstones were chosen for certain images, such as Bacchus on amethyst as a safeguard against drunkenness; the Sun god Sol is depicted on heliotrope; and Demeter, goddess of crops, on green jasper to symbolize growth and abundance.

Trade was flourishing in the vast empire with far-reaching provinces, and jewelry was being produced in Rome, Alexandria, and Antioch. Roman goldsmiths had guilds and rules existed about who could wear certain types of jewelry, but these soon diminished. During the Republic gold jewelry was reserved for the aristocracy, but by the first century C.E. its significance soon depreciated and by the second century gold was worn by those who could afford it. With adornment becoming socially acceptable for a wider public, even slaves were permitted to wear jewelry made of iron—it was mass produced, and thus plenty has survived from the Roman period. With a thriving economy by the second century, Roman jewelry became more elaborate, even heavy and gaudy—a sign of wealth and status—yet at the same time the iconography suggests the jewelry was full of symbolism and personal messages for the wearer. Deities became symbols of wealth and good fortune, the gorgon Medusa destroyed evil powers, the phallus was a popular good luck charm, and cupids with Venus or cupids riding on dolphins tokens of love. Images of clasped right hands or husband and wife facing each other alluded to the mar-

Detail from Titian's *Girl in a Fur*. The Renaissance lady in this painting wears pearls, which were a popular, if expensive, jewelry choice during the period. © BURSTEIN COLLECTION/CORBIS. REPRODUCED BY PERMISSION.

riage vows, and Latin inscriptions served as charms to protect life. Other types of jewelry such as the brooch were more decorative in character and, in fact, served a functional purpose of holding the drapery together.

By the fourth century the Roman Empire was in decline. With Christianity having been recognized by Constantine the Great, the iconography found in jewelry was relevant to the new religion, but often coded to protect the owner from being persecuted. The early Christians appear to have worn finger rings as a sign of their allegiance, and engraved on the bezels are symbols and ciphers of Christ the Saviour. In the fourth century the empire transferred to East Byzantium with its capital in Constantinople, which continued as an ecclesiastical and successful trading power until 1453 when the city fell to the Ottoman Turks. Greek goldsmiths were active there, and with their influence, despite the style being a continuation of late Roman jewelry with a love for gemstones and color, there was a greater emphasis on intricate goldwork with enamel or niello decoration. Except for bronze

gilt or gold rings, the laws were strict about who could wear jewelry. Emeralds, pearls, and sapphires were reserved for the emperor, and all the splendor of their richly embroidered and bejeweled fabrics is documented in the mosaics of the churches in Ravenna, northern Italy, as are the elaborate necklaces, earrings, and brooches. Nevertheless, the iconography was religious and the cult of saints is confirmed by the use of pectoral crosses with their images and relic inserts.

Mutual artistic influence between the Byzantine world and the expanding world of Islam is evident from the mid-seventh century onward. Byzantine and Islamic influence can also be seen in the jewelry of the Germanic tribes that occupied much of Europe after the fall of the western Roman Empire. Germanic tribesmen acquired gold from Byzantium. The jewelry of these nomadic tribes tended to be restricted to basic types and was more functional in its application, but nonetheless the jewels were a statement of status. Men wore belts, buckles, and sword harnesses; both men and women needed clasps for their dress, and these are found in the form of disc brooches or fibulae. The tribes show distinctive styles in their goldsmiths' work, but even they had many common elements, such as sophistication in the applied goldsmithing techniques, the lavish engraving, the use of garnet inlays, and the intricacy of patterns, including stylized animal themes.

During the Middle Ages cities were enlarging, the merchant classes were gaining prominence and becoming a new economic force, and with the church losing power, society became more worldly. With the rise of the middle classes and increase in wealth, sumptuary laws became necessary to restrict who was allowed to wear jewelry. Fashions determined the types of jewelry worn: with the sleeves becoming wider and more lavish, bracelets were unnecessary; high collars did not allow for earrings; cape-like coats required brooches; and the high waistlines of women's dresses made fancy belts necessary. Rings with signets or love messages were very popular.

By the twelfth and thirteenth centuries an international style in jewelry had evolved. Shapes of stone settings, designs, and decorations showed astonishing similarities in England, France, Denmark, Germany, and Italy. This phenomenon presumably can be explained by the trade routes and import of gemstones from the Near and Far East. Paris was trend-setting in the manufacturing of jewelry, whereas the ports of Venice and Genoa were influential in trade. The inscriptions on jewelry were mostly in Latin or French, the international language of the courts. The pointed arches and tracery of Gothic architecture, naturalistic rendering of foliage in sculpture, and the colors of stained glass were mirrored in the jewelry designs of the time. Devotional and secular iconography were often interlocked, gemstones in cabochon were amuletic or reflected divinity, and the images of saints had protective and healing powers, as did the emerging use of the bones of saints in reliquary pendants. Flowers and animals decorate medieval jewels as a symbol of faith, and classical gems were given Christian interpretations. Medieval jewelry was largely heraldic, religious, or expressive of courtly love.

In Europe the transition to the Renaissance period differed according to country, beginning with Italy in the fifteenth century and spreading throughout Europe by the sixteenth century. Italy, with its discoveries of ancient monuments and sculpture, was all-important in the rebirth of the cultures of ancient Greece and Rome, whereas in northern Europe Gothic styles continued much longer. With an explosion of economic trade, in particular wool and banking, many wealthy families in Italy became patrons of the arts. Goldsmiths became known as individuals by name. In the fifteenth century, Florence and the Burgundian Courts established trends in dress and jewelry; by the sixteenth and seventeenth centuries Spain became a major European power with colonies all over the world, leading to a dominant Spanish style in dress and jewelry. Religious wars raged in Europe and, often due to the circumstances, artisans traveled from one country to another—at the same time following the wealth of emerging courts in Europe. Jewelry again developed into an international style with less regional distinctions. Another factor that led to this phenomenon was the newly discovered art of printing. Artists made ornamental drawings that were printed and distributed throughout Europe, and even as far as the Spanish colonies, where jewelry was made in the style of the day for trade with Europe.

Men, in fact, showed more adornment than women. However, the function of jewels was display, as the abundance of portraits of that period document. The merchant classes were following fashions of the aristocracy, the materials used, though, were usually less precious. The heavy and dark velvets or brocades with gold embroidery were covered with jewelry, either sewn on the fabric as ornaments, or worn on the body. Pendants were fashionable for all genders, and the images were either religious or from classical mythology; exotic birds, flowers, or marine themes were also displayed as symbols of status and new wealth. Gemstones were in open settings when on the body, so that the amuletic qualities would be more effective. Heavy gold chains worn by both men and women on the breast or across the shoulder and cascading in multiple strands were undoubtedly a sign of social ranking. Men wore hat jewels, belts with sword harnesses, and jeweled buttons. The custom of wearing bracelets in pairs was revived from antiquity, as was the fashion for earrings. Decorative chains encompassed ladies' waists, often from which pomanders or pendants were suspended. Dress studs ornamented the already elaborate fabrics. To add to the display of color, Renaissance jewels often had polychrome enamels in combination with gemstones, such as rubies from Burma, emeralds from the New World, pearls off the coast of Venezuela, and diamonds from India. In contrast to the

Indian woman with nose ring. Silver and gold are signs of prestige in India, and among nomadic tribes jewelry made from these metals functions both as adornment and as portable wealth. © BRIAN A. VIKANDER/CORBIS. REPRODUCED BY PERMISSION.

cabochon cuts of the Middle Ages, during the Renaissance table cuts were common. With the renewal of classical traditions the art of cameo cutting was revived and northern Italy was an important source for this form of lapidary arts.

In the second half of the seventeenth century while Spain was in decline, France became the most important economic and cultural center. All luxury industries flourished in the France of Louis XIV. French silks from Lyon and dress fashions were exported and, with these, styles for jewelry. It was also a period when women were playing an increasingly significant role in society. For their dress, heavyweight brocades had been replaced by light silks in various pastel shades. The splendor and bright colors of the fabrics required a decrease of color in jewelry. Portraits of the period illustrate a passion for pearls, strung as necklaces or worn as pearl drops suspended from earrings, or from brooches worn on the breast, sleeve, or in the hair. Pearls were very valuable, and while pearls often were ostentatiously displayed, it is likely

Papua New Guinea native. In some parts of the world, natural and unaltered materials such as shells, feathers, and the teeth, horns, and claws of animals are worn as jewelry. © WOLFGANG KAEHLER/CORBIS. REPRODUCED BY PERMISSION.

that most of them were fake; fake pearls are known to have been produced since about 1400. Diamonds were favored. French-style enamelled settings and decorations were equally subdued in their color scheme: opaque white enamel was outlined with black, and pale pink or turquoise enamel was applied as highlights of the decoration. A source for the naturalistic floral designs of enamel decorations was the study of botany, a new science. Jewelry had the tendency of being less figural and more decorative with bows and clusters of gemstones. However, the Thirty Years War that ravaged Europe between 1618 and 1648, as well as the plague, resulted in a new type of jewelry, *memento mori*. The wearer was reminded of his or her transience and mortality, and skull's heads and skeletons were featured in all types of jewelry, which lived on in mourning jewelry of the eighteenth and nineteenth centuries with funerary ornaments and weeping maidens as motifs.

Designs in jewelry were in general more playful by the eighteenth century and the grand elegant court style

of Louis XV of France was to influence the whole of Europe, even as far as Russia. The compositions of the jewelry were more naturalistic, and thus asymmetrical; flower sprays and baskets were gem-studded, as were feathers, ribbons, and bows. Eighteenth-century jewelry moved from monochrome to polychrome; metal foils placed under the gemstones enhanced their color. Indian diamond mines had been exhausted, but with new mines found by the Portuguese in Brazil the fashion continued, and by 1720 the rose-cut diamond had been developed, allowing more light reflections. Other fashionable stones were agates, mossagate, and marcasite. Pearl strands with ornate clasps were worn like chokers; large stomachers were attached to the narrow bodices, and aigrettes to the hair; and shoe buckles were also bejewelled. With the Industrial Revolution in its beginnings towards the end of the eighteenth century, new materials for jewelry had been discovered, including cut steel. This hard metal was facetted to look like diamonds. The industrialist, Josiah Wedgewood (1730–1795), the founder of Wedgewood pottery, designed porcelain cameos to be inserted into jewelry. A special formula for making glass paste was named after Georges Frédéric Strass (1701–1773). After Marie Antoinette of France wore strass at court, it became socially acceptable to wear paste jewelry, which would have shimmered splendidly in candlelight.

In 1789 the French Revolution had dramatic effects not only in the politics and life of France, but also on Europe as a whole. Outside France the market was flooded by the jewels and gemstones of those who managed to escape, and prices fell radically. In France anybody owning jewels of aristocratic origin faced death by guillotine; only jewelry made of base metals was permitted, and this jewelry had political and patriotic inscriptions or symbols.

Luxury was revived in France with Napoleon when he proclaimed his empire in 1804. His wife Josephine was a trend-setter and wore Greek fashion, which was reflected in jewelry. Cameos, the Greek key pattern, laurel wreaths, and filigree work were reminiscent of antiquity. However the Napoleonic Wars led to quite a different and innovative type of jewelry known as Berlin iron, first developed when ladies gave their golden jewelry to finance the wars and received iron jewelry in return. The fashion spread from Germany to Austria and France; the style of this jewelry was antique or Gothic, typical of the nineteenth century with its eclectic styles.

The effects of the Industrial Revolution and the rise of the middle class became particularly evident in Britain. The middle class imitated the jewelry of the aristocracy, but instead of diamonds, rubies, sapphires, and emeralds, gemstones such as amethyst, chrysoprase, tourmaline, turquoise, and many other colourful substitutes were applied. Seed pearls were labour intensive, but as an inexpensive material replaced opulent pearl jewelry. As in dress fashions, evening and day jewelry was differentiated, the full parure consisting of necklace, bracelets, brooch, and earrings was intended for the evening, whereas the demi-parure, a brooch with matching earrings, for daytime wear. Sentimental jewelry was extremely popular: gifts with love or messages of friendship, and souvenirs of hair of the beloved or deceased were integrated in jewels. The newly acquired wealth of the middle class enabled travel, and souvenir jewelry was invented soon after, such as *pietra dura* work from Florence, coral from Naples, micromosaics from Rome, and the archaeological styles from Egypt, Assyria, and the Celtic lands. Not only were archaeological and exotic cultures reinterpreted, but so were the Middle Ages and Renaissance. By the second half of the nineteenth century the famous jewelry houses of today opened branches in the capital cities of Europe; jewelry became global.

The path to modernism in jewelry began around the turn of the twentieth century, during the *belle époque* when there was a mood for renewal and individually crafted luxury items. Paris with its exhibition of 1900 was predominant in the new aesthetic movement. The jewelry expressed emotions, and winged women were symbolic of emancipation; nature was metaphorically interpreted: themes such as birth, death, and rebirth were expressed through plants in varying stages of their life. René Lalique laid the foundation for artists' jewelry of the twentieth century and introduced novel material combinations, such as precious gold with non-precious glass. Diamonds were applied sparingly, *plique-à-jour* enamel allowed light to shine through, opals gave iridescence, and materials appeared to almost dematerialize. In contrast, silver with enamel and a few gemstones defined the Jugendstil in Germany and the Viennese Secession in Austria, both reducing nature to stylized geometric forms. Liberty of London chose Celtic inspirations, and Georg Jensen in Denmark a more sculptural rendering of nature. By 1910 platinum jewelry in the Louis XVI style with bows, tassels, and garlands enabled thin, almost invisible settings and linear designs. The costumes of the Ballets Russes in Paris were immensely inspirational for vivid color combinations in jewelry, such as emeralds with sapphires, turquoises, and coral.

Decisive innovations in jewelry were brutally interrupted by World War I. Many widows were obliged to gain employment to survive; dress and hair fashions became casual, and so did jewelry. In the golden twenties elegant lifestyle and lavish luxury prevailed again, mirrored in the jewels of the epoch. Diamonds and gemstones form stylized compositions in contrasting colors that are reminiscent of such art movements as Cubism, de Stijl and Futurism. The exoticism of Africa and Egypt attracted jewelers as well. Germany, struggling with political and economical concerns and following the artistic philosophies of the Bauhaus school of design, developed jewelry made of non-precious materials such as chrome-plated brass. Events such as the stock market crash on Wall Street in 1929 had a global economic effect in Europe, as

did World War II, when materials for jewelry were scarce, but the desire for jewelry never ceased.

In the aftermath of the wars in the twentieth century, jewelry experienced a departure from its traditional values due to radical changes in society: housewives could no longer afford staff, and young people learned to be self-sufficient. Like fashion, jewelry designs followed the movements of youth culture. Women became more independent, and began buying their own jewelry rather than traditionally having it given to them by their husbands as had been traditional. Never before had jewelry been so diverse and so independent of dress fashions.

In the 1950s and 1960s the desire for luxury was epitomized by Hollywood with its make-believe world, mink stoles, and diamonds galore. During this time jewelers in Europe were experimenting with gold surfaces, designing unconventional settings, and, thus, transforming jewelry into a free art form. After the 1960s jewelry took an almost revolutionary turn with the freelance artist jewelers in their studios boldly setting out on the path of the fine arts—by the 1980s they broke existing boundaries of dimensions and materials and used materials from gold to rubber to paper.

More than any other time in its history, by the early twenty-first century, jewelry reflected the wearers' moods and feelings, favorite colors, taste, understanding of the arts, and last, but not least, their individuality.

See also **Brooches and Pins; Earrings; Necklaces and Pendants; Rings.**

BIBLIOGRAPHY

Andrews, Carol. *Ancient Egyptian Jewelry*. New York: Harry N. Abrams, 1991.

Bury, Shirley. *Jewellery 1789–1910: The International Era.* 2 vols. Woodbridge, Suffolk, England: Antique Collectors' Club, 1991.

Daniëls, Ger. *Folk Jewelry of the World*. New York: Rizzoli, 1989.

Dormer, Peter, and Ralph Turner. *The New Jewelry: Trends and Traditions.* Revised edition. New York: Thames and Hudson, 1994.

Lightbown, Ronald W. *Mediaeval European Jewellery: With a Catalogue of the Collection in the Victoria and Albert Museum.* London: Victoria and Albert Museum, 1992.

Mack, John, ed. *Ethnic Jewelry*. New York: Abrams, 1988.

Phillips, Clare. *Jewelry: From Antiquity to the Present.* New York: Thames and Hudson, 1996.

Princely Magnificence: Court Jewels of the Renaissance, 1500–1630. London: Victoria and Albert Museum, 1980. An exhibition catalog.

Tait, Hugh, ed. *Seven Thousand Years of Jewellery.* London: British Museum Publications, 1986.

Williams, Dyfri, and Jack Ogden. *Greek Gold: Jewelry of the Classical World.* New York: Abrams, 1994.

Anna Beatriz Chadour-Sampson

JEWISH DRESS Although no specific costume was ever mandated by Jewish law, and no universal Jewish costume ever evolved, certain dress codes have been clearly identified with the Jewish people throughout the ages. In addition to the influence of Jewish law and custom on the development of these dress codes, these codes were impacted by the geography and historical setting in which the costume developed, and the extent of integration in the wider, gentile community.

Several principal factors have determined Jewish dress throughout the ages:

1. Halachah: the whole legal system of Judaism which embraces all laws and observances, from the Bible henceforth, as well as codes of conduct and customs.
2. Restrictive decrees and edicts by non-Jewish authorities in countries where Jews lived, as well as Jewish inner-communal regulations.
3. Prevailing local sartorial styles and dress codes.

Halachah
Halachah, the code of Jewish law, is based mainly on biblical precepts, which are considered the primary and most authoritative source for all Jewish laws. Since biblical precepts concerning dress are few, they determine only several aspects of Jewish costume. Later halakhic rulings regulated dress codes and interpreted the biblical injunctions.

The explicit biblical precepts refer to attaching fringes to men's dress and the prohibition of wearing a garment made of a mixture of wool and linen. Some rabbinical authorities and scholars deduce that the covering of women's hair and *peoth*—sidelocks (Leviticus 19:27) worn by Jews, which are today distinctive features of the Jewish male external appearance, were also biblical precepts. One should also mention the *tefillin*—phylacteries: these are small leather boxes containing holy and protective texts which are attached to the forehead and the left arm during morning prayer (see Exodus 13:9, 16, and Deuteronomy 6:8; 11:18). Today these are ritual accessories to which utmost importance is attributed, but in Talmudic times some scholars wore them throughout the day.

Tzitzith. In biblical times, fringes were attached to outer garments, which were probably a kind of sheetlike wraps, which had four corners. In time, when dress styles changed, two separate ritual garments evolved to fulfill this precept. The *tallith*, the prayer shawl, is a rectangular fringed shawl worn for prayer and important events in the Jewish life cycle. The *tzitzith*, which literally means fringe, or *tallith katan* (literally "small tallith"), is a poncholike undershirt worn at all times by orthodox Jewish men. According to the Torah, one tassel should be blue (Numbers 15:18), but as the process of production of the blue extracted from the *murex purpura* (a snail used for dying blue and purple in the Mediterranean) was lost, the fringes were usually white. The fringes consist of four

cords folded to produce eight ends, knotted in differing numerical combinations, equivalent to the numerical value of the letters of names of God. The religious, mystic-symbolic meaning attributed to these garments imbued them also with protective and magical powers.

Sha'atnez. Because it is not outwardly visible, *sha'atnez*, though kept to this day by certain observant Jews, is not a distinctive mark of Jewish dress. With mass-produced clothing, special laboratories are required to determine whether a particular garment contains the forbidden mixture. In the past, in many communities, tailoring became a prevalent Jewish occupation in order to be able to control the combination of fibers and textiles of clothes.

Two major tendencies direct halakhic rulings concerning dress. One is segregation from the gentile environment: "Nor shall you follow their laws" (Leviticus 18:3), as is stated generally in the Bible. More specifically relating to dress, Maimonides, the renowned medieval Jewish scholar, stated: "One must not follow in the ways of those who worship the stars nor imitate them either in dress or hairstyle" (*Mishneh Thorah, Hilkhot Avodat Kokhavim* 11:1).

Modesty
Another major concern of halakhic rulings regarding dress are various issues of modesty—for instance, the requirement to be decently dressed and covered during prayer (Tosefta Brachot 2:14, second century C.E.). This attitude was later interpreted as the separation between the upper part of the body, considered spiritual and pure, from the lower part, considered mundane and impure. Among the Hasidim of Eastern Europe (from the eighteenth century on) this division of the body acquired a rich symbolical meaning and is fulfilled by the *gartle*, a belt donned ritually before prayer.

The equivalent item among women was the apron, the purpose of which was to cover and protect their reproductive organs. These aprons, worn either under or above the skirt or both, were considered a symbol of modesty and magically protective. The wearing of aprons persisted among Eastern European Jewish women and after having almost vanished, made a comeback among some of the ultraorthodox women who wear them while lighting Shabbat candles and during festive occasions. They regard them as charms that will bring them well-mannered children.

Head covering for women. The practice of women covering their heads became pervasive and universal throughout the Jewish world. In some communities, it became customary to cut the hair or even shave it shortly before or after the wedding. Some women attempt to leave no hair uncovered while others allow some parts to be seen as is customary in each community. The custom of wearing *sheytls*, wigs, was adapted by Jewish women in Europe in the sixteenth century, when it was fashionable for both men and women, and it has lasted as an option for head covering among some Jewish orthodox groups into the twenty-first century. In several places in Morocco, in Bukhara and Georgia, Jewish women's coifs incorporated false hair that served as partial wigs. Such is the elaborate *mahdour* headgear of the Jewish women of the Sous region on the southern coast of Morocco. This is an intricate work of silver interwoven with the hair of a horse's tail, two locks of which frame the woman's forehead.

The wearing of wigs even in the twenty-first century is a highly controversial issue among the different orthodox groups. Some claim that the display of hair, even false hair, does not abide with the prohibition to conceal it, since the showing of any hair is considered erotic, and therefore immodest.

With the passing of time, both the manner and style of the head covering have taken many forms and differ immensely from place to place. In the past, prior to modernization, women's head covering attested both to her marital status as well as to her socio-economic status, her place of residence, and communal affiliation. In Sana'a, Yemenite Jewish women wore the distinctive *gargush*, a hoodlike headgear that concealed the hair, the forehead, and the neck. It identified the Jewish woman from the Muslim woman and the Jewish woman of San'a from Jewish women of other localities. Every woman had several hoods, the most sumptuous was the *gargush mezahhar merassaf* (the full golden hood), decorated with gilt, silver filigree pieces, and with several coins. All these riches formed part of the woman's dowry, which she received from her father and were used as her cash reserve.

In the early twenty-first century the distinction is less geographic and attests to religious group affiliation and degree of religiosity. Szatmar Hasidic women in New York and Jerusalem wear similar head coverings—a scarf covering their hair entirely, sometimes with a padding under it or a small piece of synthetic wig in front, or a synthetic wig worn under the scarf.

The women of the Neturei Karta, and the most extreme groups, shave their hair, and cover their head with a tight black scarf. Whereas the Belz Hasidic women wear a wig and a small cap on top of it, Sephardi-Oriental women in Israel do not wear wigs but fashionable hats and scarves.

Head covering for men. Unlike women's hair covering, men's head covering has only become obligatory in the last centuries. It is not mentioned in the Torah, and in the Babylonian Talmud it is only a custom practiced by certain people—Torah scholars—and at certain times, such as during prayers and benedictions. It is conceived as a sign of religious submission and respect to higher authorities and before God.

In the sixteenth century, when the Shulhan Aruch, the Code of Jewish Law, was written and accepted by all Jewish communities, men's head covering was not yet uni-

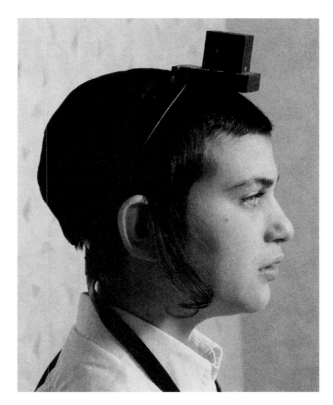

Hasidic boy wearing phylacteries. Small leather boxes called *tefillin*, phylacteries, are worn on the forehead and left arm during prayer. The boxes contain holy texts. © RICHARD T. NOWITZ/CORBIS. REPRODUCED BY PERMISISON.

versal or compulsory. The code stated that covering the head was a sign of a God-fearing Jew and especially important during study and prayer (*Orakh khayyim* 2,2; 151.6). In Christian countries, the Jewish covering of the head in the synagogue evolved as contrary to the practice of uncovering one's head as a sign of reverence, while in the Muslim world, Jews were no exception to the general practice of covering their heads. In both Christian and Muslim lands, Jews were required to wear a hat, the shape and color of which would serve to identify them as Jews.

Well known in its time was the *Judenhut*, the medieval pointed Jewish hat by which Jews were identified, and which are clearly seen in both Jewish and Christian depictions of Jewish life. The wearing of a double head covering—a *kippah* or yarmulke (skullcap) and hat—among the ultraorthodox, or a scullcap only, by orthodox Jews, evolved in nineteenth-century Europe and became part of the controversy between reformists and traditionalist groups. Among some of the reformists, the skullcap is worn during prayer and other ceremonial occasions. As for the ultraorthodox, in order to express their opposition to the reform, they started to wear a skullcap and a hat on top of it. In the early twenty-first century, especially in Israeli society, covering of the head or not

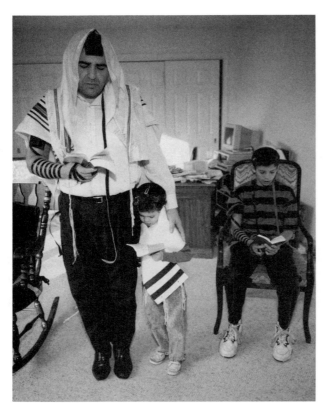

Jewish father and sons at prayer. During prayer, rectangular fringed shawls, or *tcalliths,* are worn. Some Orthodox Jews also wear small fringed talliths under their clothing at all times. © DAVID H. WELLS/CORBIS. REPRODUCED BY PERMISSION.

distinguishes between secular and observant Jews. The type of covering indicates socio-religious and ideological, even political affiliation. For instance the *kippah srugah*, a crocheted skullcap, has become an identity mark of the National Religious community and political party.

Restrictive Decrees and Edicts

Apart from the inner Halakhic rules, Jewish costume was determined by restrictive decrees issued by the gentile authorities in the countries in which Jews lived in the diaspora. These laws required Jews to wear special garment items, prohibited them from wearing particular fabrics and colors, and obliged them to mark their dress with badges.

In Muslim lands, the edicts began with the Laws of Omar (in the eighth century) that required that all non-Muslims be distinguished by their external appearance, by their clothing, the external manifestation of their lower legal status as "infidels." This distinction had far-reaching legal and social implications, and it served as a tool for keeping ethno-religious hierarchies and boundaries. These laws were the conceptual guidelines for practical restrictions imposed by different rulers. The decrees

did not deal with entire outfits, but pertained mainly to the colors and quality of fabrics, and sometimes to particular components of dress such as head gear or footwear. In Bukhara, the Jews had to wear ropelike belts as a distinction mark.

Infidels were supposed to wear dark colors such as black or dark blue (some places had specific colors for Jews and others for Christians). Green was reserved for Muslims because it is the holy color of Islam. Jews were not allowed to use luxurious fabrics, as were enumerated in the edicts. There were restrictions pertaining to the cut and size of the garment. In Turkey, the size of the turban was of great significance—the larger the turban, the higher the rank of its wearer—thus the edicts restricted the length of the turban fabric and the width of the cloak permitted to Jews. In Afghanistan in the first half of the twentieth century, Jewish men could only wear gray turbans.

Similar restrictions were imposed in medieval Europe by the church councils. In 1215, the Lateran Council issued the well-known dress restriction as a reaction to the forbidden mingling of Christians with Jews and Muslims:

> … [T]hey may not … resort to excusing themselves … for the excesses of such accursed intercourse, we decree that such [Jews and Saracens] … in every Christian province and at all times shall be distinguished in the eyes of the public from other peoples by the character of their dress. (Rubens, 1973, p. 81)

These decrees also included the wearing of a badge. The badge differed in shape and color as well as in the place where it should be displayed, either on the right shoulder or on the hat. In the duchies of Italy, a yellow patch was worn. In England, its shape was of the Tablets of the Law, and in Germany, the badge was a ring-shaped sign. The Jews were also obliged to purchase these badges from the government. "Every Jew above the age of seven must wear a yellow or red and white badge. The royal tax collectors will collect the fee for the purchase of the badge" (France, 1217–1284).

These edicts and restrictions were intended to mark the Jewish population and set them apart from others, thereby aiming at degrading and humiliating them. The spirit of this distinction did not disappear altogether and was revived by Nazi Germany by imposing the yellow badge as a race discriminator. The reaction of the Jewish population to these laws took different forms. In many cases, as can be expected, it was resented, but in some instances, it was accepted positively as described by a traveler to the Ottoman empire in the seventeenth century: "As in religion they differ from others so they do in habit: in Christendom enforcedly, here in the Turkie voluntarily" (Sandys, p. 115).

Though this may not be accurate, it does acknowledge different reactions to the humiliating restrictions. These differentiating restrictions were accepted positively, as they met with the Halakha and the desire to differentiate themselves from others by their clothing. In some cases, these restrictions were given different explanations and an inner symbolic interpretation. For example, Moroccan and Tunisian Jews and the Jews of Sana'a in Yemen held that the wearing of black, adapted by the Jews themselves, was considered as a sign of mourning commemorating the destruction of the Temple. (There are several other signs commemorating the destruction that, according to Jewish law, one has to keep).

These restrictions were at times corroborated by inner communal regulations and sumptuary laws called *takkanot*. These regulations issued by Jewish communities referred mainly to women's attire, instructing them to refrain from wearing luxurious clothes—especially with gold decorations and opulent jewelery—mainly in the public domain. Their purposes were twofold: the first, to avoid arousing jealousy among non-Jews, as it was feared that excess finery in Jewish dress might bring about additional edicts by the authorities; the second, to avoid internal tensions between rich and poor families within Jewish communities. These regulations limited excessive finery in weddings and other festive occasions but allowed some exceptions.

Such rules and regulations provide very important historical sources for a meticulous study of dress codes in each community.

We have unanimously decided that from this day forward … no woman, young or old, shall wear arm bracelets, or chains, or gold bracelets, or gold hoops, or gold rings, or any gold ornament … or pearl necklaces, or nose rings … [A woman] cannot wear any garment made of wool or silk, and [she] certainly [cannot wear] gold or silver embroidery, even if the lining is inside out, except for a head covering, which is all she is allowed to wear … and as for children and infants, neither boys nor girls may [dress] themselves [in articles made] either of gold or of silver or of silk. (From regulations pronounced by the rabbis of the community of Fez, Morocco, 1613)

Velvet for dresses, even for linings, is forbidden to women and girls, with the exception of black velvet. The bride may wear any kind of velvet under the canopy during her wedding … any type of skirt which is stiffened with a hope of wire or … other devices is forbidden to married and single women … even small children. … From today until further notice, no silk dresses of two colors should be made for women, with the exception of dark grey and brown. (Fine: 20 thalers). Whoever offends openly or in secret will be excommunicated and treated as someone who has sinned against God. (From the Jewish regulations for clothing and weddings, Hamburg, Germany, 1715)

Sartorial Styles and Dress Codes

The great variety of Jewish traditional attire prior to modernization, attests to the marked influence of the surrounding culture on each Jewish community. One can

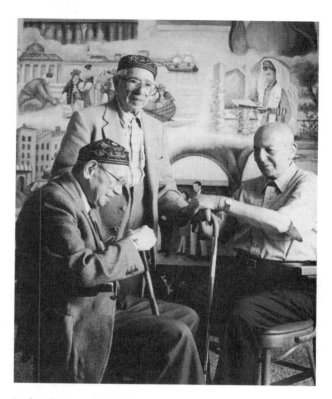

Sephardic Jews in skull caps. Covering of the head became mandatory for most orthodox Jews after publication of the *Code of Jewish Law* in the sixteenth century. © ALEN MACWEENEY/CORBIS. REPRODUCED BY PERMISSION.

safely say that the attire of the Jews resembled more that of their surrounding culture than that of Jews living in other places, notwithstanding the distinction marks imposed on them.

Yet costume was not only conceived as marking ethno-religious boundaries, but also as defining group identity within the Jewish communities; one example is the "great dress," worn as a bridal and festive dress by urban Spanish Jewish women (descendants of the Jews expelled from Spain in 1492) in Morocco. This sumptuous outfit made of metal thread–embroidered velvet, was strikingly different from the local Muslim costumes. It strongly resembled Spanish costume of the sixteenth century and preserved many of its stylistic traits. In Morocco, this dress became an identity mark of the urban Spanish Jews vis-à-vis the local rural Jews; it was one of the symbols of the preservation of the Spanish heritage, which was a source of pride to this group. However, it is not certain that this dress was worn by Jews in Spain. Within Morocco, there were also variations of this dress each belonging to a certain town, Fez, Rabat, Mogador, and others.

This rare example of the preservation of sartorial styles by an immigrant group for over 400 years leads to another feature thought to be typical or recurring in Jewish costume in different places. It has been observed that

Jews in many communities had a tendency to retain dress styles long after they have been abandoned by the gentile society. After some time, these anachronistic clothes or items of dress were appropriated by the Jews and considered later to be exclusive to them and even an identifying trait. The best known example of this phenomenon is the Hassidic or ultraorthodox costume, derived from the Polish eighteenth-century dress of nobleman and appropriated and preserved by the Jews, which became a distinctive attire exclusive to them. Another example is the sheetlike wrap-and-veil street wear worn by Jewish women in Baghdad until 1952. The custom of veiling was a norm in Muslim society. Jewish women adhered to that norm. Veiling was the prerogative of Muslim women and was not imposed on low-status women such as servants and non-Muslims. Non-Muslim women are not required to veil themselves. The Bagdadi wrap covered the whole body, while the face was hidden by a square black veil. In this period, Baghdadi Jewish women's *izar*, veils, were made of pastel-colored silk interwoven with metal thread. Prevalent among Muslim women in former times, such dress came to be considered a distinctively Jewish outfit in the early twentieth century when the customary Muslim attire changed to a plain black wrap.

The conflict between the will to integrate and the will to isolate Jewish society from the gentile surrounding cultures was strongest in Europe in the period of emancipation and modernization during the nineteenth century. As European society enabled the Jews to become equal citizens, some of the Jews wanted to assimilate and not to be distinguished by their dress, while others saw this assimilation as a great danger to Jewish religion and culture. The reform Jews changed their traditional garb to fashionable modern costume. This change was accompanied by debates over head covering and other matters. These changes and reforms caused a strong reaction among some of the East European Jews centered in Hungary, who preached to cling more strongly to tradition. Every domain of life and dress was considered a central aspect of this tradition (under the *halachic* precept that anything new is forbidden by the Torah).

The wearing of better clinging traditional attire down to the minutest detail has turned the dress of the ultraorthodox Jews into a kind of uniform by which they are recognized. It is also considered a protective mechanism against sin.

Since there are few common features of Jewish costume across time and place, it is fundamental to study it in relation to surrounding historical and cultural setting. Yet, in the confines of a given society and the bounds of limited time, Jews could still be identified by certain particularities of their dress, which were often a combination of local dress with one or two sartorial elements that they carried with them throughout time.

See also **Religion and Dress.**

BIBLIOGRAPHY
Bar'am, Ben Yossef No'am. *Brides and Betrothals: Jewish Wedding Rituals in Afghanistan.* Jerusalem: The Israel Museum, 1998.

Carrel, Goldman Barbara. "Women's Head-Coverings: A Feminised System of Hasidic Distinction." In *Religion and Dress and the Body.* Edited by Linda Boynton Arthur. Oxford: Berg, 1999, pp. 163–180.

Frankel, Giza. "Notes on the Costume of the Jewish Woman in Eastern Europe." *Journal of Jewish Art* 7 (1980): 50–57.

Goitein, Shlomo Dov. *A Mediterranean Society.* Berkeley: University of California Press, 1983, pp. 150–200.

Juhasz, Esther. *Sephardi Jews in the Ottoman Empire: Aspects of Material Culture.* Jerusalem: The Israel Museum, 1989.

Krauss, Samuel. "The Jewish Rite of Covering the Head." In *Beauty in Holiness.* Edited by Joseph Gutman. Hebrew Union College Annual XIX, 1946. Reprint, Hoboken, N.J.: Katv Publishing, 1970, pp. 420–467.

Muller-Lancet, Aviva. "Jewish Ethnographic Costume." In *Encyclopedia of Jewish History.* Israel: Masada, 1986.

———. *La vie juive au Maroc.* Jerusalem: The Israel Museum, 1973.

Rubens, Alfred. *A History of Jewish Costume.* London: Weidenfeld and Nicolson, 1967, 1973.

Sandys, George. *Travels Containing an History of the Original and Present State of the Turkish Empire.* London: Rob. Clavell, 1673.

Schwartz-Be'eri, Ora. *The Jews of Kurdistan: Daily Life, Customs, Arts and Crafts.* Jerusalem: The Israel Museum, 2000.

Slapak, Orpa, ed. *The Jews of India: A Story of Three Communities.* Jerusalem: The Israel Museum, 1995.

Stillman, Yedida K. "The Costume of the Moroccan Jewish Woman." In *Studies in Jewish Folklore.* Edited by F. Talmage. Cambridge, Mass.: Association for Jewish Studies, 1981.

Orpa Slapak and Esther Juhasz

JILBAB A plain, ankle-length garment or set of garments, the *jilbab* is worn by Muslim women in many different countries for reasons that include modesty, religious devotion, and political activism. Several other words, including *jellabib* and *djellaba*, refer to the same or similar styles of dress. The *djellaba*, a long cloak with a hood, is worn in North Africa by both men and women. In Palestine, Jordan, and Syria, the *jilbab* is a long overcoat that buttons down the front and is worn with a headscarf called a *khimar*. In Southeast Asia and East Africa, the terms *jellabib* and *jilbab* refer to a set of simple, opaque garments that, except for the face and hands, cover the body from head to toe. This new style of Muslim dress is intended as a specific change from garments (such as a sarong or *garbasaar*, a traditional head and body covering) that are part of local culture. The *jilbab* has diffused from the Middle East in conjunction with the rise of Islamism (political Islam) following the Iranian Revolution in 1979. It is also connected with more recent efforts to counteract some of the perceived negative effects of globalization such as materialism and the corruption of secular governments.

Meanings

Along with *khimar* (a head covering) and *hijab* (a more general word for something that covers), *jilbab* is a special term because it appears directly in the Qur'ān. Verse (33:59) briefly describes how the wives of the prophet Muhammad (and by extension, Muslim women) should be dressed: "O Prophet! Tell thy wives and thy daughters and the women of the believers to draw their cloaks [*jilbab*] round them [when they go abroad]. That will be better, so that they may be recognized and not annoyed" (Pickthall p. 449). This passage highlights several reasons for renewed interest in the *jilbab*. As more Muslims than ever have come into contact with non-Muslims or taken up residence in non-Muslim countries, many have wanted to make their status visible "so that they may be recognized." The *jilbab* marks a devout woman's need to pray regularly, to abstain from pork and alcohol, and to avoid compromising situations with unrelated men. For Islamist purposes, the *jilbab* speaks to an interest in "pure" Islam as exemplified by the prophet Muhammad. This is part of a pan-Islamic effort to find common ground between different sects and cultures in the Muslim world.

Construction

Although the Qur'ān does not specify the color, texture, or shape of the *jilbab*, a few basic styles have become commonplace and in the early 2000s are viewed as "authentic" dress for Muslim women. In the United States and parts of Europe, the *jilbab* is easily recognized as "religious dress" because it resembles the style of clothing worn by nuns before Vatican II. Some corporations, in an effort to comply with antidiscrimination laws, have adapted the *jilbab* as a Muslim version of their standard uniform.

Patterns for women who want to make their own Islamic clothing are widely available in books and even on the Internet. Somali women living in the United States, Europe, and Australia frequently commission or sew their own *jilbab* using cloth from local fabric stores. This requires at least four yards of material. Two yards are used for a skirt and the rest for a two-piece, tailored head covering that fits closely around the neck and hairline. Older and more devout women often prefer to have a longer head covering that extends to the waistline or even midcalf. (This requires more fabric.) As an alternative, some women wear the button-down overcoat called *jilbab* in Jordan and Palestine. This garment has a longer history in Somali culture and is called "shuka," a word for something that conceals the body.

In Iran, women often construct these garments from heavy black, navy blue, or gray fabrics. As Faegheh Shi-

"In June 1992, when a delegation of twenty-two Islamist women . . . visited Baku, Azerbaijan, their heavily-covered figures in chadors in Baku's hot summer brought stares and disdainful reactions everywhere they went. They met with the same reaction in Tajikistan and the rest of Central Asia during visits in the early 1990s. On one occasion, a middle-aged Azeri woman asked me to translate a question. . . . "Don't you feel hot under this heavy black garment in this hot summer? . . . "But the fire in hell is much hotter if one fails to follow Allah's orders," one of the Iranians replied. Baffled by her response, the Azeri woman mumbled, "What a cruel God you have! The Allah of Islam that I know of is much kinder to women" (Tohidi, p. 20)

razi notes in *Undressing Religion*, "Black, being a sign of mourning, carries a symbolic meaning in tune with the cause of the Revolution, the Iran/Iraq war and ... those who lost their lives as martyrs [in the cause of establishing an Islamic state]" (p. 120). Women in other countries wear the *jilbab* in a variety of muted colors—white (for prayers), brown, green, and rose. Somali dress in the 1970s and 1980s was very colorful, and Somali women in the early 2000s sometimes wear the *jilbab* in brighter colors such as yellow, mint green, and magenta. They might also combine the plain *jilbab* with a few touches of more colorful printed fabrics at the hemline or on a scarf worn just underneath the tailored head covering.

The Spread of Islamism

For many women, the decision to wear the *jilbab* is based on their own personal beliefs and convictions. At the same time, these garments are part of a global dialogue concerning how Muslims should live in the contemporary world. The Iranian Revolution of 1979 was an early success of Islamism, a movement to create social, economic, and political change through Islam and to establish new systems of power based on Islamic law. In the 1980s, Iranian activists who believed in Islamic dress as a symbol of this transformation traveled to parts of Central Asia, North Africa, the Persian Gulf, and Turkey to promote their ideas. The *jilbab* worn in Syria, Jordan, and Palestine is called "rupush-rusari" in Iran. There were limits to their success, however. In her essay in *Iran and the Surrounding World*, Nayereh Tohidi notes there were differences in language (Persian vs. Arabic), religious practices (Shi'a vs. Sunnī), and a general dislike for restrictive styles of dress based on the chador.

Since that time, ideas about these styles of dress have spread more indirectly through religious books and pamphlets, videos, television programs, and the Internet. In the United States and Europe, Muslims from many different countries have been brought together to worship in neighborhood mosques.

See also **Djellaba; Islamic Dress, Contemporary.**

BIBLIOGRAPHY

Arthur, Linda, ed. *Undressing Religion: Commitment and Conversion from a Cross-Cultural Perspective.* Oxford: Berg, 2000.

Berns McGown, Rima. *Muslims in the Diaspora: The Somali Communities of London and Toronto.* Toronto: University of Toronto Press, 1999.

El Guindi, Fadwa. *Veil: Modesty, Privacy and Resistance.* Oxford: Berg, 1999.

Keddie, Nikki R., and Rudi Matthi, eds. *Iran and the Surrounding World: Interactions in Culture and Cultural Politics.* Seattle: University of Washington Press, 2002.

Pickthall, Muhammad Marmaduke. *The Meaning of the Glorious Koran: Text and Explanatory Translation.* Mecca: Muslim World League, 1977.

Tohidi, Nayereh. "The International Connections of the Women's Movement in Iran." In *Islam and the Surrounding World.* Edited by Nikki R. Keddie and Rudi Matthi. Seattle: University of Washington Press, 2002.

Heather Marie Akou

JILLABA. *See* **Djellaba.**

JOCKEY SHORTS The display of Jockey shorts in the window of Marshall Field's department store in Chicago on 19 January 1935 revolutionized the men's underwear market. Over the following three months, thirty thousand were sold, and Jockey began "Changing the Underwear Habits of the Nation."

The Jockey short's Y-front with overlapping fly was patented by Coopers Inc. in 1934. Unlike other underwear of the time, it provided men with "masculine support," then only available by wearing an athletic supporter or jockstrap. In order to reinforce the idea that this new underwear would provide support, it was discreetly called the Jockey (JOCK-ey). Advertising played a key role in the awareness and massive sales of jockey shorts, and an underwear-clad Jockey statue was used both in window displays and stores. The success of the Jockey short and its massive brand recognition led the company to change its name from Coopers Inc. to Jockey.

Until the advent of Jockey Y-fronts in 1934, men's underwear consisted of loose shirts, singlets, long johns, and drawers that revealed little of the body's form. Y-fronts were revolutionary in that, owing to the way the fly was angled for modesty when urinating in public, the seams drew attention to the male genitals.

Jockey shorts, however, were not the first revolutionary underwear idea that the company had introduced. In 1910, S. T. Coopers and Sons, as the company was then known, developed one of the first closed-crotch union suits. The "Kenosha Klosed Krotch" had a seat design of two pieces of fabric that overlapped in an X to allow access for hygenic purposes and it required no buttons or ties. This new underwear made history in 1911 after the oil paintings of men in their Kenosha Klosed Krotches by *Saturday Evening Post* artist J. C. Leyendecker became the first national print advertisements for men's underwear.

Brief-style underwear quickly caught on, and many other underwear manufacturers began to produce their version of the jockey short. Traditionally these shorts had been made of white cotton, but variety was introduced in the 1950s when manufacturers began to experiment with new man-made fibers such as rayon, Dacron, and Du Pont nylon.

However, it was not until after the menswear revolution of the 1960s, spearheaded by the boutiques in London's Carnaby Street, that colored and patterned briefs and Y-fronts became popular. The increasing popularity of tight trousers in men's fashion led to an increased demand for brief underwear that did not wrinkle under trousers. Skimpier brightly colored briefs began to be produced by the major underwear companies and were overtly promoted for their erotic connotations. Magazine advertisements of the 1970s marketed underwear as a means of sexualizing the body to attract members of the opposite sex.

In 1982, Calvin Klein used an enormous billboard in New York City's Times Square to advertise his men's white briefs. It was an overtly sexual image of a perfectly formed muscular man wearing nothing but white underwear. "Klein's billboard has been credited with heralding a new era in the imagery of men in advertising and with precipitating a new fashion in men's underwear" (Cole, p. 136).

By 2004, major designers had established underwear lines, ranging from thongs to briefs to boxer shorts. Traditional companies like Jockey reacted to the competition by producing new styles and "rebranding," marketing themselves using the now almost-clichéd images of muscular, hairless models in immaculate and revealing white jockey shorts.

See also **Boxer Shorts; Underwear.**

BIBLIOGRAPHY

Carter, Alison. *Underwear: The Fashion History.* London: Batsford, 1992.

Cole, Shaun. *Don We Now Our Gay Apparel: Gay Men's Dress in the Twentieth Century.* Oxford: Berg. 2000.

Craik, Jennifer. *The Face of Fashion: Cultural Studies in Fashion.* London: Routledge 1994.

Griffin, Gary M. *The History of Men's Underwear: From Union Suits to Bikini Briefs*. Los Angeles: Added Dimensions Publishing, 1991.

Shaun Cole

JUMPER. *See* Sweater.

JUMPER DRESS
As an item of dress, the word "jumper" has referred to various garments at different points in history and in diverse sectors of society. For example, in the United States, a jumper has been a loose jacket, a sailor's overshirt, or middy blouse, a child's garment or coverall with straight-legged pants, a hooded fur jacket, or a sleeveless one-piece dress usually worn over some type of upper garment. A British jumper is a pullover sweater, and the British refer to a U.S. jumper as a pinafore dress, a pinafore, or a "pinny."

In mid- to late twentieth-century American English, a jumper is a woman's or girl's one-piece, sleeveless, dress-length garment with a low round, V, or square neckline designed to wear over a blouse, sweater, or shirt. Specific styles are described by adjectives such as "bib jumper," styled with a biblike front inspired by bib overalls, or "horseshoe jumper" referring to the low horseshoe neckline in front and back.

The origin of the word is unclear especially since "jumper" refers to many different garments. It may have come from mid-nineteenth-century English dialect "jump," meaning short coat; from Old French *juppe*, or Modern French *jupe*, meaning skirt; from Spanish *aljuba*, a Moorish garment; from Arabic *jubba*, a long garment with wide open sleeves, or *jabba*, to cut.

The evolution of the garment is also unclear. Historically, the jumper may have evolved from the four-teenth-century woman's sideless *surcote* that was worn over a gown with tight-fitting long sleeves. The sideless *surcote* had a low neckline, giving the illusion of shoulder straps and deep oval armholes extending to the hips, so the tunic worn beneath could be seen. By the early fifteenth century, when other styles replaced it, the sideless gown identified the wearer as a French queen or princess.

References to jumpers in the early twentieth century often meant a two-piece dress with a long middy-style top designed for sports, a dramatic change in sportswear for women. Jean Patou, Paul Poiret, and Coco Chanel were leaders in replacing cumbersome garments with practical and convenient clothing for sports. Patou dressed Suzanne Lenglen, the 1920s champion tennis player, in his hallmark short skirts and sleeveless long-waisted jumper blouses. Her athletic youthfulness captured the imagination of the fashion conscious (Lee-Potter), although it is unknown if this look was a predecessor to the American jumper.

While the jumper has not been at the forefront of fashion, its form has followed fashionable silhouettes such as the body skimming chemise or an exaggerated A-line resembling a tent or trapeze shapes in the 1960s. Jumpers seemed to evolve from function; and sportswear, separates, and layering are all concepts that apply to jumpers. Some jumper styles are reminiscent of children's garments or school uniforms. The ideal body for women in the 1920s was straight, undeveloped, even childlike. The *garçonne*, or waif, look also was popular in the 1960s and again in the 1980s with many images of young women wearing short, mini-length jumpers. Functional, apron-like wraparound jumpers designed to protect clothing may have inspired Claire McCardell's 1940s denim wrap-around coverall "popover dress." McCardell was famous for her sportswear designs, including jumpers to wear over jersey leotards. Bonnie Cashin is another designer also known for designing jumpers as versatile and so-phisticated sportswear.

See also **Cashin, Bonnie; McCardell, Claire; Sportswear.**

BIBLIOGRAPHY

American Heritage Dictionary of the English Language. 4th ed. Boston: Houghton Mifflin, 2000.

Blair, Joanne. *Fashion Terminology*. Englewood Cliffs, N.J.: Prentice-Hall, Inc., 1992.

Boucher, François. *20,000 Years of Fashion*. New York: Harry N. Abrams, 1987.

Calasibetta, Charlotte, and Phyllis Tortora. *The Fairchild Dictionary of Fashion*. 3rd ed. New York: Fairchild Publications, Inc., 2003.

Craig, Hazel T. *Clothing: A Comprehensive Study*. Philadelphia: J. B. Lippincott Company, 1968.

Etherington-Smith, Meredith. *Patou*. London: Hutchinson, 1983.

Lee-Potter, Charlie. *Sportswear in Vogue since 1910*. New York: Abbeville Press, 1984.

Kirkland, Sally. "McCardell." In *American Fashion*. Edited by Sarah Tomerlin Lee. New York: Quadrangle/The New York Times Book Company, 1975.

Tortora, Phyllis, and Keith Eubank. *Survey of Historic Costume*. 3rd ed. New York: Fairchild Publications, 2000.

Yohannan, Kohle, and Nancy Nolf. *Claire McCardell: Redefining Modernism*. New York: Harry N. Abrams, 1998.

Barbara Perso Heinemann

KAFFIYEH *Kaffiyeh* is used to refer to a large square head cloth, or a long rectangular head cloth, or neck scarf worn by men in the Arab world. The same term is used to refer to checkered red and white or black and white head cloths and to plain white ones. In Arabian societies all three colors are used: plain white, checkered red, and checkered black. On top of the kaffiyeh men place a band or circlet of twisted black cord made of silk or cotton thread known as agal (spoken Arabic for 'uqal).

Headgear for men in the Arab and Islamic East is variable in form, use, and terminology. Arab men of all persuasions and faiths distinctively covered their heads long before Islam. It is safe to distinguish three broad kinds of head cover for men: traditional secular, religious (Islamic or Christian), and revolutionary or resistance. These kinds not only refer to differences in form and appearance but also in function and meaning.

Historically in the region, there was as much head cover politics concerning men as concerning women. Turkey, after the fall of the Ottoman regime and the creation of a republican government, issued sartorial measures prohibiting traditional male headgear and encouraging Western hats. After the various revolutions in the Arab world in the 1950s and 1960s, particularly the 1952 Egyptian revolution led by Gamel Abdel-Nasser, the fez (*tarboush*) worn by men of the urban middle and upper classes, which had entered sartorial traditions with the reign of the Ottomans and remained, fell from favor. The fez became a symbol of classist, colonial interventionist messages which the antiroyal coups and revolutions were keen on removing. Many men who removed the fez went bareheaded permanently after that.

In the 1970s, when the Islamic movement began, urban middle-class men and college students who had until then been wearing jeans and slacks to college and work, began to wear a gallabiyya (*jellabib*) and a white kaffiyeh (pronounced *kufiyyah* in Egyptian Arabic). This new appearance marked a revitalization of Islamic identity and a desired return to forms of appearance that were innovatively envisioned, particularly by male and female college youth in urban Egypt, as reproducing historically Islamic clothing. The movement continues to this day and has spread throughout the Arab world.

The checkered kaffiyeh became internationally visible after the 1970s as a symbol of Palestine. Many people, especially students, around the world, including in Europe and the United States, showed their support for the Palestinian cause by wearing checkered kaffiyehs as neck scarves, which evoke images of Palestinian youth. The president of the Palestinian authority, Palestinian Liberation Organization (PLO), Yasir Arafat, always wears military fatigues with a checkered kaffiyeh as head cover, with a triangular fold at the center above mid-forehead. This fold is characteristic of the Palestinian style of wearing the kaffiyeh and can be seen also in Syria, Arabia, and the Gulf.

The style of solid long rectangular white kaffiyeh worn flat on the head and hanging down on both sides of the head, tends to be worn by pious Muslims or those in religious leadership positions. Seen throughout the Arab world, this style of wearing the kaffiyeh is understood as a symbol of commitment to religious values. The king of Jordan and his Hashemite royal men typically wear a kaffiyeh and *agal*. This communicates the king's identity as belonging to a long line of Hashemite bedouins indigenous to the region.

Like the "veil" or women's head cover, the kaffiyeh is not a fixed or static object of clothing. It can be manipulated to cover head or face. Thus a religious man may use the white kaffiyeh worn on his head to cover part of his face, including mouth and nose, in certain situations that need a symbolic separation in space, such as gender separation. Similarly, Muslim women in India, for example, manipulate their head covers to partially cover their faces in situations in which men who are their in-laws are nearby. In the case of Muslim Indian women, manipulating the head cover to partially veil the face communicates affinal kinship distance, whereas a Muslim man manipulating a head cover to partially veil his face communicates gender separation in public space.

Superficially resembling the kaffiyeh, the ‘*imama* (turban) is another kind of male headgear worn differently and is made of a much longer piece of cloth (118 inches, or 3 meters, or longer) wrapped around on top of one's head a number of times. It is predominantly white today, but a black ‘*imama* was worn by male members of the newly formed Islamic community in the seventh century in Arabia. This marker of male Arab identity that goes back before Islam, continues into the early 2000s.

Jordanian man in *kaffiyeh*. The *kaffiyeh* experienced a rebirth in the 1970s as a affirmation of Islamic identity and a symbol of piety. © PETER TURNLEY/CORBIS. REPRODUCED BY PERMISSION.

Early in the history of the Islamic community, the form of headgear distinguished Muslims from non-Muslims. While predominantly men's headgear, the *'imama* was worn by some women in Egypt to the consternation of religious authorities in the thirteenth century. While conservative religious authorities disapprove of sartorial gender crossing, ethnographic evidence shows that the borderline between genders in Arab clothing styles was fluid, and more importantly, the sharing of meaning and function of head covers of both sexes was often conceptually embedded in the culture.

The exact origins of the kaffiyeh are not clear. What is clear is that pious Muslims wear it as a secular head cover for marking Arab identity, as a symbol of nationalistic or revolutionary struggle, and as religious headgear.

See also **Djellaba; Hijab; Jilbab; Turban; Veils.**

BIBLIOGRAPHY

El Guindi, Fadwa. *Veil: Modesty, Privacy and Resistance.* Oxford: Berg, 1999.

Young, William C. *The Rashaayda Bedouin: Arab Pastoralists of Eastern Sudan.* Case Studies in Cultural Anthropology. Fort Worth, Tex.: Harcourt Brace College Publishers, 1996.

Fadwa El Guindi

KAIN-KEBAYA The *kain-kebaya* is a jacket-blouse and wrapper ensemble that forms the basis of national dress for Indonesian women. The long-sleeved *kebaya* comes in two lengths, at the hip (*kebaya pendek*) and near the knees (*kebaya panjang*). The five-centimeter-wide collar-lapel runs from neck to bottom hem. The *kebaya* is closed in two ways—one (*Kartini kebaya*) in which the collar-lapels meet from breast to hip and are closed with broaches or concealed pins, and the second (*kebaya kutu baru*), in which the *kebaya* is open like a jacket, with a rectangular panel bridging the collar-lapels on either side to cover the breasts. The panel is closed at center with four small buttons, or at the side with snaps by the collar-lapel. The *Kartini kebaya* style of closure is found on short and long *kebayas*, while the *kebaya kutu baru* closure style is found on short *kebayas* only. The *kebaya* is made of light-weight material in lace, cutwork, or embroidery, in printed or solid silks, cotton, and synthetics. As Javanese wedding apparel, the *kebaya panjang* comes in velvet with gold embroidery.

Kain literally means "cloth"; a traditional Indonesian *kain* is approximately 87 inches (220 cm) long by about 40 inches (100 cm) high and, when wrapped at the hips, extends to ankle length. A *kain* can be batik, silk, or other cotton. A *kain panjang* (long cloth) refers to a batik, a cloth, traditionally cambric cotton, whose surface design has been created by means of wax and dye steps. The *kain panjang* ends could be pleated or arranged in a special drape for formal wear. The *kain* can also be a batik sarong, a rectangle, shorter in length than the *kain panjang*, around 100 inches (180 cm) to 87 inches (220 cm), whose end seams are sewn together to make a tube. A woman wearing a *kebaya* and a batik sarong would still be described as wearing a kain-kebaya.

The kain-kebaya is worn for both everyday wear and formal wear, distinguished by quality of material and addition of accessories. Central to the kain-kebaya is the "belt"—a corded cotton band, *stagen*, that is 40 feet (12 m) long by 5 inches (12.5 cm) wide, that is wrapped around hips to just under the breasts. For formal wear, a solid-colored stole, or *selendang* (88.5 inches [2.25 m] by 20 inches [.5 m] wide) is draped over the right shoulder, folded to a band of about 4 inches (10 cm) wide. In everyday use, the *selendang*, generally in batik, would be worn as a baby carrier in front, or to carry a basket of goods at the back. Hair would be pulled back into a large chignon (*konde*) at the nape of the head; low-heeled sandals, earrings, a necklace, and rings would complete the formal dress.

Origin of the *Kebaya*

The *kebaya* has its origins in a garment brought over by Moslem traders from India. Prior to Moslem influence, women wore flat textiles wrapped about their body; Moslem influence required that women cover their arms and torsos. They brought over cut and sewn garments. The *baju panjang*, a long-sleeved, knee-length gusseted garment still worn in the early 2000s in the south coast of Sumatra, was the forerunner of the *kebaya* up until the late nineteenth century. The Moslem presence remained in the coastal regions of Java and nearby islands from the fifteenth century, but a central Javanese sultan was aggressive in his spread of Islam by the seventeenth. While no certain evidence exists, it's possible that the *baju panjang* was being worn even then.

As early as 1840, Eurasian women in the north coast of Java began designing and manufacturing batiks for sale to Europeans, Chinese, and other Eurasians. Their batiks made for sarongs were characterized by bold colors, an overall repeat punctuated by a wide panel of triangle border or floral bouquet. Eventually, as evidenced in late nineteenth-century photographs, the predecessor *baju panjang* shortened to the *kebaya pedek* (the short *kebaya* is the default *kebaya*) to better show off the vibrant north coast style of batiks.

The *kebaya kutu baru* (short *kebaya* with panel over the breast) seems to have developed in the late nineteenth century as well, though this subject deserves more research. Djumena states that the panel insert was an innovation developed in Yogya and Surakarta courts, but does not give a date. A photograph dated 1905 of a Javanese regent's family shows one woman in a *kebaya kutu baru* and four others in other styles of *kebaya*.

Taylor calls the kain-kebaya "a costume for all women" in the nineteenth century, because women in villages, royal courts, and European spouses of colonialists (though only at home, as morning attire) all wore them. The quality of the kain-kebaya linked women to the social status of their spouse.

National Dress

Indonesia's first president declared the Javanese kain-kebaya as Indonesia's national dress for women. In the 1950s and 1960s, it consisted of a *kebaya kutu baru* (with the panel) in sheer floral or lace, with a brassiere visible underneath, the *stagen* exposed, and a central Javanese style batik with or without pleating, the hair in a large *konde* with a jeweled hairstick, low-heeled sandals, narrow, solid-colored *selendang*, pendant on a chain, and stud earrings. This style of dress would be worn for formal occasions.

In the 1980s and 1990s, the kain-kebaya as national dress included stylistic variations as Indonesian fashion designers incorporated textile traditions throughout Indonesia and fashion trends from the Western hemisphere. Iwan Tirta introduced several variations. His *selendang* and *kain pajangs* were matching *batiks*, and were draped on the arm like the 1980s' world fashion of wearing big scarves on the shoulder. His *kebayas* were

always a solid color, and when puffed sleeves were stylish in the mid-1980s, his *kebaya* had them. He popularized the *kebaya panjang* and *Kartini kebaya* that closed in front with ornate broaches. It became acceptable to wear other textile traditions besides batik as national dress. As late as the early 2000s, Indonesian fashion designers popularized the *kebaya*, creating a variety of styles and making it part of leisure world-dress ensemble, as worn with jeans, or skirts, or shorts for middle-class Indonesian women.

See also **Asia, Southeastern Islands and the Pacific: History of Dress; Islamic Dress, Contemporary.**

BIBLIOGRAPHY

Achjadi, Judi. *Pakaian Daerah Wanita Indonesia (Indonesian Women's Costumes)*. Jakarta: Djambatan, 1976.

Djumena, Nian S. *Batik dan Mitra (Batik and Its Kind)*. Jakarta: Djambatan, 1990.

Gittinger, Mattiebelle. *Spendid Symbols: Textiles and Tradition in Indonesia*. Washington, D.C.: The Textile Museum, 1979.

Taylor, Jean G. "Costume and Gender in Colonial Java." In *Outward Appearances: Dressing State and Society in Indonesia*. Edited by Henk Schulte Nordholt. Leiden, The Netherlands: KITLV Press, 1997.

Heidi Boehlke

KAMALI, NORMA Considered one of America's most original fashion designers, Norma Kamali created innovative and influential garments during the 1970s and 1980s. In the early twenty-first century she continued to market forward-looking fashions. Born Norma Arraez in New York City in 1945, her fashion career might be said to have begun with her outrageous personal style of dressing during her teenage years. It was later refined through formal studies in illustration at the Fashion Institute of Technology (FIT) in New York. After graduating from FIT in 1964, Kamali took several jobs making sketches for Seventh Avenue buyers, only to leave in frustration

STUDENT TEACHING

The Manhattan Chamber of Commerce gave Norma Kamali the *2001 Business Outreach Award* for her outstanding work with public school students, particularly those at her alma mater, Washington Irving High School. There, in Room 741 (her former homeroom class), she has created a state-of-the-art design laboratory where she instructs students in fashion design every other week.

Kamali-designed wedding gown of parachute nylon, 1998.
Norma Kamali's fashions have extended beyond clothing design to include skin care, cosmetics, and perfume. These new avenues, however, have not detracted from the popularity of her designs. AP/WIDE WORLD PHOTOS. REPRODUCED BY PERMISSION.

at the restrictive, stifling environment. Deciding that she wanted the freedom to travel, Kamali took an office position at Northwest Orient Airlines. The airline job allowed her access to cheap travel, a benefit she exploited with frequent weekend trips to London and Paris. There she enthusiastically explored the swinging fashion scene burgeoning in the 1960s.

Her friends and associates coveted the clothes that Kamali brought back from her travels in Europe, and provided the impetus for her to open a boutique in partnership with her husband, Eddie. The shop opened in 1968 on Fifty-third Street and was stocked with garments Kamali purchased abroad. Teaching herself to sew, cut, and make patterns in a very hands-on approach to her design business, she soon began supplementing the inventory with clothes of her own creation.

From the beginning her designs were fresh, original, and entertaining. Inspired by pop culture and street fashion combined with a sense of practicality, Kamali created bold pieces, such as hot pants and leotards. When the store moved to Madison Avenue in 1974, Kamali turned to designing more refined clothing, including tailored suits. Her divorce in 1977 and subsequent

opening of OMO (On My Own) on the Upper West Side marked her true emergence as a designer. Through OMO, Kamali revealed her interest in and identification with a newly independent and creative female customer base.

Kamali is credited with introducing some of the most recognized looks of the 1970s and 1980s. She became a household name after the success of her influential 1980 collection of day and evening wear made from sweatshirt fleece. Inspired by the sleeping bag she supposedly used after her divorce, her quilted down coat design has become a fashion standard. Especially notable is Kamali's drawstring parachute jumpsuit from the mid-1970s, which was included in the Metropolitan Museum of Art's exhibition *Vanity Fair: A Treasure Trove of the Costume Institute* in 1977. In the 1980s, Kamali stressed exaggerated shoulders in her garments and is widely acknowledged as a contributor to the revival of the big shoulder look of that decade.

Kamali has also been a pioneer in swimsuit design. Her earliest pieces were daringly revealing bikinis and gold lamé maillots (one-piece swimsuits for women). She is also credited (along with Calvin Klein) with introducing high-cut bathing suits in 1976, a look that dominated swimsuit styles in the 1980s. In 1985 Kamali introduced a shirred, 1940s-inspired maillot, revealing her deep interest in retro fashions. Kamali's fresh, updated vintage styles, such as the "Ethel Mertz" wrap dress of the mid-1980s, anticipated the postmodern reprocessing of retro styles that occurred in the next decade. Even in the early 1990s Kamali was ahead of the retro curve, including flared trousers, reminiscent of those styles popular in the 1930s and 1970s, in her collection.

Kamali's creativity has been recognized through a number of awards from such fashion institutions as the Coty American Fashion Critics, Council of Fashion Designers of America, the Fashion Group, and the Fashion Walk of Fame, to name just a few. She remains in 2004 one of America's most inventive and witty designers.

See also **Retro Styles; Swimwear.**

BIBLIOGRAPHY

Baker, Therese Duzinkiewicz. "Norma Kamali." In *The St. James Fashion Encyclopedia*. Edited by Richard Martin. Detroit, Mich.: Visible Ink Press, 1997.

Diamonstein, Barbaralee. *Fashion: The Inside Story*. New York: Rizzoli, 1985.

Lencek, Lena, and Gideon Bosker. *Making Waves: Swimsuits and the Undressing of America*. San Francisco: Chronicle Books, 1989.

Milbank, Caroline Rennolds. *Couture: The Great Designers*. New York: Stewart, Tabori and Chang, 1985.

Talley, Andre Leon. "True Wit: The Zany World of Norma Kamali." *Vogue* (November 1984): 430–435.

Lauren Whitley

KANGA

KANGA Proverb cloths, called *leso*, *kanga* (*khanga*), or *lamba hoany*, are used and worn throughout coastal East Africa and Madagascar. Often worn in pairs, these lightweight cloths make a lasting impression not only for their brightly colored designs, but also for the messages that are emblazoned upon them.

History

As early as the 1850s or 1860s, women in the coastal regions of Kenya and Tanzania (perhaps around Lamu or Pate, but most likely in Mombasa or Zanzibar) began buying uncut lineal sheets of six handkerchief squares, called *leso* in Portuguese, cutting the lengths in half and sewing them together lengthwise to create larger rectangular cloths with two rows of three pattern squares each. By 1875, enterprising merchants in Zanzibar began to import modified leso from England, Switzerland, India, and the Netherlands. Leso eventually also took the name of khanga, possibly because a popular early print included small spots similar to the coloration of the guinea fowl, called *khanga* in Kiswahili. Around the turn of the century, leso/khanga became especially popular in Zanzibar, appearing at the moment that many former slaves were intent on visually separating themselves from their past and redefining themselves as newly independent, and fashionable, individuals.

In the 1920s a merchant named Kaderdina Hajee Essak (nicknamed Abdullah) in Mombasa, Kenya, began adding Arabic script to the lower center section of these brightly colored rectangular cloths. Kiswahili or English phrases in Roman script appeared in the 1960s. Inscriptions incorporate proverbs, popular sayings, greetings, warnings, and political or religious slogans. Use of proverb cloths has since spread along the coast and to the island of Madagascar, with the accompanying text in the appropriate languages. In the middle of the century, textile factories in Africa and Madagascar also began to create proverb cloths for their own markets, although factories in India became dominant cloth-producers for all the regions. Misspellings frequently occur on proverb cloths, probably because many are made abroad for a foreign market in a foreign language. In Madagascar, it is said that lamba hoany must have misspellings to be considered true lamba hoany, suggesting that this is part of their mystique.

The Cloths

Proverb cloths are traditionally cotton, but are also made of rayon, polyester, or a variety of blends. Generally three feet high by five feet wide, they have a patterned border (approximately five to nine inches deep) surrounding a patterned interior that usually includes a central design, often within a large circular orb, with four smaller versions of the central design in the four corners. Designs, in either bright and showy colors or quieter earthen tones, typically employ two to five colors upon a white base, and may incorporate virtually any-

In Tanzania, borders are called *pindo,* while the ground (or town) is *miji,* and the four corner motifs (guards of the town) are called *vilindo* (*African Textiles,* June/July and August/September, 1984).

thing, from genre scenes to a variety of objects from nature or images of technology, or food. Specific designs may or may not correspond to the accompanying text, which is located within a box just below the central motif if there is one and just above the patterned border of the long bottom edge.

Lightweight and versatile, proverb cloths are worn primarily by women, although men may also wear them, especially in Madagascar. Often worn in pairs, one may be wrapped around the upper torso and the other worn as a skirt. They can be worn singly as dresses: a girl wrapping the cloth around her body with the two ends overlapping in front and their upper corners tied behind her neck, a woman wrapping it around her body with the upper edge above her breasts and then either rolled under or over itself or the two upper corners tied in a knot. They can serve as an outer cape to protect one from cold or heat, with the top edge raised over the head to form a hood if necessary. Women often wrap proverb cloths around their waists as a protective layer over their other clothes while working. Proverb cloths can cradle a baby against one's back, with the ends either over both shoulders, under one's arms, or one over and one under an arm, the ends twisted, tied, or held in front. If twisted lengthwise and curled into a flat spiral or doughnut shape, proverb cloths make cushions when carrying a heavy or unwieldy load on one's head. They are often used to wrap objects or parcels, or to cover the contents in a basket. They are also increasingly used as wall hangings, bedspreads, curtains, or seat covers. Finally, in some regions, kangas are essential accessories when attending funerals or weddings.

Communicative Tools

A person may communicate through a proverb cloth depending on how, where, or when it is worn, displayed, or given. A person can wear a cloth so that the intended recipient of the message may see it, by walking past their house or business, by visiting a neighbor, or by wearing it at home. Messages may warn a gossiping neighbor, a rival co-wife, or an erring husband, or may indicate one's friendship or love. For example, a woman may show her affection by wearing the cloth that her husband has just removed, or she may place her cloth on her husband's pillow to indicate that she would like his attentions. Proverb cloths can also be given as gifts, by one's mother,

EXAMPLES OF PROVERBS

Utabaki na chokochoko utaambulia ukoko. "By continuing to create discord, all you'll end up with is just leftovers." Tanzania (Hassan).

Kunisalimia tu haitoshi. "It is not enough just to greet me." Kenya (Troughear).

Fanahy tsara no maha olona. "A good character makes the person." Madagascar (Green, personal translation).

spouse, parent, grandparent, lover, rival, or friend. Lovers may also send perfumed cloths to emphasize their romantic intentions.

Meanings behind messages, the identity of a message's recipient, as well as the intent of the sender can be ambiguous. However, a person can wear a proverb cloth without intending to send a message, or can wear it with a very specific person(s) in mind. Moreover, the symbolic proverbial sayings may have multiple interpretations or meanings. The responsibility of recognizing a communicative exchange, therefore, rests with the viewer, who must decide whether a message is intentional, and if so, if it applies to him or her. A woman can therefore send a rival or friend a message without risking the social stigma of inciting argument or confrontation, since she can always deny that a message was intended. The woman wearing or giving a cloth, who has the exclusive knowledge of its intent, is therefore in a position of power, and the recipient, who has the disadvantage of not knowing whether a message is intended, is disempowered (see Beck for an extended discussion). Proverb cloths, therefore, are a beautiful yet complex mode of communication and power.

See also **Africa, North: History of Dress; Africa, Sub-Saharan: History of Dress.**

BIBLIOGRAPHY
Abdullah, Fatma Shaaban. *Kanga Textiles From Tanzania: 1 June–1 July 1984.* London: Commonwealth Institute, 1984.

Anonymous. "Kanga Textiles from Tanzania." *African Textiles* (June/July 1984): 5.

Anonymous. "Kanga Textiles from Tanzania." *African Textiles* (August/September 1984): 24–25, 27.

Beck, Rose Marie. "Aesthetics of Communication: Texts on Textiles (Leso) from the East African Coast (Swahili)." *Research in African Literatures* 31, no. 4 (2000): 104–124.

Fair, Laura. "Dressing Up: Clothing, Class and Gender in Post-Abolition Zanzibar." *Journal of African History* 39 (1998): 63–94.

Green, Rebecca L. "Lamba Hoany: Proverb Cloths From Madagascar." *African Arts* (Summer 2003).

Hamid, Mahfoudha Alley. "Kanga: It Is More Than What Meets the Eye—A Medium of Communication." *African Journal of Political Science,* New Series 1, no. 1 (1996): 103–109.

Ndwiga, Robert. "Be It Love or Sorrow, Say It With Khangas." *The East African (Nairobi)* 8, part 2 (2000).

Troughear, Tony. "Khangas, Bangles and Baskets." *Kenya Past and Present* 16 (1984): 11–19.

Internet Resources
Ali, Hassan. "Kanga Writings." 1995. Available from <http://www.glcom.com/hassan/kanga.html>.

Hanbys, Jeannette and David Bygott. 1984. "The History of Kanga." Available from <http://www.glcom.com/hassan/kanga_history.html>.

Rebecca L. Green

KARAN, DONNA Donna Karan (1948–) was born Donna Ivy Faske in 1948 in New York City. Her father, Gabby Faske, was a custom tailor who died in a car accident when Donna was three years old. Her mother, Helen Faske, had been a showroom model turned fashion sales representative. Helen's second husband was Harold Flaxman, who was also involved in the garment business. The family moved to Long Island after the marriage. By the time Karan finished high school, she had already staged her first fashion show. She attended the Parsons School of Design for two years, leaving at the age of nineteen to work for the ready-to-wear designer Anne Klein. Klein fired Karan in short order, but rehired her two years later. When Anne Klein died of cancer in 1974, Karan was put in charge of Klein's Seventh Avenue sportswear company at the age of twenty-six, just days after having given birth to a baby girl.

During Karan's decade-long tenure as head designer, she built Anne Klein into the most profitable sportswear company in the United States. She launched Anne Klein II, a so-called bridge line of clothes priced slightly lower than the signature collection and meant for the working woman. So successful was the concept that the company's financial backers, Tomio Taki and Frank Mori, invested $10 million in working capital for Karan to start her own collection. She turned over the reins at Anne Klein to her assistant, Louis Dell'Olio, in 1984.

Long since divorced from Mark Karan, the father of her ten-year-old daughter, and remarried in 1983 to her business partner Stephan Weiss, Donna Karan set out to "design everything I needed, so I wouldn't have to think about it anymore" (Agins, p. 145). To this end, she devised a sophisticated twist on the mix-and-match concept and called her line Donna Karan Essentials. It consisted of a bodysuit, tights, dress, skirt, jacket, pants, and accessories—"seven easy pieces" meant to be replaceable with minimal updating. It was a modern way of dressing designed to go from day to evening, pack easily in a travel bag, and be ready to wear at a moment's notice.

"I don't like fashion," Karan once said. "To me, it's the woman, the body." She described herself not as a fashion designer but as a "doctor for women's problems." She added, "In all the chaos I live in, I always want to create calm." In the 1980s, a time when many professional women in the United States were dressing in pinstriped power suits and collared silk blouses with bows at the neck, Karan provided an attractive alternative. Her system of dressing was based on a cashmere bodysuit, on top of which could be layered silk body blouses, sweater-like jackets, unconstructed blazers, and easy-fitting skirts or trousers. "I have seen women transform themselves when they put on her clothes," said Kal Ruttenstein, fashion director of Bloomingdale's department store. "They make you look sexy and strong, a rare combination."

In addition to answering her own needs and those of many other women, Karan drew inspiration from the pace and attitude of New York City, naming her collection Donna Karan New York. Soon the label included fragrance and beauty products, a men's collection, a children's line, and a home furnishings collection. In 1989 she launched DKNY, a casual line of less expensive, more youthful fashions. Designed by Jane Chung but overseen by Karan, DKNY also quickly expanded to include a wide range of licensees.

The company was publicly traded on the New York Stock Exchange for the first time in 1996. In April 2001 Donna Karan New York was acquired for $643 million by the French luxury goods conglomerate Moët Hennessy Louis Vuitton (LVMH). What was then known as Donna Karan International had over eighty freestanding Donna Karan and DKNY retail locations worldwide, including the original two stores in London and three in New York City. Karan has been a six-time winner of awards from the Council of Fashion Designers of America.

See also **Seventh Avenue; Sportswear.**

BIBLIOGRAPHY

Agins, Teri. "Woman on the Verge." *Working Woman*, May 1993, p. 145.

Horyn, Cathy. "Review/Fashion; Up Close and Personal: Karan, Kors, Rucci." *New York Times*, 25 September 2001.

Karan, Donna. *DKNY: Soul of the City.* New York: Universe, 1999.

Singer, Sally. "Love Story." *Vogue*, September 2001.

Sischy, Ingrid. *Donna Karan: New York.* New York: Universe Books, 1998.

Liz Gessner

KENTE Kente cloth is probably the most universally recognized of all African fabrics. The word "kente" means basket, and the cloth is so-named because of its resem-

blance to a woven basket design. The Asante peoples of Ghana and the Ewe of Ghana and Togo weave it on horizontal, narrow-strip, men's treadle looms. Individual strips of kente typically feature alternating segments of warp-faced (yarn extended lengthwise in a loom) stripe patterns with weft-faced (yarn running crosswise) geometric patterns. The woven strips range from three to five inches in width and are sewn together edge-to-edge to produce men's cloths of approximately twelve feet by six feet (twenty-four strips) and women's cloths of six feet by three to four feet (nine to twelve strips). Men's cloths are worn toga style, draped around the body with the left shoulder and arm covered and the right shoulder and arm exposed. Women wear two cloths of different sizes as upper and lower wrappers and often have a third piece as a baby carrier. Queenmothers and more recently other women of stature may wear a single cloth like a man. Regardless, kente is primarily festive dress worn at a variety of annual festivals. It is also used in other traditional contexts as a drum wrapper, a palanquin liner, umbrella fabric, fan and shield covering, amulet casing, and even loincloths. More recently it has been used as a wall hanging in Ghana's Parliament House and in the United Nations. Traditional usage aside, some African and African American scholars still vehemently contend that the use of kente should be restricted to clothing for special occasions.

Weaving in what is now southern Ghana was certainly introduced from the north where strip-woven fabrics are known from at least the eleventh century in the Bandiagara escarpment region of modern Mali. There is considerable debate between the Asante and Ewe over the historical preeminence of their respective traditions. Since both are derived from more northerly practices, the argument is largely irrelevant, but for ethnic pride. Asante kente is held in high regard, and has had by far the more pervasive international significance. As the Asante kingdom rose to power in the late 1600s, the weaving of kente became the exclusive prerogative of the Asante king and his designates. Royal control of this elite fabric persisted for two hundred years, but toward the end of the nineteenth century, kente became increasingly accessible to those who could afford it. Beginning with the conquest of the Asante in 1874 by the British, the history of kente is one of increasing democratization.

Part of the appeal of Asante kente is not just visual. The Asante value the names of various cloths as much as they do their appearance. Cloths are named after their warp stripe patterns and may reference past kings, and queenmothers, historical events (for example, the "Queen comes to Ghana," commemorating Queen Elizabeth's visit in 1961), the plant and animal kingdoms ("little peppers," "guinea fowl feathers"), and other natural phenomena ("gold dust," "the rainbow," "the rising sun"). Traditional proverbs are among the most popular names. One pattern is titled "When you climb a good tree you get a push," that is, if your intentions are good people will help you. Another is called "Kindness does not travel far," referring to the idea that bad deeds attract more attention than good. The above aside, only rarely is there a visual correlation between the cloth's name and its appearance. Although the overall cloth is named after the warp pattern, weft designs are also named. Here there is more visual correspondence with the name, with designs called "comb," "hat," "knife," and "drum" being relatively descriptive. The narrative and indeed intellectual component of kente nomenclature is also undoubtedly important to its popularity in international fashion.

Kente cloth first gained exposure on the international scene with the rise of Kwame Nkrumah and the independence of Ghana in 1957. As the first sub-Saharan African country to regain its independence from colonial domination, Ghana, with Nkrumah as its first President, attained enormous symbolic stature for the rest of Africa and for African Americans—many of whom visited Ghana just before or after independence. This includes such renowned figures as Maya Angelou, Muhammad Ali, John Biggers, Ralph Bunche, W. E. B. Du Bois, Thurgood Marshall, Adam Clayton Powell, Roy Wilkins, Richard Wright, and Malcolm X, to name only a few. Most, if not all, returned with a piece of kente as a potent connection with their African heritage and identity.

Of equal or greater importance, Kwame Nkrumah visited the United States in 1958 and 1960 with an entourage of kente-adorned Ghanaian dignitaries, who appeared in photographs in many of the most important publications of the day, including *Life*, *Time*, and *Ebony* magazines, and *The New York Times* and *The Washington Post* newspapers.

Since Americans were unaccustomed to wrapped and draped clothing, kente was first used primarily as interior decoration—a furniture throw, wall hanging, or even a bedspread. But very quickly kente cloth was tailored into women's blouses, skirts, and dresses and even men's jackets, all of which otherwise followed styles prevalent in the 1960s and 70s. During this period kente wedding attire was especially popular.

The fact that handwoven kente was expensive, difficult to obtain, often uncomfortably warm and heavy, and hard to tailor led to the production of mill-woven roller-printed cloths in a variety of kente patterns beginning about 1960 and continuing into the twenty-first century. Asante and Ewe weavers naturally object to calling this material "kente," but it has entered popular parlance as such.

Both hand- and mill-woven kente have entered the contemporary fashion world in a variety of forms. Kente-covered jewelry includes earrings, pins, and bracelets, and is still popular, as are a variety of hair ornaments such as headbands, barrettes, and scrunchies. Kente hats, purses, shoes, and sandals can still be purchased in Ghanaian markets, and kente backpacks and book bags are popular tourist items.

While kente fabrics and designs can still be found internationally in a number of contexts, the use of kente in the United States persists, especially at liturgical and academic events where the robes of choirs and church leaders, as well as graduation robes, either incorporate or are augmented by a single strip of kente called a "stole." Since religion and education are of paramount importance to African American communities, it is fitting that kente still plays a profound role in these life-sustaining and family-centered institutions.

See also **Africa, Sub-Saharan: History of Dress; African American Dress; Kente; Weaving.**

BIBLIOGRAPHY
Adler, Peter and Nicholas Barnard. *African Majesty: The Textile Art of the Ashanti and Ewe*. London: Thames and Hudson, 1992. Features a stunning collection of kente.

Lamb, Venice. *West African Weaving*. London: Duckworth, 1975. Focus is on kente, but locates it in broader West African tradition.

Menzel, Brigitte. *Textilien aus Westafrica*. 3 vols. Berlin: Museum für Völkerkunde, 1972 and 1973. Catalogue of Berlin collection; Volume 1 has extensive documentation of warp and weft names.

Rattray, Robert S. *Religion and Art in Ashanti*. Oxford: Clarendon Press, 1927. First edition is remarkable for its color plates of warp patterns.

Ross, Doran H., ed. *Wrapped in Pride: Ghanaian Kente and African American Identity*. Los Angeles: UCLA Fowler Museum of Cultural History, 1998. Comprehensive study, brings history of kente up to the twenty-first century.

Doran Ross

KEVLAR. *See* **Techno-Textiles.**

KHAKIS. *See* **Trousers.**

KILT The kilt has come to signify a natural and unmistakable masculinity, but it has a long history of outside intervention and deliberate reinvention. From its origins as the basic garb of the Highlander, Scotsmen and non-Scotsmen alike have embraced it as uniform, formal and semiformal wear, and casual, everyday wear. The kilt's ability to remain recognizable while responding to changing circumstances and consumer demands has been instrumental in maintaining its popularity through successive generations and, increasingly, throughout the world.

Form and Evolution
The kilt as we know it today originated in the first quarter of the eighteenth century. Known to the Gaelic-speaking Highlander as the "little wrap" (*feileadh beag*), it evolved from the "big wrap" (*feileadh mor*), or belted

plaid, the first identifiably "Scottish" costume that emerged in the late sixteenth century. Earlier, the Scottish Gaels had worn the same clothes as their Irish counterparts, namely a shirt known in Gaelic as the *léine* and a semicircular mantle known in Gaelic as the *brat*.

The belted plaid consisted of a four- to six-yard length of woolen cloth about two yards wide. In *Highland Costume* (1977), John Telfer Dunbar explains how the belted plaid was arranged on the body. It was laid out on the ground and gathered in folds with a plain section left at each side. The man lay down on it with one selvage at about knee level, and fastened it with a belt. When he stood up, the lower part was like a kilt, and the upper part could be draped around the body in a variety of different styles. Several dress historians, however, have discounted this method on the grounds of impracticality. They propose that the most pragmatic and time-effective method was to gather the pleats in the hand, pass the plaid around the body, secure it loosely with the belt, and then tighten it after a final adjustment of the pleats.

The kilt as worn in the early 2000s is the lower half of the belted plaid with the back pleats stitched up. Its invention is credited to Thomas Rawlinson, an English ironmaster who employed Highlanders to work his furnaces in Glengarry near Inverness. Finding the belted plaid cumbersome, he conceived of the "little kilt" on the grounds of efficiency and practicality, a means of bringing the Highlanders "out of the heather and into the factory" (Trevor-Roper 1983, p. 22). However, as Dorothy K. Burnham asserts in *Cut My Cote* (1973), it is more likely that the transformation came about as the natural result of a change from the warp-weighted loom to the horizontal loom with its narrower width.

Romanticism: The Kilt as National Dress

Not long after the kilt's invention, the Diskilting Act was passed in the wake of the Jacobite Uprising of 1745. This rebellion, organized by Prince Charles Edward Stuart (Bonnie Prince Charlie), marked the final attempt by the Jacobites to regain the British throne. As in the previous Jacobite risings, the "Young Pretender" sought and won the support of many Highland chiefs and their clans. When the Jacobites were defeated at the Battle of Culloden (1746) by the duke of Cumberland and his troops, a campaign of "pacification" of the Highlands was undertaken "beginning with fire and the sword, and leading on into social engineering of various kinds" (Chapman 1992, p. 125). The latter included the proscription of Highland costume, which was seen as a symbol of rebellion and primitive savagery.

The Diskilting Act made an exception for those serving in the armed forces. Originally, the Highland regiments were dressed in the belted plaid, but in order to conform to the other regiments of the British Army they wore a red coat cut away at the skirts to allow for its voluminous folds. Other distinctive Highland features of the uniform included a round blue bonnet, a small leather sporran, red and white knee-length hose, and black buckled shoes. By about 1810, however, the Highland regiments had replaced the belted plaid with the little kilt. At the same time, the small, practical leather sporran developed into a large, hairy, decorative affair. This early-nineteenth-century military style was to have a lasting impact on civilian dress. Several dress historians have claimed that Highland costume would not have survived in civilian form had the Highland regiments not been raised and uniformed in elements of their native dress.

In 1782, through the efforts of the Highland Society of London, the Diskilting Act was repealed. By the time of the repeal, the kilt had fallen out of use as an item of ordinary dress, allowing for what Malcolm Chapman in *The Celts: The Construction of a Myth* (1992) calls the "romantic rehabilitation of Highland dress." The romantic gaze was a reaction against the urban and the industrial and a celebration of the untamed wilderness. No longer the threat from the North, the image of the Highlands could represent this wilderness within the bustling economy of the "new" Britain. Rather than dangerous, bare-legged barbarians, the Highlanders became admirable, a kilted version of the noble savage.

The romantic rehabilitation of the kilt reached its apotheosis with King George IV's carefully stage-managed state visit to Edinburgh in 1822, during which he disported himself in full Highland dress. This "publicity stunt" promoted the kilt as fashionable wear among the Scottish nobility and, in so doing, helped establish the kilt as the national dress of Scotland. However, the king's clothes, like those worn by Scottish noblemen, were far removed from those worn by the Highlanders of the previous century. Given the fact that they were largely designed for the levee, assembly, and ballroom, the emphasis was on the dramatic and spectacular. As Hugh Cheape points out in *Tartan* (1991), "'Highland dress' turned into 'tartan costume.' A practical dress with style became . . . a fashionable dress with little regard for function" (Cheape 1991, p. 52).

Throughout the nineteenth century, aristocratic patronage continued to provide cachet for this new urban-based national style, which began to have "correct" items and styles of wear for day and evening. From the 1840s, it was given new impetus through Queen Victoria's cult of the Highlands. Queen Victoria shared King George IV's romantic vision of Scotland, and in 1852 Prince Albert bought Balmoral Castle in Aberdeenshire. Parts of the interior, most notably the queen's private suites, were decorated with tartan. Queen Victoria herself wore dresses made from "Dress Stewart" or "Victoria" tartan, sparking a trend for tartan fashions worldwide. It was not until the twentieth century, however, that women embraced the kilt as fashionable attire. After World War II, a simplified version of the kilt emerged in the form of a pleated, wrap-around skirt belted at the waist and secured near the hem with a large pin. Popular with middle- and upper-class women, it also formed a component of the uniforms of private girls' schools in England and America, thus maintaining the kilt's connotations of wealth and class privilege.

Re-contextualization

As Scotland gained a new level of cultural and political confidence toward the end of the twentieth century, "a new generation of [young] radical Scots . . . reclaimed the wearing of the kilt from the embrace of nearly two hundred years of establishment, commodified gentrification" (Taylor 2002, p. 220). The Victorian styles of day wear and evening wear gave way to contemporary usage. Many younger Scotsmen began to wear their kilts for everyday use with a T-shirt or sweater, a denim or leather jacket, sneakers or chunky, heavy-soled boots, and woolly socks falling around the ankles. As Lou Taylor observes in *The Study of Dress History* (2002), "Now young Scotsmen wear their kilts according to their own cultural codes and on their own national identity terms" (Taylor 2002, p. 220).

Recently, the kilt has become increasingly popular among non-Scotsmen wishing to project a self-confidently fashionable image. This can be attributed, at least in part, to the immense success of such films as *Rob Roy* (1995) and *Braveheart* (1995). In the tradition of the Romantic movement of the late eighteenth and early nineteenth centuries, these films portray the Highlander as "warrior hero," embodying timeless, masculine values. This image has been reinforced in the arena of sport, most obviously through the Highland Games, now broadcast around the world. In putting the shot, tossing the caber, and throwing the weight, men of obvious stamina are shown competing in kilts. Most recently, however, Scottish football supporters have promoted the Highlander as a beau ideal. Their tribal antics and kilted uniforms received widespread publicity in France during the World Cup in the summer of 1998. Through such images, the kilt has come to represent a ready access to Highland male sexuality. For non-Scotsmen, it provides the means of asserting a self-consciously yet unambiguously masculine persona.

Contemporary designers have drawn heavily on the kilt's hypermasculine connotations in their attempts to appeal to the young fashion-conscious male. At the same time, various designers have attempted to blur the lines between the "kilt" and a "skirt" by re-working elements of the kilt's design. Most typically they have focused their efforts on foregrounding the cut over the culturally specific tartan, employing nontraditional "street" materials like denim or leather, and even adapting its cut, length, and construction. These "skirt-kilts" offer men a means of expressing a frank masculinity while simultaneously projecting a self-confidently unconventional persona. As such, they have proved particularly successful among youth and countercultural movements such as punks in the 1970s and new romantics in the 1980s. Since the early 1990s, kilts and skirt-kilts have entered the lexicon of gay fashion. Worn by gay men as an expression of hyper-masculinity and a flaunting of perceived femininity, the kilt has become a standard item in the masculinized gay wardrobe.

See also **Europe and America: History of Dress (400–1900 C.E.); Gender, Dress, and Fashion; Tartan; Uniforms, Military.**

BIBLIOGRAPHY

Burnham, Dorothy, K. *Cut My Cote*. Toronto: Royal Ontario Museum, 1973.

Chapman, Malcolm. *The Celts: The Construction of a Myth*. London: Macmillan, 1992.

Cheape, Hugh. *Tartan: The Highland Habit*. Edinburgh, U.K.: Weatherhill, 1991.

Dunbar, John Telfer. *Highland Costume*. Edinburgh, U.K.: Laurier Books Ltd., 1977.

——. *The Costume of Scotland*. London: B. T. Batsford, Ltd., 1981.

Scarlett, James D. *Scotland's Clans and Tartans*. Guildford, U.K.: Lutterworth Press, 1975.

Taylor, Lou. *The Study of Dress History*. Manchester, U.K.: Manchester University Press, 2002.

Trevor-Roper, Hugh. "The Invention of Tradition: The Highland Tradition of Scotland." In *The Invention of Tradition*. Edited by Eric Hobsbawm and Terence Ranger. Cambridge, U.K.: Cambridge University Press, 1983.

Andrew Bolton

KIMONO Around the world, the kimono is recognized as the national dress of Japan. Made from a single, long fourteen-inch-wide bolt of silk, the kimono has an overall T-shape, with its component parts joined mostly in straight, vertical seams. In contrast to typical Western garb, the kimono is flat rather than three-dimensional, and angular, not form-fitting. It is more an expression of surface design by means of dyed and/or embroidered patterns than a product of tailoring and weave.

The term "kimono" was coined during Japan's first era of modernization, the Meiji Period (1868–1912), in response to the heightened awareness of the Japanese to Western clothing, customs, and ideas. Japan had recently emerged from an enforced period of isolation with feelings of self-consciousness in regard to their dress as compared to that of occidentals. A dichotomy was established distinguishing Western clothing (*yōfuku*) from native dress (*wafuku*).

Kimono, the best-known article of traditional clothing, takes its name from the verb *kiru*, meaning "to wear," and *mono*, meaning "thing." In its narrowest sense, the kimono is the descendant of the *kosode*, a former undergarment that emerged prior to the Edo period (1603–1868) as the principal article of dress most sensitive to changes in styles and fashion. More broadly, kimono can refer to any traditional Japanese T-shaped garment, whether worn by men or women in any context—sacred or secular, for weddings or funerals, onstage or at festivals, or simply for relaxing at home.

Kosode/Kimono Parameters

The kosode takes its name from the adjective *ko*, meaning "small," and *sode*, for "sleeve." In that a kosode/kimono sleeve has the appearance of a large pouch, it is difficult to consider the kosode sleeve as being small. In fact, what is small relative to the overall sleeve size is the opening through which the hand passes. The kosode sleeve opening is so-named in contrast to the *ōsode* sleeve, which is entirely open and unsewn.

The kosode took precedence over the ōsode as the primary vehicle for fashion, while the ōsode was relegated to conservative milieux such as court rites, religious rituals, and the nō theater. Other variations in construction include the absence or presence of a lining, wide lapels that overlap or narrow ones that abut, a flat collar, and the occasional use of padding. When the front panels of the robe are wide enough to overlap, the left front panel is always closed over the right side. The obi is a sash used to secure the robe around the body.

Distinctions existed among kosode of the past, some of which are still current in kimonos. One type of kosode, the *furisode* (literally, "swinging sleeves") has sleeves especially long in their vertical dimension. The furisode is reserved for unmarried girls. The *katabira*, for which the nearest modern descendant is the *yukata*, was unlined and not made of silk, but rather of a bast fiber (usually hemp or ramie). Two other types of kosode, called *koshimaki* and *uchikake*, were worn as outer robes on top of another kosode. The koshimaki was densely embroidered with small auspicious motifs and draped around the hips while held in place by an obi. It became obsolete; however, the uchikake, worn like a cape and not fastened at the waist, had a thickly padded hem and was still being worn at marriage ceremonies in the early 2000s.

Early Styles

After the kosode ceased to be the plain, unpatterned silk garment worn next to the skin under layers of voluminous robes, as in the Heian Period (794–1185), it served as outerwear, initially for the lower classes and eventually for the samurai class and the aristocracy.

One of the first discernible styles in kosode, *nuihaku*, featured decoration in embroidery (*nui*) and metallic foil (*haku*). In some examples, the robe's markedly contrasting sections differ in both motifs and color schemes. Another early style, known by the poetic name *tsujigahana* (literally "flowers at the crossroads"), was technically exacting, involving careful tie-dyeing, delicate ink painting, and, occasionally, embroidery and applied metallic foil. Some kosode patterned in this fashion were only decorated at the shoulders and hem, with the midsection left empty.

Kanbun Style

The earliest style for which there is considerable pictorial and written documentation, as well as extant garments, is known as Kanbun (1661–1673) after the Japanese era of that name. Order books from the Kariganeya clothing atelier in Kyoto, which catered to samurai class and aristocratic clients, reveal an exuberant asymmetrical style often featuring large-scale motifs in a sweeping composition extending from the shoulders to the hem, with the left body panel (as viewed from the back) mostly free of decoration in its midsection. The broad, flat expanse of surface area and the T-shape, two characteristics inherent in *kosode* construction, are exploited to their full design potential in such robes.

In Kanbun kosode, tiny tie-dye spots were used extensively in the creation of individual motifs, and in combination with embroidery in polychrome silk threads and gold and silver threads. Occasionally, written characters in a flowing script were incorporated into the design scheme, adding a literary aspect and creating deeper levels of meaning in the pattern by combining words with individual design motifs.

The two most elite (and, eventually, most conservative) levels of society, the aristocracy and the samurai class, were patrons of this bold and innovative style. The earliest published kosode design books (*hinagata-bon*), printed from wood blocks to allow for wide dissemination, also featured the Kanbun style, indicating there was also a popular audience for this new fashion. Members of the nouveaux riche merchant class had the money to afford such expensive robes, although they were at the bottom of the social scale, below farmers and artisans.

Kosode design books allowed a larger public to keep pace with changing fashions. A client would select a design from such a book, then choose colors from an album of dyed fabric swatches; after which a kosode maker, in collaboration with a dyer, would produce the finished product. The concept of ready-to-wear clothes for both Western-style garments and kimono did not have an impact in Japan until after World War II. Even as late as the early twenty-first century, most finer kimonos were still made to order, like haute couture in the West.

Genroku and Yōzen Styles

The next dominant style is named for the Genroku years (1688–1704). During this time women's obi grew wider, and therefore more prominent as a fashion accessory. Many different methods were invented for tying the obi, adding another element to the repertory of styles available to fashionable women. The obi was now usually knotted at the back.

As the obi widened, the sleeves of the furisode-type kosode lengthened even more and its unpatterned space diminished, although the shoulder-to-hem Kanbun-style sweeping design composition was more-or-less preserved. The overall effect was one of opulence, as the design filled up more space and the wider obi added a further expanse of decoration.

The Kabuki theater, a new and raucous form of popular entertainment, enjoyed a wide audience in the urban centers where the merchant class was based. Since women were banned from the Kabuki stage, male actors also played the female roles. They launched fashion trends in women's kosode, particularly by popularizing certain shades of colors and individual design motifs. Woodblock print publishers had eager urbanites lining up to buy the latest images of Kabuki stars, and also of geisha, who were the female trendsetters of the moment. By this time, men's kosode were no longer interchangeable with women's dress, except within the Kabuki and brothel demimonde.

Another style that emerged during the Genroku years was named after a Kyoto painter, Yōzensai Miyazaki, and is simply referred to as *Yōzen*. He is believed to have popularized a technique that combined freehand painting and paste-resist dyeing using a wide variety of colors and allowing for the production of highly pictorial imagery and unusual shading effects on kosode.

Yōzen kosode represented a uniquely Japanese achievement in the costume arts. Whereas technological advances in textile production had previously been initiated on the Asian mainland (especially in China) and were later copied and refined by the Japanese, a new means of decoration involving the skill of the dyer and the hand of the painter had been created in Japan itself. The nearest equivalent to Yōzen in textiles outside of Japan is Indian chintz, which, however, utilizes cotton fabric rather than silk and makes less use of freehand painting and shading effects. Yōzen remains a popular technique for the decoration of kimono in the early 2000s.

Late Edo–Period Styles

Extravagance in Genroku and Yōzen-style kosode led the Tokugawa authorities to enact sumptuary laws from time to time, leading to restrictions on the use of certain colors for the lower classes and to controls on some of the more costly textile techniques. Apart from the sumptuary laws, which were randomly enforced, a reaction against flamboyance and excess became the underlying basis for a new style.

Esthetic terms such as *iki* and *shibui* were used by trendsetters who dressed in kosode with a simple striped pattern in subdued colors, or who chose a quiet ikat-patterned fabric for their robes. Other kosode were decorated only along the hem, with the remainder of the garment devoid of design except for traditional family crests arrayed across the shoulders. Subtlety, with a touch of luxury, could be conveyed by wearing a plain kosode with a richly decorated lining.

Excess was not completely forgotten during the late Edo period. The Bunka-Bunsei years (1804–1830) saw the production of many densely embroidered kosode rich in gold thread and that were often chosen by brides for their weddings. Even Buddhist monks commissioned extravagantly woven ritual robes during this period.

A trend in kosode of the Samurai class played on the juxtaposition of certain design motifs alluding to literary works from Japan's medieval period. Another style, which continued into Japan's modern era, was based on the work of the Shijō-Maruyama school of painting, whose artists were influenced by Western painting techniques such as the use of perspective. Several of these painters were recruited to work on kosode designs, and were able to successfully adapt their landscape, bird, and flower themes to the T-shaped garment.

Meiji Period (1868–1912)

In the 1850s, Japan was forced to end its policy of isolation when militarily superior Western powers demanded trading concessions. China, which had historically been the fount of culture for Japan, as ancient Greece and Rome had been for the rest of Europe, was then under the yoke of Western imperialism and was no longer considered to be a suitable role model for the Japanese.

When power was assumed by the Meiji emperor in 1868 after the shogunate collapsed, the elite of Japan embarked upon a serious program of studying and emulating Western technology and customs, including dress. In 1887, the Meiji empress issued a statement denouncing the wearing of kimono as harmful to the female body and advocated the Western blouse and skirt as a more practical form of women's wear.

However, only wealthy women who moved in international circles felt the need and had the means to dress Western style. The long kimono and its wide, tightly bound obi made chair sitting a challenge. In the traditional Japanese home, kimono-clad women sat on a tatami mat–covered floor with their lower legs folded under their thighs. Most women continued to wear kimonos, as they did not lead public lives and had no occasion to experience Western-style interior decor. The daughters of Meiji women did, however, improvise a sort of Western two-piece outfit to serve as school dress. They wore their kimonos tucked into *hakama*, the traditional skirtlike trousers, which had most recently served as part of formal dress for samurai-class men during the Edo period.

For urban men, whose lives were led in public while their wives stayed home, uniforms based on European models were worn in the exercise of certain professions. If a man had the means, he could visit a tailor and be fitted for a suit, which would invariably be made of wool, a fiber Japan itself never produced. Otherwise, at least a token article of Western dress would be worn in public, such as the bowler hat.

Meanwhile, in the West, kimonos appealed to certain sophisticates who developed a passion for things Japanese. Numerous portraits were painted of Western women in kimono during the latter part of the nineteenth century. The kimono could add both an exotic and an erotic flavor to a painting. Puccini's *Madame Butterfly* and Gilbert and Sullivan's *The Mikado* put the kimono on stage in front of large audiences in Europe and the Americas. Fashion designers such as the Callot sisters and Paul Poiret were inspired by the kimono shape.

Taishō Period (1912–1926)

Japan continued to modernize and prosper during this period. When a major earthquake seriously damaged Tokyo in 1923, much of the city was rebuilt in a more Western style, making Western attire more practical in the new modern interiors. The kimono and other traditional dress for women were further marginalized as female students started to wear blouses and skirts instead of kimono tucked into *hakama* (although such an outfit can still be seen at graduation ceremonies), and as more women entered the workforce.

Shōwa Period (1926–1989)

Militarism came to the fore in 1930s Japan, eventually leading to the disaster and devastation of World War II. Rampant nationalism did not bring about a revival of the kimono. Women were needed to fill jobs abandoned by men in the armed forces, and kimonos were impractical as work clothes. Fabric was rationed, and the kimono was seen as wasteful, requiring more material than Western-style clothes. During the occupation period following Japan's defeat, many families were forced to sell or barter heirloom kimonos for daily necessities, causing yet another setback to the tradition of kimono wearing.

However, economic recovery and prosperity created a large middle class in Japan, resulting in an increase in disposable income and leisure time. Housewives now sought to cultivate themselves by engaging in traditional arts such as flower arranging and tea ceremony, for which kimono was the appropriate dress.

Department stores became major retailers of kimonos, which were still made to order from narrow bolts of silk. Brides continued to dress in kimonos for weddings (but would also change into a Western-style wedding dress for a portion of the ceremony), and might even enroll in a school at which the proper choosing and wearing of the kimono and obi were taught. Traditional annual events, such as New Year festivals and coming-of-age ceremonies, were further occasion for kimono wearing, although primarily for women and children.

Colors and patterns in kimono did change from year to year, but the burst of creativity in surface design and dyeing of the Edo period has yet to be equaled. The modern kimono represented a middle-class rediscovery of a traditional garment. Its role is minor, or nonexistent, in the lives of Japanese women in the early twenty-first century, with the exception of the geisha, who continued to wear kimono with a sense of style while entertaining men.

However, kimonos did experience another incarnation in postwar Japan as art objects. Certain artisans who continued to practice traditional crafts, including textiles, were designated "Living National Treasures" by the Ministry of Culture. Two of the best-known Treasures in the field of textiles, Kako Moriguchi and Keisuke Serizawa, had some of their fabric production made into kimonos, which were subsequently shown at exhibitions and collected as works of art. Their work, and that of other artists of their caliber, has extended the creative life of the kimono.

The Art-to-Wear Movement led to kimono-inspired artistic production in the West. Such pieces have been worn as clothing or displayed on walls, illustrating that the scope of the kimono has broadened well beyond that of a national costume.

See also **Japanese Traditional Dress and Adornment.**

BIBLIOGRAPHY

Asian Art Museum of San Francisco. *Four Centuries of Fashion: Classical Kimono from the Kyoto National Museum.* San Francisco: Asian Art Museum, 1997.

Dalby, Liza Crihfield. *Kimono: Fashioning Culture.* New Haven, Conn.: Yale University Press, 1993.

Gluckman, Dale Carolyn, and Sharon Sadako Takeda. *When Art Became Fashion: Kosode in Edo-Period Japan.* New York: Weatherhill, 1992.

Ishimura, Hayao, and Nobuhiko Maruyama. *Robes of Elegance: Japanese Kimono of the 16th–20th Centuries.* Raleigh: North Carolina Museum of Art, 1988.

Kennedy, Alan. *Japanese Costume: History and Tradition.* Paris: Editions Adam Biro, 1990.

Kyoto National Museum. *Kyoto Style: Trends in 16th–19th Century Kimono.* Kyoto: Kyoto National Museum, 1999.

Liddell, Jill. *The Story of the Kimono.* New York: E. P. Dutton, 1989.

Peebles, Merrily A. *Dressed in Splendor: Japanese Costume 1700–1926.* Santa Barbara, Calif.: Santa Barbara Museum of Art, 1987.

Stevens, Rebecca A. T., and Yoshiko Iwamoto Wada, eds. *The Kimono Inspiration: Art and Art-to-Wear in America.* Washington, D.C.: The Textile Museum, 1996.

Stinchecum, Amanda Mayer. *Kosode: Sixteenth–Nineteenth Century Textiles from the Nomura Collection.* New York: Japan Society and Kodansha International, 1984.

Alan Kennedy

KLEIN, CALVIN Calvin Klein was born in the Bronx, New York, on 19 November 1942. He attended the High School of Industrial Arts and the Fashion Institute of Technology in New York, where he studied fashion design.

Klein's first major position in the fashion industry was with Dan Millstein, a Seventh Avenue coat and suit manufacturer. He worked there from 1962 to 1964, starting as a pattern cutter and advancing to a full-fledged designer.

Billboard featuring Calvin Klein underwear. A visually striking and sexually charged advertising campaign helped make Klein's underwear line a huge success. © BETTMANN/CORBIS. REPRODUCED BY PERMISSION.

Klein's second position was with Halldon, Ltd., where he began to be recognized in the press for his designs.

Klein soon became frustrated by the design restrictions of moderate-priced fashion manufacturers. Encouraged by his parents and financed by his boyhood friend Barry Schwartz, Klein developed a collection of coats and suits under his own label.

Klein's first line was discovered by a buyer from Bonwit Teller, who was so impressed by the collection of finely tailored coats in fresh colors that he sent Klein to meet with Mildred Custin, then president of Bonwit Teller. Custin placed a large order with Klein, giving a jumpstart to the newly formed Calvin Klein Limited.

Early on, the savvy Klein developed relationships with fashion insiders, including the designer Chester Weinberg and *Vogue* fashion editor Nicolas de Gunzburg. The publicity agent Eleanor Lambert took Klein on as a client and was instrumental in guiding his early career. Klein's first *Vogue* cover was in September 1969, with his classically cut outerwear featured prominently in the New York fall preview editorial inside. Throughout the 1970s, Klein's designs were noted for their sportswear influence, muted pastel color palettes, and simplicity of design. Looks that are considered classic Klein were introduced at this time: the pea coat, the trench coat, the shirtdress, and the wrap blouse. Klein was also an early advocate of all-occasion or "day into night" dressing, with evening pajamas being his preferred form of formal wear.

As the decade wore on, Klein eased up his tailoring for a relaxed, sexy look. Klein also began to incorporate looks from active sportswear into his collection—

swimwear and tennis outfits that could be used off the beaches and tennis courts by pairing them with wrap skirts or pants. Corduroy cargo pants, flannel shirts, and elegant fur-trimmed parkas were shown on Klein's 1970s fall runways. For all his innovations, Calvin Klein won his first Coty American Fashion Critic's Winnie Award—as the youngest recipient ever—in 1973. He won again in 1974, and in 1975 he was inducted into the Coty Hall of Fame. In 1978 Klein began designing a menswear collection that was licensed to Maurice Biderman.

The most groundbreaking piece of sportswear Klein showed on the runway first appeared in spring 1976: a slim-cut pair of jeans with his name embroidered on the back pocket. Although the idea of logo-emblazoned jeans was not brand-new, this was the first time that jeans had shown up on a designer runway. By 1978, with Puritan Fashions as manufacturer, Klein was selling 2 million pairs of jeans per month. The phenomenal success that Klein had with his jeans line was due in no small way to a brilliant and controversial advertising campaign starring a young Brooke Shields.

The 1980s

Klein's designs, even in the excessive 1980s, continued to evoke a minimalist aesthetic, with a relatively restrained use of embellishment and color. The core of the collection was, as always, made up of timeless pieces in good fabrics. The Council of Fashion Designers of America (CDFA) recognized Klein when he won designer of the year awards in 1982 and 1983 for his women's collection. Klein won a CFDA award in 1986 for both his men's and women's collections, the first time a designer had won both awards in the same year.

In 1982 Calvin Klein launched a men's underwear line. The collection revolved around a standard men's

"I didn't think I was doing anything different from what *Vogue* did when it used Brooke as a model. . . . *Vogue* put $3,000 dresses on her, but it wasn't expecting to sell those dresses to 15-year-olds. It was using her as a model and I was using her as an actress" (Quoted in Plaskin, p. 4).

With the Brooke Shields ads, Calvin Klein forever changed television commercials. Klein spent an unprecedented $5 million on marketing that year. Feminists were enraged by the jeans ads and felt that, rather than sales, the commercials—with slogans such as "You know what comes between me and my Calvin's? Nothing"—would provoke violence against women (Plaskin, p. 62).

brief, with Klein's name stamped on the waistband. Bold black-and-white photography on the packaging and an advertising campaign featuring celebrity models Antonio Sabato Jr. and Marky Mark in suggestive poses helped make the product appealing to both straight and gay men. The underwear line became a phenomenon when Klein took the same briefs and modified and marketed them for women. Warnaco purchased the underwear division in 1994.

By 1983 Calvin Klein, whose eponymous fragrance had produced a lukewarm reception four years earlier, was ready to give perfume another try. The result was Obsession and, again, with brilliant advertising—television ads directed by Richard Avedon and print ads shot by Bruce Weber—Obsession was a success. In 1986 Klein married Kelly Rector, one of his design assistants. The marriage, as well as the mid-1980s "return to family values" mood, inspired the designer's next fragrance, Eternity. A shared-gender fragrance, cK One, was launched in 1994.

The 1990s

In the 1990s Calvin Klein's worldwide expansion into Asia, Europe, and the Middle East markets brought his name international consumer recognition. The decade also saw Klein revamp the jeans/sport division of the company, creating the cK collection, made to appeal to a younger, hipper customer. Klein had been farsighted enough to realize the importance of archiving his work, so a constant recall of his roots was readily available. The cK line, largely inspired by these vintage collection pieces, was recognized by the CFDA with an award in 1993.

Klein surrounds himself with people who share his aesthetic, and he is known in the fashion world for his intensely collaborative relationships with those who work with him. Most noteworthy is Zack Carr, who was Klein's creative doppelgänger for almost thirty years. Jeffrey Banks, Isaac Mizrahi, and Narciso Rodriguez are also notable Calvin Klein alums.

The twenty-first century began with litigation between Klein and Warnaco over underwear and jeans distribution. The case was eventually settled out of court. Klein and his partner Barry Schwartz sold Calvin Klein, Inc., to Phillips–Van Heusen in December 2002. Since that time Klein has stepped down as creative head of the company that bears his name and has assumed a consultant role.

The name Calvin Klein represents so many different things—controversial advertising campaigns, the leading name in the designer-jeans phenomenon, stylish boyish underwear for women, and brilliant and ruthless business practices. So much of what Klein designed has become fundamentally what Americans wear that his clothing can rightly be called an American uniform.

See also **Avedon, Richard; Brands and Labels; Vogue.**

Calvin Klein. Considered one of the most prominent American designers, Klein launched his own clothing company in 1968, and rapidly became known for his line of designer sportswear. AP/WIDE WORLD PHOTOS. REPRODUCED BY PERMISSION.

BIBLIOGRAPHY

Carr, George. *Zack Carr.* New York: Power House Books, 2002.

Gaines, Steven, and Sharon Churcher. *Obsession: The Lives and Times of Calvin Klein.* New York: Carol Publishing Group, 1994.

Horyn, Cathy. "The Calvinist Ethic." *New York Times Magazine,* 14 September 2003, 64–69.

Marsh, Lisa. *House of Klein: Fashion, Controversy, and a Business Obsession.* Hoboken, N.J.: John Wiley and Sons, 2003.

Plaskin, Glenn. "Calvin Klein: The Playboy Interview." *Playboy,* May 1984.

Reed, Julia. "Calvin's Clean Sweep." *Vogue,* August 1994, 236–241.

Gretchen Fenston and Beth Dincuff Charleston

KNICKERS. *See* **Panties.**

KNITTING Knitwear pervades people's everyday lives; it has been estimated that one in five garments worn worldwide are knits. While comprising an essential part

Man in knitted hat. Bolivian *chullos* (caps) such as this are knitted with a very fine gauge wool, allowing for very distinctive and intricate pattern work. © HUBERT STADLER/CORBIS. REPRODUCED BY PERMISSION.

of the industrial manufacture of clothing, knitting is also a widespread leisure practice with a burgeoning literature. The titles of some publications of the late 1990s and early 2000s on the subject—*Hip to Knit, Zen and the Art of Knitting, The Urban Knitter, The Knitting Sutra*—suggest that in addition to being a craft and an expressive art form, knitting is also a lifestyle.

Techniques, Tools, and Materials

Knitting is the formation of a textile from interlocking loops (stitches) of yarn. Each stitch on a horizontal row is locked into the stitches above and below, creating a durable, pliable fabric that has been used for clothing across the world over centuries. Knitwear's elasticity enhances fit, and its structural properties of absorbency and insulation render it highly functional. Additionally, the fact that the knitter may choose from hundreds of stitches and work with multiple colors offers an aesthetic richness that has led to knitwear becoming a creative, expressive form of dress.

Knitting is formed by hand with needles or by machine. It can be created in flat-shaped pieces that are then sewn together, or worked in the round. Hand knitters have used a variety of needles, usually of metal, through sometimes of wood, bone, bamboo, ivory, and, in the twentieth century, plastic. Needles typically have pointed ends, though in some countries, such as Portugal, they are hooked. The circular needle became increasingly popular during the twentieth century. This double-ended needle with a flexible central section is used for knitting tubular pieces, but also affords greater comfort for flat knitting, as the weight of the fabric rests in the knitter's lap. Sets of smaller double-ended needles are commonly used for knitting socks or for areas with a small circumference.

Although some of the earliest knitted artifacts have been discovered in Egypt, knitting has predominantly been developed in colder climates. The most common yarn has been wool, though some exceptionally fine early pieces were knit in silk. Cotton as a less elastic yarn has not been as popular a choice for hand knitters. The explosion in availability of artificial yarns and blends during the twentieth century offered knitters unprecedented choice of materials, and some of the most innovative design has resulted from the exploitation of the structural properties of these yarns and the surface manipulation of knitted textiles.

The way the knitter holds the yarn varies by region. In America and Great Britain, the yarn is carried in the right hand and thrown over the right needle; the left is used in continental Europe. In some areas, such as the Shetland Isles off the north coast of Scotland, one needle is anchored in a sheath. In Turkey, Greece, Portugal, Peru, and Bolivia, the yarn is often looped around the neck to create tension.

History

Knitlike structures dating from the later Roman period were long thought to be the earliest extant examples of hand knitting. However, it has been determined that these pieces were made by the nalbinding method, which was practiced in Scandinavia, Africa, and other areas to make socks, gloves, bags, and even dancers' costumes. Nalbinding produces a textile resembling a knit with a single sewing needle and short lengths of yarn.

The earliest surviving true knits are Islamic socks dating from 1200 to 1500, discovered in Egypt and often decorated with bands of ornamental Arabic script, and a meticulously crafted pair of thirteenth-century cushions recovered from a royal Spanish tomb. Medieval knitting was often associated with the church; there are even a number of late medieval and early Renaissance paintings that depict the Madonna knitting. In Britain, more utilitarian applications included cap-making—a flourishing and well-regulated industry.

The Englishman William Lee invented the first hand-operating knitting frame in 1589, in response to consumer demand for imported silk stockings. He was denied a patent because of fears over the machine's impact on the hand-knitting trade. Subsequent advances enabled fabric to be produced in the round (early machines produced flat-shaped work requiring seaming), as well as with complex patterning, and use of multiple colors. But it took many centuries to produce on a machine what a skilled hand-knitter could produce on four or more needles. In fact, only as recently as 1998 was a completely seamless panty-hose product first produced.

In continental Europe, knitting guilds played an important part in regulating the industry, some of them surviving into the eighteenth century. Knits began to assume a significant role in import/export economies. During the sixteenth century, the male fashion for short full trunk hose inspired the import into Britain of expensive silk stockings from Spain, worn to display shapely legs to advantage. By the next century, wool stockings were exported from Britain to Germany, France, Italy, and Holland. While hosiery had been a mainstay of the knitting industry, other garments types such as shirts and jackets were being produced.

Despite mechanization, the hand-knitting industry continued to thrive; hand knitting could of course be executed with the minimum of equipment, at home, and between other work, and was a convenient means of supplementing income from rural industries. It was a craft practiced by women, men, and children, and could provide relief during periods of economic hardship.

Imperialism exported forms of European administration to the colonies, and also knitting. The example of Kashmiri weavers who adapted shawl motifs into knitted caps is a famous illustration of the hybridization of traditions. In America, schools were established to teach children to knit—for profit and to encourage probity—with hands and minds occupied in learning a craft, the apprentices were less likely to misbehave. By the American Civil War, knitting for soldiers became an expression of patriotism, repeated during both World Wars as well.

During the twentieth century, knitwear became an arena in which avant-garde designers experimented and excelled. It has also been a mainstay of street wear from the clinging garb of the 1950s' sweater girls to the pre-fleece cardigans of the next decades, to the ubiquitous sweat suits of the early 2000s.

Regional Traditions and Social Significance

Hand knitting has played an important role in regional economies, especially in Great Britain and Europe. Embedded as it is in the lives of local communities, the practice is rich in social significance. Many traditions have developed in response to the occupational and climactic needs of a region's inhabitants. The best known of these include the guernseys (or ganseys or jerseys), knitted for fishermen around the coasts of the British Isles. This piece of clothing is knitted in the round on the body and

sleeves and in rows on the upper torso to create a seamless garment. Typically dark blue, the guernsey makes virtuoso use of juxtapositions of knit and purl, creating rugged, utilitarian structures that aesthetically delight. Knit stitches are formed with yarn held to the back, and the loops are drawn upward, creating an appearance of vertical rows; purl stitch is created with the yarn held to the front, and the loops drawn to the face of the fabric, creating horizontal ridges. As fishing is a peripatetic occupation, and as fishermen took wives from different regions, it is fruitless to tie motifs to specific districts. What initially started as production for family consumption developed during the nineteenth century into a contract business for a much wider market, further disseminating motifs. The patterns of the guernsey reflect the inventiveness of the makers, as well as the non-local nature of the fishing industry and the role of contract work in the local economy.

An offshoot of the Guernsey tradition with a very different history is Aran knitting, produced on the three Isles of Aran off the Irish Atlantic coast. Aran sweaters are knitted in flat pieces, usually in creamy white wool, and make prodigious use of high relief cables whose boldly chiseled forms are reminiscent of ancient Celtic interlacing. It appears, though, that the Aran tradition is a relatively new one, possibly dating back no further than the early twentieth century, and more commonly produced as fashion wear than work wear.

Some regions in Spain, Russia, and the Shetland Isles became significantly known for lace knitting, and home production was often supported by philanthropic efforts to avoid displacement of rural workers. Lace knitting was practiced during the nineteenth century by the Shetland islanders after the decline in demand for mass-produced hand knitting. The fine, silky wool of the Shetland sheep benefited the production of lace shawls so delicate they could be drawn through a wedding ring. Although methods of distribution varied, home production throughout Britain was certainly assisted by the introduction of the Parcel Post in 1840.

Fair Isle, a tiny island to the south of Shetlands, became known for the production of intricate stranded-color knitting. First noted in the nineteenth century, Fair Isle knitting was absorbed into mainstream fashion when the Prince of Wales donned this style for the golf course in 1922. Many countries have stranded-color knitting traditions, and it is difficult to establish a history of precedent and derivative. Established trading between Scotland, Scandinavia, Western Russia, and the Baltic states, and the fact that all these regions have comparable knitting styles, suggests a vibrancy of cross-fertilization rather than the importation of a dominant tradition.

South American countries developed distinct styles of stranded-color knitting, often in imitation of indigenous woven textiles. Intricately patterned Bolivian *chullos*, or caps, knitted with a very fine gauge, are some of the best known. As with the Shetland Isles, availability of fine wool—in this case alpaca, llama, and vicuña—stimulated this industry. Cooperatives continue to assist South American knitters in the marketing of their work, and it is common to see sweaters from Bolivia and other South American countries for sale in the high street.

A prominent twentieth-century example of the promotion of knitting as a means of economic stimulus was the Bohus Stickning collective, created in Sweden in the 1930s to provide work for the wives of unemployed stonecutters. This company was innovative in its use of trained designers to create garments targeted at a high-end market.

Fashion Design for Hand Knitting

Despite mechanization of the craft, hand knitting continues to contribute to local economies and also functions as a fast-growing leisure pursuit. Since the 1970s, fashion designers, often trained in universities and art schools, have inspired hand knitters to take a more adventurous approach to texture, color, and construction.

Mary Walker Phillips has been at the forefront of the movement to promote knitting as a fine art, publishing books on innovative stitches and experimental structures. Patricia Roberts has revolutionized the way in which the leisure practice of hand knitting is marketed. Discouraged by the poor yarn selections in stores, she began in 1974 to sell mail-order kits with patterns and yarn. In 1976, she opened a specialized yarn shop in Knightsbridge, London—the beginning of an effort to market her line internationally. The format of her high-quality fashion publications for disseminating her designs has been much emulated.

The designer knitting boom has been fed by improvements in yarn availability for home consumption. In 1978, Stephen Sheard co-founded Rowan Yarns in Yorkshire, England, which in the early 2000s remains a prominent manufacturer of natural fiber yarn in exciting color palettes. Rowan works with some of Britain's most innovative designers such as Kaffe Fassett, originally of California, whose works inspired by Oriental ceramics, kilims, and Indian miniatures demonstrate that even inexperienced knitters may achieve results of lush, glowing color.

Many designers produce for the home knitter, as well as the fashion industry. Examples include Jean Moss, a virtuoso Fair Isle designer who has worked for Laura Ashley and Ralph Lauren; Susan Duckworth, a painter whose early clients included Joseph Tricot; and Martin Kidman, a designer of clever pictorial knits who has worked for Joseph as well.

Couture and Ready-to-Wear Knits

Certain couturier knits have become design icons—for example, Chanel's jersey-knit suits and Schiaparelli's butterfly-bow trompe-l'oeil pullover. Some design houses have built their oeuvres on knitwear. Missoni, for instance, created its unmistakable striped and zigzag motifs on the family's warp-knitting machinery, previously used for producing shawls. The Benetton company created a niche producing upliftingly colored sweaters and cardigans, often in lambswool, to a mass market.

Some designers have reinterpreted classic knitting traditions. Solveig Hisdal for Oleana transforms Norwegian folk traditions. Jean Paul Gaultier often manipulates the scale of Aran motifs, while Vivienne Westwood jests with argyles and knitted lace. The design house TSE is well-known for fine-gauge intarsia.

Perhaps the most innovative approach to contemporary knitted clothing lies in its construction. Some designers retain a couturier approach to knits, such as John Galliano, who cuts and seams with aplomb. Yohji Yamamoto manipulates garment shapes, playing with reversibility and layering. Hussein Chalayan is master of the trompe-l'oeil, creating garments that deliberately deceive as to their construction. Possibly the most radical in this field is Issey Miyake, whose concept A-POC (A Piece of Cloth) combines mass manufacture with mass customization—a potential revolution for clothing manufacture. A-POC, which has been featured in museum fine art exhibitions, creates clothing modules from enormous rolls of tubular knitted fabric.

The type of technological advance that allowed A-POC has provided fertile ground for fashion designers' experimentation. The mechanization of knitting is a complex and still-evolving subject. Developments in machinery and yarn have been symbiotic; machines are now capable of knitting "yarns" of metal wire and plastic. A further step has been the utilization of processes that permit the surface manipulation of knitted textiles—processes such as heat-bonding, laminating and rubberizing, that tend to explode the boundaries between knits as utility and art.

See also **Crochet; Knitting Machinery.**

BIBLIOGRAPHY

Black, Sandy. *Knitwear in Fashion*. New York: Thames and Hudson, Inc., 2002. A well-illustrated survey of knitwear in contemporary designer fashion.

Keele, Wendy. *Poems of Color: Knitting in the Bohus Tradition*. Loveland, Colo.: Interweave Press, 1995. Explores one example of the role of hand knitting in a regional economy, and discusses a model of manufacture and distribution, in additional to providing much clearly written technical information.

Macdonald, Anne. *No Idle Hands: The Social History of American Knitting*. New York: Ballantine Books, 1988. Explores knitting as a social practice from the Colonial period to the 1980s.

Phillips, Mary Walker. *Creative Knitting: A New Art Form*. New York: Van Nostrand Reinhold Company, 1971. Influential argument for knitting as a fine art, with instructions for experimental stitches.

Rutt, Richard. *A History of Hand Knitting.* Loveland, Colo.: Interweave Press, 1987. A comprehensive history of hand knitting with particular emphasis on Britain.

Vogue Knitting. New York: Sixth and Spring Books, 2002. A definitive single source for stitches and techniques, and a good brief history.

Lindsay Shen

KNITTING MACHINERY

KNITTING MACHINERY Knitting machinery is the primary means of producing fabrics by the knitting process outside of the crafts businesses. Mechanical production of knitted fabrics began in England in the sixteenth century with the invention of the circular knitting machine by William Lee. In the 1700s knitting machines were attached to power drives moved by water or wind for the first time and the individual production of knits as a cottage industry began to decline.

The function of an automatic knitting machine is dependent on the design and function of the knitting needles the machine uses. The knitted stitches in the fabric body are identified by component rows of needles. The stitches formed along the yarn feed direction are courses. Those formed along the position of each individual needle are the wales. There are three major categories of knitting needles for automatic machines: spring beard, latch hook, and compound (or bipartite). Each of the needle types is designed so that when it is extended, it contacts a yarn on the lower, or shank, end of the needle. It is retracted to capture the yarn inside a hollow head formed by an outer hook, and forces a previously formed loop of yarn over the outer hook to hold and form a loop with the internally held yarn inside the hook head. As the needle is extended, the internal yarn slides out of the hook interior and the head of the newly formed loop relaxes so that it cannot return into the hook interior, but rather must slide along the shank and over the hook head to capture and form the next loop of yarn in the needle. With the spring beard and latch hook needles all of the actions are entirely passive and require no external activation. The compound needle is machine activated.

Machine knitted fabric types fall into two broad categories: weft knits and warp knits. Weft knits are characterized by the use of one set of feed yarns that form loops on each successive row of previously formed loops in rows that are known as "courses." They may be produced in either circular or flat form, but require no manipulation of the weft yarns other than by the knitting needles themselves.

Warp knits are fed from warp beams very similar to those mounted on looms, but they do not require the interlacing of weft yarns for fabric formation. Like weft knits, they form interloopings of yarns in courses. Unlike weft knits, they do not interloop individually with themselves but rather require outside manipulation of their paths over or under neighboring knitting needles.

Manipulation of the warp knit yarns is effected by means of needle guide bars that hold eyelet guides used for the major motions of warp knitting—the swing (front to back) and the shog (left to right). The swing and shog motions combine to produce bindings among weft knit yarns in both the wale and course directions and may be altered to produce open, long shogs, tighter, short shogs, reverse side underlaps or looser overlap loops in the structures. These knits may have inlays of yarns that are orthogonal to the warp yarns that are known as weft yarns, but they do not act like the weft yarns in a woven fabric because they are not required for the structure to hold together.

See also **Knitting; Needles.**

BIBLIOGRAPHY

Brackenbury, T. *Knitted Clothing Technology.* Cambridge, Mass.: Blackwell Scientific, 1992.

Collier, B., and P. Tortora. *Understanding Textiles.* Upper Saddle River, N.J.: Prentice-Hall Inc., 2001.

Schwartz, P., T. Rhodes, and M. Mohamed. *Fabric Forming Systems.* Park Ridge, N.J.: Noyes Publications, 1982.

Spencer, D. J. *Knitting Technology.* Oxford: Pergamon, 1989.

Howard Thomas

KNOTTING

KNOTTING Knots by themselves are any accidental or intentional entanglement of cord, braid, ribbon, beading, fabric or other material that will create a new shape or structure by forming loops, intertwining, and weaving of the base fabric. The new structure may be used to enhance or accessorize many forms of dress. Simple knots and complex knots can be created using a few simple instructions from craft books. Using cords, beading, braiding, trims, ribbons, or other appropriate flexible material, the knowledgeable designer can enhance the appearance of any simple fabric by forming knots.

Knots are made by folding or twisting the cord over and under the standing part of the original cord. The end used to form the knot is termed the working end and the other part of the cord is the standing part. Cord may be formed into bights (a 180-degree turn with no crossing), loops (a more than 180-degree turn with crossing of the standing part), or combined into more complex shapes (a knot, bend, hitch, weave, braid, or multiple loops and bights) depending on the desired look. Fabrics may be twisted into a rope prior to knotting, whereas when ribbon is used, it is typically formed flat into bows, using bights pulled through the knot instead of pulling through the ends. Beading uses knots between the beads, to ensure that they do not all fall off if the support cord is broken.

Knotting originated with prehistoric humans tying grasses and twigs, and later using sinews, into lashings used to hold together sticks and stones to make tools.

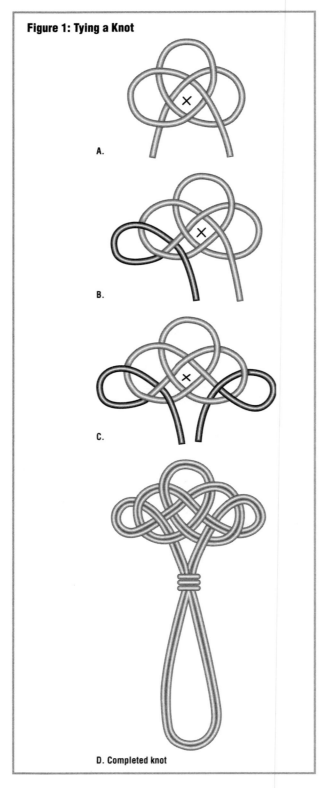

Figure 1: Tying a Knot

A.

B.

C.

D. Completed knot

Knot tying illustration. Knots can be formed by a variety of materials, from cord to beading. Both simple and more complex knots can be created by referencing instructions in craft books.

Knotting also took on survival significance in the form of knotted garments and woven fencing and roofs to keep out the cold of the Ice Age. Knotting later took on religious and political significance and appeared throughout the world as carvings in stone and wood, in the shape of magical knots and heraldry symbols.

The most well-known form of knotting is macramé. Macramé (from *miqramah* in Arabic, which means "coverlet," or *maqrama* in Turkish, which means towel), originated in the thirteenth century in what was then known as Arabia with the tying together of the cords that formed the foundation of the carpets, for which the region was already famed. Macramé work spread from there to Southern France in the fourteenth century, then fell into disuse for several more centuries, until the early part of the nineteenth century. A slightly different form of macramé was also known by sailors in the seventeenth and eighteenth centuries as McNamara's Lace, a form of pulled-thread canvas work, in which silks and ribbon were fed through in place of the weft and in which the warp threads were knotted together to form patterns of knots, after the weft threads were removed. Warp threads are those that are parallel with the salvage, the vertical edges of a fabric; weft threads are those that cross the warp threads. Sailors would weave these pieces from scraps of twine, ribbon, silk, and rope that they carried in their ditty bags, which were often highly decorated canvas bags made of macramé and McNamara's Lace combined.

Jewelry of woven gold and silver wire also produced rings, necklaces, anklets, and bracelets in adornment of simple medieval dress, while fancy knotted and braided leather belts were used to hold clothing in place, everywhere from Argentina to Canada and beyond. Knotting took on special significance in East Asian dress, where certain types of knots (usually rather elaborate ones) were considered charms capable of conferring health, wealth and well-being. Knots were used in Korea as adornments of wedding costume (*maedup*), and throughout the region as elements of Buddhist temple decorations and vestments. In Japan, special knots were used as ties to adorn gift-wrapping.

Knotting took the form of free interpretive art with the resurgence of macramé in the 1960s and again more recently with the use of macramé pieces added to enhance the look of retro fashions. European and American dress has moved beyond the look of mesh, netting, and knotted articles to a more demure and international look in knotted shoulder straps, scarves, sarongs, pareos, and sandals, imitating Grecian and South Pacific styles. The elegance of lace and tatting also has not been lost to another age, but has seen recent moves to reintroduce these fine woven and knotted fabrics to enhance or highlight evening dress necklines and cuffs. Knots used in the early 2000s include the overhand knot, the Carrick bend, plaiting and braiding, the sheet bend, and the square knot. Knotting's simplicity and its intrigue add a touch of mys-

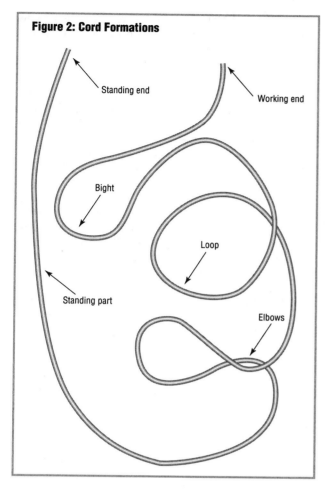

Figure 2: Cord Formations

Standing end

Working end

Bight

Loop

Standing part

Elbows

Cord formations. Cord can use several forms to create knots, including bights (180° turn, no crossing), loops (more than 180° turn, crossing the standing part), and multiple loops, as well as more complex shapes.

tery and insouciance to a wide variety of forms of modern dress, and accessories.

See also **Braiding; Weaving.**

BIBLIOGRAPHY

L'art des noeuds maedup: Tradition de la parure coréenne dans l'oeuvre de Mme. Kim Hee-Jin. Espace Pierre Cardin, Paris, 10–30 April 1986.

Ashley, Clifford W. *The Ashley Book of Knots.* 1st ed. Garden City, N.Y.: Doubleday, 1944.

Budworth, Geoffrey. *The Ultimate Encyclopedia of Knots and Rope Work.* 1st ed. London: Anness Publishing Limited, 1999.

Graumont, Raoul, and John Hensel. *Encyclopedia of Knots and Fancy Rope Work.* 2nd ed. Centreville, Md.: Cornell Maritime Press, 1939.

Lammer, Jutta. *The Reinhold Book of Needlecraft.* New York: Van Nostrand Reinhold, 1973.

Rainey, Sarita R. *Fiber Expressions.* Worcester, Mass.: Davis Publications, 1979.

Walkley, Victor. *Celtic Daily Life.* Rowayton, Conn.: Dovetail Books, 1997.

Lindsey Philpott

KOREAN DRESS AND ADORNMENT The dress of the Korean people reflects the breadth and depth of their experiences and has resulted in a continuously evolving amalgamation that includes Korean traditions as well as borrowed elements. In the twentieth century, both North and South Korean societies have experienced immense change as a result of the Korean War and the division into South and North Korea. South Korea has experienced rapid industrialization, modernization, and population shifts from rural to urban areas. Provoked by invasions and foreign occupation, South Koreans forged a strong national identity.

During its thirty-five-year annexation, Japan attempted to assimilate the Korean people into the Japanese mainstream and destroy the Korean national identity. Freed from Japanese rule and distanced from their own heritage by almost two generations of occupation, South Korea embraced the culture of their new ally, the United States, following the Korean War, to the extent that any historical customs or ideas contrary to Western culture were seen as old-fashioned and out-of-date, and the traditional culture became the subordinate one. Modernization became the goal, but new values were not securely grafted to those of the traditional. Therefore, while modernization succeeded as an economic and manufacturing goal, it failed as the basis on which to create a new national identity.

In the 1970s, South Koreans realized the necessity of rediscovering their traditional culture to create a unified and identifiable future for their country. Since then, Koreans have been more aware of their traditional values and the symbols that reflect them. They have worked diligently to redefine and reinvent their traditions.

Hobsbawm uses the term "invented tradition" to include both traditions actually invented, constructed, and instituted formally, as well as those emerging in a less traceable manner, but nonetheless establishing themselves within a brief time period. Inventing traditions is a process of formalization and ritualization characterized by reference to the past. "Invented tradition" is defined as "a set of practices, normally governed by overtly or tacitly accepted rules and of a ritual or symbolic nature," which seek to affirm certain values and norms of behavior by repetition, and automatically imply continuity with the past (Hobsbawm and Ranger, p. 1). In a society such as Korea's, with so many rapid changes taking place, tradition had become a necessity to provide a sense of integration and unity for individuals.

Korean women in traditional dress. While the retention of traditional dress is seen as important to their culture, many Koreans are not averse to the addition of contemporary elements. © ROBERT HOLMES/CORBIS. REPRODUCED BY PERMISSION.

Korean traditional dress helps Koreans define their traditional values, such as philosophy, religious attitude, and family relationships. But Koreans have not felt a contradiction in the coexistence of traditional values while adopting those of foreign cultures or searching through their own culture for new ways to express their past. The expressed need is to maintain a culture suitable to the Korean circumstance while continuing the rediscovery and rearrangement of the traditional culture. The valuing of tradition is considered not just sentimental but a necessary aspect of Korean culture.

Traditional dress has become a blend from both traditional Korean history and Western elements, and its form and definition are ever changing, but in an evolutionary process. This helps to interpret and enrich the statement of Linnekin that culture is passed on with each generation creatively adding to its construction.

Traditional Dress Defined

The term Koreans use for traditional dress is *hanbok*, which means "dress of our race," while *yangbok* is used to refer to Western dress. These two categories are worn in Korea simultaneously. Though both *hanbok* and *yangbok* have influenced each other, they appear distinct from each other in Korean society.

Korean forms of traditional dress for females and males contain many similarities. When stored flat, the parts are basic rectangular shapes, such as the full skirt of the female and the trouser of the male. The prescribed direction and manner of fastening of the parts of the *hanbok* are very specific. Fabric textures are similar and may be a smooth linen or cotton for everyday and silk or silk-like fabric for ceremony and special events.

Female *hanbok* consists of two main pieces: the full, floor-length skirt, or *chima*, which covers the lower torso and legs, and the *chogori*, which covers the upper torso. The *chima*, made of three widths of fabric gathered onto a two-and-a-half-inch-wide band, wraps tightly around the body directly under the arms and fastens just above the breasts. The middle skirt panel is placed at the center front of the body and wrapped around to overlap and open on the back left side. The tie band is brought around and secured with a front knot to fasten the skirt. The skirt is fitted to the body at the chest area, and the gathers curve from the chest and then fall to the floor.

The *chogori*, worn on the upper torso, has a V-neck and is asymmetrical, with an overlap to tie on the wearer's right side. The sleeve is a rectangular shape but with a slight curve on the underarm. The neckband, referred to as the *git*, began as a rectangle but has evolved to a curved line. The *dongjung* is a white detachable neckband made of stiff cardboard and wrapped in fabric. It is basted onto the neckband, making it both decorative and easy to replace when soiled. The *otgoreum* is a tie band that closes the *chogori* and, when fastened with a one-sided bow, results in a vertical asymmetric line that trails and extends onto the *chima*. The *norigae* is a hanging ornament, carefully selected as an accessory that attaches to the tie band. It often consists of beads, tassel, or fringe that swings freely when attached to the skirt band and *otgoreum*. A long coat, or *turumagi*, is worn over the *chogori* and *chima* in cold weather.

Traditionally the hair is arranged by pulling it back from the face, and secured in a low knot or chignon for married women or a braid for unmarried women. The resulting small, neat head shape is considered an appropriate and pleasing proportion in contrast with the voluminous skirt. A headdress, once an important aspect of traditional dress, is no longer worn. On the feet are worn padded white socks, referred to as *beoseon*. The padding provides a modified curve that relates to the gentle curves of the rest of the costume. The slipper shoe, *komusin*, is worn over the padded sock and repeats the gentle curve. Historically made of braided rice straw or silk, by the early twenty-first century the slipper was composed of rubber or leather.

Male traditional dress consists of two parts, *paji*, the trousers, and a top, *chogori*. The trousers are cut and sewn

Korean family in the early twentieth century. Korean involvement in several world conflicts helped foster a strong national identity, and traditional dress became an important factor in society. © CORBIS. REPRODUCED BY PERMISSION.

from rectangular and triangular shapes. They can be folded flat for storage but are shaped on the body by folding to the right side and fastened with a separate fabric tie. The man's *chogori*, while similar to that of the woman, is longer, with a wider neckband and shorter ribbon tie. It fastens on the right and has a V-shaped neckline, with a curved neckband and white, stiff detachable band similar to the one worn by the female. A vest of contrasting color is worn over the *chogori*, then a jacket over the vest to complete the ensemble. The vest and jacket are often of the same color, but contrast with the color of the *chogori*. A *turumagi* of dark or subdued color is worn outdoors, and a muffler added in cold weather.

Young males and females wear shapes similar to their adult counterparts, but the fabrics used are more intense primary colors and warmer in hue, such as yellow and red. Another age-based difference is seen on a young child who, for a special event such as a first birthday, wears a *chogori* with rainbow stripes on the sleeves.

Traditional colors in Korea are primary ones such as red and blue, but muted in intensity. In contrast to the West, white is the color of mourning, though it is also used for trimming the neck of the *chogori*. Traditional wedding costume is brightly colored, with red for the bride and blue for the groom.

The adoption of certain colors, such as fuchsia or hot pink, resulted from an interaction with Western culture. When Elsa Schiaparelli introduced the color in the 1930s, Koreans discovered that hot pink was flattering to their physical coloring, and thus hot pink was adopted for engagement garb of both young men and women. By the early 2000s, the use of hot pink had come to symbolize the special celebration of the engaged couple.

Some colors are traditionally worn by the elderly or by the married woman with a child, and therefore those colors have become recognized as reflecting the individual wearer and his or her respective status. The use of a color may be identified with a particular year because of

Elderly Korean man. Traditional dress in the twenty-first century is more frequently worn by older Koreans, who see it as a symbol of their heritage and value system. AP/WIDE WORLD PHOTOS. REPRODUCED BY PERMISSION.

its popularity. To be valued, Korean traditional dress must be constant in silhouette and details of layout, but have up-to-date colors and design motifs.

Intricately embroidered panels and motifs used on the elaborate wedding attire of the bride and groom are symbolic of Korean history. For example, the phoenix, a mythical bird, may be combined with clouds, animals such as tigers and deer, or recognizable flower patterns, such as the chrysanthemum. Motifs may become symbolic of cultural values such as long life, or happiness. Many of these motifs originated in China but now have been thoroughly assimilated into Korean culture. Many traditional motifs embedded in Korean history and that were worn by royalty in the past have been adopted by the modern bride or groom and worn as a part of the wedding ceremony. Many ornaments have traditionally been designed to ward off the evil eye. For example, vials of perfume or certain colors have been worn to deflect attention of the evil eye, thus acting to protect the wearer in a symbolic way.

The Role of Korean Traditional Dress
An observer walking on the streets of Seoul, South Korea, would discover that normal everyday dress is Western, or *yangbok*. There are a few differences when compared to Western dress of other cultures, especially a greater adherence to formality in the appearance of the Korean people. Both men and women in professional positions wear a coordinated suit ensemble, and men adhere to the dark formal business suit, white shirt, and tie for work. Also, because of the physical coloring of the Korean people, certain favorite colors, such as muted golds, browns, and blacks, are often worn. Because the average Korean is small-boned and between five-foot-three and five-foot-seven in height, fit is especially important in the sizing and scale of clothing.

The role of traditional dress in modern Korean society is primarily that of celebration and ritual, with traditional dress most often worn for special occasions such as birthdays, weddings, and other significant events. To serve in a celebratory manner, Korean traditional dress needed to be removed from daily use, as suggested by Hobsbawm. With its use for everyday seen as impractical and not conducive to modern life, historic Korean dress went from being a daily convention to a symbol of the traditional values of the Korean people. For those who continue to wear Korean traditional dress, such as a Buddhist monk or a waitress in a Korean folk restaurant, such modifications make it more wearable for daily use, such as shortening the skirt to ankle length or using washable and durable fabrics. However, some Koreans object to the modifications of traditional dress. Perhaps a modified Korean traditional dress doesn't function as well for celebration because it is more practical and thus loses some of that special celebratory quality.

Traditional dress is a sign and a symbol of Korean culture. To maintain its respected stature within Korean society, some changes in the formal properties of Korean traditional dress are permitted to evolve continuously and yet be perceptible to the informed eye. Shades and hues used for traditional dress may change, but these are not viewed as drastic alterations. Korea's history itself provides much of the justification for change.

Slight variations in detailing and coloration seem to be acceptable in Korean traditional dress, while changes in the silhouette are not so prevalent. The silhouette, shapes, and proportion of the *chogori* and *chima* are what make Korean traditional dress recognizable to Koreans. The neckband and asymmetrical tie are details that remain more fixed. Color is a characteristic that identifies Korean traditional dress with specific events and with an individual's selections. For example, pink is for an engagement dress and blue is a good choice for the mature woman. The use of color identification and change in some detailing does not alter the salient characteristics of silhouette, providing a clue to historical continuity and acceptance.

In Korea, traditional dress is worn to express the country's heritage and values. Korean females place importance upon their traditional dress and appearance and appreciate its symbolic nature. As in many cultures, women are usually the purveyors of culture, the arts, and traditions. The use of Korean traditional dress by females as a source of celebration is indicative of gender difference in upholding cultural traditions. Korean women wear traditional dress to show their love for their country and pride in its unique heritage. Korean males wear traditional dress more sparingly in celebration of life events, such as for a first birthday, weddings, or a sixtieth birthday.

An examination of the role historical dress plays in Korean society can illuminate those aspects that make for traditional character. To instill pride and continuity with the past, the traditional garments need to be perceived as stable, even though changes in color and surface motif do persist. Korean traditional dress changes in subtle ways, yet quite regularly, and thus is accorded a fashionable aspect. When questioned, Korean women will express the need to change their traditional dress every three to five years to keep it fashionable. However, this fashion is not determined by the United States, Paris, London, or Milan, but prescribed by Korean dressmakers and scholars of Korean traditional dress. Designers are constantly working on historic renditions of Korean traditional dress that help to interpret the past and then seem to trickle down from a couture house to being more widely available through a dressmaker or department store.

Perceptions of Korean traditional dress are a function of country of residence and age. For example, Koreans living in America have a somewhat different perspective about traditional dress than Koreans living in Korea. Age is a factor in defining perceptions of Korean traditional dress. The younger person is more accepting of modified forms and variety in wearing. These perceptions highlight the amount of change that had occurred in the late 1990s and early 2000s. However, changes in traditional practices of Koreans who live in both the United States and Korea do not seem to signify a lack of respect for traditional habits, but rather, a change in lifestyle.

Peoples of other countries use forms of traditional dress derived from their past that similarly communicate their unique history and culture. In a country where traditional and Westernized components can coexist within the same objects of tradition, its people can draw upon the influence of both. The resiliency of the Korean people has enabled a unique national character to remain paramount, while foreign elements simultaneously become deeply fused to a strong cultural base.

Present Uses of Korean Traditional Dress
Korean traditional dress has been an enduring aspect of Korean culture, historically worn every day by men, women, and children. While it is not unusual to see the elderly man or woman in traditional dress on a daily basis, the younger man or woman restricts its use to more special occasions, and unmarried youths may not wear it at all. While most men rarely dress in traditional garb, the practice of wearing it is far more prevalent for Korean women; still, evidence exists that conventions and routines are changing based upon age and other cultural ties such as marital, economic, or maternal status. With its use primarily restricted to ceremonial occasions, Korean traditional dress is still surrounded by rules of etiquette: who should wear what, how to wear it, and when it should be worn.

Certain occupations require traditional dress for everyday wear, but usually as a symbolic gesture. Those who represent the Korean culture to foreign countries often wear traditional dress. The wife of the president, flight attendants, and even the elevator operator in an international hotel in Seoul may wear traditional dress as a symbol of their country's characteristic dignity and grace.

While traditional dress remains a valued part of Korea's history, to be highly valued it also must appear fashionable. Although traditional dress by definition would seem to demand invariance, in Korea, traditional dress changes quite regularly—but in subtle ways—and is thus accorded a fashionable aspect.

See also **Ethnic Dress; Ethnic Style in Fashion.**

BIBLIOGRAPHY
Cho, Kyu-Hwa. *Aesthetics of Costume.* Seoul: Soohack Sa., 1986.
Covell, Jon Carter. *Korea's Cultural Roots* 3d ed. Salt Lake City: Moth House Publications, 1982.
DeLong, Marilyn. *The Way We Look: A Framework for Visual Analysis of Dress.* New York: Fairchild, 1998.
DeLong, Marilyn, and Key Sook Geum. "A Systematic Analysis of the Aesthetic Experience of Korean Traditional Dress." In *ITAA Special Publication Number 7.* Edited by Marilyn R. DeLong and Ann Marie Fiore. Monument, Colo.: International Textile and Apparel Association, 1994.
Geum, Key Sook. "A Study of the Korean Aesthetic Consciousness through the Choson Costume." Ph.D. diss. Ehwa Women's University, Seoul, 1988.

Geum, Key Sook, and Marilyn DeLong. "Korean Traditional Dress as an Expression of Heritage." *Dress* 19, no. 5 (1992): 57–68.

Hobsbawm, Eric, and Terence Ranger, eds. *The Invention of Tradition.* New York: Cambridge University Press, 1983.

Huh, Dong-Hwa. *Crafts of the Inner Court.* Seoul: The Museum of Korean Embroidery, 1987.

Il-sung, Park, et al. *The Identity of the Korean People.* Seoul: Research Center for Peace and Unification, 1983.

In, Dong-Hwan. *A Study on the Korean Folklore.* Seoul: Dongmyoung-moon-wha Sa., 1973.

Kahng, Hewon, and AeRan Koh. "Effect of Design Modification and Color Scheme on Impression Formation of Traditional Korean Women's Clothing." *Journal of the Korean Society of Clothing and Textiles* 15, no. 2 (1991): 211–227.

Kim, Jin-Goo. "Korean Costume: An Historical Analysis." Ph.D. diss., University of Wisconsin, 1977.

Linnekin, Jocelyn. "On the Theory and Politics of Cultural Construction in the Pacific." *Oceania* 62, no. 4 (June 1992): 249–263.

Morse, Ronald A., ed. *Wild Asters: Explorations in Korean Thought, Culture and Society.* Washington, D.C.: Asia Program, Woodrow Wilson International Center for Scholars; New York: University Press of America, 1987.

Park, Kyoung-ja, and Soon-Young Im. *Korean Clothing Construction.* Seoul: Soohack Sa, 1981.

Suk, Joo-Sun. *The History of Korean Costume.* Seoul: Bojinjae, 1971.

Marilyn Revell DeLong and Key Sook Geum

LABELING LAWS

LABELING LAWS For thousands of years, people only had natural fibers to care for and use. But with the explosion of manufactured fibers, blends, and finishes after World War II came confusion. Manufacturers gave their own products trade names that meant very little to consumers. A real need for more information was provided in the form of a series of labeling laws.

Ruling on the Weighting of Silk

In its natural state, silk has a gummy feel, and it is usual practice to remove the gum. In so doing, however, the weight of the silk is greatly reduced. To counter that loss, in the late nineteenth century, manufacturers began the weighting of silk to counteract the weight lost by degumming raw silk. Silk was subjected to metallic salts, which could be absorbed in quantities greater than the weight of the silk itself. While the immediate result was a fabric with a heavier hand, the long-term effect was to create a fabric that tended to split into shreds. Since the consumer had no way of discerning this, the U.S. Federal Trade Commission (FTC) ruled in 1938 that silk weighted more than 10 percent and black silk weighted more than 15 percent must be labeled *Weighted Silk* While this ruling remained in effect in the early twenty-first century, few silk items were weighted by then.

Wool Products Labeling Act

According to this act, most products that contain any amount of wool must be labeled by the name of the wool source and percentage weight, even if it is less than 5 percent. They must distinguish between wool (also known as "virgin wool" and "new wool") and recycled wool, wool from a textile product that has been returned to a fibrous state and remade into a different product. The manufacturer's name or number registered with the FTC must be on the label as well as (since 1984) the country of origin.

Some products, such as hats and slippers that contain some wool, must be labeled under this labeling act even though they are exempt under the Textile Fiber Products Identification Act (TFPIA). The following items, when made of wool, are exempt from the provisions of this act: carpets, rugs, mats (though these are covered by the TFPIA), upholsteries, and wool products destined for export.

In the early days of this act, the FTC assigned Wool Products Labeling (WPL) numbers to particular manufacturers or retailers of wool. Since each company would retain its number forever and some manufacturers have changed their products' fiber content from wool to such nonwool fiber as polyester, some nonwool products have a WPL number.

Fur Products Labeling Act

Fur fibers that have been removed from the animal's skin are subject to the rules set forth in the Wool Products Labeling Act and the TFPIA. Labeling of fur fibers attached to the skin is regulated by the Fur Products Labeling Act. The labels must contain the animal's species and may include the adjective form of the country (such as *Russian Mink* or *Canadian Fisher*). Labels must also provide the name or registered number (RN or WPL) of the manufacturer, importer, or other distributor. The country of origin must be given. If the fur has been colored, pointed, or bleached, the label must state this. If the fur has not been so treated, it should be labeled as *Natural.*

Flammable Fabrics Act

The original act banned the use of highly flammable materials for clothing. In 1967, the law was amended to include highly flammable household textiles. Further amendments have banned the use of all flammable materials for carpets, draperies, mattresses, upholstery, and children's sleepwear (sizes 0–14). Standards for each of these products may be found on the Web site of the Federal Trade Commission (www.ftc.gov).

Textile Fiber Products Identification Act

The TFPIA requires that the name of the fibers (natural, such as cotton, or the generic name for manufactured fibers, such as nylon) be listed in descending order by percent weight of the total. If fibers are present in quantities of less than 5 percent, they should be listed as other fiber(s). If several fibers constitute less than 5 percent each, they should be combined and listed as other fibers, even if their combined total is greater than 5 percent. Two exceptions exist: because of the Wool Products Labeling Act, all products containing wool must be listed, even if the percentage is less than 5 percent. Also, those products that provide a definite functional property in amounts of less than 5 percent may be listed as such without explaining what the functional significance is. Small amounts of spandex lend a good deal of stretch to a garment, for example.

Pile fabrics can list fibers by total weight only. However, if a label lists fibers as *100% nylon pile, 100% cotton back*, the label must also add the fibers by weight: *60% cotton, 40% nylon;* in other words, the back is 60 percent of the fabric and the pile is 40 percent. Those fibers composed of two or more chemically distinct fibers must be listed as biconstituent or multiconstituent.

The manufacturer's name or registered identification number (RN or WPL) must be given. Consumers can find out the name of the company by going to the FTC Web site (www.ftc.gov), clicking on Business Guidance, and then RN Lookup Service.

The country of origin must be listed. Products made entirely in the United States of materials from the United States must be labeled *Made in USA*. Products made in the United States of imported materials must be labeled as such: *Made in USA of Imported Fabric*. The country name for imported items must be written in English, but may be written in additional languages as well. The country of origin information must always be on the front of the label.

All of the required fiber information may be put on one tag or several as long as the information is legible, conspicuous, and accessible to the consumer. All content information must be in the same size print. Other extraneous information may be included on the fiber label as long as it is not misleading to the consumer.

Care Labeling Rule

The Care Labeling Rule of 1972 set down very specific requirements for manufacturers and importers to follow. In 1984, the rule was amended to provide a Glossary of Standard Terms. In 1999, the American Society for Testing and Materials developed care symbols intended to be understandable around the world, despite language differences. In 2000, the Care Labeling Rule was amended again. In the early 2000s the rule requires that care instruction apply to the entire garment.

According to the Care Labeling Rule, textile clothing and piece goods (fabric sold to home sewers) must carry a care label outlining safe cleaning procedures. In the case of clothing, a care label should be sewn into the garment and be easily viewed at the time of purchase. It should remain legible for the lifetime of the garment. For completely reversible garments with no pockets and for other garments where a label would ruin their appearance (such as a sheer blouse), care information may be put on a hang tag. For clothing sold to institutions such as hospitals, no label is needed, but care instructions must be given to the institution at the time of purchase. Textiles that can be cleaned safely in several ways are re-

quired to list only one method. For items that can be cleaned by the harshest methods, the label should read, *Wash or Dry Clean, Any Normal Method*. This means that the item could safely be machine-washed in hot water, bleached with any bleach, tumble-dried hot, and ironed at a hot setting. It also means that the item could be dry-cleaned using any solvent. For items that cannot be safely cleaned by any means, the label should read, *Do Not Wash—Do Not Dry Clean*.

Washing instructions include five elements, outlined below:

Washing. The label must say if hand-washing or machine-washing is recommended. Also, unless the product can be washed in hot water, a temperature must be specified.

Bleaching. If any available bleach can be used without harm, the label need not mention bleach. If chlorine bleach would damage the product, the label must say, *Only Non-Chlorine Bleach, When Needed*.

Drying. The label must indicate how the product should be dried: tumble dry, dry flat, or drip dry. If the product cannot be machine-dried at the hottest setting, then the proper temperature must be stated.

Ironing. Ironing information is required if ironing will be needed on a regular basis. If ironing cannot be done at the hottest setting, a proper temperature must be specified.

Warnings. Special warnings must be given if a consumer might reasonably use a care procedure that would result in damage. A delicate garment suitable for hand-washing might need a *Do Not Wring* warning. Products that might damage other items washed with them might need warnings such as *Wash Separately* or *Wash with Like Colors*. Warnings do not need to be used for alternative care procedures. If the label reads, *Machine Wash Cold*, it need not use the warning *Do Not Wash in Hot Water*.

If garments can be safely dry cleaned with any solvent and there are no special conditions that require warnings, then the label may say, *Dry Clean Only*. These garments can be put in a dry-cleaning machine by the consumer at a Laundromat or given to a professional dry cleaner. When a warning is needed, it should be stated after the words *Professionally Dry Clean*. For example, if steam would cause damage, the label should read, *Professionally Dry Clean—No Steam*.

See also **Dry Cleaning; Fibers; Fur; Silk; Wool.**

BIBLIOGRAPHY
Collier, Billie J., and Phyllis G. Tortora. *Understanding Textiles.* 6th ed. Upper Saddle River, N.J.: Prentice-Hall, 2000.
Humphries, Mary. *Fabric Reference.* 3rd edition. Upper Saddle River, N.J.: Prentice Hall, Pearson Education, 2004.

Internet Resources

"Care Labeling of Textile Wearing Apparel and Certain Piece Goods, as Amended, Effective September 1, 2000." U.S.

Federal Trade Commission. Available from
<http://ftc.gov/os/statutes/textile/carelbl.htm>.

"Clothes Captioning: Complying with the Care Labeling
Rule." U.S. Federal Trade Commission. Available from
<http://www.ftc.gov/bcp/conline/pubs/buspubs/
comclean.htm>.

"Threading Your Way through the Labeling Requirements
under the Textile and Wool Acts." U.S. Federal Trade
Commission. Available from <http://www.ftc.gov/bcp/
conline/pubs/buspubs/thread.htm>.

Elizabeth D. Lowe

LABOR UNIONS Clothing industry workers, severely exploited during most of the nineteenth century in countries at the forefront of the industrial revolution (such as Great Britain, France, Germany, and the United States), made powerful efforts to form effective trade unions during the latter part of the century. The initial stages of unionization saw the creation of numerous separate unions, which tended then to go through a process of amalgamation in order to increase membership and bargaining power. This process can be seen very clearly in the case of Great Britain, for example, where by the beginning of the twentieth century, clothing workers' unions included the Amalgamated Society of Journeymen Tailors, the Amalgamated Union of Clothiers' Operatives, the Amalgamated Jewish Tailors, Pressers and Machinists' Trade Union, the London Clothiers Cutters, the Shirt, Jacket and Overall Workers, and the Belfast Shirt and Collar Workers. These joined together to form the United Garment Workers' Union (UGWU) in 1912. The UGWU subsequently added other unions, including the Scottish National Association of Operative Tailors, the London Operative Tailors, and the Amalgamated Society of Tailors and Tailoresses. With the merger in 1931 of the UGWU with the United Ladies Tailors (London) and the Waterproof Garment Workers Union, the amalgamated union changed its name to the National Union of Tailors and Garment Workers. In the United States, The United Garment Workers of America (UGWA) was organized in 1891, incorporating several earlier independent unions; the more radical Amalgamated Garment Workers Union (AGWU) broke away from the UGWA in 1914. The International Ladies Garment Workers Union was founded in 1900. Textile workers, less concentrated in urban areas, were slower to unionize; the Textile Workers Union of America was organized in 1939, and later merged with the AGWU. Similar processes of organization and amalgamation marked the history of garment and textile workers unions in the countries of Western Europe.

Once a potent force in the textile and apparel industries, labor unions have been on the decline in the post–World War II period in many parts of the world, including Central and Eastern Europe, Central America, the United States, and Europe. Among the reasons for this decline are employer resistance or anti-unionism, the increasing power of multinational corporations, inadequate statutory protection for unions and union organizing in developing countries, and the inadequacy of unions to respond quickly and efficiently to labor issues. The long-term history of the garment and textile industries has been for production to move from high-wage to low-wage (which usually means from union to nonunion) countries, or regions within countries; this poses a severe challenge to labor unions in the field.

Globalization of textile and apparel production along with the dislocation of workers from industrialized countries to developing countries have meant that unions have had to reach across national boundaries to create linkages among workers for this sector. For example, members of the Union of Needletrades, Industrial and Textile Employees (UNITE) have worked through its International Trade Secretariat to organize workers and to address basic worker rights and working conditions in Central America and the Caribbean.

Internationalization of the labor movement is not a new phenomenon; it began in the late nineteenth century in Europe. Stimulated by the economic and political conditions of various countries, such as industrial growth, increased international trade, and more competitive world markets, workers in industrialized nations became apprehensive about working conditions in developing countries and sought "to establish minimum labor standards by international agreement" (Lorwin, p. xii).

The demand for international labor standards after World War I resulted in the establishment of the International Labour Organization (ILO) in 1919 under the League of Nations. The ILO became a specialized agency in the United Nations in 1946. Through a series of conventions and recommendations, labor standards to be attained worldwide were set forth by this organization. In 1998, the ILO organized a tripartite meeting for government, employer, and worker representatives to exchange views on labor practices in the textile, apparel, and footwear industries. Its report addresses labor issues concerning workers' rights to freedom of association and collective bargaining, the elimination of child labor and forced or compulsory labor, and the end of gender discrimination with respect to employment and occupation. The representatives engaged in a social dialogue about these issues.

International Labor Organizations

ICFTU. The International Confederation of Free Trade Union's regional organizational affiliates are found in Asia and the Pacific (APRO–Asia-Pacific Regional Organization), Africa (AFRO–African Regional Organization), and the Americas (ORIT–Inter-American Regional Workers' Organization). They act as channels of communication and maintain linkages with the European Trade Union Confederation and the Global Union Federation, of which the

International Textile, Garment, and Leather Workers Federation (ITGLWF) is one of ten members.

It brings together more than 200 affiliate organizations in more than 100 countries. Affiliates include UNITE in the United States and Canada, KFAT—the National Union of Knitwear, Footwear and Apparel Trades in the United Kingdom, and the BTGLWF—Bangladesh Textile, Garment and Leather Workers Federation.

Operating as an integral part of the ITGWLF are its regional organizations in Africa, Asia, Europe, and the Americas. The issues that are addressed with its regional organizations and affiliates include: (1) the elimination of forced and child labor; (2) the promotion of occupational health and safety standards; (3) the participation of women in worker-employer dialogues, especially home workers in the informal sector as well as workers in the export processing zones in different countries; and (4) the encouragement of social responsibility by multinational manufacturers, merchandisers, and retailers. It works closely with the ICFTU, the ITSs, and nongovernmental organizations (NGOs).

UNITE Formed
In 1995, the International Ladies Garment Workers Union and the Amalgamated Clothing and Textile Workers Union merged to form the Union of Needletrades, Industrial and Textile Employees (UNITE) in the United States. They joined forces to provide strength for collective bargaining and a voice concerning domestic and international labor issues. Since its inception, UNITE has been involved with: (1) initiating "Stop Sweatshop" campaigns to bring attention to working conditions in New York, California, and South America; (2) assisting university students in forming United Students Against Sweatshops—an organization to keep universities from selling garments made under sweatshop conditions; (3) demanding that labor standards be enforced in global trade agreements with developing countries during trade talks; (4) challenging retailers to improve working conditions and observe workers' rights in factories making their clothes; and (5) promoting the visibility of the "Made in the USA" label to help retain textile and apparel jobs in America. These and other activities help UNITE to fulfill its goals; that is, to bring workers together, to protect members' work contracts, to prepare a workers' agenda or a list of things to be accomplished, and advocate against sweatshops, nationally and internationally. In Canada, UNITE has more than 25,000 members and has called attention to its sweatshops and home workers which mostly employ women workers.

Summary
Garment and textile workers unions have responded to changing economic, social, and political conditions throughout the world by emphasizing international organization and cooperation. The issues that led to the formation of strong garment and textile workers unions in the industrialized world of the nineteenth century remain important throughout the world, and can only be addressed on an international level and with reference to the international labor standards promulgated and upheld by the ILO. In addition, NGOs, such as the Clean Clothes Campaign, the National Labor Committee, and the Women Workers Worldwide, have been established to draw further attention to labor issues worldwide. Unions face continuing challenges to organize industrial workers in developing countries, and to reach into informal sectors of production in many parts of the world, sectors in which women's and child labor continue to be exploited.

See also **Globalization; Sweatshops.**

BIBLIOGRAPHY

Clete, Daniel. *Culture of Misfortune: An Interpretive History of Textile Unionism in the United States.* Ithaca, N.Y., and London: Cornell University Press, 2001.

Gordon, Michael E., and Lowell Turner, eds. *Transnational Cooperation among Labor Unions.* Ithaca, N.Y., and London: Cornell University Press, 2000.

Lorwin, Lewis L. *The International Labor Movement: History, Policies, Outlook.* New York: Harper, 1953.

Nissen, Bruce, ed. *Unions in a Globalized Environment: Changing Borders, Organizational Boundaries, and Social Roles.* Armonk, N.Y., and London: M. E. Sharpe, 2002.

O'Brien, Robert. "Workers and world order: The tentative transformation of the international union movement." *Review of International Studies* 26 (2000): 533–555.

Windmuller, John P. *International Trade Secretariats: The Industrial Trade Union International.* Foreign Labor Trends Report. Washington, D.C: U.S. Department of Labor, Bureau of International Labor affairs, 1995.

Internet Resources

International Labour Office. *Business and Social Initiatives Database, 1996–2003.* Available from <http://www.oracle02.ilo.org/dyn/basi/upisearch.first?p_lang=en>.

———. *Codes of Conduct and Multinational Enterprises.* Available from <http://www.ilo.org/public/english/region/eurpro/london/download/fp3_4.pdf>.

———. *Labour Practices in the Footwear, Leather, Textiles and Clothing Industries.* Report for discussion at the Tripartite Meeting. Geneva: International Labour Organization. Available from <http://www.ilo.org/public/English/dialogue/sector/techmeet/tmlfi00/tmlfir.htm>.

International Textile, Garment and Leather Workers' Federation. *About the ITGLWF.* Available from <http://www.itglwf.org/displaydocument.asp?DocType=Background&Index=110&Language=EN>.

———. *ITGLWF Affiliates.* Available from <http://www.itglwf.org/displaydocument.asp?DocType=Background&Index=68>.

UNITE: A New Union With a Long History. Available from <http://www.uniteunion.org/research/history/unionisborn.html>.

United Nations Association of the United States of America. *Internet Resources: Worker Rights in the Global Economy, 1999–2000*. Available from <http://www.unausa.org/links/gpp99link.asp>.

Gloria M. Williams

LACE Lace has played a role in fashionable dress ever since it was developed in the sixteenth century. Loosely defined, lace can be any nonwoven, light, openwork fabric, but in historical terms it was created using two tools: the needle and the bobbin. Both techniques were time-consuming and required great skill. As a consequence, lace was extremely expensive. During the seventeenth and eighteenth centuries, when lace became an essential element of fashionable dress, the European courts spent great sums of money to acquire the finest examples. Because of this demand, new techniques were continually developed to make lace production less costly and time consuming. Unfortunately, when machine lace finally came into production in the nineteenth century, lace lost its allure and it developed into just another fashion fabric, often used in lingerie, bridal wear, and evening wear.

Needle and Bobbin Lace Origins

Before needle and bobbin lace developed in the sixteenth century, the term lace referred to the cords that laced sep-

Lace flounce. This lace piece was created using the needle and bobbin technique developed in the sixteenth century. Though this method produced lovely, unique garments, it was extremely difficult and time intensive. SECTION OF A BOBBIN-MADE LACE FLOUNCE. BRUSSELS, 1760S. LINEN. COOPER-HEWITT, NATIONAL DESIGN MUSEUM, SMITHSONIAN INSTITUTION. GIFT OF RICHARD GREENLEAF IN MEMORY OF HIS MOTHER, ADELINE EMMA GREENLEAF, 1950-121-45.

Model wearing lace dress and cape. While handmade lace continued to be produced in the twentieth century, machine lace was more widely available, and several famous designers of the period began to use it in their collections. © CONDÉ NAST ARCHIVE/ CORBIS. REPRODUCED BY PERMISSION.

arate parts of a garment together, such as the sleeves to the shoulders, or to close the back of a bodice. The cords were made in a variety of methods, including the use of bobbins to braid the threads. The term also referred to braided tapes of metallic thread that often trimmed military uniforms. This use of the word "lace" in this context continued into the eighteenth century, when it also described the woven bands that trimmed servant's livery and the furnishings found in coaches and other vehicles.

During the sixteenth century, the term "lace" found another meaning when it came to refer to bobbin-made insertions that were becoming increasingly fashionable for trimming the undergarments and household furnishings of the wealthy merchants and aristocrats of the renaissance. An insertion was a narrow band that seamed together two pieces of a garment. Like the cords or laces mentioned above, the insertions were placed between the shoulders and the sleeves, and at the shoulder seams. The bobbin technique was adapted to make these narrow flat bands with delicate openwork designs. While linen was often used to make the bobbin lace insertions, colored silk and gold- and silver-metallic thread were also employed.

Embroiderers also adapted their techniques to create insertions. Needle lace, which had its origins in cutwork, an embroidery technique in which a small square of cloth was cut away and the resulting hole filled with a structure created with needle fillings, or buttonhole stitches, became a popular technique for creating insertions. These insertions, constructed in between the grid left after square sections of the base cloth were cut away, had designs with snowflake delicacy and were referred to as *reticella* or *rosette*. *Reticella* insertions were often stitched between the seams of household furnishings, such as table covers, as well as linen undergarments that were becoming an increasingly important component of fashionable dress. *Reticella* and other forms of cutwork also stood alone or were worked into shirts and shifts, creating the elaborate cuffs, collars, and ruffs seen in portraits of the Elizabethans and their European counterparts. As fashions changed during the last decades of the sixteenth century, the rigid geometry of cutwork was replaced with more free-flowing designs. These were first created by cutting larger squares out of the base cloth and later by developing a new method of creating a base structure to hold the buttonhole stitches in place. Instead of cutting squares out of a ground cloth, narrow tapes or thread were laid on a pre-drawn pattern, and buttonhole stitches were then used to fill in the spaces between the tapes or thread, and thus true needle lace was born.

Lace as Fashion Essential

As bobbin lace, cutwork, and needle laces became more sophisticated, they developed into essential fashion accessories. During the late sixteenth and two succeeding centuries, lace collars, cuffs, borders, ruffles, and headdresses were *de rigueur* for anyone with fashionable pretensions. While most European nations developed some form of lace industry, the two most important early centers were Venice and Flanders.

Venice developed into one of the first great lace centers during the sixteenth and early seventeenth centuries. Free-flowing designs based on delicate floral vines became popular and were inspired by the textiles and other decorative arts of the countries with whom Venice traded, such as Turkey and China. The second important area for the lace trade was Flanders, where an important linen embroidery trade existed during the sixteenth century. The Flemish supplied small linen and metallic bobbin lace edgings, needle lace edgings, and cutwork, along with embroidered linens. By the seventeenth century, the Flemish became well known for their light, delicate bobbin laces.

Both the Venetian needle laces and the developing Flemish bobbin laces were well suited to new fashions of the seventeenth century that favored flat band collars instead of standing ruffs. Fashionable dress also began to feature softer, lighter fabrics, such as satins and taffetas, as opposed to the heavy velvets of the previous century. Dark colors predominated and provided a suitable surface on which to display the increasingly refined bobbin and needle laces.

In seventeenth-century France, lace became extremely important among Louis XIV's courtiers and, because of France's fashion dominance, thus all the courts of Europe. Courtiers wore flat band collars of heavy Venetian lace that showed off beautifully against the lavish fabrics then in fashion. French courtiers spent huge sums of money, most of which left France for Italy and Flanders, to prepare for obligatory visits to Versailles. Eventually Louis and his finance minister, Colbert, despaired of the large sums of money being spent on foreign lace, and they established a lace industry in France. They brought lace makers from Flanders and Italy to France and settled them in select towns including Sedans, Argentan, Valenciennes, and Alençon. These towns developed distinct styles of lace that are still identified by the names of the towns in which they were made.

By the end of the seventeenth century, fashion again impacted the lace industries as a preference grew for lighter, airier laces. The thicker needle laces of Venice went out of fashion and the bobbin laces of Flanders and the new French centers began to take prominence. One of the reasons for this change was the increasing importance of ruffles that were used to decorate the shirtfronts and cuffs of men's clothing and the skirt fronts, necklines, petticoats, headdresses, and sleeves of women's dress. Complete lace ensembles were made at extraordinary cost and worn by the elite of Europe into the eighteenth century. The 1764 probate inventory of Mme. de Pompadour, mistress of Louis XV, lists many lace accessories, including a set of Argentan-needle lace accessories for a *robe de chambre* that included dress trimmings, sleeve ruffles, stomacher, neck ruffles, and a cap. The set was valued at 3,000 French pounds, more than a set of seven buttons set with yellow diamonds and rubies that was valued at 2,600 French pounds.

Lace remained an important fashion accessory throughout the eighteenth century, although by the last quarter, designs had begun to simplify and lace with simple net grounds patterned with small floral vines became particularly fashionable. This simplification in the design of lace occurred at the same time that changes in consumerism and technology impacted the fashion and textile trades. Increasing numbers of people aspired to fashionable dress and acquired the means to afford it. This increase in demand coupled with the simplification of design led to the exploration of techniques of production to bring down the cost and the time involved in its manufacture. Along with the development of new machines to spin yarns and weave fabrics, those at the forefront of the industrial revolution experimented with ways to create machine-made nets and laces.

While lace remained a luxury good, available to few men and women before the late eighteenth century, its subsequent history is one of expansion throughout the social classes and an increasing identification with femininity. As men's clothing moved away from the colorful fabrics and luxurious accessories of the previous centuries and democratized with the development of the three-piece wool suit, lace, ribbons, and trims became the purview of women's fashion. Lace developed into a purely feminine fabric that, because of advances in technology, became widely used in lingerie, evening wear, and as accessories. The invention of machine techniques, the increasing development of new hand techniques by which to create lacelike fabrics, such as embroidered nets, crochet, and tape lace, and decreasing expectations among consumers led to lace and lacelike fabrics' widespread availability. Fine laces continued to be made, especially in Brussels, where needle, bobbin, and combination laces and lace accessories were produced. Centers in France were also celebrated for their lace, especially Chantilly, which became famous for its fine black bobbin lace accessories, such as shawls, fan leaves, and parasol covers.

Despite the continued production of handmade laces, the real story of nineteenth-century lace is the development of fine machine laces that could compete with the handmade ones. The first lace machines, developed during the eighteenth century, actually produced fine net, which was then hand-embroidered to resemble lace. It was not until the early nineteenth century, when the jacquard was attached to the net machines, that patterns became possible. Improvements to the earliest lace machines, such as the Pusher and Leavers machines, continued throughout the century. Soon machine lace could compete with some of the finest handmade laces, and lace became available to almost anyone interested in wearing it.

By the middle of the nineteenth century, when lace became a standard fashion element and no longer a lux-

ury good, a renewed interest in historic laces began. Those who could afford to started to collect historic laces and put together large collections of examples dating from the sixteenth through the eighteenth centuries. Some, like Mrs. J. Pierpont Morgan, would use their historic laces to trim their Worth gowns and would have stood out from their peers who were wearing mechanically produced laces. Other women restyled historic laces and made them into collars, cuffs, and other fashionable nineteenth-century accessories.

The interest in historic laces at the end of the nineteenth century also led to a revival of handmade lace. Italy, in particular, became a center for training young girls in needle and bobbin techniques. Schools such as Amelia Ars and the Burano Lace School taught young women to reproduce many designs from the past, especially the Renaissance. Their work was so good, that it continues to fool collectors in the early 2000s.

Lace in the Twentieth Century

Craftspeople and artists continued to make lace into the twentieth century. It was taught at art schools in Austria, Germany, Denmark, and Czechoslovakia, where designs followed the then current early-twentieth-century art movements, such as Wiener Werkstaette and the German Secession. By the middle of the twentieth century, artists began to explore the artistic potential of lace, and large hanging sculptures and hangings were made.

While artists and craftspeople continue to explore handmade lace techniques, the twentieth century is the time in which machine lace emerged as a true fashion fabric. Machine lace borders made with the Raschel, Leavers, and Pusher machines were incorporated into many fashionable dresses of the first three decades of the twentieth century. Floral and geometric designs were most common. However, novelty laces also became popular. Clowns, Greek maidens, and even one of Columbus's sailing vessels (used to commemorate the 400th anniversary of his voyage to the Americas) were incorporated into lace designs and could be found trimming women's skirts, bodices, and lingerie. During the 1920s and 1930s bolts of machine lace were produced and became a fashionable fabric out of which designers such as Gabrielle Chanel began to construct luxurious evening dresses. Lace continued to be used as a fashion fabric throughout the twentieth century, enjoying popularity during the 1950s, and again in the 1980s.

Lace continues to enjoy a place in fashionable dress and especially in lingerie. Its light, delicate, feminine qualities make it a fashion perennial, even into the twenty-first century, when the September 2003 issue of *Harper's Bazaar* proclaimed lace "fashion's most romantic fabric" (p. 364) and dedicated the fashion spread to current designs exploiting its seductive potential.

See also **Embroidery; Lingerie.**

BIBLIOGRAPHY

Levey, Santina. *Lace: A History*. London: Victoria and Albert Museum and W. S. Maney and Son, 1883.

Levey, Santina, and Milton Sonday. "Contact, Crossover, Continuity: The Emergence and Development of the Two Basic Lace Techniques." In *Contact, Crossover, Continuity: Proceedings of the Fourth Biennial Symposium of the Textile Society of America*. Earleville, Md.: Textile Society of America, 1994.

Pfannschmidt, Ernst-Eric. *Twentieth-Century Lace*. New York: Charles Scribner's Sons, 1975.

Sonday, Milton. *Lace in the Collection of the Cooper-Hewitt Museum*. New York: Cooper-Hewitt Museum, 1982.

Pamela A. Parmal

LACROIX, CHRISTIAN The creations of Christian Lacroix embody in spectacular combinations his Provençal roots, his passion for folklore, and his fascination with the history of clothing. His artfully unexpected mixtures express a new form of luxury, simultaneously youthful, baroque, and sophisticated. Lacroix mingles bright tones and extravagant materials in creations that express a refined blending of different cultures; distant and forgotten costumes form the basis, if not the raison d'être, for his work.

Christian Marie Marc Lacroix was born in 1951 in Arles, France. In early childhood Lacroix showed a flair for design by putting together little albums on theater and opera, collages assembling family portraits, and reproductions by Christian Bérard. He left his native Arles to study the history of art in Montpellier, and then enrolled at the Sorbonne in Paris in 1973. He wrote a master's thesis on French costume in the paintings of the seventeenth century while at the same time taking courses at the École du Louvre to become a museum curator. It was at this time that he met his future wife, Françoise Rosensthiel; they married in 1974.

With the encouragement of his wife, he soon turned to fashion design. In 1978 he joined Hermès, where he learned the technical aspects of the profession. Two years later he was an assistant to Guy Paulin and then succeeded Roy Gonzales as a designer for Jean Patou in 1981. In 1986 he received the Golden Thimble award for dresses designed in honor of his native region of Camargue. In December 1986 Lacroix met Bernard Arnault, chief executive officer of the multinational luxury firm Louis Vuitton Moët Hennessy (LVMH), who offered him the financial support needed to open his own couture house.

The Christian Lacroix house was inaugurated in 1987 at 73, rue du Faubourg Saint-Honoré in Paris. On 26 July 1987 Lacroix presented his first collection under his own name, and that year the Council of Fashion Designers of America awarded him the prize for Most Influential Foreign Designer. Inspired by dresses in the style of the 1880s, he designed an off-the-shoulder dress

Model in Christian Lacroix ensemble. Lacroix's creations were full of whimsy and opulence, and they often featured his trademark pouf. © JULIO DONOSO/CORBIS SYGMA. REPRODUCED BY PERMISSION.

with a high waist, the miniskirt of which became the emblematic "pouf." Completed by a short bolero jacket, the ensemble was cut in highly colored and decorative fabrics inspired by Provence. Folk and traditional elements were set off by a certain French grandeur, coquettishness, and whimsy that reflected the desires of a new generation hungry for luxury. Lacroix's style thus confirmed the taste for a typically southern opulence, instilling new life into French haute couture, which had been stigmatized as a dying art. *France Soir* described Christian Lacroix as the "Messiah," and *Time* featured him on its cover. In 1988 the profession awarded him a second Golden Thimble. The dream collapsed with the stock market crash. The pouf soon became a metaphor for the excesses of the 1980s, which gave way to the minimalism of the 1990s.

In his designs, Lacroix nevertheless remained faithful to his roots and his history in a clothing collection where east meets west, the north basks in the southern sun, and the past blends with the future. The 1980s had allowed him to define and focus these influences, and over the years he continued to quote from and vary his sources of inspiration, as he developed and refined them.

Lacroix also carried on using a glittering palette of colors. "Colors I have always liked, so much so that when

I was a child, I dreamed of swallowing tubes of yellow and vermilion paint," he said (de Bure, p. 129). His designs became more abstract and the dresses more simplified, their architecture more apparent. Previously, the decoration had been designed before the dress; now it came into play only after the dress had been constructed. "In reality, I love only what veers off course, has a defect, is heterogeneous, transitory," he said. "I think I love everything and its opposite. That is probably the key" (du Bure, p. 130).

Lacroix has turned his fashion world into a stage, designing for more than twenty ballets, operas, and plays. In 1996 he was awarded the Molière for best costume design for the Comédie Française production of *Phèdre*. In 2000 he signed a new contract with LVMH, the owner of his couture house. He divides his time between his responsibilities as artistic director of this couture house and his own company, XCLX. The list of his projects is long and varied and his commissions ever more spectacular. Among his extravagant designs are eight carriages of the TGV Méditerranée (a high-speed French train), which he "dressed" and presented as haute couture creations. "This is what now interests me: going beyond fashion to participate in ways of living, in our global environment, with uniforms [for Air France], seats for the TGV, stage costumes. Each of these areas—clothing, theater, design … helps me to express a facet of my personality" (Brébant, p. 61). Spectacle is inherent to his vision: "The Lacroix woman is staged in a theatrical fashion. She is not afraid of being noticed; for her one can imagine nothing that is bland (Alessandrini, p. 22).

In 2002 Lacroix was named artistic director of the Florence ready-to-wear house Emilio Pucci. That year he was awarded the medal of Chevalier of the Légion d'Honneur. Lacroix describes French haute couture as "eternally dying and paradoxically constantly being reborn from its ashes" (Sausson, p. 6). A great defender of couture, Lacroix does not conceive of it as an art but rather as a service rendered to his clientele: "Art is something made for love. Art is what makes life more beautiful. Something that motivates and inspires. My work has a purpose; it is not just made for the sake of it" (Lowthorpe, p. 14). His creations, brought into being by a wide range of craftsmen, knitters, corsetieres, painters, and embroiderers, overwhelm and plunge the spectator into a world located between dream and reality, where fantastic textures rival embroidered materials in elegance, where fluid fabrics wedded to richly colored costumes speak in a flamboyant vocabulary signed Christian Lacroix.

See also **Art and Fashion; Ballet Costume; Haute Couture; Paris Fashion; Pucci, Emilio; Theatrical Costume.**

BIBLIOGRAPHY

Alessandrini, Marjorie. "Christian Lacroix: La mode est un théâtre." *Le nouvel observateur*. 12–18 July 2001, p. 22.

Brébant, Frédéric. "Christian Lacroix relance la Puccicmania." *Weekend le Vif/L'Express*, 28 February 2003, p. 61.

de Bure, Gilles. "Christian Lacroix, l'homme qui comble." *Technikart* 28 (December 1998): 129.

Lowthorpe, Rebecca. "Christian Lacroix." *Independent on Sunday*, 1 July 2001.

Sausson, Damien. "Christian Lacroix, au-delà de la beauté." *L'œil*, September 2000, p. 6.

Pamela Golbin

LAGERFELD, KARL Karl Lagerfeld was born on 10 September 1938 to a wealthy family in Hamburg, Germany. He moved to Paris in 1952 and first came to the attention of the fashion world two years later when he won a competition prize for his design of a woolen coat. In 1954 he was hired as a design assistant by Pierre Balmain, one of the premier couture houses of the early postwar period. In 1958 he parted ways with Balmain and became art director at the House of Patou, where he remained until 1962. For most of the next fifteen years he designed for a number of companies and under a variety of contractual and freelance agreements.

He was associated especially with Chloë (1963–1983), where he created styles that simultaneously were elegant and focused on the young. Many of his most striking designs for Chloë had an art deco flavor, being very streamlined and body conscious. He also utilized prints to excellent effect. At the same time, he worked as a freelance designer for Krizia, Valentino, Ballantyne, and other companies. Beginning in 1965 he designed furs for Fendi. His ability to design simultaneously for several different houses has been a defining characteristic of his career; Lagerfeld became known as a man who was never content to do just one thing at a time.

In 1975 Lagerfeld formed his own company and in 1983 became artistic director of the House of Chanel. While continuing his responsibilities at Chanel and at Fendi, he formed Karl Lagerfeld S.A. and KL to market his own ready-to-wear lines. Karl Lagerfeld S.A. was acquired by Dunhill (the parent company of Chloë) in 1992, and Lagerfeld returned to Chloë at that time and held the post of chief designer until 1997, when he was replaced by Stella McCartney. When he left Chloë, he regained control of the company bearing his own name; in the early 2000s Lagerfeld was designing for Karl Lagerfeld/KL, Chanel, and Fendi. He has also designed costumes for many films and theatrical productions.

Lagerfeld probably is most admired for his work at Chanel, where in 1982–1983 he took over responsibility for a company that had become somnolent, if not moribund, and very quickly made it exciting again. Taking the basic vocabulary established by Coco Chanel, he modernized it, introducing new materials, including denim, and exaggerating such details as the "double C" logo. Remarkably, his work for Chanel has remained as vital in the twenty-first century as it was in the mid-1980s.

Karl Lagerfeld has had a wide-ranging career in the arts, achieving considerable success as a writer and photographer. Over the years he has produced many fashion photography spreads for his collections at Chanel and for his own labels and has published several books of his photographs. He also is well known as an aesthete and connoisseur of art and antiques. In 2000 he sold part of his antique furniture and art collection at auction for more than $20 million. With his signature silver-white hair and newly slim figure, he is a familiar and iconic presence on the European fashion scene.

See also **Balmain, Pierre; Chanel, Gabrielle (Coco); Paris Fashion; Patou, Jean.**

BIBLIOGRAPHY

Buxbaum, Gerda, ed. *Icons of Fashion: The Twentieth Century.* New York: Prestel, 1999.

Lagerfeld, Karl. *Karl Lagerfeld: Off the Record.* Göttingen, Germany: Steidl, 1994.

———. *Dreams.* New York: Te Neues, 2002.

Milbank, Caroline Rennolds. *Couture: The Great Designers.* New York: Stewart, Tabori, and Chang, 1985.

John S. Major

LANG, HELMUT Helmut Lang (1956–) was born on 10 March 1956 in Vienna, Austria. When he was three years old, his parents divorced; he then lived with his grandfather, who worked as a shoemaker in a village near Salzburg. Lang first took commercial courses at a local trade academy before he switched over to fashion design. Lang opened his first studio in 1977, when he was twenty-one years old, and designed T-shirts and jackets. He soon started to specialize in avant-garde fashion; by the mid-1980s, his women's ready-to-wear collections had become well known in his home country. He launched his first catwalk show in Paris in 1986, nine years after the opening of his first atelier. His minimalist approach was labeled as deconstructionist and avant-garde. In 1987 he also began to design men's wear, and promoted an essentially pure urban style. After Lang's success in Paris, he divided his time between his design studio in Vienna and his consulting agency in Paris. Lang was appointed professor of fashion design at Vienna's Universität für Angewandte Kunst, a college-level institution for the applied arts, in 1993.

Lang's core brand was the Helmut Lang Men's and Women's Collections. The brand was extended in 1995 with the addition of Helmut Lang underwear and shoes, followed by Helmut Lang jeans in the following year, as well as Helmut Lang protective eyewear and accessories. The designer achieved a high level of recognition through these extensions of his brand. He moved to New York in 1998 in order to get an international reputation in the fashion world and entered into a collaborative relationship with the Italian luxury brand Prada in 2000. Lang also launched his first perfumes in 2000.

Lang's minimalist approach was also apparent in his marketing strategy. The best example was the appearance of his Internet web page in the early 2000s. At first glance, a visitor might have thought that the designer's web domain was under construction. The page was almost completely empty; several small links provided access to his current ready-to-wear collections for women and men, accessories lines, store information, press images, and perfumes. Lang's marketing created a set of futuristic images. For example, his web page for women's perfumes featured a series of distinctive phrases in large capital letters that scrolled rapidly past the visitor's eyes: I walk in—I see you—I watch you—I scan you—I wait for you—I tease you—I breathe you—I smell you on my skin. His advertising was also minimal, with simple product shots that appeared surprisingly clean and therefore remarkable. Lang tried to make the reader "breathe" the fashionable quality in his advertising. The caption for an advertising campaign for Helmut Lang Eyewear read, "To promote an intellectual and fearless appearance," showing a "mug shot" of a model's face. While other brands put the designer himself in the foreground to promote collections, Lang avoided attracting attention to himself. When Lang was asked in an interview what his label represented, he replied, "It says Helmut Lang on it. Everything I know is in it." His catwalk shows were presented in a clean, urban minimalist style. In fact, his 1998 collection was shown only over the Internet instead of being displayed in a physical setting.

Claire Wilcox's introduction to *Radical Fashion* described Helmut Lang clothing at its simplest, as defined by a sophisticated interpretation of utilitarian wear. His clothes certainly resembled a uniform for urban living in the early twenty-first century. Lang had a preference for combining unusual materials: he blended cheap materials with expensive fabric, recycled fabrics with high technology. The fabric combinations varied from shiny to matte; they were often a mixture of natural fibers and synthetics. Lang sprayed silver and black varnish on denim in his 2000 collection, transforming basic utility into futuristic objects. His designs did not appear loud, but clearly reflected an androgynous style. A clinical look resulted from a mixture of deconstructionist and classicist forms that united contradictory elements. In "Imagining Fashion," Alistair O'Neill suggested that Lang's work could be understood as an attempt to liberate repressed attributes by concealing them under the supposedly unreadable surface of clothing. O'Neill took the advertising "Man in a Polyester Suit" as an example of Lang's suggestion that the surface of clothing is unreadable. O'Neill suggested that the phallic quality of the image reverberated in subsequent Lang campaigns, but it was the tension between the standard exterior and spectacular interior that came to the fore.

Although the era of minimalist fashion design ended in the early twenty-first century, Helmut Lang still used minimalist codes in his designs. His androgynous approach to fashion mirrored the clear distinctions between male and female dress in traditional clothing. Lang was stereotyped as the "King of Fashion Minimalism." It is true that the concept was as important to him as the clothes themselves. This concept was also reflected in his color palette, which mixed noncolors with flashy shades to produce a futuristic effect.

See also **Brands and Labels; Fashion Advertising; Fashion Marketing and Merchandising; Jeans; Unisex Clothing.**

BIBLIOGRAPHY

O'Neill, Alistair. "Imagining Fashion—Helmut Lang and Maison Martin Margiela." In *Radical Fashion*. Edited by Claire Wilcox. London: V & A Publications, 2001.

Wilcox, Claire. *Radical Fashion*. London: V & A Publications, 2001.

Internet Resource

Helmut Lang Website. 2004. Available from <http://www .helmutlang.com>.

Thomas Hecht

LANVIN, JEANNE Jeanne Lanvin (1867–1946) was born in Paris, France, and spent much of her youth as a seamstress and millinery apprentice. In 1883 she was employed to trim hats in the workshop of Madame Felix at 15, rue du Faubourg Saint-Honoré. Lanvin established her own millinery workshop at the age of eighteen in 1885. With just forty francs in cash and three hundred francs in credit, Madame Lanvin opened her millinery house in a modest apartment at 16, rue Boissy-d'Anglas in 1889.

Lanvin married the Italian aristocrat Emilio di Pietro in 1895. Although their marriage was brief, ending in 1903, the union produced a single child, Marguerite Marie-Blanche, who was born in 1897. This child inspired and supported one of the greatest design careers of the twentieth century. In 1907 Lanvin married Xavier Melet, a journalist. Lanvin's daughter married for the second time in 1925; her husband was the comte Jean de Polignac, and she became known as Marie-Blanche, comtesse de Polignac.

History of the House

In 1908 Lanvin opened a children's clothing department in the millinery shop, inspired by the wardrobe created for her own daughter, and just one year later she opened departments for ladies and girls as well. Becoming a full-fledged *couturière*, she joined the Syndicat de la Couture, the ruling body of the haute-couture industry. Her first dress designs followed the lines of the chemise frock, a long, slender, empire-waist design that offered ease of movement. By 1910, a mere two years after opening her children's department, her designs appeared in *Les modes*, a French fashion periodical.

By 1925 twenty-three ateliers operating under the Lanvin name employed up to eight hundred people. That year, branches of Lanvin were opened in Cannes and Le Touquet. Through the years the house continued to grow, with several other boutiques opening in foreign locales: In 1927 alone, additional shops were opened in Deauville, Biarritz, Barcelona, and Buenos Aires. Lanvin created departments for menswear, furs, and lingerie in 1926 and then launched several successful fragrance lines, including Arpège (1927), Scandal (1933), and Rumeur (1934).

When Jeanne Lavin died in 1946, her daughter, Marie-Blanche, became the chairman and managing director of Lanvin and Lanvin parfums; she remained at the helm of the businesses until her death in 1958.

In 1950 Marie-Blanche invited Antonio Canovas del Castillo to design the haute-couture collection. This position passed to Jules-François Crahay in 1963; to Maryll Lanvin, the wife of Jeanne Lanvin's nephew, in 1985; and, finally, to Claude Montana in 1990. He presented five haute-couture collections, two of which won the Golden Thimble Award from the Chambre Syndicale de la haute couture parisienne. By 1993 the House of Lanvin had withdrawn from haute couture to concentrate on their image as a luxury goods house.

The design career of Madame Lanvin survived sixty-one successful and productive years. Lanvin is the oldest surviving couture house in continuous existence, from 1909 to 1993. In the early 2000s, Lanvin continues to focus on ladies' ready-to-wear clothes and luxury accessories. Collections for men and made-to-measure sportswear are also produced. Fragrance remains part of the Lanvin offerings, releasing Oxygene to the masses. L'Oreal, the parent company, sold Lanvin to an unidentified Chinese owner in 2001 who focused on finding a designer who could put a modern edge on the historic, antiquated company; among designers employed during this period were Ocimar Versal Oto and Christine Ortiz. In 2003, Alber Elbaz began designing the luxury collection and has been making considerable progress in reviving the Lanvin name, gaining a more youthful clientele of models and celebrities.

Social Life

For the sole purpose of advertisement and publicity, Madame Lanvin employed the innovative technique of dressing the highly social demimondaines and actresses. Informally modeling the latest creations of the couture house, they created great interest among the social set. Demimondaines were a less respectable group of women who had lost their social standing—although they were highly social and extremely fashionable—due to sexual promiscuity or other ethically questionable activities (such as prostitution). Their male companions gave them the money to buy the finest fashions and accessories; in fact, demimondaines were notably the most fashionable women in town.

Jeanne Lanvin et sa fille, 1907. This photograph was the inspiration for the Lanvin insignia. PATRIMOINE LANVIN, DROITS RÉSERVÉS. RE-PRODUCED BY PERMISSION.

> "The longevity of this couture house may be attributed to the untiring force and determination of a woman driven by the relentless need to create, succeed, and excel within her chosen field among many worthy, predominantly male, contemporaries."
>
> *Dean L. Merceron*

Unlike her successful contemporaries, Madame Lanvin shunned the spotlight. She avoided large social settings, preferring her small, creative circle of artists, musicians, designers, and writers. On rare occasions Madame Lanvin could be seen at horse races for the sole purpose of research. Her attendance at these events enabled her to see what women were wearing, what looked good and what did not, how fabrics moved, how silhouettes looked, what was cumbersome, and what was ridiculous. In addition, by observing what the women were wearing, she could deduce what they would next be desiring to add to their wardrobes. Lanvin downplayed her image and personality, maintained a discreet background position, and rarely socialized with her clients. These habits contributed to her anonymity in the years following her death.

Inspiration
The originality of Lanvin garments, constructed in such a masterly fashion, lay in their surface detail and embellishment. Madame Lanvin extracted inspiration from various objects to be translated into viable, modern, functional design. For example, her signature color, "Lanvin blue," was inspired by the fifteenth-century Italian frescoes of Fra Angelico. Her desire to create the perfect colors for her designs prompted her to establish her own dye factories in Nanterre in 1923. This shrewd move ensured the originality and exclusivity of her colors, and, indeed, competitors who tried could never successfully duplicate them.

The beading and embroidery patterns on her designs were inspired by various exotic elements and destinations. Lanvin was an avid traveler and methodical collector of objects from various cultures around the globe; they later served as a personal library of inspiration.

Versatility
The House of Lanvin was a fashion leader and innovator in the 1920s, utilizing extraordinary beading techniques; and in the 1930s, with technically innovative surface treatment ensuring the singularity of her creations. Versatility contributed to the longevity of the couture house, as the Lanvin image was clearly defined and redefined from season to season. Marie-Blanche was her mother's muse and lent her youthful perspective to the designer's creative ideas. Consequently, the House of Lanvin forever maintained its image of youth, femininity, and beauty.

Clientele
Lanvin women typically began their association with the house as debutantes and maintained their loyalty through their weddings, motherhood, and widowhood. The youthful silhouette of the *robe de style*, synonymous with Lanvin, experienced great success, as it was offered in every collection. It flattered every figure at every age for all occasions. The *robe de style* was inspired by eighteenth-century fashions and consisted of a quasi two-dimensional silhouette created by the use of a pannier, or basket-like structure on either hip. This silhouette achieved great success during the 1920s as an option to the slender, cylindrical silhouettes promoted by other couturiers.

Madame Lanvin successfully combined romanticism and historicism in the most modern way. "Modern clothes need a certain romantic feel," she remarked (*Vogue*, 1 June 1942, p. 66). The youthful, elongated torso and romantic full skirts created a large surface that served as a canvas for any tasteful combination of beading, embroidery, or appliqué.

While the success of the vast Lanvin empire was a substantial accomplishment in itself, Madame Lanvin applied her skills to other creative areas as well. Pooling her talents with Armand Albert Rateau, a great French architect, in 1922, she completed several interior design projects, including her own homes, shops, and the Théâtre Daunou. She also opened her first interior decoration store, Lanvin Décoration. In addition, she shouldered the enormous responsibility of organizing and executing the couture exhibits at many of the great world expositions. For these efforts she was created chevalier of the Légion d'honneur on 9 January 1926. In 1938 Madame Lanvin was made an Officier of the Légion d'honneur.

Lanvin's legacy to the world of fashion is youth, beauty, and feminity—modernity softened with romance; beautiful colors in feminine silhouettes that blur the lines of age. The *robe de style* was a dress that could be worn literally by everyone. Lanvin was primarily an artist, and a businessperson second. She was guided by her artistic sensibility and supported by her fair sense of business and strong work ethic. She was an innovator and a leader, working for the industry as a whole, not just for the house of Lanvin. As one who "had it all," she was a role model for women: She started her own business, married, and had a child. Even as a single mother, she continued to run her empire and raised her daughter to be an inspirational success.

See also **Color in Dress; Dyeing; Twentieth-Century Fashion.**

BIBLIOGRAPHY

Barillé, Élisabeth. *Lanvin.* London: Thames and Hudson, Inc., 1997.

Picon, Jérôme. *Jeanne Lanvin.* Paris: Flammarion, 2002.

Vial, Franck Olivier, and François Rateau. *Armand Albert Rateau: Un baroque chez les modernes.* Paris: Éditions de L'Amateur, 1992.

Dean L. Merceron

LATIN AMERICAN FASHION Latin American dress and fashion refers to the dress, body, and culture of a large and heterogeneous world culture region that includes Mexico, Central America, the Caribbean, and South America. Given that the nature of dress in Latin America is highly diversified, one can look to overlapping socio-historical influences that have shaped the pursuit of elegance and transformed the dynamics of everyday life to elucidate some general characteristics.

When Christopher Columbus claimed the islands of Cuba as well as the Dominican Republic and Haiti for Spain in 1492, he initiated the conquest of the indigenous populations living in the region that came to be known as Latin America and the Caribbean. The first images and accounts of American natives that circulated throughout Europe reveal much about a sense of awe experienced by the first colonizers. They view the natives' nakedness with bewilderment and marvel at the presence of material goods such as cotton cloth, intricate feather work, and weavings. This "New World" would provide Europe with material goods as varied as silver, gold, sugar, chocolate, textiles, and dye. Portugal, involved in its own push for colonial power, would successfully challenge Spain for the region that makes up the country of Brazil. As Spain and Portugal quickly established colonial governments, the native populations suffered the effects of brutal conquest, incurable disease, and forced conversion to Christianity. Friar Bartolomé de Las Casas harshly condemned the exploitative practices of conquistadors and settlers who had turned to slavery and other forms of systematic violence to establish ranches, mines, and textile industries.

To maintain a sense of hierarchy and respond to increasing *mestizaje*, or racial mixing, a caste system was established throughout the region. Prior to colonization, dress and textiles had often served as indicators of social and religious identity and as a medium of exchange. The caste system forced natives and African slaves to wear Western styles of dress, thereby reinforcing the authority of the Spanish and Portuguese, and over time, their Creole descendants. Some indigenous communities gave voice to their history and religious beliefs with the help of intricate color-coding systems, as found in woven textiles or compilations of strings. In this way, the *huipil* of Guatemala and the highlands of Mexico placed deities of the sun and the underworld in dialogue with the Christian faith. Still worn today, this traditional blouse component of the Mayan *traje*, or dress, reveals information about a woman's village, status, heritage, and personal beliefs. Recent excavations in Argentina and Brazil point to the African as well as Islamic origins of some pieces of jewelry found near the sites of plantations and urban mansions, suggesting that accessories may not have been censored by colonial authorities in the same way as dress. As court records indicate, one could wear almost any design provided that it was gender specific. The selection of fabric, however, was a highly serious matter. Depending on her social status, a Mexican woman of the eighteenth century would have purchased either a silk or cotton *rebozo*, or scarf. Decrees prohibited the use of certain textiles by those who the caste system deemed as inferiors, thus leading to the prohibition of velvet or taffeta for specially fashioned Incan *unku*s, or tunics, in the Andean region.

By the early nineteenth century, the region experienced several calls for independence from Spain and Portugal that deeply affected the way people consumed fashion. For Cuba and Puerto Rico, this struggle for independence would not materialize until the end of the nineteenth century, although the description of fashion and dance in several literary works began to plot the demise of Spanish rule and to construct alternate political identities. In the visual imaginary of this period, Creole leaders such as Simón Bolívar (Venezuela) and José de San Martín (Argentina) appear in wind-swept capes and uniforms of their own design. Many women found themselves called upon to sew the accessories of war, their products in view and their identities concealed. A few, among them Juana Azurduy de Padilla (Bolivia) and Josefa Tenorio (Argentina), took on male uniforms in order to fight on the battlefield, later arguing that they merited equal status in postcolonial society. Distancing themselves from the customs of Spain, fashionable women of Buenos Aires transformed the Spanish *peineta*, or hair comb, into the three-foot-by-three-foot Argentine *peinetón* in order to assert their presence and at times obstruct the very public sphere that professed independence from oppression but which, ironically, had not yet granted all the privilege of citizenship. In satirical caricatures from the period, the enlarged crests of women's combs take to downtown Buenos Aires and quickly overpower the top hats of men.

Following the retreat of Spanish colonialism, the rhetoric of fashion provided a forum for discussions on the configuration of national identity. In some cases, fashion writing allowed intellectuals to disseminate important political agendas and evade censors. In the Southern Cone region, the regime of Juan Manuel de Rosas sought to eliminate the political opposition by requiring a scarlet insignia on a *chaleco*, or men's vest, of all citizens. In a violent push toward homogeneity, a decree prohibited light blue, the identifying color of the opposition, and green, a well-known symbol of hope. In this challenging climate, socialites introduced a secret language of fans, coded inserts for top hats, and message-revealing gloves, to state what was on a wearer's mind. Appropriating metaphors from the realm of fashion, in 1837, a group of Argentine intellectuals founded a fashion magazine, entitled *La Moda* after the audacious *La Mode* that had served as a force of violent opposition in revolutionary France. Using female pseudonyms and taking advantage of the fact that few associated fashion writing with politics, these founding fathers of modern Argentina asserted their urban, democratic ideals before seeking exile in neighboring Chile and Uruguay to avoid persecution. In an exploration of the dynamics of civilization and barbarism in his native country, Domingo Faustino Sarmiento, one of *La Moda*'s founders and a future Argentinean president (1868–1874), advocated a consolidation process that shed the nation of its traditional rural values, epitomized by the lawless poncho-clad gaucho who had long upheld Rosas's power; Sarmiento's goal was for the country to embrace an urban, and therefore more "civilized," lifestyle more conducive to the government's goals for economic growth and modernization. Economic booms at the end of the nineteenth century would earn Argentina the reputation of the Paris of South America, as its cityscape stood transformed into an allusion of luxury, consumerism, and international capitalism.

With the massive influx of European immigrants to Latin American cities at the turn of the century, luxury took on a fraudulent role. Members of the nouveaux riches and new arrivals began to imitate the styles of the upper classes in order to find work, holding in high esteem the novelties of Paris. With the emergence of the fashion lithograph, *modistas*, or tailors, copied European designs (sometimes appropriating styles for the climate of a particular region) and then commissioned seamstresses who, enduring miserable working conditions, pieced garments together with the help of sewing machines. While women's dress had become a bit more flexible, it still incorporated the corset and layered skirts and trains that required bustles. As sewing machines became more affordable, many women opted to purchase readymade clothing or to fashion their own, more comfortable, styles at home. Encouraging readers to consider individualized designs and the prospect of female emancipation, Juana Manuela Gorriti (Argentina) and Clorinda Matto de Turner (Peru) used the language of fantasy and self-transformation, or fashion writing, to enter a public debate on materialism and female economic autonomy.

During the twentieth century, Latin American dress would inspire several fashions in Europe and the United States, from the blouse with lace ruffles inspired by the Afro-Cuban rumba, to the well-known Mexican *huaraches*, or woven leather sandals, to the straw Panama hat actually created in Ecuador. *Vogue* and *Look* turned attention to trendsetting Latin American women whose visions of haute couture, as in the case of Eva Perón (Argentina), and native designs, bringing to mind the surrealist painter Frida Kahlo (Mexico) who incorporated folkloric *china poblana* costume in bright colors and with a full skirt in her self-portraits and in real life, would continue to resonate in the popular imaginary until the present day. Other, more contemporary, fashion statements have tended to revisit the past for a retro effect, such as the young Cuban American donning the *guayabera*, a lightweight, embroidered cotton shirt worn untucked throughout the Caribbean; or the Chicano zoot-suiter, whose wartime appropriations of his father's suits inspired ethnic pride in the face of racism and brutality; or the teenage club kid wearing Inca-techno styles while discotheque dancing.

The latter part of the twentieth century witnessed a horrifying backlash against democratic values when countries such as Argentina, Chile, and Uruguay installed military governments. Strict gender codes imposed clean-cut looks for men and feminine styles for women. Responding to human-rights abuses and the plight of the "disappeared" (which refers to the tens of thousands of victims who were killed or whose whereabouts still remain unknown), the Mothers of the Plaza de Mayo in Argentina began to protest near important national monuments in their morning robes and house slippers, as if to state visually that they had no one at home to care for, as the regime had taken away their sons and daughters. The Mothers wear a white scarf, embroidered with the names of their missing loved ones, during their weekly marches. Serving as living monuments for the victims of repression, mother's groups in El Salvador and throughout the world have appropriated this same white scarf in their struggles against social injustice.

The revolutionary movements of Cuba (1959–) and Nicaragua (1979–1990) signaled a turn toward socialist antifashion, which associated the elitist pursuit of luxury with the kind of capitalist domination that created dependencies on foreign goods and exploited the working classes. Indeed, much of Latin America had experienced uneven economic development throughout the twentieth century. In the garment industry, multinationals relied on the cheap labor of native workers for the weaving, assembly, and sewing of garments. But in more recent years, even revolutionary Fidel Castro (Cuba) occasionally shed his camouflage for the sartorial pleasures of a dark-blue designer suit. A heightened awareness of the sweatshop conditions of the *maquiladora*, the export-processing zones established in 1960s that continue to operate under the North American Free Trade Agreement (NAFTA), sometimes led consumers to boycott specific collections and push for a more socially conscious fashion system. Some designers, such as Carlos Miele (Brazil), have worked with women of the *favelas*, or shantytowns, and various indigenous communities to establish cooperatives that will ensure fair-trade wages for their creations.

Responding to the possibilities offered by a global marketplace and Internet connections, Hispanic designers Carolina Herrera (Venezuela), Oscar de la Renta (Dominican Republic), together with Beth Sobol (United States) and Victoria Puig de Lange (Ecuador), formed the Council of Latin American Fashion Designers in 1999. An affiliated Fashion Week of the Americas established an international platform for Latin American fashion and culture. In newspapers, a new word surfaced in popular culture that combined *fashion* and the Spanish suffix *-ista* (implying, with a tinge of sarcasm, a devotee). The dress-conscious *fashionista* scoured the ever-expanding style pages of newspapers and e-zines for information about new talents like Narciso Rodríguez (United States), the famed designer of Carolyn Bessette Kennedy's bridal gown, and faced the proliferation of fashionable identities with gusto. In the urban centers of São Paulo, Buenos Aires, and Bogotá, supermodels such as Gisele Bündchen (Brazil) and Valeria Mazza (Argentina) promoted national fashion events with international appeal. At the same time, free-trade agreements between countries, such as the Mercosur block of the Southern cone region, have enabled fashion designers to create transnational organizations, such as *Identidades Latinas*, to tap into new markets. Among others, the houses of Laurencio Adot (Argentina), Alexandre Herchcovitch (Brazil), Ronaldo Fraga (Brazil), Rubén Campos (Chile), Silvia Tcherassi (Colombia), Sitka Semsch (Peru), and Angel Sánchez (Venezuela) earned strong reputations in the category of women's wear. Lina Cantillo and Ricardo Pava (both of Colombia) seemed best known for their men's collections. Fraga and Sylma Cabrera (Puerto Rico) were noted in fashion circles for their attention to children's wear. Into the twenty-first century, the reputation of Latin American fashion designers continued to rise on the world fashion stage.

See also **Latino Style.**

BIBLIOGRAPHY

Bauer, Arnold J. *Goods, Power, History: Latin America's Material Culture.* Cambridge and New York: Cambridge University Press, 2001.

Holland, Norman. "Fashioning Cuba." In *Nationalisms and Sexualities.* Edited by Andrew Parker, Mary Russo, Doris Sommer, and Patricia Yeager. New York: Routledge, 1992.

Masiello, Francine. *Between Civilization and Barbarism: Women, Nation, and Literary Culture in Modern Argentina.* Lincoln and London: University of Nebraska Press, 1992.

Meléndez, Mariselle. "La vestimenta como retórica del poder y símbolo de producción cultural en la América colonial: De Colón a El lazarillo de ciegos caminantes." *Revista de Estudios Hispánicos* 29 (1995): 411–439.

Root, Regina A. "Tailoring the Nation: Fashion Writing in Nineteenth-Century Argentina." In *Fashioning the Body Politic.* Edited by Wendy Parkins. Oxford: Berg, 2002.

———, ed. *Latin American Fashion.* Oxford: Berg, 2004.

Regina A. Root

LATINO STYLE Latinos are people of Latin American ancestry in the United States. "Latino" is a term that embraces cultural differences among Spanish-speaking people and persons with indigenous and/or African American roots with ancestry from Latin America and the Caribbean. Thus, Latino or Latina style is a collective phrase that expresses group style for a diaspora of people.

In its broadest sense, Latino style is a contemporary manner of dressing by Latinos who pay particular attention to personal, fashion, or ethnic style that sets them apart from other ethnic groups in the United States. It is difficult to specifically characterize Latino style because Latinos as a group are not homogenous. However, Latinos tend to have high fashion interest, be brand conscious and loyal, and devote a larger percentage of household income to clothing purchases than other ethnic groups.

Latino Celebrities and Magazines

A rising Latino population and an increasing number of Latino celebrities are kindling interest in Latino cultures. Selena, the Tejana songstress, is credited with sparking widespread attention to the Latino market in the 1990s. In the early 2000s, actress and singer Jennifer Lopez (J.Lo) has influenced fashion with her clothing line and personal style. Contemporary Latina celebrities reflect strong personal styles and high fashion orientation, but minimize ethnic style compared with stereotyped Latina actresses of the past, such as Carmen Miranda.

Latino celebrities, including Jimmy Smits, Antonio Banderas, Ricky Martin, and Oscar de la Hoya, exude handsome masculinity. Latino actors are often portrayed as the "Latin lover" stereotype or a power figure. Latinos reflect less risk-taking in their appearance than Latinas, but certainly a strong sense of personal style and high fashion interest are evident.

Latina style is often illustrated as sexy, fashionable, and urban in contemporary magazines such as *Latina* and *Urban Latino*, by featuring longhaired models wearing body-revealing fashion clothing and emphasizing makeup wear. Other magazines, such as *Latina Style*, portray Latinas as educated professionals who are family-oriented *and* style-conscious. There is clearly an attention to appearance by the businesswomen featured in *Latina Style* that encompasses polished hair, makeup, and clothing styles.

Fashion

Latino style and mainstream fashion have also been shaped by noncelebrities, such as working-class Latinos. For example, in the 1980s, *cholas*, female gang members, began wearing a distinct dark lip liner and lighter lipstick that became a popular mainstream fashion.

A new phenomenon is the growth of Internet sites and product lines devoted to Latino style. Patria, a fashion house in New York City, offers fusion fashion inspired by the Latino experience. The Havanera Co. is a "Latin inspired brand" by Perry Ellis International.

CHICA, INC.

Founded by Helen Martinez, a Latina and a University of Southern California graduate, Chica, Inc. clothing company (www.chica1.com), targets Latinas from ages twelve to forty. Chica consumers are characterized as having ethnic pride, being self-assured, and connecting with the Spanish language. The company advertises its T-shirts as "having attitude." Presently, Chica clothing is sold in high-volume department stores, such as Macy's and Mervyn's.

Zalia Cosmetics promotes makeup for Latinas, and Web sites sell Latino-inspired merchandise. Increasingly, Latino youth act as fashion trendsetters, sporting branded clothing, and fueling fashion. In fact, this bicultural Latino population is becoming known as the "J.Lo generation." Moreover, institutions are highlighting Latino fashion contributions to the larger United States society.

The *Quinceañera*

Particular manifestations of Latino dress include special-occasion dress, costume for performance, unique day wear, and group dress. A *quinceañera* is a celebration for young girls of fifteen as an initiation into adulthood. With origins in pre-Columbian cultures, *quinceañeras* have spread to many Latino cultures and religions. The celebration often includes a mass followed by a reception. The *quinceañera* wears an elaborate floor-length ball gown of white, cream, or a pastel color. The ensemble can include a train, headpiece, gloves, high-heeled shoes, and elaborate hair and makeup. The celebrant is accompanied by a similarly dressed female court and male attendants wearing tuxedos.

Mariachi

Another familiar dress is that of mariachi, the "uniform" of musicians who perform a specific type of Mexican folk music. The contemporary ensemble was borrowed from the elegant suits worn by *charros* (Mexican horsemen) and gentlemen ranchers that include a close-fitting short jacket, close-fitting pants, shirt, belt with large, ornate belt buckle, wide bow-tie, boots, and sombrero. The sombrero, jacket, and pants are elegantly embroidered and may include extensive silver ornamentation.

Guayabera

A guayabera is a men's shirt style that signals Latin American heritage and is worn by men of all ages. Originating in Cuba, the guayabera is the quintessential shirt worn in hot climates. Made of lightweight fabrics, it is usually white, cream, or pastel colored, and is worn untucked. The guayabera is distinguished by its vertical rows of pin tucks or embroideries on the front and back, four symmetrical pockets, straight hem, and side vents.

Pachuco Style

In the twentieth century, group style emerged among Latino youth. The "pachucos" of the 1940s surfaced in the barrios of Los Angeles and the southwest. Pachucos were recognized by their distinct dress, mannerisms, and language. Dress for males was the adopted zoot suit, consisting of baggy, pleated pants with pegged legs and cuffs, elongated, padded shoulder jackets, long watch chains, hats, and thick-soled shoes. Hair was worn long and slicked back in a ducktail style. Females, "pachucas," wore tight, short skirts, sheer blouses, long hair, and heavy makeup. The Zoot Suit Riots of 1943 took place in Los Angeles and were the result of bias against Latinos; there was not any real provocation.

Pachucos are thought to be the precursors of low riders and of the *cholos* who emerged in the latter half of the twentieth century with their own distinct dress styles. Low riders are largely Chicano car-club members whose vehicles have been heavily customized and ride low to the ground. Multiple generations of low riding may exist within a family. Low-rider culture, cars, and persons are featured in *Lowrider* magazine, which first appeared in 1977.

Cholo Style

Cholos are urban youth who may be gang members, car-club members, or simply influenced by the *cholo* lifestyle. Gang members are called gangsters. They are identified by their unique style of dress, speech, and gestures. Although *cholo* style varies from group to group, khaki pants, white T-shirts, plaid long-sleeve shirts, and bandanas are included. Chol*as* are usually gang members who wear khaki pants, T-shirts or tank tops, plaid long-sleeve shirts, flat black shoes, extensive makeup, and long hair. Makeup includes heavy eyeliner and brown lipstick. Both *cholos* and *cholas* may signal gang membership through tattoos and the use of unique hand gestures specific to a group.

See also **Latin American Fashion; Zoot Suit.**

BIBLIOGRAPHY

Castro, Rafaela G. *Chicano Folklore: A Guide to the Folktales, Traditions, Rituals and Religious Practices of Mexican Americans.* Oxford: Oxford University Press, 2001. An excellent resource for understanding Latino terms, with an extensive bibliography.

Harris, Mary G., ed. *Cholas: Latino Girls and Gangs.* New York: AMS Press, 1987. Illustrates the importance of appearance within gangs.

Plascencia, Luis F. B. "Low Riding in the Southwest: Cultural Symbols in the Mexican Community." In *History, Culture and Society: Chicano Studies in the 1980s.* Edited by Mario T.

Garcia et al. Ypsilanti, Mich.: Bilingual Press, 1983. Scholarly understanding of the appropriation of symbols and terms to promote low-rider activities. Excellent references.

Rodríguez, Clara E., ed. *Latin Looks: Images of Latinas and Latinos in the U.S. Media.* Boulder, Colo.: Westview Press, 1997. Good overview of issues about Latinos celebrities.

Salcedo, Michele. *Quinceañera!: The Essential Guide to Planning the Perfect Sweet Fifteen Celebration.* New York: Henry Holt, 1997. Provides planning guide and traditions of *quinceañeras.*

Sands, Kathleen Mullen. *Charrería Mexicana: An Equestrian Folk Tradition.* Tuscon: University of Arizona Press, 1993. Excellent book that includes the foundations of mariachi dress.

Solomon, Michael R., and Nancy J. Rabolt. *Consumer Behavior in Fashion.* Upper Saddle River, N.J.: Prentice Hall, 2004. Brief but valuable segment devoted to Hispanic consumers.

Internet Resource

Cihlar, Kimberly. "The Good Life: Totally Shirtatious." *Cigar Aficionado Magazine,* May/June 1999. Available from <http://www.cigaraficionado.com/Cigar/CA_Features/CA_Feature_Basic_Template/0,2344,618,00.html>. Good resource for history of the guayabera.

Josephine Moreno

LAUNDRY The French word *laver,* meaning "to wash," derives from Latin. It came into English usage (*lavendry*) in the twelfth century. By the sixteenth century, "laundry" and its associated terms were commonly used to describe dirty clothes in need of washing, the place they would be washed, and the individual whose task it was to wash them.

The history of laundry, however, is much older. Ancient civilizations were familiar with many "modern" laundry practices. Archaeological evidence survives of Babylonian soap-making in 2800 B.C.E. and Egyptian laundries from around 2000 B.C.E. During the Chinese Han Dynasty (206 B.C.E.–220 C.E.) delicate silk was washed with a natural soap, probably derived from the Soapberry tree (sapindus saponaria), which was known in China as well as on the African coast at that time.

In Europe, from the classical Greek era through the time of the Roman Empire and into the Dark Ages, laundries were used by the prosperous to clean clothes, and soap-making had become a craft by the seventh century. Urine, dung, and lye formed the basis of common cleaning substances, and a variety of domestic methods, utilizing streams, tubs, or troughs, were used to clean clothes and other household items. Laundresses are regularly mentioned in records from the Middle Ages, as washing was seen as women's work, but the majority of households would have used neither soap nor laundresses. Cleanliness was still an attribute of wealth.

Lye, made by passing water through ash (potash), appears to have been the most common washing substance

Advertisement for laundry soap. In the early 1900s, several delicate new fabrics such as rayon, nylon, and acetate were introduced, creating a need for less harsh laundry detergents. © BETTMANN/CORBIS. REPRODUCED BY PERMISSION.

for clothing made of materials such as flax, hemp, cotton, and wool. The alkali in lye helped release the dirt and clean water helped restore the clothes that were later laid out in sunlight to dry and bleach. Many different types of lye mix, some made with ferns, could be found across Europe. Soap, made by heating a mixture of fat and oil with lye and salt, was known in the ancient world but later was largely forgotten. Soap reappeared in Europe again from the seventeenth century onward, but for many years to come it was regarded as a luxury item; in England there was a luxury tax on soap from 1712 to 1853. Soap thus did not begin to supplant lye as the primary cleaning substance for laundering until the late eighteenth century.

By the seventeenth and eighteenth centuries, many households had rudimentary washing equipment. Stronger materials such as wool or linen were pounded against rocks or wooden blocks with smooth or ridged implements called "bats," "beetles," or "battledores." Lye, the washing substance, was produced from a lye dropper—a wooden box with holes in the bottom fitted over the washtub. Washing "dollies"—poles with ends shaped like a cone —were used to plunge washing around in tubs of boiling water and became popular in the nineteenth century.

These women tried some of those no-rinse chemicals. Here's what they say—

FOR WHITE WHITE WASHES

"I wash 20 shirts a week!" says Mrs. L. H. Willey of Bangor, Maine. "I tried several of those no-rinse chemicals and went right back to Duz. Duz gives me snowy white washes without making my hands rough and red."

"Common-sense tells you," says Mrs. B. W. LeFave of Spokane, Wash., "that a soap so kind to hands must be safe for colored things in my machine! I've gone back to Duz—for clean, white, safe washes every time!"

WITHOUT RED HANDS

"My hands are in water so much," says Mrs. E. E. Watson of Kansas City, Kans., "I've got to give them a break! I tried some of those no-rinse chemical suds —but went back to Duz in a hurry!"

DUZ "I'VE GONE BACK TO DUZ!"

ONLY DUZ—of all leading washday products —gives you this great combination of rich, real soap and two scientifically-tested detergents for dazzling clean, white washes!

ONLY DUZ—of all leading washday package soaps or "suds"—is so kind to your hands, so safe for colors! Yet no soap known gives you a cleaner, sweeter-smelling wash!

DUZ DOES EVERYTHING

Works Wonders Even in Hardest Water!

OCTOBER, 1950

Advertisement for Duz laundry detergent. Early twentieth century advertising for laundry soaps emphasized the importance of cleanliness in middle-class society and advocated doing laundry as appropriate feminine behavior. © BETTMANN/CORBIS. REPRODUCED BY PERMISSION.

However, until the eighteenth century, laundry methods and equipment remained largely unchanged. In the eighteenth century, early washing-machine design was underway as well as laundry recipes and equipment, including handmade mangles and scrubbing boards. Washboards were becoming more popular and were used with wider bath-shaped tubs. These devices were quicker and easier to use than the dollies. Eighteenth-century chemical discoveries and nineteenth-century advances in mechanization spurred the development of improved laundry processes and services.

During the early part of the nineteenth century, laundry work remained a small-scale, technologically unsophisticated trade, often performed by women in their own home or their employer's home. Toward the end of the nineteenth century, cities and services expanded, and women's employment outside the home increased, as did the size of the "middle classes" with substantial laundry needs. The diffusion of fashionable clothing to a larger segment of the population in the nineteenth century expanded the demand for laundry services. The growth of office employment—classic "white collar" work—led to increased demand for laundry services, as clean clothes were seen as a sign of status for such workers. Other workers (such as women in domestic service) also were increasingly expected to wear clean uniforms and aprons so that by the late nineteenth century, washing expenses incurred by laboring families were sometimes equal to half the sum they spent on rent.

These social developments, and the emergence of effective machinery, improved bleaching agents, and color-fast synthetic dyes led to the increased industrialization of laundry services. By the middle of the century, laundry had become a large-scale modern industry. In Great Britain public laundries came into being in the mid-nineteenth century; in the 1890s there was a sharp increase in power laundries. By the 1890s mechanized steam, gas, and electricity helped to fuel the service-sector growth of laundries. From 1890s to World War I, there was a move toward large steam laundries in Britain and America.

Economic relations, of course, determined not only what, but *who* washed the clothes. Laundry work historically had been primarily the work of poor women, and this remained true with the industrialization of laundry work in the nineteenth century. In the United States from around 1850, Chinese men also became associated with laundry, and by the 1880s, for example, 10 percent of the men in San Francisco's Chinese community worked in the laundry trades. By 1900, when piped water became more commonplace in many parts of the United States, most large American towns had a Chinese laundry, which offered both cleaning and pressing services. Both European-style steam laundries and Chinese hand laundries in the United States were associated with poor employment conditions, and pioneering social reformers produced studies that revealed long hours and arduous labor demands in the industry.

By the nineteenth century, chlorine, detergent, water starches, and blue bleaches were in use. Around 1850–1880 hard bars of soap (brands such as *Sunlight*) became more popular. Soap was still expensive, and it was not yet differentiated into "laundry soap" and "hand soap;" one bar would be used for all cleaning purposes. Soap flakes, pioneered in 1830, became ubiquitous from the turn of the century, culminating in the introduction of Persil (1906/07) in England. Persil offered a combination of washing and bleaching agents in one powder, and was followed by Hudson's new range including Omo (1908) and Rinso (1910).

The idea that new types of gentle but effective cleaning products were needed, coincided with the emergence of new fabrics, such as rayon (1910), acetate (1927), and more significantly, nylon (1939). New materials transformed the lingerie and fashion industries, but could be neither dry-cleaned nor roughly pounded during washing. The development of easy-to-wash, stable, "drip dry" contemporary fabrics, such as polyester and nylon and so many derivatives (bri-nylon, nylon chiffon, leather-look simplex, fake fur, and more), saw the reduction of demand for public laundries, along with the expansion of the dry-cleaning industry. Dry cleaning was inadvertently invented in 1849 when Parisian tailor Jolly Bellin accidentally spilled turpentine and learned to remove stains from a table cloth. By 1866, dry cleaning was a growing business. Pullars of Perth was offering a postal dry cleaning service anywhere in the British Isles and had developed advanced cleaning methods using petroleum and benzene, as well as specialist skills to deal with unstable fabrics. Dry cleaning, as compared with laundry work, demanded new kinds of expertise about volatile materials—not just dyes, but also finishes, interfacing, linings, buttons, trims, and threads now being used in contemporary fashion.

From 1914 onward, advertisements in newspapers, magazines, and journals linked cleaning products to female users, modernity, and social improvement. More women again were doing the washing at home. Cleanliness was a sign of gentility and respectability. Middle-class anxieties about dirt brought a new focus on "hygiene" at home and in the colonies; the phrase "the great unwashed" equated dirt with lower-class status or foreignness. Unilever's advertising slogan linked cleanliness to more than godliness, declaring that "soap is civilization."

The first electric washing machine was introduced in 1906. After World War II, radio and television promotions for soap and detergent, pioneered in America by Procter & Gamble, coincided with the expanded use of washing machines; General Electric introduced a fully automatic model for home use in 1947. The rise of self-service launderettes or Laundromats in the 1950s also contributed to the laundry industry's decline and refocus on the hotel and business sector of the market. A century after it had become industrialized in the public realm, laundry moved back to the privacy of the home, where automatic washing machines became the standard way of dealing with the family wash and fueled the market for effective but clothing-friendly detergents. While the chemical dry-cleaning industry continued to prosper, industrial laundries in Britain and America continued to serve commercial clients, but no longer the family.

Postwar detergent and appliance advertising that also covertly promoted doing the laundry as appropriate and stereotypical "feminine" behavior increasingly legitimated women washing clothes at home. Toward the end of the twentieth century, major detergent and soap-powder brands owned by soap conglomerates such as Procter & Gamble and Unilever, even targeted "new" men and women without families, suggesting it is easy/sexy/enjoyable to wash clothes. These advertisements, often for phosphate-based cleaning brands, mean certain washing products continue to dominate the international supermarket shelves, with little choice between brands. The irony is that many laundry-product advertisements convey doubtful social messages, and the products themselves contribute to environmental problems; the desire for clean clothing has been largely solved in the early 2000s, but not without creating other social costs.

See also **Distressing; Dry Cleaning.**

BIBLIOGRAPHY

Davidson, Caroline. *A Woman's Work Is Never Done: A History of Housework in the British Isles, 1660–1950.* London: Chatto and Windus, 1982.

Gamman, Lorraine, and Sean O'Mara. *Dirty Washing: The Hidden Language of Soap Powder Boxes.* Catalogue to Design Museum Exhibition, July–September 2001. London: The London Institute, 2001.

Malcolmson, Patricia E. *English Laundresses: A Social History, 1850–1930.* Urbana and Chicago: University of Illinois Press, 1986.

Mohun, Arwen P. *Steam Laundries: Gender, Technology and Work in the United States and Great Britain, 1880–1940.* Baltimore and London: Johns Hopkins University Press, 1999.

Lorraine Gamman and Sean O'Mara

LAUREN, RALPH An argument can be made that Ralph Lauren is the most successful and influential designer of his time, though he is known less for the creativity of his designs than for being an astute marketer and image maker. His fascination with style began in early childhood. He was born Ralph Lifshitz in the Bronx, New York, in 1939, the fourth and last child of Frank and Frieda Lifshitz, both Jewish refugees from Eastern Europe. He was educated in both public schools and strict yeshivas and raised with high expectations.

Early Interest in Fashion
Even as a boy Lauren loved to dress well and was always a sartorial step ahead of his peers. He liked to try on his dapper father's jaunty hats, and he wore his older brothers' hand-me-downs with a notable sense of style. Even if his clothes were not expensive, he distinguished them with an unusual drape or combination. He knew how to tie a Shetland sweater around his shoulders just so and rolled the cuffs of his jeans in a particular and unique way. When he fantasized about being a teacher, he imagined himself wearing a tweed jacket with suede elbow patches. Ralph and his brother Jerry often went shopping together where they discovered thrift-shop clothing. The memories of those hunting expeditions still inform Lauren's collections: it was in thrift shops that he discovered the joys of rugged military clothes, the integrity of British tweed suits, the thrilling transformation that could take place when a socially backward Jewish kid donned a cowboy shirt and a pair of jeans and imagined himself at home on the range.

Early Career
Once out of school he became a furnishings buyer for Allied Stores, and then (having changed his surname to Lauren) a tie salesman at Brooks Brothers. After a brief stint as a supply clerk in the U.S. Army, Lauren spent the 1960s pounding the New York pavement selling gloves, men's fragrance, and ties. More importantly, however, he was refining his personal style, designing his own custom-made suits, haunting great men's stores like Paul Stuart, and gaining inspiration from custom-made suit makers like Roland Meledandri.

Lauren grew frustrated with his conservative bosses in the tie business, since they seemed unaware of the oncoming peacock revolution in men's fashion. Secretly, he designed a line of wide ties, inspired by ones made in England by the brand Mr. Fish. He sought out a backer to finance the line and others to produce it. In 1967 he launched Polo as a division of the tie-maker Beau Brummel. Soon Bloomingdale's, then America's most cutting-edge department store, discovered Ralph Lauren. Thus began an intense and mutually advantageous relationship that still thrived in the early 2000s.

Polo Brand
In 1968 Lauren left Beau Brummel, taking the name Polo with him, and went into business with the suit maker Norman Hilton. Lauren began expanding, first into a full range of clothing and furnishings for men, and then, in 1971, into women's fashions. Even in those early days, he displayed characteristics that defined his career: an innate understanding of branding (he embroidered his polo player logo on the cuffs of his first women's shirts, creating one of the most singular brand identities in the history of marketing); a fearless refusal to be reined in by finances or expectations; and a recklessness (doing too much too soon with insufficient capital and staff) that soon led to the first of several financial crises. Later crises were caused by Lau-

ren's fierce—but never entirely realized—desire to be as successful in women's fashions as he was, almost immediately, in men's wear. Still, he produced iconic clothing for both sexes after those first wide ties: his famous polo and oxford shirts, khakis, perfect Shetlands, prairie skirts, Navajo blanket coats, and men's wear–inspired women's suits. Over the years, despite nagging fit and delivery problems caused by his insistence on dressing only a certain body type and an almost paralyzing uncertainty over what to include in his lines, those styles won him a grudging respect. Clothing from his collections, which appeared in two acclaimed films from the 1970s—*The Great Gatsby* and *Annie Hall*—helped promote his name.

Print Advertising

In the late 1970s, when Lauren formed a fragrance company with Warner Communications, money began pouring in, earning him serious commercial power and financing his next and perhaps greatest innovation. In partnership with the photographer Bruce Weber, who also worked for Calvin Klein, Polo began producing extraordinary print advertisements that served as minimovies, advertising the myriad, linked product categories Lauren produced. More significantly, they hammered home Polo's most potent product, the idea that clothes not only make the man and woman, but make them whatever they want to be, whether that is a New England patrician or a Colorado cowgirl.

Retailing Legacy

In the late 1980s Lauren and his creative services department unveiled the extensive renovation and preservation project that is the Rhinelander Mansion, long one of New York's architectural treasures, and now the backdrop to Lauren's ultimate Polo retail store. It has forever redefined fashion retailing. He had become, as a biographer called him, the personification of "the commodification of status, of the democratization of symbols of the haute monde, of the perfection of luxury merchandising and the rise of 'lifestyle' marketing, and of the globalization of branding and the simultaneous Americanization of international fashion" (Gross, 2003).

Though Lauren still did not always receive the approbation of fashion editors and his peers in the fashion design world, he went on to win every award that could be bestowed on designers, as well as worldwide fame and enormous wealth. Polo grew so large that in June 1997 it became a public corporation, listed on the New York Stock Exchange.

At age sixty-five Lauren, one of the greatest businessmen-designers in fashion history, remained driven and unsatisfied, still struggling to prove himself. His attempt to reposition Polo as a premium luxury brand was a troubled one. In 2004 Polo's stock price still languished below the highs it hit the day it was first offered to the public, and investors and financiers remained skeptical not just of Polo's position in the market, but also of

Ralph Lauren. Much of Lauren's success came from his canny understanding of the importance of marketing, illustrated through his creation of instantly recognizable brands. © MITCHELL GERBER/CORBIS. REPRODUCED BY PERMISSION.

its future. As head of a company heavily dependent upon his design and marketing skills, his style intuition, and his personality, Ralph Lauren showed no signs, however, of climbing off his polo pony.

See also **Fashion Advertising; Fashion Marketing and Merchandising; Perfume.**

BIBLIOGRAPHY

Gross, Michael. *Genuine Authentic: The Real Life of Ralph Lauren.* New York: HarperCollins, 2003.

McDowell, Colin. *Ralph Lauren: The Man, the Vision, the Style.* New York: Rizzoli International, 2003.

Trachtenberg, Jeffrey A. *Ralph Lauren: The Man Behind the Mystique.* Boston: Little, Brown, 1988.

Michael Gross

LAVER, JAMES Born in Liverpool, England in 1899, James Laver was a dress historian who worked at the Victoria and Albert Museum in London as a curator from 1922 to 1959. His initial interest in dress grew out of the

Laver wrote or edited seventy books between 1921 and 1972, at least twenty-seven of which had to do with dress or costume. He explored a variety of topics, from poetry to art to the theatre. He was also the author or coauthor of seven plays.

Contemporary Authors Online

need to date accurately the pictures in his care. His instrumental relationship to costume quickly changed, and, as he writes in his autobiography, "Having studied the What and the When, I began to wonder about the How and the Why" (1963, p. 240). Laver became one of the most prolific authors in the English-speaking world to write on the history of dress and fashion as well as on the sociology of those topics. Not only did he recast the conventional narratives of European high fashion, but he also wrote about nonfashionable forms of attire, such as school and military uniforms, children's dress, and sporting clothes. He died in 1975.

Dress and Time

Laver was fascinated by the effects that the passing of time has upon people and their works. He was greatly influenced in his theory of time by a notion of *zeitgeist*, or "time spirit," a concept taken from nineteenth-century German philosophy. Zeitgeist proposes the existence of a collective psychological, or spiritual, entity that imparts a distinctive pattern of aims and emphases to a culture, nation, or historical epoch. Drawing on this idea of cultural unity, Laver concluded that every aspect of social life is permeated by the emotional and intellectual dispositions lodged within the zeitgeist. He broadened the scope of the original idea of the "time spirit" by aligning it to a theory of modernity, arguing that all things human are increasingly subject to dictates of "time consciousness." Clothing is one of the things most sensitive to changes in the zeitgeist. In dress is found an immediate physical manifestation of the patterns of the time spirit (style), while in their rapid changes (fashion) can be observed the ever widening influence of the modern form of time. As Laver observes, "Nothing illustrates the Triumph of Time more clearly than the growing dominance of fashion" (1933, p. 132).

Clothes and Style

Laver's approach to the forms of clothing was based upon his belief that there are "no accidents in the history of dress" and that "all clothes are inevitable" (1949, p.6). He explains this assertion so:

In every period costume has some essential line, and . . . [when examining previous fashions] . . . we can

see quite plainly what it is, and can see . . . that the forms of dresses, apparently so haphazard, so dependent on the whim of the designer, have an extraordinary relevance to the spirit of the age (1945, p. 250).

The task is to understand the meanings of this "essential line" as it insinuates itself into the dress styles of a culture or epoch. Some of Laver's most controversial assertions are to be found in the connections he makes between the social and political structures of an age and in the details of its dress, as indicated in *Taste and Fashion from the French Revolution until To-day*:

The aristocratic stiffness of the old regime in France is completely mirrored in the brocaded gowns of the eighteenth century.... Victorian modesty expressed itself in the multiplicity of petticoats; the emancipation of the post-War flapper in short hair and short skirts (1937, p. 250).

Laver wrote a book about the French physician and astrologer Nostradamus (1942) and also *A Letter to a Young Girl on the Future of Clothes* (1946). At times, he came close to seeing the interpretation of clothing and its changes as being akin to clairvoyance. He names this apparent ability of clothing to anticipate the future "the wisdom of forms." When, later in life, he became a media personality, he would shock audiences by asserting that links exist between the fluctuations of the stock market index and a propensity for women to abandon corsets. In his book *Style in Costume* (1949), Laver describes his method for drawing these conclusions as "to take some dominant shape of dress—a hat, a trouser-leg, or whatever it may be—and to place it beside some form of architecture or interior decoration of the same epoch, and to note the parallelism, if such exists, between them" (p. 7).

Clothes and Fashion

Laver stressed that in modern life things are increasingly subject to change, and the existence of dress fashions is evidence of the extent to which *time* has displaced *place* as the major influence on clothing. He saw the process of fashion as having two aspects. There are the broad, objective rhythms of style change in dress and the subjective, but shared, aesthetic dispositions (taste) that incline groups to prefer one type of clothing to another. Laver was convinced that neither of these sorts of change is accidental or arbitrary, and in his book *Taste and Fashion: From the French Revolution to the Present Day* (1945), he attempted to describe and explain the regularities he noticed in both these areas.

Laver's approach to taste is novel because, rather than focusing on why certain types of clothing are deemed fashionable, he instead asks the question: How can it be that what was thought of as fashionable becomes grotesque and can then start to appear charming as time passes? The answer is his list of the stages (*Taste and Fashion*, p. 258) undergone in the decay of chic.

Indecent: 10 years before its time
Shameless: 5 years before its time

Outré (daring): 1 year before its time
Smart
Dowdy: 1 year after its time
Hideous: 10 years after its time
Ridiculous: 20 years after its time
Amusing: 30 years after its time
Quaint: 50 years after its time
Charming: 70 years after its time
Romantic: 100 years after its time

Laver encountered more serious intellectual difficulties in explaining the objective shifts in dress styles. As he investigated forms of attire such as uniforms and professional dress, he realized that not all clothing changed at the same rate. To explain these different rates of change or, in some cases, their complete absence, he began to supplement his ideas about the relation between zeitgeist and dress with those of Thorstein Veblen and J. C. Flügel.

When Laver published his book *Dress* in 1950, he explained changes in dress styles using a version of the "three motives" model of the nineteenth century. Laver argued that clothing both expresses and is shaped by three fundamental principles: the hierarchical principle, the attraction or seduction principle, and the utility principle. The seduction principle plays the most significant role in fashion change, particularly as it affects women's clothes. Laver theorizes that the seduction principle is the most important because "our clothes are dictated by the fundamental desires of the opposite sex." (1950, p. 15). He goes on, "Men still choose their mates by their physical allure; that is why women's clothes follow what might be called the Attraction Principle; they are designed to make their wearers as physically attractive as possible" (1950, p. 15).

Women, according to Laver, have to compete with one another through their appearance, and wherever there is sartorial competition there will also, he argued, be fashion.

See also **Fashion, Historical Studies of; Fashion Museums and Collections; Flügel, J. C.; Veblen, Thorstein.**

BIBLIOGRAPHY

Works by James Laver

"Triumph of Time." In *Contemporary Essays: 1933.* Edited by Sylva Norman. London: Elkin Mathews and Marrot, 1933.

Nostradamus; or, The Future Foretold. London: Collins, 1942.

Taste and Fashion from the French Revolution until To-day. London: G. G. Harrap and Company, Ltd., 1937. New revised edition titled *Taste and Fashion from the French Revolution to the Present Day,* 1945.

A Letter to a Girl on the Future of Clothes. London: Home and Van Thal, 1946.

Style in Costume. London: Oxford University Press, 1949.

Dress: How and Why Fashions in Men's and Women's Clothes Have Changed during the Past Two Hundred Years. London: John Murray, 1950.

Museum Piece; or, The Education of an Iconographer. London: Andre Deutsch, 1963.

Works about James Laver

Carter, Michael. "James Laver: The Reluctant Expert." In *Fashion Classics from Carlyle to Barthes.* New York and Oxford: Berg, 2003.

Michael Carter

LAWN. *See* **Cambric, Batiste, and Lawn.**

LEATHER AND SUEDE Leather is animal skin that has been processed in various ways (generically known as tanning) to preserve and soften it for use in clothing, accessories, and other applications. Suede is a special type of leather in which the inner surface of the skin is processed to produce a pleasing texture.

History

Leather as a medium to create clothing dates back to Cro-Magnon man some 50,000 years ago. Around that time, early humans began to migrate from relatively warm regions of the earth to the more northerly and colder parts of the northern hemisphere. Although prehistoric people learned that animal skins could be used to keep warm, they would have encountered difficulties in using untreated skins: when dried, animal skins get stiff. Among the many discoveries made by our ancient ancestors, the preservation (tanning) and processing of animal skins was one of the most important to their survival. They did this through a variety of means, such as boiling the skins in tree bark and then salting them. Almost all preservation techniques concluded with rubbing the skins with animal fat to soften them, and bending and working the skins (or chewing them) until they became soft. This would render the skins soft enough so that they could be comfortably worn and tied around the body. Later, bone tools (such as needles and awls) were developed so that skins could be sewn together to create clothing.

As far back as the fifth to the third millennium B.C., there is evidence that women wore garments made of leather in Sumeria and Mesopotamia. An almost perfectly preserved gazelle skin loincloth dating from 1580–1350 B.C.E. was found in Egypt. There are also numerous references to leather found in the Bible. Tanneries were uncovered in the ruins of Pompeii.

While animal skins were usually tanned for the purpose of showing off the skin's "grain" (outer) side, eventually it was discovered that otherwise unusable skins (e.g., grain sides were scratched) could be salvaged by processing the inside of the skins. Such "inside-out" leather was the forerunner of suede.

Over time, many countries, such as Spain, England, and France, began to perfect their own tanning tech-

Versace leather dress. In the 1980s, many top designers began working with leather, and it has become a lucrative industry, garnering over $14 million a year by the early 2000s. © VAUTHEY PIERRE/CORBIS. REPRODUCED BY PERMISSION.

niques. These sometimes included novel refinements; for example, during the seventeenth century, the French would cover up the disagreeable odor left on skins after tanning by bathing the skins in perfume.

In North America, Native Americans introduced early European settlers to the technique of oil tanning. American Indians made tepees out of leather and decorated their leather clothing with beads, bones, porcupine quills, and feathers. They also painted their garments with elaborate battle scenes. Through their exceptional tanning skills, they were able to produce white leather, a particularly difficult color to achieve.

During the nineteenth century, Augustus Schultz, an American chemist, invented a newer, faster method of tanning using chromium salts. This innovation made it possible to reduce the tanning process from weeks and months to hours. Engineers in America and Europe began to invent special machines and processes that further increased tanning productivity. By 2004, tanneries around the world closely guarded proprietary techniques to give themselves a competitive advantage. Many tanneries are exploring the eco-friendly method of vegetable tanning, using extracts from quebracho wood and chestnut.

Designers throughout history have regarded leather as having a certain allure. From the earliest decorated ceremonial garments worn by tribesmen to high fashion couture collections, the wearing of leather has been synonymous with status. Because of the high cost and craftsmanship involved in the processing of leather, leather represents "luxury."

Leather has also been used for thousands of years to make sandals and shoes. In addition, it has had important industrial uses, for example to make drive belts for industrial machinery.

The Processing of Leather

Leather, for the purpose of apparel manufacturing, is a byproduct of food consumption. The animals that are consumed for food and that are most often used for clothing are: cow, goat, sheep, lamb, pig, and deer. Leather is processed by a tannery. A tannery is a factory that buys raw skins from an abattoir, makes the skins into leather, colors them, and then sells them to manufacturers. Animal skins come from all over the world and tanneries are located worldwide.

"Hides" (the pelt of large animals such as pig, deer, and cow) and "skins" (smaller animals such as goat, sheep, and lamb) are delivered to the tannery de-haired, either in a preserved dried state or in a preserved "pickled" state (i.e., chemically treated with various salts, water, and sulfuric acid). These treated hides and skins are referred to as crusts. Crusts, which are dried to a boardlike state, can be stored for several months before tanning.

Tanning is a process that is dependent on several factors: the type of skin, the desired end use, and the price the buyer is willing to pay. By using specific amounts of fat liquors, chromium salts, and other chemicals or vegetable tannins, tanneries can formulate a recipe that can create a soft, subtle expensive skin. Or by cutting out certain steps, they can produce a less expensive skin. Color can be added to skins by either adding it to the drum after tanning to produce aniline skins, or for skins of lesser quality, color can be sprayed onto the surface of the skin to produce semi-aniline skins. In the case of extremely poor quality skins, color can be applied in heavier concentrations in an attempt to hide imperfections. These are called pigmented skins. Pigmented skins are generally hard to the touch.

Leather skins can be processed utilizing different sides of the skin. When a leather skin is de-haired and tanned with the grain side out, it produces a smooth finish known as nappa. When the underside of a leather skin is buffed, it produces a velvety nap known as suede. In 1809, a leather-splitting machine was invented that could split heavy leathers to any desired thickness, producing skins known as splits, which are sueded on both sides. Cow and pig splits are less expensive than processing single-sided lamb and goat suede. The grain side of leather can also be processed to create a napped finish known as nubuck, however, this is not considered true suede.

At the tannery, skins are sorted to choose which skins will be made into suede and which will be chosen for nappa. Suede can be made from relatively lower-quality skins than nappa; however suede requires several more processing steps. The animals most often used to create garment weight suede are: lamb, sheep, goat, pig, and cow. Suede produces a nap similar to velvet and corduroy, therefore care must be taken when cutting suede into garments as color shading will occur if not properly cut. While nappa skins are generally more expensive than suede, the higher material consumption, due to cutting loss while shading, usually results in equal pricing at the retail level.

Leather Innovation

Tanneries throughout the world are constantly inventing new recipes to tan and color skins to achieve a competitive advantage over their peers. Tanneries guard their recipes and special techniques for processing leather. By working together with fashion designers, tanneries often create many innovative production techniques. Stamping, embossing, distressing, tie-dyeing, pleating, printing, beading, flocking, perforating, and embroidery are only some of the special techniques that designers have created to make leather skins even more spectacular.

Designers throughout the years have used leather much the same as they would cloth. From its main use in outerwear and sportswear, to the most elaborate eveningwear, designers have always appreciated the uniqueness of leather. Leather items such as the aviator jacket worn by General Patton in World War II and the black leather jacket worn by James Dean in the 1950s have created important trends in the fashion world. From the 1960s through the 1970s, American designer Bonnie Cashin worked extensively in leather. European designers such as Claude Montana, Versace, Armani, Ungaro, Fendi, Gucci, Alaia, and Hermès took the lead in leather apparel design through the 1980s. By the mid- to late 1980s, many of the top American designers also discovered leather's limitless possibilities, such as Ralph Lauren, Calvin Klein, Geoffrey Beene, Donna Karan, and Bill Blass.

In 2004, leather garments could be found at all price points, from the most expensive leathers used in couture to skins used in the production of mass-market clothing.

Suede Innovation

Clothing made of suede is more fragile and harder to keep clean than non-suede leathers. This is because suede tends to absorb stains. Wearing suede is considered a luxury and a symbol of status. Designers throughout history have used suede for its beauty. Many designers prefer suede to work in, especially when they are designing soft, drapey, fluid styles. Suede is used much the way a designer would use cloth. Suede can be draped, pleated, gathered, and fluted. In 1930, the French designer Paquin created a suit using goat suede and wool. Cow-slit was used by Hermès in 1957 to create a coatdress and also by Bonnie Cashin in her suede ensemble from the 1960's. Suede is also a favorite among couturiers, as demonstrated in Givenchy's suede patchwork suit from Couture Collection 1992 and Jean Paul Gaultier's suede-draped tunic from his Couture Autumn/Winter Collection 2002.

Designers often work with tanneries to develop innovations in suede such as reversible and double-faced skins, embossing to resemble hides of endangered animals, and in the creation of new perforating techniques.

Social and Political Issues

The animal-rights organization known as People for the Ethical Treatment of Animals (PETA) has a history of attacking the leather apparel industry as well the fur industry. Though they acknowledge that most leathers used in apparel are made from the byproducts of food consumption, they have accused manufacturers in developing countries of inhumane slaughtering processes as well as using toxins in the tanning of leather.

The Leather Apparel Association (LAA) is a trade association representing leather manufacturers, cleaners, suppliers, tanners, and retailers nationwide. The mission of the LAA is to continually monitor and improve the health and future of the leather apparel industry and provide support against PETA. The Leather Industries of America (LIA) is another organization that represents tanneries, sellers, and other leather-related companies. The LIA provides technical, environmental, educational, statistical, and marketing services to its members and the public.

Even with numerous attacks by PETA, the leather apparel industry remains a $14.5 million global industry. As appeal for leather clothing continues, the leather industry seeks new eco-friendly methods to process leather. Although leather apparel experiences trend cycles, it most definitely remains in 2004 a desirable commodity in the world of fashion.

See also **Cashin, Bonnie; Handbags and Purses.**

BIBLIOGRAPHY
Sterlacci, Francesca. *Leather Apparel Design.* New York: Delmar Publishing 1997.

Internet Resources

Leather Apparel Association. 2004. Available from <http://www.leatherassociation.com>.

Leather Industries of America. 2004. Available from <http://www.leatherusa.com>.

PETA. 2004. Available from <http://www.peta.org/mc/facts/fsveg.html>.

Worth Global Sourcing Network. 2004. Available from <http://www.WGSN.com>.

Francesca Sterlacci

LEGAL AND JUDICIAL COSTUME

LEGAL AND JUDICIAL COSTUME Legal and judicial costume is defined as special occupational dress worn by judges and members of the legal community to mark their membership in this professional group.

Dress in the Early Modern Period

Legal and judicial dress has its origins in royal and ecclesiastical history. Prior to the early modern period, monks and other ecclesiasts were responsible for the administration of justice in the European territories. By the fifteenth and sixteenth centuries, this group was replaced by lesser nobility appointed by European sovereigns. As direct servants of the monarch, they were charged with the administration of sovereign law, and it was important for their clothing to reflect the legitimacy and authority of the sovereign's rule. Therefore, early judicial and legal dress borrowed heavily from the styles of the church's legal representatives, while reflecting the new era now defined by royal rule.

Judicial Dress

During the fifteenth and sixteenth centuries, judicial dress varied considerably between nations due to the decentralization of ownership and rule in Europe. Ecclesiastical costume history, however, assured some general similarities in basic judicial and legal dress among European nations. Judges of the early modern period wore sleeved tunics, and over this, wide-sleeved pleated gowns or robes made from cloth, wool, or silk. This garment, previously worn by monks, was sometimes referred to as a *supertunica*. High judges might wear tabards (essentially, a sleeveless version of the supertunica) instead. Judges also wore closed mantles covering the shoulders to the middle-upper arm, and rolled hoods or casting hoods of the same fabric, lined with miniver. For ceremonial occasions, some judges wore a shorter cloak, called an *armelausa* (in France, called a *manteau*), made from the same fabric.

Despite this basic attire, there was little consistency in color of judicial uniform. James Robinson Planché summarizes this point well in his *Cyclopædia of Costume*: "Information respecting the official costume of the Bench and the Bar is abundant; but, unfortunately, the descriptions are not so clear as they are copious" (Planché, p. 426). Royalty frequently dressed judges in ornate, regal costumes of scarlet and black, although vibrant hues of pink, violet, and royal blue were also common. Color reflected royal taste, but also judicial rank or position, and lower judicial officials wore different colors than presiding judges. Justices of the peace, appointed on a local basis to police the king's laws and manage local affairs, wore lay dress associated with their middle-class rank.

Upon the head, members of the early modern judiciary typically wore a coif, a white circular lawn or silk cap, along with a black silk or velvet skullcap on top. Such head coverings bore resemblance to academic dress, which signified the possession of a doctorate degree. In fact, "The Order of the Coif" was a name given to a group of British sergeants-at-law, a special legal class who comprised the body from which high judicial offices was chosen. Judges often wore another hat on top of the coif and skullcap, particularly in France and Germany.

Early Legal Dress

Early costume for lawyers, also known as barristers, solicitors, advocates, or councillors, depending on the country, bore strong similarities to that of judges. During the Middle Ages, lawyers were considered to be apprentices to the judiciary, which explain the likeness in dress. Like their judicial counterparts, barristers in Britain also wore closed gowns made of cloth or silk. These garments, however, had raised, stuffed shoulders and elbow-length glove sleeves. Even before Queen Mary's death, these gowns were predominantly black, in accordance with the rules of the Inns of Court that organized barrister education and membership. Like judges, barristers also wore coifs and skullcaps, as well as white ruff-like bands around the neck. Solicitors, who unlike barristers, did not have the right to present in court, wore long, open black gowns with winged sleeves, although by the seventeenth century, they had lost their special dress and instead wore common business attire. French advocates wore wide, colored, bell-sleeved gowns, often in scarlet, with shoulder pieces and chaperons like their judicial counterparts. They also wore white bands and stiff black toques called *bonnets carrés*.

Regulations of the Seventeenth Century

Historically, monarchs set out complex dictates on judicial and legal dress, which reflected that individual sovereign's taste. By the seventeenth century, as countries continued to centralize and codify legal order, it became important to systemize the mélange of customs and traditions relating to legal and judicial dress. This did not, however, result in a simple, concise, framework for dress—in fact, the exact opposite! In 1602, France regulated, by royal mandate, the dress of its judges and lawyers of all ranks. Although scarlet still predominated, the monarchy dictated the specific robe fabrics, colors, and lengths for its judges, advocates, and clerks. It even made distinctions for colors by seasons and days of the week.

Britain had similarly intricate legislation, which resulted in complicated and confusing dictates. According to the 1635 Decree by Westminster, the monarch became the exclusive administrator of judicial dress. From spring to mid-autumn, it was mandatory for judges to wear a taffeta-lined black or violet silk robe with deep cuffs lined in silk or fur, a matching hood, and a mantle. Judges were also required to wear coifs, caps, and a cornered cap on top. During the winter months, the taffeta lining was replaced with miniver to keep judges warm. Special scarlet dress replaced this standard costume on holy days or the visit of the Lord Mayor.

There was no parallel code for barristers' dress at this time, and the Inns of Court governed bar costume.

WHY JUDGES WEAR BLACK

Free use of color in judicial dress lasted in European countries until the late seventeenth century, when the black robe, which many consider to be the traditional judicial color, became the preferred color for daily judicial dress. France adopted black as the color of undress for its judges, and historians believe that the British tradition of black robes began when barristers and judges adopted mourning dress for Queen Mary II in 1694. Although high court judges eventually reverted back to colors of scarlet and violet, it remained for barristers, lower-court judges, and court clerks in Britain. By the eighteenth century, American judges had followed suit, though as a symbol of liberty from British control over the American colonies, and an affirmation of Victorian values of dignity and propriety.

During the same time, Britain also regulated the judicial dress of the American colonies. Settlers followed codes and ceremonies of British law, and while little has been written on judicial and legal dress in the colonies, scarlet, which was the ceremonial and traditional color for British judges, was de rigueur for the colonial bench. American dress, however, did not mirror the same level of British complexity, given the puritan and austere circumstances and culture of the region.

Adoption of the Wig
Even the dignified and traditional dress of the legal and judicial system has not been isolated from whims of popular fashion. The wigs worn by members of the British bench and bar are perfect examples of this idea. Fashion has always influenced its styles, from changes in sleeve to ruffs and sashes. Charles II imported the wig from France in 1660, and during the seventeenth century, they were a fashionable item for all gentlemen of wealthy and established social classes. Made from human or horsehair, they sat very high at the crown, and cascaded in curls over the shoulders. Judges and barristers took to wearing these fashionable full-bottomed wigs with their robes, no doubt under the recommendation of Charles II. By the middle of the eighteenth century, wigs fell out of favor with the general public, but legal professionals adopted the wig as a vital part of the legal and judicial uniform. In the early 2000s, high-court judges and the Queen's Counsel in Britain and the Commonwealth continue to wear full-bottomed wigs for ceremonial occasions, and shorter bench wigs are customary for daily courtroom proceedings. Barristers wear an even more abbreviated version of the seventeenth-century wig, known as a tie-wig, which sits back from the forehead to expose the hairline.

Legal Dress in the Early 2000s
The styles put into place in the seventeenth century for the legal and judicial community have persisted in their basic form, although styles for sleeves, collars, and accoutrements like wigs and bands have changed, according to lay fashion and monarchial taste. Central governments rather than monarchs regulate legal and judicial dress, and complex and confusing directives, in principle, continue to exist. In Britain, judges, barristers, and court clerks sitting in high courts are generally required to wear black silk or stuff gowns over suits, and a short bench or tie-wig and bands. Black robes for judges account for more of their dress than in previous times, and high court, district, and circuit courts prescribe their use all or much of the time.

More frequently, colored mantles or sashes denote the type of case and court a judge presides over. Scarlet robes remain reserved for ceremonial occasions, as well as for some high-court criminal cases in winter. Violet is also used for certain cases according to season and court. Judges may be called to add or remove cuffs, scarves, mantles, and hoods of varying color and fabric at different times and seasons. These rules, however, are frequently amended and discarded in practice by judges in particular, who may dispense of their wigs or robes, either due to weather or due to special circumstances, such as cases involving children. Barristers' dress remains more clear-cut, and in court they continue to wear black silk or cloth gowns, tie-wigs, and bands, depending on the seniority of their position. Solicitors and lower court officials do not wear wigs. Justices of the Peace, now predominantly confined to name only, do not wear any special dress.

Like Britain, France has also retained its complex guidelines for members of the legal profession. French high court judges traditionally wear bell-sleeve cloth or silk black gowns and heavy draped manteaus lined with rabbit fur. Over the coat, they also wear fur shoulder pieces upon which they hang national medals. Like Britain, this full dress is not always abided by in daily practice. For ceremonial occasions, high-court judges may wear scarlet robes. Lower-court judges wear similar robes in black or scarlet with black satin cuffs. Unlike their British or American peers, these robes button down the front, and have trains that can be tucked up inside the robe. Additionally, they wear black moiré belts and *epitoges*, or shawls tipped in ermine or rabbit, along white cloth fichus. They also continue to wear black toques. Although French advocates wear business attire outside of the courtroom, they still wear black robes like their lower court judicial counterparts in court trials. They can, but rarely do, wear toques as well. French court clerks wear dress similar to advocates, but this depends on the formality and level of the court.

Other European countries follow similar national judicial-costume history, and even the European Community's high judges wear distinctive scarlet or royal blue judicial robes, although this is governed by tradition rather than written statute. Lawyers and advocates presenting at the European Courts of Justice wear their national legal costume, whether it be plain dress or robe.

Unlike in Europe, both national and local governments regulate judicial and legal dress in the United States, and American legal costume is confined only to judges. All levels of the judiciary wear long, black, cloth or silk gowns with bell-sleeves and yoked necklines. They wear no wig, special headdress or collar, although male judges are expected to wear a shirt and tie underneath their robes. There is no specific dress code for court clerks appearing in courts, although professional dress is assumed or required. Justices of the Peace, now largely succeeded in authority by organized lower-level courts, wear lay dress as well.

Production and Retailing

Legal and judicial dress is produced by specialized manufacturers and sold through specialty legal retailers or by companies that also cater to academic and religious vestments. Legal dress can be quite expensive, and in Britain, a black judicial gown may cost between £600 ($960) and £850 ($1,360), and a full-bottomed judicial wig, £1,600 ($2,560). Such expenses have actually resulted in a thriving market for used wigs in Britain. Some high-court judges in Britain and other European countries are given a stipend for their judicial attire, but lower-court judges, barristers, and advocates, must provide for their own. In America, judges are expected to pay for their judicial dress, but pricing is far more moderate.

Modernization

There has been considerable debate since the mid-1980s about the relevance of traditional legal and judicial dress in modern society. The United States and many European countries have relaxed regulations regarding such attire, particularly for judges, and judges have had the ability to exercise their individual judgment in such matters. Judges in Britain have chosen to disband with wigs and robes upon certain situations when they want to convey a feeling of equality to laypersons, and Muslim and Sikh judges wear their turbans instead of wigs.

Modernization has also included the exercise of individual judicial tastes as well. In 1999 American Supreme Court Justice William Rehnquist chose to wear a robe decorated with gold stripes on each sleeve at the Impeachment Trial of President William Jefferson Clinton in 1999. Justice Byron Johnson of the Idaho Supreme Court in the United States chose to wear a blue robe, rather than a black one when he sat on the bench. Although both examples are American, they reflect the questioning of relevance of judicial and legal dress in the early twenty-first century, and how it relates to the role of judges and lawyers in community organizations.

Another example of modernization is the ongoing debate regarding the relaxation of legal and judicial garb in the United Kingdom, and specifically the abolishment of wigs. In 1992, and again in 2003, the judicial system in Britain debated the redesign of judicial and legal dress in order to be more relevant to society. With this has come the question of whether to retain the wig.

In addition to being a visual guide for members of the legal profession to that of their peers, the image of judges and barristers in their traditional occupational dress for society reminds the public of the dignity and gravity of the law, and the impartiality of the judicial system. It also acts as a disguise to protect judges and barristers outside of the courtroom, as well as a tool for downplaying differences in age and gender. Hence, the decision to retain, relax, or disband with legal and judicial dress, extends beyond a discussion of the physical garments. Current debates about judicial dress are also deliberations over the function of governments and tradition in the structure of civil life, and the role of a judicial representative in the modern execution of justice.

See also **Royal and Aristocratic Dress.**

BIBLIOGRAPHY

It should be noted that there are very few books devoted to legal and judicial dress, and even fewer incorporating issues of modernization. Information can often be found in the occupational dress section in general costume histories, but books specifically dedicated to the history of judicial and legal practice too often omit dress from discussions. History journals and legal journals have been the most helpful sources, and information covering Britain and America are most predominant. Journals documenting parliamentary discussions and debates are also useful as primary source material.

Hargreaves-Mawdsley, W. N. *A History of Legal Dress in Europe until the End of the Eighteenth Century.* Oxford: Clarendon Press, 1963. An indispensable authoritative book of European legal dress before the eighteenth century.

MacClellan, Elisabeth. *Historic Dress in America, 1607–1870.* Philadelphia, Pa.: George W. Jacobs and Co., 1904. Good for judicial dress and history in the American colonies.

O'Neill, Stephen. "Why Are Judges' Robes Black?" *Massachusetts Legal History: A Journal of the Supreme Judicial Court Historical Society* 7 (2001): 119–123. Very useful for American dress.

Planché, James Robinson. *Cyclopædia of Costume or Dictionary of Dress.* Volume 8: *The Dictionary.* London: Chatto and Windus, Piccadilly, 1876. Very helpful as a detailed source of early legal garments, given the confusing nature of the dress. Extensive reference to primary sources.

Webb, Wilfred M. *The Heritage of Dress.* London: E. Grant Richards, 1907. Good discussion about the history and vestiges of early legal dress.

Yablon, Charles M. "Judicial Drag: An Essay on Wigs, Robes and Legal Change." *Wisconsin Law Review.* 5 (1995): 1129–1153. Lively, entertaining article encompassing the history, political and sociology behind judicial dress. Worth tracking down.

Leslie Harris

LEIBER, JUDITH Judith Peto was born in Budapest, Hungary, where she and her family survived World War II and the Holocaust. In 1946 she married Gerson Leiber, a Brooklyn-born American soldier serving in Budapest, and returned with him to the United States the following year. (He later became well known as an artist of the New York school.) She spent the next sixteen years working for several handbag companies, moving up the ladder from machine operator to designer, before she and her husband founded Judith Leiber, Inc., in 1963. The company became highly successful, and Mrs. Leiber's bags were avidly sought after by a growing list of clients. They sold the company in 1993, with Mrs. Leiber remaining as president and chief designer for several years thereafter; later she became a consultant to the company. She retired in 1998.

Judith Leiber's name is synonymous with a particular type of evening bag known as a minaudière. Minaudières (the name comes from a French word that means "to be charming") are small evening bags made of metal or other rigid materials and that usually have highly decorated or bejeweled surfaces. They often are fanciful or whimsical in design and can take the form of plants, animals, or trompe l'oeil objects. Minaudières, which first appeared as fashion accessories in the 1930s, have been made by a number of designers, but Judith Leiber is by far the best-known designer and manufacturer in the field. Her company has produced minaudières in hundreds of different designs, usually in very limited editions.

One of Leiber's best known designs is a bag in the shape of a ripe, red tomato, covered with thousands of hand-set red and green crystals. Each bag is handcrafted and requires several days to complete. A model is sculpted in wax and then cast in metal using the *ciré-perdu* process. The bag is then gold-plated, painted with a surface design, and covered with rhinestones, crystals, or other hand-set, faux gemstones. Other typical designs have included a white, pearl-beaded teddy bear, a slice of watermelon, and a variety of eggs.

Though Judith Leiber is best known for minaudières, she has also designed and produced a wide range of other luxurious bags. She is well known to her wealthy clientele for both day bags and evening bags, fashioned in alligator and other leathers, as well as in velvet, silk, and other fabrics, and often graced with crystal-encrusted metal handles and closures. Minaudières and other handbags by Judith Leiber are avidly collected by connoisseurs. They have been widely imitated and counterfeited, but the craftsmanship and art of the originals remain unmistakable.

See also **Handbags and Purses.**

BIBLIOGRAPHY
Nemy, Enid. *Judith Leiber: The Artful Handbag.* New York: Harry N. Abrams, 1995.

Internet Resource

Judith Leiber. Website 2004. Available from <http://www.judith-leiber.com>.

Valerie Steele

LEOTARD In January 1943, *Harper's Bazaar* hailed the leotard as "a new idea, leading toward the twenty-first century and the cosmic costumes of Flash Gordon's supergirl" (p.35). That same year's August issue urged college girls to "be the first to wear the leotard under your wool jersey jumper, a silhouette new from the ground up, a fashion so honest and sound it's bound to be a classic" (p. 65). In September of that year, *Life* magazine featured these "strange-looking garments" on its cover, declaring that "'Leotard' is a new word in fashion parlance" (p. 47).

The leotard may have been new to fashion, but it had been pioneered some eighty years before by Jules Leotard, a French gymnast who invented the flying trapeze in 1859. To show off his figure during daring aerial performances, he wore a short, close-fitting garment, cut low in the neck and gusseted between the legs. By the late nineteenth century, the worsted-wool or silk garment that acquired his name was standard wear for acrobats and gymnasts. In the early twentieth century, the leotard with tights was also the traditional rehearsal costume for ballet dancers and increasingly preferred as modern dance-performance costume. This stylized form of nudity—starkly anonymous or with minimal accessories—accentuated the line of bodies in motion in works by innovators such as Serge Diaghilev, Martha Graham, and George Balanchine.

As wartime fashion for co-eds, the leotards designed by Mildred Orrick and Claire McCardell could be snug, two-piece, wool-jersey garments with long legs, long sleeves, and high necks. Made in many colors or vividly striped, they were worn with sleeveless jumpers, skirts, or evening pants; underneath, according to *Harper's Bazaar*, went a brassiere and garterless pantie-girdle—or nothing at all.

The freedom given by leotards was appreciated in the 1960s by hip young women and by designers including Rudi Gernreich, a former dancer, as the modern concept of "body clothes" emerged. By the late 1970s, advances in technology gave active sportswear maximum comfort and fit. Made of stretchy nylon and spandex, a leotard and tights became the basic fitness fashion, sanctioned by Jane Fonda in her influential *Workout Book* of 1981. By 1985, comedian Dave Barry, in *Stay Fit and Healthy Until You're Dead* could joke that this outfit encouraged women to exercise extra vigorously since it "shows every bodily flaw a woman has, no matter how minute" and to refrain from drinking, since "there is no way to go to the bathroom in a leotard and tights."

In the body-conscious late 1970s and 1980s, many forms of the leotard—also known as the bodysuit, maillot, catsuit, unitard, body stocking, or bodytard—were everywhere or the disco or roller disco; according to the 1980 book *Sportsfashion*, leotards "stretching and moving to the beat of the music" (p. 137) adopted shimmering fabrics, Day-Glo colors, sequins, and rhinestones. The versatile garment was also seen as perfect on the beach, in town, and at the office, as dancewear companies Danskin and Capezio and designers such as Betsey Johnson made the leotard the basis of a wardrobe of separates that were "interchangeable, washable, packable, seasonless, timeless, ageless" (p. 142). To the late twentieth century, the leotard still seemed "the first dressing concept worthy of the twenty-first century" (p. 116). In the new millenium, now sometimes simply called a "body," it continues to be a streamlined second skin.

See also **Ballet Costume; Elastomers.**

BIBLIOGRAPHY

Adler, France-Michèle. *Sportsfashion*. New York: Avon Books, 1980.

Strong, Roy et al. *Designing for the Dancer*. London: Elron Press, 1981.

H. Kristina Haugland

LESAGE, FRANÇOIS François Lesage, a French embroiderer born in Chaville in 1929, is the son of Albert Lesage (1888–1949), founder of Albert Lesage and Company in 1924, and of Marie-Louise Favot, known as Yo, a designer for Madeleine Vionnet. After an apprenticeship in the family firm in Paris, François Lesage went to the United States in 1948 and opened a shop on Sunset Boulevard, Los Angeles, where he embroidered for dressmakers and Hollywood studios, but the death of his father the following year put an end to his American adventure. François Lesage returned to Paris to assist his mother in managing the renowned company.

History
At the time of his father's death, the embroidery house that Lesage inherited was among the most important and prestigious specialty companies of its type in the world.

In 1924 his father, Albert, had taken over the business of the embroiderer Michonet. Michonet's venerable firm, which was founded in 1858, had supplied the great names of couture of the belle epoque (Charles Frederick Worth, John Redfern, Jacques Doucet, Callot Soeurs) with beautiful embroidery to decorate their creations. The firm had also supplied the imperial court of Napoleon III with embroidery and had succeeded in establishing new connections with the talented generation of couturiers between World War I and World War II. François Lesage was thus familiar from a very young age with the technical and aesthetic feats accomplished by his parents for the original collections of Madeleine Vionnet and Elsa Schiaparelli, among others.

When he took charge of the firm, which possessed tens of thousands of samples, the young François continued the craft tradition and created his own collections of samples, which were immediately admired by such designers as Pierre Balmain, Cristóbal Balenciaga, Robert Piguet, Jacques Griffe, and Jean Dessès. For the *jolie Madame* (the trade name of Pierre Balmain), full of grace and delicacy expressed in muted tones, he updated the rococo ribbon. The artificial flowers, straw spangles, and planished sequins to be found in the work of several couturiers of the time are early examples of the style of the young Lesage, a subtle mixture of tradition, novelty, and a bold approach to every challenge.

Innovations
François Lesage freed himself from the weight of tradition in the 1960s. He successfully experimented with new materials, including patterns of plasticine and cellophane, bold treatments of classic materials, and uncommon arrangements that revealed a different approach to relief. Embroidery had become fabric, and fashionable dresses, cut straight and not fitted to the body, offered an ideal setting for Lesage's graphic compositions, which covered the entire surface of the design. Lesage acquired new clients, including such stellar names as Lanvin, Givenchy, Dior, Grès, Patou, and Yves Saint Laurent.

Work with Haute Couture
In the 1970s Lesage designs returned to the thematic collections that had been favored by Schiaparelli. Yves Saint Laurent was the first designer to recognize the aesthetic potential of this change. The entire industry, stimulated by lavish orders from Arab princesses, followed Saint Laurent's lead and kept the embroidery workshops operating overtime. Lesage developed embroidery on jersey and new techniques, such as precut designs attached by thermoplastic films to fabrics. In 1977 he embroidered the court dress of the wife of Jean Bedel Bokassa, which was ordered from Lanvin on the occasion of the coronation of Bokassa to the office of emperor of the Central African Empire.

In 1982 Lesage began to collaborate with the American designers Calvin Klein, Bill Blass, Geoffrey Beene, and Oscar de la Renta. Throughout the decade thematic collections provided opportunities for creation and innovation. Lesage established fruitful dialogues with Yves Saint Laurent; as well as with Karl Lagerfeld, the new artistic director of Chanel and Christian Lacroix, with whom he collaborated from the opening of his couture house in 1987. While Lacroix was still at the house of Patou, he met Lesage, whom he considered his "godfather in fashion." For all these designers, who competed with one another in erudition and historical references, Lesage revisited the entire history of art, producing masterpieces for each of them that required hundreds of hours of work. Among the most famous of his productions transposed Van Gogh's irises and sunflowers onto Yves Saint Laurent jackets in 1988, a feat requiring no fewer than six hundred hours per jacket.

Accessory Line

Encouraged by this infatuation with the magic of embroidery, Lesage launched a line of embroidered accessories in 1987, created by Gérard Trémolet and sold in the Lesage boutique opened that year on the Place Vendome on the former site of Schiaparelli's business. After the shop closed in 1992, the accessories were sold in department stores around the world.

Legacy

In 1990 Lesage joined the Comité Colbert; in 1992, in order to perpetuate his art and transmit his skill, he opened the Lesage School of Embroidery at the address of his workshop, 13 rue de la Grange Batelière in Paris.

Having attained the summit of his art, Lesage became the subject of several one-man shows: at the Fashion Institute of Technology in New York (1987), at the Musée de la mode et du costume Palais Galleria in Paris (1989), at the Fashion Foundation Hanae Mori of Tokyo (1989), and at the Los Angeles County Museum of Art (1991).

With the 1990s came an influx of new orders from creators such as Thierry Mugler and Jean Paul Gaultier, who launched their own haute couture activities. But also, paradoxically, orders for ready-to-wear clothes from houses and designers such as Chanel, Dior, and Yves Saint Laurent added to the work of the embroiderers working under Lesage.

In addition to the work done for designers, Lesage has carried out many special orders. For example, on the occasion of the World Youth Days in Paris (1997), he embroidered the chasuble and miter of Pope John Paul II. Additionally, he embroidered the costumes of Erik Orsenna and Roman Polanski for their entry into the Académie française (1999) and costumes for the new revue at the Moulin Rouge (1999). Lesage followed the long tradition of the house in working for royalty when he collaborated with Moroccan craftsmen and designed costumes for the trousseau of the bride of Mohammed VI in 2001. In 2002 the Lesage company was acquired by Chanel as part of its Paraffection group, bringing together craftsmen of elegance who possess exceptional skill.

See also **Beads; Embroidery; Spangles.**

BIBLIOGRAPHY

Kamitsis, Lydia. *Lesage.* (Paris: Editions Assouline; New York: Universe/Vendome, 2000).

White, Palmer. *The Master Touch of Lesage: Embroidery for French Fashion.* Paris: Chene, 1987.

——. *Haute Couture Embroidery: The Art of Lesage.* New York: Vendome Press, 1988.

Lydia Kamitsis

LEVI STRAUSS & CO. The name Levi Strauss is indelibly linked with a quintessential American fashion—blue jeans. The original riveted work pants, called "waist overalls," were patented by Levi Strauss in 1873 and became staples of quality, durable workingmen's garments for more than fifty years. In the 1950s blue jeans, particularly Levi Strauss classic riveted "501's" emerged as fashion statements, anticipating the skyrocketing popularity of denims worldwide in the following decades. The dominance of Levi's in this fashion phenomena transformed Levi Strauss & Co. from a successful regional company into one of the world's largest clothing brands, with $4.1 billion in total sales in 2002.

While Levi Strauss & Co. has aligned itself more closely with style and fashion in the twenty-first century, its origins were humble and rooted in the dry goods trade. Its founder, Levi Strauss, was born "Loeb" Strauss in Buttenheim, Bavaria, in 1829, one of seven children of Hirsch Strauss. In 1847, Loeb Strauss emigrated to the United States to join his stepbrothers, Jonas and Louis, owners of a dry-goods business in New York City. Loeb quickly learned the family trade and by 1850 he had changed his name to Levi.

The discovery of gold in California and the subsequent Gold Rush of 1849 brought throngs of fortune hunters west in the hopes of striking it rich. In 1853, Levi Strauss headed to San Francisco, too, not to pan for gold, but to establish his own dry-goods business catering to this new workforce.

Levi Strauss set up his wholesale business selling bolts of cloth, linens, and clothing at 90 Sacramento Street, close to the waterfront for convenient access to goods coming off ships. In the late 1850s and early 1860s, his enterprise, known merely as "Levi Strauss," profited, and its steady expansion forced him to relocate several times to other waterfront addresses. In 1863 his brother-in-law, David Stern, joined his firm, and the company was officially renamed Levi Strauss & Co. By this time, Levi Strauss was in his thirties and the firm was a profitable entity providing a variety of goods. The next decade, however, would assure Levi Strauss his place in fashion history.

Levi's advertisement, circa 1950s. Levi's gained popularity as a fashion item as Western movies romanticized the straightfoward and rugged cowboys who wore the jeans. THE ADVERTISING ARCHIVE LTD. REPRODUCED BY PERMISSION.

In 1872, Levi Strauss was contacted by one of his customers, Jacob Davis, a tailor in Reno, Nevada. Davis had discovered a practical and ingenious way to make work pants stronger by adding metal rivets to the weak points at the pocket corners and the base of the fly. Davis's rivets proved successful and his new reinforced work pants became popular among his local clients. Fearful that his idea would be copied, Davis wanted to secure a patent, but did not possess the $68 necessary to file for a patent. Instead, he turned to Levi Strauss, a successful wholesale goods purveyor from whom he often purchased fabric, and offered to share the patent if Levi Strauss & Co. would underwrite the expense.

Levi Strauss recognized the potential in this endeavor and agreed to share the patent. In 1873, Davis and Strauss received patent #139,121 from the U.S. Patent and Trademark Office for an "Improvement in Fastening Pocket-Openings." The riveted "waist overalls" (as work pants were then known) quickly achieved a reputation for strength, quality, and durability among working men. For twenty years Levis Strauss & Co. held the patent on riveted waist overalls, thereby curbing competition from other manufacturers. In 1890 the lot number 501 (which it would thereafter retain) was first used to designate the riveted waist overall. The following year, the patent expired and went into the public domain, where riveted waist overalls were quickly copied by other firms. However, the demand for Levi's waist overalls continued to grow, forcing Levi Strauss & Co. to open several manufacturing plants of its own in San Francisco.

By the turn of the century, Levi Strauss was in his early seventies and highly regarded as a successful businessman and philanthropist. He died in September 1902, a lifelong bachelor, leaving the bulk of his $6 million estate to relatives and to his favorite charities. With his four nephews running the company, Levi Strauss & Co. continued to thrive and became one of the leading companies producing work pants in the 1920s.

The company's market, however, was still restricted to predominantly western states and to the niche of work clothing. In the 1930s and 1940s, Levi Strauss & Co.'s sphere of influence got a boost from Hollywood through western movies. Popular westerns mythologized cowboys and cowboy dress, including the waist overalls. It was during this period that denims became associated with the ideals of honesty, integrity, and rugged American individualism.

After World War II, Americans enjoyed a level of prosperity marked by greater leisure time. Denims, including Levi's, began to lose their connection with manual labor and emerged as appropriate casual dress. Pivotal to the acceptance of denims was their adoption by teenagers, an increasingly vocal and important market group. When the actor James Dean wore blue jeans in the film *Rebel Without a Cause*, denims attained a completely new status as cool fashion. By this time, the term "waist overalls" was no longer used; denims were known as jean pants or simply as "Levi's."

In the 1960s denims continued their evolution as acceptable leisure wear. As a result, denim producers such as Levi Strauss & Co. and Lee (another former working-pant manufacturer) continued to expand. The 1960s was an important decade for fashion—one which witnessed challenges to the traditional haute couture system and the rising popularity of more democratic, street-inspired fashions. Denims emerged as a symbol of individualism and anti-establishment fashion, much to the benefit of Levi Strauss and its competitors. During the height of the hippie era, Levi Strauss & Co. even sponsored a competition to promote the personalized decoration of Levi's jeans.

Founder Levi Strauss could never have foreseen the meteoric rise of Levi Strauss & Co. in subsequent decades. As tastes changed in the 1970s, denims were transformed from leisure wear to high fashion at the hands of designers such as Calvin Klein. Denims now became acceptable dress for all occasions. In the 1970s and the 1980s, Levi Strauss & Co. dominated the market for blue jeans, which became a de facto uniform for youth in America and abroad. Demand for American Levi's in Europe and around the globe was widespread. In Eastern block countries American Levi's jeans even attained the status of black-market cash in the early 1980s.

The importance of the Levi Strauss brand name in the denim market has been enormous. Through clever marketing and hip advertisements, Levi's capitalized on the revival in popularity of the "classic" 501 button-fly jeans in the mid 1980s. By 1990, Levi Strauss & Co. was an international manufacturer with a global market, selling under the brands Levi's, Dockers, and Slates. Only in the late 1990s and early years of the twenty-first century has Levi Strauss & Co. seen a slight reversal of fortune. Changes in taste, from traditional blue to other colors and the revival of retro-1970s flared leg and baggy, hip-hop silhouettes has worked against Levi's classic-cut jeans in

favor of trendy styles marketed by new competitors such as Tommy Hilfiger and Guess. Since the 1990s, Levi Strauss & Co. has been forced to restructure its company to remain competitive. Ironically, Levi's "classic" denims are no longer manufactured in the United States, the production having been entirely shifted to overseas manufacturers with cheaper labor.

Despite competition from the Gap, Tommy Hilfiger, and Guess jeans, Levi Strauss & Co. remains the standard bearer in the denim world. With roots in the settling of America's west, Levi Stauss & Co. has come full circle achieving (and retaining) iconic status as the maker of the quintessential American garment, still popular throughout the world.

See also **Cowboy Clothing; Denim; Jeans; Klein, Calvin.**

BIBLIOGRAPHY

Cray, Ed. *Levi's.* Boston: Houghton Mifflin, 1978.

"Custom Fit." *W Magazine* (December 2003): 54–62.

Hambleton, Ronald. *The Branding of America: From Levi Strauss to Chrysler, from Westinghouse to Gillette: The Forgotten Fathers of America's Best Known Brand Names.* Dublin, N.H.: Yankee Books, 1987.

Internet Resources

Downey, Lynn. "Invention of Levi's 501 Jeans." About L S & Co. Available from <http://www.levistrauss.com/about/history/jeans.htm>.

"Founder Biography." About L S & Co. Available from <http://www.levistrauss.com/about/history/founder.htm>.

Lauren D. Whitley

LIBERTY & CO. In 1875, Liberty & Co.'s first small shop opened on Regent Street in London's emergent West End. It grew into a showcase for cosmopolitan goods, and the company became synonymous with exotic and avant-garde design. In particular, Liberty garments were associated with the Aesthetic movement.

Arthur Lasenby Liberty (1843–1917), the company's founder, was the son of a small provincial draper. From 1862 his formative business and aesthetic experiences were at Farmer and Rogers' Oriental Warehouse, Regent Street, specializing in fashionable Kashmir shawls and oriental goods.

At Liberty's, Middle Eastern and Asian goods determined the character of the store. Sympathetic to Arts and Crafts ideals, which rejected factory production in favor of hand craft and sought to beautify everyday things, Lasenby Liberty's ambition became the reform of dress and home furnishings along "artistic" lines. As an entrepreneur, he found ways of supplying an expanding market with exotic, handmade goods in a retail environment evoking an oriental *souk* rather than a conventional department store.

Textiles

Liberty's early catalogs, published from 1881, featured silks remarkable for their variety of color, print, and weight. By the 1880s Liberty's name had become a trademark. "Liberty Art Fabrics" were sensuous and subtly colored, widely admired and imitated. Fashionable aniline dyes were rejected in favor of natural colorings; lack of chemical adulteration, antiquity of design, and irregularity of weave, indicating hand production, were also emphasized.

Initially, dyed and printed silks were imported from India; later, silks were dyed and hand-printed in England, often by Thomas Wardle. Other companies used by Liberty include G. P. and J. Baker; David Barbour; Arthur H. Lee and Sons; Alexander Morton and Co; Turnbull and Stockdale; and Warner and Sons. Leading designers were used anonymously by Liberty. Textile printing was done increasingly by Edmund Littler at Merton, just upstream from Morris and Co.'s workshops. In 1904 Liberty bought the business; until the 1960s, the emphasis was on hand printing with wooden blocks.

Early Liberty textiles were inspired by the Middle East and Asia; by the 1890s, they had a more contemporary look. Although Lasenby Liberty expressed dislike for its more extreme forms, Art Nouveau was dubbed *Stile Liberty* in Italy. "Oriental" designs continued to sell well in the 1920s and 1930s, when small floral patterns also became associated with Liberty fabrics, which then included a huge variety of natural and synthetic materials.

Cloth and Costume

Liberty fabrics were renowned for their softness. Artists appreciated their draping qualities, and Liberty's early dress designs exploited this tendency to follow the contours of the body. This could be perceived as a challenge to propriety, particularly when used in at-home garments such as the tea gown, pioneered by Liberty and others. Early catalogs are illustrated with vignettes of women in exotic or classical costumes. Some assistants in the shop wore unusual dress; even in the 1930s, shopwalkers wore medievally inspired velvet gowns. Liberty's "artistic" styles were imitated and caricatured, notably by the cartoonist George du Maurier.

A Costume Department was established in 1884 to design and make garments suited to the fabrics; eclecticism predominated over fashionable dress. It reflected Lasenby Liberty's determination to control the entire process of design, production, and retailing. The architect E. W. Godwin was consultant designer until his death in 1886. While his earlier designs were notably Japoniste, classical models and the principles of dress reform inspired Godwin's later ideas about dress.

Liberty resisted the dominance of Paris-led styles, although a successful branch was maintained there from 1890 to 1932. Instead, the company pioneered the unstructured cut of Asian clothing as a means of liberating women from their corsets. *Tokado* was described in the company's 1884 catalog as a "Japanese robe arranged as a tea gown." Other popular garments included the *burnous* cloak, derived from North Africa, and the Greek-inspired tea gown (*Hera*, 1901–1909) was an example of Liberty's attempt to promote classical "Greek" dress well after Godwin's death. As fashion absorbed dress-reform principles, Liberty designs appeared less eccentric. By 1925, a "kimono" style floral-print coat, reminiscent of designs by the French couturier Paul Poiret, appeared highly fashionable. Poiret even used Liberty fabrics in his couture business and, following its demise, designed four collections for Liberty in the 1930s. From the 1880s, Liberty also promoted "Artistic Dress for Children," inspired by the drawings of Kate Greenaway; the "Liberty Smock" was a notable example.

The Liberty Home

Liberty also developed a reputation for furnishing fabrics, curtains, bedspreads, and upholstery. A furniture department, supported by its own workshops, opened in 1880 under the direction of Leonard F. Wyburd. At first Liberty imported goods from countries seen as "exotic" and pre-industrial, producing handmade, but relatively inexpensive, furniture and artifacts. Lasenby Liberty traveled widely, notably to Japan, to observe their production firsthand. Shrewd business instincts drove him to innovate however, and he had no scruples about modifying designs for the home market, developing hybrid, Anglo-oriental artifacts and other ersatz styles, incorporating Arts and Crafts, "Celtic," "Tudor," Art Nouveau, and oriental elements. He also invested substantially in small companies producing ceramics, metalwork, and jewelry.

During the 1920s and 1930s, Liberty goods changed little, although after both World Wars, traditional, "English" values were favored. In the 1950s and early 1960s, the company redefined itself as contemporary and European, commissioning work from world-class designers. From 1962, Bernard Nevill directed a new era of distinguished textile design; dress reflected the exuberance of the fabrics. When "ethnic" and revivalist styles became fashionable in the late 1960s and 1970s, Liberty acknowledged the exotic and Art Nouveau heritage it had earlier rejected.

The company remained in family ownership until 2000. Subsequently, the store was modernized, and fabrics and oriental goods became less prominent, while greater emphasis was placed on luxury accessories, furnishing, and "idiosyncratic" fashion by international designers.

See also **London Fashion.**

BIBLIOGRAPHY

Adburgham, Alison. *Liberty's: A Biography of a Shop.* London: Allen and Unwin, 1975. Commissioned by the company for its centenary.

Ashmore, Sonia. "Liberty's Orient: Taste and Trade in the Decorative Arts in Late Victorian and Edwardian Britain, 1875–1914." Ph.D. diss., The London Institute/The Open University, 2001.

Calloway, Stephen, ed. *The House of Liberty: Masters of Style and Decoration.* London: Thames and Hudson, 1992.

Morris, Barbara. *Liberty Design: 1874–1914.* London: Pyramid Books, 1989.

Okabe, Masayuki et al., eds. *The Liberty Style.* Tokyo: Japan Art and Culture Association, 1999.

Victoria and Albert Museum. *Liberty's 1875–1975.* London: V & A Publications, 1975. Exhibition catalog.

Sonia Ashmore

Irish Linen handkerchiefs. Ireland was one of a handful of countries producing large amounts of linen by the Middle Ages, and the name Irish Linen remains synonymous with quality. © GERAY SWEENEY/CORBIS. REPRODUCED BY PERMISSION.

LINEN Linen (flax) is considered to be one of the oldest textile fibers. Linen, the commonly used term for flax, a bast fiber, comes from the stem of the flax plant. Flax plants are either raised for their fiber or for the linseed oil harvested from flax seeds. Scientists have traced linen textiles to prehistoric times. Linen cloth was found among the artifacts of Swiss Lake Dwellers dating from 8000 B.C.E. When Tutankhamen's tomb was opened, linen curtains placed in the tomb circa 1250 B.C.E. were still identifiable. Linen was introduced to the Roman Republic by Phoenician traders who originally came from the eastern Mediterranean region. As the Roman Empire spread, so did the use of linen textiles. By the Middle Ages, German and Russian regions were major sources of fiber, while Northern Ireland, Belgium, England, Scotland, and the Netherlands established industries well known for production of linen textiles. It is from this historical development that Irish Linen became a household name and continues in 2004 as a label associated with genuine linen fiber content.

Linen production in North America, and then in Europe, became less important due to an emphasis on producing cotton that began in the eighteenth century. Argentina and Japan joined in production of linen midway into the twentieth century and production in the early twenty-first century extends to New Zealand and China. Russia, Poland, Northern Ireland, Egypt, France, and Belgium are the key producers of linen for the global marketplace. The limitation of requiring hand labor to produce linen fiber, compared to the ongoing mechanization of cotton, also contributed to limited production of linen goods.

Processing Flax Fiber

Linen is cellulosic and thus has aesthetic, comfort, and performance characteristics reminiscent of cotton and rayon textiles. These include high absorbency, low insulation, a tendency to be cool in hot temperatures. Linen textiles are additionally famous for their ability to "wick," a form of moisture transport known for providing a cooling effect in hot temperatures via drying quickly. Linen is not subject to linting, the shedding of fibers that can result in bits of fiber lying on the surface of the textile. It is therefore ideal for drying dishes and for appearance retention in apparel. While twice the strength of cotton, linen is highly subject to wrinkling and thus is reputed to produce "prestigious wrinkles." Wrinkling is diminished when fibers are long and fine, and yarns are flexible. Wrinkle-resistant finishes have been applied to many cellulosic fibers as another way to reduce this tendency to wrinkle.

Natural colors for linen fibers include buff and gray. White and pure colors are obtained through bleaching. Highly bleached textiles have lower strength and durability than those with natural color or tonal variations of color resulting when linen is not heavily bleached before dyeing. Dyeing linen is challenging because fibers resist absorbing dyes and fade easily. It has become a tradition that linen textiles are quite often in the buff, tan, and gray colors associated with the look of linen.

Dirt and stains are resisted by flattened smooth surfaces. Linen has high heat resistance, is stronger wet than dry, and withstands cleaning, pressing, and creasing very successfully. Abrasion can break fibers on creases due to low resiliency. Linen textiles are flammable and are subject to damage from mildew, perspiration, bleach, and silverfish.

Linen in Fashion Across Time

Knitwear has considerable design potential for linen apparel. The flexibility of the knit structure compensates for linen's tendency to wrinkle, yet the textile retains all the comfort factors of natural linen.

Many fabrications appear to be linen. By achieving the visual effect of linen, many textiles are called linen even when fiber content includes little or no linen fiber. For example, textiles labeled linen are often actually either rayon or polyester, or a blend of both fibers. These two fibers that have great propensity to imitate the prestigious look of linen while lowering the cost and sometimes increasing performance in terms of wrinkling and shrinkage without losing the "look of linen." Rayon textiles come a close second with regard to the absorbency, feel on the skin, and similar tendency to wrinkle. Polyester textiles can eliminate the need for ironing. Raw silk and linen suiting textiles can have a quite similar visual aesthetic, yet touching either textile reveals that linen will always have a crisper and dryer feel than silk. Linen supports keeping the body cool, while raw silk is known for keeping the body warm.

Another fiber that has been widely used in imitating linen is ramie. Ramie (also known as China grass due to its origin in China and Asia) has much of the look of linen but is not subject to import quotas, as is linen. Therefore, it is commonplace to find ramie instead of linen as the fiber content for a great many "linen" textiles. Ramie is naturally white so can be dyed a broader range of colors more easily than linen, and thus the products can be stronger since less processing is needed to reach the final product. There is a tendency for these relatively shorter fibers (from 6–8 inches) to produce textiles that have an inherent scratchiness rather than the smoothness of linen. Thus, ramie products tend to be more successful as interior textile products. With the end of fiber quotas, it is expected there will be a moderation in the use of ramie in linen-like products as designers seek creation of high-quality goods.

See also **Ramie.**

BIBLIOGRAPHY

Collier, B., and P. Tortora. *Understanding Textiles.* 6th ed. New York: Macmillan Publishing, 2000.

Hatch, K. *Textile Science.* Minneapolis: West Publishing, 1993.

Kadolph, S., and A. Langford. *Textiles.* 9th ed. New York: Prentice-Hall, 2002.

Carol J. Salusso

LINGERIE The term "lingerie" is derived from the French *linge,* or linen, and thus makes direct reference to the material from which underwear was traditionally made. By the late nineteenth century, lingerie had become a generic term commonly used to describe under-

Heidi Klum in Victoria's Secret fashion show. In the 1990s, California-based Victoria's Secret became one of the most popular and successful lingerie companies. © PETRE BUZOIANU/CORBIS. REPRODUCED BY PERMISSION.

wear that had moved beyond practical function to become a tool of erotic pleasure used for the display of the body during sexual play. The notion that women, other than prostitutes, could use underwear to designate specific occasions as sexual was particularly popularized during the Edwardian era. Under the relatively austere "tailor-made" suit, women were prepared to wear sensual camisoles and petticoats of lace, chiffon, and crepe de chine, offsetting the accusations of "mannishness" directed by the conservative press at the New Woman, a product of the suffragette movement. Lingerie was a symptom of conflicting gender relations at the turn of the century, on the one hand, the suffragette movement promoted a sea change in sexual politics, while lingerie evoked a more traditional brand of femininity, which objectified the female body. Underwear became deliberately branded as either male or female, feminine or masculine, determined by the use of delicate fabrics and applied decoration for women and practical wool and cotton for men. However, as the twentieth century progressed, the increase in the popularity and use of lingerie mirrored women's gradual freedom from the constraints of Victorian morality and notions of what constituted an appropriate femininity as they emerged as more sexually and socially independent beings. Lingerie was also set apart from the rationalist and unashamedly moralistic undergarments advocated by the Victorian Dr. Jaeger, who espoused the use of wool next to the skin for reasons of hygiene and health—lingerie was unashamedly erotic. However, caution was advocated at first: Lingerie should only be used by women within the confines of a happily married life. One female fashion journalist wrote in 1902, "'Lovely lingerie' does not belong only to the fast. . . . dainty undergarments are not necessarily [sic] a sign of depravity. The most virtuous of us are now allowed to possess pretty undergarments, without being looked upon as suspicious characters" (Steele, p. 194).

At first, handmade lingerie was a sign of social status, afforded only by the very few. Of note were those designed by English couturiere known as Lucile (Lady Duff-Gordon), who fashioned camisoles, peignoirs, and petticoats using lace, chiffon, and crepe de chine—materials that mirrored the feel of idealized flesh, deliberately appealing to the sense of touch, and evoking a new sensuality for the twentieth-century woman. Although artificial fibers such as rayon were marketed in the 1920s as a luxury fabric through the use of the name "artificial silk," their development led to a democratization of lingerie. The more body-conscious fashions of that decade also led to a new item of lingerie, the teddy, named after its inventor Theodore Baer, who combined a chemise with a short slip or attached panties. The camisole, originally derived from a decorative waist-length garment with an embroidered and pleated front and shoulder straps that were worn over the corset for warmth and modesty, became a staple garment of lingerie, eventually becoming an item of outerwear by the 1970s. Similarly the slip, a standard piece of lingerie from the 1950s and produced by the company La Perla, founded by Ada Masotti, in 1954, was used by a number of fashion designers as outerwear in the 1990s, most notably John Galliano, Dolce & Gabbana.

Sales of lingerie declined in the 1960s as the new silhouette defined by the miniskirt needed a more practical combination of matching polyester bra and panties with tights to replace stockings and suspenders. In the 1970s, however, a lingerie revival was lead by the English designer Janet Reger, whose company became one of the most renowned lingerie names of the late twentieth century. Reger was even the object of an essay by the English journalist and cultural commentator Angela Carter, who described her ranges of lingerie as "part of the 'fantasy courtesan' syndrome of the sexy exec, a syndrome reflected admirably in the pages of Cosmopolitan magazine. Working women regain the femininity they have lost behind the office desk by parading about like grande horizontale from early Colette in the privacy of their flats, even if there is nobody there to see" (Carter, p. 97). Carter was prescient in her comments, as with the rise of women entering the executive arena in the 1980s

came an exponential rise in the sales of lingerie and the power suit with a lacy camisole peeping through the jacket became the staple of many a working wardrobe. In the 1990s, a lingerie revival, attracting both male and female consumers, was led by Californian companies Victoria's Secret and Frederick's of Hollywood. Victoria's Secret was estimated in 2000 to be selling six hundred items of lingerie per minute while the simple Egyptian cotton camisole made by the Swiss firm Hanro and worn by Nicole Kidman in Stanley Kubrick's film *Eyes Wide Shut* (1999) was a major lingerie bestseller. The British company Agent Provocateur, founded by Joseph Corres and Serena Rees in 1994, has successfully integrated the glamour of 1950s underwear with the catwalk, recreating seminal garments like the baby-doll nightie and matching puff panties worn by Carroll Baker in the 1956 film *Baby Doll*. Sourcing vintage undergarments and amalgamating them with new fabrics, such as Lycra, and high-fashion design concepts, they have redefined lingerie as a luxury item with a strong appeal for a young fashion-oriented consumer. Dorothy Parker's well-known remark, "Brevity is the soul of lingerie," invokes the appeal of these most personal of undergarments.

See also **Embroidery; Lace; Lucile; Pajamas.**

BIBLIOGRAPHY

Carter, Angela. "The Bridled Sweeties." In *Nothing Sacred: Selected Writings*. London: Virago, 1982.

Saint Laurent, Cecil. *The Great Book of Lingerie*. London: Academy Editions, 1986.

Steele, Valerie. *Fashion and Eroticism: Ideals of Feminine Beauty from the Victorian Era to the Jazz Age*. New York: Oxford University Press, 1985.

Caroline Cox

LIPSTICK In many cultures, red lips are an important component of feminine beauty, and this has often prompted women to augment the redness of their lips through artificial means. The modern use of lipstick in Western society has been part of a more general development of makeup for women, one often unstated, and possibly the unconscious goal of which is the emulation of the clear skin, good blood circulation, and sexual fecundity associated with youth and good health.

Lipstick, a cosmetic product used for coloring the lips, and now usually made in the form of a cylindrical stick of waxy material encased in a metal or plastic tube, has a very long history. In ancient Egypt, powdered red ocher in a base of grease or wax was used as a lip coloring. During the time of the Roman empire, henna and carmine, in various preparations, were used for the same purpose. Other ancient lip coloring preparations were made with vermilion or mulberry juice.

Queen Elizabeth I of England made her lips crimson by using a concoction of cochineal blended with gum

Arabic and egg white; her red lips made a striking contrast with her pale powered face. In the seventeenth century artificially colored lips were denounced as immoral by the Puritan clergy; stained lips were sometimes referred to as "the devil's candy." During the eighteenth century, a moderate use of makeup was regarded as normal and attractive for members of the upper classes, but frowned upon for people of more humble status; thus the use of lip color was involved in distinctions of social class. During the nineteenth century, however, in both Europe and America, social commentators generally frowned upon the use of any cosmetics (referred to as "paint") at all; women who resorted to the conspicuous use of makeup, including lip coloring, invited social criticism. By the end of the century, in turn, many younger women rejected this socially conservative attitude and began to use cosmetics openly. The use of lip coloring came to be one of the beauty secrets of the New Woman.

Until the early twentieth century, lip coloring was often made in the form of a salve, packaged in small jars and applied with a fingertip or small brush. Lipstick as such probably derived from theatrical makeup ("greasepaint"), which was often produced in the form of a waxy crayon or pencil. The term "lipstick" itself dates from the late nineteenth century. Maurice Levy designed the first lipstick in a sliding tube in 1915. Soon thereafter, both Helena Rubinstien and Elizabeth Arden followed his lead and produced lip salve, rouge, and later lipsticks to respond to popular demand.

The influence of movie stars, heavily made up for the screen, may have prompted a shift to stronger colors of makeup, including lipstick, by the 1920s. At that time also, new clothing styles and shorter hairstyles, both of which promoted an image of fashionable youthfulness, led to new styles of makeup and more conspicuous use of lipstick and other cosmetics. By the 1920s also, cosmetic companies relied heavily on advertising to introduce new products, stimulate demand, and promote brand loyalty.

Lipstick came to be associated with other closely related products that were promoted as aids to health and good hygiene. Lip salve and lip balm, designed to protect against sunburn, dryness, and chapping, were introduced around the time of World War II and won widespread consumer approval.

Modern lipsticks typically are made from waxes (beeswax, carnauba wax, palm wax, candelilla wax), oils (olive oil, mineral oil, castor oil, cocoa butter, and others), and chemical dyes. These basic ingredients are supplemented by a range of moisturizers, vitamins, aloe vera, collagen, and other enhancers.

Recent improvements in lipstick have included lip glosses, which give the lips a moist appearance, lipstick with improved adhesion that avoids unsightly lipstick-stained cups and glasses, a wide range of colors keyed to the individual complexions of wearers, and lipsticks that also contain sunscreen. The palette of fashionable lipstick colors changes from year to year, varying from bright and vivid reds to soft pastels. Lipstick in unusual colors, such as black and dark green, is made for niche markets, such as goths and punks. In the mainstream, the continuing allure of red lips seems to assure that lipstick will be part of the beauty and fashion scene for a long time to come.

See also **Cosmetics, Non-Western; Cosmetics, Western.**

BIBLIOGRAPHY

Corson, Richard. *Fashions in Make Up: From Ancient to Modern Times.* London: Peter Owen Limited, 1972.

Ragas, Meg Cohen, and Karen Kozlowski. *Read My Lips: A Cultural History of Lipstick.* San Francisco: Chronicle Books, 1998.

Elizabeth McLafferty

LITTLE BLACK DRESS At once demure and daring, the little black dress conjures up a host of images and associations. Consistently a symbol of elegance and chic, it is an international fashion icon capable of being interpreted in myriad different styles. Since the late 1920s, some of the world's most elegant women, including Audrey Hepburn, Marlene Dietrich, Maria Callas, and Edith Piaf, have been photographed wearing a version of the little black dress. Coco Chanel claimed to have "invented"

FAMOUS CHARACTERS IN THE LITTLE BLACK DRESS

The little black dress has long been a star of page and screen, its ability to convey meaning a powerful tool. Edith Wharton's Ellen Olenska in *The Age of Innocence* wore black and shocked New York's high society when she decided to get a divorce. Majorie Morningstar, the eponymous heroine of Herman Wouk's novel, wore black, as did Mrs. Danvers of *Rebecca.* Jeanne Moreau was an image of perfection in her Chanel little black dress, chignon, and pearls in Louis Malle's *The Lovers.* But in *The Bride Wore Black,* Moreau, also in a Chanel little black dress but now a murderess, was anything but perfect. Anouk Aimee wore her signature dark glasses and little black dress in *La Dolce Vita.* Catherine Deneuve's little black dress was detailed with white in *Belle de jour,* creating an image that was at once pure and corrupt. And perhaps the most famous of all little black dresses was Audrey Hepburn's Givenchy in *Breakfast at Tiffany's.*

the little black dress, and that claim has found its way into fashion mythology. But although Chanel greatly influenced the status of the little black dress as a classic fashion item, beginning with her 1926 introduction of a simple black jersey day dress, many other designers were experimenting with the same look at the same time, and black as a fashion color has a long history.

Historically, black has been associated with mourning and asceticism. By the fourteenth century, however, black was being used to create a dramatic effect in one's appearance. In the fifteenth century, Philip the Good, duke of Burgundy, dressed exclusively in black. He was second to none in the luxury of his dress, but in black this magnificence was conveyed with much greater discretion. Black, expensive to produce with natural dyes and thought to convey an air of refinement, became the color of choice for the fifteenth-century Spanish aristocracy, and connoted wealth and social status among the Dutch commercial middle class.

By the eighteenth century black clothing was considered respectable, even dowdy, as it was associated with mourning and the dress of the clergy. Black was revived as the color of elegance, especially for men, by the dandies of the early nineteenth century. The introduction of aniline dyes later in the nineteenth century created a new vogue for bright colors for fashionable women's clothing; black clothing for women signified mourning, or was a badge of middle-class respectability. When fashionable women did wear black it was to make a statement. One of the most memorable, if controversial, examples of this was John Singer Sargent's 1884 portrait of "Madame X," Virginie Gautreau, dressed in a form-fitting black evening gown. Conventional portraiture employed colorful frilly, even demure dress that all but obscured the subject. That Mme. Gautreau, a socialite of the day whose improprieties were hardly secret, appeared in a seductively form-fitting black gown with deep décolletage was quite a departure, underscoring the subject's decision to play by a different set of rules.

In the early 1900s, black "widow's weeds" were still being sold in department stores, but black was beginning to make appearances on other occasions as well. Paul Poiret made vivid colors fashionable between 1908 and 1914. Chanel claimed to be "nauseated" by Poiret's colors and favored instead black, beige, and navy blue. Her 1926 showing of the little black dress was a milestone in the creation of this fashion icon. However, she was hardly alone. The House of Premet had already had a great success with a little black dress. Indeed, the terrible death toll in World War I had resulted in a plethora of fashionable black dresses.

The little black dress was the ideal mix of elements. It was easy, versatile, and practical; it was also chic, elegant, and sophisticated. Capable of embodying many meanings, the little black dress's chameleon-like quality enabled it to evolve with the trends, but never to be beholden to them.

Actress Audrey Hepburn in black dress. By the mid-1940s, the versatile little black dress was considered an essential part of every fashion-conscious woman's wardrobe. © SUNSET BOULEVARD/ CORBIS SYGMA. REPRODUCED BY PERMISSION.

Of the little black dress, *Vogue* declared in 1944, "Ten out of ten women have one" (MacDonell Smith, 2003, p. 14). Fashion magazines everywhere featured the new phenomenon. By 1948 Christian Dior's groundbreaking New Look was calling for hem- and necklines to drop and skirts to be fuller. The little black dress obliged. As Dior said in 1954, "You can wear black at any time. You can wear black at any age. You may wear it on almost any occasion. A little black frock is essential to a woman's wardrobe" (MacDonell Smith, 2003, p. 14).

The little black dress's versatility ensured its immortality. Parisian Left Bank intellectuals wore it for its associations with creativity and rebellion. Paired with black tights and black eyeliner, it was the uniform of the beatnik generation. Audrey Hepburn wore black in *Funny Face*, and a little black dress by Givenchy in *Breakfast at Tiffany's*.

The 1960s marked a low point in the life of the little black dress. Not only did one of its masters, Cristóbal Balenciaga, retire in 1968, but it was an era focused on a youthful sense of color and fun rather than sophistication and elegance. But a decade later, a new generation of designers began to make it once again the uniform of the modern woman. From Claude Montana's versions in leather to Azzedine Alaia's in stretch fabric, the little black dress took on a more aggressive edge during the late 1970s and 1980s. Showcased at the groundbreaking New York store Charivari, the status of the little black dress was underscored by Helmut Newton, the German-born, Australian photographer, known for his blatantly provocative erotic, sometimes violent images of women. The evolution continued and by the early 1980s a new breed of Japanese designers led by Rei Kawakubo and Yohji Yamamoto reinterpreted the little black dress according to new somber, intellectual criteria.

At the turn of the twenty-first century, the little black dress remains a mainstay of the clothing industry and a must in the wardrobe of every woman. At once impervious to and accommodating of the vicissitudes of fashion, the little black dress has become a lens through which to view the evolution of fashion and dress, since at least the late 1920's.

See also **Balenciaga, Cristóbal; Chanel, Gabrielle (Coco).**

BIBLIOGRAPHY

Hollander, Anne. *Seeing Through Clothes* New York: Viking Press, 1978.

Ludot, Didier. *The Little Black Dress: Vintage Treasure.* New York: Assouline Publishing, 2001.

MacDonell Smith, Nancy. *The Classic Ten: The True Story of the Little Black Dress and Nine Other Fashion Favorites.* New York: Penguin Books, 2003.

Mendes, Valerie. *Black in Fashion.* London: Victoria and Albert Museum Publications, 1999.

Liz Gessner

LOGOS The logo (logotype) is the emblem or device used to identify a particular company or organization. The design of a logo may be based around the name or initials of a company using a distinctive letter form, such as Coca-Cola (first used in 1887). It may also be a visual symbol of abstract or figurative design, such as the Nike swoosh (designed 1971). In order to function effectively a logo must be easily recognized in a variety of forms—on products, packaging, and advertising.

The logo is the modern equivalent of the maker's stamp; the hallmark or trademark that indicates the authenticity of a product. Logos, like monograms, heraldic devices, flags, and crests, are forms of graphical devices that have been used to indicate the origin, ownership, and status of property and people.

Law protects modern logos, so that the form, color, shape, and graphical detail of any mark cannot be copied or closely imitated without legal redress. This legisla-

tion was put into place in the mid-nineteenth century in Europe and America, and is now effective across national borders.

The logo is central to any company's concept of its brand. As the graphic designer Milton Glaser once said, "The logo is the point of entry to the brand" and is used to encapsulate all that a brand may stand for. A logo with a high recognition factor can be a major financial asset to any business, and therefore it sits at the heart of any corporate identity policy. A manufacturer's product range may change from season to season, but successful logos are rarely tampered with and, when design changes are made, they are usually subtle rather than radical. Logos also need to be adaptable to a variety of uses. The interlocking CC logo of Chanel, like many logos used by the garment industry, work well as both a repeat pattern on fabric and as an embossed button on a coat or jacket. The "Medusa head" logo used by Versace was adapted from a classical architectural motif. It can be used in print or relief, and appears on stationery, packaging, buttons, cosmetics containers, and tableware.

The use of the logo as a decorative element was traditionally the preserve of the luxury goods sector (rather than the clothing industry). Leather goods (luggage and saddlery) companies have exploited the familiarity of their logos and signature patterns as they compete in the high-fashion market. The French luggage company Louis Vuitton (founded 1854) first used its monogram in a repeat-patterned canvas in 1896, and the monogram fabric has been a staple of its collections ever since. The monogram pattern has been reinterpreted by a succession of designers from the mid-1990s, including Marc Jacobs and Stephen Sprouse. Gucci's monogrammed fabric, using the GG logo adopted in the 1960s, appeared for many years on handbags and as linings before being used for clothing.

One key factor in the development of fashion branding has been the shift of the "signature" or logo from the inside to the outside of the garment. Conventionally, the designer or manufacturer's label would be sewn inside a garment, originally to guard against the illegal copying of fashion house models. In the field of sportswear, logos began to be more prominent in the 1940s, when the brand named after the tennis star Fred Perry borrowed the idea of the team or club crest, displayed on the breast of shirts and sweaters. In the 1970s, when sportswear was worn increasingly off pitch, court, or course as leisurewear, brands such as Lacoste and Fred Perry used their logos to brand generic garments like the polo shirt. This first wave of fashion sports brands was eclipsed by the phenomenal rise of global sports corporations such as Nike in the 1980s and 1990s.

The "designer decade" of the 1980s introduced many more designer logos to the mass market, where they became adopted as part of street culture. Logos associated with status and expense, such as BMW and Mercedes car mascots in the shape of corporate logos, were worn as jewelry by American rap artists. Heavily branded sportswear by Nike and Tommy Hilfiger (where the logos became increasingly prominent) was worn with a brash, competitive attitude and an emphasis on "box-fresh" products. Between 1995 and 2000, several high-fashion brands including Gucci, Fendi, Dior, and Louis Vuitton produced collections almost entirely focused on the repeat use of the logo (dubbed "logomania" by the style press).

Reaction to this visibly over-branded culture has been strong. One economic and legal side effect has been the flourishing of a counterfeit trade in clothes and accessories where fake logos are applied to unlicensed and inferior goods. The other effect is cultural and political. Global brands have come under attack by the so-called "No Logo" generation (named after Naomi Klein's 1999 book of that title), who reject overtly branded goods as symbols of late capitalist economic exploitation and social inequality.

See also **Brands and Labels.**

BIBLIOGRAPHY
Clifton, Rita, and John Simmons, eds. *Brands and Branding.* Princeton, N.J.: Bloomberg Press, 2004.

Jane Pavitt

LONDON FASHION In the twenty-first century London ranks highly amongst the world's cities as a distinctive fashion center. Its characteristic products and sense of style compete with and complement the fashion values of other global fashion capitals including Paris, New York, Milan, and Tokyo. In the popular imagination, which is fed by the stereotyping tendencies of fashion journalism, London has become most associated with the traditional handcrafts of tailoring, shirtmaking, hatmaking, and shoemaking that underpin the image of the English gentleman, a vibrant subcultural club and street scene, and the nurturing of eccentric and innovative design talent in its famous art schools. These are largely phenomena that blossomed during the twentieth century, but London's fashion history is as old as the city itself and closely related to its economic, social, and cultural development over time.

With its thriving docks and strong mercantile economy, London operated as a natural hub for trade and cultural exchange in the late medieval period, building on a heritage that stretched back to its status as an important port on the western fringes of the Roman Empire. By the fifteenth century, it was already one of the largest cities in the world, though it could not compete with smaller European centers such as Paris, Florence, and Rome as a focus for the production and display of fashionable commodities. London operated more as a transit point in an international fashion system, exporting primary or unfinished products like wool and metal and importing luxuries such as fur and embroideries. But in a national context, the city began to exert a formidable political and cultural pressure over the rest of the country as parliament, law courts, and the crown established permanent bases there. This process drew the rich and influential into London and helped to ensure that fashionable trends originated in its streets, markets, and great houses. The palaces of Henry VIII, Elizabeth I, and Charles I at Hampton Court, Greenwich, and Whitehall thus operated as forcing houses for a very English sense of sartorial style, which nevertheless still relied largely on the pattern books, fabrics, and craftsmanship of Spain, France, and Italy for its luxurious impact.

By the early eighteenth century, the political stability afforded by the accession of the Hanoverian line of monarchs and a prosperous professional class, together with the increased income that attended London's rise as the capital of a widening network of colonies, meant that the city entered a new phase of development during which its growing confidence and urbane sophistication produced the distinctive sartorial identity that would influence world trends for the next three centuries. After the Great Fire of 1666, London's developers and architects had shifted their attention westward and the arising geography of graceful squares and parks encouraged the aristocracy to base their domestic and business affairs in the West End during those periods of the year (later known as the Season) when Parliament was sitting or the royal family was in residence. The flurry of social activity that followed, with its balls, theater visits, and court presentations, offered great incentives to entrepreneurs in the clothing trades, and it was on this basis, from the 1740s on, that the craftsmen of Savile Row, Jermyn Street, and St. James's established themselves as producers of a homegrown masculine style of dressing, replete with the genteel codes and sporting influences that have bracketed the idea of London with the identity of the dandy. The methods of tailoring developed in Savile Row in the eighteenth century also went on to inform the design of women's wear in the capital, producing the severe "tailor-mades" of the late nineteenth century and the artfully restrained creations of Norman Hartnell, Hardy Amies, and Victor Stiebel in the mid-twentieth century.

Through the nineteenth century the range and organization of the clothing industries in London expanded considerably, augmented by successive waves of immigration. As the West End became increasingly associated with the consumption of high quality, locally produced bespoke goods, so the East End or working-class districts of Aldgate and Bethnal Green played host to other, less prestigious forms of manufacturing. In the eighteenth and early nineteenth centuries, the French Huguenot community had woven high-quality figured silks for gowns, waistcoats, and ribbons in the upper floors of their tall Spitalfields houses, but by the 1870s, when the fashion for brocades had passed, the sewing of shirts and ready-made suits provided one of the few opportunities for employment in an area bedeviled by poverty and overcrowding. Even then, the infamous practice of sweating ensured that clothing production was a profession of poor pay and low esteem, associated with the exploited labor of women and Jews.

Some aspects of Victorian London's fashion scene maintained a positive gloss. In line with the city's entrepreneurial spirit, the capital witnessed several pioneering inventions such as William Perkin's discovery of synthetic (aniline) dyes in the late 1850s or Thomas Burberry's experiments with waterproofing later in the century. Perhaps the most lasting innovations to come out of London in the period were in the realm of fashion retailing. By the 1830s the West End had been transformed by the architectural renewal set in place by the Prince Regent and John Nash. The new arcades leading off of Piccadilly and the majestic sweep of Regent Street offered a fresh conception of shopping as a modish leisure activity for the middle and upper classes, where emphasis was placed on spectacular display, comfort, and escapism. Unsurprisingly the first great couturier Charles Worth learned his trade in a Regent Street emporium, and two decades later in the 1870s and 1880s Arthur Liberty perfected the selling of a lifestyle nearby, in a store that provided all the exotic accoutrements for the aesthetic movement. Napoleon's dismissive take on the English as a nation of shopkeepers would find further resonance in the development of the great London department stores such as Harrods, Selfridges, and Harvey Nichols from the Edwardian period on, and the emergence of the "happening" fashion boutique in Chelsea and West Soho in the 1950s and 1960s.

These London traits of tradition, innovation, and a certain sense of theatricality continued to inform the development of fashionable style in the city in the twentieth century. In the late 1940s and 1950s young men from chic Mayfair and working-class South and East London, with seemingly little else in common than a passionate interest in style as a means of subverting the stultifying status quo, resurrected Edwardian notions of elegance in a shocking manner of dressing that soon became associated with the "Teddy Boy" craze. Their velvet-trimmed draped jackets, drainpipe trousers, and extravagantly combed hairstyles presaged a succession of teenage poses whose influence was felt worldwide. The Mods of 1960s Carnaby Street and the Punks of 1970s King's Road all earned London a certain notoriety as the breeding ground for revolutionary acts of sartorial rebellion.

Various London designers have found their inspiration in this street-level creativity. In the 1960s Mary Quant, Barbara Hulanicki (of Biba), and Ossie Clarke were closely associated with the phenomenon of "Swinging London," famously promoted to America by *Time* magazine in 1966; while in the 1970s Zandra Rhodes and Vivienne Westwood offered a more astringent and eccentric take on contemporary mores. By the 1980s and 1990s a generation brought up in the hedo-

nistic, post-punk environment of neo-romanticism and the commercial club scene, seemed more adept at selling their London-honed individuality abroad. Central Saint Martins–trained John Galliano, Stella McCartney, and Alexander McQueen, and the Royal College protégé Julien McDonald have thus famously risen to supplant local talent at the creative helms of the great Parisian fashion houses. But behind the famous names, the studios and warehouses of London continue to support an active and influential local economy of young independent designers, stylists, photographers, publishers, and journalists (London has nurtured a wide-range of edgy fashion magazines including *The Face*, *i-D*, *Sleaze Nation*, and *Dazed and Confused*). Though there has been little concrete state support for the growth of a British fashion industry, the sheer size, diversity, and chaotic energy of the British capital still seems to foster a productive and adventurous sartorial spirit in the early twenty-first century.

See also **Amies, Hardy; Biba; Clark, Ossie; Europe and America: History of Dress (400–1900 C.E.); Galliano, John; Hartnell, Norman; McQueen, Alexander; Paris Fashion; Rhodes, Zandra; Royal and Aristocratic Dress; Westwood, Vivienne.**

BIBLIOGRAPHY

Breward, Christopher. *Fashioning London: Clothing and the Modern Metropolis*. Oxford: Berg, 2004.

Breward, Christopher, Edwina Ehrman, and Caroline Evans. *The London Look*. New Haven, Conn., and London: Yale University Press, 2004.

Tucker, Andrew. *The London Fashion Book*. London: Thames and Hudson, Inc., 1998.

Christopher Breward

LOOM Although the process of weaving has been modified and adapted to every technological advancement known to humanity, including that of computers, when one watches a contemporary weaver working at a loom in the early 2000s, what is being observed is essentially a process, and equipment, that goes back thousands of years. The loom was invented as a means to hold one set of elements, the warp (yarns extended lengthwise on the loom), under tension so that the second set of elements, the weft (yarns running crosswise), could be inserted and interlaced with the warp, to form cloth. The loom that most contemporary weavers use is called a floor loom (or a treadle loom, a shaft loom, or a harness loom). There are numerous companies making these looms in the early twenty-first century, each with its own modifications, but the essentials of the shaft looms are the same.

Elements of a Shaft Loom

The essential parts of a shaft loom are illustrated in the given diagram. The loom has a frame with both a front

Shaft Loom

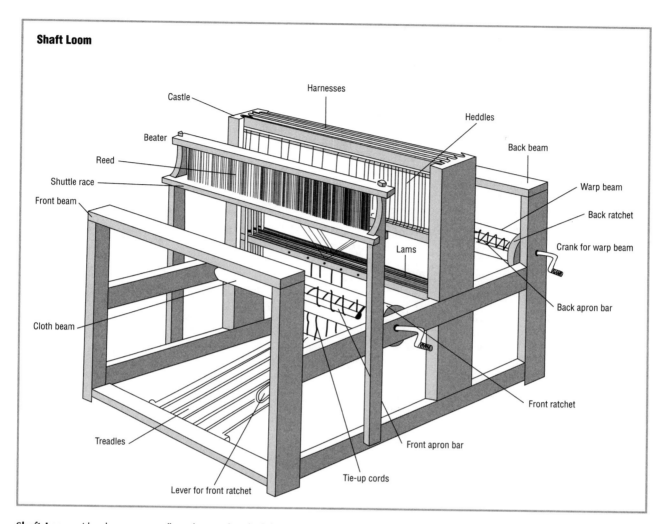

Shaft Loom. Also known as a floor loom, the shaft loom is the loom used most often by contemporary weavers.

beam and a back beam. Below the back beam lie one or two warp beams, which hold the warp or warps threads. Each warp beam will have a crank attached to it that is used to turn the beam as the warp is wound on to it. Below the front beam is the cloth beam, which holds the finished cloth as it is woven. The warp is tensioned between the back and cloth beams; the tensioning of these threads is one of the essential reasons for having a loom.

The castle is in the middle of the loom; it can be high or low, depending on the manufacturer, and the shafts (sometimes called harnesses by weavers in the United States) are seated within it. The shafts can be suspended from chains or ropes attached to levers or pulleys, or they may be riding in slots at the side of the castle.

Floor looms are generally built with anywhere from 2 to 24 shafts, though the majority of looms are 4-, or 8-, or 16-shaft looms. Shafts are movable frames that hold heddles. Heddles have eyes (holes) in their center through

which individual warp ends are threaded. In the space between the shafts and the front beam, a loom has a beater, which may be suspended from a high castle or pivoting from the bottom of the loom. The beater has a furrow in its frame in which a reed is placed. Reeds are flat metal or steel combs, with evenly spaced teeth. The spaces of a reed are called dents, and these are manufactured with different specifications. A weaver will usually have a number of different reeds (perhaps one with 8 dents per inch; one with 12 dents per inch; maybe one with 20 dents per inch). Depending on the sett (the density) of their warp, the weaver will insert the appropriate reed into the beater. When the beater is brought forward during weaving, the reed passes smoothly between the warp ends that are threaded in it, and then pushes the weft into the web of the cloth. More than one warp end can pass through a dent of the reed, as long as they are adjacent ends. The front of the beater usually extends a bit under the threads, and is called the shuttle race. When the shuttle (the device that holds a bobbin wound with the weft yarn) is thrown from edge to edge, it slides smoothly along the shuttle race.

Floor looms have treadles (pedals) that are attached to the shafts, so when a treadle is depressed the shaft will raise or lower. Lamms are the horizontal levers that reside between the treadle and the shaft and they help with the mechanics of the lifting of the shafts. Looms are usually equipped with the same number of treadles as shafts, plus two; but some four-harness looms have only four pedals. Since a weaver needs to change which shafts are tied to a pedal fairly often, the ease of changing the connection (the tie-up) is very important. Some manufacturers use string devices to make the tie-up; others use metal hooks.

At the front side of the loom, usually the right side, is another pedal, called the brake pedal. When the weaver depresses the brake pedal, it releases the ratchet that is holding the cloth beam tight, and allows the warp to be moved forward. There is a lever attached to the front ratchet, which is attached to the cloth beam, and the weaver can move this ratchet to roll the cloth forward onto the cloth beam. A weaver needs the ratchet on the warp beam to fall back into place as soon as the brake pedal is released, so she can use the front ratchet and tension the warp so weaving can proceed.

Most looms also have cloth aprons attached to both the warp beam and cloth beam. They act as extensions for the warp so there won't be too much yarn wastage at the beginning and end of the weaving. Strings can be used instead of cloth aprons.

When a loom is "dressed" with a warp, the warp is wound evenly on the warp beam, passes over the back beam, through the eyes of the heddles on the shafts, through the dents of the reed in the beater, over the front beam, and then is tied to the cloth beam. Each individual warp end passes through a different heddle, and its path should be straight from back to front. The reed not only acts as a comb to beat the weft into the cloth, it also acts to keep the warp threads in order and spaced out to their required width.

Jack-type looms
Card weaving, also known as tablet weaving, is a very ancient process. Here square cards have holes near each corner, and a warp end is threaded through each hole. When the weaver puts tension on the threaded warp, a shed forms between the ends on the two top holes and those in the bottom holes. After a weft is inserted, the cards are turned, either forward or backward, and a new shed is created. Amazingly intricate narrow bands have been woven with tablets (sometimes they are triangular or hexagonal), including Buddhist prayer bands that were woven in Burma until the early twentieth century. Card weaving can also be done using an inkle loom (band loom, a small loom that allows for a tubular warp that can be moved as weaving proceeds), or just tensioning the warp between two stationary posts or C-clamps.

Horizontal ground-loom
A dobby loom is a modified shaft loom, which uses a sequence of pegged bars to make the lifts for weaving. When the textile industry embraced the industrial revolution, electrical dobby looms and cam looms wove most of the simple fabric. These looms have now given way to computerized versions of them that can weave more than 750 picks per minute. Many handweavers also use computerized dobby looms for their weaving.

See also **Weave, Jacquard; Weaving; Weaving, Machinery.**

BIBLIOGRAPHY
Barber, E. J. W. *Prehistoric Textiles*. Princeton, N.J.: Princeton University Press, 1991.

Broudy, Eric. *The Book of Looms*. Hanover, N.H: Brown University Press: 1979.

Chandler, Deborah. *Learning to Weave*. Loveland, Colo.: Interweave Press, Inc., 1984.

Fannin, Allen A. *Handloom Weaving Technology*. New York: Van Nostrand Reinhold Company, 1979.

Hecht, Ann. *The Art of the Loom*. New York: Rizzoli, 1989.

Roth, H. Ling. *Studies in Primitive Looms*. McMinnville, Ore.: Robin and Russ Handweavers, 1981. Reprint of original edition published in 1918.

Ziek de Rodriguez, Judith, and Nona M. Ziek. *Weaving on a Backstrap Loom*. New York: Hawthorn Books, 1978.

Bhakti Ziek

LUCILE Although many of Lady Duff-Gordon's claims to originality and innovation are now discredited, her high-end dressmaking firm Lucile remains a potent example of early British couture. Although at the forefront of designing and merchanting clothes for society women at the turn of the twentieth century, these skills were eclipsed by her talent for literary biography demonstrated by the entertaining autobiography *Discretions and Indiscretions* (1932) that was intended to cement her reputation with a light, literary style of prose.

Divorced from an alcoholic husband and with little formal education, Lady Duff-Gordon persuaded her mother in 1889 to save her reputation by financially backing her as a dressmaker, capitalizing on her only practical skill of sewing. Her first design was based on a tea gown, inspired by a dress worn by an actress on stage. It became her calling card for society ladies and was worn by the Hon. Mrs Arthur Brand on the occasion of her staying with a society hostess.

The tea gown originated as a garment worn by society women when in the country, after they had de-robed from their shooting tweeds and before donning evening dress for dinner. This practice is considered to have followed on from them being solely worn for the purpose of taking tea. Set between function and formality the loose and un-corseted style of the garment implied, if not a state of undress, then at least a private and introspective state on the part of the wearer. Duff-Gordon seized on the risqué potential of the tea gown as a way of challenging late Victorian London's views on modesty and morality in women's dress, while championing her own cause for notoriety. This led her to be accused of peddling the cult of immoral dressing (Etherington-Smith 1986, p. 73).

The association of the tea gown with refreshment and sociability between women became actively embedded in the business, most notably at Maison Lucile, her Hanover Square shop at no. 17 opened in 1897 (no. 23 opened in 1901).

Duff-Gordon's belief that "nobody had thought of developing the social side of choosing clothes, of serving tea and imitating the setting of a drawing-room" informed her idea of a commercial space for the selling of clothing appearing as a space of leisure and, to some degree, domesticity. However, it was her skill in innovative sales techniques that helped to establish a glamorous cult of personality for both the designer and her committed clients.

Lucile's business was unusual in that it also was well known for designing theatrical dress for the stage. Many of the features of dress design that Lucile became renowned for, such as the delicate layering of fabrics, fusions of color, and use of filigree and trim, were very much learned from the traditions of theatrical dress design that were engineered to catch the floodlights and project the performer.

Yet it was in her efforts to create a theatrical setting in her own salon for the presentation of her latest designs for the fashionable woman that Duff-Gordon excelled. From a small stage hung with olive-colored chiffon curtains, she presented collections on models that she personally trained in deportment, each one bearing a dress with a literary title rather than a number. Duff-Gordon termed them "Gowns of Emotion," also referred to at the time as personality dresses. This oddity began in her wish to promote the idea that the clothes she made in her early career were individual to each client. As a working practice, this went against the model of practice for a couturier established by Worth, who always decided the blueprint of what all fashionable woman should wear. Duff-Gordon's approach suggested that the inspiration of what could be termed fashionable was drawn from the innate quality of each of her clients individually; a dress that could suit their personality rather than their needs.

Lucile's Gowns of Emotions were given titles such as The Captain's Whiskers, The Sighing Sound of Lips Unsatisfied, and Twilight and Memories. In associating the appearance of a dress with an inner state of mind, the disassociation of dress from social hierarchy and towards signifying a psychological state began.

What is also notable about Lucile's titles is their similarity to the themes of love found in the salacious novels written by Duff-Gordon's sister, Elinor Glyn, who also wore her sister's designs. Many of Glyn's fashionable works featured well-dressed women with descriptions that faithfully aped the latest designs of Maison Lucile. Duff-Gordon's last epic was not to be literary invention. In 1912 she survived the inaugural trip of the *Titanic*. For her husband, who also survived after joining her in a rescue boat intended for women and children only, it led to the end of his reputation. For Duff-Gordon it was the final chapter in a sensationalized career. To distance herself from the tragedy of the *Titanic*, Lady Duff-Gordon moved her career to New York where her models came to the attention of Florenz Ziegfeld in 1916. Ziegfeld persuaded Duff-Gordon to let her models wear her creations in his current Follies. She designed the costumes until 1920.

See also **Haute Couture; Tea Gown; Theatrical Costume.**

BIBLIOGRAPHY

Beaton, Cecil. *The Glass of Fashion.* London: Weidenfeld and Nicolson, 1954.

Duff-Gordon, Lady. *Discretions and Indiscretions.* London: Jarrolds, 1932.

Etherington-Smith, Meredith, and Jeremy Pilcher. *The It Girls: Lucy, Lady Duff Gordon, the Couturière 'Lucile' and Elinor Glyn, Romantic Novelist.* London: Hamilton, 1986.

Glyn, Elinor. *Three Weeks.* London: Duckworth and Company, 1907.

Alistair O'Neill

LYCRA. *See* **Elastomers.**

LYOCELL. *See* **Rayon.**

MACARONI DRESS "Macaroni" was a topical term connoting ultra-fashionable dressing in England circa 1760–1780. First use of the term appears within David Garrick's play *The Male-Coquette* (1757) that includes the foppish character the Marchese di Macaroni. Although used occasionally to refer to women noted for their conspicuous gambling—described, like fashion, as a form of ephemeral expenditure—the term generally referred to the styling of men. The famous observer of manners Horace Walpole makes numerous reference to these figures. In the first relevant letter, dated February 1764, Walpole discussed gambling losses amongst the sons of foreign aristocrats at the "Maccaroni [*sic*] club, which is composed of all the traveled young men who wear long curls and spying-glasses" (Lewis 1937, p. 306). The "Macaroni Club," was probably the Whig venue Almack's in St. James's, the court end of London.

Macaroni dress was not restricted to members of the aristocracy and gentry, but included men of the artisan and servant classes who wore examples or cheaper versions of this visually lavish clothing with a distinctive cut. To wear macaroni dress was to wear the contemporary continental court fashion of the male suit, or *habit à la française*, which consisted of a tight-sleeved coat with short skirts, waistcoat, and knee breeches. At a time when English dress generally consisted of more sober cuts and the use of monochrome broadcloth, macaronis emphasized pastel color, pattern, and textile ornamentation which included brocaded and embroidered silks and velvets, some encrusted with chenille threads and metallic sequins. Fashionable men in the late 1760s and 1770s replaced the small scratch-wig of the older generation with elaborate hairstyles that matched the towering heights of the contemporary female coiffure. For men, a tall toupée rising in front and a club of hair behind required extensive dressing with pomade and white powder. This wig was garnished with a large black satin wig-bag trimmed with bows. The use of a pigtail and wig-bag was viewed as a Francophile affectation; so much so that the visual shorthand for Frenchmen in caricature imagery was this device.

Macaroni men deployed a number of accessories that characterized court society. These included the hanger sword, which was traditionally the preserve of the nobility, and which in England was fading from general us-

age. Other Macaroni features include red-heeled and slipper-like leather shoes with decorative buckles of diamond, paste, or polished steel; a tiny *nivernais* or *nivernois* hat named after the French ambassador resident in London; large floral corsages or nosegays; chatelines or hanging watches, and seals suspended around the waist; decorative neoclassical metal snuffboxes; and eyeglasses feature in descriptions of macaronies. These objects contributed to an emphasizing of courtly artifice in posture, gesture, and speech further underlined by the use of cosmetics such as face-whiteners and rouge. According to contemporary reports, there was even a highly mannered macaroni accent and idiom, captured in popular ditties of the period. Colors particularly associated with the macaroni include those used in the contemporaneous interior design of Robert Adam: pea green, pink, and deep orange. Striped or spotted fabrics on stockings, waistcoats, and breeches appear to have been popular fashions, sometimes worn in contrasting arrangements.

Macaroni Motives

Macaroni identity was not a peripheral incident in eighteenth-century culture but a lively topic of debate in the periodical press. Motives for retaining elaborate dress requisite at court but not necessary in the streets of commercial London was various, inflected by the class interests and personal motivations of the wearers. Macaroni status was attributed to such famous figures as the Whig politician Charles James Fox (1749–1806), "the Original Macaroni;" the botanist and South Sea explorer Sir Joseph Banks (1743–1820), the "Fly Catching Macaroni;" the renowned miniature painter Richard Cosway (1742–1821); the famed landscape garden–designer Humphrey Repton (1752–1818); the St. Martin's Lane luxury upholsterer John Cobb; Julius "Soubise," the freed slave of the duchess of Queensbury, the "Mungo Macaroni;" and the Reverend William Dodd (1729–1777), the extravagantly-dressed Chaplain to George III. Aristocratic Whig adherents emphasized a version of ultra-fashionable court-dress in order to assert their preeminent wealth and privilege in the face of Tories, the English court, and its more modest Hanoverian monarchy. French and Italian goods and manners had added appeal in that travel to the Continent had not been possible and the importation of French textiles had been banned during the Seven Years War

HISTORICAL DEFINITION

"Maccaroni [sic], An Italian paste made of flour and eggs; also, a fop; which name arose from a club, called the Maccaroni [sic] Club, instituted by some of the most dressy travelled gentlemen about town, who led the fashions..."

Pierce Egan. *Grose's Classical Dictionary of the Vulgar Tongue.* Revised and corrected, with the addition of numerous slang phrases, collected from tried authorities. London, for the Editor, 1823 [revised ed. of work published 1785], n.p.

(1756–1763). Alleged macaroni status was used to attack the professional credentials of Joseph Banks within the scientific community; Cosway was similarly ridiculed as an absurd-looking parvenu. Dodd, the "Macaroni Parson," in becoming the subject of a forgery trial resulting in his execution, further highlighted the potency of the macaroni label.

Historiography

Macaroni dress was lampooned as excessive and bizarre in numerous caricature prints, plays, and satirical texts. The macaronies form the largest subset within the English graphical social satires produced in abundance from the early 1770s. The catalogers of the British Museum caricature collection, Frederic George Stephens in 1883 and Dorothy George in 1935, published a wealth of primary material relating to macaronis that has formed the basis of all further studies. Aileen Ribeiro wrote the first article devoted to them in 1978, and has included them in subsequent studies of eighteenth-century costume, where they are discussed as an amusing episode in the sartorial folly of young men. In 1985 they formed the subject of an article by Valerie Steele that broadened awareness of their social and political influence and helped lift them from the

"Such a figure, essenced and perfumed, with a bunch of lace sticking out under its chin, puzzles the common passenger to determine the thing's sex; and many a time an honest labouring porter has said, by your leave, madam, without intending to give offence."

"Character of a Macaroni." *The Town and Country Magazine* vol. IV, May 1772, p. 243

taint of triviality. Diana Donald's study of caricature indicates that a reading of the macaroni type provides important insights into eighteenth-century English society. She highlights their role in defining the English character as sane and measured in contrast to the reign of folly experienced across the Channel. Represented in a wide range of verbal and visual sources, from the press to the theater, the macaronis provided the perfect frame for critique regarding consumption and emulation, as they suggested wild expenditure, the spread of fashionability, and even the cult of gambling in late-eighteenth-century English society.

The commonly held explanation for the title "macaroni," that it was derived from a fondness for that Italian dish, may be supplemented in that "macaronic" refers also to a type of mixed language poetry known for its wit, a hallmark of the macaroni stereotype. "Macaroni" thus also suggested the world of the medieval carnival, burlesque, carousing, and excessive food. The macaroni was regularly connected with a slavish and shallow love of things continental and Catholic. The amused suspicion of the English toward these supposedly uncritical followers of fashion is linked to a hostility toward fashionable dress that had colored British life since at least the seventeenth century. This censure had generally been more strongly directed at women, and the macaroni episode shifted much of this attention toward a redefinition of effeminate men. In occasional prints, plays, and satires the macaroni was cast as an indeterminate figure who did not fit normative stereotypes of gender and sexuality. Sometimes the macaroni stereotype took on sodomitical suggestion. Fictional descriptions of "Lord Dimple," "Sir William Whiffle," and "Marjorie Pattypan" deployed the notion of a neutral or unnatural gender in which "inappropriate" feminine attributes were grafted onto male appearance, dress, and behavior. The attributes of the Regency dandy (circa 1800)—deviant masculine consumption, nonreproductive irresponsibility, a rejection of middle-class gendering, a creation of the male body and home into a work of art—are firmly evinced in the macaroni type. As a foppish type, the macaroni also shares characteristics with the precursor, the seventeenth-century Restoration fop. The macaroni fashion preferences, however, were quite different and the two should not be conflated. The macaroni remains commemorated within the song *Yankee Doodle* (1767)—"Yankee Doodle Came to Town/Riding on a Pony./Stuck a feather in his cap/And called it Macaroni"—in which the appearance and masculine identity of the American troops is ridiculed within the theater of war.

See also **Dandyism; Europe and America: History of Dress (400–1900 C.E.); Fashion, Historical Studies of.**

BIBLIOGRAPHY

Donald, Diana. *The Age of Caricature: Satirical Prints in the Reign of George III.* New Haven, Conn., and London: Yale University Press, 1996.

George, Mary Dorothy. *Catalogue of Political and Personal Satires Preserved in the Department of Prints and Drawings in the British Museum.* Vol. 5, 1771–1783, London: Trustees of the British Museum, 1935.

Lewis, Wilmarth S. *The Yale Edition of Horace Walpole's Correspondence.* Vol. 38. New Haven, Conn.: Yale University Press, 1937.

McNeil, Peter. "'That Doubtful Gender': Macaroni Dress and Male Sexualities." *Fashion Theory. The Journal of Dress, Body & Culture* 3, no. 4 (1999): 411–447.

Ribeiro, Aileen. "The Macaronis." *History Today* 28, no. 7 (1978): 463–468.

———. *Dress in Eighteenth-Century Europe, 1715–1789,* London: B. T. Batsford, Ltd., 1984.

Steele, Valerie. "The Social and Political Significance of Macaroni Fashion." *Costume,* no. 19 (1985): 94–109.

Stephens, Frederic George, and Edward Hawkins. *Catalogue of Prints and Drawings in the British Museum. Division I. Political and Personal Satires.* Vol. 14, A.D. 1761–A.D. 1770, London: Trustees of the British Museum, 1883.

Peter McNeil

MACKIE, BOB

Bob Mackie was born in Monterey Park, California, on 24 March 1940. He attended Chouinard Art Institute in Los Angeles, but left after only two years to begin his career in costume design. In 1963 he teamed up with the costume designer Ray Aghayan for the television series *The Judy Garland Show.* For this project Mackie received his first screen credit and established a long working relationship with Aghayan. Mackie went on to design all the costumes for *The Carol Burnett Show* (1967–1978), while continuing to work on other television projects, such as *The Sonny and Cher Comedy Hour* (1971–1974). Throughout his career Mackie specialized in designing wardrobes for TV specials. His celebrity clientele brought him to Las Vegas, where he designed costumes for headliners and showgirls alike. Mackie has also provided costumes for numerous theater productions. His distinguished career has included seven Emmys and three Academy Award nominations. Over the course of four decades, he has dressed a dazzling array of celebrities including Diana Ross, Tina Turner, Madonna, and RuPaul.

Costume Design

Two pervasive elements in Mackie's work are glamour and humor. His costumes for *The Carol Burnett Show* were instrumental to the program's character-driven comedy sketches. A perfect example of this is the "Starlett O'Hara" gown made of green velvet drapes—complete with curtain rod—which played a pivotal role in the "Went with the Wind" skit. The script had not called for the curtain-rod sight-gag, but the result was pure comedy genius and undoubtedly led to the skit's designation as one of "TV's Fifty All-Time Funniest Moments" by *TV Guide. The Carol Burnett Show* also provided Mackie

Designer Bob Mackie with Cher. Mackie's collaboration with Cher began in 1971 when he was hired to design the costumes for *The Sonny and Cher Comedy Hour.* © DOUGLAS KIRKLAND/ CORBIS. REPRODUCED BY PERMISSION.

with the opportunity to dress an impressive array of guest stars, including Ethel Merman, Bernadette Peters, and Sonny and Cher.

In 1971 Mackie began work on *The Sonny and Cher Comedy Hour,* a series that amply displayed his distinctive design vision. Cher had met Mackie in 1967 when she was a guest on *The Carol Burnett Show* and asked him to provide costumes for her that would create a more mature, glamorous image. Cher's physical presence and her persona enabled Mackie to showcase his flamboyant designs without seeming too extreme. About her remarkable ability to wear his designs, Mackie once remarked: "There hasn't been a woman in the limelight since Garbo or Dietrich who could pull off such outrageous visual fantasies while maintaining her individual beauty" (Mackie, p. 176). *The Sonny and Cher Comedy Hour* proved to be a ratings bonanza, since viewers tuned in weekly to see what Cher was wearing. Using nude soufflé, a soft spongy fabric and strategically placed beads, Mackie's designs drove network censors and viewers wild by showcasing her long, slender torso with cropped tops and low-slung beaded skirts. Her costumes were dripping with beads, feather, and fur, but Cher wore them with graceful nonchalance, as easily as if she were wearing a pair of blue jeans. With tongue firmly in cheek, she gamely accepted being dressed as a harem girl, an Indian princess, and even a snake. Cher is credited with making the "Mackie look" famous when she appeared on the cover of *Time* magazine in his nude soufflé gown in 1975.

Bob Mackie's collaboration with Cher continued over the decades, and his designs for her became an integral part of her image. He has provided the memorable wardrobes for her many public appearances, including her 2002 Living Proof—The Farewell Tour. Tending toward the outrageous, he dressed her as Cleopatra for the launch of her fragrance, Uninhibited, and a "Mohawk Warrior" for the 1986 Academy Awards he provided the sheer catsuit worn in her infamous "If I Could Turn Back Time" music video. This ensemble, which gave viewers a good look at Cher's tattooed derriere, was criticized as too risqué for daytime television, appearing on MTV only after 10 P.M. and sparked a national debate about decency standards. The "Mohawk Warrior," with its bare midriff and high-feathered headdress, shocked many at the Oscars presentation, but for Cher, who felt snubbed by the Academy for not being nominated for her role in the film *Mask*, it pushed all the right buttons. Creating controversy through her choice of costume, Cher stole the show. Of Mackie's designs she once remarked, "After we started working together, he just knew what I'd like. He walked the line between fashion and costume and that's my favorite place to go" (Decaro, p. 67).

Fashion Design

Mackie made the natural evolution into fashion design in 1982 when he launched a line of high-end ready-to-wear; today his empire includes furs, home furnishings, fragrance, a line of clothing sold on the cable shopping channel QVC, and a thriving made-to-order business. In 1990 Mackie began designing a highly successful line of collectible Barbie dolls for Mattel featuring his trademark style.

In 2001 Bob Mackie was honored with a special award for his "Fashion Exuberance" by the Council of Fashion Designers of America (CFDA). This was a particularly apt tribute, since Mackie's lighthearted design philosophy has often run counter to the prevailing whims of fashion. Shrewdly understanding that the public associated his name with outrageous luxury and opulence, Mackie remained true to his aesthetic even at the height of early 1990s grunge. The beads, feathers, and furs that had been such an important part of his costume designs were translated into high fashion with heavily beaded evening dresses and dramatically draped chiffon gowns. His irreverent sense of humor, seen in so many of his costume designs, is also an important element in his fashion designs. This humor has translated into bugle-beaded wetsuits and jackets adorned with miniature racing cars.

Mackie's whimsical approach to fashion is particularly apparent in a beaded minidress from 1988, which featured a trompe l'oeil beaded "bandana" at the halter-style neck. Never afraid to push a design concept to the limit, the cowboy-inspired dress was accessorized with a ten-gallon hat, boots, and gauntlets.

In 1999 Cher was honored with a CFDA award for her influence on fashion, an influence created largely by Mackie's extraordinary vision. Through the power of television, Bob Mackie has made an important contribution to popular culture and helped to keep old-fashioned Hollywood glamour alive into the twenty-first century.

See also **Celebrities; Fashion Designer; Theatrical Costume.**

BIBLIOGRAPHY

DeCaro, Frank. *Unmistakably Mackie: The Fashion and Fantasy of Bob Mackie.* New York: Universe Publishing, 1999.

Mackie, Bob, with Gerry Bremer. *Dressing for Glamour.* New York: A & W Publishers, 1979.

McConathy, Dale, with Diana Vreeland. *Hollywood Costume: Glamour, Glitter, Romance.* New York: Harry N. Abrams, 1976.

Morris, Bernadine. *The Fashion Makers.* New York: Random House, 1978.

Reilly, Maureen. *California Couture.* Atglen, Pa.: Schiffer Publishing, 2000.

Stegmeyer, Anne. *Who's Who in Fashion.* New York: Fairchild Publications, 1996.

Clare Sauro

MADONNA Whether she is wearing navel-baring miniskirts, cone bras, or Gap jeans, Madonna has been a fashion leader since she became famous in the mid-1980s. As an icon of popular culture, she has set fashion trends and boosted the careers of established as well as up-and-coming designers. She has appeared on numerous fashion-magazine covers and has been a fixture at runway shows around the world. Her chameleonlike ability to regularly transform her look reflects both the ephemeral nature of fashion and Madonna's redefinition of femininity; her styles have encompassed everything from punk to androgynous, s-m, hip-hop, geisha, western, and military looks.

Early Life and Career

Born Madonna Louise Veronica Ciccone in Bay City, Michigan, in 1958, Madonna was one of six children raised in a strict Catholic home by her father; her mother died when Madonna was only five years old. Madonna was a cheerleader in high school. She acted in school plays and trained as a dancer. She attended the University of Michigan at Ann Arbor on a full dance scholarship but dropped out to pursue a professional dancing career in New York City in the late 1970s, where she studied with choreographer Alvin Ailey. Realizing that she instead wanted to pursue a career as a singer and actor, she worked as a model, sang in the band The Breakfast Club, and starred in low-budget films such as *A Certain Sacrifice*. Her first success on the music scene came in 1983 with the release of her self-titled solo album; she released over a dozen full-length albums through 2003's *American Life*. Although best known as a singer, the multifaceted entertainer has also starred in numerous films, including the 1991 documentary *Truth or Dare*, and *Evita*, for which she won a Golden Globe in 1996; has been featured in Broadway productions; and has authored several books, including the controversial 1992 coffee-table work *Sex*.

Madonna's highly individual style was apparent in her debut on Music Television (MTV) in 1984. In her videos for "Lucky Star" and "Borderline," she wore her own version of punk—black miniskirt rolled down to expose her navel, mesh knit tank tops with her brassiere peeking through, black lace gloves, stiletto heels, a "Boy Toy" belt, rubber bracelets, teased hair with an oversized bow, and heavy makeup. Madonna's look spawned "Madonna wannabes"—legions of mostly young girls who copied her early style. The craze only heightened with her appearances in the 1985 movie *Desperately Seeking Susan* and on the MTV Music Awards ceremony the previous year, when she wore a white lace corset and "bridal" ensemble accessorized with her "Boy Toy" belt and strands of pearls, writhing onstage and singing the title track from her second album, *Like a Virgin*. Retailers like Macy's created "Madonnaland" and other Madonna-themed boutiques that sold Madonna-licensed clothing and accessories. Her look pervaded street styles of the mid-1980s and appeared in advertisements for fashion brands such as Benetton. The influence of this early look was still evident in the 1980s-inspired styles that appeared on runways almost two decades later; the popularity of navel-baring garments has only increased with the rise of young performers like Britney Spears and Christina Aguilera donning the look.

Use of Past Fashion Icons

Madonna has looked to fashion icons of the past to create a persona. In her 1985 video for "Material Girl," she copied Marilyn Monroe's look from the film *Gentlemen Prefer Blondes*, in which Monroe wears a strapless, pink evening gown with matching long gloves, adorned with a lavish diamond necklace and earrings. She again resembled Monroe at the 1991 Academy Awards in her strapless, white, sequined Bob Mackie dress and Harry Winston diamonds. In the early 1990s Madonna imitated the androgynous look of the 1930s screen siren Marlene Dietrich, wearing menswear-inspired suits both in her videos, such as "Express Yourself," and while promoting her book *Sex* and her film *Truth or Dare*. For her 1990 video "Vogue," she mimicked the famous 1939 Horst P. Horst photo of the back of a woman in a loosely laced corset.

The corset became a dominant fashion theme in Madonna's look of the early 1990s. Madonna collabo-

Madonna. Since her appearance on the pop culture scene in the 1980s, Madonna has had an impressive influence on fashion, pioneering many eclectic styles. © STEVE GRANITZ/WIREIMAGE .COM. REPRODUCED BY PERMISSION.

rated with the controversial couturier Jean Paul Gaultier for her 1990 Blonde Ambition world tour. Known for his fetishistic fashions, Gaultier designed Madonna's memorable pink corset with cone bra for her 1990 tour. Not only did Madonna's wearing of exaggerated foundation garments (sometimes worn under menswear-inspired fashions as in the "Vogue" video) toy with accepted notions of femininity, it also launched the trend of underwear as outerwear still prevalent today, seen on celebrities and in street fashions alike.

Collaborations with Designers

Madonna is known for befriending designers and for wearing and promoting the fashions of established as well as lesser-known designers. In addition to her collaboration with Gaultier, who also designed the neo-punk fashions she wore for her 2001 Drowned World tour, Madonna has worked with the Italian designers Dolce & Gabbana, who designed her clothing for the 1993 Girlie Show tour; she also wore their western styles in the videos and performances for her 2000 album *Music*. She was a

Madonna on tour, 1990. For her Blond Ambition tour performance in London, legendary music icon Madonna wears a white belted corset featuring a cone-shaped bustier, with black leggings. Rather than using the typical microphone, she employs a headset, making it easier for her to dance while singing. AP/WIDE WORLD PHOTOS. REPRODUCED BY PERMISSION.

friend to the late Gianni Versace, in whose 1995 advertising campaign she appeared, and she has often been seen in the front row of his sister Donatella's runway shows. Another close friend, the designer Stella McCartney, created a wedding ensemble for Madonna's 2000 marriage to the film director Guy Ritchie. Madonna has worn Azzedine Alaïa, Gucci, Givenchy, Alberta Ferretti, and Badgley Mischka, among others. She has also worn the fashions of designers before they were well known, such as Olivier Theyskens and Rick Owens, helping to boost their careers. In the fall of 2003 Madonna went from haute couture to mainstream, appearing in an advertising campaign for the Gap with the rapper Missy Elliot and wearing a white men's tank top, a newsboy cap, and Gap corduroy jean capris and a large amount of diamond jewelry.

Madonna's influence as a fashion leader has been consistent from the beginning of her career. Her style has been watched and followed from the moment she first appeared on MTV. She has launched style trends such as wearing navel-baring fashions and underwear as outerwear, affecting the clothing choices both of other celebrities and the public at large. Her continual repackaging of herself has reflected her evolution as a woman and a performer. She has worn haute couture, supporting both known and unknown designers, and marketed mainstream fashions, with her looks encompassing different personas. The ubiquity of her unique and highly individual style makes Madonna an icon of modern fashion.

See also **Celebrities; Gaultier, Jean-Paul; Music and Fashion.**

BIBLIOGRAPHY

Craughwell-Varda, Kathleen. *Looking for Jackie: American Fashion Icons.* New York: Hearst Books, 1999.

Faith, Karlene. *Madonna: Bawdy and Soul.* Toronto: University of Toronto Press, 1997.

Hilfiger, Tommy, with Anthony DeCurtis. *Rock Style: How Fashion Moves to Music.* New York: Universe Publishing, 1999.

McDowell, Colin. *Fashion Today.* London: Phaidon, 2000.

Rubinfeld, Jenny. "Madonna Now." *Harper's Bazaar* (September 2003): 304.

Steele, Valerie. *The Corset: A Cultural History.* New Haven, Conn.: Yale University Press, 2001.

Taraborrelli, J. Randy. *Madonna: An Intimate Biography.* New York: Simon and Schuster, 2001.

Tiffany Webber-Hanchett

MAINBOCHER Main (after his mother's Scottish maiden name and pronounced like the New England state) Rousseau Bocher (his French Huguenot surname was pronounced Bocker) was born in 1891 on Chicago's West Side. Artistically inclined from childhood, he attended the Chicago Academy of Fine Arts and had moved to New York City by 1909 to study at the Art Student's League. Broadening his pursuits to include classical voice training as well, he departed for Paris and Munich, where he celebrated his twenty-first birthday. While studying music, he began sketching dresses for fashion designers to help support his mother and sister, who had joined him abroad. They returned to America at the onset of World War I in 1914, but not before three of Main Bocher's drawings were included in an exhibition at the Paris *Salon des artistes decorateurs.* In New York he financed his studies with the career-building vocal coach Frank LaForge through the sale of his sketches to another Chicago transplant, ready-to-wear manufacturer Edward L. Mayer. This marked the true beginning of his fashion career.

Editing Career
Back abroad in 1917 with a volunteer hospital unit, Bocher enlisted in the United States Army in the Intelligence Corps. Demobilized in France in 1918, he remained there and returned to singing. A vocal failure

during a pivotal audition finally forced him to abandon his operatic aspirations and to focus all of his creative attentions on fashion. He applied to the Paris office of *Harper's Bazaar* as a sketcher, then joined French *Vogue* in 1923 as the Paris fashion editor, became editor-in-chief in 1927, and resigned over a salary dispute in late 1929. With the financial backing of a discreet group of compatriots that included Mrs. Gilbert Miller, daughter of the American banker and art collector Jules Bache, he now turned his seasoned eye and editing skills toward the realization of his own fashion vision.

Paris Salon

At a time when American designers had yet to establish credibility on their native soil, Mainbocher, his name now contracted in the manner of Paris-based couturiers Louiseboulanger and Augustabernard, opened his salon at 12, avenue George V. The impeccable designs and pristine dressmaking of this American-in-Paris proved irresistible, especially to the coterie of international hostess and taste arbiter Elsie de Wolfe. Through her influence Mainbocher was introduced to the most celebrated client of his young career, Mrs. Wallis Warfield Spencer Simpson. The international publicity surrounding the austerely classic dress he devised for her Château de Cande wedding to the Duke of Windsor in June 1937 catapulted him to celebrity status, spawning a frenzy for "Wally" dress copies and the color "Wallis blue." His couture models were imported into the United States by elite establishments, including Hattie Carnegie, I. Magnin California, Saks Fifth Avenue's Salon Moderne,

The Duke and Duchess of Windsor at their 1937 wedding. Mainbocher designed the wedding dress for the duchess, which earned him instant popularity and inspired many imitations. © BETTMANN/CORBIS. REPRODUCED BY PERMISSION.

DESIGN PHILOSOPHY

Throughout his forty-year career, Mainbocher's beliefs regarding the purpose and nature of clothing were inseparable from his work and were routinely incorporated into press coverage, providing a running philosophical commentary on his collections:

> Between the beautiful classical that has proved its worth and some new stunt, I always choose the tried and true. I like persuasive dresses that have manners and I hate aggressive ill-bred concoctions (Bocher, 1938, p. 102).
>
> A woman who has to remember to arrange any part of what she is wearing, simply cannot be smart. A well-dressed woman always appears to have forgotten what she is wearing.... To me, repose and natural ease are among the inimitable and essential attributes of the well-dressed woman (Bocher, 1950, p. 1).

and Jay Thorpe. By decade's end Mainbocher had become a pillar of the world of couture and in the process secured the adoration of a clientele who followed him back across the Atlantic upon his departure from occupied Paris in 1939.

World War II

The fashion press celebrated the opening of Mainbocher's reincarnated salon at 6 East Fifty-seventh Street and his first American-designed collection late in 1940. The November 1941 *Harper's Bazaar* applauded his rigorous attention to maintaining all the traditions of his Paris house. Innovating ingeniously around daunting governmental restrictions (his invoices stating that his designs met with L-85 standards), his work remained fresh and appealing throughout the balance of World War II. During this period he featured glamour belts, aprons, and overskirts to vary the look of concise short or long black evening dresses. He launched a sensation for plunge-backed evening gowns and "Venus pink" with his Grecian designs for the 1943 Broadway production of *One Touch of Venus* starring Mary Martin. His surprising English cashmere sweaters, lined either in fur or coordinating silk, or jeweled, elegantly addressed wartime fuel conservation.

Trademark Vision

The steadfast loyalty of his patrons and press withstood the challenge of the postwar return of French fashion and Christian Dior's triumphant "New Look" (a silhouette Mainbocher himself had presaged with his 1939 Victorian cinch-waist.) Mainbocher was as passionate about fabric as he was fastidious about craftsmanship and design. The opulent simplicity of his clothes weathered the ephemeral. His silhouettes nodded to trends yet remained true to Mainbocher. His archetypal vision of pedigreed, meticulous clothing was as readily transcribed into his polished 1950s designs as it was interpreted in architectural fabrics to relate his minimalist eloquence to the space-aged spirit of the 1960s.

Famous Clients

Mainbocher's society client list included Daisy Fellowes, Diana Vreeland, Millicent Rogers, the Duchess of Windsor, Barbara Paley, C. Z. Guest, and Gloria Vanderbilt. He designed on and offstage wardrobes for Mary Martin, Katharine Cornell, Ethel Merman, Rosalind Russell, and Ruth Gordon.

Mainbocher closed the doors of his salon at 609 Fifth Avenue in 1971. Returning to Europe, he alternated his final years between Paris and Munich, where he died in 1976.

Innovations

Although a self-described quiet innovator, Mainbocher succeeded in incrementally altering the complexion of contemporary fashion. As a fashion editor he initiated the "Vogue's Eye View" feature and introduced the terms *spectator-sports clothes* and *off-white*. As a couturier he promoted the nontraditional use of cotton gingham and lingerie crepe and glamorized cloth coats for evening use. His was the first strapless evening dress, which he executed in black satin in 1934. His wartime civilian and military contributions included "day length" evening dresses and adorned sweaters as well as uniform designs for the WAVES, the women's auxiliary of the Marine Corps, and the American Red Cross. In 1948 he designed the intermediate Girl Scout uniform.

See also **Evening Dress; Fashion Magazines; Uniforms, Military; Windsor, Duke and Duchess of.**

BIBLIOGRAPHY

Bocher, Main, "Mainbocher by Main Bocher," *Harper's Bazaar*, January 1938, 102–103.

Carter, Ernestine. *Magic Names of Fashion.* Englewood Cliffs, NJ: Prentice-Hall, 1980.

Lambert, Eleanor. *Quips and Quotes about Fashion: Two Hundred Years of Comments on the American Fashion Scene.* New York: Pilot Books, 1978.

Lee, Sarah Tomerlin. *American Fashion: The Life and Lines of Adrian, Mainbocher, McCardell, Norell, and Trigère.* New York: Quadrangle/New York Times Book Company, 1975.

Milbank, Caroline Rennolds. *Couture: The Great Designers.* New York: Stewart, Tabori and Chang, 1985.

——. *New York Fashion: The Evolution of American Style.* New York: Harry N. Abrams, 1989.

Morris, Bernadine, "Mainbocher, Fashion Designer for Notables Since the 1930's, Is Dead in Munich at 85," *New York Times*, 29 December 1976, sec. A, p. 14.

Phyllis Magidson

MAKEUP ARTISTS In the media industries of fashion, film, television, and theater, an increasing number of runway shows, photographic shoots, and film and theater productions rely on the specialized skills of the makeup artist to communicate style and image.

When Maurice Levy designed the first retractable lipstick in 1915, no one could have guessed how popular cosmetics would become or how significant the role of the makeup artist would be in such emerging new fields as fashion photography and cinema production. Indeed, the concept of "makeup artist" hardly existed at the time. Until well into the twentieth century, theatrical performers were expected to do their own makeup, as they were expected to supply their own stage costumes. The professional makeup artist, like the theatrical or cinematic costume designer, is a modern phenomenon.

For much of the twentieth century, the role of the makeup artist remained a largely anonymous one, as audiences focused on the face of the model or actor rather than the makeup techniques that enhanced it. But makeup artists in fact have a great deal to do with how an actor or model looks in any given performance or production. The looks created evoke a theme, and it is important that the makeup be correct or else the artistic theme will be obscured or inaccurate, particularly when the makeup artist's task is to evoke a particular historical era or setting. While the image created by the makeup will always be paramount, by the early twenty-first century the makeup artist's expertise was receiving greater cultural recognition, and the role of the professional makeup artist had become a more conspicuous one.

Spaces where the made-up face is viewed include theaters, films, and photographs; the makeup artist's workplace is the dressing room, the film set, and the photographer's studio. The techniques of makeup used in these spaces are quite different from those of cosmetic makeup, and the professional makeup artist's skills are typically acquired over the course of a long period of training and practice. The heavy greasepaint and panstick used for theatrical makeup require special techniques for effective use. They are designed to work in harmony with strong lighting, which the makeup artist must anticipate while doing the makeup under weaker light. What might appear exaggerated and excessive in normal lighting will appear natural to a theatrical audience watching a performance on a lit stage. The applied shading and highlighting may be deliberately over-emphasized by the makeup artist to increase the impact of the designed look for stage, screen, or catwalk.

Makeup artists build on their training, technical skills, and personal experience to develop an individual style. For example, Serge Lutens, who worked for many years with the Japanese cosmetics company Shiseido, prefers to be acknowledged as an artist who uses makeup. His style has been inspired by the cultures of China and Japan, and particularly by the highly artificial makeup of the Japanese *geisha*. He is famous for creating a geisha-like oval facial effect on the models he uses for photographic shoots. Lutens dramatically changes the faces of his models, and it is often impossible to recognize even the most famous models when he has made them up. Topolino is also recognized as an innovator in professional fashion makeup. Since the 1980s his work has broken the mold of established practice in fashion makeup, and he is known for his ability to create new looks every season for designers. Another makeup artist who has raised the prestige and visibility of the profession is Sarah Monzani, who designed the looks for the 1996 film *Evita*, starring Madonna. Some makeup artists have achieved star quality in their own right; some, such as Laura Mercier, have built upon their artistic success to become entrepreneurs in the cosmetics business. These successes have helped to establish a healthy reputation for expertise and creativity for the profession of makeup artist as a whole.

Makeup artists in the fashion industry have used conventions and techniques drawn from theater and film to expand their individual styles. The result has been a change in the face of fashion, on catwalks, in magazine editorial content, and in advertising. Prosthetic and special-effects products are used to adorn the face and the body. Feathers and crystals are used to morph the body from its human form and re-create it in statuesque or animal proportions. Makeup artists create ghostly or ghoulish looks that reference the horror film genre, and film noir is a fertile source used to create the femme fatale often seen in the pages of monthly fashion magazines.

The makeup artist today is not bound by traditional materials, styles, and conventions, but is able to call upon a wide range of techniques to create innovative effects. While new materials and techniques expand the range of possibilities available to the makeup specialist, the success of performed roles in theater, film, and fashion will continue to depend heavily on the skill and artistic vision of makeup artists.

See also **Cosmetics, Non-Western; Cosmetics, Western; Theatrical Makeup.**

BIBLIOGRAPHY
Aucoin, Kevin. *Making Faces.* New York: Little, Brown, 1999.
Delamar, Penny. *The Complete Make-up Artist: Working in Film, Television, and Theater.* 2nd edition. Evanston, Ill.: Northwestern University Press, 2002.
Kehoe, Vincent. *The Technique of the Professional Make-up Artist.* New York: Focal Press, 1995.

Elizabeth McLafferty

MALLARMÉ, STÉPHANE The French poet and critic Stéphane Mallarmé was born in Paris in 1842 into a bourgeois family of civil servants. He was expected to follow into his father and grandfather's profession but, influenced by Charles Baudelaire and Théophile Gautier, he turned to writing poetry. After leaving school he went to England, and while in London, he married Marie Gerhard. They had two children, Geneviève and Anatole, who died at the age of eight.

Mallarmé taught English in Tournon, Besançon, and Paris until his retirement in 1893. Throughout Mallarmé's life his literary output was sparse and deliberate. His first poem was published when he was twenty-four. The famous "L'après-midi d'un faune" appeared in 1865, but between 1867 and 1873 his principal poems were left unfinished. From the 1880s he was at the center of a group of French artists that included Édouard Manet and Paul Valéry. Mallarmé died in Valvins, Seine-et-Marne, in 1898. His modernist masterpiece, "Un coup de dés jamais

Stéphane Mallarmé. In his works, Mallarmé treated fashion as a unique and ever-evolving art form on the same level of importance as theater, writing, or painting. THE LIBRARY OF CONGRESS. PUBLIC DOMAIN.

n'abolira le hasard" (A throw of the dice will never abolish chance), was published posthumously in 1914.

Unique Approach to Fashion

Mallarmé's relationship with fashion is marked by his association with the exponents of two literary movements of the late nineteenth century, the Parnassians and the symbolists. However, his is not the use of clothing or accessories as mere metaphors or symbols for character or sentiment, which occupied the literary output of his contemporaries. Mallarmé's singular contribution lies in his recognition of fashion as a social, cultural, psychological, and economic force in itself, and in the way in which this recognition finds poetical expression in different forms of writing, from occasional quatrain, via complex prose poem, to journalism.

La dernière mode

Mallarmé's artistic expression found its most potent voice in journalism. In the autumn of 1874 he single-handedly wrote and edited a magazine entitled *La dernière mode* (The latest fashion). It was composed of a number of stylistically well-defined columns on such topics as couture, accessories, and hair and makeup. The poet wrote each of these columns under different female pseudonyms, slipping easily into each mode and adopting, with a mixture of reverence and irony, various poetical voices as well as mannerisms of the commercial prose of the Second Empire.

Albeit short-lived—only eight issues were published before it went into receivership—the richly illustrated *La dernière mode* became a *gesamtkunstwerk*, a total work of art on fashion and style, crossing and quoting artistic disciplines in the spirit of the *fin de siècle*.

Fashion as Cultural Form

Mallarmé's development from a symbolist poet to a modernist writer, from an esoteric style to pared-down aesthetics, finds its unique expression in his attitude to fashion, to a mode dressing as well as sociocultural existence. There are, of course, a number of central subjects around which he built respective works, but fashion—with its haptic qualities, its shaping of the human form, and its metaphoric potential—appears as one of the most significant themes in Mallarmé's oeuvre. In what proved to be the last issue of *La dernière mode* (20 December 1874), he concluded, "No! for a compendium that intends to view fashion as art, it does not suffice to say 'this is what is worn'; one has to state 'this is the reasoning behind it'" (p. 2).

Here is Mallarmé's credo in regard to fashion. It is not simply an industry that creates material objects, nor is it a medium for a merely typified, gendered, or socialized representation. Fashion is a cultural form that demands critical investigation on a par with other artistic media, like plays, paintings, or novels. Moreover, it possesses a unique structure that lends itself to a redefinition of habitual rules and expressions. Mallarmé realized

that, just as he used and reused a hermetic, musical vocabulary, where words take on very different meanings or are brought into an alternative syntax, so fashion invents its own forms anew each season. The look of a familiar piece of clothing is changed beyond recognition, or its use is radically redefined. As a structuralist before the advent of structuralism, Mallarmé found in fashion a willful and skillful reshaping of formal appearances, and thus a technique that he himself pursued from his early, fragmentary poems (such as "Hérodiade" of 1869) to the open spaces of his late, formal experiment, "Un coup de dés jamais n'abolira le hasard."

Fold and Word

Mallarmé's work is characterized by a quest for pictorial composition and at the same time by a forceful rejection of the subject. In fashion he found both his visual stimulus, through the colorful, sweeping fabric of French couture between the 1850s and 1890s, and a subject matter that was regarded as marginal within the contemporary cultural hierarchy. The topic of fashion allowed Mallarmé to work against narratives, to remain resolutely subjective within the nonlinear, associative rhythms of his verses, but, simultaneously, to remove himself from the sublime, weighty subjectivism that was considered necessary for symbolist poetry.

La dernière mode ran a dialogue with imaginary correspondents, where the poet celebrated the "profound nothingness" that pervades the life and sartorial consumption of the bourgeois female. Unlike Gustave Flaubert, Mallarmé used the seemingly empty existence and ennui of a female readership not for narrative drama, as Flaubert did with the character of Emma Bovary, but for a concentration on formal questions. Fashion, seen as insignificant and ephemeral by the cultural status quo, thus becomes a carte blanche for a poetically elaborate, yet curiously precise, description of fabrics, ribbons, pleats, and folds, as the journal aimed at fulfilling its commercial function as a source of sartorial information.

The fold in particular operates, as *pli modal*—an abstract fold that primarily exists in semantic form—in a material analogy to syntactic or stylistic innovation. Thus, a notion is either hidden within the surface of a specific word, or else one word refers to another unknown one and needs to be drawn from the depth of the linguistic fabric through combinative or connotative efforts. Fellow poets credited *La dernière mode* with the "invention of the word" (Burty, p. 587); indeed, the vocabulary in the journal surpasses the mere description of clothes or accessories and moves to constitute fashion in the abstract, as a verbal equivalent of sartorial innovations in contemporary haute couture.

Female Voices

The professed independence from the material aspect of clothing, and the deliberate ignorance vis-à-vis stylistic minutiae, rendered *La dernière mode* less than commercially viable among competitive fashion journals. However, the formal yet radical nature of its prose (such as the metaphysical musings of Marguerite de Ponty in her column, "La Mode") and the irony of its stylistic quotations (repeated references by Miss Satin to Charles Frederick Worth and Émile Pingat) create a unique and extended text that floats unconstrained by a specific stylistic period. Indeed, the prose speaks as eloquently of the sartorial as of the literary form.

A further removal from the habitual approach of the artist to fashion, whether critical or celebratory, occurs through the exclusive choice of female pseudonyms. This technique was not new in itself. Honoré de Balzac and Jules Barbey d'Aurevilly, for example, preceded Mallarmé as "female" fashion journalists in the 1830s and 1840s. Yet Mallarmé does not hide behind or subsequently disavow his feminine personae but becomes them. A mental cross-dressing allows the poet to indulge in the transitory and ephemeral, unobserved by the patriarchal mainstream, and thus free to subvert a commercial medium for the dissemination of formal experiments to a readership hitherto unaccustomed to such an approach.

Personal and Historical Impact

At the end of his life Mallarmé reminisced about the literary significance and the personal impact of the autumn of 1874. "I tried," he said, "to write up myself clothing, jewelry, furnishings, even columns on theaters and dinner menus, a journal *La dernière mode*, whose eight or ten issues still, when I undress them from their dust, help me to dream for a long time" (Correspondence, Vol. 2: Paris: Gallimard, 1965, p. 303). Such remembrance, aided by fashion's mode of existence in modernity as quotations from a past source book, prepared the ground not just for Marcel Proust's literary form, but also for Walter Benjamin's philosophy of history. The view of fashion in Mallarmé's writing, therefore, accounts for the coming hallmarks of modernity itself.

See also **Baudelaire, Charles; Benjamin, Walter; Proust, Marcel.**

BIBLIOGRAPHY
Brown, Peter. *Mallarmé et l'écriture en mode mineur.* Paris: Lettres Modernes Minard, 1998.

Burty, Philippe. Undated letter. In *Stephane Mallarmé: Correspondence.* Vol. 4: 1890–1891. Paris: Gallimard, 1973.

Deleuze, Gilles. *Le pli: Leibniz et le baroque.* Paris: Minuit, 1988.

Dragonetti, Roger. *Un fantôme dans le kiosque: Mallarmé et l'esthétique du quotidien.* Paris: Éditions du Seuil, 1992.

Faye, Jean-Pierre. "Mallarmé: l'Écriture, la mode." *Change* 4 (1969): 56–57.

Fortassier, Rose. *Les Écrivains français et la mode: De Balzac à nos jours.* Paris: Presses Universitaires de France, 1988.

Kleinert, Annemarie. "La Dernière Mode: Une tentative de Mallarmé dans la presse féminine." *Lendemains* 5, nos. 17–18 (June 1980): 167–178.

Lecercle, Jean-Pierre. *Mallarmé et la mode.* Paris: Séguier, 1989.

Lehmann, Ulrich. *Tigersprung: Fashion in Modernity.* Cambridge, Mass.: MIT Press, 2000.

Lewis Shaw, Mary. "The Discourse of Fashion: Mallarmé, Barthes, and Literary Criticism," *Substance* 68 (1992): 46–60.

Mondor, Henri. *Vie de Mallarmé.* Paris: Gallimard, 1941.

Nectoux, Jean-Michel *Un clair regard dans les ténèbres: Peinture, musique, poésie.* Paris: Editions Adam Biro, 1998.

Peyré, Yves, ed. *Mallarmé, 1842–1898, un destin d'écriture.* Paris: Gallimard/Réunion des musées nationaux, 1998.

Thibaudet, Albert. *La poésie de Stéphane Mallarmé.* Paris: Gallimard, 1912.

Ulrich Lehmann

MANNEQUINS There are several historical strands that led to the development of the modern female fashion-display mannequin. From the fifteenth century, the miniature fashion doll (known as a "milliners' mannequin") was sent by dressmakers to wealthy customers, or exhibited for money by dressmakers to customers who wanted to copy the fashions. Other precursors of the fashion-display mannequin include artists' lay figures (life-sized wooden dolls used by artists); anatomical wax models, used for teaching medicine; and, finally, tailors' dummies. These examples utilized expertise in modeling representations of the human figure in wood, cane, papier-mâché, and/or wax.

The first wickerwork mannequins appeared in the mid- to late-eighteenth century and were made to order. In 1835 a Parisian ironmonger introduced a wirework model, and it was in France in the mid-nineteenth century that the first fashion mannequins were developed. Among the first mannequins to be patented were those designed by Professor Lavigne. He had begun manufacturing tailor's dummies, but won a medal in 1848 for his patented trunk mannequin, and opened a mannequin house in France in the 1850s. He went on, together with a student of his, Fred Stockman (who founded Stockman Brothers in 1869, later Siegel and Stockman's) to develop mannequins with legs and realistic heads and hands made from wax, improving on the earlier and cruder papier-mâché ones. When clothed, these wax mannequins appeared strangely lifelike, with features detailed down to individual hairs and glass eyes. The market for fashion mannequins quickly opened up with the department stores built in Paris in the 1850s and soon after that in America and Britain.

The Fashioned Body

It was Paris that defined fashion from the mid-nineteenth until the mid-twentieth century, and the French mannequin manufacturers were able to exploit this reputation. Not only were French mannequins technologically advanced—fueled by the investment in shops and display in France—but notions of what was fashionable at any one point were centered on France, so French mannequins were considered the apex of fashion. Their new

Mannequin in Indian clothing store. As department stores opened in France, Britain, and the United States in the late nineteenth century before expanding worldwide, the fashion mannequin saw a rise in popularity. © DAVID H. WELLS/CORBIS. REPRODUCED BY PERMISSION.

designs were also regularly exhibited at the international expositions, with French models usually winning prizes, thus enhancing their fame and desirability.

The arrival of electricity was important to the appearance of the mannequin, as the faces of wax models would suffer in the heat of the window. It was imperative that new materials be found. In the 1920s, the French firm of Pierre Iman's perfected a lighter and heat-resistant material, "Carnasine," a plaster composite which would take the mannequin into a new, faster phase of change and mass production. By 1927 the French firm of Siégel and Stockman had some 67 factories in New York City, Sydney, Stockholm, and Amsterdam and had acquired agents in other parts of the world. They also employed the architect-designer René Herbst as an artistic advisor, and under his aegis the mannequin became an icon of the moderne style.

The Artistic Body

At the end of the nineteenth century, the female mannequin had become a silent muse for artists and photographers who were appropriating mass culture as subject matter. The photographer Eugene Atget photographed shop windows, and later Erwin Blumenfeld photographed mannequins as though they were human. These images resonated with the Surrealists who would use mannequins as subjects: from Man Ray's photograph of a Siégel mannequin at the 1925 Paris Exposition des Arts Décoratifs, published in the *Révolution Surréaliste* magazine, to the sixteen mannequins dressed by different artists and writers (including Salvador Dali, André Masson, and Eileen Agar) that were used as the central motif in a room at the Parisian Exposition Internationale du Surréalisme in 1938. The mannequin even became the subject of a film, *L'Inhumaine*, designed by artist Fernand Léger in 1924.

On the other hand, mannequin designers drew on ideas in works by artists such as Pablo Picasso, Marcel Duchamp, and Jean Cocteau, modeling mannequins with abstracted features and dislocated figures. The aesthetic that these extreme mannequins, usually French in origin, represented was one which appealed in particular to the elite boutiques, and it began to look outdated, as a new popular aesthetic swept in from America.

The Iconic Body

In the 1920s and 1930s the American film industry was providing an international visual language that would influence both the design of window displays and the appearance of mannequins. By the 1930s American mannequin designer Lester Gaba had produced mannequins of the film stars Marlene Dietrich and Greta Garbo, and a Shirley Temple mannequin produced by Pierre Iman's was sold on both sides of the Atlantic. Film stars imparted glamour to the window display, which was itself looking more like a film set than ever. While World War II halted mannequin production in Europe, in America production increased, and mannequins continued to reflect the American mass aesthetic. In their expansion, American firms like D.G. Williams and Lillian Greneker were aided by a material new to mannequin production—plastic.

In the 1950s, mannequins represented a sophisticated and grown-up glamour. It wasn't until 1966, when mannequin designer Adel Rootstein produced models of Twiggy and Sandie Shaw, that the emergent youth culture was reflected in shop windows.

Mannequins Now

In the late-twentieth century, supermodels and television stars served as models for fashion mannequins. Conversely, the mannequin again became a subject for artists as fashion photographer Deborah Turbeville featured mannequins extensively in her work, and fashion illustrator Ruben Toledo designed a plus-sized mannequin for manufacturer Pucci. Mannequins have also captured the interest of designers like Alexander McQueen, whose innovative shop windows provide alternatives to the ubiquitous visual merchandising of the large fashion chains.

See also **Fashion Advertising; Fashion Dolls.**

BIBLIOGRAPHY

Adburgham, Alison. *Shops and Shopping: 1800–1914.* London: Allen and Unwin, 1964.

Gronberg, Tag. *Designs on Modernity: Exhibiting the City in 1920s Paris.* Manchester: Manchester University Press, 1998.

Parrot, Nicole. *Mannequins.* New York: St. Martin's Press, 1982.

Jane Audas

MANTUA The following definition of mantua was published in a book that recorded symbols for coats of arms and was compiled in 1688 by Randle Holme, a third-generation craftsman in that field. It is the earliest known definition of the style:

> A Mantua is a kind of loose Coat without any stays in it, the body part and sleeves are of as many fashions as I have mentioned in the Gown Body; but the skirt is sometime no longer than the Knees, others have them down to the Heels. The short skirt is open before, and behind to the middle: this is called a Semmer, or Semare: have a loose Body, and four side laps or skirts; which extend to the knee, the sleeves short not to the Elbow turned up and faced.

The mantua style was introduced in the 1670s and remained fashionable until the beginning of the eighteenth century. Distinctive features of the mantua are its loose-fitting unboned bodice and the fact that it was cut in one length instead of cutting the bodice and skirt as two separate pieces. The loose-fitting over robe with a train was draped up and pulled back to reveal the petticoat. It was unboned but worn with a corset. The mantua is thought to have originated as informal dress to provide relief from the heavily boned bodices of the *grand habit* that was the style at court. The mantua had a kimono-like construction inspired by imported Indian robes worn as dressing gowns in Europe. In its earliest form, the mantua was constructed of two long pieces of fabric that ran from the front hem over the shoulders and down the back to the hem of the train. The textile was cut only minimally—at the neck and under the arm to the waist. It was recognized that styles would change and it was advantageous to have as much fabric available to convert it to the new style. Its one-piece construction formed the basis of much of women's clothing in the eighteenth century. Sack gowns of the early eighteenth century directly evolved from the mantua style.

Its loose fit and reference to dressing gowns gave the mantua an air of undress that Louis XIV considered too informal to be worn at French court functions. The mantua was supposed to be worn only in one's own chamber or at specific country residences of the court. Despite royal disapproval of the style, the mantua was the height of fashion in town and became the dominant fashionable garment for women through the beginning of the eighteenth century. Another important distinction from the *grand habit* of the court was that the mantua covered the shoulders. Ladies appreciated the warmer, more comfortable style over the off-the-shoulder cut of the *grand habit* which had to be worn no matter what the temperature.

As the mantua evolved it became more formalized and was accepted at court. The loose folds of the bodice were stitched down into pleats for a closer-fitting shape. Eventually it was allowed for all but the most formal occasions at court, and even crystalized in varied forms as court dress in England through the eighteenth century.

The overall appearance, textile, trimmings, and accessories of a mantua were far more important than the fineness of its construction. The largest portion of the cost of any new garment in that period was the fabric. Careful consideration was given to the cutting of the textile and placement of dominant motifs, but the inside stitching was sometimes quite coarse and uneven. Distinctive brocaded silk damasks now known as *bizarre* silks, fashionable from circa 1695 to 1720, were often used for the mantua. Characterized by elongated, asymmetrical patterns that combined natural and abstract motifs, bizarre silks used bold color combinations and textured gold and silver metallic threads. The combination of textures and colors of these textiles created spectacular effects in a mantua's flowing appearance. The surface of gold and silk threads change with movement, casting light and dark within the free folds of the draped train.

The interest in scientific and technical experimentation, and the influence of exoticism from imported goods from the East, coupled with the increasing demand for luxury and change of the late seventeenth century, came together to create free and dazzling bizarre silk designs. The vertical lines of the mantua complemented the long, flowing lines and large repeats of the bizarre silks. An average vertical repeat of a bizarre silk at the height of the movement was nearly 27 inches, 10 across (69 centimeters and 26 centimeters across). Commonly, the design repeated across the width of the textile twice.

Mantua makers used a combination of flat cutting and draping. First, the pieces of the garment were cut from the fabric according to measurements taken from the client. Second, the long center back seam was sewn with close stitches in the bodice, and long loose stitches below the waist. The bodice area that fits more closely and takes more stress with movement than the lower parts requires closer stitching. Side gore pieces would have been added to the sides of the main panel to make the dress wider below the waist. These seams were sewn in two different ways depending on whether the mantua was of the lined or unlined style. If the mantua was lined, the seams were sewn in the conventional manner of placing the right sides together leaving the outside with a clean finish. If the robe was unlined these seams would have been sewn wrong sides together so that the seam allowances were on the outside of the dress. The draping back of the front edge of the mantua positions the inside of the mantua to the outside in this area. Fabrics that were attractive on both sides were joined with special mantua-makers seams giving both sides a clean finish for the draped arrangement of the skirt of the mantua.

See also **Coat; Europe and America, History of Dress (400–1900 C.E.).**

BIBLIOGRAPHY
De Marly, Diana. *Louis XIV and Versailles.* New York: Holmes and Meier Publishers, Inc., 1988.

Dennita Sewell

MAO SUIT This suit comprises a front-fastening jacket, buttoned to the neck, and a pair of trousers in matching material. Its main association is with communist China. It is named in English after Mao Zedong (1893–1976), the leader of the People's Republic of China from 1949 to 1976. Its salient features are a high, turned-down collar that fits the neck closely, and four patch pockets, two large ones at waist level and two smaller ones on the breast. A classic Mao suit has expandable lower pockets, and both the top and bottom pockets close with a buttoned-down flap. The trousers have a waistband, with a fly-front fastening for men and a side fastening for women. The suit can be made from a variety of materials with cotton, polyester, or a mix of the two being the most usual. It is almost always blue, though within that spectrum the colors range from pale gray to dark blue-black. The suit is often teamed with a matching worker's cap. Mao suits can either be purchased off-the-rack or tailor-made.

Despite its name, Mao was not the first person to wear such a suit. Its precise origins are hard to pin down.

Mao Zedong. Mao wears the suit named after him. The Mao suit was nearly always a shade of blue-grey and was the preferred ensemble of government officials. HULTON/ARCHIVE. GETTY IMAGES. REPRODUCED BY PERMISSION.

In the early years of the twentieth century, as an alternative to both the long gown and the western suit with collar and tie, several different styles, similar to the Mao suit but with a high-standing collar and no patch pockets, began to be worn by Chinese men. These have been viewed as precursors of the Mao suit and are called student suits because they were first adopted in Japan by Chinese studying there. The student suit, which had derived from European, probably Prussian, military dress, became linked with those urging political and economic reform for China. Another famous Chinese leader, Sun Yat-sen (1866–1925), revered by Chinese the world over as the "Father of the Nation" for his part in creating a Chinese Republic in 1911, is credited with making adaptations to the student suit, although it still did not look like the Mao suit we know today. It was in the 1920s that Sun himself appeared in what we now perceive as a fully fledged version of the Mao suit with patch pockets. This followed on a more overt link with Soviet communist advisors, who also wore this type of suit.

See also **China: History of Dress; Politics and Fashion.**

BIBLIOGRAPHY

Roberts, Claire, ed. *Evolution and Revolution: Chinese Dress, 1700s–1900s.* Sydney: Powerhouse Publishing, 1997.

Steele, Valerie, and John S. Major, eds. *China Chic: East Meets West.* New Haven, Conn.: Yale University Press, 1999.

Verity Wilson

MARGIELA, MARTIN Martin Margiela (1957–) was born in Hasselt, Belgium. He studied fashion design at the Royal Academy of Fine Arts in Antwerp—at the same time as Ann Demeulemeester—followed by a three-year apprenticeship with Jean-Paul Gaultier (1984–1987). He established the Maison Martin Margiela in Paris in 1988, together with Jenny Meirens, a boutique owner. Margiela was categorized more than once as the deconstructivist par excellence in a period when the term was applied indiscriminately to designers whether or not it was appropriate. Margiela was probably one of the few designers in the early 2000s whose work could be fairly described as deconstructivist. His investigation into the different aspects underlying any article of clothing, such as form, material, structure, and technique, were central to his entire body of work. His work was deconstructivist because he took not only the garment itself into consideration, but also the system that produced it. Ideas about haute couture, tailoring, high or low fashion, innovation, and commercialism do not arise from any apolitical standpoint, nor are they formulated as criticisms of established fashion assumptions. Margiela's work began from a set of analyses questioning the established theories of what already exists in order to search for alternatives that can be brought to life, both within and outside the system.

Margiela's attention to tailoring often exposed the production process behind the clothing, or revealed techniques that traditionally remain hidden in its production. The experimental aspect of his clothes in fact did not take place at the expense of ease in wear or aesthetic considerations. Margiela's summer collection for 2004 included blouses and dresses whose forms were no longer determined by classic lines or cut, but rather by small black stitches that stood out sharply against the fabrics he selected. The pleating and folding techniques that formed the starting point for his 2002 and 2003 collections were further developed in the 2004 garments. The tiny stitches were applied with surgical precision in order to achieve the correct fit. The result was elegant, slightly aggressive, yet simultaneously a tribute to the work of the many professionals in the field of fashion who remain literally unseen.

The study of form was equally central to Margiela's 1998 summer collection, which was a series of "flat garments." When the pieces are not being worn, they seem to preserve the two-dimensional structure of the paper pattern. The armholes were not placed at the sides of these garments, but rather cut out of the front section. Only when the flat garments are put on does their actual three-dimensional form appear. A second collection worthy of note in this regard was Margiela's summer 1999 collection. The basic idea was to reproduce a series of doll clothes enlarged to human size. The designer retained the disproportions and finishing details, however, resulting in rather alienating pieces with giant buttons and zippers.

In 1997 Margiela based two successive semi-couture collections on an old Stockman tailor's dummy. Various elements that pointed to subsequent stages of the production process, such as the sections of a toile, for example, were permanently pinned to the bust as part of a jacket. Other jackets assumed a masculine shoulder line, with the inside of the prototype replaced with a second structure and with a feminine shoulder line. Removing the sleeves revealed both the masculine and the feminine tailoring. Shoulder pads were sometimes placed on the outside of the garment or used as a separate accessory: the inside became the outside.

This process of reversal also applied to other aspects of the designer's work. The use of recycled materials was particularly evident in Margiela's early collections. In his first winter collection, displayed in 1988, shards from broken plates were worked into shirts. Plastic shopping bags were cut to form tee-shirts and held together with brown cellophane tape. In the summer 1991 collection, secondhand ball gowns from the 1950s were dyed gray and given new life as waistcoats; old jeans and denim jackets were reworked to become elegant, full-length coats.

Margiela's reversals were more frequently a source of confusion. In his 1996 summer collection, photographs of garments, knitted goods, sequined evening wear and different fabrics were printed onto lightweight cloth with a subtle fall, which was in turn worked into simply cut designs. The very realistic printing created a trompe-l'oeil effect or optical illusion and suggested tailoring that the actual pieces did not have. The models wore cotton voile during the show to cover their faces and hair. Hiding the physical features that make a person unique increases the desire for identity and uniqueness evoked by the clothing itself.

The most noteworthy detail in Margiela's clothing was the nameless, somewhat oversized white label, identifiable on the outside of the garment by four white stitches attaching its corners. The label itself carried neither brand identification nor size indication, and therefore seemed utterly extraneous. The conspicuousness of the white stitches increased the visibility of something that at first did not seem intended to attract attention. The phenomenon of merchandise branding was thus referenced in all its complexities and ambiguities. Margiela's refusal to supply his designs with a brand name produced the opposite effect, a select in-crowd who recognized his "brand." In similar fashion, Margiela the designer wished to disappear behind his work in a decade characterized by extreme narcissism, in which other designers attained superstar status. No photographs of the designer were distributed. Communications concerning the collections consistently took place only through Maison Margiela.

Interviews were allowed only by fax, and were always answered in the first person plural. This created an ambiguous result as well. Margiela's refusal to appear in person resulted in the creation of a personality myth.

Maison Margiela seemed to rebel against the rhythm of production that the economic system imposes on designers, not by radically rejecting the system but by filling it in with its own table of contents. In the strictest sense, the house's collections and its various sideline activities are not bound to trends or seasons. Consequently, the tabi boot—a Japanese-inspired shoe in the form of a hoof—reappeared with each new season, albeit in slightly modified form. Moreover, not only were existing garments reworked into new creations, but also the "success items"—or favorite pieces from previous collections—were repeated. This method led to the evolution of different lines, each of which was given a number that referred to differences in content, working method, and technique. All the lines except 1—the main line for women—bore labels printed with a line of numbers from 0 to 23 and the relevant number was circled.

Margiela was engaged in 1997 as the in-house designer for Hermès, one of the greatest luxury houses of France, with an established reputation for quality and finishing. Here, too, Margiela succeeded in further developing the achievements of his characteristic investigations into tailoring, although he worked entirely within the Hermès atmosphere and tradition. The interpretation that Margiela contributed to Hermès was a guarantee of absolute quality and excellence in luxury productions in leather and cashmere. No busy prints were to be found, but rather a return to the article's essence, and the core of true luxury, that is, the stripping away of everything that is not essential.

Where the inside was brought outside in more experimental fashion in Margiela's own collections, the inside was also central to flawless finishing in his work for Hermès. Maison Margiela introduced line 4 in 2004, which appeared to be an in-between collection that bridged Margiela's work for his own house and his work for Hermès. Collection 4 represented a reworking of a number of pieces from line 1, with inside finishing placed on the outside of the garment but now executed in more traditional and luxurious form, as was customary in the Hermès tradition. Only the neck and shoulders of these garments were provided with a lining. Margiela left Hermès after the 2004 spring–summer collection.

See also **Belgian Fashion; Brands and Labels; Demeulemeester, Ann; Gaultier, Jean-Paul; Grunge; Hermès; Recycled Textiles.**

BIBLIOGRAPHY

Evans, Caroline. "The Golden Dustman: A Critical Evaluation of the Work of Martin Margiela and a Review of *Martin Margiela: Exhibition (9/4/1615)*." *Fashion Theory* 2 (1998): 73–93.

Gill, Alison. "Deconstruction Fashion: The Making of Unfinished, Decomposing and Reassembled Clothes." *Fashion Theory* 2 (1998): 25–49.

Street Editorial Office. *Maison Martin Margiela Street Special Edition.* Vols. 1 and 2. Tokyo, Japan: 1999.

Te Duits, Thimo, ed. *La Maison Martin Margiela: (9/4/1615).* Rotterdam, Netherlands: Museum Boijmans Van Beuningen, 1997.

Vinken, Barbara. "Mannekin, Statue, Fetisch." *Kunstforum International* 141 (Juli–September 1998): 144–153.

Kaat Debo and Linda Loppa

MARIMEKKO Marimekko, the textile, apparel, and interior design company, was founded in Helsinki, Finland, in 1951 by the husband-wife team, Armi and Viljo Ratia, as an outgrowth of Printex, their oilcloth manufacturing company purchased in 1949. As the artistic director, it was Armi's decision to use the colorful, nonfigurative patterns designed by Finnish artist Maija Isola, which were silk-screened by hand on cotton material. It was difficult to get consumers to understand these new types of designs, as they were completely different from the traditional floral fabrics. Armi came up with the idea of using the fabrics in a collection of dresses, whose bright colors and simple style were warmly embraced in post–World War II Finland.

The name Marimekko, which translated means "little dress for Mary," comes from two words: *mekko* meaning a peasant woman's simple dress and *Mari*, the Finnish form of Mary or Maria, which is the eternal name for the eternal woman. The essence of Marimekko from the beginning was a certain way of dressing—a simple, comfortable, cotton dress that exemplified the Finnish ease of lifestyle.

One of the psychological factors behind the popularity of Marimekko design is its elemental diversity. Marimekko has offered the possibility of totally contrasting associations and identifications. It has fused traditionalism and radicalism, decorativeness and asceticism, anonymity and difference, the ordinary with the festive, and pure Finnish rural with international city style. At its peak, the design managed to appeal equally to young radicals and old intelligentsia, to a new breed of career woman as well as old-school housewives.

Marimekko in the United States

Marimekko soon found a large, enthusiastic audience in the United States. Architect Benjamin Thompson, founder of Design Research (D/R) in Cambridge, Massachusetts, saw Printex fabric and Marimekko dresses at the Brussels World's Fair of 1958. When D/R prepared for an American exhibit of Finnish design in 1959, Armi Ratia arrived with two cardboard boxes of dresses and fabrics, that were an immediate hit. Ben Thompson's reaction to this was: "Marimekko certainly belonged at Design Research. Nothing like it had been seen in America.

It matched the mood of the times" (*Suhonen*, p. 110). When Jacqueline Kennedy purchased seven Marimekko dresses to wear during the 1960 Presidential campaign, it was reported in 300 U.S. newspapers, making Marimekko a household name. In the 1960s, Marimekko was celebrated worldwide for its apparel and textiles that reflected the events and current trends of the decade: Op and Pop Art, flower power, student revolts, and the conquest of space.

Marimekko Since 1979

With Armi Ratia's death in 1979, the future of Marimekko seemed uncertain. In 1985 Marimekko was sold to Amer Group Ltd., and later was acquired by Kirsti Paakkanen in 1991. By 2004 Marimekko had become a public company with some 800 retailers around the world, and was experiencing a revival with a new generation of consumers.

Designers

Maija and Kristina Isola. Maija Isola (1927–2001) started working for Printex in 1949 and for Marimekko in 1951, where she continued to design fabrics until 1987. One of her most popular designs is *Unikko*, the large and colorful flower originally designed in 1965. In more recent years, it saw a huge revival and its popularity has made it an inadvertent trademark for Marimekko. Maija's daughter, Kristina Isola, joined Marimekko in 1964 and worked with her mother until 1987. She has updated some of her mother's original designs with new adaptations and colors, as well as creating new designs of her own. In 2000, *Pieni Unikko* was created using the original flower in a smaller scale in new colorways.

ARMI RATIA AND MARIMEKKO

Armi Ratia (1912–1979) was the driving force behind the early success of Marimekko. The combination of her education as a textile artist and her work experience in public relations was a definite advantage to the company. At first Armi served as the Artistic Director, but eventually she became Marimekko's Managing Director. An idealist and a visionary, Armi was unafraid of taking risks. These assets combined with intelligence and a forceful personality made Armi capable of making Marimekko a successful business, but also of shaping it to become a cultural phenomenon. She served as an unofficial ambassador for Finland through worldwide representation of the company and by entertaining clients and guests lavishly at her summer manor house, Bökars.

Striped Marimekko cosmetic bags, 1996. Marimekko, a famous Finnish textile company, is known for having introduced modern patterns, beyond traditional floral prints, into the world of fashion. © Steve Raymer/Corbis. Reproduced by permission.

Vuokko Eskolin Nurmesniemi. Vuokko Eskolin Nurmesniemi (b. 1930) became Marimekko's chief clothing designer in 1953 and worked for the company until 1960. Vuokko's design concept for Marimekko remained into the twenty-first century: easy-to-wear clothing that has a minimum of buttons, darts, and detailing. In 1953 she designed *Piccolo*, a striped fabric that was produced in 450 colorways. A few years later, it was used in the creation of *Jokapoika*, or "Everyboy," a plain Finnish farmer's shirt, commonly known in the United States as the Finn Farmer shirt. In 2004, the *Jokapoika* shirts were still in production.

Annika Rimala. Annika Rimala (b. 1936), the main clothing designer at Marimekko from 1959 to 1982, wished to produce clothing that was timeless, that represented ease in lifestyle, that was available from one year to the next, and that was suitable for men, women, and children alike. Inspiration for her famous *Tasaraita*, "even-stripe," cotton jersey T-shirts came in the 1960s when Levi Strauss blue jeans, formerly work clothes, became that of casual, everyday wear. Hence, the colorful even-stripe T-shirt replaced that of the classic solid color

T-shirt of the miner, and was worn by the "younger generation" worldwide. It has been among Marimekko's top sellers since 1968.

Fujiwo Ishimoto. Fujiwo Ishimoto (b. 1941) began working as a textile designer for Marimekko in 1974, after first working for the company Decembre, set up by Risomatti Ratia, son of Marimekko's founders Armi and Viljo Ratia. Inspired by both Asian art and culture and Finnish traditions and nature, Fujiwo's abstract designs for textiles led the Marimekko line in the 1970s and 1980s, a change from the playful designs of the 1960s that had made Marimekko famous. Among his designs licensed for production in the United States is *Kukkaketo* (1975), a flower print used in bed linens.

Katsuji Wakisaka. Katsuji Wakisaka (b. 1944) worked as a textile designer for Marimekko from 1968 to 1976. Among his best-known designs is *Bo Boo*, a children's pattern designed in 1975 and composed of cars, buses, and trucks printed in primary colors that became an immediate Marimekko classic. Although originally designed for printed fabrics, *Bo Boo* provided the basis for a wide selection of articles ranging from towels, sheets, and bags to glassware, ceramics, and toys. It became the most popular Marimekko pattern used in licensed production in the United States.

Risomatti Ratia. Risomatti Ratia (b. 1941), son of founders Armi and Viljo Ratia, worked for Marimekko from 1973 to 1977 and its subsidiary, Marimekko Inc., from 1977 to 1984. In 1971 he designed *Olkalaukku*, one of the most beloved and widely sold canvas bags in Marimekko history. From this design came a collection of bags made in a firm cotton canvas available in the timeless colors of black, navy blue, bright red, and khaki gray. The line comprises several types of carryalls, briefcases, shoulder bags, purses, coin purses, and cosmetic cases.

See also **Art and Fashion; Traditional Dress; T-shirt.**

BIBLIOGRAPHY

Suhonen, Pekka, and Juhani Pallasmaa, eds. *Phenomenon Marimekko*. Porvoo, Finland: Marimekko Oy, 1986.

Marilee DesLauriers

MARKS & SPENCER One of the best-known United Kingdom chain stores selling its own-brand merchandise, Marks & Spencer (M&S) made a substantial contribution to the democratization of fashion in the twentieth century: the provision of competitively priced, quality clothing. Before a downturn in the company's profits at the end of the 1990s, M&S's share of the U.K. clothing market stood at 14.3 percent with a turnover of £8.2 billion and nearly 300 stores in Britain alone.

Early Development

The company's founder, Michael Marks (1863–1907) was a Jewish immigrant who left Bialystok in Russian Poland in the 1880s for England and began work as a licensed hawker selling his wares in the Yorkshire countryside. Marks then opened market stalls selling a diverse range of household and personal items, all at the uniform price of a penny (1d). Marks went into partnership with Tom Spencer and together they formed a limited company in 1903 (hence Marks & Spencer). By the eve of World War I, there were more than 140 branches of the Marks & Spencer Penny Bazaar Chain.

Marks & Spencer, November 2001. Shoppers emerge from the Marks & Spencer store on Oxford Street in London, carrying their purchases. The chain store was one of the pioneers in the democratization of fashion, with its moderately-priced, own-brand quality clothing. AP/WIDE WORLD PHOTOS. REPRODUCED BY PERMISSION.

The Launch of Clothing

During the interwar period, with the declining importance of market stalls, shops became the preferred retailing outlet. Influenced both by a fact-finding trip to the United States, and by the increasing demand for ready-made clothing from a working-class market, Michael Marks's son, Simon Marks (now leading the M&S business), concentrated on building a direct relationship with U.K. clothing manufacturers and cutting out the wholesaler in order to reduce prices and have greater control over the quality of goods. At the head office (London), a Textile Laboratory was established in 1935, followed by Merchandise Development and Design Departments in 1936 to improve the quality and design of garments. By 1939 the company was selling excellent quality underwear and an expanding range of clothing for men, women, and children.

Following World War II, M&S's emphasis was on retailing easy-care and stylish clothing manufactured from the new synthetic fabrics (for example, Nylon, Terylene, Orlon, and Courtelle). More focus was placed on design by employing designers as consultants, such as the Paris-based Anny Blatt in the 1950s (for women's jersey wear) and Italian Angelo Vitucci in the 1960s (for menswear). The company began a major phase of international expansion in the 1970s by opening stores in Europe, Canada, and later Hong Kong. For a short time, it acquired the well-known Brooks Brothers chain (1988).

Marketing and Advertising

In 1928, M&S registered the St. Michael brand name, probably the company's most successful single marketing decision. For the next 70 years, only goods with the St. Michael label would be sold in M&S stores. Advertising in the modern sense began in the 1950s. For a short time in the 1990s the company used supermodels to sell its clothing. The optimism of the early to mid-1990s and the praise M&S received for the quality and design of its clothing ranges at this time soon disappeared in the context of competition on the high street from companies with narrower and more clearly defined markets such as Gap and Jigsaw on the one hand, and the discount retailers such as Matalan on the other.

Recent Developments

Led by chairman Luc Vandevelde into the twenty-first century, and with the injection of design talent into womenswear via George Davies's Per Una range (launched autumn 2001), Marks & Spencer made a substantial recovery. Nevertheless, it is the opinion of some that "however well the company does, it will be a long time, if ever, before it regains its past reputation for unassailable excellence or is, once again, regarded as the benchmark of retailing standards" (J. Bevan, *The Rise and Fall of Marks & Spencer*, p. 262).

See also **Department Store; Fashion Marketing and Merchandising.**

BIBLIOGRAPHY

Bevan, Judi. *The Rise and Fall of Marks & Spencer.* London: Profile Books, 2002. Good on the particular circumstances leading to Marks & Spencer's fall in profits at the end of the 1990s.

Rees, Goronwy. *A History of Marks & Spencer.* London: Weiderfeld and Nicholson, 1969. Good overview of Marks & Spencer's early development from a business history perspective.

Worth, Rachel. "'Fashioning' the Clothing Product: Technology and Design at Marks & Spencer." *Textile History* 30, no. 2 (1999): 234–250. Concentrates on the clothing aspect of the business with particular focus on the role of design and technology.

Rachel Worth

MARX, KARL Karl Marx was the major critic of capitalism in the nineteenth century, and he proposed, in its place, a society organized around need rather than profit. One of his main works is a three-volume study called *Capital*, which is a study of the political economy of capitalism. Fashion is at the core of Marx's political economy. Marx identified "modes of production." These are successive epochs of technical and social arrangement, which alter the organization of production and consumption. These modes have something of fashion's logic about them, if fashion is taken to be the latest trend, against which all else is considered outmoded. More specifically, in Marx, fashion's rhythms equate with the breakneck pace and whimsicality of industrial capitalist production, which *Capital* indicts: "The murderous, meaningless caprices of fashion" (1976, p. 609), employing and dismissing workers at whim, are linked to the general "anarchy" of capitalist production. Marx mentions "the season," with its "sudden placing of large orders that have to be executed in the shortest possible time" (1976, p. 608). This phenomenon intensified with the development of railways and telegraphs. Marx quotes a manufacturer on purchasers who travel every two weeks from Glasgow, Manchester, and Edinburgh to the wholesale warehouses supplied by his factory. Instead of buying from stock as before, they give small orders requiring immediate execution: "Years ago we were always able to work in the slack times, so as to meet demand of the next season, but now no-one can say beforehand what will be in demand then" (1976, p. 608). Employment and livelihood are dependent on fashion's vagaries.

Not simply analog to the rhythm of the capitalist mode of production, fashion—or clothing—was, for Marx, the very generator of the Industrial Revolution. The textile industry inaugurated the factory system of exploitation. In the cotton mills of the mid-nineteenth century, men, women, and children labored cheaply, six days per week, spinning materials harvested by slaves in the United States. In the silk mills child labor was even more grinding: ten-hour shifts and exemption from otherwise compulsory education. The need for a light touch when working with delicately textured silk was apparently only acquired by early introduction to this work.

In another vein, Marx deployed fashion metaphorically. Discussing the first French republic, he noted how it "was only a new evening dress for the old bourgeois society" (1992, p. 48). Elsewhere, Marx described the reactionary nature of the French politicians who were establishing modern bourgeois society. They adopted "Roman costume" and "Roman slogans" (1992, p. 147). These are "self-deceptions" necessary "to hide from themselves the limited bourgeois content of their struggles and to maintain their enthusiasm at the high level appropriate to great historical tragedy" (1992, p. 148). Here costume is suspect, donned to dissimulate.

Marx's thoughts on fashion as motor, product, and metaphor of the capitalist system are echoed in the work of the German cultural critic Walter Benjamin (1892–1940). Benjamin analyzed modernity, focusing on how technology and urbanization alter experience, and, specifically, how cultural forms are affected by mechanization, industrialization, and capitalism. According to Benjamin, fashion's tempo is driven by capitalism. Capitalism needs constant novelty in order to keep sales buoyant. Benjamin named this tempo the "eternal recurrence" of the "new" (2003, p. 179). Simultaneously, Benjamin observed a modern drive toward uniformity and mass reproduction, exemplified by the standardization of women in the song-and-dance revues. Here rows of girls were identically dressed and made up, and they danced in formation. Such cabaret entertainment was extremely popular in Weimar, Germany, and along with fellow critic Siegfried Kracauer, who wrote of such shows as a cultural equivalent to the predictable and mechanistic movements of the Fordist conveyor belt, Benjamin regarded such presentation of women as socially significant. Likewise, a vignette in *The Arcades Project* noted a 1935 fashion craze: women wore initial badges made of metal, pinned to jumpers and coats. The fashion accessory signified both the alienating reduction of self to alphabetic cipher and the loss of privacy in a crowded world. Developing Marx's notion of commodity fetishism, Benjamin also analyzed fashion as a seducer of living humans into fashion's dead, inorganic world of materials and gems. Capitalism makes people increasingly thinglike; fashion dramatizes this transformation.

Peter Stallybrass's essay "Marx's Coat" develops Marx's theory of commodity fetishism in relation to the coat as useful object and as commodity or "exchange-value." He recovers the "use-value" of a coat through an examination of Marx's frequent pawning of his own overcoat, an event that prevented Marx's research in the British Library, as he could not gain entry without such a garment testifying to his respectability. Significantly, Marx called the poorest class the *lumpenproletariat; lumpen* means cloth rags. As Stallybrass shows, for the poor, even the shirts off their backs had to be exchanged for a few

Karl Marx (1818–1883). The greatest nineteenth-century critic of capitalism, Karl Marx referred to the "murderous, meaningless caprices of fashion." Marx considered the ever-changing trends of fashion to be wasteful and, combined with sweat shop-style industrialization, they epitomized for him the culture of capitalism. PUBLIC DOMAIN.

pennies at the pawn shop, however essential for living these shirts were or however sentimental their value. Marx's attack on a system that made this sort of exchange necessary, notes Stallybrass, is an attempt to stand up for human dignity and memory as it is embodied in material. Indeed, Marx's materialism can be, in this way, quite concretely linked to questions of cloth material, its mode of production, and its human meaning.

See also **Benjamin, Walter; Politics and Fashion.**

BIBLIOGRAPHY
Benjamin, Walter. *The Arcades Project.* Translated by Howard Eiland and Kevin McLaughlin. Cambridge, Mass.: The Belknap Press, 1999.
———. "Zentralpark." In *Walter Benjamin, Selected Writings, Vol. 4: 1838–1940.* Translated by Edmund Jephcott, et al. Edited by Howard Eliand and Michael W. Jennings. Cambridge, Mass.: The Belknap Press, 2003, pp. 161–199.
Marx, Karl. *Capital: A Critique of Political Economy.* Introduction by Ernest Mandel. Translated by Ben Fowkes. Hammondsworth, Middlesex, U.K.: Penguin Books, 1976.
———. "Class Struggles in France." In *Surveys from Exile.* Edited by David Fernbach. Translated by Paul Jackson. London: Penguin, 1992.

———. "The Eighteenth Brumaire of Louis Bonaparte." In *Surveys from Exile*. Edited by David Fernbach. Translated by Ben Fowkes. London: Penguin, 1992.

Stallybrass, Peter. "Marx's Coat." In *Border Fetishisms: Material Objects in Unstable Spaces*. Edited by Patricia Spyer. New York and London: Routledge, 1998.

Esther Leslie

MASKS Masks, which function to conceal a person's face, occur in a variety of forms and can be made from numerous kinds of material, including wood, cloth, and vegetable fiber (the three most common) as well as paint, metal, clay, feathers, beads, bark cloth, and plastic. Masking is an ancient tradition, dating back to the Paleolithic sculpture and cave painting of southwestern Europe (30,000–15,000 B.C.E.) and to rock paintings from the Tassilli area of northern Africa (4,000–2,000 B.C.E.). The Tassilli masks appear very similar to types that are still being worn in West Africa. Additional examples of early masking can be found in rock painting located in parts of Asia and North America.

Masks cover all or part of the face and have been used for many reasons. Some masks function to protect an individual. In the fifteenth and sixteenth centuries, Japanese, European, and Middle Eastern armor included a helmet that safeguarded the head and, in some examples, also frightened an enemy. Numerous other kinds of protection masks exist including gas masks, hockey masks, and space helmets. Yet masks usually imply a type of disguise or transformation in which a person's identity or appearance is clearly altered. Anonymity is often desired when a person acts in an antisocial or criminal manner and does not wish to be recognized. This would include bank robbers, members of terrorist organizations—including the Ku Klux Klan—and revelers that appear on festive occasions, such as Halloween, Carnival, or Mardi Gras.

In a number of examples, a mask may allow the wearer to transcend his—or in some cases her—ordinary physical nature and take on the identity of another creature, ancestor, or supernatural force. In fact, the majority of masks are associated with ceremonial or ritual activity of a social, religious, economic, or political nature. In a performance context, they often express the otherworldliness of the spirits and make visible what is invisible. Such masks tend to act dynamically when they appear either to a few initiated individuals or to a larger segment of the population—moving, speaking, or gesturing in a dramatic fashion. When considering masks of this category, it is best to employ the more inclusive concept of masquerade, since a masquerade involves more than concealing the face of a person. In most cases, it consists of a total costume functioning within a performance context. The costume may also include objects held or manipulated by the masquerader, which function as props in the performance or help clarify the character's nature. The creation of a masquerader can require the specialist talent of many individuals, and the actual performance requires the involvement of additional people, such as dancers, musicians, masquerade attendants, and audience members. The exact function and meaning of every mask is culturally determined. A mask may have different functions through time or it may have two or more functions at any given time. The focus of this entry is on what masks do and what they mean in different sociocultural systems. The structure presented below suggests one way that masks can be organized into functional categories.

Entertainment and Storytelling

In both Europe and Asia, there is a tradition of covering the face with a mask for theatrical productions. Festivals in ancient Greece used masks, made from linen, cork, or lightweight wood, for both dramas and comedies. For tragedies, masks depicted highborn men and women as well as gods. Animal, bird, and insect masks were only found in comedies. Roman culture continued to utilize theatrical masks and from the sixteenth to the eighteenth centuries, Italian and French touring troupes employed masks or half masks to exaggerate the traits of stock characters in popular theater (commedia dell'arte). The improvised performances were never subtle but usually quite bawdy. Satire or social commentary is a feature commonly associated with masking traditions.

A connection between ritual and theater is strongly evident in Asia. Indonesian face masks are used widely for dramatic performances honoring ancestors and telling stories with a moral or historical reference. A spectacular example can be seen with the Barong-Rangda dramas of Bali that depict the age-old conflict between the forces of good and evil. These masks have sacred power and when not in use must be stored in a temple. Rangda, the queen of the witches, represents the forces of evil and both her mask-image and costume are viewed as frightening. She has a long mane of hair with flames protruding from her head and a fierce face with bulging eyes, gaping mouth, huge teeth or tusks, and a long tongue. Around her waist is a white cloth, an important instrument of her magic. Rangda's opponent in the play, Barong—a defender of humanity, can be presented in a range of animal forms. The most sacred type of Barong is called Barong Ket, a shaggy-haired creature with large eyes, grinning mouth, and a huge curved tail embellished with a red flap and tiny bell. His face is overwhelmed by a huge headdress with large earflaps.

In Japan, No developed from rice planting and harvest rituals to theatrical performances that deal with social issues that spotlight past events, supernatural beings, and contemporary concerns. Men wearing lavish costumes and small wooden face masks with serene, neutral expressions perform all the roles. No masks, carved from Japanese cypress wood, represent young and old men, young and old women, deities, and demons. The specific character is brought to life through subtle movements of the actor's body. Actors have a long period of training, wearing their first mask—in a supporting role—as an early teenager. By the time he is sixty years old, an actor is permitted to play a major character that may wear more than one mask during a single performance.

Halloween has evolved from an Anglo-Saxon and Celtic ritual, to become a major American masking event involving both children and adults who wear costumes that depict aspects of popular culture, political issues, cross-dressers, social transgressions, or personal fantasies. In some communities adults have organized elaborate street fairs and parades to celebrate the holiday. For many college towns, Halloween has become a major public event associated with revelry.

Nature

Among a number of cultures, masquerades are seen as the embodiment of the vital powers of the wilderness and its inhabitants. A major concern of the Baining of New Britain (Papua New Guinea) is the transformation of the products of nature into social products through collective human activity. Baining masks, representing spirits, usually consist of a variety of large bamboo frames covered with beaten tree bark and decorated with leaves, feathers, and elaborate patterns, painted red and black against a white background. All of the designs are named, usually after different types of trees, plants, or creatures of the bush. The mask ensembles refer back to the natural domain and during the dances they mediate between the bush and community. The masks in part derive their importance from the fact that they are made out of bush material that has been transformed by human work into finished products. Although there are many types of masquerade, all can be organized into two broad categories: day dances and night dances. Day dances are associated with females and the gardens while night dances relate to males and the bush; not every village has both. These night masks, consisting of a wide variety of plank and helmet types, are named after products of the bush, especially those that men hunt and gather. The day masks, on the other hand, are usually tall, vertical structures up to forty inches high. The designs on these masks relate to the growth of domesticated plants.

The Kalabari Ijo of the delta area of Nigeria believe they share their environment with water spirits (Owu) who play an important role in providing benefits to the community. Throughout West Africa, spirits of the water are seen as more positive and more helpful than spirits associated with the forest or wilderness. For the Kalabari, wooden masks are used in the ritual cycles that honor these spirits associated with a body of water, usually a creek. Although each water spirit has its own costume, music, and dance, and appears at different points in the festival, they all dance together at the end of the ritual cycle. Water spirit masks, in the form of fish or other

Traditional Eskimo mask. Masks are often worn by shamen during dances performed to influence spirits of nature in blessing the tribe with good hunting conditions. © DANNY LEHMAN/CORBIS. REPRODUCED BY PERMISSION.

aquatic creatures and humans, are worn horizontally on the head and are characterized by a swollen forehead, a long nose, and a projecting mouth. The masqueraders also wear a costume made from different layers of cloth.

The masks of the Alaskan Eskimo populations function to provide protection from potentially dangerous nature spirits and to ensure successful hunting. For the Eskimo, animals are not just food products but spiritual beings that must be treated with respect. They believe that all natural forms have a soul (*inua*) that will usually reveal itself to a person in the form of a small, humanlike face on the back, breast, or in the eye of a creature. Masks represent supernatural beings who control the forces of nature, the spirits of particular mammals and fish, or natural phenomena such as air bubbles, a particular season, or even the wind; their specific form is based on the dream or trance of a shaman (religious leader who has an extraordinary ability to intercede with the spirits). Masks, normally made from driftwood, are created by shamans or by carvers working under their direction; they are found in a variety of shapes including a basic human

Japanese No mask. Noh is a form of stage art that combines elements of dance, drama, music, and poetry. It is performed by men wearing lavish costumes and expressive, wooden Noh masks. © REUTERS/CORBIS. REPRODUCED BY PERMISSION.

face, an oval form with some facial features, or abstract forms full of distortions and additive features. Twisted mouths, eyes of different shapes, peg teeth, encircling hoops, feathers, miniature legs, arms, small animal forms representing the shaman's spiritual helpers, sometimes frame the face and project outward into space. Masks are used in dances and elaborate winter ceremonies, which take place in the men's house and the ceremonial center of a village. A mask is usually worn by the shaman or by someone he selects and, in large part, is designed to appease the animals killed and to ensure that they continue to reproduce.

Healing and Community Well-Being

Among the Bamana of Mali, the powerful Komo association is a high-level institution, under the leadership of blacksmiths. It functions to protect the community against sorcerers and other malicious beings. The Komo horizontal helmet mask is carved and worn by a blacksmith at special secret night ceremonies. The Komo mask is a conglomerate medicinal assemblage that moves swiftly and aggressively like a wild beast. It essentially functions as a wooden support for many different kinds of power substances. Protective amulets and feathers that

symbolize the celestial realm, antelope horns that symbolize the power and mystery of the wilderness, and porcupine quills that symbolize knowledge are added to the Komo mask as they are believed to constitute the necessary ingredients to effectively combat sorcery. Moreover, the surface of the mask is impregnated with kola juice, millet, and chicken blood, all of which contribute to the awesome power and frightening appearance.

The girl's four-day puberty rite of the Apache is more than an initiation ritual as it is significantly concerned with the well-being of the entire community. This ceremony invokes the benevolence of the deity, Changing Woman, to bring good fortune to everyone in the community. On the second night of the puberty ritual, Gan masqueraders, wearing plank headdresses made of slats of yucca or agave stalk and a black cloth hood (originally buckskin), impersonate mountain spirits who bless the area and help protect the community from dangers and disease. Originally the mountain spirits lived with ordinary people, but in order to avoid death, they fled to the mountaintops to seek a world of eternal life. Before departing, the mountain spirits taught the Apache how to conduct the curing ceremonial and how to construct the appropriate costume. The headdresses are painted with black, blue, yellow, and white with patterns that protect the dancer from evil forces. During the curing ceremony, both the Gan spirits and the initiate are able to purify the community and expel illness.

The Society of Faces of the Iroquois (New York and Ontario) use masks in the communal longhouse during the mid-winter ceremonies to drive away disease and to cure those who are sick. Private curing ceremonies can also be performed in the house of a sick person. Once someone is cured by the masks, he is able to join the society. Most masks portray humanlike spirits that reveal themselves to people in dreams or by suddenly appearing in the forest. These medicine masks also participate in seasonal renewal ceremonies held in the spring and fall. At this time they run through the village, shaking rattles, to cleanse the community from all afflictions. The masks are empowered to heal an individual and to protect an entire community from the evil that supernatural powers could inflict upon it.

The carved masks are usually made from basswood, but other soft woods can be used. Ideally, a mask should be carved from a living tree. Only men are permitted to carve and wear the False Face masks. Horsehair, paint, and metal to surround the eyes are applied to the wooden face. Most masks depict capricious forest spirits that have come to serve human beings with their medicine power through gifts of food and burnt tobacco offerings. Cornhusk masks, on the other hand, worn by either men or women, are used in curing ceremonies, which follow those of the wooden masks. Iroquois women create them by sewing together coils of braided husks; they represent vegetation spirits responsible for the renewal of growth from season to season.

Agricultural Fertility

The Hopi of northern Arizona have established a yearly ceremonial cycle divided into two parts. The first from the winter solstice in December to mid-July is marked by kachina ceremonies. Five major and numerous one-day ceremonies are held during this time. The purpose of a kachina performance is the bringing of clouds and rain but it also includes promoting harmony in the universe in order to ensure health and long life to the Hopi. Kachinas, who are invisible forces that reside in the San Francisco Mountains, are associated with clouds and rainfall. All in all, there are about 250 kachinas, but only 30 are major ones. During the winter, kachinas participate in rituals held in the ceremonial center (kiva). When spring arrives, kachina dances are held in the village plaza. In the intervals between dances, when the main kachinas are resting, clown kachinas enter the plaza and afford comic relief. The cycle ends with the home dance (Niman), a sixteen-day ritual that begins just before the summer solstice. Although any kachina can participate, it is normally performed by a group of Hemis kachinas, characterized by an elaborate wooden tablita (crest form) depicting rainbow, cloud, sun, and phallic images. The tablita surmounts a case mask, usually half of it painted green while the other half is pink. The body of the impersonator is painted black and decorated with light-colored half moon motifs.

The best-known mask type of the Bamana of Mali is the Chi Wara, a graceful and decorative carved antelope, which appears when the fields are being prepared for planting. The primary purpose of the Chi Wara association, also concerned with the training of preadolescent boys, is to encourage cooperation among all members of the community to ensure a successful crop. Always performing together in a male and female pair, the coupling of the antelope masquerades speaks of fertility and agricultural abundance. The antelope imagery of the carved headdresses was inspired by a Bamana belief that recounts the story of a mythical beast (half antelope and half human) that introduced agriculture. The male antelopes are decorated with a mane consisting of rows of openwork zigzag patterns, and gracefully curved horns, while the female antelopes support baby antelopes on their backs and have straight horns. These headdresses are then attached to a wicker cap, which fits over the head of the masker, whose face is obscured by black raffia coils, hanging from the helmet.

Initiation and Coming of Age

Many societies in different parts of the world institutionalize the physical and social transformation that boys and girls undergo at the time of puberty in order to ritually mark their passage from childhood to adulthood. In the West African country of Sierra Leone, Mende girls begin an initiation process into the female Sande association where they learn traditional songs and dances and are educated about their future roles as wives and mothers. After successfully completing all initiation obliga-

Antelope masks. A Bambara man and woman in Mali dance to Chi Wara, a half man, half antelope spirit believed to bring good luck to farmers. © CHARLES & JOSETTE LENARS/CORBIS. REPRODUCED BY PERMISSION.

tions, the girls dress in fine clothing, form a procession, and parade back to town led by Sande members and a masked dancer who represents a water spirit and symbolizes the power of the Sande association. In Africa, the Sande is unique in that it is the only documented association in which women both own masks and perform masquerades. The Sande masked dancer wears a costume of black raffia and a carved helmet-type mask. The masks—characterized by fleshy neck rolls, delicately carved features, a smooth, high forehead, and an elaborate coiffure—is seen as expressing a Mende feminine ideal. The shiny black surface of the mask alludes to the flowing river, the water spirit's home when the Sande association is not in session.

Variations of *mukanda*, a male initiation association, are found in the western Congo and Angola. Here, masks are worn by both initiated novices and senior officials for final initiation celebrations and during the period of seclusion when boys are socialized into men. Taken together the initiation masks symbolize the authority of males, including the ancestors. Among the Yaka people, one type of *mukanda* mask is associated with elaborate headdresses surmounting a human face which is either naturalistic or, more commonly, a schematic interpretation where the features are abstracted and enlarged. A large and distinctive turned-up nose resembling a beak is frequently found. Lines may be incised into each cheek and refer to tear marks associated with the pain of the initiation. The headdress sometimes presents ribald sexual imagery with didactic and proverbial meaning. Worn by camp leaders these masks are said to protect the fertility of the *mukanda* members and to both demarcate and elucidate gender differences

As part of the puberty ceremony carried out among Sepik River peoples in New Guinea, boys undergo a period of seclusion during which masks depicting bush spirits appear. After appropriate training, the newly initiated boys enter a men's meetinghouse, the political and religious center of the community, and in the open space in front of the meetinghouse, initiation dances are held. Various mask types appear at this time, ranging from face masks to large fiber costumes to which wooden faces can be attached. Leaves and large orange fruits can also be attached to a costume. Most of these masquerades impersonate clan or bush spirits.

Among the Kwakiutl of the northwest coast of America, male initiation rituals take place in large ceremonial houses during the winter months. The most important Kwakiutl initiatory society is *hamatsa*, the cannibal society, which cuts across family and clan ties. After spending time in the forest and being introduced to the spirit world, a young man must be formally reintroduced back into society. This reentry is a four-day public event featuring dancing, singing, and masquerading. Masked dancers of animal and human form represent spirit beings associated with particular kinship groups or with the wilderness. The most theatrical of masks are those capable of transforming into another form. In this case, a single mask will have more than one identity. This feat is accomplished by the dancer who manipulates strings to open the outer mask to reveal another face within. An important component of this event is the appearance of large mythical cannibal bird masks, such as Raven and Crooked Beak of Heaven, who reside in the north end of the world. These enormous masks with a movable mouth are worn on the dancer's forehead at an upward angle. Kwakiutl masks, which have large bulging eyes, heavy curved eyebrows, and flat, rectangular drawn-back lips, are often embellished with broad geometric painted patterns. The most frequently used colors are black and red; blue-green and yellow are also found.

Social Control and Leadership

Masks from the Dan, a politically noncentralized group in southeastern Liberia, function primarily as agents of social control. In the nineteenth century, these masks provided the only unifying structure in a region of autonomous communities. Dan masks, known as *gle* (spirit), derive their authority from the possession of supernatural power. For the Dan, a spirit will select a man to be its owner by coming to him in a dream or vision, instructing him to have created a specific style of mask and costume. Stylistically these masks can be divided into two basic types. The first type, called Deangle is an oval face form with recognizably human features, representing a female spirit. These masks portray a gentle, peaceful spirit whose attributes of behavior are seen as feminine. The costume of the Deangle mask normally consists of a conical headdress, a commercially made cloth draped around the shoulders, and a raffia skirt. A second type of mask, Bugle, which represents male forest spirits, is grotesque and enlarged with tubular features and angular cheek planes.

In general, Bugle masks are responsible for important social control functions such as judicial decisions, law enforcement, criminal punishment, fine collection, and military supervision. Although a Deangle mask may begin its life history in an initiation camp or as an entertainment mask, its status can become elevated to that of a more powerful judge mask. Moreover, any Dan mask can function as the powerful great mask, which settles important matters like stopping wars between villages. When a mask assumes greater social control responsibility, its costume will change to reflect a new status and personality.

The Bamilike and Bamun kingdoms of the Cameroon grassfields perform masquerades owned and danced by men's regulatory associations responsible for maintaining social order. The most important regulatory society of the Bamilike is Kwifyon, which serves to support the royal establishment, but also counterbalances the power of the king by playing an important role in government, judicial administration, and policing activities. Grassfields wooden masks depicting human beings are characterized by rounded faces, prominent cheekbones, bulging almond-shaped eyes, and semicircular lateral ears. They exhibit considerable variation in form, ranging from a crest worn on top of the head to helmet forms with carved elaborate headdresses revealing symbols of authority. Attached materials, such as shells, beads, and brass, indicate high status. Animal masks symbolize important attributes of leadership and power, particularly the leopard and elephant.

The Kuba kingdom located in the Democratic Republic of the Congo has developed a masking tradition to function in a leadership context. The three principal royal masks, Mashamboy, Ngaddy a mwaash, and Bwoom, may dance separately at royal initiation and funeral ceremonies or perform together when portraying the mythological establishment of the Kuba nation. Mashamboy, the most important royal mask, represents the legendary ancestor who founded the ruling Kuba dynasty. The mask's structural frame is made of wicker, covered with leopard, and cowrie shells. The second mask (Ngaady a mwaash), which symbolizes the sister-wife of the legendary ancestor, is a more naturalistic wooden face with slit eyes. It is decorated with an overall pattern of painted striped and triangular motifs, seeds, beads, and shells. The third mask (Bwoom) represents a person of modest means or the nonroyal members of the society symbolically balancing the royal establishment. The Bwoom mask is a wooden helmet decorated with sheets of copper, hide, shells, seeds, and beads. Although the added materials enhance the mask, the carved form itself makes a powerful aesthetic statement.

See also **Carnival Dress; Ceremonial and Festival Costumes; Masquerade and Masked Balls.**

BIBLIOGRAPHY

Cole, Herbert, ed. *I Am Not Myself: The Art of African Masquerade.* Los Angeles: Museum of Cultural History, 1985.

Colleyn, Jean-Paul, ed. *Bamana: The Art of Existence in Mali.* New York: Museum for African Art, 2001.

Corbin, George. *Native Arts of North America, Africa. and the South Pacific.* New York: Harper and Row, 1988.

Fienup-Riordan, Ann. *The Living Tradition of Yup'ik Masks.* Seattle: University of Washington Press, 1996.

Jonaitis, Aldona, ed. *Chiefly Feasts: The Enduring Kwakiutl Potlatch.* New York: American Museum of Natural History, 1991.

Mack, John, ed. *Masks: the Art of Expression.* London: British Museum Press, 1994.

Napier, David. *Masks, Transformation and Paradox.* Berkeley: University of California Press, 1986.

Perani, Judith, and Fred T. Smith. *The Visual Arts of Africa: Gender, Power, and Life Cycle Rituals.* Upper Saddle River, N.J.: Prentice-Hall, 1998.

Pernet, Henry. *Ritual Masks: Deceptions and Revelations.* Columbia: University of South Carolina Press. 1992.

Fred T. Smith

MASQUERADE AND MASKED BALLS Masquerades and masked balls are linked to the celebration of Carnival and *mardi gras*. Originally part of a cycle of pagan festivities celebrating the advent of the spring planting season, in the Middle Ages, Carnival began after the winter solstice as part of the Feast of Fools, for which the congregation elected abbots and bishops from among the junior clergy who masked and dressed in women's clothes and performed a mock Mass that ended with dancing in the church and streets, and the coronation of an Abbot of Misrule. With the Reformation, Protestant countries banned Carnival, while the Feast of Fools moved into the street. The result was that in Catholic countries, Carnival revelry and masking took over the streets of towns and cities between Twelfth Night and Ash Wednesday, in anticipation of giving up all *carne*—meat and sex—for Lent. Carnival thrived in Paris, Venice, and Rome, among other cities. The last six days of Carnival were called *les jours gras* (fat days) lasting from *feudi gras*, the Thursday before Ash Wednesday through the night of *mardi gras*. *Les jours gras* were celebrated with masked balls, obscene dancing, and eating, drinking, and sex. On the morning of Ash Wednesday, this orgiastic explosion ended in a parade of exhausted, masked revelers.

Masquerades also existed in eighteenth-century London, but it is Parisian Carnival and its masked balls in the nineteenth century that have produced the most commentary, gossip, and visual images. Many European and American observers published memoirs describing their experiences at the masked balls in Paris, while lithographs of the masked balls at the opera and at other Parisian theaters and dance halls proliferated during the nineteenth century, producing countless imitations. Indeed, in popular culture masked balls and the French were so closely linked that an early American silent movie (1908) is titled *At the French Ball*—the story, of course, of adultery at a masked ball.

Court theatricals with masks and a ballet were initially introduced at the French and English courts in the seventeenth century. By the early eighteenth century, masquerades and *bals masqués* (the French term for masked balls) were attracting large crowds at the newly opened public dance halls in London and Paris, at the aristocratic balls at the Paris opera (as of 1715), and in private Parisian mansions that welcomed the masked public during Carnival. During the eighteenth century, the masked balls in public dance halls were the height of English fashion, while the French celebration of Carnival was increasingly politicized and used to attack the monarchy. In this world turned upside down, women dressed as men, frequently as soldiers, sailors, or stevedores; men as women; the poor disguised themselves as bishops, lawyers, and aristocrats; and the rich disguised themselves as beggars, peasants, fishmongers, in Oriental masquerade, and *in domino*, the classic Venetian costume of a hooded black cape and mask. Regardless of a persons gender and class, sexual license was tolerated at masked balls so that men and women were free to indulge their sexual proclivities with persons of whatever sex and class they chose. With the French Revolution, Carnival and masking were temporarily banned, while in England such permissiveness died. In 1800 Napoleon reintroduced Carnival, although by 1830 Parisian Carnival was said to be a thing of the past.

Nonetheless, from a mere three authorized public masked balls during Carnival in 1830, by 1831 Parisian Carnival exploded in the aftermath of the July Revolution (1830). The combination of a new revolutionary generation disaffected with the conservative government of the July Monarchy and the spread of romanticism infused new life into Parisian Carnival. The fashion press and the new satirical dailies, benefiting from the introduction of cheap lithographs illustrating the masked balls at the opera and at other theaters. The introduction of gossip columns and cheap newspapers, paid for by advertising instead of subscription, provided Parisians and readers everywhere a blow-by-blow account of the masked balls during Carnival after 1830. The satirical daily *Le Charivari* coined the catchwords of Carnival, "Down with the Carnival of our ancestors! Hooray for the carnival of romanticism and politics," and published lithographs by Honore Daumier and Paul Gavarni depicting the Carnival masked balls in all their glory. Hundreds of pamphlets, satires, illustrations, and fashion magazines supplied a running commentary on the pleasures to be found at the Carnival masked balls at their height in the 1830s and 1840s, including the masked balls that took place in the middle of the Revolution of 1848. It is not surprising, then, that although these balls continued until the end of the century, it was this period in the 1830s and 1840s that was mythic and that was depicted in Edouard Manet's famous painting *Le Bal masqué de l'Opéra* (1873).

What made this Carnival and its masked balls so remarkable was the confluence of political discontent and the emergence of a consumer society that fanned the flames of pleasure and desire. Many of the costumes reflected a rejection of traditional roles and a yearning for the exotic, suggesting a widespread ambivalence about the values of emerging capitalist society and its imposition of middle-class culture and domesticity. The most chic costumes of the moment worn to masked balls in eighteenth-century London were Oriental masquerades, while in nineteenth-century Paris, Spanish dancers, or couples dressed as stevedores were the most fashionable. None of these fashions lasted beyond their moment, although designers in the early twenty-first century have looked at illustrations from the masked balls of nineteenth-century Paris as an inspiration for clothes.

However, what is significant about Parisian masked balls in the nineteenth century are the technological inventions that made the balls fashionable and accessible to an expanding literate public. The introduction of the lithographic process and the rotary press made it possible for newspapers and magazines to print more newspapers with cheap illustrations, while advertising, a new capitalist invention, reduced their cost. The preeminence of Paris fashion, made more accessible through beautifully illustrated fashion magazines and the introduction of department stores and costume warehouses, offered this new consuming public fashionable disguises and cheaper clothes. Serialized novels in newspapers and gossip columns fed the aspirations and desires of increasing populations and an expanding middle class, especially the women, who now had more money to spend and places to spend it, including the masked balls during Carnival. Most of these elements already existed in England in the eighteenth century, when masquerades were the height of fashion. Missing was the French genius for publicity and seduction, which made the special pleasures and intensity of Parisian masked balls legendary and guaranteed their immortality in print and visual culture, both high and low.

See also **Carnival Dress; Ceremonial and Festival Costumes; Masks.**

BIBLIOGRAPHY
Alter, Ann Ilan. "Pursuing Pleasure at the Masked Balls at the Opera during the July Monarchy." *Laurels: The Magazine of the American Society of the French Legion of Honor* 60, no. 2 (1989): 101–118.

———. "Parisian Women at the Opera Balls." In *Masquerade and Identities: Essays on Gender, Sexuality and Marginality.* Edited by Efrat Tseëlon. London: Routledge, 2001.

Burke, Peter. *Popular Culture in Early Modern Europe.* New York: New York University Press, 1978.

Castle, Terry. *Masquerade and Civilization: The Carnivalesque in Eighteenth-Century English Culture and Fiction,* Stanford, Calif.: Stanford University Press, 1996.

Cohen, Sarah R. "Masquerade as Mode in the French Fashion Print." In *The Clothes That Wear Us: Essays on Dressing and Transgressing in Eighteenth-Century Culture.* Edited by Jessica Munns and Penny Richards. Newark: University of Delaware Press, 1999.

Flaubert, Gustave. *L'Éducation Sentimentale.* Paris: Éditions Garnier, 1984.

Ann Ilan Alter

MATELASSÉ. *See* **Weave, Double.**

MATERNITY DRESS Throughout most of history, all over the world, women's attire has of necessity been designed to adapt to the needs of pregnancy and breast-feeding, which were likely to take up a large percentage of women's lives between puberty and menopause. Before the industrial revolution, the making of fabric and clothing was labor-intensive enough to preclude the making of garments exclusive to pregnancy.

Thus, in Western Europe since medieval times, regular dress of all classes has been easily adapted for pregnancy. Laced bodices, frequently involving center panels to cover expanding waistlines, were prevalent. Petticoats, separate or integral with bodices, were tied at both sides, equally adaptable. Women appeared not to mind the rising hemline in front that resulted from the use of a normal wardrobe during pregnancy.

Beginning in the sixteenth century, styles became more restrictive. Bodices were reinforced with boning, but they were still most often laced. Writers scolded women for wearing these styles during pregnancy, accusing them of putting vanity above the health of their unborn child. But it is possible to rest the bodice or corset on the pregnant belly without constricting it, and this was probably common. Women did not abandon corsets during pregnancy, at least in public. Women of all classes wore corsets during pregnancy, tilted across their stomachs, aprons worn high to conceal the gap at the bodice's front.

Some women did contrive garments specifically for pregnancy, as a surviving set of eighteenth-century quilted garments in the collection at Colonial Williamsburg attests, in which a waistcoat expands over the belly to cover the gap in the jacket front. Possibly this sort of individualized contrivance occurred more often, at least among members of the upper class who could afford it, than surviving examples can document.

Privately, fashionable women in the seventeenth and eighteenth centuries could wear loose "wrapping gowns," popular at-home wear, worn by both sexes. Women of all classes also donned unboned sleeveless bodices, quilted or corded to support the belly and breasts. Working-class women had the added choice of loose, unconstructed jackets called "bed gowns" over a petticoat.

The sack or sacque gown, introduced in the early eighteenth century, can apparently be credited to the marquise de Montespan, mistress of Louis XIV, who strove to conceal her pregnancy to remain longer at court. This was reported at the time and may be credited more than most such anecdotes deserve. Falling loose both front and back, the sacque later became fitted in front, and thus no more suited to pregnancy than other styles.

At the turn of the nineteenth century, high-waisted styles were well suited both to pregnancy and breast-feeding. Not until waists returned to their normal level in the 1830s did pregnancy require more careful wardrobe planning.

By 1830, most dresses hooked in back; center front openings, and a "drop-front" skirt, were still occasionally used, suggesting wear during pregnancy. In the 1840s and 1850s, the "fan pleated" bodice was popular, partly because it was easily adapted. In surviving examples, gathers beginning at the shoulders extend to the waist and are gathered on drawstrings, allowing expansion and access for breast-feeding and gradual tightening as the body returned to pre-partum shape. Other innovations also existed, such as expansion of the gathers found in the era's ample skirts. Some nineteenth-century maternity garments contain linings intended to lace over the belly, providing support without constricting it, since the period's more curvilinear corsets were likelier to cause harm than earlier styles. Less constrictive corsets—less boned, or with expandable lacings over the belly—were also available.

Victorian women did not, as popular myth says, stay at home during pregnancy. Fashion magazines, with typical reticence, fail to identify maternity styles, but they can be detected by careful reading: pregnancy corsets are called "abdominal corsets," and phrases such as "for the young matron," "for the recently married lady," reveal maternity styles. An alert modern reader can easily find them, although pregnant figures are not depicted.

The 1860s brought the use of separates to aid pregnant women. For the rest of the nineteenth century, both at-home and fashionable dress offered styles that worked

Maternity wear. Fashion designer Liz Lange stands between two mannequins displaying her designs at her store on Madison Avenue, New York, in 2003. More stylish maternity clothes became available in the late twentieth century. AP/WIDE WORLD PHOTOS. REPRODUCED BY PERMISSION.

during pregnancy. Boxy jackets and amply gathered center bodice panels, for example, seen in the 1880s and 1890s, are among the obvious styles to choose.

In the twentieth century, the ready-to-wear industry strove to cater more to women by adapting current fashions to pregnancy. When catalogs finally identify maternity fashions (about 1910), they still refrain from depicting the pregnant form, revealing old discomfort with the issue but suggesting that the styles were the same as others of the time, albeit with specialized construction. Often this meant a series of fasteners at the sides, so that the dress need not be any larger than necessary in the earlier stages of pregnancy.

After World War II, specific maternity styles developed more markedly. Designers made pencil-thin skirts with elastic panels to cover a pregnant belly. Still, the tops often were made unnecessarily full, unlike regular fashions. Typical of postwar maternity fashion were oversized collars and buttons, an infantalizing effect possibly meant to balance the scale of the garment, although one may see in them a condescending attitude to women. Lucille Ball, star of *I Love Lucy*, exemplified the maternity fashions of the early 1950s, and at the time influenced many women during her 1952–1953 televised pregnancy, seen weekly by millions.

In the early 1980s, Diana, Princess of Wales' two pregnancies influenced maternity styles. Dropped-waist dresses, then in fashion, were well suited to pregnancy and a favorite of Diana's. Dresses dropping straight from the yoke with no waist at all, one of the styles favored in the

1950s and 1960s, were also worn. Long tunics and sweaters over stretchy leggings became a popular casual choice.

In the 1980s, styles for working pregnant women also emerged as a category of fashion, as garment makers, and would-be mothers, struggled to find styles apt for women in the workplace. Styles based on men's business suits still dominated, suggesting unease with the notion of women in business; pregnancy required even more cover-up. Maternity versions of masculine business suits resulted, with boxier jackets and expanded skirts. Since then, both office wear and maternity wear have developed away from closely copying men's business wear.

The 1990s saw an end to the customary attempt to conceal pregnancy. The emphasis on fit, athletic bodies, and the culture's comfort with revealing the human form, have led to adopting clinging maternity styles in place of centuries of draping and concealment, and even bare-midriff shirts are worn by pregnant women. Feminism and a body-conscious culture have taken maternity fashion in new directions.

See also **Empire Style.**

BIBLIOGRAPHY

Baumgarten, Linda. "Dressing for Pregnancy: A Maternity Gown of 1780–1795." *Dress: The Journal of the Costume Society of America* 23 (1996).

Hoffert, Sylvia D. *Private Matters: American Attitudes Toward Childbearing and Infant Nurture in the Urban North, 1800–1860* (Women in American History). Urbana: University of Illinois Press, 1989.

Leavitt, Judith Walzer. *Brought to Bed: Childbearing in America 1750–1950.* Oxford and London: Oxford University Press, 1986.

Poli, Doretta Davanzo. *Maternity Fashion.* Drama Publishers, 1997.

Alden O'Brien

METALLIC FIBERS. *See* **Fibers.**

MCCARDELL, CLAIRE Claire McCardell was one of the most influential women's sportswear designers of the twentieth century. Best known for her contributions to the "American look," she was inspired by the active lifestyle of American women. Known for casual sportswear, shirtwaist dresses, and wool jersey sheaths, as well as practical leisure clothing and swimwear, which she liked to refer to as "playclothes," McCardell designed for working women who wanted stylish, well-made clothing in washable fabrics that were easily cared for.

McCardell was born in Frederick, Maryland, in 1905, where she attended Hood College for two years in the mid-1920s before earning a degree in fashion design at the Parsons School of Design in New York City in 1928. In the course of her studies she spent one year in Paris. Working after graduation as a fit model for B. Altman and Company, McCardell later obtained a job as a salesperson and design assistant with Emmet Joyce, an exclusive, made-to-order salon on Fifth Avenue. Within a matter of months, she was lured away by the knitwear manufacturer Sol Pollack to design and oversee his Seventh Avenue cutting room, where she stayed for less than a year. By late 1929 McCardell was working as a design assistant to Robert Turk, an independent designer and dressmaker, who later took her along with him when he was employed as chief designer at Townley Frocks in the early 1930s.

Turk died unexpectedly in a boating accident in 1932, and McCardell was promoted to chief designer at Townley. McCardell remained with Townley throughout her career, with the exception of a brief hiatus in the early 1940s, and eventually became a partner. During the time that Townley's partners restructured their business, McCardell worked at Hattie Carnegie; however, Townley soon rehired her as their head designer.

Innovation

While most of McCardell's contemporaries followed the long-standing tradition of copying Paris fashion, McCardell looked instead to the lives of American women for her inspiration. Insisting that "clothes should be useful," McCardell became one of the first designers to successfully translate high-styled, reasonably priced, impeccably cut clothing into the mass-production arena. Proudly American and rebelliously innovative, McCardell (who, as a student in Paris, had admired the work of Vionnet, Chanel, and Madame Grès) turned her back on the expensive, handmade confections of the haute couture and instead promoted American mass production, readily available materials, and the form-follows-function approach to design. Insisting that heavily decorated, padded, and corseted French fashions often sacrificed comfort to style, McCardell designed clean-lined, comfortable clothes that proved such a sacrifice was not only unacceptable; it was also unnecessary.

The retail magnate Stanley Marcus once described McCardell as "the master of the line, never a slave to the sequins ... one of the few truly creative designers this country has ever produced." Shunning shoulder pads, back zippers, boning, and heavily constructed looks, McCardell became known for her self-tailoring, wrap-and-tie styles, backless halters, hook-and-eye closures, coordinated separates, racy bathing suits, and boldly printed, cotton plaid, shirtwaist dresses cut from men's shirting fabrics. Often referred to as "America's most American designer," McCardell's fresh, youthful designs were founded on logic, informed by comfort, and replete with a common sense, entirely undecorated look. As the veteran fashion model Suzy Parker once described them, McCardell's designs were "refreshingly 'unFrench.'" McCardell's first commercial hit came in 1938 with the "Monastic" dress, an

American Swimwear, 1946. Models showcase Claire McCardell's "Pantung Loincloth" (left) and Joset Walker's "Hug Me Tights" (right) swimsuits. Crafted to show off the female body, these styles were considered racy during their time. © GENEVIEVE NAYLOR/CORBIS. REPRODUCED BY PERMISSION.

unfitted, waistless shift, cut on the bias, that hung straight from the waist and was belted in any way the wearer chose. The Monastic was so resoundingly popular that it was copied by competitors into the next decade and remained in her own line in updated versions for almost twenty years. Another McCardell success story was "capsule dressing," or four- and five-piece, mix-and-match separates groups in supple wool jersey, cotton, denim, and even taffeta. These stylish, well-edited groupings offered women a convenient travel wardrobe that sold altogether for about one hundred dollars and could be tucked into a handbag. An avid champion of pants and wool jersey for both day and evening wear, McCardell's forward-looking designs and fabric sensibility provided American women with multiseasonal clothing that was easily cared for, comfortable, and stylish, but never conspicuously chic.

American designer Clare McCardell, 1940. With an eye to providing American women with comfortable, casually elegant clothing to match their active lifestyles, McCardell works at her studio in New York City. McCardell's work was essential to defining and establishing American fashion. © BETTMANN/CORBIS. REPRODUCED BY PERMISSION.

The "American Look"

McCardell's pared-down, casual American style was the hallmark of what came to be hailed as the "American look," the name under which the work of McCardell and several of her like-minded contemporaries, such as Tina Leser and Tom Brigance, was marketed at Lord and Taylor during the late 1930s and early 1940s. During World War II, McCardell's designs earned further credibility, as they reflected an acute awareness of the evolving roles of mid-century American women. Offering sportswear and daywear that were at once appropriate for the office, cocktail hour, and leisure, McCardell eliminated the fuss, decoration, and strict categorization so often encountered in women's apparel of the time. Answering practical needs, McCardell's 1942 blue denim "Popover" dress, which sold for only $6.95, was made specifically for at-home domestic work or gardening and even included an attached oven mitt. True to her problem-solving approach to fashion design, McCardell used humble fabrics such as cotton calico, denim, jersey, and even synthetics, effectively ennobling everyday materials by way of thoughtful design and deftly executed construction. And while restrained and disciplined, McCardell's work was hardly devoid of details: Her signature, even idiosyncratic, "McCardellisms"

included severe, asymmetrical, wrap necklines, yards-long sashes, spaghetti-string ties, double-needle top stitching, metal hook-and-eye closures, and even studded leather cuffs. With their sleek lines and "no-price look," McCardell's clothes became a mainstay in the wardrobe of college girls, working women, and housewives alike.

Claire McCardell achieved international fame during her lifetime, appearing on the cover of *Time* magazine and authoring a book on her fashion philosophy, *What Shall I Wear?* in 1957. In 1943 she married the architect Irving Drought Harris. McCardell was diagnosed with cancer in 1958, at the height of her success. The disease claimed her life that same year.

Looking at her own life as a starting point for her line, McCardell's casually elegant, pared-down minimalism and lifestyle-driven sportswear of the late 1930s and 1940s helped forge and define what came to be known as the "American look" and heralded the beginning of a new appreciation for American fashion. As fashion historian Valerie Steele points out in *Women of Fashion*, "without McCardell it is simply impossible to imagine a Donna Karan, Calvin Klein or a Marc Jacobs."

See also **Casual Business Dress; Ready-to-Wear; Sportswear.**

BIBLIOGRAPHY

Kirkland, Sally. "Claire McCardell." In *American Fashion: The Life and Lines of Adrian, Mainbocher, McCardell, Norell, Trigère.* Edited by Sarah Tomerlin Lee for the Fashion Institute of Technology. New York: Quadrangle/New York Times Books, 1975.

McCardell, Claire. *What Shall I Wear?* New York: Simon and Schuster, 1956.

Milbank, Caroline Rennolds. *New York Fashion: The Evolution of American Style.* New York: Abrams, 1989.

Steele, Valerie. *Women of Fashion: Twentieth Century Designers.* New York: Rizzoli International, 1991.

Yohannan, Kohle, and Nancy Nolf. *Claire McCardell: Redefining Modernism.* New York: Harry N. Abrams, 1998.

Kohle Yohannan

MCFADDEN, MARY Born in New York City in 1938, Mary McFadden spent her childhood on a cotton plantation outside Memphis, Tennessee. She moved to Paris to study at the École Lubec from 1955 to 1956 and the Sorbonne from 1956 to 1957, returning to New York to study fashion at the Traphagen School of Design in 1956. McFadden went on to study sociology at Columbia University and the New School for Social Research from 1958 to 1960.

In 1962 McFadden began working as the director of public relations for Dior New York, until 1965 when she married Philip Hariri. He was a diamond merchant, so the marriage meant a move to South Africa, where McFadden worked as a journalist for *Vogue* South Africa and the *Rand Daily Mail.*

As special projects editor for American *Vogue* in 1970, her individual and idiosyncratic style and love of handcrafts made McFadden an influential figure. She initially designed clothes for herself, which were made to her own specifications from fabrics she had found during her extensive travels, creating an eclectic look that combined designer pieces with "ethnic" garments. When *Vogue* featured McFadden's tunic ensembles, simple shapes showing her characteristic love of color and print, Geraldine Stutz, president of Henri Bendel, bought them for the store. It was possible at that time for designers to launch their careers by creating a tiny collection and selling it to a single store, and this initial success prompted McFadden to start her own designing and manufacturing business in 1973. She formed Mary Mc-Fadden Inc. in 1976 and began designing evening gowns in pleated silk using a unique "Marii" technique, resembling that used by Mariano Fortuny, which she patented in 1975. She combined this innovation with elements of hand-painting, quilting, beading, and embroidery, culling ideas and inspiration from diverse ancient and ethnic cultures. Details of the clothes were handcrafted and used passementerie and beaten brass for fastenings. Since they were made with satin-backed polyester and did not crease, these dresses were ideal for her wealthy, much-traveled customers. Her less expensive clothes, produced in the late 1970s, were still noteworthy for their use of embellishment and mix of luxurious fabrics. Later she marketed her designs on QVC, the shopping channel, where she experienced particular success with accessories. She oversaw numerous licenses of her designs for womenswear, sleepwear, footwear, eyewear, neckwear, and home furnishings.

McFadden's many career accolades include two Coty Awards and induction into the Coty Hall of Fame in 1979. In 2002 she received a Lifetime Achievement Award from Fashion Week of the Americas. She was the first non-Hispanic recipient of this tribute.

Mary McFadden has always designed her clothes to be relatively independent of trends. Her designs are concerned with an eclectic appropriation of the past and decorative elements from other cultures, which she transforms into "wearable art."

See also **Afrocentric Fashion; Fortuny, Mariano.**

BIBLIOGRAPHY

Milbank, Caroline Rennolds. *New York Fashion: The Evolution of American Style.* New York: Harry N. Abrams, Inc., 1989.

Marnie Fogg

MCQUEEN, ALEXANDER

MCQUEEN, ALEXANDER Born Lee McQueen in the East End of London in 1969, Alexander McQueen was the youngest of six children to a taxi driver and a social history teacher. He left school at the age of sixteen and started an apprenticeship with the Savile Row tailors

"He takes ideas from the past and sabotages them with his cut to make them thoroughly new and in the context of today.... He is like a Peeping Tom in the way he slits and stabs at fabric to explore all the erogenous zones of the body."

Isabella Blow, quoted in Sarajane Hoare, "God Save McQueen." *Harper's Bazaar* 30 (June 1996): 148.

Anderson and Sheppard. From there McQueen moved to the tailors Gieves and Hawkes, the theatrical costumers Bermans and Nathans, the designer Koji Tatsuno in London, and (at age twenty) to Romeo Gigli in Milan. Returning to London in 1990, he sought employment teaching pattern-cutting at Central Saint Martins College of Art and Design; instead, despite his lack of formal fashion training, he was offered a place in the fashion design course as a graduate student. He was awarded the master of arts degree in 1992. After leaving college, McQueen claimed unemployed social security benefits and feared criminal prosecution if caught working for money. He then began designing under the name of Alexander McQueen, continuing to claim benefits as Lee McQueen. His graduate collection was bought in its entirety by the influential stylist Isabella Blow, at that time a *Vogue* fashion editor, who went on to promote and encourage his work over several years.

As Alexander McQueen he immediately started his own label, first showing in autumn-winter 1993. His early collections, such as Nihilism (spring-summer 1994) and Highland Rape (autumn-winter 1995) relied on shock tactics rather than wearability, a strategy that helped him establish a strong identity. With their harsh styling, the designs in these collections explored variations on the themes of abuse and victimization. They frequently featured slashed, stabbed, and torn cloth, as well as McQueen's brutally sharp style of tailoring. He introduced extraordinary narrative and aesthetic content to his runway shows. Styling, showmanship, and dramatic presentation became as important as the design of the clothes; models walked on water, were drenched in "golden showers" on an ink-flooded catwalk, or were surrounded by rings of flame. The shows were put together on minimal budgets, assisted by models, makeup artists, stylists, and producers prepared to work for nothing. His creative director, Katy England, played an important role in both the development of his aesthetic and the design and styling of his shows. At this stage McQueen began collaborations with designers such as Dai Rees and the jewelers Shaun Leane and Naomi Filmer, whose accessories and jewelry he used in his shows. Besides these activities, he also worked with innovative film, video, and pop producers.

McQueen played up to his bad-boy reputation, opening himself to accusations of misogyny in his Highland Rape collection, which featured apparently bruised and battered models staggering along an apocalyptic, heather-strewn runway, and baring his backside to the buyers at the New York version of his Dante show (autumn-winter 1996). His commercial sense, however, was as sharp as his tailoring, and his antics and anecdotes were always to a purpose, be it to attract press, buyers, or backers. The Dante show in New York, for example, elicited an order from Bergdorf Goodman. From the start McQueen understood the commercial value of shock tactics in the British fashion industry, which had almost no infrastructure despite its reputation for innovation. After he had acquired his first backer, he toned down, while not entirely losing, the outrageous content of the shows. Other important developments for McQueen occurred in 1996. Late in that year he changed his backer to the Japanese corporate giant Onward Kashiyama, one of the world's biggest clothing production houses; it also backed Helmut Lang and Paul Smith. Its subsidiary, Gibo, produced the McQueen line. In October he was appointed designer in chief at Givenchy in Paris, replacing John Galliano, who went to Christian Dior. Also in 1996 McQueen was named the British Designer of the Year—a success he repeated in 1997 and 2001.

McQueen and Galliano thus spearheaded an assault on Paris-based fashion by young British designers in the 1990s, and their iconoclastic imagery and show techniques did much to boost a flagging French business. The appointment to Givenchy brought with it the backing of the conglomerate LVMH (Moët Hennessy Louis Vuitton), which allowed McQueen to continue his uncompromising design style for his own label. While he toned down the rougher edges of his style for Givenchy, in both the Givenchy and McQueen collections he continued to develop themes that had been with him since graduation. Darkly romantic, with a harsh vision of history and politics, McQueen's approach differed from the more straightforwardly romantic output of Galliano or Vivienne Westwood. His inspirations were as likely to be cult films by Stanley Kubrick, Pier Paolo Pasolini, or Alfred Hitchcock; seventeenth-century anatomical plates; or the photographs of Joel-Peter Witkin, as his predecessors in the pantheon of fashion design. His early designs included the low-slung and cleavage-revealing "bumster" trousers; he maintained a fascination with highly structured corsets and tailoring, as well as with historical cut and detailing. However, in the late 1990s the victimized look of his early models gave way to an Amazonian version of female glamour as a form of terror. Growing up with an older sister who was a victim of domestic violence, McQueen has said that as a designer he aimed to create a vision of a woman so powerful that no one would dare to lay a hand on her.

In tandem with his commercial work, McQueen continued to collaborate with photographers such as Nick Knight and Norbert Schoerner in publishing projects, and to work with those outside the fashion world, such as the artist Sam Taylor-Wood and the musician Björk. Whereas his sharp tailoring was sold in shops, his dramatic, unique showpieces that never went into production were in demand from art galleries and exhibitions across the world.

McQueen sold a controlling share in his business to Gucci in December 2000 and left Givenchy early in 2001, continuing to show under his own name in Paris rather than London. His role as creative director of the company permitted him to retain creative freedom as a designer, while the backing of Gucci—owner of Yves Saint Laurent, Stella McCartney, and Balenciaga—facilitated the transition of his business from a small-scale London label to a global luxury brand. In March 2001 he launched his custom-made menswear line in collaboration with the Savile Row tailors Huntsman. That year McQueen also opened a flagship store in New York and, in 2003, two more in London and Milan. He launched his perfume, Kingdom, in 2003 as well, the same year that the Council of Fashion Designers of America named him International Designer of the Year and that Britain awarded him a CBE (Commander of the British Empire) for his services to the fashion industry.

See also **Fashion Shows; London Fashion.**

BIBLIOGRAPHY

Arnold, Rebecca. *Fashion, Desire, and Anxiety: Image and Morality in the Twentieth Century.* London and New York: I. B. Tauris, 2001.

Barley, Nick, ed. *Lost and Found: Critical Voices in New British Design.* Basel, Switzerland: Birkhäuser, 1999.

Evans, Caroline. *Fashion at the Edge: Spectacle, Modernity and Deathliness.* New Haven, Conn.: Yale University Press, 2003.

Frankel, Susannah. *Visionaries: Interviews with Fashion Designers.* London: V & A Publications, 2001.

Tucker, Andrew. *The London Fashion Book.* London: Thames and Hudson, 1998.

Wilcox, Claire, ed. *Radical Fashion.* London: V & A Publications, 2001.

Caroline Evans

MEISEL, STEVEN Born in 1954, Steven Meisel became arguably the most important and prolific fashion photographer of his generation. In a body of work notable for its imaginative range and diversity, he has achieved dominance in both editorial and advertising fashion photography. He is the primary photographer for the American and Italian editions of *Vogue*, where his covers and fashion pages have regularly appeared since the late 1980s, and he has produced some of the most memorable fashion advertising ever created, including campaigns for Versace, Dolce & Gabbana, Prada, Valentino, and Yves Saint Laurent, among a long list of advertising clients. In fact, when Meisel's work for the fall 2000 Versace advertising campaign was shown at London's prestigious White Cube Gallery, it significantly bridged the gap with fine art photography, a question that had plagued fashion photography since its inception.

As a child Meisel was fascinated with fashion magazines, from which he developed an abiding love of the clothing and photographic styles of the 1960s. As a fifth grader Meisel supposedly went to the studio of fashion photographer Melvin Sokolsky and demanded to meet the famous model Twiggy, and during his high school years he photographed models he saw on the streets of New York, including Loulou de la Falaise and Marisa Berenson. After graduating with a degree in fashion illustration from the Parsons School of Design, he immediately went to work as an illustrator, first for Halston, and then for *Women's Wear Daily* (*WWD*). Since he did not want to stay at *WWD*, he got a camera, taught himself how to take photographs, and took test shots on weekends of various young models and actresses, including Phoebe Cates. Some of these shoots—on which he was responsible for the hairstyles, makeup, clothes, and photography—attracted the attention of editors at *Seventeen* magazine, resulting in work for *Mademoiselle* and, eventually, for *Vogue*. Introduced to *Vogue*'s editor-in-chief Alexander Liberman and its fashion editor Grace Mirabella, Meisel was asked to style hair, apply makeup, and take photographs, first for the French and Italian collections, and then for the New York collections.

Influences

Unlike many fashion photographers who base their work on a signature style, the character of Meisel's work is intriguingly diverse. "Inspiration comes from all over the place," the photographer said. "I'm eager to soak up new information—it can be from the nineteenth century as long as it's new to me. It can come from going to the grocery store or looking at an artist from a million years ago" (Meisel interview, 2003; as are all subsequent quotes). His influences range from 1960s fashion, Los Angeles's architecture, Nan Golden's photography, Alex Katz's paintings, and many types of film, from work by Federico Fellini, Woody Allen, and Michelangelo Antonioni to *They Shoot Horses, Don't They?* and *Blow-Up*, with David Hemmings and Verushka. "My style changes constantly," Meisel started. "Fashion is about change. In order to stay current and excited, I try new and different approaches."

Meisel is also inspired by certain women and has been credited with discovering such supermodels as Iman, Linda Evangelista, and Kristin McMenamy. "My pictures are the result of my fantasies projected onto the girl and of me trying to get the girl into my brain," Meisel said. The photographer also feels he has changed fashion photography by using models of different ethnic types, such as the African Americans Naomi Campbell and Beverly Peele, and older models such as Marianne Faithful, Benedetta Barzini, and Lauren Hutton. "I have

Steven Meisel with actress Liza Minnelli, 1991. Celebrated for producing artful and original fashion photography, Meisel has also garnered controversy for his Calvin Klein underwear advertising campaigns and for photographing pop star Madonna's *Sex* book. TIME LIFE PICTURES/GETTY IMAGES. REPRODUCED BY PERMISSION.

the greatest respect for women of all ages. The Barney's ads with Lauren Hutton made a big impact, and I used Benedetta (an Italian beauty who was an internationally-known model in the 1970s) for the Gap campaign." Meisel, like Richard Avedon before him, chooses his models to reflect the zeitgeist. Meisel's work for Calvin Klein, for example, captures the glazed-over disconnect between people of the 1990s, which is why, in the words of one critic, they "feel so subversive." Meisel's Fall 2000 advertising campaign for Versace, which features models Amber Valetta and Georgina Grenville as pill-popping, blue-eye-shadow-wearing Hollywood housewives, affectionately scrutinizes American-style luxury of the late twentieth century.

Controversy seems to swirl around Meisel, to the point that he has himself become a celebrity. "People get interested in me," he said. "In the mid-80s there was a hubbub about me." The fact that he was Madonna's choice to photograph her 1992 book, *Sex*, further fanned the flames of Meisel's notoriety. "I knew Madonna from the clubs in New York. The content was entirely her fantasies ... from her thoughts." Equally shocking to some

ENCYCLOPEDIA OF CLOTHING AND FASHION **401**

were the so-called "kiddie porn" advertisements Meisel created for Calvin Klein, which in the photographer's words "got so much grief from conservatives. I did a story for *L'Uomo Vogue* using bathing suits on young boys. Calvin came to the studio, saw those pictures and wanted it done like that." In 1999 Meisel produced an Opium perfume campaign featuring model Sophie Dahl wearing nothing but diamonds and shoes, and in January 2002 he took fashion photography close to the realm of soft porn in a twenty-two-page story for Italian *Vogue*, which featured Russian model Natalia Vodianova.

Steven Meisel's prodigious talent and extraordinary creativity, coupled with an unerring sense of the zeitgeist, make him the most important fashion photographer to have emerged in the late twentieth century. Like the greatest fashion photographers who have preceded him, Meisel continues to merge his own inventive range of ideas with an extraordinary ability to capture the moment in order to produce fashion photographs of importance and interest.

See also **Fashion Magazines; Fashion Models; Fashion Photography.**

BIBLIOGRAPHY

Klein, Rebecca. "Steven Meisel." *American Photo* 14 (May/June 2003): 58.

Lehrman, Karen. "Beyond Fashion? Steven Meisel: From the Collections to the Collectors." *Art and Auction* 22 (June 2001): 96–104.

Meisel, Steven. Telephone conversation with author, 5 September 2003.

Sischy, Ingrid. "The Shuttered Bug." *New York Times Magazine* 150, (19 August 2001 Supplement): 148.

Spindler, Amy M. "Tracing the Look of Alienation." *New York Times*, (24 March 1998): Fashion section.

Nancy Hall-Duncan

MICROFIBERS Microfibers are very fine fibers manufactured by special processes. Developed to exhibit the drape and softness of silk in fabrics, microfibers are less than 0.00004 inches in diameter, about one-tenth the size of silk fibers. Technological inprovements have made it possible to produce smaller and smaller fibers, into the range of ultrafine fibers that have diameters of less than 0.000004 inches.

The first microfibers were made by using the traditional melt-spinning process of melting a polymer, such as nylon or polyester, and extruding it through very fine holes. The disadvantage of this direct spinning method was that the filament fibers were so fine they would break during the extrusion process or during subsequent conversion into yarns and fabrics. Consequently, special manufacturing techniques are used. The most common is to spin bicomponent fibers composed of two different polymer types (for example, nylon and polyester). The bicomponent fiber may have either a citrus or an islands-in-the-sea configuration. The citrus structure has wedge-shaped segments of one polymer held within a star-shaped core of a different polymer. In the islands-in-the-sea configuration, tiny "islands" of one polymer are dispersed in a "sea" of another polymer.

For both structures the bicomponent fiber as spun is thick enough to withstand the processing. After the bicomponent fibers are spun, they are made into yarns and woven or knitted into fabrics. After the fabric is formed, one of the polymer components is dissolved, leaving the other component as microfibers.

Because they are so fine, microfibers are flexible and bend easily, so that fabrics made from them are soft and drapable. In addition, microfiber fabrics are dense, because the small fibers are able to pack closely together. This gives the fabrics a degree of water repellency, since water cannot as easily penetrate the small pores between the fibers. These properties have dictated the types of apparel in which microfibers are used.

Polyester microfiber fabrics are often seen in all-weather coats, sports coats, and soft caps for men and women. Outerwear that has a comfortable feel and also repels moisture has made these microfiber garments popular. Further, the low moisture absorbency of the polyester fibers enhances the water repellency. Nylon microfiber fabrics on the other hand are used for underwear, lingerie, and hosiery. Nylon fibers have the stretch and recovery, as well as strength, often desired for these end uses. The very fine microfibers are soft and comfortable next to the skin, and nylon has higher moisture absorbency than polyester.

The aesthetic and functional advantages of microfibers are well recognized. They are, however, more expensive than their normal-size counterparts. This is because of the more complex manufacturing processes needed to produce them. Making the precursor bicomponent fibers requires specialized equipment, and dissolution of one component after the fabric is constructed is an additional finishing step that must be conducted under carefully controlled conditions.

See also **Nylon; Outerwear; Polyester.**

BIBLIOGRAPHY

Hongu, Tatsuya, and Glyn O. Phillips. *New Fibres*. Chichester, U.K: Ellis Horwood, 1990.

Billie J. Collier

MIDDLE EAST: HISTORY OF ISLAMIC DRESS

Dress in the Islamic world has historically conveyed the wearer's rank and status, profession, and religious affiliation. Official recognition of loyal service was expressed in gifts of dress fabrics and clothing (in Arabic, *khilca*; Turkish, *hilat*; Persian, *khalat*) until the late nineteenth century.

Wearing clothing of one's social grouping signified contentment, whereas to be seen publicly in dress worn by a higher class proclaimed dissatisfaction with the prevailing order. Likewise the refusal to don the color or headwear associated with the controlling authority, whether imperial or fraternal, formally demonstrated the withdrawal of allegiance.

The ruling household was presumed to be both arbiter and custodian of "good taste," and any deviant behavior could be used to legitimize rebellion to restore "order." The theologian/jurist constantly reminded the authorities to uphold dress standards to guard against serious social repercussions; thus the 1967 Israeli occupation of Egyptian Sinai was understood by some to be a consequence of Egyptian young women adopting Western fashions. The numerous legal edicts regarding dress (such as the prohibition of cross-dressing, ostentatious female attire, and non-Muslim clothing) were difficult to police, but market regulations (hisba), concerning weaving, tailoring, and dyeing practices, were easier to enforce.

The Qur'an contains few details concerning "proper" dress; most guidance is contained in the Hadith (sayings of the prophet Muhammad) literature, an important component of Islamic law. However, it is concerned primarily with certain Muslim rituals, such as the hajj, or burial, rather than with everyday wear. Each major grouping and sect of Islam relies on its own Hadith compilation for legal guidance, and over time and in response to regional requirements historic judgements were clarified or superseded. So there is no universal ruling regarding the nature and character of "proper" dress, including female veiling. Maliki law, for example, permitted one finger's width of pure silk for (male) garment trimming, while pure silk outer garments were acceptable in Hanafi circles. All theologians, whether Sunnī or Shīcī, preferred the devout Muslim male to dress austerely in cotton, linen, or wool, and Muslim mystics were known as sufīs "wearers of wool." However, it was generally agreed that the prosperity and power of the Islamic state was best demonstrated through ostentatious dress and ceremonial; Muslim philosophers, such as Ibn Khaldun (d. 1406), acknowledged that cultured societies were recognized by their tailored garments, and not by simple Bedouin wraps.

Personal wealth was expressed by ownership of textiles and dress as recorded in the eleventh and twelfth century Cairo Geniza trousseau lists. Certain Muslim festivals were celebrated with gifts of new clothing, while other periods (e.g., the month of Muharram in Shīcī communities) were associated with mourning dress, the color of which depended on regional conventions. Cutting and tailoring of court clothing were undertaken on auspicious days determined by the royal astronomer. In the general belief that spells were more effective when secreted in clothing, the protective formula bismillah ("in the name of God…") would be uttered when dressing to deflect any evil. As further protection, many wore items decorated with talismanic designs incorporating Qur'anic verses and

Medes and Persians at Persepolis, ancient Iran. Ancient Persian soldiers dressed in *qaba*, a short, close-fitting robe, with trousers or leggings. PHOTO BY JOHN S. MAJOR. REPRODUCED BY PERMISSION.

associated symbols. Clothing of saintly persons, especially those of the prophet Muhammad, was understood to be imbued with baraka (divine blessing), and so the master's cloak (khirqa, burda) was publicly draped over the initiate's shoulders in Sufi and guild rituals.

Textile processing and production formed the mainstay of the Islamic Middle Eastern economy until the nineteenth century, so, unsurprisingly, Arabic, Persian, and Turkish literature contain numerous references to fabrics and clothing. However, meanings are imprecise and, until recently, many scholars assumed that repetition of a specific garment term over centuries and across regions signified that its meaning and appearance remained unchanged and universal; this assumption has not fostered academic interest in the subject.

Most pictorial evidence is found in post-twelfth-century manuscripts, metalwork, and other artwork, but it rarely relates to family or working life. The advent of photography in the nineteenth century resulted in valuable insights into village and rural dress, but records contain few details of the wearers' ages and social placing, and of garment and fabric structure. Textile finds have rarely been recorded in archaeological reports of excavations, and few museum pieces have been published with full seaming and decorative details.

The basic garment structure was very simple: the loom width formed the main front and back panels, with additional fabric inserts to create extra width and shaping where required, even on many Ottoman and Iranian court robes. Drawstring waists created gathers and unsewn pleats. It was not until the nineteenth century and the introduction of European fashions that shaped armholes, padded and sloping shoulders, darts, and so forth were used in garment structure.

Umayyad and Abbasid Dress

After Muhammad's death in 632 C.E., Islam spread across North Africa and into Spain, through Syria to southeastern Anatolia and Central Asia, reaching the boundaries of Imperial China and India by around 750. Chroniclers wrote extensively about such conquests, but little on dress matters. Some information is contained in Hadith compilations and in later criticisms of earlier regimes—for example ninth-century disapproval of the trailing robes of perfumed yellow silk worn by the Umayyad caliph Walid II (r. 743–744) as demonstrating a dissolute lifestyle, and the excessively large wardrobe of Hisham (r. 724–743).

With the establishment of the Islamic state, there was no immediate change in dress if only because non-Muslims, then the majority of the population, were required not to dress like Arab Muslims, and it is known that Egypt paid its annual tribute in Coptic garments. The simple wrap (*izar, thawb*) of pre-Islamic Arabia, along with a sleeved, collarless *qamis* (shirt) probably came to be recognized as "Muslim" dress for both genders. On top was worn a mantle (*caba*) formed from wide fabric, folded twice into the center along the weft and sewn along one selvage (forming the shoulder), and slit in both folds (armholes). At least six other terms for mantles were in use at this time, indicating that each differed in some way. By the eighth century the turban (*cimama*) of rolled, wound fabric became the acknowledged sign of a Muslim male, and at least sixty-six different methods of winding are mentioned.

As Muhammad disliked the color red and richly patterned fabrics, finding them distracting during prayer, devout Muslim men were advised to avoid such fabrics and colors along with green, the dress of angels. Such recommendations did not apply to Muslim women, but they were enjoined not to parade jewelry, to "cover" (*hijab*, meaning curtain or drape) themselves modestly, and to wear *sirwal* (drawers) of which, the Hadith records, Muhammad approved. Various footwear terms are mentioned, but the camel leather *nacl* sandal, worn by the Prophet, with two straps, one across the foot, the other encircling the large toe, became an enduring favorite and was required men's footwear for *hajj* pilgrims.

In his lifetime Muhammad honored certain individuals by giving an item of personal clothing or fabric length, and this became established court custom (*khilca*) in the Umayyad period from 661 to 749. An additional honor

was an embroidered or tapestry band (*tiraz*) bearing the caliph's name and other details, sewn or woven near or on the dropped shoulder positioning of the *caba* and of the *jubba*, a long centrally-fastened garment with fabric rectangles joined at right angles to form sleeves. The earliest known *tiraz* fragment in red silk (in the Victoria and Albert Museum, London) records the name of the caliph Marwan I (r. 684–685) or Marwan II (r. 744–750).

Decorative collar and cuffs were features of kingly dress and possibly formed part of the caliphal insignia. The plaster statuary depicting the ruler in Sasanid regal dress (e.g., Khirbat al-Mafjar, Qasr al-Hayr al-Gharbi) perhaps records actual Umayyad caliphal dress, but possibly it merely utilizes a recognizable regal imagery. The Umayyad dynastic color was probably white, worn with a white *cimama* for the Friday prayer, but otherwise, as depicted on coins, the "crown" was similar to the Sasanid crown (*taj*) or a tall sugar-loaf cap (*qalansuwa*).

In this period depictions of women's dress are limited to female entertainers and attendants, with few exceptions. As noted above, *sirwal* were often worn along with a *qamis*, but whether or how these differed from the male garments is unknown. The early eighth century Qusayr Amra murals show half-naked entertainers in checkered skirt wraps, but the ladies in the enthronement composition have long garments with wide necks, and head veils. The Hadith disapproves of artificial tresses, indicating a seventh- and eighth-century fashion, but these entertainers have kiss-curls and ringlets.

A favorite dress fabric at court, especially during the reigns of Sulayman (r. 715–717) and of the Abbasid caliph Harun al-Rashid (r. 786–809), was *washi* from Egypt, Iraq, and Yemen—probably a weft-ikat (tie-dyed) silk because examples, albeit in cotton, have survived. However, the man and woman of fashion avidly sought garment fabrics from across the empire: Egyptian linens, silks from Iraq and the Caucasus, Adenese mantles, Iranian silk and cotton mixtures, and so on, avoiding, if possible, noticeable textural contrast (e.g., cotton and linen) and vivid, contrasting dye shades.

With Iranian support the Abbasid family, proclaiming the right of the Prophet's family to the caliphate, seized control from the Umayyad house in 749. Within decades Spain, North Africa, and then Egypt and southern Syria broke away from direct Abbasid control while hereditary governorships in the eastern regions had virtual independence, provided they paid tribute promptly to the Baghdad court. From 945 if not earlier, the overriding cultural influences in Abbasid court ceremonies and dress were Iranian (the bureaucrats) and also Turkic (military).

As Ibn Khaldun explained, the Abbasid dynastic color was black, commemorating the violent deaths of Muhammad's son-in-law and grandsons. Failure to wear black robes at the twice-weekly audiences demonstrated the wearer's dissatisfaction with the ruler and regime. On ceremonial duty, the caliph usually wore black, with the Prophet's mantle over his shoulders (signifying his blessing) and carrying other relics associated with Muhammad, or he sometimes wore a monochrome overgarment embroidered in white wool or silk. The *qalansuwa* was still perceived as the "crown," but individual caliphs preferred one model over others.

As court ceremonial became more complex, the main professions of bureaucrat, army officer, and theologian had distinctive dress. The vizier (minister) was recognizable by his double belt, and his colleagues were known as the *ashab al-dararic* (literally, men of the *durraca*) because of their long woollen robes, buttoned neck to chest, probably with long ample sleeves. Army officers (*ashab al-aqbiyya*) wore the shorter, close-fitting *qaba*, probably introduced from Iran by Caliph al-Mansur (r. 754–775), with trousers or leggings. Its exact structure is debatable, but perhaps it was like the tailored eighth- and ninth-century silk robe, patterned with Sasanid motifs from Mochtshevaya Balka, Caucasus. The highest ranks wore black, an honor not permitted to lower ranks, but the caliphal personal guard dressed in patterned silks with gold belts. The military were allowed a form of *qalansuwa*, although by the late twelfth century the highest ranking officers displayed their Turkic origins—and indeed support for Saladin—by donning the *sharbush*, a fur-trimmed cap with a distinctive triangular central plaque. The theologian on the other hand was identifiable by his voluminous outer robe of black cotton, linen, or wool, decorated with gold-embroidered *tiraz* bands. When giving the Friday sermon, he wore a black turban, but various thirteenth-century *Maqamat al-Hariri* illustrations show him on less formal occasions in a white turban, covered by a shoulder-length black *taylasan* hood.

A lady's ensemble still consisted of *sirwal*, *qamis* under a long robe belted with a sash or cummerbund, and a similarly-colored head covering, all covered by one or more long head- and face-veils for outdoor wear. White was worn by divorced women, and blue and black were reserved for those in mourning. Multi-colored and striped fabrics were best avoided for street wear while bright monochrome colors were associated with female entertainers. Theological criticisms reveal that royal ladies spent wildly on clothing for special occasions, a single robe sometimes costing more than sixteen hundred times a doctor's monthly salary. Unfortunately, specific descriptions of such costly garments are never included.

The *Maqamat al-Hariri* illustrated manuscripts, probably produced in northern Syria or Iraq, contain valuable visual information, and occasionally peasant and working classes are shown in other illustrated works. For the earlier Abbasid period, pictorial evidence is more or less limited to early-twentieth-century archaeological drawings of excavated mural fragments from the palace complexes at Samarra. The painted ceiling of the Capella Palatina (Palermo, Sicily) is more closely related to Fa-timid (Egypt and North Africa) dress, while wall-paintings in the Xinjiang region (western China) and Lashkar-i Bazar (Afghanistan) depict regional costume styles.

Dress of the Mamluk Sultanate

With the Mongol capture of Baghdad in 1258, the Abbasid caliph fled to the Mamluk court at Cairo, where he was accorded respect but no power. It has been usual for Western historians to consider the sultanate in two periods: Bahri military rule (c. 1250–c. 1293), and Burji rule (c. 1293–1516). In the Bahri army there were at least five main ethnic groupings, and three divisions, each with distinctive dress, which were fiercely protected, as well as a special uniform for attending the sultan, and another for royal processions. At least six different types of military *qaba* are named, but none can be securely assigned to the various military garments shown in late-thirteenth-century depictions. The *sharbush* and the *sarajuq*, favorite military headgear until the late thirteenth century, were replaced by the *kalawta* or small fabric cap, sometimes costing almost two months of a doctor's salary, worn with or without a turban cloth. Army and court officers were allowed to display their own blazon (rank) on their belongings, whether shoes, pen cases, or servants' clothing; several, made of appliqué felt, have survived (for instance, those in the Textile Museum, Washington, D.C.).

As the Abbasid caliph was still theoretically the head of Muslim Sunnīs, black robes and head coverings were retained as "official" theological dress although Sultan Barquq, tiring of it in 1396 and 1397, ordered the wearing of colored woollen outer garments. Highest-ranking *qadi*s (judges) wore the *dilq*, while other magistrates had the *farajiyya*, a garment term in use since 1031; the precise characteristics of either robe are not known. That said, it is evident that there were regional differences, though undefined, as provincial theologians were recognized by their dress, perhaps in the manner of today's foreign tourists visiting another country.

Certain sultans had highly individual fashion tastes, such as al-Nasir Nasir al-Din Muhammad (r. 1294–1295; 1299–1308; 1309–1340), of Mongol parentage, who shocked court circles by wearing Arab bedouin dress. To proclaim the legality of Mamluk authority, the sultan was invested with Abbasid black by the caliph, but generally for court audiences he wore military dress, acknowledging his debt to his fellow Mamluk officers. The *khilca* or system of honorific garments, described by al-Maqrizi, offers an insight into Mamluk court complexities. Highest-ranking commanders were awarded, among other things, garments of red and yellow *Rumi* (possibly Anatolian) satin, lined with squirrel and trimmed with beaver, with a gold belt and *kalawta* clasps. A white silk *fawqani* robe, woven with gold thread and decorated with silk embroidery, squirrel, and beaver was given to chief viziers while less-costly fabrics of other colors, only hemmed in beaver, were presented to lower-ranking bureaucrats. Such *khilca* was presented to mark a new appointment, an individual's arrival and departure from court, the successful conclusion of an architectural project or medical treatment, and similar occasions.

In 1371 and 1372 the sultan ordered members of the prophet Muhammad's family, men and women, to wear a piece of green fabric in public so that due respect could be paid to them. From then on, the leaf-green color, obtained by dyeing first in blue then yellow (thus more expensive than single-dyed fabrics), was formally restricted in Sunnī circles to this grouping. In Mamluk society a bright red worn in public denoted prostitutes, although elsewhere in the Islamic Middle East it was the ceremonial color for the highest-ranking Mongol ladies, and for bridal apparel.

By this time tailored garments were the norm, formed from ten or more shaped units sewn together, as seen in garment fragments in museum collections; regrettably none has been published adequately. Many "Mamluk" dress-weight fabrics have patterns based on foliated teardrop motifs, sometimes edged with Arabic inscriptions blessing the wearer, or lobed rosette shapes surrounded by running animals.

Dress in the Ottoman Empire
From a small Anatolian principality, the Ottoman family quickly extended authority into most of Anatolia and the Balkans. In 1453 the court moved for the last time to Constantinople (Istanbul), continuing its territorial expansion into central Europe, Egypt and North Africa, the Arabian Peninsula, and western Iran.

Within the Topkapi Saray Museum (Istanbul) collections, there are more than two thousand dress items associated with the Ottoman sultans and their household; few are linked with the royal ladies and children. This source is augmented by numerous manuscript and album paintings, and other items.

Even the sultan's robes were essentially simple in construction, with shaping achieved through joining inserts to the main front and back panels. The central fastening of thread buttons with fabric loops was accentuated by horizontal lines of *chaprast* braiding, the number of rows denoting the wearer's higher status. The typical ceremonial garment, fashionable from the mid-fifteenth century to the mid-sixteenth century, was the ankle-length, elbow-length sleeved *kaftan* worn over another sleeved garment, collarless shirt, and trousers; a calf-length version was also available. A similarly tailored robe but with wide sleeves tapering sharply to a buttoned wrist-cuff was the *dolaman*, a seventeenth-century style. Over these garments, the sultan and high-ranking officials wore a long, ample mantle (*kapaniche*) with a fur-covered, shoulder-width, and shoulder-length square collar flap; for the sultan's investiture mantle, the fur was black fox, while the grand vizier, chief eunuch, and *bostanci bashi* (commander of personal guard) usually had sable. Sleeves were often extra long and worn loose to al-

low lower ranks to kiss the edge. The arm had access through a slit at the elbow or shoulder-sleeve seam. High office was also shown by excessively tall or wide headwear in various shapes, made of padded fine muslin cotton over a balsa-wood form. Breeches with drawstring waists were generously shaped, presumably to allow extra padded linings for winter wear.

There was no noticeable difference between the Ottoman ceremonial garments of the chief bureaucrat and army commander, but there were various distinct regimental uniforms, which became more ornate and less functional over the centuries. The *bostanci* was recognizable in his red, calf-length, long-sleeved outer garment worn with either a red felt cap, drooping over the right ear, or a tall, brown conical cap (perhaps denoting rank). The ceremonial archer *solak* corps wore tight-fitting *shalvar* (trousers) or hose with ankle boots, over which was worn a filmy underskirt and an elaborately patterned sleeved outer garment; an asymmetrical conical headdress with a wide gold headband completed the ensemble. The *peyk* troop of court messengers had a distinctive rounded "helmet" of gilded and incised copper, while the other Janissary regiments demonstrated their association with the Bektashi Sufi order by wearing the *keche*, a white felt "tube" rising some twelve inches from a stiff gold-embroidered band, then falling down the back; it symbolized the garment sleeve worn by the order's founder.

Muslim theologians continued to wear ample outer robes, the *cubbe* (in Arabic, *jubba*), sweeping the floor and buttoned from the waist, with very wide sleeves. The chief theologian was permitted a sable lining, but urban mullahs were restricted to ermine. In early-eighteenth-century *Sur-name* illustrated manuscripts, lower-ranking jurists are identifiable by their conical "lamp-shade" turbans, but important theologians wore the *urf*, an enormous spherically shaped rolled turban, white in color, while from the 1590s the *nakib ul-eshraf* (in Arabic, *naqib al-ashraf*), leader of the prophet Muhammad's descendants, had his in green like his outer robe. Thereafter, Europeans wearing green risked physical attack. Also depicted in various manuscripts are various Sufi (mystic) orders, whose garments and, especially, headgear had specific symbolic connotations according to the order.

There were four main grades of court honorific garments (in Turkish, *hilat*), costing the treasury each year half of what was spent on clothing the ninety-nine Janissary regiments: "most excellent," "belted," "variegated," and "plain." As the terms imply, the difference lay in fabric quality, fur lining or trimming, coloring, and number of items offered. Presentations were also made to provincial and regional governors and to visiting foreign delegates.

Status through dress was also found in the harem, conveyed in the type of fur trimming and lining, and the richness of the bejeweled "marital" belt. European reports regarding female private dress probably relate to entertainers and women in similar occupations, and to non-Muslim women, as access into the harem by a non-Muslim male was strictly curtailed. Similar constraints applied to Ottoman court painters before around 1710, so it is unclear how accurate these dress representations are. Even with the detailed album paintings of Levni (flourished 1710–1720s), there is little indication of fabric texture and seaming. The late-sixteenth-century street clothing was a long-sleeved, voluminous *ferace* (in Arabic, *farajiyya*) with its long *yaka* back-collar and two-piece *mahrama* face covering, worn with a black oblong horsehair *peche* over the eyes. This garment covered various robes, including underdrawers, ample trousers, and a fine chemise. The main visual difference between female and male attire was not the direction of fastening as in later European dress, but the revealing necklines of women's dress. Various headdresses are depicted, but it is unclear whether these were exclusive to court ladies and whether they indicated ranking. One had a tall, waisted cylindrical form, similar to that worn by fourteenth-century Mongol princesses in Iran and Mamluk ladies in Cairo. Another two frequently illustrated were a small cap with an oval metal plate placed like an angled mirror, and a truncated conical form, sometimes four inches high covered with luxurious fabric.

The choice of fabrics was staggering. Fine wools were manufactured domestically along with choice watermarked silk-mohair mixtures and printed cottons, often used for linings. Sericulture had been in full operation in Anatolia since 1500, producing superb fabrics, often with large pattern repeats highlighted in woven gold and silver thread. As yet, the fabrics manufactured elsewhere in Ottoman territories—for example the Balkans, North Africa, Syria, and Iraq—cannot be securely identified, and there are no detailed descriptions of regional dress outside eastern Europe until the late eighteenth century. The favorite sixteenth-century patterns, often in four or more colors, were based on geometric compositions, meanders, and ogival lattices, formed by or infilled with stemmed flowers, such as the carnation, rose, and tulip, perhaps reflecting the contemporary court interest in gardens; inclusion of figural representations probably denotes non-Ottoman manufacture. Plague outbreaks in the eighteenth century with subsequent loss of skilled weavers perhaps led to the increased use of embroidery and small pattern motifs carried in stripes, as in contemporary French silks.

Dress in Safavid Iran

Ismail of the Safavid family, relying on the support of some ten tribal clans (*qizilbash*), assumed control of Iran, eastern Turkey, the Caucasus, and present-day Afghanistan, sweeping aside the remnants of Timurid and other regimes. Although the majority of Iranian Muslims were then Sunnī in belief, Ismail ordered that the state religion be henceforth Shīcī Islam of the Ithna Ashari branch, which held that the twelfth descendant (Imam)

of Muhammad would return to prepare the community for the day of reckoning. Accordingly early Safavid shahs required their supporters, especially the *qizilbash* (Turkish for "red head") to wear a distinctive bloodred cap (*taj*) with twelve vertical padded folds ending in a baton-like finial, usually wound with a white turban cloth, symbolizing devotion to twelve Imams and willingness to die for the Safavid cause.

The typical early Safavid court garment retained the simple structure worn in fifteenth-century Iran under a similarly structured outer robe with loose hanging sleeves; both had horizontal chest braiding for fastening. By the 1570s, it was fashionable to don a heavier outer garment, again simply tailored but with the front left panel extended to fasten diagonally, with three or four fabric ties, under the right arm. Neither style was apparently the exclusive prerogative of any office or rank, as probably court and military officers carried identifying wands of office. As the *qizilbash* lost position to Caucasian Georgian mercenaries during the early seventeenth century, so the court turned to Georgian-styled garments with a more fitted line, still achieved by fabric insertion rather than by darts and pleats, accentuating the waist and hips with a calf-length, bell-shaped skirt and central fastening. Likewise, the *taj* was replaced by a fur-trimmed cap with a deep, upturned rim, or by various flamboyant turban forms.

As in the Ottoman court there was a rich variety of silks and velvets, many incorporating metal threads creating a shimmering background for twill weave patterns of isolated floral sprays. Unlike their Sunnī counterparts, Shīcī theologians were not overly concerned with the presence of figural representations on textiles, so motifs of people, animals, and birds were often incorporated into the pattern. Tailored within the palace, the honorific *khalat* garments were graded, according to a court administrator, on the percentage of gold used in silver-gilt metal thread. However, such rich clothing was set aside for black or dark garments during the Muslim month of Muharram, to commemorate the tragic death of the Prophet's grandson, Husain (Third Imam in Shīcī belief).

Examples of mid-seventeenth-century garment styling were described and drawn by Engelbert Kaempfer, John Chardin, and other European visitors, but without precise details of profession and status, and the pictorial accuracy of women's dress is questionable, as access would have been limited to Christian, Jewish, and Zoroastrian females. Iranian album paintings of the mid-seventeenth century depict languidly posed ladies, their heads covered by various patterned and shaped kerchiefs, and the whiteness of their faces emphasized by double strands of pearls draped over the head and under the chin. Their robes are narrow-fitting, full length, and sleeved, with fitted trousers patterned in diagonal stripes, whereas the dancing girls with their multi-plaits shown in contemporary "palace" paintings (e.g., Chihil Sutun,

Isfahan) wear hip-length, sleeved tunics and jackets over bell-shaped, calf-length drawstring skirts.

Early Ottoman and Iranian Dress

Both the nineteenth-century Ottoman sultanate and the Qajar regime in Iran from 1775 to 1924 decided that military reorganization and reequipment on European lines were vital to counter European and Russian expansionist policies. Theological antipathy was immediate, proclaiming that Islam was being betrayed, and that the wearing of European-styled uniforms signified nothing less than the victory of Christianity; a peaked army cap prohibited proper prostration required in Muslim prayer ritual, while ornate frogging on Austrian-styled military jackets signified belief in the crucified Christ. Both regimes resorted to drastic measures to achieve military reequipment, and then initiated other dress reforms alongside major changes in criminal and civic law, education, and religious endowment management.

The 1839 Gulhane edict removed legal and social differentials between Ottoman Muslim and non-Muslim subjects, including sumptuary legislation relating to non-Muslims. Thirteen years earlier, all adult males, except theologians, had been ordered to wear clothing based on European styling: straight trousers, collared shirts, cravats, and the fez, instead of multicolored long, loose silk robes and turbans. Women were not included, but by the mid-nineteenth century Ottoman ladies of status were eagerly ordering copies of the fashions worn by visiting European ladies.

After World War I Mustafa Kemal "Ataturk" undertook further dress reforms as an integral part of his modernization programs, secularizing the new Turkish Republic and linking it politically with Europe rather than the Middle East. Viewing the fez as the symbol of allegiance to Ottoman values, he ordered the wearing of brimmed hats and Western-styled suits for men, with harsh penalties for noncompliance. Once again women's clothing was not included; however, salaries were not paid to female government and public employees (for example, teachers, nurses, lawyers, and clerks) unless they dressed in European style and abandoned any face or head veiling.

In nineteenth-century Iran, similar policies were followed by the Qajar shahs. Fath Ali Shah (r. 1797–1834) had introduced a new type of *kulah* headgear of astrakhan lamb in an obliquely-cut conical form, eighteen inches high, and a close-fitting, narrow-sleeved, full-length garment designed to accentuate his height and slender form, which was worn with a dazzling array of jewelry. However, by the late 1840s, the shah's ceremonial dress was military in style with straight European trousers and shoes and a long buttoned jacket with high "mandarin" collar, embellished with gold frogging including epaulettes. Court officials followed suit. A fur-trimmed open overjacket of Kirman wool and white gloves completed the outfit.

Court ladies posed for oil paintings in richly patterned, full-length, wide "culottes" (*zir-jamah*), and a fine, filmy sleeved *pirahan* undershirt often slit vertically over each breast (symbolizing fecundity). Over this a short, hipped jacket (*chapkan*, *kurdi*), richly patterned, was worn. All this finery was concealed outdoors by a voluminous full-length dark-colored head veil (*chador*) and a fine, waist-length, white cotton or silk face veil (*ruband*). A radical change resulted from the shah's state visit to Europe in 1873. Seeing the calf-length ballerina skirts and white stockings of the Paris opera chorus, he ordered similar garments for his *anderun* (harem) which, over the years, became markedly shorter, about twelve inches.

In 1924 the military commander Reza Khan (d. 1941) took control and listened sympathetically to Iranian intellectuals, increasingly questioning the relevance of women's veiling and of social discrimination. Theological hostility erupted with the official abolition of the veil in Afghanistan in 1928, and was fanned in December that year by Reza Shah's Uniform Dress Law, which required all Iranian men, including nomadic communities but excluding licensed theologians, to wear Western suits, shirts, ties, and brimmed hats or the peaked Pahlavi *kulah*, similar to the French Foreign Legion's *kepi*. In 1934 female university students and teachers were ordered to wear hats, and by August 1935 women had be unveiled for renewal of identity documents. The Iranian queen appeared in public unveiled in early 1936, and in February of that year the *chador*, the *ruband*, and *pichah* (in Turkish, *peche*) were officially banned.

Rural and Tribal Dress

Before the 1930s, some 55 percent of the population throughout the Middle East were ruralist, and a further 25 percent were pastoralists ("nomads"), but centralized government, land legislation, economic development, and ecological changes resulted in massive migration from the land to the cities; in Iran and Turkey less than 5 percent lead a "nomadic" life in the early 2000s. Generally speaking, nineteenth- and early-twentieth-century European and Russian studies of nonurban communities were subjective, romanticizing the societies as "unchanging" and "unpolluted," although knowledge of nonurban and ethnic dress (such as Iranian Kurdish or Bakhtiari) before photography was negligible. Since the 1970s, the anthropological approach has resulted in markedly more objectivity.

Generally, after the 1930s, legislation required men to wear Western dress except during communal celebrations, but occasionally a "national" or "community" emblem was adopted, such as the distinctive felt cap of the Qashqaci (Iran) tribal subclan, introduced in 1941, or the Palestinian *kufiyya* headdress. Most married women over the age of forty continue the dress conventions of their mothers while adopting the required outer wraps for town visits but, as Shelagh Weir concludes, styles and fashions within the community are constantly changing, albeit less overtly than in the West. The variety of garment structures and dress conventions are as numerous as the clans and ethnic groups within each region.

See also **Islamic Dress, Contemporary; Religion and Dress.**

BIBLIOGRAPHY

Ahsan, Muhammad M. *Social Life under the Abbasids, 170–289 A.H., 786–902 A.D.* London: Longman, 1979.

Almegro, Martin, et al. *Qusayr Amra.* Madrid: Instituto Hispano-Arabe de Cultura, 1975. Good photographs.

Atil, Esin. *Levni and the Surname: The Story of an Eighteenth-Century Ottoman Festival.* Istanbul: Kocbank, 1999. Excellent illustrations with detailed identification of Ottoman court officials, with good bibliography.

Baker, Patricia L. "The Fez in Turkey: A Symbol of Modernization?" *Costume* (Journal of Costume Society, London) 20 (1986): 72–84.

———. *Islamic Textiles.* London: British Museum Press, 1995. Useful survey and bibliography.

———. "Politics of Dress: The Dress Reform Laws of 1920/30s Iran." In *Languages of Dress in the Middle East.* Edited by Nancy Lindisfarne-Tapper and Bruce Ingham. London: Curzon, 1997. Based on British government Foreign Office records.

Baker, Patricia L., et al. *Silks for the Sultans: Ottoman Imperial Garments from Topkapi Palace.* Istanbul: Ertug and Kocabiyik, 1996. Superb photographs with three useful essays.

Bier, Carol, ed. *Woven from the Soul, Spun from the Heart.* Washington D.C.: The Textile Museum, 1987. Excellent textile survey.

Chardin, John. *Travels in Persia, 1673–1677.* Reprint, Toronto: Dover, 1988. Informative eyewitness report.

"Clothing: XV, XVIII, XX–XXVI." *Encyclopaedia Iranica.* Costa Mesa: Mazda Publishers, 1992. Costume survey of ethnic groups in Iran, with useful bibliographies.

Dozy, Reinhart Pieter Anne. *Dictionnaire détaillé des noms des vêtements chez les arabes.* Amsterdam: Jean Muller, 1845. Reprint, Beirut: Librairie du Liban, 1969. Needs revision but shows wealth of terminology.

Golombek, L., and Veronika Gervers. "Tiraz Fabrics in the Royal Ontario Museum." In *Studies in Textile History.* Edited by Veronika Gervers. Toronto: Royal Ontario Museum, 1977. Thorough specialist survey.

Graham-Brown, Sarah. *Images of Women.* London: Quartet, 1988. Excellent study of nineteenth- and twentieth-century photographic images across Middle East.

Haldane, Duncan. *Mamluk Painting.* Warminster, U.K.: Aris and Phillips, 1978. Best available study of Mamluk manuscript painting.

Levy, Reuben. "Notes on Costumes from Arabic Sources." *Journal of Royal Asiatic Society (of Great Britain and Ireland)* (1935): 319–338.

———, trans. *The Macalim al-Qurba fi ahkam al-hisba … ibn al-Ukhuwwa.* London: Cambridge University Press, 1938. Early fourteenth-century Egyptian *hisba* regulations.

———, trans. and ed. *The Macalim al-Qurba fi ahkam al-hisba … ibn al-Ukhuwwa.* London: Cambridge University Press, 1938.

Lindisfarne-Tapper, Nancy, and Bruce Ingham, eds. *Languages of Dress in the Middle East.* London: Curzon, 1997. Articles concerning Caucasus, Iran, Turkey, and Arabia with useful bibliographies.

Mayer, Leo. *Mamluk Costume: A Survey.* Geneva: Albert Kundig, 1952. Based on literary accounts.

Rosenthal, F., and N. J. Dawood, trans. and eds. *[Ibn Khaldun] The Muqaddimah.* London: Routledge and Kegan Paul, 1978.

Rugh, Andrea B. *Reveal and Conceal: Dress in Contemporary Egypt.* Syracuse, N.Y.: Syracuse University Press, 1986. Informative study of late-twentieth-century town, village, and tribal dress styles.

Scarce, Jennifer. *Women's Costume of the Near and Middle East.* London: Unwin Hyman, 1987. Contains some drawings of garment structure.

Serjeant, Robert Betram. *Islamic Textiles: Material for a History up to the Mongol Conquest.* Beirut: Librairie du Liban, 1972. Informative literary extracts on textiles and garments, but confusing arrangement.

Sims, Eleanor. *Peerless Images: Persian Figural Painting and Its Sources.* New Haven, Conn.: Yale University Press, 2002. Contains many color illustrations, by a leading authority.

Spring, Christopher, and Julie Hudson. *North African Textiles.* London: British Museum Press, 1995. Textile-oriented but with dress information.

Stillman, Yedida K., and Nancy Micklewright. "Costume in the Middle East." *Middle East Studies Association Bulletin* 26, no. 1 (July 1992): 13–38. Informative survey of modern scholastic approaches.

Weir, Shelagh. *Palestinian Costume.* London: British Museum Publications, 1989. Excellent study.

Patricia L. Baker

MILITARY STYLE "Uniforms are the sportswear of the twentieth century," Diana Vreeland said once. Strolling through the streets of any cities in the world, one may add that military dress will be an important part of the twentieth-first-century look as well.

Teenagers in cargo pants, men in flight jackets and hooded parkas, and women in safari jackets and sailor pants are common sights on the everyday scene. Fashion runways have featured seasonal flurries of camouflage: print chiffon evening gowns, multipocket vests in bright satin, white leather cinched trench coats, and armies of military cashmere greatcoats with gilded buttons where the initials of famous fashion designers and the logos of powerful brands have taken the place of the insignia of royal families, dictators, and military empires. In the distant aftermath of the great wars, as real soldiers begin to look more and more like civilians—consider the Hollywood icon of the American soldier in plain khaki shirt, tie, and pants— "the imitation of the military uniform has triumphed over the original prototype." This was the comment of Holly Brubach in the *New York Times* on the decision of the American Navy to eliminate the bell-bottomed sailor trousers just when the fashion designers and the club kids were eager to wear them again.

The formal and technological evolution of uniforms lies at the origin of modern dress; standard military issue consists of a system of industrially produced garments in different sizes and qualities, which change according to social and weather conditions, and communicate belonging or rejection values. We may say that military uniforms are the first ready-to-wear garments, with standardized sizes and proportions to adapt to men and women with different physiques.

In a continuous process of osmosis, military uniforms and civilian dress have influenced each other over the years. An early documented case of this is, after the French Revolution, when the leg-wear of the *sans-culottes*, in revolt against the monarchy, became the model for the practical, clinging trousers worn by Napoleon and his army. The same thing happens with the new fashions of the century: the practicality of civilian clothing is continuously incorporated into military uniforms. And the garments perfected and idealized in military iconography make a triumphant return in everyday civilian dress.

The hunting dress of English country gentlemen—the Norfolk suit—is the prototype for combat gear, the fatigue jacket with deep convenient pockets and a reversible collar. The khaki color—from the Persian word *khak*, meaning dust, earth or mud—of uniforms all over the world, was borrowed from the personal wardrobe of Indian soldiers who dyed their clothing with natural pigments to disguise dirt. Perhaps the most telling of all examples is the continuous and repeated passage of the trench coat from the military to the civil sphere. Created in England, probably by the manufacturer Burberry as a garment for shepherds, farmers, and country gentlemen for protection from rain and wind, this coat became such a common feature among soldiers in the rainy trenches during War World I that it took the name "trench coat" and became a standard garment in the uniforms of many armies around the world. The practicality of this belted raincoat in certain weather conditions justified its utilization even before it became a part of the uniform. Then, between the two world wars, the trench coat returned to everyday closets and became the uniform of adventurers, spies, and rebels without a country, perfectly worn by Humphrey Bogart in *Casablanca* (1942). After being worn again by generals and colonels during World War II, the trench coat returned as the uniforms of intellectuals, writers, and journalists all over the world. It later wound up, on and off, in fashion shows, from Yves Saint Laurent to Giorgio Armani, down to the monogrammed GG, LV, and DG—Gucci, Louis Vuitton and Dolce & Gabbana—versions of recent seasons.

Dozens of familiar, common items in our everyday wardrobe have shared a similar fate: the wool pea coat of sailors, the leather flight jacket of pilots, the fur-edged hooded parka of explorers, safari jackets and cargo pants, multipocket vests, and backpacks.

The short coat known as an Eisenhower jacket is a perfect example of the way national borders become useless against the power of fashion. This garment—Wool Field Jacket M1944—was originally a combat jacket cut short at the waist for comfort and to save on fabric. First worn by the English troops during World War II, was so admired by General Eisenhower, the head of the Allied Forces in Europe and future president of the United States, and so popular among American soldiers that it became Eisenhower's most famous outfit, the most known uniform of the U.S. Army and the most common piece of sportswear in the male wardrobe. In the modern version, the buttons have been replaced by zippers, and a designer logo has taken the place of the decorations, but the proportions remain the same: wide around the chest and narrow at the waist with broad shoulders.

Soldiers in every war have come back from the front with new experiences and terrifying tales, but also with military garments that silently became a part of everyday dress. The functional quality and the comfort tested in combat, the technology used to create new, more resistant fibers and fabrics, and the economy of resources and materials represented a legacy, which the clothing industry ably transferred from military to civilian production.

While the more theatrical characteristics of uniforms are just a memory in the technologically advanced equipment issued to modern soldier, the 1990s and 2000s have seen an increase and refinement of the political, revolutionary, or conservative use of those same details. In the uniforms from the 1930s, as in the outfits of rock stars or runways models fringed epaulettes on capes, silver buckles on shiny high boots, hussar braiding on riding jackets, coats of arms, decorations, metal eagles, and gold buttons are all defining elements. Freed from their practical function—the epaulette was created as protection against blows of the sword—these elements have assumed a symbolic and at times ideological value, but increasingly serve just a decorative purpose. These include the Armani eagle, the Versace medusa head, and the crossed C's of Chanel.

See also **Camouflage Cloth; Uniforms, Military; Unisex Clothing.**

BIBLIOGRAPHY

Brubach, Holly. "Running a Fever." *New York Times Magazine*, 13 July 1997: 45.

Edwards, T. *Men in the Mirror: Men's Fashion, Masculinity and Consumer Society.* London: Cassel, 1997.

Greco, L. *Homo Militaris: Antropologia e letteratura della vita militare.* Milan: Angeli, 1999.

Finkelstein, J. *The Fashioned Self.* Cambridge, U.K.: Polity Press, 1991.

Nathan, J. *Uniforms and Non-Uniforms: Communication through Clothing.* New York: Greenwood Press, 1986.

Stefano Tonchi

MILLINERS Milliners create hats for women; hat makers make hats for men. This is the nineteenth- and twentieth-century differentiation of the two trades, which, although related, require very different technical skills and working practices.

The term "millinery" is derived from "Millaners," merchants from the Italian city of Milan, who traveled to northern Europe trading in silks, ribbons, braids, ornaments, and general finery. First chronicled in the early sixteenth century, these traveling haberdashers were received by noble aristocratic households, passing on news of the latest fashions as well as selling their wear. News of the latest styles and variations on dress was as important to men as it was to women, and milliners often acted as much sought-after fashion advisers to nobility all over Europe. One such milliner is mentioned by William Shakespeare in the historical drama *Henry IV* part 1, written in 1597, when the gallant warrior Hotspur refers to his encounter with a "trimly dress'd lord" as:

> Fresh as a bridegroom; and his chin reap'd
> Show'd like a stubble-land at harvest-home;
> He was perfumed like a milliner;
> And 'twixt his finger and his thumb he held
> A pouncet-box.

Milliners would also have traded in fine Florentine straw hats, a trade that might have been the reason for some of them to settle down as hat makers. Creating extravagant hats as well as having a flair for fashion and finery were, and still are, the trademarks of successful milliners.

The first celebrated "Marchande de Mode," or "modiste" as they were later called in France, was Rose Bertin (1744–1813). Her name is linked with Queen Marie-Antoinette of France, the most extravagant and ill-fated fashion icon of the eighteenth century. It could be argued that Marie-Antoinette and her "Ministre de Modes," Rose Bertin established haute couture in Paris and thus made it the capital of fine fashion. Elaborate hats, demure straw bonnets, and extravagant headdresses, called "poufs" were the height of fashion in the last quarter of the eighteenth century. Rose Bertin's witty creations were perched high up on the coiffure and featured rising suns, miniature olive trees, and, most famously, a ship in full sail. Her fame was enhanced by her notoriety and attracted an array of ladies of European nobility. Her salon survived the French Revolution but sadly all her hats, just like her famous clients, have disappeared and can only be traced in copies of the *Journal des modes*, which according to the custom of the period, never mentioned or credited the designer or creator of model hats.

The fashion for straw bonnets spread to the newly independent America and with it the millinery trade. Betsy Metcalf of Providence, Rhode Island, was one of the first milliners in the United States. She is said to have invented a special way of splitting locally grown oat straw, which she bleached in sulfur fumes, plaited, and sewed

Lady's portrait of gown and elaborate straw hat, 1796. Straw bonnets were popular fashion accessories throughout the eighteenth century. © HISTORICAL PICTURE ARCHIVE/CORBIS. REPRODUCED BY PERMISSION.

in spirals, creating straw bonnets intersected with fine lace and lined with silk. Having started to make hats at the age of twelve, she set the trend for new straw weaving techniques and became the founder of American millinery. The production of straw hats became an important home industry and rivaled the expensive imports of Florentine (Leghorn) straw from Italy. A bonnet that is said to be one of Betsy Metcalf's is in the collection of Rhode Island's Literary and Historical Society.

During the nineteenth century, bonnets and hats were not only fashionable, but essential in any woman's wardrobe. Bonnets were romantic and coquettish and thus the perfect accessory for women of the era. Millinery flourished, led by a strong force of Parisian "modistes," who set the tone for high fashion and demanded to be addressed reverently as "Madame." Famous names were Madame Herbault, Madame Guerin, and Madame Victorine, who created Queen Victoria's bonnets. Society ladies expected milliners to create unique models and jealously kept their sources secret. Sadly, not many hats survived, as they were often restyled or the trimmings

Milliner Frederick Fox, March 9, 1993. This famous hatmaker, shown in his studio, was a royal milliner for Queen Elizabeth II. Based in London, Fox's career peaked during the 1970s and 1980s. © TIM GRAHAM/CORBIS. REPRODUCED BY PERMISSION.

reused. Testimony of some exquisite creations can only be found in illustrations and pictures without the mention of the relevant designer or maker. However, as millinery thrived on both sides of the Atlantic, millinery designers established their personal creed and reputation.

Caroline Reboux, at the Maison Virot, was the first legendary Parisian couture modiste, making hats for the French Empress Eugénie in 1868. She reputedly created individual designs by cutting and folding felt or fabric directly on the customer's head. Her famous salon in the rue Saint Honoré survived until the 1920s. Her pupil Madame Agnes became equally sought after for her experimental surrealistic styles. Elsa Schiaparelli, the Italian-born couture designer and friend of Salvador Dali, also created surreal hats in the 1930s. She unleashed her artistic talents by creating hats using newspapers, seashells, and birdcages with singing canaries. Her Shoe Hat designs of 1937, famously worn by Daisy Fellowes, editor of *Harper's Bazaar*, made headlines on both sides of the Atlantic.

Gabrielle (Coco) Chanel was a milliner before she started her couture career. She established her first salon in the elegant apartment of her lover in Paris in 1910. An avant-garde fashion trend leader of her time, she created simple shapes and decorated sparingly to compliment her vision of modern dress. She is credited with the creation of the cloche hat, which, pulled down low over the new short hairstyles, was to become an all-time classic.

Other famous Parisian modistes of the 1930s and 1940s included Maria Guy, Rose Valois, Suzanne Talbot, Rose Descart, Louise Bourbon, and Jeanne Lanvin, who like Chanel expanded her millinery salon into haute couture. Most couture houses, like Dior, Jean Patou, or Nina Ricci, had their own millinery ateliers, all headed by a "Premiere" (Designer), a "Seconde" (Head of Workroom), with several workrooms full of "Petites Mains" (workers). Millinery hierarchy had strict rules of etiquette, with La Premiere and La Seconde always addressed as "Madame" and the inferior workers given diminutive names like Mimi, Gigi, and Flo-Flo. Milliners working in couture houses considered themselves superior to their dressmaking colleagues. The girls had a reputation for being pretty and coquettish, were always meticulously groomed, and spent more money on lipsticks and powder than on food and rent. The industry had economic importance, with top ateliers employing up to 300 milliners each.

Parisian milliners not only created hats for a selective private clientele, they also supplied a thriving wholesale export business to many stores in the United States. Lilly Daché, a Viennese-born, Parisian-trained milliner, settled in New York and led the way for talented American designers. Having opened her first tiny studio in 1926, Lilly Daché built a millinery emporium, taking over a whole building of seven floors, with a silver room for her blonde clients and a gold one for brunettes. Her devotees included the Hollywood stars Carmen Miranda, Betty Grable, and Marlene Dietrich, who all loved her chic toques, demure snoods, and stylish "profile hats," which were her trademark.

Sally Victor and Mr. John of New York later took over the reign of Lilly Daché and maintained the importance of American millinery design. Mr. John had been in partnership with Frederic Hirst since 1928 and established his own business in 1948. His famous clients included Marilyn Monroe, Lauren Bacall, and Mrs. Simpson, the future Duchess of Windsor. Toward the end of his career Mr. John of N.Y. collaborated with Cecil Beaton on the extravagant costumes for Audrey Hepburn in *My Fair Lady*.

In Europe, the most notable milliner of the interwar years was Adele List in Vienna, whose hats were an expression of aesthetics and art. She was a highly disciplined, austere-looking figure and created hats with masterly craftsmanship. Using felt, straws, silks, and feathers, she combined shape, proportion, and texture in a unique harmonious way, which never looked dated. Some of her intricate pieces took over fifty hours to make and had detachable necklaces built into the shapes. One devoted client collected and preserved 248 model hats created by Adele List, all preserved in individual hatboxes. After her death, the collection was donated to the Museum of Applied Art in Vienna, Austria, in 1983.

Aage Thaarup was a Danish milliner established in London and the first in a line of male milliners who were to dominate the second half of the twentieth century. He was self-taught and broke the established French rules of apprenticeship and gradual mastery of millinery. Having charmed the core of his high-society clientele on a voyage to India, his reputation spread quickly, and drew in ladies of the British Royal family, including the duchess of York and her daughters, Elizabeth and Margaret. When the duchess became queen of England in 1936, Aage Thaarup was officially "appointed by Her Royal Highness" and later created hats for the young Queen Elizabeth as well as for the Queen Mother.

Paris still dominated the millinery scene until the 1960s, when London took the lead with Otto Lucas, who established a most successful model wholesale business in Bond Street. His designers and ideas still came from Paris, but his flair for style created a chic, modern look much praised by millinery buyers on both sides of the Atlantic. Madame Paulette, his favorite designer, was the last of the

Headdress by Philip Treacy, 2001. Emblematic of Treacy's flamboyant style, this headdress-style hat formed part of his 2001 couture collection, shown in Paris on July 10, 2001. AP/WIDE WORLD PHOTOS. REPRODUCED BY PERMISSION.

grandes modistes of the Parisian school. With Claude Saint-Cyr, Jean Barthet, and Jean-Charles Brosseau, she was part of an era sadly in decline during the 1970s. At the height of her career Paulette had reigned over a much admired hat salon, with workrooms of 125 milliners and 8 *vendeuses mondaines*, society ladies with personal relations to important clients. Paulette created twice-yearly collections of 120 hats, presented to powerful foreign buyers as well as to her distinguished high-society clientele. Paulette's trademark was *le chapeau mou*, her draped soft turban, a sophisticated headwear for "bad hair days," popular during the 1940s and 1950s. Few of her clients knew that Algerian soldiers had inspired Paulette's original turban design during the liberation parade on the Champs Elysées in 1944.

Youth culture and the social liberation during the 1960s and 1970s brought a demise in the fashion for hats and with it a steep decline in business for milliners. The 1980s heralded a brief revival, which was partly due to Princess Diana, a fashion leader and icon of the British hat industry. London held on to its lead in millinery design, supported by royal patronage and social summer events like horse racing at Royal Ascot and Garden Parties at Buckingham Palace. John Boyd, Graham Smith, and the royal milliners Frederick Fox and Philip Somerville, a quartet of hat designers during the 1970s and 1980s, managed very successful model millinery as

Crimson hat and suit by Philip Treacy, 2000. Created for the annual London Fashion Week and modeled on September 23, 2000, this crimson hat and matching suit reveal Treacy's skill of creating art from fashion. © AP/WIDE WORLD PHOTOS. REPRODUCED BY PERMISSION.

well as wholesale businesses in London. Small factories in Luton, Bedfordshire, U.K. supported manufacture, which, historically had been the center for straw hat production in the nineteenth century. Some factories, millinery supply businesses, and block makers are left in the early 2000s, but a museum has a rich collection documenting the importance of the hat trade in the past.

During the 1980s, a new generation of millinery designers graduated from London's Fashion and Art Colleges, creating hats as pieces of art. David Shilling was the first, gaining notoriety and much press coverage with striking Ascot creations he designed and made for his mother. Mrs. Gertrude Shilling's entrance, wearing yet another extraordinary hat, was much anticipated and celebrated every year at Royal Ascot.

Patricia Underwood was a star milliner in New York during the 1980s and 1990s, with her unmistakable style of pure shape and simplicity. New York also had Eric Javits, a very successful millinery designer, who built a multimillion-dollar business and was voted Hat Designer of the Year by the Millinery Institute of America. Millinery has also declined in the United States, but the Headwear Information Bureau (HIB) founded in New York in 1989, promotes millinery with public relations and competitions for young designers.

Stephen Jones, a New Romantic of the 1980s, included men among his devoted clients, and created hats for the pop stars Boy George and Steve Strange, as well as for the Spandau Ballet. His hat salon in London's Covent Garden district was designed to be full of fun, wit, and unexpected details. Stephen Jones is a rebel with a romantic streak and designs an eclectic mix of very wearable fabric hats, which reflect his original training as a tailor. Apart from creating diffusion ranges under the label "Miss Jones" and "Jonesboy," Stephen Jones works with many of the new top designers, such as Jean-Paul Gaultier, Claude Montana, and John Galliano, creating headpieces for cutting-edge catwalk shows.

Philip Treacy, an internationally awarded accessory designer, graduated from London's Royal College of Art in 1990 and immediately hit the headlines with his flamboyant and unmistakable hat creations, lifting millinery to an even higher level of art and design. The meteoric rise of the Irish-born young designer was also much celebrated at Parisian catwalk shows, staged by top couture houses like Dior, Chanel, and Givenchy. Philip Treacy even created his own millinery show in 1993, when supermodels paraded wearing show-stopping creations, acclaimed by the fashion press. One of his famous, much-photographed pieces was a hat with a black sailing ship, which might have been inspired by Rose Bertin's design in the late eighteenth century. A true and devoted lover of his craft, Philip Treacy personally makes many of his masterpieces. His label has become a status symbol and some of his celebrated hats are collector's pieces, treasured by museums, like the Victoria and Albert Museum in London.

During the twentieth century, women's lives changed drastically and imposed a fast-living lifestyle not compatible with the ethos of beautiful hat creations. The twenty-first century has become a bare-headed era and glamorous hats have become "special occasion wear," only worn for weddings and high-society horse races. However, it is conceivable that the next generation of young designers might reinvent millinery with a new concept and purpose.

See also **Chanel, Gabrielle (Coco); Hats, Men's; Hats, Women's; Lanvin, Jeanne; Schiaparelli, Elsa; Treacy, Philip.**

BIBLIOGRAPHY
Buxbaum, Gerda. *Die Hüte der Adele List.* New York: Prestel Munchen, 1995.

Ginsburg, Madeleine. *The Hat, Trends and Traditions.* London: Studio Editions, Ltd., 1990.

Hopkins, Susie. *The Century of Hats.* London: Aurum Press, 1999.

McDowell, Colin. *Hats, Status, Style and Glamour.* London: Thames and Hudson, Inc., 1992.

Muller, Florence, and Lydia Kamitsis. *Les chapeaux, une histoire de tête.* Paris: Syros Alternatives, 1993.

Susie Hopkins

MINISKIRT The debut of the miniskirt in the early 1960s can be compared to the birth of rock'n'roll music. When rock'n'roll took hold in the 1950s, parents and clergy were up in arms, railing against it. They were hopeful that it was a fad that would play itself out and fade away. Neither the miniskirt nor rock'n'roll has faded away. They have both endured and continue to serve as chief symbols of youthful rebellion.

Fashion history is characterized by the shifting focus on one female "erogenous zone" of the body to another. The fashionable Victorian silhouette focused attention on the waist, bosom, and hips through the use of corsetry. By the beginning of the twentieth century, the "mono-bosom" was prominent. During the 1920s, the flapper-style dress, which was based on a loose tunic or tubular shift, dared to reveal more of the female leg than ever before in modern Western history. However, fashion reverted to longer hemlines by the 1930s. Just as Art Deco set the stage for modern art, so did the fashions of the Jazz Age pave the way for the miniskirt.

While the decade of the 1950s embraced prescribed rules of dressing for special occasions and time of day, there was a new freedom in the area of casual clothing. The ideal fashionable woman was a statuesque adult, and young women were expected to imitate adult styles when it came to dressing. Teenagers tended to wear grown-up versions of clothing, except for casual wear. But rumblings of change were in the air.

Mary Quant
American teenagers of the 1950s and 1960s, later dubbed baby boomers, were taking note of each other on television dance party shows spawned by Dick Clark's "American Bandstand" in Philadelphia, especially after it went nationwide in 1957. Great Britain, which lagged behind the United States in recovering from World War II, was also giving birth to its own baby boomers. Among them was the intrepid Mary Quant, whose name is forever linked with the creation of the miniskirt.

Quant was part of the restless youth culture in the Chelsea section of London. Along with her friends Alexander Plunkett Green (who later became her husband) and Archie McNair, Quant felt that clothing for her age group did not really exist, so they opened their own shop called *Bazaar* in 1955. Quant infused her de-

signs with a fresh, youthful energy, and even appeared at Buckingham Palace in a miniskirt to receive the Order of the British Empire in 1966. Along with the Beatles, Quant reinvigorated British culture, helping to launch the phenomenon known as "swinging London." Quant once noted, "London led the way to changing the focus of fashion from the Establishment to the young. As a country we were aware of the great potential of these clothes long before the Americans and the French."

Short skirts were incompatible with garters and stockings, making tights a vital new option. Already in the early 1940s, American designer Claire McCardell had presented her tunic-jumpers with dance leotards. However, the relatively high cost of producing tights kept them a novelty until the 1960s, when colored tights diffused some of the overt sex appeal of the miniskirt. Soon panty hose had largely replaced stockings and garter belts.

André Courrèges
By 1960, more than half of the world's population was under the age of 25, but it took some time before the Paris haute couture recognized the emergence of youth style. By the early sixties, however, even couture-trained designers, such as Pierre Cardin and André Courrèges, began designing youthful styles.

When Courrèges presented his autumn 1964 collection, it affected fashion as dramatically as Christian Dior's "New Look" had done in 1947. Courrèges' 1964 collection included stark, modern designs that were futuristic and electrifying. In addition to carefully sculpted tunics and trousers made out of heavy wool crepe, Courrèges created his version of the miniskirt. He paired his shorter skirts with white or colored leather, calf-high boots that added a confident flair to the ensemble. This look became one of the most important fashion developments of the decade and was widely copied. Scores of other designers embraced the miniskirt concept and strove to adapt the look for clients of various ages.

While the miniskirt did not always complement each and every figure, almost every Western woman eventually tried some version of the style during the 1960s. Young women were the first to embrace it, despite resistance from parents and school administrators. The miniskirt became a symbol of the sexual revolution, as the contemporaneous invention of the birth control pill liberated women from the specter of unplanned pregnancies.

Whereas during the early twentieth century short hemlines were associated with prostitutes and theatrical performers, by the 1960s short hemlines were also adopted by "respectable" women. The miniskirt was synonymous with Mod style. By 1969 the miniskirt evolved into the "micro-mini." As Mods gave way to hippies, however, subcultural styles increasingly emphasized long, romantic skirts. By 1970, the fashion industry had launched "midi" and "maxi" skirts, which dominated the following decade.

In the early 1980s, the miniskirt made a comeback, linked again with the power of music and the rise of MTV. Music videos promoted highly charged, sensual images of female performers wearing skimpy clothing. Rap and hip-hop performers have promoted their music by using mini-clad women in their videos. The miniskirt, first unleashed by Mary Quant and André Courrèges, has come and gone every few seasons on the fashion runways, but it has become a mainstay of popular culture.

See also **Courrèges, André; Quant, Mary; Youthquake Fashions.**

BIBLIOGRAPHY

Bond, David. *The Guinness Superlatives Guide: 20th Century Fashion.* Middlesex: Guiness Superlatives Limited, 1981.

Buxbaum, Gerda, ed. *Icons of Fashion: The 20th Century.* Munich, London and New York: Prestel, 1999.

Ewing, Elizabeth. *History of 20th Century Fashion.* 3rd ed. Lanham: Barnes and Noble Books, 1992.

Glynn, Prudence. *Skin to Skin: Eroticism in Dress.* New York: Oxford University Press, 1982.

Lehnert, Gertrud. *A History of Fashion in the 20th Century.* Cologne: Köneman, 2000.

Lobenthal, Joe. *Radical Rags: Fashions of the Sixties.* New York: Abbeville Press Publishers, 1990.

Myra Walker

MISSONI Since it was established in 1953, the Missoni company has been associated with expertly produced, lightweight, delicate knit separates. The company quickly established its image by combining innovative and fractured stripes, plaids, patchworks, ethnic effects, mosaics, zigzags, and flame stitch patterns in vivid and striking color combinations.

Young Ottavio (Tai) Missoni, a former athletic sprinter, and Rosita Jelmini, a language student, first conceived the company in 1953. Tai's workshop initially produced track suits. Through Rosita's family of manufacturers, knitting machines became available at a time when patterns were knitted only in horizontal and vertical stitches. The pair had the machines reconfigured for more modern alternatives. After the couple married, Rosita chose to become the firm's business manager. With his extraordinary eye for color, Tai focused his efforts on arranging color palettes.

Beginning with their first runway presentation in 1967, at the Pitti Palace, in Florence, the Missonis attracted attention. Fashion writers and arbiters of style such as Diana Vreeland and Bernardine Morris were the first to publicize the Missoni style. By the 1970s the rust-brown Missoni cloth label was recognized worldwide as a status symbol. Along with their artisanal approach and spirited color combinations, the Missonis developed their expertise in striping, scalloping, waves, prints, and jacquard dots. They used as many as twenty different materials, combining wool, cotton, linen, rayon, and silk in forty color selections.

In the mid-1990s Angela Missoni initiated a reinterpretation of the company's image, making her mark on her parents' label. Her intent was to update the Missoni line by creating redefined and edited collections of bright and sporty garments. Since 1998 Angela has held the position of design director, responsible for developing advertising campaigns with Mario Testino, the noted fashion photographer, in addition to retail sales and the interior design of retail stores. Her revised approach to marketing the brand emphasizes promoting the image of a more youthful, urban clientele. Her daughter, Margherita, serves as her assistant. Her brothers also are active in the family company: Vittorio is responsible for marketing and sales, and Luca directs research in fabric developments and computer technology. In 2003 he was made responsible for the development of the men's wear collection.

In the early 2000s the company employed about 250 craftspeople and technicians, designers, and administration staff at its Sumirago, Italy, enclave outside Milan. Displays of experimental knitting methods and scraps of fabric and yarn lie in a profusion of color on the factory floor. New materials and ideas are posted on the studio walls. The Missonis describe themselves as a working team of artisans and nurture that image.

The Missoni firm is identified with their collaging of unusual color combinations, patterns, and weights of sumptuous yarns. Layered knit patterns emerge from modern, computerized jacquard looms. Early in the twenty-first century the firm was producing about 150 new textiles and designs every year. The Missoni name can also be found on original collections of home furnishings, accessories, swimwear, cosmetics, and perfume.

The company owns more than twenty licensing agreements for men's wear, women's wear, accessories, children's apparel, linens, and furnishings, but the owners have been cautious about extending licensing agreements too far. The firm has ventured into fabrics for automobile interiors and also into theatrical costuming. Angela Missoni, her brothers, and their children seem eminently poised to proceed with the family love of color and their commitment to the continued success of the Missoni label.

See also **Color in Dress; Knitting Machinery.**

BIBLIOGRAPHY

Arte, Leonard, and Samuele Mazza. *Missoni (Made in Italy).* Corte Madera, Calif.: Ginko Press, 1997.

Missoni, Ottavio, et al. *Ottavio e Rosita Missoni Story.* Milan, Italy: Skira, 1995. An exhibition catalog.

Vercelloni, Isa Tutino, ed. *Missonologia: The World of Missoni.* New York: Abbeville, 1995. An exhibition catalog

Gillion Carrara

MIYAKE, ISSEY Issey Miyake was born in Hiroshima, in the southern part of Japan, in 1938. In 1965 he graduated from Tama Art University in Tokyo, where he majored in graphic design. Following graduation, he went to Paris just three months after Kenzo Takada, the first Japanese designer to became successful in France, arrived there. Miyake and Kenzo had known each other in Tokyo, and they studied together at a tailoring and dressmaking school, l'Ecole de la chambre syndicale de la couture. In 1966 Miyake worked as an apprentice under the French couturier Guy Laroche, and two years later he apprenticed at Givenchy.

He then went to New York to work with the American designer Geoffrey Beene before returning to Tokyo, where he founded the Miyake Design Studio in 1970. One of Miyake's New York friends took some of his design samples to *Vogue* magazine and a major department store, Bloomingdale's. Both *Vogue* and Bloomingdale's were enthusiastic about his work, and Bloomingdale's was so impressed that Miyake got a small section in the store. His first small collection in New York included T-shirts dyed with Japanese tattoo designs and *sashiko*-embroidered coats (*Sashiko* is a Japanese sewing technique that gives strength to the fabrics used in clothing designed for workers). In 1973, when French ready-to-wear was institutionalized for the first time as prêt-à-porter, Miyake was invited to Paris to join a group show with such other young designers as Sonia Rykiel and Thierry Mugler. He opened a boutique there two years later and continued to show his collection in Paris. Miyake later became an official member of the French prêt-à-porter organization.

Founded Japanese Avant-Garde
Miyake laid the foundation in Paris for avant-garde designers worldwide, the Japanese ones in particular. He was showing in Paris long before other Japanese designers, and his presence was further pronounced by the emergence of two influential, norm-breaking designers.

Issey Miyake fashion show. Models for avante-garde designer Issey Miyake show off his Japanese-inspired fashions. Bold fabric patterns and unusual shapes and lines typify Issey's quest to fuse his Japanese heritage with modern, Western clothing styles. AP/WIDE WORLD PHOTOS. REPRODUCED BY PERMISSION.

Rei Kawakubo, working under the label Comme des Garçons, and Yohji Yamamoto began to present their collections in Paris in 1981 along with the already-established Miyake, who is considered the founding father of the new fashion trend. These three effectively started a new school of Japanese avant-garde fashion, although it was never their intention to classify themselves as such. Kawakubo said in an interview with Olivier Séguret in *Madame Air France*, "We certainly have no desire to create a fashion threesome, but each of us has a strong urge to design new, individual clothes which are recognizably ours" (pp. 140–141). Similarly, Miyake is quoted in Dana Wood's article in *Women's Wear Daily* as follows: "In the Eighties, Japanese fashion designers brought a new type of creativity; they brought something Europe didn't have. There was a bit of a shock effect, but it probably helped the Europeans wake up to a new value" (p. 32).

Miyake was the first to redefine sartorial conventions. His clothing patterns were very different from the Western styles in that he restructured the conventional construction of a garment. As the *Time* magazine writer Jay Cocks observed:

"Issey," asks one of his friends, standing in the middle of a bustling hotel lobby, "how do I work this?" . . . "I made it like this," says the designer . . . He unbuttons a half-cape that spans the sleeves, and puts the loose ends around his friend's neck. (p. 46)

A student who worked as a dresser backstage at one of Miyake's show in the late 1980s recalled the intricate construction of his garment:

There was a garment that was totally out of shape and had four holes. You could hardly tell which holes are supposed to be for the arms to go in or the neck to go in. During the rehearsal, Issey's patternmakers would be going around the dressers making sure we knew which hole was for which part of the body. Models usually come running back from the stage to get changed to the next outfit, and it is our job to help them get dressed as quickly as possible with the right shoes, the right accessories and so on. It's a mad house at the back during the show. At that point, you have no time to think which hole goes where! Some dressers couldn't match the neck to the right hole. It was totally wrong. But who can tell?

In other words, it is up to the wearer to be creative and decide how to wear it. Miyake claims that simplicity is often the key to wearing his clothes, which are versatile enough to be worn in a variety of ways.

Western female clothes have historically been fitted to expose the contours of the body, but Miyake introduced large, loose-fitting garments, such as jackets with no traditional construction and a minimum of detail or buttons. His dresses often have a straight, simple shape, and his large coats with sweepingly oversized proportions can be worn by both men and women. He challenged not only the conventions of garment construction, but also the normative concept of fashion. All of this came at a time when women's clothes by most traditional Western designers were moving in the opposite direction, toward a tighter fit and greater formality. The avant-garde Japanese view of fashion was opposed to the conventional Western fashion. It was not Miyake's intention to reproduce Western fashion, as he pointed out in his speech at the Japan Society in San Francisco in 1984:

I realized that my very disadvantage, lack of western heritage, would also be my advantage. I was free of Western tradition or convention . . . The lack of western tradition was the very thing I needed to create contemporary and universal fashion.

Sculptor of Fabric

Miyake is best known for his original fabrics. He collaborates with his textile director, Makiko Minagawa, who interprets his abstract ideas. With Minagawa and the Japanese textile mills, he introduced his most commercially successful collection, Pleats Please, in 1993. Traditionally, pleats are permanently pressed before a garment is cut, but he did it the other way round. He cut and assembled a garment two-and-a-half to three times its proper size. Then he folded, ironed, and oversewed the material so that the straight lines remained in place. Finally the garment was placed in a press between two sheets of paper, from which it emerged with permanent pleats (Sato 1998, p. 23).

As early as 1976 Miyake began his concept of A-Piece-of-Cloth (A-POC), or clothes made out of a single piece of cloth that entirely cover the body. He introduced the line, which evolved from his earlier concept, in 1999.

Issey Miyake and Dai Fujiwara exhibit in Berlin, 2001. Japanese designers Issey Miyake and Dai Fujiwara show their A-Piece-of-Cloth (A-POC) designs at the Vitra Design Museum in Berlin, Germany. Each garment item is fashioned from one single piece of fabric. © SEIMONEIT RONALD/CORBIS SYGMA. REPRODUCED BY PERMISSION.

The A-POC clothes consist of a long tube of jersey from which individuals can cut without wasting any material. A large variety of different clothes can be made in this manner; the tubes are manufactured with an old knitting machine controlled by a computer and can be made in large quantities. His objective was to minimize waste by using all leftover material. These garments allow the buyer to size and cut out a small hat, gloves, socks, a skirt, or a dress. Depending on the way the dress is cut, it may appear in two or three pieces. In addition to Miyake's A-POC project, new techniques of sewing garments, such as heat taping and cutting by ultrasound, were also featured in his Making Things exhibition at the Fondation Cartier pour l'art contemporain in Paris in 1999.

Place in History

No history of fashion is complete without the mention of Issey Miyake, as he has made a major contribution to the world of fashion. Miyake retired from the Paris fashion scene in 1999, when Kenzo also decided to withdraw from his own brand. The Issey Miyake brand was taken over by Naoki Takizawa, who had been designing Miyake's Plantation Line since 1983 and Issey Miyake Men since 1993. Many of Miyake's former assistants, such as Yoshiki Hishinuma and Zucca (Akira Onozuka), now participate in the Paris Collection.

Every convention carries with it an aesthetic, according to which—what is conventional becomes the standard by which artistic beauty and effectiveness is judged. The conception of fashion is synonymous with the conception of beauty. Therefore, an attack on a convention becomes an attack on the aesthetic related to it. By breaking the Western convention of fashion, Miyake suggested the new style and new definition of aesthetics. It could have been taken as an offense not only against the Western aesthetic, but also against the existing arrangement of ranked statuses, a stratification system in fashion, or the hegemony of the French system.

Miyake's cutting-edge concept that there is beauty in the unfinished and the neglected has had a major influence on today's fashion. Miyake says, "I do not create a fashionable aesthetic . . . I create a style based on life" (Mendes and de la Haye 1999, p. 233). He is opposed to the words "haute couture," "mode," and "fashion," because they imply a quest for novelty; he stretched the boundaries of fashion, reshaped the symmetry of clothes, let wrapped garments respond to the body's shape and movement, and destroyed all previous definition of clothing and fashion. His concepts were undoubtedly original, especially when compared to the rules of fashion set by orthodox, legitimate Western designers such as Coco Chanel, Christian Dior, and Yves Saint Laurent. It was Miyake who set the stage for the Japanese look in the fashion establishment.

See also **Japanese Fashion; Trendsetters.**

BIBLIOGRAPHY

Cocks, Jay. "A Change of Clothes: Designer Issey Miyake Shapes New Forms into Fashion for Tomorrow." *Time*, January 27, 1986, 46–52.

Holborn, Mark. *Issey Miyake*. Cologne, Germany: Taschen, 1995.

Koike, Kazuko, ed. *Issey Miyake, East Meets West*. Tokyo, Japan: 1978.

Mendes, Valerie, and Amy de la Haye. *20th Century Fashion*. London, New York: Thames and Hudson, Inc., 1999.

Miyake, Issey. Speech delivered at Japan Today Conference in San Francisco, September, 1984.

———. *Issey Miyake and Miyake Design Studio: 1970–1985*. Tokyo, Japan: Oubunnsha, 1985.

Sato, Kazuko. "Clothes Beyond the Reach of Time." *Issey Miyake: Making Things*. Paris: Fondation Cartier pour l'art contemporain 1998, 18–62. An exhibition catalog.

Séguret, Olivier. "Les Japonais." *Madame Air France* no. 5 (1988): 140–141.

Tsurumoto, Shogo, ed. *Issey Miyake Bodyworks*. Tokyo, Japan: Shogakkan, 1983.

Wood, Dana. "Miyake's Lust for Life." *Women's Wear Daily*, December 18, 1996, p. 32.

Yuniya Kawamura

MODACRYLIC. *See* **Acrylic and Modacrylic Fibers.**

MODERN PRIMITIVES The Modern Primitive subculture exists primarily in North America and Europe. Members are known for their use of body modifications, such as blackwork tattoos (i.e., heavy black ink applied and reapplied until the color of the skin is completely obscured), three-dimensional implants, scarification, and brands. Utilizing both modern and ancient technology, members often participate in culturally authenticated rituals to achieve the desired body modifications. The subculture's basic ideology is to return to a simpler way of life, which they believe they can achieve through their body modifications.

Modern Primitive History

Modern Primitive subculture members were first evident in the latter half of the 1960s. A self-proclaimed Modern Primitive and body artist, Fakir Musafar, originally named this subculture "Modern Primitive" because "modern" represents this subculture's connection to and place in the contemporary (urban) world, and "primitive" represents the primary or initial (non-Western) cultural groups.

Fakir Musafar is one of the most recognized and publicized members of the Modern Primitive subculture. Naming himself after a nineteenth-century Sufi who wandered through India for nearly two decades with heavy metal objects hanging from his torso's flesh as a spiritual sacrifice, Musafar has numerous body modifications, such as septum, ear, and chest piercings, and blackwork tattoos. Articles in *National Geographic* and other such ethnographies about non-Western cultures, as well as personal visions, inspired many of his body modifications.

Body Modification Technology

Modern Primitive subculture members have distinct appearances because of their extreme body modifications, achieved by a variety of both modern and ancient methods. Not only do members research the design, but some also research the techniques and tools to be used for their body modification. Steve Haworth invented instruments and techniques to insert transdermally or subdermally three-dimensional Teflon and surgical steel implants (for example capture jewelry).

Body Modification Rituals

Some Modern Primitives acquire body modifications by participating in rituals, often inspired by non-Western cultures. For example, Musafar has acquired some of his most notable body modifications from participating in rituals, such as the Kavandi-bearing ceremony, where spears of Siva are placed through the skin to achieve spiritual transcendence; the Hindu Ball Dance, a ritual in which a Sadhu (i.e., an Indian holy man) is pierced by weight-bearing hooks as proof of religious fervor; and the Sun Dance, a Native American ceremony in which a participant is bodily hung from chest piercings as a token of personal sacrifice and endurance. Often the chosen rituals are modified to utilize a chosen technology, to incorporate the participant's spirituality and ideology, and to create the desired body modification. The result is a unique Modern Primitive body modification ritual.

Ideology

Modern Primitives acquire body modifications as rites of passage, spiritual transcendence, and autonomy. Members of this subculture wear their body modifications as evidence of their experiences, often in an attempt to mimic non-Western cultures. Some subculture members claim that participation in these rituals allows spiritual transcendence via enduring the associated pain. Modern Primitives believe that pain is the key to connecting the real truth and the self in the modern world. Body modifications are the link between the contemporary world and the desired "tribal," "pagan," or "primitive."

See also **Branding; Goths; Punk; Scarification; Street Style; Tattoos.**

BIBLIOGRAPHY

Mercury, M. *Pagan Fleshworks: The Alchemy of Body Modification.* Rochester, Vt: Park Street Press, 2000.

Musafar, Fakir. "Body Play: State of Grace of Sickness?" In *Bodies Under Siege: Self-Mutilation and Body Modification in Culture and Psychiatry.* Edited by A. R. Favazza, M.D. Maryland: Johns Hopkins University Press, 1996.

Vale, V. and Juno, A. *Re/Search: Modern Primitives.* Hong Kong: Re/Search Publishers, 1989.

Winge, T. M. "Constructing 'Neo-Tribal' Identities through Dress: Modern Primitives Body Modifications." In *The Post-Subcultures Reader.* Edited by D. Muggleton and R. Wienzeirl. Oxford: Berg, 2003.

Theresa M. Winge

MOHAIR The Angora goat produces a long, lustrous white fiber called "mohair." The goat originated in the Angora province of Turkey, where it has been raised for thousands of years. The word mohair stems from the Arabic word for goat's-hair fabric, *mukhayyar.* In medieval times the fabric was called *mockaire.*

Mohair varies in length depending on the number of times per year that the goats are sheared. Mohair measuring 4 to 6 inches is sheared twice per year, and 8-to-12-inch mohair fiber is sheared once per year. It grows in uniform locks, but is relatively coarse compared with sheep's wool, making it less comfortable when worn next to the skin. Unlike wool it has no crimp or waviness in the fiber length. When mohair is obtained from Angora goats less than one year old, it is called "kid mohair" and is softer and finer than fiber from adult Angora goats.

Mohair fibers have a circular cross-section, which makes them lustrous to the eye. Mohair is much smoother than wool because of its faint scale structure, making mohair more resistant to dirt than sheep's wool. The fine scales do not allow mohair to be felted. The fiber has microscopic air ducts running through the cells, giving mohair a light, airy quality. Mohair fiber is very strong and has a superior affinity for dyes.

Mohair is used in knitted sweaters, upholstery pile fabrics, summer apparel, linings, coats, and imitation furs. It is a durable, long-lasting fiber. In the twenty-first century, Turkey, Texas, and South Africa provide the majority of mohair fiber for the world market.

See also **Angora; Dyeing; Fibers.**

BIBLIOGRAPHY

Hunter, L. *Mohair: A Review of Its Properties, Processing and Applications.* West Yorkshire, England: International Mohair Association, 1993.

Ann W. Braaten

MOORE, DORIS LANGLEY Doris Langley Moore was one of the foremost scholars and collectors of historic dress in the twentieth century, a cofounder of the Costume Society, and the founder of the Museum of Costume, Bath. Born in Liverpool, England in 1902, Doris Elizabeth Langley Levy spent her youth in Johannesburg, South Africa, where her father worked as a newspaper editor. She returned to England in the early 1920s and published her first book in 1926, the same year in which she married Robin Sugden Moore.

In addition to her significant work in the field of historic clothing, Moore had a long and varied career. She was a successful designer for stage and film; a television commentator; a well-known author of fiction and nonfiction, including biography; and a Byron scholar (in 1962 at Bowood House, Wiltshire, she discovered the Albanian ensemble worn by the romantic writer in a portrait of 1814 by Thomas Phillips). Moore's many achievements were recognized during her lifetime. She was made a Member of the Order of the British Empire in 1971; a Fellow of the Royal Society of Literature in 1973; and she was awarded the Rose Mary Crawshay Prize by the British Academy in 1975. Moore died in London in 1989.

Moore's enduring contributions to the field of costume history include her outstanding collection of men's, women's, and children's dress and accessories, primarily English and Continental, dating from the sixteenth through the mid-twentieth century, and amassed over four decades beginning around 1930; her numerous books, articles, and related publications both on her collection and on the wider subject of dress; and her establishment of the Museum of Costume in 1963, and of the Costume and Fashion Research Centre (a part of the museum) in 1974. At the time of its opening, the Museum had the largest collection of fashionable historic dress on view in Britain. Both the museum and the Research Centre remain important educational and study facilities for scholars, students, and the general public.

Moore's impressive and rigorous connoisseurship encompassed all aspects of dress history, including surviving garments, visual and literary source material, display, and fashion theory. The Woman in Fashion (1949) and The Child in Fashion (1953), in particular, attest to her detailed knowledge of the silhouette and its evolution, acquired by years of close observation of objects in her own and other collections. Beyond clothing itself, Moore's expertise included the mechanics of the fashion industry and representations of costume in portraits, prints, and fashion plates. In Fashion through Fashion Plates (1971), Moore examined both the history of the fashion press and the nature of the plate as an idealized image.

Although she would later change her mind about the appropriateness of using live models for historic dress (as she did in The Woman in Fashion and The Child in Fashion), Moore felt strongly about presenting the totality of a given period silhouette, without which she felt the main garment would be meaningless and misunderstood. Her displays at the museum in Bath featured realistic, fully accessorized mannequins, complete with real or simulated hair, set in lively vignettes.

Moore was a pioneer in the study of costume history and instrumental in bringing appreciation of the subject to a popular audience. The perceptive, inquiring, and far-ranging approach of her scholarship laid the foundation for future dress historians. Moore's publications are still considered important sources of information, and her exemplary costume collection constitutes one of the most important in public institutions worldwide.

See also **Fashion, Historical Studies of; Fashion Museums and Collections.**

BIBLIOGRAPHY

Byrde, Penelope. "Doris Langley Moore, 1902–1989." *Costume* 24 (1990): 149–151.

Moore, Doris Langley. *The Woman in Fashion*. London: B. T. Batsford, 1949.

———. *The Child in Fashion*. London: B. T. Batsford, 1953.

———. *The Museum of Costume Assembly Rooms, Bath: Guide to the Exhibition and a Commentary on the Trends of Fashion*. Bath: Museum of Costume, [1969?].

———. *Fashion through Fashion Plates, 1771–1970*. London: Ward Lock, 1971.

Taylor, Lou. *The Study of Dress History*. Manchester: Manchester University Press, 2002.

Michele Majer

MORI, HANAE Hanae Mori was born Hanae Fujii in Shimane, a prefecture in the southern part of Japan, in 1926. Immediately after graduating from the Tokyo Women's Christian University in 1947, she married Ken Mori, a textile executive. She was bored by fulfilling the role that was expected of most women in Japan at the time, which was being a wife and a mother to her two sons, Akira and Kei. Consequently, she enrolled in a dressmaking school to acquire the skills that led her to establish her first shop in 1951 in the center of Tokyo. A movie theater that showed the latest films from the West was located directly across the street from her shop. Movie director Sotojiro Kuromoto noticed the window display of her store one day, walked in, and asked Mori to design costumes for his films. As a result of this chance occurrence, her career was launched, and she became Japan's first internationally known designer.

After the defeat in World War II, Mori wanted to introduce to the world the positive and beautiful aspects of the country and used fashion as the means to give Japan a new image. Mori's fashions are especially noteworthy for their use of vibrant color and lustrous textiles. She designed costumes for the opera *Madame Butterfly* at La Scala, in Milan in 1985; the ballet *Cynderella* for the Paris Opera in 1986; and the opera *Electra* at the Salzburg Music Festival 1996, among many others. She also designs costumes for the traditional Japanese theater, Kabuki. She has also made a contribution to the area of uniforms, such as the Japanese Olympics team in 1994 and the flight attendants in 1970.

In 1977 Mori was admitted to the exclusive French fashion circle of la Chambre Syndicale de la haute couture parisienne, the first Asian couturiere to be so honored. Admission to the organization is the ultimate title

For Hanae Mori, a suit made by Coco Chanel was a source of inspiration: "I was fascinated by the impeccable tailoring often found in men's suits. But it also looked elegant. . . . That experience motivated me to continue as a designer" (Mori, pp. 72–76).

Menkes, Suzy. "Hanae Mori: The Iron Butterly." *Hanae Mori Style*. Edited by Yasuko Suita. Tokyo: Kodansha International, 2001.

Mori, Hanae. *Fasshon: Chou wa Kokkyou wo Koeru* (Fashion: A butterfly crosses the border). Tokyo: Iwanami Shinsho, 1993; reprint, 2000.

Mori Hanae to Pari: Pari Oto Kuchuru Nijunen Tenran Kai (Hanae Mori and Paris: Twenty years of Paris haute couture). Tokyo: Ginza Matsuya, 1998.

Suita, Yasuko, ed. *Hanae Mori Style*. Tokyo: Kodansha International, 2001.

Yuniya Kawamura

that many prêt-à-porter designers aspire to achieve, though few realize their goals. In January 2003 the organization had only eleven members.

Mori introduced Japanese high culture, with its luxury and great beauty, to the West. She featured Japanese cultural products—such as cherry blossoms, Mount Fuji, Kabuki, and Japanese calligraphy—and applied them to Western aesthetics. One of her most famous trademarks is the butterfly, and she is therefore known as Madame Butterfly. Unlike Kenzo or the other avant-garde Japanese designers who used unconventional styles and fabrics, Mori did not attempt to break the system of Western fashion or alter its concept of clothing. What she challenged was the stereotypical, inferior image of the Orient and Japanese women that was current in the 1960s.

Mori remains exclusive among all the Japanese designers in Japan and in France because of her status as a Couturiere, the title that no other Japanese designers had attained in the early twenty-first century. She has received many prestigious awards, including the Croix de chevalier des arts et lettres (1984) and chevalier of the Légion d'honneur (1989), both from the French government. In 1989 the Japanese government designated her a Person of Cultural Merit.

Mori's enterprise was privately owned and managed by her husband, Ken, until his death in 1996, and later by her elder son, Akira. However, as the structure of the haute couture system began to change, the company was forced to go through an organizational transition. In 2001 the company announced that Mori's prêt-à-porter and licensing divisions had been sold to a British investment group, Rothschild, and a major Japanese trading company, Mitsui. Her haute couture division was sold in 2002. While Mori now designs only for her haute couture collection, which is shown biannually in Paris, her family members have completely withdrawn from her business.

See also **Costume Designer; Japanese Fashion; Textiles, Japanese.**

BIBLIOGRAPHY
Brabec, Dominique. "Hanae Mori." *L'Express* 10 (January 1977): 7.

MOSCHINO, FRANCO Franco Moschino was born in Abbiategrasso, Italy, in 1950. He attended art classes at the Academia di Belle Arti di Brera in Milan until 1969. Although he expected to be a painter, he pursued opportunities as a fashion illustrator for a variety of periodicals. He was a keen observer of the current art phenomena, from avant-garde to contemporary styles. Until 1983, Moschino collaborated with other manufacturers as a creative consultant with Aspesi, Blumarine, and Cassoli. Rather than inventing new styling, he combined existing elements in unexpected ways. His expertly tailored and classic styles, punctuated with whimsical detailing, were already apparent at the inception of his company, Moschino S.n.c., which became Moon Shadow S.r.l. in 1983. In 2000, the company was again renamed as Moschino S.p.A.

Moschino, a fashion show produced by the highly regarded Aeffe SpA, attracted media attention for the designer's persistence in appropriating garments as sign boards of irreverence and irony. In 1989, Moschino's signature line, Couture, was introduced during the "XX Olympics of Fashion." His second line, labeled Cheap and Chic, was introduced in 1988. During that unforgettable runway presentation, safety pins adorned evening clothes and garbage bags replaced woven fabric, reflecting surrealism and dadaism. Moschino previewed his Uomo menswear in 1986 and followed it with his Diffusion line in 1999. Superbly cut styling for Jeans Uomo arrived in 1996.

Business Innovations

The introduction of each of Moschino's lines featured accessories, fragrances, swimwear, eyewear, men's and women's clothing, and most notably jeans. Designs were provocatively and playfully posed in artistic vitrines, store interiors, showrooms, and even a corporate office. Vignettes are still represented as formidable instruments of communication for Moschino's acerbic wit, passions, and politics.

Theatrically dressed troubadours and character actors heralded the opening of Moschino's first boutique in Milan, in 1989. At the opening of the Cheap and Chic store, canvases painted by Moschino transformed the retail space into a fine art gallery, Una Galleria d'Arte Finta. By 1991 he had opened boutiques in Rome, Los Angeles, and New York City. The displays that launched his New York store and his Milan store, with its controversial windows, in 1992 brilliantly expressed his opinions on environmental issues, drug addiction, racism, animal causes, and violence. Stores in Bangkok and Osaka opened in 1997.

In 1999, skilled designers and artisans revisited Moschino's iconographic themes; using unorthodox methods, they updated the decor of the original showroom and the retail store. Aware of the company's historic sense of humor and irreverent approach to design, designers enlarged and renovated the Milan office space—including the corporate office, showroom, and design studios—and installed amusing sculpture and artistic, structural detailing.

Since Moschino's death in 1994, due to complications from AIDS, the company's creative force, Rossella Jardini, has preserved the Moschino traditions and message in the global market, with an emphasis on trade. In 1999, ownership of the company was transferred to the manufacturer Aeffe SpA.

Personal Image and Acknowledgments
Moschino called himself half tailor, half artist; although he did not cut or sew, he drew frequently, quickly, and spontaneously. His cuts were meticulously constructed and traditional, as well as sexy and flattering to the wearer. Yet he claimed he was in conflict with the system that produced fashion because it shamefully disregarded modern society. Moschino chose a life surrounded by mere essentials, while he provided financial support to his favorite charities, including drug rehabilitation programs and a pediatric hospice for children suffering with HIV/AIDS. In 1995, Fondazione Moschino established an organization called Smile, which offers assistance to children in developing countries.

Clothing Designs and Artistic Hallmarks
Zany theatrics have always distinguished Moschino's memorable fashion presentations, events, performances, and happenings. He produced wildly imaginative seasonal presentations, radically changing how fashion shows are conceived. The designer once bounded on stage to interrupt a runway show, exclaiming that fashion was over, although a videotape of the show kept running, all to the bemusement of journalists and buyers. On another occasion, he displayed garments on easels and orchestrated a party inspired by the atmosphere of an open-air market. Once, he paraded models on their hands and knees down the runway, all featuring his unconventional ideals of beauty, such as a crooked nose or frizzy hair. Many Moschino models have assumed the roles of clowns, madonnas, nuns, and fairies in his unusual shows.

In 1985, a sampling of his defining silhouettes was the subject of *Italia: the Genius of Fashion* exhibit at the Fashion Institute of Technology in New York. Moschino's impassioned messages appeared printed, embroidered, and otherwise stitched on garments. The strategy behind his activism can also be regarded as an ingenious ploy to motivate the customer to buy. Advertising campaigns throughout the 1990s proclaimed "Stop the Fashion System," while the clothes were brazenly printed or otherwise appliquéd with hilarious slogans and resonant symbols, including peace signs, hearts, spaghetti stains, and bar codes. Moschino's clothing has always reflected a sense of humor together with a strong sense of social justice through words and iconic patterns such as mortar and bricks, exotic opera characters, or cowboy stereotypes. In his Ecouture line he labeled fake fur as ecological and promoted "friendly garments," colored with natural dyes, since he was concerned that dress was becoming detached from humanity and nature.

Throughout the 1990s, Moschino used an abundance of props to make statements and visual puns. In his store windows he displayed mannequins in straight jackets bearing the stenciled text "For Fashion Victims Only." He posed a regal figure regally, wearing a crown fashioned from dried macaroni, illustrating his distrust for authority. Another window featured models posed among open, suspended scissors, making scraps of glamorous materials. Once he embellished a gown with the silhouette of a duck bubbling a balloon message from its beak, "I love Fashion," and through fishnet-draped windows, Venus on a Half/Shell revealed a white bathing suit stenciled with the words "Save Our Sea." A retrospective exhibition, titled XX Years of Kaos, at the Museo della Permanente, exhibited the enterprising history of Moschino. The pages of the 1993 publication, including a video, opened with an acerbic quote describing the designer's "ten years of stupidity, fantasy and me."

The city of Milan paid tribute to the designer through an exhibition titled *Moschino Forever* in 1995. Universally recognized trademark symbols, including a cow, a heart, the peace sign, and a happy face, were placed all over the city. In 1996, the *New Persona, New Universe* exhibition featured a larger-than-life, heart-shaped labyrinth created for the occasion by the design studio within Moschino's company. This exhibition formed part of the *Biennale di Firenze*, a celebration that combined art and dress for the first time in the galleries, museums, and alternative spaces of the city of Florence, Italy. A selection of Moschino designs was included in the 1998 *Fashion and Surrealism* exhibition by Richard Martin, guest curator, at the Victoria and Albert Museum in London.

Throughout his life Moschino exhibited a remarkable ability to laugh at himself. He delighted in appropriating universal symbols, playing with them as elements of dress design, and simply having fun with fashion. He claimed fashion did not exist, and if it did, its true significance would embody the freedom to wear anything.

See also **Fashion Designer; Fashion Shows; Italian Fashion; Politics and Fashion.**

BIBLIOGRAPHY

Casadio, Mariuccia. *Moschino.* Translated by Steve Piccolo. Milano: Skira, 2001.

The Fashion Book. London: Phaidon, 1998.

Steele, Valerie. *Fashion, Italian Style.* New Haven, Conn.: Yale University Press, 2003.

Mazza, Samuele, and Mariuccia Casadio. *Moschino.* Milan: Leonardo Arte s.r.l., 1997

Gillion Carrara

MOURNING DRESS In the twenty-first century, when family funerals are private and black is worn as a fashion color, it is rarely possible to recognize that a person is in mourning. But in the past, family bereavement involved a series of highly visible public rituals. The use of mourning ceremonial and dress was originally a privilege of the royal courts of Europe from the Middle Ages and was regulated by court protocol through sumptuary laws. Over a period of five hundred years, however, the use of mourning dress spread outward to the rest of society.

Court and National Mourning

At royal funerals, the hearse was accompanied for burial by a vast procession of representatives of the nation's power: the bereaved family, the aristocracy, military, church, and merchants—their mourning dress carefully coded to indicate their gender and social rank. The highest in the land, both men and women, wore the longest mourning trains and hoods in expensive dull black wool, with black or white crape or linen trimmings. Lengths of mourning and details of the requisite dress followed strict royal protocol. Widows, always deeply veiled in public, wore mourning for the longest periods.

National mourning was declared on the death of a sovereign or key political figure. This indicated that black clothing had to be worn for a specific period by established society on formal occasions and whenever royalty was present. In the eighteenth century, this could be as long as a year. After the death of Queen Elizabeth the Queen Mother, on 30 March 2002, Buckingham Palace announced ten days of national mourning in Britain.

Eighteenth Century

Efforts to restrict the use of mourning dress to court use had to be abandoned from the late seventeenth century because wealthy European merchant families, determined to copy aristocratic etiquette, defied sumptuary restrictions, paid any fines imposed, and wore versions of court mourning dress as they pleased. Mourning dress for the wealthy became increasingly fashionably styled,

with black coats and breeches for men and mantua dresses for women, in black and half-mourning mauve.

The use of mourning dress, also for reasons of social ambition, next spread slowly to the growing middle classes. Demand across Europe thus expanded and was met through the extensive manufacture of dull black mourning wools, black and white silk mourning crapes, and jewelry. Mourning dress was made up by court and private dressmakers and tailors to suit the specific styles required by these widening consumer groups.

Mourning Dress 1850–1914

By the middle of the nineteenth century, the correct fulfillment of the minutiae of family mourning became a coded and very public sign of middle-class social respectability. Etiquette rules escalated. Queen Victoria, widowed at the age of 45 in 1861, wore mourning until her death in 1901. Many other widows and families followed her example, including those of the rising industrial middle classes of Europe and North America.

The weight of participation still fell heavily on widows. A respectable widow wore mourning dress for at least two and a half years after her husband died, while a widower was required only to do so for three months. Other family bereavements were mourned for specific, graduated periods.

Widening the Market

Another reason for this rising tide of mourning wear was its successful commercial exploitation by astute manufacturers who produced etiquette-coded goods priced to suit a wide range of consumers. Thus, from the 1840s, family-mourning dress was provided by couture salons, private dressmakers working at every social level, new department stores, wholesale ready-to-wear manufacturers, and by homemade provision. Speed of supply was essential, encouraging new and well-organized wholesale manufacturing and delivery methods. Advertising struck a balance between enticing wealthy clients and encouraging the less well off. Thus, *Myra's Journal* of March 1876 reassured middle-class customers that "these extremely cheap clothes will look and wear well, a consideration for those whose means are not unlimited." This heavily feminized cult reached a peak between 1880 and 1900.

Commodification Processes

The vast array of products included widow's weeds (crape-laden bodice, skirt, and cape, with black outdoor bonnet and crape veil), indoor caps, fans, underwear, gloves, black-edged handkerchiefs, and a huge array of mourning jewelry, including black jet and "in memoriam" rings, brooches, and lockets. All of these came in three styles for use in first, second, ordinary, and half mourning. The complexities are epitomized by the finesse of descriptions for half-mourning mauve—"violet," "pansy," "scabious," and "heliotrope," none of which were to be confused with the bright purple fashion shade of "Parma violet." For wealthy women, all mourning dress also had to follow the seasonal shifts of fashion set by Paris. Styles thus went rapidly out of date and had to be replaced.

Etiquette Anxieties and Errors

Advice on all of this was offered to the anxious through books and magazines. *Sylvia's Home Journal* in 1881 advised, for example, that mothers should wear black without crape for six weeks after the death of the mothers- or fathers-in-law of their married children. Aristocratic families were advised always to travel with complete sets of mourning clothes, because they might be required to wear complementary court mourning if a death occurred in any European royal family. This practice is still maintained by the British royal family.

Altering and Making Do

At the other end of society, from the 1840s, many women purchased simpler and secondhand mourning dress. Many dyed and altered garments. Styles were modified in conformity with the less fashionable expectations of local communities. By 1900, through the growth of ready-to-wear production of women's woolen costumes, black clothing was also directed at the better-off working-class consumer. For the poorest the provision of any sort of mourning dress remained a trauma. Many, unable to afford it, even had to rely on the help of neighbors to avoid the public disgrace of a pauper funeral.

Decline of Mourning Dress

The use of black mourning crape declined steadily from the 1880s, and by the 1930s, widows' veils were already out of use except in Catholic countries and royal circles.

COURT MOURNING, FRANCE, FROM *ORDRE CHRONOLOGIQUE DES DEUILS DE LA COUR*, 1765

Widower for wife: total 6 months: first 6 weeks in black wool suit with deep weepers on cuffs; 6 weeks in black suit with silver buckles.

Widow for husband: total 1 year and 6 weeks; first 6 months in black wool trained robe with white trimmings; 6 months in black silk with white crape trimmings, 6 weeks in black and white.

First cousin: total 8 days of ordinary mourning— 5 in black and 3 in white.

Translation from Mercier, 1877.

FAMILY MOURNING, FRANCE, 1876

Widower for wife: total 3 months: black suit with black trimmings.

Widow for husband: total 2.5 years: 1 year and 1 day, black wool and crape; 9 months in black wool with less crape; 3 months in black silk; 6 months in half mourning.

First Cousin: total 6 weeks to 6 months: 3 weeks to 3 months in black silk; 6 weeks to 3 months in half mourning.

Translation from Mercier, 1877

After World War II, the provision of mourning dress was no longer a specific branch of the ready-to-wear industry. By the early 2000s family funerals had become so discreet that death barely interrupted the routine of life for both women and men alike. There are no longer "norms" of mourning dress—even among royalty. In 2002, Princess Anne's break with correct royal funeral etiquette was extreme and is so far unique. Taking on a male rather than a female role at her grandmother's funeral, she strode in the funeral procession behind the coffin, alongside the male royal mourners, wearing male military uniform complete with trousers and sword.

Conclusion

The cultural functions of mourning dress as well as the styles thus varied across society. Although Fred Davis writes that "the democratization of fashion was furthered, of course, by major technical advances in the late nineteenth and early twentieth centuries in clothing manufacture" (p. 139), the widening commodification of mourning dress by 1900 in fact reenforced existing social differences through the provision of different qualities of mourning garments and the inability of the poor to afford them at all.

Mourning dress did, however, significantly influence modern processes of garment manufacture, retailing, and consumption. The need for a rapidity of supply helped found department stores and encouraged the wholesale manufacture of women's wear. It enhanced the commercial implementation of the use of sewing machines and early forms of mail order. Mourning etiquette also contributed to the development of early forms of plastic used in imitation of jet jewelry, and finally, the careful niche marketing of mourning dress contributed to the development of modern mass-advertising techniques.

See also **Royal and Aristocratic Dress.**

BIBLIOGRAPHY

Davis, Fred. *Fashion Culture and Identity*. Chicago: University of Chicago Press, 1992.

Mercier, Louis. *Le Deuil, sons observation dans tout les temps et dans tous les pays comparée a son observation nos jours*. London: P. Douvet, 1877.

Taylor, Lou. *Mourning Dress: A Costume and Social History*. London: Allen and Unwin, 1983.

Lou Taylor

MUDCLOTH. *See* Bogolan.

MUFFS The muff, a cylindrical accessory, usually furred, into which the wearer's hands are placed on either side, was called *manchon* in French, *mouffe* in Flemish, and *manicone* in Italian, and was first called snuffkin, skimskyn, and snoskyn in England. Francis Weiss cites the first mention of a snuffkin in 1483 but the earliest image is in the illustration of L'Angloyse in *Receuil de la diversite des habits*, 1567, a small tube attached to the girdle by a cord. Furs per se were not fashionable in the English or French courts in the last thirty years of the sixteenth century, but imported skins for trims and accessories had cachet, and the muff was to prove a popular means of displaying furs and status; in 1583 a skinner named Adam Blande trimmed a velvet snuffkin with five "genette skins." Imported from Africa via Italy, the genet was exotic and expensive. The quantities of skins used suggest that the snuffkins were furred inside and out.

The rich source of fur-bearing animals inhabiting colonized Newfoundland, Canada, and North America provided quantities of beaver for hats and marten, mink, lynx, otter, and fox for dress and what were, by 1601, called muffs (also a double entendre for the female genitalia). Furs provided decoration and interest, contrasting with the undecorated silks worn following sumptuary legislation controlling the use of gold decoration in fabric. In Wenceslaus Hollar's *Winter*, 1641–1644, an English lady of fashion carries a sable or marten fur muff as befits her station, decorated with a ribbon to tie at the waist: "The cold not cruelty makes her weare/In Winter, furs and Wild beasts haire/For a smoother skinn at night/Embraceth her with more delight." Not all muffs were fur, but this contrast between smooth and hairy skins belies the notion of function over fashion and the frisson of sex; Hollar's later studies of muffs show an almost fetishistic interest in the look and feel of furs. Antoine Furetiere in his *Dictionnaire universel*, 1690, defined a muff as a fur object, "originally used only by women; at present, however, men also carry them. The finest muffs are of marten, the less expensive ones of squirrel. The muffs for horsemen are of otter or tiger." Ladies would also carry lapdogs in their *manchons*. The engrav-

Actress Ethel Barrymore with a fur muff. Fur muffs received a revival in popularity during the early twentieth century, but were then overshadowed by the fur coat. THE ADVERTISING ARCHIVE, LTD. REPRODUCED BY PERMISSION.

ings of Bonnard and Jean de St. Jean show men of fashion carrying large muffs in lynx and otter furs suspended from the waist on a belt.

The Hudson's Bay Company was formed in 1670 and provided a supply of furs to a burgeoning middle-class consumer base. In *Mundus Muliebris*, the lady has "three Muffs of Sable, Ermine, Grey (squirrel)," from the most expensive to a cheaper but pretty fur. The rococo period saw delicate muffs in sable, skunk, squirrel, and sea otter, small and barrel-shaped or large and baglike; in 1765 William Cole noted with disapproval that in Paris "all the world got into Muffs, some ridiculously large and unwieldy." The *Gallerie des modes et costumes français* showed large muffs worn by men and women of fashion in the 1780s, one style, worn to the opera, 1784, called "*d'agitation momentanee*." More prosaic is Thomas Gainsborough's portrait of the actress Mrs. Siddons depicting a large fox muff, matching the trim of her silk mantle. As a supporter of Charles James Fox, Siddons is showing her political affiliations—as well as being fashionable. The wearers of the light dress fabrics of the revolutionary and early nineteenth century required warm muffs and fashion plates depict ones made from bearskins. By the 1820s and the Romantic period, faux medieval muffs in ermine or the more luxurious chinchilla were imported from Chile and Peru. In the 1860s, the fur coat, the ultimate in conspicuous consumption, became fashionable and muffs were less prominent. Muffs enjoyed revivals in the early twentieth century, when Revillon stocked over a million muffs in their shops and *Vogue* wrote of chinchilla, sable, leopard, mole, ocelot, and monkey muffs (Sears and Roebuck advertised coney, meaning rabbit); but muffs were less of a focus. The all-important fur item, because fur now meant status, was the coat. During World War II, there was a brief return of the accessory, which added a touch of glamour, often reworked from an old fur. American *Vogue* described muffs in 1940, being in skunk, Persian lamb, blue fox, broadtail, mink, and leopard. The muff, however, did not survive the war. They were unsuited to modern women who drove cars, traveled on planes, lived in heated houses, and earned their own living.

See also **Europe and America: History of Dress (400–1900 C.E.); Fetish Fashion; Fur.**

BIBLIOGRAPHY

De Monvel, Boutet. "What's in a Muff?" *Vogue*, 1 November 1916.

Evelyn, Mary. *Mundus Muliebris, or The Ladies Dressing Room Unlock'd*. London: J. Costume Society, 1977. Published privately in 1690.

Ribeiro, Aileen. "Furs in Fashion, the Eighteenth and Nineteenth Centuries." *The Connoisseur*, December 1979.

Uzanne, Octave. *L' Ombrelle, Le Gant, Le Manchon*. Paris: A. Quantin, 1883.

Weiss, Francis. "Furred Serpents, Snuffskins and Stomachers." *Costume* (1973).

Judith Watt

MUGLER, THIERRY Known for spectacular runway shows and fetishistic fashions, Thierry Mugler came to his career in fashion design via dance and photography. Born in Strasbourg, France, in 1948, he studied at the Lycée Fustel de Coulange in Strasbourg from 1960 to 1965 and at the School of Fine Arts in 1966 and 1967. He performed as a dancer with the Rhine Opera Ballet in the 1965–1966 season. He moved to Paris and began working as a professional photographer while simultaneously freelancing as an assistant designer for a number of fashion houses in Paris, London, and Milan. Mugler showed his first ready-to-wear collection (using the brand name Café de Paris) in 1973 and obtained financial backing to open his own company, Thierry Mugler, in 1974. In 1986 he bought out his investors to obtain full ownership of the company. He opened a fragrance company in 1990 and scored considerable success with the perfume

Thierry Mugler, spring-summer haute couture collection, 1999. Reflecting Mugler's use of sexual fetishism in designing fashion, this model displays a black leather outfit consisting of a halter top, mini-skirt, and choker, as well as leather wrapped around the lower thighs and knees. © PIERRE VAUTHEY/CORBIS. REPRODUCED BY PERMISSION.

Angel in 1992. In that same year he showed his first couture collection.

Mugler's characteristic style draws heavily on the iconography of sexual fetishism, and his models frequently resemble dominatrixes, from their towering high-heeled boots and corseted curves to such accessories as neck corsets and riding crops. Among his most notorious ensembles are a hot-red "cowboy" outfit consisting of hat, corset, chaps, and heels, modeled by a black transvestite, and his famous motorcycle bustier inspired by Detroit car styles of the 1950s. Mugler frequently made garments of leather and rubber, some of which make their wearers resemble giant insects drawn from science fiction. Examples of his less-theatrical outfits, such as his colorful and sharply tailored suits, were extremely popular, especially in the 1980s. As of 2004 Mugler suspended designing both couture and ready-to-wear, although he continued to produce special costumes.

See also **Costume Designer; Cross-Dressing; Dance and Fashion; Fetish Fashion; Rubber as Fashion Fabric.**

BIBLIOGRAPHY
Baudot, François. *Thierry Mugler*. New York: Universe/Vendome, 1998.

Buxbaum, Gerda, ed. *Icons of Fashion: The Twentieth Century*. New York: Prestel, 1999.

Mugler, Thierry. *Thierry Mugler: Photographer*. New York: Rizzoli International, 1988.

———. *Fashion, Fetish, and Fantasy*. London: Thames and Hudson, Inc., 1998.

John S. Major

MUIR, JEAN Born in London, England, in 1928, Miss Muir (as she liked to be called) started her career at Liberty in Regent Street. She worked in sales and as a sketcher (1950–1954) at Liberty, followed by a brief spell at Jacqmar, before joining Jaeger, Ltd., as a designer (1956–1962). She was then invited to design a range of garments in woolen jersey for David Barnes, a collection that was so successful that he formed the company Jane and Jane for her (1962–1966). With her husband, Harry Leuckert, whom she married in 1955, she launched Jean Muir, Ltd., at 22 Bruton Street, London, in 1966. She described herself as a "dressmaker" and acknowledged no influences.

From its inception, the Jean Muir label became associated with virtually timeless designs that flattered but never dominated the wearer. The collections evolved subtly but remained true to Muir's basic ethos: to create clothing that was feminine without being fussy, and classic but devoid of nostalgia. In a 1985 article in British *Vogue*, Muir stated that her style of dressmaking had been developed through an adherence to the anatomy and techniques of dressmaking:

> On that, one diverts, exaggerates, pares down the lines to make the kind of shape and movement one wants. Then it's a natural eye in terms of shape and colour, a sense of evolving while never losing sight of the structure (p. 118).

Muir's signature fabrics were matte wool crepe and jersey, buttery-soft suede, and ultrasoft leather, which was invariably punched with small holes in decorative borders. Her fluid jersey garments were accented with precise rows of stitched or pin tucks, pleats, smocking, and shirring. Hemlines were determined by proportion rather than fashion. Although she was best known for her dark and neutral palettes, Muir was also a superb colorist. She adored beautiful buttons; for example, her tubular Perspex buttons, which were dyed to match the fabric of the garment they adorned and featured notched sides, were exquisitely restrained.

In addition to her mainline collections, Muir presented "JM in Cotton" from 1978 until about 1985 and "JM in Wool" from 1978 to 1995. In 1986 she launched her lower-priced Jean Muir Studio line, and within this, from the early 1990s, she introduced a capsule collection of well-priced separates in washable jersey called "Jean Muir Essentials." She was an ardent supporter of the United Kingdom's clothing industry.

Muir shared her knowledge of fashion and design by teaching and was a vocal spokesperson for the need to raise standards in education, training, manufacture, and design. Not surprisingly, her contribution to the catalog that accompanied a 1980 traveling exhibition of her designs was an entirely practical essay aimed at students, outlining every stage of the production process. Her many honors include the following: Royal Designer for Industry (1972), Fellow of the Royal Society of Arts (1973), and Fellow, Chartered Society of Designers (1978). She was appointed a Member of the Design Council in 1983; made a Commander, Order of the British Empire in 1984; and received a British Fashion Council Award for Services to Industry in 1985. Muir was inducted into the British Fashion Council's Hall of Fame in 1994.

Following Muir's death in 1995, the company amalgamated the Main and Studio lines under the Jean Muir label. The label's design team, in the early twenty-first century—Sinty Stemp, Joyce Fenton, Angela Gill, and Caroline Angell—jointly have some forty year's experience working with Miss Muir. Since the founder's death they have continued to evolve the line while retaining Miss Muir's signature.

See also **Jersey; Leather and Suede.**

BIBLIOGRAPHY
Bleichroeder, Ingrid. "A Certain Style: Jean Muir." *Vogue* (U.K.), August 1995, 118–119.

Miller, Beatrix. "Obituary: Jean Muir." *Vogue* (U.K.), August 1995, 98–101.

Muir, Jean. *Jean Muir*. Leeds, England: Leeds Art Galleries, 1980. An exhibition catalog.

Amy de la Haye

MUSIC AND FASHION The relationship between fashion and popular music is one of abundant and mutual creativity. Reciprocal influences have resulted in some of the most dynamic apparel visualizations ever created in popular culture. Some exist as memorable creations for the stage and music video; others become long-lasting fashion trends, which settle in the culture to become noteworthy, referential, and lasting.

Three collaborations exist. One is when fashion designers and entertainment celebrities engineer fashion to fit a declared project. Another collaboration occurs when youth subcultures articulate themselves through fashion. The third is when the fashion industry interprets a music-led theme or trend.

Music celebrities and designer collaborations have altered the course of fashion, though good examples of this relationship are few. The affects of these unions have been very significant. Outcomes include Jean Paul Gaultier's whirlpool corset dress worn by Madonna on her 1990 Blonde Ambition tour, which subsequently contributed to the trend for wearing bra tops and less clothing. Grace Jones's collaborations with the art director Jean-Paul Goude, who in the 1980s rendered Grace Jones's body a fashion object, made groundbreaking music videos and advertisements for various products. However, Grace Jones's haircut became a major trend; it became known as a "high top" when copied by young black youth.

Both Madonna and Grace Jones acted as muses for creative designers; their musical representations became reference points for widespread interpretations. The images produced by these collaborations were decisive, especially in the way they altered conceptions of traditional beauty and gestures.

The outcome of many associations of the performer and the designer or stylist is usually a confirmation of the extant youth subcultural fashion. Rather new perspectives, new methods, and new resonances of fashion are made when fashion and music are linked to subcultural expression.

Consider the partnerships of Kurt Cobain and Grunge, Marilyn Manson and Goth, and Avril Lavigne and Skater. Designer interpretations of performer and subculture expression include Jean Paul Gaultier's facsimile Marilyn Mason (Summer 2003) and Belgian designer Raf Simons's continual referencing of music-led subcultures. Simons's collections have included T-shirts emblazoned with images of the missing Manic Street Preachers guitarist Richey Edwards and a joint effort with Peter Saville, the graphic designer of Factory Records.

This article non-chronologically highlights the main collaborations since the inception of popular music. It is not a comprehensive review; Goth, Skinheads, Northern Soul, Funk, Independent Music, Rock, Grunge, Soul, Dance, and Drum & Bass cultures and collaborations are not considered. Nevertheless, it does demonstrate how innovative music and fashion expression are rooted.

Music's Influence on Fashion

Bobby-soxers. With the birth of rock'n'roll in 1951, youth culture and popular culture gained impetus. In the 1940s, American teenage girls known as bobby-soxers, became famous not only for their fashions, but for their fanatical adulation of male crooners such as Frank Sinatra. Bobby-soxers wore ankle socks, hair ribbons, denim rolled-up jeans, felt poodle skirts with an embroidered and appliquéd French poodle, and blouses with small flounced edging, sloppy sweaters, and saddle shoes. Bobby-soxers were rare in music fashion cultures because males usually led most innovations.

Mods. The idea of intra- and inter-group identification was also important to the Mods, who formed in Britain around 1965 and had a resonant influence on fashion and menswear. They sited themselves in an urban backdrop of espresso bars, Vespa scooters, the mini motorcar, and an image backdrop of Perry Como and the French look, which was influenced by the movie *Shoot the Pianist* (1960). They wore American army parkas over imported American shirts and their suits were tailored. A small number of Mods altered off-the-peg suits or tailored their own suits. Much of the allure of Mod was that fashion designers such as Mary Quant and Pierre Cardin had the term applied to their work. Graphics symbols such as targets, Union Jacks, horizontal color stripes, and cycling images were appealing to the Mods, fashion designers, and artists. Although Mods were a fusion of teenage groups that had different interests, they were sound sophisticates who had rejected the wooliness and unhewn skiffle and trad music for the poise of modern jazz, and later rhythm and blues, blues, and bluebeat. Mods were fanatical stylist who understood that nodes of change already existed and if they connected them they would become distinct from the rest of society.

In the 1980s, the new wave band the Jam illustrated the divergence of old and new Mod. The music became trashy and aggressive while the look drew on the stereotypical apparel items that already had been diluted by other Mod bands.

During the 1980s and 1990s the legacy of Mod continued in bands such as the Style Council, Blur, and Oasis though the fashion trend had begun to assume cross-cultural references. Sojourns to Ibiza and Morocco, references to Northern soul, and 1970s Regency Mod provided the visual vitality for bands such as the James Taylor Quartet, Brand New Heavies, D'Influence, and Galliano, whose clothes fused with the "ethnicity" of Mod. The new guise, Acid Jazz, became synonymous with the urban modern menswear that included formal and sportswear items.

Retro-Futurism and Neoclassicism

The German band Kraftwerk had underwritten the creative disposition for a number of British bands and the musical styles of Electro, Techno, and Rave. Kraftwerk were influenced by Stockhausen and Italian futurism. Their music encapsulated a metronomic electronic minimalism. Its austere, almost uniformed and metered beats defined a musical soundscape that challenged the conception of music in the way John Cage's ideas about music, noise, and silence did.

During the early 1980s Gianni Versace, Thierry Mugler, and Claude Montana used motifs that included asymmetry, stark bicoloration, and monochromatic uniformity. Fashion shops such as PX and Plaza in London were good examples of how fashion synchronizes with music.

Grace Jones's "hightop," 1983. A designer's "muse" and fashion trendsetter, musician Grace Jones displays her "hightop" haircut while being interviewed by nighttime television host David Letterman. © CORBIS. REPRODUCED BY PERMISSION.

Designer Anthony Price's close-fitting uniforms worn by Kraftwerk were indivisible from Price's menswear. Price's London shop, Plaza, was one of the most innovative retail concepts of its day. Price clearly referenced the Retro-Futuristic trend. From outside, neon signage was juxtaposed onto a stark white storefront, and a waist-up view of two android-like shop dummies standing behind the shop window.

These were references to Retro-Futurism and Neoclassicism that were the zeitgeists of that period. Album covers by New Order, Joy Division, and Roxy Music referenced Neoclassicism. Artists such as Gary Numan, Ultravox, and David Bowie were influenced by Kraftwerk and styled themselves in celebration of the Futurist, the Suprematist, and German and Russian Modernist.

The fashions worn by these artists varied from Numan's asymmetric all-in-one uniforms, to Bowie's mid-1970s foray in to monochromatic plain black pants and white shirt, his loose peasant shirts, pants tucked into riding boots, and exceptionally broad leather belt. Ultravox's Midge Ure captured a romantic kitsch-heroic characterization that was suitable for inclusion in a Tyrolese peasant painting by Franz von Defregger.

Rave

Techno music was an inheritor of Kratfwerk's music. Techno became a cornerstone of British Rave in the late 1980s. Rave, a loose symbiosis of Chicago House, Electro, and Balearic Beat, started as Acid House in Manchester during 1987, which became known as the second "summer of love." The label was applied to a frenetic period that ushered in the drug Ecstasy (MDMA), the ascendant of the band the Stone Roses, and Manchester's Hacienda Club, which had become acknowledged as the center of British club culture.

Known for impromptu "happenings" at motorway service stations and on farmland, raves were notorious for the popularization of the drug Ecstasy, which became the essential accompaniment to the movement.

Techno's hypnotic digitized bleeps and sampled hooks drew diverse followers from across the social and racial spectrum. Despite an indefinable constituency, Rave began to define itself as a fashion expression.

Girls wore tight leather or denim pants, waistcoats, fitted T-shirts, and long-sleeved jerkins. Accessories included large silver rings often worn on the thumb and index finger, masses of silver bracelets, and friendship bracelets and leather wristbands like those that hippies wore. Long, lank hair became de rigueur.

Boys were less definable, though many wore fashions by leading designers such as C. P Company, Stone Island, Paul Smith, John Richmond, Nick Coleman, and Armand Basi. Their clothes consisted of Polo shirts, T-shirts, jeans, anoraks, and reflected the current mood of menswear. Certainly, the "clubwear" designer label came of age between 1987 and 1993. However, these labels tended to be cheap, poorly made clothes, although they were perfect for Rave followers who were accustomed to wearing different clothes to "party" in each weekend. Rave personalities, such as Keith of the band Prodigy, communicated a visual sensibility that the second phase (mid-1990s onward) of Rave in Europe, America, and Britain continued. Rave's second phase improved on the intense colorations, silly costumes, and computer graphics that had featured Rave's first phase. Events like Berlin's annual Love Parade, which started in 1992, and designer Walter van Beirendonck's W&LT collection demonstrate how Rave has evolved into a lifestyle form.

Hip-hop and Rastafarians

Occasionally fashion draws directly on music culture for inspiration. Rastafarian music has provided popular culture with an aesthetic that is applicable in a number of forms. Fashion has been a consistent interpreter of Rastafari's fashion iconography. Fashion companies like Complice, Jean Paul Gaultier, and Rifat Ozbek have used the Rastafarian iconography such as the red, gold and green symbolism of Rastafarianism, dredlocked hair, and khaki uniforms, in what the fashion press had called "international ethno-chic." This term could also be applied to the collections of Owen Gaster and John Galliano who in 2000 appropriated Jamaican Dancehall and America Fly Girls as the themes for their respective collections.

The summer 2000 advertisements by the Italian fashion label "Versace Jeans Couture," show white models wearing multiple heavy, gold neck chains, a male model wearing a stocking hat, a gold tooth, and low-slung jeans. Here the grittiness of hip-hop fashion is reconstituted, sanitized, and made accessible for the mainstream.

New Romantics

In his 2003 spring/summer runway presentation for Dior, John Galliano referenced New Romantic personalities such as Leigh Bowery and Trojan.

The New Romantics were the most outré fashion-obsessed youth subculture London had ever witnessed. Youth subcultures tend to be motivated by class conflict and evolve fashions to counteract their position; the New Romantics lacked those anxieties. They were "Posers" who did not accept the limited propensity of glamour offered by the Punk movement. The New Romantics were led by Rusty Egan and Steve Strange, who in the late 1970s ran Billy's—A Club for Heroes—, and later Blitz,

a wine bar in London's Covent Garden, where they danced to Roxy Music, David Bowie, and Kraftwerk. They developed a series of looks based on romantic themes; in fact, almost any theme was possible if the wearer made the appropriate changes to create an outlandish and weird look. Dressing themes included Russian constructivism, Incroyables, Bonny Prince Charlie, Pirates, 1930s Berlin cabaret, and Hollywood starlet, puritans, and clowns, all heavily and inventively made-up. This alternative fashion expression became tangible and important once designers such as Vivienne Westwood, Stephan Linard, Helen Robinson, Richard Torry, Melissa Kaplan, Bell and Khan, and Rachel Auburn took notice. There were no references for this type of dressing, and no magazines except for *i-D*, *The Face*, and *Blitz*, which featured a review of what people wore in the clubs three months ago. The subculture became the catalyst for a number of new bands. In 1982 two new bands emerged, looking distinctly less weird than many die-hard New Romantics. Spandau Ballet and Duran Duran commercially crossed and became accepted by the radio stations, newspapers, and television as the palatable faces and sounds of New Romanticism.

Fashion's Influence on Music

When the British band Wham wore Katherine Hamnett's "Choose Life" T-shirts—a prompt for self-preservation in the middle of the 1980s AIDS crisis—a subtext of protest was being enacted. This call to "revolt into style" was analogous to the Hepcat's bewilderment about society's ordinariness (Cosgrove 1984, pp. 77–91).

African American youth were the first to wear zoot suits and to adopt a number of bodily gestures appropriate to the wearing of a suit, which took five yards of cloth to make. The idea of the revolt into style in youth culture is well founded (Melly 1970). Interpreters of the zoot suit were the early rock'n'roll fans from America, the Caribbean, and Europe. The drape shape of the zoot suit transferred in Britain via photographs of American rock-'n'roll stars on albums and other publicity, and through the West Indian migrants who arrived at London's Tilbury Docks in 1948. West Indian migrants to Britain were mainly young people who were influenced by American movies, music, and fashion. They wore clothes that were more vivid in shape and color than anything the British had been accustomed to. Fashion and music melded together in attempts to disengage its participants from the procession of tradition. A small number of Savile Row tailors had reintroduced the Edwardian look in 1948; it became popular with young upper-class men Londoners called Guardees. Subsequently, working-class youth groups, the Cosh boys and late in the 1950s the Teddy Boys, began to indicate their discontent with society's norms by adopting dandies narcissistic tendencies. They copied the style of the Guardees by wearing long jackets that were cut in a drape shape with velvet collars and cuffs, bright ankle socks, slim ties, and drainpipe

REBELLIOUS FASHION

In 2001 the Belgian designer Raf Simons paid homage to the Welsh band the Manic Street Preachers. The menswear collection feature oversized shirts and sweaters adorned with marxist slogans. The manics were not the first music group to wear political iconography (the Sex Pistols wore Lenin) but Simons's adoration of the Manics and of the politics of rebellion was a first in *high* fashion. (Porter, 2001)

trousers that were similar to those worn at the time of Edward VII (1901–1910). The clothes of early American rock stars such as Bill Haley, Gene Vincent, Little Richard, and Elvis Presley drew from and exaggerated the prevailing fashion aesthetic of black America, the drape silhouette. Also from the Mississippi riverboat gambler, blue-collar worker styles that included youth culture's omnipresent blue denim jeans with rolled cuffs, leather biker jackets, biker boots, a chain, and a white T-shirt were evident. Detractors labeled the status of the rock'n'roll musicians to being outside of the mainstream and to label the fashion adoptions, music and dance moves as being aligned to "the devil."

Punk

Punk rock was of the most influential and stimulating collaborations of fashion and music. It served as a pivotal catalyst for the way people in the 2000s think, create, and comment on fashion, music, and design.

Punk started in London during the 1970s and almost simultaneously became a musical genre, a fashion expression, and a way of life. Although bands such as the Slits, the Dammed, the Clash, and the Banshees were important, the Sex Pistols became the preeminent band of the genre. The fashions and the attitude of punk were on display in Malcom Maclaren's Kings Road store called Sex, and later, Seditionaries. Maclaren and his partner, Vivienne Westwood, sold clothing that was dislocated from the accepted idea of what fashion should be. The spectacle of the punk was attained by using forthright images out of context, thereby creating a distortion. Consequently, punk fashions shocked and intimidated. Punk's iconic fashion items included Maclaren and Westwood's replica of the Cambridge rapist mask, T-shirts emblazoned with corny playing card pin-up girls, homosexual cowboys, shirts with a Nazi swastika, and T-shirts of the Queen of England's face corrupted with a safety pin through her nose. All of the punk bands wore similar clothes with images that were taboo; this included

torn clothes, fetish clothes, and even clothes with simulated bloodstains.

Hippies

Punk was a reaction against the hippie culture, which became accepted as the pinnacle of youth rebellion.

The hippies were a 1960s folk- and rock-led movement that propagated an alternative perspective for living. According to one hippie commentator, "Hippy fashions originated from used-clothes bins, army/navy stores, and handmade clothes from scraps. In other words, whatever was cheap and available…" (New York Sun: 25, July, 2002). Clothes also originated from the Hippie trail, which passed through Turkey, Iran, Afghanistan, and Pakistan to India and Nepal.

During the 1980s and the 2000s, mainstream fashion design and rock music youth cultures adopted the hippie look. In the 1980s, the Italian designer Romeo Gigli used rich Indian embroideries and delicate prints and handwork to create soft and romantic themes that are seen in hippie dress. Marni, another Italian design company, has used the hippie theme exclusively in a brand that is elite and expensive and is therefore the antithesis of hippie ideology.

Fashion Catalysts

Music offers fashion more than a theme or a movement. Occasionally, a performer possesses fashion awareness that directly influences fashion.

As catalysts of fashion change (1973–1980s), David Bowie and Bryan Ferry experimented with new themes, beliefs, and values. Bowie's alter ego, Ziggy Stardust, wore elaborate costumes designed by avant-garde designer Kansai Yamamoto. The garments were not made exclusively for Bowie; they were simply part of Yamamoto's ready-to-wear collection. Bowie's fans reinterpreted the Ziggy look by wearing street clothes of the period. The ensemble consisted of high-waist pants, platform shoes, and brightly colored shirts and tank tops, which were occasionally bought from women's stores for their colors and tight fit. Ferry's various costumes included a Cosmic rocker look of a metallic leopard-skin bomber jacket and black silk trousers; the 1950s Rocker with black pants, dark blue T-shirt, and neck chain; and the lounge lizard clad in a white tuxedo, black bow tie, white shirt, and red cummerbund. He also dressed as an Army G.I., wearing khaki shirt and pants; a Neoclassic storm trooper; a gaucho, complete with gaucho pantaloons, a vest and shirt with wide sleeves and a black hat; and a 1960s soul singer, wearing a three-buttoned suit in various colors and materials, including leather and sharkskin. In many ways, 1970s disco provided exception of a music-led movement that comprehensively affected fashion. Existing at the same time as glam rock, disco had spread through much of the West. In America and Britain it had achieved the alliteration of a spectacle that fluently contorted across the age gap and from stage to the discothèque to the street.

Fashion and music proficiently and often independently create similar themes, yet the dynamic interaction between them motivates reactions that might not have otherwise occurred. The mistlike phenomenon of subcultural fashion holds apparel and popular music in totemic significance, creating fantastic fashion objects and moments from these restless forms. Formalized fashion is bound by an emphatic trepidation and terror. Its praxis and natural impulse is to conduct the activity of objectifying popular music, youth subcultures, and other "sexy" forms. This is why developments away from orthodox or formalized fashion customs can only be made when the agenda is no longer centered on the commerce of fashion, but is concerned with the irreverence and irrationality of making fashion images.

See also **Hippie Style; London Fashion; Punk.**

BIBLIOGRAPHY

Conrad, Peter. "Tommy, We Can Hear You." *Independent On Sunday.* (30 March 1997).

Cosgrove, Stuart. "The Zoot-Suit and Style Warfare." *History Workshop Journal.* 18 (Autumn 1984): 77–91.

de La Haye, Amy and Cathie Dingwall. *Surfers, Soulies, Skinheads, and Skaters: Street Styles from the Forties to the Nineties.* Woodstock, N.Y.: Overlook Press, 1996.

Graev, Nicole. "What's Next: MTA-Chic? Talks to the True Originators of Today's Fashions." *New York Sun,* (25 July 2002).

Haug, W. F. *Commodity Aesthetics, Ideology and Culture.* International General, 1987.

Lusane, Clarence. "Rap, Race, and Politics." *Race and Class: A Journal for Black and Third World Liberation* 35, no.1 (July-September 1993): 41–56.

Melly, George. *Revolt into Style: The Pop Arts.* Doubleday and Company, 1971.

Polhemus, Ted, and Lynn Procter. *Pop Styles.* London: Vermilion, 1984.

Porter, Charlie. "What a Riot." *The Guardian,* (6 July 2001).

Van Dyk Lewis

MUSLIN In the early twenty-first century muslin is an inexpensive, bleached or unbleached cotton plain-weave cloth. There is no direct connection of the name "muslin" to the earlier thin silk cloths of Mosul; rather, the name arose in the eighteenth century from the French word for foam (*mousse*), which seemed to convey the feel and texture of India's filmy cotton product. When introduced into Europe in the 1600s by the English and Dutch East India Companies, "muslin" denoted a soft, white, plain-weave cotton cloth produced in India, notably around Dacca where the constant, intense humidity eased the stress of the spinning and weaving processes on the fibers.

Muslin dress. This girl's dress, featuring a simple, princess-style cut and embroidered leaf vines, is made from sheer Indian cotton muslin fabric. AMERICAN COSTUME STUDIES. REPRODUCED BY PERMISSION.

Some muslins—their degrees of delicacy graphically identified in terms of spider webs, woven wind, and evening dew—were made from particularly fragile yarns. Less ethereal versions like *mulmul*, or mull, were sometimes embellished with embroidered and drawn-thread floral designs.

The classically-inspired white muslin dresses of the early nineteenth century are well-known, but during the eighteenth century, ladies wore muslin in the form of petticoats, aprons, and kerchiefs. French reformers like Jean-

Jacques Rousseau urged parents to dress their children in unrestrictive, washable cotton clothing better suited to their ages than the customary miniature-adult styles. Girls who grew up wearing loose muslin dresses became women who considered the *ingénue* habit worth continuing—undoubtedly encouraged by Marie Antoinette's scandalous example.

Although silks and heavier fabrics reclaimed fashion dominance by 1825, muslin continued in favor for young women's and children's dresses. Embroidered muslin accessories made pretty foils to mid-century wool, silk, and printed cotton garments. The first decade of the twentieth century saw a resurgence of enthusiasm for fine cotton dresses like those of a hundred years earlier—equally likely to be called muslin, mull, longcloth, nainsook, dimity, organdy, batiste, cambric, or lawn.

India muslins proceeded to undermine the dominance of domestic linen manufactures. At the end of the eighteenth century, European manufacturers were imitating the medium-weight India cottons and moving on to master fine ones. Delicate linen favorites like cambric and lawn increasingly came to be made of cotton instead, mainly because cotton was cheaper. In the 1830s the English exported striped and checked "muslin" for cheap clothing worn by American sailors who almost certainly would have disdained the dainty kind—an indication that utility weight domestic cotton cloth was already usurping the exotic name. By the 1870s, "muslin" was being touted for ladies' underwear, still the hard-wearing, sturdy item it had been when made of linen. Muslin has become known as a cheap, durable cloth suitable for pattern draping, upholstery, stage scenery, drop cloths and dust covers.

The world-changing influence of these imports culminated in a legacy of a few thin cotton fabrics, some of which bear names originally assigned to European linens. The once-evocative word "muslin" is now attached to an opaque, utilitarian cotton cloth that first entered the West simply designated as "calico," a name that now specifies a fairly substantial cotton fabric printed with tiny motifs.

See also **Cambric, Batiste, and Lawn.**

BIBLIOGRAPHY

Irwin, John, and P. R. Schwartz. *Studies in Indo-European Textile History.* Ahmedabad, India: Calico Museum of Textiles, 1966.

Montgomery, Florence. *Textiles in America.* New York: W. W. Norton and Co., 1984.

Paine, Sheila. *Chikan Embroidery: The Floral Whitework of India.* Aylesbury, U.K.: Shire Publications, Ltd., 1989.

Susan W. Greene

NAIL ART Beautiful nails are considered to be a precious gift to be treasured and cared for. In Greek mythology Eros is identified as the first manicurist. He cut the goddess Aphrodite's fingernails while she was sleeping and scattered them on the beaches of the earth. Seeing what had transpired, the fates collected the clippings and turned them into the semiprecious stone onyx—that is Greek for fingernail. In fact, human nails—the convex, hard horny plates covering the dorsal aspect of the fingertips and toes—have evolved from the primeval claw. In folkloric beliefs, the nails are often said to continue growing after death, temporarily evading mortal decay. Thus, long nails are characteristic of vampires, revenants, and others of "undead" status. The phenomenon is in fact due to the dehydration of the corpse which causes the skin around the nails to retract and shrink back, but the alarming effect of this particular aspect of decomposition has inspired countless morbid horror stories where sorry individuals who have been buried alive attempt to scratch their way out of the tomb. Nails, along with bones, hair, and teeth of the dead were, as Sir Thomas Browne noted in the seventeenth century, "the treasures of Old Sorcerers" and one of the oldest forms of poisoning was grated nail, which was slipped into an unsuspecting victim's food or wine. Even today people take care to disinfect a human scratch, perhaps because nails actually do contain a small percentage of arsenic.

The Origins of Manicuring

The practice of manicuring is itself extremely ancient. There is evidence that as far back as 4,000 years ago, manicures took place in southern Babylonia, and manicure instruments have been found in Egypt's royal tombs. The Romans painted their nails with a mixture of sheep fat and blood. Turkish women created a pink tint for the nails from boiled rose petals. Women in biblical times not only dyed their hair but also painted their fingernails and toenails as well as hands and feet with henna juice (as mentioned in the Song of Solomon), a practice that still forms part of Middle Eastern culture today. The custom of growing long nails relates to status, since it can preclude certain forms of manual labor. Chinese noblemen and women of the Ming Dynasty (1368–1644) were well known for their extraordinarily long fingernails, which were sometimes protected with gold and jewel-encrusted nail guards. Servants were required to feed, dress, and perform other personal chores for them so that they did not break a nail. The Chinese also used nail polish made from egg whites, beeswax, vegetable dyes, and Arabic gum.

In the Western Hemisphere colored nail polish was uncommon until the twentieth century. Instead, unstained hands with white and regularly formed nails were esteemed as part of a dominant aesthetic linking physical hygiene and moral purity. Etiquette guides from the 1800s recommend a little lemon juice or vinegar and water to whiten the nail tips and commercial products available at this time included nail polishers or buffers, crystal stones, emery boards, hand and cuticle creams, pearly white liquid, and several kinds of bleaching powders for the hands and nails. This apparent lack of adornment was an obvious indicator of wealth and enforced leisure. Emma Bovary's nails for instance are "scrubbed cleaner than Dieppe ivory and cut almond shape." Such fastidious treatment of the nails was in keeping with the anti-cosmetics stance, which professed a belief in the transparency of inner beauty and continued well into the early 1900s.

The Innovation of Nail Polish

Hollywood film did more than any other visual medium to popularize the wearing of nail polish in the West. Film actresses of the 1920s looked exotic, symbolized modernity, and flaunted nails that were painted with colorful glossy enamel that soon became commercially available. In a literal sense, the new lacquer was derived from the movies since cinematic film and nail polish originate from the same primary ingredient—nitrocellulose. One early method of making nail polish was to mix cleaned scraps of film with alcohol and castor oil and leave the mixture to soak overnight. The first tinted nail lacquers were produced in subtle shades of pink and had names like "rose," "ruby," "coral," and "natural" in an attempt both to downplay the chemical origins of the product and to overcome the monochrome format of contemporary advertising.

Deep color polishes like cardinal red were unavailable until the 1930s, when Charles Revson and his partners developed a method to add opaque pigments (rather than dyes) to polish so that it would coat the nails evenly.

Cutex brand advertisement. This "cute tomata" poster advertises a red nail color by Cutex. AP/WIDE WORLD PHOTOS. REPRODUCED BY PERMISSION.

Their company, Revlon Inc., still one of the leading producers of nail polish, became particularly famous for its legendary 1950s "Fire and Ice" advertising campaign. These ads for a range of matching nail enamels and lipsticks were groundbreaking in their use of dramatic visuals and clever text and are considered to be among the first to overtly link cosmetics with sexuality. A typical headline ran "For you who love to flirt with fire . . . Who dare to skate on thin ice." Like much cosmetic advertising of the period, Revlon's marketing exploited a range of connotations of nail decoration. Painted nails were part of the self-scrutinizing feminine masquerade that was dependent on male approbation, but they were also associated with increasingly liberal ideas about a pleasure-seeking modern woman.

Nail Art Today

The last few decades have seen further innovations and fashions in Western nail art. Manufacturers have created quick-drying polishes targeted at women with active lifestyles, and the range of colors available has multiplied. From the 1980s onward brightly colored polish has been available in unusual colors ranging from ice-cream pastels to gunmetal gray, along with polishes that contain built-in decorations such as glitter or tiny metallic stars. In 1995 Chanel brought these colors firmly into the mainstream when it launched a deep black-red polish. "Vamp" continued the Hollywood connection when the actress Uma Thurman in the film *Pulp Fiction* wore it that same year. Priced at $15 a bottle, Chanel's polish helped to create a market for high-priced nail products and paved the way for the success of companies like Urban Decay and Hard Candy—which made huge profits from manufacturing odd experimental colors for nails. In 1998 the American Jenai Lane created "mood nail polish" which is designed to change color according to body temperature—in reflection of one's mood.

Over $6 billion is spent on services in American nail salons every year and the art of the manicurist has become increasingly prized worldwide. Men as well as women are now regular clients since well-kept hands are considered to be an important part of a professional image. New technologies have also resulted in more realistic-looking acrylic nails and nail extensions, which are attached with glue adhesives and glue tabs. At the fantasy end of the market, fingernails and toenails have become a natural canvas for the expression of creative imagination. Nail art is often stunningly elaborate—nails can be sculpted, stenciled, pierced, and of course painted with intricate designs. Competitions such as the Nail Olympics held annually in Las Vegas honor the art of the manicurist—as a latter-day miniaturist painter—and indicate the growing professionalization of the industry. In Britain and the United States, contemporary nail art resonates particularly with black culture. In this context elaborately painted nails are seen to offer a highly decorative alternative to Eurocentric ideals of beauty.

See also **Cosmetics, Western; Cosmetics, Non-Western.**

BIBLIOGRAPHY

Blackmore, Colin, and Sheila Jennett. *The Oxford Companion to the Body.* Oxford: Oxford University Press, 2001.

Browne, Thomas. *Urne Buriall and The Garden of Cyrus.* Edited by John Carter. London and New York: Cambridge University Press, 1958 (originally published in 1658).

Corson, Richard. *Fashions in Makeup from Ancient to Modern Times.* London: Peter Owen, 1972.

Flaubert, Gustave. *Madame Bovary.* London: Penguin Books, 1985 (originally published in French, 1856).

Mulvey, Kate, and Melissa Richards. *Decades of Beauty: The Changing Image of Women 1890s–1990s.* London: Hamlyn, 1998.

Peiss, Kathy. *Hope in a Jar: The Making of America's Beauty Culture.* New York: Henry Holt and Company, Inc., 1998.

Sherrow, Victoria. *For Appearance's Sake: The Historical Encyclopaedia of Good Looks, Beauty and Grooming.* Westport, Conn.: Oryx Press, 2001.

Tobias, Andrew. *Fire and Ice: The Story of Charles Revson—The Man Who Built the Revlon Empire.* New York: William Morrow and Company, Inc., 1976.

Katherine Forde

NAPPING Napping is a raised surface on a textile that is a result of brushing loose staple fibers out of the fabric structure. It may also refer to the surface texture on pile-weave fabrics. The nap makes the fabric feel softer and traps air that serves as insulation. The nap is typically brushed in one direction on fabrics such as corduroy, velvet, velveteen, and flannel. Light reflects off the surface of the fabric according to the direction of the nap and produces unique aesthetic qualities on pile-weave fabrics. This aspect is important in garment construction, because if the garment pattern pieces are not laid out correctly, the end product will appear to be constructed out of fabrics of different colors.

Napping is the finishing process that raises the fibers on a fabric to produce a mat of fiber ends, or nap. It may be used on knit or woven textiles made of staple fibers, such as wool and cotton, or with fibers cut to staple length and spun into yarns such as silk, rayon, and polyester. Napped fabrics are usually made with loosely spun yarns in the filling direction so that the fibers can easily be pulled out to form the nap. Historically, napping was done with teasels—the flower heads of thistlelike plants that have many sharp, hooklike ends. Except in the case of some fine wools that are still napped by hand, napping in the early 2000s was executed with machines that mimicked the early process. The early twenty-first century napping machines involve feeding the fabric through rollers that are covered with heavy fabric that is embedded with small, brushlike wires.

Napping can be done on one or both sides of the fabric. Napping may improve durability, hide defects, or obscure the weave of the cloth. Napped fabrics may also have increased pilling, abrade more easily even with care, or flatten with wear. Common fabrics that are napped are wool and cotton flannel, flannel-back satin, polyester fleece, flannelette, and outing flannel. Sueded fabrics are also napped through a process that includes an additional step to shear the nap close to the surface of the fabric to produce a smooth, soft finish.

See also **Corduroy; Flannel; Jersey; Velvet; Wool.**

BIBLIOGRAPHY

American Fabrics Encyclopedia of Textiles. 2nd ed. Englewood Cliffs, N.J.: Prentice Hall, 1972.

Emery, Irene. *The Primary Structures of Fabric: An Illustrated Classification.* Washington, D.C.: The Textile Museum, 1966.

Gioello, Debbie Ann. *Understanding Fabrics: From Fiber to Finished Cloth.* New York: Fairchild Publishing, 1982.

Humphries, Mary. *Fabric Glossary.* 3d ed. Upper Saddle River, N.J.: Pearson Prentice Hall, 2004.

Kadolph, Sara J., and Anna L. Langford. *Textiles.* 9th ed. Englewood Cliffs, N.J.: Prentice Hall, 2002.

Linton, George Edward. *The Modern Textile and Apparel Dictionary.* 4th ed. Plinfield, N.J.: Textile Book Service, 1973.

Simpson, John A., and Edmund Weiner. *Oxford English Dictionary.* 2nd ed. Vol. 3. Oxford: Clarendon, 1989.

Wingate, Isabel, and June Mohler. *Textile Fabrics and Their Selection.* 8th ed. Englewood Cliffs, N.J.: Prentice Hall, 1984.

Marie Botkin

NATIVE AMERICAN DRESS. *See* America, North: History of Indigenous Peoples' Dress.

NAUTICAL STYLE Nautical refers to the sea and to ships. There is a romantic image of life on the sea reflected in a navy jacket with brass buttons, a crisp white sailor's uniform, a sou'wester hat and yellow slicker, or a fisherman's sweater. All sailors and those whose occupation depends on the sea deal with the unpredictable nature and allure of the sea. Protection from the salt water, wind, and sun is a primary consideration along with allowing the mobility needed to perform the duties of their job on a ship among the ropes, nets, and sails. Historic traditions in nautical dress continue to influence modern nautical apparel.

Occupational Sailing

The "Jack-tar" describes a sailor of sixteenth century Europe who wore a waist-length tarred leather jacket and hat for water protection. To facilitate movement on the ships, loose breeches called "slops" and tunics of canvas or coarse linen were worn. The slops were often striped or red in color. In addition, a tar-coated canvas petticoat called a tarpaulin was often worn over the slops during rough weather. A neckerchief and knitted woolen cap provided additional protection for the head. The tarred jacket has evolved into the classic pea coat of today, while the tarpaulin remained prevalent with fishermen through the nineteenth century.

With the birth of an official Navy uniform in England during the mid-eighteenth century, there was a more noticeable distinction between the occupational dress of a sailor and a fisherman. Blue and white with gold and silver trim for officers was the designated color palette for the Navy. This was the origination of the term "navy blue." Later in the century, American-tar wore a short blue or black-tarred jacket, cropped trousers with a knitted striped shirt, and neckerchief. Sailor hats were now made of oilcloth, a recent innovation in waterproofing that treated cotton or linen with boiled linseed oil. The oilcloth was also used in bib trousers and jackets, their yellow color serving as a safety feature for sailors who were blown overboard. A knitted wool gansey or jersey became popular during the mid-eighteenth century. These tightly knitted sweaters button on one shoulder and were patterned to represent the town of the sailor. Solid colors were reserved for naval officers, while the sailors wore stripes. The jerseys were often embroidered by the sailors with the name of the ship on the front chest.

Naval uniforms continued to evolve during the nineteenth century with the use of the sailor collar and black neckerchief that mimicked the wide collar points and black cravat worn by fashionable gentlemen. Sailors maintained variations of the blue waist-length jacket and white trousers while officers wore a gold-trimmed coat that was short in the front with tails in the back. Twenty-first-century naval officers have a white dress uniform of jacket and trousers with brass buttons and epaulets, while their service uniform is built of a navy blue jacket and pants with white shirt and black tie. The enlisted sailor wears white trousers and a tunic with a sailor collar and black tie. It is affectionately referred to as a "monkey suit" (Wilcox 1963, p. 82). Present-day commercial fishermen consider function and safety with their use of insulated layers of fleece and waterproof hooded-jackets and pants. Orange and yellow gear provides good visibility in case of a water rescue.

Recreational and Competitive Sailing

Traditional sailing garments have had a large influence on recreational and sport sailing apparel. Sailing as a competitive sport is marked by the first international yachting event, the Hundred Guineas Cup, in 1851, and its Olympic debut in 1896. The term yacht evolved from the Dutch "jaghtschiffs," which were boats designed to chase pirates. Yacht clubs developed to encourage and support the sport of sailing. Dress for most active recreational sailors needs to provide the same function and mobility required of professional sailors. Navy blue, white, red, and yellow are garment colors associated with both professional and recreational sailors. Navy jackets with brass buttons are a popular image, borrowed from the Navy, for the more social yacht-club member.

Traditional sailing garments have also been a popular influence for generations of children's garments. Sailor suits are a classic design for both boys and girls that began during the mid-nineteenth century when Queen Victoria began dressing her children in the style. It spread quickly through Europe and America, continuing to be a classic children's style in the twenty-first century along with the middy blouse.

Women in Sailing

Women have historically been on shore professionally until 1942 when the U.S. Navy began to allow women to serve in positions on ships. Their uniforms were similar in style to the men's with the addition of a skirt. A 1931 *Vogue* cover shows a woman in full bell-bottom navy slacks with a red, white, and blue striped top designed for lounging rather than rough seas. A later 1956 image shows a woman on a small dinghy wearing cropped denim jeans, a white "sloppy joe," white deck shoes, and red bandanna on her head. This outfit is intended to be comfortable and functional, but designed only for good sailing conditions. Women have dramatically increased their skill and participation in competitive sailing. Dawn Riley led the first all-women's America's Cup team in 1995 and was the first female member of the winning America3 team in 1992.

New Developments in Sailing

The garments worn by competitive sailors in the twenty-first century have the same requirements of protection from the elements and good mobility. However, innovative fiber and textile developments can now better protect the body, increase health and safety, and improve the wearer's sailing efficiency. Though wool has traditionally been the fiber used for insulation and water protection, apparel-layering systems take advantage of new fiber technology to help maintain the body's thermal balance. The first layer uses olefin to wick away moisture from the skin, while polyester fleece acts as an insulating layer to trap body heat. The outer-layer fabrics, such as Gore-Tex, provide a waterproof, yet breathable barrier from water and wind. The use of spandex, a fiber with stretch, in the first two layers allows for garments that fit closer to the body while allowing a greater freedom of mobility.

See also **Jacket; Military Style; Rainwear.**

BIBLIOGRAPHY

Cunnington, Phillis, and Catherine Lucas. *Occupational Costume in England from the Eleventh Century to 1914.* New York: Barnes and Noble, 1967.

Lee-Potter, Charlie. *Sportswear in Vogue since 1910.* New York: Abbeville Press, 1984.

Wilcox, R. T. *Five Centuries of American Costume.* New York: Charles Scribner's Sons, 1963.

Internet Resources

Naval Influences on Boys' Clothing. Naval Uniforms and Boys' Clothing. Available from <http://histclo.hispeed.com/youth/ mil-navy.html>.

Olympic History: Sailing. Available from <http://cbs.sportsline.com/u/olympics/2000/history/sailing.htm>.

Elizabeth K. Bye

NECKLACES AND PENDANTS A necklace is a form of jewelry worn suspended around the neck. It is most commonly made in flexible forms such as a chain, as a string of beads, pearls, gemstones, or other natural materials, or made of a more inflexible band of metal embellished with gemstones, pearls, beads, or other techniques such as engraving, filigree, repoussé, granulation, for example. Lengths of necklaces vary, and specific types related to extremes in length range from a short choker or dog collar necklace that fits right around the main portion of the neck to a longer neck chain or string of beads called a *sautoir*, sometimes worn hanging down to or past the waist.

As with other pieces of jewelry, the necklace has been an important site of decoration for the body but also of communication for the person. As valued material culture, necklaces communicate wealth, power, affiliation, prestige, levels of resources and skill, and elements of identity and position. The durability of jewelry like necklaces made of metal, glass beads, or gemstones provides an opportunity to appreciate and understand the technology, cultural practices, artistry, and aesthetics of other cultures and distant time periods.

A simple necklace made from a string of local organic materials such as shells, teeth, or bone beads is one of the forms of jewelry adopted by early cultures around the world. More precious materials from farther away were also valued for early necklaces, frequently in the form of beads, such as those of Mediterranean red coral found in a Neolithic burial in the Alps (circa 4200–3400 B.C.E.). Other early types of necklace included the torc or torque, an ancient Celtic neckpiece made of twisted metal, and the *lunula*, a flat, crescent-shaped and engraved variation of the torc found in Bronze Age Ireland and Scotland (circa 1800–1500 B.C.E.).

Necklaces were made to display appropriate decorative and stylistic features through each period and from region to region. Each period also has some influence upon those following, and revivals of styles, such as classical Greek and Roman necklaces or Egyptian beadwork collars, are prevalent. During the Middle Ages, jewelry became a more integral element of dress, and necklaces replaced brooches as the primary form of jewelry in the late Gothic and early Renaissance periods. Necklaces set with gemstones and heavy gold chain necklaces with pendants were in style as a distinction of wealth and social

Remembrance locket. The heart-shaped locket holds a small piece of ribbon from a September 11, 2002, remembrance ceremony. Lockets carry personal mementos are are usually worn for sentimental reasons. AP/WIDE WORLD PHOTOS. REPRODUCED BY PERMISSION.

status from the fourteenth and fifteenth centuries through the sixteenth and early seventeenth centuries.

Trends for wearing necklaces have for the most part followed the style of necklines in European and American fashionable dress. In other words, as necklines were lowered, more, as well as more elaborate, necklaces were seen. But this does not necessarily mean that necklaces were not worn when necklines were high. For example, a carcanet is a type of wide, bejeweled or enameled gold link necklace that resembles a collar. It was worn by men as a status symbol in the fifteenth through seventeenth centuries, encircling the base of the neck over a man's doublet and under the elaborate lace ruff, or worn with gold chains wrapped around the neck, or hanging over the shoulders down the front of bodices and doublets.

The necklace was a central piece in the eighteenth-century parure or matching set of jewelry for a woman, which also included brooch, earrings, bracelets, and a pendant or tiara. The necklace was meant to be worn as evening wear with a lowered décolletage bodice, while higher necklines of daywear included the brooch or the pendant instead. This concept of a matching set lasted through the early twentieth century until dress became more casual and when affordable but still attractive costume jewelry became widely available. New materials such as plastic and new technologies related to mass production and mass media have greatly expanded the social repertoire. Necklaces in the late twentieth century were

styled to follow both fashion and popular culture trends, but also to meet various needs for women's dress based on occasion, taste, or preference, and levels of fashion-ability and affordability.

Certain materials have long held reign for necklaces throughout the Western history of dress, including gold, diamonds, and pearls. The diamond necklace is one of the most expensive symbols of wealth, glamour, and prestige throughout history. Pearls were the material of choice for Roman women, and revivals of Classical period details seen in Renaissance or early-eighteenth-century neoclassical dress have included strings of pearls. The pearl was also beloved by Elizabeth I in the sixteenth century, sparking a trend for long pearl necklaces draped and pinned over elaborate stomachers. In the mid-twentieth century, the short strand of pearls became a classic gift for young American and British women on their sixteenth birthday, and it remains a popular choice for women's professional and business dress ensembles and bridal costume. The creation of imitation and synthetic diamonds and cultured pearls equalizes to some degree the concept of preciousness in jewelry and makes the look of these prestigious materials available to a wide and diverse audience today.

Both men and women throughout Western history wore necklaces until the eighteenth century, when they became primarily a feminine purview. However, American popular culture influences such as the 1960s hippie "love beads" and the 1970s disco dance craze made it more fashionable for European and American men to wear necklaces as part of popular fashion. These include gold chains, some strung with amulets or charms like the gold Italian horn or a gold cross. This trend became very prominent in the late twentieth-century hip hop music scene, when ostentatious platinum and gold chains hung with diamond-encrusted pendants displayed, as conspicuous consumption, the newly acquired wealth for African American men. Necklaces for men in certain occupations never went out of style, and higher ranks of clergy, such as Roman Catholic or Anglican bishops and cardinals have, since the Renaissance, continued to wear elaborate and expensive neck chains with large hanging pectoral crosses or crucifixes as part of their ecclesiastical regalia.

Within the broad style category of ethnic jewelry, necklaces have today transcended their original or traditional use by ethnic groups around the world and are collected and worn by European Americans of both genders as fashion or adornment regardless of, or perhaps even in reference to, their original indigenous functions or meanings. However, throughout history, the necklace as indigenous tribal or non-Western ethnic jewelry has been and continues to be a significant expression of all of the uses and meanings of jewelry outlined in this volume. In many cultures, the necklace has taken precedence over other forms of jewelry as the most important piece for adornment and communication in expressing identity or position. In addition, ethnic necklaces made from precious materials such as gold and silver, or precious organic materials like coral are frequently the repositories of a woman's or family's wealth. For example, in many nomadic cultures around the world, particularly in Central Asia, North Africa, and throughout the Middle East, heavy silver necklaces, perhaps including expensive elements such as amber or coral beads and incorporating silver coins, are portable "savings accounts" or forms of wealth and currency that could be converted to money when required. The heavy silver collar-type necklaces of the Hmong and Hmong-American ethnic group, originally from Southeast Asia and now predominantly living in the United States as political refugees, may include hundreds of silver coins and several pounds of silver metal. These necklaces serve a primary function of displaying the family's monetary wealth when worn by young women in courting rituals at Hmong New Year's celebrations. Gold necklaces, among other items of jewelry such as bangles or earrings, are purchased by women in Asia and India, for example, as their income warrants. These are put aside for future needs as investment and savings and brought out for display at weddings, for instance, especially when worn by the daughter of the family as a bride. In many instances, gold or silver jewelry is the only form of wealth that a woman may have access to. In another example, expensive Italian coral beads are collected and made into necklaces by ethnic groups in West Africa, such as the Kalabari Ijo in the Niger River delta. Worn by both men and women at ceremonial functions, these necklaces are important markers of identity but also a significant vehicle for displaying family wealth and prestige.

Pendants

A pendant is an ornament that is suspended from another piece of jewelry such as a necklace, neck chain, ribbon, brooch, bracelet, or earring. Pendants take many forms including large gems or pearls, cameos, crosses, lockets, amulets, or watches. Amulets as pendants have been most significant as one of the first forms of prehistoric jewelry. As pendants, amulets retain an unprecedented popularity in the early twenty-first century as good luck charms, as talismans, and as protection from the evil eye or any number of other perceived disasters or supernatural forces. Pendants are frequently made to be detachable so they might be used on different necklaces, or made with a pin-back so they might also be worn as a brooch.

The cross or cruciform shape is an important type of pendant in religious and amuletic categories of jewelry that has been worn since the development of early Christianity. It can carry ornamental, protective, and devotional or religious meanings. Wearing a cross can visually signify a person's religious affiliation, and different shapes of crosses can symbolize different branches or subcults of Christianity. A crucifix is a type of cross showing Christ's crucified body, worn predominantly today by religious clergy. Crosses have been made from

Amulet pendant, Thailand. This rectangular Thai amulet serves as a prayer box. Amulets as pendants were very popular in the early twenty-first century. © DAVE G. HOUSER/CORBIS. REPRODUCED BY PERMISSION.

various precious and nonprecious materials to suit a wide range of styles, tastes, and economic standings. Crosses in the Middle Ages and Renaissance were made as reliquary pendants to hold what was believed to be a relic of the true crucifix. In contemporary Western Christianity, small gold crosses on a chain are important gifts for a child's christening or first communion. Crosses have also been worn as charms or amulets to ward off evil or to protect the wearer from disease. For example, small gold crosses made with coral beads are worn in southern Italy today as an amulet that combines the amuletic protection of red coral against the evil eye with the symbolism of Christianity. This cross is seen as more socially acceptable than wearing the red or gold horn amulet called a *corno*. In the late twentieth century the cross has been appropriated as a trendy sub- or popular culture motif worn without religious overtones or with a sense of defiance against its traditional symbolism. Other types of personal pendants that might be worn to signify religious affiliation include the Roman Catholic saints' medals, the Jewish Star of David, the Islamic Hand of Fatima, the Hindu Om mantra symbol, or the phylactery or amulet case worn in Jewish, Islamic, and Tibetan Buddhist religions. This last example is a small decorated metal box enclosing a prayer or scripture passage written on paper.

A locket is a small pendant in the form of a flat, round, or oval case with a hinged cover, worn usually on a neck chain or suspended from a necklace of various styles. It is worn as a sentimental piece, meant to hold a memento such as a lock of hair, a photograph, or, before the invention of photography, a miniature portrait painted on ivory. They are made from various metals and with diverse techniques, often set with gemstones and engraved or enameled. Early lockets were worn as devotional or reliquary jewelry, made in the Middle Ages and

ENCYCLOPEDIA OF CLOTHING AND FASHION   **443**

Edith Gould wearing strands of pearls. Necklaces are made out of many materials, from the pearls shown here to beads and gemstones, and vary in length from the short choker to a longer strain called a *sautoir*. © CORBIS. REPRODUCED BY PERMISSION.

Renaissance to hold a saint's relic. In the sixteenth century, monarchs like Elizabeth I often presented gifts of lockets holding their portrait to favored courtiers. One famous example of a commemorative type of locket is Elizabeth's "Armada Jewel" (circa 1588) with a cast gold and enameled profile portrait of her on the front and an enameled depiction of Noah's Ark on the back, made to celebrate England's victory over the Spanish Armada. Lockets were very popular in the eighteenth and nineteenth centuries, and this continued into the twentieth after photography was developed. Nineteenth-century Victorian lockets were an important betrothal gift or sentimental gift of personal devotion. Lockets were frequently made as watchcases for men and worn suspended on a watch chain or fob.

See also **Brooches and Pins; Costume Jewelry; Jewelry.**

BIBLIOGRAPHY

Borel, France. *The Splendor of Ethnic Jewelry: From the Colette and Jean-Pierre Ghysels Collection.* Translated by I. Mark Paris. New York: Harry N. Abrams, 1994.

Evans, Joan. *A History of Jewellery 1100–1870.* London: Faber and Faber, 1970.

Gregorietti, Guido. *Jewelry Through the Ages.* Translated by Helen Lawrence. New York: American Heritage Press, 1969.

Kuntzsch, Ingrid. *A History of Jewels and Jewellery.* Leipzig: Edition Leipzig, 1979.

Mack, John, ed. *Ethnic Jewellery.* New York: Harry N. Abrams, 1988.

Mascetti, Daniela, and Amanda Triossi. *The Necklace from Antiquity to the Present.* New York: Harry N. Abrams, 1997.

Newman, Harold. *An Illustrated Dictionary of Jewelry.* London: Thames and Hudson, Inc., 1981.

Tait, Hugh, ed. *Seven Thousand Years of Jewellery.* London: British Museum, 1986.

Susan J. Torntore

NECKTIES AND NECKWEAR Though the origins of wearing cloth tied around the neck lie embedded in antiquity (Chaille 2001), most scholars concur that it was the Thirty Years' War (1618–1648) that cemented the practice within European cultures. Fought between Sweden and France on one side and the Hapsburg Empire on the other, the conflict introduced French soldiers to the loose-tied neckerchiefs of Croatian soldiers, which some continued to wear once they had returned home.

Nevertheless, disagreement shrouds the etymology of the word "cravat," a derivative of the French *cravate*, which denotes modern neckties, men's scarves, and neckbows. While some sources—including the Oxford English Dictionary—make a direct link between *cravate* and *croate*, others are more circumspect, looking instead to the Turkish *kyrabàc*, the Hungarian *korbàcs*, and the French *cravache*, all of which relate to long, slender or whiplike objects (Mosconi and Villarosa 1985).

Linguistic roots aside, there is consensus that 1650 was the key point at which neckwear became a distinctive feature of western men's dress. It has been suggested that its popularity was further enhanced by a climatic factor known as the "Maunder minimum," which saw temperatures dip especially low between 1645 and 1705 (Chaille 1994).

The Battle of Steinkirk in 1692 introduced the "Steinkirk" to fashionable Europeans. Consisting of a long scarflike cravat with ends of fringe or lace that were looped through the buttonhole of the jacket (Fink and Mao 1999), it was also popular with women who would sew buttonholes into their gowns to accommodate the loose ends, or simply tuck them into the laces of their corsets (Chaille 1994). The Steinkirk had a continuing presence in portraiture long after its real-life popularity had waned, for artists such as Joshua Reynolds and Thomas Gainsborough often painted their subjects wearing the attire of their predecessors (Gibbings 1990).

By the early eighteenth century the soft flamboyance of the Steinkirk was replaced by yet another style with military origins. Popularized by French and German foot soldiers at the end of the seventeenth century, by 1700 the stock had been adopted by civilians (Colle 1974). Originally consisting of a piece of white muslin folded into a narrow band, wound once or twice around the neck and fastened at the neck with tapes, buttons, or a detachable buckle (Hart 1998), the stock developed into a simple high collar stiffened with horsehair, whale-bone, pig bristle, card, or even wood covered in cloth (Gibbings 1990). While it did impart a stiff, formal posture, it was ultimately an uncomfortable and unhealthy style because it restricted the throat (Gibbings 1990). However, stylistic formality evolved into a softer, more decorative style when black ribbons used to tie the hair back were brought to the front and tied in a bow known as a solitaire, creating a contrast with the white stock beneath it (Fink and Mao 1999).

The next significant development came in the 1770s, championed by a group of young English aristocrats dubbed the Macoronis. Influenced by styles they had seen while travelling in Italy, they took to wearing white cravats with voluminous bows (Chaille 1994). In France, in the 1790s, young men known as the *Incroyables* (or Unbelievables) displayed their contempt for sartorial conventions by wearing clothing with exaggerated proportions, including huge cravats consisting of fabric wound around the neck up to ten times (Fink and Mao 1999).

The extravagance of the late 1700s gave way to a quest for simple elegance in the early nineteenth century, exemplified by dandyism in general and George Bryan Brummell (1778–1840) in particular. The key to "Beau" Brummell's style lay in understatement. Though decidedly middle-class in origin, he attained an aristocratic air through an obsessive emphasis on the cut, detail, and refinement of his clothing. Immaculate, starched cravats were central to his self-presentation and he is said to have spent hours perfecting the art of knotting, pleating, folding, and arranging them (Gibbings 1990). The popularity of cravats at this time gave rise to publications that detailed ways of tying them. Published in 1818, *Neckclothitania* presented 12 styles, *L'Art de se mettre sa cravate* described 32, and *L'Art de la toilette* outlined 72.

Around the time of Brummell's death in 1840, cravats became politicized as proponents of white cravats—affiliated with traditionalism—took on those who favored black cravats, which were associated with liberal politics (Chaille 1994). Ultimately, it was the black stock and cravat, made popular by the English monarch George IV (who reigned from 1820 to 30) that triumphed, although red ones—briefly fashionable with French and German revolutionaries in 1848—never gained much of a following in English society (Chaille 1994).

As the nineteenth century progressed, high-buttoned jackets became popular, making large, complicated cravats difficult to accommodate. Moreover, as increasing numbers of men joined the office-based workforce, few had the time to spend on the knotting and arranging of

Portrait of Robespierre wearing cravat. In the 1770s, English and French aristocrats began wearing extravagant neck bows and voluminous cravats. The trend died out by the early nineteenth century. © Archivo Iconografico, S.A./Corbis. Reproduced by permission.

neckwear. While ready-made neckwear may have offered convenience, the higher echelons of English society remained disdainful of such practices (Hart 1998). Yet the growing diversification of the workforce, prompted by the industrial revolution, fostered a proliferation of neckwear styles by the late 1800s.

Ultimately, the cravat of the nineteenth century gave rise to four main styles: the bow tie, scarves and neckerchiefs, the Ascot, and the four-in-hand or long tie (Hart 1998). Developments in photography since the mid-nineteenth century have allowed costume historians to examine neckwear from this period onward in detail, and nineteenth-century visiting cards—often showing just the head and shoulders—have proved an invaluable resource to researchers (Ettinger 1998).

Evolving from some of the popular Regency styles, the bow-tie diminished in size so that by the end of the nineteenth century, two dominant shapes were recognizable: the butterfly and the bat's wing (Fink and Mao 1999), both of which have an ongoing presence in men's attire even today, but especially in the context of formal wear.

Scarves and neckerchiefs, by contrast, tend to be associated with the working classes who originally wore them out of necessity. Popular with both men and women

Neckties on display. A woman arranges U.S. Polo neckties at a shop in Shengzhou, China, in 2003. While not as popular as they once were, neckties are still a common sight at the office and on formal occasions. Hundreds of millions of neckties are produced in Shengzhou every year to help feed this demand. AP/WIDE WORLD PHOTOS. REPRODUCED BY PERMISSION.

and typified by a square shape folded into a triangle, scarves may be knotted in dozens of ways to protect and decorate the throat (Mosconi and Villarosa 1985).

Similar to the Gordian cravat of the early nineteenth century, the Ascot became popular in the 1880s when the upper middle classes of English society started to wear it to the Royal Ascot race and other outdoor events (Hart 1998). Initially made of plain silk, the Ascot had square-ended blades that were crossed over the shirtfront and held in place with a cravat pin. Many were sold ready-made in very bright colors (Gibbings 1990).

The long tie or vertical tie originated as young men's sporting attire in the 1850s, but became widespread within a decade (Fink and Mao 1999). More than one explanation is given for its alternative name, the four-in-hand. Some believe it to be a reference to the Four-in-Hand Club, a London gentlemen's club whose members tied their neckwear using the four-in-hand knot (Fink and Mao 1999), while others suggest that its knot and trailing ends resembled the reins of four-horse carriages driven by members of the English aristocracy (Chaille 1994). Early versions of this style of tie were sim-

ple rectangular strips of material with identical square ends that reached no lower than the sternum as waistcoats were usually worn (Chaille 1994). Practical because it neither impeded movement nor came undone, it was adopted both by workers and by the leisure classes as high, stiff collars gave way to soft, turned-down ones.

As the Victorian middle class grew and male attire became increasingly homogenous (dark, somber coat and jacket and trousers in a limited range of cuts), ties became a signpost of social status (Gibbings 1990). Evolution of the club, school, and regimental ties meant that those in the know were able to identify a man's social ranking based primarily on the color and pattern of the tie they wore. Even in the twenty-first century, some sectors of British society still believe that the stripes on one's tie define an individual to himself and to others (Sells 1998), and the expression "old school tie" persists, reflecting membership of a specific, privileged class.

Although women had worn cravats and scarves in various forms alongside their male contemporaries primarily out of coquetry (Chaille 1994), it was in the late nineteenth and early twentieth century that neckwear took on a politicized significance. The evolution of Rational Dress encouraged women to adopt attire that not only allowed greater freedom of movement but also was essentially more masculine in appearance (Gibbings 1990). As the women's suffrage movement gained momentum, the tie—when worn by women—became a symbol of independence and feminist convictions (Chaille 1994).

Already established as the most popular form of men's neckwear in the early part of the twentieth century, the four-in-hand's success was cemented commercially by an American named Jesse Langsdorf. He improved the drape, elasticity, and wear of ties by cutting them diagonally (at 45 degrees) on the bias instead of cutting the fabric conventionally in an up-and-down direction. The process of constructing a tie from three separate pieces of material, known as Resilient Construction, was patented by Langsdorf's company, Resilio, in 1924 (Ettinger 1998). Though knitted ties, or Derbys, attained a degree of popularity in the early part of the twentieth century, Resilient Construction essentially brought the evolution of the modern necktie to a halt (Chaille 1994). Since then tie widths have fluctuated from two to five inches, although the usual width continues to be three to three-and-a-half inches (Fink and Mao 1999).

With shape and dimension more or less fixed since the 1920s, mass-production methods ensured that ties were readily available to men from all socioeconomic groups. With the onset of the Great Depression in the United States during the late 1920s and early 1930s, business slowed down; however, the widespread popularity of cinema contributed to a boom in tie sales as Americans sought to emulate their film idols (Ettinger 1998). Images of actresses such as Marlene Dietrich and Katharine Hepburn wearing ties remain some of the most iconic and memorable in cinematic history, demonstrating the potent impact of a woman wearing what had become a quintessentially male item (König 2001). In the United Kingdom, meanwhile, society figures such as the Duke of Windsor were influential, and the Windsor Knot became a popular method of tie-knotting (Chaille 1994).

As the twentieth century unfolded, variety in neckwear continued primarily through the changing use of fabric and color. Developments in textile technology, particularly throughout the 1930s and 1940s, meant that traditional fibers such as silk, wool, and cotton gave way to synthetic yarns including rayon, nylon, and polyester as they were cheaper and therefore well-suited for mass production (Goldberg 1997). Yet tie aficionados would argue that woven silk, possibly blended with wool, continues to be the most suitable fabric for a tie because of the "hand" that it gives (Chaille 2001).

Though wartime rationing in Europe during and after World War II (1939–1945) put a hold on nonessential manufacturing, in the United States, the tie market flourished with stripes, plaids, and other patterns making an appearance (Ettinger 1998). In the postwar years, however, men on both sides of the Atlantic sought flamboyance, leading to a proliferation of brightly colored ties known as the Bold Look (Goldberg 1997). Popular designs in the 1950s included those with an Art Deco influence, flower and leaf prints, wildlife themes, and "Wild West" designs (Ettinger 1998).

In the latter half of the twentieth century, ties ceased to be an essential component of everyday menswear, and were no longer seen as the definitive signifier of respectability. As youth culture liberated young men from the sartorial conventions of their parents, the tie became an occasional item to be worn at school (by girls as well as boys), work, and formal events (Chaille 2001). Having said this, distinctive styles, such as skinny "mod" ties and wide "kipper" ties of the 1960s, have earned their place in fashion history, complementing the stylistic characteristics of the suits they accompanied (Goldberg 1997). Despite a global drift toward casual dress, it seems likely that neckwear, and specifically the tie, will continue to have a presence in men's dress.

See also **Dandyism; Europe and America: History of Dress (400–1900 C.E.); Military Style; Sports Jacket.**

BIBLIOGRAPHY

Chaille, François. *The Book of Ties.* Paris: Flammarion, 1994.

———. *The Little Book of Ties.* Paris: Flammarion, 2001.

Colle, Doriece. *Collars, Stocks, Cravats: A History and Costume Dating Guide to Civilian Men's Neckpieces, 1655–1900.* London: White Lion Publishers Ltd., 1974.

Ettinger, Roseann. *20th Century Neckties: Pre-1955.* Atglen: Schiffer Publishing Ltd., 1998.

Fink, Thomas, and Yong Mao. *The 85 Ways to Tie a Tie: The Science and Aesthetics of Tie Knots.* London: Fourth Estate, 1999.

Gibbings, Sarah. *The Tie: Trends and Traditions.* London: Studio Editions, 1990.

Goldberg, Michael Jay. *The Ties That Bind: Neckties, 1945–1975.* Atglen: Schiffer Publishing Ltd., 1997.

Hart, Avril. *Ties.* London: V&A Publications, 1998.

König, Anna. "Tie Me Up, Tie Me Down." *The Guardian* 31 (August 2001).

Mosconi, Davide, and Riccardo Villarosa. *The Book of Ties.* London: Tie Rack Ltd., 1985.

Sells, Christopher. *Ties of Distinction.* Atglen: Schiffer Publishing Ltd., 1998.

Anna König

NEEDLES The needle is the distinctive tool of the Upper Paleolithic period that began about 40,000 years ago. The oldest known needles with eyes date from the Gravettian period, about 25,000 years ago. The needle is one of the earliest survivors of the explosion of invention that the textile archaeologist Elizabeth Wayland Barber called the String Revolution. Paleolithic needles made of animal bones, antlers, and tusks helped make possible the extension of human settlement into cooler regions after the Ice Age (until about 10,000 to 12,000 years ago), and they also were used for fashioning fishing nets and carrying bags. There is evidence that by the Gravettian, needles were used not only to stitch hides together for warmth but also for sewing and decorating textiles for social and erotic display. The needle was associated thus closely with humanity's new conceptual skills and expressions, including fashion itself.

Paleolithic needles had grooves rather than eyes to hold sinew or fiber. Some cognitive psychologists have suggested a progression in thought and design from the awl to the needle with an eye at its midpoint to the familiar form with a hole for the thread at the end opposite the point. It is much more likely that each form of needle, as today, was fashioned according to materials available for tools and sewing and the work to be done. Styles coexisted. Ancient Egyptians made ceramic double-pointed needles with an eye at each end; Heinrich Schliemann found six bone needles at Troy, most of them notched but one with an eye opposite the point. Roman needles were made of bronze and iron, with the eye on top.

The history of the needle reminds us of how recently the West achieved its technological lead. The medical texts of the Vedas—ancient and sacred Hindu texts first written about 3,500 years ago—prescribe straight and curved high-quality steel needles with today's familiar oval eyes and call attention to their care. While German cities had specialized guilds of needlemakers dating from the fourteenth century, the Persian theologian Ghazali, writing about 1100 C.E., praised as an example of human cooperation the division of the work of making a needle into twenty-five stages. Spain inherited the secrets of Islamic steel needlemaking; refugees brought these skills to England. Even in the London of Henry VIII (r. 1509–1547), the only needlemaker who could draw his own steel wire was a Spanish immigrant. Other masters imported coils from Germany and Spain. Needles were among a household's valuables, protected in special cases that women attached to their belts. Only in the eighteenth and nineteenth centuries did large needlework boxes become common, even among the affluent.

Between the death of the London master in the sixteenth century and the publication of the *Encyclopédie* in the eighteenth century, British and French needlemakers made great but largely undocumented progress in their craft. Needles were supplied for many trades outside of fashion and medicine, including clock making and goldsmithing. To escape guild restrictions on machinery in the seventeenth century, many needlemakers relocated to Redditch, England, in the Midlands, where the industry has remained ever since, with ample water power (from the Red Ditch that gave it its name) and proximity to both metalworkers and crafts using needles. While the *Encyclopédie* of 1762 illustrates a variety of stages in a single

workshop, the Redditch industry remained a network of families, each specializing in one or more stages of the process.

Eighteenth-century needlemakers developed a system of production that is still the basis of today's automated factories. (Surgical needles are still made by hand.) Steel was heated, shaped into a cylinder, and drawn through a number of dies to achieve the proper gauge, then cut into needle lengths. The end was hammered flat, the wire heated, and an eye punched and—often—grooved for easier threading; then the eye was filed smooth and the other end sharpened by filing. The needles were hardened by heating and cooling, then tempered for strength and straightened with a hammer and anvil. Up to 15,000 needles were polished by enclosure in a bag with emery dust and olive oil—a package moved back and forth between planks under a heavy weight for as long as two days—after which they were washed with hot water and soap and dried in a bran-filled box, then sorted and repointed manually with an emery stone. The water-powered scouring mills of Redditch produced such an excellent finish that the town attracted most of England's needlemakers.

During the eighteenth century, workshops grew as the operations were divided among workers of different skills. Craftsmanship may have reached an all-time peak in supplying needles for the finest embroidery and other luxury work. The Forge Mill Needle Museum in Redditch has needles from the time with hand-punched eyes so small they are visible only with a magnifying glass. Thread fine enough to pass through them is no longer made, except for some specialized sutures.

In the early industrial revolution, needle workers were both aristocrats and casualties. In the final stage, a pointer held up to 100 needles at a time against a grindstone and could finish as many as 10,000 an hour. If a grindstone broke and flew apart, it could be fatal, but the most serious threat was inhalation of tiny particles of stone and metal, which caused Pointer's Rot, an occupational pulmonary disease. Surviving pointers—their life expectancy was under thirty-five years—earned a guinea a day, and long resisted not only mechanization but also dust exhaust equipment that would have reduced their wages as well as their mortality. Nor were risks limited to the needle workshops and factories. To inhibit rust, eighteenth-century needles were (at least in France) sometimes packed in asbestos powder before the mineral was known to cause lung cancer.

The nineteenth century was the golden age of needle production. Higher disposable incomes, the new profusion of textiles, the introduction of the sewing machine, and the rise of world trade with the steamship and the British Empire all expanded markets as new machinery expanded capacity. The rule of thumb was that a nation bought three to four hand-sewing needles per year per household. Needles were now cheap enough to be lost in great numbers. By 1906, *Scientific American* reported an annual production of 3 million needles per day worldwide, with 300 million purchased each year in the United States alone. Most hand-sewing needles sold in the United States were British-made; Americans never attempted to challenge British dominance of needlemaking.

The needle industry shared the nineteenth century's enthusiasm for variety and details of finish, including gold-plated grooves. Tailors, seamstresses, and home sewers could choose from twelve sizes of "sharps," the most common style, which generally had grooved eyes to keep protruding thread from damaging fabric. There were also nine sizes of "blunts," short and thick needles for fast, uniform stitching by tailors, and a range of "betweens." Crewel needles had larger holes for stranded thread, and other styles were designed for easier work with other yarns and fabrics. For most styles and sizes there was also a range of quality and packaging. On better grades, grooved eyes were gold plated.

Threading (along with corrosion and injury risk) has long been the Achilles heel of needle design. Major nineteenth-century patents attempted to substitute tactile cues for visual hit-or-miss. The Calyx-Eye was open at the top, with two angled prongs that yielded temporarily to gentle pressure on the thread but retained it securely thereafter. Other innovations, like the Eigo and the Filtenax, guided users in threading from the side of the needle or opening the top with the thumbnail. "Primary" needles extended ease of use to schoolchildren, as sewing was still an essential skill for girls of all social classes.

At its peak in the late nineteenth century, the Redditch needle industry was producing fully 90 percent of the world's needs. But challenges were growing. German needlemakers began to assert technological leadership as early as 1850, when the Schumag company of Aachen introduced a machine that stamped and eyed needles in one operation. Even in the early 2000s, German manufacturers dominate sewing machine–needle production. With their concentration on hand sewing, British producers were also hurt by the skill's decline in the household and the school curriculum later in the century, and the factories that British firms built abroad during the empire to serve local needs with inexpensive labor have more recently come back to haunt these firms' successors with low-cost imports. Over generations, the Redditch industry has consolidated into a handful of firms producing premium hand-sewing needles for the world market.

While much of needlemaking has been a mature industry for over a century, the technological frontier continues to move in heavy industrial sewing, where stronger thread and faster machine speeds can heat needles to the point that thread and fabric are damaged. Textile engineers have been using computer models to predict these problems, and their studies are likely to lead to innovations not only in sewing procedures but in the metallurgy, production, and geometry of industrial sewing needles themselves.

See also **Pins; Sewing Machine.**

BIBLIOGRAPHY

Dennell, Robin. "Needles and Spear-Throwers." *Natural History* 90, no. 10 (October 1986): 70–78.

Gloger, Jo-Ann, and Patrick Chester. *"More to a Needle than Meets the Eye": A Brief History of Needlemaking, Past and Present.* Redditch, U.K.: Forge Mill Needle Museum, 1999.

Rollins, John G. *Needlemaking.* Aylesbury, U.K.: Shire Publications, 1981.

Edward Tenner

NEHRU JACKET The Nehru jacket worn by men in the United Kingdom, United States, and Europe differs from the upper-body garments worn by Jawaharlal Nehru, independent India's first Prime Minister (1947–1964), after whom the Western garment is named. The Nehru jacket is similar to a Western man's tailored suit jacket, but with a difference. The collar and lapels are replaced by a front-button closure rising to a high, round neckline surmounted by a narrow stand-up collar. The stand-up collar may be cut with a slight curve to set it into a well-cut neckline, evidencing the transformative effect of Western tailoring on the Indian men's collar from which it is derived. When popular in the late 1960s and early 1970s, the Nehru jacket was paired with trousers and one of several choices for shirts—turtleneck, mock turtleneck, or tunic. The design of the jacket facilitated the display of bead necklaces, a new element in the dress of male youth in that period.

The eponymous upper-body garments worn by Nehru during his public life are three in number: a *kurta* (tunic), and worn over it a *bundi* (vest) in summer or an *achkan* in winter, variously also called *jama* in Indian languages, and in Colonial English, *Pharsi-fashion coat*, or long coat (Ghurye 1996, pp. 168, 176, 188). Each of the three sports a stand-up collar atop a front-button closure, though kurta collars are optional.

In most other respects Nehru's Indian garments differed significantly from the Nehru jacket of Western men's fashion that they inspired. The kurta is a cotton or silk shirt with a broad flowing A-line silhouette, side slits, uniquely Indian inseam side pockets, inset long sleeves, stand-up collar, and a front-buttoned placket that reaches down to the wearer's lower chest. Nehru wore his kurta at below-knee length, ensembling it with *churidar payjama*—a bias cut, drawstring waist pant cut narrowly over the leg from knee down to ankle, with additional length added to the garment so that the fabric forms gathers at the ankle, mimicking the narrow *churi* glass bracelets that Indian women wear on their wrists. The churidar payjama is the ancestor of jodhpur riding pants.

Nehru's Indian bundi is a front-buttoned, high hip-length sleeveless vest with stand-up collar and three front pockets-two below and one above. It is made from cot-

Nehru with U.S. President Nixon and the First Lady. As Nehru gained prominence on the world political stage, his Indian long coat took on more Western design features, such as the besom breast pocket and vented buttoned cuff. It did retain the distinctive Indian features of A-line silhouette, below knee length, side seam slits, in-seam pockets, front buttoned closure to the neck, and standup collar. AP/WIDE WORLD PHOTOS. REPRODUCED BY PERMISSION.

ton, silk, or wool *khadi* (homespun) fabrics. Nehru wore his bundi with a knee-length kurta and churidar payjamas.

Nehru's long coat extends below the knee, and has a front opening down through the hem but closed with buttons only from neck to waist; stand-up collar; and in-set long sleeves with straight hem at the top of the hand. Unlike the aristocrats of pre-Nationalist Indian society, Nehru made his long coats from khadi fabrics, abstaining from the luxurious silk and gold brocades (*kinkhabs*) from which the Indian nobility usually made theirs. The long coat is worn with a kurta and churidar payjamas, with all its buttons closed, presenting a very finished look.

The manner in which the Western men's garment gave up its lapels and took on the stand-up collar and "Nehru jacket" name is a history of global dimensions in fashion and politics that begins before Nehru was born. Both the long coat and the kurta gained their style of inset sleeves and the kurta gained its front-button placket under European and British colonial influence. Long coats also became more tailored under the British, both during the early colonial era and, after a hiatus of rejection of western dress influence during the independence struggle, as the public officials of the new nation took their places on the global political stage.

Nehru came into public consciousness in Britain from the early decades of the twentieth century during India's long political struggle. In the United States, popular attention focused on Nehru from the mid-twentieth century, when in 1962 China attacked newly independent India. U.S. leaders courted Nehru and Pakistani leaders as allies against the spread of communism. Nehru visited Presidents Truman, Eisenhower, and Kennedy in 1949, 1956, and 1961, respectively. Jacqueline Kennedy visited Nehru in 1962. As Americans watched the first lady's dress, they also learned what Nehru wore.

Experimentation with and rejection of suit dressing for men (Bennett-England 1967) was occurring in Western fashion during this same political period. Cinema idols, such as Marlon Brando, appearing in T-shirts and black leather jackets, popularized nonsuit dressing and valorized the classes of men who could ill afford the expense of suit dressing. Inspired by advances in space travel, Pierre Cardin offered his Space Age line in 1964. The most influential piece was his collarless, lapel-free suit jacket (McDowell 1997, pp.144–145). It buttoned all the way up the front ending in an unadorned round neckline that revealed the collar of a dress shirt. Though not widely accepted, Cardin's garment found favor with the Beatles and other early 1960s British rock groups who wished to remain respectable through suit dressing, but wanted to cut an independent image. While collarless suits gained only limited popularity, Cardin's rejection of vestigial aspects of men's dress encouraged further experimentation with the suit jacket, such as the use of innovative fabrics like denim and velvet, or bright colors and prints for men's suits. A general narrowing of the entire men's suit—leg, torso, sleeve, lapel, and its accompanying necktie—also occurred. This fashion threatened to make parts of the suit disappear. It simultaneously made the suit even more uncomfortable to wear. Formal dressing in tunics à la Yves Saint Laurent and others provided nonsuit alternatives for formal male attire. After the release of the Beatles' *Sgt. Pepper's Lonely Hearts Club Band* album, stand-up collar military uniforms as featured on the album cover—with or without gold braid—as well as second hand navy pea jackets (double-breasted with lapels) became an additional popular alternative to suit dressing for youth. Within this climate of broad attack on and experimentation with suit dressing, a new type of designer arose in Britain to serve the youth who were its primary proponents in dress practice. These British boutique designers offered innovative clothing in successions of quick fads popular among youth.

The Nehru jacket appeared as one of these brief fads after George Harrison and the Beatles went to India in 1966 to learn meditation and music. They brought into fashion not only Ravi Shankar's sitar music and incense, but also paisley prints, bead necklaces (originally Indian meditation beads) for both men and women, Kolhapuri sandals, white-on-white Lucknow *Chikan* embroidered cotton kurtas, and the stand-up collar of the Nehru jacket.

Whether worn on a vest or jacket, the stand-up collar joined in the general experimentation with men's suit dressing. Marly (1985, p. 134) reports Simpson's of the United Kingdom offered a velvet lapel-free suit with Indian style stand-up collar in anticipation of a popular market they forecast with the opening of the movie *The Guru*, in 1969.

American youth were not as cognizant as British youth of Nehru and India, but they were very involved in British popular music. The Nehru jacket crossed the Atlantic and was briefly worn in the United States, too. Several entertainers, including Johnny Carson and Sammy Davis, Jr., made it a regular part of their wardrobe. However, military-style stand-up collar jackets were also redesigned and worn by youth in this period. Not all stand-up collar jackets from this period strictly trace their origins back to India via Nehru or the Beatles.

Though considered a short-lived fad on both sides of the Atlantic among sectors of Western society deriving from European roots, the Nehru jacket has achieved classic status in those sectors of global society—especially British Commonwealth countries—with significant Indian diasporas. Their tuxedo-rental agencies now routinely provide Nehru jackets with matching suit trousers as one of their options for formal attire. Conversely, the several garments that Nehru wore remain in fashion among urban upper- and upper-middle classes in India for bridal and special occasion wear. The humbler versions of these garments also continue in use in the regions of rural India whence they originated.

See also **India: Clothing and Adornment; Sports Jacket.**

BIBLIOGRAPHY

Bennett-England, Rodney Charles. *Dress Optional: The Revolution in Menswear.* London: Peter Owen, 1967.

Ghurye, G. S. *Indian Costume.* 2nd ed. Bombay, India: Popular Prakashan, 1966.

Marly, Diana de. *Fashions for Men: An Illustrated History.* New York: Holmes and Meier, 1985.

McDowell, Colin. *The Man of Fashion: Peacock Males and Perfect Gentlemen.* New York: Thames and Hudson, Inc., 1997.

Hazel Lutz

NEW LOOK The New Look was the name given to a style of women's clothing launched by Christian Dior in his first haute couture collection presented in Paris on 12 February 1947. The styles that made up the look corresponded, according to the show's program, to the shapes "8" and "Corolla," respectively described as "clear, rounded, bust emphasized, waist indented, hips accentuated," and "dancing, very full-skirted, tight-fitting bust, and narrow waist" (Musée, p. 131).

At the end of the show, Carmel Snow, editor in chief of *Harper's Bazaar*, is said to have inadvertently named

Women model Christian Dior dresses. Dior's New Look designs drastically lowered hemlines and emphasized the body's contours, frequently utilizing heavy, multilayered fabrics. AP/WIDE WORLD PHOTOS. REPRODUCED BY PERMISSION.

the style by saying to Christian Dior: "Your dresses have such a new look" (Cawthorne, p. 109). The English term was then adopted without translation by the designer himself and by many commentators in the form "New Look" or "New-Look." Christian Dior used it to define his own style between 1947 and 1952: "1952 began in solemnity … the euphoria of the New Look was finished" (Dior, p. 178–179). However, the term is more broadly applicable to all the creations inspired by Christian Dior's first collections, both his own and those of his famous or anonymous imitators. This is true regardless of the date. The New Look, a watchword in the 1950s, particularly in haute couture, had striking stylistic repercussions at least into the 1960s. It was not until 1970 that Yves Saint-Laurent dismissed the style as a thing of the past with his fall-winter 1970–1971 "Liberation" haute couture collection that celebrated the aesthetic of the World War II years that the New Look had fought against. Thereafter considered a historical style, it still inspires contemporary work that periodically quotes it (Jean-Paul Gaultier in particular) or pays it true homage (Yohji Yamamoto, "homage to French couture" collection for spring-summer 1997).

The New Look had multiple origins: the collections of the period immediately before World War II already hinted at a return to fullness in Balenciaga, Mainbocher, Lelong, and Piguet, which returned beginning in 1946; theater and film during the war revealed a clear taste for the Belle Époque and long dresses in general. The basque created by Marcel Rochas in 1942 finally opened the way to emphatic stylization of the torso. But Christian Dior was responsible for the formal, structural, and stylistic definition of the New Look, and for its economic and social impact.

In terms of form, the New Look was constructed with reference to the individual garment as a reaction against wartime style. The voluminous and composite hats in fashion in Paris under the Occupation were supplanted by those with a "deliberately simple" silhouette (Musée, p. 131). Broad shoulders were replaced during the day by the sloping profile of raglan sleeves, and in the evening by bustiers. The loose-fitting style was rejected in order to reveal the structure of the breasts.

The waist remained fitted, very often belted, to emphasize the contrast between the new width of the hips and the flare of the skirts that, "definitely lengthened" (Musée, p. 131) in the spring of 1947, and by the following fall "reached unlikely dimensions and this time went down to the ankles" (Dior, p. 49). From the spring 1947 collection, the history of fashion has preserved the styles of the "Bar" suit and the "Corolla" dress as manifestos of the New Look, reminding us that the style affected suits constructed by tailors as well as looser garments draped by dressmakers.

For the wardrobe, the New Look marked the triumphal return of the long evening dress, which the war had replaced with short formal dresses. By restoring very visible gradations between daytime clothing and evening dress, the spotlight thrown on evening gowns lastingly reestablished the fashionable dress code.

Structurally, the New Look was built on choices of material and technical procedures aimed at sculpting contours: "I wanted my dresses to be 'constructed,' shaped on the curves of the feminine body and stylizing those curves" (Dior, p. 35). Fabrics were chosen for their solidity, accentuated by lining them with percale or taffeta. In 1952, for example, *Harper's Bazaar* saw the "Cigale" style as "a masterpiece of construction" and described its watered ottoman fabric as "so heavy that it looks like pliant metal" (Martin, p. 107). Dresses were conceived as multilayered compositions supported by underpinnings, including underwired bustiers and tulle and horse-hair skirts. The body itself was, if necessary, artificially shaped by the use of girdles and basques, or by recourse to flattering padding. These artifices, modifying shape as well as bearing, characterized the fashion of the 1950s with an ultra-feminine and affected aesthetic.

In counterpoint to the tendency toward simplification and lightening, which sums up the evolution of fash-

ion from the 1910s to the 1940s, the New Look seemed in 1947 to be an anachronism. Of his second collection (fall-winter 1947–48), even more emblematic than the first, Christian Dior conceded that the "sumptuous fabrics, velvet and brocade, were heavy, but who cared!… Abundance was still too much of a novelty for people to reinvent a snobbism of poverty" (Dior, p. 49).

Considered backward-looking and extravagant, the New Look offended popular sensibility in the immediate postwar period. While the French press was indifferent or favorable to the style, it found enthusiastic support in the United States (*Life*, *Vogue*, *Harper's Bazaar*). For his very first collection, its creator was given the Neiman Marcus Award, indicating the serious commercial involvement of American buyers. A segment of the Anglo-American press, however, conducted a kind of populist anti–New Look campaign. Leagues were established in the United States against the lengthening of skirts, such as WAWS (women at war against the style) and the "little below the knee club." In England, the opposition took on a political flavor: "The long skirt is a caprice of the idle rich" (Braddock, Bessie, quoted in Steele, p. 20). These unexpected repercussions of the New Look testify to the rigor of clothing restrictions during the war. Imposed more or less drastically as part of the war effort on the American and English populations in order to contribute to victory, privations were experienced in France as despoilment by the occupying forces and had nothing of the character of patriotic sacrifice. The postwar period saw the victory of the independence of the New Look over the morality of the allies. Both liberating and respectful of custom, the style surprised and comforted bourgeois conventions. Thus, it quickly made headway in all social circles in Latin and Anglo-Saxon countries to become an international style, the popular interpretation of which was summed up in the ensemble of pleated skirt, belt, and blouse. Its diffusion was then the consensual expression of the construction of a new transatlantic social order on the ruins of European urbanity: "If I dare to refer to the style of 1947, which was called the New Look, it was successful only because it fit in with a time that was trying to escape from the inhuman in order to rediscover tradition" (Musée, p. 14).

See also **Dior, Christian; Haute Couture; Paris Fashion.**

BIBLIOGRAPHY

Cawthorne, Nigel. *Le New-look / la révolution Dior.* Paris: Celiv, 1997.

Dior, Christian, ed. *Christian Dior et moi.* Paris: Amiot-Dumont, 1956.

Martin, Richard, and Harold Koda. *Christian Dior.* New York: Metropolitan Museum of Art, 1996.

Musée des Arts de la mode. *Hommage à Christian Dior 1947–1957.* Paris: Union centrale des Arts décoratifs, 1986.

Remaury, Bruno. *Dictionnaire de la mode au XXème siècle.* Paris: Éditions du Regard, 1994.

Steele, Valérie. *Se vêtir au XXème siècle*. Paris: Adam Biro, 1998.

Veillon, Dominique. *La Mode sous l'Occupation*. Paris: Payot, 1990.

Eric Pujalet-Plaà

NEWTON, HELMUT

Helmut Newton (1920–2004) was arguably the single most inventive and influential photographer working in the realm of fashion in the second half of the twentieth century. Yet it would be selling him short to label him a fashion photographer. While he proved himself a master at this métier, his talents went far beyond the eloquent depiction of fashionable clothes. Newton's oeuvre constitutes a richly layered document of social and cultural history, intensely personal, often autobiographical, but always engaged with the world as he saw and knew it. Newton's curiosity was wide-ranging and insatiable. Within the sphere of fashion, he was instrumental in greatly extending the possibilities of what a magazine editorial photograph might be, as he wove into the equation the subtexts of his endless fascination with women and the way they lived, with status and power, and with the environments and protocols of the rich and sophisticated people who were his principal subject matter. And of course he injected sex into the mix, exploring the often-perverse erotic codes and narratives that are as integral to the processes of fashion as to life itself.

Photographic Style

Helmut Newton became an exceptional social anthropologist, constructing images that were always based on his close observations. His was a documentary project that involved reconstructing the essence of what he had seen, and doing so with the mordant wit of a satirist. While his pictures can have a theatrical extravagance of gesture or context, their incisiveness, credibility, and substance derive from their being always grounded in the realities of the worlds that he illustrated. Newton was not happy working in a studio. Like the photojournalists or documentary photographers he admired, like his heroes Dr. Erich Salomon or Brassaï, he found energy and inspiration in the world around him, on the streets, in hotels, in parks, on trains. He greatly respected the paparazzi, valuing the immediacy and energy in their way of working. Newton created a unique meld of cool, polished stylishness with authentic frontline reporting. His pictures are carefully prepared, minutely controlled and crafted, with every detail of hair, makeup, props, and accessories meticulously overseen, but they work because, however contrived and extreme, they are ultimately believable.

Early Experiences and Influences

Helmut Newton was born in Berlin into a Jewish family that enjoyed the prosperity generated by their button-manufacturing business. The pampered child of loving parents, Newton enjoyed a charmed childhood, from which date his tastes for grand cars and hotels, for elegant

Helmut Newton, 1995. Renown for his erotic black and white photography, Helmut Newton's career garnered fans, critics, and controversy. © Siemoneit Ronald/Corbis Sygma. Reproduced by permission.

fashions and other symbols of the privileged lifestyle of the old European bourgeoisie. His youthful passions were swimming, girls, and photography; he single-mindedly turned these interests into a way of life. He had little interest in academic studies and eventually persuaded his parents to allow him to abandon school in favor of an apprenticeship in the portrait and fashion studio of the Berlin photographer Yva (Elsa Simon). Newton's idyllic Berlin years were undermined by the rise of the Nazi party and the incremental persecution of Jews. In due course he had no option but to flee. Leaving his family and home in December 1938, he sailed for the Far East. He spent time in Singapore where he worked briefly, but unsuccessfully, as a photographer on the *Straits Times* and lived self-indulgently as a gigolo. In 1940 he made his way to Australia. After the war Newton set up a studio in Melbourne and worked hard towards his ambition to live by his photography. In 1948 he married June Browne, an actress he met when she visited his studio looking for modeling work.

June played a crucial role in Newton's life through more than fifty years, supporting, encouraging, editing, and protecting her husband.

Occasional assignments for the Australian supplement to British *Vogue* led to an invitation in 1957 to work for a year in London. Newton was unhappy there and found Paris far more to his liking. Work for *Jardin des modes* provided his first involvement with the world of Paris fashion. He returned to Melbourne to work for Australian *Vogue*, but he knew his destiny was to work in Europe. The big opportunity came with the offer of a contract from French *Vogue* in 1961, and his return to Europe at this date marks the beginning of his mature career. This relationship between Newton and French *Vogue* lasted until 1983. "For twenty-three years," he has said, "I did my best work for French *Vogue*." He created some of his most celebrated and admired images—such icons as the androgynous model in a Saint Laurent trouser suit in the rue Aubriot at night (1975), *Sie kommen*, naked and dressed (1981), or the first *Big Nudes* (1980)—for this magazine. Newton lived to work, and he made fashion pictures at every opportunity for numerous other magazines besides French *Vogue*, including *Elle*, *Queen*, *Nova*, *Marie-Claire*, and *Stern*.

Mature Work

If the 1961 French *Vogue* contract was a turning point, so too was an unanticipated trauma ten years later. In 1971 Newton suffered a major heart attack on the street in New York. Medical assistance was close by and he recovered, but he was severely shaken by this brush with death and determined from that moment not to waste a single day of his life. He knew he must abandon any inhibitions and concentrate on making only the pictures that he wanted to make, pushing his ideas and instincts to the limit. From this time on, he extended his range to include what he at first called his *portraits mondains* and his *sujets érotiques*. He proved himself immensely skilled in probing the boundaries of acceptability and in creating the strange mood of disquiet that pervades his pictures. Newton drew on his memories of the Weimar Berlin of his childhood and on his nostalgia for prewar Europe. He flirted with the pornographic, challenged conventions, and created a provocative, hybrid photography that embraced fashion, erotica, portrait, and documentary elements, producing a highly stylized exposé of elegant and decadent ways of life. Newton turned his attention to making powerful, confrontational nudes. He conceived witty, erotic picture stories for the American magazine *Oui*, and he gave his unique twist to the creation of pictures for *Playboy*.

Newton's portraits of celebrities became an ever-more important aspect of his work, and while these were at first mostly related to the worlds of fashion, over the years he broadened his portfolio to include countless people who intrigued him—artists, actors, film directors, politicians, industrial magnates, the powerful and the

charismatic from all spheres. Many of these photos were published through the 1980s in *Vanity Fair*.

Newton staged his first one-man exhibition in Paris in 1975. The following year he published his first book, *White Women*. Over the next twenty-five years he worked steadily and productively, publishing a series of books and creating countless exhibitions, the most impressive of which was surely the large-scale celebration of his career at the Neue National Galerie in Berlin on the occasion of his eightieth birthday in 2000, accompanied by the simply titled book, *Work*. His last major project before his death in 2004 was the planning of a foundation devoted to preserving and promoting his archive and that of his wife in his native Berlin.

See also **Fashion Magazines; Fashion Photography; Vogue.**

BIBLIOGRAPHY

Blonsky, Marshall. *Helmut Newton: Private Portraits*. Shirmer/ Mosel, 2004

Felix, Zdenek, ed. *The Best of Helmunt Newton*. New York: Thunder's Mouth Press, 1996.

Newton, Helmut. *Autobiography*. New York: Nan A. Talese/ Doubleday, 2003.

———. *Helmut Newton's Illustrated: No. 1–No. 4*. New York: Thunder's Mouth Press, 2000.

Philippe Garner

NIGHTGOWN Nightgown, now the term for women's or girls' garments worn to bed, is historically a somewhat confusing term. From the sixteenth through eighteenth centuries, it was a man's loose gown. In the seventeenth and eighteenth centuries, it was a woman's informal day dress—which was, as the name implies, originally an evening dress—hence women might quite modestly go to church in their nightgowns. While authorities believe that for much of Western history no specialized clothing—and sometimes no clothing—was worn for sleep, by the sixteenth century, nightclothes closely related to basic daywear had been adopted by both sexes.

For centuries, nightwear was cut like the male shirt and female smock or shift, with rectangular pieces for the body and sleeves and gussets under the arm, to avoid wasting fabric. It thus resembled what Lawrence Langner, in *The Importance of Wearing Clothes* of 1959 (p. 232), called "a bulky shapeless shirt hanging from the neck like a deflated balloon." As with underclothes, nightclothes absorbed perspiration, so needed to be washable; white linen, which could be boiled and bleached, was long the preferred fabric for all classes, with the quality of the linen denoting economic status.

In the nineteenth century, nightgowns became increasingly distinguishable from other feminine undergarments, featuring collars, yokes, and cuffs. *The Workwoman's Guide*, published in London in 1838, gives directions (pp. 56–57) for economically cutting out and making several types of nightdresses, and notes that the high-collared style is neater in appearance, but that nightgowns with wide necklines waste less fabric and are particularly convenient for the ill, since they are easy to don and doff and allow "blisters, leeches, &c." to be applied.

Ready-made nightwear became available in the mid-nineteenth century, but not until late in that century did nightgowns become more elaborate. Still cut loose and long, embellishment on the yoke, front placket, and cuffs could include all manner of ribbon, beading, lace, insertions, pin tucks, embroidery, and ruffles. Now usually of cotton, white remained the standard color, although the turn of the century saw occasional use of washing silk and colors, such as pink, which was said to wash well.

Pajamas entered the feminine wardrobe in the late nineteenth century, but long nightgowns remained popular, even after women's skirts shortened in the early twentieth century. During the twentieth century, glamorous and luxurious lingerie grew ever more accessible and affordable. By the twenties, straight-cut silk and rayon nightgowns in delicate colors such as "flesh," orchid, and green were popular, while the mid-century favored gowns with strappy bosom-hugging bodices above sinuous skirts. The advent of nylon allowed women to have—as the slogan for Chemstrand of the mid 1950s said—"all the luxury but none of the fuss," (*Harper's Bazar* ad, 1956) with easy-care yet washable nightgowns and peignoirs that elegantly enhanced their femininity. Nightwear, however, became increasingly more colorful and diverse, responding to new fashion impulses. Young women's "nighties" could be anything from men's pajama tops to shortie "baby-doll" gowns, sometimes with matching panties.

In the late twentieth and early twenty-first centuries, nightgowns offered by companies such as Victoria's Secret included romantic old-fashioned white cotton "nightdresses," comfortable oversize knit sleep shirts, and sexy polyester satin baby dolls, reflecting the many roles and moods of modern women.

See also **Nylon; Pajamas.**

BIBLIOGRAPHY
Cunnington, C. Willett and Phillis Cunnington. *The History of Underclothes.* London: Michael Joseph Ltd, 1951. New edition revised by A.D. Mansfield and Valerie Mansfield, published in London by Faber and Faber, 1981.
Ewing, Elizabeth. *Dress and Undress: A History of Women's Underwear.* London: B. T. Batsford, Ltd., 1978.

H. Kristina Haugland

NONWOVEN TEXTILES Nonwoven fabrics are made directly from fibers, bypassing both yarn-spinning and weaving, or knitting. Although technically fitting this description, the age-old fabric, known as felt, is not considered to be a nonwoven fabric. Specific definitions of materials that can be termed nonwovens are given by the Association of the Nonwoven Fabrics Industry (INDA) in the United States and the European Disposables and Nonwovens Association (EDANA). Nonwovens must have a fabric density of less than 0.4 grams per cubic centimeter. Felt, made from wool fibers that are entangled by heat and moisture, is usually much heavier. Another property of a nonwoven textile is that over 50 percent of its weight must be fibers with a length-to-diameter ratio of at least 300. This eliminates paper, which is made of very short fibers. Nonwovens are often called fiber webs to distinguish them from these other materials.

Properties of nonwovens are particularly dependent on the fibers and processes used. General properties are a lack of drape and an inability to shear where yarns cross over, as in woven fabrics. This often makes them stiffer and less stretchable. They are also weaker than woven and knitted fabrics.

Production Processes
Nonwoven fabrics are often classified by the production processes used to make them. The two major steps in production are web formation and bonding. Each step has a number of variants, and the combination of web forming and bonding method determine a nonwoven's properties and ultimate end-use.

There are several ways to form a fiber web. The traditional method is carding (also called dry laying), in which short, discrete, length (staple) fibers are pulled through wires to align them. This is the same process that is one of the steps in spinning yarns from staple fibers. Staple-fiber webs can also be made by air laying, where the fibers are suspended in air and collected on a moving belt; and by wet laying, a process similar to paper-making, where a mixture of fibers in water is collected on a screen, drained, and dried.

Webs can be formed from long continuous (filament) fibers as well. In these processes, spunbonding and

WHAT'S IN A DIAPER?

A disposable diaper comprises several different nonwoven fabrics. The inner liner is a spunbonded web, the outer layer is a dry-laid web bonded to a plastic film that prevents liquid from flowing through. The interior layer is a web of wood pulp and a super-absorbent fiber. There are also stretchable nonwovens in the tabs and other sections of the diaper.

meltblowing, melted polymers are extruded through many small holes and cooled and collected on a belt. The fibers in meltblown nonwovens are finer than those in spunbonded fabrics because high-velocity air is blown on the fibers as they are extruded, drawing them down to a smaller diameter.

Most webs formed by the methods described have little structural integrity, being a collection of fibers with mainly physical entanglement to hold them together. Subsequent bonding of the fibers is therefore necessary to provide that integrity. Bonding techniques used for dry- and wet-laid webs are adhesives, solutions, or heat, needle-punching, spunlacing, and stitching. Adhesives are glues that are sprayed or padded onto the webs. Alternatively, substances that dissolve the surfaces of the fibers can be applied, and when the dissolved surface areas dry, the fibers bond. A similar type of bonding can also be induced by heat if the web is composed of fibers that melt. The heat melts the fiber surfaces producing "thermal" bonds upon cooling that hold the fibers together. Spunbonded and meltblown nonwovens thermally bond when the fibers cool after being extruded. Passing the web through heated cylinders, called calender rolls, bonds them more completely.

Needle-punched nonwovens have been subjected to a process in which a set of barbed needles moves in and out of the web, entangling the fibers. Spunlaced nonwovens have a distinctive, almost lace-like, appearance because they are produced by passing the web over a set of high-force water jets to entangle the fibers. Small holes are produced where the water penetrates the web and fibers become knotted and entangled around the holes. A final method that has been used to bond fiber webs is simply stitching through them with thread.

Nonwoven Products

Many nonwoven textiles are destined for industrial uses, such as geotextiles for road reinforcement and ground and soil stabilization, roofing and insulation, dust cloths and wipes, home furnishings, and filters. They appear in garments and other wearing apparel as either durable or disposable products. One of the highest-volume disposable products is diapers, which have all but replaced cloth diapers in many countries. Nonwoven textiles are also used in other disposable items such as wipes, feminine-hygiene products, incontinence pads, surgical and medical examination gowns and masks. Surgical and other health-protection masks are often made with meltblown nonwovens that have good filtration properties due to the very fine fibers. An issue with all these disposable nonwoven products is lack of biodegradability and build-up in landfills. Some can be recycled; but, as can be imagined, recycling many of these items presents significant problems. In addition, since they are low-value, high-bulk, recycling is usually not economical.

While a great number of nonwoven textiles are disposable, there are end-uses in which a certain degree of durability is desired. An early and continuing use of such nonwovens in clothing was as interfacings and interlinings. Interfacings are placed within garments to stiffen areas such as collars, cuffs, lapels, waistbands, and parts with buttons and buttonholes. Nonwovens, due to their resistance to shearing and stretching, help to stabilize these areas. In many cases the nonwoven interfacings have heat-activated adhesives on their surfaces so that they can be thermally bonded to the outer fabric. Nonadhesive nonwovens can be included in garments to provide insulation. New stretchable nonwoven textiles are being made for use in foundation underwear and some sportswear.

See also **Felt; Yarns.**

BIBLIOGRAPHY

Oldrich, Jirsák, and Larry C. Wadsworth. *Nonwoven Textiles.* Durham, N.C.: Carolina Academic Press, 1999.

Billie J. Collier

NORELL, NORMAN The work of Norman Norell belongs within the exciting forefront of American fashion. From his first Traina-Norell collection in 1941 to the designer's death in 1972, Norell worked within a design vocabulary that presented his vision of the well-heeled American woman. While other American designers such as Claire McCardell presented an American sensibility primarily by redefining sportswear, Norell took a different approach in his career. He is credited with appropriating the quality and workmanship of French couture and applying these features to clothes produced on Seventh Avenue. Norell put an American twist on his highly sophisticated suits and dresses by adding polka dots, sailor collars, and schoolgirl bows. Fashion reports during Norell's career often claim that as an American designer Norell created certain styles, such as culottes and high-waisted dresses, ahead of his French contemporaries. Norell was a masterful fashion designer who used Seventh Avenue as the unlikely venue for his precisely made and wildly expensive clothes.

Norell was born Norman David Levinson, in Noblesville, Indiana, on 20 April 1900, the son of Harry and Nettie Levinson. As a child his attention to fashion derived from his mother's style of dress and her collection of fashion magazines; his father's haberdashery store in Indianapolis; and his early interest in clothes, interiors, and the theater. At the age of eighteen Norell went to New York City to attend the Parsons School of Design. Whether Norell actually attended Parsons or not for the year he claimed (Parsons cannot find any record of his enrollment), Norell's relationship with the school developed with his success, and Parson's claimed Norell as one of its illustrious graduates. Following a year spent back in Indianapolis opening a batik shop, Norell returned to New York to study at Pratt Institute in Brooklyn. At this time Norell created a new name for himself by combining the first syllable of his first name with the sound of the initial letter of his surname.

From his studies of fashion illustration, drawing, and painting, Norell eventually discovered his *métier* in fashion and costume design. After finishing his studies at Pratt, Norell held a progression of jobs. In 1922 he worked for the film industry in Astoria, Queens, designing costumes for Rudolph Valentino in *The Sainted Devil* and for Gloria Swanson in *Zaza*. His career in theatrical costume design continued with stints designing for the Ziegfeld Follies and the Greenwich Village Follies, and at Brooks Costume Company, where he created costumes for burlesque, vaudeville, and nightclub revues. Norell's shift to women's clothing occurred in 1924, when he was hired by Charles Armour, a manufacturer of women's apparel. During the years that Norell worked for Hattie Carnegie (1928–1940), he had the invaluable opportunities of traveling to Europe, studying the construction of French couture dresses, and working with Carnegie's glamorous clients. Following a disagreement with Hattie Carnegie over a dress for Gertrude Lawrence in *Lady in the Dark*, a Broadway production, Norell left the firm and joined Anthony Traina, owner of A. Traina Gowns. Norell is often quoted as saying, "Mr. Traina called me and asked me to join him. He offered me a larger salary if my name were not used, a smaller amount if it was" (Morris, p. 46). Norell chose recognition over financial gain. Name recognition also served Norell in 1968 when he launched his perfume, "Norell."

From its inception in 1941 to Traina's retirement in 1960, Traina-Norell produced dresses, suits, and evening wear that combined an up-to-date sensibility with a feeling of timelessness. The label of Traina-Norell was formed with Anthony Traina as businessman and Norell as his employee, solely responsible for the designs of the collections. Of the first Traina-Norell collection, Bonwit Teller declared in *Vogue*, "The House of Traina-Norell comes on the season like an electrical storm. Its designer, young Mr. Norell, creates a collection so alive that everyone's talking" (*Vogue*, 1 October 1941, p. 5). Women purchasing a Traina-Norell garment were buying, at great cost, an American-made status symbol that would likely remain in their closets for decades. The high-class status of a Traina-Norell dress is invoked in the 1957 film *Sweet Smell of Success*, a reference known to audiences of that time but likely lost on most viewers today.

During the heyday of Traina-Norell, Norell established the basic designs that carried him through his career. The designer's body-fitting, sequined gowns, known as "mermaid dresses," were first shown in the 1940s. His chic shirtwaists, suits and chemise dresses, beautifully tailored coats, and clothes featuring polka dots, white schoolgirl collars, and oversize bows all became signatures of Norell's style. A *Harper's Bazaar* caption (March 1951) to a Norell ensemble captures it well:

"American Style—sharp and clean, a parlormaid's collar and cuffs of snowy organdie on a fitted jersey top, a snowy skirt, a streak of patent leather, and a red, red rose."

Following Traina's retirement in 1960, Norell opened his own firm, Norman Norell, New York. For its first collection Norell took his inspiration from the 1920s and his favorite designer, Chanel. Slinky, spangled evening dresses combined 1920s straight silhouettes with modern opulence. Also included in this premier collection was the wool culotte suit, considered revolutionary when it appeared. *Vogue* proclaimed (1 September 1960), "Now, for the first time in the history of modern fashion, a first-rank designer has based an entire suit-collection on the divided skirt" (p. 187).

Through the 1960s until his death in 1972, Norell continued to present elegant clothes of exemplary quality. His classics of sweater tops with evening skirts, chemise dresses, sequin- paved dresses and blouses, the sailor look in various guises, and ensembles mixing dressy satins with menswear flannel, had an ongoing prestige and allure that catered to his wealthy clientele.

Norell's talents were recognized in the early years of Traina-Norell. In 1943 he was the first designer to win the Coty American Fashion Critics' award; he won it again in 1951, and in 1956 was the first designer to earn a place in the Coty Hall of Fame. Norell was a founder and first president of the Council of Fashion Designers of America in 1965. His clothes have been featured in numerous exhibitions, most recently *Norman Norell* at the Fashion Institute of Technology (1998) and *Architects of American Fashion: Norman Norell and Pauline Trigère* at the Wadsworth Atheneum (2002). Norell suffered a stroke on 15 October 1972, only one day before his retrospective at the Metropolitan Museum of Art. He died days later on 25 October 1972. A statement made by Norell in the early 1960s encapsulates the designer's career, "To qualify as a designer one should not be afraid to repeat a good design, and certainly must have his own signature" (Kellen Archive Center, Parsons School of Design, Alumni Scrapbook 5). Norell followed these maxims to great success.

See also **Chemise Dress; Film and Fashion; Shirtwaist; Spangles.**

BIBLIOGRAPHY

Baker, Therese Duzinkiewicz. "Norell, Norman." In *Contemporary Fashion*, edited by Taryn Benbow-Pfalzgraf. Detroit: St. James Press, 2002.

"Break-Through in Fashion: The Culotte Suit for City Wear." *Vogue* (1 September 1960).

Jacobs, Laura. "No One But Norell." *Vanity Fair* (October 1997): 356–367.

Lambert, Eleanor. *World of Fashion: People, Places, Resources.* New York and London: R. R. Bowker Company, 1976.

Lee, Sarah Tomerlin, ed. *American Fashion: The Life and Lines of Adrian, Mainbocher, McCardell, Norell, and Trigère.* New

York: Quadrangle/New York Times Book Company, 1975.

Levin, Phyllis Lee. *The Wheels of Fashion.* Garden City, N.Y.: Doubleday, 1965.

Milbank, Caroline Rennolds. *Couture: The Great Designers.* London: Thames and Hudson, 1985.

———. *New York Fashion: The Evolution of American Style.* New York: Harry N. Abrams, Inc., 1989.

Morris, Bernadine. "Norman Norell, Designer, Dies; Made 7th Ave. the Rival of Paris." *New York Times,* 26 October 1972.

Roshco, Bernard. *The Rag Race: How New York and Paris Run the Breakneck Business of Dressing American Women.* New York: Funk and Wagnalls, 1963.

Williams, Beryl. *Fashion Is Our Business.* Philadelphia and New York: J. B. Lippincott Company, 1945.

Donna Ghelerter

NUDISM Nudism is the practice of nonsexual social nudity, usually in mixed-sex groups, often at specially defined locations, such as nude beaches or nudist clubs. Nudism can be differentiated from the practice of spontaneous or private nude bathing ("skinny-dipping") in that it is an ongoing, self-conscious and systematic philosophy or lifestyle choice, rather than a spontaneous decision to disrobe. Nudists believe in the naturalness of the naked body, and in the medicinal, therapeutic, or relaxing properties of unself-conscious social nudity. They believe that modesty and shame are socially imposed restrictions on the freedom of the naked body, and that eroticism is not a necessary condition of nakedness. They frequently emphasize the importance of *total* nudity, arguing that partial concealment is more sexual than total exposure.

Early Nudism

Nudism arose in Germany at the turn of the twentieth century, and spread through Europe, the United States, and Australia. The so-called "father of nudism" was the German Heinrich Pudor (real name Heinrich Scham), who coined the term *Nacktkultur* ("naked culture") and whose book *Nackende Menschen* (Naked man [1894]) was probably the first book on nudism. Richard Ungewitter (author of *Die Nacktheit* [1906]) is more widely known as the founder of nudism, his reputation having survived Pudor's accusations of plagiarism.

Nudism flourished in Germany, France, England, elsewhere in Europe, and in the United States, but its advocates often had to fend off legal challenges or accusations of depravity. While nudism had distinctive national flavors, and there was occasionally some rivalry (especially between the French and the Germans), there was also considerable communication, influence, and overlap between nudist cultures. Nudism was known by many names: in Germany, as *Nacktkultur, Freikörperkultur* (free-body culture), or *Lichtkultur* (light culture); in

France as *nudisme, naturisme,* or *libre-culture* (free culture), and in England as Gymnosophy or naturism.

Germanic nudism was a proletarian movement, mostly communitarian and ascetic in style. Its constituency was largely the unemployed and the working poor. By and large however, nudism was a movement endorsed and organized by educated people—physicians, scientists, lawyers, clergy, and, in France especially, occasionally by members of the aristocracy. Nudism produced an extensive proselytizing literature. Key nudist figures or writers of the 1920s and 1930s included: in Germany, Adolf Koch, Paul Zimmerman, and Hans Surén; in France, Marcel Kienné de Mongeot, the Durville brothers, and Pierre Vachet; in the United States, Maurice Parmelee and Frances and Mason Merrill; and in England, the Reverend Clarence Norwood, John Langdon-Davies, and William Welby. Nudists often met with religious opposition, but there were also many openly Christian nudists, who argued that it was time for Christianity to rid itself of superstition.

Early nudism was a medical, philosophical, and political movement. Its key contentions were the therapeutic benefit of unhindered access to sun and air, and the psychological benefit of an open relation to the naked body. Nudist writing commonly begins with cross-cultural and historical examples demonstrating the relativity of shame and modesty, before proceeding to expound the psychological, moral, social, and physical benefits of nudity. Clothing was considered to be both an instrument of class oppression and a major cause of ill health. Nudists claimed that an excess of shame and modesty bred psychological complexes, unhealthy relations between the sexes, and produced bodies that were both unhealthy and an affront to beauty.

The contribution of nudism to the aesthetics of the race was regularly cited as one of its benefits. Maurice Parmelee, for example, argued that nudism would contribute to a more "beautiful mankind" (p. 179). Some nudist clubs banned the disabled and the corpulent as a punishment for unhygienic lifestyles, but other nudists were troubled by too strong an emphasis on the aesthetic:

> While extreme cases of deformity and mutilation can be so distressing and painful to view that there may be some justification for such exclusion, it is of supreme importance that the gymnosophy movement be maintained on a lofty humanitarian plane (*Parmelee, pp. 179–180*)

The relation between nudism and eugenics was complex, and use of an aesthetic discourse is no simple marker of eugenic thought or of fascism. Although Pudor, for example, was overtly anti-Semitic, Karl Toepfer warns that there was no "deep, inherent connection" between Germanic body culture and Nazism (p. 9).

Nudism was neither simply reactionary nor progressive. On the one hand, it was a trenchant critique of modernity. Nudist physicians lamented the soot-choked air of industrial cities and the lack of exposure to fresh air and sunlight of most working people. Socialist accounts argued that this physical malaise was compounded by the role of clothing in effecting oppressive social stratification; clothes were seen as masking the innate equality of all people. Some nudist writing is characterized by a romantic and nostalgic evocation of nature, a conception no doubt aided by the use in England and France of the euphemistic alternative "naturism" (a term that, incidentally, appears to be gaining some favor in contemporary nudism as a more "acceptable" term than nudism). For many writers, however, nudism was emphatically *not* a return to nature. As Parmelee put it, the idea that nudists want to discard anything artificial or man-made was "manifest folly" (p. 15). Scientists and physicians saw nudism not as a return to Eden (although this trope certainly occurred in nudist writing), but as a path forward to a shining new modernity in which science, rather than superstition, would lead the way.

Nudism was thus not (only) nostalgic but also saw itself as *modern* and *rational*. Nudist writing intersected with a raft of other modern discourses—heliotherapy (sun-cure), sexology, socialism, feminism, and eugenics. Caleb Saleeby, for example, was a fervent advocate of nudism, heliotherapy, and eugenics (he was Chairman of the National Birthrate Commission and author of a number of books on eugenics). Sexologist Havelock Ellis considered nudism to be an extension of the dress reform movement for women, and Maurice Parmelee saw it as a powerful adjunct to feminism. Ennemond Boniface was a socialist nudist, who fervently believed that nudism was an alternative to bloody socialist revolution, and would bring about a new naturist era in which all would be equal under the sun (see sidebar). For many, nudism was not just a therapeutic practice; it was a revolutionary plan for an egalitarian utopia.

Contemporary Nudism

There are a number of forms of contemporary organized nudism, each with a somewhat distinct culture: nude beaches, nudist resorts, nudist clubs, and swim-nights. "Clothes optional" resorts are becoming more common in some countries, as part of the growth of naturist tourism.

The utopian and political underpinning of early nudism has largely disappeared. Nudism has remained a minor practice, and it has by and large mutated into a "lifestyle" chosen by individuals rather than either a medical practice or a program for social reform. Contemporary nudists tend to be more private and less evangelical about their practice, and they are unlikely to see it as connected to any form of radical philosophy or politics. The major benefits are, they believe, a relaxed lifestyle and a healthy body image.

Body image is, in fact, the one social issue around which nudists are likely to be united in their opinion. Whereas for the early nudists, one of the prime benefits of nudism was that it would promote healthy, beautiful

NUDISM AND CAPITALISM

The French socialist Ennemond Boniface predicted that nudism would bring about the end of capitalism:

"[T]here will be an exodus . . . from the cities, and the willing return . . . to the good nourishing earth. Little by little, men will desert the monstrous, nauseating agglomerations [of our] towns, in order to found . . . new and increasingly numerous naturist towns. Then . . . the factories, those places of hard labor where decent folk are imprisoned, will progressively become empty. The ferocious reign of the industrialist and his accomplice the banker will be over" (Salardenne, p. 93).

bodies and, by social selection, contribute to the elimination of unhygienic or unappealing bodies, contemporary nudists see nudism as a way of escaping the debilitating effects of the modern obsession with the body beautiful. They believe that nudism teaches one to be comfortable with one's body, whatever it looks like.

See also **Nudity.**

BIBLIOGRAPHY

Barcan, Ruth. *Nudity: A Cultural Anatomy.* Oxford: Berg 2004.

———— "'The Moral Bath of Bodily Unconsciousness': Female Nudism, Bodily Exposure and the Gaze." *Continuum: Journal of Media and Cultural Studies* 15.3 (2001): 305–319. On contemporary female nudists' accounts of the benefits of nudism.

Clapham, Adam, and Robin Constable. *As Nature Intended: A Pictorial History of the Nudists.* Los Angeles: Elysium Growth Press, 1982. Useful history.

Clarke, Magnus. *Nudism in Australia: A First Study.* Victoria: Deakin University Press, 1982. A comprehensive study.

Merrill, Frances, and Mason, Merrill. *Nudism Comes to America.* New York: Alfred A. Knopf, 1932.

Norwood, C. E. (Rev). *Nudism in England.* London: Noel Douglas, 1933.

Parmelee, Maurice. *Nudism in Modern Life: The New Gymnosophy.* London: Noel Douglas, 1929. An account of the benefits of nudism by a nudist physician, with an introduction by Havelock Ellis.

Pudor, Heinrich [Heinrich Scham]. *Naked People: A Triumph-Shout of the Future.* Translation by Kenneth Romanes. Peterborough: Reason Books, 1998 [1894]. Earliest nudist text; little read.

Salardenne, Roger. *Le nu intégrale chez les nudistes français: Reportage dans les principaux centres.* Paris: Prima, 1931.

Saleeby, C. W. *Sunlight and Health.* London: Nisbit and Company, 1923. A eugenic view.

Toepfer, Karl. *Empire of Ecstasy: Nudity and Movement in German Body Culture, 1910–1935*. Berkeley: University of California Press, 1997.

Ruth Barcan

NUDITY Nudity is paradoxical—a bodily state that is seen as so banal or matter of fact that it is rarely given sustained conceptual or academic treatment, while all the while most societies subject it to intense regulation via customs, taboos, and laws. Nudity is customarily imagined as a "natural" state—since we are all born naked—and yet its powerful social and cultural regulation means that it is anything but simple or natural.

Nudity might seem so uncomplicated as to need no definition; it is simply the state of being without clothes. But this is too simple. In the past, the word *naked* could mean clad only in an undergarment. In fine art, the term "nude" almost always includes semiclad or lightly draped bodies. So too, in some legal jurisdictions, the erect penis is legally "nude" even when covered in an opaque fabric. Conversely, some uncovered parts of the body—an elbow, a nose, a wrist, a face—are unlikely to be considered naked. Definitions of nudity, which are subject to historical and cultural variation, rely on assumptions about what counts as clothing. Defining nudity can also be an ideological or political matter. Are ornamentation, tattooing, feathers, skins, jewelry, or even hairstyles forms of clothing? This can matter greatly, as in the colonial context, where nudity was often seen as a sign of savagery.

Nakedness versus Clothing
Nakedness and clothing help define each other. They can function as "nuclei" of humans' "sense of order" (Clark, p. 4), as in the following sample list of fundamental sense-making oppositions in the Western tradition:

> nakedness vs. clothing
> natural vs. cultural
> unchanging vs. changeable
> invisible vs. visible
> truth vs. lies
> pure vs. corrupt
> human nature vs. human society
> pre-, non-, anti-social vs. social

These terms are valued according to context, blurry at their edges, and occasionally reversible. Thus, nakedness has been able to be imagined as both an indecent state needing to be covered by "culture" (clothing) and a pure state far superior to the indecent cultural masquerade of clothing. The nakedness of "savages," for example, has been imagined as evidence of their inferior humanness—but it has also been subject to romanticization (the "naturalness" of the "noble savage").

Metaphorical Meanings of Nudity
In the Western tradition, nudity can, broadly speaking, attract both positive and negative metaphorical meanings.

"It is widely supposed that the naked human body is in itself an object upon which the eye dwells with pleasure and which we are glad to see depicted. But anyone who has frequented art schools and seen the shapeless, pitiful model which the students are industriously drawing will know that this is an illusion" (Clark, p. 3).

Mario Perniola has argued that these opposing meanings arise from the different metaphysics underlying the Greek and the Judaic traditions. In the Platonic tradition, he argues, truth was understood as something to be unveiled. Nudity, therefore, accrued metaphorical meanings of truth, authenticity, and innocence. Moreover, in sculptural and athletic practice, the ideal human figure was naked. In the Judaic tradition, however, in which the Godhead was imagined as gloriously *veiled*, nakedness was more likely to signify degradation, humiliation, or loss of personhood. It is important to stress that this is a simplification; there was internal complexity within, and interchange between, the two systems of meaning. In any case, metaphorical meanings and lived practice did not always match up; nor were the idealized meanings of nudity open to all types of naked bodies (for example, those of women, older men, or slaves).

The Naked and the Nude
English has two major terms for the state of undress: nakedness and nudity. Nakedness is the older word, coming from the Germanic family of languages. Nude is of Latin origin, entering the language in late Middle English. The original connotations of these terms persist—nakedness tends to suggest a raw, natural state, while nudity suggests a state of undress refined by culture into an aesthetic state.

Within fine arts, this etymological nuance has been elaborated into a full-fledged aesthetic distinction between the naked and the nude, a distinction most famously articulated by Kenneth Clark. Put simply, Clark's opposition is this: nakedness is the "raw" human body, the human body without clothes. Nudity results when the artist works on that raw material. Thus, the nude is not a subject of art but a form of art (p. 3). John Berger glosses it thus: nakedness is a starting point and the nude is "a way of seeing" (p. 53). Nakedness is imperfect and individual; the nude is ideal and universal. Nakedness is nature; nudity, culture. The artist's work de-particularizes the model's nakedness, lifting it into ideality.

Conceptually, the difference relies on the myth of an unmediated original bodily state—as though there were in the first place some raw "nature" untouched by cul-

"[I]n our Diogenes search for physical beauty, our instinctive desire is not to imitate but to perfect. This is part of our Greek inheritance ... 'Art,'[Aristotle] says, 'completes what nature cannot bring to a finish'" (Clark, p. 9).

ture. The opposition also depends on underlying value judgments that have made it politically unpalatable to some. Some feminists, for example, have seen much to criticize in Clark's denigration of the naked as a pitiful state. We are, says Clark, "disturbed" by the natural imperfection of the naked body, and we admire the classical scheme that eliminates flaws, wrinkles, and signs of organic process: "A mass of naked figures does not move us to empathy, but to disillusion and dismay. We do not wish to imitate; we wish to perfect" (p. 4). For many feminists, such unabashed idealism is not only conceptually untenable, it is politically suspect, since it denigrates the (traditionally feminized) body.

Clearly, the idealizing processes Clark describes are not limited to classical art. They are the backbone of the glamorizing tendencies of contemporary consumer culture, as critics such as John Berger first pointed out. Contemporary advertising favors smoothed, youthful surfaces, and it employs its own techniques, including image manipulation, to ensure that bodily ideals do not "disturb" us with signs of imperfection. It is not hard to see why feminists have by and large been less than enthusiastic about the distinction between the naked and the nude, since they are critical of the pressures that such idealization puts on women, especially, and argue that dissatisfaction with the "natural" body is a major cause of psychological and cultural malaise.

See also **Nudism.**

BIBLIOGRAPHY

Barcan, Ruth. *Nudity: A Cultural Anatomy.* Oxford: Berg, 2004.

———. "Female Exposure and the Protesting Woman." *Cultural Studies Review* 8 no. 2 (2002): 62–82.

Berger, John. *Ways of Seeing.* London: BBC; Harmondsworth: Penguin, 1972. Explores the naked/nude distinction in art and advertising.

Clark, Kenneth. *The Nude: A Study of Ideal Art.* Harmondsworth: Penguin, 1956. Classic discussion; source of naked/nude distinction.

Hollander, Anne. *Seeing through Clothes.* Berkeley: University of California Press, 1993.

Miles, Margaret R. *Carnal Knowing: Female Nakedness and Religious Meaning in the Christian West.* Boston: Beacon Press, 1989.

Nead, Lynda. *The Female Nude: Art, Obscenity, and Sexuality.* London: Routledge, 1992. Feminist text that includes an extended critique of the naked/nude distinction.

Perniola, Mario. "Between Clothing and Nudity." Translated by Roger Friedman. In *Fragments for a History of the Human Body. Part Two*, pp. 236–265. Edited by Michel Feher, with Ramona Naddaff and Nadia Tazi. New York: Zone, 1989. Outline of nakedness in Greek and Judaic traditions.

Ruth Barcan

NYLON Nylon was the first fiber to be synthesized from petrochemicals and became known as the "miracle fiber." Its inventor was American chemist Wallace Carothers of the DuPont Company. Introduced in 1931, it was first called "66." By 1938 Paul Schlack, a German chemist from the I.G. Farben Company, created a different form of the fiber known as nylon 6. In 1941, British Nylon, Inc. began nylon 6 production in Great Britain. Invented two decades after rayon and acetate, nylon opened the door for synthetic fiber inventions that revolutionized the global textile industry.

DuPont began commercial production of nylon in 1939 by featuring women's hosiery at the San Francisco Exposition. It was one of the most exciting fashion innovations of the age, and women were intrigued by the strength, beauty, and low cost of nylon stockings compared to silk stockings. World War II diverted production of nylon to the war effort as it was used in products like parachutes, ponchos, tires, ropes, tents, and even U.S. currency. When commercial production resumed after World War II thousands of women lined up in New York City to purchase nylon hosiery.

Neil Armstrong planted a nylon flag on the moon in 1969 while wearing a nylon and aramid space suit, symbolizing the futuristic aura of the "miracle fiber." Synthetic fibers can be produced in various modifications. Throughout its history special-purpose nylon fibers have been developed. The Japanese company, Kuraray, began developing leather-look microfiber nylon in 1964, which is used for high-fashion apparel, sportswear, and luggage. A lustrous and luxurious-appearing Qiana nylon was introduced in the early 1970s as an innovation with the triangular cross-sectional shape of silk. It is no longer made. Antron nylon had similar properties and continues to be produced.

Consumers found nylon to be less comfortable than natural fibers. One solution was to blend nylon with other fibers to enhance strength and improve comfort. Modifications produced Hydrofil nylon, which was engineered for increased absorbency. Recent development of microfiber nylon (fibers with exceptionally fine diameters) added a comfort dimension first appreciated in active sportswear, such as athletic wear made of Tactel microfiber nylon produced by DuPont. Designer and consumer-level fashion acceptance of microfiber products continues to grow and with it may come a resurgence of nylon in apparel fashion.

Research into possible innovations for nylon continues. One frontier is micro-encapsulation in medical applications, in which nutrients and supplements encapsulated in the apparel are released as therapy to the body. Encapsulation appeared in interior textiles as perfume in furnishings used to set the mood of a room. Nylon is produced in Asia, North America, Western Europe, and Eastern Europe, with production growth showing a marked shift to Asia. Nylon's share of fiber production has decreased from 20 percent in 1982 to 11 percent in 2002. Polyester at 58 percent has clearly become the dominant synthetic fiber.

Production of nylon
Nylon is chemically synthesized from petrochemicals by reacting an acid with an amine. The variant of amine and acid determines the resultant type of nylon (e.g. 66 or 6). The compounds form a nylon salt that is dried and heated under a vacuum to eliminate water and form a polymer known as polyamide. In the technical textile literature nylon may be referred to as polyamide. The polyamide is melted, passed through a spinneret with holes, and drawn in long continuous filaments. Variations in the steps of this process allow producers to engineer specific properties. Often yarns are texturized (treated to change the surface texture) in order to add character, stretch, or bulk. Fibers are then processed into yarns relative to use.

Characteristics of nylon textiles
Nylon is known for its high strength, abrasion resistance, durability, elongation, and versatility. These properties make nylon highly suitable for heavy poplin and taffeta upholstery and luggage fabrics. The versatility of nylon allowed for creation of the aesthetics of natural fibers with far better performance. Because of excellent elongation, nylon has been particularly well suited for knitwear. Comfort has been a challenge, though, given low absorption and a medium heat retention that contribute to sweating when physically active. Hydrophil has been engineered to provide absorption and wicking (moisture transport). Nylon taffeta has been used extensively for rainwear, umbrellas, and wind-resistant garments. Static is another outcome of low moisture absorption that can be uncomfortable and possibly unsafe in some environments. Antistatic variants have been developed to manage this problem in garments and in carpeting in which finishes or small amounts of metallic and carbon fibers are used. Nylon can be heat set, making it highly resilient and shrink resistant at normal temperatures; however, at very high heat it can wrinkle, shrink, and even melt. Nylon resists damage from chemicals and is also resistant to mold, mildew, and insects. It is less resistant to damage

from sunlight. Nylon attracts oil-based stains and performs best if treated with stain-release finishes. This is particularly needed for carpeting and upholstery.

Nylon in fashion across time
Introducing nylon through women's nylon hosiery created a fashion frenzy never seen for any other manufactured fiber. The momentum of this introduction made nylon the leading synthetic fiber until 1969 when polyester consumption overtook nylon. One major feature of these new textiles that had great appeal was "wash and wear," in which ironing became a seldom-or-never kind of expectation for relatively wrinkle-free textiles. Growth in popularity of knitwear, particularly sportswear, contributed to the fashionability of synthetic apparel. Yet, attempts to make nylon appealing in apparel have met with numerous comfort issues for typical clothing, leading to a perception that nylon is uncomfortable when worn. With ongoing innovations in sportswear and high fashion, nylon continues to be a fiber with a bit of "miracle" pending.

Common nylon textile uses
The primary demand for nylon is for carpeting; 80 percent of carpeting is nylon. Other interior-textile uses include bedspreads, window treatments, and upholstery. Within apparel, nylon is used in hosiery, particularly women's sheer hosiery, lingerie, foundation garments, raincoats, linings, windbreakers, and a wide array of athletic wear in which the stretch of nylon is an asset. Industrial uses are extensive and include tire cord, car headliners and trunk liners, car trims, clutch and brake pads, radiator and other hoses, car airbags, conveyer and seat belts, parachutes, racket strings, ropes and nets, sleeping bags, tarpaulins, tents, thread, fishing line, brushes, sports gear, luggage, and dental floss.

See also **Acrylic and Modacrylic Fibers; Rayon.**

BIBLIOGRAPHY
Braddock, Sarah, and Marie O'Mahony. *Techno Textiles: Revolutionary Fabrics for Fashion and Design.* New York: Thames and Hudson, Inc., 1998.
Collier, Billie, and Phyllis Tortora. *Understanding Textiles.* New York: Macmillan Publishing, 2000.
Hatch, Kathryn. *Textile Science.* Minneapolis: West Publishing, 1993.
Kadolph, Sara, and Anna Langford. *Textiles.* 9th ed. New York: Prentice-Hall, 2002.

Internet Resource

"Fibersource." American Fiber Manufacturers Association/Fiber Economics Bureau. Available from <http://www.fibersource .com>.

Carol J. Salusso